D1047520

South India

Sarina Singh

Amy Karafin, Adam Karlin, Anirban Mahapatra,
Amelia Thomas, Rafael Wlodarski

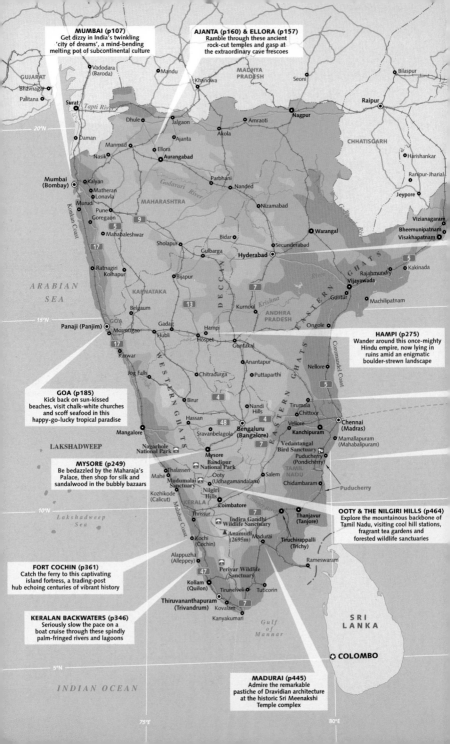

MUMBAI (p107)
Get dizzy in India's twinkling 'city of dreams', a mind-bending melting pot of subcontinental culture

AJANTA (p160) & ELLORA (p157)
Ramble through these ancient rock-cut temples and gasp at the extraordinary cave frescoes

HAMPI (p275)
Wander around this once-mighty Hindu empire, now lying in ruins amid an enigmatic boulder-strewn landscape

GOA (p185)
Kick back on sun-kissed beaches, visit chalk-white churches and scoff seafood in this happy-go-lucky tropical paradise

MYSORE (p249)
Be bedazzled by the Maharaja's Palace, then shop for silk and sandalwood in the bubbly bazaars

OOTY & THE NILGIRI HILLS (p464)
Explore the mountainous backbone of Tamil Nadu, visiting cool hill stations, fragrant tea gardens and forested wildlife sanctuaries

FORT COCHIN (p361)
Catch the ferry to this captivating island fortress, a trading-post hub echoing centuries of vibrant history

KERALAN BACKWATERS (p346)
Seriously slow the pace on a boat cruise through these spindly palm-fringed rivers and lagoons

MADURAI (p445)
Admire the remarkable pastiche of Dravidian architecture at the historic Sri Meenakshi Temple complex

GUJARAT
Vadodara (Baroda)
Bhavnagar
Palitana
Surat
Tapti River
Daman
20°N
Mumbai (Bombay)
Kalyan
Matheran
Lonavla
Murudi
Pune
Goregaon
Mahabaleshwar
Ratnagiri
Kolhapur
Belgaum
GOA
Panaji (Panjim)
Mormugao
Karwar
Jog Falls
Mangalore
LAKSHADWEEP
Lakshadweep Sea
10°N
Mahé
Kozhikode (Calicut)
KERALA
Thrissur
Kochi (Cochin)
Alappuzha (Alleppey)
Kollam (Quilon)
Thiruvananthapuram (Trivandrum)
Kovalam
Kanyakumari
5°N
INDIAN OCEAN

MADHYA PRADESH
Mandu
Khandwa
Seoni
Nagpur
Bilaspur
Raipur
CHHATISGARH
Harishankar
Ranipur-Jharial
Jeypore
Vizianagaram
Bheemunipatnam
Visakhapatnam

Dhule
Jalgaon
Amraoti
Akola
Manmad
Nasik
Ellora
Aurangabad
Ajanta
MAHARASHTRA
Godavari River
Parbhani
Nanded
Nizamabad
Warangal
Bidar
Secunderabad
Sholapur
Gulbarga
Hyderabad
Bijapur
DECCAN
KARNATAKA
Kurnool
ANDHRA PRADESH
Krishna River
Guntur
Machilipatnam
Rajahmundry
Kakinada
Gadag
Hubli
Hampi
Hospet
Guntakal
Anantapur
Chitradurga
Puttaparthi
Nellore
Birur
Nandi Hills
Tirumala
Chittoor
Hassan
Sravanabelagola
Bengaluru (Bangalore)
Vellore
Kanchipuram
Vedantangal Bird Sanctuary
Mamallapuram (Mahabalipuram)
Chennai (Madras)
Nagarhole National Park
Mysore
Bandipur National Park
Ooty (Udhagamandalam)
Salem
Puducherry (Pondicherry)
Chidambaram
Mudumalai Sanctuary
Nilgiri Hills
Coimbatore
Thanjavur (Tanjore)
Indira Gandhi Wildlife Sanctuary
Anamudi (2695m)
Madurai
Tiruchirappalli (Trichy)
Rameswaram
Periyar Wildlife Sanctuary
Tirunelveli
Tuticorin
Gulf of Mannar
SRI LANKA
COLOMBO

ARABIAN SEA

WESTERN GHATS
EASTERN GHATS
DECCAN
Malabar Coast
Konkan Coast
Coromandel Coast
TAMIL NADU

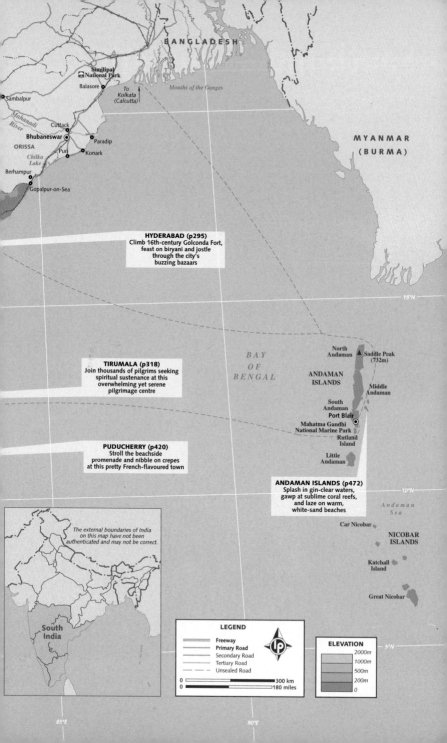

BANGLADESH

Similipal
National Park
Balasore
To
Kolkata
(Calcutta)

Sambalpur

Mahanadi River

Cuttack

Bhubaneswar

Paradip

ORISSA

Puri

Konark

Chilka Lake

Berhampur

Gopalpur-on-Sea

MYANMAR
(BURMA)

Mouths of the Ganges

HYDERABAD (p295)
Climb 16th-century Golconda Fort,
feast on biryani and jostle
through the city's
buzzing bazaars

15°N

TIRUMALA (p318)
Join thousands of pilgrims seeking
spiritual sustenance at this
overwhelming yet serene
pilgrimage centre

BAY OF BENGAL

North
Andaman

Saddle Peak
(732m)

ANDAMAN
ISLANDS

Middle
Andaman

South
Andaman
Port Blair

Mahatma Gandhi
National Marine Park

Rutland
Island

PUDUCHERRY (p420)
Stroll the beachside
promenade and nibble on crepes
at this pretty French-flavoured town

Little
Andaman

ANDAMAN ISLANDS (p472)
Splash in gin-clear waters,
gawp at sublime coral reefs,
and laze on warm,
white-sand beaches

10°N

Andaman Sea

Car Nicobar

NICOBAR
ISLANDS

Katchall
Island

Great Nicobar

*The external boundaries of India
on this map have not been
authenticated and may not be correct.*

**South
India**

5°N

LEGEND

Freeway
Primary Road
Secondary Road
Tertiary Road
Unsealed Road

0 _____ 300 km
0 _____ 180 miles

ELEVATION

2000m
1000m
500m
200m
0

85°E

90°E

South India Highlights

South India welcomes travellers with golden-sand arms, and pulls them warmly into its lush hills and backwaters, bustling urban centres and glorious ancient ruins. What constitutes a highlight for you will depend on whether you prefer lounging languidly on a palm-fringed beach, admiring the intricate carvings of rock-hewn temples, strolling through quiet hill towns or absorbing the energy of manic Mumbai. Or perhaps, like us, you'll love it all. We asked our readers for their most memorable experiences, and this is what they told us.

ANDERS BLOMQVIST

1 KERALAN BACKWATERS

On a converted rice barge, step off the backpacker circuit into India's Garden of Eden (p346). Cruising this laid-backwater world of emerald green, you'll find your lost serenity and understand why it's called God's country.

Baxter Jackson, Traveller

MUMBAI MAMBO

Blaring horns, shimmering saris and spicy, smoky heat – Mumbai (p107) has it all. Welcoming the urbane tourist, the capital's five-star hotels sit cheek-by-jowl with tenement buildings festooned with laundry.

darapinke, Traveller

2

RICHARD I'ANSON

DREAMY PALOLEM

A beautiful palm-fringed curve of sand set between rocky headlands and lined with beach-front restaurants and beach huts. Palolem (p229) strikes the perfect balance between remoteness and comforts, providing you with all you need from a beach holiday, as well as great seafood and cocktails.

Karen Burrows, Traveller

3

ANDERS BLOMQVIST

MARK DAFF

4 HAMPI

The fascinating, far-flung ruins of Vijayanagar near the village of Hampi (p275) once comprised a city of half a million. They're set in a strange and sublime boulder-strewn landscape that resonates with a magical and irresistibly seductive air.

anpl, Traveller

CRAIG PERSHO

5 MYSORE PALACE

Mysore, city of sandalwood. And home to the imposing Mysore Palace (p250), with its red domes and set in a large expanse of garden. Designed to inspire awe at the wealth of the maharajas, this is just what it achieves. It's at its most dazzling when lit up at night, or at the Mysore Dasara festival. Wander through the rooms (including the Durbah Hall, Marriage Pavilion and of course residential areas, all with their intricate architecture, and providing a break from the outside heat) for a peek into the opulence of the past.

Jeanette Wall, Lonely Planet staff

PUDUCHERRY (PONDICHERRY)

In Puducherry (p420) it is all about sun-kissed beaches and French colonial architecture. People out here are blasphemously romantic. Just like the land, the faces know no frown. Peace peeps at you from the white uniform of the cops. Preserving in itself its history, Puducherry, in the true sense of the word, is a 'time-frozen' place. You always exit with a smile.

voltavoo, Traveller

V MUTHURAMAN

HILL TRAIN FROM OOTY TO METTUPALAYAM

This tiny, slow train (p470) stops at quaint old stations with names like Wellington and Lovedale, chugs through the scenic Ketti Valley and takes you down the hills through a whole series of micro-climates, from the cool air of the tea plantations to the humid jungles of the plains.

Kate James, Lonely Planet author

ANDERS BLOMQVIST

KANNUR, NORTHERN KERALA

The beaches here are all shady palm fringing, soft white sand, lovely little lagoons dotted with fishing boats, water at just the right temperature, village women doing something scenic in the distance…divine.

Trish Pinto, Traveller, Melbourne

9

8

FORT COCHIN

The home of the Portuguese, the Dutch and then the British for over 400 years, Fort Cochin (p361) has a rich and turbulent history, and you can see it everywhere – from the crumbling Catholic churches to the dusty laneways and white-washed colonial buildings. Take a stroll through the pock-marked streets and market stalls crammed inside ancient stone houses, before heading to the beach to watch the sun set over the black Chinese fishing nets that criss-cross the shoreline.

Karl Smith, Traveller

10

VENGURLA, KONKAN COAST, MAHARASHTRA

Silvery sand. Seagulls for company. Fishnets drying on the beach. Dhows bobbing on the surf. Seashells and mother-of-pearl. A little white-washed fort covered with orange-white-magenta bougainvillea creepers (p166).

soulcurry, Traveller

Contents

Destination South India

Like a giant wedge plunging into the Indian Ocean, peninsular South India is the steamy Hindu heartland of the subcontinent, and an infinitely different place from the landlocked mountains and sun-baked deserts of the north.

Thousands of kilometres of coastline frame fertile plains and curvaceous hills, all kept deliciously lush by the double-barrelled monsoon. This is the India for those seeking the happy-go-lucky beach life of Goa; the ancient Hindu temples of Tamil Nadu and Karnataka; the upbeat urban jungles of Mumbai (Bombay) and Bengaluru (Bangalore); the breezy palm-fringed backwaters of tropical Kerala; the dramatic trekking and wildlife-watching opportunities of the hills and plains; and the unfettered rural and tribal culture of Andhra Pradesh.

NATIONWIDE FAST FACTS

Population: 1.027 billion (2001 census)

Unemployment rate: 7.2% (2008)

Average annual income: US$977

Population growth rate: 1.6%

Literacy rate: 65.38% (2001 census)

Families living in one-room homes: 42%

India's percentage of world population: 16.9%

Average cost of a big-city wedding: US$12,500

Life expectancy: 66 years (women) and 63 years (men)

Proportion of females to males: 933:1000 (2001 census)

When it comes to ethnic groups, festivals, landscapes and traditions, South India is spectacularly diverse, presenting the traveller with a scintillating smorgasbord of things to see and do. And then of course there's the food, from traditional favourites such as podgy *idlis* (rice cakes) and crisp dosas (savoury creepes) to a gamut of global fare – from sushi to nachos – found in the south's bigger cities and tourist centres.

Once you touch down on subcontinental soil, you'll quickly discover that cricket – India's sporting obsession – is one of the most spirited topics of conversation, along with the latest shenanigans in the razzle-dazzle world of Bollywood. However, it is politics – whether at the national, state or village level – that consistently dominates news headlines, with middle- and upper-class India also keenly keeping their fingers on the pulse of international events. Indeed much of the current-affairs talk on the streets of South India mirrors that up north, with political directives made in Delhi percolating down south. Economic matters frequently feature high on regional and national political agendas. With one of the world's fastest-growing economies, India has certainly made colossal strides over the past decade. However, despite averaging an annual growth rate of around 9% in recent years, vast sections of the country's billion-plus population have seen little benefit from the economic boom. Indeed the government's ongoing challenge is to spread both the burden and bounty of India's fiscal prosperity. Not an easy task given that the gap between the haves and the have-nots is far from shrinking, and poverty (see p49) is set to spiral upwards if India's population rate continues to gallop beyond that of its economic growth.

For decades, overpopulation (see p50) has been at the core of many of the country's most pressing problems. Apart from the pressure that an expanding population is placing on India's already groaning infrastructure, analysts warn that it's just a matter of time before the mounting competition for resources ignites interminable communal conflict – not to mention bringing to cracking point an already overstretched healthcare system. Analysts also predict that as the population continues to climb, so too will the number of children from low-income households who drop-out of school in order to scrape together whatever they can to supplement meagre family earnings (see p46).

When it comes to the environment, climate change, deforestation, pollution, tourism-related development (especially in Goa; see the boxed text, p194) and ever-expanding industrialisation are just some of the key issues that both the central and South Indian state governments are grappling with – for further details, see p95.

The political challenges for India's government are no less daunting, especially in relation to ongoing communal friction, with the most incessant case being that between India and Pakistan over the disputed territory of Kashmir. Unresolved since the subcontinent's partition in 1947, the Kashmir impasse has been the catalyst for intensely rocky relations between the two countries ever since. While recent years have seen promising dialogue between Delhi and Islamabad, the November 2008 commando-style terrorist attacks in Mumbai swiftly saw hope turn to suspicion – see p40.

On a more optimistic note, South India has been going from strength to strength in terms of its IT industry, with southern cities such as Bengaluru, Mumbai, Pune, Hyderabad and Chennai attracting great international interest. The south's burgeoning IT industry has played a vital role in revolutionising India's once-ramshackle economy, with analysts forecasting an even rosier future in spite of the global economic slump (see the boxed text 'A Software Superpower', p50).

Meanwhile, on the tourism front, the good news for South India is that recent years have seen an upswing in the number of foreign tourists, which not only translates to a boost in revenue for southern state coffers, but also in increased employment and benefits to associated enterprises (particularly cottage industries), as well as preservation of cultural traditions such as dance and music. Government data indicates that India's foreign tourist arrivals in 2008 was 5.37 million – a 5.7% jump from the preceding year. One of the most lucrative growth sectors for South India is that of medical tourism (travel to India for competitively priced medical treatment), which has projected earnings of a staggering US$2 billion by 2012 (also read the box 'Medical Tourism – Would you like a transplant with that?' on p341). Wellness spas – which include post-operative Ayurvedic treatments and other internationally fashionable Indian therapies – are set to mushroom in southern centres, especially Kerala and Goa, as the medical tourism sector swells.

South India offers a delightfully mellow pace of travel, with most of its sites easily accessible and the beach never too far away. No matter where your wanderings take you, you'll soon discover that India is an invigorating assault on *all* the senses, an experience that's impossible to define because it's so incredibly different for everyone. Ultimately, it's all about taking a leap of faith and surrendering to the unknown: this is the India that nothing can ever prepare you for because its very essence – its elusive soul – lies cradled in its mystery.

Getting Started

Vibrant, inspiring, mystifying, confronting, thought-provoking and frustrating in equal measure, there's no doubt that India presents the traveller with a mind-bending array of experiences. But toss aside any stereotypes you may harbour, because the South is India's 'gentler' side, with far fewer touts and scam artists than the North, and plenty of blissful beaches to flee to whenever you need some sunny seaside therapy. If you haven't visited this part of the world before, set aside the first few days to simply acclimatise to the subcontinent's bamboozling symphony of sights, sounds, tastes and smells.

As South India spans a large area and has a wealth of natural and historic attractions, deciding where to go is likely to be one of your greatest challenges (for ideas, see Itineraries, p21). The key is to try not to squeeze in too much, as travelling often involves considerable distances and stamina. Remember to allow a few weeks of pre-trip preparation to sort out your visa and immunisations. Before arriving, devise a rough itinerary – you don't want to miss that spectacular festival by three days or plan to be relaxing on a Goan beach during the sweltering summer or soggy monsoon – but also factor in a certain amount of flexibility, as things don't always run like clockwork in India. Indeed, more than a few travellers have had their holidays marred by not being able to get their preferred train seats, or being delayed by rescheduled buses and the like. Another reason to introduce flexibility into your itinerary is because India has an uncanny way of presenting unexpected surprises and guiding you off the beaten track.

Finally, read up on India as much as you can prior to your trip, especially its cultural framework (also see The Culture, p44). Doing so will enhance

DON'T LEAVE HOME WITHOUT...

- Getting a visa (p513) and travel insurance (p501)
- Seeking advice about vaccinations (p535) and taking adequate stocks of prescription medication
- Nonrevealing clothes (women *and* men) – covering up will win you more respect and is essential when visiting sacred sites
- A well-concealed money belt (p498)
- Sunscreen lotion and sunglasses
- A small torch (flashlight) for poorly lit streets and power cuts
- Good-quality earplugs to block out night din and for long bus/train trips
- Flip-flops (thongs) for shared or grotty bathrooms
- A shower cap and universal sink plug (uncommon except at top-end hotels)
- Tampons – sanitary pads are widely available but tampons are usually restricted to big (or touristy) cities
- Mosquito repellent (a mosquito net can also come in handy)
- A water bottle – if you use water-purification tablets or filters you'll help in the anti-plastic crusade (see p540 for more information on drinking water)
- Sleeping-bag sheet – if you're unsure about hotel linen (especially at budget places) and for overnight train journeys
- Expecting the unexpected – India loves to toss up surprises

> **MONSOON**
>
> Kerala is the first place the southwest monsoon strikes, around early June, drenching the state as it sweeps in eastward from the Arabian Sea. As it rises over the Western Ghats, it cools and soaks the windward slopes before dropping over the leeward side, parts of which receive only about a quarter of the rainfall dumped on the windward side. Within about 10 days the monsoon has usually travelled as far as northern Maharashtra, and by early July it has covered most of the country. Karnataka's Western Ghats are among the wettest parts of South India.
>
> A second soaking occurs in Tamil Nadu and Kerala in November and early December when the retreating monsoon (commonly referred to as the northeast or winter monsoon) blusters in from the Bay of Bengal. The coasts of Andhra Pradesh and Tamil Nadu are occasionally hit by cyclones during these months.

your appreciation of the subcontinent's sights and traditions and will better equip you to hold more informed conversations with locals.

WHEN TO GO

Except in the elevated hills of the Western Ghats, South India is hot year-round and can be roughly divided into two main seasons – dry and wet (monsoon). There are two monsoon periods – the northeast and southwest monsoons – with dates varying slightly across the region. As the climate is tropical, you won't find the large variations in temperature found in northern India.

In general, late October to early March is the best time to visit South India. It's relatively dry and cool, although in November and the beginning of December parts of Tamil Nadu and Kerala get a drenching as the northeast monsoon retreats across them. In the beach resorts of Goa, some facilities (such as beach shacks) don't open until late October or November and, in the weeks immediately after the monsoon (ie in October), there may be strong rips, which can make swimming hazardous. Accommodation prices in popular tourist places, such as Goa, Kerala and the offshore islands, peak around Christmas and New Year.

See Climate Charts (p496) for more climate information.

Temperatures start to rise rapidly in most places in late March, and by May South India sizzles. The peak travel season in the mountains is April to June, where the altitude provides cool relief from the scorching plains. Conversely, the Western Ghats can get misty and quite cold in winter (late December and January), and the nights are often cold regardless of the time of year.

The climate in the Andaman and Nicobar Islands is tropical, with temperatures averaging 29°C, but this is moderated by sea breezes. The islands receive most rain during the southwest monsoon (May to September), and during the cyclonic storms in October and November. Lakshadweep has similar tropical weather.

Apart from the weather, the timing of certain festivals or special events may also influence when you wish to visit (see p19 and the 'Festivals In...' boxes in regional chapters).

COSTS & MONEY

South India pleases all pockets. Accommodation ranges from flimsy beachside shacks to swanky five-star hotels, with some charming midrange possibilities that won't break the bank. A multi-priced array of restaurants means you can eat to your heart's content without spending a fortune, and it's also possible to zip around economically thanks to a comprehensive public transport network.

As costs vary throughout South India, the best way of ascertaining how much money you'll need for your trip is to peruse the relevant regional chapters of this book. Be prepared to pay more in the larger cities such as

Mumbai (Bombay) and Bengaluru (Bangalore), as well as at popular tourist destinations during peak season.

In regard to sightseeing, foreigners are often charged more than Indian citizens for entry into tourist sites (admission prices for foreigners are sometimes given in US dollars, payable in the rupee equivalent), and there may also be additional charges for still/video cameras.

Accommodation is likely to be your biggest expense (see p491). Costs can vary depending on the season – high-season prices for hotels can be 50% (even higher) more, but usually only at popular tourist spots – and depend on whether you're travelling solo or with a group. High season is from around November to February in most regions, with a specific peak season of mid-December to early January in coastal resorts. High season in the mountains (such as at hill stations) is from around April to June. Accommodation rates can shoot up during festivals or other special events (see p494 for details). Given the vast differences across South India, it's misleading for us to pinpoint a definitive average accommodation price – see p493 for more information, as well as the regional chapters Sleeping sections. If you've got cash to splash, some of South India's top-end hotels are among the world's finest, but be prepared to fork out *at least* US$200 per night at the better properties before even getting a whiff of room service. Surf the web for possible internet discounts.

Dining out is, overall, top value, with budget restaurant meals for as little as Rs40 (even less at the more basic street eateries), and usually from around double that for a satiating midrange restaurant meal. At the more suave urban restaurants, main dishes generally hover between Rs150 and Rs350, to which you'll need to add the cost of side dishes, such as rice, and (usually) a tax of 10% to 12.5%. As with accommodation, meal prices vary regionally (for details see the Eating sections of individual chapters).

Regarding long-distance travel, there's a range of classes on trains and several bus types, resulting in considerable flexibility vis-à-vis comfort and price – regional chapters supply specific costs; also see p523. Domestic flights have become a lot more price competitive over recent years thanks to deregulation and good internet deals (see p523). Within towns there's economical public transport (see p526), or you may like to consider hiring a car with driver, which is surprisingly good value if there are several of you to split the cost (see p525).

HOW MUCH?

Sarong: from Rs75

Toothpaste (100g): Rs28

One dozen bananas: Rs25

Bellybutton bindi: from Rs15

Sandalwood incense (15 sticks): from Rs20

TRAVEL LITERATURE

Sacred Games, by Vikram Chandra, is a skilfully crafted and gripping thriller that takes the reader on an exhilarating journey through modern-day Mumbai's seedy underworld and beyond.

William Sutcliffe's *Are You Experienced?* is the humorous tale of first-time backpacker Dave, who accompanies his best friend's girlfriend to India in an attempt to seduce her.

SCINTILLATING SOUTH INDIA

South India has far more to offer than simply sightseeing:

- Activities that span blood-pumping walks to mind-soothing meditation (see p100)
- Courses, from classical dance to specialised yoga (see p495)
- Festivals that range from the wildly upbeat to the spiritually serene (see p19)
- Shopping, shopping and more shopping! (see p506)
- Volunteering, whether it's teaching at schools or caring for injured animals (see p514)

TOP **PICKS**

SOUTH INDIA

RIVETING READS

There's no dearth of novels offering brilliant insights into India – the titles below are just a tiny selection of our favourites. For additional recommended reading, see opposite, p60 and the boxed text on p114.

- *The White Tiger* by Aravind Adiga
- *The Inheritance of Loss* by Kiran Desai
- *Shantaram* by Gregory David Roberts
- *The God of Small Things* by Arundhati Roy
- *Midnight's Children* by Salman Rushdie

FANTASTICAL FESTIVALS

South India has a glorious mix of big and small festivals – for comprehensive details see p19 and the 'Festivals In…' boxed texts in regional chapters. The following is just a drop in the vast festival ocean.

- Nehru Trophy Snake Boat Race – August; Kerala (p323)
- Ganesh Chaturthi – August/September; especially in Mumbai (Bombay; p108) and Pune (p146)
- Diwali – October/November; nationwide (p20)
- Feast of St Francis Xavier – December; Old Goa (p189)
- Festival of Carnatic Music & Dance – December/January; Chennai (Madras; p389)

TEMPTING TRIPS

With South India's diverse range of dramatic landscapes and waterways, the memories you'll gather on the road will blaze bright in your mind long after your Indian sojourn wraps up. Here are some particularly unforgettable trips.

- Toy train to Ooty (Udhagamandalam; p470) – the miniature steam train to Ooty chugs past some truly jaw-dropping mountain scenery
- Backwater cruise from Alappuzha (Alleppey) to Kollam (Quilon); see 'The Backwaters boxed' text (p346) – cruising the lush Keralan backwaters is undeniably one of the star attractions of a trip to South India
- Mumbai to Goa by train (p141) – travel down the picturesque Konkan Coast on one of India's newest stretches of rail line
- Island-hopping in the Andamans (p479) – kick back on the ferry deck and hop from one sun-kissed island to another in the tropical Andamans
- Cycling in Goa – enjoy an unhurried bike ride from chirpy Panaji (Panjim; p191) to atmospheric Old Goa (p198)

Maximum City: Bombay Lost & Found, by Suketu Mehta, is an incisively researched and elegantly written epic, equal parts memoir, travelogue and journalism, which focuses on Mumbai – gang warfare, riots, Bollywood, bar girls and more.

Chasing the Monsoon, by Alexander Frater, is an Englishman's story of his monsoon-chasing journey from Kovalam (Kerala) to Meghalaya (in the northeast states). It perceptively captures the significance of the monsoon both on the land and for the people.

Christopher Kremmer's *Inhaling the Mahatma* reveals the Australian author's multifarious encounters with India – that include a hijacking, riots, and falling in love – during and beyond his stint as a Delhi-based foreign correspondent in the early 1990s.

Geoffrey Moorhouse's *Om: An Indian Pilgrimage* provides an erudite window into the lives of a diverse group of people in South India, from coir makers to holy men.

Indian Summer, by Will Randall, is the author's personal experience of unexpectedly finding himself in Pune teaching at a school for street kids, then suddenly fighting to save the school from being shut down.

Anita Desai's *Journey to Ithaca* is the tale of two young Europeans, Matteo and Sophie, who go to India seeking spiritual enlightenment. While Matteo's ashram experience is spiritually affirming, Sophie's isn't quite so rosy.

In *Divining the Deccan,* Bill Aitken rides through the little-visited centre of South India on a motorbike, painting a lively portrait of the region and including some enlightening historical and cultural details.

Hullabaloo in the Guava Orchard, by Kiran Desai, follows a bored post-office clerk and dreamer who retreats to the branches of a secluded guava tree in search of the contemplative life, only to be pursued by crowds of people seeking enlightenment.

INTERNET RESOURCES

Events in India (www.eventsinindia.com) A handy site covering current happenings in major Indian cities.

Incredible India (www.incredibleindia.org) The official Indian government tourism site.

IndiaMike (www.indiamike.com) A popular forum that is a great place to tap into India's traveller grapevine.

Lonely Planet (www.lonelyplanet.com) Useful links, including the popular Thorn Tree travel forum, where you can swap information with fellow travellers to South India and beyond.

South India (www.southindia.com) A South India–specific portal with links to everything from hospitals to state tourist sites.

South India Tourism (www.south-india-tourism.com) Proffers information about various facets of the South Indian tourism scene, from festivals and Ayurveda to temples and beaches.

World Newspapers (www.world-newspapers.com/india.html) Provides links to India's major English-language national and regional publications, enabling you to stay tuned to what's happening where.

Events Calendar

Most festivals in India follow the Indian or Tibetan lunar calendars, tied to the moon's cycle, or the (changeable) Islamic calendar. Consequently, exact dates vary from year to year (consult tourist offices). Those listed here represent major national festivals, arranged according to the Indian lunar calendar; for details of regional festivals, see the regional chapters 'Festivals in…' boxed texts.

CHAITRA (MARCH/APRIL)

MAHAVIR JAYANTI
Jain festival commemorating the birth of Mahavir, the founder of Jainism.

RAMANAVAMI
Hindus celebrate the birth of Rama with processions, music and feasting, and readings and enactments of scenes from the Ramayana.

EASTER
Christian holiday marking the Crucifixion and Resurrection of Jesus Christ.

VAISAKHA (APRIL/MAY)

BUDDHA JAYANTI
Celebrating Buddha's birth, enlightenment and attainment of nirvana (final release from the cycle of existence); this festival can fall in April, May or early June.

JYAISTHA (MAY/JUNE)

Only regional festivals currently fall in this period; see the regional chapters 'Festivals in…' boxed texts.

ASADHA (JUNE/JULY)

RATH YATRA (CAR FESTIVAL)
Effigies of Lord Jagannath (Vishnu as lord of the world) are hauled through cities on man-powered chariots, most famously in Puri (Orissa).

SRAVANA (JULY/AUGUST)

NAAG PANCHAMI
Hindu festival dedicated to Ananta, the serpent upon whose coils Vishnu rested between uni-

verses. Snakes are venerated as totems against monsoon flooding and other evils.

RAKSHA BANDHAN (NARIAL PURNIMA)
On the full moon, girls fix amulets known as *rakhis* to the wrists of brothers and close male friends to protect them in the coming year. Brothers reciprocate with gifts. Some people also worship the Vedic sea god Varuna.

RAMADAN (RAMAZAN)
Thirty days of dawn-to-dusk fasting mark the ninth month of the Islamic calendar, when the Quran was revealed to the Prophet Mohammed. It falls around 12 August 2010, 1 August 2011 and 20 July 2012.

BHADRA (AUGUST/SEPTEMBER)

INDEPENDENCE DAY   15 Aug
This public holiday marks the anniversary of India's Independence (from Britain) in 1947. Celebrations are a countrywide expression of patriotism.

DRUKPA TESHI
A Buddhist festival celebrating the first teaching given by Siddhartha Gautama.

GANESH CHATURTHI
Hindus celebrate the birth of the elephant-headed god, Ganesh, with verve, particularly in Mumbai (see p108). Clay idols of Ganesh are paraded through the streets before being ceremonially immersed in rivers, tanks (reservoirs) or the sea.

JANMASTAMI
Hindus celebrate Krishna's birthday, particularly at his birthplace, Mathura (Uttar Pradesh).

SHRAVAN PURNIMA
On this day of fasting, high-caste Hindus replace the sacred thread looped over their left shoulder.

PATETI
Parsis celebrate the Zoroastrian new year at this time, especially in Mumbai.

ASVINA (SEPTEMBER/OCTOBER)

NAVRATRI

This Hindu 'Festival of Nine Nights' leading up to Dussehra celebrates the goddess Durga in all her incarnations. Special folk dances are held, and the goddesses Lakshmi and Saraswati also receive special praise. Festivities are particularly vibrant in Gujarat and Maharashtra.

DUSSEHRA

A Vaishnavite festival, celebrating the victory of the Hindu god Rama over the demon-king Ravana and the triumph of good over evil. Dussehra is especially big in Mysore (see the boxed text, p252), where effigies of Ravana and his cohorts are ritually burned.

DURGA PUJA

The conquest of good over evil, with the goddess Durga's victory over buffalo-headed demon Mahishasura. Celebrations occur around Dussehra.

GANDHI JAYANTI 2 Oct

This public holiday is a solemn celebration of Mohandas Gandhi's birth, with prayer meetings at Gandhi's cremation site (Raj Ghat) in Delhi.

EID AL-FITR

Muslims celebrate the end of Ramadan with three days of festivities, starting 30 days after the start of the fast.

KARTIKA (OCTOBER/NOVEMBER)

DIWALI (DEEPAVAALI)

On the 15th day of Kartika, Hindus joyfully celebrate the 'festival of lights' for five days, giving gifts, lighting fireworks, and burning butter and oil lamps to lead Lord Rama home from exile.

GOVARDHANA PUJA

A Vaishnavite Hindu festival commemorating the lifting of Govardhan Hill by Krishna; celebrated by Krishna devotees around India.

EID AL-ADHA

Muslims commemorate Ibrahim's readiness to sacrifice his son to God. It falls around 16 November 2010, 6 November 2011 and 26 October 2012.

AGHAN (NOVEMBER/DECEMBER)

NANAK JAYANTI

The birthday of Guru Nanak, the founder of Sikhism, is celebrated with prayer readings and processions.

MUHARRAM

Shi'ia Muslims commemorate the martyrdom of the Prophet Mohammed's grandson Imam. It falls around 7 December 2010, 26 November 2011 and 15 November 2012.

PAUSA (DECEMBER/JANUARY)

CHRISTMAS DAY 25 Dec

Christians celebrate the birth of Jesus Christ.

MAGHA (JANUARY/FEBRUARY)

REPUBLIC DAY 26 Jan

This public holiday commemorates the founding of the Republic of India in 1950; the most spectacular celebrations are in Delhi, which holds a huge military parade along Rajpath and the Beating of the Retreat three days later.

PONGAL

A Tamil festival marking the end of the harvest season. Families in the south prepare pots of *pongal* (a mixture of rice, sugar, dhal and milk), symbolic of prosperity and abundance, then feed them to decorated and adorned cows.

VASANT PANCHAMI

Honouring Saraswati, the goddess of learning, Hindus dress in yellow and place books, musical instruments and other educational objects in front of idols of the goddess to receive her blessing.

LOSAR

Tibetan New Year – celebrated by tantric Buddhists all over India, particularly in Himachal Pradesh, Sikkim, Ladakh and Zanskar. Dates can vary from region to region.

PHALGUNA (FEBRUARY/MARCH)

EID-MILAD-UN-NABI

Islamic festival celebrating the birth of the Prophet Mohammed. It falls around 26 February 2010, 15 February 2011 and 4 February 2012.

HOLI

One of India's most ecstatic festivals; Hindus celebrate the beginning of spring by throwing coloured water and *gulal* (powder) at anyone within range. On the night before Holi, bonfires symbolise the demise of the evil demon Holika.

SHIVARATRI

This day of Hindu fasting recalls the *tandava* (cosmic victory dance) of Lord Shiva. Temple processions are followed by the chanting of mantras and anointing of linga (phallic images of Shiva).

Itineraries
CLASSIC ROUTES

SOUTH INDIA EXPRESS
Three to Eight Weeks/Mumbai to Chennai

Start in **Mumbai** (Bombay; p107), then head northeast to **Aurangabad** (p152) to visit the amazing rock-cut caves at **Ellora** (p157) and **Ajanta** (p160). Next, scuttle south to **Pune** (p173) to meditate and play 'zennis' (Zen tennis). It's a long but easy trip to **Bijapur** (p286), with the Golgumbaz (p287), then south to the former Vijayanagar capital of **Hampi** (p275). Continue on to **Bengaluru** (Bangalore; p236), India's IT powerhouse, detouring to the pilgrimage centre of **Sravanabelagola** (p261), and the temples of **Halebid** (p260) and **Belur** (p260). Next stop is the erstwhile maharaja's capital of **Mysore** (p249) and, for a change of pace, slide down the Western Ghats to **Ooty** (Udhagamandalam; p464), with a stop at **Mudumalai National Park** (p470). Take the toy train to Mettupalayam and west to **Kochi** (Cochin; p360). From here you can travel to the **Periyar Wildlife Sanctuary** (p352) to gawk at wild animals. It's a comfortable trip from here to **Madurai** (p445) and its remarkable Sri Meenakshi Temple. After soaking up Madurai's tremendous temples, hop on a train to **Chennai** (Madras; p391).

From Mumbai to Chennai, this route includes some of the best of South India's city life and temple towns, as well as trekking and wildlife. Three weeks will cover the main stops, but add a few more weeks to tackle the 3500km.

SAVOURING THE SOUTH

Two Months/Mumbai to Hyderabad

Mumbai (p107), the rambunctious capital of Maharashtra, is a splendid jumping-off point for exploration of India's steamy south. Make sure you time your trip to avoid the sticky monsoon – the sunniest skies are from around October to February. Don't forget to pack plenty of sunscreen!

Kick off in cosmopolitan Mumbai, the beating heart of star-studded Bollywood (p120), making the most of the fabulous shopping (p138), eating (p131) and drinking (p135) before heading northeast to **Ajanta** (p160) and **Ellora** (p157) to marvel at Maharashtra's finest cave art. Sashay southwest to **Goa** (p185) to simply flop on the soft sand and splash in the cool ocean at one of the state's palm-fringed beaches before dosing up on history inland at enigmatic **Hampi** (p275), with its temple ruins and giant boulders.

Next, hang out with yuppies at the hip party bars of **Bengaluru** (p245), then get giddy on the waft of incense in spicy **Mysore** (p249) with its opulent Maharaja's Palace (p250). Tuck into a wholesome banana-leaf thali (p255), before cruising south to tropical Kerala, stopping at historical **Kochi** (Cochin; p360) to enjoy a traditional performance of Kathakali (p371). Cruise Kerala's languorous backwaters from **Alappuzha** (Alleppey; p343), before dipping your toes in the warm waters around **Varkala** (p336).

For a change of tempo, go northeast from Varkala to **Periyar Wildlife Sanctuary** (p352) to spot wild elephants before boggling at the awe-inspiring temples of **Madurai** (p445). Pop into **Trichy** (Tiruchirappalli; p438) and **Thanjavur** (Tanjore; p434) before slowing down in French-flavoured **Puducherry** (Pondicherry; p420), a cheerful coastal town where you can toss up between curries or crepes. Feast on more fine food in Tamil Nadu's chaotic capital, **Chennai** (p401), then flee north to admire intriguing Mughal-era relics in **Hyderabad** (p295).

A slice of the steamy south, this itinerary visits blissful beaches, intriguing cave temples, lush jungle reserves, a maharaja's palace and some of South India's most scintillating cities. Add on a couple of weeks if you prefer to savour the experience more slowly.

SAND, SEA & SACRED SITES   Two to Three Months/Mumbai to Chennai

This itinerary, beginning in **Mumbai** (p107) and ending in **Chennai** (p391), blends some of the south's most sublime temples with its most breathtaking beaches. If you're keen to beach it up to the max, consider tagging the sunwashed **Andaman Islands** (p472) onto the end of this itinerary.

Start at Mumbai's Chowpatty Beach (p119), overlooking the vast Arabian Sea, with a plate of delicious *bhelpuri* (p85). Take a cruise to the magnificent rock-cut temples on **Elephanta Island** (p143), then travel south by train to beach-blessed **Goa** (p185). Whether you're seeking something mellow or something party-charged, this beach-bursting state has something to suit everyone; old favourites include Arambol (Harmal; p220), Vagator (p217) and around Palolem (p229). Continue to the sacred seaside town of **Gokarna** (p272), with its more hushed appeal than touristy Goa. Next, veer inland to the ruined Vijayanagar temples at **Hampi** (p275), with its peculiar boulder-strewn landscape, and the Hoysala temples of **Belur and Halebid** (p260).

Connect through the coastal towns of **Mangalore** (p267) and **Kochi** (Cochin; p360) to Kerala's palm-packed seaside strip and indulge in some serious beach therapy in **Varkala** (p336) and **Kovalam** (p331), before taking the train northeast to the awesome Sri Meenakshi Temple in **Madurai** (p446). Continue north through the historic temple towns of **Trichy** (p438), **Thanjavur** (p434) and **Chidambaram** (p428), breaking the journey at pretty **Puducherry** (p420) where you can pick up lovely handmade paper (p427) for friends back home.

Continuing north, detour inland to the captivating **Arunachaleswar Temple** (p418) in Tiruvannamalai, and follow the coast to carving-covered **Mamallapuram** (Mahabalipuram; p407), home to the ancient Shore Temple (p408). Conclude your southern sojourn with a stroll along Chennai's **Marina Beach** (p397).

Kicking off in Mumbai and winding up in Chennai, this route brings together the best of South India's beaches and temples – you'll feel chilled out and spiritually charged at the same time! Treat yourself to an additional month to really squeeze the most out of this trip.

ROADS LESS TRAVELLED

HILL HAPPY   Three to Six Weeks/Mumbai to Periyar Wildlife Sanctuary

A great way to avoid the tourist treadmill is to ditch the coastal towns and go trekking in the beautiful national parks and hills of the Western Ghats.

From Mumbai take the toy train up to **Matheran** (p168), an appealing hilltop retreat with tranquil walks and panoramic lookouts. Head back down via Lonavla and Pune before winding your way back up into the hills to **Mahabaleshwar** (p180), a hill station popular with families and famous for its berry farms. From here it's a bit of a trek south to **Madikeri** (Mercara; p263) in the Kodagu (Coorg) hills, but worth it for the rewarding trekking and fragrant coffee plantations. Journey east to Mysore, and head back up into the hills again. Four adjoining national parks – **Mudumalai National Park** (p470) in Tamil Nadu, **Bandipur National Park** (p262) and **Nagarhole National Park** (p262) in Karnataka and **Wayanad National Park** (p380) in Kerala – form the Nilgiri Biosphere Reserve, and together they offer some of the most phenomenal wildlife viewing, trekking and jungle camps in South India. From Mudumalai it's an enjoyable trip to **Ooty** (p464), a sprawling Raj-era hill station set amid forested hills. If you still haven't had your fill of hiking and hill stations, head south from Coimbatore through the Palani Hills to **Kodaikanal** (Kodai; p456), a quainter and quieter town than Ooty. From Kodaikanal you can take a Kochi-bound bus to **Munnar** (p355), which boasts the world's highest tea plantations as well as dramatic mountain scenery. Another 70km south of here is the **Periyar Wildlife Sanctuary** (p352), a marvellous place for wildlife watching, jungle treks and lake cruises.

Verdant national parks, pretty forests and cool hill stations make a welcome change from the coast and plains. This 1500km route whisks you through impressive hill stations and wildlife-watching areas. You could wrap the trip up in just three weeks, but an extra week will give you more breathing space.

THE WORLD HERITAGE WHIRL   Four to Six Weeks/Mumbai to Thanjavur

India has close to 30 World Heritage Sites, with those in the south mostly being ancient monuments or temples.

In Mumbai, one of the newest additions to the list is the **Chhatrapati Shivaji Terminus** (p117) – better known as Victoria Terminus – the main train station, and its riotous blend of Gothic architecture makes this one of the most original train stations on the planet. **Elephanta Island** (p143), just out of Mumbai, sports rock-cut cave temples dedicated to Lord Shiva. The finest historical attractions in Maharashtra are undeniably the rock-cut cave temples at **Ellora** (p157), which were created over a period of five centuries by Buddhist, Hindu and Jain monks, and the caves and Buddhist frescoes at **Ajanta** (p160), which predate those of Ellora.

Meanwhile, the churches and convents of Goa's former capital, **Old Goa** (p198) are among India's most striking and should not be missed. They include the Basilica of Bom Jesus (p199), Sé Cathedral (Sé de Santa Catarina; p199) and the Church of St Francis of Assisi (p199). **Hampi** (p275) is a favourite as much for its atmosphere as for its eye-catching temples harking back to the Vijayanagar empire. Just north, the temples of **Pattadakal** (p286) may be less well known, but the Virupaksha Temple, with its beautifully carved columns depicting scenes from the great Hindu epics, is still worth a peek. At **Mamallapuram** (p407), the Shore Temple (p408) and Five Rathas (p408) are among a large group of monuments from the Pallava dynasty, while at **Thanjavur** (p434), the Brihadishwara Temple (p434) is the crowning glory.

India's southern World Heritage Sites include exquisite rock-cut caves, atmospheric churches, ancient temples and even a city railway station. You could manage the trip in a month, but a couple of extra weeks will make the experience more rewarding.

ISLAND MAGIC   Two to Four Weeks

If you're hankering for near-deserted beaches, snorkelling and diving, the Andamans are hard to beat. The island chain, 1000km east of the mainland in the Bay of Bengal, can be reached by boat or air from Chennai or Kolkata (Calcutta). From Chennai, you'll arrive by air or sea into the capital, **Port Blair** (p480), a busy town with little tropical allure but some commendable museums and legacies of the island's colonial past. After a visit to Port Blair's Cellular Jail National Memorial (p480) and **Ross Island** (p485), book a ferry to **Havelock Island** (p486), where you can indulge in scuba diving, snorkelling and fishing. For something quieter, stay on nearby **Neil Island** (p488). From Havelock there are ferries to **Rangat** (p489), with a possible stop at **Long Island** (p475). From Rangat a bus runs up through Middle Andaman to **Mayabunder** (p489), where you can take a boat to tiny **Avis Island** (p489). From Mayabunder, travel overland to **Diglipur** (p489) on North Andaman (or take an overnight ferry from Port Blair to Diglipur), a remote area where you can climb Saddle Peak or laze on placid beaches.

Back in Port Blair, hire a moped or catch a bus and head down to **Wandoor** (p485), the jumping-off point for the **Mahatma Gandhi Marine National Park** (p485) and Jolly Buoy and Red Skin Islands.

Travel in the beautiful Andaman Islands is a trip unto itself, with shimmering beaches, sun-warmed waters and enticing snorkelling and diving. This route covers about 800km to 1000km of land and ferry travel. You'll need a minimum of two weeks; standard permit restrictions limit you to 30 days.

TAILORED TRIPS

TEMPLES & PILGRIMAGES

If there's one thing that is bound to have a lingering impact on you during and after your South Indian wanderings, it's spirituality. To bask in South India's spiritual splendour, consider this itinerary, which follows in the footsteps of countless pilgrims and spiritual seekers. There's a particularly well-worn pilgrimage route through Tamil Nadu, which includes the temple towns of **Kanchipuram** (Kanchi; p414); **Tiruvannamalai** (p418); **Chidambaram** (p428); **Kumbakonam** (p431)); **Thanjavur** (p434); **Trichy** (p438), with the Rock Fort Temple and Sri Ranganathaswamy Temple; **Madurai** (p445) for the renowned Sri Meenakshi Temple; **Rameswaram** (p443), one of the holiest Hindu pilgrimage places in India; and **Kanyakumari** (Cape Comorin; p451), where pilgrims flock to the Kumari Amman Temple and to see the sun rise and set at the southernmost tip of India.

Over in Andhra Pradesh, the Venkateshwara Temple at **Tirumala** (p318) receives as many as 100,000 pilgrims *per day*! In Karnataka, **Sravanabelagola** (p261) is an auspicious pilgrimage centre for Jains who come to honour the statue of Gomateshvara. **Gokarna** (p272), apart from being a beach paradise, is one of South India's most sacred sites for Shaivites who gather to worship at the Mahabaleshwara Temple. Meanwhile, **Nasik** (p148) is Maharashtra's holiest pilgrimage town and host (every 12 years) to the illustrious Kumbh Mela (p54).

ASHRAM HOPPING

If you're seeking spiritual sustenance, South India has more than enough to keep you in deep contemplation for at least one lifetime. To get an insight into ashrams (spiritual retreats) see p106.

In Pune, the **Osho Meditation Resort** (p173) is the ashram of the late Bhagwan Rajneesh, which has long attracted travellers from around the globe. Serious devotees of Buddhist meditation should head for the **Vipassana International Academy** (p151) in Igatpuri. At Sevagram is the peaceful **Sevagram Ashram** (p165), established by Mahatma Gandhi in 1933.

At Puttaparthi, **Prasanthi Nilayam** (p320) is the ashram of Sri Sathya Sai Baba, while in Tiruvannamalai, the **Sri Ramana Ashram** (p419) draws devotees of Sri Ramana Maharshi. Puducherry is well known for the **Sri Aurobindo Ashram** (p421), established by a French woman known as 'the Mother'. Just outside Puducherry is **Auroville** (p428), the ashram offshoot that has developed into a large international community. The **Isha Yoga Center** (p463) in Poondi, is a little-known ashram, yoga retreat and place of pilgrimage. On the tropical Keralan backwaters near Kollam (Quilon) is the **Matha Amrithanandamayi Mission** (p346), the ashram of Matha Amrithanandamayi, known as the 'Hugging Mother' because of the *darshan* (blessing) she practices, often happily hugging thousands in a session.

CHASING THE FESTIVALS

The fantastical explosion of colour and sheer exuberance of Indian festivals make for a truly unforgettable experience – the trick is to be in the right place at the right time (see also p19).

Ganesh Chaturthi (August/September; p108) is celebrated all over South India, but is best experienced in Mumbai and Pune when these cities really burst to life. The **Ellora Dance & Music Festival** (March; p146) is a cultural event set against the stunning backdrop of the Kailasa Temple. Goa turns it on with India's most memorable Christian festivals, the biggest being the **Feast of St Francis Xavier** (3 December; p189) in Old Goa.

In Karnataka, one of the greatest **Dussehra** (September/October; p236) festivals takes place in Mysore. **Vasantahabba** (February; p236) showcases traditional and contemporary Indian dance and music. **Thrissur Pooram** (April; p323) offers spectacular elephant processions, while Alappuzha (Alleppey) hosts the inimitable **Nehru Trophy Snake Boat Race** (August; p323). The **Mamallapuram Dance Festival** (December/January; p389) is a splendid cultural event, as is the **International Yoga Festival** (January; p389) in Puducherry. The holy nine-day **Brahmotsavam** (September/October; p295) is held at Tirumala, while in Hyderabad, the **Deccan Festival** (February; p295) pays tribute to Deccan culture and includes traditional music and dance.

BLISSFUL BEACHES & BACKWATERS

Sun-worshippers will adore South India's gorgeous west-coast beaches, which have been luring travellers for decades. Throw in the postcard-perfect Keralan backwaters and you have the ultimate tropical-holiday package.

Begin with a bang in manic **Mumbai** (p107), soaking up the carnival atmosphere of Chowpatty Beach, before making your escape to India's favourite beach state, Goa. After visiting its capital **Panaji** (Panjim; p191) and the ruined former Portuguese capital of **Old Goa** (p198), select a beach that tickles your fancy for immediate sun and sand therapy. Hit the rails southwards and get off at Karwar for **Gokarna** (p272), a dusty pilgrimage town leading to a string of reasonably secluded beaches popular with the chillum-puffing crowd. If

you're visiting during the monsoon, a worthwhile detour from here is to **Jog Falls** (p271), India's highest waterfalls. Leaving Karnataka you enter the slender coastal state of Kerala. Pass through **Kozhikode** (Calicut; p378) and your next stop is the delightful island stronghold of Kochi's **Fort Cochin** (p361), reached from mainland Ernakulam. From there, head to **Alappuzha** (Alleppey; p343) for a serene houseboat journey through the dazzling backwaters of Kerala (p346). A short trip south, **Varkala** (p336) offers dramatic cliffs and beaches. Your final stop is near the southernmost tip of India: **Kovalam** (p331) is blessed with a small sweep of crescent beaches offering the perfect place to let your hair down.

History

South India has always laid claim to its own unique history, largely resulting from its insulation by distance from the political developments up north. Southern India, the cradle of Dravidian culture, has a long and colourful historical tapestry of wrangling dynasties and empires, interwoven with the influx of traders and conquerors arriving by sea. Evidence of human habitation in Southern India dates back to the Stone Age; discoveries include hand-axes in Tamil Nadu and a worn limestone statue of a goddess, believed to be between 15,000 and 25,000 years old, from an excavation in the Vindhya Range.

India's first major civilisation flourished around 2500 BC in the Indus river valley, much of which lies within present-day Pakistan. This civilisation, which continued for a thousand years and is known as the Harappan culture, appears to have been the culmination of thousands of years of settlement. The Harappan civilisation fell into decline from the beginning of the 2nd millennium BC. Some historians attribute the end of the empire to floods or decreased rainfall, which threatened the Harappans' agricultural base. The more enduring, if contentious, theory is that an Aryan invasion put paid to the Harappans, despite little archaeological proof or written reports in the ancient Indian texts to that effect. As a result, some nationalist historians argue that the Aryans (from a Sanskrit word meaning 'noble') were in fact the original inhabitants of India and that the invasion theory was invented by self-serving foreign conquerors. Others say that the arrival of the Aryans was more of a gentle migration that gradually subsumed Harappan culture, rather than an invasion. Those who defend the invasion theory believe that from around 1500 BC Aryan tribes from Afghanistan and Central Asia began to filter into northwest India. Despite their military superiority, their progress was gradual, with successive tribes battling over territory and new arrivals pushing further east into the Ganges plain. Eventually these tribes controlled northern India as far as the Vindhya Range. As a consequence, many of the original inhabitants, the Dravidians, were forced south.

India: A History by John Keay is an astute and readable account of subcontinental history spanning from the Harappan civilisation to Indian Independence.

INFLUENCES FROM THE NORTH

While the Indus Valley civilisation may not have affected South India, the same cannot be said for the Aryan invasion. The Aryanisation of the south was a slow process, but it had a profound effect on the social order of the region and the ethos of its inhabitants. The northerners brought their literature (the four Vedas – a collection of sacred Hindu hymns), their gods (Agni, Varuna, Shiva and Vishnu), their language (Sanskrit) and a social structure that organised people into castes, with Brahmins at the top (see p45).

To learn more about the ancient Indus Valley civilisations, ramble around Harappa (www.harappa .com), which presents an illustrated yet scholarly overview.

TIMELINE

2600–1700 BC	1500 BC	1000 BC
The heyday of the Indus Valley civilisation. Spanning parts of Rajasthan, Gujarat and the Sindh province in present-day Pakistan, the settlement takes shape around metropolises such as Harappa and Moenjodaro.	The Indo-Aryan civilisation takes root in the fertile plains of the Indo-Gangetic basin. The settlers here speak an early form of Sanskrit, from which several Indian vernaculars, including Hindi, later evolve.	Indraprastha, Delhi's first incarnation, comes into being. Archaeological excavations at the site, where the Purana Qila now stands, continue even today, as more facts about this ancient capital keep emerging.

Over the centuries other influences flowed from the north, including Buddhism and Jainism (see p51). Sravanabelagola (p261) in Karnataka, an auspicious place of pilgrimage to this day, is where over 2000 years ago the northern ruler Chandragupta Maurya, who had embraced Jainism and renounced his kingdom, arrived with his guru. Jainism was then adopted by the trading community (its tenet of ahimsa, or nonviolence, precluded occupations tainted by the taking of life), who spread it through South India.

Emperor Ashoka, a successor of Chandragupta who ruled for 40 years from about 272 BC, was a major force behind Buddhism's inroads into the south. Once a campaigning king, his epiphany came in 260 BC when, overcome by the horrific carnage and suffering caused by his campaign against the Kalingas (a powerful kingdom), he renounced violence and embraced Buddhism. He sent Buddhist missionaries far and wide, and his edicts (carved into rock and incised into specially erected pillars) have been found in Andhra Pradesh and Karnataka. Stupas were also built in Southern India under Ashoka's patronage, mostly along the coast of Andhra Pradesh (see the boxed text, p311), although at least one was constructed as far south as Kanchipuram in Tamil Nadu.

The appeal of Jainism and Buddhism, which arose at about the same time, was that they rejected the Vedas and condemned the caste system. Buddhism, however, gradually lost favour with its devotees, and was replaced with a new brand of Hinduism, which emphasised devotion to a personal god. This bhakti (surrendering to the gods) order developed in Southern India around AD 500. Bhakti adherents opposed Jainism and Buddhism, and the movement hastened the decline of both in South India.

MAURYAN EMPIRE & SOUTHERN KINGDOMS

Chandragupta Maurya was the first of a line of Mauryan kings to rule what was effectively the first Indian empire. The empire's capital was in present-day Patna in Bihar. Chandragupta's son, Bindusara, who came to the throne around 300 BC, extended the empire as far as Karnataka. However, he seems to have stopped there, possibly because the Mauryan empire was on cordial terms with the southern chieftains of the day.

The identity and customs of these chiefdoms have been gleaned from various sources, including archaeological remains and ancient Tamil literature. These literary records describe a land known as the 'abode of the Tamils', within which resided three major ruling families: the Pandyas (Madurai), the Cheras (Malabar Coast) and the Cholas (Thanjavur and the Cauvery Valley). The region described in classical Sangam literature (written between 300 BC and AD 200) was still relatively insulated from Sanskrit culture, but from 200 BC this was starting to change.

A degree of rivalry characterised relations between the main chiefdoms and the numerous minor chiefdoms, and there were occasional clashes

563–483 BC	326 BC	321–185 BC
The lifespan of Siddhartha Gautama – the founder of Buddhism – who attained enlightenment beneath a bodhi tree in Bodhgaya (Bihar), thereby transforming into the Buddha (Awakened One).	Alexander the Great invades India. He defeats King Porus in Punjab to enter the subcontinent, but a rebellion within his army keeps him from advancing beyond the Beas River in Himachal Pradesh.	India comes under the rule of the Maurya kings. Founded by Chandragupta Maurya, this Pan-Indian empire is ruled from Pataliputra (present-day Patna), and briefly adopts Buddhism during the reign of Emperor Ashoka.

with Sri Lankan rulers. Sangam literature indicates that Sanskrit traditions from the old Aryan kingdoms of the north were taking root in South India around 200 BC. Ultimately, the southern powers all suffered at the hands of the Kalabhras, about whom little is known except that they appeared to have originated from somewhere north of the Tamil region.

By around 180 BC the Mauryan empire, which had started to disintegrate soon after the death of Emperor Ashoka in 232 BC, had been overtaken by a series of rival kingdoms that were subjected to repeated invasions from northerners such as the Bactrian Greeks. Despite this apparent instability, the post-Ashokan era produced at least one line of royalty whose patronage of the arts and ability to maintain a relatively high degree of social cohesion have left an enduring legacy. This was the Satavahanas, who eventually controlled all of Maharashtra, Madhya Pradesh, Chhattisgarh, Karnataka and Andhra Pradesh. Under their rule, between 200 BC and AD 200, the arts blossomed, especially literature, sculpture and philosophy. Buddhism reached a peak in Maharashtra under the Satavahanas, although the greatest of the Buddhist cave temples at Ajanta (p160) and Ellora (p157) were built later by the Chalukya and Rashtrakuta dynasties.

Most of all, the subcontinent enjoyed a period of considerable prosperity. South India may have lacked vast and fertile agricultural plains on the scale of North India, but it compensated by building strategic trade links via the Indian Ocean.

> Emperor Ashoka's ability to rule over his empire was assisted by a standing army consisting of roughly 9000 elephants, 30,000 cavalry and 600,000 infantry.

THE FALL & RISE OF THE CHOLA EMPIRE

After the Kalabhras suppressed the Tamil chiefdoms, South India split into numerous warring kingdoms. The Cholas virtually disappeared and the Cheras on the west coast appear to have prospered through trading, although little is known about them. It wasn't until the late 6th century AD, when the Kalabhras were overthrown, that the political uncertainty in the region ceased. For the next 300 years the history of South India was dominated by the fortunes of the Chalukyas of Badami, the Pallavas of Kanchi (Kanchipuram; p414) and the Pandyas of Madurai (p445).

> The concepts of zero and infinity are widely believed to have been devised by eminent Indian mathematicians during the reign of the Guptas.

The Chalukyas were a far-flung family. In addition to their base in Badami, they established themselves in Bijapur, Andhra Pradesh and near the Godavari Delta. The Godavari branch of the family is commonly referred to as the Eastern Chalukyas of Vengi. It's unclear from where the Pallavas originated, but it's thought they may have emigrated to Kanchi from Andhra Pradesh. After their successful rout of the Kalabhras, the Pallavas extended their territory as far south as the Cauvery River, and by the 7th century were at the height of their power, building monuments such as the Shore Temple (p408) and Arjuna's Penance (p410) at Mamallapuram (Mahabalipuram). They engaged in long-running clashes with the Pandyas, who, in the 8th century, allied themselves with the Gangas of Mysore. This, combined with pressure

AD 319–510	610	850
The golden era of the Gupta dynasty, the second of India's great empires after the Mauryas. This era is marked by a creative surge in literature and the arts.	Prophet Mohammed establishes Islam. He soon invites the people of Mecca to adopt the new religion under the command of God, and his call is met with eager response.	The Chola empire comes to power in South India, establishing itself as an especially formidable economic and military presence in Asia under the rule of Rajaraja Chola I and his son Rajendra Chola I.

from the Rashtrakutas (who were challenging the Eastern Chalukyas), had by the 9th century snuffed out any significant Pallava power in the south.

At the same time as the Pallava dynasty came to an end, a new Chola dynasty was establishing itself and laying the foundations for what was to become one of the most significant empires on the subcontinent. From their base at Thanjavur (Tanjore), the Cholas spread north absorbing what was left of the Pallavas' territory, and made inroads into the south. But it wasn't until Rajaraja Chola I (r 985–1014) ascended the throne that the Chola kingdom really started to emerge as a great empire. Rajaraja Chola I successfully waged war against the Pandyas in the south, the Gangas of Mysore and the Eastern Chalukyas. He also launched a series of naval campaigns that resulted in the capture of the Maldives, the Malabar Coast and northern Sri Lanka, which became a province of the Chola empire. These conquests gave the Cholas control over critical ports and trading links between India, Southeast Asia, Arabia and East Africa. They were therefore in a position to grab a share of the huge profits involved in selling spices to Europe.

Rajaraja Chola's son, Rajendra Chola I (r 1014–44), continued to expand the Chola's territory, conquering the remainder of Sri Lanka, and campaigning up the east coast as far as Bengal and the Ganges River. Rajendra also launched a campaign in Southeast Asia against the Srivijaya kingdom (Sumatra), reinstating trade links that had been interrupted and sending trade missions as far as China. In addition to both its political and economic superiority, the Chola empire produced a brilliant legacy in the arts. Sculpture, most notably bronze sculpture (see p65), reached astonishing new heights of aesthetic and technical refinement.

Music, dance and literature flourished and developed a distinctly Tamil flavour, enduring in South India long after the Cholas had faded from the picture. Trade wasn't the only thing the Cholas brought to the shores of Southeast Asia; they also introduced their culture. That legacy lives on in Myanmar (Burma), Thailand, Bali (Indonesia) and Cambodia in dance, religion and mythology.

But the Cholas, eventually weakened by constant campaigning, succumbed to expansionist pressure from the Hoysalas of Halebid (p260) and the Pandyas of Madurai, and by the 13th century were finally supplanted by the Pandyas. The Hoysalas were themselves eclipsed by the Vijayanagar empire, which arose in the 14th century. The Pandyas prospered and their achievements were much admired by Marco Polo when he visited in 1288 and 1293. But their glory was short-lived, as they were unable to fend off the Muslim invasion from the north.

MUSLIM INVASION & THE VIJAYANAGAR EMPIRE

The Muslim rulers in Delhi campaigned in Southern India from 1296, rebuking a series of local rulers, including the Hoysalas and Pandyas, and by 1323 had reached Madurai.

South Indian Customs, by PV Jagadisa Ayyar, explores a range of traditional practices, from the smearing of cow dung outside homes to the formation of snake images beneath banyan trees.

Tamil Nation (www.tamil nation.org) proffers all sorts of information about Tamil culture and heritage.

1336	1498	1510
Foundation of the mighty Vijayanagar empire, named after its capital city, the ruins of which can be seen today in the vicinity of Hampi (in modern-day Karnataka).	Vasco da Gama, a Portuguese voyager, discovers the sea route from Europe to India. He arrives in (present-day) Kerala and engages in trade with the local nobility.	Sultan Adil Shah of Bijapur thwarts Portuguese attempts to take over Goa. However, a few months after Shah's death, Portuguese forces successfully capture the region under the command of Alfonso de Albuquerque.

Mohammed Tughlaq, the sultan of Delhi, dreamed of conquering the whole of India, something not even Emperor Ashoka had managed. He rebuilt the fort of Daulatabad (p156) in Maharashtra to keep control of Southern India, but eventually his ambition led him to overreach his forces. In 1334 he had to recall his army in order to quash rebellions elsewhere and, as a result, local Muslim rulers in Madurai and Daulatabad declared their independence.

At the same time, the foundations of what was to become one of South India's greatest empires, Vijayanagar, were being laid by Hindu chiefs at Hampi.

The Vijayanagar empire is generally said to have been founded by two chieftain brothers who, having been captured and taken to Delhi, converted to Islam and were sent back south to serve as governors for the sultanate. The brothers, however, had other ideas; they reconverted to Hinduism and around 1336 set about establishing a kingdom that was eventually to encompass southern Karnataka, Tamil Nadu and part of Kerala. Seven centuries later, the centre of this kingdom – the ruins and temples of Hampi (p275) – is now one of South India's biggest tourist drawcards.

The Bahmanis, who were initially from Daulatabad, established their capital at Gulbarga in Karnataka, relocating to Bidar in the 15th century. Their kingdom eventually included Maharashtra and parts of northern Karnataka and Andhra Pradesh – and they took pains to protect it.

Not unnaturally, ongoing rivalry characterised the relationship between the Vijayanagar and Bahmani empires until the 16th century when both went into decline. The Bahmani empire was torn apart by factional fighting and Vijayanagar's vibrant capital of Hampi was laid to waste in a six-month sacking by the combined forces of the Islamic sultanates of Bidar, Bijapur, Berar, Ahmednagar and Golconda. Much of the conflict centred on control of fertile agricultural land and trading ports; at one stage the Bahmanis wrested control of the important port of Goa from their rivals (although in 1378 the Vijayanagars seized it back).

The Vijayanagar empire is notable for its prosperity, which was the result of a deliberate policy giving every encouragement to traders from afar, combined with the development of an efficient administrative system and access to important trading links, including west-coast ports. Hampi became quite cosmopolitan, with people from various parts of India as well as from abroad mingling in the bazaars.

Portuguese chronicler Domingo Paez arrived in Vijayanagar during the reign of one of its greatest kings, Krishnadevaraya (r 1509–29). During his rule Vijayanagar enjoyed a period of unparalleled prosperity and power.

Paez recorded the achievements of the Vijayanagars and described how they had constructed large water tanks and irrigated their fields. He also described how human and animal sacrifices were carried out to propitiate the gods after one of the water tanks had burst repeatedly. He included

History and Society in South India, by Noboru Karashima, is an academic compilation focusing on the development of South Indian society during the Chola dynasty and the rule of the Vijayanagars.

A History of South India from Prehistoric Times to the Fall of Vijayanagar by KA Nilakanta Sastri, is arguably the most thorough history of this region; especially recommended if you're heading for Hampi.

A History of India by Romila Thapar (Volume One) and Percival Spear (Volume Two) is one of the more thorough introductions to Indian history, from 1000 BC to Independent India.

1526	**1600**	**1674**
Babur becomes the first Mughal emperor after conquering Delhi. He stuns Rajasthan by routing its confederate force, gaining a technological edge on the battlefield thanks to the early introduction of matchlock muskets in his army.	Britain's Queen Elizabeth I grants the first trading charter to the British East India Company on 31 December 1600, with the maiden voyage taking place in 1601 under the command of Sir James Lancaster.	Shivaji establishes the Maratha kingdom, spanning western India and parts of the Deccan and north India. He assumes the supercilious title of Chhatrapati, which means 'Lord of the Universe'.

ENTER THE PORTUGUESE

By the time Krishnadevaraya ascended to the throne, the Portuguese were well on the way to establishing a firm foothold in Goa. It was only a few years since they had become the first Europeans to sail across the Indian Ocean from the east coast of Africa to India's shores.

On 20 May 1498 Vasco da Gama dropped anchor off the South Indian coast near the town of Calicut (now Kozhikode; p378). It had taken him 23 days to sail from the east coast of Africa, guided by a pilot named Ibn Masjid, sent by the ruler of Malindi in Gujarat.

The Portuguese sought a sea route between Europe and the East so they could trade directly in spices. They also hoped they might find Christians cut off from Europe by the Muslim dominance of the Middle East. The Portuguese were also searching for the legendary kingdom of Prester John, a powerful Christian ruler with whom they could unite against the Muslim rulers of the Middle East. However, in India they found spices and the Syrian Orthodox community, but not Prester John.

Vasco da Gama sought an audience with the ruler of Calicut, to explain himself, and seems to have been well received. The Portuguese engaged in a limited amount of trading, but became increasingly suspicious that Muslim traders were turning the ruler of Calicut against them. They resolved to leave Calicut, which they did in August 1498.

detail about the fine houses that belonged to wealthy merchants, and the bazaars full of precious stones (rubies, diamonds, emeralds, pearls), textiles, including silk, 'and every other sort of thing there is on earth and that you may wish to buy'.

Like the Bahmanis, the Vijayanagar kings invested heavily in protecting their territory and trading links. Krishnadevaraya employed Portuguese and Muslim mercenaries to guard the forts and protect his domains. He also fostered good relations with the Portuguese, upon whom he depended for access to trade goods, especially the Arab horses he needed for his cavalry.

ARRIVAL OF THE EUROPEANS & CHRISTIANITY

And so began a new era of European contact with the East. After Vasco da Gama's arrival in 1498 came Francisco de Ameida and Alfonso de Albuquerque, who established an eastern Portuguese empire that included Goa (first taken in 1510). Albuquerque waged a constant battle against the local Muslims in Goa, finally defeating them. But perhaps his greatest achievement was in playing off two deadly threats against each other – the Vijayanagars (for whom access to Goa's ports was extremely important) and the Bijapuris (who had split from the Bahmanis in the early 16th century and who controlled part of Goa).

The Bijapuris and Vijayanagars were sworn enemies, and Albuquerque skilfully exploited this antipathy by supplying Arab horses, which had to be constantly imported because they died in alarming numbers once on Indian

The Career and Legend of Vasco da Gama, by Sanjay Subrahmanyam, is one of the better recent investigations of the person credited with 'discovering' the sea route to India.

1707	1757	1857
Death of Aurangzeb, the last of the Mughal greats. His demise triggers the gradual collapse of the Mughal empire, as anarchy and rebellion erupts across the country.	Breaking out of its business mould, the British East India Company registers its first military victory on Indian soil. Siraj-ud-Daulah, nawab of Bengal, is defeated by Robert Clive in the Battle of Plassey.	The First War of Independence against the British takes place. In the absence of a national leader, the freedom fighters coerce the last Mughal king, Bahadur Shah Zafar, to proclaim himself emperor of India.

soil. Both kingdoms bought horses from the Portuguese to top up their warring cavalries, thus keeping Portugal's Goan ports busy and profitable.

The Portuguese also introduced Catholicism, and the arrival of the Inquisition in 1560 marked the beginning of 200 years of religious suppression in the Portuguese-controlled areas on the west coast of India. Not long after the beginning of the Inquisition, events that occurred in Europe had major repercussions for European relations with India. In 1580 Spain annexed Portugal and, until it regained its independence in 1640, Portugal's interests were subservient to Spain's. After the defeat of the Spanish Armada in 1588, the sea route to the East lay open to the English and the Dutch.

Today the Portuguese influence is most obvious in Goa, with its chalk-white Catholic churches dotting the countryside, Christian festivals and unique cuisine, although the Portuguese also had some influence in Kerala in towns such as Kochi (Cochin). By the mid-16th century, Old Goa had grown into a thriving city said to rival Lisbon in magnificence, and although only a ruined shadow of that time, its churches and buildings are still a stunning reminder of Portuguese rule. It wasn't until 1961 – 14 years after national Independence – that the Portuguese were finally forced out by the Indian military.

The Dutch got to India first but, unlike the Portuguese, were more interested in trade than in religion and empire. Indonesia was used as the main source of spices, and trade with South India was primarily for pepper and cardamom. So the Dutch East India Company set up a string of trading posts (called factories), which allowed them to maintain a complicated trading structure all the way from the Persian Gulf to Japan. They set up trading posts at Surat (Gujarat) and on the Coromandel Coast in South India, and entered into a treaty with the ruler of Calicut. In 1660 they captured the Portuguese forts at Kochi and Kodungallor.

The English also set up a trading venture, the British East India Company, which in 1600 was granted a monopoly. Like the Dutch, the English were at that stage interested in trade, mainly in spices, and Indonesia was their main goal. But the Dutch proved too strong there and the English turned instead to India, setting up a trading post at Madras (now Chennai). The Danes traded off and on at Tranquebar (on the Coromandel Coast) from 1616, and the French acquired Pondicherry (now Puducherry) in 1673.

> Thousands were burned at the stake during the Goa Inquisition, which lasted more than 200 years. The judgment ceremony took place outside the Se Cathedral in Old Goa.

MUGHALS VERSUS MARATHAS

Around the late 17th century the Delhi-based Mughals were making inroads into Southern India, gaining the sultanates of Ahmednagar, Bijapur and Golconda (including Hyderabad) before moving into Tamil Nadu. But it was here that Emperor Aurangzeb (r 1658–1707) came up against the Marathas who, in a series of guerrilla-like raids, captured Thanjavur and set up a capital at Gingee near Madras.

1858	1869	1885
British government assumes control over India – with power officially transferred from the British East India Company to the Crown – beginning the period known as the British Raj, which lasts until India's Independence in 1947.	The birth of Mohandas Karamchand Gandhi in Porbandar (Gujarat) – the man who would later become popularly known as 'Mahatma' (Great Soul) Gandhi and affectionately dubbed 'Father of the Nation'.	The Indian National Congress, India's first home-grown political organisation, is established. It brings educated Indians together and plays a key role in India's enduring freedom struggle.

White Mughals by William Dalrymple tells the true story of a British East India Company soldier who married an Indian Muslim princess, a tragic love story interwoven with harem politics, intrigue and espionage.

Although the Mughal empire gradually disintegrated following Aurangzeb's death, the Marathas went from strength to strength, and they set their sights on territory to the north. But their aspirations brought them into conflict with the rulers of Hyderabad, the Asaf Jahis, who had entrenched themselves here when Hyderabad broke away from the declining Mughal rulers of Delhi in 1724. The Marathas discovered that the French were providing military support to the Hyderabadi rulers in return for trading concessions on the Coromandel Coast. However, by the 1750s Hyderabad had lost a lot of its power and became landlocked when much of its coast was lost to the British.

Down in the south, Travancore (Kerala) and Mysore were making a bid to consolidate their power by gaining control of strategic maritime regions, and access to trade links. Martanda Varma (r 1729–58) of Travancore created his own army and tried to keep the local Syrian Orthodox trading community onside by limiting the activities of European traders. Trade in many goods, with the exception of pepper, became a royal monopoly, especially under Martanda's son Rama Varma (r 1758–98).

Mysore started off as a landlocked kingdom, but in 1761 a cavalry officer, Hyder Ali, assumed power and set about acquiring coastal territory. Hyder Ali and his son Tipu Sultan eventually ruled over a kingdom that included southern Karnataka and northern Kerala. Tipu conducted trade directly with the Middle East through the west-coast ports he controlled. But Tipu was prevented from gaining access to ports on the eastern seaboard and the fertile hinterland by the British East India Company.

THE BRITISH TAKE HOLD

The British East India Company at this stage was supposedly interested only in trade, not conquest. But Mysore's rulers proved something of a vexation. In 1780 the Nizam of Hyderabad, Hyder Ali, and the Marathas joined forces to defeat the company's armies and take control of Karnataka. The Treaty of Mangalore, signed by Tipu Sultan in 1784, restored the parties to an uneasy truce. But meanwhile, within the company there was a growing body of opinion that only total control of India would really satisfy British trading interests. This was reinforced by fears of a renewed French bid for land in India following Napoleon's Egyptian expedition of 1798–99. It was the governor general of Bengal, Lord Richard Wellesley, who launched a strike against Mysore, with the Nizam of Hyderabad as an ally (who was required to disband his French-trained troops and in return gained British protection). Tipu, who may have counted on support from the French, was killed when the British stormed the river-island fortress of Seringapatam (present-day Srirangapatnam, near Mysore; p257) in 1799.

Wellesley restored the old ruling family, the Wodeyars, to half of Tipu's kingdom – the rest went to the Nizam of Hyderabad and the British East

1919	1940	1942
The massacre, on 13 April, of unarmed Indian protesters at Jallianwala Bagh in Amritsar (Punjab). Mahatma Gandhi responds with his program of civil (non-violent) disobedience against the British government.	The Muslim League adopts its Lahore Resolution, which champions greater Muslim autonomy in India. Subsequent campaigns throughout the 1940s for the creation of a separate Islamic nation are spearheaded by Mohammed Ali Jinnah.	Mahatma Gandhi launches the Quit India campaign, demanding that the British leave India without delay and allow the country to get on with the business of self-governance.

MIGHTY SHIVAJI

The name Chhatrapati Shivaji is revered in Maharashtra, with statues of the great warrior astride his horse gracing many towns, and street names and monuments being named (or renamed in the case of Mumbai's [Bombay's] Victoria Terminus, among others; see p117) after him.

Shivaji was responsible for leading the powerful Maratha dynasty, a sovereign Hindu state that controlled the Deccan region for almost two centuries, at a time when much of India was under Islamic control. A courageous warrior and charismatic leader, Shivaji was born in 1627 to a prominent Maratha family at Shivneri. As a child he was sent to Pune with his mother, where he was given land and forts and groomed as a future leader. With a very small army, Shivaji seized his first fort at the age of 20 and over the next three decades he continued to expand Maratha power around his base in Pune, holding out against the Muslim invaders from the north (the Mughal empire) and the south (the forces of Bijapur) and eventually controlling the Deccan. He was shrewd enough to play his enemies (among them Mughal emperor Aurangzeb) off against each other and, in a famous incident, he killed Bijapuri general Afzal Khan in a face-to-face encounter at Pratapgad Fort (p182).

In 1674 Shivaji was crowned Chhatrapati (Lord of the Universe) of the Marathas at Raigad Fort (p182). He died six years later and was succeeded by his son Sambhaji, but almost immediately the power Shivaji had built up began to wane.

India Company – and laid the foundations for the formation of the Madras Presidency. Thanjavur and Karnataka were also absorbed by the British, who, when the rulers of the day died, pensioned off their successors. By 1818 the Marathas, racked by internal strife, had collapsed.

By now most of India was under British influence. In the south the British controlled the Madras Presidency, which stretched from present-day Andhra Pradesh to the southern tip of the subcontinent, and from the east coast across to the western Malabar Coast. Meanwhile, a fair chunk of the interior was ruled by a bundle of small princely states. Much of Maharashtra was part of the Bombay Presidency, but there were a dozen or so small princely states scattered around, including Kolhapur, Sawantwadi, Aundh and Janjira. The major princely states were Travancore, Hyderabad and Mysore, though all were closely watched by the Resident (the British de facto governor, who officially looked after areas under British control).

In 1839 the British government offered to buy Goa from the Portuguese for half a million pounds.

THE ROAD TO INDEPENDENCE

The desire among many Indians to be free from foreign rule remained. Opposition to the British began to increase at the turn of the 20th century, spearheaded by the Indian National Congress (Congress Party), the nation's oldest political party. The fight for independence gained momentum when, in April 1919, following riots in Amritsar (Punjab), a British army contingent was sent to quell the unrest. Under direct orders of the officer in charge the

1947	1947–48	1948
India gains independence on 15 August. Pakistan is formed a day earlier. Partition is followed by cross-border exodus, as tens of thousands of Hindus and Muslims brave communal riots to migrate to their respective nations.	First war between India and Pakistan takes place not long after the (procrastinating) maharaja of Kashmir signs the Instrument of Accession that cedes his state to India. Pakistan challenges the document's legality.	Mahatma Gandhi is assassinated in New Delhi by Nathuram Godse on 30 January. Godse and his co-conspirator Narayan Apte are later tried, convicted and executed.

The Proudest Day – India's Long Road to Independence by Anthony Read and David Fisher is an engaging account of India's pre-Independence period.

army ruthlessly fired into a crowd of unarmed protesters attending a meeting, killing an estimated 1500 people. News of the massacre spread rapidly throughout India, turning huge numbers of otherwise apolitical Indians into Congress supporters. At this time, the Congress movement found a new leader in Mohandas Gandhi (see the boxed text, opposite).

After some three decades of intense campaigning for an independent India, Mahatma Gandhi's dream finally materialised. However, despite Gandhi's plea for a united India – the Muslim League's leader, Mohammed Ali Jinnah, was demanding a separate Islamic state for India's sizeable Muslim population – the decision was made to split the country.

The partition of India in 1947 contained all the ingredients for an epic disaster, but the resulting bloodshed was far worse than anticipated. Massive population exchanges took place. Trains full of Muslims, fleeing westward, were held up and slaughtered by Hindu and Sikh mobs. Hindus and Sikhs fleeing to the east suffered the same fate. By the time the chaos had run its course, more than 10 million people had changed sides and at least 500,000 had been killed.

Jawaharlal Nehru became the first prime minister of independent India while, tragically, Mahatma Gandhi was assassinated in 1948 by a Hindu fanatic. The repercussions of Partition remain apparent today: the still-disputed territory of Kashmir has witnessed bloody conflict between India and Pakistan since Independence.

A golden oldie, *Gandhi*, directed by Richard Attenborough, is one of the few films which adeptly captures the grand canvas that is India in tracing the country's rocky road to Independence.

CARVING UP THE SOUTH

While the chaos of Partition was mostly felt in the north – mainly in Punjab and Bengal – the south faced problems of its own. Following Independence, the princely states and British provinces were dismantled and South India was reorganised into states along linguistic lines. Though most of the princely states acceded to India peacefully, an exception was that of the Nizam of Hyderabad. He wanted Hyderabad to join Islamic Pakistan, although only he and 10% of his subjects were Muslims. Following a time of violence between Hindu and Islamic hardliners, the Indian army moved in and forcibly took control of Hyderabad state in 1949.

The Wodeyars in Mysore, who also ruled right up to Independence, were pensioned off. But they were so popular with their subjects that the maharaja became the first governor of the post-Independence state of Mysore. The boundaries of Mysore state were redrawn on linguistic grounds in 1956, and the extended Kannada-speaking state of Greater Mysore was established, becoming Karnataka in 1972.

Kerala, as it is today, was created in 1956 from Travancore, Cochin (now Kochi) and Malabar (formerly part of the Madras Presidency). The maharajas in both Travancore and Cochin were especially attentive to the provision of basic services and education, and their legacy today is India's most literate

1961	1962	1964
In a military action code-named 'Operation Vijay' the Indian government sends armed troops into Goa and – with surprisingly little resistance – ends over four centuries of Portuguese colonial rule in the region.	Border war (known as the Sino-Indian War) with China over the North-East Frontier Area and Ladakh. China successfully captures the disputed territory and ends the war with a unilateral ceasefire.	Prime Minister Jawaharlal Nehru dies of a heart attack. Independent India's first prime minister, he played a pivotal role in championing India's freedom from British rule.

MAHATMA GANDHI

One of the great figures of the 20th century, Mohandas Karamchand Gandhi was born on 2 October 1869 in Porbandar, Gujarat. After studying in London (1888–91), he worked as a barrister in South Africa. Here, the young Gandhi became politicised, railing against the discrimination he encountered. He soon became the spokesman for the Indian community and championed equality for all.

Gandhi returned to India in 1915 with the doctrine of ahimsa (non-violence) central to his political plans, and committed to a simple and disciplined lifestyle. He set up the Sabarmati Ashram in Ahmedabad, which was innovative for its admission of Untouchables (the lowest caste Dalits).

Within a year, Gandhi had won his first victory, defending farmers in Bihar from exploitation. It's said that this was when he first received the title 'Mahatma' (Great Soul) from an admirer. The passage of the discriminatory Rowlatt Acts (which allowed certain political cases to be tried without juries) in 1919 spurred him to further action and he organised a national protest. In the days that followed this hartal (strike), feelings ran high throughout the country. After the massacre of unarmed protesters in Amritsar (Punjab), a deeply shocked Gandhi immediately called off the movement.

By 1920 Gandhi was a key figure in the Indian National Congress, and he coordinated a national campaign of noncooperation or satyagraha (passive resistance) to British rule, with the effect of raising nationalist feeling while earning the lasting enmity of the British. In early 1930, Gandhi captured the imagination of the country, and the world, when he led a march of several thousand followers from Ahmedabad to Dandi on the coast of Gujarat. On arrival, Gandhi ceremoniously made salt by evaporating sea water, thus publicly defying the much-hated salt tax; not for the first time, he was imprisoned. Released in 1931 to represent the Indian National Congress at the second Round Table Conference in London, he won the hearts of many British people but failed to gain any real concessions from the government.

Disillusioned with politics, he resigned his parliamentary seat in 1934. He returned spectacularly to the fray in 1942 with the Quit India campaign, in which he urged the British to leave India immediately. His actions were deemed subversive and he and most of the Congress leadership were imprisoned.

In the frantic Independence bargaining that followed the end of WWII, Gandhi was largely excluded and watched helplessly as plans were made to partition the country – a dire tragedy in his eyes. Gandhi stood almost alone in urging tolerance and the preservation of a single India, and his work on behalf of members of all communities drew resentment from some Hindu hardliners. On his way to a prayer meeting in Delhi on 30 January 1948, he was assassinated by a Hindu zealot.

In 21st-century India, Mahatma Gandhi continues to be an iconic figure and is still widely revered as the 'Father of the Nation'.

---

state. Kerala also blazed a trail in post-Independence India by becoming the first state in the world to freely elect a communist government in 1957.

Andhra Pradesh was declared a state in 1956, having been created by combining Andhra state (formerly part of the Madras Presidency) with parts of the Telugu-speaking areas of the old Nizam of Hyderabad's territory.

1965	1966	1971
Skirmishes in Kashmir and the disputed Rann of Kutch in Gujarat flare into the Second India-Pakistan War, said to have involved the biggest tank battles since WWII. The war ends with a UN-mandated ceasefire.	Indira Gandhi, daughter of independent India's first prime minister, Jawaharlal Nehru, becomes prime minister of India. She has so far been India's only female prime minister.	East Pakistan champions independence from West Pakistan. India gets involved, sparking the Third India-Pakistan War. West Pakistan surrenders, losing sovereignty of East Pakistan, which becomes Bangladesh.

Tamil Nadu emerged from the old Madras Presidency, although until 1969 Tamil Nadu was known as Madras State. In 1956, in a nationwide reorganisation of states, it lost Malabar district and South Canara to the fledgling state of Kerala on the west coast. However, it also gained new areas in Trivandrum district, including Kanyakumari. In 1960, 1049 sq km of land in Andhra Pradesh was exchanged for a similar amount of land in Salem and Chengalpattu districts.

The creation of Maharashtra was one of the most contested issues of the language-based demarcation of states in the 1950s. After Independence, western Maharashtra and Gujarat were joined to form Bombay state, but in 1960, after agitation by pro-Marathi supporters, the modern state of Maharashtra was created, separating from Gujarat while gaining parts of Hyderabad and Madhya Pradesh.

The French relinquished Puducherry in 1954 – 140 years after claiming it from the British. It's a Union Territory (controlled by the government in Delhi), though a largely self-governing one. Lakshadweep was granted Union Territory status in 1956, as were the Andaman and Nicobar Islands.

Throughout most of this carve-up, the tiny enclave of Goa was still under the rule of the Portuguese. Although a rumbling Independence movement had existed in Goa since the early 20th century, the Indian government was reluctant to intervene and take Goa by force, hoping the Portuguese would leave of their own volition. The Portuguese refused, so in December 1961 Indian troops crossed the border and liberated the state with surprisingly little resistance. It became a Union Territory of India, but after splitting from Daman and Diu (Gujarat) in 1987, it was officially recognised as the 25th state of the Indian Union.

MODERN INDIA

Jawaharlal Nehru, modern India's first prime minister, tried to steer India towards a policy of nonalignment, balancing cordial relations with Britain and Commonwealth membership with moves towards the former USSR. The latter was due partly to conflicts with China and US support for its archenemy Pakistan. Adding uncertainty, wars with Pakistan in 1965 (over Kashmir) and 1971 (over Bangladesh) contributed to a sense among many Indians of having enemies on all sides.

The hugely popular Nehru died in 1964 and his daughter, Indira Gandhi (no relation to Mahatma Gandhi), was elected as prime minister in 1966. Indira Gandhi, like Nehru before her, loomed large over the country she governed. Unlike Nehru, however, she was always a profoundly controversial figure whose historical legacy remains hotly disputed.

In 1975, facing serious opposition and unrest, she declared a state of emergency (which later became known as the Emergency). Freed of parliamentary constraints, Gandhi was able to boost the economy, control inflation

1984	1991	1998
Prime Minister Indira Gandhi is assassinated by two of her Sikh bodyguards after her highly controversial decision to have Indian troops storm Amritsar's Golden Temple, the Sikhs holiest shrine.	Rajiv Gandhi is assassinated by a female suicide-bomber, a supporter of the Sri Lanka-based Liberation Tigers of Tamil Eelam (LTTE), while on the campaign trail in Tamil Nadu.	India declares itself a nuclear power after conducting underground tests near the town of Pokaran in western Rajasthan. Pakistan follows suit, and the twin tests subject the subcontinental neighbours to global condemnation.

remarkably well and decisively increase efficiency. On the negative side, political opponents often found themselves in prison, India's judicial system was turned into a puppet theatre and the press was fettered.

Gandhi's government was bundled out of office in the 1977 elections in favour of the Janata People's Party (JPP). The JPP founder, Jaya Prakash Narayan, 'JP', was an ageing Gandhian socialist who died soon after but is widely credited with having safeguarded Indian democracy. Once it was victorious, it soon became apparent that Janata lacked cohesive policies and a leader of Narayan's stature. Its leader, Morarji Desai, struggled to come to grips with the country's problems. With inflation soaring, unrest rising and the economy faltering, Janata fell apart in late 1979. The 1980 election brought Indira Gandhi back to power with a larger majority than ever before.

Indira Gandhi grappled unsuccessfully with communal unrest in several regions, violent attacks on Dalits (the Scheduled Castes or Untouchables), numerous cases of police brutality and corruption, and the upheavals in the northeast and Punjab. In 1984, following an ill-considered decision to send in the Indian army to flush out armed Sikh separatists (demanding a separate Sikh state to be called Khalistan) from Amritsar's Golden Temple, Indira Gandhi was assassinated by her Sikh bodyguards. Her heavy-handed storming of the Sikhs' holiest temple and aftermath of her assassination was catastrophic and sparked bloody Hindu-Sikh riots that left more than 3000 people dead (mostly Sikhs who had been lynched). The quest for Khalistan has since been quashed.

Indira Gandhi's son Rajiv, a former pilot, became the next prime minister, with Congress winning in a landslide in 1984. However, after a brief golden reign, he was dragged down by corruption scandals and the inability to quell communal unrest, particularly in Punjab. In 1991 he, too, was assassinated in Tamil Nadu by a supporter of the Liberation Tigers of Tamil Eelam (LTTE; a Sri Lankan armed separatist group). Over the years thousands of Tamil refugees had fled to India from war-torn Sri Lanka, most settling in Tamil Nadu.

The Nehrus and the Gandhis is Tariq Ali's astute portrait-history of these families and the India over which they cast their long shadow.

Political Resources – India (www.politicalresources.net/India.htm) provides useful links to the major players and political parties in India.

DEATH OF A BANDIT

On 18 October 2004, the elusive bandit Veerappan was shot dead by police in an ambush near a remote forest village in Tamil Nadu. It was big news given that the moustachioed outlaw had managed to evade police for more than 30 years. Dubbed the 'forest brigand', Veerappan was a notorious elephant poacher, sandalwood smuggler and cold-blooded murderer. Feared by his adversaries, he headed a loyal gang in his jungle stronghold and plied his illegal trade, dodging police task forces from three states. Veerappan was bold, very bold: in 2000 he kidnapped movie idol Rajkumar and held him hostage for three months; and in 2002 he kidnapped Karnatakan politician H Nagappa, who was later found dead. In a finale that reads like something from a movie script, Veerappan went down in true gangster style – with all guns blazing.

March 1998	May 2004	December 2004
The Bharatiya Janata Party (BJP; Indian People's Party, founded in 1980), in alliance with several other parties, wins the national elections and Atal Behari Vajpayee is installed as India's Prime Minister.	Belonging to the Sikh faith, Manmohan Singh of the Congress Party becomes the first member of any religious minority community to hold India's highest elected office.	On 26 December a catastrophic tsunami batters coastal parts of eastern and Southern India as well as the Andaman and Nicobar Islands, killing over 10,000 people and leaving hundreds of thousands homeless.

Narasimha Rao assumed the by-now-poisoned chalice that was leadership of the Congress Party and led it to victory at the polls in 1991.

The December 1992 destruction of the Babri Masjid (p108) by Hindu zealots in Ayodhya (revered by Hindus as the birthplace of Rama), in Uttar Pradesh, sparked widespread communal violence. In Mumbai alone, hundreds of people were killed after a series of bomb blasts in March 1993.

In 1997 KR Narayanan became India's president, the first member of the lowest Hindu caste (the Dalits; formerly known as Untouchables) to hold the position.

Meanwhile, Tamil Nadu also faced tumultuous times. The fiercely independent and conservative Tamils have been led alternately by the DMK (Dravida Munnetra Kazhagam) and its offshoot the AIADMK (All India Anna Dravida Munnetra Kazhagam) since 1957, both parties pushing strong Dravidian 'Tamil Nadu for Tamils' and anti-Hindi language policies, and for more independent powers.

Of all the South Indian states, Goa has probably changed most since Independence, in the rampant development of both tourism and industry (mainly petrochemicals and mining). It has also had more shifts in power since 1987 than there are sun-beds on Calangute Beach, with ministers from the Congress Party and the Hindu nationalist Bharatiya Janata Party (BJP) frequently crossing the floor (switching parties) or resigning.

On a national level, after losing the 1996 election to the BJP, the Congress Party eventually swept back to power in 2004, winning the central government elections largely on the back of major support from South Indian voters, particularly in Andhra Pradesh and Tamil Nadu. The BJP's planned national agitation campaign against the foreign origins of the Italian-born Congress leader, another Gandhi – Sonia, the Italian-born widow of the late Rajiv Gandhi – was subverted by her unexpected decision to step aside. The Congress Party's former finance minister, Manmohan Singh, was sworn in as prime minister.

The Elephant, the Tiger & the Cellphone by Shashi Tharoor 'combines hard facts and statistics with personal opinion and observations' to explore historical elements that have shaped the intriguing puzzle that is 21st-century India.

Singh was openly enthusiastic about resuming productive peace talks with Pakistan over the disputed territory of Kashmir. However these talks came to an abrupt halt when communal tensions soared following the July 2006 train bombings in Mumbai that left more than 200 people dead. The Indian government pointed the finger at Pakistan, claiming that its intelligence had played a hand in the blasts – an accusation that Islamabad vehemently denied. Singh later recommenced peace talks with Pakistan, but with suspicions running high on both sides of the border, the road to reconciliation was set to be a challenging one.

Adding further pressure to the peace process was the February 2007 terrorist bomb attack on a train travelling from Delhi to Lahore (Pakistan), which killed 68 commuters. The Indian and Pakistani governments vowed not to let the attack – suspected of being designed to specifically disrupt (improving) India–Pakistan relations – freeze bilateral peace talks. However, despite the Indian government's resolute stance, communal tension continued to fester, with 2008 proving to be one of the country's darkest years. In May 2008 a

2006	February 2007	July 2007
On 11 July seven bombs are detonated on suburban trains in Mumbai (Bombay), India's commercial capital, leaving more than 200 people dead and over 700 others wounded.	On 18 February bomb blasts on a train travelling from Delhi to Lahore kill 68 passengers. The attack is believed to have been masterminded by Islamists intent on destabilising peace talks between India and Pakistan.	The country has its first woman, Pratibha Patil, sworn in as President of India. Patil was formerly the first female Governor of Rajasthan (2004 to 2007).

series of synchronised bomb blasts in Jaipur left over 60 people dead; in July of the same year bombings in Ahmedabad killed over 55; while September saw coordinated bomb explosions in Delhi kill at least 30 people. Ongoing investigations into all of these attacks have pointed the finger at hard-line Islamist groups, with Delhi emphatically vowing to rein in terrorist activity. But for all its tough talk, the government was left speechless in late November 2008 when Mumbai, India's financial powerhouse, came under a spate of highly coordinated terror attacks – which included tourist landmarks like the iconic Taj Mahal Palace & Tower hotel (p115) – that lasted three days and left over 173 people dead. At the time of writing, investigations were still being carried out, with links to Pakistan-based Islamic militant groups being actively pursued.

On a more optimistic note, 21st-century South India has been riding the IT wave, with southern cities such as Bengaluru (Bangalore), Mumbai, Pune, Hyderabad and Chennai leading India's hi-tech push into the cyber age – see the boxed text, p50.

October 2008

On 22 October India launches the Chandrayaan-1 spacecraft – the nation's first unmanned mission to the moon for a two-year exploration of the lunar surface.

November 2008

On 26 November a series of coordinated bombing and shooting attacks on landmark Mumbai sites (primarily in the city's south) begins; the attacks last three days and kill over 173 people. One of the terrorists is caught alive.

2009

The Congress-led alliance garners a decisive victory in India's general election. Manmohan Singh is reinstated as prime minister of the world's biggest democracy.

The Culture

THE NATIONAL PSYCHE

In a land with such an astonishing melange of traditions, it might seem impossible to pin down one element that neatly defines the national psyche. However, despite the incredibly complex tapestry that is India, there is one common thread that weaves through the entire nation: religion. Whether it's a mother in Mumbai (Bombay) performing *puja* (prayers) at a little shrine tucked away in a corner of the home, or Goan children singing hymns at church, spirituality plays a paramount role in defining and guiding people of all stripes.

Along with religion, family lies at the heart of Indian society. For the vast majority of people, the concept of being unmarried and without children by one's mid-30s is unimaginable. Despite the steadily rising number of nuclear families, primarily in larger cities such as Mumbai and Bengaluru (Bangalore), the extended family remains a cornerstone in both urban and rural India, with males – usually the breadwinners – generally considered the head of the household, and two or three generations of a family often living under one roof.

With religion and family deemed so sacrosanct, don't be surprised or miffed if you're constantly grilled about these subjects, especially beyond the larger cities, and receive curious (possibly disapproving) gawps if you don't 'fit the mould'. Apart from religion and marital status, frequently asked questions include age, profession and possibly even income. Such questions aren't intended to offend, and it's also perfectly acceptable for you to echo them.

The Wonder That Was India by AL Basham offers incisive descriptions of Indian civilisations, major religions, origins of the caste system and social customs – a good thematic approach to weave the disparate strands together.

National pride has long existed on the subcontinent but has swelled in recent years as India attracts ever-increasing international kudos in the fields of information technology (IT), science, medicine, literature and film. In the sporting arena there are rising stars on the tennis front, but it is cricket that reigns supreme, with top players afforded superhero status.

The country's robust economy – one of the world's fastest growing – is another source of prolific national pride. Advancements in nuclear and space technology are also widely hailed as potent symbols of Indian honour and sovereignty. In 2008 India joined the elite global lunar club with its maiden unmanned mission to the moon.

In 21st-century India the juxtaposition of time-honoured and New Age flies in the face of some common stereotypes about the country. While you'll still come across the widely flogged clichés, from snake charmers to ox-pulled carts, there's certainly a whole lot more to modern-day India than the glossy tourist brochures may have you believe.

LIFESTYLE

Although the lifestyle of a farmer in rural Karnataka bears little resemblance to that of an IT professional in fast-paced Bengaluru, certain cultural and caste traditions are shared by most echelons of society. Indeed independent India's first prime minister, Jawaharlal Nehru, adeptly encapsulated the nation's essence by describing it as 'a bundle of contradictions held together by strong but invisible threads'.

Traditional Culture
MARRIAGE, BIRTH & DEATH

Marriage is an exceptionally auspicious event for Indians and although 'love marriages' have spiralled upwards in recent times (mainly in urban hubs), most Hindu marriages are arranged. Discreet inquiries are made within the community. If a suitable match is not found, the help of professional matchmakers may be sought, or advertisements may be placed in newspapers and/or the internet. The horoscopes are checked and, if propitious, there's a meeting between the two families. The legal marriage age in India is 18.

Dowry, although illegal, is still a key issue in many arranged marriages, with some families plunging into debt to raise the required cash and merchandise (from cars and computers to washing machines and televisions). Health workers claim that India's high rate of abortion of female foetuses (despite sex-identification medical tests being banned in India, they still clandestinely occur in some clinics) is predominantly due to the financial burden of providing a daughter's dowry.

The Hindu wedding ceremony is officiated over by a priest and the marriage is formalised when the couple walk around a sacred fire seven times. Despite the existence of nuclear families, it's still the norm for a wife to live with her husband's family once married and assume the household duties outlined by her mother-in-law. Not surprisingly, the mother–daughter-in-law relationship can be a prickly one, as portrayed in the many Indian TV soap operas which largely revolve around this theme.

Divorce and remarriage is becoming more common (primarily in India's bigger cities), however, divorce is still not granted by courts as a matter of routine and is generally frowned upon by society. Among the higher castes, widows are traditionally expected not to remarry and are admonished to wear white and live pious, celibate lives. Also see p58.

The birth of a child is another momentous occasion, with its own set of special ceremonies, which take place at various auspicious times during the early years of childhood. These include the casting of the child's first horoscope, name-giving, feeding the first solid food, and the first hair cutting.

Hindus cremate their dead, and funeral ceremonies are designed to purify and console both the living and the deceased. An important aspect of the proceedings is the *sharadda*, paying respect to one's ancestors by offering water and rice cakes. It's an observance that's repeated at each anniversary of the death. After the cremation the ashes are collected and, 13 days after the death (when blood relatives are deemed ritually pure), a member of the family usually scatters them in a holy river such as the Ganges, or in the ocean.

The Caste System

Although the Indian constitution does not recognise the caste system, caste still wields considerable influence, especially in rural India, where the caste you are born into largely determines your social standing in the community. It can also influence one's vocational and marriage prospects. Castes are further divided into thousands of *jati*, groups of 'families' or social communities, which are sometimes but not always linked to occupation. Conservative Hindus will only marry someone of the same *jati*.

According to tradition, caste is the basic social structure of Hindu society. Living a righteous life and fulfilling your dharma (moral duty) raises your chances of being reborn into a higher caste and thus into better circumstances. Hindus are born into one of four varnas (castes): Brahmin (priests and scholars), Kshatriya (soldiers or administrators), Vaishya (merchants) and Shudra (labourers). The Brahmins were said to have emerged from the mouth of Lord Brahma at the moment of creation, Kshatriyas were said to have come from his arms, Vaishyas from his thighs and Shudras from his feet.

Traditional South Indian Brahmins live with particularly stringent 'rules' of lifestyle and behaviour. These include dietary protocols (which dictate a strictly vegetarian regimen and no 'hot' foods, such as garlic or chilli), a simple

Matchmaking has embraced the cyber age, with popular sites including www.shaadi.com, www.bharatmatrimony.com and, more recently, www.secondshaadi.com – for those trying a second time.

The Indians, by Sudhir Kakar and Katharina Kakar, explores Indian identity, covering everything from caste and marriage to spirituality and attitudes towards sex.

Two insightful books about India's caste system are *Interrogating Caste* by Dipankar Gupta and *Translating Caste* edited by Tapan Basu.

dress code, and a particular social etiquette for certain occasions. Historically, Brahmin groups fled to South India to escape oppression by Muslim rulers, who often targeted Brahmins to win the support of lower Hindu castes.

Beneath the four main castes are the Dalits (formerly known as Untouchables), who hold menial jobs such as sweepers and latrine cleaners. The word 'pariah' is derived from the name of a Tamil Dalit group, the Paraiyars. Some Dalit leaders, such as the renowned Dr BR Ambedkar (1891–1956), sought to change their status by adopting another faith; in his case it was Buddhism. At the bottom of the social heap are the Denotified Tribes. They were known as the Criminal Tribes until 1952, when a reforming law officially recognised 198 tribes and castes. Many are nomadic or semi-nomadic tribes, forced by the wider community to eke out a living on society's fringes.

Contemporary Issues
HIV & AIDS IN INDIA

In 2008 there were an estimated 2.4 million HIV-positive cases in India, according to UN and NACO (National AIDS Control Organisation) reports. However some analysts believe this is a conservative estimate, as many cases go unreported.

AVERT, the UK-based international HIV and AIDS charity, says that despite the widespread belief that HIV is confined to intravenous drug users and gay men, the bulk of infections in India are actually transmitted through heterosexual sex. It claims that a significant proportion of cases are women in monogamous relationships who have been infected by husbands who have had multiple sex partners, and that there has been an increasing trend of sexually active people aged between 15 and 44 becoming infected. AVERT asserts that HIV affects a diverse spectrum of the Indian community, but those who face a proportionately elevated risk include intravenous drug users, migrant workers, truck drivers and sex workers.

AIDS Sutra: Untold Stories from India reveals the human stories behind India's AIDS epidemic, with contributions from notable writers including Kiran Desai, Salman Rushdie and Vikram Seth.

In a country of more than one billion people, health officials warn that unless the government radically increases nationwide educational programmes (especially promotion of condom use) the number of HIV-positive cases is set to dramatically spiral upwards. Campaigners purport that India's antigay laws (see p48) patently hamper treatment and education efforts.

CHILD LABOUR

Despite national legislation prohibiting child labour, human-rights groups believe India has *at least* 50 million (not the Indian government's estimation of 12.6 million) child labourers – the highest rate in the world. The International Labour Organisation (ILO) estimates that there are over 245 million children aged between five and 15 working as full-time labourers worldwide.

In India, poorly enforced laws, poverty and lack of a social-security system are cited as major causes of the problem. The harsh reality for many low-income families is that they simply can't afford to support their children, so they send them out to work in order to help make ends meet.

Recognising the need for tougher anti-child-labour laws, in 2006 the Indian government ordered a ban against the employment of children (aged below 14) as labourers in households and the hospitality trade, two areas known to have particularly high child-labour numbers (reliable statistics unavailable). The ban is an addendum to existing legislation which already forbids the employment of children under the age of 14 in what it classifies as 'hazardous jobs' (eg glass factories, abattoirs). Employers who contravene the law face possible imprisonment, a hefty monetary fine, or both. The government has promised to appropriately rehabilitate displaced

DOS & DON'TS

South India has many time-honoured traditions and while you won't be expected to get everything 'right', common sense and courtesy will take you a long way. If in doubt about how you should behave (eg at a temple), watch what the locals do, or simply ask. Refrain from kissing and cuddling in public as this isn't condoned by society.

Dress Etiquette

Dressing conservatively (women *and* men) wins a warmer response from locals. Nudity in public is not on, no matter where you are, and while bikinis may be acceptable on Goa's beaches, you should cover up (eg swim in knee-length shorts and a T-shirt) in less touristy places – use your judgement. For more advice about appropriate dress for women, see p516.

Eating & Visiting Etiquette

If you're lucky enough to be invited to someone's home it's considered good manners to remove your shoes before entering the house, and to wash your hands before and after a meal. Wait to be served food or until you are invited to help yourself – if you're unsure about protocol, simply wait for your host to direct you.

It's customary to use your right hand for eating and other social acts such as shaking hands; the left hand is used for unsavoury actions such as toilet duties and removing dirty shoes. When drinking from a shared water container, hold it slightly above your mouth (thus avoiding contact between your lips and the mouth of the container).

Photography Etiquette

Exercise sensitivity when taking photos of people, especially women, who may find it offensive – obtain permission in advance. Taking photos inside a shrine, at a funeral, at a religious ceremony or of people publicly bathing (including rivers) can also be offensive – ask first. Flash photography may be prohibited in certain areas of a shrine, or may not be permitted at all. Also see p505 and p497.

Religious Etiquette

Whenever visiting a sacred site, always dress and behave respectfully – don't wear shorts or sleeveless tops (this applies to men and women) and refrain from smoking. Loud and intrusive behaviour isn't appreciated, and neither are public displays of affection or kidding around.

Before entering a holy place, remove your shoes (tip the shoe-minder a few rupees when retrieving them) and check if photography is allowed. You're permitted to wear socks in most places of worship.

Head cover (for women and sometimes men) is required at some places of worship, so carry a scarf just to be on the safe side. There are some sites that don't admit women and some that deny entry to non-adherents of their faith – inquire in advance. Women may be required to sit apart from men. Jain temples request the removal of leather items you may be wearing or carrying, and may also request that menstruating women not enter.

Religious etiquette advises against touching locals on the head, or directing the soles of your feet at a person, religious shrine or image of a deity. Religious protocol also advises against touching someone with your feet or touching a carving of a deity.

Other Tips for Travellers

To heighten your chances of receiving the most accurate response when seeking directions from people on the street, refrain from posing questions in a leading manner. For instance, it's often best to ask, 'Which way to the museum?' rather than pointing and asking, 'Is this the way to the museum?' This is because you may well receive a fabricated answer (usually 'yes') if the person can't quite decipher your accent or simply didn't hear you properly.

It's also worth noting that the commonly used sideways wobble of the head doesn't necessarily mean 'no'. It can translate to: yes, maybe, or I have no idea.

child labourers, however, critics continue to be sceptical about its ability to effectively do so. They believe that many jobless children may well turn to begging and/or crime.

Human-rights organisations indicate that the vast majority of India's child labourers work in the agricultural industry, while others work on construction sites, or as rag pickers, household servants, carpet weavers (also see the boxed text on p507), brick makers and prostitutes. There are also believed to be some several hundred thousand children involved in the manufacture of *bidis* (small, hand-rolled cigarettes), who inhale large quantities of harmful tobacco dust and chemicals. Another hazardous industry employing children is that of fireworks manufacturing.

GAY & LESBIAN ISSUES
India has an estimated 2.5 million male homosexuals, according to the National AIDS Control Organization (NACO), however, advocacy groups claim the figure is much higher and impossible to accurately ascertain given that homosexuality is illegal in India. Some reports suggest there are roughly 100 million gay, lesbian and transgender people in the country.

Section 377 of the national legislation forbids 'carnal intercourse against the order of nature' (that is, anal intercourse) and the penalties for transgression can theoretically be up to life imprisonment, plus a steep monetary fine. There's no law against lesbian sexual relations. Although this colonial-era law, which dates back to 1861, is rarely used to prosecute, it's allegedly used by authorities to harass, arrest and blackmail gay people.

In 2006 more than 100 high-profile personalities, including Nobel prize-winning economist, Amartya Sen, and literary stalwarts, Vikram Seth and Arundhati Roy, signed an open letter supporting a legal challenge that was lodged with the Delhi High Court. The case, which sought to overturn the country's antiquated antigay law, was unsuccessful. However, the ruling has since been challenged and high courts in a number of other Indian cities were also reviewing the antigay law at the time of writing. Activists are hopeful that sustained efforts will see Section 377 repealed in the near future – surf the net to keep abreast of the latest developments.

While the more liberal sections of certain cities – such as Mumbai, Bengaluru, Delhi and Kolkata (Calcutta) – appear to be becoming more tolerant of homosexuality, gay life is still largely suppressed. As marriage is so important on the subcontinent, it's believed that most gay people stay in the closet or risk being disowned by their families and society. Nevertheless, freedom of expression is certainly growing. For instance, in 2008 there were Gay Pride marches for the first time ever in several Indian cities including Delhi, Kolkata and Bengaluru. And in 2003, Mumbai hosted the Larzish festival, India's pioneer queer film festival. This was quite a coup for the gay community, considering the hullabaloo raised by religious zealots over

HIJRAS

India's most visible nonheterosexual group is the *hijras*, a caste of transvestites and eunuchs who dress in women's clothing. Some are gay, some are hermaphrodites and some were unfortunate enough to be kidnapped and castrated. Since it has long been traditionally frowned upon to live openly as a gay man in India, *hijras* get around this by becoming, in effect, a third sex of sorts. They work mainly as uninvited entertainers at weddings and celebrations of the birth of male children, and possibly as prostitutes.

Read more about *hijras* in *The Invisibles* by Zia Jaffrey and *Ardhanarishvara the Androgyne* by Dr Alka Pande.

SUBCONTINENTAL STYLE

Widely worn by Indian women, the elegant sari comes in a single piece (between 5m and 9m long and 1m wide) and is ingeniously tucked and pleated into place without the need for pins or buttons. Worn with the sari is the choli (tight-fitting blouse) and a drawstring petticoat. The *palloo* is that part of the sari draped over the shoulder. Also commonly worn is the *salwar kameez*, a traditional dresslike tunic and trouser combination accompanied by a dupatta (long scarf). Saris and *salwar kameez* come in a range of fabrics, designs and prices.

Traditional attire for men includes the dhoti, and (in the south) the lungi and the *mundu* are also commonly worn. The dhoti is a loose, long loincloth pulled up between the legs. The lungi is more like a sarong, with its end usually sewn up like a tube. The *mundu* is like a lungi but is always white.

There are regional and religious variations in costume – for example, you may see Muslim women wearing the all-enveloping burka.

Deepa Mehta's film *Fire* (with lesbian themes), which was famously banned by the ultraconservative Shiv Sena party in 1998 (see also p61).

For details about gay support groups and publications/websites see p500.

POVERTY

Raising the living standards of India's poor has been on the agenda for governments since Independence. However, recent World Bank estimates place around a third of the global poor in India. According to Indian government sources, there are around 220 million Indians living below the poverty line, 75% of them in rural areas. Many others live in horrendously overcrowded urban slums. Non-government groups cite poverty figures closer to 250 million.

The major causes of poverty include illiteracy and a population growth level that is substantially exceeding India's economic growth rate. Although India's middle class is ballooning, there's still a marked disparity when it comes to the country's distribution of wealth. Around 25% (roughly 250 million) of India's population subsists on less than Rs20 per day, according to a 2007 report by the Government of India's 'National Commission for Enterprises in the Unorganised Sector (NCEUS)'.

In 2008 the average annual income per capita in India was US$977. India's minimum daily wage, which varies from state to state, was raised in 2007 from Rs66 per day to Rs80 per day, although this isn't always the case in reality. Wages between industries vary, with state governments setting different minimums for different vocations, and there are occupations (such as household servants) that have no minimum wage structure at all. Women are often paid less, especially in areas such as construction and farming.

Chandni Bar, directed by Madhur Bhandarkar, gives a disturbingly realistic insight into the lives of women who, driven by poverty and often family pressure, work as dancers/prostitutes in Mumbai's seedy bars.

Prostitution and poverty are closely linked. A 2007 (Indian) Ministry of Women & Child Development report indicated that India is believed to have around 2.8 million (and growing) sex workers, with about 35% entering the trade before the age of 18. Some human-rights groups believe the number of prostitutes is far more – possibly as high as 15 million – with the majority in Mumbai.

Poverty accounts for India's ever-growing number of beggars, mainly in the larger cities. For foreign visitors this is often the most confronting aspect of travelling in the subcontinent. Whether you give something is a matter of personal choice, though your money can often be put to better long-term use if given to a reputable charity. Or, you could work as a volunteer at a charitable organisation – for volunteering possibilities see p514.

POPULATION

India has the world's second-largest population, estimated at 1.15 billion in 2008, and is tipped to exceed China as the planet's most populous nation by 2030. According to the Government of India's 'India: Urban Poverty Report 2009', 40% to 50% of India's total population is likely to be urban-based by 2030.

A population census is held every 10 years in India. The most recent was in 2001 and this revealed that India's population had risen by 21.34% in the previous decade. According to this census, Mumbai is India's most populated city, with an urban agglomeration population of 16.4 million; Kolkata ranks second with 13.2 million, with Delhi (12.8 million) and Chennai (Madras; 6.6 million) third and fourth respectively. Despite India's many urban centres, the 2001 census revealed that the nation is still overwhelmingly rural, with an estimated 75% of the population living in the countryside.

Despite two South Indian cities (Mumbai and Chennai) having the country's biggest populations, the majority of India's population is concentrated in the north. Roughly 360 million people live in South India, with Maharashtra the most populous South Indian state. Nationally, men outnumber women (933 females to 1000 males), so Kerala is unique in having more women than men (1058 females to every 1000 males). For further official statistics, see the Census of India website at www.censusindia.net. For regional populations, see the Fast Facts boxes at the start of regional chapters. Throughout this book, keep in mind that we've used the official 2001 census figures, which are now close to a decade old. The next census is scheduled for 2011.

India has one of the planet's largest diasporas – over 26 million people – with Indian banks holding an estimated US$39 billion in Non-Resident Indian (NRI) accounts.

A SOFTWARE SUPERPOWER

India's burgeoning information technology (IT) industry, born in the boom years of the 1990s and founded on India's highly skilled middle class and abundance of relatively inexpensive labour, has established the country as a major player in the world of technology.

Newspaper reports peg 2007's IT (including outsourcing) industry earnings at around US$55 billion, with projections for this to at least double by 2012. However, the 2008–09 global economic slow-down has put pressure on Indian IT firms, with job cuts, wage freezes and revised investment plans on the cards. Only time will tell how the IT industry weathers the ongoing fiscal storm.

India's IT boom has transformed cities such as Hyderabad, nicknamed 'Cyberabad', and Bengaluru (Bangalore), known as 'India's Silicon Valley', into IT world leaders. Tamil Nadu, Karnataka and Andhra Pradesh now produce more than 50% of India's software exports, with emerging growth centres including Pune, Mumbai (Bombay), Delhi and Kolkata (Calcutta).

India has become an increasingly popular base for international call centres. Many of these centres put their staff through rigorous training courses to get them up to speed with the countries they'll be calling (mostly the UK, USA and Australia). These courses often include lessons on how to mimic foreign accents, and staff may also be given pseudo-Western names as another means of bridging the cultural divide. Apart from the financial carrot, another incentive used by IT companies to lure well-qualified job seekers (from call-centre operators to software engineers) is the high standard of workplace comfort (see the boxed text, 'Ground Zero of the Flat World' on p241).

Despite the IT boom playing a critical role in boosting the Indian economy, the industry does have its detractors, particularly those who claim that the country's IT growth is an entirely urban phenomenon, with little discernible impact upon the lives of the vast majority of Indians. The industry has also recently attracted negative press for various scandals, one of the most startling associated with Hyderabad-based IT giant, Satyam, which saw its chairman resign in early 2009 due to his involvement in serious accounting fraud. Despite the collective pros and cons, there is no doubt that IT will go down in history as one of India's great success stories.

ADIVASIS

India's Adivasis (tribal communities; Adivasi translates to 'original inhabitant' in Sanskrit) have origins that precede the Vedic Aryans and the Dravidians of the south. According to the 2001 census, India's Adivasis constitute 8.2% of the population (over 84 million people), with over 400 different tribal groups. The literacy rate for Adivasis, as per the 2001 census, is just 29.6%; the national average is 65.38%.

Major Adivasi communities in South India include the Lambanis and Halakkis of northern Karnataka, and the Todas of the Nilgiri Hills of Tamil Nadu (see the boxed text, p456). For information about the Andaman and Nicobar Islands tribal communities, see Island Indigenes, p476.

Historically, contact between Adivasis and Hindu villagers on the plains rarely led to friction as there was little or no competition for resources and land. However, in recent decades an increasing number of Adivasis have been dispossessed of their ancestral land and turned into impoverished labourers. Although they still have political representation thanks to a parliamentary quota system, unless more is done, the Adivasis' future is an uncertain one.

Tourism has had a mixed impact on South India's tribal communities – if you plan on taking a tribal tour, seek out culturally responsible operators who have received permission from tribal people to bring tourists into their communities.

Read more about Adivasis in *Archaeology and History: Early Settlements in the Andaman Islands* by Zarine Cooper, *The Tribals of India* by Sunil Janah and *Tribes of India – The Struggle for Survival* by Christoph von Fürer-Haimendorf.

In South India a large proportion of the population is Dravidian. Over the millennia, however, invasion, trade and settlement have made the population as diverse as anywhere in the country. Invaders and traders from the north, such as Aryans, introduced their traditions to various parts of South India over the years. Christians from the Middle East also arrived on Kerala's coast around AD 100. Arabian and Chinese people came to the Malabar and Coromandel Coasts as traders, and were followed by the Portuguese, the Danes, the French, the Dutch and the British.

RELIGION

The majority of South Indians are Hindu, although, given the region's history, there's more mixing and melding than the census figures on religious affiliation may suggest. Goa has a considerable Christian population, Hyderabad is home to a sizeable Muslim community, while Mumbai is the site of a dwindling number of Parsis (Zoroastrians), among its jumble of other religions.

Religion-based communal conflict has long been a bloody part of India's history, but tensions between religious groups, including Hindus and Muslims, are much less noticeable in the south than up north. In Goa and Kerala the Christian population lives in relative harmony with the Hindu majority, although in other states there have been isolated incidences of retribution against Christian missionaries seeking to convert Hindus.

A fantastical array of religious festivals and events are celebrated across South India, including Diwali (p20), a major Hindu festival, and Christmas as a major Christian one. For details about India's religious festivals, see the Events Calendar chapter on p19 and the 'Festivals In...' boxed texts in regional chapters.

Hinduism

India's major religion, Hinduism, is practised by approximately 82% of the population and, along with Buddhism, Jainism and Zoroastrianism, it's one of the world's oldest extant religions, with roots extending beyond 1000 BC. Hinduism has no founder or central authority and isn't a proselytising religion.

Essentially, Hindus believe in Brahman, who is eternal, uncreated and infinite; everything that exists emanates from Brahman and will ultimately return to it. The multitude of gods and goddesses are merely manifestations – knowable aspects of this formless phenomenon. Brahman is *nirguna* (without attributes), as opposed to all the other gods and goddesses, which are manifestations of Brahman and therefore *saguna* (with attributes).

Although roughly a third of India's population subsists on less than US$1 per day, the country has the world's fastest growing number of US$-millionaires; an estimated 125,000 in 2008.

GODS & GODDESSES

All Hindu deities are regarded as a manifestation of Brahman, who is often described as having three main representations, the Trimurti: Brahma, Vishnu and Shiva. Following are some prominent deities in South India.

Brahma

Only during the creation of the universe does Brahma play an active role. At other times he is in meditation. His consort is Saraswati, the goddess of learning, and his vehicle is a swan. He is sometimes shown sitting on a lotus that rises from Vishnu's navel, symbolising the interdependence of the gods. Brahma is generally depicted with four (crowned and bearded) heads, each turned towards a point of the compass.

Did you know that blood-drinking Kali is another form of milk-giving Gauri? *Myth = Mithya: A Handbook of Hindu Mythology*, by Devdutt Pattanaik, sheds light on this and other intriguing Hindu folklore.

Vishnu

The preserver or sustainer, Vishnu is associated with 'right action'. He protects and sustains all that is good in the world. He is usually depicted with four arms, holding a lotus, a conch shell (as it can be blown like a trumpet it symbolises the cosmic vibration from which all existence emanates), a discus and a mace. His consort is Lakshmi, the goddess of wealth, and his vehicle is Garuda, the man-bird creature. The Ganges is said to flow from his feet.

A renowned Vishnu pilgrimage site is the Venkateshwara Temple (p318) at Tirumala in Andhra Pradesh.

Unravelling the basic tenets of Hinduism are Shakunthala Jagannathan's *Hinduism – An Introduction, Essential Hinduism* by Steven Rosen, and *Hinduism: An Introduction* by Dharam Vir Singh.

Shiva

Shiva is the destroyer, but without whom creation couldn't occur. At Chidambaram (Tamil Nadu), he is worshipped as Nataraja, lord of the *tandava* (cosmic dance; see p429), who paces out the cosmos' creation and destruction. Shiva's creative role is phallically symbolised by his representation as the frequently worshipped lingam. With 1008 names, Shiva takes many forms, including Pashupati, champion of the animals, and Nataraja.

Sometimes Shiva has snakes draped around his neck and is shown holding a trident (representative of the Trimurti) as a weapon while riding Nandi, his bull. Nandi symbolises power and potency, justice and moral order. Shiva's consort, Parvati, is capable of taking many forms.

PILGRIMAGE

Devout Hindus are expected to go on a *yatra* (pilgrimage) at least once a year. Pilgrimages are undertaken to implore the gods or goddesses to grant a wish, to take the ashes of a cremated relative to a holy river, or to gain spiritual merit. India has thousands of holy sites to which pilgrims travel.

Most festivals in India are rooted in religion and are thus a magnet for pilgrims. This is something that travellers should keep in mind, even at festivals that may have a carnivalesque sheen (see the boxed text on p47).

THE KARMA CODE

Hindus believe that earthly life is cyclical; you are born again and again (a process known as samsara), the quality of these rebirths being dependent upon your karma (conduct or action) in previous lives. Living a righteous life and fulfilling your dharma (moral code of behaviour; social duty) will enhance your chances of being born into a higher caste and better circumstances. Alternatively, if enough bad karma has accumulated, rebirth may take animal form. But it's only as a human that you can gain sufficient self-knowledge to escape the cycle of reincarnation and achieve moksha (liberation).

Lakshmi

Lakshmi is Vishnu's consort and the goddess of wealth. In Tamil Nadu the *kolams* (rice-flour or chalk designs; see the boxed text, p68) that grace the thresholds of homes and temples are created with the hope of tempting Lakshmi, and hence prosperity, inside.

Murugan

One of Shiva's sons, Murugan is a popular deity in South India, especially in Tamil Nadu. He is sometimes identified with another of Shiva's sons, Skanda, who enjoys a strong following in North India. Murugan's main role is that of protector, and he is depicted as young and victorious.

The Hindu pantheon has around 330 million deities; those worshipped are a matter of personal choice or tradition.

Ganesh

Elephant-headed Ganesh is the god of good fortune, remover of obstacles, and patron of scribes (the broken tusk he holds was used to write sections of the Mahabharata, see below). His animal mount is a ratlike creature. How Ganesh came to have an elephant's head is a story with several variations. One legend says that he was born to Parvati in the absence of his father (Shiva), so he grew up not knowing him. One day, as Ganesh stood guard while his mother bathed, Shiva returned and asked to be let into Parvati's presence. Ganesh, who didn't recognise Shiva, refused. Enraged, Shiva lopped off Ganesh's head, only to discover, much to his horror, that he had slaughtered his own son! He vowed to replace Ganesh's head with that of the first creature he came across, which happened to be an elephant.

Ayyappan

Ayyappan is another of Shiva's sons who is identified with the role of protector. It's said that he was born from the union of Shiva and Vishnu, both male. Vishnu is said to have assumed female form (as Mohini) to give birth. Ayyappan is often depicted riding on a tiger and accompanied by leopards, symbols of his victory over dark forces. Today the Ayyappan following has become something of a men's movement, with devotees required to avoid alcohol, drugs, cigarettes and general misbehaviour before making the pilgrimage.

SACRED HINDU TEXTS
The Mahabharata

Thought to have been composed at some time around the 1st millennium BC, the Mahabharata focuses on the exploits of Krishna. By about 500 BC the Mahabharata had evolved into a far more complex creation with substantial additions, including the Bhagavad Gita (where Krishna proffers advice to Arjuna before a battle).

The story centres on conflict between the heroic gods (Pandavas) and the demons (Kauravas). Overseeing events is Krishna, who has taken on human form. Krishna acts as charioteer for the Pandava hero Arjuna, who eventually triumphs in a great battle with the Kauravas.

The Ramayana

Composed around the 3rd or 2nd century BC, the Ramayana is believed to be largely the work of one person, the poet Valmiki. Like the Mahabharata, it centres on conflict between the gods and demons.

The story goes that Dasharatha, the childless king of Ayodhya, called upon the gods to provide him with a son. His wife duly gave birth to a boy. But this child, named Rama, was in fact an incarnation of Vishnu, who had assumed human form to overthrow the demon king of Lanka, Ravana. The adult Rama, who won the hand of the princess Sita in a competition, was chosen by his father to inherit his kingdom. At the last minute Rama's stepmother intervened and demanded her son take Rama's place. Rama, Sita and Rama's brother, Lakshmana, were exiled and went off to the forests, where Rama and Lakshmana battled demons and dark forces. Ravana's sister attempted to seduce Rama. She was rejected and, in revenge, Ravana captured Sita and spirited her away to his palace in Lanka. Rama, assisted by an army of monkeys led by the loyal Hindu monkey god Hanuman, eventually found the palace, killed Ravana and rescued Sita. All returned victorious to Ayodhya, where Rama was crowned king.

> A sadhu is someone who has surrendered all material possessions in pursuit of spirituality through meditation, the study of sacred texts, self-mortification and pilgrimage. Learn more in *Sadhus: India's Mystic Holy Men* by Dolf Hartsuiker.

SACRED ANIMALS & PLANTS

Animals, particularly snakes and cows, have long been worshipped in the subcontinent. For Hindus, the cow represents fertility and nurturing, while snakes (especially cobras) are associated with fertility and welfare. Naga stones (snake stones) serve the dual purpose of protecting humans from snakes and propitiating snake gods.

KUMBH MELA

If crowds worry you, stay away. This one's big. Held four times every 12 years at four different locations across central and northern India, the Kumbh Mela is the largest religious congregation on the planet. This vast celebration attracts tens of millions of Hindu pilgrims, including mendicant nagas (naked spiritual men) from radical Hindu monastic orders. The Kumbh Mela doesn't belong to any particular caste or creed – devotees from all branches of Hinduism come together to experience the electrifying sensation of mass belief and to take a ceremonial dip in the sacred Ganges, Shipra or Godavari Rivers.

The origins of the festival go back to the battle for supremacy between good and evil. In the Hindu creation myths, the gods and demons fought a great battle for a *kumbh* (pitcher) containing the nectar of immortality. Vishnu got hold of the container and spirited it away, but in flight four drops spilt on the earth – at Allahabad, Haridwar, Nasik (p148) and Ujjain. Celebrations at each of these cities last for around six weeks but are centred on just a handful of auspicious bathing dates, normally six. The Allahabad event, known as the Maha (Great) Kumbh Mela, is even larger with even bigger crowds. Each location also holds an Ardh (Half) Mela every six years and a smaller, annual Magh Mela. For more details, visit www.kumbhamela.net.

Kumbh Mela Schedule

- 2010 – Haridwar (March–April)
- 2013 – Allahabad (27 January–25 February)*
- 2015 – Nasik (15 August–13 September)
- 2016 – Ujjain (22 April–21 May)
  *Maha (Great) Kumbh Mela

> **WORSHIP**
>
> Worship and ritual play a paramount role in Hinduism. In Hindu homes you'll often find a dedicated worship area, where members of the family pray to the deities of their choice. Beyond the home, Hindus worship at temples. *Puja* is a focal point of worship and ranges from silent prayer to elaborate ceremonies. Devotees leave the temple with a handful of *prasad* (temple-blessed food) which is humbly shared among friends and family. Other forms of worship include *aarti* (the auspicious lighting of lamps or candles) and the playing of soul-soothing bhajans (devotional songs).

Plants can also have sacred associations, such as the banyan tree, which symbolises the Trimurti, while mango trees are symbolic of love – Shiva is believed to have married Parvati under one. Meanwhile, the lotus flower is said to have emerged from the primeval waters and is connected to the mythical centre of the Earth through its stem. Often found in the most polluted of waters, the lotus has the remarkable ability to blossom above its murky depths. The centre of the lotus corresponds to the centre of the universe, the navel of the Earth; all is held together by the stem and the eternal waters. This is how Hindus are reminded their own lives should be – like the fragile yet resolute lotus, an embodiment of beauty and strength. So revered is the lotus that today it's India's national flower.

Islam

Islam was introduced to South India from around the 13th century by Arab traders who settled in coastal Kerala and Karnataka. About 10% of South India's population is Muslim, although this figure is higher in parts of Andhra Pradesh, Karnataka and Kerala. Most are Sunni, although Iranian traders and adventurers also introduced the Shiite following to the region. Although the Mughals, an Islamic dynasty whose empire encompassed a large part of India from the 16th to 18th centuries, controlled northern India for around two centuries, they never really gained a stronghold in the far south, which is one reason there are so many intact ancient Hindu temples in Tamil Nadu.

Islam, which is monotheistic, was founded in Arabia by the Prophet Mohammed in the 7th century AD. The Arabic term *islam* means to surrender, and believers (Muslims) undertake to surrender to the will of Allah (God), which is revealed in the scriptures, the Quran. God's word is conveyed through prophets (messengers), of whom Mohammed is the most recent.

Following Mohammed's death, a succession dispute split the movement, and the legacy today is the Sunnis and the Shiites. Most Muslims in India are Sunnis. The Sunnis emphasise the 'well-trodden' path or the orthodox way. Shiites believe that only imams (exemplary leaders) can reveal the true meaning of the Quran.

All Muslims, however, share a belief in the Five Pillars of Islam: the shahada (declaration of faith: 'There is no God but Allah; Mohammed is his prophet'); prayer (ideally five times a day); the zakat (tax), in the form of a charitable donation; fasting (during Ramadan) for all except the sick, the very young, the elderly and those undertaking arduous journeys; and the haj (pilgrimage) to Mecca, which every Muslim aspires to do at least once.

Christianity

Christians comprise around 2.3% of the Indian population, with around 75% living in South India. There are various theories circulating about Christ's link to the subcontinent. Some, for instance, believe that Jesus spent his 'lost years' in India, while others believe that Christianity arrived in South

India with St Thomas the Apostle in AD 52. However, many scholars say it's more likely Christianity arrived around the 4th century with a Syrian merchant, Thomas Cana, who set out for Kerala with around 400 families to establish what later became a branch of the Nestorian church. Today the Christian community is fractured into a multitude of established churches and new evangelical sects.

The Marriage of East and West, by Bede Griffiths, examines the essence of Eastern and Western thought in an attempt to forge a fresh approach to spirituality.

The Nestorian church sect survives today; services are in Armenian, and the Patriarch of Baghdad is the sect's head. Thrissur (Trichur; p375) is the church's centre. Other Eastern Orthodox sects include the Jacobites and the Syrian Orthodox churches.

Catholicism established a strong presence in South India in the wake of Vasco da Gama's visit in 1498. Catholic orders that have been active in the region include the Dominicans, Franciscans and Jesuits. The faith is most noticeable in Goa, not only in the basilicas and convents of Old Goa (p199), but in the dozens of active whitewashed churches scattered through towns and villages. Protestant missionaries are believed to have arrived in South India from around the 18th century and today most of this minority group belong to the 'Church of South India', which is comprised of various denominations including Anglican, Methodist and Presbyterian.

Evangelical Christian groups have made inroads both into the other Christian communities, and lower caste and tribal groups across South India. According to various news reports over the years, some congregations have been regarded as being aggressive in seeking converts, and in 'retaliation' a number of Christian communities have been targeted by Hindu nationalist groups.

Jainism

Jainism is followed by about 0.4% of India's population, with the majority of Jains living in Gujarat and Mumbai. Jainism arose in the 6th century BC as a reaction against the caste restraints and rituals of Hinduism. It was founded by Mahavira, a contemporary of Buddha, and evolved as a reformist movement against Brahminism. Jainism revolves around the concept of ahimsa, or nonviolence.

Apart from Mumbai, South India's small community of Jains is centred on coastal Karnataka; the 17m-high sculpture of Gomateshvara (one of the world's tallest monoliths; see p261) at Sravanabelagola is at one of Jainism's most-visited centres of pilgrimage.

Set in Kerala against the backdrop of caste conflict and India's struggle for independence, *The House of Blue Mangoes* by David Davidar spans three generations of a Christian family.

Buddhism

Buddhism developed in India when it was embraced by Emperor Ashoka during his reign (272–232 BC) and today it comprises around 0.76% of the country's population.

It appears that Buddhist communities were quite influential in Andhra Pradesh between the 2nd and 5th centuries; missionaries from Andhra helped establish monasteries and temples in countries such as Thailand. However, Buddhism's influence waned as Hinduism's waxed in South India, about 1000 years after it was first introduced. It underwent a sudden revival in the 1950s when the Dalit leader, Dr Ambedkar, converted to Buddhism and brought many Dalit followers with him. Today these Neo-Buddhists, as they are often called, number about six million and are concentrated in Dr Ambedkar's home state of Maharashtra.

There are several communities of Tibetan refugees in South India, who have established a number of new monasteries and convents since the 1960s. The Bylakuppe area of Karnataka is one of the more easily accessible Tibetan settlements – see p266 for more information.

IN PURSUIT OF NIRVANA

Buddhism arose in the 6th century BC as a reaction against the strictures of Brahminical Hinduism. Buddha (Awakened One) is believed to have lived from about 563 BC to 483 BC. Formerly a prince (Siddhartha Gautama), Buddha, at the age of 29, embarked on a quest for emancipation from the world of suffering. He achieved nirvana (the state of full awareness) at Bodhgaya (Bihar), aged 35.

Buddha taught that existence is based on Four Noble Truths – that life is rooted in suffering, that suffering is caused by craving, that one can find release from suffering by eliminating craving, and that the way to eliminate craving is by following the Noble Eightfold Path. This path consists of right understanding, right intention, right speech, right action, right livelihood, right effort, right awareness and right concentration. By successfully complying with these one can attain nirvana.

Both the current Dalai Lama and the 17th Karmapa reside in the north Indian state of Himachal Pradesh.

Judaism

Reports indicate that there are less than 5000 Jews left in India, most living in Mumbai and scattered pockets of South India. South India's Jews first settled in the region from the Middle East as far back as the 1st century. Jews became established at Kochi (Cochin), and their legacy continues in the still-standing synagogues and trading houses – see p363.

Zoroastrianism

Parsis, adherents of Zoroastrianism, today number somewhere between 60,000 and 69,600 – a mere drop in the ocean of India's billion-plus population.

Zoroastrianism, founded by Zoroaster (Zarathustra), had its inception in Persia in the 6th century BC and is based on the concept of dualism, whereby good and evil are locked in continuous battle. Zoroastrianism isn't quite monotheistic: good and evil entities coexist, although believers are enjoined to honour only the good. Humanity therefore has a choice. There's no conflict between body and soul: both are united in the good versus evil struggle. Humanity, although mortal, has components such as the soul, which are timeless; a pleasant afterlife depends on one's deeds, words and thoughts during earthly existence. But not every lapse is entered on the balance sheet and the errant soul is not called to account on the day of judgement for each and every misdemeanour.

Zoroastrianism was eclipsed in Persia by the rise of Islam in the 7th century, and its followers, many of whom openly resisted this, suffered persecution. Over the following centuries, some immigrated to India, where they became known as Parsis. For further information see the boxed text on p121.

Sikhism

South India is home to a small population of Sikhs – the majority of the country's 1.9% of Sikhs lives in North India, especially Punjab.

Sikhism, founded in Punjab by Guru Nanak in the 15th century, began as a reaction against the caste system and Brahmin domination of ritual. Sikhs believe in one god and although they reject the worship of idols, some keep pictures of the 10 gurus as a point of focus. The Sikhs' holy book, the Guru Granth Sahib, contains the teachings of the 10 Sikh gurus, among others.

Like Hindus and Buddhists, Sikhs believe in rebirth and karma. In Sikhism, there's no ascetic or monastic tradition ending the cycles of rebirth.

Handbook of Living Religions, edited by John R Hinnells, provides a succinct and readable summary of various religions in India, including Christianity and Judaism.

The Last Jews of Kerala, by Edna Fernandes, proffers an interesting window into the last remaining members of Kerala's dwindling Jewish community.

The Zoroastrian funerary ritual involves the 'Towers of Silence' where the corpse is laid out and exposed to vultures, which pick the bones clean.

Fundamental to Sikhs is the concept of Khalsa, or belief in a chosen race of soldier-saints who abide by strict codes of moral conduct (abstaining from alcohol, tobacco and drugs) and engage in a crusade for *dharmayudha* (righteousness). There are five *kakkars* (emblems) denoting the Khalsa brotherhood: *kesh* (the unshaven beard and uncut hair symbolising saintliness); *kangha* (comb to maintain the ritually uncut hair); *kaccha* (loose underwear symbolising modesty); *kirpan* (sabre or sword symbolising power and dignity); and *karra* (steel bangle symbolising fearlessness). Singh, literally 'Lion', is the name adopted by many Sikhs.

To grasp the intricacies of Sikhism read *A History of the Sikhs* by Khushwant Singh, which comes in Volume One (1469–1839) and Volume Two (1839–2004).

A belief in the equality of all beings lies at the heart of Sikhism. It's expressed in various practices, including *langar,* whereby people from all walks of life – regardless of caste and creed – sit side by side to share a complimentary meal prepared by volunteers in the communal kitchen of the gurdwara (Sikh temple).

Tribal Religions

Tribal religions have merged with Hinduism and other mainstream religions so that very few are now clearly identifiable. It's believed that some basic tenets of Hinduism may have originated in ancient tribal culture.

Village and tribal people in South India have their own belief systems, which are much less accessible or obvious than the temples, rituals and other outward manifestations of the mainstream religions. The village deity may be represented by a stone pillar in a field, a platform under a tree or an iron spear stuck in the ground. Village deities are generally seen as less remote and more concerned with the immediate happiness and prosperity of the community; in most cases they are female. There are also many beliefs about ancestral spirits, including those who died violently.

To learn more about some of South India's tribal groups, see the Nehru Centenary Tribal Museum (p302), Island Indigenes boxed text (p476) and Hill Tribes of the Nilgiri boxed text (p456).

WOMEN IN SOUTH INDIA

South Indian women have traditionally had a greater degree of freedom than their northern sisters. This is especially so in Kerala. Unique in many ways, Kerala is the most literate state in India and is also famous for its tradition of matrilineal kinship. Exactly why the matrilineal family became established in this region is subject to conjecture, although one explanation is that it was in response to ongoing warfare in the 10th and 11th centuries. With the military men absent, women invariably took charge of the household. It has also been argued that the men would very likely form alliances wherever they found themselves, and that the children of these unions would become the responsibility of the mother's family. Whatever the reason, by the 14th century a matrilineal society was firmly established in many communities across Kerala, and it lasted pretty much unchallenged until the 20th century. Kerala was also India's first state to break societal norms by recruiting female police officers in 1938. On top of that, it was the first state to establish an all-female police station (1973).

Read more about India's tribal communities at www.tribal.nic.in, a site maintained by the Indian Government's Ministry of Tribal Affairs.

In other parts of South India, such as Tamil Nadu, women also had more freedom than was the norm elsewhere in India. Matriarchy was a long-standing tradition within Tamil communities, and the practice of marriage between cousins meant that young women did not have to move away and live among strangers. Dowry deaths and female infanticide were virtually unknown in India until relatively recent times, but the imposition of consumerism on old customs and conventions, making dowries more expensive, has resulted in increased instances.

Women throughout India are entitled to vote and own property. While the percentage of women in politics has risen over the past decade, they're still notably underrepresented in the national parliament, accounting for around 10% of parliamentary members.

Although the professions are still very much male dominated, women are steadily making inroads, most noticeably in the bigger cities. For village women it is much more difficult to get ahead, and an early marriage to a suitable provider (often arranged years beforehand) is usually regarded as essential.

In low-income families, especially, girls can be regarded as a serious financial liability because at marriage a dowry must often be supplied. An Indian news report indicated that dowry-related deaths in 2006 stood at 7618 (around 12% higher than the previous year). However this is likely to be a conservative figure given that many cases go unreported. For more about dowries see p44.

For the urban middle-class woman, life is materially much more comfortable, but pressures still exist. Broadly speaking, she is far more likely to receive a tertiary education, but once married is still usually expected to 'fit in' with her in-laws and be a homemaker above all else. Like her village counterpart, if she fails to live up to expectations – even if it's just not being able to produce a grandson – the consequences can sometimes be dire, as demonstrated by the extreme practice of 'bride burning', where the husband or a member of his family inflicts pain, disfigurement or death on his wife. It may take the form of dousing with fuel and setting alight or scalding with boiling water, and is usually intentionally designed to look like an accident or suicide. Reliable statistics are unavailable, however, some women's groups claim that for every reported case, roughly 250 go unreported, and that less than 10% of the reported cases are pursued through the legal system.

According to the latest data from the Indian Home Ministry's National Crime Records Bureau (NCRB), in 2006 there was an eight-fold rise in the number of women raped since 1971 – the year rape cases were first compiled by the NCRB – jumping from seven to 53 reported cases per day (a 5.5% increase from 2005), with most incidents in Delhi. However the figure is believed to be higher, as many rape cases go unreported.

In October 2006, following women's civil-rights campaigns, the Indian parliament passed a landmark bill (on top of existing legislation) which gives women who are suffering domestic violence increased protection and rights. The new law purports that any form of physical, sexual (including marital rape), emotional and economic abuse entails not only domestic violence, but also human-rights violations. Perpetrators face imprisonment and fines.

Although the constitution allows for divorcées (and widows) to remarry, relatively few reportedly do so, simply because divorcées are traditionally considered outcasts from society, especially beyond big cities. Divorce rates in India are among the worlds' lowest, despite having risen from seven in 1000 in 1991 to 11 in 1000 in 2004. Although no reliable post-2004 statistics are available, divorce rates are reportedly growing by around 15% per annum, with most cases registered in urban India.

Women travellers should also read p516.

ARTS

Classic and contemporary artistic flourishes abound in South India, whether it's an ornately decorated elephant or a simple – yet uniquely shaped – earthenware jug. Indeed, a glowing highlight of subcontinental travel is its wealth of art treasures, from ancient temple architecture to a dynamic performing-arts scene.

Modern artists have fused historical elements with edgy modern influences, creating art, dance and music that have won acclaim on both the domestic and international arenas.

Literature

Immerse yourself in India's vibrant performing-arts scene – especially classical dance and music – at Art India (www.artindia.net).

South India's main languages – Tamil, Kannada, Telugu, Malayalam and Marathi – each have a long literary history. Tamil is considered a case apart (some early works date from the 2nd century) because it evolved independently from the others, which all have their roots in Sanskrit.

In the 19th century, South Indian literature began to reflect the influence of European genres. Where literature had once been expressed primarily in verse, now it was widely seen in prose. By the end of the 19th century, South Indian writers were pioneering new forms; among them Subramanya Bharathi and VVS Aiyar, who are credited with transforming Tamil into a modern language.

Dip into details of English-language Indian literature – from historical to contemporary times – at Indian English Literature (www.indian englishliterature.com).

India boasts an ever-growing list of internationally acclaimed authors. Some particularly prominent writers include Vikram Seth, best known for his award-winning epic novel *A Suitable Boy*, and Amitav Ghosh, who has won a number of accolades; his *Sea of Poppies* was shortlisted for the 2008 Man Booker Prize. Indeed recent years have seen a number of India-born authors win the prestigious Man Booker Prize, the most recent being Chennai-born Aravind Adiga, who won in 2008 for his debut novel, *The White Tiger*. The prize went to Kiran Desai in 2006 for *The Inheritance of Loss;* Kiran Desai is the daughter of the award-winning Indian novelist Anita Desai, who has thrice been a Booker Prize nominee. In 1997, Arundhati Roy won the Booker Prize for her novel, *The God of Small Things*, while Mumbai-born Salman Rushdie took this coveted award in 1981 for *Midnight's Children*.

Legends of Goa, by Mario Cabral E Sa, is an illustrated compilation of Goan folktales that offers an insight into the state's colourful traditions and history.

Trinidad-born Indian writer VS Naipaul has written widely about India and won many notable awards including the Booker Prize (1971) and the Nobel Prize in Literature (2001). UK-born Bengali writer Jhumpa Lahiri was awarded the 2000 Pulitzer Prize for Fiction for *Interpreter of Maladies*, a collection of short stories.

One of South India's most legendary English-language writers is Chennai-born RK Narayan (1906–2001). Many of his stories centre on the fictitious South Indian town of Malgudi; some of his most well-known works are *Swami and Friends, The Financial Expert, The Guide, Waiting for the Mahatma, The Painter of Signs* and *Malgudi Days*.

Family Matters and *A Fine Balance*, by Mumbai-born Rohinton Mistry, are expertly crafted accounts of contemporary Indian society, both set in Mumbai.

A Matter of Time, by Shashi Deshpande, centres on the problems a middle-class family faces when the husband walks out. Deshpande, who is from Karnataka, takes the reader back through several generations to demonstrate how family tradition impacts on contemporary behaviour.

Sharapanjara (Cage of Arrows), by Karnatakan author Triveni, is hailed as one of the great novels in the Kannada language (also available in English). The story centres on an upper-class Mysore woman facing the stigma of mental illness.

The Revised Kama Sutra, by Bengaluru-born Richard Crasta, takes an irreverent look at growing up in Mangalore in the 1960s and 1970s. It's a book that leaves you with a lasting insight into the local life of Mangalore and other South Indian cities.

Nectar in a Sieve, by Kamala Markandaya, is a harrowing, though at times uplifting, account of a woman's life in rural South India, and the effect of industrialisation on traditional values and lifestyles.

A LITERARY LEGEND: RABINDRANATH TAGORE

Bengalis are traditionally credited with producing some of India's most celebrated literature, a movement often referred to as the Indian or Bengal Renaissance, which flourished from the 19th century with works by Bankim Chandra Chatterjee. But the man who to this day is mostly credited with first propelling India's cultural richness onto the world stage is Rabindranath Tagore.

The brilliant and prolific poet, writer, artist and patriot Rabindranath Tagore has had an unparalleled impact on Bengali culture. Born to a prominent family in Kolkata (Calcutta) in 1861, he began writing as a young boy and never stopped (he was said to have been dictating his last poem only hours before his death in 1941).

Tagore is also largely credited with introducing India's historical and cultural splendour to the Western world. He won the Nobel Prize in Literature in 1913 with his mystical collection of poems, *Gitanjali* (Song Offerings), and in later years his lecture tours saw him carrying his message of human unity around Asia, America and Europe.

But for all his internationalism, Tagore's heart was firmly rooted in his homeland; a truth reflected in his many popular songs, sung by the masses, and in the lyrics of the national anthems of both India and Bangladesh. In 1915 Tagore was awarded a knighthood by the British, but he later surrendered it in protest to the 1919 Jallianwala Bagh Massacre in Amritsar (Punjab).

For a taste of Tagore's work, read his *Selected Short Stories*.

The first part of Salman Rushdie's *The Moor's Last Sigh* is set in Kochi, (Cochin; Kerala), while his *Midnight's Children* is a stunning story of India from Independence until the disastrous Emergency of the mid-1970s.

Karma Cola, by Gita Mehta, amusingly and cynically describes the collision between India looking to the West for technology and modern methods, and the West descending upon India in search of wisdom and enlightenment.

For more insights into southern literature see the boxed texts on p446, p399 and p403. For further reading recommendations see the boxed text on p17.

Cinema

The nation's film industry was born in the late 19th century – the first major Indian-made motion picture, *Panorama of Calcutta*, was screened in 1899. India's first real feature film, *Raja Harishchandra*, was made during the silent era in 1913 and it's ultimately from this that Indian cinema traces its vibrant lineage.

Today, India's film industry is the biggest in the world – larger than Hollywood – and Mumbai, the Hindi-language film capital, is affectionately dubbed 'Bollywood'. India's other major film-producing centres include Chennai, Hyderabad and Bengaluru, with a number of other southern centres also producing films in their own regional vernaculars.

As well as the obvious Bollywood blockbusters, most states in South India have their own regional film industry. Tamil-language films from Tamil Nadu and Telugu films from Andhra Pradesh are the most numerous, but there are strong Malayalam films from Kerala and Kannada films from Karnataka.

Big-budget films are often partly or entirely shot abroad, with some countries vigorously wooing Indian production companies because of the potential spin-off tourism revenue these films generate.

An average of 900 feature films are produced annually in India, with around 3.7 billion Bollywood movie tickets sold at the box office in 2006 alone. Apart from hundreds of millions of local Bollywood buffs, there are also millions of Non-Resident Indian (NRI) fans, who have played a significant role in catapulting Indian cinema into the international arena.

Broadly speaking, there are two categories of Indian films. Most prominent is the mainstream movie – three hours and still running, these blockbusters

Encyclopedia of Indian Cinema by Ashish Rajadhyaksha and Paul Willemen chronicles India's fascinating cinematic history, spanning from 1897 to the 21st century.

are often tear-jerkers and are packed with dramatic twists interspersed with numerous song-and-dance performances. There are no explicit sex, or even kissing, scenes (although smooching is creeping into some Bollywood movies) in Indian films made for the local market; however, lack of nudity is often compensated for by heroines dressed in skimpy or body-hugging attire.

The second Indian film genre is art house, which adopts Indian 'reality' as its base. Generally speaking they are, or at least supposed to be, socially and politically relevant. Usually made on infinitely smaller budgets than their commercial cousins, these films are the ones that win kudos at global film festivals and award ceremonies.

For the latest film fare, check out Movie South India (www.indiafilm .com), Bollywood World (www.bollywoodworld .com) and Tamil Cinema World (www.tamilcinema world.com).

Set in Mumbai, *Slumdog Millionaire*, directed by British filmmaker Danny Boyle, is the latest international success story. Adapted from the novel, *Q&A*, by Indian diplomat/author, Vikas Swarup, it scooped up eight Academy Awards in 2009, including Best Picture. However, amid the accolades, the film attracted criticism over its stereotypical depiction of India and allegedly exploitative use of child actors – accusations the filmmakers denied. In 1983, *Gandhi*, directed by Richard Attenborough, also seized eight Academy Awards, including Best Picture.

India-born Canadian filmmaker Deepa Mehta has also gained international acclaim for her trilogy, *Earth, Fire* and *Water*. Mehta faced various obstacles during and after filming, especially for *Fire*, with some nationalists burning down cinemas, claiming that the film's lesbian themes maligned Indian society and Hinduism.

For information about Bollywood and working as a film extra, read the boxed text, p120; and for more about Tamil films, see the boxed text on p402.

Music

Indian classical music traces its roots back to Vedic times, when religious poems chanted by priests were first collated in an anthology called the Rig-Veda. Over the millennia classical music has been shaped by many influences, and the legacy today is Carnatic (characteristic of South India) and Hindustani (the classical style of North India) music. With common origins, both share a number of features. Both use the raga (the melodic shape of the music) and *tala* (the rhythmic meter characterised by the number of beats); *tintal*, for example, has a *tala* of 16 beats. The audience follows the *tala* by clapping at the appropriate beat, which in *tintal* is at beats one, five and 13. There's no clap at the beat of nine; that's the *khali* (empty section), which is indicated by a wave of the hand. Both the raga and the *tala* are used as a basis for composition and improvisation.

Both Carnatic and Hindustani music are performed by small ensembles, generally comprising three to six musicians, and both have many instruments in common. There's no fixed pitch, but there are differences between the two styles. Hindustani has been more heavily influenced by Persian musical conventions (a result of Mughal rule); Carnatic music, as it developed in South India, cleaves more closely to theory. The most striking difference, at least for those unfamiliar with India's classical forms, is Carnatic's greater use of voice.

To delve into the beguiling world of Carnatic music check out www .carnaticcorner.com, www.carnatic.com and www.carnaticindia.com.

One of the best-known Indian instruments is the sitar (large stringed instrument) with which the soloist plays the raga. Other stringed instruments include the sarod (which is plucked) and the sarangi (which is played with a bow). Also popular is the tabla (twin drums), which provides the *tala*. The drone, which runs on two basic notes, is provided by the oboelike *shehnai* or the stringed *tampura* (also spelt *tamboura*). The hand-pumped keyboard harmonium is used as a secondary melody instrument for vocal music.

BHANGRA

Originating in the North Indian state of Punjab, bhangra is a wildly rhythmic and innovative form of subcontinental music and dance that has been embraced right around India, including the south. Bhangra emerged as part of Punjab's harvest-festival celebrations (dating back to around the 14th century).

This joyful, spirited dance most famously entails the arms being thrust high in the air coupled with the feisty shaking of the shoulders. The predominant musical instrument is the heart-thumping *dhol* (double-sided drum).

In the 1980s and '90s, inventive fusion versions of traditional bhangra (which include elements of hip hop, disco, techno, rap, house and reggae) exploded on the international arena, especially in the UK, rocking dance floors across the world.

Indian regional folk music is widespread and varied. Wandering musicians, magicians, snake charmers and storytellers often use song to entertain their audiences; the storyteller usually sings the tales from the great epics.

A completely different genre altogether, filmi music entails musical scores from Bollywood movies – modern (slower paced) love serenades feature among the predominantly hyperactive dance songs. To ascertain the latest filmi favourites, as well as in-vogue Indian pop singers, inquire at music stores.

Radio and TV have played a paramount role in broadcasting different music styles – from soothing bhajans to booming Bollywood hits – to even the remotest corners of South India.

Architecture

From looming temple gateways adorned with a rainbow of delicately carved deities, to whitewashed cube-like village houses, South India has a rich architectural heritage. Traditional buildings, such as temples, often have a superb sense of placement within the local environment, whether perched on a boulder-strewn hill or standing by a large artificial reservoir.

The influence of British architecture is most obvious in cities such as Chennai, Bengaluru and Mumbai, which have scores of grand neoclassical structures. British bungalows with corrugated iron roofs and wide verandahs are a feature of many hill stations, including Ooty (Udhagamandalam; p464). More memorable are the attempts to meld European and Indian architecture, such as in the great 19th-century public buildings of Mumbai and the breathtaking Maharaja's Palace in Mysore (for more details see p250).

The History of Architecture in India: From the Dawn of Civilisation to the End of the Raj, by Christopher Tadgell, is an illustrated overview of the subject that includes significant sites in South India.

RELIGIOUS ARCHITECTURE

For Hindus, the square is a perfect shape, and complex rules govern the location, design and building of each temple, based on numerology, astrology, astronomy and religious principles. Essentially, a temple represents a map of the universe. At the centre is an unadorned space, the *garbhagriha* (inner sanctum), which is symbolic of the 'womb-cave' from which the universe is believed to have emerged. This provides a residence for the deity to which the temple is dedicated.

Above the shrine rises a superstructure known as a *vimana* in South India, and a *sikhara* in North India. The *sikhara* is curvilinear and topped with a grooved disk, on which sits a pot-shaped finial, while the *vimana* is stepped, with the grooved disk replaced with a solid dome. Some temples have a *mandapa* (temple forechamber) connected to the sanctum by vestibules. These *mandapas* may also contain *vimanas* or *sikharas*.

Architecture and Art of Southern India, by George Michell, provides details on the Vijayanagar empire and its successors, encompassing a period of some 400 years.

Discover more about India's diverse temple architecture (in addition to other temple-related information) at Temple Net (www.templenet .com).

A *gopuram* is a soaring pyramidal gateway tower of a Dravidian temple. The towering *gopurams* of various South Indian temple complexes (eg Madurai's Sri Meenakshi Temple – p446) took ornamentation and monumentalism to new levels.

From the outside, Jain temples can resemble Hindu ones, but inside they're often a riot of sculptural ornamentation, the very opposite of ascetic austerity. Meanwhile, gurdwaras (Sikh temples) can usually be identified by a *nishan sahib* (flagpole flying a triangular flag with the Sikh insignia).

Stupas, which characterise Buddhist places of worship, essentially evolved from burial mounds. They served as repositories for relics of Buddha and, later, other venerated souls. A relatively recent innovation is the addition of a *chaitya* (hall) leading up to the stupa itself.

The subcontinent's Muslim invaders contributed their own architectural conventions – arched cloisters and domes among them. One of the most striking differences between Hinduism and Islam is religious imagery – while Islamic art eschews any hint of idolatry or portrayal of God, it has developed a rich heritage of calligraphic and decorative designs.

Temples of South India by Sunil Vaidyanathan is a predominantly pictorial publication covering major South Indian temples.

In terms of mosque architecture, the basic design elements are similar worldwide. A large hall is dedicated to communal prayer and within the hall is a mihrab (niche) indicating the direction of Mecca. The faithful are called to prayer from minarets, placed at cardinal points. Many large towns have at least one mosque; some fine examples of Islamic architecture in South India include Hyderabad's Mecca Masjid (p302) and Golconda Fort (p301), and Bijapur's Golgumbaz (p287).

Churches in India reflect the fashions and trends of typically European ecclesiastical architecture with many also incorporating Hindu decorative flourishes. The Portuguese, among others, made impressive attempts to replicate the great churches and cathedrals of their day. Today, Goa has some particularly impressive churches and cathedrals, especially Old Goa – see p199.

FORTS & PALACES

A typical South Indian fort is situated on a hill or rocky outcrop, ringed by moated battlements. It usually has a town nestled at its base, which would have developed after the fortifications were built. Gingee (Senji; p420), in Tamil Nadu, is a particularly good example. Vellore Fort (p417), in Tamil Nadu, is one of India's best-known moated forts, while Bidar (see p290) and Bijapur (p287) are home to great metropolitan forts.

Daulatabad (p156), in Maharashtra, is another magnificent structure, with 5km of walls surrounding a hilltop fortress. The fortress is reached by passageways filled with ingenious defences, including spike-studded doors and false tunnels, which in times of war led either to a pit of boiling oil or to a crocodile-filled moat!

Few old palaces remain in South India, as conquerors often targeted these for destruction. The remains of the royal complex at Vijayanagar, near Hampi (p275), indicate that local engineers weren't averse to using the sound structural techniques and fashions (such as domes and arches) of their Muslim adversaries, the Bahmanis. Travancore's palace of the maharajas (p336), at Padmanabhapuram, which dates from the 16th century, has private apartments for the king, a zenana (women's quarters), rooms dedicated to public audiences, an armoury, a dance hall and temples. Meanwhile, the Indo-Saracenic Maharaja's Palace (p250), in Mysore, is the best known and most opulent in the south, its interior a kaleidoscope of stained glass, mirrors and mosaic floors.

TEMPLE TANKS

Commonly used for ritual bathing and religious ceremonies, as well as adding aesthetic appeal to places of worship, temple tanks have long been a focal point of temple activity. These often-vast, angular, engineered reservoirs of water, sometimes fed by rain, sometimes fed – via a complicated drainage system – by rivers, serve both sacred and secular purposes. The waters of some temple tanks are believed to have healing properties, while others are said to have the power to wash away sins. Devotees (as well as travellers) may be required to wash their feet in a temple tank before entering a place of worship.

SCULPTURE

Sculpture and religious architecture are closely related in South India, and it's difficult to consider them separately. Sculpture is invariably religious in nature and isn't generally an art form through which individuals express their own creativity.

The 7th-century relief Arjuna's Penance (p410), at Mamallapuram (Mahabalipuram), is one of the most sublime examples of early sculpture. Its fresh, lively touch is also reflected in later 9th-century Chola shrine sculptures. The legacy and tradition of sculptors from the Pallava dynasty live on in Mamallapuram, where hundreds of modern-day sculptors work with stone to produce freestanding sculptures of all shapes and sizes (see the Sculpture Museum, p411). Some even mix the old with the spanking new – such as a sculpture of Ganesh chatting on a mobile phone!

Unlike in the north of India, a tradition of South Indian sculpture was able to develop without serious interruption from Muslim invasions. But curiously, despite a high level of technical skill, the 17th-century work often appears to lack the life and quality of earlier examples. However, South India remains famous for its bronze sculptures, particularly those of the 9th and 10th centuries, created during the highly artistic Chola dynasty (p31). Artisans employed the lost-wax technique to make their pieces, which were usually of Hindu deities, such as Vishnu and – in the south especially – Shiva in his adored form as Lord of the Dance, Nataraja. This technique, still in use in South India, involves carving a model out of wax then painting on a claylike mixture to form a mould. The wax is melted out, leaving a hollow mould into which molten bronze (or silver, copper, lead etc) is poured. Some of the most exuberant sculptural detail comes from the Hoysala period, and can be seen at the temples of Belur (p260) and Halebid (p260) in Karnataka.

Window on Goa, by Maurice Hall, is an authoritative labour of love featuring descriptions of Goa's churches, forts, villages and more.

Dance

Dance is an ancient and revered Indian art form that is traditionally linked to mythology and classical literature. Historically, accomplished artists were a matter of prolific pride among royal houses; the quality of their respective dance troupes was at one stage the cause of intense competition between the maharajas of Mysore and Travancore. Between the 2nd and 8th centuries, trade between South India and Southeast Asia brought a cultural legacy that endures in the dance forms of Bali (Indonesia), Thailand, Cambodia and Myanmar (Burma). Today dance – classical, popular and folk – thrives on city stages, on the cinema screen and in towns and villages throughout South India.

South India has many kinds of folk dance: these include the Puraviattams of Karnataka and Tamil Nadu, where dancers are dressed in horse costumes; the Koklikatai dance of Tamil Nadu, in which dancers move about on stilts that have bells attached; and the Kolyacha fishers' dance from the Konkan Coast. Goa's stylised Mando song and dance is a waltzlike blend of Indian rhythms and Portuguese melody accompanied by Konkani words.

Various forms of trance-dancing and dances of exorcism occur throughout the south, and almost all tribal peoples, including the Todas of Tamil Nadu and the Banjaras of Andhra Pradesh, retain unique dance traditions. The major classical dance forms of South India:

Indian Classical Dance by Leela Venkataraman and Avinash Pasricha is a lavishly illustrated book covering various Indian dance forms, including Bharata Natyam and Kathakali.

- Bharata Natyam (also spelt *bharatanatyam*) is Tamil Nadu's unique performing art and is believed to be India's oldest continuing classical dance. It was originally known as Dasi Attam, a temple art performed by young women called *devadasis*. After the 16th century, however, it fell into disrepute, largely because it became synonymous with prostitution. It was revived in the mid-19th century by four brothers from Thanjavur (Tanjore), who are credited with restoring the art's purity by returning to its ancient roots.

- Kathakali, one of South India's most renowned forms of classical dance-drama, is a Keralan form of play, usually based on Hindu epics; also see the boxed text, p372.

- Kuchipudi is a 17th-century dance-drama that originated in the Andhra Pradesh village from which it takes its name. Like Kathakali, its present-day form harks back to the 17th century, when it became the prerogative of Brahmin boys from this village. It often centres on the story of Satyambhama, wife of Lord Krishna.

- Mohiniyattam, from Kerala, is a semiclassical dance form that is based on the story of Mohini, the mythical seductress. Known for its gentle and poetic movements, it contains elements of Bharata Natyam and Kathakali.

- *Theyyam*, seen in Kannur (Kerala; see the boxed text, p372), is an ancient dance form practised by tribal people and villagers in the north Malabar region. The headdresses, costumes, body painting and trancelike performances are truly extraordinary. The Parasinikadavu Temple (near Kannur) stages *theyyam* performances; see p383 for details on where to catch a show.

- Yakshagana is unique to the Tulu-speaking region of Karnataka's south coast. The focus in Yakshagana is less on the dance or movement aspect of performance, since (unlike Kathakali) the actors have vocal roles to play, both singing and speaking. As in Kathakali, the

CONTEMPORARY INDIAN ART

In the 21st century, paintings by contemporary Indian artists have been selling at record numbers (and prices) around the world. One especially innovative and successful online art auction house, the Mumbai-based **Saffronart** (www.saffronart.com), has reportedly surpassed heavyweights like Sotheby's and Christie's in terms of its online Indian art sales.

Online auctions promote feisty global bidding wars, largely accounting for the high success rate of Saffronart, which also previews its paintings in Mumbai and New York prior to its major cyber auctions. Many bidders are wealthy NRIs (Non-Resident Indians) who not only appreciate Indian art, but have also recognised its investment potential. However, there is also mounting demand from non-Indian collectors, with recent years witnessing spiralling sales in Europe, the USA, UK, Southeast Asia and the Middle East.

International auction houses have been descending upon India, to either set up offices or secure gallery alliances, in order to grab a piece of what they have identified as a major growth market. Although the bulk of demand, on both the domestic and international fronts, is generally for senior Indian artists' works, such as those of Francis Newton Souza, Tyeb Mehta, Syed Haider Raza, Akbar Padamsee, Ram Kumar and Maqbool Fida Husain, there's a steadily growing interest in emerging Indian artists.

Also see the boxed text on p137.

MYSTICAL MEHNDI

Mehndi is the traditional art of painting a woman's hands (and sometimes feet) with intricate henna designs for auspicious ceremonies such as marriage. If quality henna is used, the design, which is orange-brown, can last up to one month.

In touristy areas, *mehndi*-wallahs are adept at applying henna tattoo 'bands' on the arms, legs and lower back. If you're thinking about getting *mehndi* applied, allow at least a couple of hours for the design process and required drying time (during drying you can't use your hennaed hands). Once applied, henna usually fades faster the more you wash it and apply lotion.

It's always wise to request the artist to do a 'test' spot on your arm before proceeding, as nowadays some dyes contain chemicals that can cause allergies. If good-quality henna is used, you should not feel any pain during or after the procedure.

costumes and make-up are not only visually striking but are symbolic of a particular character's personality.

Handicrafts

Over the centuries India's many ethnic groups have spawned a vivid artistic heritage that is both inventive and spiritually significant. Many crafts fulfil a practical need as much as an aesthetic one.

Crafts aren't confined to their region of origin – artists migrate and have sometimes been influenced by the ideas of other regions – which means you can come across, for example, a Kashmiri handicraft emporium anywhere in India.

There's a plethora of handicrafts produced in South India, with standouts including ceramics, jewellery, leatherwork, metalwork, stone carving, papier-mâché, woodwork and a spectacular array of textiles. To get some shopping ideas, see p506.

POTTERY

The potter's art is steeped in mythology. Although there are numerous stories that explain how potters came to be, they usually share the notion that a talent for working with clay is a gift from the god Brahma. This gives potters a very special status; on occasion they are said to act directly as intermediaries between the spiritual and the temporal worlds.

The name for the potter caste, Kumbhar, is taken from *kumbha* (water pot), which is itself an essential component in a version of the story that explains how potters found their calling. The water pot is still an indispensable item in South India. The narrow-necked, round-based design means that women can carry the water-filled pots on their heads with less risk of spillage. The shape is also symbolic of the womb and thus fertility.

Apart from water pots, potters create a variety of household items, including all manner of storage and cooking pots, dishes and *jhanvan* (thick, flat pieces of fired clay with one rough side used for cleaning the feet). The ephemeral nature of clay-made items means the potter never wants for work. Potters all over Tamil Nadu are kept especially busy at their wheels thanks to such traditions as the Pongal harvest festival (see the boxed text, p389). On the day before the festival starts, clay household vessels are smashed and replaced with new ones.

Potters are also called upon to create votive offerings. These include the guardian horse figures (which can be huge creations) that stand sentry outside villages in Tamil Nadu, images of deities such as Ganesh, and other animal effigies. Clay replicas of parts of the human body are sometimes commissioned by those seeking miraculous cures and are then placed before a shrine. Clay toys and beads are also among a potter's repertoire.

KOLAMS

Kolams, the striking and breathtakingly intricate rice-flour designs (also called *rangoli*) that adorn thresholds, especially in South India, are both auspicious and symbolic. *Kolams* are traditionally drawn at sunrise and are sometimes made of rice-flour paste, which may be eaten by little creatures – symbolising a reverence for even the smallest living things. Deities are deemed to be attracted to a beautiful *kolam,* which may also signal to sadhus (ascetics) that they will be offered food at a particular house. Some people believe that *kolams* protect against the evil eye.

Glazing pottery is rare in South Indian states; one exception is Tamil Nadu, where a blue or green glaze is sometimes applied.

TEXTILES

Textiles have always played an important role in South Indian society and trade, and are still the region's biggest handicraft industry. India is famous for *khadi* (homespun cloth) – Mahatma Gandhi's promotion of *khadi* and the symbol of the spinning wheel played a paramount part in the nation's struggle for independence. Although chemical dye is widely used nowadays, natural dyes made from plants, roots, bark and herbs are still in use.

The sari traditionally typifies Indian style, and exquisite saris brocaded with pure gold thread are still produced in the tiny village of Paithan – you can view this at the Paithani Weaving Centre (p155) in Maharashtra. Much thought is put into selecting the base fabric, style of embroidery, colour and thread for handmade saris. Sequined, beaded and salma (continuous spring thread) saris are hand-worked and the fabric is usually rayon, cotton, satin or silk.

Embroidered shawls have assumed a significant role in the culture of the Toda people from the Nilgiri Hills (see the boxed text, p456) in Tamil Nadu. Embroidered exclusively by women in distinctive red-and-black designs, these beautiful shawls are made of thick white cotton material.

SPORT

The world's second most populous nation has copped derisive criticism for its dismal performances in recent Olympic Games, with critics pointing the finger at paltry sponsorship commitment, poor infrastructure/equipment, and lack of public interest – among other things. At the 2008 Olympics in Beijing, India won just three medals (all by men) – a gold medal for shooting (10m air rifle), a bronze for boxing, and a bronze for wrestling. India only received one medal at the 2004 Athens Olympics – silver (for men's double-trap shooting). Meanwhile, at the 2000 Games in Sydney, a female weightlifter, Karnam Malleswari, was the only Indian to receive a medal (bronze), making her the first Indian woman to ever win an Olympic medal.

Cricket

In India, it's all about cricket, cricket and cricket! Travellers who show even a slight interest in the game can expect passionate conversations with people of all stripes, from taxi-drivers to IT yuppies. Cutting across all echelons of society, cricket is more than just a national sporting obsession – it's a matter of enormous patriotism, especially evident when India plays against Pakistan. Matches between these South Asian neighbours – which have had rocky relations since Independence – attract especially high-spirited support, and the players of both sides are under colossal pressure to do their countries proud.

Today cricket – especially the recently rolled out Twenty20 format (see www.cricket20.com) – is big business in India, attracting lucrative sponsorship deals and celebrity status for its players, especially for high-profile personalities such as star batsman Sachin Tendulkar and ace-bowler Harbhajan Singh. The sport has not been without its murky side though, with Indian cricketers among those embroiled in match-fixing scandals over past years.

International matches are played at various Indian centres – for venues, dates and advance online ticket bookings (advisable) click on http://indian cricketleague.in/tickets.html. Many Indian newspapers also relay details of forthcoming matches.

India's first recorded cricket match was in 1721. It won its first Test series in 1952 at Chennai against England.

Keep your finger on the cricketing pulse at **Cricinfo** (www.cricinfo.com) and **Cricbuzz** (www.cricbuzz.com).

Keeping up with Indian sporting news is just a click away on Sify Sports (www.sify.com/sports).

Football (Soccer)

In South India football has a reasonably strong following, especially in Goa and Kerala. The local newspapers carry details of major matches, and tourist offices can assist with more information if you're keen to attend as a spectator. To delve further into the sport see **Indian Football** (www.indianfootball.com). In early 2009 India occupied the 148th spot in the FIFA world rankings.

Hockey

Despite being India's national sport, field hockey no longer enjoys the same following it once did, largely due to the unassailable popularity of cricket, which snatches most of India's sponsorship funding.

During its golden era, between 1928 and 1956, India won six consecutive Olympic gold medals in hockey; it later bagged two further Olympic gold medals, one in 1964 and the other in 1980.

There have been recent initiatives aimed at generating renewed interest in the game, with high-profile hockey clubs encouraging secondary school and tertiary students to join, resulting in some success. In early 2009, India's national men's/women's hockey world rankings were 11/14 respectively.

For those keen to tap into the hockey scene, two good places to begin are **Indian Hockey** (www.indianhockey.com) and **Indian Field Hockey** (www.bharatiyahockey.org).

Cricket fans will be bowled over by *The Illustrated History of Indian Cricket* by Boria Majumdar, and *The States of Indian Cricket* by Ramachandra Guha.

Horse Racing

Horse racing, held primarily in the cooler winter months, is especially popular in large South Indian cities including Mumbai, Mysore, Hyderabad and Bengaluru; for more information, gallop straight to **India Race** (www.indiarace.com), **Equine India** (www.equineindia.com) and **Racing World** (www.racingworldindia.com).

South India's highest race course is at Ooty, where races take place from mid-April to June (see p467).

Tennis

Although nowhere near as popular as cricket, tennis is steadily generating greater interest in India. Perhaps the biggest success story for India is the doubles team of Leander Paes and Mahesh Bhupathi, who won Wimbledon's prestigious title in 1999 – the first Indians ever to do so. More recently, Bhupathi and doubles partner Sania Mirza (also of India) won the Mixed Doubles title at the 2009 Australian Open, while Paes and his partner Cara Black (Zimbabwe) nabbed the 2008 US Open Mixed Doubles title.

At the 2005 Dubai Open, Indian wild card Sania Mirza first made international waves when she convincingly defeated 2004 US Open champion Svetlana Kuznetsova. Mirza, then ranked 97th, 90 spots behind Kuznetsova, became the first Indian woman to win a Women's Tennis Association Tour title. Mirza's 2009 Australian Open Mixed Doubles win secured her a place in history as India's first woman to win a Grand Slam event.

THE GAME OF KINGS

Horse polo intermittently flourished in India (especially among Indian royalty) until Independence, after which patronage sharply declined due to lack of sufficient funds. However, today there's a renewed interest in the game thanks to beefed-up sponsorship, although it still remains an elite sport and consequently fails to attract widespread public interest.

Travellers can catch a polo match, and hobnob with high society, during the cooler winter months at centres that include Delhi, Jaipur, Kolkata and Mumbai (check local newspapers for dates and venues). Polo is also occasionally played in Ladakh and Manipur.

The origins of polo are unclear. Believed to have roots in Persia and China some 2000 years back, in the subcontinent it's thought to have first been played in Baltistan (in present-day Pakistan). Polo publications claim that Emperor Akbar (who reigned in India from 1556 to 1605) first introduced rules of the game, but that polo, as it's played today, was largely influenced by a British cavalry regiment stationed in India during the 1870s. A set of international rules was implemented after WWI. The world's oldest surviving polo club, established in 1862, is in Kolkata (Calcutta) – see **Calcutta Polo Club** (www.calcuttapolo.com).

The **All India Tennis Association** (AITA; www.aitatennis.com) has more information about the game in India.

Traditional Sports

Kambla (buffalo racing) is a local pastime in rural southern Karnataka between November and March, usually on weekends. A pair of good buffaloes and their handlers can cover about 120m in around 14 seconds! For more details, see Buffalo Surfing (p272).

Kerala is renowned for its ancient martial-arts form, Kalarippayat (see the boxed text, p372); you can watch it at the *kalari* (training school) in Thiruvananthapuram (Trivandrum) – see p327 – and at some hotels around the state.

MEDIA

According to the World Association of Newspapers (WAN) 2008 World Press Trends report, India is the second biggest market (after China) when it comes to newspaper circulation, with around 99 million copies sold daily. In 2007 there was an 11.2% jump in newspaper sales in India and a 35.5% rise in a five-year period, says WAN.

For online links to national and regional Indian newspapers, see www.onlinenewspapers.com/india.htm.

On the whole, India's extensive print media – which entails tens of thousands of newspapers and magazines in a range of vernaculars – enjoys widespread freedom of expression. According to recent surveys, India's most highly read English-language newspapers are the **Times of India** (www.timesofindia.com), **The Hindu** (www.hinduonnet.com) and the **Hindustan Times** (www.hindustantimes.com). For other English-language dailies and news magazines, see p493. Most publications have websites.

Indian TV was at one time dominated by the national (government-controlled) broadcaster **Doordarshan** (www.ddindia.gov.in); the introduction of satellite TV in the early 1990s revolutionised viewing habits by introducing hundreds of channels, from international news giants such as the BBC and CNN, to a host of Indian regional channels broadcasting in local dialects.

Programmes on the government-controlled **All India Radio** (AIR; www.allindiaradio.org), one of the world's biggest radio service providers, include news, interviews, music and sport. There are also mushrooming nationwide private FM channels that offer greater variety than the government broadcaster, including talkback on subjects, such as relationship issues, once considered taboo.

Consult local newspapers for TV and radio programme details.

Food & Drink

Traditional South Indian food is noticeably different to that of the north; however, both are comprised of regionally diverse dishes, all with their own preparation techniques and ingredients.

Although South Indian meals may at times appear quite simple – mounds of rice and side dishes of *sambar* (a soupy lentil dish with cubed vegetables), spiced vegetables, plain curd and a splodge of pickles, sometimes served on a banana-leaf plate, within this deceptive simplicity hides a sensual and complex repertoire of taste sensations and time-honoured recipes. Add to this the distinct regional variations, from the colonial-influenced fare of Goa to the traditional seafood specialities of Kerala – along with a bounty of exotic fruits and vegetables – and there's more than enough to get the tastebuds tingling.

To delve deeper into the wonderful world of South Indian cuisine see p81.

Those craving North Indian food won't have to look far to find succulent tandoori creations, *mattar paneer* (unfermented cheese and pea curry), butter chicken and piping hot naan, as they're available at numerous South Indian restaurants and hotels. Meanwhile, travellers pining for familiar fast food will find American-style burger and pizza joints scattered throughout the south, with the most variety found in the larger cities such as Mumbai (Bombay), Bengaluru (Bangalore) and Chennai (Madras). Tourist haunts, such as Goa, get special kudos when it comes to satiating foreign palates, with eateries offering everything from homemade muesli and honey-drizzled porridge for breakfast, to spinach ravioli and chicken stroganoff for dinner.

STAPLES & SPECIALITIES
Rice

Without a doubt, rice is the staple grain in South India. It's served with virtually every meal, and is used to make anything and everything from spongy *idlis* (fermented rice cakes) and dosas (large savoury crepes) to exquisite *mithai* (Indian sweets).

The Anger of Aubergines: Stories of Women and Food by Bulbul Sharma is an amusing culinary analysis of social relationships interspersed with enticing recipes.

After China, India is the world's second-largest producer and consumer of rice, and the majority of it is grown in the south. Long-grain white rice is the most common and is served boiled with any 'wet' dish, usually a thali. It can be cooked up in a pilau (or pilaf; rice cooked in stock and flavoured with spices) or in a spicy biryani, or simply flavoured with a dash of turmeric or saffron.

Spices

Spices are integral to any South Indian dish and the subcontinent boasts some of the finest. Indeed Christopher Columbus was searching for the famed black pepper of Kerala's Malabar Coast when he stumbled upon America.

Symbolising purity and fertility, rice is used in Hindu wedding ceremonies and often as *puja* (holy offerings) in temples.

Turmeric is the essence of most Indian curries, but coriander seeds are the most widely used spice, and lend flavour and body to just about every savoury dish. Most Indian 'wet' dishes – commonly known as curries in the West – begin with the crackle of cumin seeds in hot oil. Tamarind is sometimes known as the 'Indian date' and is a particularly popular souring agent in the south. The green cardamom of Kerala's Western Ghats is regarded as the world's best, and you'll find it in savoury dishes, desserts and warming chai (tea). Saffron, the dried stigmas of crocus flowers grown in Kashmir, is so light it takes more than 1500 hand-plucked flowers to yield just 1g. Cinnamon, curry leaves, nutmeg and garlic are also widely used in cooking.

A masala is a blend of dry-roasted ground spices (the word loosely means 'mixed'), the most popular being garam masala (hot mix), a combination of up to 15 spices used to season dishes.

Red chillies are another common ingredient. Often dried or pickled (in rural areas you may see chillies laid out to dry on the roadside), they are used as much for flavour as for heat.

Fruit, Vegetables & Pulses

A visit to any Indian market will reveal a vast and vibrant assortment of fresh fruit and vegetables, overflowing from large baskets or stacked in neat pyramids. The south is especially well known for its abundance of tropical fruits such as pineapples and papaya. Mangos abound during the summer months (especially April and May), with India boasting more than 500 varieties, the pick of the luscious bunch being the sweet Alphonso. Naturally in a region with so many vegetarians, *sabzi* (vegetables) make up a predominant part of the diet, and they're served in a variety of inventive ways. Potatoes, cauliflower, eggplant, spinach and carrots are some of the most commonly used vegies, but you'll rarely see them simply boiled up and plopped on your plate. They can be fried, roasted, curried, baked, mashed and stuffed into dosas or wrapped in batter to make deep-fried *pakoras* (fritters). Something a little more unusual is the bumpy-skinned *karela* (bitter gourd) which, like *bhindi* (okra), is commonly prepared dry with spices.

Pulses – lentils, beans and peas – are another major South Indian staple as they form the basis for dhal, the curried lentil-based dish served with every thali meal.

Dhal

Dhal, along with rice, is a mainstay of the South Indian diet. Dhal refers to a wide range of pulse dishes, commonly made from lentils, but also from certain beans as well as chickpeas. The pulses are boiled or simmered, then mixed with spices tempered in hot oil or ghee (clarified butter) and perhaps vegetables. The most common forms of dhal in South India are *sambar* and *tuvar* (yellow lentils).

Breads

Although traditional-style subcontinental breads are more commonly associated with North India, you'll certainly encounter them at plenty of restaurants in the south. Roti, the generic term for Indian-style bread, is a name used interchangeably with chapati to describe the most common variety: the irresistible unleavened round bread made with whole-wheat flour and cooked on a *tawa* (flat hotplate). *Puri* is deep-fried dough puffed up like a crispy balloon. Kachori is somewhat similar, but the dough has been pepped up with corn or dhal, which makes it considerably thicker. Flaky, unleavened *paratha* can be eaten as is or jazzed up with fillings such as *paneer* (soft, unfermented cheese). The thick, usually teardrop-shaped, naan is cooked in a *tandoor* (clay oven) and is especially scrummy when flavoured with garlic.

Dosas & Snacks

A much-loved classic of the south, the iconic dosa is a crepe-like mixture of fermented rice flour (or lentil flour) and dhal cooked on a griddle. It's traditionally served with a bowl of hot, orange *sambar* and another bowl of mild coconut *chatni* (chutney). The ubiquitous masala dosa is stuffed with spiced potatoes, onions and curry leaves. Don't miss it!

Breakfast in South India often consists of *idlis, vadas* (deep-fried savoury doughnuts, made of lentils) or *uttappams* (thick savoury rice-flour pancakes

---

Copra (dried coconut flesh) is pressed and made into coconut oil, a very popular cooking medium in Kerala.

Making that perfect dosa back home is just a click away on www.top-indian-recipes.com/indian-dosa-recipes.htm.

PICKLES, CHUTNEYS & RELISHES

No Indian meal is really complete without one, and often all, of the above. A relish can be anything from a little pickled onion to a delicately crafted fusion of fruit, nuts and spices. One of the most popular meal accompaniments is raita (mildly spiced yoghurt, often with shredded cucumber or diced pineapple; served chilled), which makes a tongue-cooling counter to spicy food. *Chatnis* (chutneys) can come in any number of varieties (sweet or savoury) and can be made from many different vegetables, fruits, herbs and spices. But proceed with caution before polishing off that pickled speck on your thali; it'll quite possibly be the hottest thing you've ever tasted.

with finely chopped onions, green chillies, coriander and coconut). These can also be eaten at any time of the day as tiffin, an all-purpose Raj-era term for between-meal snacks.

Meat & Fish

Although South Indian Hindus are largely vegetarian, fish is a staple food in coastal regions. South India is the undisputed 'fish basket' of the nation; in seaside areas of Goa and Kerala you can watch fishermen hauling in the day's catch, which may include tuna, mackerel, kingfish, pomfret, lobster and prawns. In Goa and Kerala, significant Christian populations mean you can find pork and even beef dishes. Chicken is widely available through the region in nonvegetarian restaurants, while goat is particularly popular in Andhra Pradesh.

Chettinad, the spicy meat-based cuisine of Tamil Nadu, hails from the Chettiars, a wealthy merchant community.

Dairy

Milk and milk products make a staggering contribution to Indian cuisine: *dahi* (curd/yoghurt) is served with most meals and is handy for countering chilli-hot food; *paneer* is a godsend for the vegetarian majority; the popular *lassi* (yoghurt-based drink) is just one in a host of nourishing sweet and savoury beverages; ghee is the traditional and pure cooking medium, and the best sweets are made with milk. About 60% of milk consumed in India is buffalo milk, a richer, high-protein version, which many prefer to cow's milk.

Sweets

India has a broad and colourful jumble of, often sticky and squishy, *mithai* (sweets), most of them sinfully sugary. The main categories are *barfi* (a fudgelike milk-based sweet), soft *halwa* (made with vegetables, cereals, lentils, nuts or fruit), *ladoos* (ball-shaped sweets made of gram flour and semolina), and those made from *chhana* (unpressed *paneer*) such as *rasgullas* (cream-cheese balls flavoured with rose water). There are also simpler – but equally scrumptious – offerings such as inimitable *jalebis* (orange-coloured coils of deep-fried batter dunked in sugar syrup; served hot) that you'll see all over the country.

Payasam (called *kheer* in the north) is one of the most popular after-meal desserts. It's a creamy rice pudding with a light, delicate flavour, enhanced with cardamom, saffron, pistachios, flaked almonds, chopped cashews or slivered dried fruit. Other favourites include *gulab jamuns*, deep-fried balls of dough soaked in rose-flavoured syrup, and *kulfi*, a firm-textured ice cream made with reduced milk and flavoured with any number of nuts (often pistachio), fruits and berries. In the hill areas of Maharashtra you'll find *chikki*, a rock-hard, ultrasweet concoction of peanuts and jaggery toffee.

Each year, an estimated 14 tonnes of pure silver is converted into the edible foil that decorates many Indian sweets, especially during the Diwali festival.

Sweet tooths will delight in *The Book of Indian Sweets*, by Satarupa Banerjee, which has goodies such as Goan *bebinca* (16-layer coconut pudding).

PAAN

Meals are often rounded off with *paan,* a fragrant mixture of betel nut (also called areca nut), lime paste, spices and condiments wrapped in an edible, silky *paan* leaf. Peddled by *paan*-wallahs, who are usually strategically positioned outside busy restaurants, *paan* is eaten as a digestive and mouth-freshener. The betel nut is mildly narcotic and some aficionados eat *paan* the same way heavy smokers consume cigarettes – over the years these people's teeth can become rotted red and black.

There are two basic types of *paan: mitha* (sweet) and *saadha* (with tobacco). A parcel of *mitha paan* is a splendid way to finish a satisfying meal. Pop the whole parcel in your mouth and chew slowly, allowing the juices to oooooooze.

DRINKS
Nonalcoholic Drinks

South India grows both tea and coffee but unlike North India, where it has only recently become all the rage to guzzle cappuccinos and lattes, coffee has long been favoured down south. In the larger cities, you'll find ever-multiplying branches of hip coffee chains, such as Barista and Café Coffee Day, widely found in what were once chai strongholds. Meanwhile, on today's tea front, you can enjoy a wide assortment, from peppermint to rosehip and good old-fashioned Indian chai – the ultrasweet milky concoction that still reigns supreme.

In cities and towns particularly you'll come across sugar-cane juice and fruit-juice vendors – be wary of hygiene standards (see the box on p76). Some restaurants think nothing of adding salt or sugar to juice to intensify the flavours; ask the waiter to omit these if you don't want them. Coconut water is also popular in the south and you'll see vendors just about everywhere standing by mounds of green coconuts, machete at the ready. Finally, there's lassi, a refreshing and delicious iced curd (yoghurt) drink that comes in sweet and savoury varieties, or mixed with fruit.

For information about safely drinking water in India, see the boxed text, p540.

Alcoholic Drinks

An estimated three-quarters of India's drinking population quaffs 'country liquor' such as the notorious arak (liquor distilled from coconut-palm sap, potatoes or rice) of the south. This is the poor-man's drink and millions are addicted to the stuff. Each year, many people are blinded or even killed by the methyl alcohol in illegal arak.

To dive into the dizzying depths of Indian wine, clink – oops we mean click – on www.indian wine.com. Cheers!

In Kerala, Goa and parts of Tamil Nadu, toddy (palm 'beer') is a milky white local brew made from the sap of the coconut palm. It's collected in pots attached to the tree by toddy-tappers and drunk either straight from the pot or distilled. In Goa toddy is called *feni* and is made either from coconut or – the more popular and potent version – from the fruit of the cashew tree. The fermented liquid is double-distilled to produce a knockout concoction that can be as much as 35% proof. Although usually drunk straight by locals, *feni* virgins should consider mixing it with a soft drink. Decorative *feni* bottles can be found in Goan shops and they make a nice gift or souvenir.

About a quarter of India's drinks market comprises Indian Made Foreign Liquors (IMFLs), made with a base of rectified spirit. Recent years have seen a rise in the consumption of imported spirits, with a spiralling number of city watering holes and restaurants flaunting a dazzling array of domestic and foreign labels.

Beer is phenomenally popular everywhere, with the more upmarket bars and restaurants stocking local and foreign brands (Budweiser, Heineken, Corona and the like). Most of the domestic brands are straightforward Pilsners around the 5% alcohol mark; travellers champion Kingfisher.

Wine-drinking is on the rise, despite the domestic wine-producing industry still being relatively new. The favourable climate and soil conditions in certain areas – such as parts of Maharasthra and Karnataka – have spawned some commendable Indian wineries including **Chateau Indage** (www.indagevintners .com), **Grover Vineyards** (www.groverwines.com) and **Sula Vineyards** (www.sulawines.com). Domestic offerings include Chardonnay, Chenin Blanc, Sauvignon Blanc, Cabernet Sauvignon, Shiraz and Zinfandel. Also see the 'Grapes of Worth' box on p150.

CELEBRATIONS

Although most Hindu festivals have a religious core, many are also great occasions for spirited feasting. Sweets are considered the most luxurious of foods and almost every special occasion is celebrated with a mind-boggling range. *Karanjis,* crescent-shaped flour parcels stuffed with sweet *khoya* (milk solids) and nuts, are synonymous with Holi, the most rambunctious Hindu festival, and it wouldn't be the same without sticky *malpuas* (wheat pancakes dipped in syrup), *barfis* and *pedas* (multicoloured pieces of *khoya* and sugar). Pongal is the major harvest festival of the south and is most closely associated with the dish of the same name, made with the season's first rice, along with jaggery, nuts, raisins and spices. Diwali, the festival of lights, is the most widely celebrated national festival, and some regions have specific Diwali sweets; if you're in Mumbai dive into delicious *anarsa* (rice-flour cookies).

Ramadan is the Islamic month of fasting, when Muslims abstain from eating, drinking or smoking between sunrise and sunset. Each day's fast is often broken with dates – considered auspicious – followed by fruit and fruit juices. On the final day of Ramadan, Eid al-Fitr, a lavish feast celebrates the end of the fast with nonvegetarian biryanis and a huge proliferation of special sweets.

WHERE TO EAT & DRINK

Restaurants in South India fall into five main categories: veg, nonvegetarian (often signposted as 'nonveg'), hotel restaurants, tourist restaurants, and restaurants specialising in regional or ethnic cuisine. The last type are really only found in major cities or tourist areas, such as Mumbai, Pune, Bengaluru, Chennai, Hyderabad and Goa, where you can also find versions of Italian, Chinese, Thai, Mediterranean, Mexican and the like. Apart from street-food vendors, the cheapest place to grab a bite is at a *dhaba* (snack bar), found throughout the country.

Veg restaurants (often called 'meals' restaurants) are simple places serving *idlis*, dosas and *vada* for breakfast, and thalis for lunch and dinner. Nonveg restaurants have both a vegetarian menu and Indian meat dishes, usually with chicken, mutton and fish, as well as Chinese offerings.

In coastal resorts, such as those at Goa and Kerala, it's hard to beat the beach shacks for a fresh seafood meal – from fried mussels, prawns and calamari to steamed fish, crab or lobster – washed down with a cold beer as you watch the sun set over the ocean. The bamboo and palm thatch shacks are usually set up in late October or early November and stay open until around late March, when they are dismantled and put away in anticipation of the summer and monsoon.

Many upmarket hotels have outstanding restaurants, usually with pan-Indian menus so you can explore various regional cuisines. Although they're

Dakshin Bhog by Santhi Balaraman offers a yummy jumble of southern stars from iconic dosas and *idlis* to *kootan choru* (vegetable rice).

not cheap, they're within splurging reach of most travellers. Some of India's more cosmopolitan cities, such as Mumbai and Bengaluru, have an especially vibrant dining-out scene, with menus sporting everything from Indian and Italian to Japanese and Mexican – peruse the Eating sections of those chapters for more details.

You'll find terrific watering holes in most major cities such as Mumbai and Bengaluru, which are usually at their liveliest on weekends. The more upmarket bars serve an impressive selection of domestic and imported drinks as well as draught beer. Many bars turn into music-thumping nightclubs anytime after 8pm although there are quiet lounge-bars to be found in some cities. In smaller towns the bar scene can be a seedy, male-dominated affair – not the kind of place thirsty female travellers should venture into alone. For details about each city's bars, see the Drinking sections of this book's regional chapters.

Stringent licensing laws discourage drinking in some restaurants, but places that depend on the tourist rupee may covertly serve you beer in teapots and disguised glasses – but don't assume anything, at the risk of causing offence. Very few vegetarian restaurants serve alcohol.

Street Food

Street Foods of India, by Vimla and Deb Kumar Mukerji, is your first-stop snack-shop with all sorts of regional favourites including *masala dosa* and *appam* (rice pancakes).

Street food is part of everyday life in South India, and the sights, smells and sounds of street cooking are a constant banquet for the senses. Whatever the time of day, food vendors are frying, boiling, roasting, peeling, simmering, mixing, juicing or baking some type of food and drink to lure peckish passers-by. Small operations usually have one special that they serve all day, while other vendors have different dishes for breakfast, lunch and dinner. The fare varies as you venture between neighbourhoods, towns and regions; it can be as simple as puffed rice or peanuts roasted in hot sand, as unexpected as a fried-egg sandwich, or as complex as the riot of different flavours known as *chaat* (savoury snack).

STREET FOOD DOS & DON'TS

Tucking into street food is one of the joys of travelling in South India – here are some tips to help avoid tummy troubles.

■ Give yourself a few days to adjust to the local cuisine, especially if you're not used to spicy food.

■ You know the rule about following a crowd – if the locals are avoiding a particular vendor, you should too. Also take notice of the profile of the customers – any place popular with families will probably be your safest bet.

■ Check how and where the vendor is cleaning the utensils, and how and where the food is covered. If the vendor is cooking in oil, have a peek to check it's clean. If the pots or surfaces are dirty, there are food scraps about or too many buzzing flies, don't be shy to make a hasty retreat.

■ Don't be put off when you order some deep-fried snack and the cook throws it back into the wok. It's common practice to partly cook the snacks first and then finish them off once they've been ordered. In fact, frying them hot again will kill any germs.

■ Unless a place is reputable (and busy), it's best to avoid eating meat from the street.

■ The hygiene standard at juice stalls is wildly variable, so exercise caution. Have the vendor press the juice in front of you and steer clear of anything stored in a jug or served in a glass (unless you're absolutely convinced of the washing standards).

■ Don't be tempted by glistening pre-sliced melon and other fruit, which keeps their luscious veneer with regular dousings of (often dubious) water.

Devilishly delicious deep-fried fare is the staple of the streets, and you'll frequently find satiating samosas (pyramid-shaped savoury pastries stuffed with spiced vegetables and less often meat), and *bhajia* (vegetable fritters) in varying degrees of spiciness. Other snacks worth sniffing out on your South Indian wanderings include the Mumbai speciality *bhelpuri; pao bhaja,* another Mumbai speciality of spiced vegetables with bread; and biryani, a Hyderabadi rice-based speciality. *Idlis* and dosas are also served at some street stalls, with the thin dosa crepe cooked on a griddle right in front of you. Much loved in Maharasthra is *vada pao,* a veg-burger of sorts, with a deep-fried potato patty in a bread bun served with hot chillies and tangy chutneys. For something simpler there are omelettes, sandwiches, or cobs of corn roasting on braziers.

Platform Food

One of the thrills of travelling by rail in India is the culinary circus that greets you at almost every station. Roving vendors accost arriving trains, yelling and scampering up and down the carriages; fruit, *namkin* (savoury nibbles), omelettes and nuts are offered through the grills on the windows; and platform cooks try to lure you from the train with the sizzle of fresh samosas. Frequent rail travellers know which station is famous for which food item: Lonavla station in Maharashtra, for example, is known for *chikki* (nut and jaggery toffee).

VEGETARIANS & VEGANS

Vegetarians will be in culinary paradise in South India. Tamil Nadu and Karnataka are predominately vegetarian, but every town will have several veg restaurants. Indian restaurants are either pure veg (no eggs or meat), veg (no meat), or non-veg (meat and veg dishes). Devout Hindus and Jains avoid foods such as garlic and onions, which are believed to heat the blood and arouse sexual desire. You may come across vegetarian restaurants that make it a point to advertise the absence of onion and garlic in their dishes for this reason. These items are also banned from most ashrams.

There's little understanding of veganism (the term 'pure vegetarian' means without eggs), and animal products such as milk, butter, ghee and curd are included in most Indian dishes. If you are vegan your first problem is likely to be getting the cook to completely understand your requirements. For further vegan-related information, surf the web – good places to begin include: **Indian Vegan** (www.indianvegan.com) and **Vegan World Network** (www.vegansworldnetwork.org).

HABITS & CUSTOMS

South Indians generally have an early breakfast, then a thali for lunch and/or several tiffin during the day. Dinner, usually large serves of rice, vegetables, curd and spicy side dishes, is eaten quite late. It's not unusual for dinner to start after 9pm and any drinking (of alcohol) is almost always done before the meal.

Food is usually eaten with the fingers in South India, or more precisely the fingers of the right hand. The left hand is reserved for toilet duties, so is considered unclean, but it's still customary to wash your hands before every meal. Rice and side dishes are mixed together with the fingers and scooped into the mouth in small handfuls using the thumb to push it in. Avoid the temptation to lick your fingers – a finger bowl filled with warm water is usually placed on the table to wash your fingers at the end of the meal and serviettes should be on hand to dry them. In most restaurants, foreigners will at least be offered a fork (and perhaps a spoon). In North Indian restaurants it is customary to scoop the food up with traditional Indian breads, such as chapati and naan.

Those curious about ayurvedic treatments that include food might be interested in *Healthy Living with Ayurveda* by Anuradha Singh.

Dakshin: Vegetarian Cuisine from South India, by Chandra Padmanabhan, is an easy-to-read and beautifully illustrated book of southern recipes.

101 Kerala Delicacies, by G Padma Vijay, is a detailed recipe book of vegetarian and non-vegetarian dishes from this tropical coast-hugging state.

COOKING COURSES

You might find yourself so inspired by local food that you want to take home a little Indian kitchen know-how by enrolling in a cooking course – some are professionally run, others are very informal, and each is of varying duration. Most require at least a few days' advance notice.

A growing number of homestays around Kerala offer cooking classes – two particularly promising places to ask around are Kumily (p354) and Fort Cochin (p366). Other possibilities include Cook & Eat (p365) and Holiday on the Menu (p195).

EAT YOUR WORDS
Food & Drink Glossary

For the low-down on Goan terms see the boxed text, 'A Goan Gourmet Glossary' on p198.

achar	pickle
aloo	potato; also *alu*
aloo tikki	mashed-potato patty
appam	rice pancake
arak	liquor distilled from coconut sap, potatoes or rice
badam	almond
baigan	eggplant/aubergine; also known as *brinjal*
barfi	fudgelike sweet made from milk
besan	chickpea flour
betel	nut of the betel tree; chewed as a stimulant and digestive in *paan;* also called areca nut
bhajia	vegetable fritter
bhang lassi	blend of lassi and bhang (a derivative of marijuana)
bhelpuri	thin fried rounds of dough with rice, lentil, lemon juice, onion, herbs and chutney
bhindi	okra
biryani	fragrant spiced steamed rice with meat or vegetables
bonda	mashed-potato patty
chaat	savoury snack, may be seasoned with *chaat* masala
chai	tea
channa	spiced chickpeas

The laudable *Complete Indian Cooking* by Mridula Baljekar, Rafi Fernandez, Shehzad Husain and Manisha Kanani contains '325 deliciously authentic recipes for the adventurous cook.' Recipes include chicken with green mango and Goan prawn curry.

The Chef's Special series has nifty (light-weight) cookbooks showcasing regional cuisines. Titles include *Goan Kitchen, Kerala Kitchen* and *South Indian Kitchen*.

USEFUL WORDS

English	Tamil	Kannada	Konkani	Malayalam	Marathi	Telugu
butter	vennai	benne	mosko	veḷḷa	lonee	wenna
coffee	kaappi	kaafi	kaafi	kaappi	kaafi	kaafee
egg	muttai	motte	taanthee	muḷḷa	aanda	guḷḷu
fruit	pazham	hannu	phala	palam	phal	paḷḷu
ice	ais	ays	jell	ays	barfu	ays/manchugaḷḷa
meat	maamisam	maamsa	maas	irachi	maas	maamsama
milk	paal	haalu	dudh	paala	dudh	paalu
rice	arisi	akki	tandul	ari	bhat/tandul (cooked/raw)	biyyam
sugar	sakkarai	sakkare	sakhar	panchasaara	sakhar	chakkera/pañcadaara
tea	teneer	tee	chay	caaya	chaha	ʃee/teneeru
vegetables	kaaykarikal	tarakaari	bhaji/verdur	pachakkaḷi	bhajee	kooragaayalu
water	neer	neeru	udhok	veḷḷam	paani	neeḷḷu

chapati	round unleavened Indian-style bread; also known as *roti*
chatni	chutney
chawal	rice
dahi	curd/yoghurt
dhal	curried lentil dish; a staple food of India
dhal makhani	black lentils and red kidney beans with cream and butter
dosa	large South Indian savoury crepe
falooda	rose-flavoured drink made with milk, cream, nuts and vermicelli
feni	Goan liquor distilled from coconut milk or cashews
ghee	clarified butter
gobi	cauliflower
gram	legumes
gulab jamun	deep-fried balls of dough soaked in rose-flavoured syrup
halwa	soft sweet made with vegetables, cereals, lentils, nuts or fruit
idli	South Indian spongy, round, fermented rice cake
imli	tamarind
jaggery	hard, brown, sugarlike sweetener made from palm sap
jalebi	orange-coloured coils of deep-fried batter dunked in sugar syrup
karela	bitter gourd
kheer	creamy rice pudding
khichdi	blend of lightly spiced rice and lentils; also *khichri*
kofta	minced vegetables or meat; often ball-shaped
korma	currylike braised dish
kulcha	soft leavened Indian-style bread
kulfi	flavoured (often with pistachio) firm-textured ice cream
ladoo	sweet ball made with gram flour and semolina; also *ladu*
lassi	refreshing yoghurt-and-iced-water drink
masala dosa	large South Indian savoury crepe *(dosa)* stuffed with spiced potatoes
mattar paneer	unfermented cheese and pea curry
mithai	Indian sweets
molee	Keralan dish; fish pieces poached in coconut milk and spices
momo	Tibetan steamed or fried dumpling stuffed with vegetables or meat
mooli	white radish
naan	*tandoor*-cooked flat bread
namak	salt
namkin	savoury nibbles
pakora	bite-sized piece of vegetable dipped in chickpea-flour batter and deep-fried
palak paneer	unfermented cheese chunks in a puréed spinach gravy
paneer	soft, unfermented cheese made from milk curd
pani	water
pappadam	thin, crispy lentil or chickpea-flour circle-shaped wafer; commonly called *pappad*
paratha	Indian-style flaky bread (thicker than *chapati*) made with ghee and cooked on a hotplate; often stuffed with grated vegetables, *paneer* etc
payasam	rice pudding (called *kheer* in the north)
phulka	a *chapati* that puffs up when briefly placed on an open flame
pilaf	see *pilau*
pilau	rice cooked in stock and flavoured with spices; also *pulau, pilao* or *pilaf*
pudina	mint
puri	flat savoury dough that puffs up when deep-fried; also *poori*
raita	mildly spiced yoghurt, often containing shredded cucumber or diced pineapple; served chilled
rasam	*dhal*-based broth flavoured with tamarind
rasgulla	sweet little balls of cream cheese flavoured with rose water
rogan josh	rich, spicy lamb curry
saag	leafy greens

sabzi	vegetables
sambar	South Indian soupy lentil dish with cubed vegetables
samosa	deep-fried pastry triangles filled with spiced vegetables, sometimes meat
sonf	aniseed; used as a digestive and mouth-freshener, usually comes with the bill after a meal; also *saunf*
tandoor	clay oven
tawa	flat hotplate/iron griddle
thali	all-you-can-eat meal; stainless steel (sometimes silver) compartmentalised plate for meals
tiffin	snack; also refers to meal container often made of stainless steel
tikka	spiced, often marinated, chunks of chicken, *paneer* etc
toddy	alcoholic drink, tapped from palm trees
upma	rava (semolina) cooked with onions, spices, chilli peppers and coconut
uttapam	thick rice-flour pancakes with finely chopped onions, green chillies, coriander and coconut
vada	South Indian doughnut-shaped deep-fried lentil savoury
vindaloo	Goan dish; fiery curry in a marinade of vinegar and garlic

Scrumptious
South India

Seafood stars in Kerala's Malabar curry, a traditional dish prepared with fresh prawns or fish

GREG ELMS

Through its legendary cuisine, you'll swiftly discover that South India is a veritable culinary carnival expressed in a symphony of colours, aromas, flavours and textures. Like so many aspects of South India, its food, too, is an elusive thing to define because it's made up of so many different dishes, all with their own special preparation techniques and ingredients. Indeed, this wonderful diversity is what makes munching your way through the steamy south so deliciously rewarding! Frying, baking, simmering, roasting, sizzling, kneading and flipping a glorious gamut of regional specialities, the hungry traveller can look forward to feasting on an adventurous array of traditional and contemporary creations – from the hushed splendour of rice dumplings and paper-thin lentil crepes to the flavours of tongue-teasing veg curries and masterfully marinated seafood.

THE GREAT SOUTH INDIAN THALI

In South India the much loved thali is the lunchtime meal of choice. Inexpensive, satiating, wholesome and downright yummy, this is Indian food at its simple best. Whereas in North India the thali is usually served on a steel plate with indentations for the various side dishes (thali gets its name from the plate), in the south a thali is traditionally served on a flat steel plate that may be covered with a fresh banana leaf.

In a restaurant, when the plate is placed in front of you, you may like to follow local custom and pour some water on the leaf then spread it around with your right hand. Soon enough a waiter with a large pot of rice will come along and heap mounds of it onto your plate, followed by servings of dhal, *sambar* (soupy lentils), *rasam* (dhal-based broth flavoured with tamarind), vegetable dishes, chutneys, pickles and *dahi* (curd/yoghurt). Using

Thali plate: a riot of colours and flavours
GREG ELMS

the fingers of your right hand, start by mixing the various side dishes with the rice, kneading and scraping it into mouth-sized balls, then scoop it into your mouth using your thumb to push the food in. It is considered poor form to stick your hand right into your mouth or to lick your fingers. Observing fellow diners will help get your thali technique just right. If it's all getting a bit messy, there should be a finger bowl of water on the table. Waiters will continue to fill your plate until you wave your hand over one or all of the offerings to indicate you have had enough.

ANDHRA PRADESH

Andhra cuisine is largely comprised of lentil, vegetable and meat or fish dishes, usually flavoured with tamarind and frequently

Hyderabadi chicken biryani is aromatic and satisfying

GREG ELMS

spiced up with bright red chillies. Popular dishes include *chapa pulusu,* a flaming red fish curry, and chicken curry in a coconut-based sauce. The state is nationally known for its fiery cuisine and unique blend of Hindu and Muslim cultures. If you visit Hyderabad, don't miss the local biryani, an aromatic baked rice dish combined with vegetables, meat (often chicken), spices and (usually) nuts. Spicy kebabs wrapped in roti and *achar gosht* (pickle-like meat dish) are other Hyderabadi favourites, while pickles and *chatnis* (chutneys made of spices, dhal and chillies) are integral to Andhra cooking. Hyderabad is also the home of the *kulcha,* a soft, leavened, Indian-style bread that is excellent for mopping up every last drop of flavoursome curry sauces.

GOA

The delectable cuisine of coast-hugging Goa largely evolved from the intermingling of the highly developed Goan culture, coupled with over four centuries of Portuguese rule. Fringing the shimmering Arabian Sea, it is little wonder that seafood is the Goan staple, with goodies such as kingfish, snapper, pomfret, tuna, lobster, sardines, mussels and prawns hauled in from the ocean. The staple meal here is simply known as 'fish curry rice' – a dish of fish served in a spicy sauce over rice. The Portuguese influence is still very much apparent in Goan cooking. This is the place to tuck into pork dishes, such as *sorpotel* (pork meat and offal stew), pork vindaloo (pickled pork curry) and chourisso (a scrummy Goan sausage). Other Goan specialities include chicken *cafrial* (pieces of chicken coated in a green masala paste) and *ambot tik* (a slightly sour but fiery curry dish), while the Portuguese influence in fish preparations can be seen in *caldeen* and *xacutí* (fish or chicken simmered in coconut

Fill up on the ocean's bounty in Goa's beach shacks

ORIEN HA

milk and spices). Meanwhile, *balchão* is fish or prawns cooked in a dark red and tangy tomato sauce. Goans specialise in mouth-wateringly good desserts; don't leave without trying the famous bebinca (layered coconut pudding) – sweet bliss!

KARNATAKA

Although you can sample almost any cuisine you'd care to think of in hip and happening Bengaluru (Bangalore), traditional Karnatakan fare is largely vegetarian, with simple rice, dhal and *rasam* making up the core diet, along with various masala rice dishes, vegetables, salads and dosas. The Mysore dosa is a real treat, spicy and crisp and stuffed with vegetables and chillies. The major exception to the popularly vegetarian diet is on the Konkan Coast of the state, where Mangalorean seafood is a speciality. Pomfret and ladyfish are some of the popular catches, often cooked in a spicy coconut sauce.

KERALA

Tropical, spice-rich Kerala has had many visitors to its shores over the centuries including Portuguese, British and Arab traders. The combination of those influences and a coastline yielding some of India's finest seafood makes Keralan cuisine some of the subcontinent's most memorable. Keralan specialities feature fish cooked in coconut oil or simmered in coconut milk

MMMMM...MANGALOREAN

The fiery cuisine of the Karnatakan coastal city of Mangalore deserves special mention because it has carved a name for itself across India, particularly for its flavour-packed seafood dishes. Mangalorean cuisine is diverse, distinct and especially characterised by its liberal use of chilli and fresh coconut – also see the boxed text on p268.

Mangalorean prawn curry packs a mighty punch

SIMON REDDY / ALAMY

and fragrant spices, lending it a Southeast Asian quality; favourites include *meen pollichathu* (fish cooked in banana leaves) and *molee* (fish or seafood cooked in coconut milk and spices). Popular ingredients in sweet fish curries include cashew nuts and mangoes, while Malabar curries (fish or prawns) are made with coconut milk, tomatoes, ginger and spices traditionally cooked in a clay pot. Dishes are often garnished with freshly scraped coconut. Vegetables are rarely overcooked, and are simply steamed or stir-fried to retain their natural flavours and nutrients.

Kerala's Syrian Orthodox community also eats chicken, mutton and even beef – a popular dish is beef fry (beef slivers cooked with spices and onions). Other dishes include the combination of chicken coconut stew and *appam* (rice pancake), or *meen,* a

Carrying coconut husks through the Keralan backwaters

MARTIN HUGHES

fish curry. Meanwhile, Keralan Muslims from the north Malabar region have a reputation for cooking tasty biryani.

MAHARASHTRA

Much of the Deccan plateau, the heart of Maharashtra, is arid and barren, giving rise to a simple diet traditionally based on pulses and grains. Marathi Brahmin food is the epitome

A world of lentils on display at the Crawford Market, Mumbai

GREG ELMS

Bhelpuris make a sensational streetside snack

ORIEN HA

of minimalist cuisine; probably nowhere else in India is dhal quite so simple – it's boiled with salt and turmeric and then flavoured with a hint of ghee, asafoetida and jaggery. Vegetables, too, are just tossed with mustard seeds, curry leaves and grated coconut. Fish is the staple of nonvegetarian Marathi food; Maharashtra's favourite fish is *bombil*, or Bombay duck, a misnomer for this slimy, pikelike fish, which is eaten fresh or sun-dried. Indeed, Marathi nonvegetarian food tends to lean towards fish – fried or curried – with the Marathi spice blend *kala* masala. Also worth sniffing out is Kolhapuri mutton, originating from Kolhapur, and served in a fiery gravy of *garam* masala, *copra* (dried coconut flesh) and red chillies.

The snack most synonymous with Maharashtra, particularly Mumbai (Bombay), is *bhelpuri*, a riotous mix of sweet, sour, hot, soft and crunchy sensations. Tossed up on a leaf plate or a square of newspaper are puffed rice, slivers of boiled potatoes, chopped onions,

THE HUMBLE IDLI

The simple *idli* is a traditional South Indian snack that can be widely found right across India; low-cal, wholesome and nutritious, it provides a welcome alternative to oil, spice and chilli. *Idlis* are spongy, round, white, fermented rice cakes that you dip in *sambar* (soupy lentils) and coconut *chatni* (chutney). *Dahi idli* is an *idli* dunked in very lightly spiced yoghurt – tremendous for tender tummies. Other top southern snacks include *vadas* (doughnut-shaped deep-fried lentil savouries) and *appams* (rice pancakes) or *uttappams* (thick rice-flour pancakes with finely chopped onions, green chillies, coriander and coconut).

peanuts, fine hairlike besan sticks, sweet tamarind *chatni*, a piquant green-coriander-and-chilli *chatni* and a generous squeeze of lime. Another all-time Maharashtrian favourite is *vada pao,* an Indian-style veg-burger of sorts – not to be missed!

Maharashtra's cosmopolitan capital, Mumbai, arguably offers South India's most diverse dining scene – a veritable melting pot of North and South Indian cuisines along with an interesting variety of global fare. Here you can gorge on a classic Gujarati thali, a succulent tandoori platter, fresh seafood from the Konkan Coast, and a medley of international creations, from Italian-style wood-fired pizzas to feisty Tex-Mex offerings. Mumbai's Parsi (Zoroastrian) community adds yet another dimension to local cuisine with dishes such as *dhansak,* which is chicken or mutton with a mild sauce of vegetables, coriander and dhal. This dish can be found in a number of city restaurants.

TAMIL NADU

Tamil Nadu largely epitomises South Indian cuisine, with veg meals generally based on rice, dhal and *sambar,* interspersed with *idlis* and dosas. The word 'curry' actually derives from the Tamil *kari* (sauce), while mango comes from the Tamil *maangaai.* Ironically, the former does not factor hugely into Tamil cuisine; in place of 'wet' dishes, the Tamils love the many varieties of rice flour: *idli, appam* (rice pancakes), *idiyappam* (rice noodles, which can be fashioned into bowls for curry or soup) and, of course, the iconic dosa; all of the above are usually served with side dishes of *sambar*, chutney and *rasam* (dhal-based broth flavoured with tamarind).

Vegetarian cuisine reigns supreme in Tamil Nadu, and in many small towns this may indeed be all you will find to eat. Chettinad cuisine is Tamil Nadu's main contribution to cooking with

Dig into dosas (large savoury crepes), served here with *sambar* and coconut chutney

GREG ELMS

The fascinating art of dosa preparation

GREG E

meat, consisting of chicken or mutton dishes in spicy gravy. You can find some particularly good Chettinad restaurants in Chennai (Madras) and other large towns.

The pretty seaside town of Puducherry (Pondicherry) offers a tantalising French-Indian fusion – a number of restaurants here whip up, with aplomb, bouillabaisse (fish and vegetable soup), baguettes, coq au vin (chicken in wine sauce), crème caramel, and other similarly enticing creations. *Bon appétit!*

THE MIGHTY DOSA

Dosas (also spelt dosais), a family of large savoury crepes usually served with a bowl of hot *sambar* and another bowl of cooling coconut *chatni*, are a South Indian breakfast speciality that can be eaten at any time of the day. The most popular is the *masala dosa* (which comes stuffed with spiced potatoes), but there are also other dosa varieties – the rava dosa (batter made with semolina), the Mysore dosa (which is like the *masala dosa* but with more vegetables and also chilli in the filling), and the *pessarettu dosa* (batter made with mung-bean dhal) from Andhra Pradesh. Nowadays, dosas are readily found far beyond South India, thanks to their widespread delish-appeal.

> ### DHAL-ICIOUS
>
> While the staple of preference divides north and south, the whole of India is merrily united in its addiction to dhal (curried lentils or pulses). You may encounter up to 60 different pulses: the most common are channa, a slightly sweeter version of the yellow split pea; tiny yellow or green ovals called *moong dhal* (mung beans); salmon-coloured *masoor* (red lentils); the ochre-coloured southern favourite, *tuvar dhal* (yellow lentils; also known as *arhar*); *rajma* (kidney beans); *kabuli channa* (chickpeas); *urad* (black gram or lentils); and *lobhia* (black-eyed peas).

Environment

THE LAND

With its mystical mix of landscapes, from lush rice paddies and breezy coconut groves to postcard-perfect beaches and mountain ranges, the great South Indian outdoors is nature at its spectacular best.

The most prominent geographical feature of the region is the range of mountains known as the ghats (literally 'steps'), running down the spine of South India, while most of Maharashtra and Andhra Pradesh sit on the dry Deccan plateau. The Vindhya Range, which stretches nearly the entire width of peninsular India (roughly contiguous with the Tropic of Cancer), is the symbolic division between the north and the south. South of the Vindhya Range lies the Deccan plateau (Deccan is derived from the Sanskrit word *dakshina*, meaning south), a triangular-shaped mass of ancient rock that slopes gently towards the Bay of Bengal. On its western and eastern borders, the Deccan plateau is flanked by the Western and Eastern Ghats. Pockets of the ghats are now protected in forest reserves and national parks.

The Western Ghats (known in Goa and Maharashtra as the Sahyadris) start to rise just north of Mumbai (Bombay) and run parallel to the coast, gaining height as they go south until they reach the tip of the peninsula. The headwaters of southern rivers, such as the Godavari and Cauvery, rise in the peaks of the Western Ghats and drain into the Bay of Bengal.

The Eastern Ghats, a less dramatic chain of low, interrupted ranges, sweep northeast in the direction of Chennai (Madras) before turning northward, roughly parallel to the coast bordering the Bay of Bengal, until they merge with the highlands of central Orissa.

At 2695m, Anamudi in Kerala is South India's highest peak. The Western Ghats have an average elevation of 915m, and are covered with tropical and temperate evergreen forest and mixed deciduous forest. The western coastal strip between Mumbai and Goa, known as the Konkan Coast, is studded with river estuaries and sandy beaches. Further south, the Malabar Coast forms a sedimentary plain into which are etched the sublime waterways and lagoons that characterise Kerala. The eastern coastline (known as the Coromandel Coast where it tracks through Tamil Nadu) is wider, drier and flatter.

Offshore from India are a series of island groups, politically part of India but geographically linked to the landmasses of Southeast Asia and islands of the Indian Ocean. The Andaman and Nicobar Islands sit far out in the Bay of Bengal (they comprise 572 islands and form the peaks of a vast submerged mountain range extending almost 1000km between Myanmar and Sumatra), while the coral atolls of Lakshadweep (300km west of Kerala) are a northerly extension of the Maldives islands, with a land area of just 32 sq km.

To keep your finger on the Indian government's green pulse, click on the Ministry of Environment & Forests site at www .envfor.nic.in.

WILDLIFE

The subcontinent has some of the richest biodiversity in the world, with 397 species of mammals, and 1232 bird, 460 reptile, 240 amphibian and 2546 fish species – among the highest counts for any country in the world. Understandably, wildlife-watching has become one of the country's prime tourist activities and there are dozens of national parks offering opportunities to spot rare and unusual wildlife. To find out where and when to get close to nature, see the boxed text, p96.

India is one of around a dozen 'megadiversity' countries, which together make up an estimated 70% of the world's biodiversity. South India has three recognised biogeographic zones: the forested, wet and elevated Western

To stay abreast of current wildlife and wilderness issues, explore Indian Jungles (www.indian jungles.com).

Ghats, which run parallel to the west coast from Mumbai to Kerala; the flat, dry Deccan plateau; and the islands, including the Andaman and Nicobar Islands and Lakshadweep.

Animals

Most people know that India is the natural home of the tiger and Indian elephant, but the forests, jungles, coastlines, waters and plains actually provide a habitat for a staggering multitude of species.

Visitors seeking an in-depth overview of India's habitats will appreciate *Ecosystems of India*, edited by JRB Alfred.

In South India, the tropical forests of the Western Ghats contain one of the rarest bats on earth – the small Salim Ali's fruit bat – as well as flying lizards (technically gliders), sloth bears, leopards, jungle cats, hornbills, parrots and hundreds of other bird species. Birders should check out the reserves listed on p100.

Offshore, the Lakshadweep in the Indian Ocean and the Andaman and Nicobar Islands in the Bay of Bengal preserve classic coral atoll ecosystems. Bottlenose dolphins, coral reefs, sea turtles and tropical fish flourish beneath the water, while seabirds, reptiles, amphibians and butterflies thrive on land. Members of the Andaman's small population of elephants have been known to swim up to 3km between islands. Another oddity found here is the coconut or robber crab, a 5kg tree-climbing monster that combs the beaches for broken coconuts.

ENDANGERED SPECIES

Despite having amazing biodiversity, India faces a growing challenge from its exploding human population. At last count, India had 569 threatened species, comprising 247 species of plants, 89 species of mammals, 82 species of birds, 26 species of reptiles, 68 species of amphibians, 35 species of fish and 22 species of invertebrates.

India's national animal is the tiger, its national bird is the peacock and its national flower is the lotus. The national emblem of India is a column topped by three Asiatic lions.

Prior to 1972 India had only five national parks, so the Wildlife Protection Act was introduced that year to set aside parks and stem the abuse of wildlife. The Act was followed by a string of similar pieces of legislation with bold ambitions but few teeth with which to enforce them. A rare success story has been Project Tiger, launched in 1973 to protect India's big mammals. The main threats to wildlife continue to be habitat loss due to human encroachment and poaching by criminals and even corrupt officials and businessmen at all levels of society. It is estimated that 846 tigers and 3140 leopards were poached between 1994 and 2008, while 320 elephants were poached from 2000 to 2008.

The bandit Veerappan (see p41 for more information) is believed to have killed 200 elephants and sold an estimated US$22 million of illegally harvested sandalwood during his 30-year crime spree.

Cheetal Walk: Living in the Wilderness, by ERC Davidar, describes the author's life among the elephants of the Nilgiri Hills and examines how they can be saved from extinction.

All of India's wild cats, from leopards to snow leopards, panthers and jungle cats, are facing extinction from habitat loss and poaching for the lucrative trade in skins and body parts for Chinese medicine. There are thought to be fewer than 3500 tigers, 1000 snow leopards and 300 Asiatic lions still alive in the wild. Spurious health benefits are linked to every part of the tiger, from the teeth to the penis, and a whole tiger carcass can fetch upwards of US$10,000. Government estimates suggest that India is losing 1% of its tigers every year to poachers.

Even highly protected rhinos are poached for the medicine trade – rhino horn is highly valued as an aphrodisiac and as a material for making handles for daggers in the Persian Gulf. Elephants are also poached for ivory – we implore you not to support this trade by buying ivory souvenirs (also see the boxed text, p92). Various species of deer are threatened by hunting for food and trophies, and the chiru, or Tibetan antelope, is nearly extinct because its hair is woven into wool for expensive shahtoosh shawls.

Other threatened species include lion-tailed macaques, glossy black Nilgiri langurs and the slender loris, an adept insect-catcher with huge eyes for nocturnal hunting. Sadly, there is still illegal trade in South India for live loris – their eyes are believed by some to be a powerful medicine for human-eye diseases, as well as a vital ingredient for love potions. South India's hilly regions are the last remaining stronghold of the endangered Nilgiri tahr (cloud goat).

In the Andaman Islands, the once-common dugong (*Dugong dugon;* a large herbivorous aquatic mammal with flipper-like forelimbs) has almost disappeared. It was hunted by mainland settlers for its meat and oil, and has also suffered from a loss of natural habitat (seagrass beds).

BIRDS

Birdlife is where South India really comes into its own, and there are several wetlands and sanctuaries supporting a large percentage of the country's water birds. Many species, including herons, cranes, storks and even flamingos, can be spotted at various sanctuaries – see p100.

In village ponds, you can often see a surprising array of birds, from the common sandpiper to the Indian pond heron, or paddy bird, surveying its domain. Waterways are particularly rich in birdlife; graceful white egrets and colourful kingfishers (including the striking stork-billed kingfisher, with its massive red bill) are common, as are smaller species, such as plovers, water hens and coots. Red-wattled and yellow-wattled lapwings can be readily recognised by the coloured, fleshy growths on their faces.

Birds of prey, such as harriers and buzzards, soar over open spaces searching for unwary birds and small mammals. Around rubbish dumps and carcasses, the black or pariah kite is a frequent visitor. Birds inhabiting forested areas include woodpeckers, barbets and malkohas (a colourful group of large, forest-dwelling cuckoos). Fruit-eaters include a number of pigeons (including the Nilgiri wood-pigeon and pompadour green-pigeon), doves, colourful parrots (including Malabar and plum-headed parakeets), minivets and various cuckoo-shrikes and mynas.

Hornbills are forest-dwelling birds, with massive curved bills, similar to toucans. The largest is the great hornbill, sporting a large bill and a horny growth on its head (called a casque); the Malabar grey hornbill is endemic to the Malabar region.

> The Wildlife Protection Society of India (www
.wpsi-india.org) is a premier wildlife conservation organisation campaigning for animal welfare via education, lobbying and legal action against poachers.

FISH

The still-pristine coral around the archipelagos of Lakshadweep, Andaman and Nicobar supports a diverse marine ecosystem that hosts a myriad of tropical fish, including butterfly fish, parrotfish, the very ugly porcupine fish and the light-blue surgeonfish. Along the Goan and Malabar coasts, mackerel and sardines are prevalent, although overfishing from mechanised trawlers is an increasing problem. Other marine life off the coast of South India includes moray eels, crabs and sea cucumbers. Migratory visitors include the sperm whale (*Physeter catodon*).

> *A Pictorial Guide to the Birds of the Indian Subcontinent,* by Salim Ali and S Dillon Ripley, is a comprehensive field reference to birds found in South India.

INVERTEBRATES

South India has some truly stunning butterflies and moths, including the Malabar banded swallowtail (*Papilio liomedon*) and the peacock hairstreak (*Thelca pavi*).

In the Andaman and Nicobar Islands, you may come across the coconut or robber crab (*Birgus latro*), a 5kg tree-climbing creature that combs the beaches for coconuts.

Leeches are common in the forests, especially during and immediately after the monsoon.

THE NOBLE INDIAN ELEPHANT

Revered in Hindu mythology and admired for its strength and stamina, the elephant traditionally appears in various guises in South India's history and culture.

Today, however, Indian elephants are exploited as well as honoured: tamed elephants are used in religious ceremonies or in logging (though they have largely been replaced by heavy machinery), while farmers fear the destructive capabilities of their wild brethren. Indian elephants weigh up to 5 tonnes and live in family groups, usually led by the oldest females. At puberty, males leave to pursue solitary lives. Elephants live in forest or grassland habitats and have voracious appetites, eating for up to 18 hours per day and wolfing down some 200kg of food, mostly grass, leaves and shrubs. While in search of food, elephants have been known to leave the forest and demolish farmers' entire crops, bringing themselves into unwanted human contact. Indeed, humans are the elephant's sole enemy. Along with loss of habitat from urban development and logging, elephants face an ongoing threat from poachers. The tusk of the male elephant is valued for its ivory, and illegal poaching has had serious effects on the gender balance.

The cultural significance of the elephant can be seen at temples and during festivals, where they may be colourfully decorated and lead processions. In Hindu creation myths, the elephant is the upholder of the universe, the foundation of life, while the elephant-headed deity Ganesh is the god of good fortune and remover of obstacles (see p53). Some temples have their own elephant, which takes part in rituals or waits patiently at the entrance with its mahout (keeper), accepting offers or coins with its trunk.

Safaris through forest reserves give you the opportunity to spot elephants in the wild, and some national parks offer elephant treks through the jungle (see p101).

MAMMALS

The nocturnal sloth bear *(Melursus ursinus)* has short legs and shaggy black or brown hair, with a splash of white on its chest. It roams in the forested areas of the national parks, and in the Nilgiris.

The gaur *(Bos gaurus)*, a wild ox (sometimes referred to as the Indian bison), can be seen in major national parks in Karnataka, Goa and Kerala. Up to 2m high, it's born with light-coloured hair, which darkens as it ages. With its immense bulk and white legs, the gaur is easily recognised. It prefers the wet *sholas* (virgin forests) and bamboo thickets of the Western Ghats.

The common dolphin *(Delphinus delphis)* is found off both coastlines of the Indian peninsula, and dugongs, although elusive, can sometimes be spotted off the Malabar Coast and the Andaman Islands.

Antelopes, Gazelles & Deer

You'll see plenty of these grazers in South India's national parks, but keep your eyes peeled for the chowsingha *(Tetracerus quadricornis)*, the only animal in the world with four horns. Also unusual is the nilgai *(Boselaphus tragocamelus)*, the largest Asiatic antelope.

The blackbuck *(Antilope cervicapra)* has distinctive spiral horns and an attractive dark coat, making it a prime target for poachers. The dominant males develop dark, almost black, coats (usually dark brown in South India), while the 20 or so females and subordinate males in each herd are fawn in colour.

The slender chinkara *(Gazella gazella*; Indian gazelle*)*, with its light-brown coat and white underbelly, favours the drier foothills and plains. It can be seen in small herds in national parks and sanctuaries in Karnataka and Andhra Pradesh.

The little mouse deer *(Tragulus meminna)* only grows 30cm tall. Delicate and shy, its speckled olive-brown/grey coat provides excellent camouflage in the forest. The common sambar *(Cervus unicolor)*, the largest of the Indian deer, sheds its impressive horns at the end of April; new ones start growing a month later. Meanwhile, the attractive chital (*Axis axis*; spotted deer) can be seen in most of South India's national parks, particularly those with wet evergreen forests. The barking deer (*Muntiacus muntjak*) is a small deer that bears tushes (elongated canine teeth) as well as small antlers, and its bark is said to sound much like that of a dog. It's a difficult animal to spot in its habitat, the thick forests of Tamil Nadu, Karnataka and Andhra Pradesh.

Tigers & Leopards

The tiger (*Panthera tigris*) is the prize of wildlife-watchers in India but, being a shy, solitary animal, it's a rare sight. India has the world's largest tiger population but most of the famous tiger reserves are in North India. Tigers prefer to live under the cover of tall grass or forest and can command vast areas of territory.

The leopard (*P pardus*) does not stick exclusively to heavy forest cover, but it is possibly even harder to find than the tiger. Leopards are golden brown with black rosettes, although in the Western Ghats they may be almost entirely black.

Dog Family

The wild dog, or dhole (*Cuon alpinus*), is a tawny predator that hunts during the day in packs that have been known to bring down animals as large as a buffalo.

The Indian wolf (*Canis lupus linnaeus*) has suffered from habitat destruction and hunting, and is now rare in South India. Its coat is fawn with black stipples, and it's generally a much leaner looking animal than its European or North American cousins. For a chance to see the Indian wolf, head to its preferred habitat of dry, open forest and scrubland of the Deccan plateau.

The Indian fox (*Vulpes bengalensis*) has a black-tipped tail and a greyish-coloured coat, and because of its appetite for rodents, it can coexist much more comfortably with farming communities than other carnivores.

Primates

You can't miss these cheeky creatures, whether it's passing through sign-posted 'monkey zones' as you traverse the Western Ghats, or fending off overfriendly macaques at temples.

The little pale-faced bonnet macaque (*Macaca radiata*) is so-named for the 'bonnet' of dark hair that covers its head. These macaques live in highly structured troops where claims on hierarchy are commonly and noisily contested. They are opportunistic feeders – barely a grub, berry or leaf escapes their alert eyes and nimble fingers – and they love to congregate at tourist spots where excited families throw fruit their way. The crab-eating macaque (*M fascicularis*), found in the Nicobar Islands, looks rather like a rhesus or a bonnet macaque, but has a longer, thicker tail. In contrast, the lion-tailed macaque (*M silenus*) has a thick mane of greyish hair that grows from its temples and cheeks.

Less shy is the common langur (*Presbytis entellus*) or Hanuman monkey, recognisable by its long limbs and black face. India's most hunted primate is the Nilgiri langur (*P johni*), which inhabits the dense forests of the Western Ghats, including the *sholas* of the Nilgiri and Annamalai ranges. This vegetarian monkey is pursued by poachers for the supposed medicinal qualities of its flesh and viscera.

The peculiar-looking slender loris (*Loris tardigradus*) has a soft, woolly, brown/grey coat and huge, bushbaby eyes. Nocturnal, this endangered species (see p91) comes down from the trees only to feed on insects, leaves, berries and lizards.

The World Wide Fund for Nature (WWF; www .wwfindia.org) promotes environmental protection and wildlife conservation throughout India.

SLITHERING THINGS

India has 460 species of reptiles, of which 50 are poisonous snakes. There are various species of cobra, including the legendary king cobra, the world's largest venomous snake, which grows up to 5m. For obvious reasons, snake charmers stick to smaller species. Nonvenomous snakes include the rat snake, the bright-green vine snake and the rock python. All live in the fear of the snake-killing mongoose, which has evolved ingenious techniques for hunting poisonous snakes; tricking the reptiles into striking repeatedly until they are exhausted, and then eating the head first to avoid being bitten.

REPTILES & AMPHIBIANS

Of the 32 species of turtles and tortoises in India, you may see the hawksbill, leatherback, loggerhead or endangered olive ridley species in the waters of South India. Turtles are protected, but it's possible to see them nesting in some areas, notably at Morjim in Goa. If you're lucky, you may see the Indian star tortoise (*Geochelone elegans*) waddling along the forest floor in Andhra Pradesh.

Three species of crocodiles are found in India, two of them in South India – the mugger, or marsh, crocodile (*Crocodylus palustris*) and the saltwater crocodile (*C porosus*). The latter lives in the Andaman and Nicobar Islands, while the mugger is extensively distributed in rivers and freshwater lakes in South India thanks to government breeding programs. If you don't see them in the wild, you certainly will at the Crocodile Bank (p407), a breeding farm 40km south of Chennai.

Plants

Once almost entirely covered in forest, India's total forest cover is now estimated to be around 20%, although the Forest Survey of India has set an optimistic target of 33%. Despite widespread clearing of native habitats, the country boasts 49,219 plant species, of which around 5200 are endemic. Species on the southern peninsula show Malaysian ancestry, while desert plants in Rajasthan are more clearly allied with the Middle East, and conifer forests of the Himalaya derive from European and Siberian origins.

Forest types in South India include tropical, wet and semi-evergreen forests of the Andaman and Nicobar Islands and Western Ghats; tropical, moist deciduous forests in the Andamans, southern Karnataka and Kerala; tropical thorn forests, found in much of the drier Deccan plateau; and montane and wet temperate forests in the higher parts of Tamil Nadu and Kerala.

Characteristic of the Nilgiri and Annamalai Hills in the Western Ghats are the patches of moist evergreen forest restricted to the valleys and steep, protected slopes. Known as *sholas*, these islands of dark green are surrounded by expansive grasslands covering the more exposed slopes. They provide essential shelter and food for animals, but their limited size and patchy distribution make *sholas* vulnerable to natural and human disturbances.

Indian rosewood (*Dalbergia latifolia*), Malabar kino (*Pterocarpus marsupium*) and teak have been virtually cleared from some parts of the Western Ghats, and sandalwood (*Santalum album*) is diminishing across India due to illegal logging for the incense and wood-carving industries. A bigger threat to forestry is firewood harvesting, often carried out by landless peasants who squat on gazetted government land.

Widely found in the south are banyan figs with their dangling aerial roots; bamboo in the Western Ghats; coconut palms on the islands and along the coastal peninsula; Indian coral trees along the coasts; and mangroves in tiny pockets. India is home to around 2000 species of orchid, about 10% of those found worldwide. The Nilgiri Hills is one of the finest places to spot orchids, such as the Christmas Orchid (*Calanthe triplicata*).

Around 2000 plant species are described in ayurveda (traditional Indian herbal medicine), while close to 100 plant species are used in *amchi* (Tibetan traditional medicine).

NATIONAL PARKS & WILDLIFE SANCTUARIES

India has 97 national parks and 486 wildlife sanctuaries, which constitute about 5% of India's territory. An additional 70 parks have been authorised on paper but not yet implemented on the ground. There are also 14 biosphere reserves, overlapping many of the national parks and sanctuaries, providing safe migration channels for wildlife and allowing scientists to monitor biodiversity. In South India, most of the parks were established to protect wildlife from loss of habitat, so entry is often restricted to tours.

We heartily recommend visiting at least one national park/sanctuary on your travels – the experience of coming face to face with a wild beast will stay with you for a lifetime, while your visit adds momentum to efforts to protect India's natural resources. Wildlife reserves tend to be off the beaten track and infrastructure can be limited – book transport and accommodation in advance, and check opening times, permit requirements and entry fees before you visit. Many parks close to conduct a census of wildlife in the off-season, while monsoon rains can make wildlife-viewing tracks inaccessible.

Almost all parks offer jeep/van tours, but you can also search for wildlife on guided treks, boat trips and elephant safaris. For the various safari possibilities, see p100.

The Kurinji shrub, which only produces bright purple-blue coloured blossoms every 12 years, is unique to the hills of South India's Western Ghats. Unfortunately the next blossom is due in 2016!

ENVIRONMENTAL ISSUES

With over a billion people, ever-expanding industrial and urban centres, and an expansive growth in chemical-intensive farming, India's environment is under tremendous threat. An estimated 65% of India's land is degraded in some way, and nearly all of that land is seriously degraded, with the government consistently falling short on most of its environmental protection goals due to lack of enforcement or willpower.

Despite numerous new environmental laws since the 1984 Bhopal disaster (for further information see www.bhopal.org), corruption continues to exacerbate environmental degradation – worst exemplified by the flagrant flouting of environmental rules by companies involved in hydroelectricity, mining, and uranium and oil exploration. Usually, the people most affected are low-caste rural farmers and Adivasis (tribal people) who have limited political representation and few resources to fight big businesses.

Between 11% and 27% of India's agricultural output is lost due to soil degradation from over-farming, rising soil salinity, loss of tree-cover and poor irrigation. The human cost is heart-rending, and lurking behind all these problems is a basic Malthusian truth: there are too many people for India to support at its current level of development.

While the Indian government could undoubtedly do more, some blame must also fall on Western farm subsidies that artificially reduce the cost of imported produce, undermining prices for Indian farmers.

As anywhere, tourists tread a fine line between providing an incentive for change and making the problem worse. Many of the environmental problems in Goa (see the boxed text, p194) are a direct result of years of irresponsible development for tourism. Always consider your environmental impact while travelling in South India, including while trekking and diving (see p102).

The Foundation for Revitalisation of Local Health Traditions has a search engine for medicinal plants at www.medicinalplants .in. Travellers with a deep interest should get CP Khare's *Encyclopedia of Indian Medicinal Plants*.

Deforestation

Since Independence, some 53,000 sq km of India's forests have been cleared for logging and farming, or damaged by urban expansion, mining, industrialisation and river dams. The number of mangrove forests has halved since the early 1990s, reducing the nursery grounds for the fish that stock the Indian Ocean and Bay of Bengal. Demand for fuel and building materials, natural fires and traditional slash-and-burn farming, destruction

Get the inside track on Indian environmental issues at Down to Earth (www.downtoearth.org .in), an online magazine that dives into subjects often overlooked by the mainstream media.

MAJOR NATIONAL PARKS & WILDLIFE SANCTUARIES

Park/Sanctuary	Page	Location	Features	Best time to visit
Calimere (Kodikkarai) Wildlife & Bird Sanctuary	p433	near Thanjavur, Tamil Nadu	coastal wetland; dolphins, sea turtles, crocodiles, flamingos, waterfowl, wading birds, mynas & barbets	Nov-Jan
Dubare Forest Reserve	p266	near Madikeri, Karnataka	interactive camp for retired working elephants	Sep-May
Indira Gandhi Wildlife Sanctuary (Annamalai)	p460	near Pollachi, Tamil Nadu	forested mountains; elephants, gaurs, tigers, jungle cats, bears, flying squirrels, civet cats	year-round, except in periods of drought
Mahatma Gandhi Marine National Park	p485	Andaman & Nicobar Islands	mangrove forests & coral reefs	Nov-Apr
Nilgiri Biosphere Reserve, including Wayanad Wildlife Sanctuary, Bandipur National Park, Nagarhole National Park, Mudumalai National Park	Wayanad p380, Bandipur p262, Nagarhole p262, Mudumalai p470	Tamil Nadu, Karnataka & Kerala	forest; elephants, tigers, deer, gaurs, sambars, muntjacs, mouse deers, chitals & bonnet macaques	Mar-May (some areas year-round)
Periyar Wildlife Sanctuary	p352	Kumily, Kerala	wooded hills; lion-tailed macaques, elephants, gaurs, otters, dholes, pythons, kingfishers & fishing owls	Oct-Jun
Ranganathittu Bird Sanctuary	p257	near Mysore, Karnataka	river & islands; storks, ibises, egrets, spoonbills & cormorants	Jun-Nov
Sanjay Gandhi National Park	p144	near Mumbai, Maharashtra	scenic city park; water birds, flying foxes & leopards	Aug-Apr
Tadoba-Andhari Tiger Reserve	p166	south of Nagpur, Maharashtra	deciduous forest, grasslands & wetlands; tigers, dholes, nilgais & gaurs	Feb-May
Vedantangal Bird Sanctuary	p413	near Chengalpattu, Tamil Nadu	forest & lake; cormorants, egrets, herons, storks, ibises, spoonbills, grebes & pelicans	Nov-Jan

Fish Curry & Rice, published by the Goa Foundation, is an incisive study of the Goan environment and the threats facing it.

of forests for mining or farmland, and illegal smuggling of teak, rosewood and sandalwood have all contributed to this drastic deforestation.

One of the most dramatic examples of deforestation is in the Andaman and Nicobar Islands where forest cover has been slashed from 90% to a mere 20%. Although protected forest reserves have been established on most islands here, illegal and sanctioned logging continues.

India's first Five Year Plan in 1951 recognised the importance of forests for soil conservation, and various policies have been introduced to increase forest cover. However, over the years there have been allegations of haphazard implementation by officials as well as cases of ordinary people clearing forests for firewood and grazing in forest areas. Try to minimise the use of wood-burning stoves while you travel (this is less of an issue in areas with fast-growing pine species in the hills).

Marine Environment

The marine life along the 3000km-long coastline of South India and around the outlying archipelagos is under constant threat from pollution, sewage and harmful fishing methods. Ports, dams and tourism all contribute to the degradation of South India's marine environment.

India's seas have been overfished to such an extent that stocks are noticeably dwindling. Trawlers and factory fishing ships have largely replaced traditional log boats, and in some areas – eg the coast of Kerala – fishing communities are struggling to find other sources of income. Over the past decade, the international demand for prawns saw a plethora of prawn farms set up in South India, resulting in vast environmental damage to the coastline and birdlife as well as to farmland. There are now laws in place to curtail the effects of prawn farming, although these are not always adhered to.

MANGROVES

About 2.5 million hectares of mangroves have been destroyed in India since 1900. Mangroves are home to migratory birds and marine life, and are the first defence against soil erosion. They also help protect the coast from natural disasters, such as tidal waves and cyclones. Destruction of South India's mangroves has been caused by cattle grazing, logging, water pollution, prawn farming and tidal changes caused by the erosion of surrounding land. On the coast of Tamil Nadu and in the Andaman and Nicobar Islands, there have been efforts to reintroduce mangroves around fishing villages as a protective barrier following the damage caused by the devastating 2004 tsunami.

CORAL REEFS

Three major coral reefs are located around the islands of Lakshadweep, Andaman and Nicobar, and the Gulf of Mannar (near Sri Lanka). Coral is a crucial part of the fragile marine ecology, but is under constant threat from overfishing and bottom-of-the-sea trawling. Other factors contributing to the onslaught against the reefs are shipping, pollution, sewage, poaching, and excessive silt caused by deforestation and urban development on the land.

Mining

Throughout South India, a considerable number of mining rights have been granted with little regard for the environment, and with no requirement to undertake rehabilitation. In 2007 the Goa Forest Department purported that more than 10,000 hectares of forest land was threatened by mining. Nearly half the iron ore exported from India comes from Goa. When open-pit mines have been fully exploited they are often simply abandoned, scarring the hinterland. In Goa and other states of South India, heavy rains flush residues from open-cut mines into the rivers and sea. Some residues seep into the local water table, contaminating the drinking water.

Some licences for the mining of gold, silver, platinum and diamonds in Karnataka, and for gold and mica in the Nilgiris, have also been issued without sufficiently considering the adverse effects on the environment.

Climate Change

Changing climate patterns – linked to global carbon emissions – have been creating dangerous extremes of weather in India. While India is a major polluter, in carbon emissions per capita it still ranks far behind the USA, Australia and Europe.

Increased monsoon rainfall has caused ever-worse flooding and destruction, including the devastating Gujarat and Maharashtra floods in 2005. In the mountain deserts of Ladakh, increased rainfall is changing time-honoured farming patterns and threatening traditional mud-brick architecture. Conversely, other areas are experiencing reduced rainfall, causing drought and riots over access to water supplies. Islands in the Lakshadweep group as well as the low-lying plains of the Ganges delta are being inundated by rising sea levels.

The popular guru Jaggi Vasudev has launched an ambitious project to plant 114 million new saplings in Tamil Nadu by 2016, increasing forest cover in the region by 10%; see www.projectgreen hands.org.

The Goa Foundation (www.goacom.com/goa foundation) is the primary environmental monitoring group in Goa.

Water

Arguably the biggest threat to public health in South India is inadequate access to clean drinking water and proper sanitation. With India's population set to double by 2050, agricultural, industrial and domestic water usage are all expected to spiral upwards, despite government policies designed to control water use. Rivers are also affected by run-off, industrial pollution and sewage contamination – the Sabarmati, Yamuna and Ganges are among the most polluted rivers on earth. At least 70% of the freshwater sources in India are now polluted in some way.

Water distribution is another volatile issue. Since 1947 an estimated 35 million people in India have been displaced by major dams, mostly built for hydroelectricity projects to provide energy for this increasingly power-hungry nation. While hydroelectricity is one of the greener power sources, valleys across India are being sacrificed to create new power plants and displaced people rarely receive adequate compensation.

Across India, ground water is being removed at an uncontrolled rate, causing an alarming drop in water-table levels and supplies of drinking water. Simultaneously, contamination from industry is rendering ground water unsafe to drink right around the country. The soft-drink manufacturer Coca-Cola faced accusations that it was selling drinks containing unsafe levels of pesticides, as well as allegations over water shortages near its plants and farmland being polluted with industrial chemicals. Although cleared of claims about the safety of its drinks, Coca-Cola has yet to be held to account on the other allegations.

Pollution

While North India is most heavily affected by pollution, the south is by no means without its share of problems. It's hard to find a river or lake that has not been polluted with sewage, rubbish and/or chemical waste. Tanneries and textile factories are often the worst polluters. Some rivers, such as the Noyyal and the Bhavani, tributaries of the Cauvery, are now virtually unusable for drinking water and irrigation.

Many of the problems experienced today are a direct result of the Green Revolution of the 1960s when a quantum leap in agricultural output was achieved using chemical fertilisers and pesticides. Pesticides used for cash crops, such as cotton and tobacco, upset the ecology – only about 1% of pesticides (which are often those banned elsewhere in the world) actually reach the pests; the rest seeps into the environment.

Read about wildlife, conservation and the environment in *Sanctuary Asia* (www.sanctuaryasia.com), a laudable publication raising awareness about India's precious natural heritage.

Noise pollution in major cities has been measured at over 90 decibels – more than one-and-a-half times the recognised 'safe' limit. Bring earplugs!

THE ANTI-PLASTIC CRUSADE

In many parts of South India plastic bags and bottles clog drains, litter city streets and beaches, and even stunt grass growth in parks. Animals choke on the waste and the plastic also clogs water courses, heightening the risk of malaria and water-borne diseases. Campaigners estimate that about 75% of plastics used are discarded within a week and only 15% are recycled.

Fed up with ineffectual government policies to address the plastic problem, an increasing number of local initiatives are being pursued. For instance, in Kodaikanal (Kodai) shopping bags are now made from paper instead of plastic, while Goa has imposed various 'plast-free' zones, including on a number of its beaches.

Tourists can assist by not buying anything in plastic bags or bottles, and encouraging hotels and shops to use environmentally-friendly alternatives. Shopkeepers almost invariably put your purchases in plastic bags, and without turning it into a battle, it does help to request they use paper bags or nothing at all. Other ways to help include buying tea in terracotta cups at train stations and purifying your own drinking water (see the boxed text, p540).

AIR POLLUTION

Air pollution from industry and vehicle emissions is an ongoing concern in South India, with Mumbai being among the world's most polluted cities, and Chennai, Hyderabad and Bengaluru (Bangalore) not that far behind. On a national level, industry and vehicle emissions in India have increased four- to eight-fold over the past 20 years, catapulting India into the ranks of countries with the most polluted air and highest levels of premature death due to air pollution. Indian diesel reportedly contains around 50 to 200 times more sulphur than European diesel, and the ageing engines of many Indian vehicles would fail most emissions tests in Europe or the USA. Unfortunately, national efforts to improve air-quality standards almost invariably fail due to lack of local enforcement. This problem occurs on the household level as well, with over half a million people a year believed to die or sustain chronic illness from indoor air pollution – a result of continuing to burn with traditional wood or animal dung rather than switching to smokeless stoves or liquid gas.

Air pollution in many Indian cities has been measured at more than double the maximum safe level recommended by the World Health Organization (WHO).

Activities

Whether it's working up a sweat on a heart-racing forest trek, or splashing in the warm waters of the Arabian Sea, South India has a truly exhilarating array of things to do. And after all those blood-pumping activities, you can stretch that aching body and nourish your weary soul by enrolling in a mind-cleansing yoga course – just one of a number of spiritual activities on offer.

It would take an entire book to cover all the possibilities out there, but this chapter should keep you content for at least one lifetime.

Choosing an Operator

Regardless of what you decide to do, you should exercise a little caution when choosing an operator. We receive regular reports of dodgy operators taking poorly equipped tourists into potentially dangerous situations. Remember that travel agents are only middlemen and the final decisions about safety and equipment come down to the people actually operating the trip. Check out all tour operators, trekking companies and activity providers carefully. Make sure that you know in advance what you're getting, then make sure you get what you paid for by having it put in writing.

Try to stick to companies that provide activities themselves, using their own guides and teaching staff. If you go through an agency, look for operators who are accredited by the Travel Agents Association of India (www.travel agentsofindia.com), the Indian Association of Tour Operators (www.iato .in) or the Adventure Tour Operators Association of India (www.atoai.org). Note that dodgy operators often change their names to sound like the trusted companies – consult official tourist offices for lists of government-approved operators and seek first-hand recommendations from fellow travellers.

Always check safety equipment before you set out and make sure you know what is included in the quoted price. If anything is substandard, let the operator know. If they refuse to make the necessary changes, go with another company. For any activity, make sure that you have adequate insurance – many travel-insurance policies have exclusions for risky activities, including such commonplace holiday pursuits as skiing, diving and trekking (see p501).

OUTDOOR ACTIVITIES

South India has an alluring array of outdoor activities, from diving and trekking to birdwatching and paragliding.

MEETING THE WILDLIFE

The subcontinent has some of the most beautiful flora and fauna on the planet – here are several ways to get up close and personal with nature in this region.

Birding in India and South Asia (www.birding .in) is a top cyber-spot to swoop into all things ornithological, right down to recommended birdwatching binoculars.

Birdwatching

Some of the world's major bird-breeding and feeding grounds are found in India. A few places offer bird-spotting by boat (see regional chapters for details). The following are prime South Indian birdwatching sites:

Andaman & Nicobar Islands Spot rare drongos and golden orioles on Havelock Island (p486).

Goa Top spots to view all sorts of species are at Cotigao Wildlife Sanctuary (p230), the Tropical

Spice Farm near Ponda (p202) and on the state's manifold river trips, and can be arranged from almost every beach resort.

Karnataka See storks, egrets, ibises and spoonbills at Karanji Lake Nature Park (p253), Ranganathittu Bird Sanctuary (p257), Bandipur National Park (p262) and Nagarhole National Park (p262).

Kerala View Indian bird species from May to July and migratory birds from October to February at Kumarakom Bird Sanctuary (p350) and Thattekkad Bird Sanctuary (p359).

Mumbai Sanjay Gandhi National Park (p144) is home to almost 300 species of birds, and Sewri Creek (p122) is big with waders and pink flamingos.

Tamil Nadu There's plenty to point binoculars at in Mudumalai National Park (p470), Calimere (Kodikkarai) Wildlife & Bird Sanctuary (p433) and Vedantangal Bird Sanctuary (p413).

Elephant Rides & Safaris

Elephant rides are a tremendous way of getting close to wildlife. Some national parks have their own working elephants, which can be hired for safaris into areas that are inaccessible to jeeps and walkers. To ascertain the best times to visit parks, see regional chapters and the boxed text, p95.

Goa Short elephant rides are possible at one of Ponda's spice plantations (p201).

Karnataka Elephant safaris go to India's largest elephant reserve at Bandipur National Park (p262) near Mysore. You can also interact with retired working elephants at Dubare Forest Reserve (p266) near Madikeri.

Kerala There are elephant rides at Periyar Wildlife Sanctuary (p352) and at Kudanadu, 50km from Kochi (p365).

Tamil Nadu There's a slim chance you'll see a tiger, and good maths for spotting gaurs and spotted deer from an elephant's back in Mudumalai National Park (p470).

Horse Rides

Horse riding is possible in various parts of South India, from gentle ambles in hill stations to more demanding trails through lowland forests. As well as these leisure rides, horses are used as transport on some *yatra* (pilgrimage) trekking routes. See the regional chapters for comprehensive details about all modes of horsing around.

Jeep Safaris

As well as elephant rides, there are many jeep safaris visiting national parks, tribal villages and remote temples. You can usually arrange a custom itinerary, either with travel agents or directly with local jeep drivers – the regional chapters have details.

Karnataka Wildlife resorts offer safaris to Nagarhole National Park (p262), Bandipur National Park (p262) and other reserves.

Kerala Wildlife-spotting jeep tours drive through the forests of Wayanad Wildlife Sanctuary (p380) as well as the areas surrounding Periyar Wildlife Sanctuary (p352).

Tamil Nadu Jeep tours are just one of several ways to scout for wildlife in Mudumalai National Park (p470).

OTHER ACTIVITIES

Apart from trekking, lovers of the great outdoors can scuba dive, paraglide, raft, kayak and more. Remember to take out adequate insurance cover before you travel.

Boat Tours

Take your pick from languid river rides, scenic lake cruises or motorboat tours of offshore islands. Some recommended tours:

Andaman & Nicobar Islands Boat and ferry trips go to outlying islands from Port Blair (p484) and Mayabunder (p489).

Goa River cruises are offered on the state's picturesque riverine stretches and from the capital, Panaji (p191). Fishing trips depart from many beaches.

Before setting off on a safari, get the lowdown on South India's wildlife sanctuaries at www .indiawildlifeportal .com/south-india-wild life-sanctuaries.html.

Karnataka Coracles unhurriedly drift up and down the meandering Tungabhadra River in Hampi (p275), while fishing boats offer sea rides in Gokarna (p272) and Malpe (p271).

Kerala Days of lazy drifting on the backwaters around Alleppey (p346), or canoe tours from Kollam (Quilon; p341) and bamboo-raft tours in Periyar Wildlife Sanctuary (p352). Houseboat trips are also available on the quieter backwaters around Kumarakom (p350) and near Bekal in northern Kerala (p384).

Maharashtra Ride out to the mid-sea island fort of Murud (p166) on a sailboat.

Mumbai Boats cruise around Mumbai Harbour and to Elephanta Island (p125).

Cultural Tours

Tours to tribal areas are permitted in limited regions and provide a window into the traditional way of life among India's Adivasis (see p51 for more details). Some tours can be quite exploitative but better ones employ tribal guides and try to minimise the effect of tourism on tribal people.

Kerala Tours to Mannakudy tribal areas of Periyar Wildlife Sanctuary (p352).

To learn more about South India's Adivasis, read *The Todas of South India – A New Look*, by Anthony Walker, and *Archaeology and History: Early Settlements in the Andaman Islands*, by Zarine Cooper.

Cycling & Motorcycling

Bicycle and motorcycle hire is widely available right across India, especially in areas that attract tourists – regional chapters have details of just some of the numerous rental places. For recommended motorcycle tours see p528.

Diving, Snorkelling & Water Sports

The Andaman Islands are India's leading destination for scuba diving, with world-class dive sites on well-preserved coral reefs, particularly around Havelock Island. Visibility is clearest from around December to March or April. Meanwhile, the Lakshadweep Islands offer more coral-atoll diving from mid-October to mid-May. Dive certification courses and recreational dives are also possible in Goa.

Dive India, an Andaman Islands' dive company, has a comprehensive list of dive sites on its website (www.diveindia .com).

Growing numbers of surfers are discovering the breaks off the island of Little Andaman (p477), with the best waves generally between mid-March and mid-May.

Andaman & Nicobar Islands India's best diving is around Havelock Island (p476).

Goa Numerous beach resorts offer diving courses, windsurfing and other holiday watersports (p186).

Kerala There is world-class diving between mid-October and mid-May on the little-visited Lakshadweep Islands (p386).

RESPONSIBLE DIVING

To help preserve the ecology and beauty of reefs, observe the following guidelines when diving:

- Never use anchors on the reef and take care not to ground boats on coral.
- Avoid touching or disturbing living marine organisms – they can be damaged by even the gentlest contact. If you must hold onto the reef, only touch exposed rock or dead coral.
- Be conscious of your fins. Even without contact, the surge from fin strokes near the reef can damage delicate organisms. Kicking up clouds of sand can smother organisms.
- Practise and maintain proper buoyancy control. Major damage can be done by divers descending too fast and colliding with the reef.
- Don't collect or buy corals or shells.
- Ensure that you take away all your rubbish and any litter you may find. Plastics in particular are a serious threat to marine life.
- Do not feed fish.
- Choose a dive company with appropriate environmental policies and practices.

Hang-gliding & Paragliding

Goa and Maharashtra are the flying capitals of South India. Safety standards have been variable in the past – consult the state tourist office for a safety update before taking the leap. The best season for flying is October to June.

Goa There are paragliding flights at Arambol (p220) and Anjuna (p214).

Kerala There are beginner paragliding classes or tandem flights in Munnar (p356).

Maharashtra You can take courses and tandem paragliding flights at Lonavla (p171).

Kayaking & River Rafting

South India doesn't have the wild river-rafting opportunities found up north, but there are still some admirable options. The rafting seasons are from around October to January in Goa and Karnataka, and July to September in Maharashtra. The level of rapids varies from modest Grade II to raging Grade IV and most operators offer multiday rafting safaris, as well as short thrill rides. Some good options:

Karnataka Kayaking and rafting trips can be organised with Bengaluru's Getoff ur ass (p242). White-water trips up to Grade IV are possible in Dubare Forest Reserve (p266).

Kerala Canoe trips on the backwaters of Kerala at Green Palms Homes (p348) near Allepey. The tourist office in Kollam (p341) also arranges canoe tours of surrounding villages.

Mumbai Rafting in Maharashtra is organised through Mumbai-based Outbound Adventure (p124) which offers rafting trips from around June to September.

Rock-Climbing

For warm-weather climbers, there exist some tremendous sandstone and granite climbing areas in Karnataka at Badami, Ramnagar, Savandurga, Anegundi and Hampi, India's premier bouldering region (see the boxed text, p278).

Climbing is on a mixture of bolts and traditional protection. Organised climbs can be arranged but serious climbers should bring gear from home – pack plenty of nuts, hexacentrics and cams, plus spare rolls of climbing tape for jamming cracks in sharp granite.

Trekking

North India is prime trekking territory; however, South India still has some worthy offerings. Most people opt for organised treks (sometimes mandatory) with local trekking agencies.

SAFETY GUIDELINES FOR WALKING

Before embarking on a walking trip, consider the following points to maximise the chances of a safe and enjoyable experience:

- Pay any fees and possess any permits required by local authorities.
- Be sure you are healthy and feel comfortable walking for a sustained period.
- Obtain reliable information about physical and environmental conditions along your intended route (eg from park authorities).
- Be aware of local laws, regulations and etiquette about wildlife and the environment.
- Walk only in regions, and on trails, within your realm of experience.
- Be aware that weather conditions and terrain vary significantly from one region, or even from one trail, to another. Seasonal changes can considerably alter any trail. These differences influence the way walkers dress and the equipment they carry.
- Ask before you set out about the environmental characteristics that can affect your walks and how local, experienced walkers deal with these considerations.

If you do make your own arrangements, tell someone where you're going and when you intend returning, and never trek alone.

Popular trekking options:

Andaman & Nicobar Islands There are birdwatching jungle treks on Havelock Island (p486).

Karnataka Interesting treks around Karnataka with Bengaluru-based Getoff ur ass (p242) and agents and guest houses in Madikeri (p264).

Kerala There are guided wildlife-spotting treks in the Periyar Wildlife Sanctuary (p352) and Wayanad Wildlife Sanctuary (p380), and hill treks at Munnar (p356) and in the surrounding areas (p359).

Tamil Nadu Guided treks in the buffer zone around Mudumalai National Park (p470), and hill and jungle treks around Indira Gandhi (Annamalai) Wildlife Sanctuary (p460), Ooty (Udhagamandalam; p467) and Kodaikanal (p458).

HOLISTIC & SPIRITUAL ACTIVITIES

Travellers with an interest in spirituality or alternative therapies will find a variety of courses and treatments that strive to heal body, mind and spirit. Meditation, ayurveda (Indian herbal medicine) and yoga, especially, are attracting an ever-increasing number of visitors to South India.

AYURVEDA

Ayurveda is the ancient science of Indian herbal medicine and holistic healing, which uses natural treatments, massage and other therapies. There are clinics, resorts and colleges across India where you can learn ayurvedic techniques and receive treatments, including the places listed below.

> Kerala is ayurveda paradise: read the boxed texts on p336 and p382.

Goa Therapies and courses in ayurveda, reflexology, aromatherapy, acupressure and yoga are run at almost every beach resort on a seasonally changing basis (p185).

Karnataka Naturopathy classes and ayurvedic therapies are offered in Bengaluru (p241), Mysore (p253) and Gokarna (p273).

Kerala You can undergo ayurvedic treatment at most towns and villages in Kerala, including around Kovalam (p331), in Varkala (p337), Kollam (p340), Alappuzha (Alleppey; p344, Fort Cochin (p365), Periyar Wildlife Sanctuary (p353) and Wayanad (p381).

Tamil Nadu Courses in ayurvedic massage are available in Puducherry (p423), as well as Mamallapuram (p411).

Spa Treatments

If you simply wish to enjoy the healing effects without the study, there are spas throughout South India, from ayurvedic hospitals to luxurious health centres at five-star resorts (see regional chapters for top-end hotel recommendations). However, be cautious of dodgy one-on-one massages by private (often unqualified) operators, particularly in tourist towns – seek advice from fellow travellers and trust your instincts.

> Over 2000 plant species are described in ancient ayurvedic texts, with at least 550 frequently used in India.

These are just a sprinkling of recommended options:

Goa Numerous beach resorts offer massages and other spa services at Calangute and Baga (p208), Anjuna (p214), Colva and Benaulim (p225), Arambol (p220) and other locations.

Karnataka Enjoy herbal rubs and scrubs in Bengaluru (p241), Mysore (p253) and Gokarna (p273).

Kerala Massages and herbal treatments at Varkala (p337) and Kochi (Cochin; p365), and therapeutic breaks at Janakanthi Panchakarma Centre (p340) and Thapovan Heritage Home (p335).

Maharashtra Massages, saunas and spa treatments at the Osho Meditation Resort (p173).

Mumbai Be pampered at one of Mumbai's finest spas, inside the ITC Maratha hotel (p131).

Tamil Nadu Try the posh hotel spas in Thanjavur (p436) and Kodaikanal (p458), and the massage sessions in Mamallapuram (Mahabalipuram; p411) and Puducherry (p423).

YOGA

Many places in South India offer classes and courses in various types of yoga, often with a meditation component. The most common yoga forms are hatha (following the *shatkarma* system of postures and meditation), *ashtanga* (following the 'eight limbs' system of postures and meditation), pranayama (controlled yogic breathing), and Iyengar (a variation of *ashtanga* yoga using physical aids for advanced postures).

Yoga Courses

There are oodles of yoga courses on offer with some outfits being more reputable than others (especially in tourist towns). Seek advice from tourist offices and other travellers and visit several to find one that suits your needs. Many ashrams (spiritual retreats) also offer yoga courses, though be aware that some centres require a minimum time commitment and stipulate that residents adhere to strict rules on silence, diet and behaviour – see the boxed text, p106.

There are many yoga opportunities across the South India region; for those that have no fees, donations are appreciated. Here are some good places to start:

Goa A huge range of yoga courses is offered at hotels, spiritual centres and retreats all around Goa, on a seasonally changing basis (p185).

Karnataka World-renowned courses in *ashtanga*, hatha and Iyengar yoga and meditation are held in Mysore (p253), and yoga classes are held in Bengaluru (p241) and the SwaSwara resort in Gokarna (p273).

Kerala Hatha yoga courses are available at Sivananda Yoga Vedanta Dhanwantari Ashram (p331) near Thiruvananthapuram (Trivandrum) (p331), as are yoga classes in Varkala (p337), Kochi (p365) and Kovalam (p331).

Maharashtra Yogic healing is held at the Kaivalyadhama Yoga Hospital (p171) in Lonalva, and advanced Iyengar yoga courses (for experienced practitioners only) are offered at Ramamani Iyengar Memorial Yoga Institute (p176) in Pune.

Mumbai Classes in various styles of yoga are held in Mumbai (p125).

Tamil Nadu Yoga classes in Chennai (Madras; p398). Various yoga classes and courses in Mamallapuram (p411) and Puducherry (p423).

Ashrams

South India has dozens of ashrams – places of communal living established around the philosophies of a guru (spiritual guide). Codes of conduct vary, so make sure you're willing to abide by them before committing. For more information, see the boxed text, p106.

Some good possibilities:

Andhra Pradesh Puttaparthi (Puttaparthi; p320) is the ashram of controversial but phenomenally popular guru Sri Sathya Sai Baba.

Kerala Matha Amrithanandamayi Mission (Alleppey; p346) is famed for its female guru Amma – 'The Hugging Mother'. Sivananda Yoga Vedanta Dhanwantari Ashram (Trivandrum; p331) is a famous yoga centre, renowned for its hatha yoga courses. Sivagiri Mutt (Varkala; p337) is the most significant ashram devoted to Shri Narayana Guru.

Maharashtra Sevagram houses the Brahmavidya Mandir Ashram (p165), established by Gandhi's disciple Vinoba Bhave, and the Sevagram Ashram (p165), founded by the Mahatma himself. There's also Anandwan (see the boxed text; p166), the ashram founded by social activist Baba Amte near Nagpur, and Pune's Osho Meditation Resort (p173), which runs on the teachings of its founder, Osho.

Tamil Nadu Sri Aurobindo Ashram (Puducherry; p421), founded by the famous Sri Aurobindo, has branches around India. The rural Isha Yoga Centre (Coimbatore; p463) offers residential courses and retreats. Sri Ramana Ashram (Tiruvannamalai; p419) is the ashram founded by Sri Ramana Maharshi.

MEDITATION

A number of centres offer courses in *vipassana*, or mindfulness meditation, and Buddhist philosophy; be aware that some courses require students to abide by a vow of silence and may also have other protocols (inquire in advance).

Yoga is one of the oldest therapies in human history, dating back 4000 years. *Light On Yoga* is by one of the world's foremost authorities, BKS Iyengar.

To delve into the world of yoga, ayurveda and other holistic therapies, click on www.indianmedicine .nic.in.

For details (including branches) about *vipassana* meditation taught by SN Goenka, go to www.dhamma.org.

ASHRAMS & GURUS

Many people visit India specifically to spend time at an ashram – literally a 'place of striving' – for spiritual and personal enrichment. There are literally hundreds of gurus (the word means 'dispeller of darkness' or 'heavy with wisdom') offering their guidance on the path to perfection to millions of eager followers. However, a little caution is required. Some ashrams tread a fine line between spiritual community and personality cult and there have been reports of questionable happenings at ashrams, often of a sexual nature. These allegations have touched some of the most popular spiritual communities.

Choosing an ashram will depend on your spiritual leanings. Every guru has their own unique take on spiritual living, often with a focus on abstinence and meditation. All ashrams have a code of conduct, and visitors are usually required to adhere to strict rules, which may include a certain dress code, a daily regimen of yoga or meditation, and charitable work at social projects run by the ashram. The diet is almost always vegetarian and you may also be asked to abstain from eggs, tobacco, alcohol, garlic, onions, and 'black drinks' – ie anything containing caffeine, including tea and coke. Sex may be prohibited or positively encouraged – make sure you are comfortable with this before you stay.

Ashrams are generally run as charitable projects – though a number of gurus are reportedly multimillionaires – and a donation is appropriate to cover the expenses of your food, accommodation and the running costs of the ashram. Most ashrams accept new residents without advance notice, but do call ahead to make sure. Some gurus move around frequently so check the guru will be in attendance when you visit. Even if you lack spiritual conviction, it's interesting to visit an ashram for the day to see the workings of a modern-day spiritual movement.

Some recommendations:

Andhra Pradesh *Vipassana* meditation courses are held in Hyderabad (p303) and Vijayawada (p316).

Maharashtra Courses of various durations are held here at the world's largest *vipassana* meditation centre at Igatpuri (p151).

Tamil Nadu Various *vipassana* courses in Chennai (p398).

Mumbai (Bombay)

Mumbai is big. It's full of dreamers and hard-labourers, actors and gangsters, stray dogs and exotic birds, artists and servants and fisherfolk and *crorepatis* (millionaires) and lots and lots of other people. It has the most prolific film industry, one of Asia's biggest slums and the largest tropical forest in an urban zone. It's India's financial powerhouse, fashion capital and a pulse point of religious tension. It's evolved its own language, Bambaiyya Hindi, which is a mix of…everything. It has some of the world's most expensive real estate and a knack for creating land from water using only determination and garbage.

But wait. Mumbai is not frantic; it's not *overwhelming*. Or at least, it doesn't have to be. Contrary to what you might think, you may not have almost just died in that taxi or been rushed by that station crowd or run over by that guy with the funny outfit and the monkey. The city just has its own rhythm, which takes a little while to hear: it's a complex but playful raga, a gliding, light-footed dance that all of Mumbai seems to know.

So give yourself some time to learn it and appreciate the city's lilting cadences, its harmonies of excess and restraint. The stately and fantastical architecture, the history hanging in the air of the markets, the scent of jasmine in the ladies' car of the train, the gardens, the street vendors, the balloon-wallahs, and the intellectuals in old libraries – it will all take you in if you let it. So sit back, develop your equanimity, and let yourself become part of the song.

HIGHLIGHTS

- Eat in one of India's best **restaurants** (p131), then watch – or be one of – the beautiful people at a posh **bar, lounge** (p135) or **club** (p136)

- Stock up on odd and exquisite things at Mumbai's ancient **bazaars** (p139) and outsource your wardrobe to its **boutiques** (p138)

- Admire the grandiose frilliness of Mumbai's colonial-era architecture: **Chhatrapati Shivaji Terminus** (p117), **University of Mumbai** (p116) and **High Court** (p116)

- Resist the urge to bow down before the commanding triple-headed Shiva sculpture at **Elephanta Island** (p143)

- Feel the city's sea breeze among playing kids, big balloons and a hot-pink sunset at **Chowpatty Beach** (p119)

FESTIVALS IN MUMBAI

Banganga Festival (Jan) A two-day classical-music festival held at the Banganga Tank (p120).

Mumbai Festival (Jan) Based at several stages around the city, it showcases the food, dance and culture of Mumbai.

Elephanta Festival (Feb) Classical music and dance on Elephanta Island (p143).

Kala Ghoda Festival (Feb) Getting bigger and more sophisticated each year, this two-week-long offering has a packed program of arts performances and exhibitions.

Nariyal Poornima (Aug) Festivals in the tourist hub of Colaba kick off with this celebration of the start of the fishing season after the monsoon.

Ganesh Chaturthi (Aug/Sep) Mumbai's biggest annual festival – a 10- to 11-day event in celebration of the elephant-headed deity Ganesh – sweeps up the entire city. On the first, third, fifth, seventh and 10th days of the festival families and communities take their Ganesh statues to the seashore and auspiciously drown them: the 10th day, which sees millions descending on Chowpatty Beach to submerge the largest statues, is particularly ecstatic.

Colaba Festival (Oct) A small arts festival in Colaba that sometimes overlaps with Diwali festivities.

Prithvi Theatre Festival (Nov) A showcase of what's going on in contemporary Indian theatre; also includes performances by international troupes and artists.

HISTORY

Koli fisherfolk have inhabited the seven islands that form Mumbai as far back as the 2nd century BC. Amazingly, remnants of this culture remain huddled along the city shoreline today. A succession of Hindu dynasties held sway over the islands from the 6th century AD until the Muslim Sultans of Gujarat annexed the area in the 14th century, eventually ceding it to Portugal in 1534. The only memorable contribution the Portuguese made to the area was christening it Bom Bahai, before throwing the islands in with the dowry of Catherine of Braganza when she married England's Charles II in 1661. The British government took possession of the islands in 1665, but leased them three years later to the East India Company for the paltry annual rent of UK£10.

Then called Bombay, the area flourished as a trading port. So much so that within 20 years the presidency of the East India Company was transferred to Bombay from Surat. Bombay's fort was completed in the 1720s, and a century later ambitious land reclamation projects joined the islands into today's single landmass. Although Bombay grew steadily during the 18th century, it remained isolated from

its hinterland until the British defeated the Marathas (the central Indian people who controlled much of India at various times) and annexed substantial portions of western India in 1818.

The fort walls were dismantled in 1864 and massive building works transformed the city in grand colonial style. When Bombay took over as the principal supplier of cotton to Britain during the American Civil War, the population soared and trade boomed as money flooded into the city.

A major player in the independence movement, Bombay hosted the first Indian National Congress in 1885, and the Quit India campaign was launched here in 1942 by frequent visitor Mahatma Gandhi. The city became capital of the Bombay presidency after Independence, but in 1960 Maharashtra and Gujarat were divided along linguistic lines – and Bombay became the capital of Maharashtra.

The rise of the pro-Maratha regionalist movement, spearheaded by the Shiv Sena (Hindu Party; literally 'Shivaji's Army'), shattered the city's multicultural mould by actively discriminating against Muslims and non-Maharashtrans. The Shiv Sena won power in the city's municipal elections in 1985. Communalist tensions increased and the city's cosmopolitan self-image took a battering when nearly 800 people died in riots following the destruction of the Babri Masjid in Ayodhya in December 1992.

They were followed by a dozen bombings on 12 March 1993, which killed more than 300 people and damaged the Bombay Stock

FAST FACTS

Population 16.4 million

Area 440 sq km

Telephone code ☎ 022

Languages Marathi, Hindi, Gujarati

When to go October to February

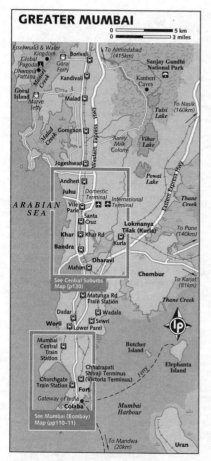

although the British names of these and most streets are still in popular local use.

ORIENTATION

Mumbai, the capital of Maharashtra, is an island connected by bridges to the mainland. The island's eastern seaboard is dominated by the city's (off-limits) naval docks. The city's commercial and cultural centre is at the southern, claw-shaped end of the island known as South Mumbai. The southernmost peninsula is Colaba, traditionally the travellers' nerve-centre with most of the major attractions, and directly north of Colaba is the busy commercial area known as Fort, where the old British fort once stood. It's bordered on the west by a series of interconnected, fenced grass areas known as maidans (pronounced may-*dahns*).

Though just as essential a part of the city as South Mumbai, the area north of here is collectively known as 'the suburbs'. The airport (p140) and many of Mumbai's best restaurants, shopping and night spots are here, particularly in the upmarket suburbs of Bandra and Juhu.

Maps

Eicher City Map Mumbai (Rs250) is an excellent street atlas, worth picking up if you'll be spending some time here.

INFORMATION
Bookshops

Vendors lining the footpaths around Flora Fountain, the maidans, and Mahatma Gandhi (MG) Rd sell new and secondhand books.

Crossword (Map pp110-11; ☎ 23842001; Mohammedbhai Mansion, NS Patkar Marg, Kemp's Corner; ⏰ 11am-8.30pm) Enormous.

Oxford Bookstore (Map p118; ☎ 66364477/88; www.oxfordbookstore.com; Apeejay House, 3 Dinsha Wachha Marg, Churchgate; ⏰ 10am-10pm) Modern, with a tea bar.

Search Word (Map p117; ☎ 22852521; Metro House, Colaba Causeway, Colaba; ⏰ 10.30am-8.30pm) Small and tidy, with a choice selection of books and magazines.

Strand Book Stall (Map p118; ☎ 22661719, www.strandbookstall.com; Cowasji Patel Rd; ⏰ 10am-8pm Mon-Sat) Old-school and smart, with good discounts.

Internet Access

Portasia (Map p118; ☎ 22032022; Kitab Mahal, Dr Dadabhai Naoroji Rd, Fort; per hr Rs20; ⏰ 9am-9pm

Exchange and Air India Building. The more recent train bombings of July 2006, which killed more than 200 people, and November 2008's coordinated attacks on 10 of the city's landmarks, which lasted three days and killed 173 people, are reminders that tensions are never far from the surface.

In 1996 the city's name was officially changed to Mumbai, the original Marathi name derived from the goddess Mumba who was worshipped by the early Koli residents. The Shiv Sena's influence has since seen the names of many streets and public buildings changed from their colonial names. The airport, Victoria Terminus and Prince of Wales Museum have all been renamed after Chhatrapati Shivaji, the great Maratha leader,

MUMBAI (BOMBAY)

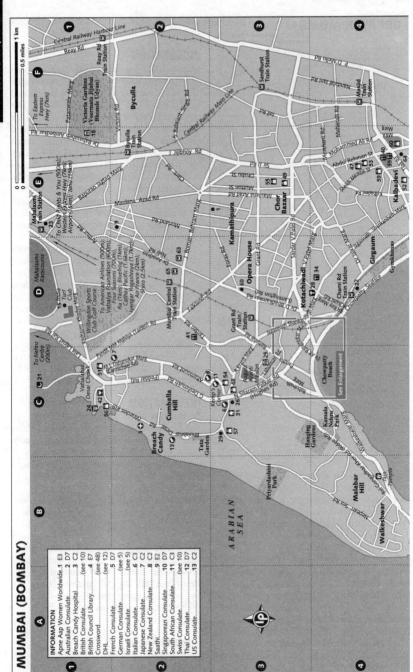

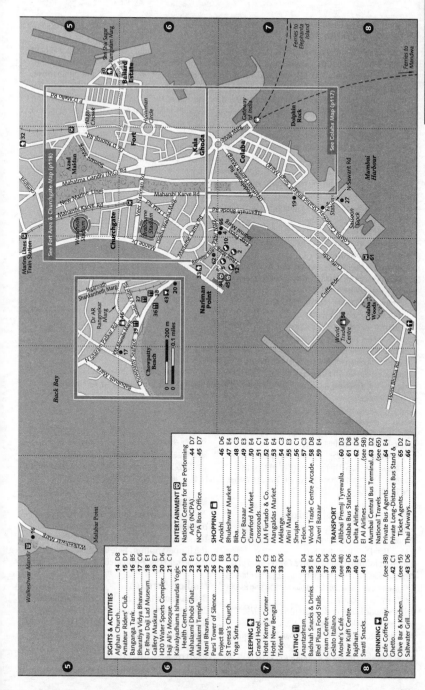

SIGHTS & ACTIVITIES
Afghan Church.....................14 D8
Amateur Riders' Club............15 D1
Banganga Tank.....................16 B5
Bharatiya Vidya Bhavan.........17 C6
Dr Bhau Daji Lad Museum......18 E1
Gallery Maskara....................19 E7
H2O Water Sports Complex....20 D6
Haji Ali's Mosque..................21 C1
Kaivalyadhama Ishwardas Yogic
  Health Centre.....................22 D4
Mahalaxmi Dhobi Ghat...........23 E1
Mahalaxmi Temple.................24 C1
Mani Bhavan........................25 C3
Parsi Tower of Silence............26 C3
Project 88............................27 E8
St Teresa's Church.................28 D4
Trident................................29 C3

SLEEPING
Grand Hotel.........................30 F5
Hotel Kemp's Corner.............31 C1
Hotel New Bengal..................32 E5
Trident................................33 D6

EATING
Anantashram........................34 D4
Badshah Snacks & Drinks........35 E4
Bhel Plaza Food Stalls............36 D6
Cream Centre.......................37 D6
Gelato Italiano......................38 D6
Moshe's Café.......................(see 48)
New Kulfi Centre...................39 E4
Rajdhani..............................40 E4
Swati Snacks.........................41 D2

DRINKING
Cafe Coffee Day....................(see 38)
Ghetto.................................42 C1
Olive Bar & Kitchen...............(see 15)
Saltwater Grill......................43 D6

ENTERTAINMENT
National Centre for the Performing
  Arts (NCPA)........................44 D7
NCPA Box Office....................45 D7

SHOPPING
Anokhi................................46 D6
Bhuleshwar Market................47 E4
Biba...................................48 C3
Chor Bazaar.........................49 E3
Crawford Market...................50 E4
Crossroads...........................51 C1
LM Furtado & Co....................52 E4
Mangaldas Market..................53 E4
Melange..............................54 C3
Mini Market..........................55 E3
Shrujan...............................56 C1
Telon..................................57 C3
World Trade Centre Arcade......58 D8
Zaveri Bazaar.......................59 E4

TRANSPORT
Allibhai Premji Tyrewalla.........60 D3
Colaba Bus Station................61 D8
Delta Airlines.......................62 D6
El Al Airlines........................(see 58)
Mumbai Central Bus Terminal...63 D2
National Travels.....................(see 65)
Private Bus Agents.................64 E4
Private Long-Distance Bus Stand &
  Ticket Agents......................65 D2
Thai Airways........................66 E7

BAMBAIYYA HINDI 101

Bambaiyya (or Mumbaiyya) Hindi, the city's own special take on India's lingua franca, is a mix of Hindi, Marathi, English, Gujarati and whatever else is on hand, which will vary from neighbour-hood to neighbourhood. Constantly evolving as it migrates across the city and the generations, it's the perfect language for Mumbai's diverse population, which loves mobility of all sorts. The dialect was once seen as an imperfect, bastardised version of Hindi, but it's increasingly gaining acceptance, in no small part because of the ubercool, rough-talking gangsters that have used it in Hindi-language films over the years. Its lack of rules also makes it beloved by all – gangsters and intellectuals alike – who come to the city with no Hindi or some other version thereof: Bambaiyya Hindi is accessible, welcoming, pliable and self-made, much like the city itself.

It's this very diversity that also makes for some exceedingly witty slang, a tiny portion of which is listed below. Note that this is *for entertainment purposes only*. We've omitted the really bad words, but some of these could still create problems for you if used inappropriately. Maybe start off using them with friends; then, once you've spent long enough on Mumbai's streets, you'll be able to speak like a real *bhai*.

Conversational Slang

baap re! – exclamation used for something surprising, good or bad.

bilkul – absolutely, exactly.

bindaas – independent, carefree; also, cool. Question: *Tum kaise ho?* (How are you?) Answer: *Bindaas, yaar.*

bhendi – literally, okra; a mild curse word, used to express frustration. *Bhendi late hogaya!* (Darn, I'm late!)

chakaas – awesome.

chhawa – a hot man or boyfriend; cf *item*.

chikna – literally, shiny; handsome.

Cutting – a half-cup of tea at streetside stalls (usually Rs3).

item – a hot woman or girlfriend, cf *chhawa*.

khallas – 'finished', often used to refer to something that didn't work out (in the underworld, this is usually a life).

locha – trouble, problem. *Kya locha hai?* (What's going on here?)

paan-patti – a stall selling cigarettes and paan.

scene – 1. a problem, issue. *Scene kya hai?* (What's going on here?); 2. a plan. *Aaj ka scene kya hai?* (What's the plan for today?)

Mon-Sat) Entrance is down a little alley; look for the 'cybercafe' sign hanging from a tree.

Sify iWay (per 3hr Rs125) Churchgate (Map p118; Prem Ct, J Tata Rd; ☽ 9am-11pm); Colaba (Map p117; Colaba Causeway; ☽ 8am-11.30pm) The Colaba branch entrance is on JA Allana Marg.

Libraries & Cultural Centres

Alliance Française (Map p118; ☎ 22035993; 40 New Marine Lines; annual membership Rs1000; ☽ 9.30am-5.30pm Mon-Fri, 9.30am-1pm Sat)

American Information Resource Center (Map p118; ☎ 22624590; http://mumbai.usconculate.gov/airc.html; 4 New Marine Lines, Churchgate; annual membership Rs400; ☽ library 10am-6pm Mon-Fri)

British Council Library (Map pp110-11; ☎ 22790101; www.britishcouncilonline.org; 1st fl, Mittal Tower A Wing, Barrister Rajni Patel Marg, Nariman Point; monthly membership Rs250; ☽ 10am-6pm Tue-Sat)

David Sassoon Library & Reading Room (Map p118; ☎ 22843703; www.davidsassoonlibrary.com; MG Rd, Kala Ghoda; 45-day/annual membership Rs500/2200; ☽ 8am-9pm)

Max Mueller Bhavan (Goethe Institut; Map p118; ☎ 22027542; www.goethe.de/mumbai; K Dubash Marg, Fort; ☽ library 11am-6pm Mon-Fri)

Media

To find out what's going on in Mumbai, check out the free **City Info**, available in hotels and restaurants, the *Hindustan Times*' **Café** insert or the hippest option, **Time Out Mumbai** (www.timeout mumbai.net; Rs30), published every two weeks.

Medical Services

Bombay Hospital (Map p118; ☎ 22067676, ambulance 22067309; www.bombayhospital.com; 12 New Marine Lines)

Breach Candy Hospital (Map pp110-11; ☎ 23672888; www.breachcandyhospital.org; 60 Bhulabhai Desai Rd, Breach Candy) Best in Mumbai, if not India.

Royal Chemists (Map p118; ☎ 22004041-3; 89A Maharshi Karve Rd, Churchgate; ☽ 8.30am-8.30pm Mon-Sat)

talli – drunk, sloshed. *Tum talli ho kya?* (Are you wasted?)

tapri – a stall, selling cigarettes and paan *(cigarette ka tapri)* or tea *(chai ka tapri)*.

time pass (TP) – to kill time.

waande – a minor problem. *Train mein seat ke waande hogaye.* (There's a problem with my train seat.)

yaar – dude. *Vo de de, yaar* (Give it to me, dude.)

Insults & Rude Talk

bewakoof – idiot. *Vo bewakoof hai* (She's an idiot.)

bol Bachchan – bullshit, smooth talk, named for the smooth-talking characters played by Bollywood legend Amitabh Bachchan. *Bol bachchan math de.* (Don't give me that bullshit.)

double battery – someone who wears thick soda-bottle glasses.

chaar-aankh – literally, four-eyes; someone who wears glasses.

Chal phut! or Chal phut yahaan se! – Get lost!

chindhi – literally, a rag; stingy, but can also mean a thief. *Mera pati chindhi hai.* (My husband's a cheapskate.)

Dimaag ka dahi math kar – shut up; literally, stop turning my brain to yoghurt.

Dimaag math kha – shut up; literally, stop eating my brain.

Dimaag ko shot math de – shut up; literally, stop shooting/fucking my brain.

khajur – literally, date (as in the dried fruit); a stupid person. *Aey Khajur!* (Hey Stupid!)

khopdi – literally, brain; a stupid person. *Aey Khopdi!*

Kya paka raha hai? – What the hell are you talking about?

sathkela – a crazy person. *Vo admi sathkela hai.* (That guy is crazy.)

Wataak yahaan se – Piss off.

Slang from the Underworld

bhai – literally, brother; a mafia don.

ghoda – literally, horse; a gun.

guest house – Arthur Rd Jail, Mumbai's largest prison.

kala coat – literally, black coat; a lawyer.

khoka – literally, box; Rs10 million (a crore).

peti – literally, trunk; Rs100,000 (a lakh).

tapori – a small-time gangster or criminal, petty thief.

Sahakari Bhandar Chemist (Map p117; ☎ 22022399; Colaba Causeway, Colaba; ◷ 10am-8.30pm)

Money

You'll never be far from an ATM in Mumbai, and foreign-exchange offices changing cash and travellers cheques are also plentiful. Nominal service charges are common.

Akbar Travels (Map p118; ☎ 22633434; 4th fl, 167/169 Dr Dadabhai Naoroji Rd; ◷ 10am-7pm Mon-Sat)

Kanji Forex (Map p118; ☎ 22040206; 40 Veer Nariman Rd, Fort; ◷ 9.30am-6pm Mon-Fri, 9.30am-4pm Sat)

Thomas Cook (◷ 9.30am-6pm Mon-Sat) Fort (Map p118; ☎ 22048556-8; 324 Dr Dadabhai Naoroji Rd) Colaba (Map p117; ☎ 22882517-20; Colaba Causeway)

Photography

Standard Supply Co (Map p118; ☎ 22612468; Image House, Walchand Hirachand Marg, Fort; ◷ 10am-7pm Mon-Sat) Everything you could possibly need for digital and film photography.

Post

The **main post office** (Map p118; ☎ 22620956; ◷ 9am-8pm Mon-Sat, 10am-5.30pm Sun) is an imposing building behind Chhatrapatri Shiraji Terminus (CST; Victoria Terminus). **Poste restante** (◷ 9am-8pm Mon-Sat) is at Counter 1. Letters should be addressed c/o Poste Restante, Mumbai GPO, Mumbai 400 001. Bring your passport to collect mail. The **EMS Speedpost parcel counter** (◷ 9am-10pm Mon-Sat, 10am-4.30pm Sun) is across from the stamp counters. Regular parcels can be sent from the parcel office behind the main building. Opposite the post office, under the tree, are parcel-wallahs who will stitch up your parcel for Rs40. The **Colaba post office** (Map p117; Henry Rd) is convenient.

Private express-mail companies:

Blue Dart (Map p118; ☎ 22822495; www.bluedart.com; Khetan Bhavan, J Tata Rd; ◷ 10am-8pm Mon-Sat)

DHL (Map pp110-11; ☎ 22837187; www.dhl.co.in; Embassy Centre, Nariman Point; ◷ 9am-8.30pm Mon-Sat).

Telephone

Justdial (☎ 69999999; www.justdial.com) and ☎ 197 provide Mumbai phone numbers.

Tourist Information

Government of India tourist office (Map p118; ☎ 22074333; www.incredibleindia.com; 123 Maharshi Karve Rd; ✆ 9am-6pm Mon-Fri, to 2pm Sat) Provides information for the entire country.

Government of India tourist office airport booths domestic (☎ 26156920; ✆ 7am-9pm); international (☎ 26829248; ✆ 24hr)

Maharashtra Tourism Development Corporation booth (MTDC; Map p117; ☎ 22841877; Apollo Bunder; ✆ 8.30am-3.30pm Tue-Sun, also 5.30-8pm weekends) For city bus tours (p125).

MTDC reservation office (Map p118; ☎ 22845678; www.maharashtratourism.gov.in; Madame Cama Rd, opposite LIC Bldg, Nariman Point; ✆ 9.30am-5.30pm Mon-Sat) Information on Maharashtra and bookings for MTDC hotels and the *Deccan Odyssey* train package.

Travel Agencies

Akbar Travels (Map p118; ☎ 22633434; Terminus View, Dr Dadabhai Naoroji Rd, Fort; ✆ 10am-7pm Mon-Sat)

Magnum International Travel & Tours (Map p117; ☎ 22838628; 10 Henry Rd, Colaba; ✆ 10am-5.30pm Mon-Fri, to 3.30pm Sat)

Thomas Cook (Map p118; ☎ 22048556-8; 324 Dr Dadabhai Naoroji Rd, Fort; ✆ 9.30am-6pm Mon-Sat)

Visa Extensions

Foreigners' Regional Registration Office (FRRO; Map p118; ☎ 22620446; Annexe Bldg No 2, CID, Badaruddin Tyabji Rd, near Special Branch) Does not officially issue extensions on tourist visas; even in emergencies they

---

MUMBAI BY NUMBERS

- Number of black taxis: about 40,000
- Population density: 29,000 people per sq km
- Average annual income: Rs48,900 (US$1000, or three times the national average)
- Number of public toilets for every 1 million people: 17
- Number of people passing through Chhattapati Shivaji Terminus (Victoria Terminus) daily: 2.5 million
- Number of people in an 1800-person-capacity train at rush hour: 7000
- Proportion of Mumbai built on re-claimed land: 60%
- Number of Bollywood movies made since 1931: 68,500

---

will direct you to Delhi (p514). However, some travellers have managed to procure an emergency extension here after much waiting and persuasion.

SIGHTS
Colaba

For mapped locations of all the following sights, see p117.

Sprawling down the city's southernmost peninsula, Colaba is a bustling district packed with street stalls, markets, bars and budget to midrange lodgings. **Colaba Causeway** (Shahid Bhagat Singh Marg) dissects the promontory

---

READING MUMBAI

Containing all the beauty and ugliness of the human condition, it's little wonder that Mumbai has inspired some of the subcontinent's best writers as well as international scribes like VS Naipaul and Pico Iyer. Leading the field are Booker Prize–winner Salman Rushdie *(Midnight's Children, The Moor's Last Sigh* and *The Ground Beneath Her Feet)* and Rohinton Mistry *(A Fine Balance* and *Family Matters),* who have both set many novels in the city.

The list of other good reads is, like Mumbai's population, endlessly multiplying.

Maximum City: Bombay Lost and Found Equal parts memoir, travelogue and journalism, Suketu Mehta's epic covers Mumbai's riots, gang warfare, Bollywood, bar dancers and everything in between. The ultimate chronicle of the city's underbelly.

Shantaram Gregory David Roberts' factional saga about an Australian prison escapee's life on the run in Mumbai's slums and jails.

Rediscovering Dharavi Kalpana Sharma's sensitive and engrossing history of Dharavi's people, culture and industry.

Bombay, Meri Jaan A heady anthology of politics, pop culture, literature and history edited by Jerry Pinto and Naresh Fernandes.

MUMBAI IN...

Two Days

Start at the granddaddy of Mumbai's colonial-era giants, the old Victoria Terminus, **Chhatrapati Shivaji Terminus** (CST; p117) and stroll up to **Crawford Market** (p139) and the maze of bazaars here. Lunch at **Rajdhani** (p133), topping it off with a juice shake from **Badshah Snacks & Drinks** (p132).

Spend the afternoon at the **Oval Maidan** (p116), checking out the cricket and the grand edifices of the **High Court** (p116) and the **University of Mumbai** (p116). Walk down to the **Gateway of India** (below) and **Taj Mahal Palace & Tower** (below) and, after the sun sets, eat street-side at **Bade Miya** (p131). Swap tall tales with fellow travellers at **Leopold's Café & Bar** (p135).

The next day, soak in the serenity of Malabar Hill's **Banganga Tank** (p120) and head to Kemp's Corner for lunch at **Moshe's Cafe** (p131) and some shopping. Make your way down to **Mani Bhavan** (p119), the museum dedicated to Gandhi, and finish the day with a **Chowpatty Beach** (p119) sunset and *bhelpuri* (crisp dough with rice, lentils, lemon juice, onions, herbs and chutney).

Four Days

See **Elephanta Island** (p143) and spend the afternoon visiting the museums and galleries of **Kala Ghoda** (p116). In the evening, head to Bandra for a candle-lit dinner at **Sheesha** (p134), followed by some seriously hip bar action at **Zenzi** (p136).

Another day could be spent visiting the **Dhobi Ghat** (p121) and the nearby **Mahalaxmi Temple** and **Haji Ali's Mosque** (p121). Lunch at **Olive Bar & Kitchen** (p136) at Mahalaxmi Racecourse and then spend the afternoon wandering the tiny lanes of **Kotachiwadi** (p120) and finish in style downtown at Indigo (p132).

and Colaba's jumble of side streets and gently crumbling mansions.

Sassoon Dock is a scene of intense and pungent activity at dawn (around 5am) when colourfully clad Koli fisherfolk sort the catch unloaded from fishing boats at the quay. The fish drying in the sun are *bombil*, the fish used in the dish Bombay duck. Photography at the dock is forbidden.

While you're here, pop into the 1847 Church of St John the Evangelist, known as the **Afghan Church** (Map pp110–11), dedicated to British forces killed in the bloody 1838–43 First Afghan War.

During the more reasonable hours of the day, nearby **Colaba Market** (Lala Nigam St) is lined with jewellery shops and fruit-and-veg stalls.

GATEWAY OF INDIA

This bold basalt arch of colonial triumph faces out to Mumbai Harbour at the tip of Apollo Bunder. Derived from the Islamic styles of 16th-century Gujarat, it was built to commemorate the 1911 royal visit of King George V. It was completed in 1924. Ironically, the gateway's British architects used it just 24 years later to parade off their last British regiment as India marched towards Independence.

These days, the gateway is a favourite gathering spot for locals and a top spot for people-watching. Giant-balloon sellers, photographers, beggars and touts rub shoulders with Indian and foreign tourists, creating all the hubbub of a bazaar. Boats depart from the gateway's wharfs for Elephanta Island and Mandwa.

The **horse-drawn gilded carriages** that ply their trade along Apollo Bunder are known as Victorias. A whirl around the Oval Maidan at night, when you can admire the illuminated buildings, should cost (after bargaining) around Rs150/250 for 15/30 minutes.

TAJ MAHAL PALACE & TOWER

This sumptuous hotel (see p131) is a fairy-tale blend of Islamic and Renaissance styles jostling for prime position among Mumbai's famous landmarks. Facing the harbour, it was built in 1903 by the Parsi industrialist JN Tata, supposedly after he was refused entry to one of the European hotels on account of being 'a native'. The palace side has a magnificent grand stairway that's well worth a quick peek, even if you can't afford to stay or enjoy a drink or meal at one of its restaurants and bars.

Kala Ghoda

'Black Horse', the area between Colaba and Fort, contains most of Mumbai's main galleries and museums alongside a wealth of colonial-era buildings. The best way to see these buildings is on a guided (p125) or self-guided (p124) walking tour.

CHHATRAPATI SHIVAJI MAHARAJ VASTU SANGRAHALAYA (PRINCE OF WALES MUSEUM)

Mumbai's biggest and best **museum** (Map p118; ☎ 22844484; www.bombaymuseum.org; K Dubash Marg; Indian/foreigner Rs15/300, camera/video Rs200/1000; ☒ 10.15am-6pm Tue-Sun), this domed behemoth is an intriguing hodgepodge of Islamic, Hindu and British architecture displaying a mix of dusty exhibits from all over India. Opened in 1923 to commemorate King George V's first visit to India (back in 1905, while he was Prince of Wales), its flamboyant Indo-Saracenic style was designed by George Wittet – who also did the Gateway of India.

The vast collection inside includes impressive Hindu and Buddhist sculpture, terracotta figurines from the Indus Valley, miniature paintings, porcelain and some particularly vicious weaponry. There's also a natural-history section with suitably stuffed animals. Take advantage of the free, multilanguage audioguides as not everything is labelled.

Students with a valid International Student Identity Card (ISIC) can get in for a bargain Rs10.

GALLERIES

The **National Gallery Of Modern Art** (Map p117; ☎ 22881969/70; MG Rd; Indian/foreigner Rs10/150; ☒ 11am-6pm Tue-Sun) has a bright, spacious and modern exhibition space showcasing changing exhibitions by Indian and international artists. **Jehangir Art Gallery** (Map p118; ☎ 22843989; 161B MG Rd; admission free; ☒ 11am-7pm) hosts interesting shows by local artists; most works are for sale. Rows of hopeful artists often display their work on the pavement outside. Nearby, the museum's contemporary-art annexe, **Museum Gallery** (Map p118; ☎ 22844484; K Dubash Marg; ☒ 11am-7pm) has rotating exhibitions in a beautiful space.

KENESETH ELIYAHOO SYNAGOGUE

Built in 1884, this sky-blue **synagogue** (Map p118; ☎ 22831502; Dr VB Gandhi Marg) still functions and is tenderly maintained by the city's dwindling Jewish community. One of two built in the city by the Sassoon family (the other is in Byculla), the interior is wonderfully adorned with colourful pillars, chandeliers and stained-glass windows – best viewed in the afternoons when rainbows of light shaft through.

Fort

For mapped locations of the following sights see p118.

Lined up in a row and vying for your attention with aristocratic pomp, many of Mumbai's majestic Victorian buildings pose on the edge of **Oval Maidan**. This land, and the **Cross** and **Azad Maidans** immediately to the north, was on the oceanfront in those days, and this series of grandiose structures faced west directly out to the Arabian Sea. The reclaimed land along the western edge of the maidans is now lined with a remarkable collection of art deco apartment blocks. Spend some time in the Oval Maidan admiring these structures and enjoying the casual cricket matches.

HIGH COURT

A hive of daily activity, packed with judges, barristers and other cogs in the Indian justice system, the **High Court** (Eldon Rd) is an elegant 1848 neo-Gothic building. The design was inspired by a German castle and was obviously intended to dispel any doubts about the authority of the justice dispensed inside, though local stone carvers presumably saw things differently: they carved a one-eyed monkey fiddling with the scales of justice on one pillar. It's permitted (and highly recommended) to walk around inside and check out the pandemonium and pageantry of public cases in progress.

UNIVERSITY OF MUMBAI (BOMBAY UNIVERSITY)

Looking like a 15th-century French-Gothic masterpiece plopped incongruously among Mumbai's palm trees, this university on Bhaurao Patil Marg was designed by Gilbert Scott of London's St Pancras Station fame. You can go inside both the exquisite **University Library** and **Convocation Hall**, but the 80m-high **Rajabai Clock Tower**, decorated with detailed carvings, is off-limits.

ST THOMAS' CATHEDRAL

Recently restored to its former glory, this charming **cathedral** (Veer Nariman Rd; ☒ 6.30am-

COLABA

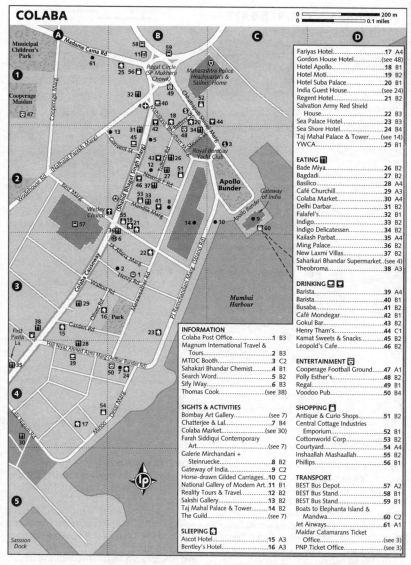

Fariyas Hotel	17	A4
Gordon House Hotel	(see 48)	
Hotel Apollo	18	B1
Hotel Moti	19	B2
Hotel Suba Palace	20	B1
India Guest House	(see 24)	
Regent Hotel	21	B2
Salvation Army Red Shield House	22	B3
Sea Palace Hotel	23	B3
Sea Shore Hotel	24	B4
Taj Mahal Palace & Tower	(see 14)	
YWCA	25	B1

EATING
Bade Miya	26	B2
Bagdadi	27	B2
Basilico	28	A4
Café Churchill	29	A3
Colaba Market	30	A4
Delhi Darbar	31	B2
Falafel's	32	B1
Indigo	33	B2
Indigo Delicatessen	34	B2
Kailash Parbat	35	A4
Ming Palace	36	B2
New Laxmi Villas	37	B2
Saharkari Bhandar Supermarket	(see 4)	
Theobroma	38	A3

DRINKING
Barista	39	A4
Barista	40	B1
Busaba	41	B2
Café Mondegar	42	B1
Gokul Bar	43	B2
Henry Tham's	44	C1
Kamat Sweets & Snacks	45	B2
Leopold's Cafe	46	B2

ENTERTAINMENT
Cooperage Football Ground	47	A1
Polly Esther's	48	B2
Regal	49	B1
Voodoo Pub	50	B4

SHOPPING
Antique & Curio Shops	51	B2
Central Cottage Industries Emporium	52	B1
Cottonworld Corp	53	B2
Courtyard	54	A4
Inshaallah Mashaallah	55	B2
Phillips	56	B1

TRANSPORT
BEST Bus Depot	57	A2
BEST Bus Stand	58	B1
BEST Bus Stand	59	B1
Boats to Elephanta Island & Mandwa	60	C2
Jet Airways	61	A1
Maldar Catamarans Ticket Office	(see 3)	
PNP Ticket Office	(see 3)	

INFORMATION
Colaba Post Office	1	B3
Magnum International Travel & Tours	2	B3
MTDC Booth	3	C2
Sahakari Bhandar Chemist	4	B1
Search Word	5	B2
Sify iWay	6	B3
Thomas Cook	(see 38)	

SIGHTS & ACTIVITIES
Bombay Art Gallery	(see 7)	
Chatterjee & Lal	7	B4
Colaba Market	(see 30)	
Farah Siddiqui Contemporary Art	(see 7)	
Galerie Mirchandani + Steinruecke	8	B2
Gateway of India	9	C2
Horse-drawn Gilded Carriages	10	C2
National Gallery of Modern Art	11	B1
Reality Tours & Travel	12	B2
Sakshi Gallery	13	B2
Taj Mahal Palace & Tower	14	B2
The Guild	(see 7)	

SLEEPING
Ascot Hotel	15	A3
Bentley's Hotel	16	A3

6pm) is the oldest English building standing in Mumbai (construction began in 1672, though it remained unfinished until 1718). The cathedral is an interracial marriage of Byzantine and colonial-era architecture, and its airy, white-washed interior is full of exhibitionist colonial memorials. A look at some of the gravestones reveals many colonists died young of malaria.

CHHATRAPATI SHIVAJI TERMINUS (VICTORIA TERMINUS)

Imposing, exuberant and overflowing with people, this is the city's most extravagant Gothic building, the beating heart of its railway network, and an aphorism for colonial India. As historian Christopher London put it, 'the Victoria Terminus is to the British

MUMBAI (BOMBAY)

FORT AREA & CHURCHGATE

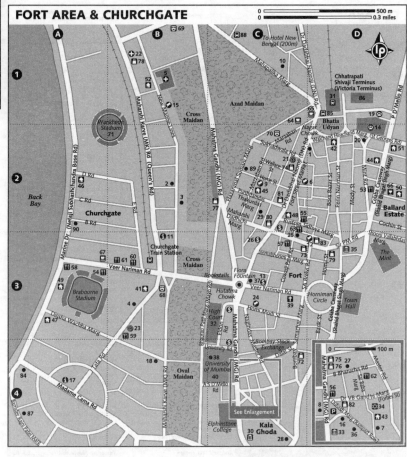

Raj, what the Taj Mahal is to the Mughal empire'. It's a meringue of Victorian, Hindu and Islamic styles whipped into an imposing, Daliesque structure of buttresses, domes, turrets, spires and stained-glass windows. Be sure to get close to the jungle-themed facade, particularly around the reservation office: it's adorned with peacocks, gargoyles, cheeky monkeys and lions.

Designed by Frederick Stevens, it was completed in 1887, 34 years after the first train in India left this site. Today it's the busiest train station in Asia. Officially renamed Chhatrapati Shivaji Terminus (CST) in 1998, it's still better known locally as VT. It was added to the Unesco World Heritage list in 2004.

MONETARY MUSEUM

While you're in the area, pop into this tiny and thoughtfully presented **museum** (☎ 22614043; www.rbi.org.in; Amar Bldg, Sir PM Rd; admission Rs10; ⏱ 10.45am-5.15pm), which is run by the Reserve Bank of India. This place offers an engrossing historical tour of India through coinage: from early concepts of cash, to the first coins of 600 BC, through Indo-European influences, and right up to today's Gandhi-covered notes. Also on display is the world's smallest coin, probably found in the crack of an ancient couch.

Chowpatty Area

For mapped locations of the following sights see pp110–11.

MARINE DRIVE & CHOWPATTY BEACH
Built on land reclaimed from Back Bay in 1920, **Marine Drive** (Netaji Subhashchandra Bose Rd) arcs along the shore of the Arabian Sea from Nariman Point past Chowpatty Beach (where it's known as Chowpatty Seaface) and continues to the foot of Malabar Hill. Lined with flaking art deco apartments, it's one of Mumbai's most popular promenades and sunset-watching spots. Its twinkling night-time lights earned it the nickname 'the Queen's Necklace'.

Chowpatty Beach (Girgaon Chowpatty) remains a favourite evening spot for courting couples, families, political rallies and anyone out to enjoy what passes for fresh air. Eating an evening time *bhelpuri* (crisp fried thin rounds of dough mixed with puffed rice, lentils, lemon juice, onions, herbs and chutney) at the throng of stalls found here is an essential part of the Mumbai experience. Forget about taking a dip: the water is toxic.

MANI BHAVAN
As poignant as it is tiny, this **museum** (☎ 23805864; www.gandhi-manibhavan.org; 19 Laburnum Rd; admission free; ☉ 9.30am-5.30pm) is in the building where Mahatma Gandhi stayed during visits to Bombay from 1917 to 1934. The museum showcases the simple room where this insightful leader formulated his philosophy of satyagraha (truth, non-violence and self-sacrifice) and launched the 1932 Civil Disobedience campaign that led to the end of British rule. Exhibitions include a photographic record of his life, along with dioramas and original documents such as

BOLLYWOOD DREAMS

Mumbai is the glittering epicentre of India's gargantuan Hindi-language film industry. From silent beginnings with a cast of all-male actors (some in drag) in the 1913 epic *Raja Harishchandra*, to the first talkie, in 1931, *Lama Ara*, today the industry churns out more than 900 films a year – more than any other industry (yes, Hollywood included). Not surprising considering they have one-sixth of the world's population as a captive audience, as well as a sizable Non-Resident Indian (NRI) following.

Every part of India has its regional film industry, but Bollywood continues to entrance the nation with its winning escapist formula of masala entertainment – where all-singing, all-dancing lovers fight and conquer the forces keeping them apart. These days, Hollywood-inspired thrillers and action extravaganzas vie for moviegoer attentions alongside the more family-orientated saccharine formulas.

Bollywood stars can attain near godlike status in India. Their faces appear in advertisements around the country, and Bollywood star-spotting is a favourite pastime in Mumbai's posher establishments.

Extra, Extra!

Studios often look for extras for background scenes and sometimes want Westerners to add a whiff of international flair (or provocative dress, which locals often won't wear) to a film. It's gotten so common, in fact, that in 2008, 100,000 junior actors nearly went on strike to protest, among other things, losing jobs to foreigners, who will work for less and come with no strings attached.

If you're still game, just hang around Colaba. Scouts, sent by the studios to conscript travellers for the following day's shooting, will usually find you. You receive Rs500 for a day's work, but it can be a long, hot day standing around on the set without promised food and water; others have described the behind-the-scenes peek as a fascinating experience. Before agreeing to anything, always ask for the scout's identification.

---

letters he wrote to Adolf Hitler and Franklin D Roosevelt. Nearby August Kranti Maidan is where the campaign to persuade the British to 'Quit India' was launched in 1942.

Kotachiwadi

For mapped locations of the following sights see pp110–11.

This *wadi* (hamlet) is a bastion clinging onto Mumbai life as it was before high-rises. A Christian enclave of elegant, two-storey wooden mansions, it's 500m northeast of Chowpatty, lying amid Mumbai's predominantly Hindu and Muslim neighbourhoods. These winding laneways allow a wonderful glimpse into a quiet life free of rickshaws and taxis. To find it, aim for **St Teresa's Church** on the corner of Jagannath Shankarsheth Marg and RR Roy Marg (Charni Rd), then duck into the warren of streets directly opposite.

Malabar Hill

For mapped locations of the following sights see pp110–11.

Mumbai's most exclusive neighbourhood of sky-scratchers and private palaces, **Malabar Hill** is at the northern promontory of Back Bay and signifies the top rung for the city's social and economic climbers.

Surprisingly, one of Mumbai's most sacred and tranquil oases lies concealed among apartment blocks at its southern tip. **Banganga Tank** is a precinct of serene temples, bathing pilgrims, meandering, traffic-free streets and picturesque old *dharamsalas* (pilgrims' rest houses). The wooden pole in the centre of the tank is the centre of the earth: according to legend, Lord Ram created the tank by piercing the earth with his arrow.

The lush and well-tended **Hanging Gardens** (Pherozeshah Mehta Gardens) on top of the hill are a pleasant but often crowded place for a stroll. For some of the best views of Chowpatty and the graceful arc of Marine Dr, visit the smaller **Kamala Nehru Park**, opposite. It's popular with couples, and there's a two-storey 'boot house' and colourful animal decorations that the kiddies like.

Byculla

Jijamata Udyan – aka Veermata Jijabai Bhonsle Udyan and formerly named Victoria Gardens –

THE PARSI CONNECTION

Mumbai has a strong – but diminishing – Parsi community. Descendants of Persian Zoroastrians who fled persecution by Muslims in the 7th century, the Parsis settled in Bombay in the 17th and 18th centuries. They proved astute businesspeople, enjoyed a privileged relationship with the British colonial powers, and became a powerful community in their own right while remaining aloof from politics.

With the departure of the British, the Parsi influence waned in Mumbai, although they continued to own land and established trusts and estates built around their temples, where many of the city's 60,000-plus Parsis still live.

Perhaps the most famous aspect of the Zoroastrian religion is its funerary methods. Parsis hold fire, earth and water sacred and do not cremate or bury their dead. Instead, the corpses are laid out within towers – known as Towers of Silence – to be picked clean by vultures. In Mumbai the **Parsi Tower of Silence** (Map pp110–11) is on Malabar Hill (although it's strictly off limits to sightseers).

The Parsi population has been declining steadily for decades; in 1940–41, the census counted 115,000 in India, Pakistan and Bangladesh, but the 2001 census recorded only 70,000 in India. (According to one survey, only 99 Parsis were born in 2007.) Their numbers are projected to fall to 23,000 by 2020, at which point they will be counted, officially, as a tribe.

is a lush and sprawling mid-19th-century garden. It's home to the gorgeous **Dr Bhau Daji Lad Museum** (Map pp110–11; ☎ 65560394, Dr Babasaheb Ambedkar Rd; Indian/foreigner Rs10/100; ⏰ 10am-5pm Thu-Tue), originally built in Renaissance revival style in 1872 as the Victoria & Albert Museum. It re-opened in 2007 after an impressive and sensitive four-year renovation. In addition to extensive structural work, the building's Minton tile floors, gilt ceiling moulding, and ornate columns, chandeliers and staircases were restored to their former, historically accurate glory. Even the sweet mint-green paint choice was based on historical research. Also restored were the museum's 3500-plus objects centring on Mumbai's history – clay models of village life, photography and maps, archaeological finds, costumes, a library of books and manuscripts, industrial and agricultural exhibits, and silver, copper and Bidriware, all set against the museum's very distracting, very stunning decor.

The gardens are also worth visiting for their green hillocks, old trees, chirping birds and – for the kids – the small playground. We don't, however, recommend the zoo.

Mahalaxmi to Worli

For mapped locations of the following sights see pp110–11.

MAHALAXMI DHOBI GHAT

If you've had washing done in Mumbai, chances are your clothes have already visited this 140-year-old **dhobi ghat** (place where clothes are washed; Map pp110–11). The whole hamlet is Mumbai's oldest and biggest human-powered washing machine: every day hundreds of people beat the dirt out of thousands of kilograms of soiled Mumbai clothes and linen in 1026 open-air troughs. The best view, and photo opportunity, is from the bridge across the railway tracks near Mahalaxmi train station.

MAHALAXMI TEMPLE

It's only fitting that in money-mad Mumbai one of the busiest and most colourful temples is dedicated to Mahalaxmi, the goddess of wealth. Perched on a headland, it's the focus for Mumbai's **Navratri** (Festival of Nine Nights) celebrations in September/October. After paying your respects to the goddess, climb down the steps towards the shore and snack on tasty *gota bhaji* (fried lentil balls) at the cliffside Laxmi Bhajiya House.

HAJI ALI'S MOSQUE

Floating like a sacred mirage off the coast, this mosque is one of Mumbai's most striking shrines. Built in the 19th century on the site of a 15th-century structure, it contains the tomb of the Muslim saint Haji – legend has it that Haji Ali died while on a pilgrimage to Mecca and his casket miraculously floated back to this spot. A long causeway reaches into the Arabian Sea, providing access to the mosque. Thousands of pilgrims, especially on Thursdays and Fridays, cross it to make their visit, many donating to the beggars who line the way; but at high tide, water covers the causeway and the mosque becomes an island.

Erosion has taken its toll on the concrete structure, and at press time, demolition of the building, along with construction of a new mosque in white Rajasthani marble, was under way. The dargah will remain open, but access may be limited.

NEHRU CENTRE

This **cultural complex** (off Map pp110-11; ☎ 24964676; www.nehru-centre.org; Dr Annie Besant Rd, Worli) includes a decent **planetarium** (☎ 24920510; adult/child Rs50/25; ☻ English show 3pm Tue-Sun), theatre, **gallery** (☎ 24963426; ☻ 11am-7pm) and the serpentine-but-interesting history exhibition **Discovery of India** (admission free; ☻ 11am-5pm). The architecture is striking: the tower looks like a giant cylindrical pineapple, the planetarium a UFO.

Central Suburbs

For mapped locations of all the following sights, see p130.

BANDRA & JUHU CHOWPATTY

Once upon a time, the luxury hotels fronting Juhu Beach, also known as **Juhu Chowpatty**, were the height of glamour for Mumbai's film crowd. The vibe is a little scruffier these days, but Juhu's reputation is still strong enough to make it a must-do for Indian tourists visiting Mumbai, and the wider neighbourhood of Juhu, along with Bandra to the south, is still home to many of Mumbai's rich and famous.

Juhu's a pleasant enough beach if you're not expecting sunbathing or a swim, and on evenings and weekends it has a carnival atmosphere as crowds of locals and tourists play cricket, ride horses, snack and drink tea, and enjoy the (sort of) fresh air. There are heaps of snack stands and fruit vendors, massage therapists, toy sellers and every other type of Indian beach entertainment. It's the suburban version of Chowpatty.

Bandra doesn't have a beach, but it does have the **Bandstand**, a seaside area with **Joggers' Park**, a sweet little green space with playgrounds and jogging paths, a 1km-long coastal **promenade**, and the ruined **Bandra Fort**. The fort, aka Castella de Aguada, was

built by the Portuguese in the 17th century at Bandra's peninsular southern tip. Concerts are sometimes held in the amphitheatre here, but mostly it's a mass foreplay festival for couples desperate for privacy. (Don't get too excited: arrests for indecent behaviour are not uncommon.) Bollywood megastar Shah Rukh Khan's estate, Mannat, is also down here.

Gorai Island

Rising up like a mirage from polluted Gorai Creek and the lush but noisy grounds of the Esselworld and Water Kingdom amusement parks, the **Global Pagoda** (Map p109; ☎ 28452261/2111; www.globalpagoda.org; admission free; ☻ 9am-6pm) is a 96m-high stupa modelled after Burma's Shwedagon Pagoda. The dome, which is designed to hold 8000 meditators and houses relics of Buddha, was built entirely without supports using an ancient technique of interlocking stones. It just took the record away from Bijapur's Golgumbaz (p287) for being the world's largest unsupported dome. The pagoda also has a museum dedicated to the life of the Buddha and his teaching (in progress at the time of writing). The pagoda is affiliated with teacher SN Goenka, and an onsite meditation centre, **Dhamma Pattana** (www .dhamma.org), offers 10-day meditation courses. The pagoda is open daily to visitors and is a nice decompression stop if you're heading to or from the amusement parks. Call ahead to let them know you're coming, and bring ID. To get here, take the train from Churchgate to Borivali, then an autorickshaw (Rs22) to the ferry landing, where boats (return Rs35) come and go every 15 minutes.

ACTIVITIES
Birdwatching

Mumbai has surprisingly good birdwatching opportunities (see the boxed text, opposite). Sanjay Gandhi National Park (p144) is popular for woodland birds, while the marshlands of industrial Sewri (pronounced *shev*-ree) swarm with birds in winter. Contact **Bombay Natural History Society** (BNHS; Map p118; ☎ 22821811; www.bnhs.org; Hornbill House, Dr Salim Ali Chowk, Shaheed Bhagat Singh Rd, Kala Ghoda) or Sunjoy Monga at **Yuhina Eco-Media** (☎ 26341531) for information on upcoming trips.

To visit Sewri on your own, check tide timings and arrive three to four hours before, or two hours after, high tide. Take the Harbour Line train from CST to Sewri, get off on the

BIRDING IN MUMBAI

Sunjoy Monga has been watching and listening to Mumbai's birds for 40 years.

When did you start birdwatching? My family first stayed downtown, in a congested area full of pigeons, and I would watch them. But then we shifted in 1968 to Kandivali in northwestern Mumbai, where at the time it was all groves, almost a forest and a little river. We could see a lot of birds from my home, and it just took off there.

I'm surprised that birds still like it here. It's so polluted. Actually, in urban areas, there's a featherfolk phenomenon happening. While some species lose out, the concentration of certain birds in the urban context – the numbers, and also the variety – is actually rising in many parts of the world, and especially the tropics.

Why? Well, the warmth of the urban world and the variety of stuff available in a limited area – the amount of garbage, all that filth, as well as, often, a wealth of introduced flowering and fruiting plants. At landfills, you have huge numbers of birds, thousands. Waders, wagtails, raptors... Certain bird species are even expanding. The cattle egret is worldwide now, I think, except for Antarctica. They're common in South Mumbai around railway tracks.

What's the deal with the pink flamingos at the Colgate Factory? At Sewri, the huge numbers of birds could actually be related to the industrialisation – the warm water and food, like algae, that arise from the pollution. The pink flamingos started to be observed in the early 1990s.

What other birds visit Sewri? Waders, gulls, terns, a lot of egrets, herons... The mangroves themselves attract birds, so wherever mangroves are surviving, you'll find a good number of birds. Most of Mumbai's mangroves are along Thane Creek. But probably as much as half of the mangroves across the Mumbai region have disappeared over the last few decades, I would say – especially in northwest Mumbai, in Manori Creek, Malad Creek, in all the small creeks around Mumbai. They're not designated protected areas.

What about the national park? We have approximately 300 species of birds there, the bulk of them woodland birds, but also many aquatic birds because of the freshwater lakes there. It has some amazing birds; we've sighted rarities like the great and malabar pied hornbills, and the malabar trogon, among others.

What are some of your favourites? My favourite would have to be the greater racket-tailed drongo. That's an absolute exhibitionist of a bird, a real flamboyant character. In the city, my favourite is the house crow.

Ugh. Really? It's a very colourful character. It's immensely adaptable, good at finding solutions to problems. The nesting material it uses is astounding, from sticks to metal wires, spectacle frames, all kinds of paraphernalia. I've got crow nests made of plastic bags, shells, dice. And we found a nest made completely – completely – of sanitary napkins.

Brilliant! Absolutely! Hugely adaptable! It's a great bird. I love it.

What are some other good birdwatching places? Thane Creek and Sewri, even the other creeks on a good day. Aarey Milk Colony, a 3000-plus-acre grassy wilderness near the park, the Powai Lake area. And little parks and gardens, especially in South Mumbai, are wintering grounds, little stopovers. Elephanta Island has a mix of waders and woodland birds, some raptors also. Overall in Mumbai, almost 400 species of birds have been recorded, just under a third of India's total count.

Wow. What is it about the city? Mumbai is wonderfully cocooned by nature on all sides. On the eastern side is forest, the Sahyadri Hills, the Western Ghats. In the central area, Mumbai lies in the fertile Konkan. Then there are the creeks, the sandy coast and also grass and scrub. Add to that the gardens and parks and all the conditions created by people.

What's your favourite place? I do a lot of good birdwatching just by the roadside. My ears and eyes are really well-attuned, I'd say, so I can pick up sounds among traffic and commotion. I'll hear a little snatch of a song and I can find the bird. But the crow remains my favourite. It will always be my favourite.

Sunjoy Monga is the author of Birds of Mumbai, The Mumbai Nature Guide *and* City Forest, Mumbai's National Park.

east side and take an autorickshaw or walk 1km to the Colgate factory. Then turn right for Sewri Bunder. Bring binoculars.

Horse Riding

The **Amateur Riders' Club** (Map pp110-11; ☎ 65005204/5; www.arcmumbai.com; Mahalaxmi Racecourse; ☎ office 9am-5.30pm Mon-Fri, 9am-1pm Sat) has horse rides for those who know how to ride for Rs1000 per 30 minutes; escorts cost Rs250 to Rs500 extra. If you don't, 10-day camps, with a half-hour lesson daily, cost Rs4500. Both require advance booking at the office.

Swimming

Despite the heat don't be tempted by the lure of Back Bay, or even the open sea; Mumbai's water is filthy. Colaba's Fariyas Hotel (p128) allows nonguests to use its tiny terrace pool (open 7am to 7pm) for Rs600.

Water Sports

H2O Water Sports Complex (Map pp110-11; ☎ 23677546/84; www.drishtigroup.com; Marine Dr, Mafatlal Beach; ⏲ 10am-10pm Oct-May) at Chowpatty Beach rents out jet skis (per 10 minutes Rs950), kayaks (per half-hour Rs150) and speed boats (per person per 'round' – about five minutes – Rs100) – all weather permitting (it often doesn't). It also operates cruises (see opposite).

Outbound Adventure (☎ 9820195115, www.out boundadventure.com) runs one-day rafting trips on the Ulhas River near Karjat, 88km southeast of Mumbai, from July to early September (Rs1500 per person). After a good rain, rapids can get up to Grade III+, though usually the rafting is much calmer, with lots of twists and zigzags. OA also organises camping and canoeing trips.

WALKING TOUR

Mumbai's distinctive mix of colonial-era and art deco architecture is one of its defining features. Look for the hard-to-find guidebook *Fort Walks* at local bookshops to learn more.

Starting from the **Gateway of India** (1; p115) walk up Chhatrapati Shavaji Marg past the members-only colonial relic **Royal Bombay Yacht Club (2)** on one side and the art deco residential-commercial complex **Dhunraj Mahal (3)** on the other towards **Regal Circle (4**; SP Mukherji Chowk). Dodge the traffic to reach the car park in the middle of the circle for the best view of the surrounding buildings, including the old **Sailors Home (5)**, which dates from

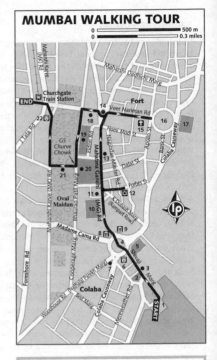

MUMBAI WALKING TOUR

WALK FACTS	
Start	Gateway of India
Finish	Churchgate train station
Distance	2.5km
Duration	3 hours minimum

1876 and is now the Maharashtra Police Headquarters, the art deco cinema **Regal (6**; p137) and the old **Majestic Hotel (7)**, now the Sahakari Bhandar cooperative store.

Continue up MG Rd, past the beautifully restored facade of the **National Gallery of Modern Art** (**8**; see p116). Opposite is the **Chhatrapati Shivaji Maharaj Vastu Sangrahalaya (9**; Prince of Wales Museum; p116); step into the front gardens to admire this grand building. Back across the road is the 'Romanesque Transitional' **Elphinstone College (10)** and the **David Sassoon Library & Reading Room (11**; p112), where members escape the afternoon heat lazing on planters' chairs on the upper balcony.

Cross back over to Forbes St to visit the **Keneseth Eliyahoo Synagogue (12**; p116) before returning to MG Rd and continuing north along the left-hand side to admire the vertical art deco stylings of the **New India Assurance Company Building (13)**. In a traffic island ahead lies the pretty **Flora Fountain (14)**, named after the Roman goddess of abundance, and erected in 1869 in honour of Sir Bartle Frere, the Bombay governor responsible for dismantling the fort.

Turn east down Veer Nariman Rd walking towards **St Thomas' Cathedral (15**; p116). Ahead lies the stately **Horniman Circle (16)**, an arcaded ring of buildings laid out in the 1860s around a circular and beautifully kept botanical garden. The circle is overlooked from the east by the neoclassical **Town Hall (17)**, which contains the regally decorated members-only Asiatic Society of Bombay Library and Mumbai's State Central Library.

Retrace your steps back to Flora Fountain and continue west past the Venetian Gothic-style **State Public Works Department (18)**. Turn south on to Bhaurao Patil Marg to see the august **High Court (19**; p116) and the equally venerable and ornately decorated **University of Mumbai (20**; p116). The facades of both buildings are best observed from within the **Oval Maidan (21)**. Turn around to compare the colonial edifices with the row of art deco beauties lining Maharshi Karve (MK) Rd, culminating in the wedding cake tower of the **Eros Cinema (22)**. End your walk at Churchgate train station.

COURSES
Yoga
Several yoga classes are held daily at the **Kaivalyadhama Ishwardas Yogic Health Centre** (Map pp110-11; ☎ 22818417; www.kdham.com; 43 Marine Dr, Chowpatty; ☒ 6.30-10am & 3.30-7pm Mon-Sat). Fees include a Rs500 (students/seniors Rs400/300) monthly membership fee and a Rs300 admission fee.

The **Yoga Institute** (Map p130; ☎ 26122185; www.theyogainstitute.org; Shri Yogendra Marg, Prabhat Colony, Santa Cruz East; per 1st/2nd month Rs400/300), near Santa Cruz station, has daily classes as well as weekend and weeklong programs.

Iyengar Yogashraya (off Map pp110-11; ☎ 24948416; www.bksiyengar.com; Elmac House, 126 Senapati Bapat Marg, Lower Parel; per class Rs276) Classes in Iyengar yoga, including some for the developmentally disabled. There is a Rs276 admission fee.

Language
Professor Shukla is based at **Bharatiya Vidya Bhavan** (Map pp110-11; ☎ 23871860; cnr KM Munshi Marg & Ramabai Rd, Girgaon) and offers private Hindi, Marathi and Sanskrit classes (Rs500 per hour). Contact this worldly octogenarian directly to arrange a syllabus and class schedule to suit your needs.

Crafts
The **Khatwara Institute** (Shri Khatwari Darbar; Map p130; ☎ 26042670, cnr Linking Rd & Khar Station Rd, Khar West) offers dozens of courses, lasting from three days to one month, for women only (sorry guys!) in Arabic mehendi, 'basic' mehendi, block printing, embroidery, sewing and cooking, among other things. Call Vanita for details.

MUMBAI FOR CHILDREN
Rina Mehta's www.mustformums.com has the Mumbai Mums' Guide, with info on crèches, healthcare and even kids' salsa classes in the city. *Time Out Mumbai* (Rs30) often lists fun things to do with kids.

Little tykes with energy to burn will love the Gorai Island amusement parks, **Esselworld** (Map p109; ☎ 28452222; www.esselworld.com; adult/child Rs480/350; ☒ 11am-7pm) and **Water Kingdom** (☎ 28452310; adult/child Rs480/350; ☒ 11am-7pm). Both are well-maintained and have lots of rides, slides and shade. Combined tickets are Rs680/550 (adult/child). Off-season weekday ticket prices are lower. It's a Rs35 ferry ride from Borivali jetty.

Several museums have kid-friendly exhibits, including **Prince of Wales Museum** (p116), with lots of stuffed animals, and **Mani Bhavan** (p119), with fascinating dioramas of Gandhi's life.

Kids usually get a kick out of the **horse-drawn gilded carriages** (p115) that ply their trade along Apollo Bunder and the **cruises** (p126) that depart from the Gateway of India.

Nature trips for kids are often conducted by BNHS (p122) and Yuhina Eco-Media (p122), while **Yoga Sutra** (Map pp110-11; ☎ 32107067; www.yogasutra.co.in; Chinoy Mansions, Bhulabhai Desai Rd, Cumballa Hill; drop-in classes Rs250-500) has kids' yoga classes, taught in English.

TOURS
Fiona Fernandez's *Ten Heritage Walks of Mumbai* (Rs395) contains excellent walking tours in the city, with fascinating historical background.

Bombay Heritage Walks (☎ 23690992; www.bombayheritagewalks.com), run by two enthusiastic architects, has the best city tours. Private guided tours are Rs1500 for up to three people, Rs500 for each additional person. Email inquiries and bookings are best.

Transsway International (☎ 26146854; traans waytours@hathway.com; per 1-/2-/3-person tour Rs2250/3100/4050) runs five-hour day or night tours of South Mumbai's sights. Prices include pick-up and drop-off.

MTDC (p114) runs one-hour open-deck **bus tours** (Rs120, weekends 7pm and 8.15pm) of illuminated heritage buildings. They depart from and can be booked near the Apollo Bunder office. **H20** (see p124) arranges 45-minute day (Rs200 per person, minimum four people) and night (Rs280, 7pm to 11pm) cruises.

Cruises (☎ 22026364; ☽ 9am-8.30pm) on Mumbai Harbour are a good way to escape the city and offer the chance to see the Gateway of India as it was intended. Ferry rides (Rs50, 30 minutes) depart from the Gateway of India.

For the luxury version, hire the **Taj Yacht** (up to 10 people per 2hr Rs48,000); contact the Taj Mahal Palace & Tower (p131) for details.

The Government of India tourist office (p114) can arrange **multilingual guides** (per half-/full day Rs600/750). Guides using a foreign language other than English will charge at least Rs200 extra.

Whether or not to visit a slum area on a tour is a delicate question. **Reality Tours & Travel** (Map p117; ☎ 9820822253; www.realitytoursandtravel.com; Unique Business Centre, 1st fl, Nawroji F Rd, Colaba; short/long tours Rs400/800) runs guided tours of Dharavi (see the boxed text, opposite) and tries to do it right. Photography is strictly forbidden and 80% of post-tax profits go to Dharavi-based NGOs.

SLEEPING

You'll need to recalibrate your budget here: Mumbai has the most expensive accommodation in India. Book ahead in Christmas and Diwali season.

Colaba is compact, has the liveliest foreigner scene and many of the budget and midrange options. Fort is more spread out and convenient to sights and the main train stations (CST and Churchgate). Most of the top-end places are dotted around the suburbs; hotels in Juhu are convenient for the trendy Bandra district.

To stay with a local family, contact the Government of India tourist office (p114) for a list of homes participating in Mumbai's **paying guest scheme** (r Rs250-2000; ☒).

Budget
COLABA
For mapped locations of the following venues see p117.

Salvation Army Red Shield House (☎ 22841824; 30 Mereweather Rd; dm with breakfast Rs195, d/tr/q with full board & without bathroom Rs600/897/1116, d with AC & full board without bathroom Rs891; ☒ ⬜) Salvy's is a Mumbai institution popular with travellers counting every rupee. The large, ascetic dorms are clean, though bed bugs make the odd cameo appearance (they seem to like the women's dorm). Rooms can be reserved in advance, but for dorm beds, come just after the 9am kick-out to ensure a spot as they can't be booked ahead.

Sea Shore Hotel (☎ 22874237; 4th fl, Kamal Mansion, Arthur Bunder Rd; s/d without bathroom Rs400/550) In a building housing several budget guest houses, the Sea Shore has a clean and friendly atmosphere that makes up for the shoe-box-size rooms and plywood walls. It's worth paying extra for a window and harbour views. On the floor below, India Guest House (☎ 22833769; singles/doubles without bathroom Rs350/450) is a less clean but passable backup, with even shoddier walls.

YWCA (☎ 22025053; www.ywcaic.info; 18 Madame Cama Rd; dm/s from Rs787/896, s/d with AC from Rs1035/1655; ☒ ⬜) The vibe here is very clean and monastic. The frosty-cold lobby has an internet and ISD booth and an overwhelming feeling of orderliness. Renovated rooms, meanwhile, including spacious three- and four-bed dorms, have geysers and immaculate bathrooms. Rooms facing front can be noisy and/or smelly, but the flip side is that they have pretty balconies. Rates include tax, breakfast, dinner and 'bed tea', and the guest house takes men and women.

Hotel Moti (☎ 22025714; hotelmotiinternational@ yahoo.co.in; 10 Best Marg; s/d/tr with AC Rs1500/2000/3000; ☒) Occupying the ground floor of a gracefully crumbling, beautiful colonial-era building, rooms are nothing special, really, but they have ghosts of charm and some nice surprises, like ornate stucco ceilings. Some are huge and all have fridges filled with soda and bottled water which is charged at cost – one of the many signs of the pragmatic and friendly management.

FORT
For mapped locations of the following venues see p118.

DHARAVI SLUM

Mumbaikers had mixed feelings about the stereotypes in 2008's runaway hit, *Slumdog Millionaire* (released in Hindi as *Slumdog Crorepati*). But slums are very much a part of – some would say the foundation of – Mumbai city life. An astonishing 60% of Mumbai's population live in shantytowns and slums, and the largest slum in Mumbai is Dharavi. Originally inhabited by fisherfolk when the area was still creeks, swamps and islands, it became attractive to migrant workers, from South Mumbai and beyond, when the swamp began to fill in as a result of natural and artificial causes. It now incorporates 1.75 sq km sandwiched between Mumbai's two major railway lines and is home to more than one million people.

While it may look a bit shambled from the outside, the maze of dusty alleys and sewer-lined streets of this city-within-a-city are actually a collection of abutting settlements. Some parts of Dharavi are mixed population, but in others, inhabitants from different parts of India, and with different trades, have set up homes and tiny factories. Potters from Saurasthra live in one area, Muslim tanners in another, embroidery workers from Uttar Pradesh work alongside metal smiths, while other workers recycle plastics as women dry pappadams in the searing sun. Some of these thriving industries export their wares, and the annual turnover of business from Dharavi is thought to top US$650 million.

Up close, life in the slums is strikingly normal. Residents pay rent, most houses have kitchens and electricity, and building materials range from flimsy corrugated-iron shacks to permanent, multistorey concrete structures. Many families have been here for generations, and some of the younger Dharavi residents even work in white-collar jobs. They often choose to stay, though, in the neighbourhood they grew up in.

Hotel New Bengal (off Map p118; ☎ 23401951-6; www.hotelnewbengal.com; Sitaram Bldg, Dr Dadabhai Naoroji Rd; s/d incl breakfast from Rs1000/1150, without bathroom Rs495/695; ✵) This well-organised Bengali-run hotel occupies a rambling, mazelike building perennially buzzing with Indian businessmen. They know a good thing when they see it: tidy rooms are an excellent deal. Look at a few, as some have lots of natural light while others flirt with pokiness.

Hotel Lawrence (☎ 22843618; 3rd fl, ITTS House, 33 Sai Baba Marg; s/d/tr without bathroom incl breakfast & tax Rs500/600/800) Modestly tucked away on a little side lane, Lawrence is a pleasant place with basic, clean rooms and affable management (ask them about their meditation practice!). The foyer has fun, original '70s styling and the location can't be beat.

Hotel Outram (☎ 22094937; Marzaban Rd; d with AC Rs1550, s/d without bathroom Rs670/830; ✵) This plain but superfriendly place is in a quiet spot between CST and the maidans. It's definitely run-down and a little dark, with unexciting shared bathrooms, but it has a tiny bit of character, some old-fashioned architectural details and peaceful, green surrounds.

Traveller's Inn (☎ 22644685; 26 Adi Marzban Rd, Ballard Estate; r from Rs780; ✵) On a quiet, tree-lined street, the tiny Traveller's Inn has well-kept rooms and professional, friendly staff. Rooms have new tiles and geysers and are small but don't feel cramped. Deluxe rooms have kooky decor, eg crown moulding, funky colours and a metal locker like from gym class! There are also singles with shared bathroom (Rs364) that are usually unavailable.

Hotel City Palace (☎ 22666666; www.hotelcitypalace .net; 121 City Tce, Walchand Hirachand Marg; s/d with AC from Rs1250/1900, with AC & without bathroom from Rs850/1350; ✵) City Palace is organised and clean and quiet, despite its location across from CST; the downside is the tininess of the rooms, which seem to increase only in height in higher price brackets. (Standard rooms have oddly low ceilings conducive to claustrophobia.) Doable if you're only in Mumbai for a night or two.

Hotel Oasis (☎ 22697887/8, fax 22697889; 276 Colaba Causeway; r Rs980, s/d with AC Rs930/1340; ✵) Rooms are incredibly small and they need some paint, but they're spick-and-span and a stone's throw from CST. The kooky pastel design scheme makes you feel like you're inside an ice cream cone. In a good way.

our pick Welcome Hotel (☎ 66314488-90; welcome _hotel@vsnl.com; 257 Colaba Causeway; s/d from Rs2530/2980, without bathroom from Rs1270/1450; ✵) You've never seen anything so clean in your life. Even rooms without bathrooms are fabulous, with segregated bathrooms that are positively spotless.

Reception and room staff are cheerful, while the common areas' grey carpeting, grey stone walls, and gleaming black-granite stairs are unintentionally high-fashion. Top-floor rooms are very bright and have awesome views of CST. Rates include breakfast and evening tea.

CST has superexcellent, always full **retiring rooms** (dm from Rs300, s/d with AC from Rs700/1400; 🕸) for those on their way in or out. Rooms have high ceilings and tall, old wooden windows and doors set with crazed glass. Check in at the office of the Deputy Station Manager (Commercial), near platform 8/9. They don't take reservations, but you may be able to book one day in advance if you're sweet.

THE SUBURBS

Hotel Kemp's Corner (Map pp110–11; 🕾 23634646; 131 August Kranti Marg; s/d from Rs1500/2000; 🕸) With the old-school price and the great spot close to the Kemp's Corner fashion bonanza, you might forgive the occasional carpet bald-spot of this old-fashioned place. It's worth forking out a bit more for the deluxe double rooms, but all rooms have tree views and a bit of old-timey character, eg white-painted furniture.

Midrange
COLABA

For mapped locations of the following venues see p117.

Bentley's Hotel (🕾 22841474; www.bentleyshotel .com; 17 Oliver Rd; s/d incl breakfast & tax from Rs1620/2010; 🕸) Bentley's definitely has the most charm of any hotel around, with old-school floor tiles and colonial wooden furniture in some rooms. Spread out over several buildings on Oliver St and nearby Henry Rd, all rooms are spotless and come with TV and optional AC (around Rs275 extra). But the welcome is a bit harsh and the service can be indifferent – definitely a weak spot. Rooms come in dozens of sizes and flavours: rooms 31 and 21 have balconies overlooking a garden (booked months in advance), while the cheaper ones on Henry Rd are a bit noisier.

Sea Palace Hotel (🕾 22854404/10; www.seapal acehotel.com; 26 PJ Ramchandani Marg; s/d with AC from Rs3500/4000; 🕸) The standard doubles here are small and the whole place is done in slightly nauseating colour schemes (eg lime yellow), but the gorgeous sea views from the pricier rooms (doubles Rs6250) redeem it. Sort of. The best part is the patio restaurant downstairs, just across from the sea.

Hotel Suba Palace (🕾 22020636; www.hotelsubapal ace.com; Battery St; r with AC incl breakfast Rs3700; 🕸 🖳) Soothing neutral tones permeate the newly renovated Suba Palace, from the tiny taupe shower tiles in the contemporary bathrooms to the creamy crown moulding and beige quilted headboards in the tastefully remodelled rooms. Comfy, quiet and central.

Regent Hotel (🕾 22871853/4; www.regentho telcolaba.com; 8 Best Marg; s/d/tr with AC incl breakfast Rs3700/3900/4200; 🕸 🖳 🛜) This stylish, Arabian-flavoured hotel has marble surfaces and soft pastels aplenty. Comfortable, freshly painted rooms all have fridge, an enclosed balcony, and a prayer mat (just in case!).

Hotel Apollo (🕾 22873312; h.apollo@gmail.com; Mahakavi Bhushan Marg; s/d with AC from Rs3700/4400; 🕸) Its recent trendy facelift hasn't kept up with its rate hikes – it feels like a less expensive place – but rooms, simple and modestly sized, are well-kept and have 'party' showers big enough for two. Some doubles have a bathtub.

Ascot Hotel (🕾 66385566; www.ascothotel.com; 38 Garden Rd; d with AC incl breakfast from Rs5500; 🕸 🖳) From the decadent marble bathrooms with bathtubs and soft lighting to the warm beiges and creams in the huge, uncluttered rooms, the Ascot is all class. Rooms have internet connection and DVD players, and front rooms get lots of natural light and tree views. The service seems a bit disorganised, though, for the price.

Fariyas Hotel (🕾 22042911; www.fariyas.com; 25 off Arthur Bunder Rd; r from Rs10,000; 🕸 🖳 🛜) Fariyas is an efficient, friendly, recently renovated (but not perfect) place. The sea-view rooms (from Rs12,000) have great views (tip: so does standard room 402), and the 1st-floor terrace cafe and pool are lovely (and open to nonguests). Fariyas also has a gym, a restaurant, a pub, a nail salon-bar and wi-fi.

FORT, CHURCHGATE & MARINE DRIVE

Residency Hotel (Map p118; 🕾 22625525-9; resi dencyhotel@vsnl.com; 26 Rustom Sidhwa Marg, Fort; s/d from Rs2000/2200; 🕸 🖳 🛜) We love how the Residency bucks the trend and doesn't double its rates every other year. It has good vibes like that. Rooms are very small but tasteful and come with fridges, flat-screen TVs and flip-flops (see what we mean?). The lobby and hallways have lots of marble and plants all around and a skylit atrium. There's free internet access.

Sea Green Hotel (Map p118; ☎ 66336525; www.sea greenhotel.com; 145 Marine Dr; s/d Rs2400/2950; ⊠) and **Sea Green South Hotel** (Map p118; ☎ 22821613; www .seagreensouth.com; 145A Marine Dr; s/d Rs2400/2950; ⊠) are identical art deco hotels with spacious but spartan AC rooms, originally built in the 1940s to house British soldiers. Ask for one of the sea-view rooms as they're the same price. Both places are great value – even with the 10% service charge.

West End Hotel (Map p118; ☎ 22039121; www.west endhotelmumbai.com; 45 New Marine Lines; s/d with AC from Rs3200/3600; ⊠ 💻 ⓢ) You'd half expect Austin Powers to be swinging in this hotel's grey velour–lined bar, Chez Nous. The hotel has a funky, unintentionally retro feel, and the old-fashioned rooms are plain but roomy, with soft beds. The buzzkill: a 20% tax is charged on rooms.

Grand Hotel (Map pp110-11; ☎ 66580500; www .grandhotelbombay.com; 17 Shri Shiv Sagar Ramgulam Marg, Ballard Estate; s/d/tr incl breakfast Rs3500/4000/5000; ⊠ 💻 ⓢ) The Grand is a good deal, with spunk – note the plaques labelling everything in the 1960s-era lobby. The place is superquiet – you can hear a pin drop in the placid, robin's egg–blue hallways – and rooms are well-kept and extremely clean. The furniture is so dated that it's coming back around to brilliant. Wi-fi and computer use are free.

Astoria Hotel (Map p118; ☎ 66541234; www.astoria mumbai.com; J Tata Rd, Churchgate; s/d with AC incl break-fast from Rs4500/5000; ⊠ 💻) This conveniently located, smart hotel has immaculate rooms that almost live up to the promise of the sleek, modern lobby. A recent tariff hike made them seriously overpriced, considering their home-liness. But some of the abodes are huge and all have wi-fi, as does the lobby, where it's free.

THE SUBURBS

There are several midrange hotels on Nehru Rd Extension in Vile Parle East near the do-mestic airport, but rooms are overpriced and only useful for early or late flights. Juhu is convenient for Juhu Beach and for the restau-rants, shops and clubs in Bandra.

For mapped locations of the following venues see p130.

Iskcon (☎ 26206860; guesthouse.mumbai@pamho .net; Hare Krishna Lane, Juhu; s/d incl tax Rs2095/2495, with AC incl tax Rs2395/2995; ⊠) Part of Juhu's lively Hare Krishna complex, this very efficiently managed guest house is spread out across two buildings – one of which is flamingo-pink.

Rooms are big and spick-and-span – those in the original building have balconies – but don't have TV or fridge. A good vegetarian buffet restaurant, Govinda's, is on site.

Hotel Suba Galaxy (☎ 26821188; www.hotelsuba galaxy.com; NS Phadke Marg, Saiwadi, Andheri East; s/d with AC incl breakfast from Rs2800/5000; ⊠) Clean lines, over-sized windows and mirrors, and lots of dark-wood laminate and bright white makes for good-looking rooms in this newish tower 4km from the international airport. The standard single is a box, but even that has all the mod cons – flat-screen TV, broadband, etc. Oh, and lots of fluffy pillows.

Hotel Columbus (☎ 26182029; hotel_columbus@rediff mail.com; 344 Nanda Patkar Rd, Vile Parle East; s/d with AC from Rs3000/3500; ⊠ 💻) One of the few decent midrange hotels in the domestic airport area, the Columbus is on a cute, tree-lined street off Nehru Rd (opposite the 'BP petrol pump'), away from the airport chaos. The gussied-up deluxe rooms (Rs4000) have stylised wood-grain accents and flat-screen TVs and aspire to high design.

Hotel New Castle (☎ 26480483; www.hotelnewcastle mumbai.com; 355 Linking Rd, Khar West; r with AC from Rs3500; ⊠ 💻) It doesn't look new or like a castle, but it's handy for the domestic airport, the train station and, more importantly, shopping! It's smack in the middle of the Linking Rd action, but set back from the street so it's quiet. Rooms are well cared for, all clean and fresh peachy-pink paint, and staff are friendly – but we're not crazy about the 10% service charge. Free wi-fi.

Hotel Metro Palace (☎ 67744555; www.uniqueho telsindia.com; Ramdas Nayak Rd, Bandra West; s/d with AC incl breakfast from Rs4000/4500; ⊠) The executive rooms here have sad little sagging bedspreads (but fridges), while the standard rooms have better bedspreads but crappier beds and paint jobs. That said, rooms, some with balconies, are comfortable and have lovingly conserved flourishes of '80s decor, like large posters of kittens. Downstairs, Pulse (a nightclub) and Temptation (a bar; aka 'the devil's alternative') can get busy.

Hotel Airport International (☎ 26182222; www .hotelairportinternational.com; Nehru Rd, Vile Parle East; s/d with AC incl breakfast from Rs5000/6500; ⊠ ⓢ) The pick of the Nehru Rd hotels, it's so close to the domestic airport you can see the runway from some rooms. Just renovated, rooms are impeccably clean, compact and tastefully done; superdeluxe rooms have bathtubs and fridges.

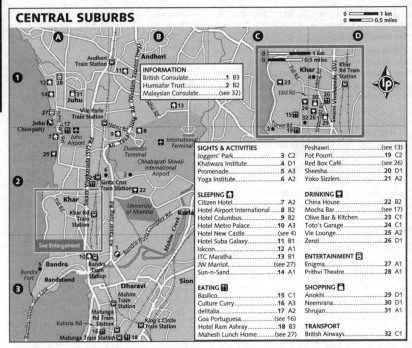

CENTRAL SUBURBS

Citizen Hotel (☎ 66932525; www.citizenhotelmum
bai.com; Juhu Tara Rd, Juhu; s/d with AC from Rs7000/7500;
❄ 🖳 🛜) The Citizen's location, right on
the beach, is what you're paying for here, but
rooms are also well-maintained, with marble
floors and marble-top furniture, flat-screen
TVs, fridges – and, of course, excellent views.
The place also has an AC restaurant and a
patio cafe, both overlooking the sea.

Sun-n-Sand (☎ 66938888; www.sunnsandhotel
.com; 39, Juhu Beach, Juhu; r with AC from Rs10,500;
❄ 🖳 🛋) The Sun-n-Sand has been offer-
ing up beachfront hospitality for decades
(cf the old-school name). The best rooms
here are the sea-facing ones (Rs12,000): lots
of silk and shades of tangerine complement
the pool, palm-tree and ocean views from
the huge window. It's off Juhu Rd, near the
old Holiday Inn.

Top End
CITY CENTRE

Gordon House Hotel (Map p117; ☎ 22871122; www.gh
hotel.com; 5 Battery St; s/d incl breakfast from US$300/325;
❄ 🖳) This self-proclaimed boutique hotel has
elegant rooms in Mediterranean, Scandinavian

or country style. Just this side of kitsch, it's
fun and has gizmos like CD players and flat-
screen TVs in all rooms. Rooms above its Polly
Esther's nightclub (see p136) are noisy but
available at a discount if you ask.

Marine Plaza (Map p118; ☎ 22851212; www.hotel
marineplaza.com; 29 Marine Dr, Nariman Point; s/d with AC
from Rs15,000/16,000; ❄ 🖳 🛋 🛜) An appealing
and showy boutique five-star hotel with art
deco flourishes and stylish rooms. The rooftop
swimming pool has a glass bottom that looks
down on the foyer five floors below! The hotel
also has wi-fi, two restaurants and the popular
Boston-style Geoffrey's Bar.

Trident (Oberoi Hotel; Map pp110-11; ☎ 66324343; www
.tridenthotels.com; Marine Dr, Nariman Point; s/d from
Rs17,250/18,500; ❄ 🖳 🛋) The Trident is, along
with the Oberoi, part of the Oberoi Hotel
complex. But the Trident wins out both on
price and on the spiffy, streamlined design
of its restaurants, bars and pool area. Plus, it
reopened like a champion less than a month
after 2008's three-day terrorist occupation.

Intercontinental (Map p118; ☎ 39879999; www.in
tercontinental.com; 135 Marine Dr, Churchgate; r incl breakfast
from Rs18,500; ❄ 🖳 🛋) You'll want to pay a

little extra for the splendid sea views at this sophisticated boutique-style hotel. Room decor is cosy but understated, with clean lines and warm tones. The stunning Dome bar and restaurant (p135) elegantly crowns the rooftop and overlooks the sea.

Taj Mahal Palace & Tower (Map p117; ☎ 66653366; www.tajhotels.com; Apollo Bunder, Colaba; tower rooms s/d from Rs18,250/19,750, palace rooms from Rs25,250/26,750; ❄ 🖥 🏊) We already loved it, but when it got back on its feet just three weeks after the November 2008 terrorist attacks (following massive construction work and blessings from leaders of seven religions), we were floored. A Mumbai landmark since 1903, this distinguished hotel, with its sweeping arches, staircases and domes, is unstoppably exquisite. Palace rooms are peaceful, heritage and plush, with separate foyer and soothing white-marble bathroom, plasma TV with internet hook-up and a separate breakfast nook (some with Gateway views). Tower rooms are gorgeous but not as special. Even if you don't stay here, have a drink or meal in one of its many excellent bars and restaurants.

THE SUBURBS

JW Marriott (Map p130; ☎ 66933000; www.marriott.com; Juhu Tara Rd, Juhu; r incl tax from Rs16,000; ❄ 🖥 🏊) Smack in the middle of Juhu Beach is this monument to luxury hotels, sporting no fewer than three pools, one of them filled with (heavily) filtered sea water. There's a bright foyer encasing a lily pond, although the rooms leave little to be desired and guests complain of overpriced extras. Its nightclub, Enigma, is big with the glitterati.

Four Seasons Hotel (off Map pp110–11; ☎ 24818000; www.fourseasons.com; Dr. E. Moses Rd, Worli; r from Rs17,650; ❄ 🖥 🏊) Great sea views and elegance at this newly opened hotel in up-and-coming Worli. The service is exceptional, the staff practically psychic, and the hotel will become a lot more convenient to town once the Bandra–Worli Sea Link is opened.

ITC Maratha (Map p130; ☎ 28303030; www.itcwelcomgroup.in; Sahar Rd, Andheri; s/d incl breakfast & tax from Rs22,000/23,500; ❄ 🖥 🏊) Easily the five-star with the most luxurious Indian character, from the Jaipur-style lattice windows around the atrium to the silk pillows on the beds and the embalmed palms in the lobby. It's right outside the international airport and has an excellent spa and two celebrated restaurants, including Peshawri (p135).

EATING

Food options in the metropolis are as diverse as the squillion inhabitants – go on a cultural history tour by sampling Parsi *dhansak* (meat with curried lentils and rice), Gujarati or Keralan thalis ('all-you-can-eat' meals) and everything from Mughlai kebabs to Goan vindaloo to Mangalorean seafood. If you find Bombay duck on a menu, remember it's actually *bombil* fish dried in the sun and deep-fried.

Don't miss Mumbai's famous *bhelpuri*, readily available at Chowpatty Beach (p119). During the Islamic holy month of Ramadan, fantastic night food markets line Mohammed Ali and Merchant Rds in Kalbadevi. Street stalls offering rice plates, samosas, *pav bhaji* (spiced vegetables and bread) and *vada pav* (deep-fried spiced-lentil-ball sandwich) for Rs5 to Rs15 do a brisk trade around the city.

For self-caterers, the **Colaba market** (Map p117; Lala Nigam St) has fresh fruit and vegies. **Saharkari Bhandar Supermarket** (Map p117; ☎ 22022248; cnr Colaba Causeway & Wodehouse Rd; ⏰ 10am-8.30pm) and, even better, **Suryodaya** (Map p118; ☎ 22040979; Veer Nariman Rd; ⏰ 7.30am-8.30pm) are well-stocked supermarkets.

Colaba

For mapped locations of the following venues see p117.

New Laxmi Vilas (19A Ram Mansion, Nawroji F Rd; light meals Rs18-55, mains Rs40-85) A budget eatery that serves great southern specialities in comfortable, modern, AC surrounds. Dosas are the speciality, one reader even wrote in 'we still dream of the meals we ate there'. The thalis (Rs43) are also high-calibre.

Bagdadi (11 Tulloch Rd; mains Rs20-70; ⏰ 7am-12.30am) Bagdadi is full of everyday guys who come for the traditional Mughlai food and nononsense service. There's lots and lots of fish, prawns and meat (including beef brain fry; Rs40) on the menu, cooked up in biryanis and daily-changing specials. The best-deal rotis in town are enormous and cost Rs7. But alas, 'food will not be served to drunken person'.

Theobroma (Colaba Causeway, Colaba; confections Rs20-100; ⏰ 8.30am-midnight) Theobrama calls its creations 'food of the gods' – and they are. Dozens of perfectly executed cakes, tarts and chocolates, as well as sandwiches and breads, go well with the coffee here. The solo hazelnut mousse cake (Rs80) or the genius pistachio-and-green-cardamom truffle (Rs25) will take you to the next plane.

Kailash Parbat (5 Sheela Mahal, First Pasta Lane; mains Rs40-78) Nothing fancy, but a Mumbai legend nonetheless thanks to its inexpensive Sindhi-influenced vegetarian snacks, mouth-watering sweets and extra-spicy masala chai. Kailash Parbat Hindu Hotel across the street is its also good, more playful, cousin.

Bade Miya (Tulloch Rd; meals Rs50-80; ☼ 7pm-3am) As Mumbai as traffic jams, this street-stall-on-steroids buzzes nightly with punters from all walks of Mumbai life lining up for spicy, fresh grilled treats. Grab a chicken tikka roll to go, or sample the *boti kebab* (lamb kebab) or *paneer masala* (unfermented-cheese and tomato curry) on the footpath.

Falafel's (Wodehouse Rd; sandwiches & salads Rs55-125; ☼ 11am-midnight) It's very chain-restaurant-like and a bit too marketing-savvy for our tastes, but there's no denying that the falafel, hummus and Greek salads are delish.

Café Churchill (103B Colaba Causeway; sandwiches Rs70-110, mains Rs170-220; ☼ 10am-midnight) This tiny, packed place does really good Western comfort food – with heavy Italian and American-diner influences – and desserts, but each time we visited, service was the pits.

Basilico (☎ 66345670; Sentinel House, Arthur Bunder Rd; mains Rs210-375; ☼ 7.30am-midnight) A très sleek, Euro-style bistro, Basilico whips up creative fresh pastas, salads and couscous that will make you melt. Veggies will flat out die – from either the wholesome green salad (mixed lettuce, corn, asparagus and sprouts with feta, lime and olive-oil dressing; Rs225) or the homemade mushroom and goat cheese cannelloni (Rs340). The coup de grâce? It's also a bakery. The Bandra branch is on St John Rd, next to HDFC, Pali Naka (Map p130, ☎ 67039999, open noon to midnight).

Indigo Delicatessen (Pheroze Bldg, Chhatrapati Shivaji Marg; mains Rs245-495; ☼ 9am-midnight) Indigo's less expensive sister is just as elegant as the original, with good jazz on, warm but sleek decor and massive wooden tables. It has breakfast any time (Rs145 to Rs265), casual meals and desserts, teas, wines (Rs360 to Rs710 per glass) and a selection of breads and imported cheeses.

Indigo (☎ 66368980; 4 Mandlik Marg; mains Rs485-985; ☼ 12-4pm & 7-11pm) Colaba's finest eating option, Indigo has inventive European cuisine, a long wine list, sleek ambience and an absolutely gorgeous roof deck lit with fairy lights. Daily specials come with wine recommendations. Favourites include the soft basil-crusted

Norwegian salmon, with asparagus, beetroot couscous and lemon and orange-caper butter (Rs985). Or lemon ricotta tortellini with fennel spinach sauce, porcini mushrooms and walnuts (Rs585). Bookings are essential.

Also recommended:

Delhi Darbar (Holland House, Colaba Causeway; mains Rs85-175; ☼ 11.30am-12.30am) Excellent Mughlai, tandoori and Middle Eastern.

Ming Palace (Colaba Causeway; mains Rs160-680; ☼ 11.30am-3.15pm & 6.45-11.30pm) Quality Chinese with gargantuan portions.

Kala Ghoda & Fort

Badshah Snacks & Drinks (Map pp110-11; opposite Crawford market; snacks Rs20-95; ☼ 7am-12.30am) Badshah been serving snacks, fruit juices and its famous *falooda* (rose-flavoured drink made with milk, cream, nuts and vermicelli) to hungry bargain-hunters for more than 100 years. It's opposite Crawford Market.

Anubhav (Map p118; 292 Shahid Bhagat Singh Marg; mains Rs40-75; ☼ 8am-9.45pm Mon-Sat) This local veg joint, aka The Veg Delite, has good South Indian food, as well as a smattering of Punjabi standbys. There are six – count 'em, six – kinds of vegetarian biryani, and a tasty lunch thali, known simply as 'lunch' (Rs45).

Ideal Corner (Map p118; Gunbow St, Fort; mains Rs40-90; ☼ 9am-4.30pm Mon-Fri) This classic Parsi cafe has the style to match its odd little spot in the crook of a funky, rounded building, with a royal-blue and mango colour scheme and wooden stairs leading to a loft space. But the most artful thing here are the fresh, homemade dishes on the daily-changing menu. Even a simple *khichdi masoor pappad* (lightly spiced rice and lentils; Thursday) is memorable.

Shivala (Map p118; Walchand Hirachand Marg; mains Rs50-110) Shivala is a working-fellas' joint with excellent North Indian food (and the requisite South Indian and Chinese offerings). The AC room upstairs is way contemporary, with lots of glass and pebbles and blue light, but also views: Shivala is just across from Bhatia Udyan, the pocket of green in front of CST.

Moshe's Cafe (Map p118; Fabindia, 1st fl, Jeroo Bldg, MG Rd, Kala Ghoda; light meals Rs60-135; ☼ 10am-7.45pm) After shopping downstairs, refuel with Moshe's excellent salads, sandwiches, baked goods, coffees and smoothies. The marinated garlic, mushroom, leek and bell-pepper open-faced sandwich with melted mozzarella on brown bread will make you collapse with pleasure on your bag of new block-printed kurtas. There's also a Moshe's in Kemp's Corner (Map pp110–11, open 11am to 8.30pm).

Mahesh Lunch Home (Map p118; ☎ 22023965; 8B Cowasji Patel St, Fort; mains Rs120-400; ⏰ 11.30am-3.30pm & 6-11.30pm) A great place to try Mangalorean seafood in Mumbai. It's renowned for its lady-fish, pomfret, lobster and crabs, and its *rawas tikka* (marinated white salmon) and tandoori pomfret are outstanding. There's also a branch on Juhu Tara Rd (Map p130, ☎ 26108848).

Trishna (Map p118; ☎ 22703213-5; Sai Baba Marg, Kala Ghoda; mains Rs160-490; ⏰ 12-3.30pm & 6.30pm-midnight) This might just be the best seafood in town. One reader wrote in to describe how a dish here sent her into deliciousness shock ('This was the best fish I have EVER had!'). It specialises in Mangalorean preparations, and the crab with butter, pepper and garlic and various shrimp dishes – all brought to your table for inspection – are outstanding.

Rajdhani (Map pp110-11; 361 Sheikh Memon St, Kalbadevi; thali Rs225; ⏰ 12-4pm & 7-10.30pm) Opposite Mangaldaas Market, Rajdhani is famous for its Gujarati and Rajasthani thalis. It's a great spot to refuel while shopping in the markets. On Sundays, dinner isn't served and lunch prices are slightly higher.

Khyber (Map p118; ⏰ 40396666; 145 MG Rd, Fort; mains Rs275-475; ⏰ 12.30-4pm & 7.30pm-midnight) Khyber serves up Punjabi and other North Indian dishes in moody, burnt-orange, Afghan-inspired interiors to a who's who of Mumbai's elite. The food is some of the city's best, with the meat-centric menu wandering from kebabs, to biryanis, to it's pièce de résistance, *raan* (a whole leg of slow-cooked lamb).

Also recommended:

Mocambo Café & Bar (Map p118; 23A Sir P Mehta Rd, Fort; mains Rs180-320; ⏰ 11.30am-11.30pm) A modern, convivial and convenient spot for sandwiches, pasta, steaks or a cold beer.

Yoko Sizzlers (sizzlers Rs270-550; ⏰ 12-11.30pm) Fort (Map p118; Gunbow St, Fort); Santa Cruz West (Map p130; ☎ 26492313; SV Rd)

Churchgate

For mapped locations of the following venues, see p118.

Tea Centre (78 Veer Nariman Rd; mains Rs115-185, veg/nonveg set lunch Rs175/195) Serving some of India's premium teas, as well as excellent light meals and snacks, this is a serene, formal, colonial-meets-contemporary place with severe AC.

Pizzeria (Soona Mahal, 143 Marine Dr; pizzas & pastas Rs145-350; ⏰ noon-midnight) Serves up pizzas and pasta, along with Indian wines, but the ocean views are the real draw.

Samrat (☎ 42135401; Prem Ct, J Tata Rd; lunch/dinner thalis Rs190/220; ⏰ 12-4pm & 7-10.45pm) A busy traditional Indian pure-veg restaurant; part of a restaurant family at the same location. Relish (mains Rs150 to Rs250, open noon to midnight) is the funkier cousin, with dishes ranging from Lebanese platters to Mexican, while 210°C is an outdoor cafe and bakery (coffees and pastries Rs20 to Rs80, open noon to 11pm).

Gaylord (☎ 22821259; Veer Nariman Rd; meals Rs190-650; ⏰ 12.30-3.30pm & 7.30-11.30pm) Great North Indian dishes served with over-the-top, Raj-era style dining replete with tuxedo-wearing waiters hanging on your every gesture. It also serves domestic and imported wines (Rs175 to Rs600 per glass).

Chowpatty & Around

For mapped locations of the following venues see pp110–11.

The evening stalls at Bhel Plaza on Chowpatty Beach are the most atmospheric spots to snack on *bhelpuri* (Rs20) or *panipuri* (small crisp puffs of dough filled with spicy tamarind water and sprouted gram; Rs15). Mobile chai-wallahs do the rounds.

New Kulfi Centre (cnr Chowpatty Seaface & Sardar V Patel Rd; kulfi per 100gm Rs18-38; ⏰ 9am-1.30am) Serves the best *kulfi* (firm-textured ice cream flavoured, often with pistachio) you'll have anywhere, which means it's the best-tasting thing in the entire world. When you order, the *kulfi* is placed on a betel-nut leaf and then weighed on an ancient scale – which makes it even better.

Anantashram (Map pp110-11; 46 Kotachiwadi; mains Rs50, thalis Rs65; ⏰ 11am-1.30pm & 7-9pm Mon-Sat) You probably won't find the place (in the gorgeous, old-timey lanes of Kotachiwadi), and if you do, you probably won't be able to read the sign outside or the menu inside or talk to the man taking the orders – unless you speak Marathi. But if you get that far, kudos: you're in for excellent old-fashioned coastal Maharashtran dishes normally only found in the kitchens of Marathi grandmas. The fish fry, prawn curry and seasonal catches can't be beat.

Swati Snacks (Map pp110-11; 248 Karai Estate, Tardeo Rd, Tardeo; mains Rs50-100; ⏰ 11am-11pm) This Mumbai institution has been revamped as a modern, high-end cafeteria (all stainless

DABBA-WALLAHS

A small miracle of logistics, Mumbai's 5000 *dabba* (food container)-wallahs (also called tiffin-wallahs) work tirelessly to deliver hot lunches to office workers throughout the city.

Lunch boxes are picked up each day from restaurants, homes, mothers and wives and carried on heads, bicycles and trains. Taken to a centralised sorting station, a sophisticated system of numbers and colours (many wallahs are illiterate) is then used to determine where every lunch must end up. More than 200,000 meals are delivered in Mumbai in this way – always on time, come (monsoon) rain or (searing) shine.

This same intricate supply-chain system has been used for centuries, and dabba-wallahs are known to take immense pride in their work. Considering that on average only about one mistake is made every six million deliveries, they've certainly earned it.

steel and smooth wood). Try out the delicious *bhelpuri* (no match for Chowpatty's though – be warned!), *panki chatni* (savoury pancake steamed in a banana leaf) and homemade ice cream in delectable flavour combinations such as coffee-orange (Rs50). The diner's across from Bhatia Hospital.

In fact, there's a lot of serious ice-cream action going on here:

Cream Centre (Chowpatty Seaface; mains Rs100-195; ☽ noon-midnight) An excellent ice-cream parlour in a bright, slick interior. Oh, and real food, too: a pure-veg hodgepodge of Indian, Mexican and Middle Eastern.

Gelato Italiano (Chowpatty Seaface; scoops Rs30-70; ☽ 11am-12.30am) Flavours like custard-apple sorbetto or limoncello, yum.

The Suburbs

North Mumbai's trendy dining joints centre on Bandra West and Juhu, while *bhelpuri*, *panipuri*, et al are served at Juhu Chowpatty. For mapped locations of the following venues see p130.

ourpick Hotel Ram Ashray (Bhandarkar Rd, Matunga East; light meals Rs12-38; ☽ 5.30am-9.30pm) We wouldn't send you to Matunga – on the Central line, no less – if this weren't something special. Tucked away in a Tamil enclave near King's Circle (a stone's throw from the station's east exit), Ram Ashray is popular with southern families for its spectacular dosas, *idli* and *upma* (semolina cooked with onions, spices and coconut). You won't taste a better coconut chutney anywhere (sorry, Chennai).

Culture Curry (Kataria Rd, Matunga West; mains Rs129-459; ☽ 12-3.30pm & 7pm-12.30am) As the Culture Curry folks rightly point out, there's a lot more to southern food than *idli* and dosas. Exquisite dishes from all over the south, from Andhra to Coorg to Kerala, are the specialty

here. Veggies are particularly well-served: the Kooru Curry (kidney and green beans in coconut gravy; Rs179) is extraordinary. The same owners run Diva Maharashtracha, down the street, and Goa Portuguesa, next door, specialising in fiery Goan dishes. Guitar-strumming musicians and singers wander between the two connected spaces.

Pot Pourri (Carlton Ct, cnr of Turner & Pali Rds, Bandra West; mains Rs150-285; ☽ noon-midnight Mon-Sat, 9am-midnight Sun) In a good spot for watching Bandra streetlife, Pot Pourri serves up sandwiches and Western- and Eastern-style cuisine. It excels with the Asian stuff: the Thai papaya salad (Rs115) and veg or meat *khau suey* (Burmese noodles with a coconut broth; Rs265) are superb.

Sheesha (☎ 66770555; 7th fl, Shoppers Stop, Linking Rd, Bandra West; mains Rs170-250; ☽ 11.30am-1.30am) With maybe the most beautiful ambiance in town, Sheesha's alfresco rooftop lair has glass lanterns hanging from wooden beams, comfy couches and coloured-glass lamps high above the city and shopping madness below. You almost forget about the food – good Indian fare (Goan fish curry; Rs245) nestling alongside 386 varieties of kebab (Rs130 to Rs220). Reserve on weekends.

Red Box Cafe (155 Waterfield Rd, Bandra West; mains Rs190-375; ☽ noon-10am) Where Bandra's beautiful people go when they want something 'simple'. Red Box does good sandwiches, salads, pizza, fondue and espresso. There's Wham! playing in the background, picture windows and sidewalk tables, and a red-and-black goth-meets-McDonald's design scheme. It works, though, on some weird level.

dellItalia (☎ 26284040; Juhu Tara Rd, opposite Juhu Beach; mains Rs280-410; ☽ 11.30am-3pm & 7.30pm-12.30am) The Italian villa decor here – the semi-alfresco terrace with hanging plants, the faux terracotta walls, the wooden pantry on the 1st floor – is a little theme-y but lovely even so, especially at night. Some of the Italian food here (ahem, pizza) is so-so, but most is sublime, for example, the artichoke and bocconcini salad with sun-dried tomato. Bottles of Italian wine start at Rs1500.

Peshawri (☎ 28303030; ITC Maratha, Sahar Rd; mains Rs500-1250; ☺ 12.30-2.45pm & 7-11.45pm) Make this Indian North-West Frontier restaurant, just outside the international airport, your first or last stop in Mumbai. You won't regret forking out for the leg of spring lamb and amazing dhal Bukhara (a thick black dhal cooked for a day!). The ITC is also home to Dakshin (open 7.30pm to 11.45pm) – better for vegetarians – serving some of Mumbai's finest southern food.

DRINKING

Mumbai's lax attitude to alcohol means that there are loads of places to drink – from hole-in-the-wall beer bars to chichi lounges to brash, multilevel superclubs. You'll pay around Rs80 to Rs130 for a bottle of Kingfisher in a bar or restaurant, a lot more in a club or fashionable watering-hole.

If it's the caffeine buzz you're after, espresso is ubiquitous.

Cafes

Kamat Sweets & Snacks (Map p117; 24 Colaba Causeway; teas & coffees Rs7-38) It's just tea, sweets and snacks and it's small and cramped, but we just can't resist the retro vibe – or the cold coffee with ice cream (Rs38).

Mocha Bar (coffees Rs30-175, light meals Rs95-175; ☺ 10am-1:30am) Churchgate (Map p118; 82 Veer Nariman Rd) Juhu (Map p130; 67 Juhu Tara Rd) This atmospheric, Arabian-styled cafe is often filled to the brim with bohemians and students deep in esoteric conversation, or just gossip. Cosy, low-cushioned seating, hookah pipes, exotic coffee varieties and world music add up to longer stays than you expected.

Samovar Café (Map p118; Jehangir Art Gallery, 161B MG Rd, Kala Ghoda; ☺ 11am-7.30pm Mon-Sat) This intimate place inside the art gallery overlooks the gardens of the Prince of Wales Museum and is a great spot to chill out over a beer, mango lassi or light meal.

Cha Bar (Map p118; ☎ 66364477; Oxford Bookstore, Apeejay House, 3 Dinsha Wachha Marg, Churchgate; ☺ 10am-9.30pm) An inspiring range of teas and tasty snacks amid lots of books.

Meanwhile, Barista and Café Coffee Day are still trying to out-Starbucks each other:

Barista (☺ 9am-1am; coffees Rs38-85) Colaba (Map p117; Colaba Causeway); Colaba (Map p117; Arthur Bunder Rd); CST (Map p118; Marzaban Rd)

Café Coffee Day (☺ 8am-12am; coffees Rs34-90) Chowpatty (Map pp110-11; Chowpatty Seaface); CST (Map p118; Marzaban Rd)

Bars
SOUTH MUMBAI

For mapped locations of the following venues see Map p117.

Leopold's Café (cnr Colaba Causeway & Nawroji F Rd; ☺ 7.30am-12am) Love it or hate it, most tourists end up at this Mumbai travellers' institution at one time or another. Around since 1871, Leopold's has wobbly ceiling fans, open-plan seating and a rambunctious atmosphere conducive to swapping tales with random strangers. Although there's a huge menu, the lazy evening beers are the real draw.

Café Universal (Map p118; 299 Colaba Causeway; ☺ 10am-11pm Mon-Sat, 7-11pm Sun) A little bit of France near CST. The Universal has an art nouveau look to it, with butterscotch-colour walls, wood-beam ceiling and lots of windows, and is a comfy, pretty place for happy hour.

Busaba (☎ 22043779; 4 Mandlik Marg; ☺ noon-3.30pm & 6pm-1am) Red walls and contemporary art of Buddhas give this loungey restaurant-bar a nouveau Tao. It's next to Indigo so gets the same trendy crowd, but serves cheaper, more potent cocktails. The upstairs restaurant serves pan-Asian (mains Rs300 to Rs750); its back room feels like a posh treehouse. Reserve ahead.

Café Mondegar (☎ 22020591; Metro House, 5A Colaba Causeway; ☺ 8am-12.30am) Like Leopold's, Café Mondegar is usually filled entirely with foreigners, but some readers find it less overwhelmingly foreign somehow. It also has more character. 'Purple Haze' seems to be always playing on the CD jukebox.

Henry Tham's (☎ 22023186; Apollo Bunder; ☺ 12.30-3pm & 7.30pm-1.30am) This superswanky bar-cum-restaurant features towering ceilings, gratuitous use of space and strategically placed minimalist decor. It's a darling of the Mumbai jet set and therefore *the* place to see and be seen. The real star here, though, is the Chinese food.

Dome (Map p118; ☎ 39879999, ext 8872; Hotel Intercontinental, 135 Marine Dr, Churchgate; ☺ 6pm-1.30am) This white-on-white rooftop lounge has awesome views of Mumbai's curving seafront. Cocktails beckon the hip young things of Mumbai nightly – get out your Bollywood star-spotting logbook.

Gokul Bar (Tulloch Rd; ⊙ 11am-midnight) This classic, working man's drinking den can get pretty lively. There's an AC section upstairs where the real boozers hang out.

THE SUBURBS

Ghetto (Map pp110-11; ☎ 23538418; 30B Bhulabhai Desai Marg, Mahalaxmi; ⊙ 7pm-1.30am) This graffiti-covered rocker's hang-out blares rock nightly to a dedicated set of regulars.

Shiro (off Map pp110-11; ☎ 66155980; Bombay Dyeing Mills Compound, Worli; ⊙ 7pm-1.30am) No lounge anywhere has ambiance as soothing as Shiro's. Water pours from the hands of towering Balinese stone goddesses into lotus ponds, which reflect shimmering light on the walls. Lighting is soft and dramatic, with lots of candles (and good Japanese food).

Toto's Garage (Map p130; ☎ 26005494; 30 Lourdes Heaven, Pali Naka, Bandra West; ⊙ 6pm-1am) Forget the beautiful people. Toto's is a local joint where you can go in your dirty clothes, drink beer and listen to '80s music with the locals. Get there early or your won't get a seat.

Vie Lounge (Map p130; ☎ 26603003; Juhu Tara Rd, Juhu; ⊙ 4.30pm-1.30am) Right on Juhu Beach is this glamorous party spot (opposite Little Italy restaurant). The drinks menu is 18 pages long and includes aged imported whiskies. It's also a nice place for an early-evening coffee and snack. Call before coming to check there isn't a private Bollywood bash on.

Zenzi (Map p130; ☎ 66430670-2; 183 Waterfield Rd, Bandra West; ⊙ 7pm-1am) This stylin' hang-out pad is a favourite among the well-heeled. Comfy lounges are sheltered by fairy lights and a tree growing out of one wall, and the burnt orange decor is bathed in soft light. It's at its best when the canopy is open to the stars.

Olive Bar & Kitchen (Map p130; ☎ 26058228; Pali Hill Tourist Hotel, 14 Union Park, Khar West; ⊙ 7.30pm-1.30am) Hip, gorgeous and snooty, this Mediterranean-style restaurant and bar has light and delicious food, soothing DJ sounds and pure Ibiza decor. Thursday and weekends are packed. The opening of a new branch at Mahalaxmi Racecourse (open for lunch and dinner, till 1.30am), next to Turf Club, made South Mumbai's rich and famous very happy.

Saltwater Grill (Map pp110-11; ☎ 23677546/84; Chowpatty Seaface; ⊙ 6pm-1am) As close as you can

get to Mumbai's ocean without swimming in it, this beach bar sits cocooned by its own palm-frond jungle. Right next to H20, it's a prime contender for the title of 'ultimate sundowner cocktail venue'. It's sometimes closed for no reason so call ahead.

China House (Map p130; ☎ 66761149; Grand Hyatt, Santacruz-Chembur Link Rd, Santa Cruz East, ⊙ 7.30-11.45pm) This latest darling of the stars is a Chinese restaurant with seating in an incredibly tranquil garden (replete with lanterns, ponds and wooden bridges) and an uberhip lounge downstairs. Come early, look hot and don't freak out if you see Abhishek and Aishwarya.

ENTERTAINMENT

The daily English-language tabloid *Mid-Day* incorporates the *List*, a guide to Mumbai entertainment. Newspapers and *Time Out Mumbai* (p112) list events and film screenings, while www.gigpad.com has live-music listings.

Nightclubs

The big nights in clubs are Wednesday, Friday and Saturday, when there's usually a cover charge. Dress codes apply so don't rock up in shorts and sandals.

Enigma (Map p130; ☎ 66933288; JW Marriott, Juhu Tara Rd, Juhu; ⊙ 9.30pm-3am Wed-Sun) For Bollywood star-spotting, Enigma is the place to see and be seen. It doesn't get going till after midnight, but then it *really* gets going. The couples cover is Rs1000.

Ra (off Map pp110-11; ☎ 66614343; Phoenix Mills, Senapati Bapat Marg, Lower Parel; ⊙ 9pm-1.30am Wed-Sat) Where the city's beautiful people come to shake their money-makers. Ra's glass roof opens wide to the stars, and your wallet will open even wider to pay for its top-notch cocktails. Cover for couples is Rs1000, but you may be able to call ahead and get on the guest list.

Polly Esther's (Map p117; ☎ 22871122; Gordon House Hotel, Battery St, Colaba; cover per couple Rs800-1500; ⊙ 9pm-2.45am Tue-Sun) Wallowing in a cheesy time-warp of retro pop, rock and disco, this mirror-plated, groovy nightclub still manages to pull a crowd. It comes complete with a *Saturday Night Fever* illuminated dance floor and waiters in Afro wigs. Wednesday is free for the gals.

Voodoo Pub (Map p117; ☎ 22841959; Kamal Mansion, Arthur Bunder Rd, Colaba; cover Rs300; ⊙ 8.30pm-1.30am) Hosting Mumbai's only regular gay night (Saturday; cover Rs300), this dark and sweaty bar has little going for it on other nights of the week.

Cinema

It would be a crime not to see a movie in India's film capital. Unfortunately, Hindi films aren't shown with English subtitles. The following all show English-language movies, along with some Bollywood.

Eros (Map p118; ☎ 22822335; MK Rd, Churchgate; tickets Rs60-100)

Metro Big (Map p118; ☎ 39844060; MG Rd, New Marine Lines, Fort; tickets Rs250-750) This grand dame of Bombay talkies was just renovated into a multiplex.

Regal (Map p117; ☎ 22021017; Colaba Causeway, Colaba; tickets Rs100-150) Check out the art deco architecture.

Sterling (Map p118; ☎ 66220016; Marzaban Rd, Fort; tickets Rs120-150)

The lesbian and gay organisation **Bombay Dost** (http://bombay-dost.pbwiki.com) organises 'Sunday High', a twice-monthly screening of queer-interest films, usually in the suburbs.

Music, Dance & Theatre

Bluefrog (off Map pp110-11; ☎ 40332300; www.bluefrog.co.in; D/2 Mathuradas Mills Compound, NM Joshi Marg, Lower Parel; admission after 9pm Sun & Tue-Thu Rs300, Fri & Sat Rs500; ☉ 7pm-1am Tue-Sun) The most exciting thing to happen to Mumbai's music scene

---

ART & THE CITY

India's contemporary art scene (see p66) has expanded in recent years along with the rising prices for art at auction. The huge sums being pumped into the art world sustained galleries old and new, allowed artists to devote more time to their work and encouraged emerging artists to pursue their passion instead of their engineering degree.

Now, even though the economy – along with those record-setting auction prices – is slowing, the art is still going strong. In fact, it will probably get better.

'This might very well end up being a good thing for the Indian art scene in the long run,' said Zehra Jumabhoy, Assistant Editor of *ART India*, the country's leading contemporary-art magazine. 'Artists might not make as much for their work, but they'll be able to focus on creating now, rather than producing works at top speed to sell to buyers eager to park their money in a "good investment".'

Mumbai, along with Delhi, is at the centre of India's art world, and a slew of recently opened galleries in Colaba, along with the old guard in Kala Ghoda, are showing incredible work in some gorgeous spaces.

To learn more, check out **Art India** (www.artindiamag.com), available at most English-language bookshops, which has news, background and criticism on work being created across the country, while **Saffronart** (www.saffronart.com) is great for scoping out artists. *Time Out Mumbai* is a good gallery-hopping guide to current shows – or just drop in at some of our favourites, listed below, when you're in the neighbourhood. They're generally open 11am to 7pm Monday to Saturday.

Bodhi Art (Map p118; ☎ 66100124; www.bodhiart.in; ITTS House, 28 K Dubash Marg, Kala Ghoda; ☉ 11am-7pm Tue-Sat, 2-7pm Mon)

Bombay Art Gallery (Map p117; ☎ 66156796; www.bombayartgallery.com; 2/19 Kamal Mansion, 1st fl, Arthur Bunder Rd, Colaba)

Chatterjee & Lal (Map p117; ☎ 22023787; www.chatterjeeandlal.com; 01/18 Kamal Mansion, 1st fl, Arthur Bunder Rd, Colaba)

Chemould Prescott Road (Map p118; ☎ 22000211/2; www.gallerychemould.com; Queens Mansion, 3rd fl, G Talwatkar Marg, Fort)

Farah Siddiqui Contemporary Art (FSCA; Map p117; ☎ 22850423; www.fsca.in; 6/18 Grants Bldg, 2nd fl, Arthur Bunder Rd, Colaba)

Galerie Mirchandani + Steinruecke (Map p117; ☎ 22023030/3434; www.galeriems.com; Sunny House, 1st fl, 16/18 Mereweather Rd, Colaba)

Gallery Maskara (Map pp110-11; ☎ 22023057; www.gallerymaskara.com; Warehouse on 3rd Pasta, 6/7 3rd Pasta Lane, Colaba; ☉ 11am-7pm Tue-Sun)

The Guild (Map p117; ☎ 22880116/95; www.guildindia.com; 02/32 Kamal Mansion, 1st fl, Arthur Bunder Rd, Colaba)

Project 88 (Map pp110–11; ☎ 22810066; www.project88.in; BMP Bldg, NA Sawant Marg, Colaba)

Pundole Art Gallery (Map p118; ☎ 22841837; www.pundoleartgallery.in; 369 DN Rd, Fort)

Sakshi Gallery (Map p117; ☎ 66103424; www.sakshigallery.com; Tanna House, 11A Nathalal Parekh Marg, Colaba)

in a long time, Bluefrog is a concert space, production studio, restaurant and one of Mumbai's most happening spaces. It hosts exceptional local and international acts, and has cool booth seating.

Not Just Jazz By the Bay (Map p118; ☎ 22851876; 143 Marine Dr; admission weekdays/weekends Rs150/200; ☺ noon-3.30am) This is the best, and frankly the only, jazz club in South Mumbai. True to its name, there are also live pop, blues and rock performers most nights, but Sunday, Monday and Tuesday are reserved for karaoke.

National Centre for the Performing Arts (NCPA; Map pp110-11; ☎ 66223737; www.ncpamumbai.com; cnr Marine Dr & Sri V Saha Rd, Nariman Point; tickets Rs200-500) Spanning eight acres, this cultural centre is the hub of Mumbai's music, theatre and dance scene. In any given week, it might host Marathi theatre, poetry readings and art exhibitions, Bihari dance troupes, ensembles from Europe or Indian classical music. The Experimental Theatre occasionally has English-language plays. Many performances are free. The box office (☎ 22824567; open 9am to 7pm) is at the end of NCPA Marg.

Prithvi Theatre (Map p130; ☎ 26149546; www.prithvitheatre.org; Juhu Church Rd, Juhu) At Juhu Beach, this is a good place to see both Hindi and English-language theatre. It hosts an excellent annual international theatre festival, too.

The **Nehru Centre** (see p122) occasionally stages dance, music and English-language theatre performances.

Sport
CRICKET
To prepare for the Cricket World Cup final in February/March 2011, **Wankhede Stadium** (Mumbai Cricket Association; Map p118; ☎ 22795500; www.mumbaicricket.com; D Rd, Churchgate) is closed until the end of 2010 for a massive renovation. When open, test matches and One Day Internationals are played a few times a year in season (October to April). Contact the cricket association for ticket information; for a test match you'll likely have to pay for the full five days.

FOOTBALL
The **Cooperage Football Ground** (Map p117; ☎ 22024020; MK Rd, Colaba; tickets Rs20-25) is home to the Mumbai Football Association and hosts national-league and local soccer matches between October and February. Tickets are available at the gate.

SHOPPING
Mumbai is India's great marketplace, with some of the best shopping in the country. Colaba Causeway is lined with hawkers' stalls and shops selling garments, perfumes and knick-knacks. Electronic gear, pirated CDs and DVDs, leather goods and mass-produced gizmos are for sale at stalls on Dr Dadabhai Naoroji Rd between CST and Flora Fountain, and along MG Rd from Flora Fountain to Kala Ghoda.

Antiques & Curios
Small antique and curio shops line Merewether Rd behind the Taj Mahal Palace & Tower (see Map p117). They aren't cheap, but the quality is a step up from government emporiums.

If you prefer Raj-era bric-a-brac, head to Chor Bazaar (Map pp110–11); the main area of activity is Mutton St, where you'll find a row of shops specialising in antiques (many ingenious reproductions, so beware) and miscellaneous junk.

Mini Market (Map pp110-11; ☎ 23472427; 33/31 Mutton St; ☺ 11am-8pm Sat-Thu) Sells original vintage Bollywood posters and other movie ephemera as well as odd and interesting trinkets.

Phillips (Map p117; ☎ 22020564; www.phillipsantiques.com; Wodehouse Rd, Colaba; ☺ 10am-7pm Mon-Sat) The 150-year-old Phillips has nizam-era royal silver, wooden ceremonial masks, Victorian glass and various other gorgeous things that you never knew you wanted. It also has high-quality reproductions of old photos, maps and paintings, and a new warehouse-shop of big antiques.

Clothes
Snap up a bargain backpacking wardrobe at Fashion St, the strip of stalls lining MG Rd between Cross and Azad maidans (Map p118), or in Bandra's Linking Rd, near Waterford Rd (Map p130); hone your bargaining skills. Kemp's Corner has many good shops for designer threads.

Fabindia (Map p118; ☎ 22626539; Jeroo Bldg, 137 MG Rd, Kala Ghoda; ☺ 10am-7.45pm) Founded as a means to get traditional fabric artisans' wares to market, Fabindia has all the vibrant colours of the country in its cotton and silk fashions, materials and homewares in a modern-meets-traditional Indian shop. The Santa Cruz outpost (Map p130) is also good.

Khadi & Village Industries Emporium (Khadi Bhavan; Map p118; ☎ 22073280/8; 286 Dr Dadabhai Naoroji

Rd, Fort; 10.30am-6.30pm Mon-Sat) All dusty and old school, Khadi Bhavan is 1940s time-warp with ready-made traditional Indian clothing, material, shoes and handicrafts that are so old they're new again.

More good shopping:

Anokhi (10am-7.30pm Mon-Sat) Chowpatty (Map pp110-11; 23685761; AR Rangnekar Marg, off Hughes Rd) Bandra West (Map p130; 26408261; Waterfield Rd) Gets the East-West balance just right, with men's and women's clothes and bedding in block-printed silk and cotton.

Biba (Map pp110-11; 23894184; 1 Hughes Rd, Kemp's Corner; 10.30am-9pm Mon-Sat) Gorgeous salwar kurtas with just the right amount of bling.

Cotton Cottage (Map p118; 22674026; Agra Bldg, MG Rd, Kala Ghoda; 10am-8.30pm) Stock up on simple cotton kurtas and various pants – salwars, *churidars*, *patiala* – for the road.

Cottonworld Corp (Map p117; 22850060; Mandlik Marg; 10.30am-8pm Mon-Sat, noon-8pm Sun) Small chain selling stylish Indian-Western-hybrid goods. Entrance is behind State Bank of India.

Courtyard (Map p117; SP Centre, 41/44 Minoo Desai Marg; 11am-7.30pm) A collection of couture boutiques. Good if you're interested in India's fashion design scene.

Kala Niketan (Map p118; 22005001; 95 MK Rd; 10am-8pm Mon-Sat) Sari madness on Queens Rd.

Mélange (Map pp110-11; 23534492; 33 Altamount Rd, Kemp's Corner; 10am-7pm Mon-Sat) High-fashion garments from 70 Indian designers in a chic exposed-brick space. Payal Singhal, next door, is also good.

Telon (Map pp110-11; 23648174; 149 Warden Rd, Kemp's Corner; 10.30am-8.30pm Mon-Sat) Fine gents tailor. Suits to order start at Rs13,000.

Neemrana (Map p130; 26469177/8; Link Sq, 2nd fl, 33rd Rd, off Linking Rd, Bandra West) Fabrics and harem pants, among other things, with exquisite Lucknow embroidery.

For the massive, modern, sterile AC shopping centre experience, get lost in **Crossroads** (Map pp110-11; 28 Pandit MM Malviya Rd, Breach Candy; 10am-8pm), Mumbai's biggest (to date).

Handicrafts & Gifts

Various state-government emporiums sell handicrafts in the World Trade Centre Arcade (Map pp110–11) near Cuffe Parade.

Bombay Store (Map p118; 40669999; Western India House, Sir PM Rd, Fort; 10.30am-7.30pm Mon-Sat, to 6.30pm Sun) A classy selection of rugs, clothing, teas, stationary, aromatherapy and brass sculptures.

Bombay Paperie (Map p118; 66358171; 59 Bombay Samachar Marg, Fort; 10.30am-6pm Mon-Sat) Sells handmade, cotton-based paper crafted into charming cards, sculptures and lampshades.

Shrujan Juhu (Map p130; 26183104; Hatkesh Society, 6th North South Rd, JVPD Scheme; 9.30am-7pm Mon-Sat) Breach Candy (Map pp110-11; 23521693; Sagar Villa, Warden Rd, opposite Navroze Apts; 10am-7.30pm Mon-Sat) Selling the intricate embroidery work of women in 114 villages in Kutch, Gujarat, the nonprofit Shrujan aims to help women earn a livelihood while preserving the spectacular embroidery traditions of the area. The sophisticated clothing, wall hangings and purses make great gifts.

Other stores worth popping into:

Central Cottage Industries Emporium (Map p117; 22027537; Chattrapati Shivaji Marg, Colaba; 10am-7pm) Easy-breezy souvenir shopping.

Chimanlals (Map p118; 22077717; Dr Dadabhai Naoroji Rd, Fort; 9.30am-6pm Mon-Sat) Writing materials made from traditional Indian paper. Enter from Wallace St.

Inshaallah Mashaallah (Map p117; 22049495; Best Marg, Colaba; 10.30am-8pm) Local oils and perfumes in antediluvian bottles; the rose is popular (Rs250 for 12ml).

Uttar Pradesh Handicrafts Emporium (Map p118; 22662702; Sir P Mehta Rd, Fort; 10.30am-6.30pm Mon-Sat)

Kashmir Government Arts Emporium (Map p118; 22663822; Sir P Mehta Rd, Fort; 10am-6.30pm Mon-Sat)

Markets

You can buy just about anything in the dense bazaars north of CST (see Map pp110–11). The main areas are Crawford Market (fruit and veg), Mangaldas Market (silk and cloth), Zaveri Bazaar (jewellery), Bhuleshwar Market (fruit and veg) and Chor Bazaar (antiques and

---

THIEVES BAZAAR

Nobody is sure exactly how Mumbai's Chor Bazaar (literally 'thieves market') earned its moniker. One popular explanation has it that Queen Victoria, upon arrival to Mumbai in her steam ship, discovered that her violin/purse/jewellery went missing while being unloaded off the ship. Having scoured the city, the missing item was supposedly found hanging in Chor Bazaar's Mutton St, and hence the name.

furniture), where Dhabu St is lined with fine leather goods and Mutton St specialises in antiques, reproductions and fine junk.

Colourful Crawford Market (officially called Mahatma Phule Market) is the last outpost of British Bombay before the tumult of the central bazaars begins. Bas-reliefs by Rudyard Kipling's father, Lockwood Kipling, adorn the Norman-Gothic exterior. The meat market is strictly for the brave.

Music

LM Furtado & Co (Map pp110-11; ☎ 22013163; 540-544 Kalbadevi Rd, Kalbadevi; ☼ 10am-8pm Mon-Sat) The best place in Mumbai for musical instruments – sitars, tablas, accordions and local and imported guitars. It also has a branch around the corner on Lokmanya Tilak Rd.

For nonpirated CDs and DVDs, visit **Planet M** (Map p118; ☎ 22071148; Dr Dadabhai Naoroji Rd, Fort; ☼ 10.30am-10.30pm) or, our fave, **Rhythm House** (Map p118; ☎ 22842835; 40 K Dubash Marg, Fort; ☼ 10am-8.30pm Mon-Sat, 11am-8.30pm Sun), which also sells tickets to concerts, plays and festivals.

GETTING THERE & AWAY
Air
AIRPORTS

Mumbai is the main international gateway to South India and has the busiest network of domestic flights. The **Chhatrapati Shivaji International Airport** (☎ domestic 26264000, international 26813000; www.csia.in), about 30km from downtown, comprises two domestic and two international terminals. However, the domestic side is accessed via Vile Parle and is known locally as Santa Cruz airport, while the international, with its entrance 4km away in Andheri, goes locally by Sahar. Both terminals have ATMs, foreign-exchange counters and tourist-information booths (p114). A free shuttle bus runs between the two every 30 minutes.

INTERNATIONAL AIRLINES

Travel agencies are often better for booking international flights, while airline offices are increasingly directing customers to their call centres.

Air France (off Map pp110-11; ☎ 1800 180033; Sarjan Plaza, 100 Dr Annie Besant Rd, Worli; ☼ 9am-1pm & 1.30-5pm Mon-Fri)

Air India (Map p118; ☎ 26818098, airport 26168000; Air India Bldg, cnr Marine Dr & Madame Cama Rd, Nariman Point; ☼ 9.30am-5.30pm)

American Airlines (off Map pp110-11; ☎ 1800 2001800; 114 Nirman Kendra, Dr E Moses Rd, Mahalaxmi; ☼ 9am-6pm Mon-Fri, 10am-2pm Sat)

British Airways (Map p130; ☎ 9892577470, 1800 10235922; Notan Plaza, Turner Rd, Bandra West; ☼ 9.30am-1pm Mon, Wed, Fri)

Cathay Pacific (off Map pp110-11; ☎ 66572222, airport 66859002/3; 2 Brady Gladys Plaza, Senapati Bapat Marg, Lower Parel; ☼ 9.30am-6.30pm Mon-Sat)

Delta Airlines (Map pp110-11; ☎ 22839712-5; Interglobe Enterprises Ltd, 12th fl, Bajaj Bhawan, Nariman Point; ☼ 9am-5.30pm Mon-Sat)

El Al Airlines (Map pp110-11; ☎ 22154701, airport 66859425/6; 57 The Arcade, World Trade Centre, Cuffe Parade; ☼ 9.30am-5.30pm Mon-Fri, to 1pm Sat)

Qantas (Map p118; ☎ 22007440; Godrej Bhavan, 2nd fl, Home St, Fort; ☼ 9am-1.15pm & 2.30-5.30pm Mon-Fri)

Thai Airways (Map pp110-11; ☎ 66373737; Mittal Towers A Wing, 2A, Nariman Point; ☼ 9.30am-5pm Mon-Fri, to 4pm Sat)

Virgin Atlantic (Map p118; ☎ 67523701-5; Poddar House, 10 Marine Dr, Churchgate; ☼ 9.15am-5.30pm)

DOMESTIC AIRLINES

The following all have ticketing counters at the domestic airport, most open 24 hours.

Go Air (☎ 9223222111)

Indian Airlines (Map p118; ☎ 22023031, call centre 1800 1801407; Air India Bldg, cnr Marine Dr & Madame Cama Rd, Nariman Point)

IndiGo (☎ call centre 1800 1803838, airport 26156774)

Jet Airways (Map p117; ☎ 39893333, airport 26266575; Amarchand Mansion, Madame Cama Rd; ☼ 9am-7pm Mon-Fri, 9am-5.30pm Sat, 9.30am-1.30pm Sun) Also handles JetLite bookings.

JetLite (☎ airport 30302020)

Kingfisher (Map p118; ☎ 40340500, airport 26262605; Nirmal Bldg, Marine Dr, Nariman Point; ☼ 9am-7pm Mon-Sat, 10am-2pm Sun)

SpiceJet (☎ call centre 9871803333, 1800 1803333)

MAJOR NONSTOP DOMESTIC FLIGHTS FROM MUMBAI			
Destination	Lowest OW Fare (Rs)	Duration (hr)	Flights per day
Bengaluru	4700	1½	32
Chennai	5100	1¾	24
Delhi	5000	2	60
Goa	4100	1	21
Hyderabad	3000	1¼	22
Jaipur	4800	1¾	6
Kochi	4800	1¾	18
Kolkata	5700	2¾	22

MUMBAI (BOMBAY)

Bus

Numerous private operators and state governments run long-distance buses to and from Mumbai.

Private buses are usually more comfortable and simpler to book but can cost significantly more than government buses; they depart from Dr Anadrao Nair Rd near Mumbai Central train station (Map pp110–11). Fares to popular destinations (like Goa) are up to 75% higher during holiday periods. To check on departure times and current prices, try **National Travels** (Map pp110-11; ☎ 23015652; Dr Anadrao Nair Rd; ☼ 7am-10pm).

More convenient for Goa and southern destinations are the private buses (Map p118) that depart twice a day from in front of Azad Maidan, just south of the Metro cinema. Ticket agents are located near the bus departure point.

Long-distance government-run buses depart from **Mumbai Central bus terminal** (Map pp110-11; ☎ 23074272/1524) by Mumbai Central train station. Buses service major towns in Maharashtra and neighbouring states. They're cheaper and more frequent than private services, but the quality and crowd levels vary.

Fares for popular routes:

Destination	Fare (Rs)	Duration (hr)
Ahmedabad	220/350-400*	13
Aurangabad	200/350	10
Mahabaleshwar	180/300-450	7
Panaji	410/550-800	14-18
Pune	120/220-250	4
Udaipur	390/550-800	16

* Fares are for private/government non-AC buses.

Train

Three train systems operate out of Mumbai, but the most important for travellers are Central Railways and Western Railways. Tickets for either system can be bought from any station, in South Mumbai or the suburbs, that has computerised ticketing.

Central Railways (☎ 134), handling services to the east, south, plus a few trains to the north, operate from CST. The **reservation centre** (Map p118; ☎ 137; ☼ 8am-8pm Mon-Sat, to 2pm Sun) is around the side of CST where the taxis gather. **Foreign tourist-quota tickets** (Counter 52) can be bought up to 90 days before travel, but must be paid in foreign currency or with rupees backed by an encashment certificate

---

MAJOR TRAINS FROM MUMBAI

Destination	Train No & name	Fare (Rs)	Duration (hr)	Departure
Agra	2137 Punjab Mail	417/1118/1528	22	7.40pm CST
Ahmedabad	2901 Gujarat Mail	235/604/816	9	9.50pm MC
Aurangabad	7057 Devagiri Exp	178/471/643	7	9.05pm CST
	7617 Tapovan Exp	103/369*	7	6.10am CST
Bengaluru	6529 Udyan Exp	377/1031/1420	25	8.05am CST
Bhopal	2137 Punjab Mail	330/872/1188	14	7.40pm CST
Chennai	1041 Chennai Exp	389/1095/1467	27	2.00pm CST
Delhi	2951 Rajdhani Exp	1495/1975/3305**	16	4.40pm MC
	2137 Punjab Mail	449/1208/1653	25½	7.40pm CST
Margao	0103 Mandavi Exp	293/796/1092	11½	6.55am CST
	2051 Shatabdi Exp	197/680*	9	5.10am CST
Hyderabad	2701 Hussainsagar Exp	317/837/1139	14½	9.50pm CST
Indore	2961 Avantika Exp	325/861/1171	14½	7.05pm MC
Jaipur	2955 Jaipur Exp	389/1039/1419	18	6.50pm MC
Kochi	6345 Netravati Exp	441/1211/1670	26½	11.40pm T
Kolkata	2859 Gitanjali Exp	517/1399/1918	30½	6.00am CST
	2809 Howrah Mail	490/1399/1918	33	8.35pm CST
Pune	2125 Pragati Exp	77/270*	3½	5.10pm CST
Varanasi	1093 Mahanagari Exp	406/1178/1623	2½	12.10am CST
Trivandrum	6345 Netravati Exp	473/1301/1795	30	11.40am T

Station abbreviations: CST (Chhatrapati Shivaji Terminus); MC (Mumbai Central); T (Lokmanya Tilak); D (Dadar)
Note: Fares are for sleeper/3AC/2AC except for: *2nd/CC, **3AC/2AC/1AC.

or ATM receipt. Indrail passes (p533) can also be bought at Counter 52. You can buy nonquota tickets with a Visa or MasterCard at the much faster credit-card counters (10 and 11) for a Rs30 fee.

Some Central Railways trains depart from Dadar (D), a few stations north of CST, or Churchgate/Lokmanya Tilak (T), 16km north of CST.

Western Railways (☎ 131, 132) has services to the north (including Rajasthan and Delhi) from Mumbai Central (MC) train station (☎ 23061763, 23073535), usually called Bombay Central. The **reservation centre** (Map p118; ⏰ 8am-8pm Mon-Sat, to 2pm Sun), opposite Churchgate train station, has a **foreign tourist-quota counter** (Counter 28) upstairs next to the Government of India tourist office. The same rules apply as at CST station. The credit-card counter is No 20.

GETTING AROUND
To/From the Airports
INTERNATIONAL

The prepaid-taxi booth at the international airport has set fares for every neighbourhood in the city; Colaba, Fort and Marine Dr are Rs325, Bandra and Juhu Rs200. There's a 25% surcharge between midnight and 5am and, at all times, a Rs10 service charge and a charge of Rs10 per bag. The journey to Colaba takes about 45 minutes at night and 1½ to two hours during the day. Tips are not required.

Autorickshaws queue up at a little distance from Arrivals, but don't try to take one to South Mumbai: they can only go as far as Mahim Creek. You can catch an autorickshaw (around Rs30) to Andheri train station, though, and catch a suburban train (Rs9, 45 minutes) to Churchgate or CST. Only attempt this if you arrive during the day outside of rush 'hour' (6am to 11am) and are not weighed down with luggage. At the very least, buy a 1st-class ticket (Rs86).

Minibuses outside Arrivals offer free shuttle services to the domestic airport and Juhu hotels.

A taxi from South Mumbai to the international airport shouldn't cost more than Rs400 with the meter, or with bargaining a fixed fare beforehand; official baggage charges are Rs10 per bag. Add 25% to the meter charge between midnight and 5am. We love the old-school black-and-yellows, but there's also **Meru** (☎ 44224422; www.merucabs.com), AC, metered call

taxis charging Rs15 for the first km and Rs13 each km thereafter (25% more at night). Colaba to the airport will cost around Rs400, and the route is tracked by GPS so no rip-offs!

DOMESTIC

Taxis and autorickshaws queue up outside both domestic terminals. There are no prepaid counters, but both queues are controlled by the police – make sure your driver uses the meter and conversion card. A taxi to Colaba costs around Rs350.

If you don't have too much luggage, bus 2 (limited) stops on nearby Nehru Rd and passes through Colaba Causeway (Rs18). Coming from the city, it stops on the highway opposite the airport.

A better alternative is to catch an autorickshaw between the airport and Vile Parle train station (Rs15), and a train between Vile Parle and Churchgate (Rs9, 45 minutes). Don't attempt this during rush hour (6am to 11am).

Boat

Both **PNP** (☎ 22885220) and **Maldar Catamarans** (☎ 22829695) run regular ferries to Mandwa (Rs110 one way), useful for access to Murud-Janjira and other parts of the Konkan Coast (p166), avoiding the long bus trip out of Mumbai. Their ticket offices are at Apollo Bunder (near the Gateway of India; Map p117).

Bus

Mumbai's single- and double-decker buses are good for travelling short distances. Fares around South Mumbai cost Rs3 for a section; pay the conductor once you're aboard. The service is run by **BEST** (Map p117; ☎ 22856262; www.bestundertaking.com), which has a depot in Colaba (the website has a useful search facility for

MAJOR BUS ROUTES	
Destination	**Bus No**
Breach Candy	132, 133
Chowpatty	103, 106, 107, 123
Churchgate	70, 106, 123, 132
Haji Ali	83, 124, 132, 133
Hanging Gardens	103, 106
Mani Bhavan	123
Mohammed Ali Rd	1, 3, 21
Mumbai Central train station	124, 125
CST & Crawford Market	1, 3, 21, 103, 124

bus routes across the city). Just jumping on a double-decker bus (such as bus 103) is an inexpensive way to see South Mumbai. Day passes are available for Rs15.

See the boxed text (opposite) for some useful bus routes; all of these buses depart from the bus stand at the southern end of Colaba Causeway and pass Flora Fountain.

Car

Cars are generally hired for an eight-hour day and an 80km maximum, with additional charges if you go over. For an AC car, the best going rate is Rs1000.

Agents at the Apollo Bunder ticket booths near the Gateway of India can arrange a non-AC Maruti with driver for a half-day of sightseeing for Rs700 (going as far as Mahalaxmi and Malabar Hill). Regular taxi drivers often accept a similar price.

Motorcycle

Allibhai Premji Tyrewalla (Map pp110-11; ☎ 23099313; www.premjis.com; 205/207 Dr D Bhadkamkar Rd, Opera House; ⏰ 10am-7pm Mon-Sat), around for almost 100 years, sells new and used motorcycles with a guaranteed buy-back option. For two- to three-week 'rental' periods you'll still have to pay the full cost of the bike upfront. The company prefers to deal with longer-term schemes of two months or more, which work out cheaper anyway. A used 350cc or 500cc Enfield costs Rs25,000 to 80,000, with a buy-back price of around 60% after three months. A smaller bike (100cc to 180cc) starts at Rs25,000. It can also arrange shipment of bikes overseas (around Rs24,000 to the UK).

Taxi & Autorickshaw

Every second car on Mumbai's streets seems to be a black-and-yellow Premier taxi (India's version of a 1950s Fiat). They're the most convenient way to get around the city and in South Mumbai drivers almost always use the meter without prompting. Autorickshaws are confined to the suburbs north of Mahim Creek.

Drivers don't always know the names of Mumbai's streets (especially new names) – the best way to find something is by using nearby landmarks. The taxi meters are out of date, so the fare is calculated using a conversion chart, which all drivers must carry. The rate during the day is around 13 times the meter reading, with a minimum fare of Rs13 for the first

1.6km (flag fall) and Rs7 per kilometre after this. Add 30% between midnight and 5am.

If you're north of Mahim Creek and not heading into the city, catch an autorickshaw. They're also metered: the fare is 10 times the meter reading, minus one. Flag fall is Rs9 (the meter will read 1.00). Add 25% between midnight and 5am.

Train

Mumbai has an efficient but overcrowded suburban train network.

There are three main lines, making it easy to navigate. The most useful service operates from Churchgate heading north to stations such as Charni Rd (for Chowpatty), Mumbai Central, Mahalaxmi (for the dhobi ghat; p121), Vile Parle (for the domestic airport), Andheri (for the international airport) and Borivali (for Sanjay Gandhi National Park). Other suburban lines operate from CST to Byculla (for Victoria Gardens), Dadar, and as far as Neral (for Matheran). Trains run from 4am till 1am. From Churchgate, 2nd-/1st-class fares are Rs6/44 to Mumbai Central, Rs9/78 to Vile Parle or Andheri and Rs11/104 to Borivali.

'Tourist tickets' are available, which permit unlimited travel in 2nd/1st class for one (Rs50/180), three (Rs90/330) or five (Rs105/390) days.

Avoid rush hours when trains are jam-packed, even in 1st class; watch your valuables, and gals, stick to the ladies-only carriages.

GREATER MUMBAI

ELEPHANTA ISLAND

In the middle of Mumbai Harbour, 9km northeast of the Gateway of India, the rock-cut temples on **Elephanta Island** (Map p109; http://asi.nic.in/; Indian/foreigner Rs10/250; ⏰ caves 9am-5pm Tue-Sun) are a Unesco World Heritage Site and worth crossing the waters for. Home to a labyrinth of cave-temples carved into the basalt rock of the island, the artwork here represents some of the most impressive temple carving in all India. The main Shiva-dedicated temple is an intriguing latticework of courtyards, halls, pillars and shrines, with the magnum opus a 6m tall statue of Sadhashiva – depicting a three-faced Shiva as the destroyer, creator and preserver of the universe. The enormous central bust of Shiva, its eyes closed in eternal contemplation, may be the most serene sight you witness in India.

The temples are thought to have been created between AD 450 and 750, when the island was known as Gharapuri (Place of Caves). The Portuguese renamed it Elephanta because of a large stone elephant near the shore, which collapsed in 1814 and was moved by the British to Mumbai's Veermata Jijabai Bhonsle Udyan (formerly Victoria Gardens).

The English-language guide service (free with deluxe boat tickets) is worthwhile; tours depart every hour on the half-hour from the ticket booth. If you explore independently, pick up Pramod Chandra's *A Guide to the Elephanta Caves* from the stalls lining the stairway. There's also a small **museum** on site, which has some informative pictorial panels on the origin of the caves.

Getting There & Away

Launches (economy/deluxe Rs100/130) head to Elephanta Island from the Gateway of India every half-hour from 9am to 3.30pm Tuesday to Sunday. Buy tickets at the booths lining Apollo Bunder. The voyage takes just over an hour.

The ferries dock at the end of a concrete pier, from where you can walk (around three minutes) or take the miniature train (Rs10) to the stairway (Rs5) leading up to the caves. It's lined with handicraft stalls and patrolled by pesky monkeys. Wear good shoes.

SANJAY GANDHI NATIONAL PARK

It's hard to believe that within 90 minutes of the teeming metropolis you can be surrounded by this 104-sq-km **protected tropical forest** (Map p109; ☎ 28866449; adult/child Rs30/15, 2-wheeler/4-wheeler

vehicle Rs15/50; ☺ 7.30am-6pm). Here, bright flora, birds, butterflies and elusive wild leopards replace pollution and crowds, all surrounded by forested hills on the city's northern edge. Urban development and shantytowns try to muscle in on the edges of this wild region, but its status as a national park has allowed it to stay green and calm.

One of the main attractions is the **lion & tiger safari** (adult/child Rs30/15; ☺ every 20min 9.20am-12.40pm & 2-5.30pm Tue-Sun), departing from the tiger orientation centre (about 1km in from the main entrance). Expect a whirlwind 20-minute jaunt by bus through the two separate areas of the park housing the tigers and lions.

Inside the main northern entrance is an **information centre** with a small exhibition on the park's wildlife. The best time to see birds is October to April and butterflies August to November.

Another big draw are the 109 **Kanheri Caves** (Indian/foreigner Rs5/100; ☺ 9.30am-5pm Tue-Sun) lining the side of a rocky ravine 5km from the northern park entrance. They were used by Buddhist monks between the 2nd and 9th centuries as *viharas* (monasteries) and *chaityas* (temples), but don't compare to the caves at Ajanta (p160), Ellora (p157) or even Lonavla (p170).

Mumbai's main conservation organisation, the Bombay Natural History Society (see p122) can provide more information on the park and occasionally offers trips here.

Getting There & Away

Take the train from Churchgate to Borivali (Rs11, one hour). From there take an autorickshaw (Rs15) or catch any bus to the park entrance. It's a further 10-minute walk from the entrance to the safari park.

Maharashtra

Stretching from the unspoilt greens of the sleepy Konkan Coast, all the way into the parched innards of India's throbbing heartland, Maharashtra packs in enough wonders to satisfy even the pickiest of travellers. Being India's second most populous state (and third largest by area), its gigantic canvas is painted with a smattering of lazy beaches, lofty mountains, virgin forests and historical hotspots, complemented by the famed sights, sounds, tastes and experiences of India.

Up north, there's Nasik, where riotous colours blend with timeless Hindu ritual. Down south, modern India comes of age in Pune, a city as famous for its sex guru as its food-and-beverage circuit. Further south still, in Kolhapur, cameras work overtime to capture overwhelming temples, extravagant palaces and grimy action in the wrestling pits. Deep in the eastern crannies, the adventurous can pitch tent in Nagpur, before setting out to spy tigers hidden in the thickets. Out west, along the shores of the Arabian Sea, the emerald greens conceal a rash of pristine, white sands that give Goa's tropical dreams a run for their money. Within spitting distance, the hills of the Western Ghats await with their stupendous views and quaint hill stations. And located in the midst of it all are the architectural and artistic wonders of the state, topped by the World Heritage–listed cave temples of Ellora and Ajanta. Whichever way you look at it, Maharashtra is truly one of the most vibrant and rewarding corners of India.

HIGHLIGHTS

- Drop your jaws at the awe-inspiring beauty of the monumental Kailasa Temple, the shining jewel of the cave temples at **Ellora** (p157)
- Choose between sipping chardonnay among the vines or losing yourself in a holy confluence of colours, faith and rituals in **Nasik** (p148)
- Gasp in wonder upon being mesmerised by antique Buddhist art in the cave galleries of **Ajanta** (p160)
- Bite into a fresh catch of marine goodies or hunt out serene beaches, elephant temples and tumbling fortresses along the **Konkan Coast** (p166)
- Gallop on a horse to Echo Point, or simply outrun the toy train chugging up the slopes in **Matheran** (p168)
- Learn how to make friends with snakes, and pick up the basics of 'zennis' (Zen tennis) in **Pune** (p173)

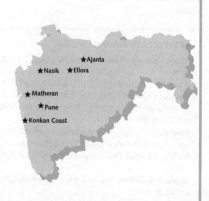

FAST FACTS

Population 96.8 million
Area 307,690 sq km
Capital Mumbai (Bombay)
Main languages Marathi, Hindi, English
When to go October to March (coast); September to mid-June (hills)

History

Maharashtra was given its political and ethnic identity by Maratha leader Chhatrapati Shivaji (1627–80) who, from his stronghold at Raigad, lorded over the Deccan and much of western India through his reign. Still highly respected among Maharashtrians, Shivaji is credited for instilling a strong, independent spirit among the region's people, apart from establishing Maharashtra as a dominant player in the power equations of medieval India.

From the early 18th century, the state was under the administration of a succession of ministers called the Peshwas who ruled until 1819, ceding thereafter to the British. After Independence, western Maharashtra and Gujarat were joined to form Bombay state, only to be separated again in 1960, when modern Maharashtra, was formed with the exclusion of Gujarati-speaking areas, with Mumbai (Bombay) as its capital.

Climate

Maharashtra is left drenched by the seasonal monsoons from May through to September. The rest of the year, you can expect the coastal and interior regions to be hot; for some respite head to the hill stations of the Western Ghats.

Information

The head office of the **Maharashtra Tourism Development Corporation** (MTDC; Map p118; ☎ 022-22845678; www.maharashtratourism.gov.in; Madame Cama Rd, Nariman Point; ⊙ 10am-5.30pm Mon-Sat) is in Mumbai. Most major towns throughout the state have offices, too, but they're generally only useful for booking MTDC accommodation and tours. For in-depth information, Mumbai remains the safest bet. While Sunday is the weekly day off, many offices are closed on alternate Saturdays.

ACCOMMODATION

In Maharashtra, rooms costing Rs1199 or less are charged a 4% tax, while those that are Rs1200 and up are slapped with a 10% tax. Some hotels also levy an extra expenditure tax (up to 10%). Rates in this chapter do not include taxes unless otherwise indicated. High-season rates are quoted, but prices might rise, sometimes unreasonably, during local holidays such as Diwali and New Year's Eve. Many places in Maharashtra also have government-approved homestays which are listed on the MTDC website www.maharashtratourism .gov.in.

Getting There & Away

Mumbai (p140) is Maharashtra's main transport hub, although Pune (p178), Jalgaon (p163) and Aurangabad (p155) are also major players.

Getting Around

Because the state is so large, internal flights (eg Mumbai to Nagpur) can help speed up your explorations. Airfares vary widely on a daily basis. Prices quoted here exclude taxes, which

---

FESTIVALS IN MAHARASHTRA

Ellora Dance & Music Festival (Mar; Ellora, p157) A popular classical music and dance festival held at the caves.

Naag Panchami (Aug; Pune, p173 & Kolhapur, p183) A slithery snake-worshipping festival.

Ganesh Chaturthi (Aug & Sep; Pune, p173) Ganesh Chaturthi is celebrated with fervour across Maharashtra, but one of the best places to be is Pune, where a host of cultural events accompany the general mayhem for the elephant-headed deity.

Dussehra (Sep & Oct; Nagpur, p164) Being a Hindu festival, this is also when thousands of Buddhists celebrate the anniversary of the famous humanist and Dalit leader Dr BR Ambedkar's conversion to Buddhism.

Kalidas Festival (Nov; Nagpur, p164) A music and dance festival dedicated to the legendary Sanskrit poet Kalidas.

Sawai Gandharva (Dec; Pune, p173) Features nightlong sessions of Indian classical music and dance performances.

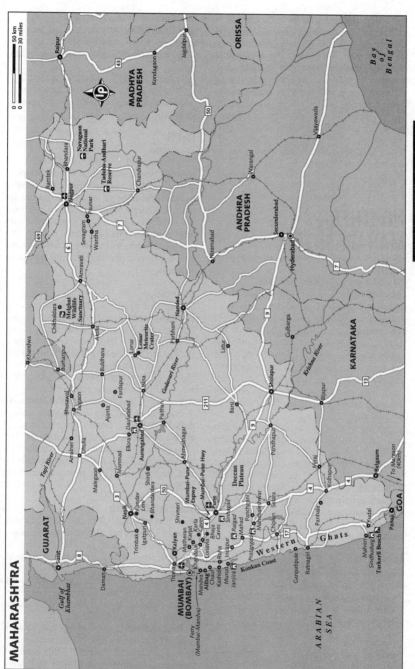

MAHARASHTRA

can sometimes be double the ticket amount. A cheaper and more exciting way to get around is by hopping onto trains or long-distance buses, of which there are plenty. The **Maharashtra State Road Transport Corporation** (MSRTC) has a superb semideluxe bus network spanning all major towns, with the more remote places being served by ordinary buses. Some private operators have luxury Volvo services connecting major cities; **Neeta Volvo** (☎ 022-28902666; www.neetavolvo.com) is highly recommended. AC Indica taxis are readily available too, and charge around Rs7 per kilometre. For long trips, factor in a minimum daily distance of 250km, and a daily driver's allowance of Rs150.

NORTHERN MAHARASHTRA

NASIK

☎ 0253 / pop 1.2 million / elev 565m

Standing on the Godavari, one of India's holiest rivers, Nasik (or Nashik) derives its name from the episode in the Ramayana where Lakshmana, Rama's brother, hacked off the *nasika* (nose) of Ravana's sister, the demon enchantress Surpanakha. True to its name, the town is an absorbing place with many associations with the Hindu epic, where you can't walk more than a few steps without chancing upon an exotic temple or colourful bathing ghat.

Adding to its religious flavour is the fact that Nasik also serves as a base for pilgrims visiting Trimbak (p151) and Shirdi (79km southeast), birthplace of the original Sai Baba. Every 12 years, Nasik plays host to the grand Kumbh Mela, the largest religious gathering on earth that shuttles between four Indian religious hotspots, and is held every three years. The next one in Nasik is due in 2015; see the boxed text, p54.

Orientation

Mahatma Gandhi Rd, better known as MG Rd, a few blocks north of the Old Central bus stand, is Nasik's commercial hub. The temple-strewn Godavari River flows through town just east of here.

Information

Cyber Café (Vakil Wadi Rd; per hr Rs20; ⏱ 10am-10pm) Near Panchavati Hotel Complex.

HDFC Bank (MG Rd) Has a 24-hour ATM.
MTDC tourist office (☎ 2570059; T/I, Golf Club, Old Agra Rd; ⏱ 10.30am-5.30pm Mon-Sat) About 700m south of the Old Central bus stand. Sells a useless city map (Rs5).
State Bank of India (☎ 2502436; Old Agra Rd; ⏱ 11am-5pm Mon-Fri, 11am-1pm Sat) Opposite the Old Central bus stand. Changes cash and travellers cheques and has an ATM.

Sights
RAMKUND

This **bathing tank** in the heart of Nasik's old quarters sees hundreds of Hindu pilgrims arriving daily to bathe, pray and, because the waters provide moksha (liberation of the soul), to immerse the ashes of departed friends and family. For a tourist, it's an intense cultural experience, which is taken a notch further by the colourful **market** just downstream. It's okay to take photographs, but try not to be intrusive.

TEMPLES

A short walk uphill east of the Ramkund, the **Kala Rama Temple** is the city's holiest shrine. Dating to 1794 and containing unusual black-stone representations of Rama, Sita and Lakshmana, the temple stands on the site where Lakshmana sliced off Surpanakha's nose. Nearby is the **Gumpha Panchavati**, where Sita supposedly hid from the evil Ravana.

The ramshackle **Sundar Narayan Temple**, at the western end of Victoria Bridge, contains three black Vishnu deities, while the modern **Muktidham Temple**, about 7km southeast of the city near the train station, has 18 chapters of the Bhagavad Gita lining its interior walls.

All temples listed here are open from 6am to 9pm.

Sleeping & Eating

Hotel Abhishek (☎ 2514201; hotabhi_nsk@sancharnet.in; Panchavati Karanja; s/d from Rs340/435) Boasting value-for-money rooms with hot showers and TV, this budget option scores over its rivals thanks to its location. A few minutes' walk uphill from the Godavari River, it sits amid all the ritualistic action, and is a vantage point from which to be totally overwhelmed by sacred India at its best (and noisiest).

Panchavati (430 Chandak Wadi, Vakil Vadi) To save yourself the hassles of scouting for a comfy bed in town, head straight for this excellent complex, comprising four hotels that cover every pocket from budget to top end, and deliver each and every penny's worth. Kicking off at the cheaper end is Panchavati Guest House (☎ 2578771; single/double Rs500/600), which has clean but cramped rooms, well enough for a couple of nights' sleep. A more inviting option is Panchavati Yatri (☎ 2578782; single/double from Rs1025/1250; AC), featuring excellent rooms with hot showers, spot-on service and an in-house health club. Hotel Panchavati (☎ 2575771; single/double from Rs1199/1499; AC) is a pricier joint with classier rooms that caters largely to business travellers. Last of all is the sumptuous Panchavati Millionaire (☎ 2312318; single/double from Rs1700/2050; AC), a moody affair where the lavish rooms are complemented by private sit-outs, perfect for the steaming morning cuppa.

Hotel Samrat (☎ 2577211; www.hotelsamratnasik .com; Old Agra Rd; s/d from Rs535/770; ⊠) The snug rooms here are tastefully done up in brown and beige, with balconies and cable TV thrown in for good measure. Located right next to the bus stands, its spick-and-span vegetarian restaurant is open 24 hours and serves as a popular refuelling stop.

Ginger (☎ 6616333; www.gingerhotels.com; plot P20, Satpur MIDC, Trimbak Rd; s/d from Rs1499/1999; ⊠ ▯) About 3km southwest of the CBS is this sleek business hotel, with a host of stylish rooms done up in a pleasant mix of cedar and pastels. It's a DIY place, so don't expect room service. But take heart, there's a water dispenser on each floor and vending machines at the restaurant, in case you're craving that late-night coffee! Near Satpur MIDC Police Station.

Gateway Hotel (☎ 6603344; www.thegatewayhotels .com; MIDC Ambad; d from Rs4680; ⊠ ▯ ▱) This is Nasik's most luxurious hotel, situated about 8km south of town off the Nasik–Mumbai Rd, close to Pandav Leni and well away from all the urban mayhem. Offering standard five-star comfort, its USPs include the delectable morsels tossed up by its multicuisine restaurant Panchratna (mains Rs150 to Rs300).

Annapoorna Lunch Home (MG Rd; snacks & meals Rs15-70) No surprises on offer here, but it would be hard to find faults with the cheap and pan-fresh eats dished out by the hospitable waiters. Peak lunch hours are a bad time to walk in; you'll have trouble finding a seat.

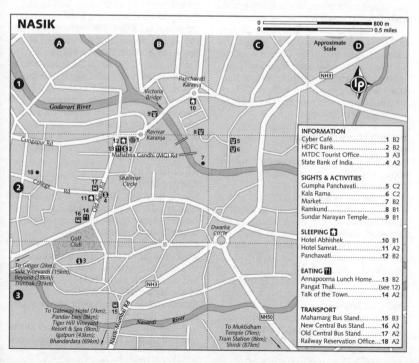

NASIK

0 — 800 m
0 — 0.5 miles

Approximate Scale

INFORMATION
Cyber Café..............................1 B2
HDFC Bank.............................2 B2
MTDC Tourist Office.................3 A3
State Bank of India..................4 A2

SIGHTS & ACTIVITIES
Gumpha Panchavati.................5 C2
Kala Rama..............................6 C2
Market...................................7 B2
Ramkund.................................8 B2
Sundar Narayan Temple...........9 B1

SLEEPING
Hotel Abhishek......................10 B1
Hotel Samrat.........................11 A2
Panchavati............................12 B2

EATING
Annapoorna Lunch Home........13 B2
Pangat Thali.....................(see 12)
Talk of the Town....................14 A2

TRANSPORT
Mahamarg Bus Stand.............15 B3
New Central Bus Stand...........16 A2
Old Central Bus Stand............17 A2
Railway Reservation Office......18 A2

MAHARASHTRA

MAHARASHTRA

GRAPES OF WORTH

So you thought chai was the only drink India churned out with zeal. Surprise, surprise! As it turns out, hilly Nasik, gifted with fertile soils and a cool climate, boasts conditions similar to Bordeaux. And over the past decade, the town has slowly but steadily been emerging as the Grand Crux of India's fledgling wine industry. Sauvignon blanc, chenin blanc, zinfandel, shiraz; Nasik produces them all. What's better, some of the wineries have now thrown their doors open for you to sample their drops, and associated luxuries, first hand!

Located 15km west of Nasik, industry pioneer **Sula Vineyards** (☎ 09970090010; www.sulawines .com; Govardhan, Gangapur-Savargaon Rd; ☒ 11.30am-5.30pm) runs a tasting room where you can round off a vineyard tour with a spirited session of wine-tasting (Rs150) in its wood-and-mosaic balcony bar. For a more lavish experience, head 3km inland to **Beyond** (☎ 09970090010; www.sulawines.com; weekdays/weekends Rs16,000/20,000), a charming three-bedroom bungalow set amid the vines, where you can ride out on bicycles past the rolling hills, picnic beside the nearby lake or skim the still waters on a kayak. Chateau Indage, another of Nasik's wine biggies, has recently joined the tourism race with **Tiger Hill Vineyards Resort & Spa** (☎ 0253-2336274; www.tigerhillvineyards.com; s/d from Rs2800/3500). A serene, stylish getaway located 8km south of town, it's the perfect place to imbibe copious amounts of chardonnay and champagne in the cosy comfort of its snazzy wine bar, and top things off with a relaxing grape-seed-oil massage in rustic bamboo huts at the spa.

Pangat Thali (Panchavati Hotel Complex; thalis Rs80) A big-eater's delight, this no-frills vegetarian restaurant cooks up an array of delicious Gujarati dishes, which liveried waiters lovingly heap on your platter quicker than you can tuck them in. Soon, you're fed up to your eyeballs, and dessert isn't served yet!

Talk of the Town (Old Agra Rd; mains Rs80-250) One of the few classy dining options in Nasik, this restaurant, next to the New Central bus stand, is a nice place to wash down sundry succulent Indian bites with a refreshing pint of lager. Don't get too adventurous with the Chinese section of the menu; your noodles might arrive smelling of raw eggs.

Getting There & Around
BUS

Nasik is a major player on the road-transport scene, with frequent state buses operating from three different stands.

The **Old Central bus stand** (CBS; ☎ 2309310) is useful mainly for those going to Trimbak (Rs20, 45 minutes). A block south, the **New Central bus station** (☎ 2309308) has services to Aurangabad (semideluxe Rs165, 4½ hours) and Pune (semideluxe/deluxe Rs180/297, 4½ hours). The **Mahamarg bus stand** (☎ 2309309) has services hourly to Mumbai (semideluxe Rs155, four hours) and twice-hourly to Shirdi (Rs75, 2½ hours).

Many private bus agents are based near the CBS and most buses depart from Old Agra Rd. Destinations include Pune, Mumbai, Aurangabad and Ahmedabad, and fares are marginally lower than those charged on state buses. Note that most of the Mumbai-bound buses terminate at Dadar.

TRAIN

Nasik Rd train station is 8km southeast of the centre, but a useful **railway reservation office** (☎ 134; 1st fl, Commissioner's Office, Canada Cnr; ☒ 8am-8pm Mon-Sat, 8am-2pm Sun) is 500m west of the CBS. The 7am *Panchavati Express* is the fastest train to Mumbai (2nd class/chair Rs66/224, 2½ hours) and the 9.35am *Tapovan Express* is the only convenient direct train to Aurangabad (2nd class/chair Rs68/240, 3½ hours). Local buses leave frequently from Shalimar Circle, a few minutes' walk northeast of the CBS, to the train station (Rs7). An auto costs about Rs60.

AROUND NASIK
Pandav Leni

Dating from the 1st century BC to the 2nd century AD, the 24 early Buddhist caves of **Pandav Leni** (Indian/foreigner Rs5/100; ☒ 8am-6pm) are located about 8km south of Nasik along the Mumbai road. There's a steep, 20-minute hike separating the caves from the highway. Caves 19 and 23 have some interesting carvings; the rest are virtually empty and of limited interest to the lay-person. Some caves bear animal figures and dice boards once engraved into the stone floors by resident monks.

Below the caves is the **Dadasaheb Phalke Memorial** (admission Rs10; ☒ 10am-9pm), dedicated to the pioneering Indian movie producer of the same name.

Local buses (Rs10) run past the caves from Shalimar Circle, near the CBS in Nasik, but the easiest way there is by autorickshaw. A return journey including waiting time costs around Rs250.

Trimbak

The moody **Trimbakeshwar Temple** stands in the centre of Trimbak, 33km west of Nasik. It's one of India's most sacred temples, containing a *jyoti linga*, one of the 12 most important shrines of Shiva. Only Hindus are allowed in; non-Hindus can get as far as peeking into the courtyard. Nearby, the waters of the Godavari River flow into the **Gangadwar bathing tank**, where earthly sins are regularly washed away by bathing pilgrims; everyone is welcome. Also try making the four-hour return hike up the **Brahmagiri Hill** behind town to the source of the Godavari. Pilgrims from across the nation clamber up to the flower-encrusted summit where the Godavari dribbles forth from a spring and into a couple of temples soaked in incense. En route you will pass a number of other temples, shrines and caves inhabited by sadhus (spiritual men). Don't attempt the ascent if rain looks imminent, as the trail can quickly become dangerous under a raging torrent.

Regular buses run from the CBS in Nasik to Trimbak (Rs20, 45 minutes).

Igatpuri

Heard of *vipassana*, haven't you? Now head to Igatpuri to see where (and how) it all happens. Located about 44km south of Nasik, this village is home to the world's largest *vipassana* meditation centre, the **Vipassana International Academy** (☎ 02553-244076; www.vri .dhamma.org), which institutionalises this strict form of meditation first taught by Gautama Buddha in the 6th century BC and reintroduced in India by teacher SN Goenka in the 1960s. The centre also serves as the apex body governing the spread of *vipassana* around the world. Ten-day residential courses (advance bookings compulsory) are held here throughout the year, though authorities warn that it requires rigorous discipline, and dropping out midway isn't encouraged. Basic accommodation, food and meditation instruction are provided free of charge, but candidates are free to make a donation once they have successfully completed their courses.

Bhandardara

A little-visited place, Bhandardara is a cute little village nestled in the Sahyadri Mountains about 70km south of Nasik. Surrounded by craggy ranges, it's a wonderful place to soak up the bounties of unpolluted nature and, in the absence of checkbox travellers, makes for a fabulous getaway from the bustle of urban India. The best thing about Bhandardara is the towering summit of **Mt Kalsubai**, scaling a height of 1646m and once used by the Marathas as an observation point, which makes for a fantastic day trek. Other sights include the **Wilson Dam** straddling nearby Pravara River, built in 1910 and known as the largest earthen dam in India; and **Arthur Lake**, a placid water body fed by the Pravara, whose banks are ideal for a lazy lunch. You could also hike about 4km past the MTDC Holiday Resort to the ruins of the **Ratangad Fort**, another of Shivaji's erstwhile strongholds, which has wonderful views of the surrounding ranges.

The **MTDC Holiday Resort** (☎ 02424-257032; PO Shendi; d from Rs800;) is a good place to camp. Located on a leafy plot by the lake, it offers a mix of well-maintained rooms ranging from standard to quite luxurious, but don't expect great food.

Bhandardara lies about 26km from Igatpuri and can be accessed by local buses connecting Nasik to Ghoti (Rs23, one hour). An auto from Ghoti costs Rs50. Alternatively, take a cab from Nasik for around Rs1000.

Shirdi

About 90km southeast of Nasik lies the town of Shirdi, known to millions of devotees across India as the home of the revered saint Sai Baba (see the boxed text, p152). The centre of all the spiritual action and drama in this holy town is the **Sai Baba Temple** (☎ 02423-258500; www.sai.org.in; 4am-11pm), in the heart of town. It houses the main *samadhi* or **shrine** of Sai Baba, flanked by other places of worship such as the **Gurusthan**, where the holy man spent most of his time after arriving in Shirdi and where the shrine of his own guru is located; the **Chavadi**, where the baba used to sleep on alternate nights late in his life; and **Dwarkmai**, the mosque from where he preached religious tolerance. Across the complex, on the other side of the Manmad–Nagar Rd, stands the Khandoba Temple, a place where Sai Baba first stopped on his journey into Shirdi, and where

HOLY MAN FROM SHIRDI

His iconic status is confirmed by the millions of posters and souvenirs bearing his calm, smiling face that one finds strewn across India. And his divinity, to some, is unquestionable. But Sai Baba, for all his popularity, remains one of India's most enigmatic figures. No one knows where he came from, what his real name was, or when he was born. His childhood veiled by obscurity, Sai Baba appeared in the town of Shirdi near Nasik around the age of 16. There, he advocated religious tolerance, and practised what he preached by sleeping alternately in a mosque and a Hindu temple and praying in them both equally. The masses took to him like fish to water, and by the time he died in 1918, the many miracles attributed to him had seen him gather a large following. Today, his temple complex in Shirdi draws an average of 40,000 pilgrims a day. Interestingly, in Andhra Pradesh, another widely respected godman called Sathya Sai Baba (born around 1926–27) claims to be the reincarnation of the original Sai Baba (see p320).

he acquired his name. All are welcome to visit and pray in the complex, irrespective of religion, caste or creed. Donations are welcome; collections go directly into funding charitable projects for the poor and the needy of the region, apart from meeting daily expenses of the temple complex.

If you want to spend a night here, contact the **Shri Sai Baba Sansthan** (☎ 02423-258500), the complex's governing body, who can arrange accommodation in one of their many guest houses. Rooms range from basic to quite luxurious (Rs50 to Rs700).

You can reach Shirdi from Nasik by taking the twice-hourly bus from the Mahamarg bus stand (Rs75, 2½ hours).

AURANGABAD

☎ 0240 / pop 892,400 / elev 513m

After lying low through most of the tumultuous history of medieval India, Aurangabad's flash-in-the-pan moment came when the last Mughal emperor, Aurangzeb, made the city his capital from 1653 to 1707. With the emperor's death, it withered away as quickly as it had bloomed, but its brief period of glory gave it some fascinating monuments, including a Taj Mahal replica, that continue to draw a steady trickle of visitors today. Coupled with other historic relics, such as a group of ancient Buddhist caves, Aurangabad makes for a fairly decent weekend excursion. But the real reason for traipsing all the way out here is because the town is an excellent base from which to explore the World Heritage Sites of Ellora and Ajanta.

Silk fabrics were once Aurangabad's chief revenue generator, but the city is now a major industrial centre with beer and bikes being the big earners.

Orientation

The train station, cheap hotels and restaurants are clumped together in the south of the town. The MSRTC bus stand is 1.5km to the north. Northeast of the bus stand is the buzzing old town with its narrow streets and Muslim quarters.

Information
BOOKSHOPS

Sharayu (☎ 2335220; 119A Kailash Market, Station Rd East; ✆ 10.30am-8.30pm) Aurangabad's best selection of English-language books.

INTERNET ACCESS

Cyber-dhaba (Station Rd West; per hr Rs20; ✆ 8am-11pm) Also changes money.
Internet Browsing Hub (Station Rd East; per hr Rs20; ✆ 8am-10pm)

MONEY

ICICI, State Bank of India and HDFC have several ATMs along Station Rd East, Court Rd, Nirala Bazaar and Jalna Rd.
Bank of Baroda (☎ 2337129; Pattan Darwaza Rd; ✆ 10.30am-3pm Mon-Fri, to 12.45pm Sat) Near the Paithan Gate; gives cash advances on Visa and MasterCard.
Trade Wings (☎ 2322677; Station Rd West; ✆ 9am-7pm Mon-Sat, to 1pm Sun) Charges a Rs50 fee on exchanges.

POST

Post office (☎ 2331121; Juna Bazaar; ✆ 10am-6pm Mon-Sat)

TOURIST INFORMATION

Government of India tourist office (☎ 2331217; Krishna Vilas, Station Rd West; ✆ 8.30am-6pm Mon-Sat) A friendly and helpful tourist office with a decent range of brochures.

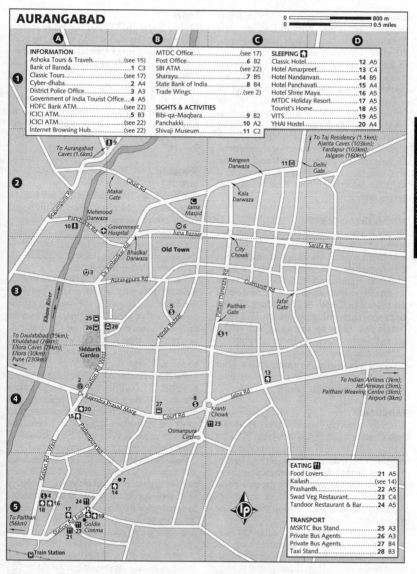

AURANGABAD

0 ——————— 800 m
0 ——————— 0.5 miles

INFORMATION
Ashoka Tours & Travels..................(see 15)
Bank of Baroda.....................................**1** C3
Classic Tours.....................................(see 17)
Cyber-dhaba......................................**2** A4
District Police Office.........................**3** A3
Government of India Tourist Office....**4** A5
HDFC Bank ATM................................(see 22)
ICICI ATM...**5** B3
ICICI ATM...(see 22)
Internet Browsing Hub.....................(see 22)
MTDC Office......................................(see 17)
Post Office..**6** B2
SBI ATM...(see 22)
Sharayu...**7** B5
State Bank of India............................**8** B4
Trade Wings.......................................(see 2)

SIGHTS & ACTIVITIES
Bibi-qa-Maqbara...............................**9** B2
Panchakki..**10** A2
Shivaji Museum.................................**11** C2

SLEEPING 🛏
Classic Hotel......................................**12** A5
Hotel Amarpreet...............................**13** C4
Hotel Nandanvan..............................**14** B5
Hotel Panchavati...............................**15** A4
Hotel Shree Maya..............................**16** A5
MTDC Holiday Resort........................**17** A5
Tourist's Home..................................**18** A5
VITS..**19** A5
YHAI Hostel.......................................**20** A4

EATING 🍴
Food Lovers..**21** A5
Kailash...(see 14)
Prashanth...**22** A5
Swad Veg Restaurant.........................**23** C4
Tandoor Restaurant & Bar.................**24** A5

TRANSPORT
MSRTC Bus Stand...............................**25** A3
Private Bus Agents.............................**26** A3
Private Bus Agents.............................**27** B4
Taxi Stand..**28** B3

MAHARASHTRA

To Aurangabad Caves (1.6km)
To Taj Residency (1.1km); Ajanta Caves (103km); Fardapur (103km); Jalgaon (160km)
Rangeen Darwaza
Delhi Gate
Chati Rd
Makai Gate
Kala Darwaza
Jama Masjid
Mehmood Darwaza
Panchakki Rd
Government Hospital
Juna Bazaar
Bhadkal Darwaza
Old Town
City Chowk
Sarafa Rd
Aurangpura Rd
Gulmandi Rd
Jafar Gate
Paithan Gate
Paithan Darwaza Rd
Nirala Bazaar
Siddarth Garden
To Daulatabad (15km); Khuldabad (26km); Ellora Caves (29km); Ellora (30km); Pune (230km)
Dr Rajendra Prasad Marg
Jalna Rd
Court Rd
Kranti Chowk
Osmanpura Circle
To Indian Airlines (3km); Jet Airways (3km); Paithani Weaving Centre (3km); Airport (8km)
Station Rd West
Padampura Rd
Station Rd East
Goldie Cinema
To Paithan (56km)
Train Station
Kham River
Beed Bypass Rd
Dr Ambedkar Rd

MTDC office (☎ 2331513, 2343169; MTDC Holiday Resort, Station Rd East; ⊙ 10am-5.30pm Mon-Sat)

TRAVEL AGENCIES
Ashoka Tours & Travels (☎ 9890340816; Hotel Panchavati, Station Rd West) City and regional tours, car hire and hotel pick-ups.
Classic Tours (☎ 2335598; www.classictours.info;

MTDC Holiday Resort, Station Rd East) Trusty place to book transport and tours.

Sights
BIBI-QA-MAQBARA
Built by Aurangzeb's son Azam Khan in 1679. A mausoleum for his mother Rabia-ud-Daurani, **Bibi-qa-Maqbara** (☎ 2400620; Indian/

foreigner Rs5/100; ⏾ dawn-10pm) is widely known as the 'Poor man's Taj'. With its four minarets flanking a central onion-domed mausoleum, the white structure bears striking resemblance to the original Taj Mahal in Agra. However, it is much less grand, and apart from a few marble adornments, most of the structure is finished in lime mortar. Apparently, the prince had conceived the entire mausoleum in white marble like the Taj, but was thwarted by his frugal father who opposed his extravagant idea of draining state coffers for the purpose. Despite the use of cheaper material and the obvious weathering, however, it remains a sight far more impressive than the average gravestone.

AURANGABAD CAVES

Strictly architecturally speaking, the **Aurangabad caves** (☎ 2400620; Indian/foreigner Rs5/100; ⏾ dawn-dusk) aren't a patch on Ellora or Ajanta. But they nonetheless throw some light onto early Buddhist architecture and, above all, make for a quiet and peaceful outing. Carved out of the hillside in the 6th or 7th century AD, the 10 caves – comprising two groups 1km apart (retain your ticket for entry into both sets) – are all Buddhist. Cave 7 with its sculptures of scantily clad lovers in suggestive positions is everyone's favourite. An autorickshaw from Bibi-qa-Maqbara shouldn't cost more than Rs100 including waiting time.

PANCHAKKI

Literally meaning 'water wheel', **Panchakki** (Indian/foreigner Rs5/20; ⏾ 6am-8pm) takes its name from the hydro-mill which, in its day, was considered a marvel of engineering. Driven by water carried through earthen pipes from the river 6km away, it once ground grain for pilgrims. You can still see the humble machine at work, but don't expect any grandeur.

Baba Shah Muzaffar, a Sufi saint and spiritual guide to Aurangzeb, is buried here. His **memorial garden** is flanked by a series of fish-filled tanks, near a large shade-giving banyan tree.

SHIVAJI MUSEUM

This dull **museum** (☎ 2334087; Dr Ambedkar Rd; admission Rs5; ⏾ 10.30am-6pm Fri-Wed), dedicated to the life of the Maratha hero Shivaji, includes a 500-year-old chain-mail suit and a copy of the Quran handwritten by Aurangzeb.

Tours

Classic Tours (p153) and the **Indian Tourism Development Corporation** (ITDC; ☎ 2331143) both run daily tours to the **Ajanta caves** (Rs300; ⏾ 8am-5.30pm Tue-Sun) and **Ellora caves** (Rs200; ⏾ 9.30am-5.30pm Wed-Mon), which include a guide but no admission fees. The Ellora tour also includes all the other major Aurangabad sites, Daulatabad Fort and Aurangzeb's tomb in Khuldabad, which is a lot to swallow in a day. Tours start and end at the MTDC Holiday Resort.

Sleeping

BUDGET

YHAI Hostel (☎ 2334892; Station Rd West; dm/d Rs70/180) This decrepit old place meets all the usual youth-hostel norms, but the lady who runs the show is a real gem, and her charming personality compensates for any shortfall on the lodging front. Breakfast is available for Rs20 and a thali dinner Rs25.

Tourist's Home (☎ 2337212; Station Rd West; s/d Rs200/300) Just why would anyone renovate the lobby before giving the rooms a much-needed coat of paint? Well, these guys surely have their own reasons, so for the moment, you're stuck with drab blue walls and squat toilets in the rooms. But it's bright and airy, so not all's lost.

Hotel Nandanvan (☎ 2338916; Station Rd East; s/d Rs350/450; ✷) This place has spacious rooms the size of mini banquet halls (joking!) and more importantly, loos that are cleaner than most other budget options in town. The friendly room-service staff here dresses in pink. Colour therapy, did someone say?

Hotel Panchavati (☎ 2328755; www.hotelpanchavati .com; Station Rd West; s/d from Rs400/650; ✷) With walls painted in floral hues and matching upholstery in its well-appointed rooms, this place seems to have buried its ghosts and redeemed its status as a premium budget option in town. The managers are efficient and friendly and it sits easily at the top of the value-for-money class.

Hotel Shree Maya (☎ 2333093; shrimaya_agd@ dataone.in; Bharuka Complex; s/d from Rs445/595; ✷) The inviting aroma of mouth-watering food wafting out of the pantry hangs heavy in the lobby here. Scent-sitive travellers can't help but check-in, and are duly rewarded with a relaxing experience in the hotel's simple but comfortable rooms, with the added advantage of exchanging notes with other travellers on the outdoor terrace, where a sumptuous all-you-can-eat breakfast (Rs40) and other meals are served.

MIDRANGE

Classic Hotel (☎ 5624314; www.aurangabadhotel.com; Station Rd East; s/d from Rs800/1000; ✖ 💻) Perched atop an automobile showroom, this shiny hotel next to Goldie Cinema is let down by shoddy housekeeping and pushy staff. Its saving grace, however, is its prime location and 24-hour room service.

MTDC Holiday Resort (☎ 2331513; Station Rd East; d from Rs900; ✖) Set amid shaded grounds, this curiously disorganised hotel is one of the better MTDC operations. The rooms, though characterless, are spacious and tidy, and there's a well-stocked bar, restaurant and a couple of travel agencies on-site. Drop in between March and July, and you pay 20% less.

Hotel Amarpreet (☎ 6621133; www.amarpreethotel .com; Jalna Rd; s/d from Rs2200/3100; ✖) A glitzy lobby leads to slightly less impressive rooms, but it's much cleaner and more professional than any other hotel in its category. New rooms were being added during research, which hopefully will conform to classier standards when completed.

TOP END

Taj Residency (☎ 2381106; www.tajhotels.com; Ajanta Rd; s/d from Rs3980/4700; ✖ 💻 🍴) Set in 2 hectares of pleasantly landscaped gardens, this palace-like hotel is a quiet oasis of well-appointed rooms on the northern fringes of Aurangabad. The more expensive rooms have romantic Mughal-style swings on the balconies. For those travelling with infants, there's a babysitting service on offer.

VITS (☎ 2350701; www.vitshotels.com; Station Rd East; s/d incl breakfast Rs5500/6500; ✖ 💻 🍴) This brand-new luxury business option, with chintzy lighting in its lobby and classy interiors (faux waterfalls!), seems to have taken all steps in the right direction. The rooms already in commission boast features such as LCD TVs and wi-fi, with comfort to boot. Other rooms are slated to follow soon.

Eating

Swad Veg Restaurant (Kanchan Chamber, Station Rd East; mains Rs30-60) As well as a pile of cheap-eat Indian staples, this place offers pizzas (Rs40 to Rs50) and lots of ice creams and shakes – all of which are gobbled up under the benevolent gaze of swami Yogiraj Hanstirth. It's quite hard to find, but if and when you do get to it, you'll realise it's worth the effort.

Prashanth (Siddharth Arcade, Station Rd East; mains Rs30-90) Prashanth wins trophies from travellers for its delightful vegetarian-only dishes, epic fruit juices and enjoyable patio setting.

Kailash (Station Rd East; mains Rs30-100) Adjacent to Hotel Nandanvan, this pure-veg restaurant is a classy glass-and-chrome place where you can sit back after a long day out and wolf down a variety of local delicacies brought to your table by smartly dressed waiters.

Food Lovers (Station Rd East; mains Rs60-200) For some lip-smacking Punjabi and Chinese fare, try this restaurant across the road from the MTDC Holiday Resort, where the decor comprises a row of aquariums (sadly dry at the time of research). Locals vouch for its quality, and say it's a reliable place to tuck into the meaty stuff.

Tandoor Restaurant & Bar (☎ 2328481; Shyam Chambers, Station Rd East; mains Rs70-220) Offering fine tandoori dishes and flavoursome North Indian and Chinese vegetarian options in a weirdly Pharaonic atmosphere, this is one of Aurangabad's top restaurants.

Shopping

Hand-woven Himroo material is a traditional Aurangabad speciality (though people have differing opinions regarding its aesthetic appeal). Made from cotton, silk and silver threads, it was developed as a cheaper alternative to Kam Khab, the more lavish brocades of silk and gold thread woven for royalty in the 14th century. Most of today's Himroo shawls and saris are mass-produced using power looms, but some showrooms in the city still run traditional workshops, thus preserving this dying art. One of the best places to come and watch the masters at work is the **Paithani Weaving Centre** (☎ 2482811; Jalna Rd; ☒ 11.30am-8pm), behind the Indian Airlines office. It's worth a visit even if you're not buying.

Himroo saris start at Rs1000 (cotton and silk blend). Paithani saris, which are of superior quality, range from Rs5000 to Rs300,000, but before you baulk at the price, bear in mind that some of them take more than a year to make!

Getting There & Away

AIR

The **airport** (☎ 2483392) is 10km east of town. En route are the offices of **Indian Airlines** (☎ 2485241;

MAHARASHTRA

Jalna Rd) and **Jet Airways** (☎ 2441392; Jalna Rd). Most domestic airlines operate daily flights from Aurangabad to Delhi, with a stopover in Mumbai. Fares start from around Rs1250.

BUS

Local buses head half-hourly to Ellora (Rs20, 45 minutes) and hourly to Jalgaon (Rs113, four hours) via Fardapur (Rs74, two hours). The T-junction near Fardapur is the drop-off point for Ajanta (see p163 for more details).

Buses leave regularly from the **MSRTC bus stand** (☎ 2240164; Station Rd West) to Pune (ordinary/ semideluxe Rs156/195, five hours) and Nasik (ordinary/semideluxe Rs95/120, five hours). For longer distances, private luxury buses are more comfortable and better value. Private bus agents congregate where Dr Rajendra Prasad Marg becomes Court Rd; a few are closer to the bus stand on Station Rd West. Deluxe overnight bus destinations include Mumbai (with/without AC Rs250/200, sleeper Rs550, eight hours), Ahmedabad (Rs350, 15 hours) and Nagpur (Rs350, 12 hours).

TRAIN

On the southern edge of town you'll find Aurangabad **train station** (☎ 131; Station Rd East). It's not on a main line, but two direct trains (often heavily booked) run daily to/from Mumbai. There's the 2.40pm *Tapovan Express* (2nd class/chair Rs94/336, six hours), and the 6am *Janshatabdi Express* (2nd class/chair Rs117/385, 5½ hours).

To Hyderabad (Secunderabad), the *Devagiri Express* departs daily at 4.05am (sleeper/2AC Rs227/836, 10 hours). To reach northern or eastern India by train, take a bus up to Jalgaon and board one of the major trains from there.

Getting Around

Autorickshaws are as common as mosquitoes in a summer swamp. The taxi stand is next to the bus stand; share jeeps also depart from here for destinations around Aurangabad, including Ellora and Daulatabad.

Ashok T Kadam (☎ 9890340816) and **Bhima** (☎ 9370246907) are trustworthy autorickshaw drivers who won't try and wrangle every rupee they can from you. Bhima carries a notebook bearing recommendations and 'thank you' notes from travellers worldwide, while Kadam owes the fact that he owns his rickshaw to a *Lonely Planet* reader!

AROUND AURANGABAD
Daulatabad

No trip to Aurangabad is complete without a pit-stop at the ruined but magnificent hilltop fortress of Daulatabad, about 15km away from town en route to Ellora. A 5km battlement surrounds this ancient **fort** (☎ 2615777; Indian/foreigner Rs5/100; ☼ 6am-6pm), a beguiling structure built by the Yadava kings through the 12th century. In 1328, it was renamed Daulatabad, the City of Fortune, by Delhi sultan Mohammed Tughlaq, who decided to shift his kingdom's capital to this citadel from Delhi. Known for his eccentric ways, Tughlaq even marched the entire population of Delhi 1100km south to populate it. Ironically, Daulatabad soon proved untenable as a capital for strategic reasons, and Tughlaq forced its weary inhabitants to slope all the way back to Delhi, which had by then been reduced to a ghost town!

The central bastion of Daulatabad sits atop a 200m-high craggy outcrop originally known as Devagiri, the Hill of the Gods. The climb to the summit takes about 45 minutes, and leads past an ingenious series of defences, including multiple doorways at odd angles with spike-studded doors to prevent elephant charges. A tower of victory, known as the **Chand Minar** (Tower of the Moon), built in 1435, soars 60m above the ground to the right; it's closed to visitors. Higher up, you can walk into the **Chini Mahal**, where Abul Hasan Tana Shah, king of Golconda, was held captive for 12 years before his death in 1699. It was once coated in blue-and-white tiles, of which only a few fractured fragments remain today. Nearby, there's a 6m **cannon**, cast from five different metals and engraved with Aurangzeb's name.

Part of the ascent to the top goes through a pitch-black, bat-infested, water-seeping, spi-ralling tunnel – down which the fort's defenders hurled burning coals and boiling water at invaders. Apparently, these were measures put in place to make the fort impregnable. Nonetheless, history records how the fort was once successfully conquered by simply bribing the guards at the gate!

Guides (Rs450) are available near the ticket counter, and their flame-bearing assistants will lead you through the dark tunnel for a small tip. But on the way down you'll be left to your own devices. Note that the crumbling staircases and sheer drops can make ascent or descent difficult for the elderly, children and those suffering from vertigo or claustrophobia.

A CONTINUOUS PRESENCE

Unlike the Ajanta Caves, which were lost to mankind only to be rediscovered in the 19th century, the caves at Ellora have interestingly never fallen prey to human neglect. Some historians attribute this to the fact that the caves were situated close to an ancient trade route linking the ports on the Arabian Sea coast to trade centres further inland, and thus attracted a steady stream of visitors. Ellora is mentioned in the chronicles of several travellers and explorers who visited India from Europe or the Middle East, starting from the 10th century right up to the 18th century. Also worth noting is the fact that the caves, despite having been under the administration of several Muslim dynasties (including the radical Aurangzeb), were never destroyed in the name of religious cleansing. Interestingly, the caves earned a reputation of being leased through auctions for religious purposes during the 19th century, when they were under the supervision of the Holkar dynasty of Indore.

If you take an organised tour from Aurangabad to Daulatabad and Ellora, you may not have time to climb to the summit.

Khuldabad

The scruffy walled town of Khuldabad, the Heavenly Abode, is a quaint and cheerful little Muslim pilgrimage village just 3km from Ellora. A number of historical figures are buried here, including Emperor Aurangzeb, the last of the Mughal greats. Despite matching the legendary King Solomon in terms of state riches, Aurangzeb was an ascetic in his personal life, and insisted that he be buried in a simple tomb constructed only with the money he had made from sewing Muslim skullcaps. An unfussy affair of modest marble in a courtyard of the **Alamgir Dargah** (7am-8pm) is exactly what he got, which, in stark contrast to the tombs of other Mughal greats, was prudent, to say the least.

Generally a calm place, Khuldabad is swamped with millions of pilgrims every April when a robe said to have been worn by the Prophet Mohammed, and kept within the dargah (shrine), is shown to the public. The shrine across the road from the Alamgir Dargah contains hairs of the Prophet's beard and lumps of silver from a tree of solid silver, which miraculously grew at this site after a saint's death.

ELLORA
☎ 02437

The saga of the hammer and chisel comes full circle at the World Heritage–listed **Ellora cave temples** (☎ 244440; Indian/foreigner Rs10/250; dawn-dusk Wed-Mon), located 30km from Aurangabad. The pinnacle of ancient Indian rock-cut architecture, these caves were chipped out laboriously through five centuries by gen-

erations of Buddhist, Hindu and Jain monks. Monasteries, chapels, temples; the caves served every purpose, and style quotient was duly met by embellishing them with a profusion of remarkably detailed sculptures. Unlike the caves at Ajanta (p160), which are carved into a sheer rockface, the Ellora caves line a 2km-long escarpment, the gentle slope of which allowed architects to build elaborate courtyards in front of the shrines as well.

Ellora has 34 caves in all: 12 Buddhist (AD 600–800), 17 Hindu (AD 600–900) and five Jain (AD 800–1000). The grandest, however, is the awesome Kailasa Temple (Cave 16), the world's largest monolithic sculpture, hewn top to bottom from the rock by 7000 labourers over a 150-year period. Dedicated to Lord Shiva, it is clearly among the very best that ancient Indian architecture has had to offer.

Historically, the site represents the renaissance of Hinduism under the Chalukya and Rashtrakuta dynasties, the subsequent decline of Indian Buddhism and a brief resurgence of Jainism under official patronage. An increasing influence of Tantric elements in India's three great religions can be seen in the way the sculptures are executed. Their coexistence at one site also indicates a lengthy period of religious tolerance.

Official guides can be hired at the ticket office in front of the Kailasa Temple for Rs600. Most relay an extensive knowledge of the cave architecture, so try not to skimp. And if you only have time to visit either Ellora or Ajanta, Ellora wins hands down.

Sights
KAILASA TEMPLE

Halfway between a cave and a religious shrine, this **rock-cut temple**, built by King Krishna I of the Rashtrakuta dynasty in AD 760, was built to represent Mt Kailasa (Kailash), Shiva's Himalayan abode. To say that the assignment was daring would be an understatement. Three huge trenches were bored into the sheer cliff face with hammer and chisel, following which the shape 'released', a process that entailed removing 200,000 tonnes of rock! All this, while taking care to leave behind those sections of rock which would later be used for sculpting. Covering twice the area of the Parthenon in Athens and being half again as high, Kailasa was an engineering marvel executed straight out of the head; modern draughtsmen can go hang their heads in shame.

Size aside, the temple is remarkable for its prodigious sculptural decoration. The temple houses several intricately carved panels, depicting scenes from the Ramayana, the Mahabharata and the adventures of Krishna. The best one depicts the demon king Ravana flaunting his strength by shaking Mt Kailasa. Unimpressed, Shiva crushes Ravana's pride by simply flexing a toe. Kailasa is a living temple, very much in use; you'll have to remove your shoes to enter the main shrine.

After you're done with the main enclosure, bypass the hordes of chip-munching day trippers to explore the temple's many dank, bat-urine-soaked corners with their numerous forgotten carvings. Afterwards take a hike up the path to the south of the complex and walk around the top perimeter of the 'cave', from where you can appreciate its grand scale.

BUDDHIST CAVES

The southernmost 12 caves are Buddhist *viharas* (monasteries), except Cave 10, which is a *chaitya* (assembly hall). While the earliest caves are simple, Caves 11 and 12 are more ambitious, on par with the more impressive Hindu temples.

Cave 1, the simplest *vihara*, may have been a granary. **Cave 2** is notable for its ornate pillars and its imposing seated Buddha figure facing the setting sun. **Cave 3** and **Cave 4** are unfinished and not well preserved.

Cave 5 is the largest *vihara* in this group, at 18m wide and 36m long; the rows of stone benches hint that it may have once been an assembly hall.

Cave 6 is an ornate *vihara* with wonderful images of Tara, consort of the Bodhisattva Avalokiteshvara, and of the Buddhist goddess of learning, Mahamayuri, looking remarkably similar to Saraswati, her Hindu equivalent. **Cave 7** is an unadorned hall, but from here you can pass through a doorway to **Cave 8**, the first cave in which the sanctum is detached from the rear wall. **Cave 9** is notable for its wonderfully carved fascia.

Cave 10 is the only *chaitya* in the Buddhist group and one of the finest in India. Its ceiling features ribs carved into the stonework; the grooves were once fitted with wooden panels. The balcony and upper gallery offer a closer view of the ceiling and a frieze depicting amorous couples. A decorative window gently illuminates an enormous figure of the teaching Buddha.

Cave 11, the Do Thal (Two Storey) Cave, is entered through its third basement level, not discovered until 1876. Like Cave 12, it probably owes its size to competition with the more impressive Hindu caves of the same period.

Cave 12, the huge Tin Thal (Three Storey) Cave, is entered through a courtyard. The (locked) shrine on the top floor contains a large Buddha figure flanked by his seven previous incarnations. The walls are carved with relief pictures, like those in the Hindu caves.

HINDU CAVES

Where calm and contemplation infuse the Buddhist caves, drama and excitement characterise the Hindu group (Caves 13 to 29). In terms of scale, creative vision and skill of execution, these caves are in a league of their own.

All these temples were cut from the top down, so it was never necessary to use scaffolding – the builders began with the roof and moved down to the floor.

Cave 13 is a simple cave, most likely a granary. **Cave 14**, the Ravana-ki-Khai, is a Buddhist *vihara* converted to a temple dedicated to Shiva sometime in the 7th century.

Cave 15, the Das Avatara (Ten Incarnations of Vishnu) Cave, is one of the finest at Ellora. The two-storey temple contains a mesmerising Shiva Nataraja, and Shiva emerging from a lingam (phallic image) while Vishnu and Brahma pay homage.

Caves 17 to 20 and also **22 to 28** are simple monasteries.

Cave 21, known as the Ramesvara Cave, features interesting interpretations of familiar Shaivite scenes depicted in the earlier temples. The figure of goddess Ganga, standing on her *makara* (mythical sea creature), is particularly notable.

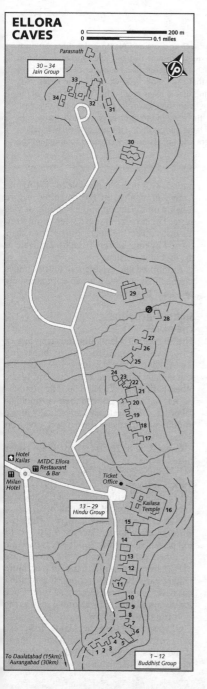

ELLORA CAVES

The large **Cave 29**, the Dumar Lena, is thought to be a transitional model between the simpler hollowed-out caves and the fully developed temples exemplified by the Kailasa. It has views over a nearby waterfall you can walk down to.

JAIN CAVES

The five Jain caves may lack the artistic vigour and ambitious size of the best Hindu temples, but they are exceptionally detailed. The caves are 1km north of the last Hindu temple (Cave 29) at the end of the bitumen road.

Cave 30, the Chhota Kailasa (Little Kailasa), is a poor imitation of the great Kailasa Temple and stands by itself some distance from the other Jain temples.

In contrast, **Cave 32**, the Indra Sabha (Assembly Hall of Indra), is the finest of the Jain temples. Its ground-floor plan is similar to that of the Kailasa, but the upstairs area is as ornate and richly decorated as the downstairs is plain. There are images of the Jain *tirthankars* (great teachers) Parasnath and Gomateshvara, the latter surrounded by wildlife. Inside the shrine is a seated figure of Mahavira, the last *tirthankar* and founder of the Jain religion.

Cave 31 is really an extension of Cave 32. **Cave 33**, the Jagannath Sabha, is similar in plan to 32 and has some well-preserved sculptures. The final temple, the small **Cave 34**, also has interesting sculptures. On the hilltop over the Jain temples, a 5m-high image of Parasnath looks down on Ellora.

Sleeping & Eating

Hotel Kailas (☎ 244446; www.hotelkailas.com; d from Rs900, cottages from Rs1500) The sole decent hotel near the site, this place should be considered only if you can't have enough of Ellora in a single day. The comfy stone cottages here come with warm showers; those with cave views are Rs500 pricier. There's a good restaurant and a lush lawn tailor-made for an evening drink.

Locals say the best food emerges from the kitchens of the **Milan Hotel** (mains Rs25-60), just across the road. Also reliable is the spotless **MTDC Ellora Restaurant & Bar** (dishes Rs40-170), which offers takeaways in case you want to picnic beside the caves.

Getting There & Away

Buses regularly ply the road between Aurangabad and Ellora (Rs20); the last bus

ART IN DARKNESS?

The first thing that gets you upon entering the caves at Ellora and Ajanta is the sheer darkness that prevails within. This leads to the niggling question: how is it possible to execute art and sculpture of such high calibre in a place with such an immense visual handicap? Historians have suggested certain theories. An obvious one is that the monks who worked in the caves used lamps to light up the interiors. Another interesting theory takes root in the fact that most of the caves in both the sites face a westerly direction, with some caves in Ajanta opening due east. The hypothesis is that monks either worked in the early morning or early evening, using light filtering directly into the caves, or that they used large mirrors during the rest of the day to reflect the light of the sun into the cave interiors, where additional mirrors were used to augment the light that was bounced in.

returns from Ellora at 8pm. Share jeeps leave when they're full and drop-off outside the bus stand in Aurangabad (Rs30). A full-day auto-rickshaw tour to Ellora with stops en route costs Rs500; taxis charge around Rs850.

AJANTA
☎ 02438

Being Ellora's venerable twin in the World Heritage listings, the **Buddhist caves of Ajanta** (☎ 244226; Indian/foreigner Rs10/250; ☉ 9am-5.30pm Tue-Sun), 105km northeast of Aurangabad and about 60km south of Jalgaon, are the Louvre of ancient India. Much older than Ellora, these secluded caves date from around the 2nd century BC to the 6th century AD and were among the earliest monastic institutions to come up in the country. Ironically, it was Ellora's rise that brought about Ajanta's downfall. As Buddhism gradually waned in the region, the site was abandoned and the focus shifted to Ellora. Upon being deserted, the caves were soon reclaimed by the greens and were forgotten until 1819, when a British hunting party led by officer John Smith stumbled upon them purely by chance. Despite their age, the paintings in these caves remain in a fine state of preservation today, and many attribute it to their relative isolation from humanity for centuries.

Information

Flash photography is banned in the caves due to its adverse effect on natural dyes used in the paintings. A video-camera permit costs Rs25. Authorities have recently installed tiny pigment-friendly lights within the dark caves, which cast a faint glow on the paintings, but bring a torch if you want to glimpse minute details.

A cloakroom near the main ticket office is a safe place to leave gear (Rs4 per item for four

hours). This makes it possible to visit Ajanta from Aurangabad in the morning, before moving on to Jalgaon in the evening, or vice versa. The caves are a short, steep climb from the ticket office; the elderly can opt for a chair carried by four bearers (Rs400), available at the foot of these steps.

Authorised and experienced tourist guides can be hired at Cave 1 for an approximately two-hour tour (Rs600).

Sights & Activities
THE CAVES

The 30 caves of Ajanta line the steep face of a horseshoe-shaped rock gorge bordering the Waghore River flowing below. They are sequentially numbered from one end to the other, baring Caves 29 and 30. The numbering has nothing to do with their chronological order; the oldest caves are actually in the middle and are flanked by newer caves on both sides.

Caves 3, 5, 8, 22 and 28 to 30 are either closed or inaccessible. Others, such as Cave 14, might be closed at times for restoration work. During rush periods, viewers are allotted 15 minutes within each cave. Some have to be entered barefoot (socks allowed).

Five of the caves are *chaityas* while the other 25 are *viharas*. Caves 8, 9, 10, 12, 13 and part of 15 are early Buddhist caves, while the others date from around the 5th century AD (Mahayana period). In the simpler, more austere early Buddhist school, the Buddha was never represented directly – his presence was always alluded to by a symbol such as the footprint or wheel of law.

Of special note are the Ajanta 'frescoes', more correctly temperas, which adorn many of the caves' interiors. It's believed that the pigments for these paintings were mixed with animal glue and vegetable gum, to bind them to the dry surface. Many caves have small, craterlike holes on their floors, which acted as colour palettes during paint jobs.

Cave 1, a Mahayana *vihara,* was one of the latest to be excavated and is the most beautifully decorated. This is where you'll find a rendition of the Bodhisattva Padmapani, the most famous of the Ajanta artworks. A verandah in front leads to a large congregation hall, housing sculptures and narrative murals known for their splendid perspective and elaborate detailing of dress, daily life and facial expressions. The colours in the paintings were created from local minerals, with the exception of the vibrant blue made from central Asian lapis lazuli. Look up to the ceiling to see the carving of four deer sharing a common head.

Cave 2 is also a late Mahayana *vihara* with deliriously ornamented columns and capitals, and some fine paintings. The ceiling is decorated with geometric and floral patterns. The murals depict scenes from the *Jataka* tales, including Buddha's mother's dream of a six-tusked elephant, which heralded his conception.

Cave 4 is the largest *vihara* at Ajanta and is supported by 28 pillars. Although never completed, the cave has some impressive sculptures, including scenes of people fleeing from the 'eight great dangers' to the protection of Avalokiteshvara.

Cave 6 is the only two-storey *vihara* at Ajanta, but parts of the lower storey have collapsed. Inside is a seated Buddha figure and an intricately carved door to the shrine. Upstairs the hall is surrounded by cells with fine paintings on the doorways.

Cave 7 has an atypical design, with porches before the verandah, leading directly to the four cells and the elaborately sculptured shrine.

Cave 9 is one of the earliest *chaityas* at Ajanta. Although it dates from the early Buddhist period, the two figures flanking the entrance door were probably later Mahayana additions. Columns run down both sides of the cave and around the 3m-high dagoba at the far end. The vaulted roof has traces of wooden ribs.

Cave 10 is thought to be the oldest cave (200 BC) and was the first one to be spotted by the

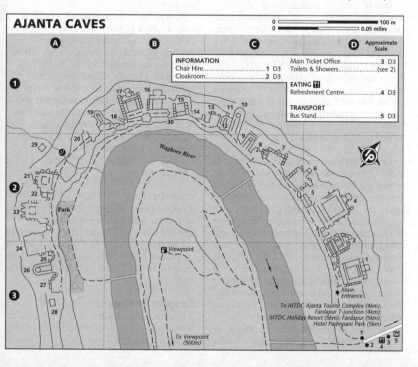

AJANTA CAVES

Waghore River

Park

Viewpoint

Main Entrance

To MTDC Ajanta Tourist Complex (4km);
Fardapur T-junction (4km);
MTDC Holiday Resort (5km); Fardapur (5km);
Hotel Padmpani Park (5km)

To Viewpoint (500m)

MAHARASHTRA

CARBON DATING AJANTA'S GOLDEN AGE

Historians worldwide have constantly been reviewing theories on major archaeological sites and their periods of existence. Unsurprisingly, the Ajanta caves are no exception.

One prominent theorist is American professor Dr Walter M Spink. With more than 40 years of research behind him, he suggests that the splendour of the later Mahayana group may have been accomplished in fewer than 20 years, rather than over centuries as previously thought.

Scholars agree that the caves had two periods of patronage: an early group was crafted around the 1st and 2nd centuries BC while a second wave of work began centuries later. Spink pinpoints the Vakataka emperor Harisena as a reigning sponsor of the incredible renaissance. Soon after his rise to the throne in AD 460, the caves began to realise their present forms, until Harisena's unexpected death in 477. The site was probably deserted in the 480s. The silver lining to the tragedy, according to Spink, is that the sudden downfall of the eminent Vakataka empire at the pinnacle of the caves' energetic crafting is solely responsible for their phenomenally well-preserved state today.

If you're interested, Spink's book *Ajanta: A Brief History and Guide* (1994) can be bought from touts near the site.

British hunting party. Similar in design to Cave 9, it is the largest *chaitya*. The facade has collapsed and the paintings inside have been damaged, in some cases by graffiti dating from soon after the rediscovery. One of the pillars bears the engraved name of Smith, who left his mark here for posterity.

Cave 16, a *vihara*, contains some of Ajanta's finest paintings and is thought to have been the original entrance to the entire complex. The best known of these paintings is the 'dying princess' – Sundari, wife of the Buddha's half-brother Nanda, who is said to have fainted at the news that her husband was renouncing the material life (and her) in order to become a monk. Carved figures appear to support the ceiling in imitation of wooden architectural details, and there's a statue of the Buddha seated on a lion throne teaching the Noble Eightfold Path.

Cave 17, with carved dwarfs supporting the pillars, has Ajanta's best-preserved and most varied paintings. Famous images include a princess applying make-up, a seductive prince using the old trick of plying his lover with wine and the Buddha returning home from his enlightenment to beg from his wife and astonished son. A detailed panel tells of Prince Simhala's expedition to Sri Lanka. With his 500 companions he is shipwrecked on an island where ogresses appear as enchanting women, only to seize and devour their victims. Simhala escapes on a flying horse and returns to conquer the island.

Cave 19, a magnificent *chaitya*, has a remarkably detailed facade; its dominant feature is an impressive horseshoe-shaped window. Two fine standing Buddha figures flank the entrance. Inside is a three-tiered dagoba with a figure of the Buddha on the front. Outside the cave to the west sits a striking image of the Naga king with seven cobra hoods around his head. His wife, hooded by a single cobra, sits by his side.

Cave 24, had it been finished, would be the largest *vihara* at Ajanta. You can see how the caves were constructed – long galleries were cut into the rock and then the rock between them was broken through.

Cave 26, a largely ruined *chaitya*, now dramatically lit, contains some fine sculptures and shouldn't be missed. On the left wall is a huge figure of the 'reclining Buddha', lying back in preparation for nirvana. Other scenes include a lengthy depiction of the Buddha's temptation by Maya.

Cave 27 is virtually a *vihara* connected to the Cave 26 *chaitya*.

VIEWPOINTS

Two lookouts offer picture-perfect views of the whole horseshoe-shaped gorge. The first is a short walk beyond the river, crossed via bridges below Caves 8 and 27. A further 20-minute uphill walk leads to the lookout from where the British party first spotted the caves.

Sleeping & Eating

Accommodation options close to the caves are limited and you're better off using Aurangabad or Jalgaon as a base.

Hotel Padmapani Park (☎ 244280; padmpani park@yahoo.co.in; Aurangabad-Jalgaon Rd; d with/without AC Rs700/500; 🔁). The small and clean rooms here come with a warm welcome. It's often booked out, so call in advance if you plan to stay over.

MTDC Holiday Resort (☎ 244230; Aurangabad-Jalgaon Rd; d with/without AC from Rs900/550; 🔁) This one's overpriced, and the staff prone to dragging their feet. The rooms, however, are clean and spacious.

MTDC Ajanta Tourist Complex (☎ 09422204326; Fardapur T-junction; cottages Rs1300; 🔁) Located just behind the shopping 'plaza' and the bus stand is this mint-fresh resort, featuring five charming and well-appointed cottages nestled amid grassy lawns overlooking the hills.

As far as tanking up goes, there is a string of cheap, unappetising restaurants in the shopping plaza – you could pack a picnic and enjoy it in the shady park below Caves 22 to 27. There's also a buzzing refreshment centre by the ticket office, which serves an overpriced vegetarian thali (Rs70).

Getting There & Away

Buses from Aurangabad (p156) or Jalgaon (right) will drop you off at the T-junction (where the Aurangabad-Jalgaon Rd meets the road to the caves), 4km from the site. From here, after paying an 'amenities' fee (Rs7), race through the shopping plaza to the departure point for the green-coloured 'pollution-free' buses (Rs7 to Rs12), which zoom up to the caves. Buses return on a regular basis (half-hourly, last bus at 6.15pm) to the T-junction.

All MSRTC buses passing through Fardapur stop at the T-junction. After the caves close you can board buses to either Aurangabad or Jalgaon outside the MTDC Holiday Resort in Fardapur, 1km down the main road towards Jalgaon. Taxis are available in Fardapur; Rs700 should get you to Jalgaon.

JALGAON

☎ 0257 / pop 368,000 / elev 208m

Apart from being a handy base for exploring Ajanta 60km away, Jalgaon is really nothing more than a convenient transit town. A grubby settlement, it stands on the passing rail trade, connecting northern Maharashtra to all major cities across India. Indeed, it's a place to consider if you're moving out of the state towards northern India, or vice versa.

Information

You can find a couple of banks, ATMs and internet cafes along Nehru Rd, which runs along the top of Station Rd.

Sleeping & Eating

Most of the hotels in Jalgaon have 24-hour check out.

our pick **Hotel Plaza** (☎ 2227354; hotelplaza_jal@ yahoo.com; Station Rd; dm/s/d from Rs150/250/350; 🔁 💻) Staying a night in this hotel is reason enough to visit Jalgaon. Nothing fancy on offer, but this cheapie has been done up with the kind of love and care that goes into building homes. The spotless rooms are simple and clean and come in a pick-and-mix range of styles and sizes. The effusive owner is a mine of useful information.

Hotel Kewal (☎ 2223949; Station Rd; d with/without AC from Rs875/625; 🔁) Another of those drab places to walk into. But it's nonetheless a decent midrange option, with motley interiors and efficient staff, which is perhaps all you need for a decidedly short stay-over.

Hotel Arya (Navi Peth; mains Rs35-70) Opposite Kelkar Market, near the clock tower. This place tosses up a long list of surprisingly tasty and well-tempered Indian fare, including some lip-smacking Punjabi delights. It's so popular you may have to queue for a table.

Silver Palace (Station Rd; mains Rs50-170) Next door to Hotel Plaza, this restaurant's claims of luxury may be stretching things too far. But the food is good, so all is forgiven.

Getting There & Away

Several express trains connecting Mumbai, Delhi and Kolkata (Calcutta) stop briefly at Jalgaon **train station** (☎ 131). Expresses to Mumbai (sleeper/2AC Rs175/632, seven hours) are readily available. The *Sewagram Express,* leaving from Jalgaon at 10.10pm, goes to Nagpur (sleeper/2AC Rs210/721, eight hours).

The first run from the **bus stand** (☎ 2229774) to Fardapur (Rs35, 1½ hours) is at 6am; buses depart every half-hour thereafter. The same bus continues to Aurangabad (Rs109, four hours).

Jalgaon's train station and bus stand are about 2km apart (Rs15 by autorickshaw). Luxury bus offices on Railway Station Rd offer services to Aurangabad (Rs120, 3½ hours), Mumbai (Rs250, nine hours), Pune (Rs250, nine hours) and Nagpur (normal/

sleeper Rs300/350, 10 hours). Rates may vary according to season and load factor.

LONAR METEORITE CRATER

If you have time on your hands, make a trip to Lonar to relive a prehistoric experience. Around 50,000 years ago, a meteorite slammed into the earth at this place, leaving behind a massive crater, some 2km across and 170m deep. In scientific jargon, it's known as the only hypervelocity natural impact crater in basaltic rock in the world. Means nothing to you? Well, then just take faith in the fact that, with a shallow green lake in its base and wilderness all around, it's as tranquil and relaxing a spot as you could hope to find. The lake itself is highly alkaline and its water supposedly excellent for the skin. Scientists suspect that the meteorite is still embedded about 600m below the southeastern rim of the crater.

The crater's edge is home to several **Hindu temples** as well as wildlife, including langurs, peacocks, gazelles and an array of birds. The **Government Rest House**, which is the starting point for the trail down to the bottom, is about 15 minutes' walk from the bus stand.

MTDC Tourist Complex (☎ 07260-221602; dm/d Rs150/550) has a prime location just across the road from the crater, and offers rather good-value rooms in a cluster of freshly painted, red-tiled cottages. Carry some mosquito repellent, and if the electricity fails at night, capitalise on the darkness by counting stars against a pitch-black sky.

Getting There & Away

There are a couple of buses a day between Lonar and Aurangabad (Rs101, 3½ hours). It's also possible to visit Lonar on a day trip from Aurangabad or Jalgaon if you hire a car and driver, and don't mind dishing out about Rs2000.

NAGPUR

☎ 0712 / pop 2.1 million / elev 305m

In the heart of India's orange country, Nagpur is located way off the main tourist routes. Nonetheless, it makes a good base for venturing out to the far eastern corner of Maharashtra. First up, it's close to Ramtek (opposite) and the ashrams of Sevagram (opposite). Besides, Nagpur is a convenient stop for those heading to the isolated **Tadoba-Andhari Reserve**, 150km south of Nagpur, which has

some of India's densest forests teeming with wildlife, including the famed Bengal tigers.

The city, however, is hopelessly devoid of sights, and gets interesting only somewhat during the **Dussehra Festival** (September or October).

Information

Computrek (18 Central Ave; per hr Rs20) Internet access on the main drag.

Cyber Zoo (54 Central Ave; per hr Rs20; ☯ 10am-10pm Mon-Sun) Another central internet cafe.

MTDC (☎ 2533325; near MLA Hostel, Civil Lines; ☯ 10am-5.45pm Mon-Sat)

State Bank of India (☎ 2531099; Kingsway; ☯ 11am-2pm Mon-Fri) A two-minute walk west of the train station. Deals in foreign exchange.

Sleeping & Eating

The majority of decent hotels are clustered along noisy Central Ave, a 10-minute walk east of the train station. An autorickshaw to Central Ave from the bus stand costs around Rs20. Most hotels cater to businesspeople rather than tourists.

Hotel Blue Diamond (☎ 2727461; www.hotelblue diamondnagpur.com; 113 Central Ave; s/d Rs345/456, with AC Rs800/912; ※) The mirrored ceiling in the reception is straight out of a bad '70s nightclub and the rooms are pretty much the type you would expect to find above a seedy '70s nightclub. But hey, it's got a Formula One–themed restaurant-cum-disco that plays blaring music and tosses up some wannabe Italian and American dishes, so you could never be bored in the evenings!

Hotel Blue Moon (☎ 2726061; fax 2727591; Central Ave; s/d from Rs450/600, with AC Rs850/950; ※) One of the closest hotels to the train station with large, plain and clean rooms that don't win any awards for imagination. But the staff is helpful, and things move at an agreeable pace.

Hotel Skylark (☎ 2724654; fax 2726193; 119 Central Ave; s/d Rs600/700, with AC Rs1150/1225; ※) Another of Nagpur's recommended budget options, which has drab rooms but scores on the assistance front, and has a good restaurant with occasional live music, serving diverse Indian and Chinese items (meals Rs70 to Rs150).

Krishnum (Central Ave; mains Rs30-60) One of the popular eateries on the main road, this place dishes out South Indian snacks and fruit juices of reasonable quality.

The dozens of *dhabas* (snack bars), food stalls and fruit stands opposite the train station rouse in the evening. Summer is the best time to sample the famed oranges.

Getting There & Away

AIR

Most domestic airlines, including **Indian Airlines** (☎ 2533962) and **Jet Airways** (☎ 5617888), operate daily flights to Delhi (from Rs1200, 1½ hours), Mumbai (from Rs500, 1½ hours) and Kolkata (from Rs1000, 1½ hours), apart from linking Hyderabad, Ahmedabad, Bengaluru, Chennai and Pune. Taxis/autorickshaws from the airport to the city centre cost Rs350/200.

BUS

The main **MSRTC bus stand** (☎ 2726221) is 2km south of the train station and hotel area. Buses head regularly for Wardha (Rs51, two hours) and Ramtek (Rs31, 1½ hours). Two buses roar off daily to Jalgaon (Rs296, 10 hours), and three go to Hyderabad (Rs164, 12 hours).

TRAIN

Nagpur **train station** (☎ 131), on the Mumbai–Howrah line, is an impressive edifice in the town centre. The overnight *Vidarbha Express* originates in Nagpur and departs at 5.15pm for Mumbai CST (sleeper/2AC Rs328/1165, 14 hours). The same train departs Mumbai at 7.10pm for Nagpur. Heading north to Kolkata the *Mumbai Howrah Mail* departs from Nagpur at 11.25am and arrives in Howrah at 5.50am (sleeper/2AC Rs366/1403, 18½ hours). Several Mumbai-bound expresses stop at Jalgaon (for Ajanta caves; sleeper/2AC Rs210/721, seven hours). There are also connections to Bengaluru, Delhi and Hyderabad.

AROUND NAGPUR
Ramtek

About 40km northeast of Nagpur, Ramtek is believed to be the place where Lord Rama, of the epic Ramayana, spent some time during his exile with his wife Sita and brother Lakshmana. The place is marked by a cluster of **temples** (☼ 6am-9pm), about 600 years old, which sit atop the Hill of Rama and have their own population of resident monkeys. Autos will cart you the 5km from the bus stand to the temple complex for Rs40; you can return to town via the 700 steps at the back of the complex. On the road to the temples you'll pass the delightful **Ambala Tank**, lined with small temples. If you're interested, you can take a boat ride (Rs20 per head) around the lake.

The **Kalidas Memorial** (admission Rs5; ☼ 8am-8.30pm), on the top of the hill beside the temple complex, is dedicated to the famous classical Sanskrit poet Kalidas. Also worth visiting is a **Jain temple** at the base of the hill and a **mosque** on the opposite hill.

On the hilltop and not far from the temples, **Rajkamal Resort** (☎ 0712-2228401; d with/without AC Rs1300/800; ☒) has large but overpriced rooms that come with TVs. There's a basic restaurant-bar.

Buses run half-hourly between Ramtek and the MSRTC bus stand in Nagpur (Rs31, 1½ hours). The last bus to Nagpur is at 8.30pm.

Sevagram
☎ 07152

Sevagram, or the Village of Service, occupies a prominent place in the history of India's Independence Movement. Chosen by Mahatma Gandhi as his base during the freedom struggle, the village played host to several nationalist leaders, who would regularly come to visit the Mahatma at his **Sevagram Ashram** (☎ 284753; ☼ 6am-5.30pm).

The peaceful ashram, built on 40 hectares of farmland, is a long way from anywhere and would motivate only die-hard Gandhi fans. The highlights of a visit are the original huts that Gandhi lived in, as well as some of his personal effects, including his walking stick. Across the road, the shoddy **Gandhi Picture Exhibition** (admission free; ☼ 10am-5.30pm Wed-Mon) traces his life through old photographs.

Very basic lodging is available in the **Yatri Nivas** (☎ 284753; d Rs100), across the road from the entry gate (advance booking recommended), and vegetarian meals are served in the ashram's dining hall.

Just 3km from Sevagram en route to Nagpur, Paunar village is home to the **Brahmavidya Mandir Ashram** (☎ 288388; ☼ 6am-noon & 2-8pm). Founded by Vinoba Bhave, a nationalist and disciple of Gandhi who participated in the Satyagraha and Quit India Movements, the ashram is now run almost entirely by women. Modelled on *swaraj* (self-sufficiency), it's operated on a social system of consensus with no central management. Basic accommodation and board (Rs100 per person) in two rooms sharing a bathroom is available; call in advance.

Sevagram can be reached by taking a Wardha-bound bus from Nagpur (Rs40, 1½ hours).

MAHARASHTRA

MAHARASHTRA

A MAN, A MISSION

Not everybody has the courage and resolve to walk out of a wealthy family and throw away a lucrative career in law, only to stand up for a social cause. But Murlidhar Devidas 'Baba' Amte (1914–2008) was an exception to the norm. Hailing from an upper-class Brahmin family in Wardha near Nagpur, Amte was snugly ensconced in the material world until he saw a leper die unattended on the streets one night.

It was an incident that changed him forever. Amte soon renounced worldly comforts, embracing an austere life through which he actively worked for the benefit of leprosy patients and those belonging to marginalised communities. In the primitive jungles of eastern Maharashtra, he set up his ashram called Anandwan (Forest of Joy). A true Gandhian, Amte believed in self-sufficiency, and his lifelong efforts saw several awards being conferred upon him, including the Ramon Magsaysay Award in 1985.

Amte's work has been carried forward by his sons Vikas and Prakash and their wives – the latter couple also won the Magsaysay Award in 2008. The family now runs three ashrams in these remote parts to care for the needy, both humans and animals. Volunteering opportunities are available; contact the ashram offices on mss@niya.org.

Tadoba-Andhari Reserve

Now under India's Project Tiger directorate, this little-explored national park lies 150km south of Nagpur. Less visited than most other forests in India, this is a place where you can get up close with wildlife, which includes gaurs, chitals, nilgais, sloth bears and the showcase Bengal tigers, without having to jostle past truckloads of shutter-happy tourists. The flipside, however, is that comfort levels are drastically low, and modern amenities unavailable. The park remains closed through the monsoons.

The **field director's office** (☎ 0712-2528953) in nearby Chandrapur can arrange for accommodation in forest rest houses and organise jungle safaris in minibuses. A better idea may be to opt for the all-inclusive weekend package trip to the reserve organised by **MTDC** (see p164) in Nagpur (Rs3750 per person), as it takes care of logistical hassles.

Several state buses ply between Nagpur and Chandrapur through the day (Rs101, 3½ hours).

SOUTHERN MAHARASHTRA

KONKAN COAST

A perfect holiday option for the intrepid kind, the Konkan Coast is a narrow strip of little-explored shoreline that runs from south of Mumbai all the way to Goa. Bordered by the Western Ghats to the east and the Arabian Sea to the west, it's a remote and rural area peppered with flawless beaches, tropic-green paddy fields, emerald hills and crumbling forts. Far from being developed, it's not the easiest of places to navigate. Accommodation is scant, the cuisine unsophisticated and monotonous, and the locals unaccustomed to tour groups, especially foreigners. Limited transport makes things more difficult; though the Konkan Railway provides access to the bigger towns, the smaller dots can only be reached by rickety local buses. A good option is to rent a taxi in Mumbai and drift slowly down the coast to Goa. Even better, get off the highway as often as you can, and try meandering your way along the back roads, which take you through uninhabited stretches of pristine mountain folds and virgin forests where few outsiders ever set foot. You may have to ask for directions often, and spend some nights sleeping in villagers' houses – be generous with how much you give. But the reward for your efforts may be an experience of which seasoned explorers would be envious!

Murud

☎ 02144 / pop 12,500

About 165km south of Mumbai, the sleepy fishing hamlet of Murud is your first port of call. Step on to its lazy beaches and feel the white surf rush past your feet, and you'll be happy you came.

More importantly, Murud is home to the commanding island fortress of **Janjira** (admission free; ⊙ 7am-5.30pm), built on an island about 500m offshore, which might just revoke your childhood memories of Long John Silver and Captain Flint. The citadel was built in 1140 by the Siddis, descendants of sailor-traders from the Horn of Africa, who settled here and allegedly made their living through piracy. Their exploits soon prompted many local kings to wage wars against them, including Shivaji and his son Sambhaji, who even attempted to tunnel to it. However, no outsider ever made it past the fort's 12m-high walls which, when seen during high tide, seem to rise straight from the sea. Unconquered through history, the fort finally fell to the spoils of nature: today, its walls are slowly turning to rubble as the forest reclaims its interiors.

The only way to reach Janjira is by boat (Rs15 return, 10 minutes) from Rajpuri Port. Boats depart from 7am to 5.30pm daily, requiring a minimum of 20 passengers. You can also have a boat to yourself (Rs400), and most oarsmen will double as guides (Rs350). To get to Rajpuri from Murud, take an autorickshaw (Rs50) or hire a bicycle (Rs5 per hour) from the shop opposite the mid-road shrine on Darbar Rd.

Back in Murud you can waste away the days on the beach, peer through the gates of the off-limits **Ahmedganj Palace**, estate of the Siddi Nawab of Murud, or scramble around the decaying mosque and tombs on the south side of town.

About 17km north of Murud lies **Kashid Beach**, which boasts a stretch of white sand that would give the Maldives an inferiority complex. Share autorickshaws (Rs10) go to Kashid from Murud all day, and shacks on the beach stock coconuts and basic snacks and have changing facilities (Rs5). However, avoid weekends, when Mumbai inc. comes calling.

SLEEPING & EATING
Several accommodation options are strung out along Murud's beach road. If you want to stay right on the sands, Kashid is a better option, where new hotels and private homestays are sprouting up by the day. Enquire in Murud.

Mirage Holiday Homes (☎ 276744; hotelmirage@san charnet.in; opposite Kumar Talkies, Darbar Rd; d with/without AC Rs1500/1000; ❄) A small and friendly hotel with a pretty garden and clean, simple rooms. The downside is it's across the road from the beach, so no sea views to wake up to.

Golden Swan Beach Resort (☎ 274078; www.gold enswan.com; Darbar Rd; d with/without AC from Rs3200/1700, cottages from Rs6400; ❄) The first place you come

to as the bus enters town is also the smartest. It's an upscale affair with plush rooms, and has a superb promenade to view the distant fishing boats.

On the food front, **Patel Inn** (☎ 274153; mains Rs40-80; ☽ 9am-10.30pm) serves fresh fish dishes that make you drool. Near the boat pier, **New Sea Rock Restaurant** (☽ 9am-10pm) is a nice place from where you can watch the sun set behind the fort. Just order yourself a cup of chai and snacks and you gain access to its excellent sea-facing sit-out!

GETTING THERE & AWAY
In Mumbai, regular ferries (Rs60, one hour) or hydrofoils (Rs110, 45 minutes) from the Gateway of India cruise to Mandva. If you take the hydrofoil the ticket includes a free shuttle bus to Alibag (30 minutes), otherwise an autorickshaw will be about Rs150. Rickety local buses from Alibag head down the coast to Murud (Rs30, two hours). Alternatively, buses from Mumbai Central bus stand take almost six hours to Murud (Rs150).

Avoid the railways. The nearest railhead is at Roha, two hours away and badly connected.

Ganpatipule
☎ 02357
Can't make it to Goa? Well, at least you can visit Ganpatipule, on the coast 375km south of Mumbai – and you won't be crying sour grapes. A sleepy but picturesque seaside village, it boasts several kilometres of almost perfect beaches and clean waters. Life generally plods along very slowly here, but heaven help anyone coming for a bit of peace and quiet during holidays such as Diwali or Ganesh Chaturthi. These are times when hordes of raucous 'tourists' turn up to visit the seaside **Ganesha Temple** (☎ 235248; ☽ 6am-9pm) housing a monolithic Ganesha (painted a lurid orange), supposedly discovered 1600 years ago.

There are several places to stay in and around town, the best bet being the **MTDC Resort** (☎ 235248; fax 235328; d with/without AC from Rs1550/1200; ❄), nicely ensconced among the palms on a prime beachside spot. On the pricier end are the sea-view cottages (Rs2650). The resort offers a variety of water sports, has a **Bank of Maharashtra** (☎ 235304) that changes travellers cheques, and the **Tarang Restaurant** (mains Rs40-110), serving local specialities such as Malvani fish curry.

For a quirkier experience, walk up a kilometre or so from the beach to **Hotel Shiv Sagar Palace** (☎ 235070; d with/without AC from Rs1800/1500; ✿). This massive pink structure, full of colonnades, domes and arches looks like a tacky Las Vegas hotel on LSD. Inside the hallowed halls is a kitsch world of orange plastic palm trees and towering chandeliers. Novelty factor apart, it's the stunning sea view, good vegetarian restaurant and a professional attitude that bring an unexpected class to the place.

GETTING THERE & AWAY
One MSRTC bus heads daily to Ganpatipule from Mumbai (semideluxe Rs345, 10½ hours), leaving the Borivali terminal at 9pm. Another bus rumbles back to Mumbai from Ganpatipule at 7pm. Frequent ordinary buses head down to Ratnagiri (ordinary/semideluxe Rs31/40, 1½ hours), from where you can catch an express train to Mumbai or Goa.

Ratnagiri
☎ 02352 / pop 70,300
Around 50km south of Ganpatipule, Ratnagiri is the largest town on the southern Maharashtra coast and the main transport hub (it's on the Konkan Railway). But for a tourist, that's about all that can be said for it. There's little to see and do apart from visiting the former home of freedom fighter Lokmanya Tilak, now a small **museum** (Tilak Alley; admission free; ◷ 9am-7pm), and the remnants of the **Thibaw Palace** (Thibaw Palace Rd; admission free; ◷ 10am-5.30pm Tue-Sun), where the last Burmese king, Thibaw, was interned under the British from 1886 until his death in 1916. A more exciting option is to take an evening stroll along the **Bhatya Beach**, but you certainly wouldn't want to step into the filthy water there.

There is no shortage of ATMs or internet cafes along the main road into town.

Just west of the bus stand, **Hotel Landmark** (☎ 220120; fax 220124; Thibaw Palace Rd; d with/without AC Rs1500/1000; ✿) has clean rooms and a restaurant serving good Indian food.

You could also try **Hotel Vihar Deluxe** (☎ 222944; fax 220544; Main Rd; d with/without AC Rs1500/900; ✿), a gigantic structure with efficient service and rejuvenating coastal food. A hearty South Indian breakfast is complimentary.

Ratnagiri **train station** (☎ 131) is 10km east of town. All express trains stop here, including the 10.45am *Janshatabdi Express* heading

south to Margao (2nd class/chair Rs122/390, 3½ hours, daily except Wednesday) and north to Mumbai (Rs132/435, four hours, daily except Wednesday). The **old bus stand** (☎ 222340), in the town centre, has ordinary state buses to Kolhapur (Rs90, four hours) and Ganpatipule (Rs26, one hour). The **new bus stand** (☎ 227882), 1km further west, has a 7.45am ordinary bus to Panaji (Panjim) in Goa (Rs160, seven hours).

Tarkarli & Malvan
☎ 02365
Don't snigger if you come across a government ad parading this place as Tahiti. Two hundred kilometres south of Ratnagiri and within striking distance of Goa, pristine Tarkarli has white sands and sparkling blue waters that any self-respectable beach resort should have, with the addition of forested hills and meandering rivers. What's lacking is a well-oiled tourist industry and urban bounties, but do you care?

There are a few places to stay on the bumpy 7km road in from Malvan, the nearest town, the **MTDC Holiday Resort** (☎ 252390; d with/without AC Rs2100/1500; ✿) being the most obvious. On offer are an array of simple but surprisingly pleasant chalets and an excellent restaurant serving some sinful Malvani seafood. Also enquire at the resort about backwater tours on its houseboats (standard/luxury including full board Rs6050/7150).

The monstrous **Sindhudurg Fort**, dating from 1664, is visible floating on an offshore island and can be reached by frequent ferries (Rs30) from Malvan. It's said that Shivaji helped build this almost impregnable island citadel; his hand- and footprints can be found in one of the turrets above the entrance.

The closest train station is Kudal, 38km west of the coast. Frequent buses (Rs20, one hour) run between here and Malvan **bus stand** (☎ 252034). An autorickshaw from Kudal to Malvan or Tarkarli is about Rs300. Malvan has several buses daily to Panaji (Rs80, four hours) and a couple of services to Ratnagiri (Rs100, five hours). An autorickshaw between Malvan and Tarkarli costs Rs60.

MATHERAN
☎ 02148 / pop 5100 / elev 803m
Within spitting distance from Mumbai's heat and grime, Matheran (Jungle Above), resting atop the craggy Sahyadri Mountains amid

a shady forest criss-crossed with foot trails and breathtaking lookouts, is easily the most elegant of Maharashtra's hill stations.

The credit for discovering this little gem goes to Hugh Malet, collector of Thane district, who chanced upon it while climbing the path known as Shivaji's Ladder in 1850. Soon it became a hill station patronised by the British. A quaint and hung-over village topped by a canopy of evergreen trees, the place owes its tranquillity to a ban on motor vehicles, making it an ideal place to rest your ears and lungs, and give your feet some exercise.

From around mid-June to early October, the monsoons hit Matheran hard, forcing it to virtually hibernate. During sunnier times, it brims over with cheerful day trippers, especially over weekends. During the true high season (summer months of May and June, Diwali and Christmas) it's nothing short of bursting at its seams with tourists.

Getting to Matheran is really half the fun. While speedier road options are available, nothing beats arriving in town on the narrow-gauge toy train (mini train) that chugs laboriously along a scenic 21km route to the heart of the village.

Information
Entry to Matheran costs Rs25 (Rs15 for children), which you pay on arrival at the train station or the car park.

Located on the main road into town, Mahatma Gandhi (MG) Rd, **Vishwa's Photo Studio** (☎ 230354; MG Rd; ⏰ 9.30am-10pm) sells useful miniguides (Rs25) and is actually a far better source of information than the so-called **MTDC Tourist Office** (☎ 230540) inside the MTDC Resort next to the car park. The **Union Bank of India** (☎ 230282; MG Rd; ⏰ 10am-2pm Mon-Fri, to noon Sat) changes travellers cheques only.

Sights & Activities
You can walk along shady forest paths to most of Matheran's viewpoints in a matter of hours, and it's a place suited to stress-free ambling. If you've got the early morning energy then **Panorama Point** is the most dramatic place to glimpse the sunrise, while **Porcupine Point** (also known as Sunset Point) is the most popular (read: packed!) as the sun drops. **Louisa Point** and **Little Chouk Point** also have stunning views of the Sahyadris and if you're visiting **Echo Point**, do give it a yell. Stop at **Charlotte Lake** on the way back from Echo Point, but don't

go for a swim – this is the town's main water supply and stepping in is prohibited. You can reach the valley below **One Tree Hill** down the path known as **Shivaji's Ladder**, supposedly trod upon by the Maratha leader himself.

Horses can be hired along MG Rd – you will certainly be approached – for rides to lookout points; they cost about Rs200 per hour.

Sleeping & Eating
Hotels in Matheran are low on quality and unreasonably high on tariff, so if you're not feeling generous, simply make a day trip from Mumbai. Most decent staying options are a short walk from the train station (1½ hours from the Dasturi car park). Check-out times vary wildly, and can be as early as 7am. Rates quoted here are standard high-season prices, but might just rise further. If you're visiting during the low-season, however, you might get a hefty discount.

MTDC Resort (☎ 230540; fax 230566; d from Rs1100; ✖) This government-run joint offers spruce, good-value rooms in a charming wooded location. The downside is it's next to Dasturi car park, so you're away from the midtown action.

Lord's Central Hotel (☎ 230228; www.matheran .com; MG Rd; s/d Rs1600/3200, valley view Rs2300/4600; ✖ 🖳 🛋) This charming colonial affair is one of Matheran's reputed establishments, but could do with the odd nip and tuck. Requisite brownie points are picked up by the stunning views, an inviting swimming pool and a rather hospitable and well-informed management. Note that they charge per person rather than per room.

Hope Hall Hotel (☎ 230253; MG Rd; d from Rs2000) 'Since 1875', says a plaque at the reception, and frankly, the age shows in the quality of the rooms! However, going by the many cheerful 'adieu' notes left by visitors, it seems that few mind the oddities such as squat toilets, hot bucket showers, or the hard-smoking, head-banging entrepreneur and his cowboy ways.

Rucha Heritage Hotel (☎ 230072; MG Rd; d from Rs2200) A grand white-pillared facade leads to less impressive rooms, but the management says they're putting in new rooms which guests are bound to love. And will pay through their noses for, obviously!

Hookahs & Tikkas (☎ 230240; MG Rd; mains Rs50-110) Operating out of a balcony overlooking the main road, this cheerful place serves

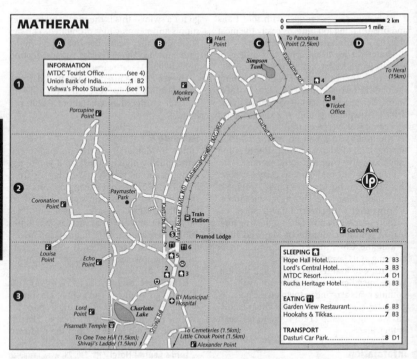

MATHERAN

INFORMATION
MTDC Tourist Office.............(see 4)
Union Bank of India.................1 B2
Vishwa's Photo Studio..........(see 1)

SLEEPING
Hope Hall Hotel.................................2 B3
Lord's Central Hotel.........................3 B3
MTDC Resort....................................4 D1
Rucha Heritage Hotel.........................5 B3

EATING
Garden View Restaurant...................6 B3
Hookahs & Tikkas.............................7 B3

TRANSPORT
Dasturi Car Park...............................8 D1

savoury Indian fare and an assortment of hookahs (Rs150), the ban on public smoking notwithstanding!

Garden View Restaurant (☎ 230550; MG Rd; mains Rs70-110) Locals insist that the tastiest meals in Matheran come from this kitchen, and might get tastier once it's done with the renovation work that was on during research time.

Getting There & Away
TAXI
Taxis run from Neral to Matheran (Rs250, 30 minutes), but might get dearer since the local cabbies have recently started demanding their pound of tourism flesh. Taxis stop at the Dasturi car park, an hour's hike from Matheran's bazaar area. Horses (Rs160) and hand-pulled rickshaws (Rs200) wait here in abundance to whisk you in a cloud of red dust to your hotel of choice. Taxis from Mumbai will take you on a daylong trip for about Rs2000.

TRAIN
The toy train (2nd class/1st class Rs36/210) trundles up to Matheran from Neral Junction five times daily, with an equal number of return journeys. During the monsoons, trains are less frequent. From Mumbai's Chhatrapati Shivaji Terminus (CST), the most convenient express train to Neral Junction is the 7.10am *Deccan Express* (2nd class/chair Rs47/167). The 9am *Koyna Express* gets to Neral Junction at 10.31am. Most expresses from Mumbai stop at Karjat, down the line from Neral, from where you can backtrack on one of the frequent local trains. Alternatively, take a suburban Karjat-bound train from CST and get off at Neral (2nd/1st class Rs20/100, 2½ hours). From Pune, you can get to Karjat by the 6.05am *Sinhagad Express* (2nd class/chair Rs48/147, two hours).

Getting Around
Apart from hand-pulled rickshaws and horses, your feet are the only other transport option in Matheran. Keep walking!

LONAVLA
☎ 02114 / pop 55,600 / elev 625m
Sorry to rain in on the party. But Lonavla, 106km southeast of Mumbai, is a cheeky little

scam masquerading under the name of a hill station. Catering to weekenders and conference groups coming in from Mumbai, this overdeveloped (and overpriced) town has no soaring peaks or quaint malls. Besides, it's a long way off from being attractive; Lonavla's main drag consists almost exclusively of garishly lit shops flogging *chikki*, the rock-hard, brittle sweet made in the area.

What saves Lonavla is its close proximity to the nearby Karla and Bhaja Caves which, after those of Ellora and Ajanta, are the best in Maharashtra.

Hotels, restaurants and the main road to the caves lie north of the train station (exit from platform 1). Most of Lonavla town and its markets are located south of the station.

It's advisable to change money in Mumbai or Pune. Internet access is available at **Balaji Cyber Café** (1st fl, Khandelwal Bldg, New Bazaar; per hr Rs20; ☾ 12.30-10.30pm), immediately south of the train station.

Activities

Those wishing for a session of yogic healing can head to the **Kaivalyadhama Yoga Hospital** (☎ 273039; www.kdham.com; Indian/foreigner from Rs9000/US$300), set in neatly kept grounds about 2km from Lonavla en route to the Karla and Bhaja Caves. Founded in 1924 by Swami Kuvalayanandji, it combines yoga courses with naturopathic therapies. Room rates cover full board, yoga sessions, programs and lectures. Rates mentioned are for a seven-day

MAHARASHTRA

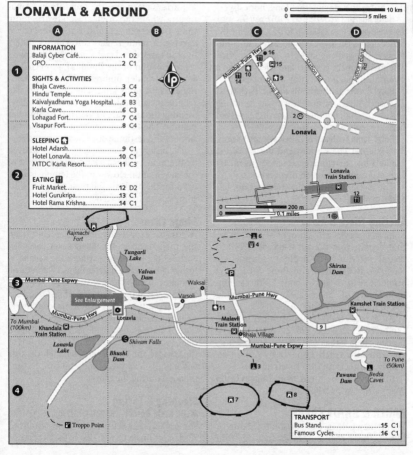

LONAVLA & AROUND

INFORMATION
Balaji Cyber Café..................1 D2
GPO..................................2 C1

SIGHTS & ACTIVITIES
Bhaja Caves.........................3 C4
Hindu Temple.......................4 C3
Kaivalyadhama Yoga Hospital.....5 B3
Karla Cave..........................6 C4
Lohagad Fort.......................7 C4
Visapur Fort........................8 C4

SLEEPING
Hotel Adarsh........................9 C1
Hotel Lonavla.......................10 C1
MTDC Karla Resort................11 C3

EATING
Fruit Market.......................12 D2
Hotel Gurukripa....................13 C1
Hotel Rama Krishna................14 C1

TRANSPORT
Bus Stand..........................15 C1
Famous Cycles......................16 C1

package, though two- and three-week sessions are also offered.

Mumbai-based **Nirvana Adventures** (☎ 022-26493110; www.nirvanaadventures.com) offers paragliding courses (three-day learner course from €250) or short tandem flights (Rs1500) at Kamshet, 25km from Lonavla.

Sleeping & Eating

Lonavla's hotels suffer from inflated prices and low standards. Most places are packed out during weekends and holidays. All hotels listed here have a 10am check-out time.

Hotel Lonavla (☎ 272914; Mumbai-Pune Hwy; d Rs995) Recently renovated, this place has small fan-only rooms, and seems a hit with corporate trainees coming for interaction programs. They insist that you clear your bills every third day, but who's staying that long, honestly?

Hotel Adarsh (☎ 272353; fax 278052; near Bus Stand; d with/without AC from Rs2000/1600; 🏊) Among the better options in town, this place has rather impressive and well-appointed rooms for the price. The management is smart and friendly, and a swimming pool is on its way to completion.

Hotel Gurukripa (Mumbai-Pune Hwy; mains Rs40-90) The dark interiors may leave you fumbling with your food, but the Punjabi dishes served here are truly worth savouring.

Hotel Rama Krishna (☎ 273600; Mumbai-Pune Hwy; dishes Rs50-120) The sleekest and busiest of the Lonavla lot, this place is famed for its meaty fare, especially the kebab preparations.

The bazaar, south of the train station, has a **fruit market**.

Getting There & Away

Lonavla is serviced by a host of MSRTC buses that depart from the **bus stand** (☎ 273842) to Dadar in Mumbai, (ordinary/semideluxe Rs58/75, two hours) and Pune (ordinary/semideluxe Rs47/60, two hours). You can hop onto luxury AC buses (about Rs100) plying the route to reach either city.

All express trains from Mumbai to Pune (2nd class/chair Rs56/190, 2½ hours) stop at Lonavla **train station** (☎ 273725). From Pune, you can also reach Lonavla by taking an hourly shuttle train (Rs14, two hours).

Bicycles can be hired from **Famous Cycles** (Mumbai-Pune Hwy; per hr Rs5).

KARLA & BHAJA CAVES

While they pale in comparison to Ajanta or Ellora, these rock-cut caves (dating from around the 2nd century BC) are definitely among the better examples of Buddhist cave architecture in India. They are also low on commercial tourism, which make them ideal places for a quiet excursion. Karla has the most impressive single cave, but Bhaja is a quieter, more enjoyable site to explore.

Karla Cave

Karla Cave (Indian/foreigner Rs5/100; 🕙 9am-5pm), the largest early Buddhist *chaitya* in India, is reached by a 20-minute climb from a mini-bazaar at the base of the hill. Completed in 80 BC, the *chaitya* is around 40m long and 15m high, and sports similar architectural motifs as *chaityas* in Ajanta and Ellora. Ellora's Kailasa Temple apart, this is probably the most impressive cave temple in the state.

Karla Cave is also the only site in Maharashtra where the original woodwork, more than two centuries old, has managed to survive. A semicircular 'sun window' filters light in towards a dagoba or stupa (the cave's representation of the Buddha), protected by a carved wooden umbrella, the only remaining example of its kind. The cave's roof also retains ancient teak buttresses. The 37 pillars forming the aisles are topped by kneeling elephants. The carved elephant heads on the sides of the vestibule once had ivory tusks.

The beauty of this cave is somewhat marred by the modern **Hindu temple** built in front of the cave mouth. However, the temple is a big draw for the pilgrims and their presence adds some colour to the scene.

Bhaja Caves

Across the expressway, it's a 3km jaunt from the main road to the **Bhaja Caves** (Indian/foreigner Rs5/100; 🕙 8am-6pm), where the setting is lusher, greener and quieter than at Karla Cave. Thought to date from around 200 BC, 10 of the 18 caves here are *viharas,* while Cave 12 is an open *chaitya,* earlier than Karla, containing a simple dagoba. Beyond this is a strange huddle of 14 stupas, five inside and nine outside a cave. From Bhaja Caves, you'll see the ruins of the **Lohagad** and **Visapur Forts**, which local kids will happily lead you to for a tip (not recommended during the rains).

Sleeping & Eating

MTDC Karla Resort (☎ 02114-282230; fax 282370; d from Rs800; 🏊 💻) Set near the access point to Karla and Bhaja Caves, this is the nicest option around Lonavla, where the silence and lush surroundings can overwhelm you. The rooms and pricier cottages are prim and well maintained, and there's a little lake where you can go boating. The resort has a restaurant, and is just off the Mumbai-Pune Hwy. Passing buses and autorickshaws can drop you within walking distance of the resort.

Getting There & Away

Karla and Bhaja can be visited over a single day from Lonavla. You can get to the access point to the caves on the highway by taking a local bus (Rs10, 30 minutes). From there, it's about a 6km return walk on each side to the two sites. A less rigorous option is to take an autorickshaw (Rs400) from Lonavla for a tour of both Karla and Bhaja, including waiting time.

PUNE

☎ 020 / pop 3.7 million / elev 457m

With its healthy mix of small-town wonders and big-city blues, Pune (also pronounced Poona) is a city that epitomises 'New India'. Once little more than a pensioners' town and an army outpost, it is today an unpretentious place with oodles of cosmopolitanism, inhabited by a cheerful and happy population. A thriving centre of academia and business, Pune is also known globally for its numero-uno export, the late guru Bhagwan Shree Rajneesh and his ashram, the Osho Meditation Resort (see the boxed text, right).

First given its pride of place by Shivaji and the ruling Peshwas who made it their capital, Pune fell to the British in 1817. Thanks to its cool and dry climate, it soon became the Bombay Presidency's monsoon capital. Globalisation knocked on Pune's doors in the 1990s, and the city went in for an image overhaul. However, the colonial charm was retained by preserving its old buildings and residential areas, bringing about a pleasant coexistence of the old and new which, despite the pollution and hectic traffic, now makes Pune a wonderful place to explore.

Orientation

The city sits at the confluence of the Mutha and Mula Rivers. Mahatma Gandhi (MG) Rd, about 1km south of Pune train station, is the main street lined with banks, restaurants and shops. Koregaon Park, northeast of the train station, is the undisputed chill-out zone, home

to some of the best restaurants and coffee shops frequented by travellers, and the city's uberchic crowd, and of course, the Osho Ashram.

MAPS

Destination Finder (Rs60) and *Geo Pune* (Rs200) are the best maps around. The former is more easily available; you can pick it up on platform 1 of the train station.

Information
BOOKSHOPS

Crossword (1st fl, Sohrab Hall, RBM Rd; ⌚ 10.30am-9pm) On Raibahadur Motilal (RBM) Rd. Offers a diverse collection of books and magazines.

Manneys Booksellers (7 Moledina Rd; ⌚ 10am-8pm)

INTERNET ACCESS

Several internet cafes dot Pune's main thoroughfares.

Cyber-Net (North Main Rd, Koregaon Park; per hr Rs20; ⌚ 8am-11.30pm) Opposite Citibank ATM; beats the competition with its lightning-fast broadband speed.

MONEY

Citibank has 24-hour ATMs on East St and North Main Rd. HSBC dispenses cash at its main branch on Bund Garden Rd. You'll find ICICI Bank and State Bank of India ATMs at the railway station and an Axis Bank ATM on MG Rd.

Thomas Cook (☎ 26346171; 2418 G Thimmaya Rd; ⌚ 9.30am-6pm Mon-Sat)

POST

Main post office (☎ 26125516; Sadhu Vaswani; ⌚ 10am-6pm Mon-Sat)

TOURIST INFORMATION

MTDC tourist office (☎ 26126867; I Block, Central Bldg, Dr Annie Besant Rd; ⌚ 10am-5.30pm Mon-Sat) Buried in a government complex south of the train station. There's an MTDC desk at the train station (open 9am to 7pm Monday to Saturday, and to 3pm Sunday).

TRAVEL AGENCIES

Rokshan Travels (☎ 26136304; rokshantravels@hot mail.com; 1st fl, 19 Kumar Pavilion, East St; ⌚ 10am-6pm) These guys shine when it comes to getting you on the right bus, train or flight without a glitch. They also book taxis.

Sights & Activities
OSHO MEDITATION RESORT

You'll either like it or hate it. A splurge of an institution, this **ashram** (☎ 66019999; www.osho

MAHARASHTRA

PUNE

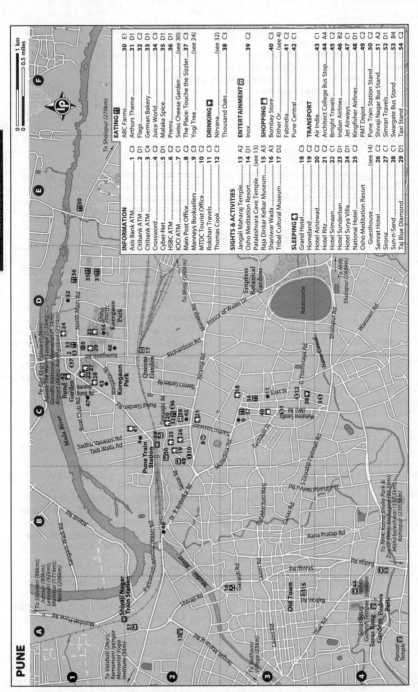

INFORMATION

Axis Bank ATM	1 C3
Citibank ATM	2 D1
Citibank ATM	3 D1
Crossword	4 C2
Cyber-Net	5 C1
HSBC ATM	6 D1
ICICI ATM	7 C1
Main Post Office	8 C3
Manneys Booksellers	9 D1
MTDC Tourist Office	10 C3
Rokshan Travels	11 C3
Thomas Cook	12 C3

SIGHTS & ACTIVITIES

Jangali Maharaj Temple	13 A2
Osho Meditation Resort	14 D1
Pataleshvara Cave Temple	(see 13)
Raja Dinkar Kelkar Museum	15 A3
Shaniwar Wada	16 A3
Tribal Cultural Museum	17 D2

SLEEPING

Grand Hotel	18 C3
Homeland	19 C3
Hotel Ashirwad	20 D1
Hotel Ritz	21 C2
Hotel Srimaan	22 C1
Hotel Sunderban	23 D1
Hotel Surya Villa	24 D1
National Hotel	25 C1
Osho Meditation Resort Guesthouse	(see 14)
Samrat Hotel	26 C2
Sirona	27 C1
Sun-n-Sand	28 C1
Taj Blue Diamond	29 D1

EATING

ABC Farms	30 E1
Arthurs Theme	31 D1
Flags	32 D1
German Bakery	33 D1
Juice World	34 C3
Malaka Spice	35 D1
Prems	36 D1
Swiss Cheese Garden	(see 30)
The Place: Touche the Sizzler	37 C3
Yogi Tree	(see 24)

DRINKING

Nirvana	(see 32)
Thousand Oaks	38 C3

ENTERTAINMENT

Inox	39 C2

SHOPPING

Bombay Store	40 C3
Either Or	(see 4)
Fabindia	41 C2
Pune Central	42 C1

TRANSPORT

Air India	43 C1
Architect College Bus Stop	44 A4
Bright Travels	45 C2
Indian Airlines	46 B2
Jet Airways	47 C1
Kingfisher Airlines	48 D1
PMT Depot	49 C2
Pune Train Station Stand	50 C2
Shivaji Nagar Bus Stand	51 A2
Simran Travels	52 C1
Swargate Bus Stand	53 B4
Taxi Stand	54 C2

.com; 17 Koregaon Park), located in a leafy, upscale northern suburb, has been drawing thousands of *sanyasins* (seekers), many of them Westerners, ever since the death of Osho (see the boxed text, p176) in 1990. With its placid swimming pool, sauna, 'zennis' and basketball courts, massage and beauty parlour, bookshop and a boutique guest house (p176), it is, to some, the ultimate place to indulge in some stress-busting meditation and rediscover one's lost spiritual self. Alternately, there are many who point fingers at the ashram's blatant commercialisation, calling it nothing short of a clever business ploy, marketing a warped version of the mystic East to gullible Westerners.

The main centre for meditation and the nightly white-robed spiritual dance is the Osho Auditorium (a cough-free and sneeze-free zone!). The Osho Samadhi, where the guru's ashes are kept, is also open for meditation. Pondering sessions apart, the commune is big business. Its 'Multiversity' runs a plethora of courses in meditation as well as New Age techniques. If you wish to take part, or even just to visit for the day to meditate, you'll have to pay Rs1300/1500 (Indian/foreigner), which covers registration, a mandatory on-the-spot HIV test (sterile needles used), introductory sessions and your first day's meditation pass. You'll also need two robes (one maroon and one white, from Rs200 per robe). For subsequent days, a daily meditation pass costs Rs200/500 (Indian/foreigner), and you can come and go as you please. If you want further involvement, you can also sign up for a 'work as meditation' program.

The curious can watch a video presentation at the visitor centre and take a 10-minute silent tour of the facilities (Rs10; adults only, cameras and phones prohibited) at 9.15am and 2pm daily. Tickets have to be booked at least a day in advance (9.30am to 1pm and 2pm to 4pm). If you decide not to enter the resort, it's worth checking out the placid 5-hectare gardens, **Osho Teerth** (admission free; 6-9am & 3-6pm), behind the commune; the gardens are accessible all day for those with a meditation pass.

RAJA DINKAR KELKAR MUSEUM
This fascinating **museum** (☎ 24461556; www .rajakelkarmuseum.com; 1377-1378 Natu Baug, Bajirao Rd; Indian/foreigner Rs50/200; 9.30am-5.30pm) is one of Pune's true delights. Housing only a fraction

of the 21,000-odd objects of daily life collected by Dinkar Gangadhar, who died in 1990, it's worth an entire day out. The quirky collection includes a suit of armour made of fish scales and crocodile skin, hookah pipes, writing instruments, lamps, toys, betel-nut cutters and an amazing gallery of musical instruments.

KATRAJ SNAKE PARK & ZOO
There's a mediocre selection of Indian wildlife on show at the **Katraj Snake Park & Zoo** (☎ 24367712; Pune-Satara Hwy; adult/child Rs3/2; 10.30am-6pm Thu-Tue). But a trip to this faraway park on Pune's southern outskirts makes sense if you want to know more about snakes, of which there are plenty. Most snakes are housed in open pits; don't lean over!

SHANIWAR WADA
The ruins of this fortresslike **palace** (Shivaji Rd; Indian/foreigner Rs5/100; 8am-6pm) stand in the old part of the city. Built in 1732, the palace of the Peshwa rulers burnt down in 1828, but the massive walls and plinths remain, as do the sturdy palace doors with their daunting spikes. In the evenings there is an hour-long **sound-and-light show** (admission Rs25; 8.15pm Thu-Tue).

PATALESHVARA CAVE TEMPLE
Set across the river is the curious rock-cut **Pataleshvara Cave Temple** (Jangali Maharaj Rd; 6am-9.30pm), a small and unfinished (though active) 8th-century temple, similar in style to the grander caves at Elephanta Island off the Mumbai coast. Adjacent is the **Jangali Maharaj Temple** (6am-9.30pm), dedicated to a Hindu ascetic who died here in 1818.

TRIBAL CULTURAL MUSEUM
About 1.5km east of the train station, at the southern end of the flyover, this obscure but excellent **museum** (☎ 26362071; Richardson Rd; admission free; 10.30am-5.30pm Mon-Sat) showcases an excellent collection of tribal jewellery sourced from remote parts of India. The section featuring ornate papier-mâché festival masks was being renovated during research, but was due to re-open soon.

GANDHI NATIONAL MEMORIAL
Set amid a sylvan 6.5-hectare plot across the Mula River in Yerwada, the grand **Aga Khan Palace & Gandhi National Memorial** (☎ 26680250; Ahmednagar Rd; Indian/foreigner Rs5/100; 9am-5.45pm)

SEX, SALVATION & THE STYLE GURU

Ever tried mixing spirituality with primal instincts, and garnishing the potent concoction with oodles of panache? Well, Bhagwan Shree Rajneesh (1931–90) certainly did – and how! Osho, as he preferred to be called, was one of India's most flamboyant 'export gurus' to market the mystic East to the world, and undoubtedly the most controversial. Initially based in Pune, he followed no particular religion or philosophy, and outraged many across the world with his advocacy of sex as a path to enlightenment. A darling of the international media, he quickly earned himself the epithet 'sex guru'. In 1981, Rajneesh took his curious blend of Californian pop psychology and Indian mysticism to the USA, where he set up an agricultural commune in Oregon. There, his ashram's notoriety as well as its fleet of (material and thus valueless!) Rolls Royces grew, until raging local paranoia about its activities running amok moved the authorities to charge Osho with immigration fraud. He was fined US$400,000 and deported. An epic journey then began, during which Osho and his followers, in their search for a new base, were deported from or denied entry to 21 countries. By 1987, he was back at his Pune ashram, where thousands of foreigners soon flocked for his nightly discourses and meditation sessions.

They still come in droves. To house them all, the capacious Osho Auditorium was unveiled in 2002, which saw the centre's name being changed from 'Osho Commune International' to 'Osho Meditation Resort'. Such is the demand for the resort's facilities that prices are continually on the rise, with luxury being redefined every day. Interestingly, despite Osho's comments on how nobody should be poor, no money generated by the resort goes into helping the disadvantaged. That, resort authorities maintain, is up to someone else.

is easily Pune's biggest crowd-puller. Built in 1892 by Sultan Aga Khan III, this lofty building was where the Mahatma and other prominent nationalist leaders were interned by the British for about two years following Gandhi's Quit India resolution in 1942. Both Kasturba Gandhi, the Mahatma's wife, and Mahadeobhai Desai, his secretary for 35 years, died here in confinement. You'll find their shrines (containing their ashes) in a quiet garden to the rear.

Within the main palace, you can peek into the room where Gandhi used to stay. Photos and paintings exhibit moments in his extraordinary career, but it's poorly presented.

RAMAMANI IYENGAR MEMORIAL YOGA INSTITUTE

To attend classes at this famous **institute** (☎ 25656134; www.bksiyengar.com; 1107 B/1 Hare Krishna Mandir Rd, Model Colony), 7km northwest of the train station, you need to have been practising yoga for at least eight years.

Sleeping

Pune's main accommodation hubs are around the train station and Koregaon Park. Many families rent out rooms to passing travellers, starting at about Rs250 (without bathroom) to about Rs600 (with bathrooms). For longer-term stays you can negotiate a room from Rs5000 to Rs12,000 per month. Rickshaw drivers will

know where to look (they get a cut from every deal) But don't go hunting after dark, especially if you're alone. Standards can vary widely.

BUDGET

Grand Hotel (☎ 26360728; grandhotelpune@gmail.com; MG Rd; d Rs770, s without bathroom Rs290) The cheapest beds here (and in all of Pune) are in cabins next to the bar, where you might get that seafaring feeling! The private rooms are in converted family homes, not the most luxurious of their kind. On the positive side, the patio bar is a good place for a beer.

National Hotel (☎ 26125054; 14 Sasson Rd; s/d/q Rs850/1000/1100, cottages s/d/q Rs650/750/950) It's a toss-up between charm and comfort at this run-down colonial mansion opposite the train station. The rooms in the main building border on suffocating, while the cottages across the garden have tiled sit-outs.

Homeland (☎ 26123203; www.hotelhomeland.net; 18 Wilson Garden; s/d from Rs800/1000; 🔣) A recent touch-up has made this place surprisingly restful. The labyrinthine corridors lead to rooms with fresh enamel-painted walls and clean sheets, and the restaurant downstairs shows movies in the evenings.

MIDRANGE

All hotels listed have a noon check out and accept credit cards.

Hotel Sunderban (☎ 26124949; www.tghotels .com; 19 Koregaon Park; d incl breakfast with/without AC from Rs1500/1000, without bathroom from Rs700; ✖ ▣) 'Wow' is the word! Located right next to the Osho Resort, this renovated art-deco bungalow effortlessly combines antiquity with style. The snug rooms, sporting a variety of classy furniture, get 30% cheaper if you drop in between April and September. The pricier rooms are across the lawns, in a sleek, glass-fronted building.

Hotel Surya Villa (☎ 26124501; www.hotel suryavilla.com; 294/1 Koregaon Park; s/d Rs1200/1500, with AC Rs1500/2000; ✖ ▣) Clearly the best among Pune's budget options, this cheerful place has bright, airy and spacious rooms and squeaky-clean loos. Managed by a spry lot, it stands just off the Koregaon backpacker hub, so you're always clued in to the coolest developments in town. Overall, a nice place to camp.

Samrat Hotel (☎ 26137964; thesamrathotel@vsnl .net; 17 Wilson Garden; s/d incl breakfast Rs1800/2200, with AC Rs2500/2900; ✖) Every Indian town has one hotel that shines above all the others and in Pune, that honour falls to Samrat. A sparkling modern hotel with excellent rooms opening around a central, top-lit foyer, this place sure knows how to make you feel at home.

Hotel Ritz (☎ 26122995; fax 26136644; 6 Sadhu Vaswani Path; s/d incl breakfast from Rs2550/2750; ✖) Plush, friendly, atmospheric: three words that sum it all up for the Ritz, a Raj-era building that holds its own in town. The pricy rooms are in the main building, while the cheaper ones are located in an annexe next to the garden restaurant, which serves good Gujarati and Maharashtrian food.

ourpick Osho Meditation Resort Guesthouse (☎ 66019900; www.osho.com; Koregaon Park; s/d Rs3000/3500; ✖) This place will allow you in only if you come to meditate at the Osho Meditation Resort (p173). The rooms in this stylish guest house are an exercise in modern aesthetics, as minimalist as they are chic. Add to that other luxe features, such as purified fresh air supply! Book well in advance; it's perpetually rushed.

Hotel Ashirwad (☎ 26128687; hotelashir@vsnl.net; 16 Connaught Rd; s/d from Rs3500/4000; ✖) A large, smooth-moving joint, this place stands out for its well-kept rooms and the popular Akshaya vegetarian restaurant downstairs, which serves a good range of Punjabi, Mughlai and Chinese fare.

Hotel Srimaan (☎ 26136565; srimaan@vsnl.com; 361/5 Bund Garden Rd; s/d Rs3500/4000; ✖ ▣) Jackson Pollock–inspired paintings lend their colour to the small but luxurious rooms in this hotel. The loos, though smart, are the size of those you'll only find on aeroplanes. A good Italian joint called La Pizzeria available on-site.

Sirona (☎ 40077000; hotelsirona@vsnl.net; 361/2 Bund Garden Rd; s/d Rs4000/4500; ✖ ▣) A sister property of Hotel Srimaan, this place has well-appointed rooms featuring all the requisite (and predictable) luxe features, but somehow there's little to tell them apart from the scores of rooms offered by other hotels in the same price bracket. DVD players and satellite radio are available on request.

TOP END

Taj Blue Diamond (☎ 66025555; www.tajhotels.com; 11 Koregaon Rd; d from Rs12,000; ✖ ▣ ♨) Being an elegant business hotel, this place possibly assumes you work on the move, so you have comfort features such as Aeron chairs at work desks in its wooden-floored rooms! It houses a stylish selection of restaurants, as well as the happening nightclub Polaris.

Sun-n-Sand (☎ 26167777; www.sunnsandhotel .com; 262 Bund Garden Rd; d incl breakfast from US$250; ✖ ▣ ♨) Centrally located on one of Pune's main thoroughfares, this luxury hotel has inviting rooms with large windows, soothing wall hues and classy upholstery. Some of the high-end rooms are fashionably built on split-levels and have gizmos such as LCD TVs.

Eating

Pune is a place with an adventurous palate. Predictably, there are a host of well-priced, high-quality eateries, many around Koregaon Park. Unless otherwise mentioned, the following are open noon to 3pm and 7pm to 11pm daily; last orders at 10.45pm.

RESTAURANTS

Vaishali (☎ 25531244; FC Rd; mains Rs30-70) The old-timers can't stop raving about this institution, known for its range of delicious snacks and meals. 'Don't miss the SPDP', notes a college student hanging out by the entrance. The scrumptious *sev potato dal puri* (Rs35), a favourite local snack, is what she means. Go find out for yourself!

Yogi Tree (☎ 26124501; 294/1 Koregaon Park; mains Rs50-150; ⏱ 8.30am-11pm) Below Hotel Surya Villa you'll find this cosy little restaurant with rainbow-coloured table linen, specialising in vegetarian organic food. Try the pizzas or

Indian curries that strike a deep chord with passing travellers.

Flags (☎ 26141617; G2 Metropole, Bund Garden Rd; mains Rs75-200) This super-popular global cuisine place was on hibernation mode during research, and should be back with its legendary Lebanese delights and dishes such as Mongolian cauliflower and *yakisoba* (fried Japanese noodles) soon.

Prems (☎ 66012413; North Main Rd, Koregaon Park; mains Rs100-250) In a quiet, leafy courtyard tucked away behind a commercial block, Prems is perfect for those lazy, beer-aided lunch sessions, and is patronised for its Indian, continental and Chinese selection.

The Place: Touche the Sizzler (☎ 26134632; 7 Moledina Rd; mains Rs120-200) As the name suggests, this long-running place specialises in sizzlers, but it also offers Indian, tandoori, seafood and continental dishes.

our pick **Malaka Spice** (☎ 26151088; Lane 6, North Main Rd; mains Rs120-350, ☿ 11am-11pm) A chic and happening restaurant that sometimes doubles as a gallery. Admire the artworks while gorging on some excellent Southeast Asian food, and wash it all down with one of the eatery's fine wines or a pint of fresh draught.

Arthur's Theme (☎ 66032710; Lane 6, North Main Rd, mains Rs150-300) A stylish place offering decent French cuisine in a slightly formal atmosphere. The dishes here have wacky names after figures such as Don Quixote. Taste for adventure, eh?

The ABC Farms is a complex of midrange restaurants in Koregaon Park, where healthy, organic food is the order of the day. One of the best restaurants here is the **Swiss Cheese Garden** (☎ 9890911923; mains Rs100-400), which, alongside delicious pastas, offers good old cheese fondues.

CAFES

German Bakery (North Main Rd, Koregaon Park; dishes Rs50-150, cakes Rs25-50; ☿ 6.30am-11.30pm) Pune's melting pot and a compulsory halt on the Koregaon Park backpacker trail, this long-running cafe is known for its light, healthy snacks and a good range of cakes and puddings.

Juice World (2436/B East St; ☿ 8am-11.30pm) As well as producing delicious fresh fruit juices and shakes, this casual cafe with outdoor seating serves inexpensive snacks such as pizza and *pav bhaji* (spiced vegetables and bread) for around Rs40 to Rs50.

Drinking & Entertainment

Pune puts a great deal of effort into nocturnal activities. But somehow, several pubs tend to shut up shop as quickly as they open. So ask around for the latest hotspots. Most are open from 7pm to around 1.30am. Some charge a weekend cover fee, around Rs200.

Nirvana (☎ 66024733; Metropole, Bund Garden Rd) Located in one of Pune's central hang-outs, this roomy, glowing lounge is a nice place to down drinks with gusto.

Thousand Oaks (☎ 26343194; 2417 East St) This one is an old favourite, featuring a cosy and quiet pub-style bar with a charming, moodily lit sit-out.

Inox (Bund Garden Rd) A state-of-the-art multiplex where you can take in the latest blockbuster, either from Hollywood or Mumbai.

Aquaa – The Water Lounge (☎ 65005566; 7th fl Tower C, Panchshil Tech Park, near Pune Golf Course, Yerwada) One of the city's newest and coolest addresses, this nightspot features funky interiors comprising aquariums and bar counters with aquamarine lights. The music is groovy; the crowd is quite sociable; and the bar shots simply keep coming!

Shopping

Pune has some good shopping options.

Bombay Store (322 MG Rd; ☿ 10.30am-8.30pm Mon-Sat) The best spot for general souvenirs.

Pune Central (Bund Garden Rd, Koregaon Park) This glass-fronted mall is full of Western high-street labels and premium Indian tags.

For modern Indian clothing, try **Either Or** (24/25 Sohrab Hall, 21 Sasson Rd; ☿ 10.30am-8pm Fri-Wed) or **Fabindia** (Sakar 10, Sasson Rd; ☿ 10am-8pm).

Getting There & Away
AIR
Airline offices in Pune:

Air India (airline code AI; ☎ 26128190; Hermes Kunj, 4 Mangaldas Rd)

Indian Airlines (airline code IC; ☎ 26052147; 39 Dr B Ambedkar Rd)

Jet Airways (airline code W8; ☎ 26123268; 243 Century Arcade, Narangi Bung Rd)

Kingfisher Airlines (airline code IT; ☎ 26059351; Koregaon Rd)

Indian Airlines, Jet Airways, Kingfisher and IndiGo fly daily from Pune to Delhi (from Rs1200, two hours), Bengaluru (from Rs750, 1½ hours), Kolkata (from Rs2300, three hours) and Goa (from Rs1000, one hour). Spicejet and

IndiGo have cheap flights to Chennai (from Rs100, 1½ hours). Kingfisher also flies daily to Ahmedabad, Chennai and Hyderabad.

BUS
Pune has three bus stands: **Pune train station stand** (☎ 26126218), for Mumbai and destinations south and west, including Goa, Belgaum, Kolhapur, Mahabaleshwar and Lonavla; **Shivaji Nagar bus stand** (☎ 25536970), for points north and northeast, including Aurangabad, Ahmedabad and Nasik; and **Swargate bus stand** (☎ 24441591), for Sinhagad, Bengaluru and Mangalore. Deluxe buses shuttle from the train-station bus stand to Dadar (Mumbai) every hour (Rs230, four hours).

Several private deluxe buses head to Panaji in Goa (ordinary/sleeper Rs300/400, 12 hours), Nasik (semideluxe/deluxe Rs150/250, five hours) and Aurangabad (Rs150, six hours). Prices can go up during rush periods. Make sure you know where the bus will drop you off (going to Mumbai, for instance, some private buses stop at Borivali). Try **Brright Travels** (☎ 26114222; Connaught Rd); its buses depart from the service station near the roundabout.

TAXI
Long-distance share taxis (four passengers) link up Pune with Dadar in Mumbai around the clock. They leave from the **taxi stand** (☎ 26121090) in front of Pune train station (per seat Rs355, 2½ hours). Several tour operators have an express Mumbai-airport drop-off scheme (Rs1600, 2½ hours). Try **Simran Travels** (☎ 26153222, 26159222; Koregaon Park).

TRAIN
Pune is an important rail hub with connections to many parts of the state. The swarming computerised **booking hall** (☎ 131) is to the left of the station as you face the entrance.

For getting to Mumbai, train is the safest option. The *Deccan Queen*, *Sinhagad Express* and *Pragati Express* are fast commuter trains to Mumbai (2nd class/chair Rs58/198, 2½ hours).

GETTING AROUND
The airport is 8km northeast of the city. An autorickshaw there costs about Rs80; a taxi is Rs250.

Turtle-paced city buses gather at the PMT depot, which is across from the train station. Useful buses include bus 4 to Swargate, bus 5 to Shivaji Nagar, and bus 159 to Koregaon Park.

Autorickshaws can be found everywhere. A ride from the train station to Koregaon Park costs about Rs30 in the daytime and Rs50 at night.

AROUND PUNE
Sinhagad
Now reduced to near-rubble, the scenic **Sinhagad** (admission free; ☉ dawn-dusk) or Lion Fort, about 24km southwest of Pune, is steeped in history. Earlier controlled by Bijapur, the fort was conquered by Shivaji after an epic battle in 1670, in which he lost his son Sambhaji. Legend has it that Shivaji used pet monitor lizards yoked with ropes to scale the craggy walls of the fort. Today, all is forgotten, and the fort's interiors are studded with telecommunication towers and ugly government buildings. However, it's worth a visit for the sweeping views it offers.

If you don't want to walk up 10km to reach the fort from Sinhagad village, jeeps (Rs30) can cart you to the base of the summit. Bus 50 runs frequently to Sinhagad village from 7am until evening, leaving from either Swargate or the Architect College bus stop opposite Nehru Stadium (Rs17, 45 minutes).

MAJOR TRAINS FROM PUNE

Destination	Train No & Name	Fare (Rs)	Duration (hr)	Departure
Bengaluru	6529 *Udyan Exp*	345/1295	21	11.45am
Chennai	2163 *Chennai Exp*	377/1372	19½	12.10am
Delhi	1077 *Jhelum Exp*	437/1654	27	5.20pm
Hyderabad	7031 *Hyderabad Exp*	250/926	13½	4.35pm
Mumbai CST	2124 *Deccan Queen*	77/270	3¼	7.15am

Express fares are sleeper/2AC; *Deccan Queen* fares are 2nd class/chair. To calculate 1st class and other fares see p532.

MAHARASHTRA

Shivneri

To history buffs, **Shivneri Fort** (admission free; ☼ dawn-dusk) holds the distinction of being the birthplace of the Maratha leader Shivaji. It's situated about 90km northwest of Pune, on an isolated and craggy hill to the south of the dusty village of Junnar. Within the triangular ramparts of the ruined fort are the old royal **stables**, a **mosque** dating back to the Mughal era and several rock-cut **water reservoirs**. Most important among them is **Shivkunj**, the house in which Shivaji is said to have been born. Situated in the northern quarters of the fort, the medieval pavilion has recently been restored; nearby, you'll find newly erected statues of Shivaji and his mother Jijabai. The approach-way to the fort is guarded by seven huge gate-ways; the fifth gate is more robust than the others and is armed with sheets of metal spikes meant to thwart elephant charges.

About 4km north of Shivneri, on the other side of Junnar, is an interesting group of Hinayana Buddhist caves known as **Lenyadri** (Indian/foreigner Rs5/100; ☼ dawn-dusk). The group comprises nearly 30 caves, of which caves 6 and 14 are *chaityas* (prayer halls), while the rest are *viharas* (monasteries/hostels). Cave 7 is the largest of the viharas, and curiously houses an image of the Hindu lord Ganesh.

You can get to Junnar by taking the 7.15am ordinary bus (Rs58, two hours) from Pune's Shivaji Nagar terminus; a return bus leaves Junnar at 11.30am. However, bus connections are infrequent thereafter, so if you want an entire day out and take in the Lenyadri caves, it's best to arrange for a day cab from Pune for around Rs1500.

MAHABALESHWAR

☎ 02168 / pop 12,700 / elev 1372m

With all due respect to its founders, Mahabaleshwar is one of the most character-less and congested hill stations you can find in India. High up in the Western Ghats, it was founded in 1828 by Sir John 'Boy' Malcolm, a British governor, after which it quickly be-came the summer capital of the Bombay presi-dency. But much of the old-world charm that the town once had has been undone today by mindless construction and lousy town plan-ning. Add to that the fact that it's a popular destination for sea-swept Mumbai weekend-ers, for whom this motor-exhaust-belching place is as good as a Himalayan getaway. What still works in Mahabaleshwar's favour, how-ever, are the delightful views it offers, but they may not be half as good in practice, given that you'll have to combat riotous tourists while appreciating them.

The hill station virtually shuts down during the monsoon season (June to September), when an unbelievable 6m of rain falls.

Orientation

The action is in the main bazaar (Main Rd, also called Dr Sabane Rd) – a 200m strip of holiday tack. The bus stand is at the western end. You have to cough up Rs15 as 'tourist tax' on arrival.

Information

Mahabaleshwar has no internet facilities. State Bank of India and Bank of Baroda have 24-hour ATMs on Masjid Rd.

Bank of Maharashtra (☎ 260290; Main Rd) Changes cash and travellers cheques.

Krsna Travels (☎ 261035; Subhash Chowk, Main Rd; ☼ 9am-8pm) Reliable onward travel information, a variety of local tours and ticketing.

MTDC tourist office (☎ 260318; Bombay Point Rd) At the MTDC Resort south of town.

Sights & Activities

The hills are alive with music, though it's usu-ally blasted out of car windows as people race by in an effort to tick off all the viewpoints as quickly as possible. If you can ignore this, or beat them by starting your day early, then fine views can be savoured from **Wilson's Point** (also known as Sunrise Point), within easy walk-ing distance of town, as well as **Elphinstone**, **Babington**, **Kate's** and **Lodwick Points**.

The sunset views at **Bombay Point** are stun-ning; but you won't be the only one thinking so! Much quieter, thanks to being 9km from town, is **Arthur's Seat**, on the edge of a sheer drop of 600m. Attractive waterfalls around Mahabaleshwar include **Chinaman's**, **Dhobi's** and **Lingmala Falls**. On the edge of Venna Lake, a **boat-house** (Temple Rd; ☼ 8am-8pm) rents out rowboats (Rs180 per hour) and pedal boats (Rs200 per hour), but the long queues can be off-putting.

A nice walk out of town is the two-hour stroll to Bombay Point, then following **Tiger Trail** back in (maps are available from the MTDC tourist office).

Tours

The MSRTC conducts sightseeing tours for the very rushed. The Mahabaleshwar round

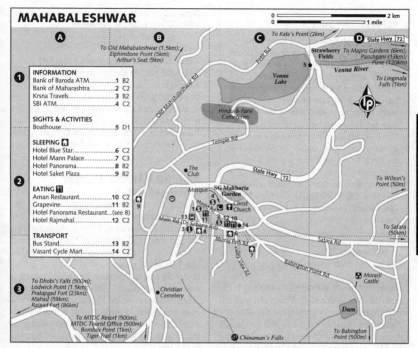

MAHABALESHWAR

0   2 km
0   1 mile

INFORMATION
Bank of Baroda ATM..............1 B2
Bank of Maharashtra..............2 C2
Krsna Travels..............3 B2
SBI ATM..............4 B2

SIGHTS & ACTIVITIES
Boathouse..............5 D1

SLEEPING
Hotel Blue Star..............6 C2
Hotel Mann Palace..............7 C3
Hotel Panorama..............8 B2
Hotel Saket Plaza..............9 B2

EATING
Aman Restaurant..............10 C2
Grapevine..............11 B2
Hotel Panorama Restaurant...(see 8)
Hotel Rajmahal..............12 C2

TRANSPORT
Bus Stand..............13 B2
Vasant Cycle Mart..............14 C2

MAHARASHTRA

(Rs65, 4½ hours) takes in nine viewpoints plus Old Mahabaleshwar, leaving the bus stand thrice from 2.15pm. Alternatively, taxi drivers will give a three-hour tour for about Rs400. Tours are also available to lookout points south of town (Rs300, 2½ hours), Panchgani (Rs400, three hours) and Pratapgad Fort (Rs450, three hours).

Sleeping & Eating

Hotel prices soar during peak holidays in Mahabaleshwar (November to June); at other times you might get heavy discounts. Most budget places are around the main bazaar, while dozens of resort-style lodges are scattered around the village – check out is usually at 8am or 9am. Single travellers can forget about camping in town; local laws bar hotels from renting out rooms to loners, especially men. Rates quoted here are high-season prices.

MTDC Resort (☎ 260318; fax 260300; d from Rs900) This large-scale operation is situated about 2km southwest from town, and comes with quieter and greener surroundings. Rooms smack of government aesthetics, but that's

no deterrent. Taxis can drop you here from the city centre for about Rs50.

Hotel Blue Star (☎ 260678; 114 Main Rd; d Rs1200) These guys offer hefty low-season discounts, which is just about the right value for the mediocre rooms. It sits on the main thoroughfare, which you might consider a bonus.

Hotel Mann Palace (☎ 261778; Murray Peth Rd; d Rs1500) This place flanks a quiet street below the main market. The neighbourhood is dingy, but the rooms are well cared for, and the staff a professional lot.

Hotel Panorama (☎ 260404; www.panoramaresorts.net; 28 MG Rd; d from Rs3500;) A midtown luxury joint, this is where business meets leisure. The rooms have recently been given a facelift, and the food at its vegetarian restaurant is recommended. If you go swimming in its pool, look out for oncoming swan-shaped paddle boats!

Hotel Saket Plaza (☎ 260583; www.saketplaza.com; Old Band Rd; d incl full board from Rs3900) Located pleasantly away from the din, this place is more of a family joint, with associated facilities such as indoor games. The beds are comfy, the food highly palatable and AC available for Rs300 extra.

MAHARASHTRA

BERRIES, ANYONE?

Fruity Mahabaleshwar is India's berry-growing hub, producing some of the country's finest strawberries, raspberries, mulberries and gooseberries. The best crops come around February, though fruits are harvested from late November through June. If you're visiting during the season, you can buy fresh berries direct from the farms, or get them from the many vendors in Mahabaleshwar's bazaar. In the absence of fresh fruits, you can always pick up fruit drinks, sweets, fudges or jams. One place to shop for farm-fresh stuff is **Mapro Gardens** (☎ 02168-240112; ⏱ 10am-1pm & 2pm-6.30pm), between Mahabaleshwar and Panchgani.

Hotel Rajmahal (80 Main Rd; meals Rs40-75) A good place to dig into some lip-smacking vegie delights.

Aman Restaurant (Main Rd; kebabs Rs50-100) Little more than a roadside stall, Aman can pull out some amazing meaty bites from the skewers.

Grapevine (Masjid Rd; dishes Rs60-180) Get ready for charming wrought-iron furniture topped with Mediterranean-themed placemats topped with the choicest Parsi and continental dishes, with a glass of wine for the added effect. Skip this place, and you've missed half the fun in town.

Mahabaleshwar is famous for its berries, which you can buy fresh (in season) or as juice, fruit bars and jams (see the boxed text; above).

Getting There & Away

From the **bus stand** (☎ 260254) state buses leave regularly for Pune (ordinary/semideluxe Rs82/100, 3½ hours), with less frequent buses rolling to Satara (Rs43, two hours), Panchgani (Rs12, 30 minutes) and Mahad (for Raigad Fort; Rs39, two hours). Two buses go daily to Kolhapur (Rs125, five hours), while eight buses ramble off to Mumbai Central Station (ordinary/semideluxe Rs156/200, seven hours).

Private agents in the bazaar book luxury buses to destinations within Maharashtra, and Goa (seat/sleeper Rs550/750, 12 hours, with a changeover at Surur). Remember to ask where they intend to drop you. Buses to Mumbai (Rs400, 6½ hours) generally don't go beyond

Borivali, while those bound for Pune (Rs200) will bid you adieu at Swargate.

Getting Around

Taxis and Maruti vans near the bus stand will take you to the main viewpoints or to Panchgani. For trips within town, the minimum charge is Rs30 (for up to 2km).

Cycling around is an option, but be careful of speeding traffic especially on the outskirts. Bikes can be hired from **Vasant Cycle Mart** (Main Rd; ⏱ 8am-9pm) for Rs10 per hour or Rs50 per day.

AROUND MAHABALESHWAR
Pratapgad Fort

Closely associated with Deccan's history, the windy **Pratapgad Fort** (maintenance fee Rs5; ⏱ 7am-7pm), built by Shivaji in 1656, straddles a high Sahyadri ridge 24km west of Mahabaleshwar. It was here that a cornered Shivaji agreed to meet Bijapuri general Afzal Khan in an attempt to end a stalemate in 1659. Despite a no-arms agreement, Shivaji, upon greeting Khan, disembowelled his enemy with a set of iron *baghnakh* (tiger's claws). Khan's tomb marks the site of this painful encounter at the base of the fort, though it's out of bounds for tourists.

Pratapgad is reached by a 500-step climb, which affords brilliant views. Guides are available for Rs150. To get here from Mahabaleshwar, you can take the 9.30am state bus (Rs72 return, one hour). It waits at the site for an hour before returning. A taxi to Pratapgad and back costs Rs450.

Raigad Fort

Some 80km northwest of Mahabaleshwar, all alone on a remote hilltop, stands **Raigad Fort** (Indian/foreigner Rs5/100; ⏱ 8am-5.30pm), a must-see for history buffs. This was Shivaji's capital, from where he held sway over his vast empire, from when he was crowned in 1648 until his death in 1680. Much of the fort was later destroyed by the British, and some colonial structures added. But monuments such as the royal court, plinths of royal chambers, the main marketplace and Shivaji's tomb still remain, and are worth a daylong excursion.

You can hike to the top; it's a 2½-hour steep haul up 1475 steps. For an offbeat experience, take the vertigo-inducing **ropeway** (☎ 02145-274831; ⏱ 8.30am-5.30pm), which zooms up the cliff and offers an eagle-eye view of the gorges below. A return ticket costs Rs150. Guides (Rs150) are available within the fort complex.

Raigad is best reached by bus from Mahad (Rs15, 45 minutes) on the Mumbai–Goa highway. Or you can take a taxi tour direct from Mahabaleshwar (Rs1200).

KOLHAPUR

☎ 0231 / pop 505,500 / elev 550m

It's surprising why people rarely visit Kolhapur, even though this historically important town offers a great opportunity to get up close and personal with the vibrant side of India. Its proximity to Goa, a friendly population and an intriguing temple complex are enough reasons why you should go, and chances are that Kolhapur will end up being the most fascinating discovery on your trip. Gastronomes take note: the town is also the birthplace of the famed, spicy Kolhapuri cuisine, especially chicken and mutton dishes.

In August, Kolhapur hosts **Naag Panchami**, a snake-worshipping festival, in tandem with Pune.

Orientation

The old town around the Mahalaxmi Temple is 3km southwest of the bus and train stations, while the 'new' palace is a similar distance to the north. Rankala Lake, a popular spot for evening strolls, is 5km southwest of the stations.

Information

Axis Bank (Station Rd) Has a 24-hour ATM below Hotel Panchsheel.

Internet Zone (Kedar Complex, Station Rd; per hr Rs20; ⏰ 8am-11pm) Internet access.

MTDC tourist office (☎ 2652935; Assembly Rd; ⏰ 10am-5.30pm Mon-Sat) Opposite the Collector's Office.

State Bank of India (☎ 2660735; Udyamnagar) A short autorickshaw ride southwest of the train station near Hutatma Park. Deals in foreign exchange.

Sights

SHREE CHHATRAPATI SHAHU MUSEUM

'Bizarre' takes on a whole new meaning at this 'new' palace, built by the Kolhapur kings in 1884. Designed by British architect 'Mad' Charles Mant, this Indo-Saracenic behemoth still serves as the royal family's private residence. The ground floor houses a wacky **museum** (☎ 2538060; Indian/foreigner Rs13/30; ⏰ 9.30am-5.30pm), with one of the most peculiar collections of memorabilia in the country.

An unconventional sort of an animal-lover, the eponymous king went on several trigger-happy trips into the jungles. The trophies he returned with were then put to some ingenious use, such as making walking sticks from tiger vertebrae, or fashioning ashtrays out of rhino feet! Then, there's an armoury, which houses enough weapons to stage a mini coup. The horror-house effect is brought full circle by the taxidermy section, where you'll see everything from tigers to African dik-diks! Don't forget to visit the durbar hall, a rather ornate affair, where the king once held court sessions. Photography is strictly prohibited.

OLD TOWN

Kolhapur's atmospheric old town is built around the lively and colourful **Mahalaxmi Temple** (⏰ 5am-10.30pm) dedicated to Amba Bai, or the Mother Goddess. The temple's origins date back to AD 10, but much of the modern structure is from the 18th century. It's one of the most important Amba Bai temples in India and therefore attracts an unceasing tide of humanity. Non-Hindus are welcome and it's a fantastic place for a spot of people-watching. Nearby, past a foyer in the Old Palace, is **Bhavani Mandap** (⏰ 6am-8pm), dedicated to the goddess Bhavani.

Kolhapur is famed for the calibre of its wrestlers and at the **Motibag Thalim**, a courtyard beside the entrance to Bhavani Mandap, young athletes train away in a muddy pit. You are free to walk in and watch, as long as you don't mind the sight of sweaty, seminaked men and the stench of urine emanating from the loos! Professional matches are held between June and December in the **Kasbagh Maidan**, a red-earth arena in a natural sunken stadium a short walk south of Motibag Thalim. Events are announced in local papers.

Finally, if you're a shopaholic, the streets of the old town are crammed with shops where the hard sale of some Indian tourist cities is unheard of. Kolhapur produces the renowned Kolhapuri leather sandals, prized the world over for their intricate needlework. You can drive a good bargain here; most designs come within Rs200 to Rs400. By the way, the sandals are notorious for blistering your feet when new!

CHANDRAKANT MANDARE MUSEUM

Dedicated to actor and artist Chandrakant Mandare (1913–2001), this well-maintained **gallery** (☎ 2525256; Rajarampuri, 7th Lane; admission Rs3;

10.30am-1pm & 1.30-5.30pm Tue-Sun) houses stills of his movies as well as his fine paintings and sketches.

Sleeping & Eating

Kolhapur's hotels are of very good value, and most of them line Station Rd, which appropriately enough is the busy main street running west of the train station.

Hotel Tourist (☎ 2650421; Station Rd; s/d incl breakfast from Rs525/675; 🗙) Known for its quality service, this place was undergoing renovation during research, and should emerge an even better place.

Hotel Vrindavan Deluxe (☎ 2664343; Station Rd; s/d from Rs550/650; 🗙) These folks have done a neat job imitating urban business hotels. The rooms sport sleek orange and buff upholstery, and open onto a breezy central vestibule. It's near Shivaji Park, and street noise is a downside.

Hotel Pavillion (☎ 2652751; www.hotelpavillion.co.in; 392E, Assembly Rd; s/d incl breakfast from Rs850/1000; 🗙) Located at the far end of a foliaged park–cum–office area, this wonderful place has large rooms with windows that open out to a splendid view of seasonal blossoms. It's very close to the MTDC office.

Hotel Pearl (☎ 6684451; hotelpearl@hotmail.com; New Shahupuri; s/d incl breakfast from Rs1700/1900; 🗙 💻) It's expensive by Kolhapur's standards, but has an ambience even city hotels would be jealous of. The rooms are large, smart and well equipped, and service is commendable.

Surabhi (Hotel Sahyadri Bldg; snacks & mains Rs20-50) This bustling eatery is the right place in town to sample some of Kolhapur's legendary snacks such as *misal* (a spicy snack not unlike *bhelpuri*), thalis and lassi.

Getting There & Around

Rickshaws are abundant in Kolhapur and most drivers are honest with their billing. Most carry conversion charts to calculate fares from outdated meters.

From the **bus stand** (☎ 2650620), services head regularly to Pune (ordinary/semideluxe Rs152/195, five hours), Mahabaleshwar (Rs125, five hours) and Ratnagiri (Rs90, four hours). For longer hauls, your body will be happier on a deluxe private bus. Most of the private bus agents are on the western side of the square at Mahalaxmi Chambers, across from the bus stand. Overnight services with AC head to Mumbai (seat/sleeper Rs350/600, nine hours) and non-AC overnighters go to Panaji (Rs180, 5½ hours).

The **train station** (☎ 2654389) is 10 minutes' walk west of the bus stand. Three daily expresses, including the 10.50pm *Sahyadri Express*, zoom to Mumbai (sleeper/2AC Rs206/750, 12½ hours) via Pune (Rs163/584, eight hours). The 2.05pm *Rani Chennamma Express* makes the long voyage to Bengaluru (sleeper/2AC Rs299/1117, 17½ hours). You can also fly cheap between Kolhapur and Mumbai on a daily basis with Kingfisher Red (from Rs450).

Goa

It's green, it's glistening and it's gorgeous: just three of the reasons why Goa has allured visitors – both of the friendly and invading varieties – for so many hundreds of years. Today, the biggest drawcard to its over two million annual visitors is the silken sand, the cocohut culture and the *sossegado* (clunkily translated as 'laid-backness') of which its residents are justifiably proud.

Nowhere else in India will you find the warmth of a Goan household and the lack of hassle when haggling for goods in its bustling marketplaces. Pour in a dash of Portuguese-influenced wine, food and crumbling colonial-era architecture, infuse with a colourful blend of Hinduism, Islam and Catholicism, pepper with parties, and you've got a happy, heady mix that proves just too enticing to long-staying foreigners, who've been clinging to its crystalline shores since the '60s.

But there's far more to discover here than the exquisite pleasure of warm sand between your toes. Pep up your stay with a wander around a vanilla-scented spice plantation, stroll the bird-filled banks of the state's gentle rivers, poke around centuries-old cathedrals, and venture out to white-water waterfalls.

All is not perfect in paradise, however, and Goa has problems aplenty – the state's environment, in particular, being today sorely taxed. Nevertheless, with a slowly growing group of environmentalists and eco-friendly individuals on the scene, the picture remains relatively rosy for this most magical of miniature states. So, come, minimise your impact as much as possible, and unwind to the swaying palms and Portuguese rhythms of Goa's still-irresistible charms.

HIGHLIGHTS

- Wander the Portuguese-flavoured old quarters of **Panaji** (Panjim; p191) and linger over lunch at one of its ravishing restaurants

- Shiver in the shadows of grand cathedrals in **Old Goa** (p198), once the ecclesiastical wonder of the Eastern world

- Indulge in barefoot luxury on quiet white-sand **beaches** (p222) in the state's sleepy southern stretches

- Dream of grand times long gone in the slowly crumbling mansions of **Chandor** (p224)

- Peruse the peppercorns and munch a banana-leaf lunch at an inland spice plantation around **Ponda** (p201)

- Worship or salute the sun away from the northern crowds on **Mandrem's beautiful beach** (p219)

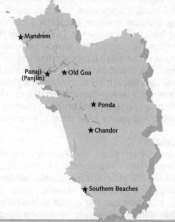

FAST FACTS

Population 1.34 million

Area 3701 sq km

Telephone code ☎ 0832

Main languages Konkani, Marathi, English and Hindi

When to go November to March

History

Probably the most influential event in Goan history, the effects of which are still evident today, was the coming of the Portuguese in 1510, who arrived seeking control of the region's lucrative spice routes by way of Goa's wide natural harbours and plentiful waterways, defeating the ruling Bijapur kings, and steadily pushing their power from their grand capital at Old Goa, out into the provinces.

Soon, the conquerors were seeing to it that not only Portuguese rule, but their religion too, was spread throughout the state – by force, if need be – and the Goan Inquisition saw repression and brutality in the name of Christianity. Though the Marathas – the central Indian people who controlled much of India at various points in history – almost vanquished the Portuguese in the late 18th century, and despite a brief occupation by the British during the Napoleonic Wars in Europe, it was not until 1961, when the Indian army marched into Goa, that almost five centuries of Portuguese occupation finally came to an end on the subcontinent.

Today Goa enjoys one of India's highest per-capita incomes and comparatively high health and literacy rates, with farming, fishing, tourism and iron-ore mining forming the basis of its economy. The legacy of the Portuguese can still be found almost everywhere, in the state's scores of crumbling mansions, its cuisine, its churches and even in its language; though it's slowly becoming rarer, if you keep an ear out you'll likely hear elderly people sitting together and conversing in Portuguese during some point in your stay.

Climate

Until recent years, the annual monsoon scoured Goa's beaches clean between June and the end of September reliably, but lately things have gone a little haywire. Sometimes the monsoon can end as late as November, while 2008 saw a poor monsoon and temperatures soaring to unusual heights well before December. In general, though, the tourist season stretches from mid-November to mid-April, with December to February proving the most pleasant (and busiest) time to visit. Temperatures and humidity increase after February, making it great for those who can stand the heat. Out of season, between April and October, you'll find most coastal resorts all but deserted, though towns like Panaji, Mapusa and Margao chug on as usual.

Information

The **Goa Tourism Development Corporation** (GTDC; www.goa-tourism.com), provides maps and information, operates (largely adequate but uncharismatic) hotels throughout the state, and runs a whole host of whirlwind one-day and multiday bus trips, as well as daily boat cruises from Panaji. Its main branches are in Panaji (p192) and at Dabolim Airport (see p189), but you can book its tours, its hotel rooms, and pick up a simple map of Goa at any of its hotel branches. Information on the state is also up for grabs at the Government of India tourist office in Panaji (p192).

ACCOMMODATION

Accommodation prices in Goa are generally higher than in most other states of India, and vary wildly depending on the season. High-season prices – often more than 100% more than mid-season rates – run from early December to early February, while prices climb higher still during the crowded Christmas and New Year period (around 22 December to 3 January). Mid-season runs from October to late November, and February to April, and low season runs throughout the monsoon, from April to October.

All accommodation rates indicated in this chapter are for high season. Budget-category double rooms come in at under Rs1000 per night. Midrange doubles range between Rs1000 and Rs2500, and top-end choices come in at over Rs2500. Note, however, that prices can fluctuate incredibly from year to year.

Most accommodation options have a standard noon checkout, except, rather inexplicably, in Panaji, where almost all hotels cruelly demand you depart at 9am.

Activities

Goa has, of late, become Activity Central, with a whole host of options for water sports,

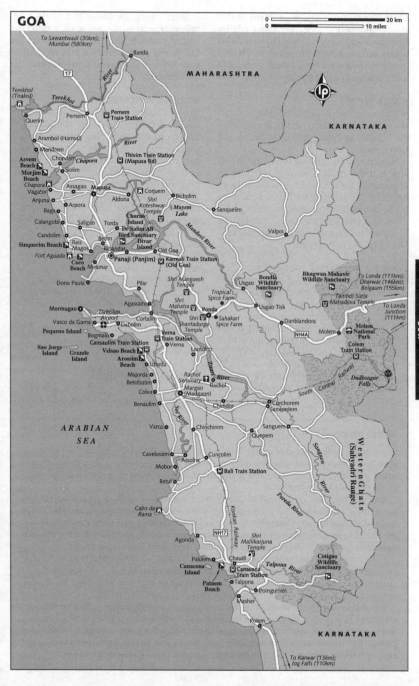

GOA

To Sawantwadi (30km);
Mumbai (580km)

Terekhol
(Tirakol)

Querim

Arambol (Harmal)

Mandrem

Asvem Beach
Morjim Beach
Vagator
Anjuna
Baga
Calangute
Candolim
Sinquerim Beach
Fort Aguada
Coco Beach
Miramar

Dona Paula

Mormugao
Vasco da Gama
Pequeno Island
Sao Jorge Island
Grande Island

Chodanem
Siolim
Assagao
Arpora
Saligao
Torda
Reis Magos
Betim
Ribandar

Banda

MAHARASHTRA

Pernem
Pernem Train Station

River

Chapora
Chapora

Mapusa

Aldona
Chorao Island
Dr Salim Ali Bird Sanctuary
Divar Island

Panaji (Panjim)

Pilar

Agassaim

Dabolim Airport
Cortalim
Dabolim
Bogmalo
Cansaulim Train Station
Velsao Beach
Arossim Beach
Utorda
Majorda
Betelbatim
Colva
Benaulim

Varca

Cavelossim
Mobor

Betul

Cabo da Rama

Agonda

Pa! olem
Canacona Island
Patnem Beach

ARABIAN SEA

Konkan Railway

Corjuem
Bicholim

Shri Koteshwar Temple
Mayem Lake

Sanquelim

Valpoi

Mandovi River

Old Goa
Karmali Train Station (Old Goa)

Shri Manguesh Temple
Shri Mahalsa Temple
Usgao
Tropical Spice Farm
Ponda
Shri Shantadurga Temple
Sahakari Spice Farm
Usgao Tisk

Danblandora

NH4A

Verna Train Station
Verna
Loutolim

Rachol Seminary
Rachol

Margao
(Madgaon)

Chandor

Corchorem
Sanvordem

Chinchinim

Sanguem

Quepem

Assolna
Cuncolim
Bali Train Station

Shri Mallikarjuna Temple

Chaudi
Canacona Train Station
Talpona

Poinguinim

Masher

Polem

KARNATAKA

KARNATAKA

Bondla Wildlife Sanctuary

Bhagwan Mahavir Wildlife Sanctuary

To Londa (111km);
Dharwar (146km);
Belgaum (155km)

Tambdi Surla Mahadeva Temple

To Londa Junction (111km)

Molem
Molem National Park
Colem Train Station

Dudhsagar Falls

South Central Railway

W e s t e r n G h a t s
(Sahyadri Range)

Sanguem River

Paroda River

Talpona River

Cotigao Wildlife Sanctuary

To Karwar (13km);
Jog Falls (110km)

0 — 20 km
0 — 10 miles

GOA

alternative therapies and yoga. Many outfits change annually – especially those run by foreigners – so it's best to head to your destination and ask around. There's no shortage of noticeboards and keen individuals on hand to bring you up to speed on current options.

WATER SPORTS
Water sports such as parasailing and jet-skiing are particularly readily available on the beaches at Baga (p209), Benaulim and Colva (p226).

You can try paragliding at Anjuna (p214) and Arambol (p220), where there's also an opportunity for kite surfing. Based in Baga, Barracuda Diving (p209), offers a range of scuba-diving opportunities, including boat dives and PADI (Professional Association of Diving Instructors) courses, as does Goa Diving (p226) in Bogmalo.

YOGA & ALTERNATIVE THERAPIES
From *ashtanga* through to Zen, every imaginable form of yoga, along with reiki, ayurvedic massage and a multitude of other spiritually orientated health regime, is practised, taught and relished in Goa. Palolem and Patnem (p229), in the south of the state, and Arambol (p220), Mandrem (p219) and Anjuna (p214) in the north are great places to take courses in reiki and manifold forms of yoga, t'ai chi and healing, and many also host retreat centres for longer meditation and yoga courses.

Since course locations and contact details change annually, we've only listed the longer-established operations here; for the full gamut of options, it's best to head to your beach of choice and scan hotel and cafe noticeboards.

WILDLIFE-WATCHING
Goa is a nature-lover's paradise, perfect for wildlife-watching, with an abundance of brilliant birdlife and a fine (but largely well-concealed) collection of fauna, including sambars, barking deer and the odd leopard. Head to Cotiago Wildlife Sanctuary (p229) to scout out birds and beasts alike, or to the Tropical Spice Plantation (p201) which offers waterborne birdwatching on its lake. Serious birding enthusiasts should consider a multi-day expedition to the jungly Backwoods Camp (p202), where dozens of dazzling species are easily spotted. Day Tripper in Calangute (p209) offers various nature-related tours, while John's Boat Tours in Candolim (p205) offers birdwatching boat trips, along with sea-based dolphin tours and crocodile-spotting trips up the Mandovi River. At almost any beach, though, you'll be sure to find someone with a boat and a strong desire to show you (on a no-show, no-pay basis) those adorable grey mammals of the waves.

Dangers & Annoyances
One of the greatest – and most deceptive – dangers in Goa is to be found right in front

---

WHERE TO GOA...
Where to go during your stay in this little beachy paradise depends very much on what you want to do when you get here, though, with enough time and possibly a scooter on which to spend some of it, you should be able to experience a little of everything that takes your fancy in this relatively tiny Indian state.

Very generally, Goa can be split up into three distinct regions: north, south and central. The north, above the Mandovi River, is the place for those seeking action, shopping and activities in equal supply, and for folks looking for the remnants of Goa's fabled trance party scene. In addition, the north boasts some beautiful stretches of almost-empty beach, along with a string of highly developed resorts with lots of choice in restaurants, hotels and water-sports outfits.

Head into central Goa, nestling between the Mandovi and Zuari Rivers, and things get decidedly more cultural. Here sits Panaji, Goa's small and loveable state capital, which slings itself lazily along the broad banks of the Mandovi River, while inland lie spice plantations and the glorious remnants of Goa's grand and glittering past in the form of mansions, temples and cathedrals.

Things slow down in the south, where the beaches grow generally quieter and the sun-lounges are spaced further apart. Not the place for partying the night away, the beaches here cater to a quieter, calmer crowd, with lots of homespun charm. This is the place to sit back, unwind, and perhaps spot a hatching turtle or two, before saddling up your scooter and heading back up the twisting National Highway (NH17) to the bright lights and big beaches of the north.

FESTIVALS IN GOA

Feast of Three Kings (6 Jan; Chandor, p224) Held in historic Chandor, local boys re-enact the story of the three kings bearing gifts for Christ.

Shigmotsav (Shigmo) of Holi (Feb/Mar; statewide) Goa's version of the Hindu spring festival Holi, this festival sees coloured water and powders thrown about with abandon, and joyous parades held in most towns.

Sabado Gordo (Fat Saturday; Feb/Mar; Panaji, p191) Part of the statewide Carnival, this festival is held on the Saturday before Lent. It's celebrated by a procession of floats and raucous street partying.

Carnival (Mar; statewide) A three-day festival heralding the arrival of spring, the party's particularly raucous in the streets of Panaji.

Procession of All Saints (Mar/Apr; Goa Velha, p198) On the fifth Monday in Lent, this is the only procession of its sort outside Rome, whereby 30 statues of saints are paraded around Old Goa and neighbouring villages.

Fama de Menino Jesus (2nd Mon in Oct; Colva, p225) Colva's biggest feast day, when the Menino Jesus (a statue of the infant Jesus said to perform miracles) is paraded through town.

Feast of Our Lady of Livrament (mid-Nov; Panaji, p195) This feast, celebrated at Panaji's diminutive Chapel of St Sebastian, culminates in a colourful street festival lining the back lanes of the capital's old Fontainhas district.

International Film Festival of India (IFFI; www.iffi.nic.in; over 10 days from the last week of Nov; Panaji, p191) Based in Goa since 2004, this is the largest film festival in India and sees the glitterati of Mumbai arrive in Panaji for premiers and parties aplenty.

Feast of St Francis Xavier (3 Dec; Old Goa, p198) Old Goa's biggest bash, this feast sees lots of festivities, processions, and huge crowds. Once every decade, an exposition involves the patron saint's body being paraded through Old Goa's streets. The next is scheduled for 2014.

Feast of Our Lady of the Immaculate Conception (8 Dec; Margao, p222, & Panaji, p191) A large fair and a church service is held at the Church of Our Lady of the Immaculate Conception in Panaji. Around the same time, Margao celebrates with a large fair.

Sunburn Festival (late Dec; www.sunburnfestival.com; Dec; Candolim, p205) Four-day dance music festival, attracting scores of international DJs and revellers to party Christmas away beside the sea.

of your beautiful bit of beach. The Arabian Sea, with its strong currents and dangerous undertows, claims dozens of lives per year, many of them foreign. Lonely Planet has received one letter from a reader whose adult daughter and her friend both drowned while paddling in the sea in north Goa.

Though some of Goa's beaches are now overseen by lifeguards during daylight hours, it's most important to heed local warnings on the safety of swimming, and don't, whatever you do, venture into the water after drinking or taking drugs.

Other dangers and annoyances are of the rather more universal kind. Be sure to keep your valuables under lock and key – especially if you're renting an easy-to-penetrate cocohut – and don't walk along empty stretches of beach alone at night. Away from the beaches,

it makes sense for visitors of both sexes to adopt the same, more modest forms of dress that they would in other parts of the country. See p516 for advice specifically for women travellers.

DRUGS

Acid, ecstasy, cocaine, *charas* (cannabis or hashish), marijuana and all other forms of recreational drugs are illegal in India (though still very much available in Goa), and purchasing or carrying drugs is fraught with danger. Goa's Fort Aguada jail is filled with prisoners, including some foreigners, serving lengthy sentences for drug offences, and being caught in possession of even a small quantity of illegal substances can mean a 10-year stay in a cockroach-infested cell.

Getting There & Away
AIR

Goa's sole and diminutive airport, Dabolim, is situated right in the centre of the state, around 29km south of Panaji, and an easy taxi ride (usually two hours, at most) from any of the state's beaches. Few international flights arrive

---

DIAL 108 IN EMERGENCIES

In any emergency in Goa, dial 108. This will connect you to the police, fire brigade or medical services.

GOA

here, and those that do are package-holiday charters, mostly from Russia and Britain: independent travellers from the UK could check Thomson (www.thomsonfly.com) and those flying from Germany can try Condor (www.condor.com) which both offer flight-only fares.

Generally, the quickest way to reach Goa from overseas is to take an international flight into Mumbai, and then a quick 45-minute hop by domestic airline down to Goa.

Numerous domestic airlines fly daily in and out of Goa, most flights taking off and landing throughout the morning and early afternoon, to a number of Indian destinations. Of them, **Indigo** (☎ toll free 18001803838; www.go indigo.in), **GoAir** (☎ toll free 1800222111; www.goair.in) and **SpiceJet** (☎ toll free 18001803333; www.spicejet .com) are the cheapest, and **Kingfisher** (☎ toll free 18001800101; www.flykingfisher.com) and **Jet Airways** (☎ toll free 1800225522; www.jetairways.com) by far the most comfortable. It is usually cheapest and easiest to book online as far in advance of your travel date as possible, and any enquiries are best made to the airlines' toll-free numbers in India.

Dabolim airport's arrivals hall is equipped with a money-exchange office, GTDC branch (see Information p186), Airtel office for purchasing mobile-phone credit, and charter-airline offices. There are two prepaid taxi booths (one in the arrivals hall and the other just outside), for heading by taxi elsewhere in the state.

BUS

Plenty of long-distance interstate buses operate to and from Panaji, Margao, Mapusa and Calangute, and you can also pick up some long-distance services from Chaudi near Palolem. See individual destination sections for detailed information.

TRAIN

The **Konkan Railway** (www.konkanrailway.com), the main train line running through Goa, connects Goa with Mumbai to the north, and with Mangalore to the south. Its main train station in Goa is Madgaon station in Margao, from which there are several useful daily services to Mumbai.

The convenient overnight *Konkan Kanya Express* (KKE; train number 0111; 1AC/2AC/ 3AC/sleeper Rs1832/1092/796/293) departs Mumbai's Dadar station at 11.05pm, arriving at Madgaon the next morning at 10.45am. In the opposite direction, the *KKE* (train number 0112) departs Madgaon at 6pm daily, and arrives at Mumbai's Dadar station at 5.20am.

From Mumbai's Chhatrapati Shivaji Terminus (CST; also known as Victoria Terminus), the daily *Mandovi Express* (train number 0103; 1AC/2AC/3AC/2nd class Rs1832/1092/796/165) departs at 6.55am and arrives at 6.45pm. In the opposite direction, the *Mandovi Express* (train number 0104) departs Madgaon at 9.40am and arrives at CST at 9.45pm.

The fastest train from Mumbai is the *Jan Shatabdi Express* (train number 2051; AC seat/ 2nd class Rs680/197) which departs Mumbai's CST at 5.10am and arrives in Madgaon at 2.10pm. In the opposite direction, the *Jan Shatabdi Express* (train number 2052) departs Madgaon at 2.30pm and arrives at Mumbai's CST at 11.20pm.

There are plenty of other rail options, too, to other parts of India. The daily *Goa Express* (train number 2780; 16½ hours) and the daily *Rajdhani Express* (train number 2432; 25 hours) both link Madgaon to Delhi's Nizamuddin station. A number of daily services link Madgaon to Trivandrum (around 20 hours); numerous daily options also head south to Mangalore (eight hours). There are also trains to Pune (14 hours) and Hospet Junction (eight hours 20 minutes), which is useful for travellers to Hampi. These services' frequencies and departure times seem to change fairly often, so check at the station or on the website for the most recent information.

Train bookings are best made at Madgaon station (p223), at the train reservation office at Panaji's Kadamba bus stand (p197) or at any travel agent vending train tickets (though you'll probably pay a small commission for the convenience). Make sure you book as far in advance as possible for sleepers, since they fill up quickly.

You can also book *Konkan Kanya Express* tickets online, subject to a long list of conditions: you can only book between seven and two days in advance of travel, only in 3AC class for a cost of Rs1500 per ticket, and with no date changes permitted.

Other smaller, useful Goan railway stations include Pernem for Arambol, Thivim for Mapusa and the northern beaches, Karmali (Old Goa) for Panaji and Canacona for Palolem.

Getting Around

BUS

Goa boasts an extensive network of buses, shuttling to and from almost every tiny town and village. There are no timetables, bus numbers, or, it seems, fixed fares, though it would be hard to spend more than Rs20 on any one single journey (and fares are usually far less). Buses range from serviceable to spluttering, and most pack passengers to bursting point, but they are a fun and colourful way to experience local life. Head to the nearest bus stand (often called the Kadamba bus stand, after the state's biggest bus company) and scan the signs posted on the bus windscreen to find the service you're after, or ask a driver who'll point you to the right old banger. Check individual destination listings for more detailed information on services.

CAR

It's easy, in most destinations, to organise a private car with a driver if you're planning on taking some long-distance day trips. Prices vary, but you should bank on paying around Rs1500 to Rs2000 for a full day out on the road.

It's also possible, if you've the nerves and the skills, to procure a self-drive car, giving you the (white-knuckled) freedom to explore Goa's highways and byways at your own pace. A small Chevrolet or Maruti will cost around Rs600 to Rs900 per day and a jeep around Rs1000, excluding petrol; there are few organised rental outlets, so ask around for a man with a car willing to rent it to you.

Note the slightly mystifying signposts posted on Goa's major National Highway 17 (NH17), which advise of different speed limits (on the largely single-carriageway road) for different types of vehicles.

MOTORCYCLE

You'll rarely go far on a Goan road without seeing an intrepid tourist whizzing by on a scooter or motorbike, and renting (if not driving) one is a breeze. You'll likely pay around Rs150 to Rs300 per day for a scooter, Rs400 for a smaller Yamaha motorbike, and about Rs500 for that most alluring, roaring symbol of mechanical freedom, the Royal Enfield Bullet. These prices can drop considerably if you're renting for more than one day, or if you've hit Goa during a less than peak period.

If you've never biked or scooted before, however, bear in mind that Goan roads are treacherous, and filled with human, bovine, canine, feline, mechanical and avian obstacles, as well as a good sprinkling of potholes and hairpin bends. Take it slowly, try not to drive at night (when black cows can prove a dangerous impediment to your progress), don't attempt a north–south day trip on a 50cc scooter, and the most cautious of riders might even consider donning a helmet or shoes.

TAXI

Taxis are widely available for hopping town-to-town, and, as with a chauffeured car, a full day's sightseeing, depending on the distance, is likely to be around Rs1500 to Rs2000. From the airport to your destination, there are two prepaid taxi stands, one inside and the other just outside the arrivals hall; buy your ticket here and you'll be ushered to a cab.

Motorcycles are also a licensed form of taxi in Goa. They are cheap, easy to find, and can be identified by a yellow front mudguard – and even the heftiest of backpacks seem to be no obstacle.

CENTRAL GOA

PANAJI (PANJIM)

pop 98,915

Panaji (also commonly known as Panjim) is an anomaly among Indian state capitals, as clean, friendly and manageable as many others are chaotic, frustrating and missable. Its Portuguese-era colonial charms make it a perfect place to lull away a day or two, strolling pretty, peaceful streets, taking a decidedly kitsch sunset river cruise, eating vindaloos and *xacutis* (spicy sauces combining coconut milk, freshly ground spices, and red chillies) to your heart's content, and ending the evening in one of dozens of hole-in-the-wall local bars. With a madcap Carnival during Lent, a growing number of 'lifestyle' stores catering to the well-heeled traveller, and a friendly, easygoing riverside vibe, it's a great base for explorations of Goa's historic hinterland, or simply a terrific option for a day trip back from the beach.

Orientation & Information

Panaji is a manageable-sized city, all the more so because only two or three distinct areas have much of interest to visitors. The central, pretty districts of Sao Tomé and Fontainhas are where you're likely to spend most of your time, with 31st January Rd providing the central spine to link them. On this road you'll find plenty of (fairly grim) budget accommodation, tiny thali joints, hole-in-the-wall bars, internet outlets, a supermarket or two, and several places for placing cheap international calls.

The wide riverside road (Dayanand Bandodkar Marg to the west, Avenida Dom Joao Castro to the east) is another good destination for eating and bar-hopping, and to the eastern end, just across the New Pato Bridge, you'll find the Santa Monica jetty for river cruises, and the local and long-distance bus stands. Further south, incongruously tucked away on the banks of Ourem Creek, is the Goa State Museum.

Back in the centre of town, clustered around the Municipal Gardens you'll find a range of cheap and cheerful joints for vegetable thalis, fish fry, and fish-curry-rice, the central, impressive Church of Our Lady of the Immaculate Conception, travel agents, shopping opportunities, and a crop of ATMs.

The other area around which you might find yourself spending time is 18th June Rd, which runs southwest from the southeast corner of the Municipal Gardens. Here are more accommodation options, eating places, ATMs, travel agents and the like, heading off down toward the nearby Kala Academy.

BOOKSHOPS
Book Fair (Hotel Mandovi, Dayanand Bahdodkar Marg; 9am-9pm) A small, well-stocked bookshop in the Hotel Mandovi lobby, with plenty of well-illustrated books on Goa.

Singbal's Book House (☎ 2425747; Church Sq; 9.30am-1pm & 3.30-7.30pm Mon-Sat) A good selection of international magazines and newspapers, and lots of books on Goa are offered at this slightly grumpy establishment.

Visionworld Book Depot (☎ 2182865; Church Sq; 9.30am-9pm) Offers a good selection of self-help and spiritual titles, novels and children's books, as well as vending an assortment of locally made snacks to provide sustenance for browsing.

INTERNET ACCESS
You'll find no shortage of internet cafes dotted across town. Most charge Rs30 per hour, have fairly slow connection times, and are open from 9am to 11pm daily.

MEDICAL SERVICES
Goa Medical College Hospital (☎ 2458700; Bambolin) Situated 9km south of Panaji on NH17.

MONEY
As with most places in Goa, you can't walk far without finding an ATM booth, with its usually icy air-conditioning and sleepy security guard. Most take international cards and you'll find a particularly bumper crop on 18th June Rd.
Thomas Cook (☎ 2221312; Dayanand Bandodkar Marg; 9.30am-6pm Mon-Sat year-round, 10am-5pm Sun Oct-Mar) Changes travellers cheques commission-free and gives cash advances on Visa and MasterCard.

POST
Main post office (MG Rd; 9.30am-5.30pm Mon-Fri, 9am-5pm Sat) Offers swift parcel services and Western Union money transfers.

TOURIST INFORMATION
Goa Tourism Development Corporation office
(GTDC; ☎ 2424001; www.goa-tourism.com; Dr Alvaro Costa Rd; 9.30am-5.45pm Mon-Fri) This GTDC office, just south of the Old Pato Bridge, is a decent place to pick up maps of Goa and Panaji, and to book GTDC's host of tours.
Government of India tourist office (☎ 2223412; www.incredibleindia.com; Communidade Bldg, Church Sq; 9.30am-1.30pm & 2.30-6pm Mon-Fri, 10am-1pm Sat) Staff here are extremely helpful, and can provide a list of qualified guides for tours and trips in Goa. A half-day tour (up to four hours) for two people, for example, costs Rs600.

Sights & Activities
Panaji is a city of long, leisurely strolls, through the sleepy Portuguese-era Sao Tomé, Fontainhas and Altinho districts, for a spot of shopping on 18th June Rd, and down along the languid Mandovi River, and if you happen to be here in November, don't miss catching a few flicks at the excellent **International Film Festival of India** (www.iffi.gov.in, www.iffigoa .org), India's largest and most glittering film festival.

CHURCH OF OUR LADY OF THE IMMACULATE CONCEPTION
Panaji's spiritual, as well as geographical, centre is its gleamingly picturesque main **church**, consecrated in 1541 and stacked like a fancy white wedding cake to the southeast of the ragged municipal gardens. When Panaji was little more than a sleepy fishing village, this

PANAJI (PANJIM)

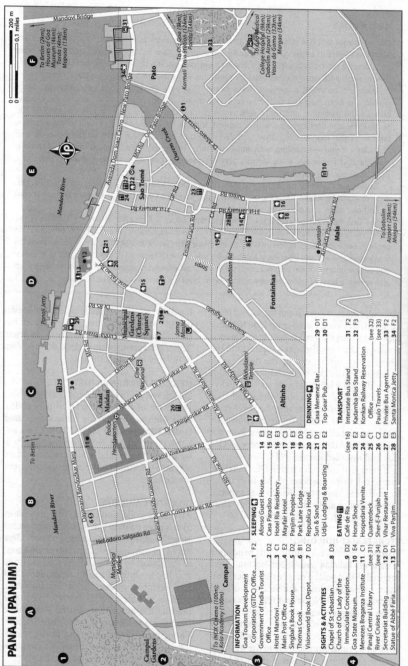

GOA

INFORMATION
Goa Tourism Development	
Corporation (GTDC) Office............**1**	F2
Government of India Tourist	
Office...**2**	D2
Hotel Mandovi................................**3**	C1
Main Post Office.............................**4**	E2
Singbal's Book House.....................**5**	D2
Thomas Cook...................................**6**	B1
Visionworld Book Depot.................**7**	D2

SIGHTS & ACTIVITIES
Chapel of St Sebastian...................**8**	D3
Church of Our Lady of the	
Immaculate Conception...............**9**	D2
Goa State Museum........................**10**	E4
Menezes Braganza Institute........**11**	C1
Panaji Central Library...........(see 31)	
River Cruises...................................(see 34)	
Secretariat Building.......................**12**	D1
Statue of Abbé Faria......................**13**	D1

SLEEPING
Afonso Guest House......................**14**	E3
Casa Paradiso................................**15**	D2
Hotel Ria Residency.......................**16**	E3
Mayfair Hotel.................................**17**	C3
Panjim Peoples..............................**18**	E3
Park Lane Lodge............................**19**	D3
Republica Hotel.............................**20**	D1
Sun & Sand....................................**21**	D1
Udipi Lodging & Boarding............**22**	E2

EATING
Café de Ria.............................(see 16)	
Horse Shoe....................................**23**	E2
Hospedaria Venite.........................**24**	E2
Quarterdeck..................................**25**	C1
Sher-E-Punjab...............................**26**	C2
Vihar Restaurant..........................**27**	E2
Viva Panjim...................................**28**	E3

DRINKING
Casa Menenez Bar........................**29**	D1
Top Gear Pub................................**30**	D1

TRANSPORT
Interstate Bus Stand.....................**31**	F2
Kadamba Bus Stand......................**32**	F3
Konkan Railway Reservation	
Office......................................(see 32)	
Paulo Travels.........................(see 33)	
Private Bus Agents........................**33**	F2
Santa Monica Jetty.......................**34**	F2

GREEN GOA?

Goa's environment has suffered from an onslaught of tourism over the last 40 years, but equally from the effects of logging, mining and local customs. Rare turtle eggs have traditionally been considered a dining delicacy; plastic bottles lie in vast glaciers (as unreceding as the real kind are the reverse); and vagrant cows feast by roadsides on refuse from unfragrant trash cans.

There are, however, a few easy ways to minimise your impact on Goa's environment. Since plastic – in both bag and bottle forms – is a major problem, bring your own nonplastic bag along while shopping, and try to refill water bottles with filtered water wherever possible. The 5L Bisleri water bottles come with a deposit and are returnable to be reused; invest in these, instead of the regular size, when you can. Don't, of course, leave litter on the beaches, and consider – if you're travelling with small children – using washable nappies, instead of the disposable kind (especially since laundry services generally cost so much less than the price of a pack of disposable nappies).

Turtles are currently protected by the Forestry Department, who operate huts on beaches, such as Agonda, where turtles arrive to lay eggs. Drop into these, or go to www.goaforest.com to find out more about the department's work.

The **Goa Foundation** (☎ 2256479; www.goafoundation.org; G-8 Feira Alta, Mapusa) in Mapusa is the state's main environmental pressure group and has been responsible for a number of conservation projects since its inauguration in 1986. Its excellent *Fish Curry & Rice* (Rs400), a rich sourcebook on Goa's environment and lifestyle, is available for sale at the Other India Bookstore (p203) in Mapusa, and online (international orders accepted) at www.otherindiabookstore.com. This excellent shop also stocks a host of other environment-related books, pamphlets and publications.

---

place was the first port of call for sailors from Lisbon, who would clamber up here to thank their lucky stars for a safe crossing, before continuing to Old Goa, the state's capital until the 19th century, further east up the river.

Entrance to its gloriously technicolour interior is along the left-hand-side wall; the itchy-fingered should try to obey the small sign requesting 'Please do not ring the bell' beside a tangle of ropes leading up to the enormous shiny church bell in the belfry, saved from the ruins of the Augustinian monastery at Old Goa and installed here in 1871.

If your visit coincides with 8 December, be sure to call in for the Feast of Our Lady of the Immaculate Conception, which sees a special church service and a lively fair spilling away from the church to mark the date.

SECRETARIAT BUILDING
Dating from the 16th century, this handsome **colonial-era building** (Avenida Dom Joao Castro) was originally the palace of Muslim ruler Adil Shah, before becoming the viceroy's official residence in 1759. Nowadays it houses rather less exciting government offices, but remains worth a gaze as the oldest building in town. It is currently under renovation and will be for quite some time. Immediately to the west, the strange and compelling **statue** of a man bearing down upon a supine female form depicts one of Goa's most famous home-grown talents, Abbé Faria, an 18th-century Goan priest, 'father of hypnotism' and friend of Napoleon, in full melodramatic throes.

MENEZES BRAGANZA INSTITUTE
On the west side of the Azad Maidan, about 1km west of the Secretariat, this beautiful early 20th-century affair houses the **Panaji Central Library** (Malaca Rd; ⊗ 9.30am-1.15pm & 2-5.30pm Mon-Fri) and is worth dropping into to see the pretty blue-and-white *azulejos* (glazed ceramic-tile compositions) in the west entrance hall.

GOA STATE MUSEUM
An eclectic collection of items awaits visitors to this large **museum** (☎ 2438006; www.goamuseum .nic.in; EDC Complex, Pato; admission free; ⊗ 9.30am-5.30pm Mon-Fri), in a strangely uncentral area southwest of the Kadamba bus stand. As well as Hindu and Jain sculptures and bronzes, and a few nice examples of Portuguese-era furniture, exhibits include an elaborately carved table used by the notoriously brutal Portuguese Inquisition in Goa, and some ancient coins. Though not exactly bursting at the seams, it's a diverting way to while away a couple of hours while waiting for a bus or river trip.

HOUSES OF GOA MUSEUM

A short taxi ride across the river to the north of Panaji, in the little village of Torda, you'll arrive at this highly worthwhile **museum** (☎ 2410711; ⏰ 10.30am-7.30pm), created by a well-known local architect, Gerard da Cunha, to illuminate the history of Goan homes, apparent statewide in various states of picturesque decrepitude. Marooned shiplike in the middle of a traffic island, it's hard to miss, and a taxi here from central Panaji should cost around Rs200.

CHAPEL OF ST SEBASTIAN

Standing at the end of a picturesque lane, this pretty chapel is home to a crucifix first brought to Panaji in 1812 from Old Goa after the Inquisition was suppressed. It's considered an unusual piece since Christ's eyes are open – rather than shut, as is customary – and legend has it that this was done to instil fear in the hearts of those being brought before the dreaded Inquisitors. If you're in Panaji in mid-November, look out for the street fair outside that accompanies the chapel's Feast of Our Lady of Livrament.

Courses

London-based **Holiday On the Menu** (www.holiday onthemenu.com) offers a range of Goan-cooking holidays, ranging from a Saturday 'Curry Morning' to a week-long program including trips out to a spice plantation and a local market, based in the picturesque village of Betim, just across the river north of Panaji. Prices start at £59 per person for the 'Curry Morning', and all courses are suitable for vegetarians.

Cruises & Tours

GTDC (see p186) operates a range of entertaining daily hour-long **cruises** (Rs150; ⏰ dusk cruise 6pm & 6.30pm, sundown cruise 7.15pm & 7.45pm) along the Mandovi River aboard the *Santa Monica* and *Shantadurga*. All include a live band – sometimes lively, sometimes lacklustre – performing Goan folk songs and dances. There are also twice-weekly, two-hour **dinner cruises** (incl snacks & buffet dinner Rs400; ⏰ 8.30pm) and regular two-hour **dolphin-watching trips** (incl refreshments Rs250; ⏰ 8.30am Wed, Sat & Sun). All cruises depart from the Santa Monica jetty next to the huge Mandovi Bridge and tickets can be purchased here.

Various other companies offer virtually identical cruises also from Santa Monica jetty.

Head down to the jetty to see what's on offer; in general, though, the GTDC cruises are a little more staid, while others – perhaps because of the promise of 'free beer' – can get a little rowdier with groups of local male tourists.

GTDC also runs a two-hour daily **Goa By Night bus tour** (Rs200; ⏰ 6.30pm), which leaves from the same jetty spot and includes a river cruise. As ever, its breakneck tour packs in as much as possible; in this case, in just two hours you'll experience a river cruise, a long string of churches, a palace, a temple and a panoramic view.

Sleeping
BUDGET

If you're looking for rock-bottom budget accommodation, lots of lodging options run the length of 31st January Rd. Don't, however, expect atmospheric old Portuguese haunts: most consist of nothing much but a cell-like room, no view, and a 9am or earlier checkout, with attached doubles going for around Rs500 or less. Wander up and down and check out a few before you decide; there's little to choose between them, though some may let you barter down the price.

Udipi Lodging & Boarding (☎ 228047; Sao Tomé; d without bathroom Rs200) For a really basic stay, without quite so much of a disturbing prison-like feel as some of the budget options along 31st January Rd, check into one of the eight rooms at the Udipi, just around the corner from the main post office. Don't expect any home comforts, but it's dingy rather than dirty and a decent enough place to lay down your backpack for a night or two.

Republica Hotel (☎ 2224630; Jose Falcao Rd; d Rs600) There are some places that promise so much and deliver so little, and the Republica, sadly, is one of them – though its dilapidation is, in part, its charm. You'll not receive a warm welcome or a well-decorated room; indeed, the service is gloomy and the decor grim, but this elderly, ramshackle wooden building is certainly no shoebox concrete cell. It's not comfy, but it's fairly cheap, and offers a central location and a stay you're unlikely to forget.

Park Lane Lodge (☎ 2227154; St Sebastian Rd; d Rs755-1025; ✷) Set in an old and rambling bungalow near the Chapel of St Sebastian, the Park Lane has been popular with travellers for years, despite its seemingly ever-extending list of rules. Current formidable warnings include

'No Laundry', 'No Internet', 'Gates Closed 10pm' and '8am Checkout'. If you can work with all this, it makes a characterful – if crumbling – place to stay.

Mayfair Hotel (☎ 2223317; Dr Dada Vaidya Rd; s/d/tr from Rs780/980/1300; 🗷) With its bright, cheerful balconies, beautiful ground-floor oyster-shell windows and general, slightly musty air of yesteryear, the Mayfair is an atmospheric central option. Note the 'hot-water timings' chart at reception, and be sure to arrange your showers accordingly.

MIDRANGE
Hotel Ria Residency (☎ 2220002; www.riaresidency .co.nr; Rua de Ourem Fontainhas; d from Rs945; 🗷) In no way spectacular, this place just off the end of 31st January Rd is perfectly acceptable for a comfortable and air-conditioned, if fairly uncharismatic, stay. However, don't believe the computer-generated image of the place on the website: the real thing is decidedly less neat and angular.

Afonso Guest House (☎ 2222359; St Sebastian Rd; d Rs1200) Run by a friendly elderly gentleman, this lovely place set in a pretty old Portuguese townhouse offers plain but comfortable rooms, and a little rooftop terrace for sunny breakfasting (dishes Rs15 to Rs25). It's a simple, serene stay in the heart of the most atmospheric part of town.

Casa Paradiso (☎ 2420297; www.casaparadiso goa.com; Jose Falcao Rd; d Rs1350-1800; 🗷) A new and terrific stay at the heart of the city, just steps away from Panaji's Church of Our Lady of the Immaculate Conception, with friendly staff and modern, well-decorated rooms.

TOP END
Sun & Sand (☎ 240000; www.sunsandhotel.com; Bairo Alto Dos Pilotos, Jose Falcao Rd; d with/without river view Rs5500/6500, ste Rs12,000; 🗷 🖳 🖳) Perched high above Panaji, with lovely views from its terrace and small pool, this is a great option for a little bit of luxury in the midst of the city. The price includes breakfast and pick-up/drop-off at the airport or railway station, for stays of over two nights.

Panjim Peoples (☎ 226523, 2435628; www.panjiminn .com; 31st January Rd; d Rs7500; 🗷) Undeniably atmospheric, if rather pricey for the standard of facilities on offer, this lovely option sports rooms with mosaic-covered bathrooms, deep baths and lots of quaint antiques, arranged around a serene indoor courtyard.

Eating
You'll never go hungry in Panaji, where food is enjoyed fully and frequently. A stroll down 18th June or 31st January Rds will turn up a number of great, cheap canteen-style options, as will a quick circuit of the Municipal Gardens.

Vihar Restaurant (MG Rd; veg thalis Rs30-60) A vast menu of 'pure veg' food, great big thalis and a plethora of fresh juices make this clean, simple canteen a popular place for locals and visitors alike. Sip a hot chai, invent your own juice combination, and dig into an ice cream for afters.

Café de Ria (Rua de Ourem; mains from Rs40) Just beneath the Hotel Ria Residency (left) sits the unassuming Café de Ria, another 'pure veg' place that dishes up delicious, diverse South Indian dishes.

Viva Panjim (31st January Rd; mains Rs50-160; 🕑 11.30am-3pm & 7-11pm) Though it might be more than a touch touristy these days this little side-street eatery, with a couple of tables out on the street itself, nevertheless still delivers tasty Goan staples, as well as the standard range of Indian fare. Keep an eye out in the dim interior for Mrs Linda de Souza, restaurant founder and doughty matriarch.

Sher-E-Punjab (18th June Rd; mains Rs60-150) A cut above the usual lunch joint, Sher-E-Punjab caters to well-dressed locals with its generous, carefully spiced Indian dishes. There's a pleasant garden terrace out back, and an icy AC room if you're feeling sticky. Try the delicious paneer tandoori tikka (Indian cheese coated in red spice paste, and baked in a tandoor oven; Rs90) but note, if you're hungering for snacks, that the fish fingers and chicken fingers are 'seasonal only'.

Hospedaria Venite (31st January Rd; mains Rs65-110) Along with Viva Panjim, this is without a doubt the lunch address to which most tourists head, and, though the food isn't exactly excellent, the atmosphere warrants the visit. Its tiny, rickety balcony tables, looking out onto pastel-washed 31st January Rd, make the perfect lunchtime spot, and the Goan chourisso (spiced sausages; Rs145) and vegetable vindaloo (Rs95) are actually pretty tasty. Order a cold beer or two, munch on a slightly '70s-style salad (think cold boiled vegetables in vinaigrette) and watch lazy Panaji slip by.

Quarterdeck (Dayanand Bandodkar Marg; mains from Rs80) Watch crammed passenger ferries and hulking casino boats chug by from a waterside table at this open air 'multi-cuisine' restaurant perched on the Mandovi banks. There's a small playground for children and the food is tasty enough, though the location is without doubt the restaurant's biggest drawcard.

Horse Shoe (☎ 2431788; Ourem Rd; mains Rs150-350; ☺ 7-10.30pm) A well-respected, sweet little Goan-Portuguese place, this is a simple but romantic choice for some traditional dishes and a nice bottle of Portuguese wine. At the time of research Horse Shoe was open for dinner only (bookings advised) but this might change, so call ahead to be sure.

Drinking

Panaji's got pick-me-up pit stops aplenty, and a visit to 31st January Rd or Dayanand Bandodkar Marg will take you hopping in and out of lots of them. Mostly simple little bars with a few plastic tables and chairs and a friendly barman presiding, they're a great way to escape the midday heat and the best place to get chatting to locals on a balmy evening.

Casa Menenez Bar (Dayanand Bandodkar Marg; ☺ 11am-3pm & 7-10.30pm) A down-to-earth drinking hole on the river road, open to the street and with just a scattering of plastic tables, this place is great for grabbing a cool Kingfisher.

Top Gear Pub (Dayanand Bandodkar Marg; ☺ 11am-3pm & 6.30pm-midnight) A few doors down from Casa Menenez, there's a tiny, cool, retro bar hidden behind Top Gear's unassuming doors. There's no food here, so don't come hungry, but it's a great place to wet your whistle or whet your appetite.

Entertainment

Casino boats ply the Mandovi waters each night, offering lose-your-savings fun to all who step aboard; most leave from the Panaji jetty, so head there to make preparations for blowing your budget. **Casino Royale** (☎ 6659400; www.casinoroyalegoa.com; entry Mon-Thu Rs1500, Fri-Sun Rs1800; ☺ 6pm-8am) is the newest and largest; various age and dress restrictions apply.

INOX Cinema (☎ 2420999; www.inoxmovies.com; Old GMC Heritage Precinct; tickets Rs100-170) This comfortable and even plush multiplex cinema, which shows Hollywood and Bollywood blockbusters alike, is near the Kala Academy. If you've internet access, you can even try your hand at online booking and choose your seats in advance.

Kala Academy (☎ 2420451; www.kalaacademy .org; Dayanand Bandodkar Marg) On the west side of the city at Campal is Goa's premier cultural centre, which features a program of dance, theatre, music and art exhibitions throughout the year. Many shows are in Konkani, but there are occasional English-language productions; call to find out what's on when you're in town.

Getting There & Away

AIR

A taxi from Panaji to Dabolim airport takes 1½ hours, and costs Rs800.

BUS

All local services depart from Panaji's Kadamba bus stand, with frequent local services (running to no apparent timetables) heading out all over the state every few minutes. To get to South Goan beaches, take a bus to Margao (Rs15, 45 minutes) and change there. State-run long-distance services also depart from the Kadamba bus stand, but since the prices offered by private operators are about the same, and levels of comfort are far greater, it makes sense to go private instead.

Many private operators have booths outside the entrance to the Kadamba bus stand, but most private interstate services depart from the interstate bus stand next to the Mandovi Bridge.

One reliable private operator is **Paulo Travels** (☎ 2438531; www.paulotravels.com; G1, Kardozo Bldg) with offices just north of the Kadamba bus stand. It operates a number of services with varying levels of comfort to Mumbai (Rs350 to Rs700; 11 to15 hours), Pune (Rs450 to Rs600, 10 to 12 hours), Hampi (Rs450 to Rs650, 10 hours), Begaluru (Rs450 to Rs750, 14 to 15 hours) and various other long-distance destinations.

TRAIN

The closest train station to Panaji is Karmali (Old Goa), 12km to the east, at which a number of long-distance services stop. Note, though, that Panaji's **Konkan Railway reservation office** (☺ 8am-8pm Mon-Sat) is on the 1st floor of the Kadamba bus stand. You can also check times, prices and routes online at www .konkanrailway.com.

Getting Around

It's easy enough to get around Panaji itself on foot, and it's unlikely you'll need even as much as an autorickshaw. To Old Goa, a taxi costs around Rs300, and an autorickshaw

A GOAN GOURMET GLOSSARY

With its infinite combinations of coconut, chillies, rice and spice, Goan cuisine is one of the original fusion foods, rich in Portuguese and South Indian heritage. 'Prodham bhookt, magi mookt' (You can't think until you've eaten well), say the locals in Konkani and we wholeheartedly agree.

- **Bhaji-pau:** The classic Goan breakfast: pau (a fluffy bread roll) dunked into a small dish of bhaji (spicy, coconut-based vegetable curry). Look out for tasty variations on the bhaji, using cashew nuts, black eye beans or chunks of tomato, or try idli (steamed rice cakes) or puri (puffed up, fried breads) in place of the pau.

- **Fish-curry-rice:** What bhaji-pau is to a Goan breakfast, fish-curry-rice is to a Goan lunch. Usually a piece of fried mackerel steeped in a thin coconut and red chilli sauce and served with rice, this is the cheap and filling formula that keeps many Goans going until dinnertime.

- **Vindalho:** Not the sole preserve of something-to-prove British curry house lads, this Vindalho vindaloo's the real thing – a uniquely Goan derivative of Portuguese pork stew that traditionally combines wine vinegar, garlic and spices.

- **Chourisso:** Dried spicy red pork sausages flavoured with feni, palm-sap vinegar and chillies, and served with bread rolls for lunch.

- **Sorpotel:** One for the strictly carnivorous, this is a rich stew made at Christmas, incorporating almost every part and internal organ of the pig – even tossing in an ear or two.

- **Feni:** A clear and fiery liquor made from distilled cashew fruit or coconut sap, sure to help you sink into that Goan sosegado spirit.

- **Balchão:** A deliciously rich and tangy dark red tomato and chilli sauce, often used to cook tiger prawns or fish, and eaten with fresh, fluffy pau.

- **Xacutí:** A spicy sauce (pronounced sha-coo-tee) frequently used to make vegetarian dishes, combining coconut milk, freshly ground spices and red chillies.

- **Rechead:** A spicy paste used to marinade seafood, which is then fried, grilled or baked in a tandoori oven.

- **Cafrial:** Spicy pieces of dry-fried fish or chicken, marinated in a green masala paste and sprinkled with toddy vinegar.

- **Ambot tik:** A hot-and-sour curry, usually made with chicken, fish or seafood.

- **Sanna:** Traditional steamed bread rolls, similar to crumpets, made with sugar, rice flour and fermented toddy.

- **Bebinca:** Rich and delicious, this 16-layer coconut cake is whipped up with sugar, nutmeg, cardamom and egg yolks and often served at Christmas.

- **Batica:** A squidgy coconut cake best served piping hot from the oven.

- **Dodol:** A gorgeous, gooey fudgelike treat made from litres of fresh coconut milk, mixed with rice flour and jaggery, and boiled gently for hours on end.

should take you there for Rs150 to Rs200. Lots of taxis hang around at the Municipal Gardens, making it a good place to haggle for the best price.

OLD GOA

Gazing at the crumbling cathedral-filled remains of Old Goa today it's hard to believe that it was, from the 16th to the 18th centuries, the 'Rome of the East'. But travel back five centuries, to a time when Old Goa's population exceeded that of Lisbon or London, and that's exactly what this fallen city, then capital of Goa, was considered. Its reign, however, was as short as it was glorious, and devastating outbreaks of cholera and malaria finally forced the abandonment of the city in 1835. By 1843, the capital had been shifted to Panaji, further along the river, and the towering city was inhabited only by ghosts and the occasional grim hanger-on.

These days, Old Goa makes for an interesting outing, particularly if you're there to mill among the weekend crowds, and in the 10 days leading up to the **Feast of St Francis Xavier** on 3 December.

Sights

SÉ CATHEDRAL

The largest church in Old Goa, the **Sé de Santa Catarina**, as it's known by its full name, is also the largest in Asia, standing at over 76m long and 55m wide. Construction here begun in 1562, under orders from King Dom Sebastio of Portugal, and the finishing touches to the altars weren't made until 1652, some 90 years later.

Fairly plain all-round, the cathedral has three especially notable features: the first, up in the belfry, is the **Golden Bell**, the largest bell in Asia; the second is in the little screened chapel inside to the right, known as the **Chapel of the Cross of Miracles**, wherein sits a cross said to have miraculously – and vastly – expanded in size after its creation by a group of local shepherds in 1619. The third point of particular interest is the massive gilded *reredos* (ornamental screen behind the altar) which depicts the life of St Catherine, to whom the cathedral is dedicated,

and who came to a sticky end in Alexandria, Egypt, where she was eventually beheaded.

CHURCH OF ST FRANCIS OF ASSISI

A beautifully fading **church** built in 1661 over an earlier 16th century chapel, its lovely interior is filled with gilded and carved woodwork, murals depicting the life of St Francis, 16th-century Portuguese tombstones, and another stunning *reredos*. Note the sign inside that reads 'No Photography of Persons'. Presumably, they've no problem with you clicking pictures of any heavenly hosts that decide to put in an appearance.

Just behind the church, its former convent houses an **archaeological museum** (entrance free; ⏰ 10am-5pm Sat-Thu), whose small but worthwhile collection includes a portrait gallery of Portuguese viceroys, a couple of bronze statues, fragments of Hindu temple sculpture, and some interesting 'hero stones', carved to commemorate Hindu warriors who perished in combat.

BASILICA OF BOM JESUS

Famous throughout the Roman Catholic world for its rather grizzled and grizzly long-

GOA

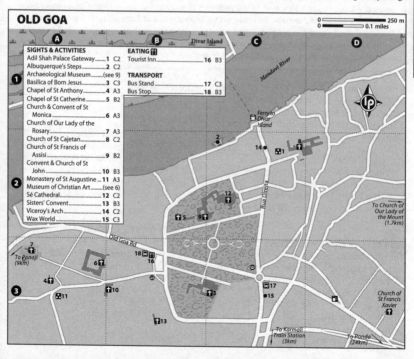

OLD GOA

SIGHTS & ACTIVITIES	
Adil Shah Palace Gateway	1 C2
Albuquerque's Steps	2 C2
Archaeological Museum	(see 9)
Basilica of Bom Jesus	3 C3
Chapel of St Anthony	4 A3
Chapel of St Catherine	5 B2
Church & Convent of St Monica	6 A3
Church of Our Lady of the Rosary	7 A3
Church of St Cajetan	8 C2
Church of St Francis of Assisi	9 B2
Convent & Church of St John	10 B3
Monastery of St Augustine	11 A3
Museum of Christian Art	(see 6)
Sé Cathedral	12 C2
Sisters' Convent	13 B3
Viceroy's Arch	14 C2
Wax World	15 C3

EATING	
Tourist Inn	16 B3

TRANSPORT	
Bus Stand	17 C3
Bus Stop	18 B3

Divar Island
Mandovi River
Ferry to Divar Island
Rua Direita
Old Goa Rd
To Panaji (9km)
To Church of Our Lady of the Mount (1.7km)
Church of St Francis Xavier
To Karmali Train Station (3km)
To Ponda (24km)

0 ——— 250 m
0 ——— 0.1 miles

HOLY RELICS!

Though Goa's patron saint, Francis Xavier, 'the Apostle of the Indies' spent 10 years as a tireless missionary trudging Asia in search of souls ripe for conversion, it was – rather unfortunately for him – only his death on 3 December 1552 that sparked his remarkable rise to fame throughout the region.

Having breathed his last while on his way to China, St Francis's mortal remains were buried on the deserted island of Sancian, off the Chinese coast, and covered in piles of quicklime to hasten the body's decomposition. Several months later, however, the exhumed corpse was found to be in tip-top, Sleeping Beauty–like condition, and the following year it was returned to Goa, where it was received in 1554 to far greater local excitement than the live version ever witnessed.

A medical examination, ordered by suspicious clerics, confirmed that the body had not been embalmed, and the viceroy's physician declared that all internal organs were still intact and preservative-free. On noticing a small wound in the chest, and having a Jesuit priest stick a couple of fingers in for closer examination, the physician declared that, 'When they withdrew them, they were covered with blood which I smelt and found to be absolutely untainted'. Moreover, almost a century later, so the story goes, an over-zealous Portuguese noblewoman who bit off the corpse's little toe in the throes of religious fervour, experienced an outpouring of fresh, unclotted blood from the wound.

Despite the 'miracle,' it took another 70 years for St Francis to achieve canonisation, by which time holy relic–hunters had already been hard at work on what became known as the saint's 'incorrupt body'. In 1614 his right arm had been removed and divided between Jesuits in Japan and Rome, and by 1636 parts of one shoulder blade and most of his internal organs had been liberally distributed through Southeast Asia, while his diamond-encrusted fingernail found its way to a family chapel in the Goan village of Chandor (see p224). By the end of the 17th century, the body had finally desiccated, and the Jesuits decided it was high time to coffin up the corpse and store it out of sight. However, in the mid-19th century St Francis was once again hauled out for public viewing, and remains so today in Old Goa's Basilica of Bom Jesus. Every 10 years on 3 December, he's carried in his glass-sided palanquin from the Basilica across the road to the Sé Cathedral, with pilgrims travelling for miles to get a better look at the shrivelled saint. The next such procession, with its attendant funfair and festivities, is sadly not scheduled until 2014.

term resident, the Basilica's vast, gilded interior forms the last resting place of Goa's patron saint, St Francis Xavier (except for his diamond-encrusted fingernail, which sits in Chandor – see p224) who, in 1541, embarked on a mission to put right the sinful, heady lifestyles of Goa's Portuguese colonials.

Construction of the imposing red-stone basilica was completed in 1605; St Francis himself is housed in a **mausoleum** to the right, in a glass-sided coffin amid a shower of gilt stars.

MONASTERY OF ST AUGUSTINE

The melancholy, evocative ruins of this once vast and impressive **Augustinian monastery** are all that remains of a huge structure founded in 1572 and finally abandoned in 1835. The building's facade came tumbling down in 1942; all that remains, amid piles of rubble, is the towering skeletal belfry, though the bell itself was rescued and now hangs in Panaji's

Church of Our Lady of the Immaculate Conception.

WAX WORLD

If you're a fan of kooky representations of obscure historical figures, look no further than this brand new **waxworks** (☎ 9970126202; admission Rs30; ⏱ 9.30am-7pm), which boasts of a host of 'Life-Size Look-Alike Wax Statues' including a full, waxen version of Michelangelo's *Last Supper*.

CHURCH OF ST CAJETAN

The pretty Church of St Cajetan sports the only surviving domed roof in Old Goa, and was modelled in miniature on St Peter's in Rome. It was built between 1612 and 1661 by Italian friars of the Order of Theatines, who were sent to India by Pope Urban III to preach Christianity in the Sultanate of Golconda (near Hyderabad). After being refused entry to Golconda, the friars settled instead for

Old Goa, where they created a church rich in woodcarvings, and where the remains of deceased Portuguese governors were kept in lead caskets until they were shipped back home to Europe. Goa's last few late governors, forgotten for more than three decades, were finally sent back to Lisbon in 1992.

CHURCH & CONVENT OF ST MONICA
Once the only convent in the whole of Old Goa, this huge, three-storey **laterite building** was completed in 1627, only to burn down just nine years later. Reconstruction started the following year, and it's from this time that the scuffed and scruffy buildings date. Ring the bell and you might receive a guided visit of the convent by its current inhabitants, nuns of the Mater Dei Institute. Behind the high altar, look out for the 'miraculous' **cross** on which, in 1636, Christ allegedly opened his eyes and dripped blood from his thorny crown.

Next to the convent, the interesting **Museum of Christian Art** (adult/child Rs15/free; ✆ 9.30am-5pm) contains ornate and antique statuary, crosses, icons and robes aplenty, and is definitely worth a wander.

OTHER HISTORIC SITES
There are plenty of other monuments, sprinkled throughout Old Goa, to explore, including the **Church & Convent of St Monica**, **Church of St Catejan**, **Viceroy's Arch**, **Adil Shah's Palace Gateway**, **Chapel of St Anthony**, **Chapel of St Catherine**, **Albuquerque's Steps**, the **Convent & Church of St John**, **Sisters' Convent** and the **Church of Our Lady of the Rosary**. For a wonderful view of the city hike up to the hilltop **Church of Our Lady of the Mount**, 2km east of Sé Cathedral, especially worth the trip for a spectacular sunset.

Sleeping & Eating
There's no real reason to visit Old Goa for anything more than a day trip, and it's best to base yourself in Panaji or beyond.

A little string of tourist restaurants on the corner near the bus stand make perfect pit stops for a cold drink and a snack; the basic **Tourist Inn** (Old Goa Rd; mains from Rs90) on the corner offers simple, tasty Indian dishes, cold Kingfishers, and a 1st-floor vantage point for watching Old Goa comings and goings.

Getting There & Away
Frequent buses to Old Goa depart from the Kadamba bus stand at Panaji (Rs7, 25 min-

utes) and stop at the 'Bus Stand-cum-ATM' just beside the Tourist Inn restaurant and from the main roundabout to the east.

LOUTOLIM
Relics of Goa's grand Portuguese heritage can be found with a wander around the unhurried village of Loutolim, around 10km northeast of Margao. The village hosts a number of impressive Portuguese-era mansions, but just one, the 252-year-old **Casa Araujo Alvares** (admission Rs125; ✆ 10am-6pm), is officially open to the public. Though it's not as brimming with atmosphere as some other examples you'll find scattered across the state, it's still well worth looking in on.

The best reason to visit Loutolim, though, is to bask in slow, sleepy, Goan village life and gaze at the privately owned jewels of mansions scattered along the foliage-thick lanes.

With just four lovely, antique-filled rooms, each with a private terrace, **Casa Susegad** (✆ 2106341; www.casasusegadgoa.com; s/d from Rs3685/5170), a spot of civilisation in the depths of the countryside, is just the place to relax, recuperate and replenish from hard weeks, or months, on the Indian road. An organic vegetable garden supplies delicious dinners in the formal dining room; parakeets, monkeys, cats and dogs inhabit the extensive gardens; a swimming pool awaits on the umbrella-shaded terrace. What better a definition of *susegad* could you possibly ask for?

Without your own wheels, Loutolim is best accessed by taxi from Margao; a one-way fare should be in the range of Rs120.

PONDA & AROUND
The workaday inland town of Ponda, 29km southeast of Panaji, has two big drawcards in the vicinity: Hindu temples and spice plantations, and, if either appeal to you, are well worth a day away from the beach. If you're a temple aficionado, however, you might be a little disappointed; most were built or rebuilt after the originals were destroyed by the Portuguese, so they're not as ancient as in other parts of India.

The 18th-century hilltop **Manguesh Temple** at Priol, 5km northwest of Ponda is an architecturally mixed-up composition dedicated to Manguesh, a god known only in Goa, while 1km away at Mardol is the **Mahalsa Temple**, also dedicated to a specifically Goan deity. The 1738 **Shantadurga Temple**, meanwhile, is

GOA

dedicated to Shantadurga, the goddess of peace, and is one of the most famous shrines in Goa.

One of the best spice plantations to visit is the **Tropical Spice Farm** (☎ 2340329; admission Rs300; ☽ 9am-5pm), 5km northeast of Ponda. An entertaining (especially so if your guide happens to be Martin) 45-minute tour of the spice plantation, followed by a banana-leaf buffet lunch is included in the price, and elephant rides/bathings are available for Rs500/600 extra.

Nearby, the 200-year-old **Savoi Plantation** (☎ 2340272; www.savoiplantations.com), whose motto is 'Organic Since Origin', is less touristed and elephant-free, but you'll find a warm welcome from knowledgeable guides keen to walk you through the 40-hectare plantation at your own pace. Local crafts are for sale, and you're welcomed with fresh pomegranate juice, cardamom bananas and other organic treats.

There are regular buses to Ponda from Panaji and Margao (Rs15, 45 minutes), after which you'll need to arrange an onward taxi to visit the temples or spice farms. Far better, if you can, is to potter out to this scenic area under your own steam.

NORTH GOA

BHAGWAN MAHAVIR WILDLIFE SANCTUARY

The forlorn, mining truck–riddled village of Molem is the gateway to the Bhagwan Mahavir Wildlife Sanctuary, the largest of Goa's protected wildlife areas, which covers 240 sq km and incorporates the 107-sq-km Molem National Park.

Unless you're on a guided tour courtesy of your hotel, travel agent or the GTDC, you might have problems actually gaining access to the park's quiet, shady trails. In theory, tickets are available at the Forest Interpretation Centre, 2km before the park entrance, close to Molem town. In practice, there's usually only a couple of bewildered-looking men sitting about, who will have enough trouble interpreting your request to purchase a ticket, let alone finding the keys to the park gates.

If you persist, you'll be rewarded with lush and deserted tracts of forest populated by jungle cats, deer and Malayan giant squirrels, although the wildlife is confoundedly shy and hard to spot.

Another way to visit the park is to stay at Molem's sole accommodation option, the upscale **Azuska Retreat** (☎ 2612319; www.azuska retreat.com; d/tent incl breakfast Rs3750/7500; ☒ ⬜ ☒), a newly renovated and luxurious series of bungalows and huge luxury tents set up around a lovely, if slightly municipal-feeling, garden. Azuska's (which means 'clean and green' in Sanskrit) tents are a delight, set on the quiet side of the site amid monkey-clad trees, with huge beds, sleek modern furnishings and gorgeous deep baths. Situated near the Molem forest checkpoint, the highly obliging folks here can organise all sorts of excursions into the park, including elephant rides and nighttime forest forays, in addition to trips out to Dudhsagar Falls. There's also a spa with steam baths and sauna, three restaurants and a nice garden pool.

Molem and the gateway to the sanctuary lie southeast of Panaji (54km from Margao), with its main entrance on NH4A. To reach here by public transport, take any bus to Ponda, then change to a bus to Belgaum or Londa, getting off at Molem.

DUDHSAGAR FALLS

On the eastern border with Karnataka, **Dudhsagar Falls** (603m) are Goa's most impressive waterfalls, and the second highest in India, best seen as soon as possible after the end of the monsoon. To get here, take a train to Colem from Margao (several trains run daily; check at the station, p223, for train times) and from there, charter a jeep for the bumpy 40-minute trip to the Falls (Rs800 to Rs1000 per person). It's then a short but rocky clamber to the edge of the falls themselves. A simpler (but less exciting) option is to take a full-day **GTDC tour** (without/with AC per person Rs700/800; ☽ 9am-6pm Wed & Sun from Panaji & Calangute) to the falls (see p186), or to arrange an excursion with the Day Tripper travel agency in Calangute (p209).

TAMBDI SURLA

Any serious temple buffs won't want to miss the atmospheric remains of the unusual little Hindu **Mahadeva Temple** at Tambdi Surla, 12km north of the truck-stop town of Molem. Built around the 12th century by the Kadamba dynasty, who ruled Goa for 400 years between the 10th and 14th centuries, it's the only temple of its type to have survived both the years and the various conquerings by Muslim and

Portuguese forces, and probably only made it thus far due to its remote jungle setting.

Dedicated to Shiva and constructed from long-lasting black basalt, the temple sports intricate bas-relief carvings around its sides and interior, and faces east, so that the rays of each sunrise illuminate its deity. The temple's sides sport images of Shiva, Vishnu and Brahma, along with their consorts; look out for the image inside the *mandapa* of an elephant crushing a horse, thought to be a symbol of the Kadambas's own military power at the time of the temple's inauguration.

A temple day trip is easiest with your own wheels (though GTDC tours also stop here; see p186); otherwise, take a bus to Molem via Ponda, and negotiate a taxi fare from there. If you roll up on a weekday, when it's not inundated with quick-stopping, fast-snapping day trippers, this remote place remains a solitary and stirring memorial to a once grand and glorious era.

For birdwatching enthusiasts, quiet, rustic **Backwoods Camp** (☎ 9822139859; www.backwoodsgoa .com) in the village of Matkan near Tamdi Surla offers one of Goa's richest sources of feathered friends, with everything from Ceylon frogmouths and Asian fairy bluebirds, to puffthroated babblers and Indian pittas putting in regular appearances. Accommodation comes in the form of tents on raised forest platforms, bungalows and farmhouse rooms, and the camp makes valiant attempts to protect this fragile bit of the Goan ecosystem through measures including waste recycling, replanting indigenous tree species and employing local villagers. Three-day birdwatching excursions, including guide, transport, accommodation at the camp and all meals, cost from Rs5500 per person.

MAPUSA
pop 40,100

The market town of Mapusa (pronounced Mapsa) is the largest town in northern Goa, and is most often visited for its busy **Friday Market** (☻ 8am-6.30pm) which attracts scores of buyers and sellers from neighbouring towns and villages, and a healthy intake of tourists from the northern beaches. It's a good place to pick up the usual slew of embroidered bedsheets and the like, at prices far lower than in the beach resorts.

There's not a lot else to see here, though it's a pleasant, bustling and typically Indian town

to wander for a while, and if you're interested in learning more about the admirable work of El Shaddai, International Animal Rescue, (for both, see Getting Involved, p204) or the Goa Foundation (see Green Goa?, p194), which all have their headquarters here or very close by.

Information

There are plenty of ATMs scattered about town, and you won't have any trouble locating one. There's a bumper crop around the Municipal Gardens and the market area.

Mapusa Clinic (☎ 2263343; ☻ consultations 10am-noon & 4-6pm) A well-run medical clinic, and the place to go in an emergency.

Other India Bookstore (☎ 2263306; www.otherindia bookshore.com; Mapusa Clinic Rd; ☻ 9am-5pm Mon-Fri, to 1pm Sat) A little hard to find, go up the steps on the right as you walk down Mapusa Clinic Rd, and follow signs: this friendly and rewarding little bookshop is at the end of a highly dingy corridor.

Pink Panther Travel Agency (☎ 2250352, 2263180; panther_goa@sancharnet.in) A very helpful agency, selling bus, train and air tickets (both international and domestic) as well as offering currency exchange and property consultancy services.

Softway (☎ 2262075; Rs20 per hr; Chandranath Apts, opposite Police Station) In a small shopping complex to the left just after the post office, this place has fast internet connections, and vends ice creams to keep you cool while surfing.

Sleeping

Sleeping options are pretty grim in Mapusa, and there's little reason to stay the night when the beaches of the north coast are all so close.

Hotel Vilena (☎ 2263115; Feira Baixa Rd; d Rs450, without bathroom Rs300) Friendly owners run Mapusa's best budget choice, though don't bring a cat since there won't be room in any of the 14 plain double rooms to swing it. The hotel's quaint Obsession Pub is open for bar-propping each evening.

Hotel Satyaheera (☎ 2262849; hotelsatyaheera@ hotmail.com; d without/with AC from Rs700/1000; ☒) Just next to the little Maruti Temple, this is widely considered Mapusa's best hotel – and don't they know it. Uninterested staff dole out dated, though comfy, rooms and the most thrilling thing about the entire experience is the forest-scene wallpaper in the elevator. Note the 9am check-out time and the stipulation that children up to age 12 will be

GET INVOLVED

'Never work with children or animals', so the old thespian adage goes, but for those with the opportunity to volunteer while in the sunny state, three opportunities exist for helping small creatures with two or four – and sometimes even three – legs who need help most.

■ **El Shaddai** (☎ 2266520, 6513286, 6513287; www.childrescue.net; El Shaddai House, Socol Vaddo, Assagao) A British-founded charity, El Shaddai aids impoverished and homeless children throughout Goa and beyond, running a number of day and night shelters, an open school and children's homes throughout the state. Volunteers (who undergo a rigorous vetting process) able to commit to more than four weeks work with El Shaddai are encouraged to contact James d'Souza (☎ 9225901266). This is an undertaking to arrange in advance, since it can take up to six months to complete the vetting process. You can also sponsor a child, and make a difference to a young life, for less than £1 per day: check El Shaddai's website for details.

■ **International Animal Rescue** (IAR; ☎ 2268328/272; www.iar.org.uk/india/goa; Animal Tracks, Mandungo Vaddo, Assagoa) An internationally active charity, helping Goa's furry and feathery sick, unwanted and strays, IAR runs its Animal Tracks rescue facility in Assagao, near Mapusa, in north Goa. Visitors and volunteers (both short- and long-term) are always welcome, and IAR's website includes a 'Needs List' of things you might be able to fit into your backpack and bring from home, including antiseptic ointment, flea powder and puppy toys. You'll also find online blogs written by current volunteers, and a downloadable PDF of information for willing volunteers. If you find an animal in distress in Goa, call the shelter for help.

■ **Goa Animal Welfare Trust** (GAWT; ☎ 2653677; www.gawt.org; Old Police Station, Curchorem) Based in South Goa, GAWT operates an animal shelter at Curchorem (situated in the Old Police Station on the main road), helping sick, stray and injured dogs, cats and even a calf or two, and is open daily from 9am to 5pm for visits. GAWT, like IAT, undertakes extensive dog sterilisation projects throughout Goa, offers low-cost veterinary care, deals with animal cruelty cases, and finds homes for stray puppies. Volunteers are welcome, if only for a few hours to walk or play with the dogs, and even your old newspapers (all those you've bought from beach vendors) will be gratefully received for lining kennel floors, as will old sheets, towels and anything else you might not be taking home. GAWT also operates a shop and information centre in Colva (see p226).

---

charged Rs50 per day to share a room with their parents, though 'no extra linen will be provided'.

Eating & Drinking

There are plenty of nice, old-fashioned cafes within the market area, serving simple Indian snacks, dishes and cold drinks to a local clientele. Thalis come in at the Rs40 mark, and chai at Rs5.

Hotel Vrundavan (dishes Rs8-50; 7am-late) An all-veg place bordering the Municipal Gardens, this is a great place for a hot chai and a quick breakfast. Dip your *pau* (fluffy white Portuguese bread roll) or *puri* (flat savoury dough that puffs up when deep fried) into a cashew-nut *bhaji* (small vegetable-based curry) for just Rs10, or try the tomato version for a more modest Rs9.

Ruchira Restaurant (mains Rs30-100; 11am-11pm) On the top floor of Hotel Satyaheera, Ruchira

is widely deemed to be one of Mapusa's best restaurants and is very popular with tourists. Serving Indian and Continental dishes, the views alone make a visit worthwhile, though beware the slightly bewildered, lacklustre service.

The Pub (9am-10.30pm; mains from Rs70) Don't be put off by the dingy entrance or stairwell; this place is great for watching the milling market crowds over a cold beer or long glass of *feni* (Goan liquor distilled from coconut milk or cashews). Eclectic daily specials (Rs108) include roast beef and goulash with noodles.

Getting There & Away

If you're coming to Goa by bus from Mumbai, Mapusa's Kadamba bus stand is the jumping-off point for the northern beaches. Private operators vend tickets to Mumbai (normal/AC Rs500/700, 14 hours) and Bengaluru (normal/AC Rs500/700, 12 hours) from just next to the bus stand. There's generally little difference in prices, comfort or duration between services, but shop around for the best fare.

Frequent local services – express and regular – also arrive and depart from the Kadamba bus stand; just look for the correct destination on the sign in the bus windscreen. Express services to Panaji (Rs9, 25 minutes), Calangute (Rs8, 20 minutes) and Anjuna (Rs8, 20 minutes), all depart every 30 minutes or so. For buses to the southern beaches, take a bus to Margao (Rs10, 1½ hours) and change there.

An autorickshaw to Anjuna or Calangute should cost Rs150; a taxi will charge at least Rs250.

Thivim, about 12km northeast of town, is the nearest train station on the Konkan Railway. Local buses meet trains (Rs10); an autorickshaw into Mapusa from Thivim costs around Rs120.

CANDOLIM, SINQUERIM & FORT AGUADA
pop 8600

Candolim's long, clean and narrow beach, which curves round as far as smaller Sinquerim beach in the south, is largely the preserve of slow-roasting package tourists from the UK, Russia and Scandinavia, and is fringed with an unabating line of beach shacks, all offering sun beds and shade in exchange for your custom. There are, however, some great independent budget hotels, which make for great stays in the area if you've got your own transport.

None of the most interesting attractions here, however, are directly beach-related. The most astonishing is the hulking wreck of the *River Princess* tanker, which ran aground in the late 1990s. Nothing can quite prepare you for the surreal sight of this massive industrial creature, marooned just a few dozen metres offshore, with tourists sunbathing in its sullen shadow.

The post office, supermarkets, travel agents, pharmacies and plenty of banks with ATMs are all located on the main road, known as Fort Aguada Rd, which runs parallel to the beach. Ask around for the season's latest internet outfit.

Sights & Activities

Aside from lazing on the beach, the Candolim area boasts a number of noteworthy attractions. First, guarding the mouth of the Mandovi River and hugely popular with Indian tour groups, is **Fort Aguada**, constructed by the Portuguese in 1612 and the most impressive of Goa's remaining forts. It's worth braving the crowds and hawkers at the moated ruins on the hilltop for the views, which are particularly good from the four-storey **Portuguese lighthouse**, built in 1894 and the oldest of its type in Asia. It's a pleasant 2km ride along a hilly, sealed road to the fort, or you can walk via a steep, uphill path past Marbella Guest House. Beneath the fort, facing the Mandovi, is the **Fort Aguada Jail**, whose cells were originally fort storehouses.

A highlight of Candolim for those interested in Goan heritage is **Calizz** (☎ 325000; Fort Aguada Rd; admission Rs300; ◷ 10am-7pm), an impressive compound filled with traditional Goan houses. Tours, which last for 45 minutes, are conducted by historians to bring the state's cultural history to life, in this National Tourism Award–winning project.

Throughout town there are numerous boat cruises on offer, the best known of which are **John's Boat Tours** (☎ 5620190, 9822182814; www.johnsboattours.com), offering a variety of boat and jeep excursions, and arranging wonderful houseboat cruises (Rs4300 per person per day, full board). A dolphin-watching trip costs Rs795; a boat trip to Anjuna Market and back costs Rs500, and a 'Crocodile Dundee' river trip, to catch a glimpse of the Mandovi's 'muggers' (crocodiles), costs Rs1000. If you're looking to haggle for a dolphin-spotting trip, head up to the **excursion boat jetty** along the Nerul River, from which lots of independent local boatmen operate.

For the last couple of years, the stellar **Sunburn Festival** (www.sunburn-festival.com), which bills itself as 'Asia's biggest music festival', has set up camp in Candolim over Christmas and New Year. Check the website for details and, if it continues to run to form, don't miss it for a four-day dance-music extravaganza filled with international DJs and all-day partying.

Sleeping

Though Candolim is largely frequented by package tourists bussed straight in from Dabolim Airport, there's a great range of accommodation for the independent traveller, with the added bonus that many midrange places include nice little swimming pools. Most of the best-value budget choices are situated either in the northern part of Candolim

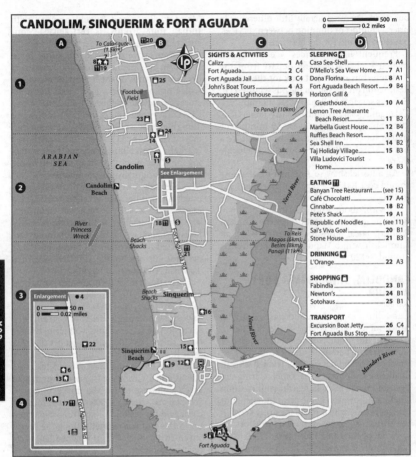

CANDOLIM, SINQUERIM & FORT AGUADA

SIGHTS & ACTIVITIES	
Calizz	1 A4
Fort Aguada	2 C4
Fort Aguada Jail	3 C4
John's Boat Tours	4 A3
Portuguese Lighthouse	5 B4

SLEEPING	
Casa Sea-Shell	6 A4
D'Mello's Sea View Home	7 A1
Dona Florina	8 A1
Fort Aguada Beach Resort	9 B4
Horizon Grill &	
Guesthouse	10 A4
Lemon Tree Amarante	
Beach Resort	11 B2
Marbella Guest House	12 B4
Ruffles Beach Resort	13 A4
Sea Shell Inn	14 B2
Taj Holiday Village	15 B3
Villa Ludovici Tourist	
Home	16 B3

EATING	
Banyan Tree Restaurant	(see 15)
Café Chocolatti	17 A4
Cinnabar	18 B2
Pete's Shack	19 A1
Republic of Noodles	(see 11)
Sai's Viva Goa!	20 B1
Stone House	21 B3

DRINKING	
L'Orange	22 A3

SHOPPING	
Fabindia	23 B1
Newton's	24 B1
Sotohaus	25 B1

TRANSPORT	
Excursion Boat Jetty	26 C4
Fort Aguada Bus Stop	27 B4

or in the Sinquerim area further south; the little road up to Marbella (see opposite) has lots of private houses offering double rooms for around Rs500 per night.

BUDGET

Villa Ludovici Tourist Home (☎ 2479684; Fort Aguada Rd; d incl breakfast Rs650) For 30 years, Ludovico's has been welcoming travellers into its well-worn, creaky rooms in a grand old Portuguese villa. This is the place for a four-poster bed on a budget; rooms are vast, if definitely faded, and the hosts (and ghosts) are kind and amiable.

D'Mello's Sea View Home (☎ 2489650; dmellos_sea view_home@hotmail.com; d small/large Rs700/1200) Lovely breezy rooms are the principle attraction at D'Mello's, which has the advantage of being just a stone's throw from the beach. A great choice for a simple, serene stay, especially when nearby Dona Florina is fully booked.

our pick **Dona Florina** (☎ 2489051; www.donaflorina .com; Monteiro's Rd; s/d/sea view Rs750/850/1000) It's hard to get better value in Candolim than friendly Dona Florina, just a quick walk from the sea and situated in the quiet northern part of the village. Front-facing rooms have spectacular sea views, there's daily yoga on the roof terrace, and the lack of vehicle access ensures a quiet night's repose.

Sea Shell Inn (☎ 2489131; seashellgoa@hotmail .com; Fort Aguada Rd; d Rs850) You won't miss this beautiful white-painted Portuguese mansion, just opposite the massive Newton's supermarket. Its eight plain rooms might come as a bit of a disappointment, however, after visiting the reception; they're in a '70s-style annexe around the back. Still, they're clean, fan-cooled and reasonable value, and rates include breakfast.

MIDRANGE

Casa Sea-Shell (☎ 2479879; seashellgoa@hotmail.com; Fort Aguada Rd; d without/with AC Rs1150/1850; ✖ 🔲 🖳) This modern, rather characterless choice, run by the same people as the Sea Shell Inn, nevertheless represents good value with its efficient service, nice little pool and comfortable rooms.

Horizon Grill & Guesthouse (☎ 2479727; www.horizon view.co.in; d without/with AC Rs1200/1800; ✖ 🖳) One of the few midrange places in town catering solely to independent tourists, this small hotel is a good-value new option run by British expats, with simple rooms set around a small swimming pool. Don't expect luxury, but for the price tag, it can't be beat.

Ruffles Beach Resort (☎ 6641039; www.rufflesgoa .com; Fort Aguada Rd; d/tr Rs1500/1800; ✖ 🖳) 'Welcome to your abode in Paradise', declares Ruffles' website; that might be a bit much, but this decent place does have a pleasant courtyard pool and good-value, well-equipped rooms.

TOP END

Marbella Guest House (☎ 2479551; www.marbellagoa .com; d from Rs2700, presidential ste Rs4700; ✖) You might be put off by the name – particularly if you've already noticed the similarities on the sands – but this place has not a touch of Spain's Costa del Sol about it. A stunning Portuguese villa filled with antiques and backed by a peaceful courtyard garden, this place is a romantic, redolent old-world remnant. Its kitchen serves breakfast, lunch and dinner daily, with some imaginative touches, and its penthouse suite is a dream of polished tiles and four-posters. Sadly for kids with a keen sense of style, no guests under 12 are permitted.

Fort Aguada Beach Resort (☎ toll-free 1 800 111825; www.tajhotels.com; d from Rs9000; ✖ 🔲 🖳) Dominating the headland above Sinquerim beach, the Taj Group's sprawling beach resort isn't the best the Taj name has to offer, but its service is still top-notch even where its rooms are showing signs of wear and tear. Its Jiva Spa offers a host of soothing balms and palms, and there's a gym, pool and even adventure sports on offer.

Taj Holiday Village (☎ toll-free 1 800 111825; www .tajhotels.com; cottages from Rs10,000; ✖ 🔲 🖳) Next door to the Fort Aguada Beach Resort, this newly renovated set of cottages – also owned by the Taj Group – is a smart variation on a five-star theme, possessing all the luxuries, though lacking all the individual character, you'd expect from this top-end chain. Its Banyan Tree restaurant (open from 7.30pm to 10.30pm) deserves a special mention for its gorgeous Thai food, served in suitably upscale surroundings.

Lemon Tree Amarante Beach Resort (☎ 3988188; www.lemontreehotels.com; Fort Aguada Rd; r Rs10,500-21,000; ✖ 🔲 🛜 🖳) Squeezed in on the main strip, this boutiquey, luxey place conjures up a strange mixture of Thai-spa style and medieval motifs intended to echo, apparently, 'the history and romance of 15th-century Portugal'. Whatever the mix, it works, with swish rooms equipped with wi-fi and DVD players, a luxurious spa and a roomy courtyard pool with swim-up bar.

Eating & Drinking

Candolim's drinking scene is largely hotel-based, but its plentiful beach shacks are popular places for a lunchtime beer or a happy-hour sunset cocktail or two. Look out for **Pete's Shack** (mains from Rs80) on the northern end of the strip, which is one of the sleekest, coolest beachfront operations.

Cinnabar (coffees from Rs40; 🕑 9am-late) This corner joint set in Acron Arcade shopping centre makes a calm pull-up for a pit stop on the shady terrace. Snack from an uncomplicated bistro menu of pastas, soups and salads, then top it off with a Black Forest ice cream and a frothy cappuccino.

Sai's Viva Goa! (Fort Aguada Rd; mains from Rs60; 🕑 11am-midnight) This cheap, locals-oriented little place serves flipping-fresh fish and Goan seafood specialities such as a spicy mussel fry.

our pick **Café Chocolatti** (Fort Aguada Rd; cakes from Rs80; 🕑 9am-7pm) When you're tired of thalis, or simply seeking sanctuary, there's nowhere better to treat yourself in Candolim than this lovely tearoom, set in a green garden light years from the bustle of the beach. Though the cafe serves sandwiches and salads, the clue to its speciality is in the name. Order a ginger lime fizz (Rs60) and a slice of double-chocolate cake (Rs80) and sink back into cocoa heaven.

L'Orange (Fort Aguada Rd; mains from Rs90; 🕑 midday-midnight) A cute, and largely orange, bar, restaurant and art gallery just beside John's Boat Tours, head here on Tuesday and Thursday nights for 'live music by Elvis', who's apparently alive and well and living in Candolim.

Stone House (Fort Aguada Rd; mains Rs90-240; ☺ 6pm-midnight) Surf 'n' turf's the thing at this venerable old Candolim venue, inhabiting a stone house and a leafy front courtyard, and the improbable sounding 'Swedish Lobster' tops the list. There's live music most nights of the week, amid the twinkle of fairy lights.

Republic of Noodles (Fort Aguada Rd; appetisers Rs200, mains from Rs425; ☺ 11.30am-3pm & 7-11pm) For a sophisticated dining experience, the RoN delivers with its dark bamboo interior, Buddha heads and floating candles. Delicious, huge noodle plates are the order of the day, and if you're feeling flush there's an exquisite brunch on Sunday mornings: Rs1200 buys you an extensive southeast Asian buffet, along with unlimited Mimosas and Bloody Marys.

Shopping

Sotohaus (☎ 2489983; www.sotodecor.com) Offering cool, functional items dreamed up by a Swiss expat team, this is the place to invest in a natural form–inspired lamp, mirror or dining table to add a twist of streamlined India to your pad back home. It's near the football ground.

Fabindia (Seashell Arcade) Part of a nationwide chain selling tempting textiles, home furnishings, jewellery and toiletries, this place has a thorough fair-trade policy. It's opposite the Canara Bank.

Newton's (☺ 9.30am-midnight) If you're desperately missing tinned spaghetti hoops, corned beef or Ribena, don't delay in dashing to Newton's to stock up on pricey, but satisfyingly homely, goods of all descriptions. This vast supermarket also stocks a good line in toiletries, wines and children's toys. Expat folks travel miles just to peruse its goodie-lined shelves.

Getting There & Away

Buses run about every 10 minutes to and from Panaji (Rs7, 45 minutes), and stop at the central bus stop near John's Boat Tours. Some continue south to the Fort Aguada bus stop at the bottom of Fort Aguada Rd, then head back to Panaji along the Mandovi River road, via the villages of Nerul and Betim.

Frequent buses also run from Candolim to Calangute (Rs3, 15 minutes) and can be flagged down on Fort Aguada Rd.

CALANGUTE & BAGA
pop 15,800

Once the summertime preserve of wealthy Goans escaping the oppressive heat of the premonsoon hinterlands, and later the heady '60s hotspot for naked, revelling hippies, the Calangute of today is India's 'Kiss Me Quick' capital, and, if you're not expecting pristine tropical sands, can prove just the place for fun-in-the-sun akin to a quick trip to Blackpool in a heatwave.

While Calangute's northern beach area is very much bucket-and-spade territory, its southern beach is more relaxed, refined, and upscale. Baga to the north, meanwhile, is the place for drinking and dancing with – unusually these days for Goa – clubs open until 4am, and a younger beach-shack based crowd. To escape the Baga heat, head north across the Baga River to some budget accommodation bargains clinging to the coast.

Orientation & Information

Currency-exchange offices, ATMs, supermarkets and pharmacies cluster around Calangute's main market and bus-stand area, continue north up to Baga, and head south too along the main road leading to Candolim. Here you'll also find international brand stores such as Levis, Lee and even a dedicated Crocs shop.

There are plenty of internet cafes (most charging Rs40 to Rs60 per hour) and prices tend to drop as you go further inland from the beach.

Literati Bookshop & Café (☎ 2277740; www.literati-goa.com; ☺ 10am-6.30pm Mon-Sat) Tucked away down a dusty lane leading to the beach at the far southern end of Calangute is this refreshingly different bookshop. Piles of good reads are stacked onto shelves throughout the owner's home, and there's a good line in strong Karnatakan coffee to keep you focused.

MGM International Travels (☎ 2276249; www.mgmtravels.com; ☺ 9.30am-6.30pm Mon-Sat) A long-established and trusted travel agency near Calangute's central roundabout, this travel agency offers competitive prices on domestic and foreign air tickets.

Mubli Cybercafé (Tito's Rd; per hr Rs60; ☺ 9am-late) Order a simple breakfast or a strong cup of Italian coffee, surf and watch the beach crowds mill by.

Oxford Bookstore (☎ 9326060647; www.oxfordbookstore.com; ☺ 10am-7pm) Just opposite St Anthony's Chapel, this is a well-stocked and well-run branch of the countrywide bookshop chain.

Activities

Aside from frolicking in the waves with scores of other holidayers, there's a host of activities on offer in both Calangute and Baga, including a highly respectable diving school.

WATER SPORTS

You'll find numerous jet-ski and parasailing operators on Baga Beach, and it pays to compare a few to find the most competitive rate. Parasailing usually costs around Rs1500 per ride; jet-skis cost Rs900 per 15 minutes, and water-skiing can be had for about Rs800 per 10 minutes.

Barracuda Diving (☎ 2182402; www.barracudadiving .com; Sun Village Resort, Baga) a longstanding diving school, offers a vast range of classes, dives and courses, including a free 'Try Scuba' family session every Monday. It's also exceptional for its 'Project A.W.A.R.E' which undertakes marine-conservation initiatives and annual underwater and beach clean-ups.

YOGA & AYURVEDA

Ayurvedic Natural Health Centre (☎ 2409275; www .healthandayurveda.com; Chogm Rd, Saligao) a highly respected centre 5km inland, offers a vast range of courses, in reflexology, aromatherapy, acupressure, yoga and various other regimes. There's also a range of herbal medicines on offer and treatments available by an ayurvedic doctor.

Pousada Tauma (☎ 2279061; www.pousada-tauma .com; d from €225; 🐕 🖳 🐾) If you're looking for luxury with your ayurvedic regime, check right into this gorgeous little boutique hotel in Calangute. Costs for treatments range from €45 for a 1½-hour treatment, up to €495 for a 14-day 'Pizhichil' course to treat complaints such as arthritis and sciatica.

BOAT TRIPS

Local fishermen congregate around the northern end of Baga beach, offering dolphin-spotting trips (Rs350 per person), visits to Anjuna Market (Rs270 per person) and whole-day coastal excursions up to Arambol, Mandrem and back (Rs800 per person). To pre-arrange and negotiate a trip, call friendly fisherman Eugenio (☎ 9226268531).

OTHER ACTIVITIES

Kerkar Art Complex (☎ 2276017; www.subodhkerkar .com; 🕑 10am-11pm) Showcases the colourful paintings, photographs and sculptures of local artist Dr Subodh Kerkar; the complex is most notable for its soothing weekly open-air **Indian music and dancing recitals** (Rs300 per person; 🕑 6.45-8pm Tue).

Jungle Guitars (☎ 9823565117; www.jungleguitars .com) If you've always been one to strum to your own tune, Jungle Guitars might just be the place for you. Fifteen- to 20-day courses will allow you to build your very own steel-string or classical guitar from scratch, overseen by master guitar-builder, Chris. Courses cost Rs55,000, including all materials and a case for the finished product.

Tours

Day Tripper (☎ 2276726; www.daytrippergoa.com; Calangute–Anjuna Rd; 🕑 9am-6pm end Oct–end Apr), with its head office in south Calangute, is one of Goa's best tour agencies. It runs a wide variety of trips around Goa, including to Dudhsagar Falls (p202), and also interstate to Hampi and the Kali River (for rafting and birdwatching trips) in Karnataka.

GTDC tours (see p186) can be booked at the '70s monstrosity **Calangute Residency** (☎ 2276024) beside the beach.

Sleeping

Calangute and Baga's sleeping options are broad and varied, though most decent budget options are towards the top end of the budget range. Generally, the quietest, most laid-back hotels lie in south Calangute, and across the bridge north of Baga.

BUDGET

Calangute

Johnny's Hotel (☎ 2277458; s/d Rs400, d Rs600-900) Twelve basic rooms in this backpacker-popular place make for a sociable stay, with regular classes available in yoga, ayurveda, reiki, and the tantalisingly titled 'metamorphic technique'. A range of apartments and houses are also available for longer-stayers: ask at reception for current prices. Johnny's is also home to a popular cafe: stop in for baked beans on toast for breakfast (Rs100) or spice up lunchtime with a Goan 'veg vindaloo' (Rs60).

our pick **Indian Kitchen** (☎ 2277555; ikitchen2602@ yahoo.co.in; off Calangute–Baga Rd; d Rs880; 🖳 🛜 🐾) If a colourful stay is what you're after, look no further than this family-run guest house, which offers basic, rather ramshackle rooms with lots of attempts at individual charm, around a sparkly, spangly central courtyard.

BOUNTIFUL BEACHES: THE NORTHERN NAMES

Goa's northern beaches vary dramatically in character within short distances. Whether you're looking for backpacker-filled beach huts, silent sands or plenty of party people, you'll likely find what you're looking for.

Arambol (Harmal) & Querim

Backpacker central, little Arambol (p220), with its simple huts scattered across a rocky headland, is the most northerly of Goa's developed beaches, and is a popular choice for long-stay hippies and travellers, as well as for those looking for somewhere cheap and chilled to rest up for a while. A little further north, quiet Querim is still just a fishing village with a scattering of beach shacks, and makes a nice change of pace if you're looking to bask in peace.

Mandrem

South from Arambol, Mandrem (p219) is a long, palm-backed ribbon of clean, uncluttered sand. Although it's certainly been discovered, it still makes a great choice for getting away from it all. The best digs here are found in the midrange budget, with many offering yoga courses, ayurvedic massage and other ways to help you relax, release and rejuvenate.

Morjim & Asvem

Stretching down to the Chapora River, the sandy beaches of Morjim and Asvem might be beautiful, but the village resorts behind them are decidedly lacklustre. Morjim, particularly popular with young Russians, has a somewhat desolate aura, though it's a scenic place for a walk along the mouth of the Chapora River and is a breeding site for endangered olive ridley sea turtles. Asvem's beach, meanwhile, is wide and lovely, but the strip of development behind it is distinctly lacking atmosphere, and some of its sandy stretches these days are getting very grubby indeed. Nevertheless, Asvem, like Arambol, is very popular with long-stayers.

Vagator & Chapora

Once the centre of Goa's trance party scene, things are quieter these days on Vagator's (p217) three small and characterful covelike beaches ranged around a rocky headland, though remnants of the state's fabled parties do still put in an appearance over Christmas and New Year. Small Chapora, just north of Vagator and dominated by the hilltop remains of a Portuguese fort, has more puff than a magic dragon, and the scent of charas hangs thick in the air at the centre of the village.

Anjuna

Famed for its weekly Wednesday flea market, slightly scruffy Anjuna (p214) remains a firm backpacker favourite week-round, with its nice rocky beaches, great eating options and general sense of chilledness. It might not be as hip or hippie as in years past, but it still makes a terrific place to hang out, eat and drink into the wee hours with travellers and long-stayers from across the globe.

Calangute & Baga

If you're in Goa for the action, or are in the mood for a good dose of 'Oh, I do like to be beside the seaside,' Calangute and Baga (p208) are without doubt the places for you. Here you'll find bars open until 4am, unbroken lines of beach shacks, international brand shops, scores of tourist-orientated restaurants, and some pretty classy dining and accommodation options tucked in between. The beaches are busy (think sun-lounger central), but the bustle appeals to the many who've been returning annually for decades.

Candolim & Sinquerim

Busy Candolim (p205) is a favourite with British package tourists, who set up camp for their fortnightly dose of sun 'n' sand at one of its dozens of beach shacks. Away from the beach, you'll find some surprisingly good budget accommodation options, making Candolim a good base for exploring the coast if you've your own set of wheels. Sinquerim, at its north end, is dominated by the Taj Hotel's two resorts, and is a little less buzzing, but a popular location for arranging water sports through ever-changing independent operators.

Each room has its own terrace or sit-out, but what really tips the budget scales in its favour is the small, sparklingly clean swimming pool out the back and the free wi-fi. Roomy air-conditioned apartments are also available for long-stayers, for Rs15,000 to Rs18,000 per month.

Coco Banana (☎ 2279068; www.cocobananagoa.com; d from Rs950) A quiet place run by a friendly Swiss-Goan family, colourful Coco Banana proves a soothing retreat from the mayhem outside. If you're looking for something roomier than their big double rooms, consider one of the two apartments at their nearby Casa Leyla, which both have a separate sitting room and kitchen area.

Baga

Melissa Guest House (☎ 2279583; d Rs500) Neat little rooms, all with attached bathroom and hot-water showers, comprise this quiet, good-value little place, pleasantly situated just past Nani's & Rani's.

Divine Guest House (☎ 2279546; www.indivinehome .com; d from Rs800;) You'll get the general optimistic air of this place as soon as you see the 'Praise the Lord' gatepost, and the happiness continues indoors with quietly cheerful rooms embellished with the odd individual touch amid a quiet riverside location.

Nani's Bar & Rani's Restaurant (☎ 2276313; www .naniranigoa.com; r Rs1000;) Situated on the tranquil north side of the Baga River, just a short hop from the Baga beach action, Nani's is as charming as it is well situated, with simply furnished rooms set around a garden and a gorgeous colonial bungalow. Be sure to try the restaurant's food, cooked, its website claims, by the 'inmates', and look out for the heritage room equipped with such mod cons as an 'inverter'.

MIDRANGE & TOP END
Calangute

Hotel Seagull (☎ 2179969; www.villatheresagoa.com; Holiday St, Calangute; d without/with AC Rs2300/2500;) Bright, friendly and welcoming, the Seagull's rooms, set in a cheerful orange-painted house in quieter South Calangute, are light and airy, with antique bits and pieces of furniture to give them character. There's a popular bar-restaurant downstairs with meals served all day.

Vila Goesa (☎ 2277535; www.vilagoesa.com; d without/with AC from Rs2750/3250;) Nicely situated between south Baga and north Calangute and

hidden in the palm thickets 200m back from the beach, this is a great place for lingering with a good book by the pool. Rooms are simple but pleasantly furnished; the higher the tariff, the closer you get to the beach.

Nilaya Hermitage (☎ 2276793; www.nilaya .com; Arpora; d incl breakfast & dinner €320;) Ultimate Goan luxury, set 6km inland from the beach at Arpora, a stay here will see you signing the guestbook with the likes of Giorgio Armani, Sean Connery and Kate Moss. Beautiful red-stone laterite structures undulate around a swimming pool, around which are set 11 luxury rooms and four stunning tents. The food is as dreamy as the surroundings, and the spa will see you spoiled rotten.

BAGA

Cavala Seaside Resort (☎ 2276090; www.cavala.com; s/d without AC from Rs850/1100, d with AC from Rs2200;) Idiosyncratic, ivy-clad Cavala has been charming Baga-bound travellers for over 25 years, and continues to deliver clean, simple, nicely furnished rooms, ranged about a large complex with two central swimming pools. Rates include a hearty breakfast, and the bar-restaurant cooks up a storm most evenings.

Casa Baga (☎ 2253205; www.casaboutiquehotels.com; d Rs6000-7000;) Twenty Balinese-style rooms, some with huge four-poster beds, make for a classy and tranquil stay, with all the little stylish touches the Casa boutique team are so adept at providing.

Eating

Calangute and Baga boast probably the greatest concentration of dining options of anywhere in Goa, with everything on offer from the simplest curbside *bhelpuri* (thin fried rounds of dough with rice, lentils, lemon juice, onion, herbs and chutney) to the finest Scottish smoked salmon.

For the best of the area's street food, try the main Calangute beach strip, which is thick with vendors grilling sweetcorn, serving up *bhaji pau* (spicy vegetable curry with a white bread roll for dipping, served for breakfast), and spinning luminescent candyfloss. Dining gets more sophisticated to both the north and south, with a number of Mediterranean stunners, while all along the beach, you'll find the usual gamut of beach-shack cuisine. The market area, meanwhile, is filled with little local chai-and-thali joints, where an all-veg lunch can be had for a mere Rs30 or so.

GOA

CALANGUTE & BAGA

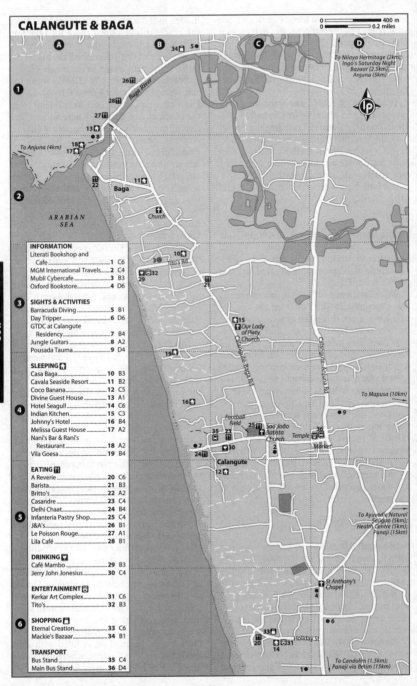

0 —————— 400 m
0 —————— 0.2 miles

GOA

CALANGUTE

Delhi Chaat (snacks from Rs20; ⊙ 8am-late) In the thick of the seaside action, this highly popular takeaway joint dispenses all manner of spicy, savoury snacks to the milling masses, as well as delicious hot, sweet chai (Rs10). A *bhaji pau* comes in at Rs40; an *aloo fry masala chaat* at Rs20.

Barista (Calangute–Baga Rd; coffee Rs45-79; ⊙ 10am-4am) For a cup of Joe around the clock, rest weary feet on the pleasant terrace of this countrywide coffee chain, and kick back with a cappuccino.

Infanteria Pastry Shop (Calangute–Baga Rd; cakes Rs50-100; ⊙ 7.30am-midnight) Next to the Sao João Batista church is this scrummy bakery, loaded with home-made cakes, croissants and little flaky pastries. The noticeboard here is a hotbed for all things current and counter-current.

Casandre (mains from Rs100; ⊙ 9am-midnight) Housed in an old Portuguese bungalow, this dim and tranquil retreat seems mightily out of place amid the tourist tat of Calangute's main beach drag. With a long and old-fashioned menu encompassing everything from 'sizzlers' to Goan specialities, and a cocktail list featuring the good old gimlet, this is a loveable time warp, with a pool table to boot.

our pick **A Reverie** (Holiday St; mains from Rs320; ⊙ 7pm-late) A gorgeous lounge bar, all armchairs, cool jazz and sparkling crystals, this is the place to spoil yourself, with the likes of Serrano ham, grilled asparagus, French wines and Italian cheeses. Try the delectable forest-mushroom soup with truffle oil (Rs255) or go for a bowl of wasabi-flavoured guacamole (Rs215).

BAGA

Britto's (mains Rs70-250; ⊙ 8am-late) Long-running, usually packed-to-the-gills, and sometimes open as late as 3am, this Baga institution tumbles out onto the beach, serving up a healthy mixture of Goan and Continental cuisines, satisfying cakes and desserts, and live music several nights a week.

J&A's (mains from Rs250) A pretty cafe set around a gorgeous little Portuguese villa, this little slice of Italy is a treat even before the sumptuous, if rather pricey, food arrives. Owned by a wonderful couple originally from Mumbai, the jazz-infused garden and twinkling evening lights makes for a place as drenched in romance as a tiramisu is in rum. Add to this triple-filtered water, electric car and composted leftovers, and

you've got an experience almost as good for the world as it is for your tastebuds.

Le Poisson Rouge (dishes from Rs250; ⊙ 7pm-late) Baga manages to do fine dining with aplomb, and this French-slanted experience is one of the picks of the place. Simple local ingredients are combined into winning dishes such as beetroot carpaccio and red-snapper masala, and served up beneath the stars.

Lila Café (mains from Rs70; ⊙ 8.30am-6pm Wed-Mon) Airy, white and enticing is this roomy semi-open air place along the river, run by German long-term expats and with a great line in home-baked breads and perfect, frothy cappuccinos. The restful river view is somewhat obscured by the cafe's own guest parking places, but it still makes for a soothing place for a quiet cuppa.

Drinking & Entertainment

Boisterous, brash and booming, Baga's club scene somehow manages to bubble on long after the trance parties of further north have been locked down for good by late-night noise regulations. Just how this little strip of night-owls' nirvana has managed to escape the lockdown is anybody's guess, but escape it has, and if you're up for a night of decadent drinking or dancing on the tables, don your gladrags and hit the hot spots with the best of them.

If you're seeking something lower-key, go for the main Calangute seaside road, where simple bars are populated with a captivating mix of frazzled foreigners, heavy-drinking locals, and tipsy out-of-towners.

Jerry John Jonesius (JJJ; ⊙ 7am-10.30pm) Largely the preserve of locals, JJJ is a suitably dingy and atmospheric bar to down a few beers. Snacks and basic Indian meals (from Rs50) are also available, if you need to line your stomach with something more substantial than *feni*.

Tito's (☎ 9822765002; www.titos.in; Tito's Rd; cover charge men/women from Rs300/free; ⊙ 8pm-3am) Tito's, the titan on Goa's clubbing scene, is trying its hardest to escape the locals-leering-at-Western-women image of yesteryear, though it's still hardly the place for a hassle-free girls' night out. Thursday's Bollywood Night and Friday's hip hop are the pick of the bunch, for the closest thing to Ibiza this side of Star TV.

Café Mambo (☎ 9822765002; www.titos.in; before/after 10pm free/Rs200; ⊙ 8pm-late) Owned and managed by Tito's, this is a – very slightly – more sophisticated version of the same thing, with nightly DJs pumping out commercial house, hip hop and Latino tunes.

Shopping

At the time of writing, the future of both the area's famous night markets – alternatives to Anjuna's weekly Wednesday market – looked uncertain. Both **Mackie's Saturday Nite Bazaar** (Map p212) and **Ingo's Saturday Nite Bazaar** (off Map p212), held each Saturday night from 6pm to midnight, had been cancelled and opinion was divided on whether they might be reinstated. Ask around to make sure.

A worthwhile stop if you're shopping in town is **Eternal Creation** (www.eternalcreation.com; Holiday St) which produces Australian-designed, fair-trade clothes, jewellery and children's wear up north in Dharamsala, and sells them here in its cheerful, colourful little store.

Getting There & Away

There are frequent buses to Panaji (Rs7, 45 minutes) and Mapusa (Rs6) from the bus stand near the beach, and some services also stop at the bus stop near the temple. A taxi from Calangute or Baga to Panaji costs around Rs350 and takes about 45 minutes. A prepaid taxi from Dabolim Airport to Calangute costs Rs645.

ANJUNA

Dear old Anjuna, that stalwart on India's hippie scene, still drags out the sarongs and sandalwood each Wednesday for its famous – and once infamous – flea market. Though it continues to pull in droves of backpackers and long-term hippies, midrange tourists are also increasingly making their way here for a dose of hippie-chic without the beach-hut rusticity of Arambol further up the coast. The town itself is might be a bit ragged around the edges these days, but that's all part of its charm, and Anjuna remains a favourite of long-stayers and first-timers alike.

Orientation & Information

Anjuna is spread out over a wide area, its most northerly point being the main Starco crossroads – where most buses stop and around which many eating options are dotted – and the southernmost being the flea-market site, about 2km south. Most accommodation and other useful services are sprinkled along the beach, or down shady inland lanes, in between.

Internet access in Anjuna – away from the midrange hotels – is perilously slow and unreliable, and internet joints thus open and close down regularly. Ask around for the best new option on the scene, or head to the German Bakery which offers wireless access for those with their own laptops.

Something important to consider – especially on market day – is that there are no ATMs in Anjuna. The **Bank of Baroda** (9.30am-2.30pm) gives cash advances on Visa and MasterCard, but won't exchange currency. For this, try one of the travel agents below.

There are plenty of reliable travel agents in town. Try **Speedy Travels** (2273266) near the post office, or the excellent **MGM Travels** (2274317; www.mgmtravels.com; Anjuna-Mapusa Rd; 9.30am-6pm Mon-Sat).

Activities

Anjuna's charismatic, rocky beach runs for almost 2km from the northern village area to the flea market. The northern end shrinks to almost nothing when the tide washes in, when it's fun to watch local tourist ladies hopping perilously from rock to rock in strappy sandals and saris, in search of a scenic photo opportunity. When the tide goes out, it becomes a lovely – and surprisingly quiet – stretch of sand, with lots of room to escape the presence of other sunbathers.

There's lots of yoga, reiki and ayurveda on offer, seasonally, in town; look out for notices posted at Café Diogo and the German Bakery (see Eating below), while the popular upscale **Purple Valley Yoga Retreat** (www.yogagoa.com) in nearby Assagao village offers one- and two-week residential courses in *ashtanga* yoga; rates begin at £390 for one week.

For an adrenalin rush, **paragliding** usually takes place off the headland at the southern end of the beach on market days; tandem rides cost Rs1500. And if you're looking to embellish yourself while in town, try **Andy's Tattoo Studio** (www.andys-tattoo-studio-goa.com; 11am-7pm), attached to San Francisco Restaurant, just where the Anjuna cliffside slides down to meet the beach. Drop in to make an appointment and receive a price quote for your permanent souvenir.

Sleeping
BUDGET

Dozens of rooms of the large concrete cell variety string themselves along Anjuna's north-

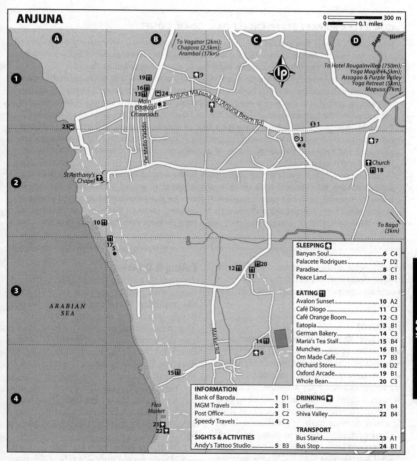

ANJUNA

	0 — 300 m
	0 — 0.1 miles

To Vagator (2km);
Chapora (2.5km);
Arambol (17km)

To Hotel Bougainvillea (750m);
Yoga Magic (1.5km);
Assagao & Purple Valley
Yoga Retreat (5km);
Mapusa (7km)

Anjuna Mapusa Rd (Anjuna Beach Rd)

Main
(Starco)
Crossroads

St Anthony's
Chapel

ARABIAN
SEA

Church

To Baga
(3km)

Market Rd

Flea
Market

SLEEPING 🛏
Banyan Soul	..6 C4
Palacete Rodrigues	..7 D2
Paradise	..8 C1
Peace Land	..9 B1

EATING 🍴
Avalon Sunset	.10 A2
Café Diogo	.11 C3
Café Orange Boom	.12 C3
Eatopia	.13 B1
German Bakery	.14 C3
Maria's Tea Stall	.15 B4
Munches	.16 B1
Om Made Café	.17 B3
Orchard Stores	.18 D2
Oxford Arcade	.19 B1
Whole Bean	.20 C3

DRINKING 🍸
Curlies	.21 B4
Shiva Valley	.22 B4

TRANSPORT
Bus Stand	.23 A1
Bus Stop	.24 B1

INFORMATION
Bank of Baroda	..1 D1
MGM Travels	..2 B1
Post Office	..3 C2
Speedy Travels	..4 C2

SIGHTS & ACTIVITIES
Andy's Tattoo Studio	..5 B3

GOA

ern clifftop stretch; most come in at Rs250 to Rs500 per night. There are also plenty of small, family-run guest houses tucked back from the main beach strip, offering nicer double rooms for a similar price; take your pick from the dozens of signs announcing 'Rooms To Let'. Below, though, are three exceptional choices for something a little bit different.

ourpick Peace Land (☎ 2273700; s/d Rs300/500; 🖳) You can't get better on a budget than Peace Land, run by a friendly couple and arranged around a tranquil courtyard garden. Rooms are small but spotlessly clean and comfortable, and their little restaurant cooks up some great Indian food. There's internet access for Rs30 per hour, and a small shop selling basic provisions.

Paradise (☎ 9922541714; janet_965@hotmail.com; Anjuna–Mapusa Rd; d without AC Rs400-800, with AC Rs1500) A paradise for animal-lovers particularly, since proprietor Janet is a keen collector of all things canine, feline and avian, this friendly place fronted by an old Portuguese home offers good, clean rooms with particularly well-decorated options in the newer annexe. And Janet doesn't stop at accommodation: her enterprising family can service your every need, with its pharmacy, general store, restaurant, internet access (Rs40 per hour), Connexions travel agency, money exchange, Western Union services and beauty parlour. You name it and Janet can probably arrange it for you.

Palacete Rodrigues (☎ 273358 ; www.palacetegoa .com; s/d without AC Rs850/950, d with AC Rs1050; 🗙) This

---

GOA'S FLEA MARKET EXPERIENCE: GOAN, GOAN, GONE?

Wednesday's weekly **flea market** at Anjuna is as much part of the Goan experience as a day on a deserted beach. More than two decades ago, it was still the sole preserve of hippies smoking jumbo joints and convening to compare experiences on the heady Indian circuit.

Nowadays, however, things are far more staid and mainstream, and package tourists seem to beat out independent travellers both in numbers and purchasing power. The market sprawls on vending stuff that is much of a muchness: a couple of hours here and you'll never want to see a mirrored bedspread, peacock-feather fan, or floaty Indian cotton dress again in your life. That said, though, it's still a great place for a spot of people-watching, and you can find some interesting one-off souvenirs and pieces of clothing in among the tourist tat. Remember to bargain hard and take along equal quantities of patience and stamina, applicable to dealing with local and expat vendors alike.

Until recently, great evening-time alternatives to the Anjuna experience were Mackie's and Ingo's Saturday 'Nite Bazaars,' both set up in the region of Calangute and Baga. At the time of research, however, both had been cancelled. Reasons for the cancellations remained unclear – reports range from licenses being revoked to the ongoing threat of terrorism – but ask around to double-check, since in seasons past they made for a pleasant evening mix of live music, food and shopping.

---

beautifully old-fashioned mansion, filled with antiques, odd corners and bags of charm, is as cool and quirky as you could hope Anjuna to come.

MIDRANGE

Banyan Soul (☎ 9820707283; sumityardi@thebanyansoul .com; d Rs1500; ❄) A slinky new 12-room option, tucked just behind Anjuna's scrummy German bakery, lovingly conceived and run by a young escapee of the Mumbai technology rat race. Rooms are chic and well equipped, the decor is flawless, and there are plans afoot for a rooftop restaurant. It's without a doubt the best midrange choice in town, and staff are extremely keen to please.

Hotel Bougainvillea (☎ 2273270; www.granpasinn .com; d incl breakfast & tax Rs1950-3250; ❄ ☑) An old-fashioned hotel housed in a centuries-old mansion, this place – also known as Granpa's Inn – offers charm with a touch of luxury with a lovely pool and well-decorated rooms.

TOP END

Yoga Magic (☎ 6523796; www.yogamagic.net; tent/villa per person Rs2750/3500) Solar lighting and compost toilets are just some of the worthy initiatives practiced in this ultraluxurious bamboo hut-and-villa village, where hand-printed textiles, locally made ironwork furniture and organic gourmet vegetarian food are the order of the day. Prices are based on two sharing and include breakfast and afternoon tea; daily yoga classes cost an extra Rs300 per session.

Eating & Drinking

Anjuna has a whole host of great eating options, with jostling cliffside cafes sporting the standard traveller-orientated menus, happy hours and stunning coastal views. The area around the Starco crossroads is also thick with dining options, as is Anjuna Beach Rd. Inside the flea market on market days, you'll find a number of boozy bars with stages full of cover version–singing foreigners. For a quick market shopping stop, look out for teensy **Maria's Tea Stall** (☺ market day; Flea Market; snacks from Rs10), selling tasty chai and snacks made by colourful elderly local Maria herself.

Café Orange Boom (mains from Rs40) Just past Café Diogo on the opposite side of the road, this nice little place has the same good food and friendly service at equivalent prices, with a useful noticeboard for catching up on Anjunan goings-on.

Avalon Sunset (dishes from Rs60; ☎) Good food, a pool table, a chill-out area, free wi-fi and rooms for rent (from Rs400) make this a great representative of Anjuna's clifftop restaurant parade. There's daily yoga on the roof, too; call in for class times.

German Bakery (dishes from Rs60; ☎) Leafy, and filled with prayer flags and jolly lights, this is a perfect place for a huge lunch from its equally huge menu. Tofu balls in mustard sauce with parsley potatoes and salad is a piled-platter winner at Rs150; wireless internet is available for a fairly steep Rs100 per hour.

Café Diogo (dishes from Rs70; ☼ 9am-4pm) Probably the best fruit salads in the world are sliced and diced at Café Diogo, a small locally run cafe on the way down to the market. Also worth a munch are the generous toasted avocado, cheese and mushroom sandwiches.

Whole Bean (Rs70-130) This simple, tasty, tofu-filled health-food cafe – which proudly announces itself as 'Anjuna's premier soy destination' – focuses on all things created from that most versatile of beans.

At the time of writing, **Curlies** (mains from Rs50; ☼ till late) and nearby **Shiva Valley** (☼ till late) were the best-hidden places for an evening drink, an alternative crowd and the odd impromptu party. Head down to either to find out what's on.

our pick Om Made Café (dishes Rs90-190; ☼ 8.30am-sunset) A highlight on Anjuna's clifftop strip, this cheery little place offers striped deckchairs from which to enjoy the views and the simple, sophisticated breakfasts, sandwiches and salads. Go for a raw papaya salad with ginger and lemongrass (Rs170), accompanied by a *chickoo* (Sapodilla fruit)–and–coconut smoothie or a glass of 'perfumed water' (Rs20).

Munches (mains from Rs40; ☼ 24 hr) Near the Starco Crossroads, this 24-hour place, serving up the full list of travellers' favourites, is popular for when an attack of the munchies demands you munch. Next door, Eatopia (mains from Rs40) also offers a wide range of pastas, pizzas and seafood, with the benefit of a movie screened nightly.

Two popular shops service the needs of Anjuna-based travellers missing home: the first, Oxford Arcade, near the Starco Crossroads, sells everything from peppermints to pesto, and has grown into a fully-fledged supermarket complete with trolleys and check-out scanners. You'll also find a great big wine section and a good range of toiletries, fresh bakery goods, pet food and children's toys. The smaller, jam-packed (in both senses of the phrase) Orchard Stores does much the same thing, with more of a village-shop vibe.

Getting There & Away

There are buses every half-hour or so from Mapusa to Anjuna (Rs6), stopping at the end of the road to the beach and continuing on to Vagator and Chapora, while some continue to Arambol. Plenty of motorcycle taxis gather at the main crossroads and you can also hire scooters and motorcycles easily from here.

VAGATOR & CHAPORA

Dramatic red-stone cliffs, dense green forests and a crumbling 17th-century **Portuguese fort** provide Vagator and its diminutive neighbour Chapora with one of the prettiest settings on the north Goan coast. Once known for their wild trance parties and heady, hippie lifestyles, things have slowed down considerably these days, though Chapora – reminiscent of Star Wars' Mos Eisley Cantina – remains a fave for smokers, with the smell of charas hanging heavy in the air.

If you're keen to see the remnants of the trance scene, hang around long enough in Vagator and you'll likely be handed a flyer for a party (many with international DJs) which can range from divine to dire. You may also catch wind of something going down in a hidden location – if you're lucky, it won't have been closed down by the time you get there.

Information

In Vagator, the lovely little **Rainbow Bookshop** (☎ 2273613; ☼ 9.30am-10pm), run by a charming elderly gentleman, stocks a good range of second-hand and new books, including this very guide. Plenty of internet places are scattered along the road to Little Vagator beach; **Tanu Communications** (Ozran Beach Rd; Rs50 per hr; ☼ 9am-late) just before the Alcove Resort at Little Vagator, is one reliable option.

Sleeping
VAGATOR

Budget accommodation, much of it in private rooms, ranges along Ozran Beach Rd in Vagator; you'll see lots of signs for 'rooms to let' in the side roads, too, in simple private homes and guest houses. Most charge Rs300 to Rs500 per double room.

Paradise On the Earth (☎ 2273591; www.moondance .co.nr; huts without bathroom Rs300) Simple bamboo huts with shared bathrooms clinging to the cliff above Little Vagator Beach offering great value for the beachside location, though the name might be a little overkill. The website boasts, intriguingly, of a 'well-stocked bare', something to certainly bear in mind come sunset.

Bean Me Up Soya Station (☎ 2273479; www.myspace .com/beanmeupindia; d Rs550, without bathroom Rs350) The rooms around a leafy, parachute-silky

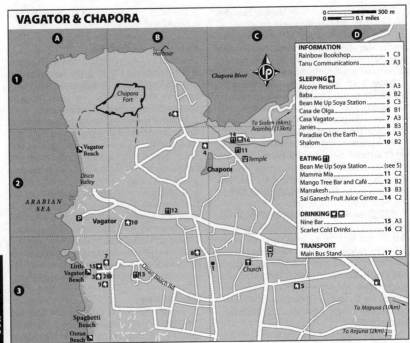

VAGATOR & CHAPORA

courtyard might look a bit cell-like from the outside, but step in and you'll be pleased to find that the billowing silks and mellow, earthy shades follow you there. Bicycles (Rs1000 deposit and Rs100 per day) and motorbikes (Rs250 per day) are both available for rent, and there's a nice vegetarian restaurant (see Eating, opposite).

our pick Shalom (☎ 2273166; d without/with TV & fridge Rs800/1500, 2-bedroom apt per month Rs25,000) Arranged around a placid garden not far from the path down to Little Vagator Beach, this place, run by a friendly family (whose home is on-site), offers a variety of well-kept rooms, and a two-bedroom apartment for long-stayers.

Janies (☎ 2273635; janiesricardo@hotmail.com; d Rs800, 1-/2-bedroom bungalow Rs1000/1200) A great choice for long-stayers, run by a very friendly lady and with a simple but homely vibe. The three double rooms each come equipped with small kitchen, bathroom and TV, and there are two large bungalows, the first with one double bedroom and the second with two.

Alcove Resort (☎ 2274491; www.alcovegoa.com; Ozran Beach Rd; d without/with AC Rs1800/2200, cottages without/with AC Rs2000/2500, ste without/with AC Rs3000/3500;

🐶 🖭) Attractively furnished rooms, slightly larger cottages, and four suites within easy striking distance of Little Vagator Beach, this place is for those who want a touch of luxury at surprisingly reasonable prices. When you tire of the sands there's a cool central pool.

Casa Vagator (☎ 2416738; www.casaboutiquehotels .com; d Rs7000-13,000; 🐶 🖳 🖭) A successfully rendered outfit in the deluxe Casa boutique mould, this is Vagator's most stylish accommodation option, with gorgeous rooms offering equally gorgeous views out to the wide blue horizon. The only downside is its proximity to techno-heavy Nine Bar, which pumps out Goa Trance every night until the 10pm shutdown; great, if you like that sort of thing, gruesome if you don't.

CHAPORA

Head down the road to the harbour and you'll find lots of rooms – and whole homes – for rent, far nicer than setting yourself up in the congested village centre; be sure to thoroughly trawl what's on offer before you land your catch.

Baba (☎ 2273213; d Rs300, without bathroom Rs150) The gaggle of men who own this place, with simple,

GOA

dingy, but serviceable rooms, seem a little like rulers of their own small empire. Nevertheless, they're a one-stop destination for most material needs, with their restaurant (serving the usual menu hodgepodge of Indian, Italian and just about everything else), internet cafe (Rs40 per hour) and money-exchange service.

Casa de Olga (☎ 2274355, 9822157145; d from Rs250) This welcoming choice arranged around a nice garden offers clean rooms of a variety of sizes with some better equipped than others. You'll pay more for the best of them, which come with hot showers, kitchenette and balcony.

Eating

VAGATOR

There are a few eating options clustered around the entrance to Little Vagator Beach, along with the usual slew of much-of-a-muchness beach shacks down on the sands themselves.

Mango Tree Bar & Café (mains Rs70-120) An ever-popular place for its big breakfasts and far-ranging menu, with films screened here most nights around 7.30pm.

Marrakesh (mains Rs120-160; 11am-11pm) Billing itself as the 'Heart of Moroccan cuisine', this is the place to pick up a tasty tagine or a delectable veg couscous (Rs150), in what seems to be Goa's only Moroccan restaurant.

Bean Me Up Soya Station (Ozran Beach Rd; mains from Rs150) A delicious, all-vegetarian restaurant at this popular place to stay, with lots of carefully-washed salads and a wealth of tasty tofu and tempeh.

CHAPORA

our pick **Mamma Mia** (paninis & pizza Rs100; 8am-9pm Tue-Sun) The best of the Chapora bunch is Mamma Mia, run by Marco who makes his own focaccia fresh every night ready for the next day. The cappuccinos are perfect, the pizza is simple and filling, and the smoke is strong and heady.

Two long-lived local institutions are **Scarlet Cold Drinks** (drinks & desserts Rs15-50) and the **Sai Ganesh Fruit Juice Centre** (juices Rs15-30), both offering juices, snacks and lassis, in close proximity to the thickest gusts of charas smoke. The former has an exceptionally good noticeboard, to keep you abreast of local developments.

Drinking & Entertainment

Aside from secretive parties, there's not too much going on in Vagator and Chapora these days. The once heaving **Nine Bar** (Sunset Point, Little Vagator Beach; till 10pm), however, is still thumping on; gone, though, are the all-nighters and the trance is now turned off promptly at 10pm.

> **WHERE'S THE PARTY?**
>
> Though Goa was long legendary among Western visitors for its all-night, open-air Goan trance parties, a central government 'noise pollution' ban on loud music in open spaces between 10pm and 6am has largely curbed its often notorious, drug-laden party scene. With a tourist industry to nurture, however, authorities tend to turn a blind eye to parties during the peak Christmas–New Year period, and seem to allow the monster mainstream clubs of Baga to carry on regardless. If you're looking for the remainder of the real party scene, though, you'll need to cross your fingers, keep your ear close to the ground, and wait out for word in Vagator or Anjuna.

Getting There & Away

Fairly frequent buses run to both Chapora and Vagator from Mapusa (Rs12) throughout the day, many via Anjuna. The bus stand is near the road junction in Chapora village. Many people hire a motorcycle to buzz back and forth; enquire wherever you see a man with a scooter. Prices tend to be around Rs150/200 per day for a scooter/motorbike.

MANDREM

Lovely, hidden Mandrem has in recent years become an in-the-know bolt hole for those seeking respite from the relentless traveller scene of Arambol and Anjuna. The beach is beautiful, and there's little to do but laze on it; the narrow lane leading down to the sea is filled with accommodation options to suit most budgets. There are also lots of cocohuts to be had for Rs400 or thereabouts on the beach, and there's a plethora of yoga and ayurveda on offer, mostly taught by foreigners, each season. It's not easy to get here by public transport; the best bet is to rent a scooter at Arambol.

Sleeping & Eating

Oasis on the Beach (huts Rs500-700) One of the many tip-top beach-hut options, with the added advantage of an excellent ayurvedic massage parlour, run by the delightful Shanti (massages Rs800 to Rs1000), whose claim to fame is having massaged Dawn French. Oasis's beachfront restaurant gets rave reviews, too, especially for its seafood and tandoori dishes.

Cuba Retreat (☎ 2645775; www.cubagoa.com; d without/with AC Rs1050/1500; ✕) Those people from Cuba seem to get everywhere, including to this spick-and-span set of suites just a few moments' walk from the beach. Though it didn't seem too pricey to us, Cuba's website claims it serves up 'exorbitant seafood delicacies' in its great courtyard bar-restaurant.

Villa River Cat (☎ 2247928; www.villarivercat.com; d Rs1700-3600; ✕ 💻) This fabulously unusual circular guest house, filled with art, light and antiques, makes for a wonderful – and extremely popular – stay. Because of this, the management advises to book an astonishing eight months ahead during high season.

Shree Gopal Supreme Pure Juice Centre & Café (juice Rs30-35; ⏰ 7am-10pm) On the road down to the beach, thirst-quenching juicy combinations are squeezed and served up in a cute little chill-out area. Lots of notices are posted in the vicinity, with info on the latest yoga class locations.

ARAMBOL (HARMAL)

Arambol first emerged in the 1960s as a mellow paradise for long-haired long-stayers. Today, things are still decidedly cheap and cheerful, with much of the village's mostly budget accommodation ranged in simple little huts along the cliff sides. However, it's a bit more mainstream festivalish than in days gone by and you have a feeling that many of today's 'hippies' shave off their fortnight's beards and take off their tie-dye once they're back to the nine-to-five.

Some people love Arambol for all this; others turn up their pierced noses and move along, leaving today's long-stayers to enjoy the pretty beach and extensive 'alternative' shopping opportunities provided by nonstop stalls all the way down the beach road and along round the cliff. If you're looking for a committed traveller vibe, this is the place to come; if you're seeking laid-back languidness, you might be better heading on down the coast to Mandrem.

Information

Everything you'll need in the way of services – dozens of internet outfits, travel agents, money changers and the like – you'll find in abundance on 'Glastonbury Street', the road leading down to Arambol's beach. Internet access here generally costs Rs30 to Rs40 per hour, and money-changing commission rates are all comparable. There are also several agencies towards the top of the road offering parcel services with Federal Express and DHL deliveries, and by air and sea mail.

Activities

The **Himalayan Iyengar Yoga Centre** (www.hiyoga centre.com) is a popular spot for a spot of yoga, with five-day courses, intensive workshops, children's classes, and teacher training all available.

Aside from yoga and beach lounging, the most popular pursuits in Arambol these days are **paragliding** and **kite surfing**. Several operators give lessons and rent equipment on the very south of Arambol beach; walk down there, or check out some noticeboards, to find out who's renting what this season.

Sleeping

Accommodation in Arambol is almost all of the budget variety, and it pays to trawl the cliffside to the north of Arambol's main beach stretch for the best of numerous hut options. Here you can expect simple accommodation, mostly without private bathroom but with the benefit of incredible sea views (along with attendant breezes). Most come in at Rs350 to Rs500 in high season, and it's almost impossible to book in advance – simply turn up early in the day to check out who's checking out of your dream hut.

Chilli's (☎ 9921882424; Glastonbury St; d Rs300) This clean and simple place, owned by friendly and helpful Derek Fernandez, is one of Arambol's best nonbeachside bargains. Chilli's offers 10 nice, no-frills rooms on the beach road, all with attached bathroom, fan and a hot-water shower, and there's an honour system for buying bottled water, self-service, from the fridge on the landing.

Om Ganesh (☎ 2297675; r Rs350-400) Popular huts, especially those on the sea-side of the coastal path, as well as a great place for lunch or dinner, with almost everything you can think of on the menu (if you can manage to decode entries such as 'Gokomadi' in the Mexican section). Some huts have no attached bathroom.

Shree Sai Cottages (☎ 2262823; shreesai_cottages@ yahoo.com; huts without bathroom Rs400) A good ex-

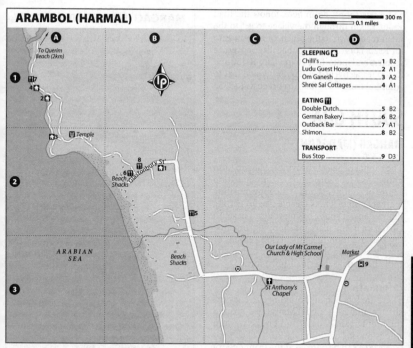

ARAMBOL (HARMAL)

SLEEPING	
Chilli's	1 B2
Ludu Guest House	2 A1
Om Ganesh	3 A2
Shree Sai Cottages	4 A1

EATING	
Double Dutch	5 B2
German Bakery	6 B2
Outback Bar	7 A1
Shimon	8 B2

TRANSPORT	
Bus Stop	9 D3

ample of what's on offer, Shree Sai has simple sea-facing huts a short walk north from the main Arambol beach, with lovely views out over the water, and a calm, easygoing vibe.

Ludu Guest House (☎ 2242734; r Rs700-1000) A cut above many other Arambol options, Ludu offers simply decorated, clean and bright cliffside rooms with attached cold-water showers. Hot water can be ordered by the bucketful. Some huts have no attached bathroom.

Eating & Drinking

Aside from myriad standard shacks lining the sands, plenty of cute, sparkly little places are dotted along the top part of the road curving down toward the beach. Many change annually; stroll along and see which organic, glitter-ball and parachute-silk destination takes your fancy. For simpler fare, head up to the village, where chai shops and small local joints will whip you up a chai for Rs4 and a thali for Rs40.

German Bakery (Welcome Inn; 'Glastonbury St'; cakes from Rs40; ☼ 7am-late) This rather dim and dingy corner cafe is exceptionally popular, with great

cakes including lemon cheese pie (Rs50) and a scrummy chocolate biscuit cake (Rs40), as well as big breakfasts coming in at around the Rs90 mark.

Outback Bar (mains from Rs50) Seafood's a speciality at this nice place tucked away from the Arambol action; it also makes a fantastic spot for a sundown cocktail or two.

Double Dutch (mains from Rs70) An ever-popular option for its steaks, salads and famous apple pies, this is a great place to peruse the noticeboard for current affairs, while munching on a plateful of cookies or a huge, tasty sandwich.

Shimon ('Glastonbury St'; snacks from Rs70; ☼ 8am-midnight) If you can navigate the surly service, Israeli-owned Shimon's is a good place to fill up on a tasty falafel (Rs70) before hitting the beach. For something more unusual, go for *sabich* (Rs70), crisp slices of aubergine stuffed into pita bread along with boiled egg, boiled potato, salad and spicy relishes.

Getting There & Away

Buses from Mapusa stop on the main road at Arambol (Rs12), where there's a church, school and a few shops. From here, follow the road about 1.5km through the village to get to the main road down to the beach, or take an auto for Rs20. Lots of places in the village advertise scooters and motorbikes to rent, for Rs150 and Rs200 respectively, per day. A prepaid taxi to Arambol from Dabolim Airport costs Rs975.

SOUTH GOA

MARGAO (MADGAON)
pop 94,400

The capital of Salcete province, Margao (also known as Madgaon) is the main population centre of south Goa and is a happy, bustling market town of a manageable size for getting things done. If you're basing yourself in south Goa, it's a useful place for shopping, organising bus and train tickets, checking emails or simply enjoying the busy energy of big-city India in manageable small-town form.

Information

There are lots of banks offering currency exchange and 24-hour ATMs ranged around the Municipal Gardens, and on the western extension of Luis Miranda Rd. GTDC trips (see p186) can be booked at the front desk of the Margao Residency Hotel.

Golden Heart Emporium (Confidant House, Abade Faria Rd) One of Goa's best bookshops, crammed with fiction, nonfiction and illustrated books on the state's food, architecture and history.

Grace Cyber Café (1st fl, Reliance Trade Centre, V V Rd; per hr Rs20; 9.30am-7.30pm Mon-Sat) A new place in the centre of town, Grace has reliable, fast connections and a number of other services including CD writing and DVD burning direct from USB.

Maharaja Travels (2732744; Luis Miranda Rd; 9am-1pm & 3-6pm Mon-Sat) A great source of long-distance bus tickets.

Main post office (9am-1.30pm & 2-4pm) On the north side of the municipal gardens, the post office also arranges Western Union money transfers.

The Cyberlink (Caro Centre, Abade Faria Rd; per 20min Rs8, per hr Rs20; 8.30am-7pm Mon-Sat) Reasonably swift internet access on the central square; be sure to heed the notice that requests you to 'Register yourself before sitting on the PC'.

Sights

Margao has plenty of workaday, practical shopping opportunities, and the daily **covered market** in the town centre is one of the

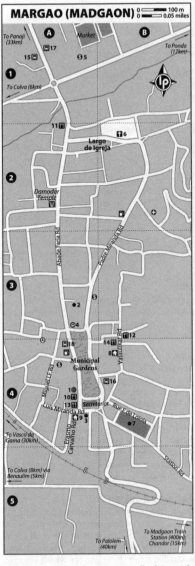

MARGAO (MADGAON)

most colourful and raucous in all of Goa. It's also worth a walk around the lovely, small northern **Largo de Igreja** district, home to lots of atmospherically crumbling old Portuguese homes. Stop in, too, at the quaint and richly decorated 17th-century **Church of the Holy Spirit**, particularly impressive when a Sunday morning service is taking place.

INFORMATION			SLEEPING			TRANSPORT		
Cyberlink	1	A4	Hotel Tanish	8	B4	Bus Stand	15	A1
Golden Heart Emporium	2	A3	Margao Residency	9	A4	Buses to Palolem,		
Grace Cyber Café	(see 8)					Colva, Benaulim &		
Maharaja Travels	3	A4	EATING			Betul	16	B4
Main Post Office	4	A3	Casa Penguim de Gelados	10	A4	Kadamba Bus Stand	17	A1
UTI Bank ATM	5	A1	Casa Vaz Tea Shop	11	A2	Old Bus Stand	18	A4
			Gaylin	12	B3			
SIGHTS & ACTIVITIES			Longhuino's	13	A4			
Church of the Holy Spirit	6	B2	Tato	14	B4			
Covered Market	7	B4						

Sleeping

With the southern beaches all so close, there's little, if any, reason to stay in Margao.

Hotel Tanish (☎ 2735656; Reliance Trade Centre, Valaulikar Rd; s/d without AC Rs900/1500, s/d/ste with AC Rs1300/1900/2500) Without doubt the best place to stay in town, this top-floor hotel offers great views of the surrounding countryside, with stylish, well-equipped rooms. Suites come with a bathtub, a big TV and a view all the way to Colva.

Eating

Casa Vaz Tea Shop (Abade Faria Rd; dishes from Rs8; ☯ breakfast & lunch) Run by a lovely local lady, this teensy tea joint serves up the best, caramelised-oniony *bhaji pau* we've ever tasted for an equally tiny Rs12.

Casa Penguim de Gelados (opposite municipality, Abade Faria Rd; veg thali Rs30; ☯ 8.30am-8pm Mon-Sat) Tea and ice creams are really their thing, but this clean, fan-cooled place does a decent vegetarian thali and an array of dosas and *idlis* (South Indian spongy, round, fermented rice cakes) too.

our pick **Longhuino's** (Luis Miranda Rd; mains from Rs40) Since 1950, quaint old Longhuino's has been serving up tasty Indian and Chinese dishes, popular with locals and tourists alike. To thoroughly hark back to the '50s, order the tongue roast for Rs80 (and that doesn't mean a very spicy masala) and follow it up with a rum ball (Rs15).

Gaylin (mains from Rs40; ☯ noon-3pm & 6.30-11pm) Hidden behind opaque glass doors decorated with dragon motifs, generous, garlicky renditions of Chinese favourites are dispensed here by the friendly Darjeeling-derived owners, with recipes suitably spiced up to cater to resilient Indian palates.

Tato (Apna Bazaar Complex, Varde Valualikar Rd; veg thali Rs40-45; ☯ 7am-10pm Mon-Sat) This is a favourite local lunch spot, offering tasty vegetarian fare, including a vegie thali. It's located in a bustling backstreet canteen.

Getting There & Around

BUS

Local buses all arrive and depart at the busy Kadamba bus stand about 2km north of the Municipal Gardens, though many services also stop at the old bus stand in the centre of town. Buses to Palolem, Colva, Benaulim and Betul stop at the Kadamba bus stand and at the bus stop on the east side of the Municipal Gardens. Services run to no timetable at all, but are cheap and frequent.

Though there are daily public buses to Mumbai (Rs700, 16 hours) and Bengaluru (Rs400, 14 hours), a better bet is to take a long-distance private bus, which is more comfortable, quicker and about the same price. You'll find booking offices all over town; Maharaja Travels (see Information opposite) is one helpful choice.

Private buses to Mumbai (with/without AC Rs750/650, 12 hours), Bengaluru (with/without AC Rs700/350, 12 hours), Pune (with/without AC Rs750/650, 11 hours) and Hampi (sleeper/luxury Rs750/650, eight hours) all leave from the bus stand opposite the Kadamba bus station.

TAXI

Taxis are plentiful around the municipal gardens and Kadamba bus stand, and are a quick and comfortable means to reach any of Goa's beaches, including Palolem (Rs650), Calangute (Rs1000), Anjuna (Rs1000) and Arambol (Rs1700). Be sure to wear your best bargaining cap for negotiating your fare.

TRAIN

Margao's well-organised train station, about 1.5km south of town, serves both the Konkan Railway and local South Central Railways routes. Its **reservation hall** (☯ 8am-2pm & 2.15-8pm Mon-Sat, 8am-2pm Sun) is on the 2nd floor of the main building. See p190 for details of Konkan Railway services.

GOA

A taxi or autorickshaw from the town centre to the station should cost Rs50.

CHANDOR

The lush village of Chandor, 15km east of Margao, makes a perfect day away from the south Goan beaches, and it's here, more than anywhere else in the state, that the once opulent lifestyles of Goa's former landowners, who found favour with the Portuguese aristocracy, are still visible in its strings of quietly decaying colonial-era mansions.

A kilometre east past the church and open to the public is the **Fernandes House** (☎ 2784245; ☑ 10am-5pm Mon-Sat), whose original building dates back more than 500 years, while the Portuguese section was tacked on by the Fernandes family in 1821. The secret basement hideaway, full of gun holes and with an escape tunnel to the river, was used by the family to flee attackers. A minimum Rs100 donation per visitor is expected.

The best way to reach Chandor is with your own transport, or by taxi from Margao (Rs200 for the round trip). On 6 January, Chandor hosts the colourful **Feast of the Three Kings**, during which local boys re-enact the arrival of the three kings from the Christmas story.

BETELBATIM

Though the beaches along this entire strip – from Mobor in the south right up to Velsao further north – are actually just different patches of one long and continuous stretch of sand, each place manages to retain its own very distinct and individual character. Betelbatim, just to the north of Colva, is a good example of what a difference a few hundred metres can make – it's as calm, quiet and pastoral as Colva is touristed and dust-blown. And even Betelbatim itself consists of several different smaller strips of beach – try Sunset Beach or Lovers' Beach, which is suitably lovely, though the only lovers to be seen when we visited were a pair of wheeling seagulls, along with the odd solitary dog and a lone lovelorn sea eagle. To get to Lovers' Beach, follow signs from the main road, passing a less lovely rash of timeshares on the way.

As well as Sunset and Lovers', there are a couple of other entrance points onto Betelbatim beach from the village, all more or less guaranteeing peace and quiet.

A local legend and popular with Indian tourists, **Martin's Corner** (www.martinscornergoa .com; mains from Rs60; ☑ 11am-3pm & 6.30-11pm), near Sunset Beach, is a great place to try out Goan

---

CHANDOR'S COLONIAL JEKYLL AND HYDE

Braganza House, built in the 17th century and stretching along one whole side of Chandor village square, is possibly the best – and worst – example of what Goa's scores of once grand and glorious mansions have today become. Built on land granted by the King of Portugal, the house was divided from the outset into the east and west wings, to house two sides of the same big family.

The **West Wing** (☎ 2784201; ☑ 10am-5pm) belongs to one set of the family's descendents, the Menezes-Braganza, and is filled with gorgeous chandeliers, Italian marble floors and antique treasures from Macau, Portugal, China and Europe. The elderly, rather frail, Mrs Aida Menezes-Braganza nowadays lives here alone, but will show you around with the help of her formidable lady assistant. Between them, they struggle valiantly with the upkeep of a beautiful but needy house, whose grand history oozes from every inch of wall, floor and furniture.

Next door at the **East Wing** (☎ 2784227; ☑ 10am-5pm), prepare for a shock. Owned by the Pereira-Braganza family, descendents of the other half of the family, it's as shabby and decaying as the other is still grand. Paint peels from windows; ceilings sag; antiques are mixed in willy-nilly with a jumble of cheap knick-knacks and seaside souvenirs. The only high point here is the small family chapel, which contains a carefully hidden fingernail of St Francis Xavier (see p199), and even this – the chapel, not the fingernail – is beginning to show signs of neglect. A starker architectural contrast at such close quarters you're unlikely to see for quite a while, and it's a moving, if melancholy, experience.

Both homes are open daily, and there's almost always someone around to let you in. Though there are no official entry fees, the owners rely on contributions for the hefty costs of maintenance: Rs100 per visitor per house is reasonable, though anything extra would, of course, be welcome.

cuisine in a relaxed and quite upmarket setting. The *xacutís* and *vindalhos* are superb, and there are plenty of tasty vegetarian options on offer. There's live music most nights from 8pm; plump for, or avoid, Wednesdays, depending on your relationship with karaoke.

COLVA & BENAULIM
pop 10,200

Colva and Benaulim might between them comprise the biggest resorts on the south coast, but they're certainly not the first place for backpackers to head, and most tourists here are of the domestic or ageing European varieties. Of the two, Benaulim has the greater charm, though out of superduper high season still gives off the sad sort of feel of a deserted Welsh seaside town, were global warming to get that far. Perhaps the biggest reason to stay at either is if you're keen to explore this part of southern coast (which stretches north as far as Velsao and south as far as the mouth of the Sal River at Mobor), which in many parts is empty and gorgeous. The inland road that runs this length is perfect for gentle scootering, with lots of picturesque Portuguese mansions and whitewashed churches along the way.

Information

Colva has plenty of banks and ATMs strung along Colva Beach Rd, and a post office on the lane that runs past the eastern end of the church. Benaulim has a single Bank of Baroda ATM – which professes to be

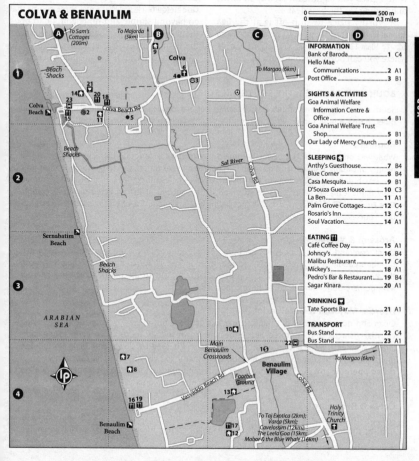

COLVA & BENAULIM

| 0 | 500 m |
| 0 | 0.3 miles |

24-hour but is sometimes locked – at the top of Vasvaddo Beach Rd, and most of its useful services (pharmacies, supermarkets and travel agents) are clustered around the main crossroads.

Hello Mae Communication (Colva Beach Rd; for 15min Rs10, per hr Rs30; 8am-10pm) Internet access, money exchange and weekly Wednesday trips to Anjuna Market for Rs150 per person. Keep in mind the stern warning: 'No Surfing of Porn Websites'.

Sights & Activities

The beach entrances of Colva and Benaulim throng with young men keen to sell you **parasailing** (per ride Rs500), jet-skiing (per 15min Rs700), and **dolphin-watching trips** (per person around Rs250). There's little to choose between operators, which gives you significant leeway in terms of haggling for the best deal.

A worthy place to stop off is at the **Goa Animal Welfare Trust Shop** (www.gawt.org; Colva Beach Rd; 10am-12.30pm & 5-7pm Mon-Sat) in Colva where you can borrow books from its lending library, or peruse the new and second-hand goods on offer. There's also a newly opened **Information Centre & Office** (Below Infant Jesus Church Hall; 9.30am-1pm & 3-5pm Mon-Sat), also in Colva, where you can find out more about the work of this wonderful organisation.

Sleeping

It's hard to recommend many budget or midrange options in Colva, since the majority are either horribly overpriced or, more simply, horrible. Indeed, unless you're lying low in one of the town's groovier top-end choices, you're far better off heading down to Benaulim or pushing on further south.

BUDGET
Colva

Casa Mesquita (r Rs300) With just three rooms that go beyond simple and no telephone to book them by, this atmospheric old mansion on the main coast road is certainly the place to go if you thrive on the atmosphere that Colva

---

BOUNTIFUL BEACHES: THE SOUTHERN STRETCH

South Goa conceals the state's best beaches, perfect for picnicking, paddling and peace and quiet. Here's a brief run-down of the south's secrets, to help make your selection.

Bogmalo

What was once a small but perfectly formed bay roared to life (quite literally) with the arrival nearby of Dabolim Airport and its attendant hoards of weekenders, not to mention a rather ugly five-star hotel dipping its toes in the shallows. Nevertheless, if you've a night to kill before an early flight it makes an acceptable stop and is best known for its respected diving operation, **Goa Diving** (2555117; www.goadiving.com), which offers a long list of dives, tours and certification courses.

Arossim & Velsao

Quiet, cool and happily undeveloped, both Velsao and Arossim make perfect places for a picturesque paddle with just seabirds and the occasional shack for company. The only blight on the horizon is the scowling, spluttering petrochemical plant to the north, something only Mr Montgomery Burns himself could have conceived.

Utorda, Majorda & Betelbatim

Clean and quiet stretches of sand, offering lots of space to frolic away from the sun-lounging crowds, characterise these three villages heading down south towards Colva. Perfect for exploring by scooter, they're dotted with beach shacks and backed by slowly crumbling Portuguese mansions. If you're keen to explore on four legs rather than two wheels, Frank, Goa's only **horse-riding operator** (9822586502), organises sunset and sunrise rides from Rs600 per hour. Call in advance, or drop into the Treat Yourself Health Centre in Majorda village.

Colva & Benaulim

Not the loveliest, nor the liveliest, of Goa's bigger resorts, Colva (p225) is a hit with domestic tourists, though its busy beach and raggle-taggle beach road are distinctly lacking in charm.

lacks. Goodness knows when rooms were last cleaned; nevertheless, the elderly inhabitants are friendly and the ghosts of better days linger lovingly in the shadows.

Sam's Cottages (☎ 2788753; r Rs350) Up where the countryside begins you'll find Sam's, painted a cheerful bright orange and with decent, clean rooms. If your name happens to be Sam too, prepare yourself for a particularly ebullient welcome.

La Ben (☎ 2788040; www.laben.net; Colva Beach Rd; r without/with AC Rs575/965; 🕸) Neat, clean and not entirely devoid of atmosphere, this place is particularly known for its rooftop restaurant, though its rooms represent reasonable value.

Benaulim

There are lots of village homes along the Vasvaddo Beach Rd, and in among the lanes off it, advertising simple rooms to let for tourists. This, combined with a couple of really decent budget options, make Benaulim a far better bet for backpackers than Colva.

Rosario's Inn (☎ 2770636; r Rs300, without bathroom Rs150; 🕸) Across a football pitch flitting with young players and dragonflies, Rosario's is a large, motel-like establishment with clean, simple rooms. There's a nice bar-restaurant in the garden, and two AC rooms (Rs500 each).

D'Souza Guest House (☎ 2770583; d Rs400) As you'd guess from the name, this traditional blue house is run by a local Goan family and comes with bundles of homey atmosphere, a lovely garden and just three spacious, clean rooms – making it best to book ahead.

Blue Corner (☎ 9850455770; www.blue-cnr-goa.com; huts from Rs600) One of only a handful of truly beachside places on this entire strip of coast, Blue Corner offers simple beach huts, and a nice beachfront restaurant that gains stellar reviews from guests.

MIDRANGE & TOP END
Colva

Soul Vacation (☎ 2788144/7; www.soulvacation.in; d from Rs5500; 🕸 🖫 🖭) Thirty restful white rooms

---

Benaulim next door is quieter, though a little wind-blown and desolate, and offers better options for the budget and midrange travellers. The sands aren't exceptional, but both make decent bases for exploring this stretch of southern coast.

Varca, Cavelossim & Mobor

A string of luxury resorts running south from Varca to the river mouth at Mobor (p229) front relatively empty, undeveloped beaches, with lots of room to stretch out unhassled by crowds. Cavelossim, while not a pretty development, sports a good range of eating and drinking options for night-time satiation.

Palolem

Palolem's golden crescent of sand remains one of Goa's gems, despite the hut-to-hut development along its entire length. The seas are shallow and swimmable, the days are long and languid, and there's little to do except indulge in a slow pace and perhaps a spot of beach volleyball, if you're feeling energetic.

Agonda, Rajbag, Colomb & Patnem

Patnem, a short distance south, is a quieter, if less picturesque, alternative to Palolem, with a wide sand beach and good surf on windy days. South of here, small Rajbag beach is dominated by the presence of the Intercontinental Hotel, but makes a nice jaunt across the rocky headland. While here, see if you can seek out tiny **Vernekar Restaurant** (Rajbag; 🕑 lunch & dinner) which serves some of the tastiest Indian food in the entire area. Colomb, meanwhile, a tiny bay between Patnem and Palolem, makes for relaxed beach-hut repose, though it's too rocky to be good for swimming. Agonda to the north, is gorgeous, expansive, idyllically undeveloped, and shuts up shop well before 10pm.

Polem

Tucked away at the southern end of the state, this empty little bay of golden sand (p231), though notorious as a smugglers' den, makes for a nice day trip, by bus or scooter, from Palolem.

COLVA'S MENINO JESUS

If the only miracle you've experienced in Colva is finding a nice budget bed, the village's 18th-century **Our Lady of Mercy Church** has been host to several miracles of its own, of the rather more celestial kind. Inside, closely guarded under lock and key, lives a little statue known as the 'Menino' (Baby) Jesus, which is said to miraculously heal the sick and which only sees the light of day during the **Fama de Menino Jesus festival**, on the second Monday in October. Then, the little image is paraded about town, dipped in the river, and installed in the church's high altar for pilgrims, hoping for their own personal miracle, to pray to.

---

arranged around nice gardens and a great pool are the trademarks of sleek Soul Vacation, set 400m back from Colva Beach. Equipped with all the mod cons, it's a great – if slightly pretentious – place to unwind without ever even having to venture out of the resort itself.

Benaulim

Anthy's Guesthouse (☎ 2771680; anthysguesthouse@ rediffmail.com; r Rs1300-1800) One of just a handful of places lining Benaulim's beach, Anthy's is a firm favourite with travellers for its warm service (manager Prabot is friendly and helpful), good restaurant and its well-kept, chalet-style rooms, which stretch back from the beach surrounded by a pretty garden. Ayurvedic massage is available for Rs500 per, um, squeeze.

Palm Grove Cottages (☎ 2770059; www.palmgrove goa.com; d without/with AC from Rs1460/1575; ✹) Old-fashioned, secluded charm is to be had amid the dense foliage at Palm Grove Cottages, hidden among a thicket of trees on a road winding slowly south out of Benaulim. Guest rooms are atmospheric, and the ever-popular Palm Garden Restaurant graces the garden.

Taj Exotica (☎ 2771234; www.tajhotels.com; d from US$300; ✹ 🖥 ⚑) If your budget runs to it, don't hesitate: here's one of Goa's plushest resorts, set in 56 acres of tropical gardens, and just aching to pander to your every whim. It's probably best to just relinquish the struggle and let it.

Eating & Drinking
COLVA

There are plenty of wooden beach shacks lining the Colvan sands, offering the long, and standard range of fare, and you'll spot this season's best by the crowds already dining within. For simpler eating, head up to the roundabout just before the church, where tourist joints are replaced by simple chai shops and thali places, and there's plenty of fruit, vegetable and fish stalls for self-caterers. At night, *bhelpuri* vendors set up camp here, dishing up big portions of the fried noodle snack for just a few rupees.

Café Coffee Day (cakes & coffees from Rs40; ✹ 8am-midnight) A pleasant enough place to escape the heat, this wannabe sleek joint offers a half-decent cappuccino (Rs44) along with a range of cakes, including the suitably '70s Black Forest Gateau (Rs44), reminiscent of the era when Colva was still cool.

Mickey's (Colva Beach Rd; mains from Rs60) An ever-popular place to drink the afternoon away or munch lunch from the extensive Indian/Continental/Chinese menu, Mickey's is usually busy and the food dispensed is fresh and filling.

Sagar Kinara (Colva Beach Rd; mains Rs30-100) A pure-veg restaurant with tastes to please even committed carnivores, this great place is clean, efficient and offers cheap and delicious North and South Indian cuisine all day long.

Tate Sports Bar (✹ 8am-midnight) Hearty English breakfasts, draught Kingfisher on tap and football on TV inhabit a comfier, more cosmopolitan drinking option than Colva is used to.

BENAULIM

Johncy (Vasvaddo Beach Rd; mains Rs60-120) Like Pedro's beside it, Johncy dispenses standard beach-shack favourites from its location just back from the sands themselves. Staff are obliging and food, if not exciting, is fresh and filling.

Pedro's Bar & Restaurant (Vasvaddo Beach Rd; mains Rs60-120) Set amid a large, shady garden on the beachfront and popular with local and international tourists alike, Pedro's offers standard Indian, Chinese and Italian dishes, as well as a good line in Goan choices and some super 'sizzlers'.

Malibu Restaurant (mains Rs90-150) With a secluded garden setting, this place, a short walk back from the beach, offers one of Benaulim's more sophisticated dining experiences, with great renditions of Italian favourites and live jazz and blues on Tuesday evenings.

Getting There & Away

Buses run from Colva to Margao roughly every 15 minutes (Rs12, 20 minutes) from

7.30am to about 7pm, departing from the parking area at the end of the beach road.

Buses from Margao to Benaulim are also frequent (Rs8, 15 minutes); some continue on south to Varca and Cavelossim. Buses stop at the crossroads quite a distance from the main action (such as it is) and beach; it's best to hail a rickshaw (Rs20) for the five-minute ride to the sea.

BENAULIM TO PALOLEM
Immediately south of Benaulim are the beach resorts of **Varca** and **Cavelossim**, both boasting wide, pristine sands and a line of roomy five-star hotel complexes set amid extensive landscaped grounds fronting onto the beach. The most luxe of all is **Leela Goa** (☎ 2871234; www .theleela.com; d from Rs8500; ✕ ▢ ▣) at Mobor, 3km south of Cavelossim. Stray just beyond it, however, to the end of the peninsula, and you'll find one of the most picture-perfect spots in the whole of Goa, at the simple **Blue Whale beach shack** (mains from Rs50; ☯ 8.30am-late), run by friendly local Roque Coutinho.

If you're heading down this coast under your own steam, you can cross the Sal River to continue south, at Cavelossim, by taking the rusting tin-tub ferry. To reach it, turn at the sign saying 'Village Panchayat Cavelossim' close to Cavelossim's whitewashed church, then continue on for 2km to the river. From here you can ride on to the fishing village of **Betul**; ferries run approximately every half-hour between 8am and 8.30pm. They're free for pedestrians and cost Rs7 for cars; outside those hours, you can charter the ferry for a princely Rs50.

From Betul on south to Agonda, the road winds over gorgeous, undulating hills thick with palm groves. It's worth stopping off at the bleak old Portuguese fort of **Cabo da Rama** (look for the green, red and white signposts leading the way), which has a small church within the fort walls, stupendous views and several old buildings rapidly becoming one with the trees.

Back on the main road there's a turn-off to **Agonda**, a small village with a wide, empty beach on which rare olive ridley turtles sometimes lay their eggs, and which remains the silent, idyllic secret of south Goa. There's plenty of accommodation to choose from, but don't come here looking for any sort of action: the pace is slow and the only bright lights at night are the stars. **Chattai** (☎ 9822481360; www.chattai

.co.in; huts Rs1200), at the north end of the beach, offers lovely, simple huts on the sands, while **Praia de Agonda** (☎ 9763129429; praiadeagonda@gmail .com; huts from Rs1200) is a well-run and child-friendly set-up at the south end, with fun jam sessions and live bands several evenings per week.

There's lots of yoga and ayurveda about in Agonda – look out for notices – and plenty of beach restaurants serving up good grub. For a simpler local breakfast, *bhaji pau* and chai are to be had at the cluster of tiny eateries beside the church.

PALOLEM & AROUND
Palolem's stunning crescent beach was, as recently as 10 years ago, another of Goa's undiscovered gems, with few tourists and even fewer facilities to offer them. Nowadays, it's no longer quiet or hidden, but remains one of Goa's most beautiful spots, with a friendly, laid-back pace, and lots of budget accommodation ranged along the sands. Nightlife's still sleepy here – there are no real clubs or pubs and the place goes to sleep when the music stops at 10pm. But if you're looking for a nice place to lay up, rest a while, swim in calm seas and choose from an infinite range of yoga, massages and therapies on offer, this is the place for you.

If even Palolem's version of action is all too much for you, head south, along the small rocky cove named **Colomb Bay**, which hosts several basic places to stay, to **Patnem Beach** beyond, where a fine selection of beach huts, and a less pretty – but infinitely quieter – stretch of sand awaits.

Information
Palolem's beach road is lined with travel agencies, internet places, and money changers. There are no ATMs in Palolem itself, but two in the nearby workaday village of Chaudi, which also boasts a supermarket, several pharmacies, and all the other amenities you might require. An autorickshaw from Palolem to Chaudi costs Rs100, or you can walk the flat 2km in a leisurely 45 minutes.
Butterfly Book Shop (☎ 9341738801; ☯ 9am-late) The best of several good bookshops in town, this cute and cosy place with resident cat stocks bestsellers, classics and a good range of books on yoga, meditation and spirituality.

Sights & Activities
Palolem and Patnem are, these days, the places to be if you're keen to yoga, belly dance,

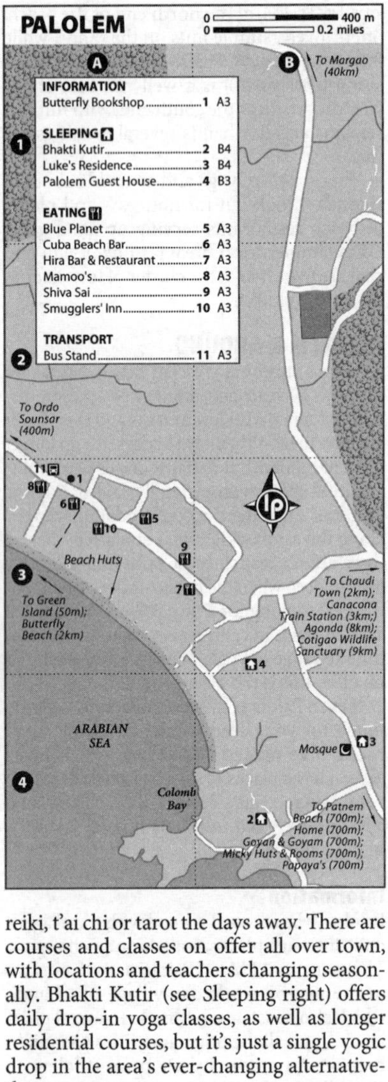
PALOLEM
0 400 m
0 0.2 miles
INFORMATION
Butterfly Bookshop 1 A3
SLEEPING
Bhakti Kutir 2 B4
Luke's Residence 3 B4
Palolem Guest House 4 B3
EATING
Blue Planet 5 A3
Cuba Beach Bar 6 A3
Hira Bar & Restaurant 7 A3
Mamoo's 8 A3
Shiva Sai 9 A3
Smugglers' Inn 10 A3
TRANSPORT
Bus Stand 11 A3
To Margao (40km)
To Ordo Sounsar (400m)
Beach Huts
To Green Island (50m); Butterfly Beach (2km)
To Chaudi Town (2km); Canacona Train Station (3km;) Agonda (8km); Cotigao Wildlife Sanctuary (9km)
ARABIAN SEA
Mosque
Colomb Bay
To Patnem Beach (700m); Home (700m); Goyan & Goyam (700m); Micky Huts & Rooms (700m); Papaya's (700m)

reiki, t'ai chi or tarot the days away. There are courses and classes on offer all over town, with locations and teachers changing seasonally. Bhakti Kutir (see Sleeping right) offers daily drop-in yoga classes, as well as longer residential courses, but it's just a single yogic drop in the area's ever-changing alternative-therapy ocean.

Kayaks are available for rent on both Patnem and Palolem beaches; an hour's paddling will cost Rs300.

About 9km south of Palolem, and a good day trip, is the beautiful, remote-feeling **Cotigao Wildlife Sanctuary** (☎ 2965601; admission/camera Rs5/25; ⌚ 7am-5.30pm). Don't expect to bump into its more exotic residents (including gaurs, sambars, leopards and spotted deer), but frogs, snakes, monkeys, insects, and blazingly plumed birds are in no short supply. Marked trails are hikable; set off early in the morning for the best sighting prospects from one of the sanctuary's two forest watchtowers.

Sleeping

PALOLEM

Most of Palolem's accommodation is of the simple beach-hut variety, with little to distinguish where one outfit stops and next door's begins. Since the huts are dismantled and rebuilt with each passing season, standards can vary greatly from one year to the next. It's best to walk along the beach and check out a few before making your decision; a simple hut without attached bathroom will usually cost Rs400 to Rs600, while something more sophisticated can run to Rs2000 and beyond. If bamboo beach huts aren't your thing, however, below are some solid alternatives.

Palolem Guest House (☎ 2644879; www.palolemguesthouse.com; d Rs600-1200; ❄) If you pale at the thought of another night in a basic beach hut, this splendid place a quick walk from the beach offers lots of plain but comfortable rooms with solid, brick walls arranged around a nice leafy garden.

Ordo Sounsar (☎ 9822488769; www.ordosounsar.com; huts Rs2000, without bathroom Rs1500) Beach huts they might be, but set as far north up Palolem beach as it's possible to go, across a rickety bridge spanning a wide creek, this hidden haven makes a cool, quiet alternative to some of the elbow-to-elbow options further on down the sands.

Bhakti Kutir (☎ 2643472; www.bhaktikutir.com; cottages from Rs2500; 💻) Ensconced in a thick wooded grove between Palolem and Patnem Beaches, Bhakti's well-equipped rustic cottages are a little on the pricey side these days, but still offer a unique junglish retreat. There are daily drop-in yoga classes, and the outdoor restaurant, beneath billowing parachute silks, turns out yummy, imaginative, healthful stuff.

Luke's Residence (☎ 2643003; www.lukesresidence.com; d Rs2500) Set in a quiet, green part of Palolem, about 10 minutes' walk from the beach, Luke's is praised by its oft-returning guests for its warm, helpful hospitality and great food. The beds are comfy, most rooms would easily fit three or four beach huts inside, and rates include a simple breakfast.

PATNEM

Long-stayers will revel in Patnem's choice of village homes and apartments available for rent. A very basic house can cost Rs10,000 per month while a fully equipped apartment will go for anything up to Rs50,000.

Micky Huts & Rooms (☎ 9850484884; huts Rs200) If you don't blanche at basic, this is the best bargain on the whole of Patnem beach, run by the friendliest and most obliging local family you could imagine. There's no signpost: just head for the huge patch of bamboo beside the small stream towards the northern end of the beach, and enquire at the restaurant.

Papaya's (☎ 9923079447; www.papayasgoa.com; huts Rs1500) Lovely, rustic huts head back into the palm grove from Papaya's popular restaurant. Each is lovingly tended to, with lots of wood and floating muslin, and the staff are incredibly keen to please.

Goyam & Goyam (☎ 9822685138; www.goyam.net; huts with/without sea view Rs3000/2500) Comfortable, cute and well-equipped pastel-shaded huts are the trademark here, with plenty of character and lots of room to breathe between each one.

Eating & Drinking

Both Palolem and Patnem's beaches are lined with beach shacks, offering all-day dining and fresh, fresh seafood as the catch comes in and the sun goes down. As with accommodation, places here change seasonally, but below are a few well-established options.

Hira Bar & Restaurant (breakfast from Rs12; ☺ breakfast & lunch) The best place to start the morning in Palolem with a simple *bhaji pau* and a glass of chai, along with locals on their way out to work.

our pick Mamoo's (mains from Rs40) Don't be put off by the rather dark, cavernous interior: here's where you'll find Palolem's very best Indian food, in delicious and generous portions. For a taste sensation, explore the variety of vegetarian tandoori options; you'll likely be back the following night to continue trawling the extensive menu.

Shiva Sai (vegetable thali Rs40; ☺ breakfast & lunch) A thoroughly local lunch joint, knocking out tasty thalis of the vegie, fish and Gujarati kinds, and a good line, too, in breakfasts such as banana pancakes (Rs40).

Blue Planet (dishes from Rs60) Tasty vegan and organic treats served up with love by a local couple at this shady retreat from the hot

Palolem day. Bring your water bottles here to be refilled with safe, filtered drinking water for just Rs3 per litre (free to restaurant patrons), to do your little bit towards reducing Palolem's plastic problem.

Home (☎ 2643916; home.patnem@yahoo.com; mains from Rs80) This hip, relaxed restaurant, run by a lovely British couple, serves up unquestionably the best food in Patnem. Fill up for breakfast with a thick, delicious rosti topped with fried eggs, cheese and tomatoes, or stop in for coffee and the best chocolate brownies in India. Home also rents out nicely decorated, light rooms (Rs1000 to Rs2500); call to book or ask at the restaurant.

Cuba (mains from Rs100) For scrambled eggs, soups and sundowners alike, perennially popular Cuba, down on the beach and with a bar on the beach road, has it all. Its Indian food is tasty and filling, as are its Chinese specialities, and the Cuba experience is enhanced by a great music collection, and a laid-back, lazy vibe.

Smugglers' Inn (mains from Rs120) If you're craving full English breakfasts or Sunday dinner with all the trimmings, the Smugglers' Inn, with its football on TV and weekly quiz nights, provides that little bit of Britain in the midst of beachside India.

Getting There & Away

There are hourly buses to Margao (Rs25, one hour) from the bus stand on the main road down to the beach. There are also regular buses to nearby Chaudi (Rs5), the nearest town, from which you can get frequent buses to Margao and Panaji or south to Karwar and Mangalore. The closest train station is Canacona.

An autorickshaw from Palolem to Patnem costs Rs50; an autorickshaw from Palolem to Chaudi costs Rs100. A prepaid taxi from Dabolim airport to Palolem/Patnem costs Rs1005/1080.

POLEM

In the very far south of the state, just a hop, skip and a jump to Karnataka, lies Goa's southernmost beach, ranged around a beautiful small bay on the seafront of the small village of Polem. Though the village itself seems to have been lumbered with an unsavoury reputation – due to its secretive, lucrative line in interstate liquor smuggling – it's actually a fine, friendly spot for a seaside stroll or a picnic on the deserted and pristine sands, with a beautiful view of a cluster of rocky islands out towards the horizon. Tourist development thankfully hasn't yet made it as far as Polem, and the beach retains a decidedly local feel, with a handful of fishermen bringing in their catch to the northern end and nothing much else to keep you company except scuttling crabs and circling seabirds.

For a fishy lunch so fresh it's still dithering, stop off at the **Kamaxi Hotel** (☎ 2640145; ⏰ lunch & dinner) in among the palms, run by

the eccentric local Laxaman Raikar. He stocks Kingfisher, if you're in need of something cold and frothy, and also has three exceedingly grim and grotty rooms for rent – in case you get seriously stranded – for Rs200 apiece.

To get to Polem, take a bus from Chaudi (the nearest town to Palolem) and get off at the bus stop around 3km after the petrol station. The stop is directly opposite the turning to the beach, after which it's a 1km walk to the village and beach.

Karnataka

'One state, many worlds', goes the slogan currently peddling Karnataka's tourism wonders to the world. And that's kidding you not! Rounding off the southern extent of the Deccan Plateau, this sprawling South Indian state exemplifies natural and cultural variety. And complemented by its ultra-professional tourism industry and inherent friendliness, Karnataka has, in recent times, surged ahead to redefine itself as a travellers' haven. It's fun, stress-free and thoroughly enjoyable all the way, and you're unlikely to return disappointed.

The epicurean silicon-capital Bengaluru (Bangalore), overfed with the good life, is your entry point to the state. Within arm's length is Mysore, the royal jewel in Karnataka's crown, with its spectacular palace and vibrant markets. Dodge the herds of grumpy tuskers in the Nilgiri Biosphere Reserve to arrive at the rock-cut temples of Belur and Halebid, and you've probably already sniffed the heady aroma of coffee and spices from the lush plantations of hilly Kodagu (Coorg). A stone's throw away is the shimmering Karnataka coastline, dotted with beaches and fascinating temple towns. If history is your forte, head to the centre of the state, studded with ancient architectural gems including the World Heritage–listed monuments of Hampi and Pattadakal. Finally, sign off by visiting the forgotten battlements and monuments of Bijapur and Bidar, where you'll be bowled over by a true blast from the state's glorious past.

HIGHLIGHTS

- Be dazzled by the Maharaja's Palace and the technicolour Devaraja Market in **Mysore** (p249)
- Savour aromatic coffee while recharging your spirit in the lush, cool highlands of the **Kodagu region** (p263)
- Drink yourself under the table, or stab into top-notch global cuisine in **Bengaluru** (p244)
- Stride across the deserted ramparts of the romantic 15th-century fort in **Bidar** (p290)
- Marvel at the gravity-defying boulders, and wander amid the melancholic ruins of **Hampi** (p276)
- Survey the sensuous carvings in the ancient caves and temples of **Badami** (p284)
- Play Robinson Crusoe and wave at passing boats along the deserted beaches of **Gokarna** (p272)

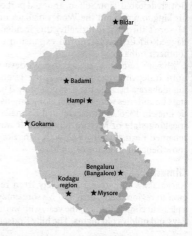

KARNATAKA

History

A playfield of religions, cultures and kingdoms galore, Karnataka has been ruled by a string of rulers through history. India's first great emperor, Chandragupta Maurya, made the state his retreat, when he embraced Jainism at Sravanabelagola in the 3rd century BC. From the 6th to the 11th century, the land was under a series of dynasties such as the Chalukyas (who built some of the earliest Hindu temples near Badami), the Cholas and the Gangas. From the 11th to the 14th century, the Hoysalas shaped the state in their own way, leaving a lasting mark with their stunning temples at Somnathpur, Halebid and Belur.

In 1327, Mohammed Tughlaq's Muslim army sacked Halebid. In 1347, Hasan Gangu, a Persian general in Tughlaq's army led a rebellion to establish the Bahmani kingdom, which was later subdivided into five Deccan sultanates. An attempt to counter the growing Islamic presence in the area saw the rise of the Vijayanagar kingdom, with its capital in Hampi. The dynasty peaked in the early 1550s, but fell in 1565 to a combined effort of the sultanates.

Following Vijayanagar's downfall, the Hindu Wodeyars (former rulers of Mysore state) quickly grew in stature, extending their rule over a large part of southern India. Their power remained largely unchallenged until 1761 when Hyder Ali (one of their generals) deposed them. Backed by the French, Hyder Ali and his son, Tipu Sultan, set up the capital in Srirangapatnam and consolidated their rule in the region. However, in 1799, the British defeated Tipu Sultan, annexed part of his kingdom and put the Wodeyars back on Mysore's throne. Historically, this incident flagged off British territorial expansion in southern India.

Mysore remained under the Wodeyars until Independence; post-1947, the reigning maharaja became the first governor. The state boundaries were redrawn along linguistic lines in 1956 and the extended Kannada-speaking state of Mysore was born. It was renamed Karnataka in 1972, with Bangalore (now Bengaluru) as the capital.

Climate

Karnataka's climate varies widely from region to region. Bengaluru and Mysore enjoy a pleasant climate through the year, with warm days and mildly cold nights. The hilly Kodagu

---

FAST FACTS

Population 52.7 million
Area 191,791 sq km
Capital Bengaluru (Bangalore)
Main languages Kannada, English
When to go October to March

---

region is damp through most of the year except for winter, when sunny skies make trekking a pleasure. The coastal stretch remains muggy most of the time; the conditions up north towards Bijapur and Bidar are drier, though notoriously hot through the summer months. The monsoons hit the state in late May.

Information

The website of **Karnataka State Tourism Development Corporation** (KSTDC; www.karnatakatourism.org) has a lot of relevant information.

The government-run **Jungle Lodges & Resorts Ltd** (Map p240; ☎ 080-25597021, 25597944; www.junglelodges.com; 2nd fl, Shrungar Shopping Complex, MG Rd, Bengaluru; ⏰ 10am-5.30pm Mon-Sat) is an excellent outfit that manages sustainable ecotourism in the state's many wildlife parks and reserves. It's worth contacting them if you want to go on a jungle jaunt. Bookings have to be made in Bengaluru, or through credit-card payment online.

Note that several government offices in Karnataka remain closed on alternate Saturdays.

ACCOMMODATION

In Karnataka luxury tax is 4% on rooms costing Rs151 to Rs400, 8% on those between Rs401 and Rs1000, and 12% on anything over Rs1000. Some midrange and top-end hotels may add a further service charge. Rates quoted in this chapter do not include taxes unless otherwise indicated.

Getting There & Away

The main gateway to Karnataka is Bengaluru. The city is serviced by most domestic airlines, including some international carriers. Airfares listed in this chapter are indicative only. Taxes are extra, and can sometimes be almost twice the actual fare.

Coastal Mangalore is a transit point for those going north to Goa, or south to Kerala. Hubli, in central Karnataka, is a major railway junction for routes going into Maharashtra and northern India.

KARNATAKA

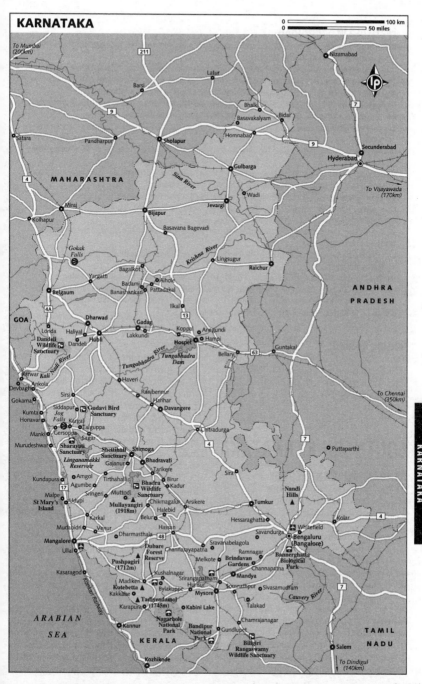

FESTIVALS IN KARNATAKA

Udupi Paryaya (Jan; Udupi, p270) Held in even-numbered years, with procession and ritual marking the handover of swamis at the town's Krishna Temple.

Classical Dance Festival (Jan/Feb; Pattadakal, p286) Features some of India's best classical dance performances.

Tibetan New Year (Feb; Bylakuppe, p266) Lamas in the Tibetan refugee settlements take shifts leading non-stop prayers that span the week of celebrations, which also include special dances and a fire ceremony.

Vasantahabba (Feb; Nrityagram, p249) The largest free classical dance and music event in India, hosted by the dance village of Nrityagram, featuring traditional and contemporary Indian dance and music.

Shivaratri Festival (Feb/Mar; Gokarna, p272) Two gargantuan chariots barrel down Gokarna's main street on 'Shiva power' amid much colourful ritual.

Muharram (Feb/Mar; Hospet, p281) This Shi'ia Muslim festival sees fire walkers in action, to the accompaniment of mass hoopla.

Vairamudi Festival (Mar/Apr; Melkote, p258) Lord Vishnu is adorned with jewels at Cheluvanarayana Temple, including a diamond-studded crown belonging to Mysore's former maharajas.

Ganesh Chaturthi (Aug/Sep; Gokarna, p272) Families quietly march their Ganeshas to the sea at sunset.

Dussehra (Sep/Oct; Mysore, p252) Also spelt 'Dasara' in Mysore. The Maharaja's Palace is lit up in the evenings and a vibrant procession hits town to the delight of thousands.

Vijaya Utsav (Nov; Hampi, p275) Traditional music and dance re-creates Vijayanagar's glory among Hampi's temples and boulders.

Lakshadeepam (Nov; Dharmasthala, p270) A hundred thousand lamps light up this Jain pilgrimage town, offering spectacular photo-ops.

Huthri (Nov/Dec; Madikeri, p263) The Kodava community of Kodagu celebrates the start of the season's rice harvests with ceremony, music, traditional dances and much feasting for a week, beginning on a full-moon night.

Mastakabhisheka (Feb; Sravanabelagola, p261) Held once every 12 years, when the 58ft monolithic statue of Bahubali is swathed in colourful offerings. The next date is in 2018.

Getting Around

Karnataka State Road Transport Corporation (KSRTC) has a superb bus network across the state. Taxis with drivers are readily available in major towns. For long trips, most charge around Rs7 per kilometre for a minimum of 250km, plus a Rs150 allowance for the driver.

SOUTHERN KARNATAKA

BENGALURU (BANGALORE)

☎ 080 / pop 5.7 million / elev 920m

Strategically located at the southern tip of the Deccan and within close range of Kerala and Tamil Nadu, cosmopolitan Bengaluru (formerly Bangalore) makes a great base and starting point for venturing out across southern India. The hub of India's booming IT industry, the city has experienced a mad surge of urban development of late, which shows in its crazy traffic, rising pollution levels and civic congestion. However, it's also a city that has taken care to preserve its green spaces and colonial heritage. Add to that a benevolent climate, some interesting sights and a progressive dining, drinking and shopping scene, and Bengaluru promises a few great nights on the town.

History

Literally meaning 'Town of Boiled Beans', Bengaluru supposedly derived its name from an ancient incident involving an old village woman, who served cooked pulses to a lost and hungry Hoysala king. Kempegowda, a feudal lord, was the first person to earmark Bengaluru's extents by building a mud fort in 1537. However, the town remained obscure until 1759, when it was gifted to Hyder Ali by the Mysore maharaja.

The British came to town in 1809, and made it their regional administrative base in 1831, thus renaming it Bangalore. During the Raj era, the city played host to many a British officer, including Winston Churchill, who enjoyed life here during his greener years and famously left a debt (still on the books) of Rs13 at the Bangalore Club!

That Bengaluru was a city with a knack for technology became apparent quite early; in 1905, it was the first Indian city to have electric street lighting. Since the 1940s, it has been home to Hindustan Aeronautics Ltd (HAL), India's premier aerospace company. And if you can't do without email today, you owe it all to a Bangalorean too; Sabeer Bhatia, inventor of the pioneering Hotmail service, grew up here!

A nominal step backward was taken when the city's name was changed back to Bengaluru in November 2006, though few care to use it in practice. Home to a swanky new international airport and a rush of software, electronics and business process outsourcing firms, Bengaluru's skyline is increasingly being dotted by skyscrapers today, each of which seems to be reaching for the sky, literally as well as figuratively.

Orientation

Increasing development continues to push Bengaluru's boundaries outward by the day. However, the central part remains more or less unchanged. Of interest to travellers are Gandhi Nagar (the old quarters); Mahatma Gandhi (MG) Rd, the heart of British-era Bangalore; and the Central Business District (CBD), north of MG Rd, across the greens.

Known as Majestic, Gandhi Nagar is a crowded area where the Central bus stand and the City train station are located. A few historical relics lie to its south, including Lalbagh Botanical Gardens and Tipu Sultan's palace.

About 4km east are the high streets bounded by Mahatma Gandhi (MG), Brigade, St Mark's and Residency (FM Cariappa) Rds. This is Bengaluru's cosmopolitan hub, with parks, churches, grand houses and military establishments. In between are sandwiched the golf club, racecourse and cricket stadium.

Finding directions in Bengaluru can be slightly disorienting at times. In certain areas, roads are named after their widths (eg 80ft Rd). The city also follows a system of mains and crosses; 3rd cross, 5th main, Residency Rd, for example, refers to the third lane on the fifth street branching off Residency Rd.

MAPS

The tourist offices (p238) give out decent city maps. The excellent *Eicher City Map* (Rs200) is sold at Bengaluru's many bookshops.

Information
BOOKSHOPS

Blossom (Map p240; 84/6 Church St; ☉ 10.30am-8pm Mon-Sat) The excellent collection here gets even better when you know the books often come at bargain prices!

Crossword (Map p240; ACR Tower, Residency Rd; ☉ 10.30am-9pm Mon-Sat) Offers a great selection of books, magazines, CDs and DVDs.

Premier Bookshop (Map p240; 46/1 Church St; ☉ 10am-1.30pm & 3-8pm Mon-Sat) It's tiny but somehow has everything; enter from Museum Rd.

CULTURAL CENTRES

Alliance Française (Map p238; ☎ 41231340; www .afindia.org/bangalore; 108 Thimmaiah Rd; ☉ 10am-7pm Mon-Sat) French cultural hub offering courses, events, a cafe and a library.

British Library (Map p238; ☎ 22489220; www.library .britishcouncil.org.in; 23 Kasturba Rd Cross; ☉ 10.30am-6.30pm Mon-Sat) English newspapers, books and magazines, and free internet access for members (annual membership Rs1000).

Max Mueller Bhavan (off Map p238; ☎ 25205305; www.goethe.de; 716 CMH Rd, opposite MK Retailers, Indiranagar 1st Stage; ☉ 9am-5pm Mon-Fri) Has a good cafe and library of German titles; runs exhibitions and courses.

INTERNET ACCESS

For an IT city, internet cafes are plentiful in Bengaluru, as is wi-fi access in hotels.

LEFT LUGGAGE

Both the City train station (Map p238) and Central bus stand (Map p238), located either side of Gubbi Thotadappa Rd, have 24-hour cloakrooms (per day Rs10).

MEDIA

City Info (www.explocity.com) is a bimonthly listings booklet that's available free from tourist offices and many hotels. *Ticket Bengaluru* (Rs350) is a great handbook and is available in major bookstores.

MEDICAL SERVICES

Most hotels in Bengaluru have doctors on call.

Chetak Pharma (Map p238; ☎ 22212449; Basement, Devatha Plaza, Residency Rd; ☉ 9am-9pm Mon-Sat, 9.30am-2pm Sun) Well-stocked pharmacy.

Mallya Hospital (Map p238; ☎ 22277979; www.mallya hospital.net; Vittal Mallya Rd) With a 24-hour pharmacy.

MONEY

ATMs are common.

Monarch (Map p240; ☎ 41123253; 54 Monarch Plaza, Brigade Rd; ☉ 10am-8pm Mon-Sat) Deals in foreign exchange, travellers cheques and ticketing.

TT Forex (Map p238; ☎ 22254337; 33/1 Cunningham Rd; ☉ 9.30am-6.30pm Mon-Fri, 9.30am-1.30pm Sat) Changes travellers cheques with no commission.

PHOTOGRAPHY

Digital services are easy to come by.

GG Welling (Map p240; 113 MG Rd; ☉ 9.30am-1pm & 3-7.30pm Mon-Sat)

GK Vale (Map p240; 89 MG Rd; ☉ 10am-7pm Mon-Sat).

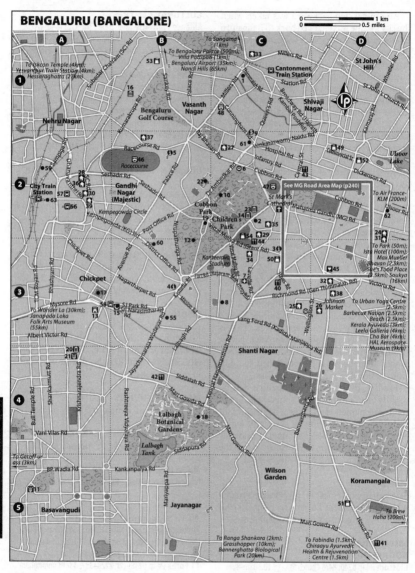

BENGALURU (BANGALORE)

0 _____ 1 km
0 _____ 0.5 miles

POST
Main post office (Map p238; ☎ 22892211; Cubbon Rd; ☒ 10am-7pm Mon-Sat, 10am-1pm Sun).

TOURIST INFORMATION
Government of India tourist office (Map p240; ☎ 25585417; 48 Church St; ☒ 9.30am-6pm Mon-Fri, 9am-1pm Sat)

Karnataka State Tourism Development Corporation (KSTDC; Map p238) Badami House (☎ 22275883; Badami House, Kasturba Rd; ☒ 10am-7pm Mon-Sat); Karnataka Tourism House (☎ 41329211; 8 Papanna Lane, St Mark's Rd; ☒ 10am-7pm Mon-Sat) Bookings can be made for KSTDC city and state tours, as well as for luxury holidays such as the Golden Chariot (p531).

INFORMATION

Alliance Française	1	C1
British Library	2	C2
Chetak Pharma	(see 40)	
Karnataka State Tourism Development Corporation	3	B3
Karnataka State Tourism Development Corporation	4	C3
Karnataka Tourism	5	B2
Main Post Office	6	C2
Mallya Hospital	7	C3
Skyway	(see 3)	
STIC Travels	(see 9)	
Swabhava	8	C3
TT Forex	9	C2

SIGHTS & ACTIVITIES

Attara Kacheri (High Court)	10	C2
Bull Temple	11	A5
Cubbon Park	12	B3
Dodda Ganesha Temple	(see 11)	
Fort	13	A3
Government Museum	14	C2
Jama Masjid	15	B3
Karnataka Chitrakala Parishath	16	B1
Krishnarajendra (City) Market	17	A3
Lalbagh Botanical Gardens	18	B4
State Central Library	19	B2
Tipu Sultan's Palace	20	A4
Venkatappa Art Gallery	(see 14)	
Venkataraman Temple	21	A4
Vidhana Soudha	22	B2

Visvesvaraya Industrial and Technical Museum	23	C2

SLEEPING

Ashley Inn	24	D2
Casa Piccola Cottage	25	C3
Casa Piccola Service Apartments	26	D3
Chevron Hotel	27	C2
Hari International	28	A2
Homestead Serviced Apartments	29	D3
Hotel Adora	30	A2
Hotel Ajantha	31	D2
Hotel Vellara	32	D3
Jayamahal Palace	33	C1
Mélange	34	C3
Regaalis	35	C2
Sandhya Lodge	36	A2
Taj West End	37	B2
Tom's	38	D3
Tricolour Hotel	39	A2

EATING

Casa del Sol	40	C3
Gramin	41	D5
Harima	(see 40)	
Mavalli Tiffin Rooms (MTR)	42	B4
Samarkand	43	C2
Sunny's	44	C3

DRINKING

Fuga	45	D3

ENTERTAINMENT

Bangalore Turf Club	46	B2
M Chinnaswamy Stadium	47	C2

Nani Cinematheque	48	C1
PVR Cinema	(see 51)	

SHOPPING

Fabindia	49	D2
Ffolio	50	C3
Forum	51	D5
Mysore Saree Udyog	52	D2
Raintree	53	B1
UB City Mall	54	C2

TRANSPORT

Air India	55	B3
Central Bus Stand	56	A2
City Bus Stand	57	A2
City Market Bus Stand	58	A3
Divisional Railway Office	59	A2
Indian Airlines	60	B3
Jet Airways	(see 55)	
Kingfisher Airlines	61	C2
KSRTC Booking Counter	(see 40)	
Lufthansa	62	D2
Train Reservation Office	63	A2

Karnataka Tourism (Map p238; ☎ 22352828; 2nd fl, 49 Khanija Bhavan, Racecourse Rd; ☺ 10am-5.30pm Mon-Sat)

TRAVEL AGENCIES

Skyway (Map p238; ☎ 22111401; www.skywaytour .com; 8 Papanna Lane, St Mark's Rd; ☺ 9am-6pm Mon-Sat) A thoroughly professional outfit with satellite offices in Mysore and Madikeri. Reliable for booking long-distance taxis and air tickets.

STIC Travels (Map p238; ☎ 22202408; www.stictravel .com; Imperial Court, 33/1 Cunningham Rd; ☺ 9.30am-6pm Mon-Sat)

Dangers & Annoyances

For information about safety on local buses, see p248.

Sights

LALBAGH BOTANICAL GARDENS

Spread over 96 acres of landscaped terrain, **Lalbagh** (Map p238; ☎ 26579231; admission Rs10; ☺ 5.30am-7.30pm) or the Red Garden was laid

out in 1760 by Hyder Ali, and is now one of Bengaluru's most famous greens. Ten-seater ecofriendly buggies (per head Rs100) take you on a guided tour across the garden, telling you more about the centuries-old trees and collections of plants from around the world. A beautiful glasshouse, modelled on the original Crystal Palace in London, is the venue for flower shows in the weeks preceding Republic Day (26 January) and Independence Day (15 August). Walk in early on Sundays, and you can also hear the police band perform at the Police Bandstand.

BENGALURU PALACE

The private residence of the Wodeyar family, **Bengaluru Palace** (off Map p238; ☎ 23315789; Palace Rd; Indian/foreigner Rs100/200, camera/video Rs500/1000; ☺ 10am-6pm) preserves a slice of the bygone royal life for you to see. Aged retainers show you around the building, designed to resemble Windsor Castle, and you can marvel at the lavish interiors and galleries featuring family photos and a collection of nude portraits. Ask

KARNATAKA

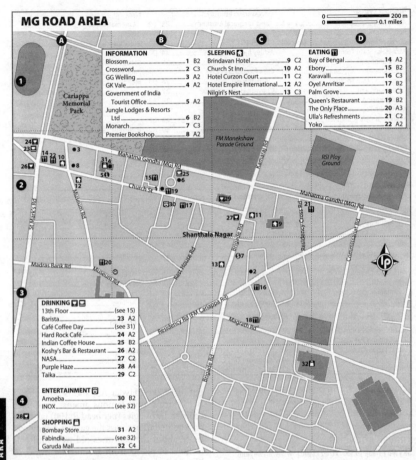

MG ROAD AREA

0 ———— 200 m
0 ———— 0.1 miles

INFORMATION
Blossom **1** B2
Crossword **2** C3
GG Welling **3** A2
GK Vale **4** A2
Government of India
    Tourist Office **5** A2
Jungle Lodges & Resorts
    Ltd **6** B2
Monarch **7** C3
Premier Bookshop **8** A2

SLEEPING
Brindavan Hotel **9** C2
Church St Inn **10** A2
Hotel Curzon Court **11** C2
Hotel Empire International ... **12** A2
Nilgiri's Nest **13** C3

EATING
Bay of Bengal **14** A2
Ebony **15** B2
Karavalli **16** C3
Oye! Amritsar **17** B2
Palm Grove **18** C3
Queen's Restaurant **19** B2
The Only Place **20** A3
Ulla's Refreshments **21** C2
Yoko **22** A2

DRINKING
13th Floor .... (see 15)
Barista **23** A2
Café Coffee Day .... (see 31)
Hard Rock Café **24** A2
Indian Coffee House **25** B2
Koshy's Bar & Restaurant **26** A2
NASA **27** C2
Purple Haze **28** A4
Taika **29** C2

ENTERTAINMENT
Amoeba **30** B2
INOX .... (see 32)

SHOPPING
Bombay Store **31** A2
Fabindia .... (see 32)
Garuda Mall **32** C4

---

before you get clicking. The palace grounds, interestingly, are now Bengaluru's hottest concert arena, having hosted everyone from Iron Maiden, Rolling Stones, Aerosmith and Deep Purple in the past!

KARNATAKA CHITRAKALA PARISHATH

This **visual arts gallery** (Map p238; ☎ 22261816; www .chitrakalaparishath.org; Kumarakrupa Rd; admission Rs10; ⏰ 10.30am-5.30pm Mon-Sat) is Bengaluru's definitive art institution. A wide range of Indian and international contemporary art is on show at its exhibition galleries (open 10.30am to 7pm), while permanent displays showcase lavish gold-leaf works of Mysore-style paintings and folk and tribal art from across Asia. A section is devoted to the works of Russian master

Nicholas Roerich, known for his vivid paintings of the Himalaya, and his son Svetoslav.

CUBBON PARK

Named after former British commissioner Sir Mark Cubbon, the leafy boughs of the 120-hectare **Cubbon Park** (Map p238) provide a few moments' respite to the city's stressed-out residents. On its fringes are the red-painted Gothic-style **State Central Library** and two municipal museums. For the gadget-oriented kind, there's the **Visvesvaraya Industrial & Technical Museum** (☎ 22864009; Kasturba Rd; admission Rs15; ⏰ 10am-6pm Mon-Sat), which showcases a wide range of electrical and engineering displays, from a replica of the Wright brothers' 1903 flyer to 21st-century virtual-reality

GROUND ZERO OF THE FLAT WORLD

You'll be pardoned for mistaking it for the sets of a Utopian movie. In reality, however, it's only the lush and modern campus of Indian IT giant Infosys, located on the southeastern edge of Bengaluru. A pioneer in India's booming software industry, the company has almost single-handedly ushered in India's IT revolution through its years of operation. In 2005, it was also responsible for cementing Bengaluru's reputation as the silicon-coated heart of India, when Pulitzer Prize–winning writer Thomas L Friedman wrote *The World Is Flat* after visiting its campus and being inspired by the company's progressive principles.

Established by seven software engineers in 1981, Infosys today has over 100,000 employees and revenues of over US$4 billion – its client list currently includes nearly 100 Fortune 500 companies. Its campus (not open to the public) represents an alternative, enterprising India existing in the form of shiny glass and steel structures sprouting amid rolling lawns. The workforce (average age 26) cycle or use electric golf carts to get around the 32-hectare campus, passing five food courts (serving 14 types of cuisine), banks, a supermarket, basketball courts, putting green and state-of-the-art gyms, and even a hotel!

The point, perhaps, is to prove that Infosys can compete on equal terms with the Western world – thus putting India on a level playing field with other nationalities in Friedman's 'flat world'.

games. The **Government Museum** (☎ 22864483; Kasturba Rd; admission Rs4; ☯ 10am-5pm Tue-Sun) to the south of Cubbon Park houses a collection of stone carvings and relics, including some good pieces from Halebid. Your ticket also gets you into the attached **Venkatappa Art Gallery** (☯ 10am-5pm Tue-Sun), where you can see several works and personal memorabilia of K Venkatappa (1887–1962), court painter to the Wodeyars.

At the northwestern end of Cubbon Park are the colossal neo-Dravidian-style **Vidhana Soudha**, built in 1954, and the neoclassical **Attara Kacheri**, opposite, that houses the High Court. Both are closed to the public.

TIPU SULTAN'S PALACE

In the heart of the vibrant Krishnarajendra City Market stands the elegant **palace** (Map p238; Albert Victor Rd; Indian/foreigner Rs5/100, video Rs25; ☯ 8.30am-5.30pm) of Tipu Sultan, notable for its teak pillars and ornamental frescoes. Though not as beautiful (or well-maintained) as Tipu's summer palace in Srirangapatnam, it's an interesting monument, and definitely worth an outing when combined with other nearby sights such as the **Krishnarajendra (City) Market**, the massive **Jama Masjid** (Map p238; Silver Jubilee (SJ) Park Rd; admission free), the remains of Kempegowda's **fort** (Map p238) and the ornate **Venkataraman Temple** (Map p238; Krishnarajendra Rd; ☯ 8.30am-6pm).

BULL TEMPLE & DODDA GANESHA TEMPLE

Built by Kempegowda in the 16th-century Dravidian style, the **Bull Temple** (Map p238; Bull Temple Rd, Basavangudi; ☯ 7am-8.30pm) contains a huge granite monolith of Nandi and is one of Bengaluru's most atmospheric temples. Nearby is the **Dodda Ganesha Temple** (Map p238; Bull Temple Rd, Basavangudi; ☯ 7am-8.30pm), with an equally enormous Ganesh idol.

ISKCON TEMPLE

Built by the International Society of Krishna Consciousness (Iskcon), better known as the Hare Krishnas, this shiny **temple** (off Map p238; Hare Krishna Hill, Chord Rd; ☯ 7am-1pm & 4-8.30pm), 8km northwest of the town centre, is lavishly decorated in a mix of ultra-contemporary and traditional styles. The Sri Radha Krishna Mandir has a stunning shrine to Krishna and Radha.

HAL AEROSPACE MUSEUM

For a peek into India's aeronautical history, visit this wonderful **museum** (off Map p238; ☎ 25228341; Airport-Varthur Rd; admission Rs20; ☯ 9am-5pm Tue-Sun) past the old airport, where you can see some of the indigenous aircraft models designed by HAL, sometimes with a little help from other nations. Interesting exhibits include the infamous MIG-21, indigenous models such as the Marut and Kiran, and a vintage Canberra bomber. You can also engage in mock dogfights at the simulator machines (Rs10) on the top floor.

Activities

AYURVEDA & YOGA

Chiraayu Ayurvedic Health & Rejuvenation Centre (off Map p238; ☎ 25500855; 6th block, 17th D Main, Koramangala;

(☾ 8.30am-6pm) These people take their practice seriously, so don't make vague demands like 'I'd like a massage'. Make an appointment, discuss your problems, and the resultant therapy could range from a day-long spa session (from Rs700) to long-term programs.

Based in the eastern part of town, **Kerala Ayurveda** (off Map p238; ☎ 25262515; 3282 12th Main, HAL 2nd Stage), a veteran in the wellness industry, offers holistic ayurvedic treatment through its centres across Bengaluru. Prices kick off from around Rs600. For a more lavish experience, try **Soukya** (off Map p238; ☎ 25318405; www.soukya.com; Soukya Rd, Samethanahalli, Whitefield; ☾ 6am-8.30pm), an internationally renowned place set on a picture-perfect 30-acre organic farm, that offers some of the best programs in ayurvedic therapy and yoga (per hour therapy Indian/foreigner Rs2200/US$55).

Stylish **Urban Yoga Centre** (off Map p238; ☎ 32005720; www.urbanyoga.in; 100ft Rd, Indiranagar; ☾ 6.30am-9pm) has a smart yoga studio offering a range of classes, and sells yoga clothes, accessories and books.

OUTDOOR ADVENTURE
Getoff ur ass (off Map p238; ☎ 26722750; www.getoffurass.com; 858 1D Main Rd, Giri Nagar 2nd Phase) has perfect recipes for outward-bound adventures, including rafting, kayaking, trekking and mountaineering in Karnataka and elsewhere. It also sells and rents outdoor gear.

WATER RIDES
Wonder La (off Map p238; www.wonderla.com; adult/child weekdays Rs450/350, weekends Rs570/420; ☾ 11am-6pm weekdays, 11am-7pm weekends) is located 30km out of town on the Mysore highway; this massive aqua park offers dozens of water rides.

Tours
Bangalore Walks (☎ 9845523660, 9880671192; www.bangalorewalks.com) is a must-do! Choose between a traditional walk, garden walk or Victorian walk to get under Bengaluru's skin. Held on Saturdays and Sundays (7am to 10pm), the walks (Rs495 including breakfast) teach you to love Bengaluru in a way that many locals have forgotten. Book in advance; each walk takes a maximum of 15 people.

KSTDC runs a couple of city bus tours, all of which begin at Badami House. The basic city tour runs twice daily at 7.30am and 2pm (ordinary/deluxe Rs170/190), while a 16-hour tour to Srirangapatnam, Mysore and

Brindavan Gardens departs daily at 7.15am (ordinary/deluxe Rs525/675). There are longer tours to other destinations; enquire at the KSTDC offices (see p238).

Sleeping
With demands for a decent bed rising by the day, accommodation in Bengaluru is pricey and in short supply. A decent night's sleep could set you back by at least Rs1000. Anything under Rs500, and you're possibly courting asphyxia. Serviced apartments are frequently a better deal than many midrange (Rs1500 to Rs5000) and top-end hotels. Most hotels have 24-hour checkout. Book early.

BUDGET
Stacks of hotels line the loud and seedy neighbourhood of Subedar Chatram (SC) Rd, east of the bus stands and City train station. It's an unpleasant area, but convenient if you're in transit. For longer stays, consider moving into town, preferably closer to MG Rd. All hotels listed here have hot water, at least in the mornings.

Hotel Adora (Map p238; ☎ 22200024; 47 SC Rd; s/d from Rs400/600) A largish and popular budget option near the stations, this place has non-fussy rooms with clean sheets. Downstairs is a good veg restaurant, Indraprastha.

Hotel Ajantha (Map p238; ☎ 25584321; fax 25584780; 22A MG Rd; s/d from Rs450/700, with AC from Rs999/1050; ☒) Old Indian tourism posters and stacks of potted foliage welcome you into this place with a range of par-for-the-course rooms in a semi-quiet compound off MG Rd. It's popular with local tourists; book in advance.

Brindava Hotel (Map p240; ☎ 25584000; 108 MG Rd; s/d from Rs550/850, with AC from Rs1250/2550; ☒) Another place where advance booking is recommended. Its central position is a definite advantage, and the rooms are clean, bright and airy (with balconies). There's an in-house astro-palmist, if you're interested.

Sandhya Lodge (Map p238; ☎ 22874071; 70 SC Rd; d from Rs555, with AC Rs1450; ☒) Functionality overrides comfort at this place with unimaginative rooms, but at least they're tidy and the loos well-scrubbed. Try for a room on the upper floors; it gets brighter the higher you climb.

Tom's (Map p238; ☎ 25575875; 1/5 Hosur Rd; s/d Rs999/1299, with AC Rs1800/2100; ☒ ▢) Clearly the best of Bengaluru's low-cost brigade. The spacious modern rooms here come with freshly painted walls, moody lighting, large windows and spotless linen. Add to that its prime location and a warm, friendly management – need we say more?

Hotel Vellara (Map p238; ☎ 25369116; fax 25369775; 283 Brigade Rd; s/d from Rs1000/1050; ✗ ▣) Slapbang in the middle of town you'll find this little patch of quiet. The Vellara isn't what you might call lavish, but you'll sense the human touch and warmth in the way you're made to feel at home by its management. The rooms are spacious, prim and extremely well serviced. Some look out on to the busy road below.

MIDRANGE
Hotel Curzon Court (Map p240; ☎ 25582997; 10 Brigade Rd; s/d from Rs1400/1600; ✗) Not too elaborate on the decor front, but this place has well-appointed and neat rooms with AC comfort. A sumptuous range of vegie delights are served at their restaurant, Aathithya.

Hotel Empire International (Map p240; ☎ 25593743; www.hotelempire.in; 36 Church St; s/d incl breakfast from Rs1550/1850; ✗ ▣) The modern rooms here are spacious and bright, and it's in the heart of all the action and nightlife. The reception desk is staffed by a professional lot, and the travel desk does a good job at booking tours.

Nilgiri's Nest (Map p240; ☎ 25588401; www .nilgiris1905.com; 171 Brigade Rd; s/d from Rs1650/2150; ✗) An air of freshness hangs in the snug rooms of this centrally located hotel. Below is an upmarket ration store run by the same company, which stocks some great ready-to-eat delights.

Ashley Inn (Map p238; ☎ 41233415; www.ashleyinn .in; 11 Ashley Park Rd; s/d incl breakfast from Rs1800/2200; ✗ ▣) Seconds away from the MG Rd mayhem is this charming island of quiet. With eight pleasant rooms done up in soothing colours, this sweet guest house evokes that homey feeling you sometimes desperately yearn for while on the move.

Church Street Inn (Map p240; ☎ 30577190; www .churchstreetinn.in; 46/1/1 Church St; s/d Rs1900/2100; ✗) It's perfect for a longish stay. Guess why? The tariff goes down by 10% every successive day! The rooms, some with wooden floors and tinted windows looking down on Church St, are comfy. The bookshelf at the reception is worth a thumbing.

Casa Piccola Service Apartments (Map p238; ☎ 22270754; www.casapiccola.com; Wellington Park Apartments, Wellington St; r with/without AC Rs2300/2000;

✗) A wonderful range of two- and three-bedroom apartments are available in this building on a shared basis. Tastefully done up in pastel shades, they are stocked up with all amenities. It's owned by the Oberoi family which runs the Casa Piccola Cottage across the lane.

Tricolour Hotel (Map p238; ☎ 41279090; www.ibc hotels.co.in; 15 Tank Bund Rd; s/d incl breakfast Rs2000/2500; ✗ ▣) Built back-to-back against a shopping mall, this place is both classy and contemporary, with lavishly laid-out rooms and cheerful, sky-lit foyers. Convenient for both the bus and train stations.

Hari International (Map p238; ☎ 40214021; www .hotelhariinternational.com; 68/68/1 SC Rd; d incl breakfast Indian/foreigner from Rs2400/US$60; ✗ ▣) More of a business joint, this place, despite its noisy surroundings, makes for a pleasant stay. Rooms meet requisite luxury standards, and the amiable staff is always ready to meet your requirements.

our pick Casa Piccola Cottage (Map p238; ☎ 22270754; www.casapiccola.com; 2 Clapham St; r incl breakfast from Rs3000; ✗ ▣) The rates may have gone up considerably, but this beautifully renovated 1915 cottage still scores on the comfort front. A tranquil sanctuary from the madness of the city, its studio rooms are high on old-world charm, and the gazebo in the garden across the tiny lawn is a nice place to tuck into your complimentary breakfast.

Villa Pottipati (off Map p238; ☎ 23360777; www .neemranahotels.com; 142 8th Cross, 4th Main, Malleswaram; s/d from Rs3500/5000; ✗ ▣ ✗) Located a little off-centre, this heritage building packs in dollops of quaintness (read antique four-poster beds and arched doorways); adding to its ambience is a garden full of ageless tress, seasonal blossoms and a dunk-sized pool.

Homestead Serviced Apartments (Map p238; ☎ 22220966; www.homesteadbangalore.com; 12/12 7th Cross, Lavelle Rd; apt incl breakfast from Rs4200; ✗ ▣) One among several of Bengaluru's stylish new serviced-apartment options, this place stands out for its central location, and is positioned primarily to cater to corporate jet-setters. The apartments are a riot of bright colours and comfy furnishings, with fully loaded kitchenettes for you to try your gourmet skills.

Jayamahal Palace (Map p238; ☎ 23331321; www.jayamahalpalace.com; 1 Jayamahal Rd; s/d from Rs5000/6000; ✗ ▣) Once an Englishman's residence, this heritage structure is now royal property, owned by the former royal family of the Gujarati princely state of Gondal.

KARNATAKA

Thoughtfully renovated, its rooms are stacked with relics from the past; the more expensive suites house things like brass swings and excellent stained glass-work.

Chevron Hotel (Map p238; ☎ 22356000; www.the chevronhotel.com; 147 Infantry Rd; d Indian/foreigner from Rs5550/US$160; ✕ ⬜) A glitzy player in Bengaluru's midrange scene, this boutique place ups its style quotient with ocean-blue lighting, and serves a host of succulent bites at its multi-cuisine restaurant, Ground Pepper. The snug rooms are well-appointed, and house everything you require for a good night's sleep.

Also recommended:

Mélange (Map p238; ☎ 22129700; www.melange bangalore.com; 21 Vittal Mallya Rd; apt from Rs3250; ✕) A range of designer serviced apartments.

Regaalis (Map p238; ☎ 41133111; www.ushalexus hotels.com; 40/2 Lavelle Rd; d incl breakfast from Rs5000; ✕ ⬜) A midrange option in the heart of town.

TOP END

Ista Hotel (off Map p238; ☎ 25558888; www.istahotels.com; 1/1 Swami Vivekananda Rd, Ulsoor; s/d from Rs6500/13,000; ✕ ⬜ ✉) Its name meaning 'Sacred Space', Ista delivers accommodation happiness in a cool, minimalist style. The smallish but elegant rooms with king-size windows offer sweeping vistas across Ulsoor lake and the city, and the bar and restaurant, opening on to the rooftop pool, are heavenly.

Taj West End (Map p238; ☎ 66605660; www.tajhotels.com; 23 Racecourse Rd; s/d from Rs8000/9200; ✕ ⬜ ✉) These guys have done a swell renovation job – the rooms, though new, still look old! A charming property set amid a luscious 8-hectare garden, this place offers rooms that ooze character. Each room comes with a private verandah, and boasts butler service.

Park (off Map p238; ☎ 25594666; www.bangalore .theparkhotels.com; 14/7 MG Rd; s/d from Rs15,000/17,000; ✕ ⬜ ✉) This Terence Conran–styled hotel dares to defy the norms. You have psychedelic red-and-white chairs in its bar, yellow-and-black upholstery in its ultramodern rooms and romantic candle-lit tables in its futuristic poolside club, Aqua. The Italian restaurant i-t.alia is a premium dining address in town.

Eating

Bengaluru's delicious dining scene keeps pace with the whims and rising standards of its hungry, moneyed masses. Unless mentioned otherwise, all restaurants are open from noon to 3pm, and 7pm to 11pm. If there's a telephone number, it's advisable to book.

MG ROAD AREA

All the following venues can be found on Map p240.

Ullas Refreshments (1st fl, Public Utility Bldg, MG Rd; mains Rs40-70; ✆ 9am-10pm) On a quiet terrace overlooking the MG Rd mad rush, this place serves simple North and South Indian snacks that can fuel your lazy chat sessions. A hit with students and young executives.

Palm Grove (Ballal Residency, 74/3 3rd Cross, Residency Rd; mains Rs60-100; ✆ 7am-10.30pm) This cheerful eatery has earned a name for itself thanks to its wide and delicious range of Kannada vegie dishes, including staples such as dosas and *vadas*, as well as expansive veg thalis for lunch and dinner.

Queen's Restaurant (Church St; mains Rs100-150) The rustic, tribal decor in this cosy restaurant complements its lip-smacking Indian fare, especially the vegie dishes.

Bay of Bengal (☎ 25320332; 48/1 St Mark's Rd; mains Rs100-150) Run by a Kolkata catering heavyweight, this place has some delightful Bengali dishes on offer. Recommended for treats of the fishy kind.

The Only Place (☎ 32718989; 13 Museum Rd; mains Rs100-250) Burgers, steaks, apple pies or the classic shepherd's pie – no one serves them better than this oldie, which boasts semi-alfresco interiors and a relaxed vibe.

Ebony (☎ 41783344; 13th fl, Barton Centre, 84 MG Rd; mains Rs120-300) Rated highly by Bengaluru's foodies, this place high up on a skyscraper serves the best Parsi food in town, along with some delectable Thai and French dishes.

Oye! Amritsar (☎ 41122866; 4th fl, Asha Enclave, Church St; mains Rs200-250) Get a feel and taste of good old Punjab at this place with funky interiors and wacky graffiti. Don't forget to wash down your meals with that frothy glass of yoghurt-based lassi!

Yoko (☎ 41266588; 42 Church St; mains Rs300-400) Walk into this non-fussy joint to gorge on sumptuous sizzlers, choosing from one of its many cracking offerings. The downside: you'll miss that cold pint of beer to go along with the meat.

Karavalli (☎ 66604545; 66 Residency Rd; mains Rs400-600) Mangalore's some 500km away, but you'll have to come only as far as this fine-dining spot to savour its famous coastal cuisine. Adorned with dark wood interiors, this classy restaurant at the Gateway Hotel serves some of the best seafood in town.

OTHER AREAS

Mavalli Tiffin Rooms (MTR; Map p238; Lalbagh Rd; dishes Rs20-80; ☒ 6.30-11am, 12.30-2.45pm, 3.30-7.30pm & 8-9.30pm) This legendary joint, commonly called MTR, has been feeding Bengaluru its stock South Indian fare such as *masala dosas* for more than seven decades. The queues can get long during lunch hours.

Gramin (Map p238; ☎ 41104103; 20, 7th Block Raheja Arcade, Koramangala; mains Rs100-150) A wide choice of flavourful and breezy North Indian fare is on offer at this extremely popular all-veg place. Try the excellent range of lentils, best had with oven fresh roti.

Sue's Food Place (off Map p238; ☎ 25252494; Subedar Garden, Sri Krishna Temple Rd, Indiranagar; mains Rs150-250) Run by the charming proprietor Sue, this Jamaican restaurant has lacy curtains, kitschy plastic creepers and football shirts as part of its decor, and serves Caribbean cuisine to die for. The lunch buffet (Rs225) is not to be missed!

Casa del Sol (Map p238; ☎ 41510101; 3rd fl, Devatha Plaza, 131 Residency Rd; mains Rs200-350; ☒ 11am-11pm) This is a relaxed Mediterranean-style bistro with a semi-alfresco area. Wednesday is disco night, Thursday has free salsa classes and Sunday has an opulent brunch (Rs600) with unlimited drinks and children's activities.

Sunny's (Map p238; ☎ 22120496; 34 Vittal Mallya Rd; mains Rs250-450) Missing those Mediterranean flavours? Well, just head to Sunny's and pamper yourself with a wide range of salads, mains and desserts. It's particularly popular with Bengaluru's expat community, and the food is simply divine.

Barbeque Nation (off Map p238; ☎ 32504455; 100Ft Rd, Indiranagar; set meal Rs400) Good news for kebab lovers! This stylish new place makes your dreams come true by serving a set meal of select barbeques, of which you can have unlimited portions! What's better, you can have them skewered at your table to suit your tastes. Eat till you're beat.

ourpick **Grasshopper** (off Map p238; ☎ 26593999; 45 Kalena Agrahara, Bannerghatta Rd; multi-course meal Rs1000) Save this one for a special occasion. Some 15km south of town, this leafy boutique restaurant run by a designer couple has no menu; you just have to go by what it tosses up for the day. Besides, you have to book at least a day in advance and inform them about

your food preferences. The upside of all this is a scrumptious, heart-warming meal, which you'll remember for a long time to come.

Also recommended:

Samarkand (Map p238; ☎ 41113364; Gem Plaza, Infantry Rd; mains Rs150-300) For Peshawari food.

Harima (Map p238; ☎ 41325757; 4th fl Devatha Plaza, 131 Residency Rd; mains Rs250-400) For Japanese food.

Drinking

BARS & LOUNGES

Despite Bengaluru's rock-steady reputation of getting sloshed in style, local laws require pubs and discos to shut shop at 11.30pm (opening time is usually 7.30pm). That's the bad news. The good news is that given the wide choice of chic watering holes, you can indulge in a spirited session of pub-hopping in this original beer town of India. The trendiest spots will typically charge you a cover of between Rs500 and Rs1000 per couple, but it's often redeemable against drinks or food.

Beach (off Map p238; 1211 100ft Rd, HAL 2nd Stage, Indiranagar) Feel the sand between your toes – literally – at this fun beach-bums' bar in the happening Indiranagar area. Women drink for free on Wednesday.

Fuga (Map p238; 1 Castle St, Ashoknagar) This eye-poppingly slick bar-club-lounge is where the beautiful people dance the evening away to groovy music, aided by a steady supply of absinthe from the bar.

Koshy's Bar & Restaurant (Map p240; 39 St Mark's Rd; ☒ 9am-11.30pm) Don't step into the AC section; it's considered a place for wannabes. The seasoned guys gather in its buzzy old wing, where they put away pints of beer and classic British meals (mains Rs50 to Rs250) in between fervent discussions. It's an institution that has a reputation for serving Bengaluru's intelligentsia.

NASA (Map p240; 1A Church St; ☒ 11am-11pm) This old favourite is decked out like a spaceship, with laser sparks adding to your Spaceman Spiff experience. Three drinks later, you're speeding through the galaxy of faux stars that decorate the pub's walls!

Hard Rock Café (Map p240; 40 St Mark's Rd) Eric Clapton or Jimi Hendrix? The guitar-god debate continues here, and you're free to join in. Or just sit quietly and drink, while the PA system comes alive with your classic rock favourites.

Taika (Map p240; Church St) This one is twice as much fun, and comprises two clubs playing

KARNATAKA

different strains of music. You can flit from one to the other, and choose the right kind of music to go with your drink.

13th Floor (Map p240; 13th fl, Barton Centre, 84 MG Rd) Come early to grab a spot on the terrace sit-out, with all of Bengaluru glittering at your feet. The atmosphere is that of a relaxed cock-tail party, and you can tap your feet to a good selection of retro music.

Purple Haze (Map p240; 17/1 Residency Rd) The name is a dead giveaway. A favourite watering hole for Bengaluru's headbangers, Purple Haze gives rock 'n' roll aficionados their daily dose of shreds and riffs to go with their tipples. The interiors are electric, to say the least, and you'll have decent company while hanging out here.

CAFES & TEAHOUSES

Bengaluru is liberally sprinkled with good chain cafes; those such as **Café Coffee Day** (Map p240; MG Rd; ☽ 8am-11.30pm) and **Barista** (Map p240; 40 St Mark's Rd; ☽ 8am-11.30pm) have several outlets across town. For something different, try one of the following.

Indian Coffee House (Map p240; 78 MG Rd; ☽ 8.30am-8.30pm) On par with Koshy's in terms of herit-age value, this charming old-timer churns out the best java, South Indian style, which is brought to your table by noddy waiters in turbans and fabulous buckled belts.

Brew Haha (off Map p238; 5th block Koramangala; ☽ 11am-11pm) A hit with youngsters, this hip cafe in Bengaluru's stylish southern quarters has a neat collection of board games and a selection of books to go with your coffee.

Cha Bar (off Map p238; Oxford Bookstore, Leela Galleria, Airport Rd; ☽ 10am-10pm) Offering more than 20 different types of tea, Cha Bar allows you to hunker down with a book or magazine from the attached bookshop.

Entertainment

BOWLING

Amoeba (Map p240; ☎ 25594631; 22 Church St; ☽ 11am-11pm) A date with the lanes at this state-of-the-art bowling alley costs Rs100 to Rs150 per person, depending on the time of day.

CINEMA

English-language films are popular, and tick-ets range from Rs80 to Rs250, depending on your theatre of choice and the show-time. **INOX** (Map p240; ☎ 41128888; www.inoxmovies.com; 5th fl, Garuda Mall, Magrath Rd) Bollywood movies are shown here.

Nani Cinematheque (Map p238; ☎ 22356262; 5th fl, Sona Tower, 71 Millers Rd) Classic Indian and European films are screened here Friday, Saturday and Sunday.

PVR Cinema (Map p238; ☎ 22067511; www.pvrcinemas .com; Forum, 21 Hosur Rd) A megacinema with 11 screens. Bollywood movies are shown here.

SPORT

Bengaluru's winter horse-racing season runs from November to February; summer season is from May to July. Races are generally held on Friday and Saturday afternoons. Contact the **Bangalore Turf Club** (Map p238; ☎ 22262391; www .bangaloreraces.com; Racecourse Rd) for details.

For a taste of India's sporting passion up close, attend one of the regular cricket matches at **M Chinnaswamy Stadium** (Map p238; ☎ 22869970; MG Rd). Details can be found on the **Karnataka Cricket Association** (www.cricketkar nataka.com) website.

THEATRE

Ranga Shankara (off Map p238; ☎ 26592777; www .rangashankara.org; 36/2 8th Cross, JP Nagar) All kinds of interesting theatre (in a variety of languages) and dance are held at this cultural centre.

Shopping

Bengaluru's shopping options are abun-dant, ranging from teeming bazaars to glitzy malls. Some good shopping areas include Commercial St (Map p238), Vittal Mallya Rd (Map p238) and the MG Rd area (Map p240).

Ffolio (Map p238; 5 Vittal Mallya Rd; ☽ 10.30am-8pm) A good place for high Indian fashion. There's also a branch at Leela Galleria (23 Airport Rd, Kodihalli).

Fabindia (off Map p238; 54 17th Main Koramangala; ☽ 10am-8pm) Commercial St branch (Map p238); Garuda mall branch (Map p240; McGrath Rd) This flagship shop contains Fabindia's full range of stylish clothes and homewares in traditional cotton prints and silks.

Raintree (Map p238; 4 Sankey Rd; ☽ 10am-7pm Mon-Sat, 11am-6pm Sun) This early-20th-century villa has been turned into a stylish gift shop, fashion shop and cafe; it includes a branch of ethnic clothes shop Anokhi, which is also found at the Leela Galleria (23 Airport Rd, Kodihalli).

UB City Mall (Map p238; Vittal Mallya Rd; ☽ 11am-9pm) Global haute couture and high Indian fashion come to roost at this towering new complex in the heart of town.

KARNATAKA

Bombay Store (Map p240; 99 MG Rd; ⊙ 10.30am-8.30pm) A one-stop option for gifts ranging from ecobeauty products to linens.

Mysore Saree Udyog (Map p238; 1st fl, 294 Kamaraj Rd; ⊙ 10.30am-8.30pm Mon-Sat) Located near Commercial St, Mysore Saree Udyog is great for top-quality silks and saris.

Some good malls in town include **Garuda Mall** (Map p240; McGrath Rd), **Forum** (Map p238; Hosur Rd; Koramangala) and **Leela Galleria** (off Map p238; 23 Airport Rd, Kodihalli).

Getting There & Away

AIR

Airline offices are generally open from 9am to 5.30pm Monday to Saturday, with a break for lunch. Domestic carriers serving Bengaluru include the following:

Indian Airlines (Map p238; ☎ 22978406, 22978484; www.indian-airlines.nic.in; Housing Board Bldg, Kempegowda Rd)

Jet Airways (☎ 39893333, 39899999; www.jetairways.com; Unity Bldg, JC Rd)

Kingfisher Airlines (Map p238; ☎ 41979797; www.flykingfisher.com; 35/2 Cunningham Rd)

Spice Jet (☎ 9871803333; www.spicejet.com)

Some international airline offices and helplines in Bengaluru:

Air France-KLM (off Map p238; ☎ 66783110, 180011 0088/4777; www.airfrance.in, www.klm.com; 21 Ulsoor Rd)

Air India (Map p238; ☎ 22277747/8; www.airindia.in; Unity Bldg, JC Rd)

British Airways (☎ 18001021213; www.britishairways.com)

Lufthansa (Map p238; ☎ 66784050; www.lufthansa.com; 44/2 Dickenson Rd)

DAILY FLIGHTS FROM BENGALURU

Destination	Starting price (INR)	Duration (hr)
Ahmedabad	2100	3½
Chennai (Madras)	480	¾
Delhi	1330	2½
Goa	480	1
Hyderabad	180	1
Kochi	950	1½
Kolkata (Calcutta)	1850	3
Mangalore	1335	1
Mumbai (Bombay)	1180	2
Pune	480	1½
Trivandrum	800	1½

BUS

Bengaluru's huge, well-organised **Central bus stand** (Map p238; Gubbi Thotadappa Rd), also known as **Majestic**, is directly in front of the City train station. **Karnataka State Road Transport Corporation** (KSRTC; ☎ 22870099, 22872050) buses run throughout Karnataka and to neighbouring states. Other interstate bus operators:

Andhra Pradesh State Road Transport Corporation (APSRTC; ☎ 22873915)

Kadamba Transport Corporation (☎ 22351958) Goa.

State Express Transport Corporation (SETC; ☎ 22876974) Tamil Nadu.

Computerised advance booking is available for most buses at the station; **KSRTC** (Map p238; Devantha Plaza, Residency Rd) also has convenient booking counters around town, including one at Devantha Plaza. It's wise to book long-distance journeys in advance.

MAJOR BUS SERVICES FROM BENGALURU

Destination	Fare (Rs)	Duration (hr)	Frequency
Chennai	251 (R)/423 (V)	7-8	15 daily
Ernakulam	377 (R)/637 (V)	10-12	6 daily
Hampi	301 (R)	8½	1 daily
Hospet	370 (V)	8	1 daily
Hyderabad	667 (V)	10-12	3 daily
Jog Falls	328 (R)	9	1 daily
Mumbai	1060 (V)	19	4 daily
Mysore	121 (R)/212 (V)	3	every 30min
Ooty	237 (R)	8	6 daily
Panaji	779 (V)	12-14	3 daily
Puttaparthi	220 (V)	4	3 daily

R – Rajahamsa, V – Airavath Volvo AC

KARNATAKA

Numerous private bus companies offer comfier and only slightly more expensive services. Private bus operators line the street facing the Central bus stand, or you can book through an agency (see p239).

Major KSRTC bus services from Bengaluru are listed on p247.

TRAIN

Bengaluru's **City train station** (Map p238; Gubbi Thotadappa Rd) is the main train hub and the place to make reservations. **Cantonment train station** (Map p238; Station Rd) is a sensible spot to disembark if you're arriving and headed for the MG Rd area, while **Yesvantpur train station** (off Map p238; Rahman Khan Rd), 8km northwest of downtown, is the starting point for Goa trains.

Rail reservations in Bengaluru are computerised. If the train is fully booked, foreign travellers can get into the emergency quota; first, buy a wait-listed ticket, then fill out a form at the **Divisional Railway Office** (Map p238; Gubbi Thotadappa Rd) building immediately north of the City train station. You'll know about 10 hours before departure whether you've got a seat (a good chance); if not, the ticket is refunded. The **train reservation office** (Map p238; ☎ 139; 🕒 8am-8pm Mon-Sat, 8am-2pm Sun), on the left as you face the station, has separate counters for credit-card purchases (Rs30 fee), for women and foreigners. Luggage can be left at the 24-hour cloakroom on Platform 1 at the City train station (Rs10 per bag per day).

See below for information on major train services.

Getting Around
TO/FROM THE AIRPORT

The swish new **airport** (off Map p238; ☎ 23540000; www.bengaluruairport.com) is in Hebbal, about 40km north from the MG Rd area. Prepaid taxis can take you from the airport to the city centre (Rs600). You can also take the shuttle AC bus service to Majestic or MG Rd (Rs150).

AUTORICKSHAW

The city's autorickshaw drivers are legally required to use their meters; few comply in reality. After 10pm, 50% is added onto the metered rate. Flag fall is Rs14 for the first 2km and then Rs7 for each extra kilometre.

BUS

Bengaluru has a thorough but crowded local bus network, operated by the **Bangalore Metropolitan Transport Corporation** (BMTC). Pickpockets abound and locals warn solo women against taking buses after dark. Most local buses (light blue) run from the City bus stand (Map p238), next to Majestic; a few operate from the City Market bus stand (Map p238) to the south.

To get from the City train station to the MG Rd area, catch any bus from Platform 17 or 18 at the City bus stand. For the City market, take bus 31, 31E, 35 or 49 from Platform 8.

CAR

Several places around Bengaluru offer car rental with driver. Standard rates for a long-haul Tata Indica cab are Rs7 per kilometre for a minimum of 250km, plus an allowance of Rs150 for the driver. For an eight-hour

MAJOR TRAINS FROM BENGALURU

Destination	Train No & Name	Fare (Rs)	Duration (hr)	Departures
Chennai	2658 *Chennai Mail*	195/662	6	10.45pm
	2028 *Shatabdi*	510/1105	5	6am Wed-Mon
Delhi	2627 *Karnataka Exp*	559/2083	39	7.20pm
	2649 *Sampark Kranti Exp*	547/2036	35	10.20pm Mon, Wed, Fri, Sat & Sun
Hospet	6592 *Hampi Exp*	203/738	9½	10.30pm
Hubli	6589 *Rani Chennamma Exp*	206/750	8	9pm
Kolkata	2864 *YPR Howrah Exp*	517/1918	35	7.35pm
Mumbai	6530 *Udyan Exp*	369/1389	22	8.10pm
Mysore	2007 *Shatabdi*	305/590	2	11am Wed-Mon
	2614 *Tippu Exp*	67/228	2½	2.15pm
Trivandrum	6526 *Kanyakumari Exp*	312/1165	17	9.45pm

Shatabdi fares are chair/executive; Express (Exp/Mail) fares are 2nd class/chair for day trains and sleeper/2AC for night trains.

day rental, you're looking at around Rs1100. Luxury Renault cabs are also available for around Rs15 per kilometre.

We recommend:
Meru Cabs (☎ 44224422)
Skyway (☎ 22111401)

AROUND BENGALURU
Bannerghatta Biological Park

The attached zoo is a little grim, but it's worth making the 25km trek south of Bengaluru to this **nature reserve** (off Map p238; ☎ 080-27828425; weekday/weekend Rs25/30, video Rs100; ☼ 9am-5.30pm Wed-Mon) to take its hour-long **grand safari** (weekday/weekend Rs65/80; ☼ 11am to 4pm) in a minibus through an 11,330-hectare enclosure. Here the Karnataka Forest Department rehabilitates tigers, lions and sloth bears rescued from circuses or the wilds. To get here, take bus 366A from City Market (Rs20, one hour).

Hessaraghatta

Located 30km northwest of Bengaluru, Hessaraghatta is home to **Nrityagram** (☎ 080-28466313; www.nrityagram.org; ☼ 10am-5.30pm Tue-Sat, 10am-3pm Sun), the living legacy of celebrated dancer Protima Gauri Bedi, who died in a Himalayan avalanche in 1998. Protima established this dance academy in 1990 to revive and popularise Indian classical dance.

Designed in the form of a village by Goa-based architect Gerard da Cunha, the attractive complex offers long-term courses in classical dance within a holistic curriculum. Local children are taught for free on Sundays. Self-guided tours cost Rs20 or you can call ahead to book a tour, lecture-cum-demonstration and vegetarian meal (Rs1250, minimum 10 people). A month-long beginners' workshop is held in July for US$1000. Earmark the first Saturday in February for the free dance festival **Vasantahabba** (p236).

Opposite the dance village, **Taj Kuteeram** (☎ 080-28466326; www.tajhotels.com; d from Rs4000; ☒) combines comfort with rustic charm. It also offers ayurveda and yoga sessions.

Learn how to drive a bullock cart and how to milk a cow at **Our Native Village** (☎ 080-41140909; www.ournativevillage.com; Survey 72, Kodihalli, Madurai Hobli; s/d incl breakfast Rs7000/8500; ☒), an ecofriendly organic farm and resort. The resort generates its own power, harvests rainwater, and processes and reuses all its waste.

From Bengaluru's City Market, buses 253, 253D and 253E run to Hessaraghatta (Rs20,

one hour), with bus 266 continuing on to Nrityagram.

Nandi Hills

Rising to 1455m, the **Nandi Hills** (admission Rs5; ☼ 6am-10pm), 60km north of Bengaluru, were once the summer retreat of Tipu Sultan. Today, it's Bengaluru's favourite weekend getaway, and is predictably congested on Saturdays and Sundays. It's a good place for hiking, with stellar views and two notable **Chola temples**. A recommended retreat out here is **Silver Oak Farm** (☎ 9342510445; www.silveroakfarm .com; Sultanpet Village; s/d incl full board from Rs3250/4750), which has a beautiful hillside position. Buses head to Nandi Hills (Rs40, two hours) from Bengaluru's Central bus stand.

Janapada Loka Folk Arts Museum

Situated 53km south of Bengaluru, this **museum** (admission Rs10; ☼ 9am-1pm & 2.30-5.30pm Wed-Mon) has a wonderful collection of folk art objects, including 500-year-old shadow puppets, festival costumes and musical instruments. Mysore-bound buses (one hour) can drop you here; get off 3km after Ramnagar.

Channapatna

About 60km southwest of Bengaluru, on the highway to Mysore, is the bustling little village of Channapatna, a traditional handicrafts manufacturing centre that makes for a fine outing. Home to several hundred local Kannada artisans, the village is famous for its exquisitely carved wooden toys and colourful lacquerware, apart from being a silk manufacturing hub. You can wander the lanes of this pretty village, soaking in the sights and sounds, and the friendly villagers are always on hand to engage in conversations over steaming chai. Several shops and emporiums line the village streets, where you can pick up a wide range of souvenirs to take back home. Refrain from haggling; the traders here are an honest bunch.

Regular buses plying the highway can drop you at Channapatna from Bengaluru (ordinary/semideluxe Rs35/58, two hours). Onward or return connections can be found through the day.

MYSORE
☎ 0821 / pop 799,200 / elev 707m

The historic headquarters of the Wodeyar maharajas, Mysore is a city that bowls you over with its fascinating regal heritage. That apart, it's one of the most flamboyant places you could visit in South India, known for its bustling markets, magnificent monuments and a friendly populace. A thriving centre for the production of premium silk, sandalwood and incense, Mysore also flaunts a considerable expertise in yoga and ayurveda, two trades that it has recently begun to market worldwide. So stretch your body in a traditional yoga pose or take a gentle stroll through the city's magnificent palace and bazaars; Mysore is a place that will surely reward your languid pace.

History

Mysore owes its name to the mythical Mahisuru, a place where the demon Mahisasura was slain by the goddess Chamundi. Its regal history began in 1399, when the Wodeyar dynasty of Mysore was founded, though they were to remain in service of the Vijayanagar empire until the mid-16th century. With the fall of Vijayanagar in 1565, the Wodeyars declared their sovereignty, which – apart from a brief period in the late 18th century, when Hyder Ali and Tipu Sultan claimed power – remained un-scathed until 1947.

Orientation

The train station is northwest of the city centre, about 1km from the main shopping street, Sayyaji Rao Rd. The Central bus stand is on Bengaluru–Mysore (BM) Rd, on the northeastern edge of the city centre. The Maharaja's Palace sits in the heart of the buzzing quarters southeast of the city centre. Chamundi Hill is an ever-visible landmark to the south.

Information

BOOKSHOPS
Ashok Book Centre (396 Dhanvanthri Rd; 🕑 10am-8pm Mon-Sat, 10am-2pm Sun) Stocks books on religion, ayurveda and yoga.
Geetha Book House (KR Circle; 🕑 10am-1pm & 5-7.30pm Mon-Sat)
Sapna Book House (1433 Narayan Shastry Rd; 🕑 10.30am-8.30pm)

INTERNET
Internet cafes are sprinkled around town.
Reliance Webworld (115D Devaraj Urs Rd; per hr Rs30; 🕑 10am-8pm) Has lightning-fast internet connections with webcam facility.

LEFT LUGGAGE
The City bus stand has a cloakroom open from 6am to 11pm; it costs Rs10 per bag for 12 hours.

MEDICAL SERVICES
Basappa Memorial Hospital (☎ 2512401; 22B Vinoba Rd, Jayalakshmipuram)

MONEY
ATMs are common.
State Bank of Mysore (☎ 2538956; cnr Irwin & Ashoka Rds; 🕑 10.30am-2.30pm & 3-4pm Mon-Fri, 10.30am-12.30pm Sat) Changes cash and Amex travellers cheques.
Thomas Cook (☎ 2420090; Silver Tower, 9/2 Ashoka Rd; 🕑 9.30am-6pm Mon-Sat) For foreign exchange.

PHOTOGRAPHY
Danthi (44 Devaraj Urs Rd; 🕑 10am-8pm)
Rekha Colour Lab (142 Dhanvanthri Rd; 🕑 9am-9.30pm)

POST
Main post office (cnr Irwin & Ashoka Rds; 🕑 10am-6pm Mon-Sat)

TOURIST INFORMATION
Karnataka Tourism (☎ 2422096; Old Exhibition Bldg, Irwin Rd; 🕑 10am-5.30pm Mon-Sat) Extremely helpful.
KSTDC Transport Office (☎ 2423652; 2 Jhansi Lakshmi Bai Rd; 🕑 8.30am-8.30pm) KSTDC has counters at the train station and Central bus stand, as well as this transport office next to KSTDC Hotel Mayura Hoysala.

Sights
MAHARAJA'S PALACE
Among the grandest of India's royal buildings, the fantastic **Mysore Palace** (☎ 2421051; www .mysorepalace.in; Indian/foreigner Rs20/200; 🕑 10am-5.30pm) was the former seat of the Wodeyar maharajas. The old palace was gutted by fire in 1897; the one you see now was completed in 1912 by English architect Henry Irwin, at a cost of Rs4.5 million.

The interiors of this Indo-Saracenic marvel – a kaleidoscope of stained glass, mirrors and gaudy colours – is undoubtedly over the top. The decor is further added to by the awe-inspiring carved wooden doors, mosaic floors, and a series of paintings depicting life in Mysore during the Edwardian Raj. The way into the palace takes you past a fine collection of sculptures and artefacts. Don't forget to check out the armoury, which houses

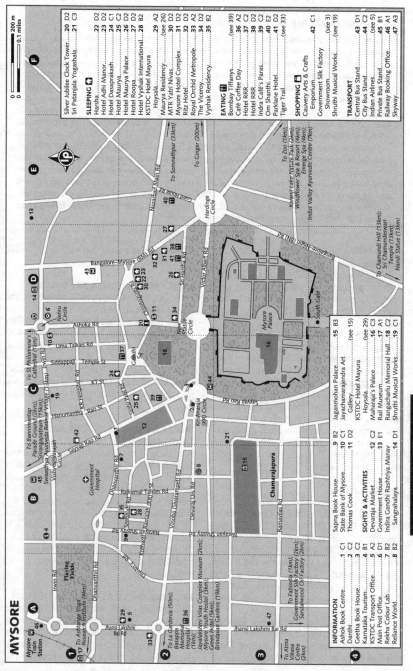

DUSSEHRA JAMBOREE

Mysore is at its carnivalesque best during the 10-day Dussehra (locally spelt 'Dasara') festival. During this period, the Maharaja's Palace lights up in the collective glow of more than 96,000 light bulbs every evening (7pm to 9pm), while the town is transformed into a gigantic fairground, with concerts, dance performances, sporting demonstrations and cultural events running to packed houses. On the last day, the celebrations are capped off in grand style. A dazzling procession of richly costumed elephants, garlanded idols, liveried retainers and cavalry kicks off around 1pm, marching through the streets to the rhythms of clanging brass bands, all the way from the palace to the Bannimantap parade ground. A torchlight parade at Bannimantap and a spectacular session of fireworks then closes the festival for the year.

Mysore is chock-a-block with tourists during the festival, especially on the final day. To bypass the suffocating crowds, consider buying a Dasara VIP Gold Card (Rs6000 for two). Though expensive, it assures you good seats at the final day gala and helps you beat the entry queues at all the other events and performances, while providing discounts on accommodation, dining and shopping. It's also possible to buy tickets (Rs250 to Rs1000) just for entering the palace and Bannimantap for the final day's parades. Contact the local KSTDC office or the **Dasara Information Centre** (☎ 2418888; www.mysoredasara.com) for more details.

an intriguing collection of more than 700 weapons!

While you are allowed to snap the palace's exterior, photography within is strictly prohibited. Cameras must be deposited in lockers (Rs5) at the palace entrance.

DEVARAJA MARKET

Dating from Tipu Sultan's reign, the spellbinding **Devaraja Market** (Sayyaji Rao Rd; 🕑 6am-8.30pm) is a lively bazaar that combines both the ancient and Indian faces of India. International brands compete for space here with local traders selling traditional items such as flower garlands, spices and conical piles of *kumkum* (coloured powder used for bindi dots), and their unique co-existence makes for some great photo-ops. Refresh your bargaining skills before shopping!

CHAMUNDI HILL

At a lofty height of 1062m, on the summit of Chamundi Hill, stands the **Sri Chamundeswari Temple** (☎ 2590027; 🕑 7am-2pm & 3.30-9pm), dominated by a towering 40m-high *gopuram* (entrance gateway). It's a fine half-day excursion, offering spectacular views of the city below; you can take bus 201 (Rs10, 30 minutes) that rumbles up the narrow road to the summit. A return autorickshaw trip will cost about Rs250.

On your way down, you can also take the foot trail comprising 1000-plus steps that Hindu pilgrims use to visit the temple. One-third of the way down is a 5m-high statue of **Nandi** (Shiva's bull) that was carved out of solid rock in 1659.

JAYACHAMARAJENDRA ART GALLERY

Built in 1861 as the royal auditorium, the **Jaganmohan Palace**, just west of the Maharaja's Palace, houses the **Jayachamarajendra Art Gallery** (☎ 2423693; Jaganmohan Palace Rd; adult/child Rs20/10; 🕑 8.30am-5pm), where large crowds gather to check out a collection of kitsch objects and regal memorabilia. The collection includes some fantastic and rare musical instruments, Japanese art, and paintings by the noted artist Raja Ravi Varma.

INDIRA GANDHI RASHTRIYA MANAV SANGRAHALAYA

A branch of the Bhopal-based **Indira Gandhi Rashtriya Manav Sangrahalaya** (National Museum of Mankind; ☎ 2448231; www.museumofmankindindia.gov.in; Wellington House, Irwin Rd; admission free; 🕑 10am-5.30pm Tue-Sun), this museum functions primarily as a cultural centre and exhibition space showcasing arts from rural India. Housing excellent rotating exhibitions and a souvenir shop, the centre organises two-week workshops in traditional art forms, which are open to the public.

JAYALAKSHMI VILAS COMPLEX MUSEUM

This **museum** (☎ 2419348; Mysore University Campus; admission free; 🕑 10am-5.30pm Mon-Sat, closed alternate Sat), housed in a grand mansion, specialises in folklore. A wooden puppet of the 10-headed demon Ravana, leather shadow puppets, rural costumes and a 300-year-old temple cart are part of its curious collection.

RAIL MUSEUM

A must-see. Located behind the train station, this **museum** (KRS Rd; adult/child Rs5/2, camera/video Rs10/25; ⏱ 9.30am-6.30pm Tue-Sun) bears testimony to the stylish way in which the royals rode the railways in the past. The chief exhibit is the Mysore maharani's saloon, a wood-panelled beauty dating from 1899. There are also five steam engines, each with its own story, and a sprinkling of instruments and memorabilia from the Indian Railways' chequered past.

OTHER SIGHTS

For architecture buffs, Mysore has quite a handful of charming buildings. Dating from 1805, **Government House** (Irwin Rd), formerly the British Residency, is a Tuscan Doric building set in 20 hectares of **gardens** (admission free; ⏱ 5am-9pm). Facing the north gate of the Maharaja's Palace is the 1927 **Silver Jubilee Clock Tower** (Ashoka Rd); nearby stands the imposing **Rangacharlu Memorial Hall**, built in 1884. The beauty of towering **St Philomena's Cathedral** (☎ 2563148; St Philomena St; ⏱ 5am-6pm, English mass 7am), built between 1933 and 1941 in neo-Gothic style, is emphasised by beautiful stained-glass windows.

Mysore's **zoo** (☎ 2440752; Indiranagar; adult/child Rs25/10, camera/video Rs10/150; ⏱ 8.30am-5.30pm Wed-Mon), set in pretty gardens on the eastern edge of the city, dates from 1892. A range of primates, tigers, elephants, bears, birds and rhinos live here.

Activities
BIRDWATCHING

Karanji Lake Nature Park (Indiranagar; admission Rs10, camera/video Rs10/25; ⏱ 8.30am-5.30pm), next to the zoo, is a place to spy on sundry bird species, including great and little cormorants, purple and grey herons, egrets, black ibises, rose-ringed parakeets, green bee-eaters and painted storks, as well as several kinds of butterfly.

AYURVEDA

Mysore's spa operations are spearheaded by the slick **Emerge Spa** (☎ 2522500; www.emergespa.co.in; Windflower Spa & Resort, Maharanapratap Rd, Nazarbad), where you can drop by for an hour's ayurvedic massage starting at around Rs750, or choose from a range of Balinese massage, hydrotherapy and beauty treatments.

Set on 6.5 hectares of gardens, the classy **Indus Valley Ayurvedic Centre** (☎ 2473437; www.ayurindus.com; Lalithadripura) is a place that derives its therapies from ancient scriptures and pre-scriptions. A wide range of treatments are on offer, as well as basic training programs. It's wise to visit with some time on your hands; the best deals are the overnight-stay packages (Indian/foreigner from Rs9300/US$269).

For an exceptionally peaceful and refreshing ayurvedic vacation, head about 12km towards Srirangapatnam to the **Swaasthya Ayurveda Retreat Village** (☎ 6557557, 08236-217476; www.swaasthya.com; 69 Bommaru Agrahara; s incl full board Rs1500), where you can spend some time in quiet meditation and feel your senses feast on the lush greenery, the aromatic herb gardens, the simple vegetarian food and the gurgling sounds of the Cauvery River. Daily rates include basic yoga sessions; for specific ayurvedic treatments, there is a range of special packages on offer. Book well in advance.

Courses
YOGA

The following places have put Mysore on the international yoga map. Unlike casual centres, they are all austerely committed to the art, and require at least a month's commitment on your part. You'll also need to register far in advance, since they are often booked out. Call or write to the centres for details.

Ashtanga Yoga Research Institute (AYRI; ☎ 2516756; www.kpjayi.org; 3rd Stage, 235 8th Cross, Gokulam) Founded by the renowned Ashtanga teacher K Pattabhi Jois, who taught Madonna her yoga moves.

Atma Vikasa Centre (☎ 2341978; www.atmavikasayoga.com; Kuvempunagar Double Rd) 'Backbending expert' Yogacharya Venkatesh offers courses in yoga, Sanskrit and meditation. Opposite State Bank of India.

Sri Patanjala Yogashala (Yoga Research Institute; Sri Brahmatantra Swatantra Parakala Mutt, Jaganmohan Palace Circle; ⏱ 6-8am & 5-7pm) The baby of well-respected Ashtanga practitioner BNS Iyengar (not to be confused with BKS Iyengar, famed exponent of Iyengar yoga).

MUSIC

The folks at **Shruthi Musical Works** (☎ 2529551; 1189 3rd Cross, Irwin Rd; ⏱ 10.30am-9pm Mon-Sat, 10.30am-2pm Sun) get good reviews for their tabla instruction (Rs200 per hour).

Tours

The KSTDC runs a daily Mysore city tour (Rs155), which takes in the entire city, along

KARNATAKA

with Chamundi Hill, Srirangapatnam and Brindavan Gardens. It starts daily at 8.30am, ends at 8.30pm and is likely to leave you breathless!

Other KSTDC tours include one to Belur, Halebid and Sravanabelagola (Rs400) on Tuesdays and Thursdays from 7.30am to 9pm. There's also a three-day tour of Ooty, Kodaikanal, Doddabetta and Coonoor every Monday, Thursday and Saturday (per person including accommodation is Rs2200) that starts off from Bengaluru; you can join at Mysore. These tours generally run during the high season.

All tours leave from the **KSTDC Hotel Mayura Hoysala** (2 Jhansi Lakshmi Bai Rd). Bookings can be made at the nearby KSTDC Transport Office (p250) or at travel agencies around town.

Sleeping

Mysore attracts tourists through the year and can fill up very quickly during Dussehra. Booking early is recommended. Check with the tourist office about the local government-approved homestays, which offer rooms from around Rs400 per person.

BUDGET

The following have hot water (at least in the morning) and 24-hour checkout.

Mysore Youth Hostel (☎ 2544704; www.yhmysore .com; Gangothri Layout; dm from Rs45) Despite the usual rules and regs, including a 10.30pm curfew, this well-run hostel set amid green lawns is exceptionally clean and tidy. Breakfast costs Rs17; dinner is Rs24. Don't forget to bring a proof of age and identity document.

Hotel Dasaprakash (☎ 2442444; www.mysore dasaprakashgroup.com; Gandhi Sq; s/d from Rs250/470; 🖳) This long-time favourite is a tried and tested sleeping option, popular with local tourists. Rooms are well maintained; some get a touch of antiquity with old wooden furniture. An inexpensive veg restaurant, an ice-cream parlour and an astro-palmist are available within the complex.

MTR Yatri Nivas (☎ 2521148; 2747 Chandragupta Rd; s/d from Rs300/450, d with AC Rs800; 🖳) So what if the windows of the rooms here open out to the walls of other buildings at close range? For the price, this cheapie is more than just a good deal in town. The management is friendly, the sheets are clean and you're within close range of all of Mysore's major attractions. Nuff said.

Hotel Maurya (☎ 2426677; Hanumantha Rao St; s/d from Rs350/500) In the process of upgrading its well-kept rooms, this justifiably popular place has obliging staff and a great location among Mysore's winding alleys. There are also a few dirt-cheap beds (singles/doubles Rs140/260) on-site, but they're – well – dirty.

Mysore Hotel Complex (☎ 2426217; BM Rd; s/d from Rs350/500; 🖳) A giant affair, this place comprises row after row of pleasant, non-fussy rooms, where you'll be made to feel at home by a friendly staff. Scattered across the property is a travel agent and a few souvenir shops.

Ritz Hotel (☎ 2422668; BM Rd; d/q Rs500/900) A quaint, ramshackle place in the heart of town, the Ritz makes little effort to latch on to its heritage. The lack of enthusiasm shows in its mediocre rooms, which are charming but a tad run-down. The shaded restaurant-bar downstairs is a good place for an unhurried evening drink.

MIDRANGE

KSTDC Hotel Mayura Hoysala (☎ 2425349; www.nic .in/kstdc; 2 Jhansi Lakshmi Bai Rd; s/d incl breakfast Rs650/800, with AC Rs800/1000; 🖳) With lace-lined curtains and heavy wooden doors in its rooms, and an assortment of cane furniture and potted plants in the corridors, this place sure brings back the memories. The bar downstairs is popular with Mysore's tipplers.

Hotel Roopa (☎ 2443370; 2724C BM Rd; d from Rs775; 🖳) A surprisingly cheerful hotel, this place boasts spacious modern rooms done up in fresh upholstery, and is often one of the first places to fill up. The pure-veg restaurant Nakshatraa is a good place to start the day, with a sumptuous buffet breakfast (Rs40).

Hotel Vyshak International (☎ 2421777; vyshak international@yahoo.com; 19 Seebaiah Rd; d from Rs 800; 🖳) Clean, efficiently run and welcoming – what more could you want? The management also runs the Vyshak Residency (double from Rs850) across the road, which is equally good.

Maurya Residency (☎ 2523375; www.sangrouphotel .com; Sri Harsha Rd; d from Rs835; 🖳) The best of the Sri Harsha Rd midrange gang, this ultra-friendly place has snug beds, offers a refreshing welcome drink of grape juice and has ecofriendly directives smattered across its rooms. Sister property, Hotel Maurya Palace (☎ 2435912; double from Rs725), is next door.

Hotel Adhi Manor (☎ 4001000; L20 Chandragupta Rd; s/d from Rs1400/1600; 🖳) This one's a trifle overpriced, and the biggest beef happens to be the loos which, though relatively new, show signs of seepage and staining. Nonetheless, the rooms are spacious and stylishly painted in shades of lavender, ochre or moss green, and the management often gives discounts during lean periods, which might happen to coincide with your visit!

Ginger (☎ 6633333; www.gingerhotels.com; Nazarbad Mohalla; s/d Rs1499/1999; ☒ ▣) An ultramodern business hotel, Ginger has sleek and comfortable rooms painted in warm orange tones. Features include self check-in, a gymnasium, wi-fi and LCD TVs, and its location away from the city centre makes for a peaceful stay.

Viceroy (☎ 2424001; www.theviceroygroup.com; Sri Harsha Rd; s/d from Rs1895/2295; ☒ ▣) Sporting an all-new look with spacious, cosy and warmly lit rooms, this swish place is worth considering if you desire a combination of both luxury and location. Some of the rooms – and the rooftop restaurant – have million-dollar views of the Maharaja's Palace just across the road!

TOP END

Green Hotel (☎ 4255000; www.greenhotelindia.com; 2270 Vinoba Rd, Jayalakshmipuram; s/d incl breakfast garden from Rs2250/2750, palace from Rs2950/3250) You're largely paying for the quaint ambience here, which is more prominent in the themed and moody palace rooms. The garden rooms, though fronted by blooming antirrhinum beds, are characterless (and a trifle overpriced).

Windflower Spa & Resort (☎ 2522500; www .thewindflower.com; Maharanapratap Rd, Nazarbad; s/d incl breakfast from Rs3900/4500; ☒ ▣ ☲) Bali comes to Mysore at this stylish and relaxing resort, where the elegant rooms are complemented by the world-class Emerge Spa, and Olive Garden, a top-of-the-line fine-dining restaurant and bar. Other activities at the resort include cycling, trekking and golfing.

our pick **Royal Orchid Metropole** (☎ 4255566; www.royalorchidhotels.com; 5 Jhansi Lakshmi Bai Rd; s/d incl breakfast from Rs5000/5600; ☒ ▣ ☲) This recently renovated hotel was originally built by the Wodeyars to serve as the residence of the maharaja's British guests. A fascinating colonial structure with bona-fide old-world charm, it has 30 rooms oozing heritage, and a stay here is spiced up with several add-ons such as occasional magic, music and dance performances. The friendly and efficient management is among the best that Karnataka's hotels have to offer.

Eating

Mysore is well served by Indian restaurants, but for Western food you're best sticking with the major hotels. Unless otherwise mentioned, restaurants are open from noon to 3pm and 7pm to 11pm.

Bombay Tiffanys (Sayyaji Rao Rd; sweets Rs5-40; ☾ 7.30am-10pm) For traditional Indian sweets, Bombay Tiffanys has a solid reputation. Those with a sweet tooth could try the local delicacy *Mysore pak* (a sweet made from chickpea flour, sugar and ghee).

Indra Café's Paras (1740 Sayyaji Rao Rd; mains Rs30-60; ☾ 7.30am-10pm) Take your pick from South (Rs30) or North (Rs60) Indian-style thalis at this popular joint opposite the main market. It's perpetually crowded.

Parklane Hotel (☎ 2430400; www.parklanemysore .com; 2720 Sri Harsha Rd; mains Rs40-150) Choose from a wide selection of Indian, Continental, Chinese and Mexican dishes at this popular restaurant-bar, where food is served by candlelight at night, with occasional live music. Occasional barbeque nights have a special range of kebabs and grills on offer.

Hotel RRR (Gandhi Sq; mains Rs40-70) Classic Andhra-style food is belted out at this ever-busy eatery, and you might have to queue for a table if you walk in during lunch. One item to try is the piping-hot veg thali (Rs43) served on banana leaves. Some meaty options are available, too. There's a second branch on Sri Harsha Rd.

Om Shanthi (Hotel Siddhartha, Guest House Rd; mains Rs40-100; ☾ 7.30am-10pm) Om Shanthi is a byword for excellent veg food in Mysore. Its special South Indian thali (Rs80) is really quite special, as is the hearty breakfast platter of *puris* and vegetables (Rs25).

La Gardenia (☎ 2426426; Hotel Regaalis, 3-14 Vinoba Rd; mains Rs100-180) This place serves tasty and well-presented food in a sophisticated environment. In case you've tired of the local Indian options, this is a nice place to dig into some tasty Continental fare.

Tiger Trail (☎ 4255566; Royal Orchid Metropole, 5 Jhansi Lakshmi Bai Rd; mains Rs100-250) This delightful restaurant specialising in tandoori dishes serves decent food in a courtyard that twinkles with torches and fairy lights at night. There's often live classical Indian music performances.

Café Coffee Day (Devaraj Urs Rd; snacks Rs30-50; ☾ 10am-11pm) Part of the pan-Indian chain of coffee shops, this is currently where Mysore's young generation hangs out. The open-air terrace is a particularly good spot for that steaming cup of cappuccino.

Shopping

Mysore is a great place to shop for its famous sandalwood products, silk saris and wooden toys. It is also one of India's major incense-manufacturing centres, peppered with scores of little family-owned *agarbathi* (incense) factories.

Souvenir and handicraft shops are dotted around Jaganmohan Palace and Dhanvanthri Rd, while silk shops line Devaraj Urs Rd.

Cauvery Arts & Crafts Emporium (Sayyaji Rao Rd; ☯ 10am-7.30pm) Not the cheapest place, but the selection is extensive and there's no pressure to buy.

Government Silk Factory (☎ 2481803; Mananthody Rd, Ashokapuram; ☯ 10am-noon & 2-4pm Mon-Sat) It's the best place to shop for Mysore silk, given that the exclusive fabric is made at this very place and thus comes at its cheapest. Behind the showroom is the factory, where you can drop by between 7.30am and 4pm to see how the fabric is made. There's also a factory showroom on KR Circle, open from 10.30am to 7.30pm, barring Sundays.

Sandalwood Oil Factory (☎ 2483531; Ashokapuram; ☯ 9.30am-11pm & 2-4pm Mon-Sat) Buy authentic incense sticks and pure sandalwood oil (Rs650 for 5ml!) at this factory, located about 2km southeast of the Maharaja's Palace, off Mananthody Rd. Guided tours are also available to show you around the factory, and explain how the products are made.

Fabindia (☎ 4259009; 451 Jhansi Lakshmi Bai Rd, Chamrajpuram; ☯ 10am-8pm) There's a branch of the ever-reliable clothing and homewares shop on the way to the silk and sandalwood factories.

Shruthi Musical Works (☎ 2529551; 1189 3rd Cross, Irwin Rd; ☯ 10.30am-9pm Mon-Sat, 10.30am-2pm Sun) Sells a variety of traditional musical instruments; you can view the workshop across the road from the shop.

Getting There & Away

AIR

Mysore's new airport was nearing completion at the time of research and should be ready by mid-2009. **Indian Airlines** (☎ 2421846; Jhansi Lakshmi Bai Rd; ☯ 10am-1.30pm & 2.15-5pm Mon-Sat) has an office next to KSTDC Hotel Mayura Hoysala where you can book tickets for routes starting from Bengaluru, Mangalore or elsewhere. For booking on other carriers, try **Skyway** (☎ 2444444; 370/4 Jhansi Lakshmi Bai Rd; ☯ 10am-6pm Mon-Sat).

BUS

The **Central bus stand** (☎ 2520853; BM Rd) handles all KSRTC long-distance buses. The **City bus stand** (☎ 2425819; Sayyaji Rao Rd) is for city, Srirangapatnam and Chamundi Hill buses. KSRTC bus services from Mysore include those listed on opposite.

For Belur, Halebid or Sravanabelagola, the usual gateway is Hassan. For Hampi, the best transfer point is Hospet.

The **Private bus stand** (Sayyaji Rao Rd) has services to Hubli, Bijapur, Mangalore, Ooty and Ernakulam. You'll find several ticketing agents around the stand.

TRAIN

At the **railway booking office** (☎ 131; ☯ 8am-8pm Mon-Sat, 8am-2pm Sun), located within the train station, you can reserve a seat on the 6.45am *Chamundi Express* or the 11am *Tippu Express* to Bengaluru (2AC/chair Rs67/198, three hours), or on the high-speed *Shatabdi Express* (chair/executive Rs275/550, two hours), departing at 2.20pm daily except Tuesday. The *Shatabdi* continues to Chennai (chair/executive Rs690/1315, seven hours). Several passenger trains also go daily to Bengaluru (Rs30, 3½ hours), stopping at Srirangapatnam (Rs10,

---

SANDAL FACTS

Used in different forms in Indian society through the ages, sandal plays an essential role in the lives of millions of Indians. In its most basic application, sandalwood powder is mixed with water to form a paste that is ritually used to embalm temple idols, as well as being applied to the foreheads of priests and worshippers visiting temples to offer *pujas*. Sandalwood oil, due to its antiseptic and antimicrobial qualities, has been a vital ingredient in traditional Indian medicine and ayurveda; several therapeutic practices that have evolved from Vedic scriptures use sandalwood oil as a basic healing component. The modern cosmetic industry makes liberal use of sandal extracts as well, to manufacture soaps, perfumes and a range of aromatherapy products, which you can pick up in Mysore's bazaars.

BUSES FROM MYSORE

Destination	Fare (Rs)	Duration (hr)	Frequency
Bandipur	47 (O)	2	hourly
Bengaluru	121 (R)/212 (V)	3	every 30min
Channarayapatna	55 (O)	2	hourly
Chennai	742 (V)	12	3 daily
Ernakulam	388 (R)	11	5 daily
Gokarna	290 (O)	12	1 daily
Hassan	68 (O)	3	hourly
Hospet	247 (O)	10	4 daily
Mangalore	147 (O)/224 (R)	7	10 daily
Nagarhole	55 (O)	3	4 daily
Ooty	75 (O)/114 (R)	5	6 daily

O – Ordinary, R – Rajahamsa, V – Airavath Volvo

20 minutes). Two passenger and three express trains go daily to Arsikere and Hassan. The 8.10pm *Swarna Jayanthi Express* goes to Hubli (sleeper/2AC Rs457/1684, nine hours).

Getting Around

Agencies at hotels and around town rent cabs for about Rs7 per kilometre for an AC Indica, with a minimum of 250km per day, plus Rs150 for the driver.

Flag fall on autorickshaws is Rs16, and Rs6 per kilometre is charged thereafter. Autorickshaws can also be hired for a day's sightseeing (Rs850). Try the polite and energetic **Ganesh** (☎ 9342201774).

AROUND MYSORE
Srirangapatnam
☎ 08236

Steeped in bloody history, the fort town of Srirangapatnam is built on an island straddling the Cauvery River 16km from Mysore. The seat of Hyder Ali and Tipu Sultan's power, this town was the de-facto capital of much of southern India during the 18th century. Srirangapatnam's glory days ended when the British waged an epic war against Tipu Sultan in 1799, when he was defeated and killed. However, the ramparts, battlements and some of the gates of the fort still stand, as do a clutch of monuments.

Close to the bus station is a handsome twin-tower mosque built by the sultan, and within the fort walls you can also find the dungeon where Tipu held British officers captive, and the handsome **Sri Ranganathaswamy Temple** (☹ 7.30am-1pm & 4-8pm). Srirangapatnam's star at-

traction, however, is Tipu's summer palace, the **Daria Daulat Bagh** (☎ 252023; Indian/foreigner Rs5/100; ☹ 9am-5pm), which lies 1km east of the fort. Built largely out of wood, the palace is notable for the lavish decoration that covers every inch of its interiors. The ceilings are embellished with floral designs, while the walls bear murals depicting courtly life and Tipu's campaigns against the British. There's a small museum within, which houses several artefacts including a portrait of Tipu Sultan aged 30, painted by European artist John Zoffany in 1780.

About 2km further east, the remains of Hyder Ali, his wife and Tipu are housed in the impressive onion-domed **Gumbaz** (☎ 252007; ☹ 8am-8pm), which stands amid serene gardens. Head 500m east of Gumbaz for the river banks to end your trip with a refreshing 15-minute **coracle ride** (per boat Rs100).

Three kilometres upstream, the **Ranganathittu Bird Sanctuary** (☎ 0821-2481159; Indian/foreigner Rs25/75, camera/video Rs25/100; ☹ 8.30am-6pm) is on one of three islands in the Cauvery River. The storks, ibises, egrets, spoonbills and cormorants here are best seen in the early morning or late afternoon on a short **boat ride** (per person Rs100). There's also a maze made from herbal plants and a restaurant on-site.

SLEEPING & EATING
Royal Retreat New Amblee Holiday Resort (☎ 217474; www.ambleeresort.com; d from Rs1200; ☒ ☒) A menagerie of rabbits and ducks, and the owner's (covered) Rolls-Royce greets you at the Amblee, which offers relatively good accommodation, a pleasant riverside setting and a reasonably priced restaurant.

KARNATAKA

THE CAUVERY DISPUTE

While it lends its matchless beauty to the regional landscape, the waters of the Cauvery River have been the subject of a heated dispute between the states of Karnataka and neighbouring Tamil Nadu in the past. The origins of the discord go way back to 1892, when a water-sharing agreement was struck between the Madras Presidency and the Mysore state. Post Independence, Karnataka claimed that the agreement was a raw deal, given that Tamil Nadu got access to most of the river's waters, despite the fact that the Cauvery originated in Karnataka. Tamil Nadu, on the other hand, stood its ground, maintaining that any reduction in its share of water could potentially spell disaster for the state's agricultural sector. The debate soon reached a deadlock, and after decades of raucous argument, the matter was taken to court in 1990. Finally, in 2007, a verdict was passed, which worked out an equal and fair distribution of water between both states, while allotting some of the water to Kerala and Puducherry (Pondicherry). However, frayed nerves are yet to be soothed, as all four states seem disappointed with the verdict and have indicated their desire to pursue further legal action on the matter.

Mayura River View (☎ 217454; d Rs1750; ✗) Set on a quiet patch of riverbank, this government outfit has a handful of cute bungalows, each well appointed and comfortable, along with a bug-themed children's park. The restaurant (mains Rs30 to Rs100) has a wonderful sit-out from where you can gaze at the river.

GETTING THERE & AWAY

Take the frequent buses 313 or 316 (Rs10, one hour) from Mysore's City bus stand. Passenger trains travelling from Mysore to Bengaluru (Rs10, 20 minutes) also stop here. The stand for private buses heading to Brindavan Gardens (Rs15, 30 minutes) is just across from Srirangapatnam's main bus stand.

GETTING AROUND

The sights are a little spread out, but walking isn't out of the question. For a quicker tour, tongas (two-wheeled horse carriages) cost about Rs150 for three hours, and an autorickshaw from Mysore is about Rs300 (three hours).

Brindavan Gardens

If you're familiar with Bollywood, these ornamental **gardens** (☎ 08236-257247; adult/child Rs20/15, camera/video Rs50/100; ✆ 8am-8.30pm) might just give you that sense of déjà vu – they've indeed been the backdrop to many a shimmying musical number. The best time to visit is in the evening, when the fountains are illuminated and made to dance to the accompaniment of popular film tunes!

Within the gardens are two hotels: the no-frills **Hotel Mayura Cauvery** (☎ 08236-215876; d Rs400) and the swanky **Royal Orchid Brindavan Garden**

(☎ 08236-257257; www.royalorchidhotels.com; s/d incl breakfast from Rs4500/5000; ✗), with lavish rooms and the strategically located Elephant Bar, the best spot from which to view the sound-and-light shows while sipping on your poison.

The gardens are 19km northwest of Mysore. One of the KSTDC tours stops here, and buses 301, 304, 305, 306 and 365 depart from Mysore's City bus stand hourly (Rs10, 45 minutes).

Melkote

Life in the devout Hindu town of Melkote, about 50km north of Mysore, revolves around the 12th-century **Cheluvanarayana Temple** (☎ 08236-298739; Raja St; ✆ 8am-1pm & 5-8pm), with its rose-coloured *gopuram* (gateway tower) and ornately carved pillars. Get a work-out on the hike up to the hilltop **Yoganarasimha Temple**, which offers fine views of the surrounding hills. The town comes alive for the **Vairamudi Festival** in March or April (p236).

Three KSRTC buses a day shuttle between Mysore and Melkote (Rs40, 1½ hours).

Somnathpur

The astonishingly beautiful **Keshava Temple** (☎ 08227-270010; Indian/foreigner Rs5/100; ✆ 9am-5.30pm) is one of the finest examples of Hoysala architecture, on par with the masterpieces of Belur and Halebid. Built in 1268, this star-shaped temple, located some 33km from Mysore, is adorned with superb stone sculptures depicting various scenes from the Ramayana, Mahabharata and Bhagavad Gita, and the life and times of the Hoysala kings.

On a tree in the temple grounds there's a red postbox, where prestamped mail posted by you will be collected by the local post office and marked with a special postmark bearing the temple's image – this is a great memento to send back home.

Somnathpur is 7km south of Bannur and 10km north of Tirumakudal Narsipur. Take one of the half-hourly buses from Mysore to either village (Rs12, 30 minutes) and change there.

Sivasamudram

About 60km east of Mysore is Sivasamudram, home to the twin waterfalls of Barachukki and Gaganachukki. The site of the first hydroelectric project in India, in 1902, it's a place where you can spend a quiet time while indulging in natural bounties. The relaxing **Georgia Sunshine Village** (☎ 9448110660; www.georgiasunshine .com; d incl full board from Rs3700; ✗ ☞) is a wonderful place to camp; accommodation is in bungalows and the home-made food is delicious. The dog-loving hosts can arrange treks to the waterfalls and fishing trips on request.

Frequent buses run from Mysore (Rs25, one hour) to Malavalli, 14km away. Call ahead and they'll arrange an autorickshaw to pick you up for around Rs100.

HASSAN

☎ 08172 / pop 133,200

With a good range of hotels, a railhead and other conveniences, Hassan is a handy base for exploring Belur (38km), Halebid (33km) and Sravanabelagola (48km). Situated not far from either Mysore or Bengaluru, it's a bustling town with friendly people, and promises a good night's sleep in between hectic days of sightseeing.

Orientation & Information

The train station is 2km east of the town centre on busy Bengaluru–Mangalore (BM) Rd. The Central bus stand is on the corner of AVK College and Bus Stand Rds. The **tourist office** (☎ 268862; AVK College Rd; ✆ 10am-5.30pm Mon-Sat), 100m east of the bus stand, is one of Karnataka's more helpful. There are plenty of ATMs and internet cafes. It's advisable to change foreign currency in Bengaluru or Mysore.

Sleeping

Vaishnavi Lodging (☎ 263885; Harsha Mahal Rd; s/d Rs 190/270) Located across a quiet courtyard in a building close to the bus stands. It's cheap, tidy and the sheets are clean.

Hotel Sri Krishna (☎ 263240; BM Rd; s/d from Rs350/725; ✗) Hugely popular with local tourists, this place has biggish rooms done up in red and black checks. The staff is efficient, and there's a quality veg restaurant downstairs (mains Rs30 to Rs60).

Jewel Rock (☎ 261048; BM Rd; d with/without AC Rs950/600; ✗) Close to the rail station, this place is a steal. The spacious rooms, with floral curtains, are comfortable, and the hotel houses two popular eateries: the pure-veg Annapurna, and Chalukya, a reliable place for meaty delights.

Hotel Suvarna Regency (☎ 266774; www.hotel suvarnaregency.com; BM Rd; d with/without AC Rs1025/705; ✗ ☞) This place, just south of Gandhi Sq, is frequented by businessmen, and is one of Hassan's trusted oldies. Get over the stiff smell of sanitisers that welcomes you into its well-kept rooms, and the rest is a breeze.

Hotel Hassan Ashhok (☎ 268731; www.hassanashok .com; BM Rd; s/d from Rs3000/3350; ✗ ☞) Clearly the classiest of Hassan's hotels, this superbly renovated place offers you luxe features such as minibars in its plush rooms and baskets full of herbal toiletries in the showers. The soft, cotton-white beds and stacks of fluffy pillows are simply irresistible!

our pick **Hoysala Village Resort** (☎ 256764; www.trailsindia.com; Belur Rd; d incl breakfast from Rs4800; ✗ ☞) Located 6km from town on the road to Belur, this rustic and relaxing place is set amid a patch of manicured gardens. Its cosy rooms have a country feel, with large windows looking out onto the palms and hedges. There's a tree house where you can laze away the evening, beer in hand, or flex your pectorals in the aqua-blue pool. The resort also has an ayurvedic massage centre, where sessions kick off for around Rs400.

Eating

Hotel Sanman (Municipal Office Rd; meals Rs15-20; ✆ 7am-10pm) Pay upfront and take your pick from *masala dosas* (curried vegetables inside crisp pancakes) or a thali at this busy joint located a block south of the bus station.

Hotel GRR (Bus Stand Rd; meals Rs20-50; ✆ 11am-11pm) Top-of-the-line Andhra-style thalis (Rs25) are on offer at this busy place, as is the popular chicken biryani (Rs50).

Suvarna Gate (Hotel Suvarna Regency, BM Rd; mains Rs40-120; ✆ noon-3.30pm & 6.30-11.30pm) You might have to wait a while for your food but it's worth it. The chicken tandoori masala is

KARNATAKA

delicious and the terrace dining room overlooking neatly trimmed hedges has ambience. It's located to the rear of Hotel Suvarna Regency.

Getting There & Away

BUS

Buses leave from the Central bus stand, situated on the corner of AVK College and Bus Stand Rds. Buses to Halebid (Rs15, one hour) run half-hourly starting at 6am, with the last bus back leaving Halebid at 7.30pm. Frequent buses connect Hassan and Belur (Rs20, one hour); the first leaves Hassan at 6am, and the last bus from Belur is at 10pm.

To get to Sravanabelagola, you must take one of the many buses to Channarayapatna (Rs20, 45 minutes) and change there.

There are frequent services to Mysore (Rs68, three hours), Bengaluru (semideluxe/deluxe Rs159/190, four hours) and Mangalore (Rs148, five hours).

TAXI

Taxi drivers hang out on AVK College Rd, north of the bus stand. A tour of Belur and Halebid will cost you about Rs800 for the day. A return taxi to Sravanabelagola will cost the same. Firmly set the price before departure.

TRAIN

The well-organised **train station** (☎ 268222) is about 2km east of town (Rs15 by autorickshaw). The main building should be fully renovated by now; and cloakroom services available again. Three passenger trains head to Mysore daily (2nd class Rs27, three hours). For Bengaluru, take one of the four daily trains to Arsikere (Rs15, one hour) and change there.

BELUR & HALEBID

☎ 08177 / elev 968m

The Hoysala temples at Halebid (also known as Halebeedu) and Belur (also called Beluru), along with the temple at Somnathpur (p258), are the apex of one of the most artistically exuberant periods of ancient Hindu cultural development. Architecturally, they are South India's answer to Khajuraho in Madhya Pradesh and Konark, near Puri in the state of Orissa.

Only 16km lie between Belur and Halebid, and the towns are connected by frequent shuttle buses from 6.30am to 7pm (Rs15, 30 minutes). See above for details of buses to/from Hassan. Belur also has ordinary buses to Bengaluru (Rs120, five hours). To get to Hampi, it's best to return to Bengaluru and take an overnight bus to Hospet.

Belur

The **Channakeshava Temple** (Temple Rd; admission free; ☉ dawn-dusk) was commissioned in 1116 to commemorate the Hoysalas' victory over the neighbouring Cholas. It took more than a century to build, and is currently the only one among the three major Hoysala sites still in daily use – try to be there for the *puja* (offerings or prayer) ceremonies at 9am, 3pm and 7.30pm. Some parts of the temple, such as the exterior lower friezes, were not sculpted to completion and are thus less elaborate than those of the other Hoysala temples. However, the work higher up is unsurpassed in detail and artistry, and is a glowing tribute to human skill. Particularly intriguing are the angled bracket figures depicting women in ritual dancing poses. While the front of the temple is reserved for images depicting erotic sections from the Kamasutra, the back is strictly for gods. The roof of the inner sanctum is held up by rows of exquisitely sculpted pillars, no two of which are identical in design.

Scattered around the temple complex are other smaller temples, a marriage hall which is still used and the seven-storey *gopuram*, which has sensual sculptures explicitly portraying the *après*-temple activities of dancing girls.

Guides can be hired for Rs150; they help to bring some of the sculptural detail to life.

Vishnu Regency (☎ 223011; Kempegowda Rd; d with/without AC Rs1000/500; ☒ ▯) is clearly the best of Belur's none-too-salubrious hotels. Its simple rooms are clean and fresh, and it has a pleasant **restaurant** (mains Rs30-80; ☉ 11.30am-10.30pm) serving North Indian and Chinese food. From the bus stand, walk up Temple Rd and turn left at the statue of Kempegowda.

Near Kempegowda's statue is **Shankar Hotel** (Temple Rd; meals Rs27; ☉ 7am-9.30pm), a busy place serving fine South Indian thalis, *masala dosas,* Indian sweets, snacks and drinks.

Halebid

Construction of the **Hoysaleswara Temple** (admission free; ☉ dawn-dusk), Halebid's claim to fame, began around 1121 and went on for more than 80 years. For some reason, it was never completed, but nonetheless stands today as a masterpiece of Hoysala architecture. The interior of its inner sanctum, chiselled out of black stone, is marvellous. On the outside, the temple's richly sculpted walls are covered with a flurry of Hindu deities, sages, stylised animals and friezes depicting the life of the Hoysala rulers. A huge statue of Nandi (Shiva's bull) sits to the left of the main temple, facing the inner sanctum.

The temple is set in large, well-tended gardens, adjacent to which is a small **museum** (admission Rs2; ☺ 10am-5pm Sat-Thu) housing a collection of sculptures.

If the pesky touts get on your nerves, take some time out to visit the nearby, smaller **Kedareswara Temple**, or a little-visited enclosure containing three **Jain temples**, which also have fine carvings.

If you're really stuck in Halebid for the night, count away the hours in the drab rooms of the shoddy **KSTDC Mayura Shanthala** (☎ 273224; d/q without bathroom Rs250/350).

SRAVANABELAGOLA
☎ 08176

Atop the bald rock of Vindhyagiri Hill, the 17.5m-high statue of the Jain deity Gomateshvara (Bahubali), said to be the world's tallest monolithic statue, is visible long before you reach the pilgrimage town of Sravanabelagola. Viewing the statue close up is the main reason for heading to this sedate town, whose name means 'the Monk of the White Pond'. Sravanabelagola also played hermitage to emperor Chandragupta Maurya, who came here in the 3rd century BC after renouncing his kingdom.

Information
The defunct **tourist office** (☎ 257254; ☺ 10am-5.30pm) sits in a new complex at the foot of Vindhyagiri Hill. The grand plans to have an audiovisual display, a cafe and a gift store have sadly not materialised. There are no entry fees to the sites in Sravanabelagola, though donations are encouraged.

Sights
GOMATESHVARA STATUE
A steep climb up 614 steps takes you to the top of Vindhyagiri Hill, the summit of which is lorded over by the towering naked statue of **Gomateshvara** (Bahubali; ☺ 6am-6.15pm). Commissioned by a military commander in the service of the Ganga king Rachamalla and

carved out of a single piece of granite by the sculptor Aristenemi in AD 981, its serenity and simplicity are in stark contrast to the Hoysala sites at Belur and Halebid.

Bahubali was the son of emperor Vrishabhadeva, who became the first Jain *tirthankar* (revered teacher) Adinath. Initially embroiled fiercely with his brother Bharatha to succeed his father, Bahubali soon realised the futility of material gains and renounced his kingdom. As a recluse, he meditated in complete stillness in the forest until he attained enlightenment. His lengthy meditative spell is denoted by vines curling around his legs and an ant hill at his feet.

Shoes have to be left at the foot of the hill, but it's fine to wear socks. If you want it easy, you can hire a *dholi* (portable chair) with bearers for Rs150, from 7am to 12.30pm and 3pm to 5.30pm.

Every 12 years, millions flock here to attend the Mastakabhisheka ceremony, when the statue is doused in holy waters, pastes, powders, precious metals and stones. The next ceremony is slated for 2018.

TEMPLES
Apart from the Bahubali statue, there are several interesting Jain temples in town. The **Chandragupta Basti** (Chandragupta Community; ☺ 6am-6pm), on Chandragiri Hill opposite Vindhyagiri, is believed to have been built by Emperor Ashoka. The **Bhandari Basti** (Bhandari Community; ☺ 6am-6pm), in the southeast corner of town, is Sravanabelagola's largest temple. Nearby, **Chandranatha Basti** (Chandranatha Community; ☺ 6am-6pm) has well-preserved paintings depicting Jain tales.

Sleeping & Eating
The local Jain organisation **SDJMI** (☎ 257258; d/tr Rs135/160) handles bookings for its 15 guest houses. The office is behind the Vidyananda Nilaya Dharamsala, past the post office.

Hotel Raghu (☎ 257238; d with/without AC Rs800/500; ✸) It's the only privately owned hotel around, and offers basic but clean rooms. The real bonus is its vegetarian **restaurant** (mains Rs20-40; ☺ 6am-9pm) downstairs, which works up an awesome thali (Rs40), sometimes served caringly by the owner himself.

Getting There & Away
No buses go direct from Sravanabelagola to Hassan or Belur – you'll need to go to

Channarayapatna (Rs10, 20 minutes) and catch an onward connection there. Three direct buses a day run to both Bengaluru (Rs78, 3½ hours) and Mysore (Rs52, 2½ hours). Long-distance buses clear out before 3pm. If you miss these, catch a local bus to Channarayapatna, which is on the main Bengaluru–Mangalore road and has lots of connections.

NILGIRI BIOSPHERE RESERVE

The pristine forests of the **Nilgiri Biosphere Reserve** are one of India's best-preserved wildernesses, and span about 5500 sq km across the states of Karnataka, Kerala and Tamil Nadu. Human access to the reserve is through a number of national parks, such as Wayanad (see p380) in Kerala and Mudumalai (see p470) in Tamil Nadu. In Karnataka, the best access points are the national parks of Bandipur and Nagarhole, and the super-green forested region around the Kabini Lake.

Home to over 100 species of mammals and some 350 species of birds, the reserve is also a natural habitat for the prized but endangered Bengal tigers and Asiatic elephants; more than a fifth of the world's population of jumbos live here.

Bandipur National Park

About 80km south of Mysore on the Ooty road, the **Bandipur National Park** (☎ 08229-236021; Indian/foreigner Rs60/200) covers 880 sq km and was once the Mysore maharajas' private wildlife reserve. The park is noted for its herds of gaurs (Indian bison), chitals (spotted deer), sambars, panthers, sloth bears and langurs, apart from tigers and elephants. Despite its rich wildlife, however, Bandipur isn't the best place for animal sightings; unrestricted traffic hurtling down the busy highway that cuts through the forest has made the animals wary of venturing close to safari areas of late.

Brief **elephant rides** (Indian/foreigner Rs50/150) are available for a minimum of four people. For a **safari** (Indian/foreigner Rs25/175; ⏰ 6am, 7am, 8am, 4pm & 5pm) there's the forest department's minibus, the rumbling of which further puts off the shy creatures. Resort vehicles are permitted to go into the forest; they are quieter and thus a better bet.

SLEEPING & EATING

Forest Department Bungalows (d Indian/foreigner from Rs490/840) It's all pretty basic, but you'll love

it when the chitals spill onto the grounds at night. Meals are available upon advance notice. Book early with Project Tiger (☎ 0821-2480901, Aranya Bhavan, Ashokapuram) in Mysore.

Tusker Trails (☎ 080-23618024, 09845326467; per person incl full board Indian/foreigner Rs2200/US$80; 🏊) A lovely resort located on the eastern edge of the park, this place provides accommodation in simple huts, with good food and an inviting pool to splash about in. Rates include two daily safaris.

GETTING THERE & AWAY

Buses between Mysore and Ooty will drop you at Bandipur (Rs47, three hours). You can also book an overnight taxi from Mysore (about Rs2000).

Nagarhole National Park

West of the Kabini River is the 643-sq-km wildlife sanctuary of **Nagarhole National Park** (Rajiv Gandhi National Park; Indian/foreigner Rs50/150), pronounced *nag*-ar-hole-eh. The lush forests here are home to tigers, leopards, elephants, gaurs, muntjacs (barking deer), wild dogs, bonnet macaques and common langurs. The park can remain closed for long stretches between July and October, when the rains transform the forests into a giant slush pit.

The park's main entrance is 93km southwest of Mysore. If you're not staying at a resort nearby, the only way to see the park is on the forest department's bus **tour** (per person Rs95; ⏰ 6-8am & 3-5.30pm). The best time to view wildlife is during summer (April to May), though winter (November to February) is kinder.

Decent sleeping options are limited in Nagarhole. An OK place to camp is **Jungle Inn** (☎ 08222-246022; www.jungleinnnagarhole.com; Hunsur-Nagarhole Rd; per head incl full board Indian/foreigner from Rs1800/US$60) about 35km from the park reception on the Hunsur road. With a welcoming atmosphere, evening campfires and simple, clean rooms, it also serves good food made from organic produce. Rates for safaris are extra.

Kabini Lake

About 70km south of Mysore lies **Kabini Lake**, a giant forest-edged reservoir formed by the damming of the Kabini River. Endowed with rich and unspoilt vegetation, the area is rapidly growing as one of Karnataka's best wildlife destinations. Positioned midway between the animal corridors of Bandipur and Nagarhole, the Kabini forests are also the habitat for a large variety of wildlife, and give you the chance to view the animals up close.

Tourism around Kabini is managed by a few resorts, most of which are founded on ecofriendly principles. Jungle safaris and other activities such as boat rides and birdwatching are conducted by the resorts, generally from 6.30am to 9.30am, and 4pm to 7pm.

SLEEPING & EATING

our pick Kabini River Lodge (☎ 08228-264402; per person tents/r/cottages Indian Rs3000/3750/4250, foreigner US$160) No sooner than you've entered will you be told that Goldie Hawn was here! Rated among the world's best wildlife resorts, this fascinating government-run eco-getaway is located on the grounds of the former Mysore maharaja's hunting lodge beside Kabini Lake. Run by an excellent staff, it offers accommodation in a choice of large canvas tents, regular rooms and cottages. Rates include full board, safaris, boat rides and forest entry fees. Book through Jungle Lodges & Resorts Ltd (Map p240; ☎ 080-25597021, 25597944; www.junglelodges.com).

Cicada Kabini (☎ 080-41152200, 9945602305; www .cicadaresorts.com; s/d from Rs8000/12,000;) Another highly recommended ecoresort, this well-conceived luxury option brings a dash of contemporary chic to the lakeside. The rates are for accommodation and meals only; safaris (Rs750) and kayaks and pedal boats (Rs250) are extra.

GETTING THERE & AWAY

A few buses depart daily from Mysore and can drop you at Kabini village. However, it's better to have your own taxi. Enquire with the resorts while making a booking.

KODAGU (COORG) REGION

Nestled amid the verdant, ageless hills that line the southernmost edge of Karnataka is the luscious Kodagu (Coorg) region, gifted with emerald green landscapes and acre after acre of plantations. A major centre for coffee and spice production, this rural expanse is also home to the unique but numbered Kodava race, believed to have descended from migrating Persians and Kurds or perhaps Greeks left behind from Alexander the Great's armies. The uneven terrain and cool climate make it a fantastic area for trekking, birdwatching or lazily ambling down little-trod paths that

wind their way around the carpeted hills. All in all, Kodagu is rejuvenation guaranteed.

The best season for trekking is October to March. Guides are available for hire and can arrange food, transport and accommodation; see p264 for recommendations. Treks can last from two to three days to a week; the most popular routes are to the peaks of Tadiyendamol (1745m) and Pushpagiri (1712m), and to smaller Kotebetta. Adventure activities are conducted between November and May; the rest of the year is too wet for traipsing around.

Kodagu was a state in its own right until 1956, when it merged with Karnataka. The region's chief town and transport hub is Madikeri, but for an authentic Kodagu experience, you have to venture into the plantations. Avoid weekends, when places can quickly get filled up by Bengaluru's IT and call-centre crowd.

Madikeri (Mercara)
☎ 08272 / pop 32,400 / elev 1525m
Also known as Mercara, this congested market town is spread out along a series of ridges. The only reason for coming here is to organise treks or sort out the practicalities of travel. The Huthri festival (see the boxed text, p236), which falls sometime between November and December, is a nice time to visit.

ORIENTATION & INFORMATION
In the chaotic centre around the KSRTC and private-bus stands, you'll find most of the hotels and restaurants and several ATMs.

A semi-functional **KSTDC Office** (☎ 228580; near Raja's Seat; ☺ 10am-5.30pm Mon-Sat) offers basic tourist information about the region. If you need to change money, cash travellers cheques or get a credit-card advance, try **Canara Bank** (☎ 229302; Main Rd, Gandhi Chowk; ☺ 10.30am-2.30pm Mon-Fri) or **ICICI Bank** (☎ 645380; College Rd; ☺ 10am-6pm Mon-Sat). Internet cafes are plentiful.

SIGHTS
Madikeri's **fort**, now the municipal headquarters, was built in 1812 by Raja Lingarajendra II. There's an old church here, housing a quirky **museum** (admission free; ☺ 10am-5.30pm Tue-Sun) displaying dusty, poorly labelled artefacts. Panoramic views of the hills and valleys can be taken in from **Raja's Seat** (MG Rd; admission free; ☺ 5.30am-7.30pm). Behind are gardens, a toy train line for kids and a tiny Kodava-style **temple**.

CALL OF THE WILD

Its flagship resort at Kabini Lake continues to earn rave reviews as one of the world's finest ecotourism resorts today. But the inception, objective and success of the **Jungle Lodges & Resorts Ltd** (Map p240; ☎ 080-25597021, 25597944; www.junglelodges.com) group of eco-getaways can be singularly attributed to the passion and dreams of one man. Born to British-Indian parents in Bihar in 1916, Col John Wakefield's fascination for the jungles began early in his life. A trained hunter, he shot his first leopard when he was nine; however, he was to give up the gun soon after and devote himself to conservation. In 1967, after a stint with the army, he began his career in wildlife tourism, working with a safari company in Uttarakhand. Reputed for his knowledge and exhaustive experience in India's forests, he was soon given an invitation by the Karnataka government to introduce wildlife tourism to the South Indian state. Wakefield took up the challenge, and his tireless work and enthusiasm soon bore fruit with the foundation of the Kabini River Lodge (p263) in 1980. Many more resorts were to follow in subsequent years.

Wakefield now resides in the Kabini River Lodge as resident director. He occupies a part of the former viceregal hunting lodge on-site, where he spends his time feeding the sparrows and planning new projects and resorts for the future.

On the way to **Abbi Falls**, a pleasant 7km hike from the town centre, visit the quietly beautiful **Raja's Tombs**, better known as Gaddige. An autorickshaw costs about Rs150 return.

ACTIVITIES

A trekking guide is essential for navigating the labyrinth of forest tracks. Most of the estates in Kodagu also offer trekking programs.

Raja Shekhar and Ganesh at **V-Track** (☎ 229974; Crown Towers, College Rd; ⏰ 10am-2pm & 4.30-8pm Mon-Sat) can arrange one- to 10-day treks including guide, accommodation and food. Rates are around Rs600 per person per day, and can vary depending on the duration and number of people. Short walks take only a day or two to prepare. For long treks, trips on obscure routes or big groups, it's best to give a week's notice.

Coorg Trails (☎ 320578; coorgtrails@yahoo.co.in; Main Rd; ⏰ 9am-8.30pm) can arrange day treks for Rs400 per person, and a 22km trek to Kotebetta, including an overnight stay in a village, for Rs1200 per person. The office is near the town hall.

Located in Kirudale, about 25km from Madikeri, **Coorg Planters' Camp** (☎ 08276-320500; www.coorgplanterscamp.com; d incl full board Rs2400) is a fantastic ecoresort featuring tented accommodation, which treats guests to activities such as a tour of coffee plantations and nature walks through Kodagu's dense forests. Day-long treks to the summits of Pushpagiri and Kotebetta, the region's second- and third-highest peaks respectively, require a nominal extra charge.

Ayurjeevan (☎ 224466; Kohinoor Rd; ⏰ 9am-6pm), a short walk from ICICI Bank, offers a whole range of rejuvenating ayurvedic packages, with 30-minute sessions kicking off at around Rs400.

SLEEPING

Many hotels reduce their rates in the off season (June to September); all of those listed below have hot water, at least in the morning, and 24-hour checkout.

Hotel Cauvery (☎ 225492; School Rd; s/d Rs250/500) This ageing hotel behind Hotel Capitol opposite the private bus stand is slowly going through a facelift. The decor is a mix of printed upholstery and plastic creepers, which lend a rather kitschy character to the place.

Hilltown Hotel (☎ 223801; www.hilltownhotel.com; Hill Town Rd; s/d from Rs350/700; ❷) Down the lane running past Hotel Chitra, the Hilltown is a spruce place with fish tanks on the stairs and a pretty garden opposite. Singles are small; some have damp walls. It also has a restaurant (mains Rs30 to Rs60).

Hotel Hill View (☎ 223808; Hill Rd; s/d Rs850/1000) Situated at a far corner of the new town, this cosy place has small but well-kept rooms. The wall shades and the pruned hedges in the tiny sit-outs are perfectly colour coordinated with the green hills that overlook the rooms.

Hotel Mayura Valley View (☎ 228387; near Raja's Seat; d incl breakfast from Rs1200; ❷) It's recently been renovated, but the lack of maintenance has already begun to tell. However, nothing beats the stunning views that you get from the floor-to-ceiling windows of its rooms.

Service is patchy, and the restaurant-bar (mains Rs30 to Rs100, open 7am to 10pm) with a terrace is certainly the best place in town for a drink.

Hotel Coorg International (☎ 228071; www.coorg international.com; Convent Rd; s/d incl half-board from Rs3200/4000; 🔀 🖭) Madikeri's classiest option isn't a bad deal considering rates include fixed-menu breakfast and dinner, snacks through the day, and facilities such as cable TV, a small pool, a gym and an ayurvedic massage room.

EATING

Popular Guru Prasad (Main Rd; meals Rs25-30; ⏰ 7am-10pm) The aptly named Popular Guru Prasad serves a range of vegie options, including a value-for-money veg thali (Rs30) and breakfast snacks.

Athithi (mains Rs30-50; ⏰ 7am-10pm) The best vegetarian option in town, Athithi is known for its lip-smacking vegetarian thali (Rs40), an elaborate affair served on banana leaves. Near the police station.

Hotel Capitol (School Rd; mains Rs30-70; ⏰ 7am-9.30pm) Don't mind the shabby interiors. This is one of the best places in town to sample the local speciality, the flavourful and spicy *pandhi* (pork) curry (Rs60), best had with a pint of cold beer.

East End Hotel (GT Circle; mains Rs35-80; ⏰ 7am-10pm) An assortment of South Indian staples and local chicken and mutton dishes are offered at this eatery, its popularity seconded by the locals who converge here during meals.

GETTING THERE & AWAY

Five deluxe buses a day depart from the KSRTC **bus stand** (☎ 229134) for Bengaluru (Rs279, six hours), stopping in Mysore (Rs140, three hours) on the way. Deluxe buses also go to Mangalore (Rs160, three hours, three daily), while ordinary buses head to Hassan (Rs65, three hours) and Shimoga (Rs151, eight hours).

GETTING AROUND

Madikeri is a small town easy to negotiate on foot. For excursions around the region, several places rent out motorcycles for around Rs300 a day, with an initial refundable deposit of Rs500. Try **Spice's Mall** (☎ 9449275669; opposite KSRTC bus stand) or **Coorg The Guide** (☎ 9448184829; Chethana Complex). Carry your driving licence, tank up on gas and off you go!

SPICE OF LIFE

If you're passing through Madikeri and have space in your backpack, don't forget to pick up some local spices and natural produce from its main market. There's a whole range of spices on offer at the shops which line the streets, including vanilla, nutmeg, lemongrass, pepper and cardamom, apart from the unbranded aromatic coffee that comes in from the neighbouring plantations. Look out for fruit juices and squashes, bottles of fresh wild honey sourced from the forests and packets of ready-made curry masala to flavour your dishes back home. Most items cost between Rs50 to Rs150.

The Plantations

Spread around Madikeri town are Kodagu's quaint and leafy spice and coffee plantations. Many estates here offer homestays, ranging from basic to quite luxurious, while high-end resorts have begun to spring up recently. The following are our pick of places within easy reach of Madikeri; also see p266. Unless otherwise mentioned, rates include meals and trekking guides. Advance bookings should be made. Some options remain closed during the monsoons. Most arrange transport to/from Madikeri; enquire while booking.

our pick **Rainforest Retreat** (☎ 08272-265636; www.rainforesttours.com; Gallibeedu; s/d from Rs1750/3000) is located on an organic plantation. These eco-chic cottages are run by the friendly owners Sujata (a botanist) and Anurag (a molecular biologist) who are a fount of regional knowledge. The trekking is excellent, or you can just lie in a hammock and watch the birds. All proceeds go to the couple's NGO, which promotes environmental awareness and sustainable agriculture.

The snug, earth-coloured cottages at the **Alath-Cad Estate Bungalow** (☎ 08274-252190; www .alathcadcoorg.com; Ammathi; d incl breakfast from Rs1900), set on a 26-hectare coffee plantation 28km southeast of Madikeri, are a good place to give in to unadulterated nature. Activities include plantation tours and picnics, while treks and fishing trips can be arranged upon request. Lunch and dinner cost Rs150 each.

Plantation Trails (☎ 08274-251428; www.tatacoffee .com/plantation_trails; Pollibetta; d incl breakfast Indian/foreigner from Rs3080/US$105) rides on its parent company Tata Coffee's heritage to throw open a number of old planters' bungalows scattered among their plantations, all luxuriously renovated but still sporting antique features such as wooden floors, teak furniture and fireplaces. Guests get to use facilities reserved for company officials, including the minigolf course. Meals are Rs280 each.

A German-owned organic plantation, **Golden Mist** (☎ 08272-265629; www.goldenmist.4t.com; Kaloorvillage; d Rs3500), is one of the nicest options near Madikeri town, with cottage accommodation for up to six people. Similar in atmosphere to Rainforest Retreat, it offers nature walks and plantation tours. For larger groups, the price drops to Rs1200 per person per day.

Green Hills Estate (☎ 08274-254790; www.neem ranahotels.com; Virajpet; r incl breakfast Rs5000) is another quaint planter's bungalow that houses stacks of family memorabilia within its rosewood panelled interiors. The rooms have quirky names such as Lord Jim and Lady Madcap, supposedly named after racing thoroughbreds once owned by the planter's family. Lunch and dinner are Rs350 each.

Kadkani (☎ 08274-254186; www.kadkani.com; Ammathi; r from Rs14,500; 🕸 🔊), an uber-luxury retreat nestled in a dale amid silent forests by the Cauvery River, effortlessly matches the best of modern comforts and rustic charm in its classy ecocottages. An excellent place to unwind in style, the sprawling resort also offers activities such as golf, river crossing and river rafting (Rs300 per person). The evenings are reserved for listening to the cicadas.

Kakkabe
☎ 08272

About 40km from Madikeri, the region around the village of Kakkabe is an ideal base if you're planning an assault on Kodagu's highest peak, Tadiyendamol. At the bottom of the summit, 3km from Kakkabe, is the picturesque **Nalakunad Palace** (admission free; 🕘 9am-5pm), the restored hunting lodge of a Kodagu king dating from 1794. Within walking distance are several excellent places to camp.

our pick **Honey Valley Estate** (☎ 238339; d from Rs700, s without bathroom from Rs300) is a wonderful place 1250m above sea level where you can wake to a chirpy dawn and cool, fresh air. The owners' friendliness, ecomindedness and scrumptious organic food make things even better (meals Rs95). The estate is only accessible by jeep or by a one-hour uphill walk. Advance bookings are essential.

The name of tiny **Misty Woods** (☎ 238561; www .coorgmisty.com; cottages from Rs2799), immediately uphill from Nalakunad Palace, aptly sums up the landscape that surrounds it. The *vastu shastra* (ancient science similar to Feng Shui)–style cottages are both comfortable and stylish. Meals are extra.

Regular buses run to Kakkabe from Madikeri (Rs20, 1½ hours) and from Virajpet (Rs14, one hour).

Dubare Forest Reserve

En route to Kushalnagar, Kodagu's second-largest town, is the Dubare Forest Reserve on the banks of the Cauvery River, where about a dozen elephants retired from forest department work live on pension. Cross the river (Rs25) to participate in an **elephant interaction programme** (Indian/foreigner Rs270/550; 🕘 8.45am-noon), where you can bathe, feed and then ride the jumbos.

Bookings can be made through **Jungle Lodges & Resorts Ltd** (Map p240; ☎ 080-25597021, 25597944; www.junglelodges.com), which also runs the reserve's rustic but good **Dubare Elephant Camp** (☎ 9449599755; per person Indian/foreigner Rs2250/ US$90). Rates include the elephant-interaction program.

White-water rafting (per person Rs850) is also organised from here, over an 8km stretch that features rapids up to grade 4.

Bylakuppe
☎ 08223

Tiny Bylakuppe, 5km southeast of Kushalnagar, was among the first refugee camps set up in South India to house thousands of Tibetans who fled from Tibet following the 1959 Chinese invasion. Comprising several clusters of settlements amid 1200 hectares of rolling sugarcane fields that rustle in the breeze, it's among the few camps where many Tibetans have been able to return to their agrarian ways of life. That apart, it has all the sights and sounds of a Tibetan colony, with resident maroon-and-yellow-robed monks and locals selling Tibetan food and handicrafts. The atmosphere is heart-warmingly welcoming. The settlement is also home to much festivity during the Tibetan New Year celebrations (see the boxed text, p236).

Foreigners are not allowed to stay overnight in Bylakuppe without a Protected Area Permit (PAP) from the Ministry of Home Affairs in Delhi. Contact the **Tibet Bureau Office**

(☎ 26474798, 26439745; 10B Ring Rd, Lajpat Nagar IV, New Delhi) for details.

The area's highlight is the **Namdroling Monastery** (☎ 254036; www.palyul.org/eng_centers), home to the jaw-droppingly spectacular **Golden Temple** (Padmasambhava Buddhist Vihara; ☺ 7am-8pm), presided over by an 18m-high gold-plated Buddha. The temple is at its dramatic best when school is in session and it rings out with gongs, drums and chanting of hundreds of young novices. You're welcome to sit and meditate; look for the small blue guest cushions lying around. The **Zangdogpalri Temple** (☺ 7am-8pm), a similarly ornate affair, is next door.

Opposite the Golden Temple is a shopping centre, where you'll find the simple **Paljor Dhargey Ling Guest House** (☎ 258686; pdguesthouse@yahoo.com; d Rs280). Add Rs100 if you want a TV.

In the same shopping centre is **Shanti Family Restaurant** (mains Rs30-60; ☺ 7am-9.30pm), offering a decent range of Indian meals and Tibetan dishes such as *momos* (dumplings) and *thukpa* (noodle soup).

If you cannot manage a PAP, a good place is the lovely **Shri Kalpa Farm** (☎ 9886776923; per person per day Rs500), just outside the settlement on the approach way, where the friendly Kaveriappa family can accommodate up to four people in the pleasant terrace room of their plantation villa. Meals are extra.

Autorickshaws (shared/alone Rs10/30) travel to Bylakuppe from Kushalanagar. Buses frequently do the 34km run to Kushalnagar from Madikeri (Rs20, 1½ hour) and Hassan (Rs70, four hours); most buses on the Mysore–Madikeri route stop at Kushalnagar.

KARNATAKA COAST

MANGALORE
☎ 0824 / pop 539,300

Situated at the estuaries of the Netravathi and Gurupur Rivers on the Arabian Sea coast, Mangalore has been a major pit stop on international trade routes since the 6th century AD. The largest city on the Karnataka coast, it's a nice place to break long-haul journeys along the western shoreline, go shopping for amenities or move inland.

Once the main port of Hyder Ali's kingdom, Mangalore now ships out a bulk of the region's spice, coffee and cashew crops from the modern port, 10km north of the city.

Apart from a few tourist charms, such as the quiet Ullal Beach, 12km south, the city also has a pleasant cosmopolitan air about it and, with a sprinkling of pubs and restaurants, makes for a relaxing stay.

Orientation
Mangalore is hilly, with winding, disorienting streets. Luckily, most hotels and restaurants, the bus stand and the train station are in or around its frenzied centre. The KSRTC bus stand is 3km to the north.

Information
ATMs and internet cafes are everywhere, and several banks in town also have foreign-exchange facilities.

Athree Book Centre (Balmatta Rd; ☺ 8.30am-1pm & 2.30-8pm Mon-Sat)
Bookmark (PM Rao Rd; ☺ 8.30am-8.30pm Mon-Sat, 8.30am-1pm Sun)
KSTDC tourist office (☎ 2453926; Lalbagh Circle; ☺ 10am-5pm Mon-Sat) Kind of useless.
Trade Wings (☎ 2427225; Lighthouse Hill Rd; ☺ 9.30am-5.30pm Mon-Sat) Travel agency. Changes travellers cheques.

Sights
Catholicism's roots in Mangalore date back to the arrival of the Portuguese in the early 1500s, and today the city is liberally dotted with churches. One of the most impressive is the Sistine Chapel–like **St Aloysius College Chapel** (Lighthouse Hill Rd; ☺ 8.30am-6pm Mon-Sat, 10am-noon & 2-6pm Sun), with its walls and ceilings painted with brilliant frescoes. Also worth checking out is the imposing Roman-style **Milagres Church** (Falnir Rd; ☺ 8.30am-6pm) in the city centre.

Sultan's Battery (Sultan Battery Rd; admission free; ☺ 6am-6pm), the only remnant of Tipu Sultan's fort, is 4km from the centre on the headland of the old port; bus 16 will get you there. The Kerala-style **Kadri Manjunatha Temple** (Kadri; ☺ 6am-1pm & 4-8pm) houses a 1000-year-old bronze statue of Lokeshwara, if you're interested.

The real ace up Mangalore's sleeve is serene **Ullal Beach**, which is best enjoyed from Summer Sands Beach Resort (p268). If you're not staying there, the resort charges you Rs25 to access its beach, but it's well worth it if you drop by at sunset. You can also use the pool for Rs100. An autorickshaw is Rs170 one way, or the frequent bus 44A (Rs10) from the City bus stand will drop you right outside the gate. Buses 44C and 44D also go to Ullal.

KARNATAKA

Sleeping

BUDGET

Hotel Surya (☎ 2425736; Balmatta Rd; s/d/tr from Rs225/360/425; 🏠 🖳) The rooms in this basic joint set back from the main road look a little bombed out. But the dirt-cheap rates help it barely make the cut. It's behind Lalith Bar & Restaurant.

Hotel Manorama (☎ 2440306; KS Rao Rd; s/d from Rs250/360; 🏠) A motley collection of sculptures welcomes you into its lobby, and the spartan rooms with squat loos have an air of quaintness to them. It's the best of the budget brigade.

Hotel Srinivas (☎ 2440061; GHS Rd; s/d from Rs450/600; 🏠) It's central and reasonably clean, but characterless and really nothing to write home about.

MIDRANGE & TOP END

Hotel Poonja International (☎ 2440171; www.hotel poonjainternational.com; KS Rao Rd; s/d from Rs750/900; 🏠) This well-managed place has faux sunflowers and creepers lining its lobby, and the rooms offer standard comfort with few frills. It's huge; 154 rooms, for the record!

Nalapad Residency (☎ 2424757; www.nalapad.com; Lighthouse Hill Rd; s/d incl breakfast from Rs800/900; 🏠) It's one of Mangalore's best midrange options. The rooms are spruce, with floor to ceiling windows and heavy red curtains. The rooftop restaurant, Kadal, is a definite bonus.

Moti Mahal (☎ 2441411; www.motimahalmangalore .com; Falnir Rd; d incl breakfast Indian/foreigner from Rs950/US$25; 🏠 🖳) The rooms here are average, but the selling points include its clean outdoor pool, a gym and three restaurants.

The Gateway Hotel (☎ 6660420; www.thegateway hotels.com; Old Port Rd; s/d from Rs3500/4000; 🏠 🖳 🖳)

Head and shoulders above the rest of Mangalore's hotels, this business hotel offers all the services you would expect with four stars. Some of the superior rooms have sea views.

Summer Sands Beach Resort (☎ 2467690; www .summersands.in; d from Rs4000; 🏠 🖳) Set amid the greens on a remote patch along Ullal Beach, Summer Sands offers a series of ethno-chic bungalows done up in earth and floral shades and is the ideal place for a quiet retreat. Memories of Joanna, its restaurant, sometimes organises food galas with candle-lit dinner on the beach (buffet per person Rs350).

Eating & Drinking

While in town sample some Mangalorean delights such as *kane* (ladyfish) served in a spicy coconut curry, or the spicy deep-fried prawn *koliwada*.

Janatha Deluxe (Hotel Shaan Plaza, KS Rao Rd; mains Rs20-45; ⏱ 7am-11pm) This local favourite serves good thalis (Rs30) and a range of North and South Indian veg dishes.

Lalith Bar & Restaurant (Balmatta Rd; mains Rs30-110; ⏱ 9am-3pm & 5.30-11pm) Unwind in the Lalith's cool, subterranean interior while enjoying a cocktail combined with prawns, crab or king-fish from its extensive menu. The day's special seafood is usually the best bet.

Naivedyam (Hotel Mangalore International, KS Rao Rd; mains Rs40-90) Probably the best place in town to sample some vegetarian delicacies. It also has an interesting range of tandoori dishes.

Pallkhi (☎ 2444929; 3rd fl, Tej Towers, Balmatta Rd; mains Rs80-180; ⏱ noon-3pm & 7-11pm) This relatively smart and easy-going place, with stylish interiors and efficient service, has a good reputation for its seafood.

SAVOURY SOUTH

Apart from all its touristy attractions, what really gives southern Karnataka its pride of place on the national stage is its diverse and distinctive cuisine. The highest flying of them all are the spicy, tangy non-vegetarian dishes that emerge from the kitchens of the Kodagu region (p263). One delicacy that foodies can't stop raving about is *pandhi* curry, the flavourful signature dish of the Kodavas, made of pork and tempered with a mix of local spices. Mangalore out on the coast, refurbishes its regional identity with fiery Mangalorean cuisine, which features a train of dishes made from fresh marine catches of prawns, fish and crabs. Prawn *koliwada* is one of Mangalore's many dishes to have gathered a pan-Indian following, while typically indigenous delights such as the sinful chicken ghee roast can only be sampled if you happen to be passing through town.

Vegans take heart: southern Karnataka isn't only about exercising the canines. The temple town of Udupi (p270) has been nothing short of trademarked by thousands of restaurateurs peddling its legendary vegetarian thalis across India. Made fresh, these simple but lip-smacking spreads are bound to leave your taste buds tingling for more. *Bon Appétit!*

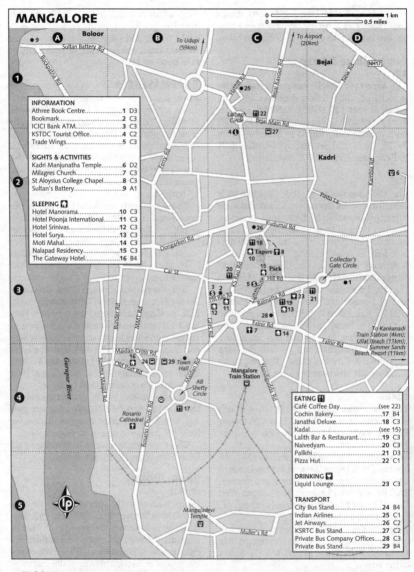

MANGALORE

KARNATAKA

Kadal (Nalapad Residency, Lighthouse Hill Rd; mains Rs80-250; ⏰ noon-3.30pm & 7.30-11pm) This high-rise restaurant has elegant and warmly lit interiors, with sweeping views of town and the sea beyond. Try the spicy chicken *varval* (a coastal Karnataka style of curry) or the fresh prawn dishes. Also enquire about the day's specials.

Liquid Lounge (☎ 4255175; Balmatta Rd; ⏰ 7-11.30pm) The coolest (and loudest) pub in town, this place has funky posters and neon-lit interiors, including a backlit Les Paul guitar replica above the bar! It has a good selection of beers and its staff in floral shirts are a courteous lot.

For Western food, head to **Bharath Mall** (Bejai Main Rd; ⏰ 10am-10pm), with branches of Pizza

Hut and Café Coffee Day. For desserts, there's **Cochin Bakery** (AB Shetty Circle; cakes Rs10-20; ☻ 9.30am-9pm Mon-Sat), with its delicious puffs and cakes.

Getting There & Away

AIR

The **airport** (☎ 2254252; www.mangaloreairport.com) is in Bajpe, about 20km northeast of town. **Indian Airlines** (☎ 2254254; Hathill Rd) and **Jet Airways** (☎ 2253432; Ram Bhavan Complex, KS Rao Rd) both operate daily flights to Mumbai (from Rs725, 1½ hours). Jet Airways also flies daily to Bengaluru (from Rs725, one hour).

BUS

The **KSRTC bus stand** (☎ 2211243; Bejai Main Rd) is 3km north of the city centre; an autorickshaw there costs about Rs20. Be warned, however, that bus rides in or out of Mangalore can be harsh on your posteriors, as the roads are pothole hell, especially during the monsoons.

Several deluxe buses depart daily to Bengaluru (Rs421, eight hours), via Madikeri (Rs139, 3½ hours) and Mysore (Rs305, six hours). Semideluxe buses go daily to Hassan (Rs148, five hours). A 9.30pm semideluxe bus heads to Panaji (Rs305, 10 hours). Private buses heading to destinations including Udupi, Dharmasthala and Jog Falls run from opposite the City bus stand. Tickets can be purchased at offices near Falnir Rd.

TRAIN

The main **train station** (☎ 2423137) is south of the city centre. The 12.15am *Netravati Express* stops at Margao in Goa (sleeper/2AC Rs197/715, 5½ hours), and continues to Mumbai (sleeper/2AC Rs369/1389, 16 hours). The 6.15pm *Malabar Express* heads to Thiruvananthapuram (Trivandrum; sleeper/2AC Rs261/966, 15 hours). The 9.30pm *West Coast Express* heads to Chennai (sleeper/2AC Rs322/1206, 18 hours).

Several Konkan Railway trains (to Mumbai, Margao, Ernakulam or Trivandrum) use **Kankanadi train station** (☎ 2437824), 5km east of the city.

Getting Around

To get to the airport, take bus 47B or 47C from the City bus stand, or catch a taxi (Rs400). Indian Airlines has a free airport shuttle for its passengers.

The City bus stand is opposite the State Bank of India, close to The Gateway Hotel.

Flag fall for autorickshaws is Rs10, and they cost Rs6 per kilometre thereafter. For late-night travel, add on 50%. An autorickshaw to Kankanadi station costs around Rs40, or take bus 9 or 11B.

DHARMASTHALA

Move inland from Mangalore, and you'll come across a string of Jain temple towns, including Venur, Mudabidri and Karkal. The most interesting is Dharmasthala, 75km east of Mangalore on the banks of the Netravathi River. Some 10,000 pilgrims pass through this town every day; during major holidays and major festivals (see p236), the footfall can go up tenfold.

Three elephants trunk out blessings to pilgrims outside the **Manjunatha Temple** (☎ 08256-277121; ☻ 6.30am-2pm & 5-9pm); men have to enter bare-chested, with legs covered. Simple free meals are available in the temple's **kitchen** (☻ 11.30am-2.15pm & 7.30-10pm), attached to a hall that can seat up to 3000.

If you're passing through town, also check out the 12m-high **statue of Bahubali** at Ratnagiri Hill; the **Manjusha Museum** (admission Rs2; ☻ 10am-1pm & 4.30-7pm Mon-Sat) housing a collection of Indian stone and metal sculptures, jewellery and local craft products; and, best of all, the **Car Museum** (admission Rs3; ☻ 8.30am-1pm & 2-7pm), home to 48 vintage autos, including a 1903 Renault and a monster 1954 Cadillac!

Should you wish to stay, contact the helpful **temple office** (☎ 08256-277121; www.shridharmasthala .org), which can arrange accommodation for Rs50 per person in one of its pilgrim lodges.

There are frequent buses to Dharmasthala from Mangalore (Rs35, two hours).

UDUPI (UDIPI)

☎ 0820

Udupi is home to the atmospheric, 13th-century **Krishna Temple** (☎ 2520598; Car St; ☻ 3.30am-10pm), which draws thousands of Hindu pilgrims through the year. Surrounded by eight *maths* (monasteries), it's a hive of activity, with musicians playing at the entrance, elephants on hand for *puja,* and pilgrims constantly coming and going. Non-Hindus are welcome inside the temple; men must enter bare-chested. Elaborate rituals are also performed in the temple during the Udupi Paryaya festival (see boxed text, p236).

Near the temple, above the Corp Bank ATM, the **tourist office** (☎ 2529718; Krishna Bldg,

Car St; 10am-5.30pm Mon-Sat) is a useful source of advice on Udupi and the surrounding area.

Udupi is famed for its vegetarian food – it's particularly well known for its vegetarian thali. A good place to sample the local fare is **Woodlands** (Dr UR Rao Complex; mains Rs30-45; 8am-9.30pm), a short walk south of the temple.

Udupi is 58km north of Mangalore along the coast; regular buses ply the route (Rs30, 1½ hours).

MALPE
☎ 0820

A laid-back fishing harbour on the west coast 4km from Udupi, Malpe has fabulous beaches ideal for flopping about in the surf. A good place to stay is the **Paradise Isle Beach Resort** (☎ 2538777; www.theparadiseisle.com; s/d from Rs2500/3000;), right on the sands, which has comfortable rooms and offers a host of water sports for guests, such as bumpy rides and jet skiing (Rs450 to Rs1600), and scuba diving on request. Also enquire about its **house boats** (d incl full board Rs4000) in the backwaters of Hoode nearby.

From Malpe pier, you can take a boat (Rs70 per person) at 10.30am and 3.30pm out to tiny **St Mary's Island**, where Vasco da Gama supposedly landed in 1498. Over weekends the island is busy with locals inspecting the curious hexagonal basalt formations that jut out of the sand; during the week you might have it to yourself. An autorickshaw from Udupi to Malpe is around Rs50.

DEVBAGH

About 50km north of Gokarna, on one of the many islands that dot the Arabian Sea near the port town of Karwar, is the heavenly **Devbagh Beach Resort** (☎ 08382-221603; d incl full board Indian/foreigner from Rs2500/US$90;). It's the perfect place to cosy up with your favourite paperback or stroll aimlessly along the sands, while the roar of the breakers and the rustle of the forests work their sonic magic on you. Accommodation comes in a choice of cute and comfy fishermen's huts, cottages, log huts and houseboats. Water sports such as snorkelling and scooter rides cost extra.

You can reach Karwar by taking a slow bus from Gokarna (Rs29, 1½ hours) or Panaji (Rs42, three hours). Alternatively, take a taxi from either place. Call the resort in advance to arrange for a ferry to the island. Bookings can be made through **Jungle Lodges & Resorts**

Ltd (Map p240; ☎ 080-25597021, 25597944; www.jungle lodges.com).

MURUDESHWAR
☎ 08385

Apart from its pleasant and clean beaches, Murudeshwar is popular among travellers for its pretty little Shiva temple, which is towered over by a stupendous 83m-tall *gopuram*, and an immense 40m-high idol of the eponymous Hindu deity, said to be the tallest of its kind in the world. It's a quiet place with a friendly population, and can prove to be a nice stopover during your journey along the Karnataka coast.

The best places to put up in town are the **RNS Residency** (☎ 260060, 268901; www.naveenhotels .com; d with/without AC from Rs2200/1100;) and the **Naveen Beach Resort** (☎ 260415, 260428; www .naveenhotels.com; d from Rs1600;), both offering comfortable, well-furnished and breezy rooms with sea views. Perched over the waves, the Naveen Beach Restaurant tosses up excellent Punjabi and South Indian thalis (Rs35 to Rs60), as well as desserts and ice-cream sundaes.

Murudeshwar is just off the coastal highway, 163km north of Mangalore and 70km south of Gokarna. Trains on the **Konkan Railway** (www.konkanrailway.com), which connects Goa with Mumbai and Mangalore, stop here.

JOG FALLS
☎ 08186

Nominally the highest waterfalls in India, the Jog Falls only come to life during the monsoon. At other times, the Linganamakki Dam further up the Sharavati River limits the water flow. The tallest of the four falls is the Raja, which drops 293m.

To get a good view of the falls, bypass the scrappy area close to the bus stand and hike to the foot of the falls down a 1200-plus step path. It takes about an hour to get down and two to come up. Watch out for leeches in the wet season.

The **tourist office** (☎ 244732; 10am-5pm Mon-Sat) is above the food stalls close to the bus stand. On-site is the **KSTDC Hotel Mayura Gerusoppa** (☎ 244732; s/d Rs300/400), about 150m from the car park, with enormous, musty rooms.

Stalls near the bus stand serve omelettes, thalis, noodles and rice dishes, plus hot and cold drinks. KSTDC's mediocre **restaurant** (meals Rs30-50) is just next door.

BUFFALO SURFING

Call it an Indian take on the ancient Roman chariot race. Kambla, the traditional sport of buffalo racing, is a hugely popular pastime among villagers along the southern Karnataka coast, and indeed worth a watch, time and place permitting. Kambla first became popular in the early part of the 20th century, born out of the local farmers' habit of racing their buffaloes home after a day in the fields. Today the best of the races have hit the big time, with thousands of specta-tors attending. Valuable racing buffaloes are pampered and prepared like thoroughbreds for the occasion; a good animal can cost more than Rs300,000!

Kambla events are held in the Dakshina Kannada region between November and March, usu-ally on weekends. Parallel tracks are laid out in a paddy field, along which buffaloes hurtle towards the finish line. There are two versions: in one, the man runs alongside the buffalo; in the other, he rides on a board fixed to a ploughshare, literally surfing his way down the track behind the beasts!

Keep your cameras ready, but don't even think of getting in the buffaloes' way to take that prize-winning photo. The faster creatures can cover the 120m-odd distance through water and mud in around 14 seconds!

Jog Falls has buses roughly every hour to Shimoga (Rs45, three hours), and three daily to Karwar via Kumta (Rs43, three hours), where you can change for Gokarna (Rs12, one hour). For Mangalore, change at Shimoga.

DANDELI

Located in the wilderness of the Western Ghats about 130km from Goa, Dandeli is an up-and-coming nature and wildlife getaway that is rapidly striking a chord with travellers of the intrepid kind. And for good reason too! To begin with, a rich variety of animal life, including sloth bears, panthers, elephants, Indian bisons, wild dogs and flying squir-rels, inhabit the greens within the **Dandeli Wildlife Sanctuary** (Indian/foreigner Rs20/80, camera/video Rs15/150; ⏱ 6am-6pm). The park is also a chosen destination for birders, who come here to spot various species of birds residing in the park, including grey hornbills, great pied hornbills, golden-backed woodpeckers, serpent eagles and white-breasted kingfishers.

Dandeli is also a vantage point for in-dulging in a slew of **adventure activities**, ranging from canoeing, boating and crocodile-spotting trips, to bowel-churning white-water rafting on the swirling waters of the Kali River. You could also indulge in more restrained activities, such as nature walks and ethnic tours to nearby tribal villages.

The government-owned **Kali Adventure Camp** (☎ 08284-23336091; per person incl full board Indian/for-eigner Rs2250/US$90) is a lovely place to stay in Dandeli. You can choose from a mix of tents and cottages, all done up rather lavishly while

adhering to ecofriendly principles. Charges include forest entry fees, jeep safaris and boat rides, while rafting charges are extra. Rafting charges for the 9km stretch along the river are about Rs900 per person. Book through **Jungle Lodges & Resorts Ltd** (Map p240; ☎ 080-25597021, 25597944; www.junglelodges.com).

Frequent buses connect Dandeli to both Hubli (Rs40, two hours) and Dharwad (Rs28, 1½ hours), from where you can find onward connections to Panaji, Gokarna or Bengaluru.

GOKARNA
☎ 08386

The quaint village of Gokarna, 50km south of Karwar, provides a fantastic glimpse into vi-brant Hindu rituals and a medieval way of life. A low-key settlement on the coast, Gokarna is where hordes of pilgrims gather through the year to pay their respects in the ancient temples. During Hindu festivals such as Shivaratri and Ganesh Chaturthi (see boxed text, p236), the village is at its dramatic best. While the main village is rather conservative in its outlook, a few out-of-town beaches provide an ideal op-portunity for some carefree sunbaking.

Information

There are lots of places to access the internet, including many of the guest houses.
Pai STD Shop (Main St; ⏱ 9am-9pm) Changes cash and travellers cheques and gives advances on Visa.
Shree Radhakrishna Bookstore (Car St; ⏱ 10am-6pm) Good selection of new and second-hand books.
Sub post office (1st fl, cnr Car & Main Sts; ⏱ 10am-4pm Mon-Sat)

Sights & Activities

TEMPLES

Foreigners and non-Hindus are not allowed inside Gokarna's temples. However, there are plenty of colourful rituals to be witnessed around town. At the western end of Car St is the **Mahabaleshwara Temple**, home to a revered lingam (phallic representation of Shiva). Nearby is the **Ganapati Temple**, while at the other end of the street is the **Venkataraman Temple**. About 100m further south is **Koorti Teertha**, the large temple tank (reservoir) where locals, pilgrims and immaculately dressed Brahmins perform their ablutions next to washermen on the ghats (steps or landings).

BEACHES

Gokarna's 'town beach' is dirty, and not meant for casual bathing. The best sands are due south, and can be reached via a footpath that begins south of the Ganapati Temple and heads down the coast (if you reach the bathing tank – or find yourself clawing up rocks – you're on the wrong path).

A 20-minute hike on the path brings you to the top of a barren headland with expansive sea views. On the southern side is **Kudle** (koodlay), the first of Gokarna's pristine beaches. Basic snacks, drinks and accommodation are available here.

South of Kudle Beach, a track climbs over the next headland, and a further 20-minute walk brings you to **Om Beach**, with a handful of chai shops and shacks. South of Om Beach lie the more isolated **Half-Moon Beach** and **Paradise Beach**, which come to life generally between November and March. They are a 30-minute and one-hour walk, respectively.

Depending on demand, fishing boats can ferry you from Gokarna Beach to Kudle (Rs100) and Om (Rs 200). An autorickshaw from town to Om costs around Rs150.

Don't walk around after dark, and not alone at any time – it's easy to slip on the paths or get lost, and muggings have occurred. For a small fee, most lodges in Gokarna will safely store valuables and baggage while you chill out in the beach huts.

AYURVEDA

Quality ayurvedic therapies and packages are available at specialist ayurvedic centres in SwaSwara (right) and Om Beach Resort (right).

Sleeping

With a few exceptions, the choice here is between a rudimentary beach shack or a basic but more comfortable room in town. Some hotels in town cater to pilgrims, and may come with certain rules and regs. Prices quoted here are for the high season (November to March), but may increase depending on demand.

BEACHES

Both Kudle and Om beaches have several shacks offering budget huts and rooms – shop around. Places also open up on Half-Moon and Paradise beaches from November to March. Most places provide at least a bedroll; bring your own sheets or sleeping bag. Padlocks are provided and huts are secure. Communal washing and toilet facilities are simple.

Namaste Café (☎ 257141; Om Beach; s without bathroom Rs150, deluxe hut Rs600) In and out of season, Namaste is the place to hang. Its restaurant-bar cooks up great bites and is the premier Om chill-out spot. In season it also offers basic huts (Rs50) at Paradise Beach and cottages at Namaste Farm (from Rs400) on the headland.

Nirvana Café (☎ 329851; Om Beach; s without bathroom Rs250, cottage Rs600) Located on the southern end of Om is this pleasant option, with a handful of cute and rustic cottages with little sit-outs, nestled amid shady palms and groves.

Hotel Gokarna International Kudle Resort (☎ 257843; Kudle Beach; d with/without AC Rs1500/1200; ❄) Run by the same management that owns Hotel Gokarna International in town, this midrange option has smart rooms and a lovely garden in front overlooking the sea. The waves wash up to its gates during high tide!

SwaSwara (☎ 257132, 0484-2668221; www.swaswara.com; Om Beach; d per week Indian/foreigner Rs120,000/US$2300; ❄ ☐ ☑) No short stays on offer here, but you can chill out at this elegant and superbly designed red laterite resort for a full week, and enjoy a holiday based around yoga and ayurvedic treatments. Rates include full board, transport, leisure activities and daily yoga sessions. Week-long ayurvedic treatment packages kick off at around US$570.

GOKARNA

Vaibhav Nivas (☎ 256714; off Main St; d Rs200, s/d without bathroom Rs100/150; ☐) The cell-like rooms at this place tucked away from the main drag

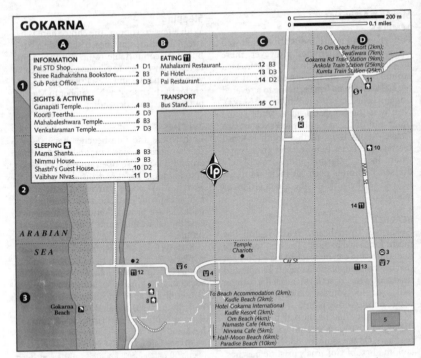

GOKARNA

INFORMATION	
Pai STD Shop	1 D1
Shree Radhakrishna Bookstore	2 B3
Sub Post Office	3 D3

SIGHTS & ACTIVITIES	
Ganapati Temple	4 B3
Koorti Teertha	5 D3
Mahabaleshwara Temple	6 B3
Venkataraman Temple	7 D3

SLEEPING	
Mama Shanta	8 B3
Nimmu House	9 B3
Shastri's Guest House	10 D2
Vaibhav Nivas	11 D1

EATING	
Mahalaxmi Restaurant	12 B3
Pai Hotel	13 D3
Pai Restaurant	14 D2

TRANSPORT	
Bus Stand	15 C1

To Om Beach Resort (2km);
SwaSwara (7km);
Gokarna Rd Train Station (9km);
Ankola Train Station (25km);
Kumta Train Station (25km)

ARABIAN SEA

Gokarna Beach

Temple Chariots

Car St

To Beach Accommodation (2km);
Kudle Beach (2km);
Hotel Gokarna International
Kudle Resort (2km);
Om Beach (4km);
Namaste Cafe (4km);
Nirvana Cafe (5km);
Half-Moon Beach (6km);
Paradise Beach (10km)

---

come with mosquito nets and hot water in the morning. There's also a rooftop restaurant.

Mama Shanta (☎ 256213; r without/with bathroom Rs120/150) Just past Nimmu House is this rather gloomy and basic homestay, but the kindly old lady of the house does her best to make you feel at home. It's right next to the beach.

Shastri's Guest House (☎ 256220; dr_murti@rediff mail.com; Main St; s/d Rs150/200) This place has a hostel-like feel to it. The singles are tiny; the doubles in the new block out back are bright and airy, with squat loos. Some have balconies and palm-tree views.

Nimmu House (☎ 256730; nimmuhouse@yahoo.com; s/d old block Rs250/500, new block Rs300/1000; ☐) Just off the foot trail along the beach is this pleasant option run by a friendly family. The rooms in the new block are nice, with tiled floors and balconies.

our pick Om Beach Resort (☎ 257052; www.om beachresort.com; Bangle Gudde; d incl breakfast Indian/foreigner Rs2100/US$80; ☒ ☐) This little jewel sits on a headland 2km out of Gokarna off the Om Beach road. Set amid lawns and shady trees, its red-brick cottages are excellently designed, and its restaurant serves some delectable sea-

food. There's a professional ayurvedic centre on-site, offering short sessions (from Rs750) as well as longer treatment packages.

Eating

The chai shops on all of the beaches rustle up basic snacks and meals.

Pai Hotel (Car St; mains Rs20-35; ☒ 6am-9.30pm) A good place for veg food.

Pai Restaurant (Main St; mains Rs25-40; ☒ 6.30am-9.30pm) This place draws in visiting pilgrims with its vegetarian fare.

Mahalaxmi Restaurant (meals Rs30-70) This popular hang-out promises 'all types of world famous dishes' (ie banana pancakes and cornflakes!) in myriad ways. The ambience, however, is relaxing.

Namaste Café (meals Rs30-80; ☒ 7am-11pm) Om Beach's social centre serves decent Western stand-bys – pizzas and burgers – and some Israeli specials.

Getting There & Away
BUS

From Gokarna's rudimentary **bus stand**, rickety buses rumble out to Karwar (Rs29, 1½ hours), which has connections to Goa. Direct buses run to Hubli (Rs92, four hours), where you can change for Hospet and Hampi. There are two direct evening buses to Bengaluru (semi-deluxe/sleeper Rs256/456, 12 hours).

TRAIN
Only slow passenger trains stop at **Gokarna Rd train station** (☎ 279487), 9km from town. A 10.40am train heads daily to Margao in Goa (Rs21, three hours). For Mangalore (Rs42, five hours), a train departs daily at 4.20pm.

A better idea is to head out by local bus to **Kumta station** (☎ 223820) 25km away, to board one of the expresses which stop there. From Kumta, the 2.14am *Matsyagandha Express* goes to Mangalore (sleeper Rs168, four hours); the return train leaves Kumta at 6.38pm for Margao (sleeper Rs141, 3½ hours). Many of the hotels and small travel agencies in Gokarna can book tickets. Ankola Station, 25km south of Gokarna, is also a convenient railhead.

Autorickshaws charge Rs100 to go to Gokarna Rd station. Buses go hourly (Rs7) and also meet arriving passenger trains. A bus to Kumta station is Rs12.

CENTRAL KARNATAKA

HAMPI
☎ 08394
Unreal and bewitching, the forlorn ruins of Hampi lie scattered over a landscape that leaves you spellbound the moment you cast your eyes on it. Heaps of giant boulders perch precariously over miles of undulated terrain, their rusty hues offset by jade-green palm groves, banana plantations and paddy fields, while the azure sky painted with fluffy white cirrus only adds to the magical atmosphere. A World Heritage Site, Hampi is a place where you can lose yourself among the ruins that come alive with a fascinating tale, or simply be mesmerised by the vagaries of nature, wondering how millions of years of volcanic activity and erosion could have resulted in a landscape so fascinating.

Hampi is a major pit stop on the traveller circuit, with the cooler months of November to March being the peak season. While it's possible to see the main sites in a day or two, this goes against Hampi's relaxed grain; plan on lingering for a while.

History
Hampi and its neighbouring areas find mention in the Hindu epic Ramayana as Kishkinda (see Anegundi, p280), the realm of the monkey gods. In 1336, Telugu prince Harihararaya chose Hampi as the site for his new capital, Vijayanagar which, over the next couple of centuries, grew into one of the largest Hindu empires in Indian history. By the 16th century, it was a thriving metropolis of about 500,000 people, its busy bazaars dabbling in international commerce, brimming with precious stones and merchants from faraway lands. All this, however, ended in a stroke in 1565, when a confederacy of Deccan sultanates razed Vijayanagar to the ground, striking it a death blow from which it never recovered.

A different battle rages in Hampi today, between conservationists bent on protecting Hampi's architectural heritage and the locals who have settled there. A master plan is being prepared to notify all of Hampi's ruins as protected monuments, while resettling villagers at a new commercial-cum-residential complex away from the architectural enclosures. However, implementation is bound to take time, given the resistance from the locals who fear their livelihoods might be affected by the relocation process. **Global Heritage Fund** (www.globalheritagefund.org) has more details about Hampi's endangered heritage.

Orientation
Hampi Bazaar and the southern village of Kamalapuram are the two main points of entry to the ruins. Kamalapuram has the KSTDC Hotel and the archaeological museum. But the main travellers' scene is Hampi Bazaar, a village crammed with budget lodges, shops and restaurants, all dominated by the majestic Virupaksha Temple. The ruins are divided into two main areas: the Sacred Centre, around Hampi Bazaar; and the Royal Centre, towards Kamalapuram. To the northeast across the Tungabhadra River is the village of Anegundi (see p280).

Information
Andhra Bank (Map p279) Has an ATM off the entrance to Hampi bazaar.

Aspiration Stores (Map p279; ☀ 10am-1pm & 4-8pm) For books on the area. Try *Hampi* by John M Fritz and George Michell, a good architectural guide.

Canara Bank (Map p279; ☎ 241243; ☀ 11am-2pm Mon, Tue, Thu & Fri, 11am-12.30pm Sat) Changes travellers cheques and gives cash advances on credit cards.

Hampi Heritage Gallery (Map p279; 10am-1pm & 3-6pm) Sells books and offers half-day walking or cycling tours for Rs200.

Sree Rama Cyber Café (Map p279; per hr Rs30; 7am-11pm) The best of Hampi's internet cafes. It also burns CDs of digital snaps for Rs50.

Tourist Office (Map p279; ☎ 241339; 10am-5.30pm Sat-Thu) Can arrange guides for Rs300/500 for a half-full day.

Dangers & Annoyances

Hampi is generally a safe, peaceful place. However, don't wander around the ruins after dark or alone, as muggings are not unreported. Besides, it's a dangerous terrain to get lost in, especially at night.

Sights & Activities

VIRUPAKSHA TEMPLE

The focal point of Hampi Bazaar is the **Virupaksha Temple** (Map p279; ☎ 241241; admission Rs2; dawn-dusk), one of the city's oldest structures. The main *gopuram*, almost 50m high, was built in 1442, with a smaller one added in 1510. The main shrine is dedicated to Virupaksha, a form of Shiva.

If Lakshmi (the temple elephant) and her attendant are around, she'll smooch (bless) you for a coin. The adorable Lakshmi gets her morning bath at 8.30am, just down the way by the river ghats.

To the south, overlooking Virupaksha Temple, **Hemakuta Hill** (Map p279) has a scattering of early ruins, including monolithic sculptures of Narasimha (Vishnu in his manlion incarnation) and Ganesha. It's worth the short walk up for the view over the bazaar. At the east end of Hampi Bazaar is a monolithic **Nandi statue** (Map p279), around which stand some of the colonnaded blocks of the ancient marketplace. This is the main location for **Vijaya Utsav**, the Hampi arts festival held in November (see p236).

VITTALA TEMPLE

From the eastern end of Hampi Bazaar, a track, best covered on foot, leads left along the riverbank to the **Vittala Temple** (Map p277; Indian/foreigner Rs10/250; 8.30am-5.30pm), about 2km away. The undisputed highlight of the Hampi ruins, the 16th-century temple is in fairly good condition, though a few cement scaffolds have been erected to keep the main structure from collapsing.

Work possibly started on the temple during the reign of Krishnadevaraya (1509–29) but it was never finished or consecrated. Yet, the temple's incredible sculptural work remains the pinnacle of Vijayanagar art. The outer 'musical' pillars reverberate when tapped, but authorities have placed them out of tourists' bounds for fear of further damage, so no more do-re-mi. Don't miss the temple's showcase piece: the ornate stone chariot that stands in the temple courtyard, whose wheels were once capable of turning.

Retain your ticket for same-day admission into the Zenana Enclosure and Elephant Stables in the Royal Centre (see below).

SULE BAZAAR & ACHYUTARAYA TEMPLE

Halfway along the path from Hampi Bazaar to the Vittala Temple, a track to the right leads over the rocks to deserted **Sule Bazaar** (Map p277), one of ancient Hampi's principal centres of commerce. At the southern end of this area is the **Achyutaraya Temple** (Map p277). Its isolated location at the foot of Matanga Hill makes it quietly atmospheric, doubly so since it is visited by few tourists.

ROYAL CENTRE

While it can be accessed by a 2km walking trail from the Achyutaraya Temple, the Royal Centre is best reached via the Hampi–Kamalapuram road. It's a flatter area compared to the rest of Hampi, where the boulders have been shaved off to create stone walls. A number of Hampi's major sites stand here, within the walled ladies' quarters called the **Zenana Enclosure** (Map p277; Indian/foreigner Rs10/250; 8.30am-5.30pm). There's the **Lotus Mahal** (Map p277), a delicately designed pavilion which was supposedly the queen's recreational mansion. The Lotus Mahal overlooks the **Elephant Stables** (Map p277), a grand building with domed chambers where state elephants once resided. Your ticket is valid for same-day admission to the Vittala Temple (see left).

Further south, you'll find various temples and elaborate waterworks, including the **Underground Virupaksha Temple** (Map p277; 8.30am-5.30pm) and the **Queen's Bath** (Map p277; 8.30am-5.30pm), deceptively plain on the outside but amazing within.

ARCHAEOLOGICAL MUSEUM

The **archaeological museum** (Map p277; ☎ 241561; Kamalapuram; admission Rs5; 10am-5pm Sat-Thu) has well-displayed collections of sculptures from local ruins, Neolithic tools, 16th-century weaponry and a large floor model of the Vijayanagar ruins.

ROCK-CLIMBING

Some of the best low-altitude climbing in India can be had near Hampi. For more information, see p278.

Sleeping

There's little to choose from between many of the basic rooms in Hampi Bazaar and Virupapur Gaddi. If you need AC and cable TV, stay in Kamalapuram (p279). Prices listed can shoot up by 50% or more during Christmas, and drop just as dramatically in the low season (April to September).

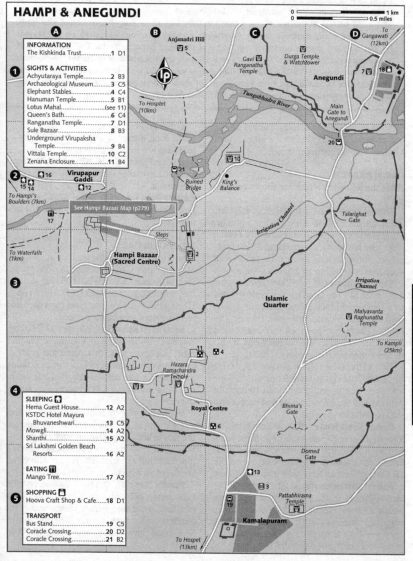

HAMPI & ANEGUNDI

INFORMATION
The Kishkinda Trust...............1 D1

SIGHTS & ACTIVITIES
Achyutaraya Temple..............2 B3
Archaeological Museum..........3 C5
Elephant Stables....................4 C4
Hanuman Temple..................5 B1
Lotus Mahal.......................(see 11)
Queen's Bath.......................6 C4
Ranganatha Temple...............7 D1
Sule Bazaar...........................8 B3
Underground Virupaksha
  Temple..............................9 B4
Vittala Temple.....................10 C2
Zenana Enclosure................11 B4

SLEEPING
Hema Guest House...............12 A2
KSTDC Hotel Mayura
  Bhuvaneshwari...................13 C5
Mowgli...............................14 A2
Shanthi................................15 A2
Sri Lakshmi Golden Beach
  Resorts.............................16 A2

EATING
Mango Tree.........................17 A2

SHOPPING
Hoova Craft Shop & Cafe......18 D1

TRANSPORT
Bus Stand...........................19 C5
Coracle Crossing..................20 D2
Coracle Crossing..................21 B2

0 — 1 km
0 — 0.5 miles

To Gangawati (12km)

Anjanadri Hill

Gavi Ranganatha Temple

Durga Temple & Watchtower

Anegundi

Tungabhadra River

Main Gate to Anegundi

To Hospet (10km)

Ruined Bridge

King's Balance

Irrigation Channel

Talarighat Gate

Virupapur Gaddi

To Hampi's Boulders (7km)

See Hampi Bazaar Map (p279)

To Waterfalls (1km)

Steps

Hampi Bazaar (Sacred Centre)

Islamic Quarter

Irrigation Channel

Malyavanta Raghunatha Temple

To Kampli (25km)

Hazara Ramachandra Temple

Royal Centre

Bhima's Gate

Domed Gate

Pattabhirama Temple

Kamalapuram

To Hospet (13km)

KARNATAKA

CLIMBING IN KARNATAKA

Karnataka is a place which promises that perfect high, on the rocks! Magnificent bluffs and rounded boulders stand tall all over the state, offering some of India's best rock-climbing opportunities. However, bolting is limited, so bring a decent bouldering mat and plenty of gear from home – see p103.

Hampi is the undisputed bouldering capital of India, and **Anegundi** (p280), across the Tungabhadra River, is a place to indulge in some hassle-free climbing (rocks are graded and equipment provided). Through the rest of the state, routes and grades are still being assigned, so it's all pretty much old-fashioned. Challenging rock faces can be found in **Badami** (p283), where the perfect horseshoe of red sandstone cliffs with some magnificent bolted and traditional routes is any climber's dream. **Ramnagar**, about 40km from Bengaluru on the Mysore Rd, has outsized granite boulders, with some of the more popular climbs. The granite massif at **Savandurga**, 50km west of Bengaluru near Magadi, and the boulders of **Turalli**, 12km south of Bengaluru towards Kanakapura, are other places you might want to flex your muscles. Both are accessible by bus or taxi from Bengaluru. For more information on climbing in Karnataka, log on to **Dreamroutes** (www.dreamroutes.org/etc/allclimbs.html).

Most guest houses display notices saying use of narcotics and alcohol are strictly prohibited. Trip on nature instead!

HAMPI BAZAAR
All of the following places are shown on Map p279.

Shanthi Guest House (☎ 241568; s/d Rs250/300, without bathroom Rs150/250) An oldie but a goodie, Shanthi offers a peaceful courtyard with a swing chair, and has plastic creepers and divine posters decorating its basic rooms. There's a small shop that operates on an honour system.

Gopi Guest House (☎ 241695; kirangopi2002@yahoo .com; d Rs300; ▨) The Gopi empire has expanded to a renovated block across the road, which contains four pleasant en-suite rooms. The rooftop room, equipped with a carom board and guitar, is a nice place to hang out. It also makes a mean cup of espresso (Rs30).

Vicky's (☎ 241694; vikkyhampi@yahoo.co.in; d Rs350; ▨) One of the village's larger operations done up in pop purple and green, with 10 brightly painted and tiled rooms, internet access and the requisite rooftop cafe.

Pushpa Guest House (☎ 241440; d/tr Rs400/500) The fresh new rooms here have pink walls and brightly printed upholstery, with a cordial family playing host. The lovely sit-out on the 1st floor gives it an edge over its competitors.

Padma Guest House (☎ 241331; d Rs400-800) The astute Padma might have got her spellings wrong ('Recommendation by Lovely Plant', reads her business card!), but the tidy rooms are more than inviting. Try one upstairs for great views of the Virupaksha Temple.

Other good options:

Sudha Guest House (☎ 652752; d from Rs200) Has a good family vibe and a riverside location.

Rama Guest House (☎ 241962; s/d Rs300/400) Some rooms are a little low on light, but the cool rooftop cafe seals the deal.

Ranjana Guest House (☎ 241696; d Rs400-600) On par with Padma Guest House. The terrace rooms have great views and TV.

VIRUPAPUR GADDI
Many travellers prefer the tranquil atmosphere of Virupapur Gaddi, across the river from Hampi Bazaar. A small boat (Rs10) shuttles frequently across the river from 7am to 6pm. During the monsoon, the river runs high and ferry services may be suspended.

Hema Guest House (Map p277; ☎ 9449103008; dm/ bungalows Rs100/500) One of Virupapur Gaddi's most popular spots, this place has rows of cute and comfy cottages laid out in a shady grove, and scores with its informal restaurant in a beautiful wooden belvedere overlooking the river.

Mowgli (Map p277; ☎ 329844; hampimowgli@hotmail .com; d from Rs250; ▨) With prime views across the rice fields, shady gardens sheltering hammocks, and thatched-roof bungalows, this is a top-class chill-out spot. The rooms with views are the most expensive, around Rs500.

Shanthi (Map p277; ☎ 325352; d without bathroom Rs300, cottages Rs600) Shanthi's bungalows have rice-field, river and sunset views, and front porches with couch swings. The restaurant does good thalis (Rs45) and pizzas (Rs70 to Rs85).

Sri Lakshmi Golden Beach Resorts (Map p277; ☎ 08533-287008, 9448436537; d incl breakfast from Rs2000; 🛏 🔁) A welcome change from Hampi's basic sleeping options, this resort-style place amid paddy fields has a range of cosy cottages. The pool, sadly, won't be in commission until early 2010.

Hampi's Boulders (off Map p277; ☎ 08539-265939, 9448034202; Narayanpet; d incl full board with/without AC from Rs8000/6000; 🛏 🔁) The only luxury option in these parts, this ecowilderness resort sits amid leafy gardens in Narayanpet, 7km west of Virupapur Gaddi. Accommodation is in chic cottages designed like boulders, and the food is good. The downside: you're way removed from the buzz.

KAMALAPURAM

KSTDC Hotel Mayura Bhuvaneshwari (Map p277; ☎ 08394-241574; d/tr from Rs825/1125; 🔁) This tidy government place, about 3km south of the Royal Centre, has well-appointed rooms (though the murals make you go bleh!) and creature comforts such as TV and AC. A huge plus is the bar – the only legal one close to Hampi – and ayurvedic sessions (from Rs1550) on request.

Eating

With one exception, Hampi is not renowned for its restaurants. Due to Hampi's religious significance, meat is usually off the menu, and alcohol is banned. Places are open from 7am to 10pm.

New Shanthi (Map p279; mains Rs30-50) A hippie vibe, complete with trance music and acid-blue lights, hangs over this popular option serving a good selection of juices and shakes. The bakery churns out passable cookies and crumbles.

our pick Mango Tree (Map p277; mains Rs30-90) Creativity blends with culinary excellence at this rural-themed chill-out joint, spread out under the eponymous mango tree by the riverbanks. The walk out here is through a banana plantation, and the food is delicious – the restaurant does lip-smacking dosas for breakfast and dinner. The ambience is simply overwhelming, and the terraced seating perfect for whiling away a lazy afternoon, book in hand.

Shiv Moon (Map p279; mains Rs35-90) This friendly place with pleasant views sits by the river to the east of Hampi Bazaar. It gets good reviews

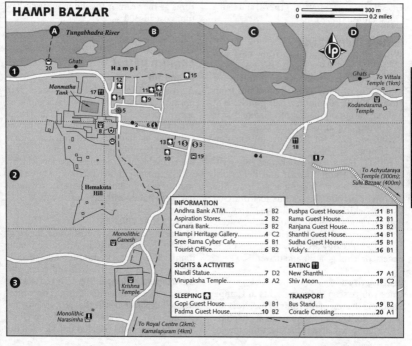

HAMPI BAZAAR

0 — 300 m
0 — 0.2 miles

INFORMATION	
Andhra Bank ATM	1 B2
Aspiration Stores	2 B2
Canara Bank	3 B2
Hampi Heritage Gallery	4 C2
Sree Rama Cyber Cafe	5 B1
Tourist Office	6 B2

SIGHTS & ACTIVITIES	
Nandi Statue	7 D2
Virupaksha Temple	8 A2

SLEEPING	
Gopi Guest House	9 B1
Padma Guest House	10 B2

Pushpa Guest House	11 B1
Rama Guest House	12 B1
Ranjana Guest House	13 B2
Shanthi Guest House	14 B1
Sudha Guest House	15 B1
Vicky's	16 B1

EATING	
New Shanthi	17 A1
Shiv Moon	18 C2

TRANSPORT	
Bus Stand	19 B2
Coracle Crossing	20 A1

To Vittala Temple (1km)

To Achyutaraya Temple (300m); Sule Bazaar (400m)

To Royal Centre (2km); Kamalapuram (4km)

KARNATAKA

VIJAYANAGAR'S TWILIGHT YEARS

While the battle of 1565 effectively put an end to the glory days of the Vijayanagar empire, its ruling dynasty was to survive for nearly another 100 years, though severely weakened and reduced to utter ignominy. Following the routing of Hampi by the Deccan sultanates, Tirumala Raya – the sole surviving commander of the Vijayanagar army – decided to abandon the plundered city and shift what was left of the empire to a place called Penukonda, in the Anantapur district of Andhra Pradesh. Legend has it that he gleaned every bit of treasure that had managed to escape the invaders' eyes before he left, which was apparently still enough to load the backs of more than 500 elephants! However, Penukonda soon proved untenable as a capital, and the Rayas were left with no option but to scout for a new base once again. A third capital was founded in 1592 at the base of the Chandragiri Hill, also in Andhra Pradesh, about 14km from the temple town of Tirupathi (p318). It was here that the Vijayanagar empire whimpered away its last years before finally fading into oblivion. Chandragiri was annexed by the Golconda sultans sometime in the mid-17th century, only to be passed on to Mysore in due course.

for the quality of its food, though the owners often tend to get politely pushy.

Waterfalls (off Map p277; mains Rs40-60) Around a 2km walk west of Hampi Bazaar is this appealing operation tucked away beside shady banana plantations en route to a group of small waterfalls. The tasty Indian fare justifies the walk out of town.

Several of Hampi's lodges sport rooftop restaurants; good ones include those at Gopi Guest House (p278), Vicky's (p278) and Rama Guest House (p278).

Getting There & Away

While some private buses from Goa and Bengaluru will drop you at the bus stand in Hampi Bazaar, you have to go to Hospet to catch most buses out. The first bus from Hospet (Rs10, 30 minutes, half-hourly) is at 6.30am; the last one back leaves Hampi Bazaar at 8.30pm. An autorickshaw costs around Rs100. See p282 for transport information for Hospet.

KSRTC has a daily Rajahamsa bus service between Hampi Bazaar and Bengaluru (Rs301, 8½ hours) leaving at 8.45pm. The overnight private sleeper bus to/from Goa (Rs550), which runs November to March, is a popular option – but don't expect a deep sleep. Numerous travel agents in Hampi Bazaar are eager to book onward bus, train and plane tickets, or arrange a car and driver.

Getting Around

Once you've seen the main sights in Hampi, exploring the rest of the ruins by bicycle is the thing to do. The key monuments are haphazardly signposted all over the site; while they're

not adequate, you shouldn't get lost. Bicycles cost about Rs30 per day in Hampi Bazaar; mopeds can be hired for around Rs200, plus petrol. You can take your bicycle or motorbike (extra Rs10) across the river on the boat.

Walking is the only way to see all the nooks and crannies, but expect to cover at least 7km just to see the major ruins. Autorickshaws and taxis are available for sightseeing, and will drop you as close to each of the major ruins as they can. A five-hour autorickshaw tour costs Rs300.

Organised tours depart from Hospet; see opposite for details.

AROUND HAMPI
Anegundi

Across the Tungabhadra River, about 5km northeast of Hampi Bazaar, sits Anegundi, an ancient fortified village that's part of the Hampi World Heritage Site but predates Hampi by way of human habitation. Gifted with a landscape similar to Hampi, quainter Anegundi has been spared the blight of commercialisation, which is why it remains a chosen getaway for those who want to soak up the local atmosphere without having to put up with the touristy vibe.

SIGHTS & ACTIVITIES

Mythically referred to as Kishkinda, the kingdom of the monkey gods, Anegundi retains many of its historic monuments, such as sections of its defensive wall and gates, and the **Ranganatha Temple** (Map p277; admission free; ☼ dawn-dusk) devoted to Rama. The whitewashed **Hanuman Temple** (Map p277; admission free; ☼ dawn-dusk), accessible by a 570-step climb atop the Anjanadri Hill, has fine views of the rugged terrain around. Many believe this is the birthplace of Hanuman, the Hindu monkey god who was Rama's devotee and helped him in his mission against Ravana. The hike up is pleasant, though you'll be courted by impish monkeys, and within the temple you'll find a horde of chillum-puffing resident sadhus!

The **Kishkinda Trust** (TKT; ☎ 08533-267791, 9449284496; www.thekishkindatrust.org), a non-profit organisation that manages tourism in Anegundi, has a slew of nature and adventure activities that you can indulge in. Events include rock climbing, camping, trekking, rappelling and zoomering. Equipment and trained instructors are provided. A string of cultural events, such as performing arts sessions, and classical and folk music concerts, are also conducted from time to time. For more information on TKT, see the boxed text, below.

SLEEPING & EATING

Anegundi has several homestays, managed by TKT. Contact the trust for bookings.

Champa Guest House (d incl breakfast Rs600) Champa offers basic but pleasant accommodation in two rooms, and is looked after by an affable village family.

TEMA Guest House (d incl breakfast Rs600; 🖳) For an alternative experience try the two rooms here, attached to the trust's information centre, where you can read up on local heritage and sit in during community interaction programs.

Naidile Guest House (r Rs1000) A charmingly rustic air hangs over this place, a renovated village home in the heart of Anegundi where you can savour all the sights and sounds of the ancient village. It can sleep up to five people.

The **Hoova Craft Shop & Café** (dishes Rs20-40; ☯ 9.30am-5pm Mon-Sat, 9.30am-2pm Sun) is a lovely place for a laid-back meal or snack. You can also pick up sundry souvenirs made by women's self-help groups of the village here.

Meals are also provided by the guest houses upon prior notice.

GETTING THERE & AWAY

Anegundi can be reached by crossing the river on a coracle (Rs10) from the pier east of the Vittala Temple. If and when the new concrete bridge at the site is completed, you can simply cycle across.

Alternately, you can get to Anegundi by taking a bus (Rs20, one hour) from Hospet.

HOSPET

☎ 08394 / pop 164,200

This busy regional centre is the transport hub for Hampi. There's no reason to linger unless you desire an air-conditioned hotel room and cable TV. The Muslim festival of Muharram (see boxed text, p236), however, brings things to life in this otherwise mundane place.

Information

Internet joints are common, with connections costing Rs30 per hour. ATMs are common too. The bus-stand cloakroom holds bags for Rs10 per day.

KSTDC tourist office (☎ 228537, 221008; Shanbag Circle; ☯ 10am-5.30pm Mon-Sat) Offers a Hampi tour (Rs175) daily from 9.30am to 5.30pm. The quality of guides varies. Call ahead as tours won't run with fewer than 10 people.

State Bank of India (☎ 228576; Station Rd; ☯ 10.30am-4pm Mon-Sat) Changes currency.

KARNATAKA

THE KISHKINDA TRUST

Since 1995, the **Kishkinda Trust** (TKT; ☎ 08533-267791, 9449284496; www.thekishkindatrust.org) has been actively involved in promoting rural tourism, sustainable development and women's empowerment in Anegundi, apart from preserving the architectural and living heritage of the Hampi World Heritage Site. The first project in 1997 created a cottage industry of crafts using locally produced cloth, banana fibre and river grass. It now employs over 600 women, and the attractive crafts produced are marketed in ethnic product outlets across India, along with the village outlet at the **Hoova Craft Shop & Café**.

The trust's other projects include holding cottage industry workshops and sensitising the village folk in regard to self-help and sustainable ecotourism. Its homestay program has met with enormous success, and the revenue generated through tourism now goes into community welfare, training and empowerment of village personnel as well as running interaction programs in village schools. An information and interpretation centre has also been set up, while more self-help projects have recently taken their positions at the starting line.

'THIS PLACE NATURALLY CASTS ITS SPELL ON YOU'

At 36, H Virupaksha, a proud resident of Anegundi, comes across as a personification of enthusiasm. Cross the Tungabhadra River from Hampi and amble down the road towards Anegundi, and there's every chance you'll run into this spry son-of-the-soil patrolling the magical landscape on his motorbike, camera slung across his shoulder, going about his mission to put his native village firmly on the tourism map. He's out to make a difference, and there's simply no stopping him.

Born to a humble family, Virupaksha – like any other aspiring youth – had left his birthplace in 1991 to pursue big city dreams. 'But I just couldn't stay away', he admits, sitting by the river, his gaze fixed on the boulder-strewn horizon far away. 'I was craving for the sense of peace this place gives you. I realised that this was the only place on earth where I could be truly happy and at peace with myself. It's one of those few places still largely out of mobile phone coverage; no ringtones to disturb the sound of the flowing waters. You know what I mean?' he smiles.

Ever since he returned in 1997, Virupaksha has trained himself in the tourism trade. Fluent in English, he's now a qualified guide, and plans to pursue a further course in front-office management. 'Tourism is our chief source of income, and we have to know how to best make use of our natural and historic resources to draw in people', he says. Now associated with **The Kishkinda Trust** (see the boxed text, p281), Virupaksha goes about informing his fellow villagers about the benefits of sustainable ecotourism, and hopes that his village will wake to a new and prosperous dawn very soon. 'This place naturally casts its spell on you', he says. 'With a little bit of organisation, we can extend its charm to many more people, don't you think?'

A keen nature lover and photographer, Virupaksha also offers professional services related to camping, trekking, birdwatching and documentary filmmaking. He scouted for the 2005 Jackie Chan production *The Myth*, a part of which was shot in Hampi, and is now making a string of short films on Anegundi to upload on YouTube! So if you touch base at The Kishkinda Trust, get in touch with him for that really memorable excursion in Hampi's magical backyards. 'I'm also a trained snake-catcher; I rescue snakes trapped within the village and release them in the wilds', he grins. Feeling adventurous, anyone?

Sleeping & Eating

Hotel Malligi (☎ 228101; www.malligihotels.com; Jabunatha Rd; d with/without AC from Rs1500/650; ❄ 🖳 ☎) Only the more expensive rooms here are worth it. A couple of decent restaurants, a pool (Rs35 for nonguests and guests in the cheapest rooms) and a gym on-site.

Hotel Priyadarshini (☎ 228838; www.priyainhampi .com; Station Rd; s/d from Rs1300/1500; ❄ 🖳) Handily located between the bus and train stations, the fresh rooms here have balconies and TV. The outdoor non-veg restaurant-bar Manasa (mains Rs60 to Rs120) has a good menu.

Udupi Sri Krishna Bhavan (meals Rs15-45; ⏲ 6am-11pm) Opposite the bus stand, this clean spot dishes out Indian vegie fare, including thalis for Rs27.

Getting There & Away

BUS

The **bus stand** (☎ 228802) has services to Hampi from Bay 10 every half-hour (Rs 10, 30 minutes). Express buses run to Bengaluru (ordinary/deluxe Rs320/400, nine hours); two overnight buses go to Panaji (Rs215, 11 hours) via Margao.

Two buses go to Badami (Rs130, six hours), or take a bus to Gadag (Rs52, 2½ hours) and transfer. There are buses to Bijapur (Rs130, six hours) and overnight services to Hyderabad (Rs340, 10 hours). For Gokarna, take a bus to Hubli (Rs82, 4½ hours) and change. For Mangalore/Hassan, take a morning bus to Shimoga (Rs145, five hours) and change.

TRAIN

Hospet's **train station** (☎ 228360) is a Rs15 autorickshaw ride from town. The daily *Hampi Express* heads to Hubli at 7.50am (2nd class Rs43, 3½ hours) and then to Bengaluru at 7.50pm (sleeper/2AC Rs193/738, 10 hours). Every Monday, Wednesday, Thursday and Saturday, a 6.30am express heads to Vasco da Gama (sleeper/2AC Rs178/643, 8½ hours).

To get to Badami, catch a Hubli train to Gadag and change there.

HUBLI

☎ 0836 / pop 786,100

The prosperous city of Hubli is a hub for rail routes from Mumbai to Bengaluru, Goa and northern Karnataka. Several hotels and restaurants sit close to the train station; others surround the old bus stand, a 15-minute walk from the train station. Long-distance buses usually stop here before heading to the new bus stand 2km away, where there are few amenities.

Information

ATMs are easy to find. There are several internet cafes too, charging around Rs20 per hour.

Sleeping & Eating

Hotel Ajanta (☎ 2362216; Jayachamaraj Nagar; s/d from Rs150/210) This well-run place near the train station has basic, functional rooms. Its ground-floor restaurant (thalis Rs27) is packed at lunchtime.

Hotel Samrat Ashok (☎ 2362380; Lamington Rd; s/d from Rs425/810; 🍴) Above a bookshop on Lamington Rd, this tidy place is handy for both the train station and old bus stand.

Sagar Palace (Jayachamaraj Nagar; mains Rs30-70; 🕙 11am-3.30pm & 7-11.30pm) A pure-veg restaurant and bar serving good food, including rum-spiked ice-cream sundaes!

Getting There & Away

BUS

Long-distance buses depart from the **new bus stand** (☎ 2221085). There are numerous semideluxe services to Bengaluru (Rs370, 10 hours) and Hospet (Rs85, four hours); one bus goes daily to Mangalore (Rs331, 10 hours). Buses also head to Borivali in Mumbai (semideluxe/sleeper Rs484/531, 14 hours, four daily), Mysore (Rs231, 12 hours, one daily), Bijapur (Rs100, six hours, several daily), Gokarna (Rs92, five hours, two daily) and Panaji (Rs113, six hours, six daily), as well as Vasco da Gama and Margao.

Private deluxe buses to Bengaluru (Rs335) run from opposite the **old bus stand** (Lamington Rd), 2km away.

TRAIN

From the train station, which has a **reservation office** (☎ 2345333; 🕙 8am-8pm), three expresses head to Hospet (2nd class Rs47, 3½ hours). Five expresses run daily to Bengaluru (sleeper/2AC Rs241/936, 11 hours); and there's one direct train to Mumbai (sleeper/2AC Rs276/1026, 14 hours). Trains run on Monday, Wednesday, Thursday and Saturday

to Vasco de Gama (via Margao; sleeper/2AC Rs134/468, six hours).

NORTHERN KARNATAKA

BADAMI

☎ 08357 / pop 25,800

Now in a shambles, scruffy Badami is a far cry from its glory days, when it was the capital of the mighty Chalukya empire. Its importance lasted from the 6th to the 8th century AD, when the Chalukya kings shifted the capital here from Aihole, with a satellite capital in Pattadakal. The relocation of power saw Badami being scattered with several temples and, most importantly, a group of magnificent rock-cut cave temples, which are the main reason for coming to the village today.

History

Badami was the Chalukyan capital from about AD 540 to 757. At its height, the empire was enormous, stretching from Kanchipuram in Tamil Nadu to the Narmada River in Gujarat. Badami eventually fell to the Rashtrakutas, and changed hands several times thereafter. Everyone from the Chalukyas of Kalyan (a separate branch of the Western Chalukyas), the Kalachuryas, the Yadavas of Devagiri, the Vijayanagar empire, the Adil Shahi kings of Bijapur and the Marathas held sway over Badami in the years to come. The handing-down of Badami is chronicled by the numerous temples, fortifications, carvings and inscriptions that stand around the village, dating not just from the Chalukyan period but also from other times when the site was occupied.

The sculptural legacy left by the Chalukya artisans in Badami includes some of the earliest and finest examples of Dravidian temples and rock-cut caves. During Badami's heydays, Aihole and Pattadakal served as trial grounds for new temple architecture; the latter is now a World Heritage Site.

Orientation & Information

Station Rd, Badami's busy main street, has several hotels and restaurants; the old village is between this road and the hilltop caves. The **tourist office** (☎ 220414; Ramdurg Rd; 🕙 10am-5.30pm Mon-Sat), in the KSTDC Hotel Mayura Chalukya, is not very useful.

Mookambika Deluxe hotel changes currency for guests, but at a lousy rate.

Internet is available at **Hotel Rajsangam** (Station Rd; per hr Rs60) in the town centre.

State Bank of India has an ATM on Ramdurg Rd.

Sights
CAVES

Badami's highlight is its beautiful **cave temples** (Indian/foreigner Rs5/100; ☉ dawn-dusk). Non-pushy and informed guides ask Rs200 for a tour of the caves, or Rs300 for the whole site. Watch out for pesky monkeys!

Cave One

This cave, just above the entrance to the complex, is dedicated to Shiva. It's the oldest of the four caves, probably carved in the latter half of the 6th century. On the wall to the right of the porch is a captivating image of Nataraja striking 81 dance poses.

On the right of the porch area is a huge figure of Ardhanarishvara. The right half of the figure shows features of Shiva, such as matted hair and a third eye, while the left half has aspects of his wife Parvati. On the opposite wall is a large image of Harihara;

the right half represents Shiva and the left half Vishnu.

Cave Two

Dedicated to Vishnu, this cave is simpler in design. As with Caves One and Three, the front edge of the platform is decorated with images of pot-bellied dwarfs in various poses. Four pillars support the verandah, their tops carved with a bracket in the shape of a *yali* (mythical lion creature). On the left wall of the porch is the bull-headed figure of Varaha, an incarnation of Vishnu and the emblem of the Chalukya empire. To his left is Naga, a snake with a human face. On the right wall is a large sculpture of Trivikrama, another incarnation of Vishnu. The ceiling panels contain images of Vishnu riding Garuda, *gandharva* (demigod) couples, swastikas and 16 fish arranged in a wheel.

Between the second and third caves are two sets of steps to the right. The first leads to a **natural cave**, where resident monkeys laze around. The eastern wall of this cave contains a small image of Padmapani (an incarnation of the Buddha). The second set of steps – sadly, barred by a gate – leads to the hilltop **South Fort**.

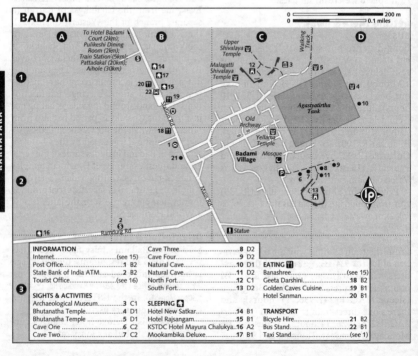

BADAMI

Cave Three

This cave, carved in AD 578 under the orders of Mangalesha, the brother of King Kirtivarma, contains some sculptural highlights.

On the left-hand wall is a carving of Vishnu, to whom the cave is dedicated, sitting on a snake. Nearby is an image of Varaha with four hands. The pillars have carved brackets in the shape of *yalis;* the sides are also carved. The ceiling panels contain images, including Indra riding an elephant, Shiva on a bull and Brahma on a swan.

Cave Four

Dedicated to Jainism, Cave Four is the smallest of the set and was carved between the 7th and 8th centuries. The pillars, with their roaring *yalis,* are of similar design to the other caves. The right wall has an image of Suparshvanatha (the seventh Jain *tirthankar*) surrounded by 24 Jain *tirthankars.* The inner sanctum contains an image of Adinath, the first Jain *tirthankar.*

OTHER SIGHTS

The caves overlook the 5th-century **Agastyatirtha Tank** and the waterside **Bhutanatha temples** (admission free). On the other side of the tank is an **archaeological museum** (☎ 220157; admission Rs2; ◷ 10am-5pm Sat-Thu), which houses superb examples of local sculpture, including a remarkably explicit Lajja-Gauri image of a fertility cult that once flourished in the area. The stairway just behind the museum climbs through a dramatic sandstone chasm and fortified gateways to reach the various temples and ruins of the **north fort** (admission free).

It's also worth exploring Badami's **laneways**, where you'll find old houses with brightly painted and carved wooden doorways, the occasional Chalukyan ruin and, of course, flocks of curious children.

Activities

Badami offers some great low-altitude climbing. For more information, see p278.

Sleeping

Many of Badami's hotels offer discounts in the low season.

Hotel New Satkar (☎ 220417; Station Rd; s/d from Rs250/350; ☒) Not the best of places, but at least the rooms are clean and the staff efficient. The best holes, painted in beige and cream, are on the 1st floor.

Mookambika Deluxe (☎ 220067; fax 220106; Station Rd; s/d from Rs350/550; ☒) Faux antique lampshades hang in the corridors of this friendly hotel, leading to comfy rooms done up in matte orange and green. It's Badami's de-facto tourist office, and can arrange taxis and guides.

KSTDC Hotel Mayura Chalukya (☎ 220046; Ramdurg Rd) This place with large and pleasant rooms, located in a quiet compound away from the bustle, was undergoing renovation at the time of research, and should be open by November 2009.

Hotel Rajsangam (☎ 221991; www.hotelrajsangam .com; Station Rd; d Indian/foreigner from Rs800/US$20; ☒ ▯ ▣) This midrange place with good rooms (the best are the quieter deluxe ones at the back) is a useful addition to Badami's hotel scene. The defunct plunge pool on the roof should be back in commission by now – brilliant views on offer here.

Hotel Badami Court (☎ 220230; Station Rd; s/d incl breakfast from Rs2500/3200; ☒ ▣) As good as it gets for Badami, this one sits in pastoral countryside 2km from the noisy town centre. Rooms are more functional than plush. Nonguests can use the pool for Rs100.

Eating

Geeta Darshini (Station Rd; snacks Rs6-15; ◷ 7am-9pm) South Indian bites such as *idlis* (South Indian spongy, round, fermented rice cakes) and *masala dosas* come out thick and fast at this popular joint, all washed down with milky chai (Rs5).

Golden Caves Cuisine (Station Rd; mains Rs30-80; ◷ 9am-11pm) Desperately missing your Continental breakfast platter? You'll find it here, along with several other tasty non-veg bites. The manager is a picture of politeness.

Hotel Sanman (Station Rd; mains Rs35-60; ◷ 10am-11.30pm) You might call it ropey, but it feels kind of nice to disappear behind a curtain in the booths and sip on your beer in peace. The food is average.

Banashree (Station Rd; mains Rs40-70; ◷ 7am-10.30pm) In front of Hotel Rajsangam, this tidy pure-veg place makes one of the best North Indian thalis (Rs65) to be found in these parts. It's tasty to the last morsel.

Pulikeshi Dining Room (mains Rs60-150; ◷ 24hr) People rave about the good range of Continental and Indian dishes at this silver-service restaurant in Hotel Badami Court.

Getting There & Away

Direct buses shuffle off from the Badami **bus stand** (Station Rd) to Bijapur (Rs84, four hours, two daily), Hubli (Rs65, three hours, seven daily) and Bengaluru (semideluxe/sleeper Rs276/453, 12 hours, four daily). Three buses go direct to Hospet (Rs130, six hours), or you can catch any of the buses to Gadag (Rs46, two hours) and transfer. The tarmac's rough down this lane; mind your bum!

The medium-gauge train line to Badami was being upgraded to broad-gauge during research. If and when it meets its 2009 deadline, direct trains should begin travelling to Hubli and Hospet.

Getting Around

Exploring the surrounding area by local bus is easy, since they're moderately frequent and usually run on time. You can visit both Aihole and Pattadakal in a day from Badami if you get moving early; it's best to start with Aihole (Rs18, one hour). Frequent buses then run between Aihole and Pattadakal (Rs12, 30 minutes), and from Pattadakal to Badami (Rs15, one hour). The last bus from Pattadakal to Badami is at 8pm. Take food and water with you.

Taxis cost around Rs800 for a day trip to Pattadakal, Aihole and Mahakuta. Badami's hotels can arrange taxis; alternatively, go to the taxi stand in front of the post office. You can hire bicycles from Station Rd in Badami for Rs10 per day.

AROUND BADAMI
Pattadakal

A secondary capital of the Badami Chalukyas, Pattadakal is known for its group of **temples** (☎ 08357-243118; Indian/foreigner Rs10/250; ⏰ 6am-6pm), which are collectively a World Heritage Site. Barring a few temples that date back to the 3rd century AD, most others in the group were built during the 7th and 8th centuries AD. Historians believe Pattadakal served as an important testing ground for the development of South Indian temple architecture.

Two main types of temple towers were tried out here. Curvilinear towers top the Kadasiddheshwara, Jambulinga and Galaganatha temples, while square roofs and receding tiers are used in the Mallikarjuna, Sangameshwara and Virupaksha temples.

The main **Virupaksha Temple** is a massive structure, its columns covered with intri-

cate carvings depicting episodes from the Ramayana and Mahabharata. A giant stone sculpture of Nandi sits to the temple's east. The **Mallikarjuna Temple**, next to the Virupaksha Temple, is almost identical in design. About 500m south of the main enclosure is the Jain **Papanatha Temple**, its entrance flanked by elephant sculptures. The temple complex also serves as the backdrop to the annual Classical Dance Festival (see boxed text, p236), held sometime between January and February.

Pattadakal is 20km from Badami. See left for transport details.

Aihole

Some 100 temples, built between the 4th and 6th centuries AD, dot the ancient Chalukyan regional capital of Aihole (ay-ho-leh). However, most are either in ruins or have been engulfed by the modern village. Aihole documents the embryonic stage of South Indian Hindu architecture, from the earliest simple shrines such as the most ancient Lad Khan Temple, to the later and more complex buildings, such as the Meguti Temple.

The most impressive of them all is the 7th century **Durga Temple** (☎ 08351-284533; Indian/foreigner Rs5/100; ⏰ 8am-6pm), notable for its semicircular apse (inspired by Buddhist architecture) and the remains of the curvilinear *sikhara* (temple spire). The interiors house intricate stone carvings. The small **museum** (admission Rs2; ⏰ 10am-5pm Sat-Thu) behind the temple contains further examples of Chalukyan sculpture.

To the south of the Durga Temple are several other temple clusters, including early examples such as the Gandar, Ladkhan, Kontigudi and Hucchapaya groups – pavilion type with slightly sloping roofs. About 600m to the southeast, on a low hillock, is the Jain **Meguti Temple**. Watch out for snakes!

The unappealing **KSTDC Tourist Home** (☎ 08351-284541; Amingad Rd; d/tr Rs300/500), 1km from the village centre, is the only accommodation in town. You're better off staying in Badami.

Aihole is about 40km from Badami. See left for transport information.

BIJAPUR
☎ 08352 / pop 253,900 / elev 593m

A fascinating open-air museum dating back to the Deccan's Islamic era, dusty and tattered Bijapur tells a faded but glorious tale that dates back some 600 years. Blessed with a heap of mosques, mausoleums, palaces and fortifications, the town is a must-visit on the historical circuit.

The capital of the Adil Shahi kings from 1489 to 1686, Bijapur was one of the five splinter states formed after the Bahmani Muslim kingdom broke up in 1482. Despite its strong Islamic character, Bijapur is also a centre for the Lingayat brand of Shaivism, which emphasises a single personalised god. The **Lingayat Siddeshwara Festival** runs for eight days in January/February.

Orientation

Bijapur's prime attractions, the Golgumbaz and the Ibrahim Rouza, are at opposite ends of town. Between them runs Station Rd (also known as MG Rd), dotted with the town's major hotels and restaurants. The bus stand is a five-minute walk from Station Rd; the train station is 2km east of the centre.

Information

Cyber Park (MG Rd; per hr Rs20; ☯ 9am-10pm) Internet access.

State Bank of India (☎ 251182; Station Rd; ☯ 10.30am-4.30pm Mon-Fri, 10.30am-1.30pm Sat) Changes travellers cheques and is super-efficient.

Tourist office (☎ 250359; Station Rd; ☯ 10am-5.30pm Mon-Sat) A poorly serviced office behind KSTDC Hotel Mayura Adil Shahi Annexe.

Sights

GOLGUMBAZ

Set in tranquil gardens, the magnificent **Golgumbaz** (☎ 240737; Indian/foreigner Rs5/100, video Rs25; ☯ 6am-5.40pm) is big enough to pull an optical illusion on you; despite the perfect engineering, you might just think it's ill-proportioned. Golgumbaz is actually a mausoleum, dating back to 1659, and houses the tombs of emperor Mohammed Adil Shah (r 1627–56), his two wives, his mistress (Rambha), one of his daughters and a grandson.

Octagonal seven-storey towers stand at each corner of the monument, which is capped by an enormous dome, 38m in diameter. In fact, it's said to be the largest dome in the world after St Peter's Basilica in Rome. Climb the steep, narrow stairs up one of the towers to reach the 'whispering gallery' within the dome. An engineering marvel, its acoustics are such that if you whisper into the wall, a person on the opposite side of the gallery can hear you clearly. Unfortunately people

like to test this out by hollering, so come early in the morning before any school groups or vocal tourists arrive.

Set in the lawns, fronting the monument, is a fantastic **archaeological museum** (admission Rs2; ☯ 10am-5pm Sat-Thu). Skip the ground floor and head upstairs; there you'll find an excellent collection of artefacts, such as Persian carpets, china crockery, weapons, armours, scrolls and objects of daily use, dating back to Bijapur's heydays.

IBRAHIM ROUZA

The beautiful **Ibrahim Rouza** (Indian/foreigner Rs5/100, video Rs 25; ☯ 6am-6pm) is clearly among the most elegant and finely proportioned Islamic monuments in India. Its tale is rather poignant: the monument was built by emperor Ibrahim Adil Shah II (r 1580–1627) as a future mausoleum for his queen, Taj Sultana. Ironically, he died before her, and was thus the first person to rest there. Interred here with Ibrahim Adil Shah and his queen are his daughter, his two sons, and his mother, Haji Badi Sahiba.

Unlike the Golgumbaz, which is impressive for its immensity, the emphasis here is on grace and architectural finery. Its 24m-high minarets are said to have inspired those of the Taj Mahal. For a tip (Rs150 is fine), caretakers will show you around the monument, including the dark labyrinth around the catacombs where the actual graves are located.

CITADEL

Surrounded by fortified walls and a wide moat, the **citadel** once contained the palaces, pleasure gardens and durbar (royal court) of the Adil Shahi kings. Now mainly in ruins, the most impressive of the remaining fragments is the **Gagan Mahal**, built by Ali Adil Shah I around 1561 as a dual-purpose royal residency and durbar hall.

The ruins of Mohammed Adil Shah's seven-storey palace, the **Sat Manzil**, are nearby. Across the road stands the delicate **Jala Manzil**, once a water pavilion surrounded by secluded courts and gardens. On the other side of Station Rd are the graceful arches of **Bara Kaman**, the ruined mausoleum of Ali Roza.

JAMA MASJID

The finely proportioned **Jama Masjid** (Jama Masjid Rd; ☯ 9am-5.30pm) has graceful arches, a fine dome and a vast inner courtyard with room for more than 2200 worshippers. It was

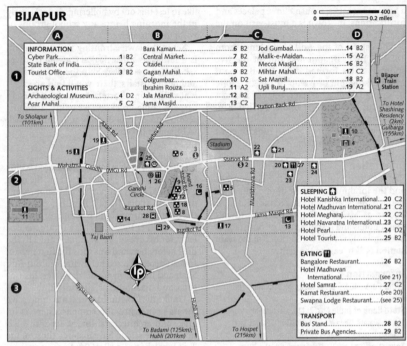

BIJAPUR

0 —————— 400 m
0 —————— 0.2 miles

INFORMATION			SIGHTS & ACTIVITIES	
Cyber Park	1 B2	Archaeological Museum	4 D2
State Bank of India	2 C2	Asar Mahal	5 C2
Tourist Office	3 B2		

Bara Kaman	6 B2
Central Market	7 B2
Citadel	8 B2
Gagan Mahal	9 B2
Golgumbaz	10 D2
Ibrahim Rouza	11 A2
Jala Manzil	12 B2
Jama Masjid	13 C2

Jod Gumbad	14 B2
Malik-e-Maidan	15 A2
Mecca Masjid	16 B2
Mihtar Mahal	17 C2
Sat Manzil	18 B2
Upli Buruj	19 A2

SLEEPING
Hotel Kanishka International	20 C2
Hotel Madhuvan International	21 C2
Hotel Megharaj	22 C2
Hotel Navaratna International	23 C2
Hotel Pearl	24 D2
Hotel Tourist	25 B2

EATING
Bangalore Restaurant	26 B2
Hotel Madhuvan International	(see 21)
Hotel Samrat	27 C2
Kamat Restaurant	(see 20)
Swapna Lodge Restaurant	(see 25)

TRANSPORT
| Bus Stand | 28 B2 |
| Private Bus Agencies | 29 B2 |

constructed by Ali Adil Shah I (r 1557–80), also responsible for erecting the fortified city walls and the Gagan Mahal. You can take a silent walk through its assembly hall, which still retains some of the elaborate murals. Women should make sure to cover their heads and not wear revealing clothing.

OTHER SIGHTS

On the eastern side of the citadel is the tiny, walled **Mecca Masjid** (admission free), thought to have been built in the early 17th century. Some speculate that this mosque, with high surrounding walls, may have been for women. Further east, the **Asar Mahal** (admission free), built by Mohammed Adil Shah in about 1646 to serve as a Hall of Justice, once housed two hairs from the Prophet Mohammed's beard. The rooms on the upper storey are decorated with frescoes, and a square tank graces the front. It's out of bounds for women. The stained but richly decorated **Mihtar Mahal** (admission free) to the south serves as an ornamental gateway to a small mosque.

Upli Buruj (admission free) is a 16th-century, 24m-high watchtower near the western walls of the city. An external flight of stairs leads

to the top, where you'll find two hefty cannons and good views of other monuments around town. A short walk west brings you to the **Malik-e-Maidan** (Monarch of the Plains), a huge cannon over 4m long, almost 1.5m in diameter and estimated to weigh 55 tonnes. Cast in 1549, it was supposedly brought to Bijapur as a war trophy thanks to the effort of 10 elephants, 400 oxen and hundreds of men!

In the southwest of the city, off Bagalkot Rd, stand the twin **Jod Gumbad** tombs with handsome bulbous domes; an Adil Shahi general and his spiritual adviser, Abdul Razzaq Qadiri, are buried here. The surrounding gardens are a popular picnic spot.

Don't forget to spend a few hours in Bijapur's colourful **central market**, with its spice sellers, florists and tailors.

Sleeping

Hotel Tourist (☎ 250655; MG Rd; d with/without TV Rs250/160) Bang in the middle of the bazaar, with scrawny (but clean) rooms. Service is apathetic, so bring that DIY manual along.

Hotel Megharaj (☎ 254458; Station Rd; d with/without AC Rs540/300; ❄) The cost-cutting is evident in the poor quality of the washrooms. But it's a friendly place, and the yellow and pink walls might just cheer you up!

Hotel Navaratna International (☎ 222771; fax 222772; Station Rd; d from Rs400; ❄) A touch of class is provided by paintings in the style of Kandinsky and Chagall that hang in the lobby here. Rooms are sparkling clean, with shiny floor tiles.

Hotel Pearl (☎ 256002; fax 243606; Station Rd; d Indian/foreigner from Rs450/600; ❄) Across the road from the Golgumbaz is this orderly business hotel, with a central atrium and clean, brightly painted rooms. Ask for one to the rear to avoid street noise.

Hotel Kanishka International (☎ 223788; fax 243131; Station Rd; s/d from Rs500/600; ❄) One of Bijapur's trusted options, this place has spacious and clean rooms, some with balconies. There's a small gym for guests' use, and the deal-maker is the excellent vegetarian restaurant downstairs.

Hotel Madhuvan International (☎ 255571; fax 256201; Station Rd; d from Rs600; ❄) Freshly renovated, this pleasant hotel boasts lime-green wall shades, tinted windows and an amiable management. The garden restaurant is a hit with locals, but watch out for those boisterous wedding receptions that are often thrown there!

Hotel Shashinag Residency (☎ 260344; www.hotel shashinagresidency.com; Sholapur-Chitradurga Bypass Rd; s/d incl breakfast Indian Rs650/1000, foreigner US$50/60; ❄ ▢ ❄) The most upmarket choice in Bijapur, this hotel has large rooms with frilly curtains and floral blankets! Bonuses are a small pool (Rs30 per hour for nonguests), a gym and a snooker room.

Eating

Unless otherwise mentioned, all places are open from around 6pm to 10pm.

Kamat Restaurant (Station Rd; mains Rs15-60; ❄ 9am-11pm) Below Hotel Kanishka International, this popular vegetarian eatery churns out superb food in clean surroundings. Try the elaborate and delicious Kamat special thali (Rs55).

Hotel Samrat (Station Rd; mains Rs15-60; ❄ 9am-11pm) On par with Kamat Restaurant and located just beside it, Samrat scores with its North Indian (Rs55) and South Indian (Rs44) thalis, which begin with tomato soup and end with ice cream!

Bangalore Restaurant (MG Rd; meals Rs20) This modest little pink-painted place does a decent

South Indian veg thali. Don't fuss over its skeletal appearance; just refuel and leave!

Swapna Lodge Restaurant (MG Rd; mains Rs30-110; ❄ 11am-11pm) It's located two floors up a dingy staircase in the building next to Hotel Tourist, and has good grub, cold beer and a 1970s lounge feel. Its open-air terrace is perfect for evening dining, though it does get a little noisy with the maddening traffic below.

Hotel Madhuvan International (Station Rd; mains Rs35-70) Delicious vegie food is served here either in the garden or inside in AC relief. Try the yummy *masala dosa* or the never-ending North Indian thalis dished out by waiters in red turbans. The downside is that you'll sorely miss the booze.

Getting There & Away

BUS

From the **bus stand** (☎ 251344), buses run direct to Bidar (Rs155, seven hours, four daily). Buses head frequently to Gulbarga (Rs85, four hours) and Hubli (Rs100, five hours). Three evening buses go to Bengaluru (Rs372, 12 hours) via Hospet (Rs100, five hours), four buses a day go to Hyderabad (ordinary/semideluxe Rs196/288, 10 hours), while two go to Pune (Rs226, 10 hours).

TRAIN

From **Bijapur train station** (☎ 244888), there are four daily passenger trains to Sholapur (Rs23, 2½ hours), which has connections to Mumbai, Hyderabad and Bengaluru. A daily express to Bengaluru (sleeper/2AC Rs286/1125, 17 hours) also passes through, as do 'fast passenger' trains to Mumbai (chair/sleeper Rs70/143, 12 hours, four weekly) and Hyderabad (sleeper Rs123, 15½ hours, daily).

Getting Around

Autorickshaws are oddly expensive in Bijapur, so be prepared to haggle. From the train station to the town centre should cost Rs60. Between the Golgumbaz and Ibrahim Rouza they cost about Rs40. Tonga drivers are eager for business but charge around the same. Autorickshaw drivers ask for about Rs250 for four hours around town.

GULBARGA

☎ 08472

Obscured from urban eyes, dusty Gulbarga wallows in neglect about 140km northeast of Bijapur, and is today only a faint shadow of its former self. Nonetheless, historians remember it as a thriving metropolis that once served as the capital city of the mighty Bahamani sultans. The history of the settlement goes way back to the 6th century, when the Rashtrakutas first came to power in the region. In 1347, while the region was still under the Delhi sultanate, a revolt broke out under the leadership of a general named Hassan Gangu, who seized power in the area and founded the Bahamani kingdom, with Gulbarga as its seat of power. However, the empire was to later shift its capital to Bidar (right), a move that robbed Gulbarga of much of its importance. Subsequently, in the early 16th century, the Bahamani empire disintegrated to form five independent sultanates, none of whom ever considered either relocating to Gulbarga or restoring it to its former glory.

Quite a few sites of historical importance now lie scattered around Gulbarga, though few are visited by outsiders. The 14th century **Gulbarga Fort** (admission free; ☾ dawn-dusk) is a must-see. Built by a Hindu king and later fortified by the Bahamani sultans, it is a fascinating heap of ruins, and houses the elegant **Jama Masjid** (admission free; ☾ dawn-dusk). Capped by a large dome to the west and four smaller domes on each of its corners, the medieval structure is known to have been designed by a Moorish architect along the lines of the Cordoba Mosque in Spain. You can also walk across town to its eastern quarters to visit the serene compound of **Haft Gumbaz**, which is studded by seven massive domes, each one being the mausoleum of an erstwhile Bahamian king. Gulbarga is also an important stop for Sufi pilgrims, who come here to pay their tributes at the dargah or **shrine** of 14th-century Sufi saint Khwaja Bande Nawaz Gesu Daraz, which stands about 2km northeast of the fort.

Most staying options in Gulbarga are rather basic, owing to an abject lack of tourists. You could try camping at **Hotel Pariwar** (☎ 221421; 1-73/1 Station Rd; s/d from Rs375/490, d with AC Rs1100; ❄), which offers clean and well-kept rooms and stands out for its friendly service.

Gulbarga is serviced by buses through the day which run to Bidar (Rs68, 2½ hours), Bijapur (Rs93, four hours) and Hyderabad (Rs115, eight hours). Four trains run from Gulbarga daily to Bengaluru (sleeper/2AC Rs281/996, 12 hours), while three trains go daily to Hyderabad (sleeper/2AC Rs128/448, five hours).

BIDAR

☎ 08482 / pop 174,200 / elev 664m

Tucked away in Karnataka's far northeastern corner, Bidar is a little gem that most travellers choose to ignore, and no one quite knows why. At most an afterthought on some itineraries, this old walled town – first the capital of the Bahmani kingdom (1428–87) and later the capital of the Barid Shahi dynasty – is drenched in history. That apart, it is home to some amazing ruins and monuments, including the colossal Bidar Fort – the largest fort in South India. Wallowing in neglect, Bidar sure commands more than the cursory attention it gets today.

Orientation & Information

The modern town centre is strung along Udgir Rd, down which you'll also find the bus station. Fast internet access is available at **Arien Computers** (per hr Rs20; ☾ 9.30am-10.30pm) near Hotel Krishna Regency, and at **iWeb World** (per hr Rs20; ☾ 11am-11pm), off Ambedkar Circle. There are several ATMs around town.

Sights
BIDAR FORT

Keep aside a few hours for peacefully wandering around the remnants of the magnificent 15th-century **Bidar Fort** (admission free; ☾ dawn-dusk). Sprawled across rolling hills 2km east of Udgir Rd, this fort was once the administrative capital of much of southern India. Surrounded by a triple moat hewn out of solid red rock and 5.5km of defensive walls (the

---

BIDRI: THE ART OF BIDAR

Highly prized for its intricate designs, *bidriware* is a traditional art-form that was invented around the 14th century by the Persian craftsmen of Bidar. Heavily influenced by medieval Islamic decorative motifs, *bidriware* is produced by moulding metals such as zinc, copper, lead and tin, and blackening them by applying a mixture containing dark clay typically found in the region. Then, after being embossed, the objects are overlaid or inlaid with pure silver. Finely crafted pieces, such as hookahs, goblets, and jewellery boxes, are exquisitely embellished with interwoven creepers and flowing floral patterns, occasionally framed by strict geometric lines.

THE LEGEND OF GAWAN

A key character behind the development and flourishing of the Bahamani empire was a man named Mahmud Gawan. Born in Iran in 1411, Gawan – originally a merchant by profession – first came to India in 1453 to trade in huge consignments of fabrics, jewels and horses he had brought with him. However, he soon found refuge in the Bahamani court, and in an odd twist of fate, was installed as an administrator. Not a man to baulk at challenges, Gawan quickly proved himself to be an able courtier, and was appointed chief minister in 1463. Under his direction, the empire reached its greatest size and supremacy. He executed successful military campaigns, and introduced administrative reforms which were intended to centralise power in a region where provincial governors often attempted to wrest autonomy from the sultanate. A noted educationist, he also established the Khwaja Mahmud Gawan Madrasa (below), aimed at furthering advanced religious and scientific studies in the empire.

Yet, despite all his achievements, Gawan scored few brownie points with his administrative colleagues, many of whom were of the opinion that he had been given undue privileges as a naturalised outsider. Dissent against Gawan built up rapidly, and in 1481, a group of conspirators brought trumped-up false charges against him, and convinced the emperor Muhammad III to try him for treason. Gawan was summarily convicted and executed, but the emperor soon realised his mistake, and allegedly grieved himself to death.

second longest in India), the fort has a fairy-tale entrance on a roadway that twists in an elaborate chicane through three gateways.

Inside the fort are many evocative ruins, including the **Rangin Mahal** (Painted Palace) which sports elaborate tilework, woodwork and panels with mother-of-pearl inlay, and the **Solah Khamba Mosque** (Sixteen-Pillared Mosque). There's also a small **museum** (admission free; ☾ 9am-5pm) in the former royal bath. Clerks at the **archaeological office** (☎ 230418) beside the museum often double as guides. It helps to ask one of them to show you around; for a small tip (Rs100 is fine) they can show you many hidden places within the fort that ordinarily remain locked.

BAHMANI TOMBS

The huge domed **tombs** (admission free; ☾ dawn-dusk) of the Bahmani kings, in Ashtur, 3km east of Bidar, have a desolate, moody beauty that strikes a strange harmony with the sunny hills around them. These impressive mausoleums were built to house the remains of the sultans – their graves are still regularly draped with fresh satin and flowers – and are arranged in a long line along the edge of the road. The painted interior of Ahmad Shah Bahman's tomb is the most impressive, and is regularly prayed in.

About 500m prior to reaching the tombs, to the left of the road, is **Choukhandi** (admission free; ☾ dawn-dusk), the serene mausoleum of Sufi saint Syed Kirmani Baba, who trav-elled here from Persia during the golden age of the Bahmani empire. An uncanny air of calm hangs within the monument, and its polygonal courtyard houses rows of medieval graves, amid which women in *hijab* sit quietly and murmur inaudible prayers. You are welcome to sit or walk around, and soak up the ambience.

Both places are best visited during afternoons, as it's difficult to find transport back to Bidar after dark.

OTHER SIGHTS

Dominating the heart of the old town are the ruins of **Khwaja Mahmud Gawan Madrasa** (admission free; ☾ dawn-dusk), a college built in 1492. To get an idea of its former grandeur, check out the remnants of coloured tiles on the front gate and one of the minarets that still stands intact.

Bidri artists (see opposite) still tap away at their craft in the back streets on and around Chowbara Rd, near Basveshwar Circle.

Sleeping & Eating

Don't expect much in the way of pampering – the best you can hope for is a clean room with AC and hot shower. Places listed below are all within a few minutes' walk of the bus stand.

Krishna Regency (☎ 221991; fax 228388; Udgir Rd; s/d from Rs350/450; ﹖) A friendly place by the bus stand that you can identify by the glass elevator running up outside. The rooms are

KARNATAKA

tidy though unimaginative. Some lack natural light, and there's no food available.

Sapna International (☎ 220991; fax 226824; Udgir Rd; s/d from Rs400/450; 🔀) On a par with the Krishna Regency in terms of rooms – but not as friendly. In its favour are its two restaurants: the pure-veg Kamat and the Atithi, which offers meat dishes and booze. Mains cost Rs25 to Rs70.

Hotel Mayura (☎ 228142; Udgir Rd; d with/without AC Rs550/350; 🔀) Across from the bus station and set back from the road is this non-fussy hotel, with rooms decent enough for a comfortable night's stay.

Jyothi Udupi (Udgir Rd; meals Rs20-45; 🕑 6.30am-11pm) This place opposite the bus stand has 21 kinds of dosa (Rs16 to Rs32), filling South Indian thalis (Rs25) and an ice-cream dessert called Easy Sunday!

Getting There & Away

From the **bus stand** (☎ 228508), frequent services run to Gulbarga (Rs65, three hours), which has good express-train connections to Mumbai and Bengaluru. Buses also run to Hyderabad (Rs70, four hours), Bijapur (Rs180, seven hours) and Bengaluru (semideluxe/AC Rs470/700, 12 hours).

The train station, around 1km southwest of the bus stand, has daily services to Hyderabad (2nd class/sleeper Rs27/80, 5½ hours) and Bengaluru (sleeper Rs295, 17 hours).

Getting Around

Rent a bicycle at **Sami Cycle Taxi** (Basveshwar Circle; per day Rs15; 🕑 7am-10pm) against your proof of identity. Or simply arrange a day tour in an autorickshaw for around Rs300.

Andhra Pradesh

Andhra Pradesh is not going to hit you over the head with its attractions. It doesn't brag about its temples or talk about its colourful history. It does not name streets after its long roster of enlightened beings. It's forgotten most of its palaces and royal architecture – the extreme wealth of most of the last 500 years is apparently no big deal – and if you don't purposely seek them out, they'll be missed. No, to travellers, Andhra Pradesh is not flirtatious.

Andhra prefers to play hard to get: its charms are subtle. But if you look closely, you'll find a long, fascinating history of arts and culture, spiritual scholarship and religious harmony. In Hyderabad's Old City, Islamic monuments, Persian-inspired architecture and the call of the muezzin speak of the city's unique history, created most notoriously by two wealthy family dynasties that loved Allah, diamonds and, above all, beauty.

Dig a little deeper and you'll find another Andhran history, peopled by the good life's renunciates: the region was an international centre of Buddhist thought for several hundred years from the 3rd century BC. Today ruins of stupas and monasteries defy impermanence at 150 sites around the state.

Meanwhile, deep in the countryside, more than eight million tribal people practise ancient religious, cultural and farming traditions, writing their own quiet history away from the compulsively modernising cities nearby.

So come, but only if you're prepared to dig: the jewels here have to be earned. But if you keep your eyes open and your curiosity sharp, you're bound to find something that even Andhrans, in their modesty, hadn't thought to mention.

HIGHLIGHTS

- Find out how many bangles and sequinned slippers one person can buy at Hyderabad's 400-year-old **Laad Bazaar** (p300)
- Absorb the meditative vibrations of monks past at **Sankaram** (p315), **Bavikonda** and **Thotlakonda** (p315), destinations on a 2300-year-old monastic trail
- Eat cotton candy, drink chai, and ride the kitschy Kailasagiri ropeway with local tourists at Visakhapatnam's **beaches** (p313)
- Get hypnotised by the lush intricacy and rich colours of kalamkari paintings in **Sri Kalahasti** (p320)
- Notice how death doesn't seem so bad before the sublime beauty of Hyderabad's **Paigah tombs** (p301) and **tombs of Qutb Shahi kings** (p301)

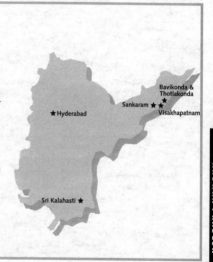

History

From the 2nd century BC, the Satavahana empire, also known as the Andhras, reigned throughout the Deccan plateau. It evolved from the Andhra people, whose presence in southern India may date back to 1000 BC. The Buddha's teaching took root here early on, and in the 3rd century BC the Andhras fully embraced it, building huge edifices in its honour. In the coming centuries, the Andhras would develop a flourishing civilisation that extended from the west to the east coasts of South India.

From the 7th to the 10th century the Chalukyas ruled the area, establishing their Dravidian style of architecture, especially along the coast. The Chalukya and Chola dynasties merged in the 11th century to be overthrown

> **FAST FACTS**
>
> **Population** 75.7 million
> **Area** 276,754 sq km
> **Capital** Hyderabad
> **Main languages** Telugu, Urdu, Hindi
> **When to go** September to February

by the Kakatiyas, who introduced pillared temples into South Indian religious architecture. The Vijayanagars then rose to become one of the most powerful empires in India.

By the 16th century the Islamic Qutb Shahi dynasty held the city of Hyderabad, but in 1687 was supplanted by Aurangzeb's Mughal empire. In the 18th century the post-Mughal

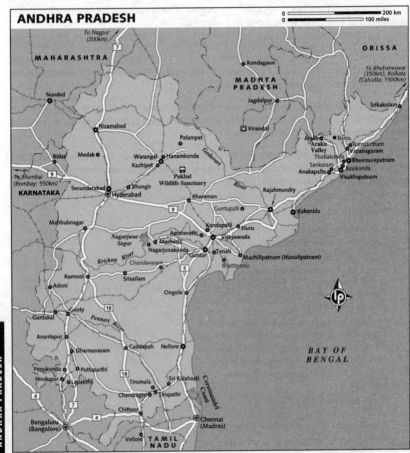

FESTIVALS IN ANDHRA PRADESH

Sankranti (Jan; statewide) This important Telugu festival marks the end of harvest season. Kite-flying abounds, women decorate their doorsteps with colourful *kolams* (or *rangolis* – rice-flour designs), and men decorate cattle with bells and fresh horn paint.

Industrial Exhibition (Jan/Feb; Hyderabad, below) A huge exhibition with traders from around India displaying their wares, accompanied by a colourful, bustling fair.

Deccan Festival (Feb; Hyderabad, below) Pays tribute to Deccan culture. Urdu *mushairas* (poetry readings) are held, along with Qawwali (Sufi devotional music) and other local music and dance performances.

Shivaratri (Feb/Mar; statewide) During a blue moon, this festival celebrates Shiva with all-night chanting, prayers and fasting. Hordes of pilgrims descend on the auspicious Shiva temples at Sri Kalahasti, Amaravathi and Lepakshi.

Muharram (Feb/Mar; Hyderabad, below) Muharram commemorates the martyrdom of Mohammed's grandson for 14 days in Hyderabad. Shiites wear black in mourning, and throngs gather at Mecca Masjid.

Ugadi (Mar; statewide) Telugu new year is celebrated with *pujas* (offerings or prayers), mango-leaf *toranas* (architraves) over doorways, and sweets and special foods.

Mahankali Jatra (Jun/Jul; statewide) A festival honouring Kali, with colourful processions in which devotees convey *bonalu* (pots of food offerings) to the deity. Secunderabad's Mahankali Temple goes wild.

Mrigasira (Jun/Jul; Hyderabad, below) Also known as Mrugam, this event marks the start of the monsoon with a feast of local fish and a fascinating medical treatment for asthma sufferers; more than 150 years old, it involves swallowing live fish that have consumed a herbal remedy. It's believed that the remedy was revealed by a sage to the ancestors of the physicians who now dispense it.

Batakamma (Sep/Oct; Hyderabad, below & Warangal, p312) Women and girls in the north of the state celebrate womanhood with dancing, feasting and making elaborate flower arrangements in honour of the goddess Batakamma, which they then set adrift on rivers.

Brahmotsavam (Sep/Oct; Tirumala, p318) Initiated by Brahma himself, the nine-day festival sees the Venkateshwara temple adorned in decorations. Special *pujas* and colourful chariot processions are a feature of the festivities, and it's considered an auspicious time for *darshan* (deity viewing).

Pandit Motiram–Maniram Sangeet Samaroh (Nov; Hyderabad, below) This four-day music festival, named for two renowned classical musicians, celebrates Hindustani music.

Lumbini Festival (2nd Fri in Dec; Hyderabad, below & p310) The three-day Lumbini Festival honours Andhra's Buddhist heritage.

Visakha Utsav (Dec/Jan; Visakhapatnam, p313) A celebration of all things Visakhapatnam, with classical and folk dance and music performances; some events are staged on the beach.

rulers in Hyderabad, known as nizams, retained relative control as the British and French vied for trade, though their power gradually weakened. The region became part of independent India in 1947, and in 1956 the state of Andhra Pradesh, an amalgamation of Telugu-speaking areas, plus the predominantly Urdu-speaking capital, was created.

Information

ACCOMMODATION

Hotels charge a 5% 'luxury' tax on all rooms over Rs300; it's not included in the prices quoted in this chapter. All hotels listed have 24-hour checkout unless stated otherwise.

HYDERABAD & SECUNDERABAD

☎ 040 / pop 5.5 million / elev 600m

Hyderabad, City of Pearls, is like an elderly, impeccably dressed princess whose time

has past. Once the seat of the powerful and wealthy Qutb Shahi and Asaf Jahi dynasties, the city has seen centuries of great prosperity and innovation. Today, the 'Old City' is full of centuries-old Islamic monuments and even older charms. In fact, the whole city is laced with architectural gems: ornate tombs, mosques, palaces and homes from the past are tucked away, faded and enchanting, in corners all over town. Keep your eyes open.

In the last decade, with the rise of Hyderabad's west side – our aged princess's sexy and popular granddaughter – a new decadence has emerged. 'Cyberabad', with Bengaluru (Bangalore) and Pune, is the seat of India's software dynasty and generates jobs, wealth and posh lounges like she was born to do it. Opulence, it seems, is in this city's genes.

A sizeable percentage of Hyderabad's population is Muslim, and the city is known for

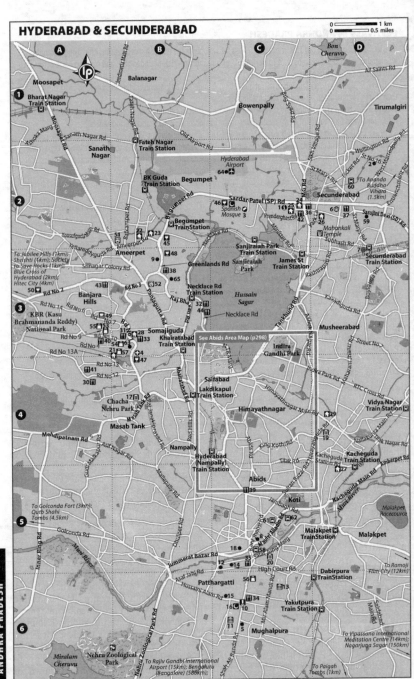

HYDERABAD & SECUNDERABAD

0 ————— 1 km
0 ————— 0.5 miles

its tolerance. You'll probably be taken aback by the chilled-out kindness of Hyderabadis, and many find the city delightful: lots to see and do with almost no hassle.

History

Hyderabad owes its existence to a water shortage at Golconda in the late 16th century. The reigning Qutb Shahis were forced to relocate, and so Mohammed Quli and the royal family abandoned Golconda Fort for the banks of the Musi River. The new city of Hyderabad was established, with the brand-new Charminar as its centrepiece.

In 1687 the city was overrun by the Mughal emperor Aurangzeb, and subsequent rulers of Hyderabad were viceroys installed by the Mughal administration in Delhi.

In 1724 the Hyderabad viceroy, Asaf Jah, took advantage of waning Mughal power and declared Hyderabad an independent state with himself as leader. The dynasty of the nizams of Hyderabad began, and the traditions of Islam flourished. Hyderabad became a focus for the arts, culture and learning, and the centre

of Islamic India. Its abundance of rare gems and minerals – the world-famous Kohinoor diamond is from here – furnished the nizams with enormous wealth. (Get a copy of William Dalrymple's *White Mughals* for a fascinating portrait of the city at this time.)

When Independence came in 1947, the then nizam of Hyderabad, Osman Ali Khan, considered amalgamation with Pakistan – and then opted for sovereignty. Tensions between Muslims and Hindus increased, however, and military intervention saw Hyderabad join the Indian union in 1948.

Orientation

Hyderabad has four distinct areas. The Old City by the Musi River has bustling bazaars and important landmarks, including the Charminar.

North of the river is Mahatma Gandhi (Imlibun) bus station, Hyderabad (Nampally) station and the main post office. Abids Rd runs through the Abids district, a good budget-accommodation area.

Further north, beyond the Hussain Sagar, lies the British-founded Secunderabad. Technically

ANDHRA PRADESH

it's Hyderabad's sister city, but it's generally considered part of the Hyderabad metropolitan area. Here you'll find Jubilee bus station and the huge Secunderabad train station.

Jubilee Hills and Banjara Hills, west of Hussain Sagar, are where the well heeled – and their restaurants, shops and lounges – reside, and further west is Cyberabad's capital,

Hitec (Hyderabad Information Technology Engineering Consulting) City.

Information
BOOKSHOPS
On Sunday, second-hand books are sold on Abids Rd; a few gems nestle among the computer books.

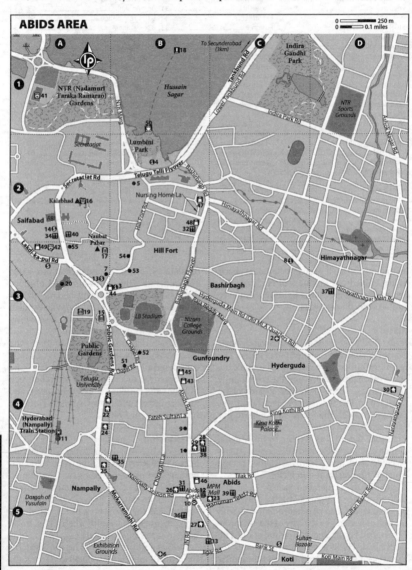

ABIDS AREA

0 — 250 m
0 — 0.1 miles

AA Husain & Co (Map p298; ☎ 23203724; Abids Rd; ⓥ 10am-8.30pm Mon-Sat) Heaps of Indian and foreign authors.

MR Book Centre (Map p298; ☎ 23205684; Abids Rd; ⓥ 10am-9pm) New and second-hand novels; magazines from back home.

Walden Banjara Hills (Map p296; ☎ 23551613; Trendset Towers, Rd No 2; ⓥ 10.30am-9pm); Begumpet (Map p296; ☎ 23413434; Greenlands Rd; ⓥ 9am-9pm) Hyderabad's megastore.

CULTURAL CENTRES & LIBRARIES
Alliance Française (Map p296; ☎ 27700734; www.afindia.org; St No 16, West Marredpally, Secunderabad; ⓥ 9am-1pm & 2-6pm Mon-Fri, 9am-1pm Sat)

British Library (Map p298; ☎ 23483333; www.britishcouncilonline.org; Secretariat Rd; ⓥ 11am-7pm Tue-Sun) Membership costs Rs1200.

Goethe-Zentrum (Map p298; ☎ 65526443; www.goethe.de/hyderabad; Hill Fort Rd; ⓥ 9.30am-5pm Mon-Sat)

State Library (Map p296; ☎ 24600107; Maulvi Allaudin Rd; ⓥ 8am-8pm Fri-Wed) Beautiful old building with 700,000 books.

INTERNET ACCESS
Both Hyderabad (Map p298) and Secunderabad stations (Map p296) have a **Railtel Cyber Express** (per hr Rs23; ⓥ 9am-7pm).

Reliance Web World (Map p298; ☎ 30339991; MPM Mall, Abids Circle; per 3hr Rs100; ⓥ 9am-10pm)

LEFT LUGGAGE
All three train stations, as well as Mahatma Gandhi bus station, have left-luggage facilities, charging Rs10 per bag per day, or Rs15 for a locker.

MEDIA
Good 'what's on' guides include *Channel 6*, *GO Hyderabad* and *City Info*. The juiciest is **Wow! Hyderabad** (www.wowhyderabad.com; Rs25). The *Deccan Chronicle* is a good local paper; its *Hyderabad Chronicle* insert has info on happenings.

MEDICAL SERVICES
Apollo Pharmacy (Map p298; ☎ 23431734; Hyderguda Main Rd; ⓥ 24hr) Delivers.

Care Hospital Banjara Hills (Map p296; ☎ 30418888; Rd No 1); Nampally (Map p298; ☎ 66517777; Mukarramjahi Rd) Reputable hospital with a 24-hour pharmacy.

Mor Chemists (☎ 23297111; Bashirbagh Rd; ⓥ 10am-9pm Mon-Sat) Helpful and well-stocked.

MONEY
The banks offer the best currency-exchange rates here. ATMs are everywhere.

ANDHRA PRADESH

State Bank of India (Map p298; ☎ 23231986; HACA Bhavan, Saifabad; ⏰ 10.30am-4pm Mon-Fri)
Thomas Cook (Map p298; ☎ 23296521; Nasir Arcade, Saifabad; ⏰ 9.30am-6pm Mon-Sat) Changes travellers cheques with no commission.

POST
Post office (⏰ 8am-8.30pm Mon-Sat, 10am-6pm Sun) Secunderabad (Map p296; Rashtrapati Rd); Abids (Map p298; Abids Circle)

TOURIST INFORMATION
Andhra Pradesh Tourism Development Corporation (APTDC; ☎ 24-hr info 23450444; www.aptdc.in; ⏰ 7am-8pm) Bashirbagh (Map p298; ☎ 23298456; NSF Shakar Bhavan, opposite Police Control Room); Secunderabad (Map p296; ☎ 27893100; Yatri Nivas Hotel, SP Rd); Tankbund Rd (Map p298; ☎ 65581555) Organises tours.
Indiatourism (Government of India; Map p298; ☎ 23261360, 23260770; Netaji Bhavan, Himayathnagar Rd; ⏰ 9.30am-6pm Mon-Fri, to noon Sat) Information for Hyderabad and beyond.

Sights
CHARMINAR & BAZAARS
Hyderabad's principal landmark, the **Charminar** (Four Towers; Map p296; Indian/foreigner Rs5/100; ⏰ 9am-5.30pm) was built by Mohammed Quli Qutb Shah in 1591 to commemorate the founding of Hyderabad and the end of epidemics caused by Golconda's water shortage. Standing 56m high and 30m wide, the dramatic four-column structure has four arches facing the cardinal points. Minarets sit atop each column. The 2nd floor, home to Hyderabad's oldest mosque, and upper columns are not usually open to the public, but you can try your luck with the man with the key. The structure is illuminated from 7pm to 9pm.

West of the Charminar, the incredible, crowded **Laad Bazaar** (Map p296) is the perfect place to get lost. It has everything from fine perfumes, fabrics and jewels to musical instruments, second-hand saris and kitchen implements. Artisans are tucked away creating jewellery and scented oils, large pots and burkas. The lanes around the Charminar also form the centre of India's pearl trade. Some great deals can be had – if you know your stuff.

SALAR JUNG MUSEUM
The huge collection of the **Salar Jung Museum** (Map p296; ☎ 24523211; Salar Jung Marg; Indian/foreigner Rs10/150; ⏰ 10am-5pm Sat-Thu), dating back to the

1st century, was put together by Mir Yusaf Ali Khan (Salar Jung III), the grand vizier of the seventh nizam, Osman Ali Khan (r 1910–49). The 35,000 exhibits from every corner of the world include sculptures, wood carvings, devotional objects, Persian miniature paintings, illuminated manuscripts, weaponry and more than 50,000 books. The impressive nizams' jewellery collection is sometimes on special exhibit. Cameras are not allowed. Avoid visiting the museum on Sunday when it's bedlam. From any of the bus stands in the Abids area, take bus 7, which stops at Afzal Gunj bus stop on the north side of the nearby Musi River bridge.

Just west of the bridge are the spectacular **Osmania General Hospital** (Map p296), on the north side, and, on the south, the **High Court** (Map p296) and **Government City College** (Map p296) buildings, all built under the seventh nizam in the Indo-Saracenic style.

CHOWMAHALLA PALACE
In their latest act of architectural showmanship, the nizam family has sponsored a restoration of this dazzling **palace** (Khilwat; Map p296; ☎ 24522032; www.chowmahalla.com; Indian/foreigner Rs25/150, camera Rs50; ⏰ 10am-5pm Sat-Thu) – or, technically, four (char) palaces (mahalla). Begun in 1750, it was expanded over the next 100 years, absorbing Persian, Indo-Saracenic, Rajasthani and European styles. The southern courtyard has one mahal with period rooms that have been reconstructed with the nizams' over-the-top furniture; another mahal with an exhibit on life in the zenana (women's quarters) that includes bejewelled clothes, carpets and a bride palanquin; antique cars (one nizam allegedly used a Rolls Royce as a garbage can); and curiosities like elephant seats, a clock with a miniature dancing band, and a Remington Urdu typewriter.

In the northern courtyard is the Khilwat Mubarak, a magnificent durbar hall where nizams held ceremonies under 19 enormous chandeliers of Belgian crystal. Today the hall houses exhibitions of photos, arms and clothing. Hung with curtains, the balcony over the main hall once served as seating for the family's women, who attended all durbars in purdah.

HEH THE NIZAM'S MUSEUM
The 16th-century Purani Haveli was home of the sixth nizam, Fath Jang Mahbub Ali Khan

(r 1869–1911), rumoured to have never worn the same thing twice. His 72m-long, two-storey wardrobe of Burmese teak is on display at this **museum** (Purani Haveli; Map p296; ☎ 24521029; adult/student Rs70/15; ⏰ 10am-5pm Sat-Thu). Also on exhibit, in the palace's former servants' quarters, are personal effects of the seventh nizam and gifts from the Silver Jubilee celebration of his reign. The pieces are unbelievably lavish and include some exquisite artwork. The museum's guides do an excellent job putting it all in context.

The rest of Purani Haveli is now a school, but you can wander around the grounds and peek in the administrative building, the nizam's former residence.

GOLCONDA FORT
Although most of this 16th-century **fortress** (off Map p296; ☎ 23513984; Indian/foreigner Rs5/100; ⏰ 9am-6pm) dates from the time of the Qutb Shah kings, its origins, as a mud fort, have been traced to the earlier reigns of the Yadavas and Kakatiyas.

Golconda had been the capital of the independent state of Telangana for nearly 80 years when Sultan Quli Qutb Shah abandoned the

GOLCONDA FORT
0 ___ 200 m
0 ___ 0.1 miles

Suggested Route

To Qutb Shahi Tombs (1.5km)

Well

Bus Stand

Tank

Nagina Bagh

Mortuary Baths

Grand Portico

Entrance

Barracks

Ambar Khana

Viewpoint

Balahisar Gate

Mahakali Temple

Ramdas Jail

Arsenal

Ibrahim Masjid

Taramati Mosque

Durbar Hall

Camel Stables

Dad Mahal

Fountain

Tank

Harem

Rani Mahal

Shahi Mahal

Langer Khana

Approximate Scale

fort in 1590 and moved to the new city of Hyderabad.

In the 17th century, Mughal armies from Delhi were sent to the Golconda kingdom to enforce payment of tribute. Abul Hasan, last of the Qutb Shahi kings, held out at Golconda for eight months against Emperor Aurangzeb's massive army. The emperor finally succeeded with the aid of a treacherous insider.

It's easy to see how the Mughal army was nearly defeated. The citadel is built on a granite hill, 120m high and surrounded by crenellated ramparts constructed from large masonry blocks. Outside the citadel there stands another crenellated rampart, with a perimeter of 11km, and yet another wall beyond this. The massive gates were studded with iron spikes to obstruct war elephants.

Survival within the fort was also attributable to water and sound. A series of concealed glazed earthen pipes ensured a reliable water supply, while the acoustics guaranteed that even the smallest sound from the Grand Portico would echo across the fort complex.

Knowledgeable guides around the entrance charge Rs500 for a 1½-hour tour. Check for their shirt badge, or better yet, go through the AP Tourism table in front of the entrance. Small guidebooks to the fort are also sold near the entrance.

An autorickshaw from Abids costs around Rs150. Mornings are best for peace and quiet.

A trippy **sound-and-light show** (admission Rs50; ⏰ English version 6.30pm Nov-Feb, 7pm Mar-Oct) is also held here.

QUTB SHAHI TOMBS
These graceful domed **tombs** (off Map p296; admission Rs20, camera/video Rs20/100; ⏰ 9am-5pm) sit serenely in landscaped gardens about 1.5km northwest of Golconda Fort's Balahisar Gate. You could easily spend half a day here taking photos and wandering in and out of the mausoleums and various other structures. The upper level of Mohammed Quli's tomb, reached via a narrow staircase, has good views of the area. *The Qutb Shahi Tombs* (Rs20) is sold at the ticket counter.

The tombs are an easy walk from the fort, but an autorickshaw ride shouldn't be more than Rs25. Bus 80S also stops right outside.

PAIGAH TOMBS
The aristocratic Paigah family, purportedly descendents of the second Caliph of Islam,

were fierce loyalists of the nizams, serving as statespeople, philanthropists and generals under and alongside them. From 1797, the two families began intermarrying as well, solidifying their close bond. The Paigahs' **necropolis** (off Map p296; Phisalbanda, Santoshnagar, 🕑 9am-5pm), tucked away in a quiet neighbourhood 4km southeast of the Charminar, is a small compound of exquisite mausoleums made of marble and lime stucco. The main complex contains 27 tombs with intricate inlay work, surrounded by delicately carved walls and canopies, stunning filigree screens with geometric patterning and, overhead, tall, graceful turrets. The tombs are down a small lane across from Owasi Hospital. Look for the Preston Junior College sign. *The Paigah Tombs* (Rs20) booklet is sold at the AP State Museum (below), but not here.

BUDDHA STATUE & HUSSAIN SAGAR

Hyderabad has one of the world's largest free-standing **Buddha statues** (Map p298), completed in 1990 after five years of work. However, when the 17.5m-high, 350-tonne monolith was being ferried to its place in the **Hussain Sagar** (Map p298), the barge sank. Fortunately, the statue was raised – undamaged – in 1992 and is now on a plinth in the middle of the lake.

Frequent **boats** (adult/child Rs45/25) make the 30-minute return trip to the statue from both **Eat Street** (Map p296; 🕿 9848354440; 🕑 2-9pm) and **Lumbini Park** (Map p298; 🕿 65510372; admission Rs5; 🕑 9am-9pm), a pleasant place to enjoy sunsets and the popular musical fountain. The Tankbund Rd promenade, on the eastern shore of Hussain Sagar, has great views of the Buddha statue.

AP STATE & HEALTH MUSEUMS

The continually renovated **AP State Museum** (Map p298; 🕿 23232267; Public Gardens Rd, Nampally; admission Rs10, camera/video Rs100/500; 🕑 10.30am-5pm Sat-Thu) hosts a collection of important archaeological finds from the area, as well as a Buddhist sculpture gallery, with some relics of Buddha and an exhibit on Andhra Pradesh's Buddhist history. The ever-expanding museum also houses Jain and bronze sculpture galleries, a decorative-arts gallery, an exhibition of paintings by Lahore painter AR Chughtai, and an Egyptian mummy. The museum, like the gorgeous **Legislative Assembly building** (Map p298) down the road

(both commissioned by the seventh nizam), is floodlit at night.

Also in the Public Gardens area is the **Health Museum** (admission free; 🕑 10.30am-5pm Sat-Thu), where you'll see a bizarre collection of medical and public-health paraphernalia.

NEHRU CENTENARY TRIBAL MUSEUM

Andhra Pradesh's 33 tribal groups, based mostly in the northeastern part of the state, comprise several million people. This **museum** (Map p296; 🕿 23391270; Masab Tank; admission free; 🕑 10.30am-5pm Mon-Sat), run by the government's Tribal Welfare Department, exhibits photographs, dioramas of village life, musical instruments and some exquisite Naikpod masks. It's basic, but you'll get a glimpse into the cultures of these fringe peoples. There's a small, interesting library here, and next door is the tiny Girijan Sales Depot, selling products made in tribal communities. Both are across from Chacha Nehru Park.

MECCA MASJID

This **mosque** (Map p296; Shah Ali Banda Rd, Patthargatti; 🕑 9am-5pm) is one of the world's largest, with space for 10,000 worshippers. Women are not allowed inside.

Construction began in 1614, during Mohammed Quli Qutb Shah's reign, but the mosque wasn't finished until 1687, by which time the Mughal emperor Aurangzeb had annexed the Golconda kingdom. Several bricks embedded above the gate are made with soil from Mecca – hence the name. To the left of the mosque, an enclosure contains the tombs of Nizam Ali Khan and his successors.

Since the 2007 bomb blasts here, security is tight; no bags are allowed inside.

BIRLA MANDIR & PLANETARIUM

The Birla **temple** (Map p298; 🕑 7am-noon & 2-9pm), constructed of white Rajasthani marble in 1976, graces Kalabahad (Black Mountain), one of two rocky hills overlooking the Hussain Sagar. Dedicated to Venkateshwara, it's a popular Hindu pilgrimage centre and affords excellent views over the city, especially at sunset. The library here is worth a visit (open 4pm to 8pm).

Next door are the **Birla Planetarium & Science Museum** (Map p298; 🕿 23235081; museum/planetarium Rs20/25; 🕑 museum 10.30am-8pm, till 3pm Fri, planetarium shows 11.30am, 4pm, 6pm) and the **Birla Modern Art Gallery** (Map p298; admission Rs10; 🕑 10.30am-6pm).

RAMOJI FILM CITY

Movie fans can't miss the four-hour tour of **Ramoji Film City** (off Map p296; ☎ 23412262; www.ramojifilmcity.com; adult/child Rs300/250; ☉ 9.30am-5.30pm), an 800-hectare movie-making complex for Telugu, Tamil and Hindi films. This place has everything – dance routines, gaudy fountains, flimsy film sets – and the whole thing wraps up with a Wild West song-and-dance number. Buses 205 and 206 from Koti Women's College, northeast of Koti station, take an hour to get here.

PT REDDY ART MUSEUM

The late PT Reddy (1915–96) was a prolific painter whose art career spanned 60 years and many styles. He is best-known for his neo-Tantric work, full of hypnotic symmetries and evocative symbols. Many of his paintings, along with several others by major Andhran contemporary artists, are on display at this **museum** (☎ 9440652340, 27561866; http://ptreddy.org/introduction.html; Narayanguda Main Rd), also known as Sudharma, which is his former home. His daughter, Lakshmi, offers tours on weekends; call for an appointment.

Activities

The Theravada **Ananda Buddha Vihara** (Map p296; ☎ 27733160; www.buddhavihara.in; Mahendra Hills; ☉ 6am-12.30pm & 4-8.30pm) is the first South Indian monastery to emerge in Andhra Pradesh after a lapse of 1000 years. It will eventually include an art museum and a library, but at the time of writing, only the temple – on a hill with incredible views – was complete. Meditation sessions are held daily at 6am and chanting at 7pm; Sunday meditation is at 4pm, followed by a Dharma talk. And the friendly monks are available anytime to give instruction. Call to inquire about special programs.

To get here, take East Maredpally Main Rd through Trimurthy Colony. An autorickshaw from Abids will cost around Rs100.

Courses

The **Vipassana International Meditation Centre** (off Map p296; Dhamma Khetta; ☎ 24240290; www.khetta.dhamma.org; Nagarjuna Sagar Rd, 12.6km) has intensive 10-day meditation courses at its peaceful grounds 20km outside the city. Apply online or at the Hyderabad **office** (☎ 24732569). A shuttle runs to/from Hyderabad on the first and last day of courses.

Tours

APTDC (see p300) conducts tours of the city (Rs270), Ramoji Film City (Rs500), Nagarjuna Sagar (weekends, Rs450) and Tirupathi (three days, Rs1750). The Sound & Light tour (Rs200) takes in Hitec City, the botanic gardens and Golconda Fort's sound-and-light show, but you may spend much of it in traffic.

Society To Save Rocks (off Map p296; ☎ 23552923; www.saverocks.org; 1236 Rd No 60, Jubilee Hills) organises monthly walks through the Andhran landscape and its surreal-looking boulders.

Sleeping

Rooms tend to fill up, so call ahead.

BUDGET

Youth Hostel Hyderabad (Map p298; ☎ 66758393; www.yhaindia.org; YMCA Circle, Narayanguda; dm/d Rs80/300; 🏠) There doesn't seem to be a reception desk here, per se, and the staff may be confused by your presence – all a bit mysterious, really. But it's clean, damn cheap and worth exploring if you don't mind the 10pm curfew and 8am checkout. It's opposite the Shanti Theatre.

Hotel Suhail (Map p298; ☎ 24610299; www.hotelsuhail.in; Troop Bazaar; s/d/tr from Rs375/475/650; 🏠) If all budget hotels were like the Suhail, we'd all be much better off. Staff is friendly and on top of it, and rooms are large and quiet and have balconies and constant hot water. It's tucked away on an alley behind the main post office and the Grand Hotel – away from the Hyderabad bustle, but it's also unlit at night; some readers find it sketchy.

Hotel Sri Brindavan (Map p298; ☎ 23203970; fax 23200204; Nampally Station Rd; s/d from Rs400/600; 🏠) Sri Brindavan is full of staff who don't speak English and curious gents in tank tops who look like they should be doing something else. But put that aside for now. It's great value and (unwittingly) has style: the curved balconies and lemon-yellow paint are vaguely art deco. Rooms are tidy and compact, the grounds leafy and the AC rooms in the back are so peaceful, you'll almost forget you're in Abids.

Nand International (Map p296; ☎ 24657511; www.nandhotels.com; Kacheguda Station Rd; s/d/tr from Rs450/550/650; 🏠) The Nand is a pleasant surprise near Kacheguda Station. It has a roof garden (with chai on order and potted geraniums), sitting areas and water coolers on each floor, and well-looked-after peach rooms hung with weird mixed-media art.

Hotel Gaayatri Resiidency (Map p298; ☎ 66742288; Public Gardens Rd; s/d from Rs600/750; ☒) It's called Gaayatri Resiidency and not Gayatri Residency for numerology reasons. If you stay here, then, consider yourself protected. And there are other curiosities, like the surveillance TV in the restaurant. But otherwise, the Gaayatri's a straightforward place. Rooms don't win the prize for best personality, but they're neat and have subtle touches like top sheets. It's right near Nampally station.

Hotel Jaya International (Map p298; ☎ 24752929-39; hoteljaya2007@yahoo.com; Hanuman Tekdi Rd; s/d from Rs650/750; ☒) The Jaya's capacious, sunny rooms have stained-glass lamps and arched balconies with apple-green trim and tree views. It all blends harmoniously to create a Brady-Bunch-meets-the-Mughals look. It's also clean as anything and runs like a champion. But you absolutely must book ahead.

Hotel Rajmata (Map p298; ☎ 66665555; fax 23204133; Public Gardens Rd; s/d Rs690/790; ☒) A recent reno freshened the Rajmata up and added huge and shiny (but overpriced) AC rooms. Since the place is set back from Public Gardens Rd, rooms are quiet – but some are better than others so check out a few. Staff is very professional, and there's a helpful travel desk. The place is popular with families.

Two budget Taj Mahal Hotels (there are 11 brothers) just east of the heritage Taj (see right) on King Kothi Rd are shabby but well run, with a dash of character. **Taj Mahal Hotel (#2)** (Map p298; ☎ 40048484; fax 66827373; King Kothi Rd; s/d from Rs650/1000; ☒) is better value and just behind **Taj Mahal Hotel (#3)** (Map p298; ☎ 24758221; fax 24760068; King Kothi Rd; r from Rs600; ☒).

If you arrive late at Secunderabad train station, try their good-deal **retiring rooms** (dm/s/d from Rs100/250/450; ☒).

MIDRANGE
APTDC (p300) can help arrange rooms from Rs1000 in private homes.

Hotel Ambassador (Map p296; ☎ 27843760; fax 27899095; SD Rd, Secunderabad; s/d from Rs850/1000; ☒) At the possibly misnomered Paradise Circle, the Ambassador's doorman (yes, it has a doorman) will show you to reception, where friendly staff will greet you under arty halogen lights. Non-AC rooms face environmentally challenged SD Rd, unfortunately, but they're compact, tidy and well tended to. AC rooms are a step up: a little bigger and a lot quieter. Convenient for Secunderabad station.

ourpick Taj Mahal Hotel (Himayathnagar) (Map p296; ☎ 27637836-9; tajcafe@gmail.com; Himayathnagar; s/d from Rs900/1200; ☒) Don't everybody all go here – we don't want them to get cocky – but this Taj is, for now, Hyderabad's best deal. Despite its unfortunate location in front of an overpass on Himayathnagar Rd, it's a peaceful, sunny, stylish place where the staff are warm and welcoming and the hallway floors look like Jaipuri marble. Rooms are surprisingly tasteful, with sleek lamps and chunky, contemporary wooden furniture. Comfy and classy for less than the going rate.

Taj Mahal Hotel (Map p298; ☎ 24758250, 66511122; fax 24758253; cnr Abids & King Kothi Rds; s/d with AC from Rs1050/1475; ☒) This rambling 1924 heritage building has a magnificent exterior, plants peppered about, and some exceedingly charming rooms. Each is different so ask to see a few: the better ones have boudoirs, crystal-knobbed armoires and wood-beam ceilings. The standard singles are small, with less personality, but all rooms are peaceful.

Athidhi Guesthouse (Map p296; ☎ 9246544051; www.athidhiguesthouse.com; Rd No 13A, Happy Valley Rd, Banjara Hills; s/d with AC incl breakfast Rs1200/1500; ☒) Rooms in Athidhi's three-bedroom serviced apartments, on a tranquil lane in chichi Banjara Hills, are homey, spotless and close to Hyderabad's best shopping and dining (but not transport).

Hotel Harsha (Map p298; ☎ 23201188; www.hotel harsha.net; Public Gardens Rd; s/d incl AC & breakfast from Rs1400/1600; ☒) The formerly budget Harsha now aspires to being high class. Rooms don't have tonnes of character, but they're bright, with fridges, the furniture is in good taste and the art is a step up from the usual schlock. The overall effect is polished but comfy. The lobby smells like success, with lots of glass and marble. One of the city's best deals.

Yatri Nivas Hotel (Map p296; ☎ 23461855; SP Rd, Secunderabad; s/d with AC incl breakfast Rs1400/1600; ☒) Indian families mill about the Yatri Nivas compound, which is set back from the road among lots of trees strung with lights. Meanwhile, back at the room, your remote control, soap, coconut oil and towel sit in an obedient pile on your bed. The hotel is practically its own small town, which is a good thing since SP Rd is kind of horrible. This way, you don't technically have to leave campus: there's an ice-cream parlour, a shop, three restaurants and a bar, and the APTDC office is just out front.

Athithi Inn (Map p296; ☎ 23739091-8; www.athithi
inn.com; DK Rd, Ameerpet; s/d with AC incl breakfast from
Rs2000/2200; 🛰) Overpriced, but with an enchanting, over-the-top South Indian design
scheme: colonnaded hallways, unusual antique furniture in suites, and golden swings
in the rooftop restaurant.

Other good options:

Hotel Saiprakash (Map p298; ☎ 24611726; www
.hotelsaiprakash.com; Nampally Station Rd; s/d with AC
from Rs1400/1600; 🛰) Good value, but slipping.

Hotel Annapoorna Residency (Map p296;
☎ 27891221/22/33; www.annapoornaresidency.com;
PG Rd, Paradise, Secunderabad; s/d with AC incl breakfast
Rs1400/1550; 🛰) A miracle in Paradise: organised, clean,
and downright tranquil in a nonparadisial neighbourhood
of honking autorickshaws, rushing people and screaming
mopeds.

Hotel Minerva (Map p298; ☎ 66994747; minerva@
nettlinx.com; Himayatnagar; r with AC from Rs1875;
🛰) Almost perfect, but could be better maintained.

TOP END

The following have central AC, wi-fi access, complimentary breakfast and noon
checkout.

Green Park (Map p296; ☎ 66515151; www.hotelgreen
park.com; Greenlands Rd, Begumpet; s/d from Rs5250/6250;
🛰 💻) Don't bother going beyond the
standard rooms here, which are comfy and
classy, with flower petals in the bathroom
and bamboo flooring. The lobby is a paragon
of peace and gentle lighting, while smiley
staff look on.

Minerva Grand (Map p296; ☎ 66117474; www.minerva
grand.com; SD Rd, Secunderabad; s/d from Rs4000/4400;
🛰 💻) It's rare to find a hotel that has genuine style; the Minerva Grand has nailed it.
Standard rooms (one wheelchair-accessible)
have striking deep-fuchsia walls, white furniture, tasselled bedspreads and piles of pillows.
More expensive rooms are similarly bold in
design, and all rooms have hardwood floors,
gentle lighting and sleek, spacious bathrooms.
A diamond in the rough of SD Rd.

ITC Hotel Kakatiya (Map p296; ☎ 23400132; www
.itcwelcomgroup.in; Begumpet; s/d from Rs16,500/18,000;
🛰 💻 🍽) All rooms here have hardwood
or lushly carpeted floors, interesting art
like architectural drawings of Kakatiya-era
buildings, and a homey sumptuousness. But
the Sheraton Towers rooms have the most
character, with pewter onion-dome posts on
furniture, silver-legged bathroom furniture
and other touches that evoke a bygone nizam's

> **BEATING THE BHATTIS**
>
> If you're travelling around Andhra Pradesh
> during Ramadan (known locally as Ramzan),
> look out for the clay ovens called *bhattis*.
> You'll probably hear them before you see
> them. Men gather around, taking turns to
> vigorously pound *haleem* (a mixture of
> meat, ghee, wheat and spices) inside pur-
> pose-built structures. Come nightfall, the
> serious business of eating begins. The taste
> is worth the wait.

palace. Downstairs the pool has wicker chaise
longues surrounded by palms.

Taj Krishna (Map p296; ☎ 66664242; www.tajhotels
.com; Rd No 1, Banjara Hills; s/d from Rs22,000/23,500;
🛰 💻 🍽) The gardens of the Taj Krishna are
where Hyderabad's beautiful people come to
have their fashion shows. But they're likely to
be upstaged by the lush, artful gardens. Or the
rooms, with their elegant furniture, antique
parquet floors, and piles of taffeta pillows. The
opulence you expect for the price.

Eating

Andhra Pradesh's cuisine has two major influences. The Mughals brought tasty biryanis,
haleem (pounded, spiced wheat with mutton;
see the boxed text, above) and kebabs. The
Andhra style is vegetarian and famous for
its spiciness.

Per local usage, we use the term 'meal' instead of 'thali' in this chapter.

CITY CENTRE

Mozamjahi Market (Map p296; cnr Mukarramjahi &
Jawaharlal Nehru Rds; ☽ 6am-6pm) A great place to
buy fruit and veggies (or ice cream), while
enjoying the alluring architecture of the stone
building, commissioned by the seventh nizam
and named after his son.

G Pulla Reddy (Map p296; Patthargatti; sweets Rs8-25
☽ 10am-9pm) Sweets so good you'll die. Also has
branches in Abids (Map p298) and Begumpet
(Map p296).

Karachi's (Map p298; Mahaprabhu House, JN Rd; snacks
Rs12-40; ☽ 11.30am-10.30pm) A tacky, fun fast-food
joint with good *chaat* (snacks), vegie burgers,
pizza and the enigmatic 'Chinese dosa'.

Kamat Hotel (Map p296; SD Rd, Secunderabad; mains
Rs45-75; ☽ 7.30am-10pm) How much do we love
Kamat Hotel? Words can't say. Each Kamat
is slightly different, but they're all cheap and

good. There are two branches on SD Rd; the others are in Saifabad and on Nampally Station Rd (Map p298). Meals (from Rs36) are reliably delish.

Kamat Andhra Meals (Map p298; Troop Bazaar; meals Rs45; noon-3.30pm & 7-10.30pm) Excellent authentic Andhra meals on banana leaves, topped up till you almost faint with pleasure, and finished off with a banana. Its sister restaurants in the same compound – Kamat Jowar Bhakri (Maharashtran), Kamat Restaurant (North and South Indian) and Kamat Coffee Shop – are likewise friendly family joints full of happy diners. No relation to Kamat Hotel.

Sagar Papaji Ka Dhaba (Map p298; Hanuman Tekdi Rd; mains Rs45-110; noon-4pm & 7-11pm) Always busy, Papaji's has profoundly delicious veg and nonveg biryanis, curries and tikkas. Watch the guys making naan and throwing it in the tandoor while you wait for a table.

Hotel Shadab (Map p296; High Court Rd, Patthargatti; mains Rs60-145; noon-2am) One meal at Shadab and you'll be forever under its spell. The hopping restaurant is *the* place to get biryani and, during Ramadan, *haleem* (see p305). It has even mastered veg biryani (!) and hundreds of other veg and nonveg delights (if you try the chocolate chicken or pineapple mutton, let us know how it goes). Packed with Old City families and good vibes.

Minerva Coffee Shop (Map p298; Himayathnagar Rd; mains Rs105-150; 7am-10.30pm) You can depend on this old-school coffee shop with contemporary decor for excellent meals, dosas (thin lentil pancakes) and masala chai (Rs27). Both this and the Somajiguda branch (Map p296) are popular with old friends catching up over lunch.

Palace Heights Restaurant & Bar (Map p298; ☎ 24754483; 8th fl, Triveni Complex; mains Rs165-275; 12-11pm) This pearl in the dirty shell of an old city-centre building has a palatial interior and incredible views. The service is excellent, the booze relatively cheap and the nonveg menu – steak, pulau, tandoori, Chinese, Continental – extensive.

Gufaa (Map p298; ☎ 23298811; Ohri's Cuisine Court, Bashirbagh Rd; mains Rs175-275; 11.30am-3.30pm & 7pm-midnight) The eccentric Gufaa has faux-rock walls with African masks, leopard-print upholstery, twinkling stars on the ceiling and red roses on the tables. And it serves Peshawari food. But somehow it works, and even 'dhal with roti' (black dhal stewed with fresh cream and tomatoes, and roti made with chillies) is extraordinary here.

Waterfront (Map p296; ☎ 65278899; Necklace Rd; mains Rs175-450; noon-11pm) Just next to Eat Street, the outdoor deck here on the water (dinner service only) may have the best ambience in all of Hyderabad, with soft lighting overhead and the Buddha Statue, the entire Hussain Sagar and the Birla Mandir all twinkling in the distance. Eating indoors, alongside enormous picture windows, isn't bad either. But it's the Chinese, Indian and Thai food that's to die for – their take on *phad kea mou* (noodles with tasty bok choy) is a must-eat.

Eat Street (Map p296; Necklace Rd; 7am-11pm) This food court has good coffee and fast food, kids' rides, boat launches to the Buddha Statue (see p302) and tables on a waterfront boardwalk. It could be cheesy, but instead it's delightful.

Also recommended:

Paradise Persis Restaurant (Map p296; ☎ 27843115; cnr SD & MG Rds, Secunderabad; mains Rs125-200; 11am-11pm) Ask any Hyderabadi about biryani, and they'll mention Paradise.

Ming's Court (Map p298; ☎ 23298811; Ohri's Cuisine Court, Bashirbagh Rd; mains Rs190-280; 11.30am-3.30pm & 7pm-midnight)

Sukha Sagara (Map p298; AG's Office Rd; mains Rs65-110; 7am-10pm)

BANJARA HILLS

Ofen (Map p296; ☎ 23372205; Rd No 10; desserts Rs15-110; 8am-11pm) Two words: Linzer torte. Scrumptious desserts (even some vegan and sugar-free), fresh-baked bread and comfort food like sandwiches and pasta (Rs90 to Rs195).

Le Café d'Art (Map p296; ☎ 65506661/2; Rd No 1; light meals Rs115-185; 9am-11pm) Beautiful young people come here to smoke hookahs (Rs250) in antique-chic surrounds. We like it for the salads, sandwiches and espresso, though the service charge – for slow service – is a downer.

Angeethi (Map p296; ☎ 66255550; 7th fl, Reliance Classic Bldg, Rd No 1; mains Rs150-275; 12.30-3.30pm & 7-10.30pm) The setting, designed to resemble an old Punjabi *dhaba* (snack bar), is over the top. But Angeethi does truly outstanding North Indian and Punjabi dishes, such as corn *methi malai* (sweet-corn stew with fenugreek leaves; Rs170).

Fusion 9 (Map p296; ☎ 65577722; Rd No 1; mains Rs325-425; 12-3.30pm & 7pm-midnight) Soft lighting and cosy decor set off pan-fried Norwegian salmon (Rs750) or Brazilian tenderloin steak (Rs1200). There's also (less expensive) Mexican, Thai, pizzas and veg dishes and lots of imported liquor.

Healthy people will appreciate **24-Lettered Mantra** (Map p296; ☎ 23300303; Rd No 12; ◷ 9.30am-9.45pm), a tiny grocery shop with organic produce, snacks and juices.

Other recommendations:

Southern Spice (Map p296; ☎ 23353802; Rd No 2; mains Rs85-260; ◷ 12.15-3.30pm & 7.15-10.30pm) Spicy goodness.

Ohri's Far East (Map p296; ☎ 23302200; Rd No 12; mains Rs185-350; ◷ 12.30-3.30pm & 7-11.30pm) Pan-Asian.

Drinking
CAFES

Café Coffee Day (Map p296; Eat Street, Necklace Rd; coffees Rs28-85; ◷ 7.30am-11pm)

Barista (Map p296; Rd No 1, Banjara Hills; coffees Rs30-95; ◷ 8am-10pm)

Mocha (Map p296; Rd No 7, Banjara Hills; coffees Rs30-180, light meals Rs75-150; ◷ 9am-11pm) Full of 20-somethings smoking hookahs. The decor, the garden and the coffee are fabulous.

BARS & LOUNGES

Hyderabad's scene is growing, but drinking establishments are limited by a midnight-curfew law. Unless stated otherwise, the following are open noon to midnight (but don't get going till 9pm). All serve food and charge covers (Rs500 to 1000) on certain nights – for couples, that is: guys usually need a gal to enter. Beer starts at Rs150, cocktails at Rs300.

Liquids Again (Map p296; ☎ 66259907; Bhaskar Plaza, Rd No 1, Banjara Hills) Regularly featured in the papers' society pages, Liquids is the reigning queen of Hyderabad nightlife.

Touch (Map p296; ☎ 23542422; Trendset Towers, Rd No 2, Banjara Hills) Touch is all about image. It's a stylish, comfy place to watch the beautiful people.

Awana (Map p296; ☎ 23300427; Rd No 12, Banjara Hills) Awana has fun theme nights and a low-key restaurant next door.

Marco Polo Bar (Map p296; ☎ 23400132; ITC Hotel Kakatiya, Ameerpet) With views of the pool and palm trees, stools with antler-esque backrests, and old maps of the world, it's the perfect place for a twilight drink. The ITC also has Dublin, a popular 'Irish' pub.

Begumpet bars club on weekends:

10 Downing Street (Map p296; ☎ 66629323; My Home Tycoon Bldg)

Bottles & Chimney (Map p296; ☎ 27766464; SP Rd)

Entertainment
ARTS

Ravindra Bharati Theatre (Map p298; ☎ 23233672; www.artistap.com; Public Gardens Rd) Regular music, dance and drama performances. Check local papers.

Hyderabad has a burgeoning contemporary-art scene:

ICCR Art Gallery (Map p298; ☎ 23236398; Ravindra Bharati Theatre, Public Gardens Rd; ◷ 11am-7pm)

Kalakriti (Map p296; ☎ 66564466; www.kalakriti.in; Rd No 10, Banjara Hills; ◷ 11am-7pm)

Shrishti (off Map p296; ☎ 23540023; www.shrishtiart .com; Rd No 15, Jubilee Hills; ◷ 11am-7pm)

CINEMA

Mega-cinemas have taken over Hyderabad's English-language movie scene:

Prasad's Multiplex (Map p298; ☎ 23448989, booking 39895050; www.prasadz.com; NTR Marg) A monstrous IMAX theatre.

PVR Cinemas (Map p296; ☎ 66621115; www.pvr cinemas.com; Hyderabad Central, Panjagutta Rd)

Hyderabad Film Club (Map p296; ☎ 9391020243; Ameerpet Rd) Shows foreign films, sometimes in conjunction with the Alliance Française (p299). Membership is Rs750.

Shopping

The bazaars near the Charminar (see p300) are the most exciting places to shop: you'll find exquisite pearls, silks, gold and fabrics alongside billions of bangles.

Hyderabad Perfumers (Map p296; ☎ 24577294; Patthargatti; ◷ 10am-8pm Mon-Sat) The family-run Hyderabad Perfumers, which has been in business for four generations, can whip something up for you on the spot.

Meena Bazar (Map p298; ☎ 24753566; Tilak Rd; ◷ 10.30am-8.30pm Mon-Sat) Gorgeous saris, *salwar* (trouser) suits and fabrics at fixed prices. Even if you're not in the market, come here to sightsee.

Kalanjali (Map p298; ☎ 23423440; Public Gardens Rd; ◷ 10am-9.30pm Mon-Sat) With a huge range of arts, crafts, fabrics and clothing, Kalanjali has higher prices than the bazaar, but you can get a feel for what things cost in a relaxed environment.

Sangeet Sagar (Map p298; ☎ 23225346; Bashirbagh Rd; ◷ 10.30am-9pm Mon-Sat) Great little music shop.

Nursing Home Lane is a sweet little street with kurta stores and our favourite bangle shop,

New Fashion Ladies Emporium (Map p298; ☎ 66688867; Bashirbagh; ⏰ 11am-10pm Mon-Sat, 2-10pm Sun).

A world away in Banjara Hills, Rd No 4 has several high-end boutiques worth visiting. **Creative Bee** (Map p296; ☎ 23357887; ⏰ 11am-7.30pm Mon-Sat) has subtle cotton fabrics ready to be coordinated and taken to the tailor, while both **GoodluM's** (Map p296; ☎ 9848555821; ⏰ 10.30am-7.30pm Mon-Sat) and the cooperative **United Designers** (Map p296; ☎ 9866155189, 9966950503; ⏰ 10.30am-8pm) have exciting designs by a new wave of young Hyderabadi fashion designers. Expect to pay Rs1000 and up per piece.

Other places for crafts and clothes:

Anokhi (Map p296; ☎ 23350271; Rd No 10, Banjara Hills; ⏰ 10.30am-7.30pm Mon-Sat) Sophisticated clothes in hand-block prints.

Bidri Crafts (Map p298; ☎ 23232657; Gunfoundry; ⏰ 11am-9pm Mon-Sat)

Fabindia (Map p296; ☎ 23354526; Rd No 9, Banjara Hills; ⏰ 10am-9pm Tue-Sun) Hip clothes in traditional artisanal fabrics.

Lepakshi (Map p298; ☎ 23212902; Gunfoundry; ⏰ 10am-8pm Mon-Sat) Andhra crafts.

Utkalika (Map p296; ☎ 23240510; Lakdi-ka-pul; ⏰ 11am-7.30pm Mon-Sat) A tiny Orissa State Emporium with some lovely saris, fabrics & handicrafts.

Getting There & Away

Hyderabad's massive new **Rajiv Gandhi International Airport** (☎ 66546370, 1800 4192008; http://hyderabad.aero) is 22km southwest of the city in Shamshabad.

AIR

You'll get the best fares online or with a travel agent. Try **Neo Globe Tours & Travels** (Map p298; ☎ 66751786; Saifabad; ⏰ 10am-7.30pm Mon-Sat) beside the Nizam Club.

Airline offices are generally open from 9.30am to 5.30pm Monday to Friday, with a one-hour lunch break, and to 1.30pm Saturday.

Domestic Airlines

GoAir (☎ airport 9223222111, 1800 222111; Rajiv Gandhi International Airport)

Indian Airlines (Map p298; ☎ 23430334, 1800 1801407, airport 24255161/2; HACA Bhavan, Saifabad)

IndiGo (Map p298; ☎ 23233590, airport 24255052; Interglobe Air Transport, Chapel Rd; ⏰ 8.30am-6pm Mon-Sat)

Jet Airways (Map p298; ☎ 39824444, airport 39893322; Hill Fort Rd; ⏰ 9am-7pm Mon-Sat) Also handles bookings for JetLite.

JetLite (☎ call centre 30302020, 1800 223020; Rajiv Gandhi International Airport)

Kingfisher Airlines (Map p298; ☎ 23210985/8, 1800 2333131; Summit House, Hill Fort Rd)

Paramount Airways (☎ airport 66605220-2, 1800 1801234; Rajiv Gandhi International Airport)

SpiceJet (Map p296; ☎ 27904796, 1800 1803333; Begumpet)

International Airlines

Air India (Map p298; ☎ 1800 227722, airport 24255161/2; HACA Bhavan, Saifabad)

Cathay Pacific (Map p296; ☎ 27704310; SD Rd, Secunderabad)

Emirates (Map p296; ☎ 66234444; Rd No 1, Banjara Hills)

GSA Transworld Travels (Map p298; ☎ 66102781; Chapel Rd) For Qantas.

Interglobe Air Transport (Map p298; ☎ 23233590; Chapel Rd) For Air New Zealand, Delta, South African, Turkish, United and Virgin Atlantic.

KLM (☎ airport 66605102; Rajiv Gandhi International Airport)

Lufthansa (Map p296; ☎ 44331000; Begumpet) Next to the Lifestyle Building.

Qatar Airways (Map p296; ☎ 0124 4566000; Rd No 1, Banjara Hills)

Sri Lankan Airlines (Map p296; ☎ 23372429/30; Raj Bhavan Rd, Somajiguda) Opposite the Yashoda Hospital.

Thai Airways (Map p296; ☎ 23333030; Rd No 1, Banjara Hills)

BUS

Hyderabad's long-distance bus stations are mind-bogglingly efficient. **Mahatma Gandhi bus**

MAJOR DOMESTIC FLIGHTS FROM HYDERABAD			
Destination	**Lowest one-way fare (Rs)**	**Duration (hr)**	**Flights per day**
Bengaluru	3500	1	18
Chennai	3500	1	20
Delhi	5700	2	24
Kolkota	6000	2	16
Mumbai	3500	1¼	22
Tirupathi	3500	1	3
Visakhapatnam	3500	1	10

ANDHRA PRADESH

BUSES FROM IMLIBUN

Destination	Fare (Rs)	Duration (hr)	Departures (daily)
Bengaluru	358/695	12/10	34 (evening)
Bidar	70	4	half-hourly
Chennai	390-660	12	5 (evening)
Hospet	305	12	10
Mumbai	430/810	16/12	8 (evening)
Mysore	480	13	4
Nagarjuna Sagar	63-85	4	8
Tirupathi	255-560	12	12
Vijayawada	160-275	6	half-hourly
Warangal	65	3	half-hourly

station (Map p296; ☎ 24614406, 23434268/80), better known as Imlibun, has **advance booking offices** (🕐 8am-11pm). For trips to Karnataka, go with **KSRTC** (☎ 24656430).

Secunderabad's **Jubilee bus station** (Map p296; ☎ 27802203) operates Volvo AC buses to Bengaluru (Rs685, 10 hours, three daily), Chennai (Rs700, 12 hours, one daily) and Visakhapatnam (Rs701, 13 hours, one daily).

Private bus companies with AC services are on Nampally High Rd, near the train station entrance.

TRAIN

Secunderabad (Map p296), Hyderabad (Map p298) – also known as Nampally – and Kacheguda (Map p296) are the three major train stations. Most through trains stop at Secunderabad and Kacheguda, which is convenient for Abids. See the boxed text, p310, for key routes. You can book at Hyderabad and Secunderabad stations from 8am to 8pm Monday to Saturday (to 2pm Sunday). Both stations have a tourist counter. For general inquiries, phone ☎ 131; for reservation status, ☎ 135.

Getting Around
TO/FROM THE AIRPORT

The new airport is fabulous, but until the express highway is completed, it's a 1½-hour schlep from town. Free shuttle buses run to the airport's Public Transportation Centre (PTC).

Bus

Frequent public buses depart from the PTC for Jubilee and Imlibun stations. More comfy are AC **Aeroexpress** (☎ 1800 4192008; Rs120-150; 🕐 24hr) buses, which run half-hourly to five loca-

tions: Charminar, Secunderabad, Begumpet, Mehdipatnam, and Hitec City.

Taxi

For prepaid taxis, pay at the counter inside the terminal, then get your cab at the PTC. **Meru** (☎ 44224422) and **Easy** (☎ 43434343) 'radio taxis' queue up outside arrivals and charge Rs15 per kilometre, Rs18.75 at night. The trip to Abids or Banjara Hills shouldn't exceed Rs450. Going to the airport, try **Yellow Taxi** (☎ 44004400).

AUTORICKSHAW

Flag fall is Rs12 for the first kilometre, then Rs7 for each additional kilometre. Between 10pm and 5am a 50% surcharge applies. Unfortunately, the new electronic meters often don't work and lots of drivers won't use them: be prepared to negotiate.

BUS

Lots of local buses originate at **Koti bus station** (Map p296; ☎ 23443320; Rani Jhansi Rd), so if you come here you might get a seat. The 'travel as you

MAJOR BUS ROUTES FROM HYDERABAD & SECUNDERABAD

Bus No	Route
20D	Jubilee station–Nampally
1P/25	Secunderabad station–Jubilee station
2/2V, 8A/8U	Charminar–Secunderabad station
1K, 1B, 3SS, 40	Secunderabad station–Koti
20P, 20V, 49, 49P	Secunderabad station–Nampally
65G/66G	Charminar–Golconda, via Abids
87	Charminar–Nampally
1190R, 142M	Nampally–Golconda
142K	Koti–Golconda

MAJOR TRAINS FROM HYDERABAD & SECUNDERABAD

Destination	Train No & Name	Fare (Rs)	Duration (hr)	Departure Time & Station
Bengaluru	2430 *Rajdhani*	3AC/2AC 1065/1410	12	6.50pm Secunderabad (Tue, Wed, Sat & Sun)
	2785 *Secunderabad–Bangalore Exp*	sleeper/3AC/2AC 291/731/1036	11	7.05pm Kacheguda
Chennai	2604 *Hyderabad–Chennai Exp*	sleeper/3AC/2AC 301/792/1076	13	4.55pm Hyderabad
	2760 *Charminar Exp*	sleeper/3AC/2AC 317/837/1139	14	6.30pm Hyderabad
Delhi	2723 *Andhra Pradesh Exp*	sleeper/3AC/2AC 473/1275/1747	26	6.25am Hyderabad
	2429 *Rajdhani*	3AC/2AC 1725/2245	26	7.50am Secunderabad (Mon, Tue, Thu & Fri)
Kolkata	2704 *Falaknuma Exp*	449/1208/1653	26	4pm Secunderabad
	8646 *East Coast Exp*	sleeper/3AC/2AC 437/1200/1654	30	10am Hyderabad
Mumbai	2702 *Hussainsagar Exp*	sleeper/3AC/2AC 317/837/1139	15	2.45pm Hyderabad
	7032 *Hyderabad–Mumbai Exp*	sleeper/3AC/2AC 297/807/1109	16	8.40pm Hyderabad
Tirupathi	2734 *Narayanadri Exp*	sleeper/3AC/2AC 288/756/1026	12	6.05pm Secunderabad
	2797 *Venkatadri Exp*	sleeper/3AC/2AC 281/704/996	12	8.05pm Kacheguda
Visakhapatnam	2728 *Godavari Exp*	sleeper/3AC/2AC 299/785/1106	13	5.15pm Hyderabad

like' ticket (ordinary/express Rs28/40), available from bus conductors, permits unlimited travel anywhere within the city on the day of purchase. The tiny *City Bus Route Guide* (Rs10) is available at bookshops around Koti.

CAR
There are several car-rental places around Hyderabad station. **Links Travels** (☎ 9348770007, 9885460531) is reliable for local or long-distance day rental.

TRAIN
MMTS trains are convenient, particularly for the three main train stations. There are two main lines: Hyderabad (Nampally) to Lingampalli (northwest of Banjara Hills) has 11 stops, including Lakdikapul, Khairatabad, Necklace Rd, Begumpet and Hitec City; the Falaknuma (south of Old City) to Begumpet line passes by Yakutpura, Dabirpura, Malakpet, Kacheguda and Secunderabad, among others. Trains will be labelled with their start and end point: so, HL is Hyderabad–Lingampalli, FS is Falaknuma–Secunderabad and so on. Trains are efficient but only run every 30 to 40 minutes. Tickets are Rs2 to Rs7.

NAGARJUNAKONDA
☎ 08680
The Hill of Nagarjuna, 150km southeast of Hyderabad, is a peaceful island in the mid-

dle of the Nagarjuna dam peppered with ancient Buddhist structures. From the 3rd century BC until the 4th century AD, the Krishna River valley was home to powerful empires that supported the sangha (Buddhist community of monks and nuns), including the Ikshvakus, whose capital was Nagarjunakonda. It's estimated that this area alone had 30 monasteries.

The remains here were actually discovered in 1926 by archaeologist AR Saraswathi in the adjacent valley. In 1953, when it became known that a massive hydroelectric project would soon create the **Nagarjuna Sagar** reservoir, flooding the area, a six-year excavation was launched to unearth the area's many Buddhist ruins: stupas, *viharas*, *chaitya-grihas* (assembly halls with stupas) and *mandapas* (pillared pavilions), as well as some outstanding examples of white-marble depictions of the Buddha's life. The finds were reassembled on Nagarjunakonda.

AP Tourism (☎ 276634; ⊗ 9am-6pm Mon-Sat) has an office at Project House, across from the bus stand.

Sights
NAGARJUNAKONDA
The thoughtfully laid-out **Nagarjunakonda Museum** (Indian/foreigner Rs5/100; ⊗ 9.30am-3.45pm Sat-Thu) has Stone Age tools on exhibit, but more exciting are its Buddha statues and

carved stone slabs that once adorned stupas. Most are from the 3rd century AD and depict scenes from the Buddha's life, interspersed with *mithuna* (paired male and female) figures languorously looking on. The re-assembled **monuments** are spread around the hilltop outside.

Launches (Rs75, one hour) depart from Vijayapuri, on the banks of Nagarjuna Sagar, at 9.30am and 1.30pm, and stay for one hour. To do the place justice, take the morning launch out and the afternoon one back. Extra morning launches usually run on weekends and holidays.

NAGARJUNA SAGAR
Buddha Park
Construction has slowed on this APTDC project 2km north of the Nagarjuna Sagar bus stand, but if completed, it will be a 285-

acre park dedicated to Buddhism in Andhra Pradesh. It's slated to include a Garden of Stupas, with large models of the state's many stupas; the eponymous Buddha Park; and a museum on local Buddhist history. At the time of writing, only the meditation centre, **Dhamma Nagajjuna** (☎ 9440139329; www.dhamma nagajjuna.org; Hill Colony), is functioning, hosting one intensive 10-day *vipassana* course a month.

Sleeping & Eating
Nagarjunakonda is popular, and accommodation can be tight during weekends and holidays. **Nagarjuna Resort** (☎ 08642-242471; r from Rs630; 🖭) is the most convenient place to stay, across the road from the boat launch. It has spacious, slightly shabby rooms with geysers, balconies and good views. Two kilometres up the hill from the bus stand is the fancy **Vijay Vihar Complex** (☎ 277362; fax 276633; r with AC

STATE OF GOOD KARMA

In its typically understated way, Andhra Pradesh doesn't make much of its vast archaeological – and karmic – wealth. But in fact, the state is packed with impressive ruins of its rich Buddhist history. Only a few of Andhra's 150 stupas, monasteries, caves and other sites have been excavated, turning up rare relics of the Buddha (usually pearl-like pieces of bone) with offerings like golden flowers. They speak of a time when Andhra Pradesh – or Andhradesa – was a hotbed of Buddhist activity, when monks came from around the world to learn from some of the tradition's most renowned teachers, and when Indian monks set off for Sri Lanka and Southeast Asia via the Krishna and Godavari Rivers and the Bay of Bengal to spread the teaching of the Buddha.

Andhradesa's Buddhist culture, in which sangha (community of monks and nuns), laity and statespeople all took part, lasted around 1500 years from the 6th century BC. There's no historical evidence for it, but some even say that the Buddha himself visited the area.

Andhradesa's first practitioners were likely disciples of Bavari, an ascetic who lived on the banks of the Godavari River and sent his followers north to bring back the Buddha's teaching. But the dharma really took off in the 3rd century BC under Ashoka (see p30), who dispatched monks out across his empire to teach and construct stupas enshrined with relics of the Buddha. (Being near these was thought to help progress on the path to enlightenment.)

Succeeding Ashoka, the Satavahanas and then Ikshvakus were also supportive. At their capital at Amaravathi, the Satavahanas adorned Ashoka's modest stupa with elegant decoration. They built monasteries across the Krishna Valley and exported the dharma through their sophisticated maritime network.

It was also during the Satavahana reign that Nagarjuna lived. Considered by many to be the progenitor of Mahayana Buddhism, the monk was equal parts logician, philosopher and meditator, and he wrote several ground-breaking works that shaped contemporary Buddhist thought. Other important monk-philosophers would emerge from the area in the following centuries, making Andhradesa a sort of Buddhist motherland of the South.

Today, the state's many remains are ripe for exploring; even in ruins, you can get a sense of how large some of the stupas were, how expansive the monastic complexes must have been, and how the monks lived, sleeping in caves and fetching rainwater from stone-cut cisterns. Plus, most of the sites have stunning views across seascapes and countryside. Head to the area around Vijayawada for Chandavaram, Guntupalli or Bhattiprolu, and near Visakhapatnam for Thotlakonda and Bavikonda (p315), Sankaram (p315) and Ramatirtham.

from Rs1650; ⊠ ⓐ) overlooking the lake. Room balconies have excellent views. Both hotels have restaurants.

Getting There & Away

The easiest way to visit Nagarjunakonda is with **APTDC** (☎ 040-65581555) in Hyderabad. Tours (Rs450) depart on weekends at 7am from Yatri Nivas Hotel (see p304) and 7.30am from APTDC in Bashirbagh (see p300), returning at 9.30pm.

You can also make your own way there from Hyderabad or Vijayawada. From Hyderabad, take a bus to Nagarjuna Sagar (or to Macherla or Vinukonda, which will stop at Nagarjuna Sagar). From there, it's a Rs10 shared rickshaw to Pylon, and another Rs10 to the boat launch. The nearest train station is 22km away at Macherla, where buses leave regularly for Nagarjuna Sagar.

WARANGAL

☎ 0870 / pop 528,570

Warangal was the capital of the Kakatiya kingdom, which covered the greater part of present-day Andhra Pradesh from the late 12th to early 14th centuries until it was conquered by the Tughlaqs of Delhi. The Hindu Kakatiyas were great builders and patrons of Telugu literature and arts, and it was during their reign that the Chalukyan style of temple architecture reached its pinnacle. If you are interested in Hindu temple development, then it's worth the trip to Warangal and Palampet (see opposite). It's possible to visit both places on a long day trip from Hyderabad, 157km away.

Most buses and trains will stop en route at Bhongir, 60km from Hyderabad. It's worth jumping down for a couple of hours to climb the fantastical-looking 12th-century Chalukyan **hill fort** (Rs3). Looking like a gargantuan stone egg, the hill is mostly ringed by stairs.

Orientation & Information

Warangal, Hanamkonda and Kazhipet are sister towns. The Warangal train station and bus stand are opposite each other, and the post office and police station are on Station Rd. Main Rd connects Warangal and Hanamkonda.

Lots of ATMs and **Apple Computers** (per hr Rs8) are near Hotel Ratna on JPN Rd. The **Department of Tourism** (☎ 2459201; Hanamkonda-Kazhipet Rd; ⏰ 10.30am-5pm Mon-Sat), opposite REC, is helpful.

Sights

Warangal's **fort** (Indian/foreigner Rs5/100; ⏰ dawn-dusk) was a massive construction with three distinct circular strongholds surrounded by a moat. Four paths with decorative gateways, set according to the cardinal points, led to the Swayambhava, a huge Shiva temple. The gateways are still obvious, but most of the fort is in ruins. It's easily reached from Warangal by bus or autorickshaw (Rs100 return).

Built in 1163, the **1000-Pillared Temple** (⏰ 6am-6pm) on the slopes of Hanamkonda Hill, 400m from Hanamkonda crossroads, is a fine example of Chalukyan architecture in a peaceful, leafy setting. Dedicated to three deities – Shiva, Vishnu and Surya – it has been carefully restored with intricately carved pillars and a central, very impressive Nandi (bull; Shiva's mount) of black basalt.

Down the hill and 3km to the right is the small **Siddheshwara Temple**. The **Bhadrakali Temple**, featuring a stone statue of Kali seated with a weapon in each of her eight hands, is high on a hill between Hanamkonda and Warangal.

Sleeping & Eating

Vijaya Lodge (☎ 2501222; fax 2446864; Station Rd; s/d from Rs150/240) About 100m from the train station, the Vijaya is well organised with helpful staff, but the rooms are becoming a little dreary.

Hotel Ratna (☎ 2500645; fax 2500555; MG Rd; s/d from Rs400/600; ⊠) The Ratna has shiny floors, fresh paint and professional staff, and it accepts credit cards. Oh, and it's super-clean. Its veg restaurant, Kavya (open 6.30am to 10pm, mains Rs65 to Rs100), makes insanely delicious, enormous meals (Rs48) that will leave you feeling fully satisfied and slightly intoxicated.

Hotel Surya (☎ 2441834; fax 2441836; Station Rd; s/d incl breakfast from Rs450/575; ⊠) Near the stations, the Surya has smart rooms, which are only just beginning to fade, and constant hot water. The restaurant downstairs, Surabhi (mains Rs75 to Rs140), has good Chinese food and kebabs, and plenty of nonveg.

Hotel Ashoka (☎ 2579260; Main Rd, Hanamkonda; s/d from Rs450/600; ⊠ ⓐ) Good-value rooms near the Hanamkonda bus stand and the 1000-Pillared Temple. Also in the compound are a restaurant, a bar-restaurant, a pub and the veg Kanishka (mains Rs40 to Rs110).

The train station has a few **retiring rooms** (r without/with AC Rs100/200; ⊠).

Getting There & Around

Buses head to Vijayawada (express/deluxe Rs115/150, seven hours, seven daily) from **Warangal bus stand** (☎ 9959226057). Frequent buses to Hyderabad (express/deluxe/luxury Rs66/74/85, four hours) depart from **Hanamkonda bus stand** (☎ 9959226056), a Rs6 bus ride away.

Warangal is a major rail junction. Trains go regularly to Hyderabad (2nd class/chair Rs68/232, three hours), Vijayawada (2nd class/chair Rs80/282, four hours) and Chennai (sleeper/3AC/2AC Rs281/735/996, 11 hours). Many trains go to Delhi daily.

Shared autorickshaws ply fixed routes around Warangal (including to the fort), Kazhipet and Hanamkonda. A shared autorickshaw ride costs Rs5 to Rs7.

AROUND WARANGAL
Palampet

About 65km northeast of Warangal, the stunning **Ramappa Temple** (✆ 6am-6.30pm), built in 1234, is an attractive example of Kakatiya architecture, although it was clearly influenced by Chalukya and Hoysala styles. Its pillars are ornately carved and its eaves shelter fine statues of female forms.

Just 1km south, the Kakatiyas constructed **Ramappa Cheruvu** to serve as temple tank. The lake, along with nearby Pakhal Lake 20km south, is popular with migrating birds.

The easiest way to get here is by private car (Rs1200), but frequent buses also run from Hanamkonda to Palampet (Rs28). The temple is about 500m from here.

VISAKHAPATNAM

☎ 0891 / pop 1.3 million

Visit Visakhapatnam – also called Vizag (*viezag*) – during the holiday season and you'll see domestic tourism in rare form: balloons, cotton candy and, of course, weddings! But the crowds only enhance the area's kitschy coasts: the run-down boardwalk along Ramakrishna Beach has lots of spunk, and the beach at nearby Rushikonda is one of Andhra's best.

The old beach-resort vibe exists despite the fact that Vizag is Andhra Pradesh's second-largest city, famous for shipbuilding, steel manufacturing and now, call centres, software and film production. It's a big, dusty city, but it's surrounded by little gems: sweet beaches, a gorgeous temple and, further out, the Araku Valley (see p315) and several ancient Buddhist sites (p315 and p315).

Orientation

Vizag's train station sits in a hive of shops and hotels on the western edge of town, near the port. Dwarakanagar, Vizag's commercial centre, is 2km east of the train station, and RTC Complex, the bus stand, is just southeast of here. Waltair and its Ramakrishna Beach are about 3km south of RTC.

Information

ATMs are everywhere. RTC Complex has several internet cafes, some open 24 hours.

Apollo Pharmacy (☎ 2788652; Siripuram Junction; ✆ 24hr)

APTDC RTC Complex (☎ 2788820; ✆ 6am-9pm); Train station (☎ 2788821; ✆ 5am-10pm) Information and tours.

Cloak rooms RTC Complex (per day Rs8); Train station (per day Rs10, locker per day Rs15; ✆ 24hr)

Pages Book Shop (☎ 6450555; Old Jail Rd, Daba Gardens; ✆ 9.30am-9.30pm) Opposite State Bank of India. Stocks the English-language what's-on mag, *Yo! Vizag* (Rs40).

Thomas Cook (☎ 2588112; Eswar Plaza, Dwarakanagar; ✆ 9am-6.30pm Mon-Sat) Near ICICI Bank.

Sights & Activities

The long beaches of **Waltair** overlook the Bay of Bengal, with its mammoth ships and brightly painted fishing boats. Its coastal **Beach Rd**, lined with parks and weird sculptures, is great for long walks.

The best beaches for swimming are at **Rushikonda**, 8km north. On the way, **Kailasagiri Hill** has gardens, playgrounds and a gargantuan Shiva and Parvati. The views from the hill and the **Kailasagiri Passenger Ropeway** (☎ 6510334; admission Rs55; ✆ 11am-1pm & 2-8pm) are awesome. Movies or cricket matches are sometimes shown across Beach Rd, at the festive **Tenetti Beach**.

At Simhachalam Hill, 10km northwest of town, is a fine 11th-century **Vishnu Temple** (✆ 6-10am & 4-6pm) in Orissan style. You can give *puja* to the deity, who's covered with sandalwood paste. Bus 6 A/H (Rs13) goes here.

Tours

APTDC operates full-day tours of the city (from Rs300) and Araku Valley (see p315).

Sleeping

Prices rise for Dussehra/Diwali holidays, when Bengalis swarm to Vizag.

Sree Kanya Lodge (☎ 5564881; Bowdara Rd; s/d from Rs200/450; ▒) Near the train station but out of the bustle, Sree Kanya is mostly characterless and a little dirty, but it's the best of the sorry lot. On the flip side, most rooms have balconies and the restaurant downstairs is good. Go for the 'deluxe' singles (Rs250) if you like daylight.

Sai Priya Resort (☎ 2790333; www.saipriya beachresorts.com; cottages/r from Rs700/1300; 🔀 🔊) Modern rooms, some with sea views, and cottages of bamboo and cane on Rushikonda beach. The grounds are lush and *almost* really beautiful, but like the rest of the place, they fall short of their potential. Also, checkout's a rude 8am. Nonguests can use the pool for two hours for Rs100.

Haritha Hotel (☎ 2562333; Beach Rd; Appughar; r incl breakfast from Rs850; 🔀) This APTDC hotel, formerly Punnami, is near Kailasagiri Hill and right across from the beach. The lowest-priced rooms (with no views) are only so-so; bump yourself up if you can. Checkout is 10am.

Hotel Daspalla (☎ 2564825; www.daspallahotels.com; Suryabagh; s/d incl breakfast from Rs1900/2300; 🔀 🖥) Looking like the inside of an Ambassador car and evoking an age when travel was a rare and special occasion, the Daspalla is Vizag's classic. It's professionally run and has a bar named Dimple. Free wi-fi.

Park (☎ 2754488; www.theparkhotels.com; Beach Rd; s/d from Rs7000/9000; 🔀 🖥 🔊) Vizag's only five-star is very elegant, very high-design. Even if you don't stay here, visit Bamboo Bay, its beachfront restaurant, for a drink. Checkout is noon.

Dumpy budget hotels huddle around the train station, which has **retiring rooms** (dm/r from Rs50/250; 🔀). Waltair has better vibes, but few inexpensive hotels.

Other recommendations:

YMCA Tourist Hostel (☎ 2755826; ymca_visakha@ yahoo.com; Beach Rd; dm/s/d from Rs150/550/650; 🔀) Best value in town, with superb views, but always full. Call anyway; you might get lucky.

Gateway Hotel (☎ 6623670; www.tajhotels.com/gate way; Beach Rd; s/d from Rs6500/7500; 🔀 🖥 🔊) The usual Taj classiness, with great views. Checkout is noon.

Eating & Drinking

At night, the snack stalls on Ramakrishna Beach and the beachfront restaurants at Rushikonda, next to Punnami, are hopping.

New Andhra Hotel (Sree Kanya Lodge, Bowdara Rd; mains Rs25-75; 🕙 11am-3.30pm & 7-10.30pm) An unassuming little place with *really* good, *really* hot Andhra dishes. Meals (Rs40/100 for veg/non-veg) and biryani are top-notch.

our pick **Vaisakhi** (☎ 2564825, Hotel Daspalla, Suryabagh; mains Rs55-100; 🕙 11.30am-3pm & 7-10.30pm) Words don't do justice to the super-deliciousness of the meals (Rs72) at this family vegetarian restaurant. *And* they come with ice cream. Yes, we're still dreaming of them.

Masala (☎ 2750750, Signature Towers, 1st fl, Asilmetta; mains Rs70-130; 🕙 11am-3.30pm & 7-11pm) Near Sampath Vinayaka Temple, Masala does out-of-this-world Andhra, tandoori and Chinese. Try the *chepa pulusu* (Andhra-style fish; Rs100).

Café Coffee Day (coffees Rs20-50; 🕙 9.30am-10.30pm) Up the road from Masala.

Getting There & Around

You'll have to negotiate fares with autorick-shaw drivers here. Most in-town rides will be around Rs20. **Guide Tours & Travels** (☎ 2754477), reliable for car rental, is opposite the RTC Complex 'out gate'.

AIR

Take an autorickshaw (Rs150), taxi (Rs225) or bus 38 (Rs6) to Vizag's airport, 13km west of town.

Domestic airlines and their daily services:
Indian Airlines (☎ 2746501, 1800 1801407; LIC Bldg) Chennai (except Sunday), Delhi (except Sunday), Hyderabad, Mumbai (via Hyderabad).

Jet Airways (☎ airport 2741092) Delhi, Hyderabad, Kolkota, Mumbai.

Kingfisher (☎ 2503285, airport 2517614; Ardee Bldg, Siripuram Junction) Bengaluru, Chennai, Hyderabad, Kolkota, Tirupathi.

Paramount (☎ airport 2010400) Bengaluru, Chennai (via Hyderabad), Hyderabad.

SpiceJet (☎ airport 2010422) Hyderabad; Delhi and Mumbai via Hyderabad.

BOAT

Boats depart every month-ish for Port Blair in the Andaman Islands (see p480). Bookings for the 56-hour journey (Rs2000) can be made at the **Shipping Office** (☎ 2565597, 2562661, 9866073407; Av Bhanoji Row; 🕙 9am-5pm Mon-Sat) in the port complex. Bring your passport.

BUS

Vizag's well-organised **RTC Complex** (☎ 2746400) has frequent bus services to Vijayawada (de-luxe/Volvo Rs193/402, eight/six hours) and, in the afternoon, Hyderabad ('superluxury'/Volvo Rs395/700, 14/12 hours).

TRAIN

Visakhapatnam Junction station is on the Kolkata–Chennai line. The overnight *Coromandel Express* (sleeper/3AC/2AC Rs338/896/1220, 13½ hours) is the fastest of the five daily trains running to Kolkata. Heading south, it goes to Chennai (sleeper/3AC/2AC Rs300/796/1131, 12½ hours). Frequent trains head to Vijayawada including 2717, the *Ratnachalam Express* (2nd-class/chair Rs109/386).

AROUND VISAKHAPATNAM
Araku Valley

Andhra's best train ride is through the magnificent Eastern Ghats to the **Araku Valley**, 120km north of Vizag. The area is home to isolated tribal communities, and the tiny **Museum of Habitat** (admission Rs10; ☻ 10am-1pm & 2-5pm) has fascinating exhibits of indigenous life. APTDC runs tours from Vizag (see p313; Rs500), which take in a performance of Dhimsa, a tribal dance, and the million-year-old limestone **Borra Caves** (Rs25; ☻ 10am-5.30pm), 30km from Araku.

The **Punnami Hill Resort** (☎ 958936-249204; cottages from Rs650; ✖), near the museum, has cottages with good views. But it's more fun to stay at the forest retreat of **Jungle Bells** (Tyda; cottages from Rs800; ✖), 45km from Araku, with cottages tucked away in woods. Book at APTDC (see p313).

The Kirandol passenger train (Rs28, five hours) leaves Vizag at 6.50am and Araku at 3pm. It's a slow, spectacular ride; sit on the right-hand side coming out of Vizag for best views. For Jungle Bells, get off at Tyda station, 500m from the resort.

Bavikonda & Thotlakonda

The Vizag area's natural harbours have long been conducive to dropping anchor, which helped monks from Sri Lanka, China and Tibet come here to learn and practise meditation. **Bavikonda** (☻ 9am-6pm) and **Thotlakonda** (☻ 10am-3pm) were popular hilltop monasteries on the coast that hosted up to 150 monks at a time – with the help of massive rainwater tanks and, at Thotlakonda, a natural spring.

The monasteries flourished during the Theravada period (Bavikonda, from the 3rd century BC to the 3rd century AD, and Thotlakonda, from the 2nd century BC to 2nd century AD) and had votive stupas, congregation halls, *chaitya-grihas* (assembly halls

enclosing stupas), *viharas,* and refectories. Today only the ruins of these massive monastic compounds remain, but they're impressive nonetheless, with a placid, almost magical, air, and sea views to meditate on. Bavikonda and Thotlakonda are 14km and 16km, respectively, from Vizag on Bheemli Beach Rd. Vizag's autorickshaw drivers charge around Rs400 return to see both.

Sankaram

Forty kilometres southwest of Vizag is this stunning **Buddhist complex** (☻ 9am-6pm), better known by the name of its two hills, Bojjannakonda and Lingalakonda. Used by monks from the 1st to 9th centuries AD (see the boxed text on p311), the hills are covered with rock-cut caves, stupas, ruins of monastery structures, and reliefs of the Buddha that span the Theravada, Mahayana and Vajrayana periods. Bojjannakonda has a two-storey group of rock-cut caves flanked by *dwarapalakas* (doorkeepers) and containing a stupa and gorgeous carvings of the Buddha (some restored). Atop the hill sit the ruins of a huge stupa and a monastery; you can still make out the individual cells where monks meditated. Lingalakonda is piled high with stupas, some of them enormous. Each hill requires some climbing and hiking – better to take in the spectacular views of palms and rice fields below.

A private car from Vizag costs around Rs800. Or, take a bus to Anakapalle (Rs24, one hour, every 20 minutes), 3km away, and then an autorickshaw (Rs150 return including waiting time).

VIJAYAWADA
☎ 0866 / pop 1 million

Vijayawada is a busy, rapidly growing city and an important port at the head of the delta of the mighty Krishna River. It's bustling, but it's also intersected by canals, lined with ghats and ringed by fields of rice and palm. The surrounding area is intensely lush and green.

Vijayawada is considered by many to be the heart of Andhra culture and language and has an important Durga temple. Nearby Amaravathi, meanwhile, was a centre of Buddhist learning and practise for many centuries.

Orientation

The Krishna River cuts across the city's southern end. The bus station is just north of the

ANDHRA PRADESH

river, and the train station is in the centre of town, near the Hanumanpet and Governorpet neighbourhoods, which are separated by Eluru Rd. **Om Art Print** (☎ 2578333; JD Hospital Rd, cnr Besant Rd; ☷ 10am-8.30pm Mon-Sat) sells maps.

Information
Apollo Pharmacy (☎ 2432333; Vijaya Talkies Junction, Eluru Rd; ☷ 24hr)
APTDC (☎ 2571393; MG Rd, opposite PWD Grounds; ☷ 8am-8pm) Don't bother, unless you need brochures.
Care Hospital (☎ 2470100; Siddhartha Nagar)
Cloakrooms (per day Rs10; ☷ 24hr) At the train and bus stations.
MagicNet (☎ 2570956; Swarnalok Complex, Eluru Rd; per hr Rs20; ☷ 9.30am-9pm)
Department of Tourism (☎ 2577577; train station; ☷ 10am-5pm)
State Bank of Hyderabad (☎ 2574832; 1st fl, Vijaya Commercial Complex, Governorpet; ☷ 10.30am-3pm Mon-Fri) Changes currency and travellers cheques.

Sights
CAVE TEMPLES
Four kilometres southwest of Vijayawada, the stunning **Undavalli cave temples** (Indian/foreigner Rs5/US$2; ☷ 9am-5pm) cut a fine silhouette against the palm trees and rice paddies. Shrines are dedicated to the Trimurti – Brahma, Vishnu and Shiva – and one cave on the third level houses a huge, beautiful statue of reclining Vishnu while seated deities and animals stand guard out front. The caves, in their Hindu form, date to the 7th century, but they're thought to have been constructed for Buddhist monks 500 years earlier. Bus 301 goes here.

VICTORIA JUBILEE MUSEUM
The best part of this **museum** (☎ 2574299; MG Rd; admission Rs3; ☷ 10.30am-5pm Sat-Thu) is the building itself, built in 1877 to honour Queen Victoria's coronation jubilee. Later, in 1921, it hosted the Congress meeting where a new tricolour flag was introduced: Mahatma Gandhi added a wheel to the design and made it the Indian National Congress's official flag.

The interesting architecture outshines the museum's small collection of art and arms. But the garden, where temple sculptures from around the state line shady paths, is lovely.

GHATS
Vijayawada's Krishna River has 10 ghats running along its shores. The Krishnaveni ghat, just across from the bus stand, is a fascinating place to sit and watch the world – and its swimming kids, laundry and prayers – go by.

KANAKA DURGA TEMPLE
This **temple** (Indrakila Hill; ☷ 5am-9pm) is dedicated to Kanaka Durga, the goddess and protector of the city. Legend has it that she eradicated powerful demons from the area. She now receives continual gratitude from her followers, who credit her with Vijayawada's prosperity. Avoid mornings and bring coins for blessings.

Courses
Dhamma Vijaya (Vipassana Meditation Centre; ☎ 08812-225522, 9441449044; www.dhamma.org; Eluru-Chintalapudi Rd) offers intensive 10-day *vipassana* meditation courses free of charge in lush palm-and cocoa-forested grounds. Frequent buses (Rs33, 1½ hours, every 15 minutes) and trains (2nd-class/chair Rs52/197, one hour) run from Vijayawada to Eluru. The centre is 15km from Eluru; call for details.

Sleeping
Hotel Sri Ram (☎ 2579377; Hanumanpet; s/d from Rs320/450; ☒) This cheapie has bright, clean, nondescript rooms near the train station. A conveniently located safe bet.

Hotel Raj Towers (☎ 2571311; Eluru Rd, Governorpet; s/d from Rs410/510; ☒) Raj Towers seems to be confused, acting like an expensive hotel when it's not. Staff is super-helpful, rooms are scrubbed daily and have constant hot water, and there are laundry bags and stationery(!). The restaurant downstairs isn't bad, either.

Vijayawada's two best midrange places, **Swarna Palace** (☎ 2577222; fax 2574602; Eluru Rd, Governorpet; s/d with AC from Rs1400/1500; ☒) and **Hotel Ilapuram** (☎ 2571282; fax 2575251; Prakasam Rd; s/d with AC from Rs1500/1700; ☒), both fall short of the sleekness they aspire to. But they're professionally run – and a little bit sleek anyway.

The train station's clean and spacious **retiring rooms** (dm/s/d from Rs50/120/250; ☒) are a great option. The bus station has **dorms** (☎ 3097809; from Rs100) for gents.

Eating
Sree Lakshmi Vilas Modern Cafe (Besant Rd, Governorpet; meals Rs30; ☷ 6.30am-10.30pm) With black-and-white-check floors and mismatched wooden chairs, this gritty, down-home veg joint has a heavy 1940s vibe. The meals are great, as are the fresh juices (Rs12).

Cross Roads (Prakasam Rd; mains Rs65-135; ☻ 11am-10.30pm) There's sometimes a wait at this popular family place specialising in quality nonveg kebabs, biryani and North Indian dishes. Save room for ice cream.

our pick **Minerva Coffee Shop** (Museum Rd; mains Rs70-105; ☻ 6am-11.30pm) Just around the corner from Big Bazaar, this outpost of the fabulous Minerva chain has great North and South Indian, including top-notch dosas (Rs21 to Rs45). Its *rava masala dosa* is the best thing *ever*.

Getting There & Around
The bus stand has a helpful **inquiry desk** (☎ 2522200). Frequent services run to Hyderabad (deluxe/Volvo Rs132/273, six hours), Amaravathi (Rs21, two hours) and Warangal (deluxe Rs120, four hours) and Visakhapatnam (deluxe/Volvo Rs192/370, 10 hours).

Vijayawada is on the main Chennai–Kolkata and Chennai–Delhi railway lines. The daily *Coromandel Express* (2841) runs to Chennai (sleeper/3AC/2AC Rs205/522/733, seven hours) and, the other way, to Kolkata (2842; sleeper/3AC/2AC Rs401/1073/1466, 20 hours). Speedy *Rajdhani* (Thursday and Saturday) and *Jan Shatabdi* (daily except Tuesday) trains also ply the Vijayawada–Chennai route. Trains galore run to Hyderabad (2nd-class/chair Rs109/386, 6½ hours) and Tirupathi (sleeper/3AC/2AC Rs201/510/685, seven hours). The **computerised advance-booking office** (☎ inquiry 2577775, reservations 2578955) is in the basement.

The train station has a prepaid autorickshaw stand marked 'Traffic Police'.

AROUND VIJAYAWADA
Amaravathi
Amaravathi, 60km west of Vijayawada, was once the Andhran capital and a significant Buddhist centre. India's biggest **stupa** (Indian/foreigner Rs5/100; ☻ dawn-dusk), measuring 27m high, was constructed here in the 3rd century BC, when Emperor Ashoka sent monks south to spread the Buddha's teaching. All that remains are a mound and some stones, but the nearby **museum** (admission Rs2; ☻ 10am-5pm Sat-Thu) has a small replica of the stupa, with its intricately carved pillars, marble-surfaced dome and carvings of scenes from the Buddha's life. It also has a reconstruction of part of the surrounding gateway, which gives you an idea of the stupa's massive scale. It's worth the trip, but many of Amaravathi's best sculptures are

in London's British Museum and Chennai's Government Museum (p393).

About 1km down the road is the **Dhyana Buddha**, a 20m-high seated Buddha built on the site where the Dalai Lama spoke in the 2006 Kalachakra.

Buses run from Vijayawada to Amaravathi every half-hour or so (Rs21, two hours), but it may be quicker to head to Guntur (Rs9, 45 minutes) and take another bus from there.

Kondapalli
Situated strategically on the old Machilipatnam–Golconda trade route, **Kondapalli fort** (admission Rs5; ☻ 10.30am-5pm) was built in 1360 by the Reddy kings, and was held by the Gajapathis, the Qutb Shahis, the Mughals and the nizams before becoming a British military camp in 1767. Today it's a quiet, lovely ruin. On weekdays, you'll likely have the place to yourself and you can easily spend a few hours hiking around. Kondapalli village, 1km downhill, is famous for its wooden dolls. The fort is 21km from Vijayawada; an auto costs Rs400 return.

Guntupalli
Getting here is an adventure – a very scenic one. The former **monastic compound** (Indian/foreigner Rs5/100; ☻ 10am-5pm), high on a hilltop and overlooking a vast expanse of forest and paddy fields, is noteworthy for its circular rock-cut *chaitya-griha*. The cave's domed ceiling is carved with 'wooden beams' designed to look like those in a hut. The *chaitya-griha* also has a lovely, well-preserved stupa and, like the many monk dwellings that line the same cliff, a gorgeous arched facade also designed to look like wood (note the 'rafters'). The monastery was in use from the 3rd or 2nd century BC to the 3rd century AD, and the aesthetic is in keeping with the Theravada (early Buddhist) architectural style found in Bihar and Maharashtra. Also be sure to check out the beds and rainwater drains in the monks' cells, as well as the compound's 60-plus votive stupas.

Guntupalli is best reached from Eluru, which is on the main Vijayawada–Visakhapatnam train line. From Vijayawada, buses run half-hourly to Eluru (Rs33, 1½ hours), and from Eluru, hourly buses make the 35km trip to Kamavarapukota (Rs24, one hour). Guntupalli is about 10km west of Kamavarapukota, which you can travel to by local bus or autorickshaw. The easiest option,

ANDHRA PRADESH

a private taxi from Eluru, will cost you Rs600 to Rs700 including waiting time.

TIRUMALA & TIRUPATHI

☎ 0877 / pop 302,000

The holy hill of Tirumala is, on any given day, filled with tens of thousands of blissed-out devotees, many of whom have endured long journeys to see the powerful Lord Venkateshwara here, at his home. It's one of India's most visited pilgrimage centres: on average, 40,000 pilgrims come each day (the total often exceeds 100,000), and *darshan* (deity-viewing) runs 24/7. Temple staff alone number 12,000, and the efficient **Tirumala Tirupathi Devasthanams** (TTD; ☎ 2277777; www .tirumala.org) brilliantly administers the crowds. As a result, although the throngs can be overwhelming, a sense of order, serenity and ease mostly prevails, and a trip to the Holy Hill can be fulfilling, even if you're not a pilgrim.

'It is believed that Lord Sri Venkateshwara enjoys festivals', according to the TTD. And so do his devotees: *darshan* queues during October's Brahmotsavam can run up to several kilometres.

Orientation & Information

Tirupathi is the service town at the bottom of the hill, with hotels, restaurants, and transport; a fleet of buses constantly ferries pilgrims the 18km up and down. You'll find most of your worldly needs around the Tirupathi bus station (TP Area) and, about 500m away, the train station. G Car St becomes Tilak Rd further from the train station.

Anu Internet Centre (☎ 3202119; APSRTC Commercial Complex; per hr Rs15; ☷ 8am-11pm) Next to the bus stand.

Apollo Pharmacy (☎ 2252314; G Car St; ☷ 24hr)

APTDC (☎ 2289120; Sridevi Complex, 2nd fl, Tilak Rd; ☷ 9am-7pm)

Cloakrooms (per day Rs10; ☷ 24hr) At the train and bus stations.

Cybermate (☎ 3293968; Tilak Rd; per hr Rs15; ☷ 9am-9pm) Internet access.

Police station (☎ 2289006; Railway Station Rd)

Reliance Webstore (☎ 3042993; Tilak Rd; per 3hr Rs50; ☷ 9.30am-10.30pm) Opposite municipal office; internet access.

Sights

VENKATESHWARA TEMPLE

Devotees flock to Tirumala to see Venkateshwara, an avatar of Vishnu. Among the many powers attributed to him is the granting of any wish made before the idol at Tirumala. Many pilgrims also donate their hair to the deity – in gratitude for a wish fulfilled, or to renounce ego – so hundreds of barbers attend to devotees. Tirumala and Tirupathi are filled with tonsured men, women and children.

Legends about the hill itself and the surrounding area appear in the Puranas, and the temple's history may date back 2000 years. The main **temple** is an atmospheric place, though you'll be pressed between hundreds of devotees when you see it. The inner sanctum itself is dark and magical; it smells of incense, resonates with chanting and may make you religious. There, Venkateshwara sits gloriously on his throne, inspiring bliss and love among his visitors. You'll have a moment to make a wish and then you'll be shoved out again.

'Ordinary *darshan*' requires a wait of several hours in the claustrophobic metal cages ringing the temple. 'Special *darshan*' tickets (Rs50) can be purchased a day in advance in Tirupathi. These come with a *darshan* time and get you through the queue faster – in theory.

Foreigners are advised to have VIP 'cellar' *darshan*, which involves minimal waiting. Bring your passport, photocopies of your visa and passport, and Rs100 to the Joint Executive Officer's (JEO) office at Tirumala, about 2km from the Tirupathi bus drop-off. The free red buses go here.

Tours

If you're pressed for time, APTDC runs three-day tours (Rs1750) to Tirumala from Hyderabad. KSTDC (see p238) and TTDC (see p392) offer the same from Bengaluru and Chennai, respectively. APTDC also has a full-day tour (Rs340) of temples in the Tirupathi area.

Sleeping & Eating

The TTD runs *choultries* (guest houses) for pilgrims in Tirumala and Tirupathi, but most non-Hindu visitors stay in one of Tirupathi's many hotels.

TIRUMALA

Vast **dormitories** (beds free) and **guest houses** (Rs100-2500) surround the temple, but these are intended for pilgrims. To stay, check in at the Central Reception Office. Huge **dining halls** (meals free) serve thousands of pilgrims daily. Veg restaurants also serve meals for Rs15.

TIRUPATHI

Hotel Mamata Lodge (☎ 2225873; fax 2225797; 1st fl, 170 TP Area; s/d/tr & q Rs150/250/300) A friendly, spick-and-span cheapie. Some of the sheets are stained, but they're tucked in tight and lovingly patched with white squares. Avoid the downstairs lodge of the same name.

Hotel Woodside (☎ 2284464; 15 G Car St; s/d from Rs375/500; ❄) The cheerful Woodside is beginning to furl at the edges, but its clean rooms have peach-and-royal-blue walls and plaid curtains (unlike the dreary Woodside Annexe down the road). The restaurant downstairs has great, exceedingly spicy meals (Rs35) and big windows perfect for people-watching.

Hotel Annapurna (☎ 2250666; 349 G Car St; r from Rs750; ❄) The Annapurna is a wee bit overpriced, but it's convenient and well-organised. Rooms are clean, compact and pink, with constant hot water. Since it's on a corner (across from the train station), non-AC front rooms can be noisy. Its veg restaurant has fresh juices and Tirupathi's best food (mains Rs45 to Rs80) in sublime air-conditioning.

Hotel Mayura (☎ 2225925; mayurahotels@yahoo.co.in; 209 TP Area; s/d from Rs1000/1150; ❄) Across from the bus stand, the Mayura is somehow strangely peaceful, with super-tidy, spacious rooms, cool stone floors, and serene views of the surrounding hills from some rooms.

Hotels are clustered around the bus stand and train station, which has super-value **retiring rooms** (dm/r from Rs45/150, with AC Rs400; ❄). **Hotel Universal Deluxe** (49 G Car St; mains Rs20-50; ❤ 5.30am-11.30pm), near the train station, and **Hotel Vikram** (☎ 2225433; TP Area; mains Rs35-65; ❤ 5am-11pm) by the bus stand both serve hearty meals and juices.

Other digs:

Bhimas Deluxe (☎ 2225521; www.thirupathibhimas hotels.com; 34-38 G Car St; r from Rs850; ❄)

Hotel Sindhuri Park (☎ 2256430; www.hotelsindhuri .com; 119 TP Area; r from Rs1530; ❄ ▯)

Getting There & Away

It's possible to visit Tirupathi on a (very) long day trip from Chennai. If travelling by bus or train, buy a 'link ticket', which includes transport from Tirupathi to Tirumala.

AIR

Indian Airlines (☎ 2283992; Tirumala Bypass Rd; ❤ 9.30am-5.30pm), 2km from town, has daily flights to Delhi (Rs7840, two hours) via Hyderabad (Rs3675, one hour). **Kingfisher Red** (☎ 9849677008) plies the same route, including Bengaluru and Visakhapatnam. Book with **Mitta Travels** (☎ 2221135; Prakasam Rd; ❤ 9am-7.30pm Mon-Sat, 9am-12.30pm Sun), next to Manasa Fast Foods, 2km from the train station.

BUS

Tirupathi's mega **bus station** (☎ 2289900) has frequent buses to Chennai (Rs56, four hours) and Hyderabad (deluxe/Volvo Rs276/560, 12/10 hours). Tonnes of APSRTC and KSTDC buses go to Bengaluru (deluxe/Volvo Rs140/325, six/five hours), and seven buses head to Puttaparthi daily (express/deluxe Rs136/160, eight hours).

Private buses depart from TP Area, opposite the bus stand.

TRAIN

Tirupathi station is well served by express trains. The **reservation office** (☎ 2225850; ❤ 8am-8pm Mon-Sat, 8am-2pm Sun) is across the street.

Getting Around

BUS

Tirumala Link buses have two bus stands in Tirupathi: next to the main bus stand and outside the train station. The scenic 18km trip to Tirumala takes one hour (Rs44 return); if you don't mind heights, sit on the left side for views. A prepaid taxi is Rs350.

WALKING

TTD has constructed probably the best footpath in India for pilgrims to walk up to Tirumala. It's about 15km and takes four to six hours. Leave your luggage at the toll gate at Alipiri near the Hanuman statue. It will be transported free to the reception centre. It's best to walk in the cool of the evening, but there are shady rest points along the way, and a few canteens.

AROUND TIRUMALA & TIRUPATHI
Chandragiri Fort

Only a couple of buildings remain from this 15th-century **fort** (☎ 2276246; Indian/foreigner Rs7/100; ❤ dawn-dusk), 14km west of Tirupathi. Both the Rani Mahal and the Raja Mahal, which houses a small **museum** (❤ 10am-5pm Sat-Thu), were constructed under Vijayanagar rule and resemble structures in Hampi's Royal Centre. There's a nightly **sound-and-light show**

TRAINS FROM TIRUPATHI			
Destination	**Fare (Rs)**	**Duration (hr)**	**Daily Departures**
Bengaluru	sleeper/3AC/2AC 166/437/596	7	2
Chennai	2nd-class/chair 61/209	3	2
Hyderabad/Secunderabad	sleeper/3AC/2AC 288/756/1026	12	7
Vijayawada	sleeper/3AC/2AC 201/510/685	7	11

(admission Rs30; ☼ 8pm Mar-Oct, 7.30pm Nov-Feb), narrated by Bollywood great Amitabh Bachchan. Buses for Chandragiri (Rs6) leave Tirupathi train station every half-hour. A prepaid taxi is Rs400 return.

Sri Kalahasti

Around 36km east of Tirupathi, Sri Kalahasti is known for its important **Sri Kalahasteeswara Temple** and for being, along with Machilipatnam near Vijayawada, a centre for the ancient art of *kalamkari*. These paintings are made with natural ingredients: the cotton is primed with *myrabalam* (resin) and cows' milk; figures are drawn with a pointed bamboo stick dipped in fermented jaggery and water; and the dyes are made from cow dung, ground seeds, plants and flowers. You can see the artists at work in the Agraharam neighbourhood, 2.5km from the bus stand. **Sri Vijayalakshmi Fine Kalamkari Arts** (☎ 08578-230701) is an old family business with 40 artists. Call for an appointment to visit their studio.

Buses leave Tirupathi for Sri Kalahasti every 10 minutes (Rs18, 45 minutes); a prepaid taxi is Rs650 return.

PUTTAPARTHI
☎ 08555

Prasanthi Nilayam (Abode of Highest Peace) is the main ashram of Sri Sathya Sai Baba, who has a huge following in India and around the globe. He set up this ashram in Puttaparthi, his hometown, 60 years ago and lives here most of the year.

When he was 14, Sai Baba declared himself to be the reincarnation of another Sai Baba, a saintly figure who died in 1918 (p152). Today, millions of devotees regard Sai Baba as a true avatar and believe that he performs miracles. They come for the ashram's program of *darshan* (here, that means seeing Baba), chanting and prayer.

Everything about Sai Baba is big: the Afro hairdo; the big-name devotees; and the millions of dollars pumped into the nearby hos-

pital, schools and university. And there's the big controversy: serious allegations of sexual misconduct have led some devotees to lose faith. Others, however, regard the controversy as simply another terrestrial test for their avatar.

Sleeping & Eating

Most people stay at the **ashram** (☎ 287390; www .srisathyasai.org.in), a small village with all amenities. Accommodation and food are cheap but basic. Advance bookings aren't taken, and visitors under 25 must be in a family or group.

Non-ashram options include the clean and simple **Sri Pratibha Guest House** (☎ 289599; Gopuram Rd, 1st Cross; r from Rs350), on an alley behind the ashram's vehicle entrance, and the excellent-value **Sri Sai Sadan** (Meda's Guest House; ☎ 287507; srisaisadan@gmail.com; Gopuram Rd; s/d from Rs630/810; ✷), near Venugopalaswamy Temple, with a roof garden, and spacious rooms with fridges and balconies.

The rooftop **World Peace Café** (German Bakery; Main Rd; mains Rs55-115; ☼ 7.30am-9.30pm) is an old favourite for saffron lassis, good filter coffee and healthy food. The Tibetan **Bamboo Nest** (Chitravathi Rd, 1st fl; mains Rs55-80; ☼ 9.30am-2pm & 4.30-9pm) has a memorable veg wonton soup (Rs45) and good *momos* (dumplings).

Getting There & Around

Puttaparthi is most easily reached from Bengaluru; nine KSRTC buses (express/ Volvo Rs107/243, four hours) and eight trains (sleeper/3AC/2AC Rs145/351/464, three hours) head here daily. The **KSRTC office** (☎ 288938) is next to the bus station.

From the **APSRTC bus station** (☎ 287313), uncomfortable buses run to/from Tirupathi (express/ deluxe Rs136/160, eight hours, seven daily) and Chennai (Rs277, 12 hours, two daily).

The bus station has a **train reservation booth** (☼ 8am-noon & 5-7pm Mon-Sat, 8am-2pm Sun). For Hyderabad, an overnight train goes daily to Kacheguda (7604; sleeper/3AC/2AC

Rs230/592/846, 10 hours). Overnight train 8564 runs to Visakhapatnam (sleeper/3AC/2AC Rs330/901/1239, 20 hours), stopping at Vijayawada. The daily *Udyan Express* (6530) heads to Mumbai (sleeper/3AC/2AC Rs341/930/1279, 21 hours).

A free shuttle for ashram visitors runs from the train station. An autorickshaw is Rs50.

LEPAKSHI

About 70km from Puttaparthi is Lepakshi, site of the **Veerbhadra Temple**. The town gets its name from the *Ramayana*: when demon Ravana kidnapped Rama's wife, Sita, the bird Jatayu fought him and fell, injured, at the temple site. Rama then called him to get up; 'Lepakshi' derives from the Sanskrit for 'Get up, bird'.

Look for the 9m-long monolithic Nandi – India's largest – at the town's entrance. From here, you can see the temple's Naga-lingam,

a lingam (image of Shiva) crowned with a spectacular seven-headed cobra. The temple is known for its unfinished Kalyana Mandapam (Marriage Hall), which depicts the wedding of Parvati and Shiva, and its Natyamandapa (Dance Hall), with its carvings of dancing gods. The temple's most stunning feature, though, are the Natyamandapa's ceiling frescoes.

Ramana, an excellent guide, brings the temple to life (Rs100 is an appreciated offering). Bring change for the friendly priests giving blessings in the inner sanctum.

To get here, take a Puttaparthi–Bengaluru bus and alight at Kodakonda Checkpost. From there, take a Hindupur-bound bus (Rs6) or an autorickshaw (Rs300 return) to Lepakshi. A private car from Puttaparthi is Rs1000.

You can also go from Hindupur, a main stop on the Puttaparthi–Bengaluru train line with a few hotels. It's 11km from the temple.

Kerala

Kerala's deliberate and thoughtful pace of life is as contagious as the Indian head-wobble – just setting foot on this sliver of green will slow your stride to an intoxicatingly slow amble. Consisting of a skinny strip of land running between the Arabian Sea and the Western Ghats, Kerala is, at the same time, one of India's most beautiful and successful states.

The spindly network of rivers, lakes and canals that make up the breathtaking backwaters of Kerala is the region's star attraction. Here, one can meander through an infinite network of rice paddies, coconut groves and bucolic villages, viewed from the comfort of an elegant houseboat. Further south, the golden beaches of Kovalam and Varkala are where Kerala's green interior flirts with the azure shore, making an ideal destination for the sun-worshipping crowd. Higher inland, the mountainous Ghats lie covered in a thick blanket of spices and tea plantations, also home to thousands of species of exotic bird and wildlife.

Adventurers and traders have been exploring this thriving land for eons. Serene Fort Cochin is a melange of colonial influences, with dozens of buildings paying homage to Chinese visitors, Portuguese traders, Jewish settlers, Syrian Christians and Muslim merchants. Yet even with all these colonial distractions, Kerala still clings to vibrant traditions of its own: Kathakali – a blend of religious play and dance; *kalarippayat* – a gravity-defying martial art; and *theyyam* – a trance-induced ritual. Mix that with some of the most tastebud-tingling cuisine in India and you can imagine how hard it will be to leave before you even get here.

HIGHLIGHTS

- Soak in 500 years of colonial history and stay in a restored heritage home in laid-back **Fort Cochin** (p361)

- Slowly meander your way through the famed **backwaters** (p346) of Kerala on a houseboat, handmade in the style of traditional rice barges

- Sneak in some serious R & R time at one of Kerala's beach-side resort towns – **Kovalam** (p331) or **Varkala** (p336)

- Frolic in the tea-plantation–filled green hills of **Munnar** (p355), high in the lush mountains of Kerala's Western Ghats

- Go elephant spotting at **Wayanad** (p380) or **Periyar Wildlife Sanctuary** (p352)

- Really get off the beaten track to explore the little-visited beaches of **Kannur** (p383) and **Bekal** (p384)

History

Traders have been drawn to the whiff of Kerala's spices and to the shine of its ivory for more than 3000 years. The coast was known to the Phoenicians, the Romans, the Arabs and the Chinese, and was a transit point for spices from the Moluccas (eastern Indonesia).

The kingdom of Cheras ruled much of Kerala until the early Middle Ages, competing with kingdoms and small fiefdoms for territory and trade. Vasco da Gama's arrival in 1498 opened the floodgates to European colonialism as Portuguese, Dutch and English interests fought Arab traders, and then each other, for control of the lucrative spice trade.

The present-day state of Kerala was created in 1956 from the former states of Travancore, Kochi and Malabar. A tradition of valuing the arts and education has resulted in a post-

Independence state that is one of the most progressive in India.

Kerala had the first freely elected communist government in the world, coming to power in 1957 and holding power regularly since. The participatory political system has resulted in a more equitable distribution of land and income, and impressive health and education statistics (see boxed text, p334). Many Malayalis (speakers of Malayalam, the state's official language) work in the Middle East, and remittances play a significant part in the economy.

FAST FACTS

Population 31.8 million
Area 38,864 sq km
Capital Thiruvananthapuram (Trivandrum)
Main language Malayalam
When to go October to March

FESTIVALS IN KERALA

Across the state on any night in Kerala you can find temple festivals being celebrated enthusiastically. Some highlights:

- **Ernakulathappan Utsavam** (Jan/Feb; Shiva Temple, Ernakulam, Kochi (Cochin), p360) Hugely popular in Kochi, this eight-day festival climaxes with a procession of 15 splendidly decorated elephants, ecstatic music and fireworks.
- **Bharni Utsavam** (Feb/Mar; Chettikulangara Bhaghavathy Temple, Chettikulangara village, near Kayamkulam, p343) This one-day festival is dedicated to the popular Keralan goddess Bhagavathy. It's famous for its *kootiattam* (traditional Sanskrit drama) ritual and a spectacular procession of larger-than-life effigies.
- **Thirunakkara Utsavam** (Mar; Thirunakkara Shiva Temple, Kottayam, p348) There's all-night Kathakali dancing on the third and fourth nights of this 10-day festival; with processions of caparisoned elephants marking the finale.
- **Pooram Festival** (Apr; Asraman Shri Krishna Swami Temple, Kollam (Quilon), p340) Full-night Kathakali performances are common during this 10-day festival; with a procession of 40 ornamented elephants marking the end of festivities.
- **Thrissur Pooram** (Apr/May; Vadakkumnatha Temple, Thrissur (Trichur), p375) This festival boasts the elephant procession to end all elephant processions.
- **Nehru Trophy Snake Boat Race** (2nd Sat in Aug; Punnamadakalyal, Alappuzha (Alleppey), p343) The most popular of Kerala's boat races.
- **Aranmula Boat Race** (Aug/Sep; near Shri Parthasarathy Temple, Aranmula, p351) This water regatta recreates a ritualistic journey in honour of Krishna. It's a spectacular event, with crowds cheering as rowers shout along with the songs of the boatmen.
- **Onam** (Aug/Sep; statewide) Kerala's biggest cultural celebration is the 10-day Onam, when the entire state celebrates the golden age of mythical King Mahabali.
- **Ashtamudi Craft & Art Festival** (Dec/Jan; Asraman Maidan, Kollam (Quilon), p340) This festival, held every second year, features folk art from all over India, with workshops, demonstrations and exhibitions.

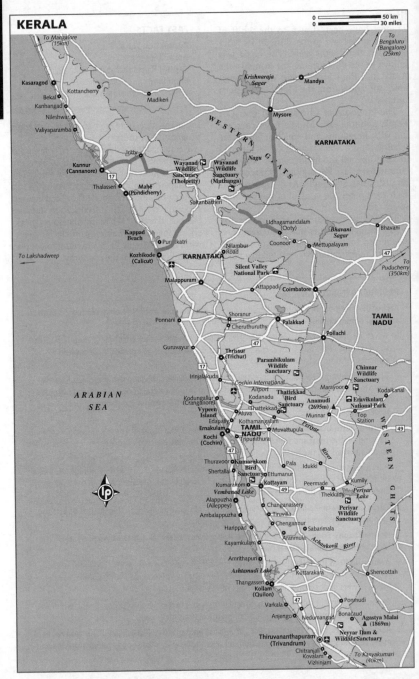

KERALA

| 0 | 50 km |
| 0 | 30 miles |

Information

Kerala Tourism (☎ 0471-2321132; www.keralatourism .org) is a government tourism promotion body with information offices – usually called District Tourism Promotion Council (DTPC) or Tourist Facilitation Centres – in most major towns.

ACCOMMODATION

Parts of Kerala – particularly the beachside towns and backwater hubs – have a distinct high season around November to March. Around the mid-December to mid-January peak season, prices creep up again, though great deals are to be had during the monsoon season (April to September). Homestays are a popular alternative to dowdy hotels in areas like Fort Cochin and Periyar Wildlife Sanctuary.

National Parks

All national parks mentioned in this chapter close for one week for a tiger census during the months of January or February. The dates differ, so check with Kerala Tourism for exact dates.

Getting Around

The Kerala State Road Transport Corporation (KSRTC) runs an extensive network of buses between most Keralan cities. They're not the fastest or most comfortable things on earth, but are reliable and nearly always punctual. Private buses ply the same routes, plus some the KSRTC don't cover, and can be more comfortable – though departure times are more erratic.

SOUTHERN KERALA

THIRUVANANTHAPURAM (TRIVANDRUM)
☎ 0471 / pop 889,191

For obvious reasons, Kerala's capital Thiru-vananthapuram is still often referred to by its colonial name: Trivandrum. Most travellers merely springboard from here to the nearby beach-side resorts of Kovalam and Varkala, though laid-back and hill-enclosed Trivandrum can muster enough appeal to keep you entertained for a day or two. All you have to do is get off Trivandrum's racing-drag of a main street to find yourself immersed in old Kerala: surrounded by pagoda-shaped buildings, red-tiled roofs and narrow, winding lanes.

Orientation

Mahatma Gandhi (MG) Rd, the town's main artery and unofficial speedway, runs 4km north–south from the museums and zoo to the Sri Padmanabhaswamy Temple area.

Information

BOOKSHOPS & LIBRARIES

Alliance Française (☎ 2320666; www.afindia.org /trivandrum; Forest Office Lane, Vazhuthacaud; ☺ 9am-1pm & 2-6pm Mon-Sat) Library and cultural events.
DC Books (☎ 2453379; www.dcbooks.com; Statue Rd; ☺ 9.30am-7.30pm Mon-Sat) Kerala's excellent bookshop chain, with a respectable selection of fiction and nonfiction books.

INTERNET ACCESS

Almikkice (Capital Centre; MG Rd; per hr Rs20; ☺ 7.30am-11.30pm) One of several good internet places in this small mall.
Yahoo Internet City (Manjalikulam Rd; per hr Rs20; ☺ 9am-9.30pm) Fast connections in cartoon-coloured cubicles.

MEDICAL SERVICES

KIMS (Kerala Institute of Medical Sciences; ☎ 2447676; Kumarapuram) With the best medical facilities Trivandrum has to offer, it's about 3km northwest of Trivandrum.

MONEY

There are ATMs that accept foreign cards all along MG Rd.
Thomas Cook (☎ 2338140-2; MG Rd; ☺ 9.30am-5.30pm Mon-Sat) Changes cash and travellers cheques.

PHOTOGRAPHY

Paramount Digital Colour Lab (☎ 2331643; MG Rd; ☺ 8.30am-9pm) Burns photo CDs; sells memory cards and digital accessories.

POST & TELEPHONE

There are several STD/ISD kiosks around town.
Main post office (☎ 2473071; MG Rd)

TOURIST INFORMATION

Tourist Facilitation Centre (☎ 2321132; Museum Rd; ☺ 24hr) Supplies maps and brochures.
Tourist Reception Centre (KTDC Hotel Chaithram; ☎ 2330031; Central Station Rd; ☺ 6.30am-9.30pm Tue-Sun) Arranges KTDC-run tours (see p327) and car hire.

Sights & Activities

ZOOLOGICAL GARDENS & MUSEUMS

This collection of museums, a gallery and the excellent zoo make a peaceful retreat from the flurry of the city.

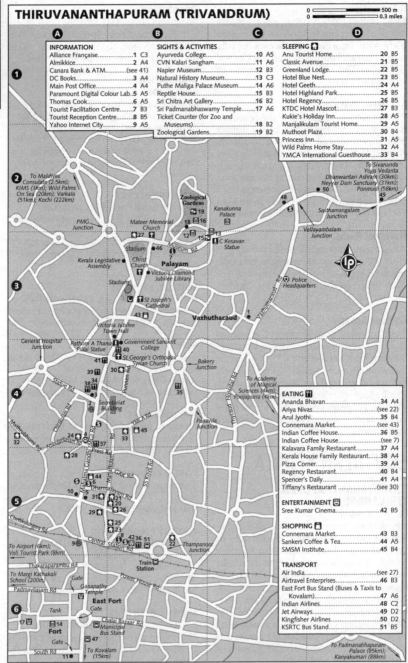

THIRUVANANTHAPURAM (TRIVANDRUM)

0 ————— 500 m
0 ————— 0.3 miles

INFORMATION
Alliance Française..............1 C3
Almikkice..........................2 A4
Canara Bank & ATM..........(see 41)
DC Books.........................3 A4
Main Post Office................4 A4
Paramount Digital Colour Lab.5 A5
Thomas Cook....................6 A5
Tourist Facilitation Centre.....7 B3
Tourist Reception Centre......8 B5
Yahoo Internet City............9 A5

SIGHTS & ACTIVITIES
Ayurveda College...............10 A5
CVN Kalari Sangham...........11 A6
Napier Museum..................12 B3
Natural History Museum.......13 C3
Puthe Maliga Palace Museum.14 A6
Reptile House....................15 B3
Sri Chitra Art Gallery...........16 B2
Sri Padmanabhaswamy Temple.17 A6
Ticket Counter (for Zoo and
    Museums)...................18 B2
Zoological Gardens.............19 B2

SLEEPING
Anu Tourist Home...............20 B5
Classic Avenue..................21 B5
Greenland Lodge................22 B5
Hotel Blue Nest.................23 B5
Hotel Geeth.....................24 A4
Hotel Highland Park............25 B5
Hotel Regency..................26 B5
KTDC Hotel Mascot.............27 B3
Kukie's Holiday Inn.............28 B4
Manjalikulam Tourist Home....29 A5
Muthoot Plaza...................30 B4
Princess Inn.....................31 A5
Wild Palms Home Stay.........32 A4
YMCA International Guesthouse..33 B4

To Maldives
Consulate (2.5km);
KIMS (3km); Wild Palms
On Sea (20km); Varkala
(51km); Kochi (222km)

To Sivananda
Yoga Vedanta
Dhanwantari Ashram (30km);
Neyyar Dam Sanctuary (31km);
Ponmudi (58km)

PMG
Junction

Zoological
Gardens

Kanakunna
Palace

Sasthamangalam
Junction

Mateer Memorial
Church

Museum Rd

Vellayambalam
Junction

C Kesavan
Statue

Stadium

Museum Rd

Kerala Legislative
Assembly

Christ
Church

Palayam

Stadium

Victoria Diamond
Jubilee Library

Police
Headquarters

St Joseph's
Cathedral

Vazhuthacaud

Victoria Jubilee
Town Hall

General Hospital
Junction

Rathon A Thanu
Pillai Statue

Government Sanskrit
College

St George's Orthodox
Syrian Church

Bakery
Junction

Statue Rd

To Academy
of Magical
Sciences (4km);
Poojapura (4km)

EATING
Ananda Bhavan..................34 A4
Ariya Nivas......................(see 22)
Arul Jyothi.......................35 B4
Connemara Market.............(see 43)
Indian Coffee House............36 B5
Indian Coffee House............(see 7)
Kalavara Family Restaurant....37 A4
Kerala House Family Restaurant.38 A4
Pizza Corner.....................39 A4
Regency Restaurant............40 B4
Spencer's Daily.................41 A4
Tiffany's Restaurant ....(see 30)

Secretariat
Building

Panavila
Junction

Press Rd

Dharmalayam Rd

ENTERTAINMENT
Sree Kumar Cinema............42 B5

SHOPPING
Connemara Market.............43 B3
Sankers Coffee & Tea..........44 A5
SMSM Institute..................45 B4

Central Station Rd

Thampanoor
Junction

To Airport (6km);
Veli Tourist Park (8km)

Thakaraparambu Rd

To Margi Kathakali
School (200m);
Padmavilasom St

Train
Station

Power House Rd

TRANSPORT
Air India.........................(see 27)
Airtravel Enterprises............46 B3
East Fort Bus Stand (Buses & Taxis to
    Kovalam).....................47 A6
Indian Airlines...................48 C2
Jet Airways......................49 D2
Kingfisher Airlines..............50 D2
KSRTC Bus Stand...............51 B5

Ganapathy
Temple

East Fort
Gate

Tank

Gate

Fort

Chalai Bazaar Rd
Manicipal
Bus Stand

Gate

South Rd

To Kovalam
(15km)

To Padmanabhapuram
Palace (85km);
Kanyakumari (88km)

The modern **zoological gardens** (☎ 2115122; admission Rs10, camera Rs25; ◷ 9am-6pm Tue-Sun) are among the most impressive in India. There are shaded paths meandering through woodland and lakes, where animals, such as tigers, macaques and lots of bird-life, happily frolic in massive, open enclosures that mimic their natural habitats. There's a separate **reptile house** (entrance with zoo ticket), where dozens of the slithery things do their thing and cobras frequently flare their hoods – just don't ask what the cute guinea pigs are here for.

A single Rs10 entry ticket, purchased at the **ticket counter** (◷ 9am-5.15pm), covers the **gallery and two museums** (◷ 10am-5pm Tue & Thu-Sun, 1-5pm Wed) in the park. Housed in a fetching Keralan-style wooden building from 1880, the **Napier Museum** has an eclectic display of bronzes, Buddhist sculptures, temple carts and ivory carvings. The brightly painted, carnivalesque interior is stunning and worth a look in its own right. The dusty **Natural History Museum** has hundreds of stuffed animals and birds, a fine skeleton collection and the odd mysteriously empty display case. The **Sri Chitra Art Gallery** has paintings by the Rajput, Mughal and Tanjore schools, and works by Ravi Varma.

SRI PADMANABHASWAMY TEMPLE

This 260-year-old **temple** (◷ 4am-7.30pm) is Trivandrum's spiritual heart. Spilling over 2400 sq metres, its main entrance is the 30m tall, seven-tier eastern *gopuram* (gateway tower). In the inner sanctum, the deity Padmanabha reclines on the sacred serpent and is made from over 10,000 *salagramam* (sacred stones) that were purportedly, and no doubt slowly, transported from Nepal by elephant.

The temple is officially open to Hindus only, but the path around to the right of the gate offers good views of the *gopuram*.

PUTHE MALIGA PALACE MUSEUM

The **Puthe Maliga Palace Museum** (admission Rs20; ◷ 8.30am-1pm & 3-5pm Tue-Sun) is housed in the 200-year-old palace of the Travancore maharajas. The traditional Keralan palace has carved wooden ceilings, marble sculptures and even imported Belgian glass. Inside you'll find Kathakali images, an armoury, portraits of maharajas, ornate thrones and other artefacts.

The annual **classical music festival** is held here in January/February.

VELI TOURIST PARK

At the junction of Veli Lake and the Arabian Sea, 8km west of the city, this unique **park** (☎ 2500785; admission Rs5; ◷ 8am-7.30pm) showcases oversized modern sculptures by local artist Kanai Kunhiraman. It is well designed, and the ponds, mammoth concrete conches and quasi-erotic curves of the statues make quite an interesting backdrop for a picnic or a stroll. Kids will love the paddle boats available for rent on the small lake (Rs50 to Rs75 per hour).

AYURVEDA

Students at **Ayurveda College** (☎ 2460190; MG Rd; ◷ 8am-1pm) perform massage and cleansing and purification treatments (after consultation with a doctor) free of charge. Expect to wait in line, and expect rudimentary Indian hospital, rather than Western resort-style, ambience.

Courses

Margi Kathakali School (☎ 2478806; Fort) conducts courses in Kathakali (see the boxed text, p372) and *kootiattam* (traditional Sanskrit drama) for beginner and advanced students. Fees average Rs200 per 1½-hour class. Visitors can peek at uncostumed practice sessions held 10am to noon Monday to Friday. It's in an unmarked building behind the Fort School.

CVN Kalari Sangham (☎ 2474182; South Rd; ◷ 9.30am-12.30pm & 4.30-6.30pm) offers three-month courses (Rs1000 per month) in *kalarippayat* (see boxed text, p372) for serious students with some experience in martial arts. Contact **Sathyan** (☎ 2474182; sathyacvn@vsnl.net) for details. On Monday to Saturday at 7am to 8.30am, training sessions are open for public viewing.

Tours

The Kerala Tourism Development Corporation (KTDC) runs several tours, all leaving from the Tourist Reception Centre at the KTDC Hotel Chaithram on Central Station Rd. The **Kanyakumari Day Tour** (per person Rs350; ◷ 7.30am-9pm Tue-Sun) visits Padmanabhapuram Palace (p336), Kanyakumari (p451) and the nearby Suchindram Temple. The **Thiruvananthapuram City Day Tour** (half-/full-day tours Rs100/175) visits Trivandrum's major sights plus Kovalam beach (half day 8.30am to 1pm and 2pm to 7pm; full day 8.30am to 7pm). Avoid Monday, when some places are closed.

Sleeping

BUDGET

The best hunting ground is along the quieter Manjalikulam Rd – some streetside rooms at MG Rd hotels are subject to ear-splitting noise.

Kukie's Holiday Inn (☎ 2478530; Lukes Lane; s/d Rs180/300) This meticulously maintained little gem lies enveloped in verdant silence at the end of a small lane. The rooms are very simple but thoughtfully maintained and offer frilly bits, like wicker chairs and bright paintwork. Excellent bang for your buck.

Greenland Lodge (☎ 2328114; Thampanoor Junction; s/d Rs231/296, r with AC Rs805; 🏵) Greenland lays out lots of serenity-inducing pastel colours to greet you. Inside, the spick-and-span rooms are great value, have lots of space and come with hybrid squat/sit-down toilets. It's efficiently run by smiling staff – though expect to pay a hefty two-night deposit upon arrival.

Princess Inn (☎ 2339150; Manjalikulam Rd; s/d Rs250/325, r with AC Rs600; 🏵) In a modern (read: 80s) glass-fronted building, the Princess Inn promises a relatively quiet sleep in spotless surrounds. Satellite TV and immaculate green-tiled bathrooms are thrown in for good measure.

YMCA International Guesthouse (☎ 2330059; YMCA Rd; s/d Rs330/440) On a quiet street well off MG Rd. Our value-ometer went off the scale when we saw this place. The rooms here are spacious, spotless and come with flawless tiled bathrooms and TV as standard. Both men and women accepted.

MIDRANGE

Manjalikulam Tourist Home (☎ 2330776; www.mthkerala.com; Manjalikulam Rd; s/d Rs400/500, r with AC Rs750-850; 🏵) The rooms here are massive and tidy but ruthlessly austere, except for a few odd grandmotherly touches like pink floral curtains.

Anu Tourist Home (☎ 2329777; at_homeanu@hotmail.com; Manjalikulam Rd; s/d Rs400/500, r with AC Rs900; 🏵) The cookie-cutter rooms here are modern and clean, though fairly austere and guarded by seemingly bored staff.

Hotel Regency (☎ 2330377; www.hotelregency.com; Manjalikulam Rd; s/d Rs490/650, with AC Rs800/1000; 🏵) With small, cosy rooms boasting satellite TV, a leafy entryway, lots of hush and plenty of smiles, this is a solid choice for a solid night's rest.

Hotel Highland Park (☎ 2338800; Manjalikulam Rd; s/d Rs500/750, with AC Rs950/1150; 🏵) Relatively new and in very good nick, only the single rooms here are really cramped. Don't mistake this for its older sister-hotel, Hotel Highland, across the road.

Hotel Blue Nest (☎ 3012800; www.hotelbluenest.com; Manjalikulam Rd; s/d Rs700/800, s/d with AC Rs1000/1150; 🏵) Clean and dull, this standard-issue mid-range joint has little to differentiate it from the competition, though it still makes for a comfy night's kip.

Wild Palms Home Stay (☎ 2471175; www.wildpalmsonsea.com; Mathrubhumi Rd; s Rs1095-1795, d Rs1395-2195; 🏵) Even thought this is the only place in town with any real character, recent price hikes are probably not justified. Still, nowhere else has a *Venus de Milo* statue greeting you in the front garden. The ornate, comfortable family home here has several spacious rooms, all handsomely furnished and offering a welcoming vibe. The same owners also have a beach-side property, Wild Palms On Sea, a more resorty place 20km from town, that can be booked here.

Hotel Geeth (☎ 2471987; www.geethinternational.in; Ambujarilasam Rd; s/d from Rs1200/1500; 🏵) This place will teach you not to judge a hotel by its drab cover. The Geeth comes to you fresh from a round of drastic renovations that have left the rooms fetchingly decked out in stylish modern furniture, IKEA-inspired wooden panelling, huge bathrooms and flat-screen TVs. Top value.

TOP END

KTDC Hotel Mascot (☎ 2318990; hotelmascot@vsnl.net; Mascot Sq; s/d from Rs3000/3500; 🏵 🖳 🖳) Lots of period touches, massive hallways and an imposing reception area lend this place an aura of old-world charm. It has a monster pool and ayurvedic spa, and is convenient for visits to the zoo, museums and galleries.

Classic Avenue (☎ 2333555; www.classicavenue.net; Manjalikulam Rd; s/d from Rs3000/4500; 🏵 🖳 🖳 🛜) Even though the foyer flirts with gaudy kitsch, the rooms here are absolutely lovely, with wood panelling, huge bathrooms, bathtubs, fluffy pillows and a soothing burgundy colour scheme. Best of all there's a rooftop pool, a gym, free wi-fi and airport pickups. The price even includes three square meals for the double rooms (breakfast for single rooms).

Muthoot Plaza (☎ 2337733; www.themuthootplaza.com; Punnen Rd; s/d from Rs5400/6200, ste from Rs8500; 🏵 🖳 🛜) Even though the arctic-level AC would make penguins shiver, this ultrachic business-focused hotel is still a great place to stay. Expect 3m chandeliers in the lobby, zealous staff and plush rooms stuffed with pillows, couches and all mod cons.

Eating

For some unusual refreshments with your meal, look out for *karikku* (coconut water) and *sambharam* (buttermilk with ginger and chilli).

Ananda Bhavan (☎ 2477646; MG Rd; dishes Rs15-25; ☽ lunch & dinner) A classic Keralan sit-down-and-dig-in-with-your-hands type situation.

Indian Coffee House (Maveli Cafe; Central Station Rd; dishes Rs15-45) This branch of the Indian Coffee House chain serves its yummy coffee and snacks in a unique, four-storey, spiralling tower lined inside by bench tables. Equal parts funhouse and Indian diner, it's a must-see. There's also a traditional branch (open 8.30am to 6pm) in Museum Rd, opposite the zoo.

Kerala House Family Restaurant (Statue Rd; mains Rs25-75) Don't expect much in the way of decor (think Formica), but do expect a decent serving of traditional South Indian cuisine with fish *pollichathu* (baked in banana leaf), with ginger, vegetables and spices.

Kalavara Family Restaurant (Press Rd; dishes Rs30-150; ☽ lunch & dinner) A bustling favourite of Trivandrum's middle class, this place does commendable lunchtime biryanis (Rs40 to Rs80) and a range of Keralan fish dishes. Our money's on the fish *molee* (fish pieces in co-conut sauce, Rs90).

Arul Jyothi (Bakery Junction; meals Rs32; ☽ lunch & dinner; ☒) Thali action can be found at this particularly clean place offering an AC dining room and exceptionally eager, friendly staff.

Ariya Nivaas (Manorama Rd; meals Rs42; ☽ 7am-9pm) Close to the train station and convenient for a quick feed between trains, this popular thali (traditional 'all-you-can-eat' meal) place gets positive reports from travellers. It's sparkling and run with efficiency.

Pizza Corner (MG Rd; small pizzas Rs85-170; ☽ lunch & dinner) A bit of East meets West, with tasty pizzas sporting everything from traditional toppings (margherita) to Indian twists on a theme (ie Punjabi chicken tikka).

There's a choice of decent hotel buffets at places like **Tiffany's Restaurant** (Muthoot Plaza; lunch/dinner Rs600/750) and **Regency Restaurant** (South Park Hotel; MG Rd; lunch/dinner Rs325/250). **Spencer's Daily** (MG Rd; ☽ 9am-9pm) is a well-stocked supermarket with lots of Western food (and even tampons!). Stock up on fruit and veg at Connemara Market.

Entertainment

For a quick Bolly- or Holly-wood fix, try **Sree Kumar Cinema** (☎ 2331222; Central Station Rd; admission Rs30-35; ☽ 11am-11pm).

If you ever wanted to learn how on earth they do that Indian rope trick, the **Academy of Magical Sciences** (☎ 2358910; www.magicmuthukad .com; Poojapura; show Rs350 per person) is the place for you. This academy works to preserve traditional Indian magic, give recognition to street magicians and train students in the art of illusion. It holds regular shows and has a shop selling magic kits. A little pricey, but fun.

Shopping

Wander around **Connemara Market** (MG Rd) to see vendors selling vegetables, fish, live goats, fabric, clothes, spices and more bananas than you can poke a hungry monkey at.

Sankers Coffee & Tea (☎ 2330469; MG Rd; ☽ 9am-9pm Mon-Sat) You'll smell the fresh coffee well before you reach this dainty little shop. It sells Nilgiri Export OP Leaf Tea (Rs250 per kg) and a variety of coffees and nuts.

SMSM Institute (☎ 2330298; YMCA Rd; ☽ 9am-8pm Mon-Sat) No, this place is not dedicated to the study of text messaging, but is a Kerala Government–run handicraft emporium with an Aladdin's cave of well-priced goodies.

Getting There & Away

AIR

Some airlines with offices in Trivandrum:
Air India (☎ 2317341; Mascot Sq; ☽ 9am-5.30pm Mon-Sat)
Indian Airlines (☎ 2314781; Museum Rd; ☽ 10am-1pm & 1.45-5.35pm Mon-Sat)
Jet Airways (☎ 2728864; Sasthamangalam Junction; ☽ 9am-5.30pm Mon-Sat)
Kingfisher Airlines (☎ 18002333131; Star Gate Bldg; TC 9/888, Vellayambalam)

Between them these airlines fly daily to Mumbai (from US$150) and several times a day to Kochi (US$85). There are at least four flights a day to Bengaluru (Bangalore, US$74), two to Chennai (Madras, US$75) and one direct flight to Delhi (US$180).

There are regular flights from Trivandrum to Colombo and Male; see p521.

All airline bookings can be made at the efficient **Airtravel Enterprises** (☎ 3011412; www .ategroup.org; New Corporation Bldg; MG Rd; ☽ 9.30am-6pm Mon-Sat, to 5pm Sun).

BUSES FROM TRIVANDRUM (KSRTC BUS STAND)

Destination	Fare (Rs)	Duration (hr)	Frequency
Alleppey	98	3½	every 15min
Chennai	325	17	8 daily
Ernakulam (Kochi)	135	5	every 20min
Kanyakumari	40	2	6 daily
Kollam	45	1½	every 15min
Kumily (for Periyar)	161	8	2 daily
Madrai	180	7	9 daily
Neyyar Dam	22	1½	every 40min
Puducherry	280	16	1 daily
Thrissur	183	7½	every 30min
Udhagamandalam (Ooty)	305	14	1 daily
Varkala	36	1¼	hourly

BUS

For buses operating from the **KSRTC bus stand** (☎ 2323886), opposite the train station, see the table, above.

For Tamil Nadu destinations, the State Express Transport Corporation (SETC) buses leave from the eastern end of the KSRTC bus stand.

Buses leave for Kovalam beach (Rs9, 30 minutes, every 20 minutes) between 5.40am and 10pm from the southern end of the East Fort bus stand on MG Rd.

TRAIN

Trains are often heavily booked, so it's worth visiting the **reservation office** (☎ 139; ☼ 8am-8pm Mon-Sat, to 2pm Sun). See the table, below, for major long-distance services.

Within Kerala, there are frequent trains to Varkala (2nd class/AC chair Rs22/142, one hour), Kollam (Rs26/142, one hour) and

Ernakulam (Rs56/238, 4½ hours), with trains passing through either Alleppey (Rs45/180, three hours) or Kottayam (Rs46/188, 3½ hours). There are also several daily services to Kanyakumari (Sleeper/3AC/2AC Rs101/188/258, 2½ hours).

Getting Around

The **airport** (☎ 2501424) is 6km from the city and 15km from Kovalam; take local bus 14 from the East Fort bus stand (Rs6). Prepaid taxi vouchers from the airport cost Rs206 to the city and Rs313 to Kovalam.

Autorickshaws patrol the streets and are the easiest way to get around. Standard rates are Rs10 flagfall, then Rs5 per kilometre, but all rules go out the window at night – 50% over the meter is fair. Agree on a fare beforehand. A cheap way to get around is to hop on and off any of the crowded buses plying the length of MG Rd (Rs4).

AROUND TRIVANDRUM
Neyyar Dam Sanctuary

This **sanctuary** (☎ 2272182; Indian/foreigner Rs10/100; ☼ 9am-4pm Tue-Sun), 32km north of Trivandrum, lies around an idyllic lake created by the 1964 Neyyar Dam. The fertile forest lining the shoreline is home to gaurs, sambar deer, sloth, elephants, lion-tailed macaques and the occasional tiger.

The sanctuary office organises one-hour **lion safaris** (per person Rs250) by boat and bus, though you're more likely to see monkeys than any big cats. For improved spotting opportunities it's better to sneak around on a guided **trek** (per person per hr Rs100). Nearby there's a **Crocodile Protection Centre** (Indian/foreigner Rs5/10). Get here from Trivandrum's KSRTC bus stand by frequent bus (Rs22, 1½ hours). A taxi is Rs700 to

MAJOR TRAINS FROM TRIVANDRUM

The following are some of the major long-distance trains departing from Trivandrum.

Destination	Train no & name	Fare (Rs*)	Duration (hr)	Departures
Bengaluru	6525 Bangalore Exp	322/868/1234	18	12.55pm
Chennai	2696 Chennai Exp	356/938/1271	16½	5.25pm
Coimbatore	7229 Sabari Exp	204/534/722	9¼	7.15am
Delhi	2625 Kerala Exp	614/165/2281	50	11.15am
Mangalore	6347 Mangalore Exp	270/724/985	14½	8.45pm
	6347 Malabar Exp	270/724/985	15½	6.30pm
Mumbai	6346 Netravathi Exp	483/1320/1814	30½	10.00am

*Sleeper/3AC/2AC

Rs800 return (with two hours waiting time), a very bumpy rickshaw about half that.

Sivananda Yoga Vedanta Dhanwantari Ashram

Just before Neyyar Dam, this superbly located **ashram** (☎ /fax 0471-2273093; www.sivananda .org/ndam), established in 1978, is renowned for its hatha yoga courses. Courses start on the 1st and 16th of each month, run for a minimum of two weeks and cost Rs600 per day for accommodation in a double room (Rs450 in dormitories). Low season (May to September) rates are Rs100 less. There's an exacting schedule (5.30am to 10pm) of yoga practice, meditation and chanting; and students rave about the food (included in the rates). Bookings are required. Month-long yoga-teacher training and ayurvedic massage courses are also available.

KOVALAM
☎ 0471

Holding the dubious title of India's most 'developed' resort, these days Kovalam's sliver of beach plays second fiddle to the bumper-to-bumper development onshore. After it was discovered by backpackers in the '70s, it didn't take too long for European package-tour operators, looking for the next Goa goldmine, to descend en masse on this once-calm fishing village. Nevertheless, shreds of charm do remain – particularly outside the peak season, when sky-high prices subside and resident touts and male gawkers seem to go into hibernation.

Orientation

Kovalam consists of two coves (Lighthouse beach and Hawah beach) separated from less-populated beaches north and south by rocky headlands. The town proper is at Kovalam Junction, about 1.5km from the beaches.

Information

Just about every shop and hotel will change money – ask around for the best rate. In Kovalam, near the Leela resort there's a **National Bank of India** (⏱ 10.30am-1.30pm Mon-Fri, to noon Sat) that changes cash and, near the hospital, a CBS ATM taking Visa cards. Otherwise, there are Federal Bank and ICICI ATMs at Kovalam Junction. There are lots of small, uniformly slow internet places charging Rs30 to Rs50 per hour, as well as numerous STD/ISD facilities around.

Bookshop (⏱ 7am-11pm) A great range of books to rent/buy/exchange, next to the German Bakery.
Post office (⏱ 9am-1pm Mon-Sat)
Top Shop Cyber Cafe (per hr Rs30; ⏱ 9.30am-8.30pm) Off the beach up a steep hill, this is the only dedicated internet joint.
Tourist Facilitation Centre (☎ 2480085; ⏱ 10am-5pm) Very helpful, inside the entrance to the Kovalam Beach Resort.
United Books (NUP Beach Rd; ⏱ 9am-9pm) A random collection of books on Kerala, Indian spirituality and English-language trash lit.
Upasana Hospital (☎ 2480632; ⏱ 9.30am-1pm & 5-8.30pm) Has two English-speaking doctors who can take care of minor injuries.

Dangers & Annoyances

Women are likely to grow tired of the parade of male Indian day-trippers stalking the beach in hope of glimpsing female flesh – though it's more annoying than dangerous. Theft does occur, both from hotels and the beach – watch your possessions at the beach.

There are strong rips at both ends of Lighthouse beach that carry away several swimmers every year. Swim only between the flags in the area patrolled by lifeguards.

Kovalam has frequent blackouts and the footpaths further back behind Lighthouse beach are unlit, so carry a torch (flashlight) after dark.

Activities

For ayurvedic treatments that won't break the bank, **Gopal's** (☎ 2480833; www.sarisafari.com/gopals; ⏱ 8am-5pm) is a government approved ayurveda centre. A massage costs US$3 to US$6, with longer, multi-day treatments available. Don't expect resort-style ambience – this is a basic clinic that specialises in authentic treatments.

Sleeping

Kovalam is chock-a-block with hotels, though budget places here cost more than usual and are becoming a dying breed. Beachfront properties are the most expensive and have great sea views, though many cater solely to package groups. Look out for smaller places tucked away in the labyrinth of paths behind the beach among the palm groves and rice paddies; they're much better value. For more top-end accommodation choices, also check out Around Kovalam, p335.

Prices quoted are for the November to March high season when you'll need to book

KERALA

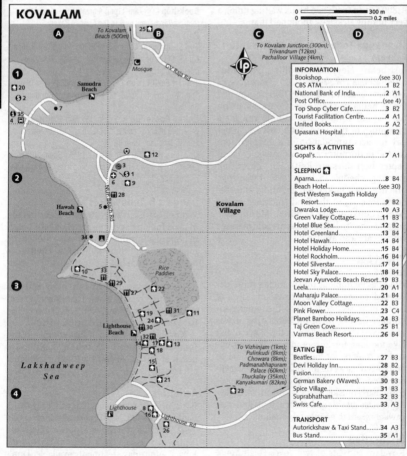

KOVALAM

0 ─────── 300 m
0 ─────── 0.2 miles

INFORMATION

Bookshop	(see 30)
CBS ATM	1 B2
National Bank of India	2 A1
Post Office	(see 4)
Top Shop Cyber Cafe	3 B2
Tourist Facilitation Centre	4 A1
United Books	5 A2
Upasana Hospital	6 B2

SIGHTS & ACTIVITIES

Gopal's	7 A1

SLEEPING

Aparna	8 B4
Beach Hotel	(see 30)
Best Western Swagath Holiday Resort	9 B2
Dwaraka Lodge	10 A3
Green Valley Cottages	11 B3
Hotel Blue Sea	12 B2
Hotel Greenland	13 B4
Hotel Hawah	14 B4
Hotel Holiday Home	15 B4
Hotel Rockholm	16 B4
Hotel Silverstar	17 B4
Hotel Sky Palace	18 B4
Jeevan Ayurvedic Beach Resort	19 B3
Leela	20 A1
Maharaju Palace	21 B4
Moon Valley Cottage	22 B3
Pink Flower	23 C4
Planet Bamboo Holidays	24 B3
Taj Green Cove	25 B1
Varmas Beach Resort	26 B4

EATING

Beatles	27 B3
Devi Holiday Inn	28 B2
Fusion	29 B3
German Bakery (Waves)	30 B3
Spice Village	31 B3
Suprabhatham	32 B3
Swiss Cafe	33 A3

TRANSPORT

Autorickshaw & Taxi Stand	34 A3
Bus Stand	35 A1

ahead; outside of these times expect huge discounts. During the Christmas and New Year rush prices can double.

BUDGET

Hotel Holiday Home (☎ 2486382; newholidayhome@ yahoo.com; s/d Rs300/500; 🖳) Recently spruced up with a fantastic face-lift, this top-value place offers spacious and cheerily coloured bungalow-style rooms surrounding a small, quiet garden. There's a tangible chill-out vibe, helped along by its tranquil setting in a maze of paths behind the main beach. It's popular with long-term travellers.

Pink Flower (☎ 2383908; d Rs350) It's worth seeking this place out, at least for the look of surprise on friendly Mr Sadanandan's face

that you managed to find his little guest house. Tucked away in the palms behind several hotels, this well-kept place has several humble, clean rooms that may just be the cheapest digs in Kovalam. Yoga classes are held on the rooftop.

Dwaraka Lodge (☎ 2480411; d Rs500) With regular licks of paint helping cover up the war wounds of this tired old-timer, Dwaraka remains among the cheapest ocean-front property out there. There's nothing flash inside, just clean sheets, a loo and a room with a view.

Moon Valley Cottage (☎ 9446100291; sknair kovalam@yahoo.com; d from Rs500, upstairs apt per week Rs5000) There's nothing but swaying palms all the way back here, and this place makes the most of it with a top-floor hang-out where you can practically reach out and fondle the coconuts. The rooms are a decent size and come well finished, with lots of hush on offer for all.

Hotel Sky Palace (☎ 9349083949; s Rs500; d Rs800-1000) This little two-storey place lies sandwiched down a small lane and has just a few lovely rooms – all have small patios or balconies – with a sliver of garden at the front. It's relaxed and central without being too noisy.

Hotel Greenland (☎ 2486442; hotelgreenlandin@yahoo.com; r Rs600/1200) Family run and as friendly as they come. The well-kept refurbished rooms in this multilevel complex have lots of natural light – some even have small kitchenettes for self-catering. Will cook up yummy food on request.

Hotel Silverstar (☎ 2482983; www.silverstar-kovalam.com; d incl breakfast Rs750-1100) The spick-and-span rooms here have loads of space, though the place is set quite a way back in the heart of the palm-frond jungle. It's quiet, but the large balconies don't have much of a view.

Green Valley Cottages (☎ 2480636; indira_ravi@hotmail.com; r Rs800) Also way back in the paddy fields, this serene spot is the place to revel in serious shush time. The rooms are ruthlessly austere, perfect for monks-in-training looking to escape pesky distractions like room furnishings.

MIDRANGE & TOP END

Planet Bamboo Holidays (☎ 9946477929; www.planetbambooholidays.com; r Rs1000) At least these guys are trying for a slightly different angle – here you can stay in bamboo-clad bungalows set around a little grassy patch, complete with a small pond and a dwarf-sized bamboo bridge. Rooms are nothing fancy, but it's quiet and very rustic.

Maharaju Palace (☎ 2485320, 9895012129; www.maharajupalace.in; d Rs1500-1700) More of a quiet retreat than a palace, this boutiquey place has far more character than anything else in its class. The few medium-sized rooms are decorated with artsy touches and have a large shared balcony with comfortable lounging chairs. There's a secluded little garden out the front.

Aparna (☎ 2480950; www.aparnahotelkovalam.com; s/d Rs1500/1750) Aparna has just a handful of cute, oddly-shaped little rooms. All are cosy, with bright blue bathrooms, private balconies, excellent sea views and welcome sea breezes.

our pick **Beach Hotel** (☎ 2481937; www.thebeachhotel-kovalam.com; s/d Rs1500/2500; ☒) Brought to you by the long-running German Bakery, this uberhip beach-front property has just a few rooms, though all are designed with minimalist flair and finished with smart, arty touches. Throw in some bright orange/burgundy tones, bamboo window shutters, and the crown for 'affordable Kovalam chic' is theirs for the taking. Best of all, the German Bakery is right upstairs.

Varmas Beach Resort (☎ 2480478; www.calanguetebeach.com; Lighthouse Rd; d Rs1650, with AC Rs2300; ☒) This is one of the nicest-looking places in Kovalam, with a wood-panelled, Kerala-style facade and rooms adorned with wooden furniture. Throw in comfy sitting areas on private balconies, some exceptional views and access to an isolated beach and, bingo – we have a winner!

Best Western Swagath Holiday Resort (☎ 2481148; www.swagathresorts.com; r Rs1700-3900, with AC Rs2000-4200, ste Rs6000; ☒ ☒ ☒) Set in a cultivated, fairytale-perfect garden overlooking coconut palms. The rooms are big and well furnished, though with a whiff of the hotel-chain about them. The place is kid-friendly, with a small playground and kiddie pool, and there is one ridiculously charming garden villa (Rs2400), complete with a white-picket fence.

Hotel Rockholm (☎ 2480306; www.rockholm.com; Lighthouse Rd; s/d Rs1850/2000, with AC Rs2250/2500; ☒ ☒) Overlooking crashing waves and near a secluded beach, this place bravely clings to remnants of leftover '80s chic. AC rooms are slightly bigger and have romantic window seats, though the whole place is really beginning to show its age.

Hotel Blue Sea (☎ 9349991992; www.hotelbluesea.net; r Rs2500, with AC Rs4000; ☒ ☒) Something different: great rooms inside circular, three-storey towers with polished floors and round verandahs. They also offer plain-old square rooms for Rs1000.

Jeevan Ayurvedic Beach Resort (☎ 2480662; www.jeevanresort.com; d Rs3000-4500; ☒ ☒) This resort has a neat colour scheme, ageing, decent-sized rooms with bathtubs and an alluring pool that practically plays footsies with the ocean. Upstairs rooms have balconies with sea views.

Hotel Hawah (☎ 2481951; www.hawahbeach.com; r Rs2000, with AC Rs3500-5500; ☒) While it comes up a little short in the character department, at least Hawah has immaculately clean and

KERALA

LEADER OF THE PACK

In 1957 Kerala was first in the world to freely elect a communist government. While communism's hammer and sickle hasn't had much luck in running other parts of the world, Kerala's unique blend of democratic-socialist principles has a pretty impressive track record.

Kerala has been labelled 'the most socially advanced state in India' by Nobel prize–winning economist Amartya Sen. Land reform and also a focus on infrastructure, health and education have played a large part in Kerala's success. The literacy rate (91%) is the highest of any developing nation in the world, though a strong history of education stretches back centuries to the days of magnanimous Rajas and active missionaries. The infant mortality rate in Kerala is one-fifth of the national average, while life expectancy stands at 73 years, 10 years higher than the rest of the country.

The picture is not all rosy, however. Lack of any industrial development or foreign investment means that the ambitions of many educated youth are curtailed. This might explain why Kerala also has the highest suicide rates and liquor consumption in the country. A big hope for the economy's future is the recent boom in tourism, with Kerala emerging as one of India's most popular new tourist hot spots. So, thanks for coming, and congratulations on being a part of the solution.

---

humongous rooms right near the beach. Only a couple of the rooms come with any real sea views.

Leela (☎ 2480101; www.theleela.com; s/d from US$295/320; ❇ 🏊) The only real top-end option right in Kovalam, the Leela comes jam-packed with a ridiculous amount of facilities. Glamorously located around extensive grounds on the headland north of Hawah beach, there are three (three!) swimming pools, an ayurvedic centre, a gym, two private beaches, several restaurants and more. Rooms aren't huge, but are sumptuously decorated with period touches, colourful textiles and Keralan artwork.

Eating

Dozens of open-air restaurants line the beach area displaying the catch of the day nightly – just pick a fish, settle on a price (per serve around Rs150, tiger prawns over Rs400) and decide how you want it prepared. Menus and prices are indistinguishable, so it's more about which ambience takes your fancy.

Devi Holiday Inn (mains Rs40-120) A tiny, family run eatery a little off the beach, this hotel has whips up great veg and non-veg Indian food for refreshingly reasonable prices.

Suprabhatham (meals Rs45-80) This cosy little veggie place dishes up excellent, dirt-cheap and truly authentic Keralan cooking in a rustic setting. Out in the palm groves, it's secluded and intimate, with an option to dine under the stars to a nightly orchestra of crickets.

Spice Village (dishes Rs50-220) Run by a squad of local Rastas, this small lily-pond oasis calls itself 'traditional Keralan' – though the requisite pasta and Chinese dishes do make cameo appearances. It serves decent Keralan goods like fish *pollichathu* (Rs150).

Beatles (mains Rs90-270) You can't miss Beatles, with it's funky gnarled wood decor and vines dripping from every corner. Nepalese run, you'll find Himalayan specials like *momos* (Tibetan dumplings) on the menu (Rs90 to Rs120) among other standard-issue Western/Indian victuals.

Swiss Cafe (mains Rs140-230) While the setting here is lovely, with an upstairs balcony and lots of wicker seating, the menu offers pretty much the same choices as everywhere else, with a few token Swiss dishes (ie schnitzel) thrown in to justify the name.

Fusion (mains Rs140-450) This funky eatery has an inventive menu where dishes from the East meet dishes from the West – and it seems like they get along pretty well. You can get regular Indian or Western meals, but the fun part is trying their fusion options where the two cuisines collide to form yummy new taste combinations. Also serves French press coffee and herbal teas.

German Bakery (Waves) (mains Rs140-700) In a swanky new location on an airy, sunburnt-orange balcony, this remains the most popular hang-out in town. Finger-licking pastries still take pride of place on the menu, as do a huge range of winning breakfasts, strong coffees and quiches. It's easy to spend the entire day relaxing here, with a varied selection of classy main courses featuring curries, seafood, tofu and pizzas taking you into your evening meal.

Entertainment
During the high season, an abridged version of Kathakali is performed most nights somewhere – enquire about locations and times at the Tourist Facilitation Centre (p331).

Hollywood film fodder is shown nightly in some restaurants. Dedicated bars are thin on the ground, but beer is available in most restaurants (around Rs80), with some serving cocktails (Rs80 to Rs120) to a repetitive soundtrack of reggae, trance and classic rock.

Getting There & Away
BUS
There are local buses connecting Kovalam and Trivandrum every 20 minutes between 5.30am and 10.10pm (Rs9, 30 minutes); catch them from the entrance to Leela resort. Buses to Ernakulam leave at 6am and 2.30pm (Rs140, 5½ hours), stopping at Kallambalam (for Varkala, Rs39, 1½ hours), Kollam (Rs44, 2½ hours) and Alleppey (Rs87, four hours). There's another 6.30am bus to Ernakulam via Kottayam that bypasses Varkala.

TAXI & AUTORICKSHAW
A taxi between Trivandrum and Kovalam beach is around Rs300. Autorickshaws should be about Rs120. Prepaid taxis from Trivandrum airport to Lighthouse beach cost Rs313.

Voyager Travels (☎ 9847065093) rents out scooters/Enfields for around Rs450/550 per day. It has no fixed office address.

AROUND KOVALAM
Samudra Beach
Samudra beach, about 4km north of Kovalam by road, has seen a growing number of resorts edge out what was until recently a small fishing village. Although more peaceful, the steep and rough beach here is not as good as Lighthouse Beach for swimming.

Taj Green Cove (☎ 2487733; www.tajhotels.com; r from Rs11,000-30,000; ❷ 🖳 🏊) The Kovalam branch of this swanky Indian hotel chain is set among lolling, green grounds and has direct access to a private beach. The individual chalets here are simply but tastefully adorned,

some with private gardens and others with primo sea views. Several restaurants and the usual top-end amenities are all here for the taking.

Pulinkudi & Chowara
Around 8km south of Kovalam are some luxury alternatives to Kovalam's crowded beaches.

Dr Franklin's Panchakarma Institute (☎ 2480870; www.dr-franklin.com; Chowara; s €15-38, d €20-55; 🖳) For those serious about ayurvedic treatment, here is a reputable and less expensive alternative to the flashier resorts. Daily treatment costs €35, with a full meal plan an additional €16. Accommodation is tidy and comfortable but not resort style. There are therapy packages for whatever ails you, including spine problems, purification/detox treatments, as well as general rejuvenation and stress relief. A one-off relaxation or rejuvenation massage costs €12 to €17.

Thapovan Heritage Home (☎ 2480453; www .thapovan.com; s/d Rs3300/4125) This place is the way to live the simple life (no pool, AC or TV) in complete, understated luxury. The gorgeous Keralan teak cottages here are filled with handcrafted furniture and are set among perfectly manicured grounds overlooking breathtaking swaying palm groves. Ayurvedic treatments available range from one-hour massages to 28-day treatment marathons. It's a few kilometres from the nearest beach.

Bethsaida Hermitage (☎ 2267554; www.bethsaida hermitage.com; Pulinkudi; r €80-140) A resort with a difference: this is a charitable organisation that helps support a nearby orphanage. As a bonus, it's also a luxurious and remote beachside escape, with sculpted gardens, seductively slung hammocks, putting-green perfect lawns, palms galore and shade in spades. It offers a variety of cottages, from rainbowpainted, half-ovals to spacious, cool Keralastyle huts.

The luscious, small resort of **Surya Samudra Beach Garden** (☎ 2480413; www.suryasamudra.com; Pulinkudi; r incl breakfast €120-350; ❷ 🏊) has several types of cottages, many of which are transplanted traditional Keralan homes, with spectacular carved ceilings and open-air bathrooms. There are private beaches, an infinity pool and ayurvedic treatments – all on 8.5 hectares of wonderfully cultivated grounds. It was closed for extensive renovations at the time of our last visit.

PADMANABHAPURAM PALACE

With dozens of lumberyards worth of carved ceilings and polished-teak beams, this **palace** (☎ 04651-250255; admission Indian/foreigner Rs25/200, camera/video Rs25/1500; ⏲ 9am-5pm Tue-Sun) is considered the best example of traditional Keralan architecture today. Parts of it date back to 1550 though, as the egos of successive rulers left their mark, it expanded into the magnificent conglomeration of 14 palaces it is today.

The largest wooden palace complex in Asia, it was once the seat of the rulers of Travancore, a princely state taking in parts of Tamil Nadu and Kerala. Fetchingly constructed of teak and granite, the exquisite interiors include carved rosewood ceilings, Chinese-style screens, and floors finished to a high black polish.

Padmanabhapuram is about 60km southeast of Kovalam. Catch a local bus from Kovalam (or Trivandrum) to Kanyakumari and get off at Thuckalay, from where it's a short autorickshaw ride or 15-minute walk. Alternatively, take one of the tours organised by the KTDC (see p327), or hire a taxi (about Rs1500 return from Trivandrum or Kovalam).

VARKALA

☎ 0470 / pop 42,273

With a gaggle of guest houses and restaurants perched almost perilously along the edge of breathtaking cliffs, Varkala is a sight to behold. This beach-side resort town is considerably more laid back than its Kovalam cousin, valiantly clinging to its backpacker roots in the face of ongoing development. The strand of golden beach here nuzzles Varkala's cliff edge, where restaurants play more Bob Marley music that you can poke a dreadlocked backpacker at. Even though more hotels mushroom every year and prices creep that little bit higher, this is still a great place to while away some time and watch the days slowly turn into weeks.

Orientation & Information

The main beach is accessed from either Beach Rd or by several steep stairways cut into the north cliff. Varkala town and the train station are about 2km from the beach.

A 24-hour SBI ATM at the temple junction takes Visa cards, otherwise there's a State Bank of India ATM in Varkala town. Many of the moneychangers and travel agents lining the cliff do cash advances on credit cards and change travellers cheques. There are plenty of places to update your Facebook profile along the cliff top (around Rs40 per hour) – save emails often, as power cuts are not uncommon.

Police aid post (⏲ Nov-Feb) At the helipad, rarely staffed.

Post office (⏲ 10am-2pm Mon-Sat) North of Temple Junction.

Dangers & Annoyances

The beaches at Varkala have strong currents; even experienced swimmers have been swept away. This is one of the most dangerous beaches in Kerala, so be careful and swim

---

AYURVEDA

With its roots in Sanskrit, the word ayurveda is derived from *ayu* (life) and *veda* (knowledge); it is the knowledge or science of life. Principles of ayurvedic medicine were first documented in the Vedas some 2000 years ago, but it may even have been practised centuries earlier.

Ayurveda sees the world as having an intrinsic order and balance. It argues that we possess three *doshas* (humours): *vata* (wind or air); *pitta* (fire); and *kapha* (water/earth), known together as the *tridoshas*. Deficiency or excess in any of them can result in disease: an excess of *vata* may result in dizziness and debility; an increase in *pitta* may lead to fever, inflammation and infection. *Kapha* is essential for hydration.

Ayurvedic treatment aims to restore the balance, and hence good health, principally through two methods: *panchakarma* (internal purification, see boxed text, p382) and herbal massage. The herbs used in ayurveda grow in abundance in Kerala's moist climate, and every village has its own ayurvedic pharmacy.

Having an occasional ayurvedic massage, something offered at tourist resorts all over Kerala, is relaxing, but you'll have to go in for the long haul to reap any real benefits – usually 15 days or longer. Expect a thorough examination followed by an appropriate ayurvedic diet, exercises and a range of treatments.

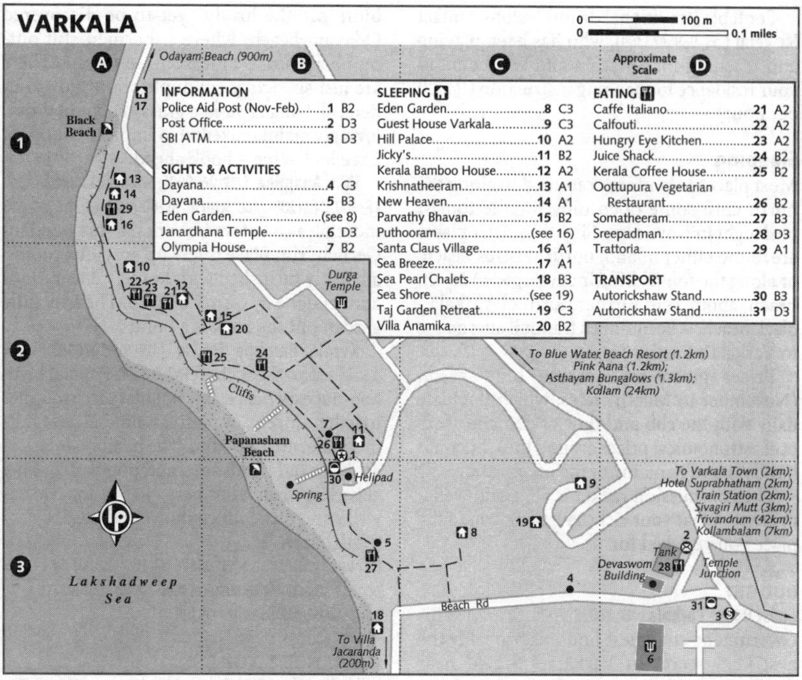
VARKALA
0 100 m
0 0.1 miles
Approximate Scale
A B C D
1 2 3
Odayam Beach (900m)
INFORMATION
Police Aid Post (Nov-Feb)........1 B2
Post Office........2 D3
SBI ATM........3 D3
SIGHTS & ACTIVITIES
Dayana........4 C3
Dayana........5 B3
Eden Garden........(see 8)
Janardhana Temple........6 D3
Olympia House........7 B2
SLEEPING
Eden Garden........8 C3
Guest House Varkala........9 C3
Hill Palace........10 A2
Jicky's........11 B2
Kerala Bamboo House........12 A2
Krishnatheeram........13 A1
New Heaven........14 A1
Parvathy Bhavan........15 B2
Puthooram........(see 16)
Santa Claus Village........16 A1
Sea Breeze........17 A1
Sea Pearl Chalets........18 B3
Sea Shore........(see 19)
Taj Garden Retreat........19 C3
Villa Anamika........20 B2
EATING
Caffe Italiano........21 A2
Calfouti........22 A2
Hungry Eye Kitchen........23 A2
Juice Shack........24 B2
Kerala Coffee House........25 B2
Oottupura Vegetarian Restaurant........26 B2
Somatheeram........27 B3
Sreepadman........28 D3
Trattoria........29 A1
TRANSPORT
Autorickshaw Stand........30 B3
Autorickshaw Stand........31 D3
Black Beach
Durga Temple
Cliffs
Papanasham Beach
Helipad
Spring
Lakshadweep Sea
To Blue Water Beach Resort (1.2km) Pink Aana (1.2km); Asthayam Bungalows (1.3km); Kollam (24km)
To Varkala Town (2km); Hotel Suprabhatham (2km) Train Station (2km); Sivagiri Mutt (3km); Trivandrum (42km); Kollambalam (7km)
Tank
Devaswom Building
Temple Junction
Beach Rd
To Villa Jacaranda (200m)

between the flags or ask the lifeguards for the best place to swim.

Indian male gawkers are starting to discover the many bikini-clad attractions at Varkala. However, with police patrolling beaches to keep male starers a-walkin' and the hawkers at bay, this is more of a nuisance than a danger. It still pays to dress sensitively, especially if you're going into Varkala town.

It seems like every man and his dog has an ayurvedic-related product to sell, from treatments, to massage, to ayurvedic tea and even, wait for it, ayurvedic toilets. Most aren't qualified practitioners – ask for recommendations before you go to get herbalised. Women should always be treated by a female practitioner.

Sights & Activities

Varkala is a temple town, and **Janardhana Temple** is the main event – its technicolour Hindu spectacle sits hovering above Beach Rd. It's closed to non-Hindus, but you may be invited into the temple grounds where there is a huge banyan tree and shrines to Ayyappan, Hanuman and other Hindu deities.

Sivagiri Mutt (☎ 2602807; www.sivagiri.org) is the headquarters of the Sree Narayana Dharma Sanghom Trust, the ashram devoted to Shri Narayana Guru (1855–1928), Kerala's most prominent guru. This is a popular pilgrimage site and the resident swami is happy to talk to visitors.

Practically everyone in town offers ayurveda, yoga or massage (see also Dangers & Annoyances, opposite). A recommended place for ayurvedic beauty treatments is **Dayana** (☎ 2609464; manicure & pedicure Rs250, facials Rs400-1000; 9am-7pm), which has a shack on the beach and a shop on Beach Rd (women only). Mr Omanakuttan at **Olympia House** (☎ 9349439675) is a qualified massage instructor, in both ayurveda and other schools, and has a sound reputation. The excellent **Eden Garden** (☎ 2603910; www.eden-garden.net) is a popular ayurvedic resort offering single treatments and packages; see p339 for accommodation details. Yoga is offered at several guest houses for around Rs200 to Rs300 per hour.

Boogie boards can be hired from places along the beach for Rs100, but be wary of very strong currents.

For tabla (traditional drum) lessons contact **Mr Venu** (☎ 9895473304), who has been playing and teaching for 15 years and will come to your residence for banging instruction (Rs300 per hour).

Sleeping

Most places to stay are crammed in along the north cliff; some open only for the tourist onslaught in November. Slightly quieter places are found either inland, north at Black beach, or along the south cliff. Undeveloped Odayam beach, about 1km further north of Varkala's black beach, is becoming a tranquil alternative to Varkala's bustle.

Prices given are average high-season (November to March) rates, which fluctuate daily with the ebb and flow of demand – expect astronomical prices around the Christmas holidays and bargains in the off season.

The commission racket is alive and well – make sure that your rickshaw takes you to the place you've asked for.

BUDGET

Guest House Varkala (☎ 2602227; s/d Rs165/220) This government-run guest house is probably the best kept secret in Varkala. Located near the Taj hotel, it has several rooms in huge Keralan-styled bungalows that were once part of a palace complex. Though spartan, each bargain-basement abode is finished with lots of polished wood and has high ceilings.

Jicky's (☎ 2606994; www.jickys.com; s Rs350, d Rs500-1000) Way back in the palm groves, family run Jicky's is as friendly as they come. There is a range of spotless rooms available in a large two-storey building here, all surrounded by oodles of green and piles of hush.

New Heaven (☎ 9846074818; newheavenbeachresort@yahoo.com; r Rs500-700) Just back from the northern cliffs, New Heaven has easy access to Black beach and great top-floor views. Bedrooms are roomy, basic and tidy, with big blue bathrooms and hanging wicker chairs out the front for lazing.

Sea Shore (☎ 9746550396; r Rs500-800) The Sea Shore occupies a barbie-pink building that's been smothered in other pastel shades throughout. Inside it is predictably basic and clean, with the top-floor rooms offering good sea views and welcome breezes. It's a short walk to Black beach.

Asthamay Bungalows (☎ 2663613; www.asthamay.com; s/d Rs500/1000) Asthamay crowns a small bluff on the lovely, yet-to-be-discovered Odayam beach, where fishermen still outnumber tourists at least three-to-one. There are just six octagonal duplex bungalows out here, all lying around a grassy coconut grove, lovingly maintained and in immaculate order. Excellent value – book ahead.

Villa Anamika (☎ 2600096; www.villaanamika.com; s Rs600, d Rs1200-1400, with AC Rs2000; 🖳) One of the more pleasant stays in Varkala, this Keralan/German run place offers up spacious rooms, all neatly furnished with homely decorations and art done by owner Chicku. The trim little garden out the back is a bonus.

Kerala Bamboo House (☎ 9895270993; www.keralabamboohouse.com; huts d Rs750-1500) For that bamboo-hut experience, this popular place squishes together dozens of pretty, Balinese-style huts in a massive compound. The bamboo interiors are basic but handsome, and popular cooking classes are run from here (Rs500 for two) as well as regular culture shows and yoga.

Also try:

Parvathy Bhavan (☎ 9847616410; r Rs600) Barebones homestay with austere, tiled rooms that makes a good back-up if elsewhere is full.

MIDRANGE & TOP END

Hill Palace (☎ 2610142; www.hillpalaceresort.com; r Rs750-1000) Chintzy decor will greet you here, but the place is always sparkling clean and freshly painted, with balconies facing the ocean and a decent sea breeze.

Santa Claus Village (☎ 9249121464; www.santaclausvillageresort.com; r Rs800-2000, with AC Rs1800-2500; 🖳 🖳) Even though the cheesy name is only apt once a year, this place is surprisingly well designed – with traditional Keralan-themed buildings, fetching bits of furniture and lots of teak-wood flair. The two deluxe rooms at the front are the money shot, with huge bay windows facing out to sea.

Sea Pearl Chalets (☎ 2660105; www.seapearlchalets.com; d Rs1300) Precariously dangling off a bluff at Varkala's southern cliff, these small, basic and charismatic wigwams have unbeatable views. They're definitely worth checking out before they tumble into the ocean.

Krishnatheeram (☎ 2601305; www.krishnatheeram.com; r Rs1400, with AC from Rs2750; 🖳) The octagonal bungalows here make for a slightly more interesting kip than normal. The place sits right on the quiet Black beach, is fronted by a carpet of shaded green lawn and has a breezy upstairs restaurant with great views.

Eden Garden (☎ 2603910; www.edengarden.in; r €23-33, luxury ste €105) Delightfully situated overlooking peaceful paddy fields, this place has a few small, orderly and well-decorated double rooms set around a lush lily pond. Recently added phantasmagoric luxury suites are organically shaped like white space-mushrooms and decked out with intricate paintwork, curvy windows and an opulent shower room. A recommended ayurvedic resort is based here, with both short- and long-term treatments available.

Sea Breeze (☎ 2603257; www.seabreezevarkala.com; r Rs1500, with AC Rs2000-3000; ✴) The large and orderly rooms in this hefty pink building all offer great sea views and share a large verandah – perfect for nightly sunset adulation. While the rooms here are achingly nondescript, the friendly owners and quiet location give this place a slight edge over the competition.

Puthooram (☎ 3202007; www.puthooram.com; r Rs2000-3000) If garden gnomes were looking for a holiday destination, they'd probably come here. Puthooram has cute bungalows that are panelled with wood both inside and out, all set around a charming little garden. Budget rooms are also available, though they're not nearly as nice.

Blue Water Beach Resort (☎ 9446848534; www .bluewaterstay.com; r Rs3000) These pretty, all-wood bungalows are lined up on a small bluff on Odayam Beach, all offering tiny verandahs with massive vistas. Several rooms are in a large wooden house further back, though they still promise the good views.

Pink Aana (☎ 9746981298; www.pinkaana.at; r €50) On the quiet Odayam beach north of Varkala, there are just four sturdily-constructed bungalows at the 'Pink Elephant'. Made of coconut wood and bamboo, they're sparse but very stylish and great value. Each has a private verandah and they're right on the beach, enjoying uninterrupted sunset views.

Villa Jacaranda (☎ 2610296; www.villa-jacaranda. biz; d Rs3600-5000) The ultimate in understated luxury, this romantic retreat has just a handful of huge, bright, gracious rooms in a large house, each with a balcony and individually decorated with a chic blend of minimalist modern and period touches. It's all kept refreshingly simple, and the solitude here is all-encompassing. The delicious complimentary breakfast is served on your verandah.

Taj Garden Retreat (☎ 2603000; www.tajhotels.com; r Rs6500-9000; ✴ ▣ ✴) Luxury, '80s-style: this ritzy-but-dated resort has big fancy rooms, an ayurvedic centre, a bar and health club. The Sunday lunch buffet (12.30pm to 3pm; Rs600) is deservedly popular – particularly since you get to use the pool. Poolside cocktails all round, then?

Eating

Most restaurants in Varkala offer pretty much the same predictable mix of Indian, Asian and Western fare. It's best to join in the nightly Varkala cliff-side saunter till you find a place that suits your mood. The following places have stood the test of time and offer reliably decent victuals.

Oottupura Vegetarian Restaurant (mains from Rs30) Bucking the trend and serving only veggie options, this budget eatery has a respectable range of yummy dishes, including breakfast *puttu* (flour with milk, bananas and honey) and lots of lunch and dinner options.

Sreepadman (meals Rs30-45) For dirt cheap and authentic Keralan fare – think dosas (paper-thin lentil-flour pancakes) and thalis – where you can rub shoulders with rickshaw drivers rather than tourists, hit Sreepadman. This is a real hole-in-the-wall with a view: there is neat seating out the back with temple tank views.

Juice Shack (juices Rs50, snacks Rs30-150; ☺ 7am-7.30pm-ish) A funky little health-juice bar that doubles as Varkala's informal intranet – this is where long-termers come to gossip and share the latest news the old way.

Caffe Italiano (meals Rs50-200) Enjoy leafy, vineside munching on relatively authentic Italian pizza and pasta.

Somatheeram (meals Rs60-150) This bare-bones beach-side restaurant whips up consistently tasty Indian fare. The location, right on the main beach where you can dig your toes into the sand, is about as good as it gets.

Hungry Eye Kitchen (meals Rs60-160) We love the stepped, multilevel design of Hungry Eye – this way everyone gets uninterrupted sea views. Very diplomatic. Thai food is a speciality here, and the kitchen can whip up red and green curries as well as the usual suspects of Varkala dishes.

Kerala Coffee House (breakfast/mains around Rs70/100) With oodles of atmosphere and top service, this perennially popular hang-out has tableclothed dining under the swaying palms. It serves cocktails (around Rs80) and has particularly flavoursome pizzas (Rs70 to Rs90), all served to a dancy, reggae soundtrack.

Trattoria (meals Rs70-150) Don't let the name fool you, the menu has lots of Asian meals as well as dishes from every other point of the compass – *momos* are a specialty (Rs60 to Rs100).

Calfouti (meals Rs70-200) The menu here doesn't look that different from everywhere else, but the setting is a notch swishier than most places, with an upper level balcony, colourful lamps and more than its fair share of dinnertime fairy lights.

Drinking

Although most of the places along the cliff aren't licensed, many will serve beer (around Rs80) in a discreet teapot and with a watchful eye for patrolling police.

Entertainment

Kathakali performances are organised during December and January; look out for signs advertising location and times.

Getting There & Away

There are frequent trains to Trivandrum (2nd class/AC chair Rs22/142, one hour) and Kollam (Rs18/142, 30 minutes), as well as three daily services to Alleppey (Rs35/155, two hours). It's feasible to get to Kollam in time for the morning backwater boat to Alleppey (see the boxed text, p346). From Temple Junction, four daily buses pass by on their way to Trivandrum (Rs36, 1½ hours), with one heading to Kollam at around 11am (Rs32, one hour). Alternatively you can catch a bus or autorickshaw to the highway junction at Kollambalam (7km away) for more frequent express buses rumbling north.

Getting Around

It's about 2.5km from the train station to Varkala beach, with autorickshaws covering the distance for between Rs30 and Rs50, taxis for Rs80. Local buses also travel regularly between the train station and the temple junction (Rs5). Beware that many drivers will try to shoehorn you into the hotel that pays them the highest commission – it's often best to be dropped off at the Helipad and walk to your chosen hotel.

Many places along the cliff hire out scooters/Enfields for Rs300/450 per day.

KOLLAM (QUILON)

☎ 0474 / pop 380,100

Tiny Kollam (Quilon) is the sleepy southern approach to Kerala's backwaters. One of the oldest ports in the Arabian Sea, it was once a major commercial hub that saw Roman, Arab, Chinese and later Portuguese, Dutch and British traders jostle ships into port – eager to get their hands on spices and the region's valuable cashew crops. The town's shady streets and antediluvian market are worth a wander, and the calm waterways of the surrounding Ashtamudi Lake are still fringed with coconut palms, cashew plantations and traditional villages.

Information

There are several ATMs around town.

DTPC information centre (☎ 2745625; info@dtpckol lam.com; ☽ 7am-7pm) Very helpful; near the KSRTC bus stand and boat jetty.

Post office (☎ 2746607; Alappuzha Rd)

Silver Net (per hr Rs15; ☽ 9.30am-9pm Mon-Sat) The most convenient of numerous internet cafes at the Bishop Jerome Nagar Complex.

UAE Exchange (☎ 2751240-1; Alapuzha Rd; ☽ 9.30am-6pm Mon-Sat, to 1pm Sun) For changing cash and travellers cheques.

Sights

If you have the time, it's well worth visiting **Kollam beach** to stroll past picturesque Keralan fishing hamlets and watch fishermen mending nets while their bright fishing boats colour the shoreline. There's a rowdy **fish market** here where customers and fisherfolk alike pontificate on the value of the catch of the day – get there early in the morning. The beach is 2km south of town, a Rs20 rickshaw ride away.

South of Main Rd, the **Mukkada Bazaar** has been a commercial hub of activity for hundreds of years. Here, spice merchants sit atop bags of bright powders, porters ferry goods deftly on their heads and shop fronts are draped in mysterious herbs (many used for ayurvedic treatments).

The lively **Shrine of Our Lady of Velankanni** is dedicated to a patron saint from Tamil Nadu. There aren't many places in the world you can see sari-clad Christian iconography worshipped with such Hindu exuberance.

Activities

Janakanthi Panchakarma Centre (☎ 2763014; www .santhigiri.co.in; Vaidyasala Nagar, Asraman North) is an

MEDICAL TOURISM – WOULD YOU LIKE A TRANSPLANT WITH THAT?

Some tourists come to India to see the Taj Mahal, others the Kerala backwaters – and now a new breed of traveller is visiting the subcontinent to experience the joys of liposuction and knee-reconstructive surgery.

In Western countries lacking socialised medicine, or with long public hospital waiting lists, the costs of private health care alternatives is spiralling out of affordability for the average patient. The most obvious example remains the US, where heart-bypass surgery can cost upwards of US$100,000 and where patients are desperately seeking viable alternatives for both essential and elective surgery. Enter the emerging economies. Southeast Asian countries like Singapore and Thailand have been offering international-standard hospital facilities at a fraction of international prices for years, attracting a growing number of globetrotting patients. With the number of Americans travelling overseas for medical treatment expected to increase six-fold in the next few years (to 6 million per year), India also looks poised to profit from the international search for affordable medical care.

Medical tourist numbers have been shooting up as rapidly as India's private hospital standards – which in some cases surpass those of their Western counterparts. Large national care providers, like India's Apollo and Wockhardt chain of hospitals, are often staffed by Western-trained doctors, filled with the latest high-tech equipment, and yet still manage to charge around 15% of the US price for many of their surgical procedures. These facts, coupled with cheap air fares and the extra possibility of tacking on a free holiday in an exotic destination, means that, for many, the decision to head overseas for some 'sun and scalpel' time is an easy one. In fact, it's such an enticing idea that several large American corporations (and even US health-providers!) are looking into outsourcing expensive procedures for staff and patients overseas to save costs.

---

ayurvedic resort, 5km from Kollam, popular for its seven- to 21-day treatment packages (seven-day packages including basic accommodation start at around Rs9000). You can also just visit for a rejuvenation massage and herbal steam bath (Rs750). An autorickshaw from Kollam should cost around Rs100.

Tours

Excellent **canoe-boat tours** (per person Rs300; ☼ 9am & 2pm) through the canals of Munroe Island and across Ashtamudi Lake are organised by the DTPC. On these excursions (with knowledgeable guides) you can observe daily village life, see *kettuvallam* (rice barge) construction, toddy (palm beer) tapping, coir-making (coconut fibre), prawn and fish farming, and also do some birdwatching and spice-garden visits.

Festivals & Events

The **Pooram festival** (p323) is held in Kollam every April, while the **Ashtamudi Craft & Art festival** (December/January) is every two years.

Sleeping

BUDGET

The DTPC office keeps a list of **homestays** (d Rs200-500) in and around Kollam.

Lekshmi Tourist Home (☎ 2741067; Main Rd; s/d Rs150/250) About as basic as they come, this primitive pilgrims' lodge at least has clean sheets and plenty of light. Some rooms have balconies facing a relatively quieter street.

Government Guest House (☎ 2743620; r Rs220, with AC Rs440; 🗷) In a splendid colonial-era relic that still wafts in the remnants of faded grandeur, this guest house offers immense, crumbling rooms with high ceilings and wooden floors. They're a bargain, but isolated 3km north of the centre on Ashtamudi Lake.

Karuna Residency (☎ 3263240; Main Rd; s/d Rs350/450, r with AC Rs600; 🗷) This little budgeter is starting to show its age, but is still maintained in decent condition. The central location close to the train station is probably its single biggest asset.

Kodiyil Residency (☎ 3018030; Main Rd; s/d Rs399/499, with AC Rs699/799; 🗷) This new hotel brings a mild touch of class to the budget category. Bright red walls are lit by mood lighting; rooms come in shades of lime and have stylishly modern furniture and TVs. Shame about the complete lack of windows. Check-out is 24 hours.

MIDRANGE

Valiyavila Family Estate (☎ 2701546, 9847132449; www .kollamlakeviewresort.com; Panamukkom; r Rs750-1500, with

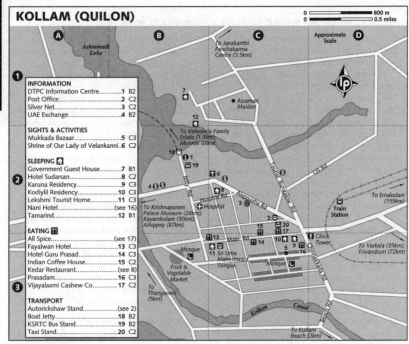

KOLLAM (QUILON)

0 — 800 m
0 — 0.5 miles

Approximate Scale

INFORMATION
DTPC Information Centre..............**1** B2
Post Office...............................**2** C2
Silver Net................................**3** C2
UAE Exchange..........................**4** B2

SIGHTS & ACTIVITIES
Mukkada Bazaar........................**5** C3
Shrine of Our Lady of Velankanni..**6** C2

SLEEPING
Government Guest House.............**7** B1
Hotel Sudarsan........................**8** C3
Karuna Residency......................**9** C3
Kodiyil Residency....................**10** C3
Lekshmi Tourist Home..............**11** C3
Nani Hotel............................(see 16)
Tamarind.............................**12** B1

EATING
All Spice..............................(see 17)
Fayalwan Hotel.......................**13** C3
Hotel Guru Prasad...................**14** C3
Indian Coffee House.................**15** C2
Kedar Restaurant.....................(see 8)
Prasadam.............................**16** C3
Vijayalaxmi Cashew Co............**17** C2

TRANSPORT
Autorickshaw Stand..................(see 2)
Boat Jetty............................**18** B2
KSRTC Bus Stand......................**19** B2
Taxi Stand............................**20** C2

Ashtamudi Lake

To Janakanthi Panchakarma Centre (3.5km)

Asraman Maidan

To Valiyavila Family Estate (1.5km); Munroe Island

To Ernakulam (159km)

Train Station

To Krishnapuram Palace Museum (28km); Kayamkulam (30km); Alleppey (87km)

Hospital

Hospital Rd

Alappuzha Rd

Main Rd

Clock Tower

To Varkala (35km); Trivandrum (72km)

Mosque

Sri Uma Maheshwara Temple

Mosque

Fruit & Vegetable Market

To Thangassen (5km)

Kollam Canal

To Kollam Beach (2km)

AC Rs2500;) The pick of Kollam's sleeping bunch, this estate crowns a breezy peninsula surrounded by leisurely backwaters on three sides. The enormous rooms are a little sparse, but come with lots of windows to enjoy the views, the morning breeze and the extraordinary sight of large bosoms (belonging to a misshapen sculpture – the *Goddess of Light*). Call ahead for a boat pick-up, catch a public ferry from Kollam (Rs3), or grab an autorickshaw (Rs100) to get here.

Hotel Sudarsan (2744322; Alappuzha Rd; www .hotelsudarsan.com; s/d with AC from Rs900/1000, executive Rs1500/1750;) Sudarsan is welcoming enough, but a little institutionally designed for our taste. The non-AC rooms in the front wing are spacious but very noisy, while the executive rooms at the back are smaller, quieter and probably a little overpriced.

Nani Hotel (2751141; Chinnakada Rd; r Rs1200-3000;) This brand spanking new boutique hotel boasts some of the best bang for buck in India. Built by a cashew magnate, it's gorgeously designed and mixes traditional Keralan elements and modern chic like it's not even trying. Even the cheaper rooms have

mod cons you'd expect at double these prices, including flat panel TVs, feathery pillows and sumptuous bathrooms.

Tamarind (2745538; r Rs2000;) Fresh from a life-changing set of renovations, this once-rusty government guest house has gone all upmarket and now has big, airy, bright orange rooms offering pleasant views over backwaters. An autorickshaw from town is around Rs50.

Eating

Fayalwan Hotel (Main Rd; meals Rs10-45) This is a real Indian working-man's diner, packed to the rafters come lunchtime. There are concrete booths and long benches for sitting and tucking in – try the mutton biryani (Rs45).

Hotel Guru Prasad (Main Rd; meals Rs18) In a neat colonial building still clinging to remnants of a once-cheery paint job, this busy lunchtime place draws the punters with dirt-cheap set meals.

All Spice (Musaliar Bldgs; mains Rs30-110; lunch & dinner) Desperate for a Western fast-food fix? Burgers (Rs29 to Rs55), pizzas (Rs50 to Rs90), hot dogs (Rs35) and good tandoori items can be followed up with ice-cream desserts – all served in a disconcertingly shiny cafeteria-style atmosphere.

Prasadam (☎ 2751141; Chinnakada Rd; meals Rs60-175) The restaurant at the swish Nani Hotel has a comely setting amidst intricate copper-relief artwork depicting Kollam history. The meals are well prepared, and dishes range from Western fare, salads and pastas to lots of typical Indian victuals. The massive thalis are Rs80.

Kedar Restaurant (Hotel Sudarsan, Alappuzha Rd; mains Rs65-125) The restaurant at Hotel Sudarsan makes a fine attempt at Indian food, though the dining room is a tad gloomy. The tangy fish curry (Rs75) is excellent.

Also recommended:

Indian Coffee House (Main Rd) Reliable for a decent breakfast and strong coffee.

Vijayalaxmi Cashew Co (Main Rd; ⏱ 9.30am-8pm) A major exporter of Kollam's famous cashews; quality nuts are around Rs250 per 500g.

Getting There & Away
BOAT
See the boxed text, p346, for information on cruises to Alleppey. From the main boat jetty, there are frequent public ferry services across Ashtamudi Lake to Guhanandapuram (one hour) and Perumon (two hours). Fares are around Rs10 return.

BUS
Kollam is situated on the well-trodden Trivandrum–Kollam–Alleppey–Ernakulam bus route, with superfast/superexpress (but sadly no super-duper-double-fast-express) buses departing every 10 or 20 minutes to Trivandrum (Rs45, 1½ hours), Alleppey (Rs55, two hours) and Ernakulam (Kochi,

Rs91, 3½ hours). Buses depart from the **KSRTC Bus Stand** (☎ 2752008) near the boat jetty.

TRAIN
There are frequent trains to Ernakulam (2nd class/AC chair Rs46/188, 3½ hours, 12 daily) and Trivandrum (Rs26/142, one hour) via Varkala (Rs18/142, 30 minutes). Four daily trains go to Alleppey (Rs33/142, 1½ hours).

Getting Around
Most autorickshaw trips should cost around Rs20, but drivers will ask for more at night. There's a prepaid stand opposite the post office.

AROUND KOLLAM
Krishnapuram Palace Museum
Two kilometres south of Kayamkulam (between Kollam and Alleppey), this restored **palace** (☎ 0479-2441133; admission Rs10, camera Rs25, video Rs250; ⏱ 10am-1pm & 2-5pm Tue-Sun) is a fine example of grand Keralan architecture. Now a museum, inside are paintings, antique furniture, sculptures, and a renowned 3m-high mural depicting the Gajendra Moksha (the liberation of Gajendra, chief of the elephants) as told in the Mahabharata. The **Bharni Utsavam Festival** is held at the nearby Chettikulangara Bhaghavathy Temple in February/March.

Buses (Rs24) leave Kollam every few minutes for Kayamkulam. Get off at the bus stand near the temple gate, 2km before Kayamkulam.

ALAPPUZHA (ALLEPPEY)
☎ 0477 / pop 282,700
Almost Venice-like, the shady streets of Alappuzha (Alleppey) are set around a grid of canals that spill into the vast watery highways

---

NEHRU TROPHY SNAKE BOAT RACE

This famous regatta on Vembanad Lake in Alleppey takes place on the second Saturday of August each year, with scores of giant, low-slung *chundan vallam* (snake boats) competing. Each boat is over 30m long with a raised, snaking prow, and is crewed by 100 rowers singing in unison, all shaded by gleaming silk umbrellas. Watched avidly by thousands of cheering spectators, the annual event celebrates the seafaring and martial traditions of ancient Kerala with floats and performing arts.

Tickets entitle you to seats on bamboo terraces, which are erected for the races. Prices range from Rs75 to Rs500 for the best seats in the Tourist Pavilion, which offers views of the finishing point and separates you from gatherings of rowdy men. Take food, drink and an umbrella.

Other less famous but no less spectacular boat races are held around the backwaters between June and September. Ask at any KTDC office for details.

of the region. As the gateway to the famed backwaters, this is the place in Kerala to organise some houseboat action and is home to the famous Nehru Trophy Snake Boat Race (p343). It's worth stopping in Alleppey to soak up some tropical village life before making a beeline for the backwaters.

Orientation

The bus stand and boat jetty are close to each other; the hotels spread far and wide. The train station is 4km southwest of the town centre. There's a beach about 2km west of the city centre.

Information

There are several ATMs around town.

Danys Bookshop (Hotel Royale Park; YMCA Rd; ☎ 2237828; ☉ 10am-9pm, 10am-1pm Sun) Tiny bookshop in the Hotel Royal Park.

DTPC Tourist Reception Centre (☎ 2253308; www .alappuzhatourism.com; ☉ 8.30am-6pm) Barely offers rudimentary tourist info.

Mailbox (☎ 2339994; Boat Jetty Rd; internet per hr Rs40; ☉ 9am-8pm)

National Cyber Park (☎ 2238688; YMCA Compound; internet per hr Rs30; ☉ 10am-10pm Mon-Sat)

Tourist Police (☎ 2251161; ☉ 24hr)

UAE Exchange (☎ 18004259585; cnr Cullan & Mullackal Rds; ☉ 9.30am-6pm Mon-Sat, to 1pm Sun) For changing cash and travellers cheques.

Activities

For ayurvedic treatments, **Ayurveda: Sree Krishna** (☎ 3290728, 9847119060; www.krishnayurveda.com), near Fishing Point, does one-hour rejuvenation massages for Rs600. For more serious health issues, the ayurvedic doctor here has over 20 years' experience and will suggest a course of multiday treatment suitable to your ailments. It's near the Nehru race finishing point.

Tours

Any of the dozens of travel agencies in town, or the KTDC, can arrange canoe-boat tours of the backwaters; see also the boxed text, p346.

Sleeping

Look out for guest-house and heritage home accommodation in Alleppey; they're better that the town's uninspiring hotels.

There are several relaxed sleeping options on the backwaters a few kilometres north of Alleppey; all can arrange pick-ups and drop offs from town.

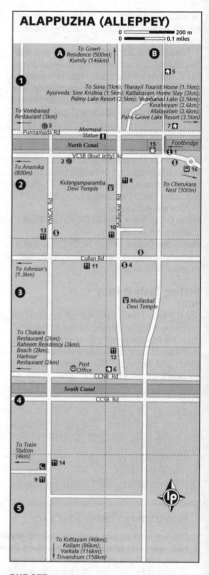

BUDGET

St George Lodgings (☎ 2251620; CCNB Rd; s/d Rs105/200, without bathroom Rs75/155) While this place might look a little sketchy, the fresh lick of yellow paint and spacious rooms at rock-bottom prices are hard to ignore. It's uberbasic – the communal bathrooms have quite a waft about them.

INFORMATION		SLEEPING 🛏		Indian Coffee House................10 B2
Danys Bookshop...................(see 13)		Palmy Residency........................5 B1		Kream Korner............................11 A3
DTPC Tourist		St George Lodgings..................6 B4		Kream Korner............................12 B4
Reception Centre...................1 B2		Springs Inn................................7 B1		Royal Park Hotel......................13 A2
Mailbox......................................2 A2				Thaff..14 A5
National		EATING 🍴		
Cyber Park..............................3 A1		Hot Kitchen...............................8 B2		TRANSPORT
Tourist Police.........................(see 1)		Indian		Boat Jetty................................15 B2
UAE Exchange...........................4 B3		Coffee House..........................9 A5		KSRTC Bus Stand.....................16 B2

Palmy Residency (☎ 2235938; www.palmyresort.com; r Rs300-500) Run by the super-friendly folk of Palmy Resort, this central little place has four absurdly neat and quiet rooms of varying size – all with mosquito netting, flyscreens and free bicycles. It's just north of the footbridge.

Johnson's (☎ 2245825; www.johnsonskerala.com; r Rs300-750) On a quiet street just west of town, Johnson's homestay takes up several rooms in a large quirky mansion. Captained by the zealous Johnson Gilbert, this rambling residence is filled with funky furniture and loads of plants. It offers just a few big, bright upstairs rooms with enormous balconies. The cheaper bamboo and thatch huts are a bit dowdy for our tastes.

Springs Inn (☎ 9847750000; Punnamada Rd; r Rs500, with AC Rs800) The Springs Inn has three nifty rooms in a comely Keralan-style house. They're darned cute from the outside, though plain on the inside.

Gowri Residence (☎ 2236371; www.gowriresidence .com; r Rs500-800, with AC Rs1000-1800; 🖳) What started as a small heritage home has turned into a huge complex of great rooms and bungalows. There's a bewildering selection of abodes here, ranging from traditional wood-panelled rooms in the main house to several types of bungalows made from either stone, wood, bamboo or thatch. Good food is served in gazebos in the garden or on your veranda.

Cherukara Nest (☎ 9947059628; www.cherukara nest.com; d incl breakfast Rs550, with AC Rs1200; 🖳) This commendably maintained heritage home has the sort of welcoming family atmosphere that makes you miss your grandma. There are four large rooms filled with character, each sporting lots of polished wood touches and antediluvian doors with ornate locks. Great value.

MIDRANGE & TOP END

Kattakayam Home Stay (☎ 2232380; www.kattakayam homestay.com; Punnamada; r Rs600, with AC Rs1000; 🖳) The friendliness of this place is a big hit with readers, though the rooms, either above a family home or bright bungalows, are a little plain-Jane.

Tharayil Tourist Home (☎ 2233543; www.tharayil touristhome.com; Punnamada; r Rs600-850, with AC Rs1300-1500; 🖳 🖳) With a few rooms either above a family abode or in small bungalows out front, Tharayil offers a comfy, if unexciting, place to bed down for the night. Internet is available for Rs60 per hour.

Palmy Lake Resort (☎ 2235938; www.palmyresorts .com; Punnamada Rd East; cottages d Rs750) With six handsome cottages, some in bamboo and some in concrete, there's loads of charm and peace at this small homestay, 3.5km north of Alleppey. It's set among palm groves near the backwaters, with gracious owner Bigi and his wife Macy providing delicious meals on request.

Sona (☎ 2235211; www.sonahome.com; Shornur Canal Rd; r Rs800, with AC Rs1100; 🖳) Run by an affable family, this charming old heritage home has cool, spacious rooms with loads of character, high rosewood ceilings, four-poster beds and secluded verandahs overlooking a well-kept garden.

Malayalam (☎ 2234591; malayalamresorts@yahoo .com; Punnamada; r Rs1000) With one of the best locations in Alleppey, this little family-run pad has a handful of cute cottages that practically play footsies with the backwaters. And if your front porch is still not close enough to the water for you, you can laze on two bamboo sit-outs that jut out over the lake. It lies surrounded by the Keraleeyam resort.

Keraleeyam (☎ 2231468; www.keraleeyam.com; Punnamada; s/d from Rs1140/1425; 🖳) This mini-resort is laid out along the backwaters a few kilometres north of Alleppey. There are several comfortable AC rooms inside the main building, which is a traditional Keralan home, but our money's on the charming, two-storey, deluxe thatch bungalows (single/double Rs1425/1710) with porches that practically hang over the backwater lake. Also offers ayurvedic treatments.

Palm Grove Lake Resort (☎ 2235004; www .palmgrovelakeresort.com; Punnamada; cottages d Rs1500-1750) Close to the starting point of the Nehru Trophy Snake Boat Race on Punnamada Lake,

KERALA

THE BACKWATERS

The undisputed main attraction of a trip to Kerala is travelling through the 900km network of waterways that fringe the coast and trickle far inland. Long before the advent of roads, these waters were the slippery highways of Kerala, and many villagers today still use paddle-power as their main form of transport. Trips through the backwaters traverse palm-fringed lakes studded with cantilevered Chinese fishing nets, and wind their way along narrow, shady canals where coir (coconut fibre), copra (dried coconut kernels) and cashews are loaded onto boats. Along the way are isolated villages where farming life continues as it has for eons.

Kerala Tourism (www.keralatourism.org) produces a *Backwater Map*.

Tourist Cruises

The popular tourist cruise between Kollam and Alleppey (Rs400) departs at 10.30am, arriving at 6.30pm, daily from August to March and every second day at other times. Generally, there are two stops: a 1pm lunch stop (with a basic lunch provided) and a brief afternoon chai stop. The crew has an ice box full of fruit, soft drinks and beer to sell. Bring sunscreen and a hat.

It's a scenic and leisurely way to get between the two towns, but as a backwater experience the cruise is limited by the fact that the boat travels along the major highways of the canal system – you won't see much of the close-up village life that makes the backwaters so magical. Travellers have reported getting bored with the eight-hour trip.

Another option is to take the trip halfway (Rs200) and get off at the **Matha Amrithanandamayi Mission** (☎ 0476-2897578; www.amritapuri.org; Amrithapuri), the incongruously pink ashram of Matha Amrithanandamayi. One of India's few female gurus, Amrithanandamayi is also known as Amma (Mother), or 'The Hugging Mother', because of the *darshan* (blessing) she practises, often hugging thousands of people in marathon all-night sessions. The ashram runs official tours at 5pm each day. It's a huge complex, with about 2000 people living here permanently – monks, nuns, students, Indian families and Westerners. It offers food, ayurvedic treatments, yoga and meditation, as well as souvenirs from the cult of Amma – everything from books to postcards of her toes. Amma travels around for much of the year, so you might be out of luck if you're in need of a cuddle.

Visitors should dress conservatively and there is a strict code of behaviour. With prior arrangement, you can stay at the ashram for Rs150 per day (including simple vegetarian meals) and pick up an onward or return cruise a day or two later. Alternatively, you can take the free ferry to the other side of the canal and grab a rickshaw to Karunagappally 10km away (around Rs100), from where you can catch buses to Alleppey (Rs32, 1½ hours).

Houseboats

Renting a houseboat designed like a *kettuvallam* (rice barge) could be one of your most expensive experiences in India, but it's worth every darned rupee. Drifting through quiet canals lined with coconut palms, eating deliciously authentic Keralan food, meeting local villagers and sleeping on the water under a galaxy of stars – it's a world away from the clamour of India.

Houseboats cater for couples (one or two double bedrooms) and groups (we've seen seven bedroom boats being constructed!). Food (and an onboard chef to cook it) is generally included

this isolated upmarket option has stylish, airy double cottages right on the lake. Made of natural materials, each skilfully finished hut has a secluded verandah, eye-catching outdoor showers and perfect patio views of the lake.

Anamika (☎ 242044; www.anamikahome.com; VCSB (Boat Jetty) Rd; d incl breakfast Rs1800-2200) This elegant Syrian Christian home has four massive, breezy rooms sparsely decorated with

traditional furniture and glistening polished floorboards. The simple yet elegant ambience is helped along by moody lamp lighting.

Raheem Residency (☎ 2239767; www.raheemresidency.com; Beach Rd; s/d from €140/170; ❄ ⌘) This thoughtfully renovated 1860s heritage home is an absolute delight to visit, let alone stay in. All the rooms here have been restored to their former glory and boast bathtubs, dash-in the quoted cost. Houseboats can be chartered through a multitude of private operators in Kollam and Alleppey. Be warned that this is the biggest business in Kerala, and some operators are unscrupulous. The quality of boats varies widely, from veritable rust buckets to floating palaces – try to lay eyes on the boat you'll be travelling in before agreeing on a price. Travel-agency reps will be pushing you to book a boat as soon as you set foot in Kerala, though most of the bad experiences we hear about are from people who booked their trip outside the backwater hub towns. Your choice is greater in Alleppey (500 boats and counting), but it's a ridiculously popular activity there and you're likely to get caught in backwater-gridlock in the high season. It's not possible to travel by houseboat between Alleppey and Kollam, or between Alleppey and Kochi.

Prices are hugely variable. Expect a boat for two people for 24 hours to cost anything from Rs4500 to Rs7000, more for larger boats or for AC. Shop around to negotiate a bargain; but in the peak season you'll definitely pay more.

Village Tours & Canoe Boats

Village tours usually involve small groups of five to six people, a knowledgeable guide and an open canoe or covered *kettuvallam*. The tours (from Kochi, Kollam or Alleppey) last from 2½ to six hours and cost between Rs300 and Rs650 per person. They include visits to villages to watch coir-making, boat building, toddy (palm beer) tapping and fish farming. On longer trips a traditional Keralan lunch is often provided. The Munroe Island trip from Kollam (see p341) is an excellent tour of this type; and the tourist desk in Ernakulam (p360) also organises recommended tours.

In Alleppey, rented canoe boats offer a nonguided laze through the canals on a small, covered canoe for up to four people (two people for four hours Rs600) – a great way to spend a relaxing afternoon.

Public Ferries

If you want the local backwater transport experience, there are State Water Transport boats between Alleppey and Kottayam (Rs12, 2½ hours, five boats daily from 7.30am to 5.30pm). The trip crosses Vembanad Lake and has a more varied landscape than the Alleppey cruise.

Environmental Issues

Environmental problems, such as pollution, land reclamation, and industrial and agricultural development, seriously threaten the backwaters and the communities that live on their banks. It's estimated that water levels have dropped by two-thirds since the mid-19th century and many migratory birds no longer visit the area.

Pollution from houseboat motors is becoming a major problem as boat numbers swell every season. The Keralan authorities have introduced an ecofriendly accreditation system for houseboat operators. Among the criteria an operator must meet before being issued with the 'Green Palm Certificate' are the installation of solar panels and sanitary tanks for the disposal of waste. Although the system is still new, you can ask operators whether they have the requisite certification. There's been talk of running boats on cleaner natural gas, though we've yet to see this being implemented. Seriously consider choosing one of the few remaining punting, rather than motorised, boats if possible to reduce pollution.

---

ing antique furniture and period fixtures. The common areas are airy and comfortable, there are pretty indoor courtyards, a well-stocked library and a great little pool. This is the ideal luxury getaway.

Eating

Hot Kitchen (Mullackal Rd; thali Rs22-28) With a small AC dining area for those scorching hot days,

this place comes highly recommended for veg meals and South Indian breakfasts. It's packed come lunchtime.

Kream Korner (Mullackal Rd; dishes Rs30-130) This relaxed place is popular with Indian and foreign families and offers a tasty multicuisine menu. The yummy cold coffee with ice cream (Rs25) beats a frappuchino any day. There's another branch on Cullan Rd.

Thaff (YMCA Rd; meals Rs35-110) An absurdly popular joint that has scrumptious Indian bites, with some Arabic flavours mixed in, to boot. It does succulent roast spit-chicken (Rs90), scrumptious *shawarma* (Rs25) and brain-freezing cold ice-cream shakes (Rs25).

Royal Park Hotel (YMCA Rd; meals Rs70-210) The extensive menu at this swish hotel restaurant is heavily meat-centric, but the food is excellent. You can order from the same menu in the upstairs bar and wash down your meal with a cold Kingfisher. Try the yummy butter chicken masala (Rs75).

Harbour Restaurant (☎ 2230767; Beach Rd; meals Rs80-200; ✹ lunch & dinner) This beach-side, casual Euro-style eatery is run by the swish Raheem Residency Hotel. It's a little more casual and budget conscious than the hotel's main restaurant, but promises equally well prepared Indian and Western cuisine.

Chakara Restaurant (☎ 2230767; Beach Rd; 3 course lunch/dinner €12/17; ✹ lunch & dinner) The restaurant at Raheem Residency is the most expensive, and best, place in town. The menu is creative, combining elements of traditional Keralan and European cuisine. Local Indian wine is available by the bottle.

Others to try:

Vembanad Restaurant (Alleppey Prince Hotel; AS Rd; mains Rs40-170) Fine dining pool-side to nightly live music shows.

Indian Coffee House (snacks Rs4-12) Branches on Mullackal Rd and YMCA Rd.

Getting There & Away

BOAT

Ferries run to Kottayam from the boat jetty on VCSB (Boat Jetty) Rd; see p347.

BUS

From the KSRTC bus stand, frequent buses head to Trivandrum (Rs98, 3½ hours, every 20 minutes), Kollam (Rs55) and Ernakulam (Kochi, Rs39, 1½ hours). Buses to Kottayam (Rs30, 1¼ hours, every 30 minutes) are considerably faster than the ferry. One bus daily leaves for Kumily at 6.30am (Rs90, 5½ hours). For Varkala you can catch certain Trivandrum-bound buses, which will drop you off at Kollambalam (Rs76, 2½ hours), 7km from Varkala.

TRAIN

There are several trains to Ernakulam (2nd class/AC chair Rs25/135, 1½ hours) and Trivandrum (Rs45/180, three hours) via Kollam (Rs33/142, 1½ hours). Three trains a day stop at Varkala (2nd class/AC chair Rs35/155, two hours). The train station is 4km west of town.

Getting Around

An autorickshaw from the train station to the boat jetty and KSRTC bus stand is around Rs50. Several guest houses around town hire out scooters for Rs200 per day.

AROUND ALLEPPEY

Kerala's backwaters snake in all directions from Alleppey and, while touring on a houseboat is a great experience, taking time to slow down and stay in a village can be even more rewarding.

Just 10km from Alleppey, and run by the erudite and ever-helpful Thomas, **Green Palms Homes** (☎ 0477-2724497, 9495557675; community .greenpalms@gmail.com; Chennamkary; s/d/tr with full board Rs1100/1800/2250) is a series of homestays that seem a universe away, set in a typical, achingly picturesque backwater village, where you will sleep in basic rooms in villagers' homes among the rice paddies. Your host will double as a guide to the village and its traditions, and will prepare three Keralan meals a day. It's splendidly quiet, there are no roads in sight and you can hire bicycles (Rs25 per hour) and canoes (Rs50 per hour) or take cooking classes with your hosts (Rs150). If you have the time, you can stay longer and learn local trades like rice farming, carpentry, coconut collecting and more. Book ahead during the high season.

To get here, call ahead and catch one of the hourly ferries from Alleppey to Chennamkary (Rs5, 1¼ hours). Please remember this is a traditional village; dress appropriately.

KOTTAYAM

☎ 0481 / pop 172,867

Sandwiched between the Western Ghats and the backwaters, Kottayam is more renowned for being Kerala's centre of the spice and rubber trade than for its aesthetic appeal. For most travellers it's a hub town, well connected to both the mountains and the backwaters.

Kottayam has a bookish history: the first Malayalam-language printing press was established here in 1820, and this was the first district in India to achieve 100% literacy. A place of churches and seminaries, Kottayam was a refuge for the Orthodox church when the Portuguese began forcing Keralan Christians to switch to Catholicism in the 16th century.

The **Thirunakkara Utsavam Festival** is held in March at the Thirunakkara Shiva Temple.

Orientation & Information

The KSRTC bus stand is 1km south of the centre, the boat jetty a further 2km (at Kodimatha), while the train station is 1km north of Kottayam. There are a handful of ATMs around.

DC Books Heritage Bookshop (☎ 2300501; Good Shepherd St; ⏰ 9.30am-7.30pm Mon-Sat) Excellent collection of literature, philosophy and culture titles.

DTPC office (☎ 2560479; dtpcktm@sancharnet.in; ⏰ 10am-5pm Mon-Sat) At the boat jetty.

Sify iWay (☎ 2563418; KK Rd; per hr Rs25; ⏰ 8.30am-8.30pm Mon-Sat) Internet.

UAE Exchange (☎ 2303865; 1st fl, MC Rd; ⏰ 9.30am-6pm Mon-Sat, to 12.30pm Sun) Changes cash and travellers cheques.

Sleeping

Accommodation options are pretty dire in Kottayam – you're better off heading to Kumarakon for some great top-end hotels. Also try checking for homestays at the **DTPC office** (☎ 2560479), which range from the basic (Rs1000 per person full board) to deluxe (up to US$100).

Ambassador Hotel (☎ 2563293; KK Rd; www.fhrai .com; s/d from Rs250/325, d with AC Rs650; ✷) A very respectable budget sleeping option, the rooms here are spartan but spotless, spacious and quiet. It has a bakery, an AC bar, an adequate restaurant and a huge painting of the *Last Supper* to greet you in the lobby.

Homestead Hotel (☎ 2560467; KK Rd; s/d from Rs317/502, d with AC Rs1483; ✷) Easily the pick of the budget litter, this place has painstakingly maintained rooms in a blissfully quiet building off the street. The foyer sports '60s-style decor that's accidentally stumbled into vogue again, and there are two great eateries right out front.

Hotel Aida (☎ 2568391; MC Rd; s/d Rs350/700, with AC Rs500/850; ✷) Looking like a very lost ski chalet from the outside, the rooms inside are comfortable, but on the dark and dowdy side.

Pearl Regency (☎ 2561123; www.pearlregencyktm .com; MC Rd; s/d from Rs1500/1900; ✷ 🖥) This slick business-focused contender has roomy-but-dull abodes. It's all run very efficiently, and

there's an internet centre, coffee shop and restaurant on site. It's decent value.

Windsor Castle (☎ 2363637; www.thewindsorcastle .net; MC Rd; s/d from US$80/100, cottages RsUS$150; ✷ 🖥) This grandiose carbuncle of a building has some of the better rooms in Kottayam – minimally furnished, spacious and with bathtubs, though they're still overpriced by our measure. You may as well go for the deluxe cottages lying strewn around the private backwaters.

Eating

Hotel Suryaas (TB Rd; dishes Rs20-60) It's no surprise this cosy dining room is packed to the rafters with hungry families come mealtime – the North and South Indian food here is excellent. Thalis cost Rs45.

Hotel Green Park (Nagampadon; meals Rs30-90; ✷) The restaurant at the hotel of the same name serves up great Indian victuals, both veg and nonveg, in either its fan-cooled room or in AC comfort.

Meenachil (2nd fl, KK Rd; dishes Rs50-110; ⏰ lunch & dinner) This is our favourite place in Kottayam for scrumptious Indian fare. The family atmosphere is friendly, the dining room modern and tidy and the menu expansive – biryanis, veg and nonveg dishes and tandoori.

Thali (1st fl, KK Rd; meals Rs53-63) This place is a slightly swankier version of the typical Keralan set-meal place. Spotlessly kept. The food here is great

Nalekattu (Windsor Hotel; MC Rd; dishes Rs60-125; ⏰ lunch & dinner) The traditional Keralan restaurant at the Windsor Castle is in an open-walled pavilion and serves tasty Keralan specialities like *chemeen* (mango curry) and *tharavu mappas* (duck in coconut gravy).

Indian Coffee House (TB Rd) We just can't get enough of this South Indian institution serving the whole gamut of tasty Indian snacks.

Also try:

Hotel Basant (TB Rd; meals Rs25-30) Popular lunchtime place with set meals.

Getting There & Away

BOAT

Ferries run to Alleppey; see p347.

BUS

The **KSRTC bus stand** has buses to Trivandrum (Rs86, four hours, every 20 minutes), Alleppey (Rs30, 1¼ hours, every 30 minutes) and Ernakulam (Kochi, Rs46, two hours, every 20 minutes). There are also frequent buses

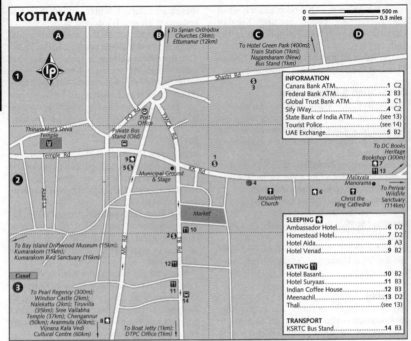

KOTTAYAM

INFORMATION	
Canara Bank ATM.................................1 C2	
Federal Bank ATM...............................2 B3	
Global Trust Bank ATM......................3 C1	
Sify iWay..4 C2	
State Bank of India ATM.............(see 13)	
Tourist Police...............................(see 14)	
UAE Exchange....................................5 B2	

SLEEPING	
Ambassador Hotel..............................6 D2	
Homestead Hotel................................7 D2	
Hotel Aida...8 A3	
Hotel Venad..9 B2	

EATING	
Hotel Basant.....................................10 B2	
Hotel Suryaas...................................11 B3	
Indian Coffee House........................12 B3	
Meenachil...13 D2	
Thali..(see 13)	

TRANSPORT	
KSRTC Bus Stand...............................14 B3	

to nearby Kumarakom (Rs8.50, 30 minutes, every 15 minutes), to Thrissur (Rs81, four hours), Calicut (Rs162, seven hours, 13 daily), Kumily for Periyar Wildlife Sanctuary (Rs69, four hours, every 30 minutes) and Munnar (Rs101, five hours, five daily). Certain buses to Trivandrum pass by Kollamballam, 7km from Varkala (Rs80, three hours).

TRAIN
Kottayam is well served by frequent trains running between Trivandrum (2nd class/AC chair Rs46/188, 3½ hours) and Ernakulam (Rs26/142, 1½ hours).

Getting Around
An autorickshaw from the jetty to the KSRTC bus stand is around Rs30, and from the bus stand to the train station about Rs20. Most trips around town cost Rs15.

AROUND KOTTAYAM
Kumarakom
☎ 0481
Kumarakom, 16km west of Kottayam and on the shore of Vembanad Lake, is an un-

hurried backwater town with a smattering of dazzling, top-end sleeping options. You can arrange houseboats through Kumarakom's less-crowded canals, but expect to pay considerably more than in Alleppey.

Arundhati Roy, author of the 1997 Booker Prize–winning *The God of Small Things,* was raised in the nearby Aymanam village.

SIGHTS
Kumarakom Bird Sanctuary (☎ 2525864; Indian/foreigner Rs5/45; ⏲ 6am-5.30pm) is on the 5-hectare site of a former rubber plantation and is the haunt of a variety of domestic and migratory birds. October to February is the time for travelling birds like the garganey teal, osprey, marsh harrier and steppey eagle, while May to July is the breeding season for local species like the Indian shag, pond herons, egrets and darters. Early morning is the best viewing time.

Buses between Kottayam's KSRTC stand and Kumarakom (Rs8.50, 30 minutes, every 15 minutes) stop at the entrance to the sanctuary.

It's worth stopping by the **Bay Island Driftwood Museum** (☎ 2517530; www.bay-island

-museum.com; admission Rs50; 🕙 10am-5pm Tue-Sat, 11.30am-5pm Sun), not least for owner Raji Punnoose's animated explanations of her life's work. Inside is a motley collection of driftwood from the Andaman Sea which has been cleaned up and arranged to resemble all manner of shapes and wildlife. Some pieces have striking resemblances to real life objects, while others take a lot more imagination and prompting from the convincing Ms Punnoose.

SLEEPING

Mooleppura Guest House (☎ 2525980; www.kailasam househoat.com; s/d Rs500/1000) If you are on a budget, this welcoming homestay has just two small, very rudimentary rooms in a family home 500m south of the sanctuary entrance.

Cruise 'N Lake (☎ 2525804; www.homestaykuma rakom.com; Puthenpura Tourist Enclave; r Rs1000-1500, with AC Rs1500-2000; 🗷) As any estate agent will tell you, it's all about location, location, location. Crowning the tip of a small peninsula surrounded by backwaters on one side and a lawn of rice paddies on the other, this is the ideal affordable getaway. The rooms are plain, but it's lovely and secluded out here, surrounded by bucolic villages where houseboats are made by hand. To get to it, go several kilometres past the sanctuary and take a left, it's then 2km down a dirt road. Pickups from Kottayam cost Rs350.

Tharavadu Heritage Home (☎ 2525230; www .tharavaduheritage.com; r Rs2000, with AC Rs1400; 🗷) Tharavadu means 'large family house', an apt description. Rooms are either in the superbly restored 1870s teak family mansion or in equally comfortable individual creekside cottages. All abodes are excellently crafted and come with arty touches – some have glistening teak beams while others have big bay windows and relaxing patios. It's 4km before the bird sanctuary.

Taj Garden Retreat (☎ 2524377; www.tajhotels .com; cottages from Rs11,500, r from Rs13,000, villas Rs23,000; 🗷 🗷) Shrouded in seclusion and relative luxury, this great example of a Taj resort has rooms in an expertly restored colonial house, in individual cottages, or in luxury villas on their own private lagoon. The grounds abut the bird sanctuary, so wannabe ornithologists don't even have to leave their porch.

Coconut Lagoon (☎ 2524491; reservations 0484-2668221; coconutlagoon@cghearth.com; cottages €200-380;

🗷 🗷 🗷) Spread languidly over 9 hectares of grounds, this luxurious resort offers the ultimate in seclusion: it's reachable only by private boat. Surrounded by backwaters and with perfect sunsets guaranteed, the different *tharawad* (ancestral home) cottages on offer here are variously filled with polished wood, classy antique-style furnishings and neat open-air bathrooms. This place might be familiar to those who have read Arundhati Roy's *The God of Small Things*.

Ettumanur

The **Shiva Temple** at Ettumanur, 12km north of Kottayam, has inscriptions dating from 1542, but parts of the building may be even older than this. The temple is noted for its exceptional woodcarvings and murals, similar to those at Kochi's Mattancherry Palace. The annual **festival**, involving exposition of the idol (Shiva in his fierce form) and elephant processions, is held in February/March.

Sree Vallabha Temple

Devotees make offerings at this temple, 2km from Tiruvilla, in the form of traditional, regular all-night **Kathakali** performances that are open to all. Tiruvilla, 35km south of Kottayam, is on the rail route between Ernakulam and Trivandrum.

Vijnana Kala Vedi Cultural Centre

This French-run **centre** (☎ 0468-2214483; www .vijnanakalavedi.org; Tarayil Mukku) at Aranmula, 10km from Chengannur, offers highly recommended courses in Indian arts with expert teachers. You can choose from a range of 15 subjects to study, including ayurveda, Kathakali, classical dances, Carnatic music, Keralan cooking, languages (Malayalam, Sanskrit and Hindi) and *kalarippayat*. Classes are generally individual and are held for a minimum of three hours per day, Monday to Friday.

Fees, which include lessons, accommodation in the village and all meals, are Rs10,120/28,600 per week/month – less for longer stays. You can volunteer to teach English to children in the village schools, which will entitle you to a discount on your fees. Short stays of one to three nights are also possible (Rs2000 per night), though you will need to book well ahead.

The **Aranmula Boat Race** is held here in August/September.

THE WESTERN GHATS

PERIYAR WILDLIFE SANCTUARY
☎ 04869

Periyar (☎ 224571; www.periyartigerreserve.org; Indian/foreigner Rs25/300; ⊙ 6am-6pm), South India's most popular wildlife sanctuary, encompasses 777 sq km and a 26-sq-km artificial lake created by the British in 1895. The vast region is home to bison, sambar, wild boar, langur, over 1000 elephants and about 46 tigers. Firmly established on both the Indian- and foreign-tourist trails, the place can sometimes feel a bit like Disneyland-in-the-Ghats, but its mountain scenery and neat jungle walks make for an enjoyable visit. Bring warm and waterproof clothing.

Orientation
Kumily, 4km from the sanctuary, is a growing strip of hotels, spice shops and Kashmiri emporiums. Thekkady is the actual sanctuary centre with the KTDC hotels and boat jetty. Confusingly, when people refer to the sanctuary they tend to use Kumily, Thekkady and Periyar interchangeably.

Information
DC Books (☎ 222548; ⊙ 9.30am-8.30pm) Has a small but excellent selection of fiction and nonfiction books.
DTPC office (☎ 222620; ⊙ 10am-5pm Mon-Sat) Behind the bus stand, not as useful as the Ecotourism Centre.
Ecotourism Centre (☎ 224571; ⊙ 9am-5pm) For park tours and walks.
IR Communications (internet per hr Rs40; ⊙ 7am-10pm)
Spider-Net Cafe (per hr Rs30; ⊙ 10am-10pm)
State Bank of Travancore (⊙ 10am-3.30pm Mon-Fri, to 12.30pm Sat) Changes travellers cheques and currency; has an ATM accepting foreign cards.
Wildlife Information Centre (☎ 222028; ⊙ 6am-6pm) Above the boat jetty in Thekkady.

Sights & Activities
VISITING THE PARK
Two-hour **KTDC boat trips** (lower/upper deck Rs75/150; ⊙ departures 7am, 9.30am, 11am, 2pm & 4pm) around the lake are the usual way of touring the sanctuary. The trips can be enjoyable enough, though they are often packed, rowdy, and not an ideal way to spot wildlife. The smaller, more decrepit **Forest Department boats** (per person Rs40; ⊙ departures 9.30am, 11.30am, 2pm & 4pm) offer a chance to get a bit closer to the animals, and are driven by

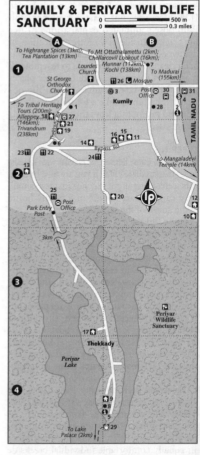

sanctuary workers who may offer commentary. Entry to the park doesn't guarantee a place on the boat; get to the **ticket office** (⊙ 6.30am-4pm) one hour before each trip to buy tickets. The first and last departures offer the best wildlife-spotting prospects, and October to March are generally the best times to see animals.

Guided three-hour **jungle walks** (up to 5 people Rs500; ⊙ departures 7am, 10.30am & 2pm) cover 4km or 5km and are a better way to experience the park close up, accompanied by a trained tribal guide. Note that leeches are common after rain.

A number of more adventurous explorations of the park can be arranged by the Ecotourism Centre (left). These include two-/three-day **'tiger trail' treks** (per person Rs3000/5000),

INFORMATION			
DC Books	1 A1	Benny's Bamboo Village	10 B2
DTPC Office	2 B1	Chrissie's Hotel	11 B2
IR Communications	(see 19)	Claus Garden	12 B2
Spider-Net Cafe	3 B1	Coffee Inn	13 A2
State Bank of Travancore	4 B1	Green View Homestay	14 A2
Wildlife Information Centre	5 B4	Kairali Palace	15 B2
		Mickey Homestay	16 B2
		Periyar House	17 A3
SIGHTS & ACTIVITIES		Silver Crest	18 A1
Ecotourism Centre	6 A2	Spice Village	19 A2
Santhigiri Ayurveda	7 B1	Tranquilou	20 B2
Ticket Office	8 B4	Wildernest	21 A2

SLEEPING		EATING	
Aranya Nivas	9 B4	Ambadi Restaurant	22 A2

Chrissie's Cafe	(see 11)		
Coffee Inn	(see 13)		
French Restaurant & Bakery	23 A2		
Pepper Garden Coffee House	24 A2		
Periyar Cafe	25 A2		
Sree Krishna	26 B1		
ENTERTAINMENT			
Mudra	27 A1		
TRANSPORT			
Bicycle Hire Shacks	28 B1		
Boat Jetty	29 B4		
Bus Stand	30 B1		
Tamil Nadu Bus Station	31 B1		

full-day **hikes** (per person Rs750), three-hour **night treks** (per person Rs500), elevated **cloud walks** (per person Rs200) and full-day **bamboo rafting** (per person Rs50; 8am-4pm) are engaging 45-minute tours through Mannakudy tribal village inside the sanctuary, which include visits to a small village museum. See www.periyartigerreserve.org for more information on what's available.

Most hotels and agencies around town can arrange all-day 4WD **Jungle Safaris** (per person Rs1600-2000; 5am-6pm), which cover over 40km of trails in jungle bordering the park. Tours include meals as well as a paddleboat trip.

SPICE GARDENS & PLANTATIONS

Interesting spice tours cost around Rs400/600 by autorickshaw/taxi (two to three hours) and can be arranged by most hotels. If you want to see a tea factory in operation, do it from here – tea-factory visits are not permitted in Munnar.

If you'd rather do a spice tour independently, you can visit a few excellent gardens outside Kumily. **Abraham's Spice Garden** (222919; 6.30am-7.30pm) has been going for 56 years and does tours of its one-hectare garden for Rs100. **Highrange Spices** (222117; 7am-7pm), 3km from Kumily, has 4 hectares of spice garden and you can see ayurvedic herbs and vegetables growing. A one-hour tour is Rs100. A rickshaw to either spice garden and back will be around Rs200 to Rs250. About 13km away from Kumily is a working **tea plantation** (8am-5pm) where you can wander around the grounds and see displays of the tea-making process for free.

INDEPENDENT TREKKING

If you want to escape the tourist hordes of Periyar and don't mind some independent, DIY exploration, options abound.

For spectacular views of Kumily and the sanctuary, you can take a one-hour hike up **Mt Ottathalamettu** past some lovely bucolic villages. To get there, grab a bus or rickshaw 2km out of town along Munnar Rd and get off at the College of Teacher Education, taking the dirt road turn-off past the college all the way to the summit.

A little further, 16km from Kumily, **Chellarcovil** is a stunning lookout with sweeping vistas of Tamil Nadu's Western Ghats. It's an idyllic setting for a picnic, with rolling hillocks thick with grass and bubbling creeks aplenty. To get here grab a rickshaw for around Rs300 round trip (most rickshaw drivers know it).

OTHER ACTIVITIES

You can arrange **elephant rides** (per 30 min Rs350) at most hotels and agents in town. If you want the extended elephant experience, you can pay Rs2000 for a two-hour ride that includes elephant feeding and cleaning. **Cooking classes** (around Rs250) are offered by many of the homestays in town.

AYURVEDA

One recommended place for the ayurvedic experience is **Santhigiri Ayurveda** (223979; Vandanmedu Junction), offering both massage (Rs650 to Rs750) and long-term treatments including 21-day panchakarma cleansing (Rs30,000).

Sleeping

INSIDE THE SANCTUARY

The Ecotourism Centre can arrange accommodation in a basic **forest cottage** (d with dinner Rs2000), a one-hour hike in from the forest checkpoint.

The KTDC runs three steeply priced hotels in the park. It's a good idea to make reservations (at any KTDC office), particularly for weekends. Note that there's effectively a curfew at these places – guests are not permitted to roam the sanctuary after 6pm.

Periyar House (☎ 222026; periyar@sancharnet.in; s/d with breakfast & dinner from Rs1275/1850) This fauxbrick, school camp–like complex has bland, slightly musty and highly overpriced rooms (although it's still the most affordable place to stay inside the sanctuary).

Aranya Nivas (☎ 222023; aranyanivas@sancharnet.in; s/d incl breakfast & dinner from Rs4000/4900; 🏊) Bright, clean abodes in an imposing, pseudo-stone building with a few token period touches. There are lots of games and activities to keep you entertained, and the pool is in a lush forest setting.

Lake Palace (☎ 222023; aranyanivas@sancharnet.in; r with all meals Rs16,000-20,000) Located on an island in the middle of the Periyar Lake, this is the best value of the government hotels inside the park. It is a stunningly restored old palace that has a handful of charismatic rooms, all restored with flair using antique furnishings and a selection of modern conveniences (like flat-screen TVs). Staying in the midst of the sanctuary gives you the best chance of actually seeing wildlife, right from your private patio. Transport is by boat across the lake.

KUMILY

The growing homestay scene in Kumily offers far better bang for your rupee than the uninspiring hotels.

Coffee Inn (☎ 222763; coffeeinn@sancharnet.in; Thekkady Rd; huts Rs150-500, r Rs500-1500) While still keeping its original range of rustic bamboo huts, tree houses and cottages, Coffee Inn has recently expanded to include much swankier digs. The deluxe rooms here have great antique features like enormous brass-studded doors and colourful interiors, several offering balconies with sweeping private views of the sanctuary.

Mickey Homestay (☎ 223196; www.mickeyhomestay .com; Bypass Rd; r Rs300-750) Mickey has just a handful of intimate rooms in their family house, all with homely touches that make them some of the most comfortable in town. Balconies have rattan furniture and hanging bamboo seats and the whole place is surrounded by greenery.

Green View Homestay (☎ 224617; sureshgreenview@ yahoo.com; Bypass Rd; r incl breakfast Rs300-900) Grown from its humble homestay origins to be practically hotel-size today, Greenview manages

to retain the friendly family welcome that has made it so popular with travellers over the years. The multistorey buildings house several classes of immaculately maintained rooms with private balconies, bamboo or wood furniture and loads of greenery.

Kairali Palace (☎ 224604; Bypass Rd; r Rs700) There are just two comfy rooms here, sitting above an affable family home. It's a neat place for a night's kip, with each spacious, plain room boasting polished wood panelling on the outside and a small verandah.

Claus Garden (☎ 222320; www.homestay.in; r Rs700-1000) This lovely big building sports gently curving balconies and has warm, bright colours in spades. The excellent rooms are spacious and have neat touches like colourful blankets, rugs, artwork and funky bathrooms. Top value.

Chrissie's Hotel (☎ 224155; www.chrissies.in; Bypass Rd; r Rs1400-1800) This four-storey building behind the popular expat-run restaurant of the same name somehow manages to blend in with the forest green surrounds. The chic rooms are refreshingly spacious and bright, with cheery furnishings, lamps and colourful pillows. Yoga is held on the rooftop.

Wildernest (☎ 224030; www.wildernest-kerala.com; Thekkady Rd; r Rs2750) We have a soft-spot for this hotel. Located in two arc-shaped stone-walled buildings, the ten rooms here have radical amounts of space and come in funky, unique shapes. Depending on the room, you can have either a private garden or a rooftop balcony at your disposal. An excellent breakfast is included. Book way ahead.

Silver Crest (☎ 222481; www.sealordhotels.com; Thekkady Rd; r Rs3000-4000; ☒) With lots of polished wood interiors and a small pool, these decent rooms are all set around a small indoor courtyard. The place is efficiently run and a huge hit with travelling groups.

Spice Village (☎ 222314; spicevillage@cghearth .com; Thekkady Rd; villas €190-295, breakfast/lunch/dinner Rs375/675/800; ☒) This place has captivating, spacious cottages in pristinely kept grounds. Its restaurant does lavish buffets and you can find the Wildlife Interpretation Centre here (open 7.30am to 7.30pm), which has a resident naturalist showing slides to guests and answering questions about the park.

Also recommended:

Benny's Bamboo Village (☎ 321919; www.bamboo village.in; r Rs300-1000) Six neat rooms flavoured with either rattan walls, concrete or wood panelling.

Tranquilou (☎ 223269; tranquilouhome@hotmail.com; Bypass Rd; r Rs800-1000; ☐) Friendly family homestay huddled among some hush.

Eating

There are plenty of good cheap veg restaurants in the bazaar area.

Pepper Garden Coffee House (breakfast Rs30-100) In the tiny back garden of a local house, the Pepper Garden specialises in the best choice of breakfast options in town, including coconut pancakes (Rs60) and porridge with milk and honey (Rs60). They also have a handful of spices growing here, like cardamom and pepper, and coffee. Be prepared for a hard-sell of their tours.

Ambadi Restaurant (meals Rs35-100) At the hotel of the same name, the North and South Indian victuals here are expertly prepared and served in an airy indoor dining room.

Periyar Cafe (meals Rs35-110) Painted in blindingly bright colours, this cheery eatery serves up loads of North Indian and local dishes at very sensible prices. Located right near the park entrance, it's perfect for an early breakfast or quick lunch between animal spotting trips.

Chrissie's Cafe (Bypass Rd; snacks Rs40-80, meals Rs110-180) A perennially popular haunt that satisfies travellers with yummy cakes and snacks, excellent coffee, and well-prepared Western faves like pizza and pasta. Try the spinach lasagne (Rs130).

Coffee Inn (meals Rs75-200) This laid-back restaurant, in a peaceful spice-garden setting, serves just a few Indian and Western meals in what might just be the cosiest setting in Kumily. The food is OK, and can take quite a while to arrive, but the relaxing dining room, filled with arty and soulful music, makes it all worthwhile.

Also worth a try:

Sree Krishna (meals Rs35-85) Modern, clean veg place serving several versions of thali.

French Restaurant & Bakery (meals Rs60-120) Friendly and rustic shack with good snacks and brown bread.

Entertainment

For Kathakali performances, visit **Mudra** (☎ 9447157636; admission Rs125; ☼ shows 4pm & 8pm), which has shows twice a day, with make-up starting 30 minutes before each show. One-hour **Kalaripayattu demonstrations** (admission Rs200) are held in Kumily at 6pm daily, though the location changes – ask around.

Getting There & Away

Buses originating or terminating at Periyar start and finish at Aranya Nivas, but they also stop at the Kumily bus stand, at the eastern edge of town.

Eight buses daily operate between Ernakulam (Kochi) and Kumily (Rs115, five hours). Buses leave every 30 minutes for Kottayam (Rs69, four hours), with two direct buses to Trivandrum at 8.45am and 11am (Rs161, eight hours) and at least one daily bus to Alleppey (Rs90, 5½ hours). One KSRTC bus goes to Munnar at 8.25am (Rs79, 4½ hours), though several private buses also make this trip throughout the day from the same bus stand.

Tamil Nadu buses leave every 30 minutes to Madurai (Rs42, four hours) from the Tamil Nadu bus stand just over the border.

Getting Around

Kumily is about 4km from Periyar Lake; you can catch the bus (almost as rare as the tigers), take an autorickshaw (Rs40) or set off on foot; it's a pleasant, shady walk into the park. **Bicycle hire** (per hr Rs5; ☼ 6.30am-8pm) is available from a couple of shacks near the bus stand and many guest houses.

MUNNAR

☎ 04865 / elev 1524m

Scruffy little Munnar town may not be much to look at, but wander just a few kilometres outside the city and you'll be engulfed in a sea of stunning green. The lolling hills all around here are covered by a thick carpet of tea-trees, with breathtaking mountain scenery and fresh crisp air aplenty. Once known as the High Range of Travancore, today Munnar is the commercial centre of some of the world's highest tea-growing estates.

Information

There are ATMs near the bridge, south of the bazaar.

DTPC Tourist Information Office (☎ 231516; ♥ 8.30am-7pm) Marginally helpful.

Forest Information Centre (☎ 231587; enpmunnar@ sify.com; ♥ 10am-5pm)

Olivia Communications (internet per hr Rs35; ♥ 8.30am-10pm). Surprisingly fast internet.

State Bank of Travancore (☎ 230274; ♥ 10am-3.30pm Mon-Sat, to noon Sun) Has an ATM.

Tourist Information Service (☎ 231136; ♥ 9am-6pm) Run by local legend Joseph Iype, a walking Swiss Army knife of Munnar information. His office has maps, local history, travel tips and more.

Sights & Activities

The main reason to be in Munnar is to explore the lush, tea-filled hillocks that surround it. Hotels, travel agencies, autorickshaw drivers and practically every passer-by will want to organise a day of sightseeing for you: shop around.

The **Tata Tea Museum** (☎ 230561; adult/child Rs75/35; ♥ 10am-4pm Tue-Sun) is, unfortunately, about as close as you'll get to a working tea factory around Munnar. It's a slightly sanitised version of the real thing, but it still shows the basic process. A collection of old bits and pieces from the colonial era, including photographs and a 1905 tea-roller, are also kept here. The short walk to here from town is lovely, passing some of the most accessible tea plantations from Munnar town.

Most guest houses can arrange one-day or half-day trekking trips around the region. **Edelweiss Adventures** (☎ 09447876751; www.edelweiss adventures.com; Mattupetty Rd; ♥ 9am-7.30pm) also does full-day 17km treks (Rs900 per person), as well as other adventure sports like rock-climbing/rapelling (Rs300) and even paragliding with their professional flyers (Rs2500 for a tandem flight).

You can do your own 12km day-trek around the patchwork of plantations surrounding Munnar to visit the gorgeous

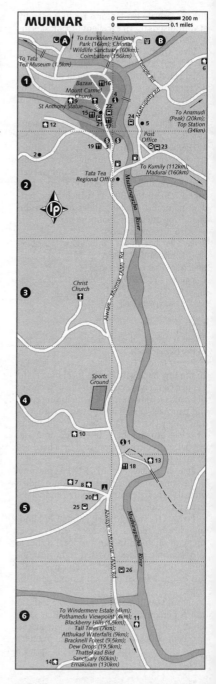

Pothamedu Viewpoint and the roaring **Atthukad Waterfalls**. To start, head south on the road towards Ernakulam, cross the bridge just after the government checkpoint, take a right and continue up the road. Take a path leading to the viewpoint just after Copper Castle Resort. From here, continue down towards the waterfalls, from where you can take a shortcut to the Ernakulam-Munnar Rd and either walk, or catch one of the frequent buses, back to Munnar. A rickshaw to the waterfalls or to the viewpoint and back costs Rs150.

Tours

The DTPC runs a couple of fairly rushed full-day tours to points around Munnar. The **Sandal Valley Tour** (per person Rs300; ☉ 9am-6pm) visits its Chinnar Wildlife Sanctuary (p359), several viewpoints, waterfalls, plantations, a sandalwood forest and villages. The **Tea Valley tour** (per person Rs250; ☉ 10am-6pm) visits Echo Point, Top Station and Rajamalai (for Eravikulam National Park), among other places.

Sleeping

There are several basic-and-cheap hotels right in Munnar town, but these are best avoided. Prices are a bit higher than in comparable Indian towns and there are several great options outside of Munnar.

AROUND TOWN

Westend Cottages (☎ 230954; satish_cbe@sify.com; d Rs300-500) In a small family house – there are nice homely touches in the rooms here, though it's dark and damp in the wet season.

Kaippallil Homestay (☎ 230203; www.kaippallil.com; r Rs300-1000) Up the hill and away from (most of) the clatter of the bazaar, Kaippallil is the best place to stay in town, with several unique rooms set in attractively landscaped gardens. There are sitting areas out the front, and the rooms are eclectically but tastefully decorated,

some with balconies and sweeping views. The budget room shares a bathroom and is a bit dingy.

JJ Cottage (☎ 230104; jjcottagemunnar@sancharnet .in; d Rs350-800) The mothering family at this superb homestay will go out of its way to make sure your stay is comfortable. The varied and uncomplicated rooms are ruthlessly clean, bright and have TV and geyser hot water. The one deluxe room has frilly pink curtains and sweeping views.

Green View (☎ 230940; www.greenviewmunnar .com; r Rs500-700) Next door to JJ Cottage, this place feels more like a hotel than homestay, but otherwise offers similar standard rooms. Lots of trekking trips can be organised from here (Rs400 to Rs750 per person for four- to seven-hour treks).

Kanan Devan Hills Club (☎ 230252; kdhclub@rediff mail.com; r Rs550-850) With a whiff of the colonial-era still hanging in the air, these aged government buildings have pretty vanilla rooms, and are surrounded by a perfectly kept little garden and great tea-plantation views. The staff seems a little bewildered by walk-in visitors.

Zina Cottages (☎ 230349; r incl tax Rs700-900) Just on the outskirts of town but immersed in lush tea plantations, with a cute garden. The cosy rooms in this hospitable homestay are an outstanding deal. Frilly touches in the rooms and stunning vistas come as standard, as do the piles of information provided by gregarious owner Mr Iype from the Tourist Information Service.

Government Guest House (☎ 230385; Colony Rd; r Rs1150) If no visiting dignitaries are in town, travellers are welcome to stay at this Government Guest House, with a trim front garden, perched above the town. The five ageing rooms here are top value: absolutely huge, with high wood-panelled ceilings.

Royal Retreat (☎ 230240; www.royalretreat.co.in; r Rs1599-3999) These comfortable rooms are OK value by Munnar's standards, with the better rooms fronted by a small and manicured little garden. Decorations are a bit chintzy, though the comfy mattresses and TV in the rooms help.

Westwood Riverside Resort (☎ 230884-6; www.westwoodmunnar.com; Alwaye-Munnar (AM) Rd; r Rs2200-3200) You might be forgiven for thinking you'd stumbled onto a lost ski lodge. It has lots of polished wood, heartfelt murals on the walls, and rooms that are refreshingly inviting for a midrange hotel.

MUNNAR HILLS

There are some excellent top-end accommodation options in plantations in the hills around Munnar, where the mountain serenity is unbeatable.

Dew Drops (☎ 0484-231555; wilsonhomes2003@yahoo.co.in; Kallar; r incl breakfast Rs1000-1200) Set in the thick forest far below Munnar, this fantastic guest house lies on 97 hectares of spice plantation and farmland. The resplendent building is expertly constructed, with modern and bright rooms that are finished with finely crafted furnishings and bits of artwork. Each room has a verandah on which you can sit and enjoy the hush and the small restaurant has 280-degree views. It's 20km from Munnar, call for a pick-up (Rs50).

Windermere Estate (☎ 230512; www.windermeremunnar.com; Pothamedu; s incl breakfast Rs3750-7650, d Rs5000-10,250) Windermere is a boutique-meets-country-retreat and manages to be both luxurious and intimate at the same time. There are farmhouse rooms and newer, swankier cottages with spectacular views, and it's surrounded by shush and 26 hectares of cardamom and coffee plantations. Book ahead.

Blackberry Hills (☎ 232978; www.blackberryresorts.com; Puthameda; r Rs4000-5500) Multistorey cottages spilling down a steep cliff, Blackberry Hills boasts comfy, modern and airy rooms with bright blankets and handmade wood furniture. All cottages have balconies to enjoy the sensational valley views. It's 4.5km from Munnar.

Bracknell Forest (☎ 231555; www.bracknellforestmunnar.com; Ottamaram; r Rs4500) Located 9.5km from Munnar, this compact two-storey building houses several lovely rooms overlooking a lush valley. It's surrounded by deep forest on all sides and makes for a remote getaway. The rooms are very neat, spacious and handsomely furnished.

Tall Trees (☎ 230641; Pothamedu; cottage incl breakfast & dinner Rs8000-12,000) Spread around thick forest and far away from the clamour of the world, this massive, back-to-nature resort has comfy cottages with natural-wood finishes, each with balconies opening to infinite nature views. There's a kids' playground and sprawling grounds dotted with cardamom trees. It's 7km from Munnar.

Eating

Early-morning food stalls in the bazaar serve breakfast snacks and cheap meals.

Hotel Saravan Bhavan (dishes Rs25-60) Try this popular, upstairs place for top-value veg banana-leaf meals (Rs35).

SN Restaurant (AM Rd; meals Rs30-80) Serving some of the best-value Indian food in town, SN seems to be perpetually full of people digging into morning dosas (Rs15 to Rs25) and other Indian dishes.

Surya Soma (dishes Rs35-60) Surya Soma is a modern and bright eatery that dishes up cheap North Indian, local and Chinese dishes in a welcoming, modern dining area. Good tunes can usually be heard playing on the crackle-free sound system.

Rapsy Restaurant (Bazaar; dishes Rs35-70) This hole-in-the-wall is packed at lunchtime, with locals lining up for Rapsy's famous *paratha* or biryani (from Rs40). It also makes a decent stab at fancy international dishes like Spanish omelette (Rs25) and Israeli *shakshuka* (scrambled eggs with tomatoes and spices; Rs35).

Silver Spoon (AM Rd; meals Rs50-140; ☽ lunch & dinner) Probably the swankiest joint in town, this family eatery has tables overlooking the river and whips up a fantastic Keralan fish-curry set meal (Rs75).

Shopping

Shops all over town sell local tea and spices grown in the surrounding hills. Also worth visiting is the excellent **Kurinji Gift Shop** (☎ 230561; near KSRTC Bus Stand; ☽ 9.30am-5.30pm Wed-Mon) for an excellent selection of pretty and delicate paper products and hand-dyed fabrics. All proceeds go to support local charities.

Getting There & Away

Roads around Munnar are in poor condition and can be affected by monsoon rains, so bus times may vary. The main **KSRTC bus station** (AM Rd) is south of town, but it's best to catch buses from stands in Munnar town (where more frequent private buses also depart).

There are around 10 buses a day to Ernakulam (Kochi, Rs80, 5½ hours) and a few services to Kottayam (Rs101, five hours), Kumily (Rs79, 4½ hours) and Trivandrum (Rs193, nine hours). There are two daily Tamil Nadu buses to Coimbatore (Rs82, six hours), and one bus to Madurai (Rs89, six hours) at 2.30pm.

Getting Around

The government tourist office rents out bicycles for Rs15 per hour. **Gokulam Bike Hire** (☎ 9447237165; per day Rs250; ⏰ 7.30am-7pm) has several motorbikes for hire, as does SN Restaurant (per day Rs250).

Autorickshaws ply the hills around Munnar with bone-shuddering efficiency; they charge from Rs150 to nearby places and up to Rs650 for a full day's sightseeing.

AROUND MUNNAR

Eravikulam National Park (Indian/foreigner Rs15/200; ⏰ 7am-6pm Sep-May), 16km from Munnar, is home to the rare, but almost tame, *Nilgiri tahr* (a type of mountain goat). From Munnar, an autorickshaw/taxi costs Rs150/300 return; a government bus takes you the final 4km from the checkpoint (Rs20).

Chinnar Wildlife Sanctuary (⏰ 7am-6pm), about 10km past Marayoor and 60km northeast of Munnar, hosts deer, leopards, elephants and the endangered grizzled giant squirrel. Trekking (Rs100 for three hours) and tree house (single/double Rs1000/1250) or hut stays (single Rs1500 to Rs2500, double Rs1800 to Rs3000) within the sanctuary are available, as well as ecotour programs like river-trekking, cultural visits, and waterfall treks (around Rs100). For details contact the Forest Information Centre in Munnar. Buses from Munnar heading to Coimbatore can drop you off at Chinnar (Rs31, 1½ hours).

Top Station, on Kerala's border with Tamil Nadu, has spectacular views over the Western Ghats. From Munnar, four daily buses (Rs26, from 7.30am) make the steep 32km climb in around an hour. Taxis (Rs800) and rickshaws (Rs400) also make the return trip from Munnar.

Thattekkad Bird Sanctuary (☎ 0485-2588302; Indian/foreigner Rs10/100; ⏰ 6am-6pm) is a serene 25-sq-km park, home to over 270 species, including Malabar grey hornbills, jungle nightjar, grey

drongo, darters and rarer species like the Sri Lankan frogmouth. You can hire private guides (Rs100 to Rs150) in the sanctuary, and there's a canteen with basic food and drinks just inside the gate. To stay in the **Treetop Machan** (d incl meals Rs2500) in the sanctuary contact the assistant wildlife warden (☎ 0485-2588302) at Kothamangalam. Otherwise, **Hornbill Inspection Bungalow** (☎ 0484-2310324; www.thehornbillcamp.com; s/d Rs1200/2400) has basic rooms outside the sanctuary. A better option is staying in the **homestay** (per person incl meals Rs700) of eager Ms Sudah, who greets most foreign visitors at the sanctuary gate. For accommodation with a little more style, visit the lovely **Birds Lagoon Resort** (☎ 0485-2572444; www.birdslagoon.com; Palamattom, Thattekad; r incl breakfast Rs2500-3500; 🛏 🖥). Set deep in the villages near Thattekkad, this low-key resort lies on a seasonal lake among spacious and manicured grounds. The basic rooms here are roomy and very comfy, with lots of wood trim and lamp lighting. The whole place feels refreshingly remote and is particularly popular with visiting ornithologists. It's 16km from Kothamangalam.

Thattekkad is on the Ernakulam–Munnar road. Take a direct bus from either Ernakulam (Rs29, two hours) or Munnar (Rs51, three hours) to Kothamangalam, from where a Thattekkad bus travels the final 12km (Rs6, 25 minutes).

PARAMBIKULAM WILDLIFE SANCTUARY

Possibly the most protected environment in South India – it's nestled behind three dams in a valley surrounded by Keralan and Tamil Nadu sanctuaries – **Parambikulam Wildlife Sanctuary** (www.parambikulam.org; Indian/foreigner Rs10/100, camera Rs25; ⏰ 7am-6pm) constitutes 285 sq km of Kipling-storybook scenery and wildlife-spotting goodness. It's home to elephants, bison, gaur, sloths, sambar, crocodiles, tigers, panthers and some of the largest teak trees in Asia. The sanctuary is best avoided during monsoon (June to August) and it sometimes closes in March and April.

Contact the **ecocare centre** (☎ 04253-245025) in Palakkad to arrange tours of the park, hikes and stays on the reservoir's freshwater island (Rs600 to Rs4000). There are 150 beds in **tree-top huts** (from Rs2500) throughout the park; book through the ecocare centre.

You have to enter the park from Pollachi (40km from Coimbatore and 49km from

Palakkad; see p460) in Tamil Nadu. There are at least two buses in either direction between Pollachi and Parambikulam via Anamalai daily (Rs15, 1½ hours). The nearest train station is Coimbatore, Tamil Nadu, from where you can board buses to Pollachi.

CENTRAL KERALA

KOCHI (COCHIN)
☎ 0484 / pop 1.36 million

Serene Kochi has been drawing traders and explorers to its shores for over 600 years, and today stands as a living homage to a vibrant past unlike any other. Nowhere in India could you find such a melange: giant fishing nets from China, a 400-year-old synagogue, ancient mosques, Portuguese houses built half a millennium ago, all mixed in with the crumbling residuum of the British Raj. The result is an unlikely blend of medieval Portugal, Holland and an English country village grafted onto the tropical Malabar Coast. It's a delightful place to spend some time, soak in the history, peruse art galleries and nap in some of the finest heritage accommodation in India.

Mainland Ernakulam is the hectic transport and cosmopolitan hub of Kochi, while the historical towns of Fort Cochin and Mattancherry remain wonderfully serene – thick with the smell of the past where goats still outnumber rickshaws on the history-laden streets.

Orientation
Kochi is made up of a gaggle of islands and peninsulas that includes mainland Ernakulam; the islands of Willingdon, Bolgatty and Gundu; Fort Cochin and Mattancherry on the southern peninsula; and Vypeen and Vallarpadam Islands. All are linked by bridges or ferry services. The main train station, the bus stand and KTDC Tourist Reception Centre are in Ernakulam, while Fort Cochin and Mattancherry have all the historical sites and most of the better-value accommodation.

Information
BOOKSHOPS
Current Books (Map p364; ☎ 3231590; Market Rd; ◔ 9.30am-7.30pm Mon-Sat) A branch of DC Books.
DC Books (Map p364; ☎ 2391295; Banerji Rd, Ernakulam; ◔ 9.30am-7.30pm Mon-Sat) A typically great English-language selection.

Idiom Bookshop Fort Cochin (Map p362; ☎ 2217075; Bastion St; ◔ 9am-9pm Mon-Sat, 10am-6pm Sun); Mattancherry (Map p362; ☎ 2225604; opposite boat jetty; ◔ 10am-6pm) Huge range of quality new and used books.

INTERNET ACCESS
Cafe de Net (Map p362; Bastion St, Fort Cochin; per hr Rs30; ◔ 9am-10.30pm) This old-timer may have DOS-era computers, but the breezy upstairs location is hard to beat.
Experience (Map p362; per hr Rs30; ◔ 10am-midnight) Flat-screen computers in tiny, cubicled rooms.
Net Park (Map p364; Convent Rd, Ernakulam; per hr Rs15; ◔ 9am-9pm)
Net Point (Map p364; Carrier Station Rd, Ernakulam; per hr Rs20; ◔ 9.30am-9.30pm)
Sify iWay (Map p362; per hr Rs30; ◔ 9.30am-10pm) Fast computers in a spacious upstairs cafe setting above the Shop-n-Save.

MEDICAL SERVICES
Lakeshore Hospital (Off Map p364; ☎ 2701032; NH Bypass, Marudu) Has the best medical facilities in the city. It's 8km southeast of central Ernakulam.

MONEY
There are scores of ATMs along Mahatma Gandhi (MG) Rd in Ernakulam, and a few in Fort Cochin.
Thomas Cook (Map p364; ☎ 2369729; Palal Towers, MG Rd; ◔ 9.30am-5.30pm Mon-Sat)
UAE Exchange (◔ 9.30am-6pm Mon-Sat, to 1.30pm Sun); Ernakulam (Map p364; ☎ 2383317; Perumpillil Bldg, MG Rd); Fort Cochin (Map p362; ☎ 2216231; Amravathi Rd) A reliable place for foreign exchange and changing travellers cheques.

POST
College post office (Map p364; ☎ 2369302; Convent Rd, Ernakulam; ◔ 9am-4pm Mon-Fri, to 9pm Sat)
Ernakulam post office branches Hospital Rd (Map p364; ☎ 2355467; ◔ 9am-8pm Mon-Sat, 10am-5pm Sun); Broadway (Map p364); MG Rd (Map p364)
Main post office (Map p362; Post Office Rd, Fort Cochin; ◔ 9am-5pm Mon-Fri, to 3pm Sat)

TOURIST INFORMATION
There's a tourist information counter at the airport. Many places distribute a brochure that includes a neat map and walking tour entitled 'Historical Places in Fort Cochin'.
Government of India Tourist Office (Map p362; ☎ 2668352; indtourismkochi@sify.com; Willingdon Island; ◔ 9am-5.30pm Mon-Fri, to 1pm Sat) Range of brochures and maps of India.

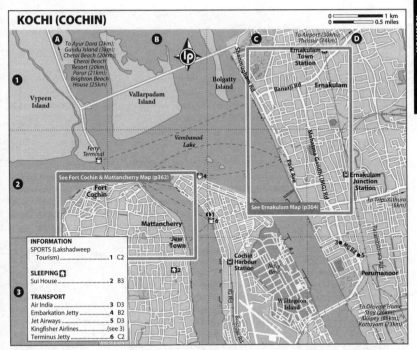

KOCHI (COCHIN)

0 —— 1 km
0 —— 0.5 miles

To Ayur Dara (2km);
Gundu Island (3km);
Cherai Beach (20km);
Cherai Beach
Resort (20km);
Parur (21km);
Brighton Beach
House (25km)

Ernakulam
Town
Station

Bolgatty
Island

Banerji Rd   Ernakulam

Vypeen
Island

Vallarpadam
Island

Shanmugham Rd

Vembanad
Lake

Mahatma Gandhi (MG) Rd

Park Ave

Ferry
Terminal

See Fort Cochin & Mattancherry Map (p362)

Fort
Cochin

Ernakulam
Junction
Station

To Tripunithura
(6km)

See Ernakulam Map (p364)

Mattancherry

Jew
Town

INFORMATION
SPORTS (Lakshadweep
Tourism)................................**1** C2

SLEEPING 🏠
Sui House...............................**2** B3

TRANSPORT
Air India..............................**3** D3
Embarkation Jetty.................**4** B2
Jet Airways...........................**5** D3
Kingfisher Airlines...........(see 3)
Terminus Jetty......................**6** C2

Cochin
Harbour
Station

Navy
Base

Willingdon
Island

MG Rd

Perumanoor

To Olavipe Home
Stay (30km);
Allepey (56km);
Kottayam (73km)

IG Rd

Bristow Rd

Palarvathom Rd

To Airport (30km);
Thrissur (74km)

KTDC Tourist Reception Centre Ernakulam (Map p364;
☎ 2353234; Shanmugham Rd, Ernakulam; ⏰ 8am-
7pm); Fort Cochin (Map p362; ☎ 2216567; Calvathy Rd;
⏰ 10am-5pm Mon-Sat) Very helpful, also organises tours.
Tourist Desk Information Counter Ernakulam
(Map p364; ☎ 2371761; touristdesk@satyam.net.in;
⏰ 8.30am-6pm); Fort Cochin (Map p362; ☎ 2216129)
A private tour agency knowledgeable about Kochi and
beyond.
Tourist Police Ernakulam (Map p364; ☎ 2353234; 8am-
6pm); Fort Cochin (Map p362; ☎ 2215055; ⏰ 24hr)

VISAS
Depending on the type of visa you have, with
some wrangling it may be possible to arrange
visa extensions at the office of the **City Police
Commissioner** (Map p364; ☎ 9744060421; Banerji Rd,
Ernakulam; ⏰ 10.15am-5.15pm Mon-Fri). You'll need
your passport, copies of the identity and visa
pages of your passport, four photographs and
oodles of patience.

Sights
FORT COCHIN
At the very tip of Fort Cochin sit the unofficial emblems of Kerala's backwaters: can-

tilevered **Chinese fishing nets** (Map p362). A
legacy of traders from the 1400 AD court
of Kubla Khan, these enormous, spiderlike
contraptions require at least four people to
operate their counterweights at high tide.
Unfortunately, modern fishing techniques
are making these labour-intensive methods
less and less profitable.

The **Indo-Portuguese Museum** (Map p362;
☎ 2215400; Indian/foreigner Rs10/25; ⏰ 9am-1pm &
2-6pm Tue-Sun), in the garden of the Bishop's
House, preserves the heritage of one of India's
earliest Catholic communities, including vest-
ments, silver processional crosses and altar-
pieces from the Cochin diocese. The basement
contains remnants of the Portuguese Fort
Immanuel.

Believed to be India's oldest European-built
church, **St Francis Church** (Map p362; Bastion St) was
originally constructed in 1503 by Portuguese
Franciscan friars. The stone edifice that stands
here today was built in the mid-16th century to replace the original wooden structure. Adventurer Vasco da Gama, who died
in Cochin in 1524, was buried on this spot
for 14 years before his remains were taken

KERALA

FORT COCHIN & MATTANCHERRY

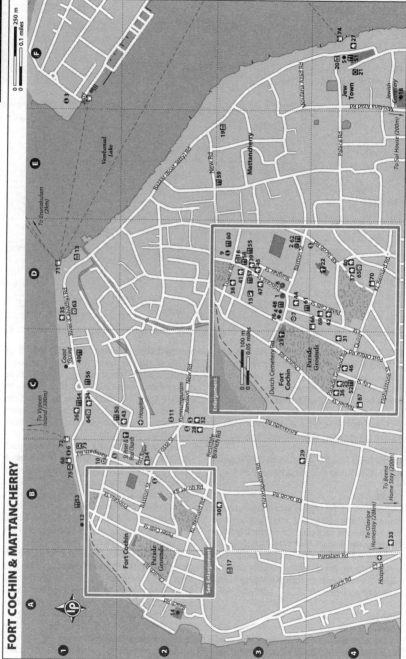

to Lisbon – you can still visit his tombstone in the church.

The **Dutch Cemetery** (Map p362; Beach Rd), consecrated in 1724, contains the worn and dilapidated graves of Dutch traders and soldiers; its gates are normally locked but you can ask the caretaker at St Francis Church if you want to have a look around.

The imposing Catholic **Santa Cruz Basilica** (Map p362; cnr Bastion St & KB Jacob Rd) was originally built on this site in 1506, though the current building dates to 1902. Inside you'll find artefacts from the different eras in Kochi and a striking pastel-coloured interior.

MATTANCHERRY PALACE
Built by the Portuguese in 1555, **Mattancherry Palace** (Dutch Palace; Map p362; ☎ 2226085; Bazaar Rd; admission Rs2; ☾ 10am-5pm Sat-Thu) was a rather generous gift presented to the Raja of Kochi, Veera Kerala Varma (1537–61), as a gesture of goodwill. More probably, it was a used as a sweetener to securing trading privileges. The Dutch renovated the palace in 1663, hence its alternative name, the Dutch Palace.

The star attractions here are the astonishingly preserved Hindu **murals**, depicting scenes from the Ramayana, Mahabharata and Puranic legends in intricate detail. The central hall on the 1st floor is now a portrait gallery of maharajas from 1864. There's an impressive collection of palanquins (hand-carried carriages), bejewelled outfits and splendidly carved ceilings in every room. The ladies' bedchamber downstairs features a cheerful Krishna using his six hands and two feet to engage in foreplay with eight very happy milkmaids.

Photography is prohibited.

PARDESI SYNAGOGUE & JEW TOWN
This **synagogue** (Map p362; admission Rs2; ☾ 10am-noon & 3-5pm Sun-Thu, closed Jewish holidays) was originally built in 1568, partially destroyed by the Portuguese in 1662, and rebuilt two years later when the Dutch took Kochi. It features an ornate gold pulpit and intricate, hand-painted, willow-pattern floor tiles from Canton, China. It's magnificently illuminated by chandeliers (from Belgium) and coloured-glass lamps. The graceful clock tower was built in 1760. There is an upstairs balcony for women who worshipped separately according to Orthodox rites. Note that shorts or sleeveless tops are not allowed inside.

KERALA

ERNAKULAM

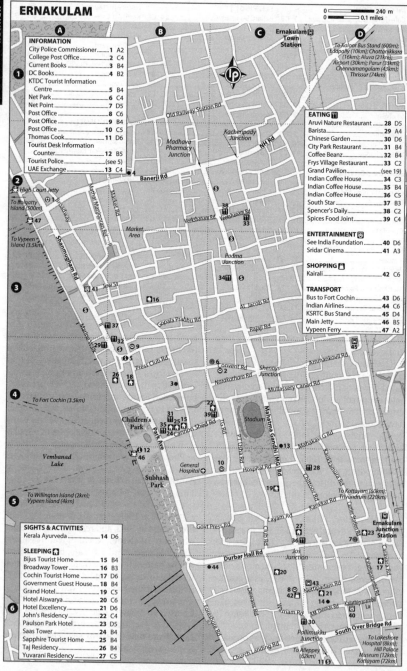

0 — 240 m
0 — 0.1 miles

INFORMATION
City Police Commissioner 1 A2
College Post Office 2 C4
Current Books 3 B4
DC Books 4 B2
KTDC Tourist Information
  Centre 5 B4
Net Park 6 C4
Net Point 7 D5
Post Office 8 C6
Post Office 9 B4
Post Office 10 C5
Thomas Cook 11 D6
Tourist Desk Information
  Counter 12 B5
Tourist Police .... (see 5)
UAE Exchange 13 C4

SIGHTS & ACTIVITIES
Kerala Ayurveda 14 D6

SLEEPING
Bijus Tourist Home 15 B4
Broadway Tower 16 B3
Cochin Tourist Home 17 D6
Government Guest House 18 B4
Grand Hotel 19 C5
Hotel Aiswarya 20 C6
Hotel Excellency 21 D6
John's Residency 22 C4
Paulson Park Hotel 23 D5
Saas Tower 24 B4
Sapphire Tourist Home 25 B4
Taj Residency 26 B4
Yuvarani Residency 27 C5

EATING
Aruvi Nature Restaurant 28 D5
Barista 29 A4
Chinese Garden 30 D6
City Park Restaurant 31 B4
Coffee Beanz 32 B4
Frys Village Restaurant 33 C2
Grand Pavilion .... (see 19)
Indian Coffee House 34 C3
Indian Coffee House 35 B4
Indian Coffee House 36 C5
South Star 37 B3
Spencer's Daily 38 C2
Spices Food Joint 39 C4

ENTERTAINMENT
See India Foundation 40 D6
Sridar Cinema 41 A3

SHOPPING
Kairali 42 C6

TRANSPORT
Bus to Fort Cochin 43 D6
Indian Airlines 44 C6
KSRTC Bus Stand 45 D4
Main Jetty 46 B5
Vypeen Ferry 47 A2

The synagogue is smack bang in the middle of **Jew Town** (Map p362), a bustling port area and centre of the Kochi spice trade. Scores of small firms huddle together in old, dilapidated buildings and the air is filled with the biting aromas of ginger, cardamom, cumin, turmeric and cloves. These days the lanes around the Dutch Palace and synagogue are packed with more antique and tourist-curio shops than pungent spices. Look out for the Jewish names on some of the buildings.

Around the corner lies the old **Jewish cemetery** (Map p362). Though it is not open to visitors, one enterprising shop owner lets visitors climb on his rooftop for views of the overgrown necropolis.

ART GALLERIES
Kochi is a leader in encouraging contemporary local artists.

Draavidia Art & Performance Gallery (Map p362; ☎ 3096812; Bazaar Rd; ☉ 9am-5pm) Shows off art by Keralan artists in an airy upstairs gallery. It also holds classical music concerts (Rs100) from November to March at 6pm.

Kashi Art Gallery (Map p362; ☎ 215769; Bazaar Rd, Mattancherry; ☉ 10am-12.30pm & 2-6pm) The pioneer of Fort Cochin's art revival, Kashi displays changing exhibitions of local artists.

Heritage Art (Map p362; Tower Rd; ☉ 10am-6pm) A tiny little gallery showing a small selection of works by local artists.

Activities
SWIMMING
Non-guests can swim at the small pool of **Grande Residencia Hotel** (Map p362; Princess St, Fort Cochin) for Rs500 per person. For a dip in the ocean, you can make a day trip out to the attractive **Cherai beach** on Vypeen Island (see p374).

AYURVEDA
Ayur Dara (☎ 2502362; www.ayurdara.com; Murikkumpadam, Vypeen Island; treatment €20 per day; ☉ 9am-5pm) Run by third-generation ayurvedic practitioner Dr Subhash, this delightful waterside treatment centre specialises in long-term treatments. It's 4km from the Vypeen Island ferry (autorickshaw Rs40). By appointment only.

Ayush (Map p362; ☎ 6456566; KB Jacob Rd, Fort Cochin; massage from Rs700; ☉ 8.30am-7pm) Part of an India-wide chain of ayurvedic centres, this place also does long-term treatments.

Kerala Ayurveda (Kerala Ayurveda Pharmacy Ltd; Map p364; ☎ 2378198; www.kaplayurveda.com; AM Thomas Rd, Ernakulam; massage from Rs500; ☉ 7am-7pm) This

government-approved centre comes recommended for all types of ayurvedic treatments.

Courses
Mrs Leelu Roy runs a popular cooking class called **Cook & Eat** (Map p362; ☎ 2215377; simonroy@hotmail.com; Quiros St; Rs500; ☉ 11am & 6pm) in her great big family kitchen. Several of the homestays in towns are also happy to organise impromptu cooking demonstrations and classes for their guests.

The Kerala Kathakali Centre (p371) has lessons in classical **Kathakali** dance, music and make-up (from Rs350 per hour). Contact Suji (☎ 09895860646) for more details.

For a crash course in the martial art of **kalarippayat**, head out to Ens Kalari (p371), a famed training centre. Short courses from one week to one month cost Rs2500 to Rs8500 (including accommodation).

Tours
The private Tourist Desk Information Counter (p360) runs popular full-day, **houseboat backwater tours** (Rs550) through local canals and lagoons. A canoe trip through smaller canals and villages is included, as is lunch and hotel pick-ups. See the boxed text, p347, for more information.

The KTDC (p360) also has half-day backwater tours (Rs350) at 8.30am and 2pm, and tourist **motor-boat tours** around Fort Cochin (Rs100) at the same times. It has full-day houseboat backwater trips at 8.30am (Rs650), where you stop at local weaving factories, spice gardens and, most importantly, toddy tapping!

Most hotels and tourist offices can arrange a day trip out to the **elephant training camp** (☉ 7am-6pm) at Kudanadu, 50km from Kochi. Here you can go for a ride (Rs200) and even help out with washing the gentle beasts if you arrive at 8am. Entry is free, though the elephant trainers will expect a small tip. A return trip out here in a taxi should cost around Rs900 to Rs1000.

Festivals & Events
In January/February, the eight-day **Ernakulathappan Utsavam festival** culminates in a procession of 15 decorated elephants, ecstatic music and fireworks.

Sleeping
Fort Cochin is an ideal place to escape the noise and chaos of the mainland – it's tranquil

and romantic, with some excellent accommodation choices. Its homestay scene has ballooned recently, with hundreds of family houses offering near-identical, large and clean, budget rooms.

Ernakulam is much cheaper and more convenient for onward travel, but the ambience and accommodation choices there are less than inspiring. Regardless of where you stay, book ahead during December and January.

FORT COCHIN
Budget
Royal Grace Tourist Home (Map p362; ☎ 2216584; Amaravathi Rd; r Rs350-500) This old-timer is one of the rare budget stalwarts still left in Fort Cochin. There are loads of rooms on offer in a large multistorey building, each with little more than a bed, four walls and a teeny-tiny bathroom.

Princess Inn (Map p362; ☎ 2217073; princessinnfort kochi@gmail.com; Princess St; s Rs350, d Rs400-600) One of the few places that sticks valiantly to its budget guns, the exceptionally friendly Princess Inn is a shining example of what a fresh lick of paint can do: sprucing up what would otherwise be dull, tiny rooms with cheery bright colours. The comfy communal spaces are a treat, and the three large, front-facing rooms are particularly excellent value.

Santa Cruz Tourist Home (Map p362; ☎ 2216250; santacruzhome@vsnl.net; Peter Celli St; r Rs474-675, with AC Rs1250; 🗶) This friendly, family-run affair has immaculate little rooms, though it's unfortunate that many of them only have windows to the corridor and can get a little stuffy.

Mother Tree (Map p362; ☎ 3220996; www.hotelmother tree.com; KL Bernard Master Rd; r Rs600, with AC Rs800; 🗶) There are just a few miniscule rooms in this compact homestay, but the hip and colourful paint job, immaculate cleanliness and neat rooftop chill-out space make this place worth seeking out.

Hanna's Haven (Map p362; ☎ 2215634; norma_nevis@ yahoo.com; Fort Nagar, r from Rs600, with AC Rs1000) Friendly owner Herman will happily fill you in on his family history as he's checking you into one of his several clean rooms. The decor here is nothing to write home about, but it's kept in excellent condition and there's a restaurant on the rooftop.

Green Woods Bethlehem (Map p362; ☎ 3247791; greenwoodsbethlehem1@vsnl.net; opp ESI Hospital; r Rs800-900) Owner Sheeba looks ready to sign your adoption papers the minute you walk through

her front door. What might just be the cutest guest house in Kochi lies in a quiet residential area cocooned in its own thick jungle of plants and soaring palms. The rooms in this multistorey building are humble but cosy, all lovingly decorated with homely bits and bobs. The included breakfast is served in the fantastic, leafy rooftop cafe, where cooking classes/demonstrations are often held.

Sonnetta Residency (Map p362; ☎ 2215744; www .sonnettaresidency.com; Princess St; r Rs800, with AC Rs1200; 🗶) Right in the thick of the Fort Cochin action, the plain rooms at this Portuguese-era building are pretty small, but come with nice touches like curtains and indoor plants to make you feel at home.

Oy's Homestay (Map p362; ☎ 9947594903; www.oys .co.in; Burgher St; r Rs800-1200) What used to be a scruffy budget den has recently re-invented itself as a hip midranger. There are just three large rooms here, all sparsely fitted out with a few decorations and set over a tiny courtyard. Though the bathrooms are a little scruffy, the central location is hard to beat.

Two other homestays worth checking out:

Costa Gama Home Stay (Map p362; ☎ 2216122; www.stayincochin.com; Thamaraparambu Rd; r Rs550-600) Cosy little place that gets rave reviews from travellers.

Beena Home Stay (Kadathanad; ☎ 2215458; www .homestaykochi.com; KB Jacob Rd; s Rs600, d Rs800-1000, d with AC Rs1300-1500; 🗶) Offers simple rooms and a ridiculously friendly welcome.

Midrange
Oy's La Homestay (Map p362; ☎ 6521384; www.oys.co.in; KB Jacob Rd; r Rs800-1000, with AC Rs1800-2000; 🗶) An extension of the original Oy's on Burgher St, this large guest house occupies a brand new building and has several large rooms happily painted in bold colours. Some of the abodes have balconies facing the street, so expect a fair bit of street-noise to drift up. Manager Tresa cooks up feasts for guests on demand.

Delight Home Stay (Map p362; ☎ 2217658; www .delightfulhomestay.com; Post Office Rd; r Rs1000-1500, with AC Rs2500; 🗶) And delightful it is. The uniquely styled rooms here have been marvellously remodelled and are eminently alluring. There's frilly white woodwork all around, a charming little garden, and an imposing sitting room covered in wall-to-wall polished teak.

Spencer Home (Map p362; ☎ 2215049; spencerhome styfc@rediffmail.com; Parade Ground Rd; d Rs1200) This handsomely restored heritage home has top-value, snug rooms set around a charming little garden courtyard. It has great period highlights, like high wood-beam ceilings and amazingly intricate antique locks, and breakfast is served garden-side, in front of your room.

Walton's Homestay (Map p362; ☎ 2215309; www .waltonshomestay.com; Princess St; r Rs1200-2000; ✕) The fastidious Mr Walton offers big and light rooms in his guest house, all decked out in white with blue trim. There's a lush garden out the back, a large secondhand bookshop downstairs, and a communal breakfast is included in the price. The bird-filled garden has one lovely AC garden cottage available for rent (double, Rs2000).

Chack Inn (Chackupurakal; Map p362; ☎ 2217504; Kunnumpuram Junction; r Rs1500, with AC Rs2000; ✕) Housed in a large white mansion fronted by a trim lawn (complete with a statue of three angry looking swans), the rooms at Chack Inn are equally grandiose. Inside it's all spacious and bright, immaculately kept and trimmed with frilly bits like curtains and a few knick-knacks. Breakfast is included and served on a large communal balcony.

Raintree Lodge (Map p362; ☎ 3251489; www.fort cochin.com; Peter Celli St; r Rs2000; ✕) The intimate and comfortable rooms at the Raintree flirt with boutique-hotel status. Each room has a great blend of modern and period decor fused with well-design flair. Try to get an upstairs room with a (tiny) balcony.

Bernard Bungalow (Map p362; ☎ 2216162; www .bernardbungalow.com; Parade Ground Rd; r Rs2500-3500; ✕) This gracious place is in a generously sized 350-year-old house that boasts a large collection of interesting rooms. The house has polished floorboards, wooden window shutters, balconies and verandahs, and is filled with lovely period furniture that gives it that 1940s summer cottage look.

Hotel Fort House (Map p362; ☎ 2217103; www.hotel forthouse.com; Cavathy Rd; r Rs2500-3800; ✕) In a prime spot right on the water, it's a shame most of the rooms here don't get to partake in the sea views. Still, abodes here have modern and thoughtful interiors, with colourful bed-spreads and funky lamp-shades to jazz them up. There's a dining area that juts out into the water – an idyllic spot for a nibble or your morning breakfast (included).

Ballard Bungalow (Map p362; ☎ 2215854; www .cochinballard.com; River Rd; r Rs3000-4000; ✕ 🖳) This gorgeous colonial-era building has airy, spa-

cious rooms with tall ceilings, lots of polished floorboards, elongated lounging chairs and poster beds. Lovely.

Sui House (Off Map p361; ☎ 2227078; suihouse@ gmail.com; Maulana Azad Rd; r Rs3500; ✕) This luxury homestay is the home of the owner of gorgeous Caza Maria (p368). There are just two mammoth AC en-suite rooms in this large family villa, painted either turquoise or yellow. Both rooms are breezy and bright, each filled with a range of elegant antique pieces. The sumptuous communal drawing room is filled with more fetching antiques, and a hearty breakfast is served in the outdoor courtyard.

Also worth checking out:

Daffodil Home Stay (Map p362; ☎ 2218686; www .daffodilhomestay.com; Njaliparambu Junction; r Rs800, with AC Rs1500-2000; ✕) Big and brightly painted modern rooms, with an upstairs carved-wood Keralan balcony.

Fort Heaven Residency (Map p362; ☎ 2215588; www.fortheavenresidency.com; Amravathi Rd; r Rs950, with AC Rs1350; ✕) Massive rooms in a very spacious and comfy house with a huge lawn.

Top End

our pick **Old Harbour Hotel** (Map p362; ☎ 2218006; www.oldharbourhotel.com; Tower Rd; r incl tax Rs7500-14600; ✕ 🖳 🖳) Set around an idyllic garden, with lily ponds and a small pool, the dignified Old Harbour is housed in a 300 year old Dutch-Portuguese heritage building and is one of the best luxury deals around. The elegant mix of period and modern styles and bright colour accents are luxurious without being over the top, lending the place a much more intimate feel than some of the more grandiose competition. Many rooms here face directly onto the garden, and some sport plant-filled, open-air bathrooms.

Malabar House (Map p362; ☎ 2216666; www.mala barhouse.com; Parade Ground Rd; r €220, ste incl breakfast €300-360; ✕ 🖳 🖳) What may just be one of the fanciest boutique hotels in Kerala, Malabar flaunts its uberhip blend of modern colours and period fittings like it's not even trying. It has a restaurant, wine bar and tapas bar on the premises. While the suites are huge and lavishly appointed, the standard rooms are a little short on space.

Brunton Boatyard (Map p362; ☎ 2215461; brunton boatyard@cghearth.com; River Rd; r Rs17,500-25,000; ✕ 🖳 🖳) This imposing hotel faithfully re-produces 16th- and 17th-century Dutch and Portuguese architecture in its grand complex.

KERALA

All of the rooms look out over the harbour, and have bathtub and balconies with a refreshing sea breeze that beats AC any day.

MATTANCHERRY & JEW TOWN

Caza Maria (Map p362; ☎ 3258837; cazamaria@rediffmail.com; Jew Town Rd; r incl breakfast Rs3000-4500; ☒) Right in the heart of Jew Town, this unique place has just two enormous and sumptuously decorated heritage rooms overlooking the bazaar. Fit for a maharaja, the idiosyncratic style here has to be seen to be believed – with each high-ceilinged room painted in bright colours, filled to the brim with first-rate antiques and with tall windows looking onto the bustling market street below.

ERNAKULAM
Budget

Cochin Tourist Home (Map p364; ☎ 2377577; Caravara Rd; s/d from Rs175/275, r with AC Rs750; ☒) This ultra-budget cheapie opposite Ernakulam Junction train station is fine for an emergency kip if you arrive late or have to leave early. Rooms are scruffy but reasonably hygienic.

Broadway Tower (Map p364; ☎ 2361645; www.broadwaytowers.com; Marie Drive; s/d Rs250/350, with AC Rs500/650; ☒) With cookie-cutter standard rooms, this place is one of the better deals in Ernakulam's busy market area. Slightly tucked away, it's surprisingly quiet and has a handy, modern cheap-eats restaurant downstairs.

Sapphire Tourist Home (Map p364; ☎ 2381238; Cannon Shed Rd; d Rs350-450, with AC Rs1000; ☒ 🖵) The very trim and bright little rooms here are darned good budget value – all well maintained and very efficiently run. There's one computer downstairs offering internet access.

Saas Tower (Map p364; ☎ 2365319; www.saastower.com; Cannon Shed Rd; s/d Rs350/550, with AC from Rs650/1000; ☒) They say they have 'facilities to match your fantasies' – but you'd need pretty dull fantasies to justify that tagline. The predictably standard and straightforward rooms, filled with almost-pink wooden furniture, are made more attractive by the handy location near the boat jetty and above a decent restaurant.

John's Residency (Map p364; ☎ 2355395; TG Rd; r Rs400-600, with AC Rs1200; ☒) It's a shame that the funky, almost boutiquey, yellow foyer design isn't replicated throughout this small hotel. Still, the rooms are fastidiously clean and come with red curtains that give it a moody, almost arty, feel during the day.

Bijus Tourist Home (Map p364; ☎ 2361661; www.bijustouristhome.com; Market Rd; s/d from Rs440/690, d with AC Rs1300; ☒) This friendly, popular choice is handy for the main jetty and has slightly dated, though excellently maintained rooms that still manage to look smart. The place is very efficiently run.

Midrange & Top End

Hotel Aiswarya (Map p364; ☎ 2364454; www.aiswaryahotel.com; Warriam Rd; s/d Rs450/650, d with AC Rs975; ☒) Aiswarya gets top marks for its central location, with a respectable score for its clean, bright rooms. This is a decent, though unexciting, midrange choice.

Paulson Park Hotel (Map p364; ☎ 2378240; www.hotelpaulsonpark.com; Carrier Station Rd; s/d from Rs495/800, d with AC Rs1200; ☒) Right near the station, this quiet, spick-and-span place stands out for its fantasy-inspired, plasticky indoor garden. The cheaper rooms are pretty bare, but the pricier rooms have just enough decoration to make them feel welcoming.

Hotel Excellency (Map p364; ☎ 2378251; www.hotelexcellency.com; Nettipadam Rd; s/d from Rs650/750, with AC Rs950/1050; ☒ 🖵) This businesslike hotel has white-tiled and sterile hallways more reminiscent of a hospital, but the lamp-lit rooms are more welcoming and come with spotless bathrooms.

Government Guest House (Map p364; ☎ 2360502; Shanmughan Rd; s/d Rs850/1200; ☒) We secretly love Kerala's government guest houses – they always manage to be the best deal in town. Right in the city's heart and near the sea, this massive eight-storey monolith of a building has huge, perfectly neat rooms. The place probably won't win any style awards soon, but considering some of the upper-floor rooms have balconies with sweeping sea vistas, this is still unbeatable value.

Yuvarani Residency (Map p364; ☎ 2377040; www.yuvaraniresidency.com; MG Rd; s/d from Rs950/1200, with AC Rs1500/1850; ☒) Even though all that glitters is not gold here, these almost-swanky rooms are perfectly comfortable and finished with all the stylish dark-wood fixtures your heart desires. It's set back from MG Rd enough to shield the noise.

Grand Hotel (Map p364; ☎ 2382061; www.grandhotelkerala.com; MG Rd; s/d from Rs1800/2100; ☒) This funky 1960s hotel oozes the sort of retro styling that modern hotels would kill to re-create. The large rooms are very neat, with parquet floors and large modern bathrooms, and the foyer has cool lounges and groovy art deco chairs. One of the more interesting places to stay in Ernakulam.

Top End

Taj Residency (Map p364; ☎ 2371471; www.tajhotels.com; Marine Drive; s/d incl breakfast from Rs6500/7000; 🔀 🔃 🖳) This branch of the Taj chain is a businessman's mecca, with understated dark-wood interiors in the rooms and all the pre-requisite modern conveniences. There's a gym, pool and sauna here, and their cafe is in a fantastic atrium with views out to sea.

AROUND KOCHI

our pick Olavipe Homestay (Map p362; ☎ 0478-2522255; www.olavipe.com; Olavipe; s/d incl meals Rs7000/1000) This gorgeous 1890s traditional Syrian-Christian home is on a 16-hectare farm surrounded by backwaters, 28km south of Kochi. A restored mansion of rosewood and glistening teak, it has several large and breezy rooms – all skilfully finished with original period decor (only the ceiling fans are new). There are lots of shady awnings and sitting areas, a fascinating archive with six generations of family history, and the gracious owners will make you feel like a welcome friend rather than a guest. A taxi to/from Fort Cochin is Rs600 to Rs700.

Eating & Drinking

Covert beer consumption is *de rigueur* at most of the Fort Cochin restaurants, and more expensive in the licensed ones (Rs80 to Rs165).

FORT COCHIN

Cake Shop Cafe (Map p362; Calvathy Rd; cakes Rs6-35; 🔀) This modern little cake shop sells yummy Western-style cookies and tarts alongside espresso coffee. Try and resist the butterscotch tart (Rs25). Go on, just try.

Café Coffee Day (Map p362; Bastion St; snacks Rs10-65; coffee Rs22-60, 🕑 8am-11pm; 🔀) This modern cafe is India's answer to the Starbucks call to arms. Expect comfy couches, a bewildering array of espresso options, blaring MTV and almost no soul.

Teapot (Map p362; Peter Celli St; snacks Rs30-50, meals Rs125-175) This stylish haunt is the perfect venue for 'high tea', with quality teas, sandwiches and full meals served in chic-minimalist, airy rooms. Witty tea-themed accents include loads of antique teapots, tea chests for tables

and a gnarled, tea-tree-based glass table. The death by chocolate here (Rs50) is truly cocoa homicide. Trust us.

Solar Cafe (Map p362; Bazaar Rd; meals Rs30-75; 🕑 10am-6pm) This arty and funky cafe at Draavidia Gallery (p365) serves up organic breakfasts and lunches in a brightly coloured and friendly setting. There's a fun open kitchen and upstairs verandah seating overlooks the hubbub of the street below.

Oy's Restaurant (Map p362; Burgher St; meals Rs60-175) This new addition to the dining scene is one of the hippest looking restaurants in Kochi. The setting is groovy lounge-like: with low-slung couches backed by bamboo; low glass-topped tables; and a bass-heavy chillout soundtrack. The Southeast Asian–focused dishes are original and reasonably good – try the grilled prawns with crunchy vegetables (Rs145).

Casa Linda (Map p362; Dispensary Rd; mains Rs65-250) This modern dining room above the hotel of the same name might not be much to look at, but it's all about the food here. Chef Dipu once trained with a Frenchman and whips up delicious local Keralan dishes alongside French imports like Poisson de la Provencale (fish fried in oil and herbs, Provence style). The Keralan dry-fried coconut prawns (Rs140), made to a loving mother's recipe, are scrumptious.

our pick Dal Roti (Map p362; Lily St; meals Rs70-170; 🕑 lunch & dinner) You'll hear the buzz about this place before you even arrive in Fort Cochin – it's the best food in town. Friendly and knowledgeable owner Ramesh will hold your hand through his expansive North Indian menu, which even sports its own glossary, and will help you dive in to his delicious range of vegetarian, eggetarian and nonvegetarian options. The setting is chic minimalist, with whitewashed walls and bench seating, helping you focus on the yummy dishes here.

Kashi Art Cafe (Map p362; Burgher St; breakfast/lunch Rs85/90; 🕑 8.30am-7.30pm) An institution in Fort Cochin, this place has a hip-but-casual vibe, along with hip-but-casual service. The coffee is as strong as it should be and the daily Western breakfast and lunch specials are excellent. A small gallery shows off local artists.

Upstairs (Map p362; ☎ 6452922; Bastion St; mains Rs140-300) With a real Italian cook, a classy, Mediterranean-white upstairs dining room and an impressive Italian menu boasting imported ingredients (like gorgonzola cheese

---

SYRIAN CHRISTIANS IN SOUTH INDIA

Tradition has it that Christianity was first brought to India in the first century, when St Thomas (one of the original apostles) found his way to the subcontinent and evangelised a family of Brahmins. With strong early ties to the Middle East, Christians in Kerala aligned themselves with the Syrian Patriarch from around the 4th century onwards.

The 16th century brought the Portuguese to Kerala, along with missionaries eager to convert locals to their Roman brand of Catholicism. Then the arrival of the Anglican British in the 18th century led to further challenges to India's unique Christianity. Today, small communities of Syrian Christians still survive in Kerala, professing a faith that dates all the way back to one adventurous apostle.

---

and Parma ham), you'd think this place had it made. Unfortunately the food just doesn't live up to the hype. Still, it remains one of the most romantic places for an evening meal.

Old Courtyard (Map p362; ☎ 2216302; Princess St; mains Rs180-320) This restaurant is set in a lovely open courtyard surrounded by white marble arches. The menu is seafood-centric and comes highly rated by readers and pundits alike.

Malabar Junction (Map p362; ☎ 2216666; Parade Ground Rd; mains Rs280-1000) Set in an open-sided pavilion, the classy restaurant at Malabar House is movie-star cool. There's a seafood-based, European-style menu and Grover's Estate wine (quaffable, Indian) is served. The signature dish is the impressive seafood platter with grilled vegetables (Rs980).

History Restaurant (Map p362; ☎ 2215461; River Rd; mains Rs350-550) Brunton Boatyard's restaurant with a historical menu tracing Kochi's Jewish, Syrian, Arabic and Portuguese history.

Also recommended:

New Ananda Bhavan (Map p362; River Rd; dishes Rs14-40) Herbivores: make a beeline for this basic but spotless veggie hole-in-the-wall restaurant.

Salt 'n' Pepper (Map p362; Tower Rd; dishes Rs40-120; ☯ 24hr) Superbly average food, but the street-side tables bustle nightly with punters having a 'special teapot' tipple (Rs100).

Behind the Chinese fishing nets are a couple of **fishmongers** (Map p362; seafood per kg Rs50-300), from whom you can buy fish (or prawns, scampi,

lobster). Then take your selection to a shack where they will cook it and serve it to you (fish about Rs40 per kg).

MATTANCHERRY & JEW TOWN

Ramathula Hotel (Map p362; Kayees Junction, Mattancherry; biryani Rs35-40; ☯ lunch & dinner) This place is legendary among locals for its chicken and mutton biryanis – get here early or you'll miss out. It's better known by the chef's name, Kayees.

Caza Maria (Map p362; Bazaar Rd; mains Rs100-200) With cooks trained by a travelling Frenchman, this is an enchanting, bright blue space with funky music and a changing daily menu of North Indian, South Indian and French dishes.

ERNAKULAM

Spices Food Joint (Map p364; Cannon Shed Rd; dishes Rs20-80; ☯ 5am-12pm) A family-run hole-in-the-wall restaurant captained by the gregarious Sherief. The tasty chicken and meat biryanis (Rs65 to Rs85), as well as fish-curry meals (Rs35), are deservedly popular.

Coffee Beanz (Map p364; Shanmugham Rd; breakfast Rs30-75; ☯ lunch & dinner; ☒) Come here for a hip hit of coffee, with trendy, loud students and arctic AC for company.

Frys Village Restaurant (Map p364; Veekshanam Rd; dishes Rs35-100; ☯ lunch & dinner; ☒) This cavernous family restaurant is one of the best places in town for authentic Keralan food, especially for seafood like *pollichathu* (fish in banana leaves) or crab roast (Rs50 to Rs100).

Aruvi Nature Restaurant (Map p364; Chittoor Rd; meals around Rs50) An interesting twist on the traditional Keralan set meal – the whole menu here is created according to ayurvedic principles and contains no dairy, spicy peppers or salt. And it's still damned tasty – definitely worth a try!

South Star (Map p364; Shanmughan Rd; meals Rs50-100; ☒) This upmarket version of the Bimbis chain of restaurants is in a dark, moodily lit space that's plushed out in nice chairs and dark-wood tables. The bulky menu has North and South Indian victuals, as well as a massive choice of Chinese dishes.

City Park Restaurant (Map p364; Cannon Shed Rd; dishes Rs60-90) City Park has a well-prepared and varied menu spanning the usual Indian, Chinese and Continental gamut.

Grand Pavilion (Map p364; MG Rd; meals Rs80-350; ☒) This is the restaurant at the Grand Hotel and is as retro-stylish as the hotel itself. It serves a tome of a menu that covers dishes from the

West, North India, South India and most of the rest of the Asian continent. The *meen pollichathu* (fish cooked in banana leaves, Rs150) here gets the thumbs up.

Other options:

Spencer's Daily (Map p364; Veekshanam Rd; 7.30am-10.30pm) Well-stocked supermarket.

Indian Coffee House (Map p364; Cannon Shed Rd) Also has branches on Jos Junction and MG Rd near Padma Junction.

Coffee Beanz (Map p364; Shanmugham Rd; breakfasts Rs30-75; lunch & dinner;) For a hip coffee hit.

Barista (Map p364; Bay Pride Mall; Marine Walk; snacks Rs50-70; lunch & dinner;) Branch of the Indian coffee chain with great location on the sea.

Entertainment
CINEMAS
Sridar Cinema (Map p364; Shanmugham Rd, Ernakulam; tickets Rs40) Screens films in Malayalam, Hindi, Tamil and English.

KATHAKALI
There are several places in Kochi where you can view Kathakali (see the boxed text, p372). The performances are certainly made for tourists, but they're also a good introduction to this intriguing art form. The standard program starts with the intricate make-up application, followed by a commentary on the dance and then the performance.

See India Foundation (Map p364; 2376471; Kalathiparambil Lane, Ernakulam; admission Rs150; make-up 6pm, show 7-8pm) One of the oldest Kathakali theatres in Kerala, it has small-scale shows with an emphasis on the religious and philosophical roots of Kathakali.

Kerala Kathakali Centre (Map p362; 2217552; www.kathakalicentre.com; KB Jacob Rd, Fort Cochin; admission Rs150; make-up 5pm, show 6.30-8pm) In a massive new theatre, this place specialises in grand, showy performances and provides useful translations of the night's story.

Greenix Village (Map p362; 2217000; www.greenix .in; Calvathy Rd, Fort Cochin; admission Rs350; make-up 5.15pm, show 6.15pm) In a very kitschy, purpose-built complex, this three-hour show mixes Kathakali with other types of classical dance performances and music. Don't expect a whole lot of authenticity, but do expect a fast, colourful show that will keep the kiddies enthralled.

KALARIPPAYAT
Examples of this fast-paced traditional martial art can now be easily seen in Fort Cochin. The

Kerala Kathakali Centre (left) holds one-hour performances at its old theatre (Map p362) opposite Brunton Boatyard nightly at 7pm (Rs150).

If you want to see real professionals have a go at it, it's best to travel out to **Ens Kalari** (Off Map p364; 2700810; www.enskalari.org.in; Nettoor, Ernakulam), a renowned *kalarippayat* learning centre 8km southeast of Ernakulam. They hold one-hour demonstrations Monday to Saturday at 7pm (one day's notice required, admission by donation).

Greenix Village (Map p362; 2217000; www.greenix .in; Calvathy Rd, Fort Cochin; Rs250) also holds one-hour Kalarippayat shows at 7.30am and 2pm.

Shopping
Broadway in Ernakulam (Map p364) is good for local shopping, spice shops, clothing and a bazaar feel. Around Convent and Market Rds there's a huddle of tailors, and on and around Market Rd, between Jew St and Press Club Rd, is the textiles centre. On Jew Town Rd in Mattancherry (Map p362) there's a plethora of Kashmiri-run shops selling everything from genuine antiques to cheap knock-offs. Many shops in Fort Cochin operate lucrative commission rackets, with rickshaw drivers getting huge kickbacks (which are added to your price) just for dropping tourists at their door.

Fabindia (Map p362; 2217077; www.fabindia .com; Napier St, Fort Cochin; 10am-8pm) This popular chain of stores has oodles of fine Indian fabrics, clothes and home linens as well as accessories, personal care products and homewares.

Cinnamon (Map p362; 2217124; Post Office Rd, Fort Cochin; 10am-7pm Mon-Sat) Cinnamon sells gorgeous Indian-designed clothing, jewellery and homewares in an ultrachic white retail space.

Niraamaya (Map p362; 3263465; Quiros St, Fort Cochin; 10am-5pm) Popular throughout Kerala, Niraamaya sells 'ayurvedic' clothing and fabrics – all made of organic cotton, coloured with natural herb dyes, or infused with ayurvedic oils. The clothing is very simple, but makes for an original gift.

Kairali (Map p364; 2354507; MG Rd, Ernakulam; 9am-8pm Mon-Sat) This handicraft shop is a government emporium with quality items at fixed prices. There's a much smaller **Kairali** (Map p362; 221544; River Rd; 9am-7pm Mon-Sat) in Fort Cochin.

TRADITIONAL KERALAN ARTS

Kathakali

The art form of Kathakali crystallised at around the same time as Shakespeare was scribbling his plays, though elements of it stem from 2nd-century temple rituals. The Kathakali performance is the dramatised presentation of a play, usually based on the Hindu epics the Ramayana, the Mahabharata and the Puranas. All the great themes are covered – righteousness and evil, frailty and courage, poverty and prosperity, war and peace.

Drummers and singers accompany the actors, who tell the story through their precise movements, particularly mudras (hand gestures) and facial expressions. Traditionally, performances took place in temple grounds and went from 8pm until dawn; shorter performances in other locales are now also popular.

Preparation for the performance is lengthy and disciplined. Paint, fantastic costumes, ornamental headpieces and meditation transform the actors both physically and mentally into the gods, heroes and demons they are about to play.

You can see cut-down performances in tourist hot spots all over the state, and there are Kathakali schools in Trivandrum (see p327) and near Thrissur (see p378) that encourage visitors.

Kalarippayat

Kalarippayat is an ancient tradition of martial training and discipline, still taught throughout Kerala. Some believe it is the forerunner of all martial arts, with roots tracing back to the 12th-century skirmishes among Kerala's feudal principalities.

Masters of kalarippayat, called Gurukkal, teach their craft inside a special arena called a kalari. The kalari is part gymnasium, part school and part temple. Its construction follows traditional principles: its rectangular design is always aligned east–west and Hindu deities are represented in each corner.

Kalarippayat movements – the foundation of choreography that uses the actors' bodies and gestures as tools of expression – can be traced in Kerala's performing arts, such as Kathakali and kootiattam, and in ritual arts such as theyyam.

Theyyam

Kerala's most popular ritualistic art form, theyyam, is believed to pre-date Hinduism, originating from folk dances performed during harvest celebrations. An intensely local ritual, it's often performed in kavus (sacred groves) throughout northern Kerala.

Theyyam refers both to the shape of the deity/hero portrayed, and to the actual ritual. There are around 450 different theyyams, each with a distinct costume; face paint, bracelets, breastplates, skirts, garlands and especially headdresses are exuberant, intricately crafted and sometimes huge (up to 6m or 7m tall).

During performances, each protagonist loses his physical identity and speaks, moves and blesses the devotees as if he were that deity. There is frenzied dancing and wild drumming, and a surreal, otherworldly atmosphere is created, the kind of atmosphere in which a deity indeed might, if it so desired, manifest itself in human form.

The theyyam season is October to May, during which time there will be an annual ritual at each of the hundreds of kavus. Theyyams are often held to bring good fortune to important events, such as marriages and housewarmings. See p383 for details on how to find one.

Traveller's Paradise (Map p362; ☎ 2218633; KL Bernard Master Rd, Fort Cochin; ✆ 9.30am-7pm) Originally started by a French expat, this place sells intricate gifts of handmade postcards, silk bedcovers, tablecloths, bags and accessories made by disenfranchised local women, with all proceeds going to charity.

Getting There & Away

AIR

The following airlines have offices in Kochin:
Air India (Map p361; ☎ 2351295; MG Rd; ✆ 9.30am-1pm & 1.45-5.30pm Mon-Sat)
Indian Airlines (Map p364; ☎ 2370238; Durbar Hall Rd; ✆ 9.45am-1pm & 1.45-5pm)

Jet Airways (Map p361; ☎ 2358582; MG Rd; ⏰ 9am-5pm Mon-Sat, to 1.30pm Sun)
Kingfisher Airlines (Map p361; ☎ 2351144; 2nd fl, Sreekandath Rd; ⏰ 9.30am-6pm Mon-Sat)

Low-cost airlines **Paramount Airways** (☎ 2610404-5), **IndiGo** (☎ 4029316) and **Spice Jet** (☎ 18001803333) have offices at the airport. See the table, below, for sample fares and flights.

BUS
The **KSRTC bus stand** (Map p364; ☎ 2372033; ⏰ reservations 6am-10pm) is in Ernakulam next to the railway halfway between the two train stations. Many buses passing through Ernakulam originate in other cities – you may have to join the scrum when the bus pulls in. You can make reservations up to five days in advance for buses originating here. There's a separate window for reservations to Tamil Nadu. See p374 for more information on buses from Ernakulam.

Several private bus companies have super-deluxe, AC, video buses that go to Bengaluru, Chennai, Mangalore and Coimbatore; prices for these are around 75% higher than government buses. There are stands selling tickets all over Ernakulam. **Kaloor bus stand** is the main private bus station; it's 1km north of the city.

TRAIN
Ernakulam has two train stations, Ernakulam Town and Ernakulam Junction, with reservations for both made at the Ernakulam Junction **reservations office** (☎ 132; ⏰ 8am-8pm Mon-Sat, to 2pm Sun).

There are lots of trains to Trivandrum (2nd class/AC chair Rs56/238, 4½ hours), via Alleppey (Rs25/135, 1½ hours), Kollam (Rs46/188, 3½ hours) or Kottayam (Rs6/142, 1½ hours). Several trains also run to Thrissur (Rs29/131, 1½ hours), Calicut (Rs55/180, 4½ hours) and Kannur (Rs70/276, 6½ hours). For long-distance trains, see p375.

Getting Around
TO/FROM THE AIRPORT
Kochi International Airport (Off Map p364; ☎ 2610113; www.cochin-airport.com) is at Nedumbassery, 30km northeast of Ernakulam. Taxis to/from Ernakulam cost around Rs500, and to/from Fort Cochin around Rs650. Ernakulam's mad traffic means that the trip can take over 1½ hours in the daytime, though usually less than one hour at night.

DOMESTIC FLIGHTS FROM ERNAKULAM

Destination	Airline	Fare (US$)	Duration (hr)	Frequency
Agatti	IT	145	1½	5 weekly
Bengaluru	9W	84	1¼	1 daily
	IT	84	1¼	3 daily
Chennai	IC	88	1	3 weekly
	9W	85	1½	1 daily
	IT	85	1½	3 daily
	I7	81	1	3 daily
Delhi	IC	200	3	1 daily
	9W	136	3	2 daily
	IT	121	4	1 daily
	6R	89	4	1 daily
Goa	IT	75	4	1 daily
Kozhikode	IC	85	1	1 daily
	IT	85	1	1 daily
Mumbai	IC	120	2	1 daily
	9W	111	2	2 daily
	IT	85	2	2 daily
	SG	77	2	1 daily
Trivandrum	IC	85	¾	2 daily
	IT	85	¾	1 daily

Note: Fares are one-way. Airline codes: IC – Indian Airlines; 9W – Jet Airways; IT – Kingfisher; I7 – Paramount Airways; 6E – IndiGo; SG – SpiceJet.

BOAT

Ferries are the fastest form of transport between Fort Cochin and the mainland. The jetty on the eastern side of Willingdon Island is called **Embarkation** (Map p361); the west one, opposite Mattancherry, is **Terminus** (Map p361); and the main stop at Fort Cochin is **Customs Jetty** (Map p362), with another stop at the **Mattancherry Jetty** near the synagogue (Map p362). One-way fares are all around Rs3.

Ernakulam

There are services to both Fort Cochin jetties (Customs and Mattancherry) every 25 to 50 minutes (5.55am to 9.30pm) from Ernakulam's **main jetty** (Map p364).

Ferries also run every 20 minutes or so to Willingdon and Vypeen Islands (6am to 10pm).

Fort Cochin

Ferries run from Customs Jetty to Ernakulam between 6.20am and 9.50pm. Ferries also hop between Customs Jetty and Willingdon Island 18 times a day from 6.40am to 9.30pm (Monday to Saturday).

Car and passenger ferries cross to Vypeen Island from Fort Cochin virtually nonstop from 6am until 10pm.

LOCAL TRANSPORT

There are no real bus services between Fort Cochin and Mattancherry Palace, but it's an enjoyable 30-minute walk through the busy warehouse area along Bazaar Rd. Autorickshaws should cost around Rs20, but you'll need to haggle. Most autorickshaw trips around Ernakulam shouldn't cost more than Rs25.

To get to Fort Cochin after ferries stop running, catch a bus in Ernakulam on MG Rd (Rs8, 45 minutes), south of Durbar Hall Rd. From Fort Cochin, buses head out to Ernakulam from opposite the Vypeen Island ferry jetty. Taxis charge round-trip fares between the islands, even if you only go one way – Ernakulam Town train station to Fort Cochin should cost around Rs170.

Scooters/Enfields can be hired for Rs250/450 per day from **Vasco Tourist Information Centre** (Map p362; ☎ 2216215; vascoinformations@yahoo.co.uk; Bastion St, Fort Cochin).

AROUND KOCHI
Tripunithura

Hill Palace Museum (Off Map p364; ☎ 0484-2781113; admission Rs20; ⏰ 9am-12.30pm & 2-4.30pm Tue-Sun) at Tripunithura, 12km southeast of Ernakulam en route to Kottayam, was formerly the residence of the Kochi royal family and is an impressive 49-building palace complex. It now houses the collections of the royal families, as well as 19th-century oil paintings, old coins, sculptures and paintings, and temple models. From Ernakulam catch the bus to Tripunithura from MG Rd or Shanmugham Rd, behind the Tourist Reception Centre (Rs5, 45 minutes); an autorickshaw should

MAJOR BUSES FROM ERNAKULAM

The following bus services operate from the KSRTC bus stand (Map p364).

Destination	Fare (Rs)	Duration (hr)	Frequency
Alleppey	39	1½	every 20min
Bengaluru	249 (AC 448)	14	8 daily
Calicut	129	5	hourly
Chennai	425 (AC 650)	16	1 daily
Coimbatore	118	4½	9 daily
Kannur	146	8	7 daily
Kanyakumari	197	8	2 daily
Kollam	91	3½	every 20min
Kothamangalam	29	2	every 30min
Kottayam	46	2	every 20min
Kumily (for Periyar)	115	5	8 daily
Madurai	174	9	2 daily
Mangalore	270	12	1 daily
Munnar	80	5½	every 45min
Thrissur	51	2	every 15min
Trivandrum	135	5	every 20min

MAJOR TRAINS FROM ERNAKULAM

The following are major long-distance trains departing from Ernakulam Town.

Destination	Train No & Name	Fare* (Rs)	Duration (hr)	Departures
Bengaluru	6525 *Bangalore Exp*	270/724/986	13	6.05pm
Chennai	2624 *Chennai Mail*	303/791/1066	12	7.15pm
Delhi	2625 *Kerala Exp***	599/1621/2220	46	3.40pm
Goa	6312 *Bikaner Exp*	320/862/1179	15	8pm (Sat only)
Kanyakumari	6526 *Kanyakumari Exp*	167/431/580	8	10.10am
Mangalore	6329 *Malabar Exp*	200/525/711	10½	11.45pm
Mumbai	6382 *Mumbai Exp*	473/1320/1815	40	1pm

*Sleeper/3AC/2AC
**Departs from Ernakulam Junction

cost around Rs250 return with one-hour waiting time.

Cherai Beach

On Vypeen island, 25km from Fort Cochin, **Cherai beach** might just be Kochi's best-kept secret. It's a lovely stretch of as-yet undeveloped white sand, with miles of lazy backwaters just a few hundred metres from the seafront. Best of all, it's close enough to visit on a day trip from Kochi.

If you plan on staying for more than a day, there are a few low-key resorts here.

Brighton Beach House (☎ 0484-221855, 9947440449; www.brightonbeachhouse.org; r Rs850, with AC Rs1200; ☺ Nov-Mar) is run by the same folk who own Salt 'n' Pepper restaurant in Fort Cochin. This place has a few basic rooms in a small building right near the shore. The beach is rocky here, but the place is wonderfully secluded, filled with hammocks to loll in, and has a neat, elevated stilt-restaurant that serves perfect sunset views with dinner.

Cherai Beach Resort (☎ 0484-2416949; www .cheraibeachresorts.com; Vypeen Island; r Rs2000-3000, with AC Rs4200-4500; ☺ ▣) is an excellent collection of distinctive cottages lying around a meandering lagoon, with the beach on one side and backwaters immediately on the other. Bungalows are individually designed using natural materials, with either curving walls or split-levels, or lookouts onto the backwaters. There's even a tree growing inside one room. The restaurant serves daily buffets (breakfast/lunch/dinner Rs150/300/350). Check out a few different rooms to find one to your liking.

To get here from Fort Cochin, catch a vehicle ferry to Vypeen Island (per person/scooter Rs1.50/3) and either hire an autorickshaw

from the jetty (around Rs270) or catch one of the frequent buses (Rs14, one hour).

Parur & Chennamangalam

Nowhere is the tightly woven religious cloth that is India more apparent than in Parur, 35km north of Kochi. Here, a **synagogue** (Rs2; ☺ 9am-5pm Tue-Sun), one of the oldest in Kerala, at Chennamangalam (8km from Parur), has been fastidiously renovated. Inside you can see notable door and ceiling wood reliefs in dazzling colours, while just outside lies the oldest tombstone in India – inscribed with the Hebrew date corresponding to 1269. The Jesuits first arrived in Chennamangalam in 1577 and there's a **Jesuit church** and the ruins of a Jesuit college nearby. Nearby are a **Hindu temple** on a hill overlooking the Periyar River, a 16th-century **mosque**, and Muslim and Jewish **burial grounds**.

In Parur town, you'll find the **agraharam** (place of Brahmins) – a small street of closely packed and brightly coloured houses originally settled by Tamil Brahmins.

Parur is compact, though Chennamangalam is best visited with a guide. **Indoworld** (Map p362; ☎ 2218947; www.indoworldtours.com; Princess St; ☺ 8am-8pm Mon-Sat, to 2.30pm Sun) can organise tours (around Rs600 plus guide).

Buses for Parur leave from the KSRTC bus stand in Kochi (Rs16, one hour, every 10 minutes). From Parur catch a bus (Rs3) or autorickshaw (Rs50) to Chennamangalam.

THRISSUR (TRICHUR)

☎ 0487 / pop 330,100

While the rest of Kerala has its fair share of celebrations, Thrissur remains the cultural cherry on the festival cake. With a list of energetic and highly spirited festivals as long as a temple-elephant's trunk, the region supports several institutions that nurse the dying classical Keralan performing arts back to health. This busy, bustling place is home to a community of Nestorian Christians, whose denomination dates back to the 3rd century AD. The popular Sri Krishna Temple (33km northwest of Thrissur; p378) and performing-arts school Kerala Kalamandalam (p378) are nearby. Plan to get here during the rambunctious festival season (November to mid-May).

Orientation & Information

There are several ATMs around town.
DTPC office (District Tourism Promotion Council; ☎ 2320800; Palace Rd; ✆ 10am-5pm Mon-Sat)

Lava Rock Internet Cafe (Kuruppam Rd; per hr Rs25; ✆ 8.30am-9.30pm)
Paragon Web Inc (2nd fl, High Rd; per hr Rs20; ✆ 8.30am-9.30pm)
UAE Money Exchange (☎ 2445668; TB Rd; ✆ 9am-5.30pm Mon-Sat, 9.30am-1pm Sun)

Sights & Activities

One of the oldest in the state, **Vadakkunathan Kshetram Temple** crowns the hill at the epicentre of Thrissur. Finished in classic Keralan architecture, only Hindus are allowed inside, though the mound surrounding the temple has sweeping metropolis views and is a popular spot to loiter. Thrissur is also famed for its numerous churches, including **Our Lady of Lourdes Cathedral**, a massive cathedral with an

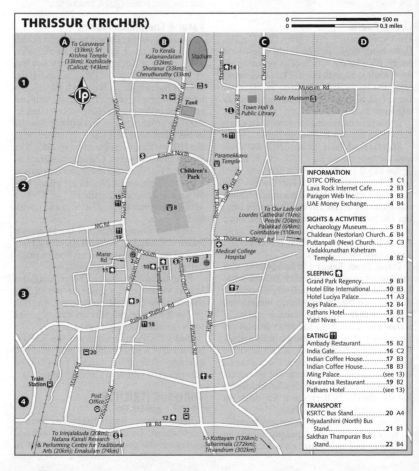

THRISSUR (TRICHUR)

INFORMATION	
DTPC Office	1 C1
Lava Rock Internet Cafe	2 B3
Paragon Web Inc	3 B3
UAE Money Exchange	4 B4

SIGHTS & ACTIVITIES	
Archaeology Museum	5 B1
Chaldean (Nestorian) Church	6 B4
Puttanpalli (New) Church	7 C3
Vadakkunathan Kshetram Temple	8 B2

SLEEPING ⌂	
Grand Park Regency	9 B3
Hotel Elite International	10 B3
Hotel Luciya Palace	11 A3
Joys Palace	12 B4
Pathans Hotel	13 B3
Yatri Nivas	14 C1

EATING ⊞	
Ambady Restaurant	15 B2
India Gate	16 C2
Indian Coffee House	17 B3
Indian Coffee House	18 B3
Ming Palace	(see 13)
Navaratna Restaurant	19 B2
Pathans Hotel	(see 13)

TRANSPORT	
KSRTC Bus Stand	20 A4
Priyadarshini (North) Bus Stand	21 B1
Sakthan Thampuran Bus Stand	22 B4

underground shrine; **Puttanpalli (New) Church** with its towering, pure-white spires; and the **Chaldean (Nestorian) Church**, which is unique in its complete lack of pictorial representations of Jesus.

The **Archaeology Museum** (admission Rs6; ☼ 9am-1pm, 2pm-4.30pm Tue-Sun) is housed in the 200-year-old Sakthan Thampuran Palace. Wandering through its arrow-guided maze you get to see some neat artefacts, including 12th-century Keralan bronze sculptures, earthenware pots big enough to cook children in, and an extraordinary 1500kg wooden treasury box covered in locks and iron spikes.

Festivals & Events

In a state where festivals are a way of life, Thrissur still manages to stand out for temple revelry. Highlights include **Thrissur Pooram** (April/May), Kerala's biggest and most colourful temple festival with processions of elephants; **Uthralikavu Pooram** (March/April), whose climactic day sees 20 elephants circling the shrine; and **Thypooya Maholsavam** (January/February), with a spectacular *kavadiyattam* (a form of ritualistic dance) procession in which dancers carry tall, ornate structures called *kavadis*.

Sleeping

Pathans Hotel (☎ 2425620; www.pathansresidentialhotel.com; Round South; s/d from Rs275/395, with AC 585/788; 🖳) With no-frills rooms at no-frills prices, this is probably the best budget value in town. The basic and clean rooms are on the 5th and 6th floors here and have TV and occasional hot water.

Hotel Elite International (☎ 2421033; mail@hotel eliteinternational.com; Chembottil Lane; r incl breakfast from Rs420, with AC Rs800; 🖳 🖳) Not quite elite, but better than average and it has decent rooms with balconies – though some are noisy. The staff here seems to get ruder each time we visit.

Yatri Nivas (☎ 2332333; Stadium Rd; r Rs460, with AC Rs690; 🖳) This government-run hotel is opposite the town stadium on a refreshingly quiet street. Set around scruffy gardens, it has large, plain rooms and service as slow as molasses.

Hotel Luciya Palace (☎ 2424731; luciapalace@hotmail .com; s/d Rs666/777, with AC Rs888/999; 🖳) In a cream, colonial-themed building, this is one of the few places in town that has some character. Sitting in a quiet cul-de-sac, this grandiose-looking hotel has comfortable and spacious

rooms, though some of the non-AC rooms are nicer than the AC ones.

Grand Park Regency (☎ 2428247; www.grand parkregency.com; Kuruppam Rd; s/d from Rs700/850; 🖳) This businessy place offers very good bang-for-buck: all rooms come with AC, are filled with furniture and have separate sitting areas. Don't mind the peeling hallways, the rooms are in much better nick.

Joys Palace (☎ 2429999; www.joyshotels.com; TB Rd; s/d from Rs1500/1800; 🖳) This showy tower that looks like a like an ornate 10-storey meringue caters to Thrissur's jet set. Thankfully, the rooms are not too over the top, are quite comfy and have big windows to enjoy the upper floor's sweeping views. There's a 2nd-floor restaurant with an outdoor balcony (buffet breakfast/lunch/dinner Rs205/240/260) and cool glass-fronted elevator that feels like a fun-park ride.

Eating

Pathans Hotel (1st fl, Round South; dishes from Rs25) A little cafeteria-like, this atmospheric place is popular with families for lunch (thali Rs40) and has a sweets counter downstairs.

Ambady Restaurant (Round West; dishes Rs25-60) A little way off the street, this breezy semi-outdoor place is a huge hit with families tucking into several different varieties of set meals.

India Gate (Town Hall Rd; dishes Rs25-60) In the same building as the HDFC Bank, this is a bright, pure-veg place serving an unbeatable range of dosas (Rs45 to Rs60), including jam, cheese and cashew versions, and *uttappams* (thick savoury rice pancake – a Tamil Nadu version of a pizza; Rs25 to Rs40).

Navaratna Restaurant (Round West; dishes Rs45-90; ☼ lunch & dinner) Cool dark and intimate, this is the classiest joint to eat at in town. Expect lots of veg and nonveg dishes from North India served in arctic AC surrounds. Great lunchtime meals for Rs70.

Ming Palace (Round South; dishes Rs50-90; 🖳) This red-lantern lit and plush-looking upstairs restaurant makes a decent attempt at Chinese and Thai dishes – we like the tomyum sour soup (Rs48). Note that it can be sweltering when their AC is not working.

The Indian Coffee House has branches at Round South and Railway Station Rd.

Getting There & Away
BUS

KSRTC buses leave around every 30 minutes from the KSRTC bus stand bound for

Trivandrum (Rs183, 7½ hours), Ernakulam (Kochi, Rs51, two hours), Calicut (Rs80, 3½ hours), Palakkad (Rs41, 1½ hours) and Kottayam (Rs81, four hours). Hourly buses go to Coimbatore (Rs68, three hours). From here there are buses to Ponnani (Rs31, 1½ hours) and Prumpavoor (Rs37, two hours), where you can connect with buses bound for Munnar.

Regular services also chug along to Guruvayur (Rs22, one hour), Irinjalakuda (Rs15, one hour) and Cheruthuruthy (Rs18, 1½ hours). Two private bus stands (Sakthan Thampuran and Priyadarshini) have more frequent buses to these destinations, though the chaos involved in navigating each station hardly makes using them worthwhile.

TRAIN
Services run regularly to Ernakulam (2nd class/AC chair Rs29/131, 1½ hours) and Calicut (Rs39/157, three hours). There are also trains running to Palakkad (sleeper/3AC/2AC Rs101/188/258, 1½ hours) via Shoranur.

AROUND THRISSUR
The Hindu-only **Sri Krishna Temple** at Guruvayur, 33km northwest of Thrissur, is perhaps the most famous in Kerala. Said to have been created by Guru, preceptor of the gods, and Vayu, god of wind, the temple is believed to date from the 16th century and is renowned for its healing powers. An annual and spectacular **Elephant Race** is held here in February or March.

Kerala Kalamandalam (☎ 04884-262418; www .kalamandalam.org), 32km northeast of Thrissur at Cheruthuruthy, is a champion of Kerala's traditional-art renaissance. Using an ancient Gurukula system of learning, students undergo intensive study in Kathakali, *mohiniyattam* (classical dance), *kootiattam*, percussion, voice and violin. Structured **visits** (per person incl lunch US$25; ⏱ 9.30am-1pm) are available, including a tour around the theatre and classes. Individually tailored introductory courses are offered one subject at a time (between six and 12 months; around Rs1500 per month, plus Rs1500 for accommodation).

Natana Kairali Research & Performing Centre for Traditional Arts (☎ 0480-2825559; natanakairali@gmail .com), 20km south of Thrissur near Irinjalakuda, offers training in traditional arts, including rare forms of puppetry and dance. Short appreciation courses lasting up to a month are

sometimes available to keen foreigners (about Rs250 per class). In December each year, the centre holds five days of *mohiniyattam* (dance of the temptress) performances, a form of classical Keralan women's dance.

Regular bus services connect each of these destinations with Thrissur (see p377).

NORTHERN KERALA

KOZHIKODE (CALICUT)
☎ 0495 / pop 880,168

Always a prosperous trading town, Calicut was once the capital of the formidable Zamorin dynasty. Vasco da Gama first landed near here in 1498, on his way to snatch a share of the subcontinent for king and country (Portugal that is). These days, trade depends mostly on exporting Indian labour to the Middle East. There's not a lot for tourists to see, though it's a nice break in the journey and the jumping-off point for Wayanad Wildlife Sanctuary.

Information
There are HDFC and State Bank of India ATMs in town.

Cat's Net (Mavoor Rd; internet per hr Rs25; ⏱ 9am-9pm) Fast computers.

KTDC Tourist Information (☎ 2373862; GH Rd) Cursory tourist information.

LogOn (Ansari Park; internet per hr Rs25; ⏱ 9am-9pm)

Thomas Cook (☎ 2762681; Bank Rd; ⏱ 9.30am-5.30pm Mon-Sat)

UAE Exchange (☎ 2762772; Bank Rd; ⏱ 9.30am-6pm Mon-Sat, to 1.30pm Sun)

Sights
Mananchira Square was the former courtyard of the Zamorins and preserves the original spring-fed tank. The 650-year-old **Kuttichira Mosque** is in an attractive four-storey wooden building supported by wooden pillars and painted brilliant aqua, blue and white. Burnt down by the Portuguese in 1510, it was rescued and rebuilt to tell the tale. The **Church of South India** was established by Swiss missionaries in 1842 and has unique Euro-Keralan architecture.

Sleeping
Alakapuri (☎ 2723451-54; www.alakapurihotels.com; MM Ali Rd; s/d from Rs200/550, with AC Rs500/650; ⏏) Built motel-style around a green lawn (complete with fountain!) this place is off the road and

quieter than most. Rooms come in different sizes and prices and, while a little scuffed, are tidy and reasonable value.

Hotel Maharani (☎ 2723101; www.hotelmaharani .com; Taluk Rd; d from Rs550, with AC from Rs1200; ⚡) This massive, hospital-like block lies secluded at the eastern end of town, surrounded by palms and greenery. Rooms are big, though spartan and a bit worn. Some hush time is almost guaranteed.

Hyson Heritage (☎ 4081000; www.hysonheritage .com; Bank Rd; s/d from Rs750/850, with AC from Rs1000/1300; ⚡) At this business-focused place you get a fair bit of swank for your rupee. The standard rooms are tidy, spacious and comfortable, while the massive deluxe AC rooms come with bathtubs and average art.

Beach Hotel (☎ 2762055; www.beachheritage.com; Beach Rd; r Rs1750; ⚡) Built in 1890 to house the Malabar British Club, it's now a delightful 10-room hotel. Some rooms have bathtubs and secluded verandahs; others have original polished wooden flooring and private balconies. All are tastefully furnished and drip with character. Dinner is often served in the trim little garden. Easily the best place to stay in Calicut.

Eating

Hotel Sagar (Mavoor Rd; dishes Rs10-80; ⚡ 6am-2am) With a dark-wood interior and latticework on the front, this eatery is a tad more stylish than the competition. Veg and nonveg thali meals are served, with yummy biryanis (including fish, Rs60) and other dishes offered at lunchtime.

Coffee Beanz (RC Rd; snacks Rs25-80, meals Rs40-180; ⚡ noon-10pm) The local franchise of our favourite coffee-chain, this jazzy, modern AC joint offers the usual gamut of coffee options (Rs20 to Rs70), as well as great-value lunchtime-special meals (from Rs45 to Rs60). Snacks and full meals also available.

French Bakery (off Convent Rd; dishes Rs35-85) There ain't much French left about this place, but that doesn't bother the legions of fans that pack this upstairs hole-in-the-wall to sample their lunch meals and massive, delicious meat biryanis (Rs85).

Paragon Restaurant (Kannur Rd; dishes Rs40-195) Bypass the slightly dingy old section of this always-packed restaurant and head straight to the bright-yellow, modern and swish dining area with separate AC room. The menu is

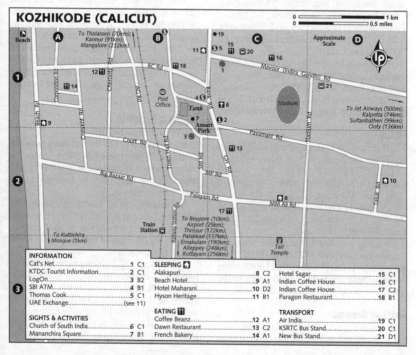

KOZHIKODE (CALICUT)

embarrassingly vast, with lots of fish, chicken and veg options. The food is scrumptious.

Dawn Restaurant (GH Rd; dishes Rs75-180, lunch buffet Rs200) The restaurant at the Hotel Malabar does multicuisine well, serving inventive Indian dishes and Keralan specials to a soundtrack of dull muzak.

For tasty, cheap snacks and great coffee, hit the Indian Coffee House on Mavoor Rd or GH Rd.

Getting There & Away

AIR

Air India (☎ 2771974; Eroth Centre, Bank Rd) flies daily to Mumbai (US$110), Chennai (US$85) and Kochin (US$85). **Jet Airways** (☎ 2740518; 29 Mavoor Rd) has one daily flight to Mumbai (US$95), while **Kingfisher** (☎ 18002333131; Airport) flies to Chennai (US$75), Mangalore (US$85) and Kochi (US$85).

BUS

The **KSRTC bus stand** (Mavoor Rd) has buses to Bengaluru (Bangalore, via Mysore, Rs210, AC Rs351, eight hours, 10 daily), Mangalore (Rs163, seven hours, three daily) and to Ooty (Rs86, 5½ hours, four daily). There are frequent buses to Thrissur (Rs80, 3½ hours), Trivandrum (via Alleppey and Ernakulam; Rs268, 10 hours, eight daily) and Kottayam (Rs162, seven hours, 13 daily). For Wayanad district, buses leave every 15 minutes heading to Sultanbatheri (Rs62, three hours) via Kalpetta (Rs48, two hours).

The New Bus Stand, further east along Mavoor Rd, has long-distance private buses.

TRAIN

The train station is 1km south of Mananchira Sq. There are trains to Mangalore (sleeper/3AC/2AC Rs108/305/423, five hours), Kannur (Rs32/130, two hours), Ernakulam (2nd class/AC chair Rs55/180, 4½ hours) via Thrissur (Rs39/157, three hours), and all the way to Trivandrum (sleeper/3AC/2AC Rs190/505/691, 11 hours).

Heading southeast, there are trains to Coimbatore (sleeper/3AC/2AC Rs101/271/388, 4½ hours), via Palakkad (Rs101/216/300, three hours). These trains then head north to the centres of Bengaluru, Chennai and Delhi.

Getting Around

Calicut has a glut of autorickshaws and, curiously, most are happy to use the meter. It costs about Rs10 from the station to the KSRTC bus stand or most hotels.

WAYANAD WILDLIFE SANCTUARY
☎ 04936 / pop 780,200

Ask any Keralan what the prettiest part of their state is and most will whisper: Wayanad. Encompassing part of a remote forest reserve that spills into Tamil Nadu, Wayanad's landscape is a green medley of rice paddies, untouched forests and the odd spice plantation. With only rudimentary tourist infrastructure, the region gets surprisingly few visitors, a shame since it's one of the few places you're almost guaranteed to spot wild elephants.

Orientation & Information

The sanctuary, covering an area of 345 sq km, consists of two separate pockets – **Muthanga** in the east and bordering Tamil Nadu, and **Tholpetty** in the north bordering Karnataka. Three major towns in Wayanad district make good bases for exploring the sanctuary – **Kalpetta** in the south, **Sultanbatheri** (also known as Sultan Battery) in the east and **Mananthavadi** in the northwest.

The somewhat disorganised **DTPC office** (☎ 04936-202134; www.dtpcwayanad.com; Kalpetta; 🕙 10am-5pm Mon-Sat) at Kalpetta can help organise tours, permits and trekking. There are UAE Exchange offices in Kalpetta and Sultanbatheri, and Federal Bank and Canara Bank ATMs can be found in each of the three main towns, as can a smattering of internet cafes.

Sights & Activities

VISITING THE SANCTUARY

Entry to both parts of the **sanctuary** (Indian/foreigner Rs10/100, camera/video Rs25/150; 🕙 7am-5pm) is only permitted as part of a guided trek or **jeep safari**, both of which can be arranged at the sanctuary entrances.

At **Tholpetty** (☎ 04935-250853; jeep tour incl guide Rs500), the 1½-hour jeep tours (7am to 9am and 3pm to 5pm) are a great way to spot wildlife. Rangers organise **guided treks** (up to 5 people Rs1600; 🕙 8am-2pm) from here.

At **Muthanga** (☎ 271010; jeep tour incl guide Rs350), two-hour jeep tours are available in the mornings and afternoons, and, at the time of research, all day guided walks (Rs500 to Rs800) were being planned for the near future.

The DTPC, as well as most hotels, arranges guided jeep tours (up to five people Rs1500 to Rs1800) of the Muthanga sanctuary and surrounding Wayanad sights.

AYURVEDA

For ayurvedic treatments, visit the **Kannur Ayurvedic Centre** (☎ 0436-203001; www.ayurvedawayanad.com; Kalpetta; r Rs500), a small, government-certified and family-run clinic in Kalpetta. Ayurvedic massage starts at Rs500, longer treatments like full 21-day panchakarma cleansing cost around Rs9100, plus Rs120 for food and Rs500 for accommodation per day. There are also daily yoga classes.

OTHER SIGHTS & ACTIVITIES

There are some top opportunities for independent **trekking** around the district, including a climb to the top of Chembra Peak, at 2100m the tallest summit; Vellarimala, with great views and lots of wildlife-spotting opportunities; and Pakshipathalam, a formation of large boulders deep in the forest. Permits are necessary and can be arranged at forest offices in South or North Wayanad. The DTPC office in Kalpetta organises trekking guides (Rs600 per day), camping equipment (around Rs250 per person) and transport – pretty much anything you might need to get you hiking. It also runs four-hour bamboo **rafting trips** (Rs1000) from June to September.

Thought to be one of the oldest on the subcontinent, **Thirunelly Temple** (dawn-dusk) is 10km from Tholpetty. While non-Hindus cannot enter, the ancient and intricate pillars and stone carvings, set against a soaring backdrop of mist-covered peaks, is an astounding sight no matter what your creed.

The 13th-century **Jain temple** (8am-noon & 2-6pm), near Sultanbatheri, has splendid stone carvings and is an important monument to the region's strong historical Jain presence. Close by, near Ambalavayal, are the **Edakal Caves** (admission Rs10; 9am-5pm), with petroglyphs thought to date back over 3000 years and jaw-dropping views of Wayanad district. In the same area, **Wayanad Heritage Museum** (Ambalavayal; admission Rs10; 9am-5pm) exhibits headgear, weapons, pottery, carved stone and other artefacts dating back to the 15th century that shed light on Wayanad's significant Adivasi population.

The picture-perfect **Pookot Lake** (admission Rs10; 9am-6pm) is 3km before Vythiri. Geared up for visitors, it has well-maintained gardens, a cafeteria, playground and paddle/row boats for hire (Rs30/50 per 20 minutes). It gets packed on the weekends, though feels quite peaceful during the week.

Sleeping & Eating

There are forest serambys (wooden huts; double without bathroom Rs1000) near the entrances of both Tholpetty and Muthanga, though you'll have to bring your own food. Contact either sanctuary office for bookings, or the **wildlife warden** (☎ 04936-220454; 10am-5pm Mon-Sat) at Sultanbatheri.

PPS Tourist Home (☎ 04936-203431; www.ppstouristhome.com; Kalpetta; s/d Rs250/340, deluxe r Rs500-600;) This agreeable and friendly place in the middle of Kalpetta has budget rooms in a motel-like compound that are clean, fair sized and comfy. Management can arrange trips around Wayanad (Rs1700 per carload) and hikes up Chembra Peak (Rs600 plus permit fees, six hours).

Hotel Regency (☎ 04936-220512; www.issacsregency.com; Sultanbatheri; s/d from Rs495/750, with AC from Rs1100/1200;) The pick of Sultanbatheri's bunch of hotels, this quiet and no-nonsense place has routine, large and relatively tidy rooms in a U-shaped building. The deluxe rooms differ from the standard ones in price only.

Kannur Ayurvedic Centre (☎ 0436-203001; www.ayurvedawayanad.com; Kalpetta; r Rs500) This small, family-run ayurvedic clinic also offers great-value accommodation in a large, airy house surrounded by their small ayurvedic herb garden. Rooms are big, have balconies and some boast lovely Wayanad views. As a bonus, it's a little off the main drag in Kalpetta and feels more villagey than other places. It's behind Haritagiri resort.

Woodlands Hotel (☎ 04936-202547; www.thewoodlandshotel.com; Kalpetta; r Rs950, with AC Rs1400-2250;) Smack-bang in the middle of Kalpetta's main drag, this business-focused hotel is convenient for a night's kip if you arrive late into town. It has comfortable though unexciting digs, filled with big walk-in closets and cheesy art.

Pachyderm Palace (☎ reservations 0484-2371761; touristdesk@satyam.net.in; Tholpetty; r per person incl meals Rs1250-1500) This rambling house lies just outside the gate of Tholpetty Wildlife Sanctuary – very handy for early morning treks, tours and ad hoc wildlife viewing. The varied rooms are very simple and tidy, with one great stilt-bungalow on offer that's surrounded by forest. The Keralan food served here is excellent, and

PANCHAKARMA – DETOX THE HARD WAY

Ayurveda, Kerala's ancient approach to health and wellbeing, proposes two fundamental methods of healing: *shaman chikitsa* and panchakarma *chikitsa*. While *shaman chikitsa* uses external herbal-medicinal preparations to heal the body of minor ills, the more intense system of panchakarma *chikitsa* (bodily purification) is used to treat more serious ailments.

In what is essentially an intense detox regime, panchakarma uses a combination of five types of different therapies (*panchakarma* means 'five actions') to rid the body of built-up endotoxins. These include: *vaman* – therapeutic vomiting; *virechan* – purgation; *vasti* – enemas; *nasya* – elimination of toxins through the nose; and *raktamoksha* – detoxification of the blood. Before panchakarma begins, the body is first prepared over several days with a special diet, oil massages *(snehana)* and herbal steam-baths *(swedana)*. Only then can real treatment begin. Depending on the patient's ailments, vomiting may be induced using herbal concoctions, diarrhoea provoked using natural laxatives, the nasal passages may be flushed with oils, herbs may be inserted into the rectum as enemas, and the blood may be flushed through bloodletting (cutting) and the use of leeches. Treatment lasts for a minimum of 15 days, with 21 days the norm.

Although it may sound pretty grim, panchakarma purification might only use a few of these treatments at a time, with therapies like bloodletting and leeches only used in rare cases. Still, this is no spa holiday. Many tourist-geared ayurvedic clinics offer basic oil massage and the like, but for genuine panchakarma you will need to visit an ayurvedic doctor who can prescribe a cleansing treatment individually tailored to your needs. Conveniently located clinics that offer three-week purification regimes include Dr Franklin's Panchakarma Institute in Kovalam (p335), Eden Garden in Varkala (p337), Janakanthi Panchakarma Centre in Kollam (p340), Ayurveda: Sree Krishna in Alleppey (p344) and Kannur Ayurvedic Centre in Wayanad (p381). Expect to pay from around Rs800 to Rs2000 per day for treatment, with accommodation charges extra.

free morning/night animal-spotting safaris are included in the price.

Ente Veedu Homestay (☎ 0435-220008; www.ente veedu.co.in; Panamaram; r incl breakfast Rs2000-2500; 🖳) In a stunning location overlooking sprawling banana plantations and rice paddies, this isolated homestay halfway between Kalpetta and Manthavady is definitely worth seeking out. Surrounded by bucolic villages, it has several large rooms that come thoughtfully and colourfully furnished. Two rooms are bamboo lined and offer private balconies. There are hammocks and wicker lounges here to enjoy the sensational views. Call to arrange a pick-up.

our pick **Stream Valley Cottages** (☎ 04936-255860; www.streamvalleycottages.com; Vythiri; d Rs3000) These wonderful modern cottages lie on the banks of a small stream, several hundred metres off the main road (2.5km before Vythiri). Each cottage has loads of space, separate sitting areas, large private verandahs, stylish dark-wood interiors and comes with a hushed sound-track of singing birds and bubbling brooks. Traditional Keralan meals are available (Rs300 per day).

Vythiri Resort (☎ 0436-255366/7; www.vythiriresort .com; Vythiri; s/d from Rs5900/6500; 🖳) This massive, sprawling eco-resort lies hidden in the forest on the edge of sprawling tea plantations. The styling of the resort is refreshingly unobtrusive, with rooms hidden among trees or spread out among the lush grounds. Inside, each pretty abode is large, filled with raw-wood furniture, and often has a private balcony looking into the wild. Popular with Indian groups, there are loads of activities and facilities on offer here to keep you entertained.

Tranquil (☎ 04936-220244; www.tranquilresort .com; Kuppamudi Estate, Kolagapara; s/d Rs10,100/12,750, deluxe s/d Rs14,350/18,000; 🖳) This truly charming and luxurious homestay is in the middle of 160 hectares of pepper, coffee, vanilla and cardamom plantations. The elegant house has sweeping verandahs filled with plants and handsome furniture. The owners are excellent hosts and arrange tours of the area (included). Prices include meals and tax.

Getting There & Around

Buses brave the winding roads between Calicut and Sultanbatheri (Rs62), via Kalpetta (Rs48), every 30 minutes. Private buses also run between Kannur and Mananthavadi every 45 minutes (Rs53, 2½ hours). From Sultanbatheri, one 8am bus heads out for

Ooty (Rs84, four hours), with a second one passing through town at around 1pm. Buses for Mysore (Rs75, three hours) leave every 30 minutes or so.

Plenty of private buses connect Mananthavadi, Kalpetta and Sultanbatheri every 10 to 20 minutes during daylight hours (Rs14 to Rs26, 45 minutes to 1¼ hours). From Mananthavadi, regular buses also head to Tholpetty (Rs12.50, 45 minutes). You can hire jeeps to get from one town to the next for around Rs400 to Rs600 each way.

There are plenty of autorickshaws for short trips within the towns, and the DTPC can help arrange car hire (from around Rs1500 per day).

KANNUR (CANNANORE)

☎ 0497 / pop 498,200

Under the Kolathiri rajas, Kannur was a major port bristling with international trade – explorer Marco Polo christened it a 'great emporium of spice trade'. Since then, the usual colonial suspects, including the Portuguese, Dutch and British, have had a go at exerting their influence on the region. Today it is an unexciting though agreeable town known mostly for its weaving industry and cashew trade, with an excellent beach at Costa Malabari and incredible *theyyam* possession performances (see p372).

Information

The **DTPC Office** (☎ 2706336; ۷ 10am-5pm Mon-Sat), opposite the KSRTC bus stand, supplies basic maps of Kannur. There are Federal Bank and State Bank of India ATMs adjacent to the bus stand. A **UAE Exchange** (☎ 2709022; City Centre, Fort Rd; ۷ 9.30am-6pm Mon-Sat, to 1.30pm Sun) office changes travellers cheques and cash; it's located in City Centre mall, five minutes from the train station.

Sights

Kannur is the best place to see the spirit-possession ritual called **theyyam** (see the boxed text, p372); on most nights of the year there should be a *theyyam* ritual on somewhere in the vicinity. The easiest way to find out about *theyyam* is to contact Kurien at Costa Malabari (see right). Alternatively, you can visit the **Kerala Folklore Academy** (☎ 2778090), near Chirakkal Pond Valapattanam, 20km north of Kannur, where you can see costumes up close and sometimes catch a performance.

The Portuguese built **St Angelo Fort** (admission free; ۷ 9am-6pm) in 1505 from brilliantly red laterite stone on a promontory a few kilometres south of town. It has a serene garden and excellent views of nearby palm-fringed beaches.

Established in 1955, the **Loknath Weavers' Co-operative** (☎ 2726330; ۷ 8.30am-5.30pm Mon-Sat) is one of the oldest in Kannur and occupies a large building busily clicking with the sound of looms. You can stop by for a quick tour and visit the small shop here that displays the fruits of their labours. It's 4km south of Kannur.

This region is also known for the manufacture of *beedis*, those tiny Indian cigarettes deftly rolled inside green leaves. One of the largest, and purportedly best, manufacturers is the **Kerala Dinesh Beedi Co-Operative** (☎ 2835280; ۷ 8am-5pm Tue-Sat), with a factory at Thottada, 7km south of Kannur. Either of these cooperatives is a Rs80 to Rs100 (return) autorickshaw ride from Kannur town.

Kairali (☎ 0460-2243460), located 20km north of Kannur, offers rice-barge trips on the unspoilt northern Kerala backwaters. Day cruises (10am to 4pm) for up to 10 people cost Rs3500, or you can rent a barge by the hour (Rs1500 per hour).

Sleeping & Eating

Government Guest House (☎ 2706426; d Rs220, with AC Rs575; 🍴) As usual, a government guest house comes through with the goods. This place has several buildings near the water, but rooms in the 'new block', which are enormous, simply and tastefully furnished and sport balconies looking right onto the sea, are phenomenal value.

Hotel Meridian Palace (☎ 2761676; Bellard Rd; s Rs225-500, d Rs275-550, d with AC Rs700-1000; 🍴) Located in the market area opposite the main train station. There's a bewildering array of budget rooms on offer here. If you manage to decide on one, chances are it will be clean, basic and convenient for an early train departure.

Mascot Beach Resort (☎ 2708445; www.mascotresort.com; s/d Rs700/900, with AC from Rs1000/1200; 🍴 🍹) A few hundred metres south of the Government Guest House, this place also has grand views of the ocean from its neat and comfy AC rooms, though the budget options are a bit dowdy and filled with '80s bling.

KK Heritage (☎ 9447067408; Thottada Beach; s/d incl meals from Rs800/1300) This little guest house is much more basic than the competition on this secluded beach (Costa Malabari and Kannur Beach House) and has just a few tiny rooms, either in a red-brick cottage or above a family home.

Kannur Beach House (☎ 0497-2708360, 9847184535; www.kannurbeachhouse.com; Thottada Beach; r per person incl meals Rs1100) Near Costa Malabari and in an idyllic spot right behind the beach, the large rooms in this traditional Keralan building are presentably furnished and boast handsome large wooden shutters – though unfortunately no mosquito screens or nets. Each room comes with either a balcony or porch to enjoy the sensational ocean sunset views through swaying palms. It's 8km from Kannur.

ourpick Costa Malabari (☎ reservations 0484-2371761; touristdesk@satyam.net.in; Thottada Beach; r per person incl meals Rs1250) In a small village and five minutes' walk from an idyllic beach, Costa Malabari pioneered tourism in this area with its spacious rooms in an old hand-loom factory. There's a huge communal space, comfy lounging areas outside, and extra rooms now offered in two other nearby houses – one perched dramatically on a sea cliff. The home-cooked Keralan food is plentiful and, frankly, might just be some of the best in the country. Kurien, your gracious host, is an expert on the astonishing *theyyam* ritual (see boxed text, p372) and can help arrange a visit. It's 8km from Kannur town; a rickshaw/taxi from the train station is around Rs100/200.

Getting There & Away

There are frequent daily buses to Mysore (Rs186, eight hours) and a few to Mangalore (Rs107, four hours). Most departures for Calicut (Rs51, 2½ hours) and Ernakulam (Rs186, eight hours) leave in the afternoon and evening. There's one daily bus to Ooty (via Wayanad, Rs113, nine hours) at 10pm. Frequent private buses to Mananthavadi (for Wayanad, Rs53, 2½ hours) leave from the private bus stand between the KSRTC stand and the train station.

There are several daily trains to Mangalore (sleeper/3AC/2AC Rs101/220/306, three hours), Calicut (2nd class/AC chair Rs32/130, two hours) and Ernakulam (Rs70/276, 6½ hours).

BEKAL & AROUND

☎ 0467

Bekal and nearby Palakunnu and Udma, in Kerala's far north, host a handful of white-sand beaches begging for DIY exploration. As yet there are few decent places to stay and getting around can be a real pain, though off-the-beaten-track adventurers may revel in discovering the place before it's turned into the next Kovalam. Because it's a predominantly Muslim area, it's important to keep local sensibilities in mind, especially at the beach.

The laterite-brick **Bekal Fort** (Indian/foreigner Rs5/100; ☯ 8am-5pm), built between 1645 and 1660, sits on Bekal's rocky headland and houses a small Hindu temple and plenty of goats. Next door, **Bekal beach** (admission Rs5) encompasses a grassy park and a long, beautiful stretch of sand that turns into a circus on weekends and holidays when local families descend here for rambunctious leisure time. Isolated **Kappil Beach**, 6km north of Bekal, has fine sand and calm water, but beware of shifting sandbars.

Located 22km south of Bekal, **Bekal Boat Stay** (☎ 0467-2282633; www.bekalboatstay.com; Kottappuram, Nileshwar) is one of the first enterprises in the region to offer overnight houseboat trips around the Valiyaparamba backwaters (Rs7000/9500 per 24 hours for two/four people). It has just four boats – all considerably more rustic than those on offer in Alleppey.

Sleeping & Eating

Sleeping options are pretty dire in the area, with lots of cheap, poor quality hotels scattered between Kanhangad (12km south) and Kasaragod (10km north).

K-Tees Residency (☎ 2275633; www.kteesresidency .com; Bekal; s/d from Rs200/350, with AC Rs500/900; ☒) The only place near Bekal passing muster in the hygiene department, it's squished between the railway and the road and has big, clean rooms.

Hotel Bekal International (☎ 0467-2204271; www .hotelbekal.com; Kanhangad; s/d from Rs200/350, d with AC from Rs700; ☒) A relatively comfortable, if unexciting, midrange option 10km south of Bekal Fort. This huge complex has a green fetish, in everything from walls to '70s chairs, and a big choice of spacious, immaculate (green) rooms.

Gitanjali Heritage (☎ 9447469747; www.gitanjali heritage.com; s/d with meals Rs2500/3500) Five kilometres from Bekal, this lovely homestay lies surrounded by rice paddies, deep among Kasaragod's inland villages. It's an intimate heritage home with comfortable, higgledy-piggledy rooms filled with ancestral furniture and polished wood. Call ahead for pick-ups.

Bekal Beach Camp (☎ 0946267792; www.bekalbeach camp.com; Pallikara; r incl meals & taxes Rs3500) This is the hands-down winner for Bekal's 'most atmospheric place to stay' award. It's camping in style here, with luxury canvas cabins scattered around the secluded end of Bekal beach among a small grove of palms. Each cabin has lots of space and is fitted out with comfy beds, lamps and fun en-suite toilets. Constant sea breezes and perfect sunset vistas come standard, as do hammocks on its private beach.

Getting There & Around
A couple of local trains stop at Fort Bekal station, right on Bekal beach. Kanhangad, 12km south, is a major train stop, while Kasaragod, 10km to the north, is the largest town in the area. Both Kanhangad and Kasaragod have frequent buses running to and from Bekal (around Rs10, 20 minutes). An autorickshaw from Bekal Junction to Kappil beach is around Rs30.

LAKSHADWEEP

pop 60,700

Comprising a string of 36 palm-covered coral islands 300km off the coast of Kerala, Lakshadweep is as stunning as it is isolated. Only 10 of these islands are inhabited, mostly with Sunni Muslim fishermen, and foreigners are only allowed to stay on a few of these. With fishing and coir production the main sources of income, local life on the islands remains highly traditional, and a caste system divides the islanders between Koya (land owners), Malmi (sailors) and Melachery (farmers).

The real attraction of the islands lies under the water: the 4200 sq km of pristine archipelago lagoons, unspoiled coral reefs and warm waters are a magnet for flipper-toting travellers and divers alike. Lakshadweep can only be visited on a pre-organised package trip – all listed accommodation prices are for the peak October to May season and include permits and meals. Diving, snorkelling, kayaking, boat trips, sailing and jaunts to nearby islands can be arranged by most resorts.

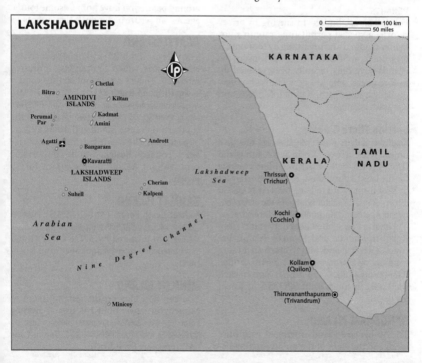

DIVING

Lakshadweep is a diver's dream, with excellent visibility and an embarrassment of marine life living on undisturbed coral reefs. The best time to dive is between mid-October and mid-May when the seas are calm and visibility is 20m to 40m. During the rough monsoon many dive outfits close up shop.

Lacadives (☎ 022-66627381-82; www.lacadives.com; E-20 Everest Bldg, Taredo Rd, Mumbai) runs dive centres on Bangaram and Kadmat Islands. Costs can vary: a CMAS one-star course costs US$500, while experienced divers pay from US$50 per dive (including equipment hire), with discounts available for multiple dives. Information is available through the hotels or directly through Lacadives in Mumbai. The diving school on Agatti Island is run by **Goa Diving** (☎ 0832-2555117; www.goadiving.com).

From Kadmat Island, dives range from 9m to 40m in depth. Some of the better sites include North Cave, the Wall, Jack Point, Shark Alley, the Potato Patch, Cross Currents and Sting Ray City. Around Bangaram good spots include the 32m-deep wreck of the *Princess Royale*, Manta Point, Life, Grand Canyon and the impressive sunken reef at Perumal Par.

For a guide to environmentally friendly diving, see the boxed text, p102.

Information

SPORTS (Society for the Promotion of Recreational Tourism & Sports; Map p361; ☎ 0484-2668387; www.lakshadweeptourism.com; IG Rd, Willingdon Island; ⏰ 10am-5pm Mon-Sat) is the main tourism organisation.

PERMITS

Foreigners are limited to staying in pricey resorts; a special permit (one month's notice) is required and organised by tour operators, hotels or SPORTS in Kochi. Most of the islands have only recently been opened up to foreigners, who are now allowed to stay on Bangaram, Agatti, Kadmat, Minicoy and Kavaratti islands.

Getting There & Away

Kingfisher Airlines (www.flykingfisher.com) flies five times a week between Kochi and Agatti Island (US$145 each way) – check the airline's website for the latest information. A 1½-hour transfer by boat from Agatti to Bangaram costs US$50 return. A fast 25-seater boat plies the waters between Agatti and Kadmat for Rs750 each way.

There are scheduled boat departures from Kochi to Kadmat and Minicoy islands between October and May (return including food in AC seat/4-berth/2-berth cabins, Rs3500/6000/8000, 18 to 20 hours each way). Get in touch with SPORTS in Kochi for details.

BANGARAM ISLAND

The 50-hectare island is fringed with pure sand, and the sight of the moon slipping beneath the lagoon horizon is very nearly worth the expense.

Bangaram Island Resort (☎ 0484-2668221; www.cghearth.com; r full board Oct-Apr €300, 4-person deluxe cottages €550) is run by the CGH Earth group and administered from its hotel in Kochi. Shop around before you leave home – some tourist agents can secure better deals than others.

AGATTI ISLAND

The village on this 2.7-sq-km island has several mosques, which you can visit if dressed modestly. There's no alcohol on the island.

Agatti Island Beach Resort (☎ 0484-2362232; www.agattiislandresorts.com; s/d full board €100/140, with AC €140/190; ❄) sits on two beaches at the southern tip of the island and offers a range of packages. The resort has simple, low-rise beach cottages, designed to be comfortably cool without AC, and a restaurant for 20 people.

KADMAT ISLAND

Kadmat Beach Resort (☎ 0484-2668387; laksports_2004@vsnl.net; s/d Rs2500/4000, with AC Rs3000/5000; ❄) is administered by SPORTS (left) and can be reached by overnight boat from Kochi (left).

MINICOY ISLAND

You can now stay on the remote island of Minicoy in newly built cottages at **Swaying Palm** (☎ 0484-2668387; laksports_2004@vsnl.net; s/d Rs2500/4000, with AC Rs3000/5000; ❄). See left for boat transport from Kochi.

Tamil Nadu

Many foreign travellers come to India seeking something 'old', a sense of living connection to traditions older than the culture they've left.

For many Indians, that same sense of age is achieved in Tamil Nadu, homeland of one of humanity's living classical civilisations, a people whose culture has grown, but in many ways not fundamentally altered, since the Greeks sacrificed goats to Zeus.

Here you can listen to one of the oldest dialogues in the human conversation: that of South India and its Dravidian inhabitants, whose cultural heart beats here at the tip of the subcontinental triangle. Haggle with a local merchant and they're using the same slang Roman sailors heard on the streets of Mamallapuram almost 2000 years ago.

But this state is as dynamic as it is drenched in history. In Tamil Nadu's famous temples, fire-worshipping devotees smear tikka on their brows before heading to IT offices to develop new software applications. Deep green rice paddies, sandstone rock carvings, ubiquitous white sarongs and next-generation Windows; here, India has one foot in the 21st century and the other in the poetry of one of the oldest literary languages on Earth.

When you visit, try to reach the ends of India, where three oceans mingle and avatars of God worship God on the beach. See the tiger-prowled hills of the Nilgiris, the Mother Temple of the triple-breasted, fish-eyed goddess and the Mountain of Fire, where the Destroyer and Dancer of the Universe manifests himself as a pillar of flame. It's all packed into a state that manages to remain fiercely distinct from India, while exemplifying its oldest and most adventurous edges.

HIGHLIGHTS

- Explore the past in one of India's most ancient states and temples of **Thanjavur** (Tanjore; p434)

- Breathe in the cool air, the colonialism, the quirkiness of **Ooty** (Udhagamandalam; p464)

- Enjoy steak. Or yoga. Or steak *and* yoga in the former French colony of **Puducherry** (Pondicherry; p420)

- Join the pilgrims and devotees filing into Madurai's **Sri Meenakshi Temple** (p446), a riot of Dravidian sculpture.

- Pick through the ruins of **Mamallapuram** (Mahabalipuram; p407) by sunset, then gorge on fresh seafood

History

It's ironic that the bearers of the torch of South Indian identity may have their origins in Punjab and Pakistan. The early Indus civilisations display elements of Dravidian thought, language, culture and art, including a meditating god seated in the lotus position. This may be the world's first depiction of the yogi archetype, who has come to symbolise, for many, Asian spirituality.

The nomadic Aryans drove the Dravidians south around 1500 BC. Here, a classical language and classical civilisations developed, cushioned by geography against North Indian invasion. By 300 BC the region was controlled by three major dynasties – Cholas in the

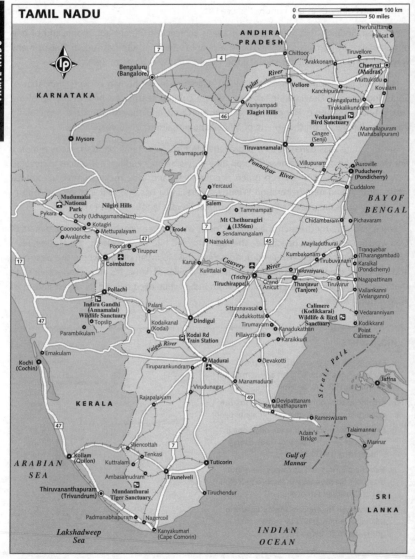

east, Pandyas in the central area and Cheras in the west. This was the classical period of Tamil literature and myth – the Sangam Age – when kingdoms were ruled by feuding poet-kings and romantic epics; a visitor at the time described the Tamils as favouring rose petals over gold.

The Tamils developed their own aesthetic style, constructing huge cities that rivalled population centres in China and Europe and magnificent stepped temples that wouldn't look out of place in Mayan Central America. Although each kingdom left notable achievements, the Cholas deserve some special mention. This remarkable nation maintained one of the great maritime empires of history, extending its influence to Cambodia, Vietnam and Indonesia and spreading Tamil ideas of reincarnation, karma and yogic practice to Southeast Asia. The end result of this cross-

pollination was architectural wonders like Angkor Wat, the intellectual gestation of Balinese Hinduism and much of the philosophy associated with classical Buddhism.

Before the Mughals could fully extend their reach to India's tip, in 1640 the British negotiated the use of Madraspatnam (now Chennai) as a trading post. Subsequent interest by the French, Dutch and Danes led to continual conflict and, finally, almost total domination by the British, when the region became known as

FAST FACTS

Population 62.1 million
Area 130,058 sq km
Capital Chennai (Madras)
Main language Tamil
When to go November to March

TAMIL NADU

FESTIVALS IN TAMIL NADU

Many of Tamil Nadu's most colourful festivals revolve around temples – there's something going on somewhere in the state all year round.

International Yoga Festival (4-7 Jan; Puducherry, p420) Puducherry's ashrams and yoga culture are put on show with workshops, classes and music and dance events. Held throughout the city, the event attracts yoga masters from all over India.

Pongal (mid-Jan; statewide) As the rice boils over the new clay pots, this festival symbolises the prosperity and abundance a fruitful harvest brings. For many, the celebrations begin with temple rituals, followed by family gatherings. Later it's the animals, especially cows, which are honoured for their contribution to the harvest.

International Music festival (Jan; Thiruvaiyaru, p437) Held near Thanjavur, this music festival is held in honour of the saint and composer Thyagaraja.

Teppam (Float) Festival (Jan/Feb; Madurai, p449) A popular event held on the full moon of the Tamil month of Thai, when statues of deities are floated on the huge Mariamman Teppakkulam Tank.

Natyanjali Dance Festival (Feb/Mar; Chidambaram, p428) This five-day festival attracts performers from all over the country to the Nataraja Temple to celebrate Nataraja (Shiva) – Lord of the Dance.

Chithrai Festival (Apr/May; Madurai, p445) The main event on Madurai's busy festival calendar is this 14-day event that celebrates the marriage of Meenakshi to Sundareswarar (Shiva). The deities are wheeled around the Sri Meenakshi Temple in massive chariots that form part of long, colourful processions.

Summer festivals (May/Jun; Ooty, p464 & Kodaikanal, p456) Tamil Nadu's hill stations both hold similar festivals which feature boat races on the lake, horse racing (in Ooty), flower shows and music.

Bastille Day (14 Jul; Puducherry, p420) Street parades and a bit of French pomp and ceremony are all part of the fun at this celebration.

Karthikai Deepam Festival (Nov/Dec; statewide) Held during full moon, Tamil Nadu's 'festival of lights' is celebrated throughout the state with earthenware lamps and firecrackers, but the best place to see it is Tiruvannamalai (see boxed text, p419), where the legend began.

Festival of Carnatic Music & Dance (mid-Dec–mid-Jan; Chennai, p402) One of the largest of its type in the world, this festival is a celebration of Tamil music and dance.

Mamallapuram Dance Festival (Dec & Jan; Mamallapuram, p407) A four-week dance festival showcasing dances from all over India, with many performances on an open-air stage against the imposing backdrop of Arjuna's Penance. Dances include the Bharata Natyam (Tamil Nadu), Kuchipudi (Andhra Pradesh) tribal dance, and Kathakali (Kerala drama); there are also puppet shows and classical music performances. Performances are held only from Friday to Sunday.

the Madras Presidency. Small pocketed areas, including Puducherry (Pondicherry) and Karaikal, remained under French control.

Many Tamils played a significant part in India's struggle for independence, which was finally won in 1947. In 1956 the Madras Presidency was disbanded and Tamil Nadu was established as an autonomous state.

Information

The state tourism body is **Tamil Nadu Tourism** (www.tamilnadutourism.org), which runs tourist offices of varying uselessness in most cities and large towns plus a reliably average chain of hotels. You can also check www.tamilnadu -tourism.com for package-tour options.

ACCOMMODATION

Accommodation costing more than Rs200 in Tamil Nadu (but not Puducherry) is subject to a government 'luxury' tax – 5% on rooms between Rs200 and Rs500, 10% on rooms between Rs501 and Rs1000, and 12.5% on rooms over Rs1000. There's often an additional 'serv-

ice tax' at upmarket hotels. Prices throughout this chapter do not include tax, unless stated otherwise. The best lodging in the state is in Mamallapuram, which boasts some excellent quirky backpacker lodges; Puducherry, with its old colonial villages (and some newer, more stylish digs); and the Victorian guest houses of Ooty and Kodaikanal.

PERMITS

As well as for the areas listed following, permits are required for trekking in some areas of the Nilgiri Hills around Mudumalai National Park (see p470). Reputable guides should have the required permits for tourist trekking; researchers and academics need to apply separately.

Conservator of Forests (Map pp394-5; ☎ 24321139; 8th fl, Panangal Bldg, 1 Jeenis Salai, Saidapet, Chennai) The Conservator of Forests issues permits for all areas other than the Vedantangal Bird Sanctuary, but will only do so for researchers.

Wildlife Warden's Office (WWO; Map pp394-5; ☎ 24321471; 4th fl, DMS Office, 259 Anna Salai, Teynam-

---

DEFINING DRAVIDIANS

The Tamils consider themselves the standard bearers of Dravidian – pre-Aryan Indian – civilisation. Their culture, language and history are distinctive from North India (although more related than some Tamil nationalists claim), and their ability to trace Tamil identity to classical antiquity is a source of considerable pride.

During the Indus Valley period (2600–1900 BC), the nomadic Aryans drove the city-dwelling Dravidians south while incorporating elements of the latter's beliefs into their holy texts, the Vedas. Take vegetarianism; before contact, the Aryans were known to have a penchant for meat (especially beef). The marriage of Aryan rituals and Dravidian concepts like renunciation, karma and reincarnation laid the groundwork for the development of early Hinduism.

But the Aryan insistence on segregating their dark-skinned Dravidian subjects may have been the foundation of caste as well. Early edicts make it clear: the paler the complexion, the higher the caste. South–North and class tensions were encouraged by the British, who used these strains to facilitate divide-and-conquer policies.

Ever since Indian Independence in 1947, Tamil politicians have railed against caste (which they see as favouring light-skinned Brahmins) and Hindi (as unrelated to Tamil as Russian). The post-Independence 'Self Respect' movement, influenced by Marxism, mixed South Indian communal values with class-warfare rhetoric and spawned Dravidian political parties that remain major regional powers today. Anti-Hindi riots have defaced thousands of Hindi street signs here, and for a period in the late 1950s activists called for Dravida Nadu (Home of the Dravidians), an independent South Indian nation.

Although calls for separatism are past, Tamil nationalism is still in vogue. Many Tamil politicians loudly defend the Tamil Tigers, the same organisation that assassinated Rajiv Gandhi in 1991 (imagine a viable, sitting opposition party in your country openly supporting a group that killed your president or prime minister to get an idea of how separate some Tamil parties still consider themselves from India), and there is an unfortunate prejudice among the generally tolerant Tamils towards anything Sinhalese. Throughout the state, male politicians don a white shirt and white *mundu* (sarong), the official uniform of Tamil pride.

TOP FIVE TEMPLES

Tamil Nadu is nirvana for anyone wanting to explore South Indian temple culture and architecture. Many of the temples are important places of pilgrimage for Hindus, where daily *puja* (offering or prayer) rituals and colourful festivals will leave a deep impression on even the most temple-weary traveller. Other temples stand out for their stunning architecture, soaring *gopurams* (gateway towers) and intricately carved, pillared *mandapas* (pavilions in front of the temple). Almost all have free admission. There are so many that it pays to be selective, but the choice is subjective. Here's our top five:

- Sri Meenakshi Temple, Madurai (p446)
- Arunachaleswar Temple, Tiruvannamalai (p418)
- Brihadishwara Temple, Thanjavur (Tanjore; p434)
- Sri Ranganathaswamy Temple, Trichy (Tiruchirappalli; p438)
- Nataraja Temple, Chidambaram (p429)

---

pet, Chennai) Issues permits in advance for accommodation at Vedantangal Bird Sanctuary.

Dangers & Annoyances

The big draw in Tamil Nadu is the some 5000 temples, but this is a very religious state, and non-Hindus are generally not allowed inside inner sanctums. This can be frustrating, as large areas of the best temples are essentially inaccessible to many travellers. Even non-resident Indians can be subject to scrutiny, and non-Indian Hindus may have to provide proof of conversion. Temple touts are fairly common and can be a nuisance, but don't dismiss every one as a scammer. There are many excellent guides here and they deserve both your time and rupees; use your best judgement, ask other travellers which guides they'd recommend and be on the lookout for badge-wearing official guides, who tend to be excellent resources.

Don't expect the Hindi slang you picked up in Rishikesh to go over well here. The Tamils are fiercely proud of their language and some consider Hindi to be North Indian cultural imperialism (see boxed text, opposite). North Indian tourists are often as confused as you are down here; more Tamils speak English than Hindi.

CHENNAI (MADRAS)

☎ 044 / pop 6.6 million

No matter how determined you are, you'd be pretty hard pressed to find much to gush about when it comes to Chennai. The streets are clogged with traffic, the weather oppres-sively hot, the air heavy with smog, and sights of any interest are uncooperatively thin on the ground. Even the movie stars, as one Chennaiker put it, are 'not that hot'.

While it may not boast the money of Mumbai (Bombay) or the buzz of Bengaluru (Bangalore), Chennai does feel friendlier than most cities its size. Chennai is so modest you wouldn't even know it's an economic power-house, much less a queen of showbiz: India's fourth-largest city is most humble.

The major transport hub of the region, this 70-sq-km city is a conglomerate of urban vil-lages connected by a maze of roads ruled by hard-line rickshaw drivers. Its central location and excellent plane, train and bus connec-tions actually make it an interesting alterna-tive entry point into India. If you do happen to be caught here between connections, it's certainly worth your while poking around the markets of George Town or taking a sunset stroll along pretty Marina Beach.

HISTORY

Chennai and surrounds have been attracting seafaring traders for centuries. As long as 2000 years ago, its residents traded and haggled with Chinese, Greek, Phoenician, Roman and Babylonian merchants. The Portuguese and the Dutch muscled in on this lucrative trade in the 16th century. The British, initially content to purchase spices and other goods from the Dutch, soon had enough of that and in 1639 established a settlement in the fishing vil-lage of Madraspatnam. The British East India Company erected Fort St George in 1653.

By the 18th century, the British East India Company had to contend with the French.

Robert Clive (Clive of India), a key player in the British campaign, recruited an army of 2000 sepoys (Indian soldiers in British service) and launched a series of military expeditions which developed into the Carnatic Wars. Facing defeat, the French withdrew to Pondicherry (now Puducherry) in 1756.

In the 19th century, the city became the seat of the Madras Presidency, one of the four divisions of British Imperial India. After Independence, growth continued until the city became the significant southern gateway it is today.

ORIENTATION

Bordered on the east by the Bay of Bengal, Chennai is a sprawling combination of several small districts. George Town, a jumble of narrow streets, bazaars and the court buildings, is in the north, near the harbour. To the southwest is the major thoroughfare of Anna Salai (Mount Rd) and the two main train stations: Egmore, for destinations in Tamil Nadu, and Central, for interstate trains.

INFORMATION
Bookshops

Higginbothams (Map p396; ☎ 28513519; 116 Anna Salai; ☽ 9am-8pm Mon-Sat, 10.30am-7.30pm Sun) Decent English-language book selection. Has a branch at the airport.
Landmark (☽ 9am-9pm Mon-Sat, 10.30am-9pm Sun) Anna Salai (Map p396; ☎ 28495995; Spencer Plaza, Phase II); Nungambakkam (Map pp394-5; ☎ 28221000; Apex Plaza, Nungambakkam High Rd)

Cultural Centres

The following centres have libraries and sometimes sponsor concerts, films and events.
Alliance Française de Madras (Map pp394-5; ☎ 28279803; www.af-madras.org; 24/40 College Rd, Nungambakkam; ☽ 9am-7pm Mon-Fri, 9.30am-1.30pm Sat)
American Information Resource Center (Map pp394-5; ☎ 28112000; http://americanlibrary.in.library .net; Gemini Circle, Anna Salai; ☽ 9.30am-5pm Mon-Fri) Bring ID.
British Council Library (Map p396; ☎ 42050600; www.britishcouncilonline.org; 737 Anna Salai; ☽ 11am-7pm Mon-Sat) Monthly membership is Rs200.
Goethe-Institut (Max Mueller Bhavan; Map pp394-5; ☎ 28331314/2; 4 5th St, Rutland Gate, Nungambakkam; ☽ 9am-4pm Mon-Fri, library 11am-6pm Tue-Sat)

Internet Access

Internet Zone (Map p396; ☎ 42145885; 1 Kennet Lane, Egmore; per hr Rs25; ☽ 8am-10pm)

Log In Net Cafe (Map p396; ☎ 52141648; 35 Triplicane High Rd, Triplicane; per hr Rs15; ☽ 9am-11pm)
SGee (Map p396; ☎ 42310391; 20 Vallabha Agraharam St, Triplicane; per hr Rs20; ☽ 24hr)
Sify i-way (Map pp394-5; ☎ 6551755; 59 Dr Radhakrishnan Salai, Royapettah; per hr Rs20; ☽ 24hr)

Left Luggage

Egmore and Central train stations have left-luggage counters, as do the international and domestic airports (Rs10 per 24 hours).

Medical Services

Apollo Hospital (Map p396; ☎ 28293333, emergency 28290792; www.apollohospitals.com; 21 Greams Lane) Cutting-edge hospital popular with international 'medical tourists'.
St Isabel's Hospital (Map pp394-5; ☎ 24662611; 18 Oliver Rd, Mylapore)

Money

State Bank of India George Town (Map pp394-5; 22 Rajaji Salai; ☽ 10am-4pm Mon-Fri, 10am-1pm Sat); Anna Salai (Map p396; Anna Salai; ☽ 10am-4pm Mon-Fri, 10am-1pm Sat)
Thomas Cook Anna Salai (Map p396; ☎ 28492423/4; Spencer Plaza, Phase I; ☽ 9.30am-6.30pm); Egmore (Map p396; ☎ 28553276; 45 Montieth Rd; ☽ 9.30am-6pm Mon-Sat); George Town (Map pp394-5; ☎ 25342374; 20 Rajaji Salai; ☽ 9.30am-6pm Mon-Sat); Nungambakkam (Map pp394-5; ☎ 28274941; Eldorado Bldg, 112 Nungambakkam High Rd; ☽ 9.30am-6.30pm Mon-Fri, 9.30am-noon Sat) Changes currency and travellers cheques with no commission.

Post

DHL (Map p396; ☎ 4214886/7; 85 Pantheon Rd, Egmore; ☽ 8am-11pm) For secure international parcel delivery.
Post office Anna Salai (Map p396; ☽ 8am-8.30pm Mon-Sat, 10am-4pm Sun, poste restante 10am-6pm Mon-Sat); Egmore (Map p396; Kennet Lane; ☽ 10am-6pm Mon-Sat); George Town (Map pp394-5; Rajaji Salai; ☽ 8am-8.30pm Mon-Sat, 10am-4pm Sun)

Tourist Information

The free **CityInfo** (www.explocity.com), available at the tourist office and at some hotels, has information on restaurants, nightlife and what's on. Also check out **Chennai Best** (www.chennaibest .com) and **Chennai Online** (www.chennai online.com).
India Tourism Development Corporation (ITDC; Map p396; ☎ 28281250; www.attindiatourism.com; 29 Cherian Cres, Egmore; ☽ 10am-5.30pm Mon-Sat) Hotel and tour bookings only.

Indiatourism (Map p396; ☎ 28460285; indtour@vsnl .com; 154 Anna Salai; ☑ 9am-6pm Mon-Fri, 9am-1pm Sat) Good for maps and information on all of India.
Tamil Nadu Tourism Complex (TTDC; Map p396; ☎ 25367850; www.tamilnadutourism.org; 2 Wallajah Rd, Triplicane; ☑ 10am-5.30pm Mon-Fri) Brochure-filled state tourist offices from all over India. The tour-booking desk at the Tamil Nadu office (☎ 25383333) is open 24 hours.

Travel Agencies
Madura Travel Service (Map p396; ☎ 28192002; www.maduratravel.com; Kennet Lane, Egmore; ☑ 24hr)
SP Travels & Tours (Map p396; ☎ 28604001; sptravels1@eth.net; 90 Anna Salai, Triplicane; ☑ 9.30am-6.30pm Mon-Sat)

Visa Extensions
Foreigners' Regional Registration Office (Map pp394-5; ☎ 28251721; Shastri Bhavan, Haddows Rd, Nungambakkam; ☑ 9.30am-noon Mon-Fri) With some complicated wrangling and copious doses of patience, some travellers have managed to procure visa extensions here. Theoretically, they take 10 days to process.

DANGERS & ANNOYANCES
While it may seem that Chennai autorickshaw drivers take pride in being the city's biggest annoyance, this is probably just a coincidence: convincing a driver to use the meter is a Vatican-certified miracle; fares border on the astronomical; and post-arrival disputes over pre-agreed fares are not uncommon. Avoid paying up front.

Tempting offers of Rs50 'tours' of the city sound too good to be true. They are. Expect to spend the day being dragged from one shop or emporium to another.

If you have a serious problem with a driver, mentioning a call to the **traffic police** (☎ 103) can defuse the conflict. See p405 for details on other modes of transport.

SIGHTS
Egmore & Central Chennai
GOVERNMENT MUSEUM
Housed across several British-built buildings known as the Pantheon Complex, this excellent **museum** (Map p396; ☎ 28193238; www.chennaimuseum.org; 486 Pantheon Rd, Egmore; Indian/foreigner Rs15/250, camera/video Rs200/500; ☑ 9.30am-5pm Sat-Thu) is Chennai's best.

The main building has a respectable **archaeological section** representing all the major South Indian periods, including Chola, Vijayanagar, Hoysala and Chalukya. Don't

miss the intricate marble reliefs on display from Amaravathi temple in Andhra Pradesh (p317). Further along is a **natural history and zoology** section with a motley collection of skeletons and stuffed birds and animals.

In Gallery 3, the **bronze gallery** has a superb and beautifully presented collection of Chola art. Among the impressive pieces is the bronze of Ardhanariswara, the androgynous incarnation of Shiva and Parvati.

The same ticket gets you into the **National Art Gallery**, the **children's museum** and a small **modern art gallery**, all located in the same complex.

VALLUVAR KOTTAM
This **memorial** (Map pp394-5; Valluvar Kottam High Rd, Kodambakkam; ☑ 9am-7.30pm) honours the Tamil poet Thiruvalluvar and his classic work, the *Thirukural*. A weaver by trade, Thiruvalluvar lived around the 1st century BC in what is present-day Chennai and wrote this famed poem, providing a moral code for millions of followers. The three-level memorial replicates ancient Tamil architecture and boasts an immense 35m chariot, as well as an enormous auditorium and inscriptions of the *Thirukural*'s 1330 couplets.

VIVEKANANDAR ILLAM
The **Vivekananda House** (Map pp394-5; ☎ 28446188; Kamarajar Salai, Triplicane; adult/child Rs2/1; ☑ 10am-1pm & 3-7pm Thu-Tue) is interesting not only for the displays on the famous 'wandering monk', but also for the semicircular structure in which it's housed (see boxed text, p397). Swami Vivekananda stayed here briefly in 1897 and preached his ascetic philosophy to adoring crowds. The museum houses a collection of photographs and memorabilia from the swami's life, a gallery of religious historical paintings and the 'meditation room' where Vivekananda stayed. Free one-hour meditation classes are held on Wednesday nights at 7pm.

South Chennai
Chennai's most active and impressive temple, the ancient Shiva **Kapaleeshwarar Temple** (Map pp394-5; Kutchery Rd, Mylapore; ☑ 4am-noon & 4-8pm) is constructed in the Dravidian style and displays the architectural elements – rainbow-coloured *gopuram* (gateway tower), *mandapas* (pavilions in front of a temple) and a huge tank – found in the famous temple cities of Tamil Nadu.

TAMIL NADU

TAMIL NADU

CHENNAI (MADRAS)

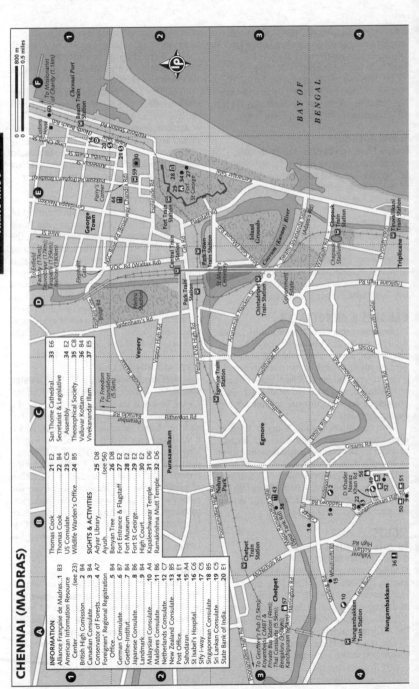

INFORMATION
Alliance Française de Madras...1 B3
American Information Resource Center.........(see 23)
British High Comission...2 B4
Canadian Consulate...3 B4
Conservator of Forests...4 A7
Foreigners' Regional Registration Office...5 B4
German Consulate...6 B7
Goethe-Institut...7 B4
Japanese Consulate...8 B6
Landmark...9 B4
Malaysian Consulate...10 A4
Maldives Consulate...11 B6
Netherlands Consulate...12 C7
New Zealand Consulate...13 B5
Post Office...14 E1
Sahodaran...15 A4
St Isabel's Hospital...16 C6
Sify i-way...17 C5
Singaporean Consulate...18 B5
Sri Lankan Consulate...19 C5
State Bank of India...20 E1
Thomas Cook...21 E2
Thomas Cook...22 B4
US Consulate...23 C5
Wildlife Warden's Office...24 B5

SIGHTS & ACTIVITIES
Adyar Library...25 D8
Ayush...(see 56)
Banyan Tree...26 D8
Fort Entrance & Flagstaff...27 E2
Fort Museum...28 E2
Fort St George...29 E2
High Court...30 E2
Kapaleeshwarar Temple...31 D6
Ramakrishna Mutt Temple...32 D6
San Thome Cathedral...33 E6
Secretariat & Legislative Assembly...34 E2
Theosophical Society...35 C8
Valluvar Kottam...36 B4
Vivekanandar Illam...37 E5

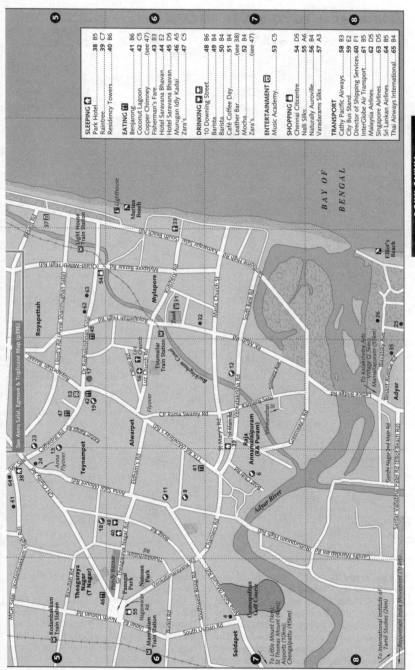

TAMIL NADU

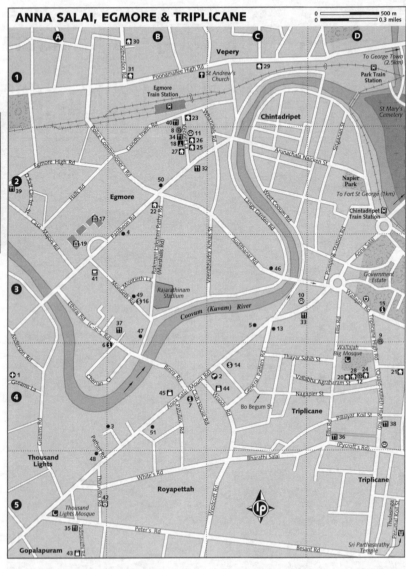

ANNA SALAI, EGMORE & TRIPLICANE

The tranquil, leafy grounds of the **Ramakrishna Mutt Temple** (Map pp394-5; RK Mutt Rd; ⏰ 4.30-11.45am & 3-9pm, puja 8am) are a world away from the chaos and crazy rickshaw drivers outside. Orange-clad monks glide around and there's a reverential feel here. The temple itself is a handsome shrine constructed in themes paying homage to India's major religions. It's open to followers of any faith for meditation.

Originally built by the Portuguese in 1504, then rebuilt in neo-Gothic style in 1893, **San Thome Cathedral** (Map pp394-5; ☎ 24985455; Kamarajar Salai) is a soaring Roman Catholic church between Kapaleeshwarar Temple and Marina Beach. In the basement is a chapel housing

TAMIL NADU

the tomb of St Thomas the Apostle (Doubting Thomas), who it is said brought Christianity to the subcontinent in the 1st century.

During an early morning or evening stroll along the 13km sandy stretch of **Marina Beach** (Map pp394–5) you'll pass cricket matches, kids flying kites, fortune-tellers, fish markets and families enjoying the sea breeze. This beach was especially hard hit during the 2004 tsunami, with around 200 recorded casualties, most of them children. Don't swim here – strong rips make it dangerous.

Between the Adyar River and the coast, the 100 hectares of the **Theosophical Society** (Map pp394-5; Lattice Bridge Rd; 8-10am & 2-5pm Mon-Fri, 8-10am Sat) provide one of the few peaceful retreats from the city. The sprawling grounds contain a church, mosque, Buddhist shrine and Hindu temple. There's a huge variety of native and introduced trees, including a famed 400-year-old **banyan tree** whose branches offer reprieving shade for over 3700 sq metres. The **Adyar Library** (9am-5pm) here has an immense collection of books on

THE ICE HOUSE

Before it was a shrine to Swami Vivekananda (see p393), this beautiful, pink wedding-cake building on Chennai's promenade served as the town's sole refrigerator.

From Boston, USA, Frederic Tudor – known as the 'Ice King' – was the first to bring the cooling magic of ice to the subcontinent in 1833. Chipped off in huge blocks from New England's wintry slopes and cleverly wrapped in insulating woodchips, nearly two-thirds of the precious cargo survived its maiden sea voyage to Calcutta aboard the clipper *Tuscany*. These precious and ephemeral goods (the first real whitegoods) were highly prized by British expatriates of the East India Company. Soon, insulated depots were being built in Calcutta, Bombay and Madras to store the ice upon its arrival; Madras' dainty Victorian-style 'Ice House' was built for this purpose around 1842. The Ice King's business was successful for decades, until the discovery of ice-making through steaming led to its eventual collapse in 1880, when the Ice House was sold to Biligiri Iyengar of Madras.

In 1897, Swami Vivekananda had returned from the USA, passing through Madras and spending nine days as a guest at the Ice House. After his departure, a short-lived shrine was established in the basement of the building with the help of its owner. The government then acquired the building in 1917 and used it variously as different hostels and a school until 1997, when the Tamil government dedicated the building as a permanent exhibit of Swami Vivekananda's life.

religion and philosophy, from 1000-year-old Buddhist scrolls to intricate, handmade 19th-century Bibles. If you're interested in the Theosophical Society's philosophy, call into the public relations office and chat with the director.

George Town
FORT ST GEORGE

Finished around 1653 by the British East India Company, the **fort** (Map pp394-5; ○ 10am-5pm) has undergone many facelifts over the years. Inside the vast perimeter walls is now a precinct housing the **Secretariat & Legislative Assembly**. The 46m-high **flagstaff** at the main entrance is a mast salvaged from a 17th-century shipwreck.

The **Fort Museum** (☎ 25670389; Indian/foreigner Rs5/100, video Rs25; ○ 10am-5pm Sat-Thu) has military memorabilia from the British and French East India Companies, as well as the Raj and Muslim administrations.

HIGH COURT

Built in 1892, this red Indo-Saracenic structure at Parry's Corner is said to be the largest judicial building in the world after the Courts of London. You can wander around the court buildings (Map pp394-5) and sit in on sessions.

Other Sights
LITTLE MOUNT & ST THOMAS MOUNT

It's believed that from around AD 58, St Thomas lived in hiding at **Little Mount** (Chinnamalai; off Map pp394-5; Saidapet). The cave still bears what some believe to be Thomas' handprint, left when he escaped through an opening that miraculously appeared. Three kilometres on, **St Thomas Mount** (Parangi Malai) is thought to be the site of Thomas' martyrdom in AD 72. Both mounts are about 1km from the Saidapet and St Thomas Mount train stations, respectively.

ACTIVITIES

Have an *abhyangam* (oil treatment; Rs650) or ayurvedic treatment at **Ayush** (Map pp394-5; ☎ 65195195; www.leverayush.com; 6 Khader Nawaz Khan Rd, Nungambakkam; ○ 7am-7pm). Yoga classes (Rs150) or 21-day courses (Rs1200) also offered.

COURSES
Language
International Institute of Tamil Studies (off Map pp394-5; ☎ 22540992; www.ulakaththamizh.org; Central Polytechnic Campus, Adyar) Runs intensive one-month courses in Tamil.

Meditation
Mahabodhi Society of Sri Lanka (Map p396; ☎ 28192458; 12 Kennet Lane, Egmore) Dharma talks,

A MODERN CLASSIC – THE ENFIELD BULLET

The classic lines, the guttural purr – to motoring enthusiasts India's Enfield motorcycle is as unmistakable as the silhouette of the Taj Mahal. The iconic Enfield Bullet has been manufactured in India since 1955, boasting the longest production run of any bike anywhere in the world.

The Enfield story begins in country England, where the factory of George Townsend Jr first took a stab at making newfangled bicycles in the 1880s. The following decade the company also started supplying rifle parts to a factory in Enfield, assuming the name Royal Enfield and stamping the slogan 'made like a gun' on their bicycles. Their first twin-engine motorbike was introduced in 1909.

During WWI demand for Enfield's two-wheeled transport boomed. The famous 'Bullet' moniker was first applied to Enfield's 1931 four-valve, single-cylinder bike, a machine that was in high demand during WWII.

The 350cc Bullet was first manufactured in India by Madras Motors in 1955 to supply the Indian Army. During the 1970s increasing competition from Japan's light and compact scooters forced Enfield's UK factories to close up shop. By this time, Enfield India was still soldiering on, a practically independent company that made their own modifications to the original Bullet design to better suit the subcontinent. By 1989, Enfield India was exporting their sought-after vintage-styled bikes – made to the same specifications for over 30 years – back to the UK and Europe.

The original Bullet remains in production today at the **Enfield Factory** (☎ 42230245; www.royalenfield.com; Tiruvottiyur), 17km outside of Chennai. Half-hour tours (Rs600) run on Saturdays at 10.30am. Enfield's legendary motorbikes, designed in 1955 but manufactured just last week, truly give meaning to the term 'modern-day classic'.

TAMIL NADU

TAMIL LITERATURE

The Tamil language is the oldest and purest of India's four Dravidian languages, and Tamil literature boasts an illustrious history spanning over two millennia.

The earliest era of Tamil writing was the Sangam period (from the 1st century BC to the 5th century AD); remains of the writing of this era have been gathered into two collections known as the Eight Anthologies and the Ten Idyls. Secular writing of this time was rich with images of everyday life – seasons, plants, animals and places.

The medieval period that followed saw Jain, Buddhist and Muslim influences take control of the Tamil region, with didactic Tamil texts of the time leading a religious renaissance. Tamil literature from this period was famed for its wealth of ancient morals and values, and is still considered some of the most important world literature of the era.

The changing socio-political scene of Tamil Nadu continued to inspire Tamil writing, with the most recent, modern period of Tamil literature owing its roots to influences from colonial British writers of the 19th century.

---

meditation and special *pujas* (offerings or prayers) on full-moon and other days.

Vivekanandar Illam (Map pp394-5; ☎ 28446188; Kamarajar Salai, Triplicane) Free one-hour classes on Wednesday nights at 7pm.

TOURS

TTDC (p392) conducts half-day city tours (non-AC/AC Rs125/180) and day trips to Mamallapuram (non-AC/AC Rs350/500), Puducherry (non-AC Rs400) and Tirupathi (AC Rs665). Book at ITDC (p392) or TTDC.

SLEEPING

Hotels in Chennai are pricier than in the rest of Tamil Nadu and don't as a rule offer much bang for your buck.

Egmore, on and around chaotic Kennet Lane, is best for budget accommodation, as is the Triplicane High Rd area, which is a little further out and mildly less chaotic. Egmore is also where you'll find the majority of midrange sleeping options, while the top-end hotels lie further out in leafy, south-west Chennai.

Many hotels in Chennai fill up by noon.

Budget
EGMORE

Salvation Army Red Shield Guest House (Map p396; ☎ 25321821; 15 Ritherdon Rd; dm/r Rs100/300; 🗙) Though bordering on the dingy, this surprisingly popular cheapie lies in a quiet spot north of Egmore Station. The bathrooms make only the most basic concessions to hygiene, though the staff here are helpful. Checkout is 9am.

Hotel Regent (Map p396; ☎ 28191801; 11 Kennet Lane; s/d Rs200/350) The pick of the litter when it comes to budget digs in them 'ere parts. The frequently cleaned rooms are located around a courtyard and blissfully set back from much of Kennet Lane's mayhem.

Masa (Map p396; ☎ 28193954; 15 Kennet Lane; s/d from Rs270/460) The grotty and windowless abodes here will usually reward a last-ditch effort of finding a room if all other places are full (as they often are).

YWCA International Guest House (Map p396; ☎ 25324234; ywcaigh@indiainfo.com; Poonamallee High Rd; s/d/tr from Rs600/750/1000; 🗙) Set around sprawling, green and shady grounds right near the train station, the YWCA still manages to offer up healthy doses of hush. Rooms are housed in an oversized building, where the dregs of colonial-era charm still hang around the hallway lounge. The old rooms adhere to the most demanding levels of cleanliness.

TRADITIONAL TRADERS

George Town, the area that grew around the fort, retains much of its original flavour. This is the wholesale centre of Chennai (Madras). Many backstreets, bordered by NSC Bose Rd, Krishna Koil St, Mint St and Rajaji Salai, are entirely given over to selling one particular type of merchandise as they have for hundreds of years – paper goods in Anderson St, fireworks in Badrian St and so on. Even if you're not in the market for anything, wander the mazelike streets to see another aspect of Indian life flowing seamlessly from the past into the present.

TRIPLICANE

Cristal Guest House (Map p396; ☎ 28513011; 34 CNK Rd; s/d Rs150/200) In a modern building adhering to the white-tile-on-every-surface school of interior design, the clean abodes here win our 'cheapest rooms in Chennai' award.

Paradise Guest House (Map p396; ☎ 28594252; paradisegh@hotmail.com; 17 Vallabha Agraharam St; s/d/tr from Rs250/300/400; 🕱) Travellers agree that the Paradise boasts some of the best-value digs on this street. Expect sparkling white tiles, a breezy rooftop, friendly staff and hot water by the steaming bucket.

Broad Lands Lodge (Map p396; ☎ 28545573; broadlandshotel@yahoo.com; 18 Vallabha Agraharam St; s/d from Rs300/400, without bathroom from Rs270/300) At this old-school favourite of the dreadlocked brigade, the warrens of rooms puncture a creaky colonial-era building like holes in Swiss cheese. Strangely, visitors don't seem to mind the bare-bone, idiosyncratic rooms, the plain concrete floors or the dank shared bathrooms – perhaps the leafy, subdued courtyards and happy communal vibe trumps these shortcomings.

Midrange

EGMORE

Hotel Pandian (Map p396; ☎ 28191010; 15 Kennet Lane; s/d from Rs700/1100; 🕱) This decent pad bridges the budget and midrange categories with slightly dated, wood-panelled rooms that are kept in reasonably good nick.

Hotel Chandra Park (Map p396; ☎ 28191177; www.hotelchandrapark.com; 9 Gandhi Irwin Rd; s/d with AC incl breakfast from Rs850/950; 🕱) With other hotels practically doubling their prices every year, the Chandra Park prices remain mysteriously low. Standard rooms are small but have clean towels and tight, white sheets. Throw in a hearty buffet breakfast and classy front lobby, and this place offers superb value by Chennai standards.

Hotel Ashoka (Map p396; ☎ 28553377; www.ballalgrouphotels.com; 47 Pantheon Rd; s/d Rs905/1250, with AC Rs1250/1500; 🕱) If a 1950s Miami architect was asked to design a space-age hotel on Mars, the Ashoka might be what he'd come up with. The novelty of the funky design will soon wear off, however, and you'll be left with old-school rooms covered in 1000 layers of paint and filled with musty air. The cottages (single/double Rs2400/2800) have more of an Austin Powers ambience: lush red carpeting, fridges and cocoonlike tubs.

Royal Regency (Map p396; ☎ 2561 1777; www.royalregency.co.in; 26-27 Poonamallee High Rd; r from Rs2300; 🕱) The splashes of colour adorning the outside of this hotel, smack-bang between Central and Egmore train stations, cannot be missed. It's all very businesslike inside, sparsely furnished and offering the minimum needed for a solid night's sleep.

TRIPLICANE

Hotel Comfort (Map p396; ☎ 28587661; www.hotelcomfortonline.com; 22 Vallabha Agraharam St; s/d from Rs1100/1200; 🕱) Fresh from a major round of renovation, the immaculate rooms here now offer goodies like flat-screen TVs and bright-orange bathrooms. Perfectly comfy.

Top End

The following hotels have central AC and multicuisine restaurant and bar, and they accept credit cards. Unless stated otherwise, checkout is noon.

Residency Towers (Map pp394-5; ☎ 28156363; www.theresidency.com; Sir Theagaraya Nagar Rd, T Nagar; s/d from Rs5000/5500; 🕱 🖥 🛋) At this price, it's like Residency Towers doesn't know what a good thing it has going: five-star elegance with a lot more personality. Every floor is decorated differently, but rooms all have sliding doors in front of windows to block out light and noise, dark-wood furniture and thoughtful touches.

** our pick** **Raintree** (Map pp394-5; ☎ 24304050; www.raintreehotels.com; 120 St Mary's Rd, Mylapore; s/d from Rs7500/8500; 🕱 🖥 🛋) A rarity in Chennai, this ecofriendly lodge oozes personality from every pore. Floors are made of bamboo, wastewater is treated and used for gardening, and electricity conservation holds pride of place. But then the sleek, minimalist rooms are some of the most stylish and comfortable around, and the rooftop infinity pool (which doubles as insulation) has a gorgeous wooden terrace with views of the sea.

Park Hotel (Map pp394-5; ☎ 42676000; www.theparkhotels.com; 601 Anna Salai; s/d from Rs11,000/13,000; 🕱 🖥) We love this uberchic boutique hotel, which flaunts stylish elements like frosted-glass partitions, towering indoor bamboo gardens and oversized doors. The rooms are petite but have all the mod cons, including funky bathrooms separated from the boudoir by an opaque glass wall. It's all pretty swish, and as a bonus you have the trendy Leather Bar (p402) on the premises.

EATING

Chennai is packed with classic 'meals' joints, which serve thalis (traditional South Indian 'all-you-can-eat' meals) for lunch and dinner, and tiffin (snacks) such as *idlis* (rice dumplings) and dosas (paper-thin lentil-flour pancakes) the rest of the day. It's tempting – and feasible – to eat every meal at one of Chennai's dozen Saravana Bhavan restaurants (below), where you can count on quality vegetarian food.

The Mylapore area has many good independent restaurants, so head there if you're looking for something more refined.

Restaurants

EGMORE

Vasanta Bhavan (Map p396; 33 Gandhi Irwin Rd; mains Rs40-60; ☾ 5am-11pm) Excellent 'meals' (Rs40). The older Vasantha Bhavan down the street at No 10 is not as good but has more charm and also sweets.

Annapurna (Map p396; ☎ 28523037; 23 Pantheon Rd; mains Rs40-60; ☾ lunch & dinner Mon-Sat, lunch Sun) A bustling hole-in-the-wall that serves up a lip-smacking taste of Bengal in Chennai's Egmore district. Try the *bhetki paturi* (fish baked in banana leaves). Yum.

Ponnusamy Hotel (Map p396; Wellington Estate, 24 Ethiraj Rd; mains Rs40-85; ☾ lunch & dinner) This well-known non-veg place serves curry, biryani (steamed rice with meat or vegetables) and Chettinad specialities. Look out for interesting options like pigeon fry and rabbit masala.

Hotel Saravana Bhavan Egmore (Map p396; 21 Kennet Lane; ☾ 6am-10.30pm); George Town (Map pp394-5; 209 NSC Bose Rd); Mylapore (Map pp394-5; 101 Dr Radhakrishnan Salai; ☾ 7am-11pm); Thousand Lights (Map p396; 293 Peter's Rd; ☾ lunch & dinner); Triplicane (Map p396; Shanthi Theatre Complex, 48 Anna Salai; ☾ 7am-11pm) Dependably delish, 'meals' at the Saravana Bhavans run around Rs50, though the Mylapore locale has some 'special meals' for Rs95 and up. The Thousand Lights branch is more upscale, with a Rs180 buffet and silver cutlery.

Fisherman's Fare (Map pp394-5; ☎ 28362071; Major Ramanathan Salai (Spur Tank Rd); meals Rs110-300; ☾ 11am-10pm) This small, spotless, AC dining room gets packed to the rafters come lunchtime with punters digging into well-prepared fish fare ranging from shrimp to fish curries to tandoori fish. There's a great lunchtime special for Rs155.

Sparky's Diner (Map p396; ☎ 42144206; Ramanathan Salai (Spur Tank Rd); meals Rs140-250; ☾ lunch & dinner) Sparky's is a wall-to-wall homage to kitsch.

This expat-run 'American' diner is plastered with US state licence plates and movie posters, has Sinatra crooning on the radio, and decks its waiters out in baseball shirts. Look out for OK American specials like deep-fried chicken or Cajun gumbo.

TRIPLICANE

Ratna Cafe (Map p396; ☎ 28487181; 255 Triplicane High Rd; dishes Rs25-60) Though often crowded and cramped, Ratna is renowned in Triplicane and beyond for its scrumptious *idlis* and the hearty doses of *sambar* (soupy lentil dish with cubed vegetables) that go with it.

Hotel Comfort (Map p396; 22 Vallabha Agraharam; mains Rs30-100; ☾ dinner) The menu is typical Indian and Chinese, but the rooftop garden is green, cosy and relaxed. Beer is served.

GOPALAPURAM

Amethyst (Map p396; ☎ 28353581; 14 Padmavathi Rd; meals Rs105-260; ☾ 10am-10pm) Set in a stunning lemon-coloured, colonial-era building, this place is comfortably posh. The lush garden setting and patio dining takes the cake for restaurant ambience. Expect comfy couches, tasteful antique furniture and afternoon tea with cucumber-and-mint-chutney sandwiches.

MYLAPORE & AROUND

Murugan Idly Kadai (Map pp394-5; ☎ 42025076; 77 GN Chetty Rd, T Nagar; dishes Rs30-60) Those in the know generally agree this particular branch of the small chain serves some of the best *idli* and South Indian meals in town. We heartily concur.

Coconut Lagoon (Map pp394-5; ☎ 42020428; cnr Cathedral & TTK Rds, Alwarpet; mains Rs55-200; ☾ noon-3pm & 7-11.45pm) Excellent Keralan and Goan fare with a focus on seafood delicacies, such as *kari meen polli chathu* (fish masala steamed in banana leaf).

Zara's (Map pp394-5; ☎ 28111462; 74 Cathedral Rd, Teynampet; tapas Rs70-250; ☾ 1-3pm & 6.30-11pm) Though this tiny place is a little tough to find, seekers will be rewarded by this ultra-cool tapas bar. Expect genuine Spanish flavour: everything from squid and olives to tortilla and sangria. Three-course lunch specials with wine or beer are a decent deal at Rs225/245 for veg/non-veg. The bar here doubles as a popular hang-out in it's own right (see p402).

Copper Chimney (Map pp394-5; ☎ 28115770; 74 Cathedral Rd, Teynampet; mains Rs140-250; ☾ noon-3pm & 6-11.30pm) Vegetarians might want to give this

TAMIL NADU

meat-centric place a wide berth, but others will drool over the yummy North Indian tandoori dishes served among plush furnishings.

Benjarong (Map pp394-5; ☎ 24322640; 537 TTK Rd, Alwarpet; mains Rs140-500; ⓥ lunch & dinner) From the finely crafted furniture and calming ambience to the attentive service and superbly presented food, this Thai restaurant is an experience. Most mains are around Rs200.

Self-Catering

Jam Bazaar (Map p396; cnr Ellis Rd & Bharathi Salai, Triplicane) Animated market bursting with fruit, vegetables and spices.

Spencer's Daily (Map p396; ☎ 42140784; Spencer Plaza, Anna Salai; ⓥ 9.30am-9pm)

DRINKING
Cafes

Mocha (Map pp394-5; D Khader Nawaz Khan Rd, Nungambakkam; coffee Rs20-180; ⓥ 11am-11pm) The young and beautiful come here for coffee, hookahs (water pipes; Rs195 to Rs245) and snacks (Rs50 to Rs150). Lovely outdoor garden.

Chennai is very much in the throes of India's cappuccino addiction.

Barista (Map pp394-5; Rosy Towers, Nungambakkam High & D Khader Nawaz Khan Rds, Nungambakkam; coffee Rs20-50; ⓥ 7.30am-11.30pm)

Café Coffee Day (coffee Rs20-50; ⓥ 10am-11pm) Egmore (Map p396; Alsa Mall, Montieth Rd); Nungambakkam (Map pp394-5; 123/124 Nungambakkam High Rd)

Bars & Nightclubs

Chennai's nightlife scene throbs that little bit more every year, though it's no Bengaluru

or Mumbai yet. It doesn't help that bars and clubs are supposed to close at midnight and are restricted to hotels.

Zara's (Map pp394-5; ☎ 28111462; 74 Cathedral Rd, Teynampet; cocktails Rs230-350; ⓥ 1-3pm & 6.30-11pm) Where the cool people come on weekends for tapas (see p401), sangria, house-infused vodka (jalapeño, almond, cinnamon) and inventive mocktails. Dress nice.

Geoffrey's Pub (off Map pp394-5; ☎ 24757788; Radha Park Inn Hotel, 171 Jawaharlal Nehru Salai, Arumbakkam; ⓥ 6-11pm Wed-Mon) This modern version of the English pub is one of the few places in Chennai that hosts live music nightly. Not always great music, but music nonetheless. The atmosphere is casual, with Kollywood types occasionally gracing the place with their presence.

Leather Bar (Map pp394-5; ☎ 42144000; Park Hotel, 601 Anna Salai; ⓥ 6-11pm) Thankfully 'leather' refers to floor and wall coverings rather than kinky jock-straps and dungeons. This modish pad has talented mixologists dishing up fancy drinks and DJs spinning happy dance tunes.

10 Downing Street (Map pp394-5; ☎ 43546565; North Boag Rd, T Nagar; ⓥ 6-11pm) Also worth checking out, this English-themed pub is often packed with a mixed bag of punters.

ENTERTAINMENT
Classical Music & Dance

If you happen to be in Chennai around mid-December to mid-January, you're in for a treat: the Festival of Carnatic Music & Dance (see the boxed text, p389) is a massive showcase of classical Tamil music and dance. Turn up to hear

---

KOLLYWOOD BLING

Tamil film fans – and they're known for their fanaticism – will tell you that their movies have always been technically superior to Hindi films. Far from living in Bollywood's shadow, Kollywood – named for Kodambakkam, the neighbourhood preferred by many studios and film people – has its own tradition of film-making founded on high-quality production, slightly more realistic plot lines and much more realistic heroes (ie they like them chubby and moustachioed).

Kollywood style, though, is changing. Bollywood's famous 'masala' format – that crowd-pleasing mix of drama, comedy, romance and action – is rubbing off on Tamil films, and vice versa. Bollywood's been remaking Tamil blockbusters, while the big-name celebs in Mumbai (Bombay) are working in Kollywood.

Kollywood comes second to Bollywood for revenue, and some say it even rivals it for distribution – with obsessed Tamil fans queuing up not only in Tamil Nadu's 1800 cinemas, but also in Sri Lanka, Malaysia, South Africa, Europe and the USA. Meanwhile, some Hindi film studios, hearing the ch-ching of Kollywood's success, have begun to get in on the action and produce Tamil films themselves – films which, to be sure, will be remade someday in Bollywood. And the circle begins again.

lectures, see demonstrations and view numerous concerts held around the Tamil capital.

Music Academy (Map pp394-5; ☎ 28115162; cnr TKK & Cathedral Rds) This is Chennai's most popular public venue for Carnatic classical music and Bharata Natyam dance. Many performances are free.

Kalakshetra Arts Village (off Map pp394-5; ☎ 24521169; kshetra@vsnl.com; Dr Muthulakshmi Rd, Tiruvanmiyu; ☺ 10am-6pm) Founded in 1936, Kalakshetra is committed to reviving classical dance and music. Check out one of their regular performances, or a class (9am to 11am and 2pm to 4.30pm Monday to Friday). Four-month courses in music and dance cost Rs750 per month.

Cinema

Chennai has more than 100 cinemas, a reflection of the vibrant film industry here (see boxed text, opposite). Most screen Tamil films, but **Sathyam Cinema** (Map p396; ☎ 28512425; 8 Thiruvika Rd, Royapettah; tickets Rs65-120) often shows English-language films alongside local fare.

SHOPPING

Theagaraya Nagar (T Nagar; Map pp394–5) has great shopping, especially at Pondy Bazaar and around Panagal Park. Nungambakkam's shady D Khader Nawaz Khan Rd (Map pp394–5) is an exceedingly pleasant lane of shops, cafes and galleries.

Most of the finest Kanchipuram silks turn up in Chennai (and Bengaluru), so consider doing your silk shopping here.

Amethyst (Map p396; ☎ 28351627; 14 Padmavathi Rd, Gopalapuram; ☺ 11am-8pm) See what's the latest at this collection of shops in Sundar Mahal, a lovely heritage building. Clothes, Indo-Western jewellery, lacquer-ware and other home decor by India's hottest designers.

Fabindia Spencer Plaza (Map p396; ☎ 42158015; Anna Salai; ☺ 11am-8pm); Woods Rd (Map p396; ☎ 42027015; ☺ 10am-8pm) The Woods Rd shop has home and food sections, along with fabulous clothes.

Naturally Auroville (Map pp394-5; ☎ 28330517; D Khader Nawaz Khan Rd, Nungambakkam; ☺ 10.30am-8pm Mon-Sat, 11.30am-7pm Sun) *Objets* (pottery, bedspreads, candles) and fine foods (organic coffees, breads and cheeses) from Auroville.

The best commercial shopping malls include **Spencer Plaza** (Map p396; Anna Salai) and **Chennai Citicentre** (Map pp394-5; Dr Radhakrishnan Salai, Mylapore).

For silks, check out the following:

Nalli Silks (Map pp394-5; ☎ 24344115; 9 Nageswaran Rd, T Nagar; ☺ 9.30am-9.30pm) The granddaddy of silk shops.

Varadarams Silks (Map pp394-5; ☎ 28363867; 88 Harrington Rd, Chetpet; ☺ 10am-7.30pm Mon-Sat) Low-priced Kanchipuram silk.

GETTING THERE & AWAY
Air
AIRPORTS

Anna International Airport (☎ 22560551) in Tirusulam, 16km southwest of the centre, is efficient and not too busy, making Chennai a good entry or exit point. **Kamaraj domestic terminal** (☎ 22560551) is next door.

CRASH! BANG! BOOKS!

We go on a lot about the ancient culture of the Tamils and their sacred texts and classical epics, but we shouldn't overlook the other side of cultural life, one that appreciates detectives who can catch their man through a casually observed cigarette butt, reincarnated warrior princesses and scientist-slaying fembots.

We speak, of course, of pulp fiction. Not the kind with John Travolta blasting people in a dark suit; we mean real-deal pulp fiction – simple stories, not a lot of plot, lurid murders, sex etc, all printed on paper that could double as toilet roll and sold for next to nothing in small shops, bus stands and railway stations. Tamils are mad for pulp fiction, and their authors are simply mad, full stop (but in a good way). Rajesh Kumar has (wait for it) 1250 novels and over 2000 short stories to his name; quite a few other authors take up similar space on the bibliography shelf. Does some of this writing seem to follow, shall we say, easily repeatable templates? Yes – but a lot of it original, inventive and amusing as hell to read.

Which you can do, in English, if you find the *Blaft Anthology of Tamil Pulp Fiction*, put together by a small Chennai publishing house which is planning follow-up collections. Show the locals you meet your pulp covers – they'll realize what you're reading and are almost always enthusiastically approving.

TAMIL NADU

DOMESTIC AIRLINES

Domestic airlines with offices in Chennai include the following:

Indian Airlines (Map p396; ☎ 28578153/4, airport 22561906; 19 Rukmani Lakshmi Pathy Rd (Marshalls Rd), Egmore)

IndiGo (☎ 22560286; airport)

Jet Airways (Map p396; ☎ domestic 39893333, international 1800 225522; 41/43 Montieth Rd, Egmore; ❍ 9am-8pm Mon-Sat, 9am-7pm Sun) Also flies internationally.

Kingfisher Airlines (Map p396; ☎ 28584366; 19 Rukmani Lakshmi Pathy Rd (Marshalls Rd), Egmore) Also has international flights.

Paramount Airways (☎ 22561667-70; airport)

SpiceJet (☎ 1800 1803333; airport)

INTERNATIONAL AIRLINES

Air Canada (Map p396; ☎ 28582817; 8 Audithanar Rd, Egmore)

Air France (Map p396; ☎ 1800 1800033; 42 Pantheon Rd, Egmore)

Air India (Map p396; ☎ 1800 1801407; 19 Rukmani Lakshmi Pathy Rd (Marshalls Rd), Egmore)

American Airlines (Map p396; ☎ 18001807300; Prince Centre, 248 Pathari Rd, Thousand Lights)

Cathay Pacific Airways (Map pp394-5; ☎ 42988400; 47 Major Ramanathan Salai (Spur Tank Rd), Chetpet)

Gulf Air (☎ 28554417; airport)

InterGlobe Air Transport (Map pp394-5; ☎ 28226149; Maalavika Centre, MGR Salai (Kodambakkam High Rd), Nungambakkam) For Air New Zealand, South African, United, Delta and Virgin Atlantic ticketing changes.

KLM (Map p396; ☎ 1800 1800044; 42 Pantheon Rd, Egmore)

Lufthansa (Map p396; ☎ 30213500, airport 22569393; 167 Anna Salai) No walk-ins.

Malaysia Airlines (Map pp394-5; ☎ 42191919; 90 Dr Radhakrishnan Salai, Mylapore)

DOMESTIC FLIGHTS FROM CHENNAI (MADRAS)

Destination	Airline	Fare (US$)	Duration (hr)	Frequency
Bengaluru	IC	86	¾	2 daily
	9W	76	1	4 daily
	I7	71	¾	2 daily
	6E	63	1	1 daily
Delhi	IC	128	2½	4 daily
	9W	123	2½	4 daily
	6E	95	2½	3 daily
Goa	IC	130	1¼	3 weekly
	I7	101	1¼	1 daily
	6E	77	2½	1 daily
Hyderabad	IC	79	1	2 daily
	9W	74	1	3 daily
	I7	71	1	3 daily
	6E	56	1	1 daily
Kochi	IC	98	1	3 weekly
	9W	85	1	1 daily
	I7	81	1	3 daily
Kolkata	IC	138	2	1 daily
	9W	123	2	1 daily
	6E	82	2	2 daily
Mumbai	IC	145	2	4 daily
	9W	115	2	6 daily
	SG	84	2	2 daily
Port Blair	IC	136	2	1 daily
	9W	98	2	2 daily
Trivandrum	IC	95	1½	1 daily
	I7	91	1¼	2 daily
	9W	75	1½	1 daily

Note: Fares are one-way only.
Airline codes: 6E – IndiGo, 9W – Jet Airways, I7 – Paramount, IC – Indian Airlines, SG – SpiceJet.

Singapore Airlines (Map pp394–5; ☎ 28473976; Westminster, 108 Dr Radhakrishnan Salai, Mylapore)
Sri Lankan Airlines (Translanka Air Travels; Map pp394–5; ☎ 43921100; 4 Kodambakkam High Rd, Nungambakkam)
Thai Airways International (Map pp394–5; ☎ 42173311; 31 Haddows Rd, Nungambakkam)

Boat
Passenger ships sail from the George Town harbour to Port Blair in the Andaman Islands (see p478) every 10 days or so. The **Director of Shipping Services** (Map pp394–5; ☎ 25226873; fax 25220841; Shipping Corporation Bldg, Rajaji Salai, George Town; ☽ 10am–4pm Mon-Sat) sells tickets (Rs1932 to Rs6221) for the 60-hour trip. You'll need two photos and three photocopies each of your passport identity page and visa.

Bus
Most Tamil Nadu (SETC) and other government buses operate from the insanely chaotic **Chennai Mofussil Bus Terminus** (CMBT; off Map pp394–5; ☎ 23455858, 24794705; Jawaharlal Nehru Salai, Koyambedu), better known as Koyambedu CMBT, 7km west of town.

Buses 15 or 15B from Parry's Corner or Central train station, and 27B from Anna Salai or Egmore train station, all head there (Rs4, 45 minutes). An autorickshaw charges around Rs150 for the same ride.

Frequent SETC, Karnataka (KSRTC) and Andhra Pradesh (APRSTC) buses cover the destinations listed in the boxed text (below), usually in the morning and late afternoon.

Several companies operate Volvo AC buses to the same destinations from the less over-whelming private-bus station next door; try **KPN** (☎ 24797998) or **Rathi Meena** (☎ 24791494). There's another, smaller private bus stand (Map p396) opposite Egmore train station. These super-deluxe buses usually leave at night and cost two to three times more than ordinary buses.

Train
Interstate trains and those heading west generally depart from Central train station (Map pp394–5), while trains heading south depart from Egmore (Map p396). The **Train Reservation Complex** (☎ general 139, reservations 1361; ☽ 8am–8pm Mon-Sat, 8am–2pm Sun) is in a separate 10-storey building just west of Central station; the Foreign Assistance Tourist Cell is on the 1st floor. Egmore's **booking office** (☎ 28194579) keeps the same hours.

GETTING AROUND
To/From the Airport
The cheapest way to reach the airport is by MRTS train to Tirusulam station, 300m across the road from the terminals (Rs6). An auto-rickshaw will cost you at least Rs200/300 for a day/night trip.

Both terminals have prepaid taxi kiosks, where tickets are Rs270/450 for non-AC/AC to Egmore or Anna Salai/Triplicane.

Autorickshaw
Rickshaw drivers in Chennai have the scru-ples of a scorpion, with astronomical fares

TAMIL NADU

BUS SERVICES FROM CHENNAI (MADRAS)

Destination	Fare (Rs)	Duration (hr)	Frequency
Bengaluru	170-260	9	every 30min
Chidambaram	80-90	7	18 daily
Coimbatore	210-290	11½	every 30min
Ernakulam (Kochi)	425-650	16	1 daily
Hyderabad	350-400	12	5 daily
Kodaikanal	200-220	14	1 daily
Madurai	155-190	10	every 20min
Mamallapuram	40	2	every 15-30min
Mysore	200-235	11	10 daily
Ooty	250-310	14	2 daily
Puducherry	50-85	4	every 20min
Thanjavur	120-135	9	hourly
Tirupathi	60-70	4	every 30min
Trichy	120-185	8	every 15-30min
Trivandrum	325-425	17	6 daily

TAMIL NADU

MAJOR TRAINS FROM CHENNAI (MADRAS)

Destination	Train No & name	Fare (Rs)	Duration (hr)	Departure
Bengaluru	2007 Shatabdi Exp*	530/1015	5	6am CC
	2609 Bangalore Exp	121/412	6½	1.20pm CC
Delhi	2615 Grand Trunk Exp	547/1504/2017	35	7.15pm CC
	2621 Tamil Nadu Exp	547/1504/2017	33	10pm CC
Coimbatore	6627 West Coast Exp	225/594/806	8½	11.30am CC
Goa	7311 Vasco Exp**	359/973/1329	22	1.40pm CC
Hyderabad	2759 Charminar Exp	326/857/1159	14	6.10pm CC
	2603 Hyderabad Exp	311/812/1095	13	4.45pm CC
Kochi	6041 Alleppey Exp	283/761/1036	11¾	9.15pm CC
Kolkata	2842 Coromandel Exp	479/1284/1751	27	8.45am CC
	2840 Howrah Mail	479/1284/1751	28½	11.35pm CC
Madurai	6127 MS Guruvayur Exp	225/594/806	8½	7.50am CE
	2635 Vaigai Exp	145/499	8	12.25pm CE
Mumbai	1042 Mumbai Exp	399/1085/1486	26	11.45am CC
	2164 Chennai Exp	419/1114/1517	23	6.50am CE
Mysore	2007 Shatabdi Exp*	675/1284	7	6am CC
	6222 Mysore Exp	224/594/806	10½	11.30pm CC
Tirupathi	6053 Tirupathi Exp	71/229	3	1.50pm CC
Trichy	2605 Pallavan Exp	115/392	5½	3.30pm CE
Trivandrum	2695 Trivandrum Exp	356/938/1272	15¾	4pm CC

Departure codes: CC – Chennai Central, CE – Chennai Egmore
*Daily except Tuesday; ** Fridays only
Shatabdi fares are chair/executive; Express and Mail fares are 2nd class/chair for day trains, sleeper/3AC/2AC for overnight trains

routinely quoted for both locals and tourists alike. Since you have no chance of getting a driver to use the meter, expect to pay at least Rs25 for a short trip down the road. From Egmore to George Town, Triplicane or Anna Salai will cost around Rs50, to Nungambakkam Rs60. Prices are at least 25% higher after 10pm. There's a prepaid booth outside Central station.

See p393 for more details on Chennai's autorickshaws.

Bus

Chennai's bus system is worth getting to know. The main city bus stand (Map pp394–5) is at Parry's Corner, and fares are between Rs4 and Rs10.

Car & Taxi

For an extended hire, organise a driver through a travel agent or large hotel. You might pay a little more, but the driver should be reliable and you'll have a point of contact should something go wrong. Non-AC rates are around Rs500 per half-day (five hours) within the city, and Rs5 per kilometre (with a daily 250km minimum) beyond city limits.

For slightly more expensive and reliable AC cabs, you can call **Manjoo Cabs** (☎ 23813083; manjoocabs@yahoo.com), a drivers' cooperative.

Train

Efficient MRTS trains run every 15 minutes from Beach station to Fort, Park (at Central Station), Egmore, Chetpet, Nungambakkam, Kodambakkam, Mambalam, Saidapet, Guindy, St Thomas Mount, Tirusulam (for the airport), and on down to Tambaram. The second

CHENNAI BUS ROUTES

Bus No	Route
1	Parry's-Central-Triplicane
5D	Koyambedu CMBT-Guindy-Adyar-Mylapore
9, 10	Parry's-Central-Egmore-T Nagar
11/11A	Parry's-Anna Salai-T Nagar
15B	Parry's-Central-Koyambedu CMBT
18	Parry's-Saidapet
19S	Parry's-Central-Adyar
27B	Egmore-Chetpet-Koyambedu CMBT
31	Parry's-Central-Vivekananda House
32	Central-Triplicane-Vivekananda House
51M	T Nagar-St Thomas Mount

line branches off at Park and hits Light House and Tirumailar (at Kapaleeshwarar Temple). Tickets cost between Rs5 and Rs10.

NORTHERN TAMIL NADU

CHENNAI TO MAMALLAPURAM

Chennai's sprawl peters after an hour or two heading south, at which point Tamil Nadu becomes open road, red dirt, khaki sand and blue skies. Currently this stretch of sand – known as the Coromandel Coast – is the only area of Tamil Nadu's 1076km coastline that's being developed for traditional beachside tourism. Small resorts, artist colonies and roadside plazas dot the way to Mamallapuram, and real-estate development signs sprout like mushrooms.

There's a tropical bohemian groove floating around Injambalkkam village, site of the **Cholamandal Artists' Village** (☎ 044-4926092; admission free; ☺ 9.30am-6.30pm). This 4-hectare artists' cooperative (18km south of Chennai) is a serene muse away from the world and a quiet chance to both see and purchase contemporary Indian art direct from the source. There are two simple studio-cum–guest houses available for visiting artists only (Rs500 per day; book well in advance).

As Cholamandal is to contemporary Indian expression, **DakshinaChitra** (☎ 044-27472603; www .dakshinachitra.net; Indian adult/student Rs75/30, foreign Rs200/75; ☺ 10am-6pm Wed-Mon) is to traditional arts and crafts. Located about 12km south of Cholamandal, this is a jumble of open-air museum, preserved village and artisan workshops – another well-worth-it stop (especially for the kids) for learning about the Dravidian crafts of Tamil Nadu, Kerala, Karnataka and Andhra Pradesh. Of special note are 17 refurbished heritage houses and recreated village-scapes. DakshinaChitra means 'A Picture of the South', which is essentially what you're provided via local pottery, silk-weaving, puppet-building and basket-making workshops, traditional theatre performances and art studios. A delightfully cool 12-room **guest house** (☎ 98414 22149; r Rs550, with AC Rs800; ☒) is in the grounds, though you might want to check your visit is not coinciding with a school overnight excursion.

You can ditch the inimitable cultural heritage of one of India's oldest states for a day at one of India's largest amusement parks: **MGM Dizzee World** (☎ 044-24981005; www.mgmdizzeeworld .com; adult/child Rs350/300; ☺ 10am-7.30pm), just north of the Crocodile Bank.

One of the best institutions of its kind in India, **Crocodile Bank** (☎ 044-27472447; www.madras crocodilebank.org; adult/child Rs30/15, camera/video Rs10/75; ☺ 8am-5.30pm Tue-Sun), 40km south of Chennai, is a fascinating peek into a world of reptiles culled from your best dinosaur dreams, and an incredible conservation trust to boot. The Bank does crucial work towards protecting the critically endangered gharial, an enormous but harmless (to humans) species of crocodilian with a long, thin nose that feeds on fish. There are thousands of other reptiles here, including the Indian mugger and saltwater crocs of the Andaman and Nicobar Islands. If you've got an open evening on the weekend, come for the **night safari** (adult/child Rs60/20; ☺ 7-8.30pm Sat & Sun), when you can shine a flashlight over the water and catch the staring eyes of thousands of the Bank's local residents.

We weren't able to visit on our last trip, but if you love your dolphins (or water slides), **Dolphin City** (☎ 04114-46370; ☺ 10am-7pm), 6km south of Crocodile Bank, is a huge water-park complex that features daily dolphin and sea-lion shows, plus a nice range of water slides, pools and kiddie rides.

About 5km north of Mamallapuram in the village of Salavankuppam, beside the East Coast Rd, the **Tiger Cave** is a rock-cut shrine, possibly dating from the 7th century. It's dedicated to Durga and has a small *mandapa* featuring a crown of carved *yali* (mythical lion creature) heads.

To reach these places, take any bus heading south from Chennai to Mamallapuram and ask to be let off at the appropriate destination. An AC taxi for a full-day tour costs about Rs1500; an autorickshaw will run Rs650 to Rs800. You can swim along the coast, but beware of strong currents and tides as there are no lifeguards around.

MAMALLAPURAM (MAHABALIPURAM)
☎ 044 / pop 12,345
Mamallapuram is a tossed salad: ancient archaeological wonders, a fine, if windy strip of sand, good biryani in local *dhabas* (snack bars) and cheap internet in the traveller ghetto, one of the few in Tamil Nadu. But don't think of it as only the latter; this World Heritage Site was

once a major seaport and second capital of the Pallava kings, and a saunter through the town's great carvings and temples at sunset, when the sandstone turns bonfire orange and blood red and modern carvers *tink-tink* with their chisels on the street, enflames the imagination.

And then…you wander down Othavadai Cross St. There are the mellow trills of Jack Johnson. Bob Marley flags hang from the balconies. Stores sell things from Tibet, 'Indian' clothes that few Indians would probably ever wear, toilet paper, hand sanitiser and used books, and you know you have landed, once again, in the Kingdom of Backpackistan.

'Mal', as many travellers call it, is less than two hours by bus from Chennai. Its beach, cheap accommodation, handicraft shops and Tamil Nadu's most highly regarded dance festival (see boxed text, p389) make it easy to see why many travellers make a beeline here straight from Chennai.

Orientation
Mamallapuram village is tiny and laid-back, with most of the action on East Raja, Othavadai and Othavadai Cross Sts; the last runs parallel to the beach. The surrounding sites of interest can be explored on foot or by bicycle.

Information
BOOKSHOPS
JK Bookshop (☎ 9840442853; 144 Othavadai St; ☺ 8.30am-9pm) A small bookshop where you can buy or swap books in several languages, including English, French and German. Proceeds support village schools established by the owner.

EMERGENCY
All Women Police station (GK Mandapa St)
Police station (Kovalam Rd)

INTERNET ACCESS
Internet access is everywhere.
AM Communication (cnr Othavadai and East Raja St; per hr Rs40; ☺ 9am-9pm)
Lakshmi Lodge Internet (5 Othavadai Cross St; per hr Rs40; ☺ 9am-10pm)

MEDICAL SERVICES
Suradeep Hospital (☎ 27442390; 15 Thirukkulam St; ☺ 24hr) Recommended by travellers.

MONEY
LKP Forex (East Raja St; ☺ 9.30am-6.30pm Mon-Sat)
State Bank of India ATM (East Raja St; ☺ 24hr)

POST
Post office (☺ 8am-4pm Mon-Fri) Located just down and to the east of the tourist office.

TOURIST INFORMATION
Tourist office (☎ 27442232; Kovalam Rd; ☺ 10am-5.45pm Mon-Fri)

Sights
You can easily spend a full day exploring the temples, *mandapas* and rock carvings around Mamallapuram. Apart from the Shore Temple and Five Rathas, admission is free. Official guides from the Archaeological Survey of India can be found at archaeological sites and hired for Rs50 (give more if the tour is good); they're well worth the money.

SHORE TEMPLE
Standing like a magnificent fist of rock-cut elegance overlooking the sea, the **Shore Temple** (combined ticket with Five Rathas Indian/foreigner Rs10/250, video Rs25; ☺ 6.30am-6pm) symbolises the heights of Pallava architecture and the maritime ambitions of the Pallava kings. Its small size belies its excellent proportion and the supreme quality of the carvings, many of which have been eroded into vaguely Impressionist embellishments. Originally constructed in the 7th century, it was later rebuilt by Narasimhavarman II and houses two central shrines to Shiva. The layout is meant to resemble the perfect cosmic body, with the head and heart located over the spire that dominates the structure. Facing east and west, the original linga (phallic images of Shiva) captured the sunrise and sunset. The temple is believed to be the last in a series of buildings that extended along a since submerged coastline; this theory gained credence during the 2004 tsunami, when receding waters revealed the outlines of what may have been sister temples. The building is now protected from further erosion by a huge rock wall, and like many of Mamallapuram's sights, it's spectacularly floodlit at night.

FIVE RATHAS
Carved from single pieces of rock, the **Five Rathas** (Five Rathas Rd; combined ticket with Shore Temple Indian/foreigner Rs10/250, video Rs25; ☺ 6.30am-6pm), are low-laying monoliths that huddle in more ancient subtlety than grandeur. Each temple is dedicated to a Hindu god and named for one of the Pandavas, the five hero-brothers of the epic Mahabharata, plus their common wife,

TAMIL NADU

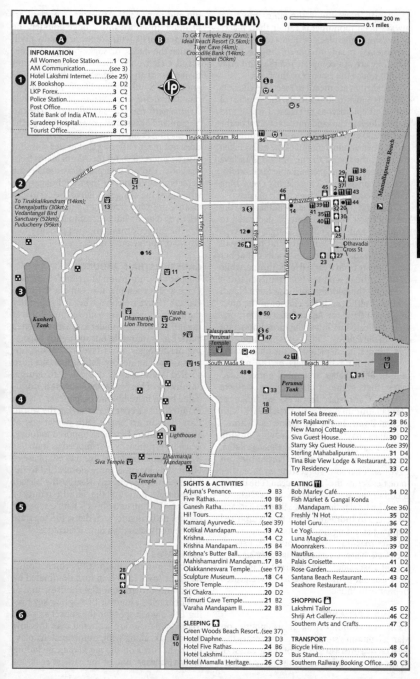

MAMALLAPURAM (MAHABALIPURAM)

0 _____ 200 m
0 _____ 0.1 miles

INFORMATION
All Women Police Station.......**1** C2
AM Communication............(see **3**)
Hotel Lakshmi Internet.......(see **25**)
JK Bookshop.........................**2** D2
LKP Forex..............................**3** C2
Police Station.......................**4** C1
Post Office............................**5** C1
State Bank of India ATM.......**6** C3
Suradeep Hospital................**7** C3
Tourist Office.......................**8** C1

To GRT Temple Bay (2km);
Ideal Beach Resort (3.5km);
Tiger Cave (4km);
Crocodile Bank (14km);
Chennai (50km)

To Tirukkalikundram (14km);
Chengalpattu (30km);
Vedantangal Bird
Sanctuary (52km);
Puducherry (95km)

Tirukkalikundram Rd

GK Mandapam St

Othavadai St

Othavadai
Cross St

Kanheri
Tank

Dharmaraja
Lion Throne

Varaha
Cave

Talasayana
Perumal
Temple

South Mada St

Beach Rd

Perumal
Tank

Lighthouse

Dharmaraja
Mandapam

Siva Temple

Adivaraha
Temple

Mamallapuram Beach

SIGHTS & ACTIVITIES
Arjuna's Penance....................**9** B3
Five Rathas.........................**10** B6
Ganesh Ratha.....................**11** B3
Hi! Tours............................**12** C2
Kamaraj Ayurvedic............(see **39**)
Kotikal Mandapam.............**13** A2
Krishna...............................**14** C2
Krishna Mandapam.............**15** B4
Krishna's Butter Ball..........**16** B3
Mahishamardini Mandapam..**17** B4
Olakkannesvara Temple......(see **17**)
Sculpture Museum..............**18** C4
Shore Temple......................**19** D4
Sri Chakra..........................**20** D2
Trimurti Cave Temple.........**21** B2
Varaha Mandapam II..........**22** B3

SLEEPING
Green Woods Beach Resort..(see **37**)
Hotel Daphne.....................**23** D3
Hotel Five Rathas...............**24** B6
Hotel Lakshmi....................**25** D2
Hotel Mamalla Heritage......**26** C3

Hotel Sea Breeze.................**27** D3
Mrs Rajalaxmi's...................**28** B6
New Manoj Cottage............**29** D2
Siva Guest House................**30** D2
Starry Sky Guest House.......(see **39**)
Sterling Mahabalipuram.......**31** D4
Tina Blue View Lodge & Restaurant..**32** D2
Try Residency.....................**33** C4

EATING
Bob Marley Café..................**34** D2
Fish Market & Gangai Konda
  Mandapam.......................(see **36**)
Freshly 'N Hot....................**35** D2
Hotel Guru.........................**36** C2
Le Yogi..............................**37** D2
Luna Magica.......................**38** D2
Moonrakers........................**39** D2
Nautilus.............................**40** D2
Palais Croisette...................**41** D2
Rose Garden.......................**42** C4
Santana Beach Restaurant....**43** D2
Seashore Restaurant............**44** D2

SHOPPING
Lakshmi Tailor....................**45** D2
Shriji Art Gallery.................**46** C2
Southern Arts and Crafts.....**47** C3

TRANSPORT
Bicycle Hire........................**48** C4
Bus Stand...........................**49** C4
Southern Railway Booking Office..**50** C3

Draupadi. Interestingly, the *rathas* may have always been monuments rather than places of worship – their lack of finials (central roof ornaments) means that according to Vedic law, they are not complete temples and ergo cannot house the essence of the gods.

The shrines are meant to resemble chariots (*ratha* is Sanskrit for chariot), the vehicles of gods and epic heroes in classical India, and were hidden in the sand until excavated by the British 200 years ago. Outside each *ratha* is a carving of an animal mount of the gods. Taken together, the layout theme of God, Pandava and animal mount is remarkable for its architectural consistency, considering everything here was cut from one big chunk of rock.

The first *ratha*, **Draupadi Ratha**, on the left after you enter the gate, is dedicated to Draupadi and the goddess Durga, who represents the sacred femineity and fertility of the Indian soil. The goddess looks out at her worshippers from a carved lotus throne, while outside, a huge sculpted lion stands guard.

Behind the goddess shrine, a huge Nandi (Shiva's bull) heralds the chariot of the most important Pandava. **Arjuna Ratha** is appropriately dedicated to Shiva, the most important deity of the Pallavas. Other gods, including the Vedic Indra, are depicted on the outer walls.

Look around the lintels of the middle temple, **Bhima Ratha**, and you'll notice faded faces that some archaeologists believe possess Caucasian features, evidence of Mamallapuram's extensive trade ties with ancient Rome. Inside is a shrine to Vishnu.

Guides may tell you the carving of king Narasimhavarman outside **Dharmaraja Ratha**, the tallest of the chariots, resembles an Egyptian pharaoh, suggesting even earlier trade ties across the Indian Ocean. The theory is tantalising, but not terribly well substantiated. The final *ratha*, **Nakula-Sahadeva Ratha**, is dedicated to Indra and has a fine sculptured elephant standing nearby. As you enter the gate approaching from the north you see its back first, hence its name **gajaprishthakara** (elephant's backside). The life-sized image is regarded as one of the most perfectly sculptured elephants in India.

ARJUNA'S PENANCE

As if we couldn't wax more poetic on Mamallapuram's stonework, along comes this **relief carving** (West Raja St), one of the greatest of its age and certainly one of the most convinc-

ing and unpretentious works of ancient art in India. Inscribed into a huge boulder, the penance bursts with scenes of Hindu myth (notice the *nagas*, or snake-beings, that descend a cleft once filled with water, meant to represent the Ganges) and everyday vignettes of South Indian life. A herd of elephants marches under armies of angels, while Arjuna performs self-mortification so he can be granted Shiva's most powerful weapon, the god-slaying Pasupata. In Hinduism, 'penance' does not mean suffering that erases sins, but distress undertaken for the sake of boons from the gods. Another interpretation: the carving depicts the penance of the sage Bhagaritha, who asked the Ganges to fall to the earth and cleanse the ashes (and ergo, sins) of his dead relatives. There's humour amid the holy: notice the cat performing his own penance to a crowd of appreciative mice.

GANESH RATHA & AROUND

This *ratha* is northwest of Arjuna's Penance. Once a Shiva temple, it became a shrine to Ganesh (Shiva's elephant-headed son) after the original lingam was removed. Just north of the *ratha* is a huge boulder known as **Krishna's Butter Ball**. Immovable, but apparently balancing precariously, it's a favourite photo opportunity. The nearby **Kotikal Mandapa** (also spelled Mandapam) is dedicated to Durga. Southwest of here is **Varahu Mandapa II**, dominated by an incredibly active panel of Vishnu manifested as a boar avatar saving the world. Early Hindu art is rife with depictions of Vishnu in animal form, as opposed to today, when he is primarily worshipped as Rama or Krishna, which suggests this nascent phase of Hindu theology was more closely tied to the tribal worship of Adivasis. Nearby, the **Trimurti Cave Temple** honours the Hindu trinity – Brahma, Vishnu and Shiva – with a separate section dedicated to each deity; the separate shrine for Brahma is a rare occurrence.

MANDAPAS

Mamallapuram's main hill, which dominates the town (and is in turn dominated by a red-and-brownstone lighthouse), makes for an excellent hour or two of low-key hiking (it's a good spot for the sunset as well). Many *mandapas* are scattered over this low rise of rock, along with, unfortunately, plastic trash. Focus on the *mandapas*, including **Krishna Mandapa**, one of the earliest rock-cut temples around. The famous carving depicts both a rural pastiche and Krishna lifting up Govardhana mountain to protect his kinsfolk from the wrath of Indra. Other shrines include **Mahishamardini Mandapa**, just a few metres southwest of the lighthouse. Scenes from the Puranas (Sanskrit stories dating from the 5th century AD) are depicted on the *mandapa* with the sculpture of the goddess Durga considered one of the finest.

Above the *mandapa* are the remains of the 8th-century **Olakkannesvara Temple**, and spectacular views of Mamallapuram. Photography is forbidden here for 'security reasons' – there's a nuclear power station a few kilometres south.

SCULPTURE MUSEUM

This **museum** (East Raja St; adult/child Rs2/1, camera Rs10; ⊗ 9am-5.30pm) contains more than 3000 sculptures and paintings that run the gamut from interesting stonework to still-life depictions of fruit bowls that could have been found in grandma's basement. We can safely say: you get your Rs2 worth.

Activities

BEACH

Mamallapuram's beach, or at least the bit that fronts the village, isn't exactly pristine and gets downright dingy in some spots, but if you walk a bit north or south of the Shore Temple it clears into very fine sand. You'll also be further away from the leers of men who love spending their days out here gawking at tourists. It's not a great place for swimming – there are dangerous rips – but it's possible to go fishing in one of local outriggers; negotiate a price with the owner.

THERAPIES

There are numerous places offering massage, reiki, yoga and ayurvedic practices. Sessions cost around Rs350 for 30 to 45 minutes. **Krishna** (Siesta; Othavadai St) is recommended by both male and female travellers, as is Kamaraj Ayurvedic, which can be contacted through Moonrakers restaurant (p412).

Sri Chakra (Othavadai St; massage per hr Rs300; ⊗ 8am-9pm) offers ayurvedic massage as well as yoga sessions (Rs150) at 7am.

There are many other operators in town with similar rates and timings. As always, and especially for such an intimate service, ask fellow travellers, question the massage thera-

pist carefully and if you have any misgivings, don't proceed.

Tours

Hi! Tours (☎ 27443360; www.hi-tours.com; 123 East Raja St) runs bicycle tours to sights like the Tiger Cave. Tours run from 8am to 2pm and include guide and lunch. Hi! Tours also organises day trips to Kanchipuram (p414) and Vedantangal Bird Sanctuary (p413).

Sleeping

BUDGET

Hotel Five Rathas (r from Rs100) Tucked into the alleys across from the Five Rathas, this place has clean concrete rooms that have been livened up with murals that look like Hindu temple art pressed through an acid trip. It's an idiosyncratic place run by a sweet old man, but be aware the psychedelic character doesn't just apply to the decor.

Mrs Rajalaxmi's (☎ 27442460; from r Rs150) Like many of the family-run hotels near the Five Rathas, this is a friendly and homey spot. The rooms are basic, but fresh coats of paint and a transitory clientele of eccentrics give this spot a bit of character.

Tina Blue View Lodge & Restaurant (☎ 27442319; 34 Othavadai St; r Rs150-300) Tina is one of Mamallapuram's originals and kind of looks it, but remains deservedly popular for its whitewashed walls, pale-blue accents and tropically pleasant garden, if not its facilities, which are getting a bit rusty.

Green Woods Beach Resort (☎ 27442212; green woods_resort@yahoo.com; 7 Othavadai Cross St; d without/with AC Rs 300/750; ✷) You enter off of the side of Othavadai cross into…well, not Green Woods, but quite a nice garden that makes for a sweet communal area, assuming enough guests are staying. If not, it's still a leafy place to pass a lazy hot day. The rooftop rooms are the best deal in the house.

Lakshmi Lodge (☎ 27442463; 5 Othavadai Cross St; d Rs200-500, with AC Rs850; ✷ ▢ ✷) The Lakshmi is a backpacker standard with a huge number of rooms on offer and a plethora of travel services (internet, taxi booking etc) available on the ground floor. There's a tanklike swimming pool (empty in the low season) and friendly (if slightly overbearing) owners thrown in free of charge.

Starry Sky Guest House (☎ 27443726; 2B Othavadai Cross St; d from Rs250; ✷) The title isn't a misnomer – you can get nice views of the night sky from the rooftop verandah of this hotel, which otherwise offers clean and cheap rooms that are good value for money.

Siva Guest House (☎ 27443234; sivaguesthouse@ hotmail.com; 2 Othavadai Cross St; d Rs250, with AC Rs800; ❂) Deservedly popular with travellers, Siva gets consistently good reports. Rooms are spotless and each has a small verandah.

ourpick **Hotel Daphne** (☎ 27442811; hoteldaphne1@ yahoo.com; 17 Othavadai Cross St; d Rs350, with AC Rs750; ❂) This cubist complex conceals spotless rooms that resemble Ikea showpieces that somehow stumbled into India. It's a decided step above the rest of the backpacker-blah accommodation, and the upper-floor rooms are great spots for lazing about and generally vegetating.

MIDRANGE & TOP END

New Manoj Cottage (☎ 9840387095; newmanojcottage@ yahoo.com; 136 Fisherman Colony; r Rs500-700) The un-signed Manoj (it's across from New Papillon Le Bistro restaurant) is a family-run homestay with three spacious and well-kept rooms that are the easy equivalent of most midrange ac-commodation in town.

Hotel Sea Breeze (☎ 27443035; www.nivalink .com/seabreeze; Othavadai Cross St; r from Rs900; ❂ 🏊) The Sea Breeze is a nice hotel of the reliably middle-class beachfront-escape school of design, but the real draw is the pool, which nonguests can use for Rs150.

Try Residency (☎ 27442728; tryresidency@gmail .com; East Raja St; r Rs800, with AC Rs1300; ❂) Rooms are exceptionally large and some overlook Mamallapuram's algae-laden tank (mmm). There's not a lot of character, but if you need some Western-style amenities, it's not a bad option.

Hotel Mamalla Heritage (☎ 27442060; www.hotel mamallaheritage.com; 104 East Raja St; s/d with AC from Rs1100/1900; ❂ 🏊) In town, this corporate-y place has large comfortable rooms, all with fridge, and charmingly friendly service. The pool's a decent size, and there's a quality veg and rooftop restaurant.

Sterling Mahabalipuram (☎ 27443914; http:// mahabalipuram.indecohotels.com; Shore Temple Rd; d Rs 4950; ❂ 🏊) The grounds and lobby of this gardeny resort are green and lovely – very much the whole India heritage hotel thing gussied up and paraded in chintzy glory. Unfortunately the same can't be said for the rooms, which, while serviceable, are overpriced. You'll get much the same amenities for half the cost at

the other high-end and even midrange resorts in town, although the packaging here is ad-mittedly a lot nicer.

Ideal Beach Resort (☎ 27442240; www.idealresort .com; s/d Rs4000/5000, cottages from Rs5000; ❂ 🖥 🏊) With a landscaped garden setting and com-fortable rooms or cottages, this low-key beachfront resort is popular with package tours and Chennai expats. The design is small and secluded enough to have an intimate atmosphere and there's a lovely open-air poolside restaurant. It's about 3.5km north of town.

GRT Temple Bay (☎ 27443636; www.grttemplebay .com; r from Rs8000; ❂ 🖥 🏊) This is the best of the luxury resorts that lie to the north of town. It's got everything you need to feel like water-front royalty, including 24-hour service, a spa, sauna, health club and prices that are probably a little much all things considered.

Eating & Drinking

Restaurateurs near Othavadai Cross St have realised travellers want open-air ambience, soft music and humble service, and generally provide all of the above, along with decent Western mains and bland Indian curries. If you want real Indian food, there are some genuinely good biryani (rice cooked in stock and flavoured with spices) stalls and cheap thali joints near the bus stand. The third op-tion is seafood, which is generally fresh, tasty and (relatively) pricey. Most places – licensed or not – serve beer, but be sensitive to the 11pm local curfew; if you persuade a restau-rant to allow you to linger over last drinks, it's the owner, not you, who faces a hefty fine. That said, on an almost rotating basis one restaurant in town will break curfew and this place ends up being where the party is come 11pm. All places listed are open for breakfast, lunch and dinner.

Palais Croisette (8 Othavadai St; mains 40-120) On the roof of Hotel Ramakrishna, the Palais manages very nice pasta (put it this way: it came recommended by an Italian traveller) and similarly good fresh seafood.

Rose Garden (Beach Rd; mains around Rs50) This is one of the better biryani shops in a town that's surprisingly full of joints serving this tasty treat. The other spot locals recommend for similar fare (and prices) is the unaffiliated Hotel Guru, located behind the fish market. Expect a barren atmosphere and great food at both spots.

Freshly 'N Hot (Othavadai Cross St; mains from Rs50) Yes, the name makes no sense, and we're not sure it's some cute misspelling either, considering the guys who run this open-air cafe have so many other Western standards down. Especially the ice coffee: hands down the best in town.

Nautilus (Othavadai Cross St; mains from Rs50) The Nautilus seems perpetually buzzing with every traveller you've ever met talking about how much they loved/hated/got-ripped-off-in Goa/Varanasi/Hampi/Cochi while eating eggs on toast and drinking smoothies.

Moonrakers (34 Othavadai St; mains Rs60-150) Like it or not, you'll likely end up here at some stage; it's the sort of place that draws travellers. Probably because it's a three-storey resto-bar complex that dominates the backpacker-ghetto streetscape. Food is OK, ambience is better and beer is enjoyable from the top-floor verandah.

Le Yogi (☎ 27442571; Othavadai St; mains Rs70-150) This is without doubt the best Western food in town. The steaks, pastas and pizzas are genuine and tasty (if small), service is stellar, and the airy dining area, with wooden accents, flickering candlelight and billowing fabrics, is romantic as all get out.

Beachside Bob Marley Café, Seashore Restaurant, Santana Beach Restaurant and Luna Magica are all recommended for fresh seafood; you'll get a good plate of fish for around Rs150.

Shopping

Mamallapuram wakes to the sound of sculptors' chisels on granite, and you'll inevitably be approached by someone trying to sell you everything from a Rs90 stone pendant to a Rs400,000 Ganesh that needs to be lifted with a mobile crane. There are lots of good art galleries, tailors and antique shops here. For clothes, we recommend **Lakshmi Tailor** (Othavadai St), across from Moonrakers. Nice prints and original art can be found at **Shriji Art Gallery** (11/1 Othavadai St), and expensive but beautiful curios culled from local homes at **Southern Arts and Crafts** (☎ 27443675; 72 East Raja St).

Getting There & Away

There are at least 30 buses a day running to/from Chennai (Rs25, two hours, 30 daily). To Chennai airport take bus 108B (Rs25, two hours, four daily). There are also at least nine daily buses to Puducherry (Rs35, two hours)

and Kanchipuram (Rs20, two hours, 11 daily) via Tirukkalikundram.

Taxis are available from the bus station. Long-distance trips require plenty of bargaining. It's about Rs900 to Chennai or the airport.

You can make train reservations at the **Southern Railway Booking Office** (East Raja St).

Getting Around

The easiest way to get around is on foot, though on a hot day it's quite a hike to see all the monuments. Bicycles or mopeds (we recommend the former; Mamallapuram is pretty small) can be rented through most guest houses and at numerous stalls along East Raja St.

AROUND MAMALLAPURAM

About 14km west of Mamallapuram in Tirukkalikundram is the hilltop **Vedagirishvara Temple** (admission Rs2; ⏰ 8.30am-1pm & 5-7pm) dedicated to Shiva. It's often called the Eagle Temple; according to legend two eagles come here each day at noon from Varanasi, a good 2000km away (they often don't turn up on time). It might also be called the Eagle Temple because that's what you should be if you want to visit the shrine.

You climb (and climb and climb) the 550 smooth steps to the hilltop bare-footed. Once there, the temple contains two beautiful shrines and incredible views over the rich green rice paddies in every direction. It's lovely – if busy – in the late afternoon, but the middle of the day (while making for a hot climb) is very peaceful when the temple itself is closed. You can get here by bus or bicycle from Mamallapuram.

VEDANTANGAL BIRD SANCTUARY

Located about 52km from Mamallapuram, this wildlife **sanctuary** (admission Rs5; ⏰ 6am-6pm) is one of the best birdwatching places in South India and is an important breeding ground for waterbirds – cormorants, egrets, herons, ibises, spoonbills, storks, grebes and pelicans – that migrate here from October to March. At the height of the breeding season (December and January) there can be up to 30,000 birds nesting in the mangroves, and the best viewing times are early morning and late afternoon; head for the watchtower and look down on the noisy nests across the water.

Big and comfortable rooms are available at the **Forest Department Resthouse** (d Rs 300), a lovely quiet spot 500m before the sanctuary. You're supposed to book in advance with the **Wildlife Warden's Office** (WWO; Map pp394–5; ☎ 24321471; 4th fl, DMS office, 259 Anna Salai, Teynampet) in Chennai – good luck – but in practice the caretaker will probably find a room for you if one's available. You may be offered food if you arrive unexpectedly; come with snacks just in case, or if you have transport be prepared to drive 10km or so to the nearest evening food stall.

To get there by public transport, first get to Chengalpattu, an hour's bus ride from Mamallapuram (see p413). From here you can take a bus to Vedantangal via Padalam, where you may have to change buses at the road junction. Most Vedantangal buses go directly to the sanctuary entrance, others to the village bus station, from where the sanctuary is a 1km walk south. Visitors also often make a day trip by AC taxi from Mamallapuram; this should cost around Rs1000.

KANCHIPURAM
☎ 044 / pop 188,763

The old capital of the Pallava dynasty is a typical Tamil Nadu temple town: modern India at its frenetic best dappled with houses of worship that form a veritable dialogue with history in stone. Kanchi (as it's often called) is also famed for its silk production and quality saris. It's best visited as a day trip from Mamallapuram or Chennai, as there's not a lot to see outside of the justifiably famous temples.

Orientation & Information

The city is on the main Chennai–Bengaluru road, 76km southwest of Chennai. There's no tourist office, but for information online check out www.hellokanchipuram.com. On Kamaraja St there's a small cluster of cheap internet cafes. Changing travellers cheques can be a hassle, so it's best to use local ATMs.

Googly (144 Kamaraja St; per hr Rs25; ☉ 9am-9pm) Internet access.

ICICI Bank ATM (Gandhi Rd)

Netcafé (148 Kamaraja St; per hr Rs25; ☉ 9am-9pm) Internet access.

State Bank of India ATM (Hospital Rd)

Sights

All temples are open from 6am to 12.30pm and 4pm to 8.30pm. Most have free admission.

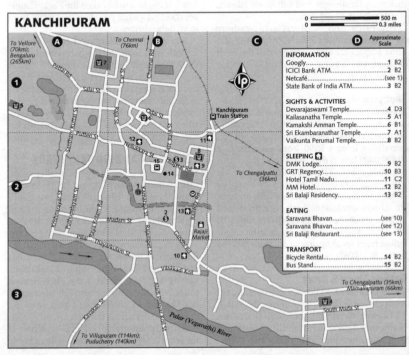

KANCHIPURAM

| 0 | 500 m |
| 0 | 0.3 miles |

Approximate Scale

INFORMATION
Googly...................................1 B2
ICICI Bank ATM.......................2 B2
Netcafé...............................(see 1)
State Bank of India ATM............3 B2

SIGHTS & ACTIVITIES
Devarajaswami Temple..............4 D3
Kailasanatha Temple.................5 A1
Kamakshi Amman Temple...........6 B1
Sri Ekambaranathar Temple........7 A1
Vaikunta Perumal Temple...........8 B2

SLEEPING
DMK Lodge............................9 B2
GRT Regency.........................10 B3
Hotel Tamil Nadu....................11 C2
MM Hotel.............................12 B2
Sri Balaji Residency.................13 B2

EATING
Saravana Bhavan..................(see 10)
Saravana Bhavan..................(see 12)
Sri Balaji Restaurant..............(see 13)

TRANSPORT
Bicycle Rental.......................14 B2
Bus Stand............................15 B2

Kanchipuram & Kung Fu?

One of Asia's most famous historical personalities is Bodhidharma, a Buddhist monk credited with bringing Chan Buddhism – better known by its Japanese title, 'Zen' – to China. Like King Arthur, Bodhidharma's historical origins are lost to legend, and he may actually be an amalgamation of several real-life individuals, but many sources say he was born in the 5th century in Kanchipuram. Supposedly, Bodhidharma travelled to China, where he taught and popularised Chan Buddhism, which later spread to Korea and Japan. Legends also say Bodhidharma instructed disciples at the Shaolin Monastery (of Every Kung Fu Movie Ever fame) in Varma Kalai (The Art of Vital Points), a South Indian martial art that is practised in Tamil Nadu today. In China, the self-defence style evolved into Kung Fu. We should note this version of events is disputed by many Chinese, although it carries a lot of weight in this corner of South India, where Tamil action heroes fight using moves inspired by Varma Kalai, along with good old Indian cinematic moustache-fu.

KAILASANATHA TEMPLE

The oldest temple in Kanchi is the most impressive, not for its size or grandeur but weight of historical presence. Dedicated to Shiva, the Kailasanatha Temple was built by the Pallava king Rajasimha in the 7th century. The low-slung sandstone compound is chock-a-block with fascinating carvings, including many half-animal deities that were in vogue during the period of early Dravidian architecture.

The remaining fragments of 8th-century murals are visible reminders of how magnificent the original temple must have looked. There are 58 small shrines honouring Shiva and Parvati and their sons, Ganesh and Murugan.

It's worth your while to hire an official guide from the Archaeological Survey of India (Rs50). Non-Hindus are allowed into the inner sanctum here, where there is a prismatic lingam – the largest in town and third-largest in Asia.

SRI EKAMBARANATHAR TEMPLE

This Shiva temple is one of the largest in the city, covering 12 hectares and dominated by a 59m-high *gopuram*. The carvings feel alive and beautiful, but still weighted with five centuries of history; they were first chiselled out by artisans in 1509 during the Vijayanagar empire. The temple's name is said to derive from Eka Amra Nathar – Lord of the Mango Tree – and there is an old mango tree, with four branches representing the four Vedas (sacred Hindu texts) on-site.

Non-Hindus cannot enter the inner sanctum, but here's an idea of what you'd find inside: according to legend, the goddess Kamakshi worshipped Shiva here in

the form of a lingam made of sand, which still lies at the heart of the temple. Thus, Sri Ekambaranathar is the temple of Earth and one of the five elemental temples of Shiva. The sand linga is inscribed with carvings of 108 smaller lingam. Also of note is the mirror chamber, an electricity-free room that worshippers enter with candles. The central image of Shiva is reflected in the candlelight across the mirrored walls, creating countless images of the god that allude to his infinite presence.

KAMAKSHI AMMAN TEMPLE

This imposing temple is dedicated to the goddess Parvati in her guise as Kamakshi (She Whose Eyes Awaken Desire). To the right of the temple's entrance is the marriage hall, with wonderful ornate pillars, and directly ahead is the main shrine topped with a golden *vimana* (legendary flying chariot). Again, non-Hindus cannot enter the sanctum, where Kamakshi/ Parvati is depicted, uncharacteristically, in the lotus position. Each February/March carriages housing statues of the temple deities are hauled through the streets; this procession should not be missed if you're in the vicinity.

DEVARAJASWAMI TEMPLE

Dedicated to Vishnu, this enormous **monument** (admission Rs2, camera/video Rs 5/100) was built by the Vijayanagars and is among the most impressive of Kanchipuram's temples. It has a beautifully sculptured '1000-pillared' hall (only 96 of the original 1000 remain) as well as a marriage hall commemorating the wedding of Vishnu and Lakshmi. One of the temple's most notable features is a huge chain carved from a single piece of stone which can be seen at each corner of the *mandapa*. The annual temple festival is in May. This temple is supposedly the best around to receive cures from lizard-related illnesses thanks to twin silver- and gold-plated reptiles that crawl over the temple ceiling, where they devour platinum cockroaches (kidding).

Every 40 years the waters of the temple tank are drained, revealing a huge wooden statue of Vishnu which is worshipped for 48 days. You may like to hang around for the next viewing – in 2019. Otherwise, float festivals (when deities are literally floated cross the reservoir) are held on the tank three times a year.

VAIKUNTA PERUMAL TEMPLE
Roughly 1200 years old and dedicated to Vishnu, this temple was built shortly after the Kailasanatha. The cloisters inside the outer wall consist of lion pillars and represent the first phase in the architectural evolution of the grand 1000-pillared halls. The main shrine, rather uniquely spread over three levels, contains images of Vishnu in standing, sitting and reclining positions, as well as riding his preferred mount, the Garuda (eagle). There's another monitor lizard icon here that, if touched, cleanses worshippers of lizard-related sins.

Sleeping & Eating
Kanchi's cheap pilgrims' lodges are shabby, but there are a few decent midrange options.

DMK Lodge (☎ 9380913144; Nellukkara St; r from Rs150) Basically a lodge for members of the DMK political party, this is a friendly spot but the rooms are pretty tatty (like every other budget place in town).

Sri Balaji Residency (☎ 47203868; sribalajiresidency@ gmail.com; 124 Railway Rd; s/d from Rs300/500; 🍽) This is your best bet in town: big clean rooms at a cutthroat price with polished floors, colour TVs and an excellent restaurant downstairs.

Hotel Tamil Nadu (☎ 27222553; d Rs490, with AC Rs800; 🍽) A study in government-run mediocrity, this hotel opposite the railway station has wide, airy rooms set off with scrubbed tile floors, and the character of a blank piece of paper.

MM Hotel (☎ 27227250; www.mmhotels.com; 65 Nellukkara St; d Rs650, with AC Rs990; 🍽) A good-value, busy and clean hotel, frequented by Indian businesspeople. A Saravana Bhavan veg restaurant is next door, with a welcome AC dining room.

GRT Regency (☎ 27225250; www.grthotels.com; 487 Gandhi Rd; s/d Rs1750/2250; 🍽 💻) While it's not the

best setting on the noisy main road, the rooms here are the probably the cleanest and most comfortable you'll find in Kanchi. There is yet another Saravana Bhavan – we like to think of it as the vegetarian McDonald's (well, a lot better) of Tamil Nadu – located here.

Getting There & Away
The busy bus stand is in the centre of town. See the boxed text (below) for services.

Regular suburban trains leave from Beach, Fort or Egmore stations in Chennai direct to Kanchipuram.

Getting Around
Bicycles can be hired (per hour/day Rs3/40) from stalls around the bus station. An auto-rickshaw for a half-day tour of the five main temples (around Rs200) will inevitably involve a stop at a silk shop.

VELLORE
☎ 0416 / pop 386,746
For a dusty bazaar town, Vellore feels both cosmopolitan and majestic, thanks to its massive Vijayanagar fort and the Christian Medical College (CMC) Hospital, one of the finest hospitals in India. The hospital attracts international medical students as well as patients from all over India, and the town is worth a day for soaking up both its historical ambience and small-town-but-international vibe.

Information
There are several internet cafes along Ida Scudder Rd in front of the hospital.

State Bank of India (102 Ida Scudder Rd) Money can be exchanged here and there's an ATM.

Surfzone (Ida Scudder Rd) Internet cafe next to the State Bank of India.

Tourist office (🕙 10am-5.45pm Mon-Fri)

BUSES FROM KANCHIPURAM			
Destination	Fare (Rs)	Duration (hr)	Frequency
Bengaluru	120-150	5	2 daily
Chennai	20-24.50	2	every 10min
Mamallapuram	25	2	9 daily
Puducherry	35	3	12 daily
Tiruvannamalai	40	3	22 daily
Trichy	105	7	5 daily
Vellore	20	1½	every 15min

Sights

The solid walls and dry moat of the splendid **Vellore Fort** dominate the west side of town. It was built in the 16th century and passed briefly into the hands of the Marathas in 1676 and the Mughals in 1708. The British occupied the fort in 1760 following the fall of Srirangapatnam and the death of Tipu Sultan. These days it houses various government offices, parade grounds, a university, a church, an ancient mosque and a police recruiting school.

At the west side of the fort complex, the small **national government museum** (admission free; 9am-5pm Sat-Thu) contains sculptures dating back to Pallava and Chola times. Next door, pretty **St James' Church** (1846) is only open for Sunday services.

On the east side, the **Tamil Nadu government museum** (Indian/foreigner Rs5/100; 9am-5pm Sat-Thu) displays hero stones in the forecourt dating from the 8th century and depicting the stories of war heroes in battle. The dusty exhibits have seen much better days, but the small collection of tribal clothes and artefacts is interesting.

Near the fort entrance, **Jalakanteshwara Temple** (6am-1pm & 3-8pm), a gem of late Vijayanagar architecture, was built about 1566. Check out the small detailed sculptures on the walls of the marriage hall. During the invasions by the Adil Shahis of Bijapur, the Marathas and the Carnatic nawabs (Muslim ruling princes), the temple was occupied by a garrison and temple rituals ceased. Now it's once again a place of worship.

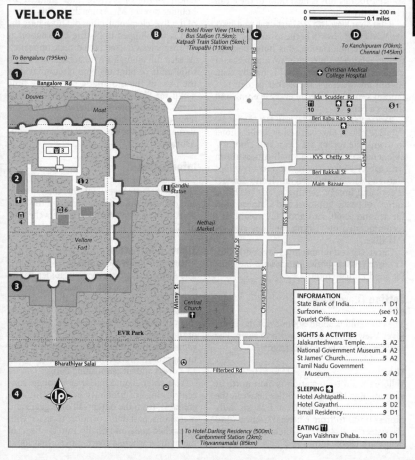

VELLORE

To Hotel River View (1km); Bus Station (1.5km); Katpadi Train Station (5km); Tirupathi (110km)

To Bengaluru (195km)

To Kanchipuram (70km); Chennai (145km)

Bangalore Rd

Christian Medical College Hospital

Douves

Moat

Ida Scudder Rd

Beri Babu Rao St

KVS Chetty St

Gandhi Statue

Beri Bakkali St

Main Bazaar

Nethaji Market

Vellore Fort

EVR Park

Central Church

Bharathiyar Salai

Filterbed Rd

To Hotel Darling Residency (500m); Cantonment Station (2km); Tiruvannamalai (85km)

INFORMATION	
State Bank of India	1 D1
Surfzone	(see 1)
Tourist Office	2 A2

SIGHTS & ACTIVITIES	
Jalakanteshwara Temple	3 A2
National Government Museum	4 A2
St James' Church	5 A2
Tamil Nadu Government Museum	6 A2

SLEEPING	
Hotel Ashtapathi	7 D1
Hotel Gayathri	8 D2
Ismail Residency	9 D1

EATING	
Gyan Vaishnav Dhaba	10 D1

TAMIL NADU

Sleeping & Eating

Vellore's cheapest hotels are concentrated along the roads south of and parallel to the hospital, mostly catering to people in town for treatment; there are many to choose from on Beri Babu Rao St. Decent midrange hotels are scattered further afield.

Hotel Gayathri (☎ 2227714; 22 Beri Babu Rao St; s/d Rs150/230) This dingy place has impersonal service and squat toilets, but at least the shared balconies let in some light.

Hotel Ashtapathi (☎ 2224602; Ida Scudder Rd; r Rs400, with AC Rs520; 🕃) It's small, clean and good value here, but ask for a room off the noisy roadside. There's a decent veg restaurant attached.

Ismail Residency (☎ 2223216; Ida Scudder Rd; s/d Rs420/575; 🕃) A five-room lodge with tatty but spotless rooms, this is next door to the clean Hotel Arthy restaurant.

Hotel River View (☎ 2225251; Katpadi Rd; d Rs900, with AC Rs1300; 🕃) North of the town centre and close to the bus station, this hotel benefits from a relatively quiet location and pleasant gardens, but the 'river view' is hardly that. Rooms are spacious, the Shikar garden restaurant serves a barbecue every evening and there's a bar.

Darling Residency (☎ 2213001; 11/8 Officers Line; s/d Rs1300/1400; 🕃) Recognised as the best hotel in town. The rooms are clean and comfortable, and there's even a small fitness room with exercise bike. The rooftop Aranya Roof Garden Restaurant (open lunch and dinner) is cool and breezy, serving salads (Rs25), a variety of pasta, tandoori and Chinese food for around Rs60, and good ice cream. It's recommended by visiting medicos and locals alike.

Cheap veg restaurants line Ida Scudder Rd. Try **Gyan Vaishnav Dhaba** (Ida Scudder Rd; thalis Rs25) for good Punjabi food.

Getting There & Away
BUS

The bus stand is about 500m from the Hotel River View, 1.5km to the north of town. For services, see the boxed text (right).

TRAIN

Vellore's main train station is 5km north at Katpadi. Bus 192 (Rs2) shuttles between the station and town. There are at least six daily express trains to/from Chennai Central (2nd class/sleeper Rs45/67), which continue to Bengaluru (Rs65/120).

BUSES FROM VELLORE

Destination	Fare (Rs)	Duration (hr)	Frequency
Chennai	46-60	3	every 10min
Bengaluru	80-95	5	every 30min
Kanchipuram	20	2	every 15min
Tiruvannamalai	40	2	every 5min
Trichy (direct)	110	7	4 daily

TIRUVANNAMALAI
☎ 04175 / pop 130,567

There are temple towns, there are mountain towns, and there are temple-mountain towns where God appears as a phallus of fire. Welcome to Tiruvannamalai. About 85km south of Vellore and flanked by boulder-strewn Mt Arunachala, this is one of the five 'elemental' cities of Shiva; here the god is worshipped in his fire incarnation as Arunachaleswar (see boxed text, opposite). At each full moon Mt Arunachala swells with thousands of pilgrims who circumnavigate the base of the mountain, but at any time you'll see Shaivite priests, sadhus (spiritual men) and devotees gathered around the temple. Tiruvannamalai is also home to the Sri Ramana (also known as Sri Ramanasramam) Ashram.

Information

The main post office is just off the road to Gingee; there are several internet cafes in town and opposite the ashram. Although the State Bank of India won't change travellers cheques, its ATM accepts international cards.

Sights & Activities
ARUNACHALESWAR TEMPLE

The Arunachaleswar is awash in golden flames and the roasting scent of burning ghee, as befits the fire incarnation of the Destroyer of the Universe. Covering some 10 hectares, this vast **temple** (🕙 6am-1pm & 5.30-10pm) is one of the largest in India. Four large unpainted *gopurams*, one for each cardinal point, front the approaches, with the eastern tower rising 13 storeys and an astonishing 66m.

You enter Arunachaleswar through concentric rings of profanity evolving into sacredness, from the outer wall of beggars and merchants, past dark corridors recessed with bejewelled gods, and finally, into the heart of the temple, where a roaring oven that looks like a fire-spewing walnut shell is tended by temple Brahmins in front of a lingam. *Puja* is performed daily at 8am, 10am, 6pm, 8pm and 9.30pm.

MT ARUNACHALA
Known as Sonachalam (Red Mountain) in Sanskrit, this 800m-high extinct volcano dominates Tiruvannamalai and local conceptions of the element of fire, which supposedly finds its sacred abode in Arunachala's heart. On full-moon and festival days thousands of pilgrims circumnavigate the 14km base of the mountain. If you're not quite that devoted, an autorickshaw will take you around – stopping at small temples and shrines along the way – for around Rs150. An alternative is to pick up a circle map from the ashram office, hire a bicycle (per hour Rs3) from the road near the entrance, and bike your way around.

You can make a sort of phallus pilgrimage here by visiting eight famous linga dotted around the mountain's cardinal and subcardinal spokes. The names of the linga shrines (which share names with Hindu deities), from east to west, are Indra, Agni, Yama, Niruthi, Necrannamla, Varuna, Vaya, Kubera and Esanya. Also, watch out for the field of a thousand linga, 'planted' by domestic and overseas donators from Malaysia to America.

For a superb view of the Arunachaleswar Temple, climb part or all the way up the hill (about four hours return). There's a signed path that leads up through village homes near the northwest corner of the temple, passing two caves, **Virupaksha** and **Skandasramam**. Sri Ramana Maharshi lived and meditated in these caves for more than 20 years from 1899 to 1922, after which he and his growing band of spiritual followers established the ashram.

SRI RAMANA ASHRAM
This tranquil **ashram** (☎ 237292; www.ramana -maharshi.org; ☽ office 8-11am & 2-5pm), 2km southwest of Tiruvannamalai, draws devotees of Sri Ramana Maharshi, a guru who died in 1950 after nearly 50 years in contemplation. It's a very relaxed place, set in green surrounds, where visitors are able to meditate or worship the shrine where the guru achieved samadhi (conscious exit from the body). Day visits are permitted but *devotees only* may stay at the ashram by applying in writing, preferably at least three months in advance.

Sleeping & Eating
Tiruvannamalai is best visited as a day trip from Puducherry. There are budget lodges around the temple, but quality is lacking. During festival time (November/December) prices can rise by a staggering 1000%.

Arunachala Ramana Home (☎ 236120; www .arhometvm.com; 70 Ramana Nagar, Chengam Rd; s/d from Rs200/300) Basic, clean and friendly, it's close to the fabulous Manna Café which answers any need for non-Indian food, including salads (Rs25), pastas and cakes. Plenty of chai stalls and veg cafes are nearby.

Hotel Ganesh (☎ 2226701; 111A Big St; d Rs245, with AC Rs645; ✖) On the busy bazaar road running along the north side of the temple, Ganesh is a little haven of peace and value. Some rooms are poky, but they're clean enough and the inner-courtyard balcony is pleasant. There's a decent veg restaurant downstairs.

Hotel Arunai Anantha (☎ 237275; www.arunaianan tha.com; s/d from Rs1500/2000; ✖ ☑) The big draws at this fairly deluxe hotel, about 1km beyond the ashram, are the landscaped gardens and swimming pool. For deluxe rooms add Rs300; they're worth it for the extra size and comfort.

THE LINGAM OF FIRE
Legend has it that Shiva appeared as a column of fire on Mt Arunachala, creating the original symbol of the lingam. Each November/December full moon, the **Karthikai Deepam Festival** celebrates this legend throughout India but becomes particularly significant at Tiruvannamalai. Here, a huge fire, lit from a 30m wick immersed in 2000L of ghee, blazes from the top of Mt Arunachala for days. In homes, lamps honour Shiva and his fiery lingam. The fire symbolises Shiva's light, which eradicates darkness and evil.

At festival time up to half a million people come to Tiruvannamalai. In honour of Shiva, they scale the mountain or circumnavigate its base. On the upward path, steps quickly give way to jagged and unstable rocks. There's no shade, the sun is relentless and the journey must be undertaken in bare feet – a mark of respect to the deity. None of this deters the thousands of pilgrims who quietly and joyfully make their way to the top and the abode of their deity.

Getting There & Away

There are buses every half-hour to Chennai (Rs62, 3½ hours) and Vellore (Rs40, two hours). There are at least three daily buses to Puducherry (Rs31, three hours). A taxi to Puducherry (via Gingee) costs around Rs800.

Only local passenger trains use Tiruvannamalai train station – two trains a day pass through between Vellore and Villupuram (where you can change for Puducherry).

GINGEE (SENJI)

☎ 04145

Somewhere 37km east of Tiruvannamalai, nature sprinkled a smattering of marbles – rounded boulders and lumpy rocks – in shades of grey, brown and red over the flat green paddies of Tamil Nadu. Then man turned two of these stony protrusions into the King and Queen of Forts: **Rajagiri & Krishnagiri** (King & Queen Fort; Indian/foreigner Rs5/100; ⏲ 9am-5pm). Constructed mainly in the 16th century by the Vijayanagars (though some structures date from the 13th century), these edifices, which poke out of the Tamil plain like castles misplaced by the *Lord of the Rings*, have been occupied by the Marathas, the Mughals, the French and finally, the British.

It's a good hike to the top of either fort, but along the way you'll pass through several monuments, from *gopurams* to granaries. And hassle is almost non-existent (besides a few wandering sadhus); when you're here, it's you, a few friendly Indian tourists and lots of monkeys. A walk around will take half a day, especially if you cross the road and make the steep ascent to Krishnagiri. Buildings within Rajagiri (on the south side of the road) include a Shiva temple, a mosque and – most prominent – the restored audience hall. Almost all have been marred by graffiti.

It's easy to take a day trip to Gingee from Puducherry (67km) or Tiruvannamalai (37km). Buses leave every 30 minutes from Tiruvannamalai (Rs11.50, one hour). Ask to be let off at 'the fort', 2km before Gingee town. An autorickshaw from Gingee to the fort costs about Rs70 one way.

PUDUCHERRY (PONDICHERRY)

☎ 0413 / pop 220,749

Let's get something clear: if you came to Puducherry (which used to be called Pondicherry and is almost always referred to

as 'Pondy') expecting a Provençal village in South India, you're in for some sore disappointment, *mon ami*. Most of Pondy is Tamil Nadu: honk-scream-screech-honk-chaos Tamil Nadu. Running through Tamil Nadu is a thin trickle of colonial Pondy: some cobblestones, mustard-yellow townhouses, and here and there a shady boulevard that could put you in mind of gendarmes marching past sari-clad belles – HONK.

On top of everything are hotels, restaurants and 'lifestyle' shops that sell a vision of *vieux Asie* created by savvy entrepreneurs and embellished by Gallic creative types who arrived here on the French hippie trail. Their presence has in turn attracted Indian artists and designers, and thus, Pondy's vibe: less faded colonial *ville*, more contemporary bohemian, vaguely New Age – but also faintly Old World – node on the international travel trail.

Enjoy the shopping, the French food (helloooo steak!), the beer (goodbye Tamil Nadu alcohol taxes – Pondy is a Union Territory) and, if you like, yoga and meditation at the Sri Aurobindo Ashram. Have a stroll past the police, who still wear red Gallic *kepi*, and imagine another time when – HONK.

Orientation

Puducherry is split from east to west by a partially covered sewer…we mean, canal. The more 'French' part of town is on the east side (towards the sea), the more typically Indian portion to the west. Nehru St and Lal Bahadur Sastri, better known as Rue Bussy, are the main east–west streets; Mahatma Gandhi (MG) Rd and Mission St are the north–south thoroughfares. Pondy's grid design makes it relatively easy to follow, although many streets have one name at one end and another at the other, while others use the French 'Rue' instead of 'Street'.

Information

Puducherry keeps European hours and takes a long lunch break; expect most businesses to be closed from about 1pm to 3.30pm. Besides the usual Indian and Tamil Nadu festivals, Puducherry celebrates its Gallic roots with a nice fete come Bastille Day (p389).

BOOKSHOPS

French Bookshop (☎ 2338062; Suffren St; ⏲ 9am-12.30pm & 3.30-7.30pm) This small shop next to the Alliance Française carries many French titles.

Librairie Kailash (☎ 331872; 169 Lal Bahadur Shastri St; ☉ 9.30am-1.30pm & 3.30-9pm Mon-Sat) Another excellent collection of titles, particularly coffee-table books, in French.

Vibe (☎ 4500250; 6 Rue Surcouf; ☉ 10am-7.30pm Mon-Sat) Has a decent selection of books by Indian authors.

CULTURAL CENTRES

Alliance Française (☎ 2338146; afpondy@satyam.net .in; 58 Suffren St; ☉ 9am-noon & 3-6pm Mon-Sat) The French cultural centre has a library, computer centre and art gallery, and conducts French-language classes. Films are shown on Sunday at 6pm. The monthly newsletter, *Le Petit Journal*, details forthcoming events. Maison Colombani, its associated exhibition and performance space, is on Dumas St.

INTERNET ACCESS

You won't lack for internet cafes.

Coffee.Com (236 Mission St; per 30min Rs20; ☉ 10am-1am) A popular, hip cafe, but service has suffered as it has grown in popularity.

Wi Corner (1 Caziavar St, cnr Lal Bahadur Shastri Street;. per hr Rs30; ☉ 10am-10pm) Our favourite, run by the overwhelmingly friendly Mohamed. Has rocket-fast connections and wi-fi.

MEDICAL SERVICES

Lal Bahadur Shastri St between Bharathi St and MG Rd is packed with clinics and pharmacies.

New Medical Centre (☎ 2228890; 470 MG Rd; ☉ 24hr)

MONEY

ATMs are plentiful.

Canara Bank ATM (45 Gingy St)

Citibank ATM (cnr Lal Bahadur Shastri & Labourdonnais Sts)

ICICI Bank ATM (47 Mission St)

LKP Forex (☎ 2224008; 2A Labourdonnais St; ☉ 9.30am-7.30pm Mon-Fri, 9.30am-6.30pm Sat)

State Bank of India (15 Suffren St)

UTI/Axis Bank ATM (164 Bussy St)

POST

Main post office (Rangapillai St; ☉ 9am-7pm Mon-Sat, 10am-5pm Sun)

TOURIST INFORMATION

Puducherry tourist office (☎ 2339497; 40 Goubert Ave; ☉ 9am-5pm) Enthusiastic staff; decent free map.

Sights & Activities

FRENCH QUARTER

Pocketed away in the eastern alleys is a series of cobbled roads, white and mustard buildings

in various states of romantic *déshabillé*, and a slight sense of Gallic glory gone by, otherwise known as the French Quarter. The best way to explore these streets is via Puducherry's **heritage walk**. Start at the north end of Goubert Ave, the seafront promenade, and wander south past the **French consulate** and the **Gandhi Statue**. Turn right at the **Hôtel de Ville** (**town hall**) on Rue Mahe Labourdonnais, past the shady **Bharathi Park**. From there it's a matter of pottering south through **Dumas**, **Romain Rolland** and **Suffren Sts**. **Focus Books** (☎ 2345513; 204 Mission St; ☉ 9.30am-1.30pm & 3.30-9pm Mon-Sat) sells heritage walking-trail brochures (Rs9). You may also want to take a look down Vysial St, between MG Rd and Mission St; locals say this tree-lined block is one of the last faithfully maintained slices of old Pondy.

SRI AUROBINDO ASHRAM

Founded in 1926 by Sri Aurobindo and a Frenchwoman known as 'the Mother' (whose visage, which you'll either find benevolent or vaguely creepy, is *everywhere* here), this **ashram** (cnr Marine St & Manakula Vinayagar Koil St) seeks to synthesise yoga and modern science. After Aurobindo's death spiritual authority (and minor religious celebrity) passed to the Mother, who died in 1973 aged 97. A constant flow of visitors files through the **main ashram building** (☉ 8am-noon & 2-6pm Mon-Sat), which has the flower-festooned *samadhi* (tomb venerated as a shrine) of Aurobindo and the Mother in the central courtyard.

PUDUCHERRY MUSEUM

Goodness knows how this cute little **museum** (15 St Louis St; adult/child Rs2/1; ☉ 9.40am-1pm & 2-5.20pm Tue-Sun) keeps its artefacts from rotting, considering there's a whole floor of French-era furniture sitting in the South Indian humidity. As you amble through the colonial-era building, keep an eye peeled for Pallava and Chola sculptures, a small Versailles' worth of French Union–era bric-a-brac, and coins and shards of pottery excavated from Arikamedu, a once-major seaport a few kilometres south of Puducherry that traded with the Roman Empire during the 1st century BC.

CHURCHES & TEMPLES

Puducherry has one of the best collections of over-the-top cathedrals in India. *Merci*, French missionaries. The **Church of Our Lady of the Immaculate Conception** (Mission St),

TAMIL NADU

PUDUCHERRY (PONDICHERRY)

completed in 1791, is a robin's-egg-blue-and-cloud-white typically Jesuit edifice, while the brown-and-white grandiosity of the **Sacred Heart Church** (Subbayah Salai) is set off by stained glass and a Gothic sense of proportion. The mellow pink-and-cream **Notre Dame de Anges** (Dumas St), built in 1858, looks sublime in the late-afternoon light. The smooth limestone

interior was made using eggshells in the plaster.

But this is still India, and the Hindu faith still reigns supreme. Don't miss the chance to watch tourists, pilgrims and the curious get a head pat from the temple elephant who stands outside **Sri Manakula Vinayagar Temple** (Manakula Vinayagar Koil St; ☯ 5.45am-12.30pm & 4-9.30pm), dedi-

INFORMATION	Sri Manakula Vinayagar	Grinde Sridharan General
Alliance Française......................**1** C5	Temple..............................**27** C2	Merchants........................**48** D3
Canara Bank...........................**2** C3		Hotel Aristo......................**49** B2
Citibank ATM..........................**3** C4	**SLEEPING**	kasha ki aasha..................**50** C4
Coffee.Com.............................**4** B4	Ajantha Beach	La Coromandale................**51** D4
Focus Books............................**5** C3	Guest House...................**28** D5	La Terrasse.......................**52** C5
French Bookshop......................**6** C5	Ajantha Sea View.................(see 28)	Le Café............................**53** D3
French Consulate......................**7** D2	Calve................................**29** C2	Le Club............................(see 37)
ICICI Bank..............................**8** C1	Devaki Ellite.......................**30** A4	Madame Shante's................**54** C4
Libraire Kailash.......................**9** B4	Dumas Guest House...............**31** D5	Nilgiri
LKP Forex.............................(see 59)	Family Guest House...............**32** B5	Supermarket....................**55** C3
Main Post Office.....................**10** C3	French Villa........................**33** C5	Rendezvous.......................**56** C4
New Medical Centre.................**11** B4	Ganga Guest House...............**34** A4	Satsanga..........................**57** C5
Puducherry Tourist Office.........**12** D4	Hotel Continental.................**35** C5	Surguru...........................**58** C3
State Bank of India..................**13** C4	Hotel De L'Orient..................**36** C5	
UTI Bank ATM........................**14** B1	Hotel	**DRINKING**
Vibe...................................(see 64)	de Pondichery...................**37** C5	Le Café............................(see 53)
Wi Corner.............................**15** C4	New Guest House..................**38** D5	Promenade.......................(see 41)
	Park Guest House..................**39** D5	Space Coffee & Arts.............**59** C4
SIGHTS & ACTIVITIES	Patricia Coloniale Heritage Guest	
Ayurvedic Holistic Healing	House............................**40** C5	**SHOPPING**
Centre.............................**16** C1	Promenade.........................**41** D3	Auroboutique....................(see 25)
Botanical Gardens...................**17** A5	Richmond...........................**42** C5	Fabindia............................**60** C5
Church of Our Lady of the	Santhi Inn..........................**43** C2	Geethanjali........................**61** C4
Immaculate Conception........**18** C3	Sri Aurobindo Information	kasha ki aasha..................(see 50)
Gandhi Statue........................**19** D3	Centre...........................(see 26)	La Boutique
Hôtel de Ville (Town Hall)........**20** D4	Surya Swastika	d'Auroville.......................**62** C2
Jayalakshmi Fine Arts Academy..**21** C3	Guest House....................**44** C2	Pondy Cre'Art...................(see 60)
Notre Dame de Agnes.............**22** D4	Villa Helena........................**45** C4	Sri Aurobindo Handmade Paper
Puducherry Museum................**23** D3		Factory...........................**63** C1
Sacred Heart Church.................**24** B5	**EATING**	Vibe................................**64** C4
Sri Aurobindo Ashram..............**25** D2	Adyar Ananda	
Sri Aurobindo Information	Bhavan..........................**46** C3	**TRANSPORT**
Centre.............................**26** C3	Au Feu de Bois.....................**47** C4	Bicycle Hire.......................**65** C5

cated to Ganesh and tucked down a backstreet just south of the Sri Aurobindo Ashram; the temple also contains over 40 skilfully painted friezes.

BOTANICAL GARDENS
Established by the French in 1826, the **botanical gardens** (admission free; 10am-5pm) form a green, if somewhat litter-strewn, oasis on the southwest side of town.

BEACHES
Pondy is a seaside town, but that doesn't make it a beach destination; the city's sand is a thin strip of dirty brown blah that slurps into a seawall of jagged rocks. With that said, Goubert Ave (Beach Rd) is a killer stroll, especially at dawn and dusk when everyone in town takes a constitutional or romantic stroll. There are a few decent beaches to the north and south of town. Quiet, Reppo and Serenity Beaches are all north of the centre, within 8km of Puducherry. Chunnambar, 8km south, has Paradise Beach, water sports and backwater boat cruises. Both areas are becoming inundated with high-end resorts. The tourist office (p421) has details.

Courses
ARTS
Jayalakshmi Fine Arts Academy (2342036; goodsin@vsnl.net.in; 221 Mission St; 9.30am-1.30pm & 3.30-8.30pm Mon-Sat, 7am-12.30pm Sun) is an established place with classes in *bharatanatyam* (dance), singing, *veena* (Indian stringed instrument), tabla (drums) and a range of other musical instruments. Private tuition fees start at Rs200 per hour for a minimum of five hours, and there's a one-off registration fee (Rs350).

YOGA & AYURVEDA
Puducherry's International Yoga Festival (p389) is held annually in early January.
Ayurvedic Holistic Healing Centre (6537651; 6 Sengeniammal Koil St) Performs detox services, back procedures, varna point massage, skin treatment and offers ayurvedic massages and yoga courses.
International Centre for Yoga Education & Research (ICYER; 2241561; www.icyer.com; 16A Mettu St, Chinnamudaliarchavady, Kottukuppam) Also known as the Ananda Ashram, this renowned centre conducts annual six-month yoga teacher-training courses and 10-day summer courses.
Sri Aurobindo Ashram (23396483; bureaucentral@sriaurobindoashram.org; 3 Rangapillai St) Study and/or practise yoga (see also p421).

Tours

The tourist office (p421) runs half-day sightseeing tours (Rs100, 2pm to 6pm) to the water-sports complex at Chunnambar, Auroville and Sri Aurobindo Ashram. Full-day tours (Rs200, 9am to 6pm) cover the same area plus the botanical gardens, paper factory (p427), Sacred Heart Church and a couple of Hindu temples; both tours need a minimum of six people to operate.

Sleeping

If you've been saving for a special occasion, splurge here, because Puducherry's lodgings are as good as South India gets. Local heritage houses manage to combine colonial romanticism with modern spoilage and dare we say French playfulness, like vintage movie posters and colour schemes that run from monochrome to neon-bright; these same rooms would likely run to hundreds of dollars in the West.

BUDGET

New Guest House (☎ 2221553; 64 Romain Rolland St; d Rs100) Spare, huge and packed with the ashram faithful; this is a great spot for those who love the monastery cubicle school of lodging.

Surya Swastika Guest House (☎ 2343092; 11 Iswaran Koil St; d Rs140-150, without bathroom Rs100) It's (decidedly) not the Ritz, but if you need clean, cheap rooms and no curfew, this is your best bet.

Hotel Continental (☎ 2225828; 48 Labourdonnais St; s/d Rs350/500; 🏵) The Continental may not have much charm, but it does have clean, polished rooms and AC for a bargain price.

Family Guest House (☎ 2228346; 526 MG Rd; s/d Rs400/500) A two-storey complex of balconies, smart verandahs and peeling colonial-era rot gives this place some faded elegance, but it gets a little too faded in some spots. Also, and it needs to be said: while the rooms are perfectly pleasant and service is as charming as you please, it sucks to share squat toilets at this price.

Park Guest House (☎ 2334412; 1 Goubert Ave; d Rs400, with AC Rs600; 🏵) This is the most sought-after ashram address in town thanks to its wonderful seafront position. All front rooms face the sea and have their own porch or balcony, and there's a large lawn area for morning yoga or meditation.

Sri Aurobindo Ashram runs a lot of local budget accommodation. They're clean and you'll be around like-minded souls (ie the budget and karma conscious). But they come

with rules: 10.30pm curfew and no smoking or alcohol. For information and reservations, contact the **Sri Aurobindo information centre** (☎ 2339646/8; bureaucentral@sriaurobindoashram.org; cnr Rangapillai St & Ambour Salai; 🕑 6am-8pm).

MIDRANGE & TOP END

Ganga Guest House (☎ 2222675; www.gangaguest.com; 479 Bharathi St; r Rs400-750) This old colonnaded house, swathed in red, yellow and chocolate browns feels like the antique set of a period-piece Bollywood blockbuster – posters for which decorate every room. Aim for a terrace room; they get a bit of breeze and some have balconies.

Dumas Guest House (☎ 2225726; 31 Dumas St; s/d Rs600/750; 🏵) A tall, thin rabbit warren of nooks and crannies, this tidy six-room guest house has a good beach and restaurant-accessible location, as well as hip managers who seem to know what the independent traveller wants out of their holiday – ie they'll steer you away from the tackier tourism activities. It's one of the few places we'd say was equally good for families or single travellers – everyone should feel comfy.

Santhi Inn (☎ 2220946; www.santhinn.com; 57 Nehru St; r Rs600-850; 🏵) The multistorey Santhi certainly isn't a heritage house, but it's a clean, corporate-y kinda spot with comfy beds and a conveniently central location.

Ajantha Beach Guest House (☎ 2338898; 1 Rue Bazar St Laurent; d with sea view Rs600-1200; 🏵) The location is the main selling point – right on the beachfront promenade. The four sea-view rooms are plain but comfortable and have balconies; others are drab and windowless.

Villa Pondicherry (☎ 2356253; www.pondy.org; 23 Dr Ambedkar Salai; d from Rs650, without bathroom from Rs550; 🏵) This ageing but charming colonial residence is about 1km south of the train station next to St Francis Xavier Church. The five rooms and central lounge certainly have character and fun decor, but some may find it a little too homely. Look for the red door and small brass plaque under the verandah.

Devaki Elite (☎ 2224700; 225 Lal Bahadur Shastri; r Rs1150; 🏵) Clean and vaguely businesslike, with scrubbed floors, flat-screen TVs and chilly aircon, Devaki is a good place for those who'd rather have some Western corporate comfort in a place full of heritage quirks. It may not have a ton of character, but you're guaranteed peace, quiet and cool (temperatures), which isn't the worst trade-off.

Hotel de Pondichery (☎ 2227409; 38 Dumas St; r from Rs1350-2450; ❄) Yet another heritage home, this recently renovated place has lovely colonial-style rooms and outdoor terraces. It's more Old World than luxurious, but rooms are private and quiet.

French Villa (☎ 4201545; www.thefrenchvilla.in; 51 Suffren St; r Rs1500) We're not quite sure what a 'traveller's house of colours and flavours', as the brochure states, is supposed to be, but we do think this villa – more of a cottage – is immaculately cute. The smallish scale and seashore-bright rooms are a pleasant break from Pondy's more baroque heritage-style hotels.

Ajantha Sea View (☎ 2349032; www.ajanthaseaview hotel.com; 50 Goubert Ave; r from Rs1750; ❄) Pondy may not be a beach town, but that doesn't mean you can't enjoy a bit of salt breeze from your room. Ajantha Sea View provides the above gust of fresh air (along with other earthier scents rolling out of town) thanks to its full beachfront balconies: these rooms have the best views in town. Go for the corner deluxe rooms, full of light thanks to windows on two sides. There are ice-cream shops nearby for beating the heat.

Patricia Coloniale Heritage Guest House (☎ 2224 720; colonialeheritage@rediffmail.com; 54 Romain Rolland St; r incl breakfast Rs1800-3000; ❄) For an intimate, peaceful stay, Patricia's is hard to beat. The delightful colonial-era home is run by a friendly family and the six rooms all have exotic but original character with stained-glass window panes, traditional Indian furniture and a lovely central garden where breakfast is served in a sunken courtyard. If it's full, ask the owners about their other properties around town.

our pick **Villa Helena** (☎ 2226789; villahelena@ satyam.net.in; 13 Lal Bahadur Shastri St; r Rs2200-2800; ❄) What sits Helena apart from her heritage siblings is the dash of vintage fun she overlays on respectable colonial facades. With 1930s-era Chinese movie posters, luxurious beds and high-ceilinged rooms, you feel caught between a black-and-white colonial noir flick and a modern designer's dream.

Hotel De L'Orient (☎ 2343067; www.neemranahotels .com; 17 Romain Rolland St; r Rs3000-6000; ❄) This is as grand as it gets in Puducherry: a restored colonial mansion with rooms that appeal to your inner pith-helmeted aristocrat. Should you need a sense of columned regal importance, the hush of breezy verandahs and the scurry-

ing service of men in clean white uniforms, this is the place to book.

Richmond (☎ 2346363; www.theresidency.com; 12 Labourdonnais St; r incl breakfast Rs3500-4000; ❄ ▯) The Richmond, located in an attractive yellow colonial-era edifice, manages the whole heritage with a twist of modern aesthetic very well; rooms are dark-wood accented but sleek enough to stand out to the contemporary conscious.

Calve (☎ 2224261; www.calve.in; 36 Vysial St; r incl breakfast Rs3555-5355; ❄) This excellent heritage option, located on a quiet, tree-shaded boulevard, combines a soaring sense of high-ceilinged space with egg-white walls, flat-screen TVs, huge niche-embedded mattresses groaning under soft cushions and a warm backdrop of Burmese teak floors and banisters.

Promenade (☎ 2227750; www.sarovarhotels.com; 23 Goubert Ave; r incl breakfast Rs5200-6900; ❄) The Promenade is a supremely modern beachfront boutique dripping with contemporary design flash. It's owned and operated by the swish Hidesign group, and is trying to magnetise itself as a centre for Puducherry's small social scene.

Eating

Puducherry is a Tamil Nadu culinary highlight; you get the best of South Indian cooking plus several restaurants specialising in well-prepped French and Italian cuisine. If you've been missing cheese, and think cows are only sacred when seared medium rare, you're in luck. There's a string of cheap street stalls open past 11pm on Anna Salai and Lal Bahadur Shastri St

La Coromandale (30 Goubert Ave; mains Rs40) Tasty South Indian thalis, rice, noodles and cold drinks and a relaxed atmosphere for meeting and chatting are the attractions of this open-fronted restaurant, situated on the promenade. Beware of eccentric opening hours.

Le Café (Goubert Ave; mains Rs40-150) Situated near the Gandhi statue, this is a good spot for sandwiches, coffee (hot or ice) and clean views over the Bay of Bengal. As waterfront cafes go, this is pretty much Pondy's only option.

Adyar Ananda Bhavan (☎ 2223333; cnr Nehru & Gingy Sts; up to Rs100) This a modern, clean Indian fast-food place that sells everything from curries to pakoras to samosas to sweets, plus a nice line of fresh juices. It's always humming with customers, and you'll be hard pressed to spend more than Rs100 on a meal. If you're nervous about giving street food a go, this might be the spot for you – the amount of mothers with children inside suggests this is a very sanitary spot.

kasha ki aasha (☎ 2222963; www.kasha-ki-aasha.com; 23 Rue Surcouf; Rs60-120; ◷ 8am-7pm Mon-Sat) You'll get a great pancake breakfast, good lunches (try the European-style thali) and delicious cakes served on the pretty rooftop of this colonial-house-cum-craftshop-cum-cafe.

Surguru (☎ 4308082; 99 Mission St; mains Rs40-100; ◷ lunch & dinner) Simple South Indian served in a posh setting. Surguru is the fix for thali addicts who like their veg accompanied by the strongest AC this side of Chennai.

Hotel Aristo (Nehru St; mains around Rs80-150; ◷ lunch & dinner Sat-Thu) The rooftop restaurant at Aristo continues to be a great choice and is usually crowded in the evenings with tourists, both domestic and foreign. Dishes include walnut chicken with brown rice (delicious but generally made with cashews!) and grilled prawns, and there's a bit of an East-meets-West vibe going on throughout the entire menu. A small Kingfisher (known here as 'secret tea') is Rs40, which is as good a deal boozehounds can likely sniff out.

La Terrasse (☎ 2220809; 5 Subbayah Salai; pizzas Rs80-175; ◷ Thu-Tue) This simple semi-open-air place near the southern end of the promenade has a wide menu but is best known for good pizzas and safe salads, as opposed to their Indian food (which is, frankly, wanting). No alcohol is served.

Madame Shante's (40 Romain Rolland St; mains Rs90-170; ◷ lunch & dinner) This rooftop option, which does its stock-in-trade in French, with a focus on seafood (try the garlic squid), isn't quiet as polished looking as the competition, but the food is still excellent and the ambience decidedly open-air and alluring.

Au Feu de Bois (☎ 2341821; 28 Lal Bahadur Shastri St; pizzas Rs140-230; ◷ lunch & dinner Tue-Sun) Wood-fired pizza and only wood-fired pizza is the name of the game here, and it's a damn decent game.

Le Club (☎ 2339745; 38 Dumas St; mains Rs140-325; ◷ lunch & dinner) This club wraps three restaurants into one, with heavy French fare, a simple garden terrace and – unique to Pondy as of our writing – Vietnamese and Southeast Asian fare in the attached Indochine.

Satsanga (☎ 2225867; 30-32 Labourdonnais St; mains Rs150-250; ◷ lunch & dinner) This very popular

backyard spot serves excellent continental cuisine and, like most places in this genre, a full Indian menu as well. The large variety of sausages and lovely homemade bread and butter goes down a particular treat, as does any of the steaks.

Rendezvous (☎ 2339132; 30 Suffren St; mains Rs150-500; ◷ lunch & dinner Wed-Mon) The steaks here are superb, but then again, so is just about anything at this suitably romantic restaurant, where diners can lounge in AC comfort or pick at their coq au vin under the stars on the lush garden terrace.

SELF-CATERING

Nilgiri Supermarket (cnr Mission & Rangapillai Sts; ◷ 9.30am-9pm) A well-stocked, modern place in which to shop for groceries in air-conditioned comfort. Credit cards are accepted.

Grinde Sridharan General Merchants (☎ 2221232; grspondy@sify.com; 25 St Louis St; ◷ 9am-1pm & 4-9pm Mon-Sat) An excellent, long-established grocery store with plenty of imported goods and an exchange facility for cash and travellers cheques.

Neighbouring bakeries Your Daily Bread and Hot Breads are on Ambour Salai, selling terrific French bread, croissants and other baked goodies from 7am daily. The main fresh-produce market is west of MG Rd, between Nehru and Rangapillai Sts.

Drinking & Entertainment

Although this is one of the better spots in Tamil Nadu to sink a beer, closing time is a decidedly un-Gallic 11pm. If you're here on Friday or Saturday, get ready for some late-night fun, when Pondy stays open until (drum roll)…11.30pm! Break out the champagne! With low taxes on alcohol, Puducherry has a reputation for cheap booze. The reality is you'll really only find cheap beer (Rs30) in 'liquor shops' or the darkened bars attached to them. While you can sometimes get a large Kingfisher for Rs60, the better restaurants charge up to Rs100.

Space Coffee & Arts (☎ 2356253; 2 Labourdonnais St; ◷ 6pm-11pm) A funky little semi-open-air cafe for juice, coffee, beer, a bite and some damn fine cocktails (hello, Blue Lemonade). Staff are friendly, locals and tourists congregate here, and all in all it's the most social traveller spot in Pondy.

The Promenade (p425) hotel bar also occasionally gets buzzing in the evenings.

Shopping

With all the yoga yuppies congregating here, Pondy is starting to specialise in the sort of boutique-chic-meets-Indian-bazaar school of fashion, accessories and souvenirs.

Sri Aurobindo Handmade Paper Factory (☎ 2334 763; 50 SV Patel Salai; ⏲ 8.30am-noon & 1.30-5pm Mon-Sat) Fine handmade paper is sold here, and you can ask at the counter about tours of the factory. There's a wider choice of goods at Auroboutique near the ashram; all sales support ashram work.

Fabindia (☎ 2226010; www.fabindia.com; 59 Suffren St; ⏲ 9.30am-7.30pm) Opposite Alliance Française, this shop has a good variety of quality woven goods and furnishings, traditionally made but with a contemporary feel. In operation since 1960, one of its selling points is its 'fair, equitable and helpful relationship' with village producers.

Geethanjali (☎ 4200392; 20 Lal Bahadur Shastri St; ⏲ 10am-7pm Mon-Sat) The sort of place where Indiana Jones gets the sweats, this antique and curio shop sells statues, sculptures, paintings and furniture culled from Puducherry's colonial, and even pre-colonial history.

La Boutique d'Auroville (38 Nehru St; ⏲ 9.30am-1pm & 3.30-8pm Mon-Sat) It's fun browsing through the crafts here, including jewellery, batiks, *kalamkari* (similar to batik) drawings, carpets and woodcarvings.

kasha ki aasha (☎ 2222963; www.kasha-ki-aasha .com; 23 Rue Surcouf; ⏲ 8am-7pm Mon-Sat) Fabulous fabrics and gorgeous garments and crafts that are sourced directly from their makers are sold by an all-women staff in this lovely old colonial house. There's a breezy rooftop eatery on-site.

Pondy Cre'Art(☎ 4200258; 53 Suffren St; ⏲ 10am-7.30pm Mon-Sat) Local and European designers get their creativity going on here with leather handbags, handmade paper journals and the sort of clothes that look like they got caught between an Indian flea market and a Soho outlet.

Vibe (☎ 4500250; 6 Rue Surcouf; ⏲ 10am-7.30pm Mon-Sat) There's a lot of made-for-travellers Indian fashion here; think breezy but flattering *salwar kameez*-inspired blouses for women and mandarin-collared cotton shirts for men. It also does a good stock-in-trade of the sleek designer homeware that screams conspicuous consumption, and sells some good books on the side, but the staff can be overbearing, following you around every room in the shop.

Getting There & Away

BUS
The bus stand is 500m west of town. See the boxed text (below) for details of services.

TAXI
Air-conditioned taxis from Puducherry to Chennai cost around Rs2700, and to Chennai airport Rs2500.

TRAIN
There are two direct services a day to Chennai (Rs58, five hours), and one to Tirupathy. There's a computerised booking service for southern trains at the station.

Getting Around

One of the best ways to get around Pondy is by walking. Large three-wheelers shuttle between the bus stand and Gingy St for Rs5, but they're hopelessly overcrowded. Cycle- and autorickshaws are plentiful – an autorickshaw across town costs about Rs40.

Since the streets are broad and flat, the most popular transport is pedal power. Bicycle-hire shops line many of the streets, especially MG Rd and Mission St. You'll also find hire shops

TAMIL NADU

BUSES FROM PUDUCHERRY (PONDICHERRY)

Destination	Fare (Rs)	Duration (hr)	Frequency	Type
Bengaluru	150	8	6 daily	Deluxe
Chennai	55	3½	83 daily	Express
Chidambaram	25	1½	50 daily	State
Coimbatore	170	9	8 daily	Deluxe
Kanchipuram	40	3	5 daily	State
Kumbakonam	35	4	6 daily	State
Mamallapuram	35	2	5 daily	State
Tiruvannamalai	40	3½	9 daily	State
Trichy	75	5	4 daily	Deluxe & State

in Subbayah Salai and Goubert Ave. The usual rental is Rs5/20 per hour/day, but some places ask Rs70 per day.

Mopeds or motorbikes are useful for getting out to the beaches or to Auroville and can be rented from a number of shops and street stalls. The going rate is Rs150 a day for a gearless scooter and Rs175 for a motorbike.

AUROVILLE
☎ 0413 / pop 1800

Auroville is one of those ideas anyone with a whiff of New Age will love: an international community built on handfuls of soil donated by 124 countries, where dedicated souls, ignoring creed, colour and nationality, work to build a universal township and realise interconnectedness, love and good old human oneness.

On paper. In execution, Auroville is both its high ideals and some not-as-glamorous reality. Imagine over 80 rural settlements encompassing scrubby Tamil countryside, where harmony is strived for if not always realised between 1800 residents representing almost 40 nationalities. Two-thirds of Aurovillians are foreign, and outside opinions of them range from positive vibes to critics who say the town is an enclave for expats seeking a self-indulgent rustic escape.

Ultimately, Auroville encompasses all of the above, and anyone interested in the experiment may want to visit on a day trip from Puducherry. Be prepared for lots of posters celebrating 'The Mother', the French traveller-turned-guru, and founder of the Sri Aurobindo Ashram (p423). Be warned: Auroville is not that tourist-friendly. Each settlement has its own area of expertise and most Aurovillians are busy simply getting on with their work. Still, you may get a sense of the appeal of the place after a visit to the visitor centre and the **Matrimandir**, Auroville's spiritual heart. One of those unfortunate buildings that tries to look futuristic and ends up coming off dated, this giant golden golf ball/faux Epcot Center contains an inner chamber lined with white marble that houses a solid crystal (the largest in the world) 70cm in diameter.

Which you won't actually see, since the Matrimandir is not open to casual visitors. But there is a pleasant plot of **gardens** (10am-1pm & 2-4.30pm daily except Sun afternoon), from which you can spy the structure while listening to piped-in Enya-esque music; you need to pick up a pass (free) from the information service (right).

Information

There's a photographic exhibition and video room at the **Auroville Information Service** (www .auroville.org; admission free; 9am-1pm & 1.30-5.30pm), which also issues garden passes for external views of the Matrimandir (from 9.45am to 12.30pm and 1.45pm to 4pm only). In the same complex, the **visitor centre** (☎ 2622239; www .auroville.org; 9am-6pm) contains a bookshop, a nice cafe and Boutique d'Auroville, which sells Aurovillian handicrafts.

Sleeping & Eating

You can only stay in Auroville if you're serious about contributing to it. A stay of no shorter than a week is preferred and while work isn't obligatory, it's much appreciated. Accommodation isn't offered in exchange for work; rooms range from Rs150 to Rs1000, and guests are also required to contribute around Rs60 per day for the 'maintenance and development' of Auroville.

There are more than 40 guest houses in Auroville, each tied to communities with specific work missions (women's education, farming etc). The best way to match your interests with the community you'll stay in is to check out the website and, preferably, get suggestions from and make arrangements with the **Auroville Guest Service** (☎ 2622704; avguests@ auroville.org.in) before arriving.

Although there are stores and small roadside eateries in Auroville, and communities have communal dining areas, many Aurovillians gather at the Solar Kitchen – powered by solar energy – which dishes out more than 400 meals daily from its buffet. The cafe at the visitor centre is open to day visitors.

Getting There & Away

The best way to enter Auroville is from the coast road, at the village of Periyar Mudaliarchavadi. Ask around as it's not well signposted. A return autorickshaw ride from Puducherry is about Rs250, but a better option is to hire a moped or bicycle. It's about 12km from Puducherry to the visitor centre.

CENTRAL TAMIL NADU

CHIDAMBARAM
☎ 04144 / pop 67,795

There's basically one reason to visit Chidambaram: The Lord of the Dance. No, put away your Michael Flatley posters – we mean the great temple complex of Nataraja, Shiva as the Dancer of the Universe. The greatest Nataraja temple in India also happens to be a Dravidian architectural highlight and one of the holiest Shiva sites in South India. Chidambaram can be visited as a day trip from Puducherry, or as a stopover between Puducherry and Kumbakonam or Trichy.

Of the many festivals, the two largest are the **10-day chariot festivals**, which are celebrated in April/May and December/January. In February/March the five-day **Natyanjali Dance Festival** (p389) attracts performers from all over the country to celebrate Nataraja (Shiva) – Lord of the Dance.

Orientation & Information

The small town is developed around the Nataraja Temple with streets named after the cardinal points. Accommodation is close to the temple and the bus stand a five-minute walk to the southeast. The train station is about 1km further south.

Cybase (Pillaiyar Koil St; per hr Rs30; ☼ 9am-9pm) Fast internet access.

ICICI Bank ATM (Hotel Saradharam; South Car St)

Post office (North Car St; ☼ 10am-3pm Mon-Sat)

Tourist office (☎ 238739; Railway Feeder Rd; ☼ 9am-5pm Mon-Fri) Frequently deserted.

UAE Exchange (Pillaiyar Koil St; ☼ Mon-Sat) Best place in town to exchange money.

Sights

NATARAJA TEMPLE

The legend goes: one day, in a nearby forest, Shiva and Kali got into a dance-off that was judged by the assembled gods. Shiva finished his routine with a high kick to the head that Kali could not duplicate and won the title Nataraja, or Lord of the Dance. It is in this form he is worshipped at the great **Shiva temple** (☼ courtyard & shrines 6am-12.30pm & 4-4.30pm-10.30pm), which draws a regular stream of pilgrims and visitors. The region was a Chola capital from 907 to 1310 and the temple was erected during the later time of the administration, although local guides claim some of the complex was built by the Pallavas in the 6th century. The high-walled 22-hectare complex has four towering *gopurams* a-decked out in schizophrenic Dravidian stonework.

The main entrance, through the east *gopuram*, off East Car St, depicts the 108 sacred positions of classical Tamil dance. In the northeast of the complex, to the right as you enter, is the 1000-pillared **Raja Sabha** (King's Hall), open only on festival days, and to the left is the **Sivaganga** (Temple Tank), which is thick with mudfish and worshippers performing ritual ablutions. To the west of the entrance to the inner sanctum is a depiction of Shiva as Nataraja that is underlined by a

CHIDAMBARAM
0 ——— 300 m
0 ——— 0.2 miles

INFORMATION	
Cybase	(see 4)
ICICI Bank ATM	1 A4
ICICI Bank ATM	(see 8)
Post Office	2 A4
Tourist Office	3 B5
UAE Exchange	4 B5

SIGHTS & ACTIVITIES	
Main Temple Entrance	5 A4
Nataraja Temple	6 A4

SLEEPING 🏠	
Hotel Akshaya	7 A4
Hotel Saradharam	8 B5

EATING 🍴	
Anuupallavi	(see 8)
Ishwarya	9 B5

TRANSPORT	
Bus Stand	10 B5

To Cuddalore (50km); Puducherry (71km); Chennai (232km)

North Main Rd

North Car St

West Car St East Car St

VOC St

South Car St

Pillaiyar Koil St

To Pichavaram (15km)

Hospital

Railway Feeder Rd

Khan Sahib Canal

To Vaitheeswarankoil (25km); Kumbakonam (69km)

Train Station

SOUTHERN STYLE

Even Indians are often overwhelmed by the number of temples in Tamil Nadu; if you're a tourist with only a small (or no) grasp on Hinduism and Dravidian culture, temple exhaustion can set in quickly here. Try to keep this in mind: throughout history Indian art has been wrapped up in religion. As a result, temples here (especially religious Tamil Nadu) are more than houses of worship. They're the collected, preserved and maintained aesthetic – sculpture, painting, architecture, even music and literature in the form of hymns and *puja* (offerings or prayers) – of a classical civilization, the primary place where Dravidian culture has preserved, and sometimes reinvented, itself.

That said, it can be a lot easier to appreciate all the temples in South India if you know a little a bit about what to expect. Southern styles differ from the north, which is a point of some pride down here. Tamil temples are dominated, not by their inner shrine (as in the North), but the *gopuram*, or entrance gateway, some of which are as tall as 70m. Each *gopuram* marks the transition space between this world and the sacred (also often marked by candy-striped red and white stripes) and is decked out to the point of almost being obscured by gods, goddesses, mythological characters etc. The *gopurams* enclose a square (always square) that includes a *chawadi*, or thousand-pillared (well, many pillars) halls, used for multiple purposes, *mandapas*, which are porches set over the most sacred nodes and finally, in the centre, the ruling deity itself. The cell for said deity is housed in a building called the *vimana* (principal part of Hindu temple). Reaching the centre of the shrine, no matter how small or large the temple, is the fulfilment of a spiritual quest for millions.

distinctly European pair of cherubic angels. In the southwest corner of the second enclosure is the Dance Hall, decorated with 56 pillars, that marks the spot where Shiva outdanced Kali.

Cameras are not allowed inside the temple, and non-Hindus cannot enter the inner sanctum, although you can glimpse its golden roof and its 21,600 tiles (one for every breath a human takes a day). Note the lions that top the columns; symbols of Chola royalty and a reminder of who acted as patron for the temple. Also look out for temple Brahmins, who sport a specific lopsided-to-the-left-half shaved head. Nataraja images abound, wherein Shiva holds the drum that beats the rhythm of creation and the fire of destruction in his outstretched hands, ending one cycle of creation, beginning another and uniting all opposites – light and dark, good and evil.

Try to catch the fire ceremony, which occurs six times a day and pulls in hundreds of worshippers who watch a ritual essentially unchanged for thousands of years. The entire complex erupts in drum beats and bells, while fires of clarified oil and butter are passed under the image of the deity, thus ensuring the cycle of creation continues.

Brahmin priests will usually guide you for a fee (anywhere from Rs30 up to Rs300, depending on the language skills and knowledge of the guide) around the temple complex.

Since the Brahmins work as a cooperative to fund the temple you may wish to support this magnificent building by way of donation or hiring a guide (but don't feel bound to do so).

Sleeping & Eating

Chidambaram has many cheap pilgrims' lodges clustered around the temple; you can usually get an AC room for between Rs500 and Rs800, and non-AC for as low as Rs150, but some of these spots come off as pretty dire.

Hotel Akshaya (☎ 220192; 17/18 East Car St; r Rs300-800) Close to the temple, this hotel has a wide range of rooms that run the gamut from boxy singles to quite good-value AC 'suites'.

Hotel Saradharam (☎ 221336; www.hotelsaradharam .co.in; 19 VGP St; d Rs650, with AC Rs1200; ✷) The busy and friendly Saradharam is the top hotel in town and conveniently located across from the bus stand. It's a bit worn in corners, but it's clean and comfortable and a welcome respite from the frenzy of the town centre.

Predictably, the best places to eat are in hotels. **Anuupallavi** (mains Rs25-70; ✷ lunch & dinner) is an excellent AC multicuisine restaurant in the Saradharam. Just across the bus stand is vegetarian **Ishwarya** (thalis Rs25), which does very fine thalis. There are lots of cheap veg eats in the area immediately surrounding the temple complex.

Getting There & Away

The bus stand is very central – within walking distance to the temple and accommodation. There are hourly buses to Chennai (Rs90, seven hours), and buses to Puducherry (Rs40, two hours) and Kumbakonam (Rs35, 2½ hours) run regularly. There are also five direct buses daily to Madurai (Rs150, eight hours).

Chidambaram now stands on the Chennai–Trichy gauge line; trains and services are open to Kumbakonam, Thanjavur and once a day to Rameswaram. The station is a 20-minute walk southeast of the temple (Rs40 by autorickshaw).

AROUND CHIDAMBARAM

About 15km east of town, **Pichavaram** is peaceful backwater of mangroves and tidal flats. You can spend a pleasant hour or two being rowed around the waterways and enjoying the bird life and calm surrounds. Boat hire (per hour Rs125; maximum five people) is available every day, and is busy with local visitors at the weekend. A basic three-room **guest house** (per room Rs300) is available beside the boat-hire place, and you can order food there.

KUMBAKONAM
☎ 0435 / pop 160,767

At first glance Kumbakonam is another Indian junction town, but then you notice the temples that sprout out of this busy city like mushrooms, a reminder that this was once a seat of medieval South Indian power. It's an easy day trip from Thanjavur, and makes a good base for exploring the coastal towns of the Cauvery Delta.

There's no tourist office in Kumbakonam, and road names and signs here are more erratic than usual. The best place to exchange travellers cheques is at the **UAE Exchange** (☎ 2423212; 134 Kamarajar Rd) near the train station. You'll find an ICICI Bank ATM almost opposite **Ashok Net Café** (☎ 2433054; 24 Ayikulam Rd; per hr Rs20; 9am-10.30pm).

Sights

Dozens of colourfully painted *gopurams* point skyward from Kumbakonam's 18 temples, most of which are dedicated to Shiva or Vishnu, but probably only the most dedicated temple-goer would tackle visiting more than a few. All temples are open from 6am

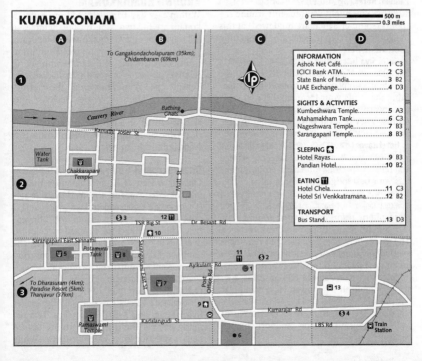

KUMBAKONAM

0 ——— 500 m
0 ——— 0.3 miles

To Gangakondacholapuram (35km);
Chidambaram (69km)

Cauvery River

Bathing Ghats

Kamatri Josier St

Water Tank

Chakkarapani Temple

Mutt St

TSR Big St
Dr Besant Rd

Sarangapani East Sannathi

Potamurai Tank

Ayikulam Rd

Post Office Rd

To Dharasuram (4km);
Paradise Resort (5km);
Thanjavur (37km)

Kadalangudi St

Kamarajar Rd

LBS Rd

Ramaswami Temple

Train Station

to noon and 4pm to 10pm, and admission is free.

The largest Vishnu temple in Kumbakonam, with a 50m-high east gate, is **Sarangapani Temple**, just off Ayikulam Rd. The temple shrine, in the form of a chariot, was the work of the Cholas during the 12th century.

Kumbeshwara Temple, about 200m west and entered via a nine-storey *gopuram*, is the largest Shiva temple. It contains a lingam said to have been made by Shiva himself when he mixed the nectar of immortality with sand.

The 12th-century **Nageshwara Temple**, from the Chola dynasty, is also dedicated to Shiva in the guise of Nagaraja, the serpent king. On three days of the year (in April or May) the sun's rays fall on the lingam. The main shrine here is in the form of a chariot.

The huge **Mahamakham Tank**, 600m southeast of the Nageshwara Temple, is the most sacred in Kumbakonam. It's believed that every 12 years the waters of the Ganges flow into the tank, and at this time a festival is held; the next is due in 2016.

Sleeping & Eating

Pandian Hotel (☎ 2430397; 52 Sarangapani East St; s/d Rs140/250) You might want to sniff around the rooms (some of which are mildewed) at this budget standby, but in general you're getting good value here.

Hotel Siva International (☎ 2424013; Periya St; d from Rs300, with AC from Rs800; ☒) Given the sheer size of this complex you're likely to find something that suits your taste amid the labyrinthine warren of clean budget and midrange rooms. They're a bit boxy, but comfortable for their lack of character.

Hotel Rayas (☎ 2422545, 2423170; 18 Post Office Rd; d from Rs700, with AC from Rs900; ☒) Friendly service and reliably spacious (and clean) rooms make this your best lodging option in town.

Paradise Resort (☎ 2416469; www.paradiseresort india.com; Tanjore Rd, Darasuram; r from Rs2000; ☒) An atmospheric resort constructed around heritage buildings and thatch and teak cottages. The rooms here have cool tiles and verandahs overlooking quiet and spacious gardens, and a plethora of ayurvedic spa treatment options.

Hotel Sri Venkkatramana (TSR Big St; thalis Rs25) serves good fresh veg food and is very popular with locals. At **Hotel Chela** (9 Ayikulam Rd; mains Rs30-80; ☺ lunch & dinner) there's a decent North Indian restaurant serving tandoori chicken (Rs80).

BUSES FROM KUMBAKONAM			
Destination	**Fare (Rs)**	**Duration (hr)**	**Frequency**
Chennai (No 303)	113	7	every 30min
Chidambaram	22	2½	every 20min
Coimbatore	110	10	1 daily (7pm)
Madurai	65	5	8 daily
Puducherry	40	4½	every 20min
Thanjavur	14.50	1½	every 10min

Getting There & Away

The bus stand and train station are about 2km east of the town centre. For details of bus services, see the boxed text (above).

For the Cauvery Delta area there are buses running every half-hour to Karaikal (Rs16, two hours), via Tranquebar and then on to Nagapattinam.

The overnight *Rock Fort Express* is the only major train to/from Chennai (sleeper/3AC Rs130/365), going via Thanjavur and Trichy. Passenger trains run to Chidambaram (Rs31, two hours) and Thanjavur.

AROUND KUMBAKONAM

Within easy day-trip distance from Kumbakonam are the two superb Chola temples of Dharasuram and Gangakondacholapuram. They are comparatively unvisited and beautifully constructed, and can be enjoyed in relative peace. Along with Brihadishwara Temple (p434) in Thanjavur, these structures are a Unesco World Heritage Site: the Great Living Chola Temples. They can also be visited on a day trip from Thanjavur (for Dharasuram) and Chidambaram (for Gangakondacholapuram).

Dharasuram & Gangakondacholapuram

Only 4km west of Kumbakonam in the village of Dharasuram, the **Airatesvara Temple** (☺ 6am-noon & 4-8pm), constructed by Rajaraja II (r 1146–63), is a superb example of 12th-century Chola architecture. Fronted by columns overflowing with miniature sculptures, the temple art depicts Shiva in the rare incarnation as Kankalamurti, the mendicant.

At Gangakondacholapuram, 35km north of Kumbakonam, you'll find a Shiva **temple** (☺ 6am-noon & 4-8pm) that's only slightly smaller than Thanjavur's Brihadishwara Temple; many believe the quality of the sculpture here is superior to its sister structure. While that's a subjective opinion, the temple, built by Rajendrea I (son of Rajaraja I, builder of Brihadishwara), does represent a later, somewhat more developed phase of Chola art. Note the 49m-tall *vimana* (tower) that tops the temple; its elegant up-sloping curves stand in stark contrast to the Brihadishwara's angular lines, and as a result the Gangakondacholapuram is often described as the feminine counterpart to the Thanjavur edifice.

Buses go from Kumbakonam bus stand to Gangakondacholapuram every half-hour (Rs15, 1½ hours). A rickshaw to Dharasuram will run you about 75 Rd round trip. Frequent buses head to Dharasuram as well; ask at the bus stand, as these tend to be village buses that will have to drop you off on their way out of the city.

CAUVERY DELTA

The Cauvery River is the beating heart of South Indian agriculture and, back in the day, connected the entire region via riverine routes. Today the Cauvery's delta, which spills into Tamil Nadu's east coast, is one of the prettiest and poorest parts of the state. This green and pleasant region can be visited on a lovely day drive (expect to pay Rs2000 to Rs3000 for a return taxi from Kumbakonam), although Nagapattinam, the capital of the district of the same name, can be given a pass unless you love traffic and drying fish.

Tourism infrastructure is generally of a low standard. Nagapattinam district was the worst affected part of Tamil Nadu when the 2004 tsunami struck, with up to 7000 lives lost and thousands more left homeless. Life seems to have returned to normal, although international aid projects were still very much in evidence at the time of writing.

Tranquebar (Tharangambadi)
☎ 04364

About 80km south of Chidambaram, Tranquebar was a Danish post established in 1620 by the Danish East India Company. The solid, pink-hued seafront **Danesborg Fort** (Indian/foreigner Rs5/50; ☿ 10am-1pm & 2-5.45pm Sat-Thu), occupied by the British in 1801, houses a small but fascinating **museum** on the region's Danish history. The quiet roadway leading to the fort is entered by an impressive 1792 gateway, and an exuberant Sunday service is held in the nearby 1718 church. Danish NGOs are restoring some of the colonial row houses nearby.

Stay directly opposite the fort in the exquisitely plush **Bungalow on the Beach** (☎ 288065; www.neemranahotels.com; r from Rs3000; ❇ ❇); rooms and views are fabulous, as is the villa-like heritage setting. Just next door – and still with sea views – is the pleasant **Hotel Tamil Nadu** (☎ 288065; dm/r Rs150/600), run by the owners of Bungalow on the Beach. To get here, take a bus from Chidambaram (Rs30, 2½ hours).

Vailankanni (Velanganni)
☎ 04365 / pop 10,151

In the 15th century, a buttermilk boy glimpsed the Virgin Mary as Our Lady of Good Health here, and her **basilica** remains one of the great cross-cultural religious icons in South India.

Housed in a neo-Gothic cathedral (elevated to the status of basilica when the Pope popped by in 1962), the Catholic Our Lady is the recipient of some distinctly Hindu worship. While one hall displays the Crucifixion and the Last Supper, the main event is the altar of Our Lady, where Mary is dressed in a golden sari, adorned with garlands of flowers and anointed with the milk of smashed coconuts.

Behind the basilica is a small **museum** (admission free) that houses offerings to Mary; small gold leg icons from those who've healed a bad leg, silver heart lockets from newlyweds, even silver-and-gold stethoscopes from medical students who have passed their exams. It's an almost medieval display of reverence.

An annual nine-day festival culminates on 8 September, the celebration of Mary's birth. There's a hectically devout but amiable atmosphere, with many interested Hindu visitors.

In town there are many lodges, especially in the square by the bus station and around the basilica. **SPT Lodge** (☎ 264288; r Rs250, with AC Rs500; ❇) – with a car on the roof…huh? – is a clean option, as is **Dayana Lodge** (☎ 263116; r Rs350, with AC Rs650; ❇). Or ask at the Church Rooms Booking Office, also on the square.

Daily bus services travel between Vailankanni and Chennai, Coimbatore, Bengaluru, Kanyakumari and Thiruvananthapuram (Trivandrum).

Calimere (Kodikkarai) Wildlife & Bird Sanctuary

This 333-sq-km **sanctuary** (☎ 04365-253092; per person/vehicle Rs5/15; ☿ 6am-6pm) 90km southeast of Thanjavur is noted for vast flocks of migratory curlews, terns, plovers, sandpipers, shanks and more that nest in the tidal mud flats from October to March. Unfortunately, in 2008 it also became a smuggling point for Tamil Tigers, and we weren't able to visit due to security concerns.

In the past the forest department ran two lodges here, charging Rs100 for two people. Other options included **Thambusamy Rest House** (r Rs100), 1km or so off the main road and beside the new lighthouse; you can walk to a watchtower and there's a shady, neglected garden. You'll need to bring food.

The easiest way to get to Calimere is by bus (Rs6, every hour) or taxi from Vedaranniyam, which is 12km away and linked by frequent buses to Nagapattinam or Thanjavur.

THANJAVUR (TANJORE)

☎ 04362 / pop 215,314

Here are the ochre foundation blocks of one of the most remarkable nations of Dravidian history, one of the few kingdoms to expand Hinduism beyond the Black Waters that surround India, a bedrock for aesthetic styles that spread from Madurai to the Mekong. A dizzying historical legacy was once administered from Thanjavur, ancient capital of the great Chola Empire, which today…is a chaotic, messy, modern Indian town. Oh, how the good times have gone. But their presence is still remarkably evident; past the honking buses and happy public urination are the World Heritage–listed Brihadishwara Temple and the sprawling Maratha palace complex.

Information

BBC Net (18/12 MKM Rd; per hr Rs25; ☺ 9.30am-9.30pm) Fast internet access in the basement of the Nallaiyah Shopping Complex.

ICICI Bank ATM (South Main Rd; New Bus Station)

Indian Bank ATM (Vallum Rd)

Main post office (☺ 9am-7pm Mon-Sat, 10am-4pm Sun) Near the train station.

Sify i-way (East Main Rd; per hr Rs20; ☺ 9am-11pm) Broadband goodness.

State Bank of India ATM (Hospital Rd)

Tourist office (☎ 230984; Gandhiji Rd; ☺ 10am-5.45pm Mon-Fri) On the corner of the Hotel Tamil Nadu complex.

VKC Forex (Golden Plaza, Gandhiji Rd; ☺ 9.30am-9pm) Changes cash and travellers cheques.

Sights

BRIHADISHWARA TEMPLE & FORT

Come here twice: in the morning, when the tawny sandstone begins to assert its dominance over the white dawn sunshine, and in the

evening, when the rocks capture a hot palette of reds, oranges, yellows and pinks. Alright; there's no single light that best illuminates the **Brihadishwara Temple** (☺ 6am-1pm & 3-8pm), the crowning glory of Chola temple architecture. The temple was commissioned in 1010 by Raja Raja (whose name literally means 'king of kings'), a well-regarded monarch so organised he had the names and addresses of all his dancers, musicians, barbers and poets inscribed into the temple wall – better than many modern Indian institutions can manage.

Note the covered statue of Nandi (Shiva's sacred bull) – 6m long by 3m high – that faces the inner sanctum. Created from a single piece of rock, it weighs 25 tonnes and is one of India's largest Nandi statues. There's also a well-executed interpretive centre set along the side alcoves, which includes sculptures and paintings culled from the temple walls (including a particularly energetic Shiva slaying an army of demons while Buddha hovers above. Not for enlightenment either – the demons were Shiva-worshippers, and the Buddha took them on as devotees so the Destroyer could justify killing them).

Unlike most South Indian temples where the *gopurams* are the highest towers, here the 13-storey, 66m *vimana* (centre tower) dominates.

THANJAVUR ROYAL PALACE & MUSEUMS

The pink walls hold court for crows; the queen's courtyard is overrun with weeds; the inner corridors stink of bat guano. And yet…amid the decay are expertly carved bodies of gods and goddesses, sky-bright tile work, massive columns of preserved, chocolate teak and the incredible murals of one of the great dynasties of South Indian royalty. The labyrinthine complex was constructed partly by the Nayaks of Madurai and partly by the Marathas.

Walk by a local school to enter the main hall of the **palace** (Indian adult/child Rs5/2, foreign adult/child Rs50/25, incl entry to the Durbar Hall & bell tower; ☺ 9am-6pm), and follow the signs to the elegantly faded **Durbar Hall** (Royal Court). An incredible profusion of murals erupts here, unrestored and elegantly faded, bursting with geometric designs, scenes of Hindu legend and a flock of vaguely European yet almost Indian cherubs. With a torch you can peek into a 6km secret passage that runs under the palace and reeks of bat poo.

THE SOUTH INDIAN–SOUTHEAST ASIAN CONNECTION

If you're a fan of Southeast Asian temples, art and architecture, going to South India is like retracing Western art back to Greece. Which would make Tamil Nadu, the cultural cradle of South India, and Thanjavur, the heartland of the Cholas, something like Athens. Under Rajaraja (r 985–1014) and his son, Rajendra (r 1012–44), the Chola Empire expanded into Sri Lanka and Southeast Asia, annexing much of Sumatra and the Indo-Malay kingdom of Srivijaya. Beyond the military influence, South Indian Hindus expanded their cultural umbrella, sometimes literally: the Southeast Asian use of umbrellas as royal regalia traces directly back to South India. So do the statues of *apsaras* (heavenly nymphs), the richly embellished jewellery of court fashions from Angkor in Cambodia to Ayutthaya in Thailand (the latter name derived from the Ramayana kingdom of Ayodyah), the centrality of temples to daily life, the sense of form and space used in stone and bronze sculptures, and a common usage of Sanskrit in classical literature. Bali remains a Hindu island thanks to the cross-cultural connections of this period, and every Thai king for the past 200 years has been named Rama in honour of the prince of the Indian epic.

There's a legend of the founding of Angkor Wat, with its Chola-esque step pyramids and bas reliefs of enormous Khmer faces, which elegantly sums up this link: a Cambodian *naga* (serpent-dragon) princess would not marry any suitor until she was approached by an Indian warrior, who cast his spear into her fertile paddies (no, really). The story doesn't just link two nations, it weds their religions as well, indigenous Southeast Asian nature cults (which venerated *nagas* and other animal deities) blending with the classical Hinduism of South India.

In the former Sadar Mahal Palace is the **Raja Serfoji Memorial Hall** (admission Rs2) with a small collection of thrones, weapons and photographs; there's a similar collection in the **Royal Palace Museum** (admission Rs1, camera/video Rs30/250). Many of the artefacts date from the early 19th century when the enlightened and far-sighted scholar-king Serfoji II ruled. His sixth descendant still lives here; pick up *Raja Serfoji II* (Rs25), his very readable monograph about his extraordinary ancestor, from any of the ticket desks.

An extensive **gallery** (admission Rs15, camera/video Rs30/250) of Chola bronzes sits between the Royal Palace Museum and the bell tower. Admission to a small tower is included with this fee, wherein you can see an incongruous whale skeleton and a lovely lotus-style ceiling, plus a few peeling murals. Nearby, the **bell tower** is worth a climb for views right across Thanjavur and the palace itself. The spiral stone staircase is dark, narrow and slippery; watch your head and your step.

Perhaps Serfoji II's greatest contribution to posterity is the **Saraswati Mahal Library** (admission free; ⏱ 10am-1pm & 1.30-5.30pm Tue-Thu) between the gallery and the palace museum. It's a monument to both universal knowledge and an eclectic mind that collected prints of Chinese torture methods, Audubon-style sketches of Indian flora and fauna, sketches of the old London skyline and a collection of some

60,000 palm-leaf and paper manuscripts in Indian and European languages. Like few of his contemporaries, Serfoji II understood the need to preserve the Indian written canon, and today the library has converted 243 Tamil and 183 Sanskrit palm-leaf records into printed material.

Just down the road, the uninspiring **Tamil Museum** (East Main Rd; admission free; ⏱ 10am-1pm & 1.30-5.30pm Tue-Thu) houses a blasé collection of coins, carvings and cannonballs.

Sleeping

BUDGET

There's a bunch of nondescript cheap lodges opposite the central bus stand with rooms for Rs150 to Rs300 a double.

Ashoka Lodge (☎ 230022; 93 Abraham Pandithar Rd; dm/s/d Rs130/140/300, r with AC Rs525; ✶) The Ashoka has been in business for 42 years, and is, frankly, looking its age. That said, the rooms are, if a little tattered, surprisingly spacious for the cost and kept clean.

Hotel Yagappa (☎ 230421; 1 Trichy Rd; d Rs195-420, with AC Rs770; ✶) Yagappa is close to the train station and an ATM; this is a good thing. It's also getting a bit faded; this is a bad thing. But the interior is still well maintained, and rooms are clean enough for the budget-and-rail-proximate conscious.

Manees Residency (☎ 271574; www.manees residency.com; 2905 Srinivasam Pillai Rd; s/d Rs275/425, with

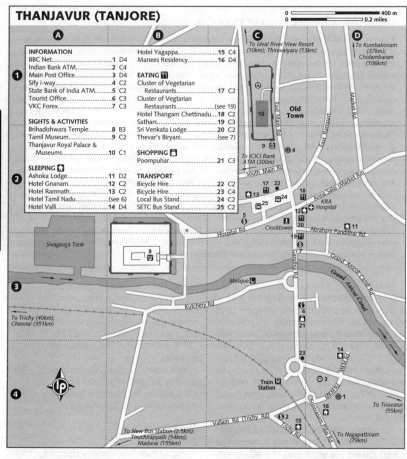

THANJAVUR (TANJORE)

0 — 400 m
0 — 0.2 miles

INFORMATION
BBC Net.................................1 D4
Indian Bank ATM....................2 C4
Main Post Office.....................3 D4
Sify i-way.............................4 C2
State Bank of India ATM..........5 C2
Tourist Office........................6 C3
VKC Forex............................7 C3

SIGHTS & ACTIVITIES
Brihadishwara Temple............8 B3
Tamil Museum.......................9 C2
Thanjavur Royal Palace &
    Museums........................10 C1

SLEEPING
Ashoka Lodge.....................11 D2
Hotel Gnanam....................12 C2
Hotel Ramnath...................13 C2
Hotel Tamil Nadu.............(see 6)
Hotel Valli........................14 D4

Hotel Yagappa...................15 C4
Manees Residency..............16 D4

EATING
Cluster of Vegetarian
    Restaurants..................17 C2
Cluster of Vegtarian
    Restaurants...............(see 19)
Hotel Thangam Chettinadu....18 C2
Sathars............................19 C3
Sri Venkata Lodge..............20 C2
Thevar's Biryani...............(see 7)

SHOPPING
Poompuhar........................21 C3

TRANSPORT
Bicycle Hire.......................22 C2
Bicycle Hire.......................23 C4
Local Bus Stand..................24 C2
SETC Bus Stand..................25 C2

To Ideal River View Resort (10km); Thiruvaiyaru (13km)

To Kumbakonam (37km); Chidambaram (106km)

Old Town

To ICICI Bank ATM (300m)

South Main Rd

Hospital Rd

Sivaganga Tank

Clocktower

Anna Salai (Market Rd)

KRA Hospital

Abraham Pandithar Rd

Grand Anicut Canal Rd

Mosque

Kutchery Rd

Gandhiji Rd

Grand Anicut Canal

To Trichy (40km); Chennai (351km)

Train Station

To New Bus Station (2.5km); Tiruchirappalli (54km); Madurai (155km)

Vallam Rd (Trichy Rd)

Trichy Rd

To Tiruvarur (55km)

To Nagapattinam (79km)

AC Rs426/625; ✪) The best high-budget/low-midrange option around, Manees provides energetic service, sparkling cleanliness and rooms that are almost shockingly sparkly for the price.

Hotel Valli (☎ 231580; arasu_tnj@rediffmail.com; 2948 MKM Rd; s/d from Rs260/500, r with AC Rs600; ✪) Near the train station, Valli is another great bet for budget travellers. Staff are personable and the rooms themselves are spick and span. It's in a reasonably peaceful location beyond a bunch of greasy backyard workshops.

MIDRANGE & TOP END
Hotel Ramnath (☎ 272567; 1335 South Rampart; s/d from Rs400/450, with AC Rs650/700; ✪) Just across from the bus stand, the Ramnath is a nice 'upmar-

ket budget' option for those who want a little bit of spoiling – fresh rooms and credit-card acceptance – with their savings.

Hotel Tamil Nadu (☎ 231325; Gandhiji Rd; d from Rs450, with AC from Rs800; ✪) The Tamil Nadu has cleaned up its act (and hiked its prices) as of late, making this former government guest house a cool spot for those hovering between price categories. The architecture is sultan-chic (makes sense, given this is a former royal guest house), an atmosphere accentuated by a quiet, leafy courtyard, big rooms and wide balconies.

Hotel Gnanam (☎ 278501; www.hotelgnanam.com; Anna Salai; s/d Rs1050/1250; ✪ 🖳) It's a bit of a corporate hotel, but the Gnanam is perfect for anyone needing wireless internet and other modern amenities while plopped in Thanjavur's geographic centre.

Ideal River View Resort (☎ 250633; www.idealresort .com; s/d from Rs3000/3500; ❄ 🖳 🗪) About 10km northwest of the city, this tranquil resort is by far the nicest place to stay near Thanjavur. Set in beautiful gardens beside the Vennar River are immaculate, brightly furnished cottages with roomy balconies.

Eating
There's a cluster of simple veg restaurants, open for breakfast, lunch and dinner, near the local bus stand and along Gandhiji Rd.

Sri Venkata Lodge (Gandhiji Rd; thalis Rs25) A few minutes from the bus station, this veg-only place does a nice thali.

Thevar's Biryani (☎ 270979; Gandhiji Rd; mains Rs30-60) Thevar's specialises in exactly what the name suggests, and it specialises in the Mughal rice dish (done up with southern influences here, like sour tamarind sauce) well.

Hotel Thangam Chetttinadu (☎ 272755; Old Bus Station, Anna Salai Rd; mains Rs30-80) A conveniently located, often locally stuffed spot that should satisfy any mixed group of vegetarians and carnivores.

Sathars (☎ 331041; 167 Gandhiji Rd; mains Rs40-95) Good service and quality food make this place popular. Downstairs is a veg restaurant with lunchtime thalis, upstairs is an AC section with great-value non-veg food.

Shopping
Thanjavur is a good place to shop for handicrafts and arts, especially around the palace. Numerous shops along East Main Rd and Gandhiji Rd sell everything from quality crafts and ready-made clothes to inexpensive kitsch. For fixed prices and hassle-free shopping, try **Poompuhar** (Gandhiji Rd; ⏰ 10am-8pm Mon-Sat).

To see bronze-casters at work, call craftsman **Mr Kathirvel** (☎ 098432-35202), whose extended family has, for several generations, used the lost-wax method to make bronze artefacts in a backyard kiln; it's a window into the small cottage industries on which Indian craft still thrives. He lives out towards Vallam Rd; call for directions.

Getting There & Away
BUS
The two city bus stands are for local and SETC buses. SETC has a computerised **reservation office** (☎ 230950; ⏰ 7.30am-9.30pm). The New

BUSES FROM THANJAVUR (TANJORE)			
Destination	Fare (Rs)	Duration (hr)	Frequency
Chennai	105-135	8	20 daily
Chidambaram*	50	4	every 30min
Kumbakonam*	15	1	every 30min
Madurai*	50	4	every 15min
Ooty	125	10	8.30pm only
Trichy*	20	1½	every 5min
* New Bus Station			

Bus Station, 2.5km south of the centre, services local areas and destinations south. Bus 74 shuttles between the three bus stations (Rs3.50). For details of services, see the boxed text (above).

TRAIN
The station is conveniently central at the south end of Gandhiji Rd. Thanjavur is off the main Chennai–Madurai line, so there's only one express train direct to Chennai – the overnight *Rock Fort Express* (sleeper/3AC Rs181/485, 9½ hours) departing at 8.30pm. For more frequent trains north or south, including to Madurai, take a passenger train to Trichy (Rs20, 1½ hours, eight daily) and change there. There's one daily express (6.50am) and a couple of passenger trains to Kumbakonam (Rs10, one hour).

The *Thanjavur-Mysore Express* leaves daily at 7.15pm for Bengaluru (sleeper/3AC Rs205/493, 11 hours) and Mysore (sleeper/3AC Rs220/598, 14½ hours).

Getting Around
The main attractions of Thanjavur are close enough to walk between, but this can make for a tiring day depending on your fitness. Bicycles can be hired from stalls opposite the train station and local bus stand (per hour Rs3). An autorickshaw into town from the New Bus Station costs around Rs200.

AROUND THANJAVUR
About 13km north of Thanjavur, **Thiruvaiyaru** hosts the January **international music festival** (p389) in honour of the saint and composer Thyagaraja, whose birthplace is at Tiruvarur, 55km east of Thanjavur. The **Thyagararajaswami Temple** here boasts the largest temple chariot in Tamil Nadu, which is hauled through the streets during the 10-day **car festival** in

April/May. Regular buses run from Thanjavur to Thiruvaiyaru for Rs4.

TRICHY (TIRUCHIRAPPALLI)

☎ 0431 / pop 866,354

Welcome to (more or less) the geographic centre of Tamil Nadu. Fortunately, this hub isn't just a travel junction, although it does make a good base for exploring large parts of central Tamil Nadu. But Tiruchirappalli, universally known as Trichy, also mixes up a throbbing bazaar with several major must-see temples, including the dramatic Rock Fort and mind-boggling Sri Ranganathaswamy complex. It's popular with Indian tourists, especially during auspicious marriage seasons when gorgeously clothed families abound in every hotel.

Trichy's long history dates back to before the Christian era when it was a Chola citadel. Since then it's passed into the hands of the Pallavas, Pandyas, Vijayanagars and Deccan sultans. The modern town and the Rock Fort Temple were built by the Nayaks of Madurai.

Orientation

Trichy's places of interest are scattered over a large area from north to south, but for travellers the city is conveniently split into three distinct areas. The Trichy Junction, or Cantonment, area in the south has most of the hotels and restaurants, the bus and train stations, the tourist office and the main post office. This is where you'll likely arrive and stay. The Rock Fort Temple and main bazaar area is 2.5km north of here; the other important temples are in an area called Srirangam, a further 3km to 5km north again, across the Cauvery River. Fortunately, the whole lot is connected by a good bus service.

Information

INTERNET ACCESS

Mas Media Internet (Map p440; Williams Rd; per hr Rs10; ☒ 24hr)

Sify i-way (per hr Rs30; ☒ 9am –9pm) Chinnar Bazaar (Map p439); Royal Rd (Map p440); Williams Rd (Map p440)

MEDICAL SERVICES

Seahorse Hospital (Map p440; ☎ 2462660; Royal Rd) A large hospital in the Cantonment.

MONEY

Canara Bank (Map p439; Chinnar Bazaar)
Delight Forex (Map p440; Williams Rd; ☒ 9.30am-5.30pm Mon-Sat)

ICICI Bank ATM Junction Rd (Map p440); West Boulevard Rd (Map p439)
UTI Bank ATM Chinnar Bazaar (Map p439); Junction Rd (Map p440)

TOURIST INFORMATION

Tourist office (Map p440; ☎ 2460136; 1 Williams Rd; ☒ 10am-5.45pm Mon-Fri) One of the more helpful tourism info offices in the state.

TRAVEL AGENCIES

Indian Panorama (☎ 2433372; www.indianpanorama.in) Trichy-based and covering all of India, this professional and reliable agency/tour operator is run by a New Zealand couple.

Sights

ROCK FORT TEMPLE

The **Rock Fort Temple** (Map p439; admission Rs2, camera/video Rs10/50; ☒ 6am-8pm), perched 83m high on a massive outcrop, lords over Trichy with stony arrogance. The ancient rock was first hewn by religious-minded Pallavas, who cut small cave temples into the southern face, but it was the war-savvy Nayaks who later made strategic use of the naturally fortified position. There are two main temples: **Sri Thayumanaswamy Temple**, halfway to the top (there may be some bats snoozing in the ceiling), and **Vinayaka Temple**, at the summit, dedicated to Ganesh. There are 437 stone-cut steps to climb, and the hike is worth the effort – the view is wonderful, with eagles wheeling beneath and Trichy sprawling all around into the greater Cauvery. Non-Hindus are not allowed into either temple, but occasionally – for a small fee – temple priests waive this regulation, although the inside of the Vinayaka temple isn't that impressive.

SRI RANGANATHASWAMY TEMPLE

Alright temple-philes, here's the one you've been waiting for: quite possibly the biggest temple in India. Actually, even if you're feeling templed-out, we have a feeling this **temple complex** (Map p439; camera/video Rs50/150; ☒ 6am-1pm & 3-9pm) is going to knock your socks off. Located about 3km north of the Rock Fort, it feels more like a self-enclosed city than a house of worship, and in truth, that's the idea: entering this temple's inner sanctum requires passing through seven *gopuram* (the largest is 73m high). Inside the fourth wall is a kiosk where you can buy a ticket (Rs10) and climb the wall for a semi-panoramic view of the complex that delineates levels of existence and consciousness. You'll proceed past rings of beggars, merchants and Brahmins, then plazas of *devas* (angels) and minor deities before reaching the inner chamber, dedicated to Vishnu. Here, the god is worshipped as Sheshashayana, Vishnu who sleeps on a bed made of the king of *nagas*.

Take note of the numerous carvings and statues of *vanaras* (literally 'forest people'), monkey warriors and princesses from the Ramayana, as well as avatars (incarnations) of Vishnu in one of his animal forms, such as the half-lion Nairarishma. These may have been tribal pre-Hindu deities that were folded into the religion, and remain popular objects of worship.

A **Temple Chariot Festival**, where statues of the deities are paraded aboard a fine chariot, is held here each January, but the most important festival is the 21-day **Vaikunta Ekadasi** (Paradise Festival) in mid-December, when the celebrated Vaishnavaite text, Tiruvaimozhi, is recited before an image of Vishnu.

Bus 1 from Trichy Junction or Rock Fort stops right outside this temple.

SRI JAMBUKESHWARA TEMPLE

If you're visiting the five elemental temples of Shiva, you need to visit **Sri Jambukeshwara Temple** (Map p439; camera/video Rs20/150; ☉ 6am-1pm & 3-9pm), dedicated to Shiva, Parvati and the medium of water. The liquid theme of the place is realised in the central shrine, which houses a partially submerged Shiva lingam. The outer chambers are full of carvings, including several of an elephant being freed from a spider web by Shiva, which provoked the pachyderm to perform *puja* for the Destroyer.

If you're taking bus 1, ask for 'Tiruvanakoil'; the temple is about 100m east of the main road.

OTHER SIGHTS

Lourdes Church (Map p439) is heavily decked out in Gallo-Catholic design, from neo-Gothic spires to the anguished scenes of crucifixion and martyrdom painted inside. The hush of the nave makes an interesting contrast to the frenetic activity that characterises Trichy's Hindu temples, but note the cross-religious pollination: icons of the Virgin Mary are garlanded in Hindu flower necklaces. The **Feast of Our Lady of Lourdes** is held on 11 February.

The entrance to Lourdes is on Madras Trunk Rd, and when you're finished you can escape into the green and cool campus of

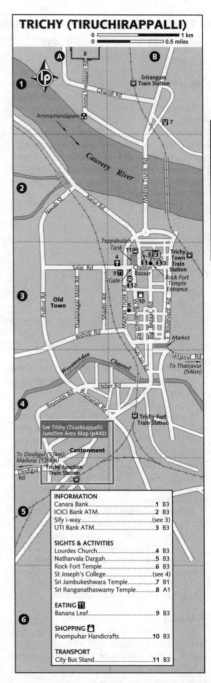

TRICHY (TIRUCHIRAPPALLI)

INFORMATION	
Canara Bank................................1	B3
ICICI Bank ATM..........................2	B3
Sify i-way..............................(see 3)	
UTI Bank ATM............................3	B3

SIGHTS & ACTIVITIES	
Lourdes Church..........................4	B3
Natharvala Dargah......................5	B3
Rock Fort Temple........................6	B3
St Joseph's College.................(see 4)	
Sri Jambukeshwara Temple..........7	B1
Sri Ranganathaswamy Temple.......8	A1

EATING	
Banana Leaf...............................9	B3

SHOPPING	
Poompuhar Handicrafts..............10	B3

TRANSPORT	
City Bus Stand...........................11	B3

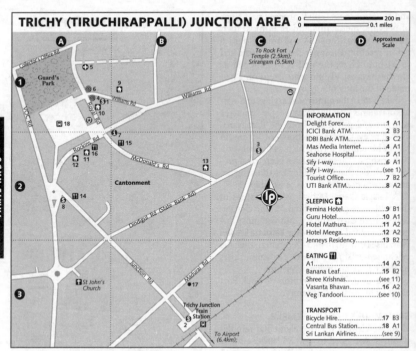

TRICHY (TIRUCHIRAPPALLI) JUNCTION AREA

INFORMATION
Delight Forex	1 A1
ICICI Bank ATM	2 B3
IDBI Bank ATM	3 C2
Mas Media Internet	4 A1
Seahorse Hospital	5 A1
Sify i-way	6 A1
Sify i-way	(see 1)
Tourist Office	7 B2
UTI Bank ATM	8 A2

SLEEPING
Femina Hotel	9 B1
Guru Hotel	10 A1
Hotel Mathura	11 A2
Hotel Meega	12 A2
Jenneys Residency	13 B2

EATING
A1	14 A2
Banana Leaf	15 B2
Shree Krishnas	(see 11)
Vasanta Bhavan	16 A2
Veg Tandoori	(see 10)

TRANSPORT
Bicycle Hire	17 B3
Central Bus Station	18 A1
Sri Lankan Airlines	(see 9)

Jesuit **St Joseph's College** (where classes run from Intro to Javascript to Comparative Theology). You might notice signs that display a syncretic icon: a Hindu temple overlaid by a Christian cross underlined by the Muslim crescent and star. An eccentric and dusty **museum** (admission free; ⏰ 10am-noon & 2-4pm Mon-Sat) contains the natural history collections of the Jesuit priests' summer excursions to the Western Ghats in the 1870s. Bang on the door and the caretaker will let you in – or not, depending on if he's there.

Natharvala Dargah (Map p439) is another example of India's masalafication of religion. It's Islam's turn, in the form of the tomb of popular Muslim saint Natther. From a distance the mausoleum is a minaret-ensconced compound with distinctly Arab sea-green embellishments, but the *puja*-like worship of Natther has strong Hindu overtones.

Sleeping

Most of Trichy's accommodation is in the Junction-Cantonment area around the bus station and a short walk north of the train station.

BUDGET

Hotel Meega (Map p440; ☎ 2414092; hotelmeega@rediff mail.com; 3 Rockins Rd; d Rs325, with AC Rs500; ❄️) This is a good-value hotel – the rooms are smallish but clean, bright and more midrange than budget standard. There's a popular veg restaurant downstairs.

Hotel Mathura (Map p440; ☎ 2414737; www.hotel mathura.com; 1 Rockins Rd; s/d Rs325/415, with AC Rs595/685; ❄️) The Mathura is quite good value, as long as you can score a room that isn't on the bus-stand side of the building (or if you can sleep through the honk of a dozen Indian air horns). Rooms are all clean and spacious.

Guru Hotel (Map p440; ☎ 2415881; guruhotel@yahoo .com; 13A Royal Rd; s/d without AC Rs500/600, with AC Rs700/900, ste Rs1300; ❄️) Like the Mathura, the Guru is a lovely midrange option; if anything, it comes off as cleaner and posher (especially the marble lobby) than its competitor.

MIDRANGE & TOP END

Femina Hotel (Map p440 ☎ 2414501; try_femina@san charnet.in; 104C Femina Rd; d from Rs550, with AC from Rs1300; ❄️ 🖥️) Femina is one of those Indian business hotels that manages to be affordable even if you're on a budget – and the staff doesn't look at travellers as if they've just crawled out of a swamp. Nonguests can use the pool and small gym (per hour Rs75).

Jenneys Residency (Map p440; ☎ 2414414; jenneys@satyam.net.in; 3/14 McDonald's Rd; r from US$50; ☒ ☒) Jenneys is enormous, semi-luxurious and in a relatively quiet location. The best rooms are on the top floors but all are well appointed; be aware that a 25% luxury tax will be added. Hotel facilities include a health club and a truly bizarre Wild West theme bar.

Eating

Veg Tandoori (Map p440; Royal Rd; Rs15-40; ☒ breakfast, lunch & dinner) It may look tatty, but this spot adjacent to the bus stand does a reliable line in all kinds of veg cuisine, and the best dosas we tried in Trichy. Plus, it's open late (well, past 11pm).

Shree Krishnas (Map p440; 1 Rockins Rd; mains Rs20-40; ☒ breakfast, lunch & dinner) On the lower floor of Hotel Mathura, with a nice view of the buses playing plough-the-pedestrian across the road, this is a reliable spot for veg goodness and milky-sweet desserts.

Vasanta Bhavan (Map p440; Rockins Rd; Rs20-40) Just next door to Shree Krishnas, you can pop in here for North Indian veg – that of the paneer and naan genre – if you're tired of dosas and *idlis*.

A1 (Map p440; Junction Rd; Rs25-80; ☒ lunch & dinner) The waiters clearly graduated from the Keystone Cops School of Food Service, but otherwise this pleasant AC restaurant does very tasty veg and non-veg.

Banana Leaf (Map p439; ☎ 271101; Madras Trunk Rd; mains Rs30-90; ☒ lunch & dinner) The Leaf is the best thing going in Trichy, with an enormous menu that plucks off regional favourites from Kashmir to Kanyakumari. With that said, the speciality is the fiery, vaguely vinegary cuisine of Andhra Pradesh; if you can handle your heat, fall in love with the chicken Hyderabadi. Another branch is next to the Hotel Tamil Nadu in Trichy Junction.

Shopping

The main bazaar, which runs by the entrance to the Rock Fort, is as chaotic and crowded as you like; it constantly feels like all of Trichy is strolling the strip. The usual Indian array of plastic toys and ripped-off Bollywood VCDs is on sale. Try **Poompuhar Handicrafts** (Map p439; West Boulevard Rd; ☒ 9am-8pm) for fixed-price crafts.

Getting There & Away

Trichy is virtually in the geographical centre of Tamil Nadu and it's well connected by air, bus and train.

AIR

As well as domestic flights, Trichy's airport has flights to Sri Lanka. **Sri Lankan Airlines** (Map p439; ☎ 2412582; ☒ 9am-5.30pm Mon-Sat, 9am-1pm Sun), with an office at Femina Hotel, flies daily to Colombo (US$175).

BUS

Most buses head to the central bus station (Map p440) on Rockins Rd. If you're travelling to Kodaikanal, a good option is to take one of the frequent buses to Dindigul (Rs25, two hours) and change there. For details of services, see the boxed text (p442).

TRAIN

Trichy is on the main Chennai–Madurai line so there are lots of rail options in either direction. Of the nine daily expresses to Chennai, the quickest are the *Vaigai Express* (2nd/chair class Rs85/312, 5½ hours) departing Trichy at 9.10am, and the *Pallavan Express,* which leaves at 6.30am. The best overnight train is the *Rock Fort Express* (sleeper/3AC Rs145/392, 7½ hours) at 9.40pm.

For Madurai the best train is the *Guruvaya Express* (2nd class/sleeper Rs47/75, three hours), which leaves at 1pm. The *Mysore Express* goes daily to Bengaluru (sleeper/3AC Rs160/450, 11½ hours) and Mysore (sleeper/3AC Rs212/562, 15 hours).

Getting Around

TO/FROM THE AIRPORT

The 7km ride into town is Rs1400 by taxi and Rs80 by autorickshaw. Otherwise, take bus 7, 59, 58 or 63 to/from the airport (30 minutes).

BICYCLE

Trichy lends itself to cycling as it's flat; it's a reasonably easy ride from Trichy Junction to the Rock Fort Temple, but a long haul to Srirangam and back. There are a couple of places on Madurai Rd near the train station where you can hire bicycles (per hr Rs5).

BUS

Trichy's local bus service is easy to use. Bus 1 (any letter) from the central bus station

TAMIL NADU

BUSES FROM TRICHY (TIRUCHIRAPPALLI)			
Destination	Fare (Rs)	Duration (hr)	Frequency
Bengaluru	150	8	3 daily
Chennai	110-142	7	every 5min
Chidambaram	51	3½	hourly
Coimbatore	73	7	every 30min
Kodaikanal	62	6	3 daily
Madurai	35	3	every 10min
Ooty	100	8	1 daily
Puducherry	70	5	3 daily
Thanjavur	15	1½	every 5min

on Rockins Rd goes every few minutes via the Rock Fort Temple, Sri Jambukeshwara Temple and the main entrance to Sri Ranganathaswamy Temple (Rs4). To see them all, get off in that order (ask the conductor or driver where the stops are), as it runs in a one-way circuit.

SOUTHERN TAMIL NADU

TRICHY TO RAMESWARAM

In between Trichy and Rameswaram is Tamil Nadu's best example of cave art, the homeland of the region's greatest traders and bankers, and a few other stop-offs that make for a good road trip (or day tour from Trichy, Madurai or Rameswaram). The following sites are, unless otherwise noted, listed in order of encounter from Trichy south to Rameswaram.

Some 34km south of Trichy is the nondescript town of Pudukkottai, which has historical importance in inverse proportion to its current obscurity. From 1680 to 1947 this was one of the great princely states of South India, and the relics of bygone days are on display in the wonderful **Pudukkottai Museum** (Indian/foreigner Rs3/100; ⊗ 9.30am-5pm), located in a renovated palace building in Pudukkottai town. Its eclectic collection includes musical instruments, megalithic burial artefacts and some remarkable paintings and miniatures.

About 16km north of Pudukkottai is **Sittannavasal** (admission Rs100), where you'll find a small Jain cave temple that conceals magnificent vegetable-oil frescoes. The shrine is small, but the cave is widely ignored by day trippers,

which means you'll likely get to appreciate these masterpieces of Jain art on your own. Note the Edenic garden paradise painted on the main ceiling, which conceals fish, mythical sea monsters and beautiful water maidens. Or try making your 'Om' echo across an acoustic masterpiece of a meditation chamber, where statues of Jain saints sit in cross-legged repose.

Simple and imposing, the renovated **Tirumayam Fort** (Indian/foreigner Rs5/100; ⊗ 9am-5pm), located about 17km south of Puddukotai, is worth a climb for the 360-degree views from the battlements onto the surrounding countryside. Or you can take a shady rest with local goats under a banyan tree.

In the backstreets of small **Kanadukathan**, 10km south of Tirumayam, are the weddingcake houses of the Chettiars, an interrelated clan of bankers, merchants and traders. The mansions of the community are decked out in the cosmopolitan goods brought home by Chettiars during their extensive trading forays: Belgian chandeliers, Italian granite, Burmese teak and artwork from around the world. To get a feel for the royal life, book a night in the **Chettinadu Mansion** (☎ 04565-273080; www.chettinadumansion.com; r from Rs3300; ⊠ ▯ ▣) or **Visalam** (☎ 04843-011711; www.cghearth.com /visalam; from €170; ⊠ ▯ ▣), both restored and frankly fantastic heritage houses. They're pricey, but hey: you get to spend the night in a living Indian palace.

Another important stop made by Rama during the epic Ramayana, **Devipattanam**, some 25 minutes north of Rameswaram, marks the spot where Rama prayed before embarking to (Sri) Lanka to rescue his wife. As part of his ablutions, the avatar of Vishnu fashioned nine idols out of the sand, meant to represent the nine Navagrahas, or planets (worshipped as deities in classical Hinduism). Rama placed the Navagrahas in the sea, where they stand to this day, visited by pilgrims who wade into an enclosed pool of waist-high water at the end of a small pier. The **shrine** is a very sacred pilgrimage spot, but the rubbish in the water might make you think twice about circumnavigating the holy solar system, although doing so will endear you to local Hindus.

It's an easy day tour from Trichy (taxi with/ without AC Rs1500/1000) or Madurai (a little more). Otherwise catch one of the many daily buses from Trichy to Karaikkudi (Rs52, three hours) and get on and off at the sights along the way. Coming from Madurai, get a bus to Karaikkudi and take a local bus or hire a taxi. Kanadukathan is about a 500m walk off the main road.

Regular buses run between Karaikkudi, via Ramanathapuram, to Rameswaram.

RAMESWARAM
☎ 04573 / pop 37,968

In the past, one did not go past here. Rameswaram was the southernmost point of sacred India; to leave the boundaries was to abandon caste and fall below the status of the lowliest skinner of sacred cows. Then Rama, incarnation of Vishnu and hero of the Ramayana, led an army of monkeys and bears to the ocean and crossed into the kingdom of (Sri) Lanka, where he defeated the demon Ravana and rescued his wife, Sita. Afterwards, prince and princess came to this spot to offer thanks to Shiva.

If all this seems like so much folklore, it's honest but for millions of Hindus, who flock to the Ramanathaswamy Temple to worship where God, essentially, worshipped God.

Apart from these pilgrims, Rameswaram is a sleepy fishing village. It's also an island, connected to the mainland by the Indira Gandhi bridge, and used to serve as a ferry link to Sri Lanka – until the Tamil Tigers went on the prowl. Tamil Sri Lankan refugees still come here by the boatload.

Orientation & Information

Most hotels and restaurants are clustered around the Ramanathaswamy Temple. The bus stand, 2km to the west, is connected by shuttle bus to the town centre.

You can't change money here but the **State Bank of India** (East Car St) has an ATM accepting international cards.

Sights
RAMANATHASWAMY TEMPLE

When Rama decided to worship Shiva, he figured he'd need a lingam to do the thing properly. Being a God, he sent a flying monkey to find the biggest lingam around – in this case, a Himalayan mountain. But the monkey took too long, so Rama's wife Sita made a simple lingam of sand, which Shiva approved of, and which is enshrined today in the centre of this **temple** (camera Rs25; ⏱ 4am-1pm & 3-8.30pm). Besides housing the world's holiest sand-mound, the structure is notable for

its horizon-stretching thousand-pillar halls and 22 *theerthams* (tanks), which pilgrims are expected to bathe in and drink from. The number of *theerthams* corresponds to the number of arrows in Rama's quiver, which he used to generate water on the island. Only Hindus may enter the inner sanctum.

Even when the temple is closed, it is possible to take a peaceful amble through the extensive corridors. In the evening, before the temple is closed, you may see temple Brahmins take some of the residing deities on a parade through the halls of Ramanathaswamy.

DHANUSHKODI & ADAM'S BRIDGE

Kanyakumari may technically be India's land's end, but **Dhanushkodi** plays the part better. About 18km southwest of town, this is a long, low sweep of sand, dust devils, fishing hamlets, donkeys and green waves. It's tempting to swim here, but be careful of strong rips. You can ride a passenger truck for a few rupees, or walk 2½ hours (one way!) to the edge: **Adam's Bridge**, the chain of reefs, sandbanks and islets that almost connects India with Sri Lanka, 33km away, was supposedly built by Rama and his monkey army. Buses (Rs5, hourly) from the local bus stand on East Car St stop about 4km before the beach so you have to walk the rest of the way, and an autorickshaw costs Rs250 return.

About 10km before Dhanushkodi, the **Kothandaraswamy Temple** is the only structure to survive a 1964 cyclone that destroyed the village. Legend has it Rama, overcome with guilt at having killed Ravana, performed a *puja* on this spot and thereafter the temple was built. It is also believed Vibhishana, brother of Sita's kidnapper Ravana, joined Rama here, prompting one of the great ethical debates in Indian literature: is it right to betray your family to be true to yourself?

GANDAMADANA PARVATHAM

This **temple**, located 3km northwest of Rameswaram, is a shrine reputedly containing Rama's footprints. The two-storey *mandapa* is on a small hill – the highest point on the island – and has good views out over the coastal landscape. Pilgrims visit at dawn and dusk.

Activities

Childrens Park Beach is a neglected splash of sand with fishing boats and some swings which might distract a wee one for a little.

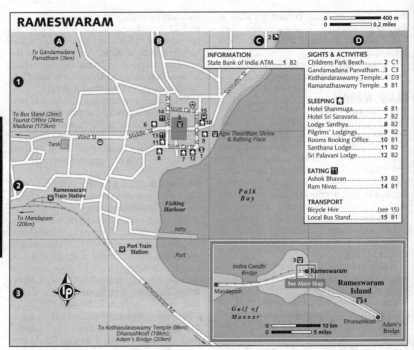

RAMESWARAM

INFORMATION
State Bank of India ATM......1 B2

SIGHTS & ACTIVITIES
Childrens Park Beach............2 C1
Gandamadana Parvatham...3 C3
Kothandaraswamy Temple...4 D3
Ramanathaswamy Temple...5 B1

SLEEPING
Hotel Shanmuga....................6 B1
Hotel Sri Saravana...............7 B2
Lodge Santhya.....................8 B2
Pilgrims' Lodgings...............9 B2
Rooms Booking Office.......10 B1
Santhana Lodge.................11 B2
Sri Palavani Lodge............12 B2

EATING
Ashok Bhavan.....................13 B2
Ram Nivas...........................14 B1

TRANSPORT
Bicycle Hire......................(see 15)
Local Bus Stand................15 B1

Festivals & Events

Car Festival (Feb/Mar) During the festival, a huge decorated chariot with idols of the deities installed is hauled through the streets in a pulsating parade.

Thiru Kalyana (Jul/Aug) This festival celebrates the celestial marriage of Shiva and Parvati.

Sleeping & Eating

Budget travellers should call in at the **rooms booking office** (East Car St) opposite the main temple entrance, which can score beds as low as Rs120. Many hotels here are geared towards pilgrims, which means staff can be conservative, often refusing to take in single travellers (because, you know, the nightlife in Rameswaram is so hot). Cheap rooms tend to be dire, but there's a string of good midrange (Rs400 to Rs800) hotels around; book ahead before festivals.

Santhana Lodge (☎ 221229; West Car St; r Rs200-300) This is a decent (and we're using the term relatively) budget option, with requisite bad sheets but acceptably clean rooms and squat toilets.

Lodge Santhya (☎ 221329) Next door to Santhana Lodger, this grotty spot offers singles for as low as Rs150. You get what you pay for, but if you must pinch that penny...,

Hotel Shanmuga (☎ 222984; 7 Middle St; d Rs380, with AC Rs750; ✖) This is another nice midrange place, just removed from the western (main) temple entrance. Rooms are large and connected to the outside world via HBO and CNN.

Hotel Sri Saravana (☎ 223367; South Car St; r from Rs450, with AC from Rs750; ✖) This is a friendly, clean hotel with great service and spacious rooms, and they're not averse to single travellers. Rooms have TVs, and the ones towards the top have sea views (and increased rates).

Sri Palavani Lodge (☎ 223367; South Car St; r from Rs500, with AC from Rs800; ✖) Next door to Shanmuga, this place offers almost identical rooms, layout and friendly service.

A number of inexpensive vegetarian restaurants such as **Ashok Bhavan** (West Car St) serve thalis for around Rs35. As you might guess there's a focus on South Indian food here, but **Ram Nivas** (West Car St; Rs15-40) does a nice line in North Indian veg like paneer and dhal fry. You can find fish in a few restaurants, but if you track down anything else befitting carnivores, let us know.

Getting There & Away

BUS

Buses run to Madurai every 10 minutes (Rs49, four hours). There are SETC buses to Chennai (Rs240, 12 hours, one daily), Kanyakumari (Rs120, 10 hours, two daily) and Trichy (Rs82, seven hours) every half-hour.

There are also private buses and minibuses from the town centre to Chennai (Rs400) and Madurai (Rs125).

TRAIN

The *Rameswaram Express* leaves for Chennai daily at 7.55pm.

Getting Around

Town buses (Rs1) travel between the temple and the bus stand from early morning until late at night. Cycling is a good way to get around, with many stalls renting old rattlers for Rs5 per hour.

MADURAI

☎ 0452 / pop 1.2 million

Do you not feel the southern breeze blowing from the city... This breeze comes laden with the odours of saffron, chives, sandal paste, and musk... It brings us the smell of good food, for it went through the fumes of bazaars, where pancakes are fried in countless stalls... It is thick with smoke of sacrifices... The wealthy city is not far off, and you need have no fear. Even if you go there alone, you will meet no danger on your way.

Silappatikaram

Chennai may be the heart of Tamil Nadu, but Madurai claims the soul. No European-built port town this; Madurai is Tamil-borne and Tamil-rooted, one of the oldest cities in India, a metropolis that traded with ancient Rome and outlasted its destruction. Now Madurai competes with the Italian capital for 'worst traffic ever', and while the smells described in the *Silappatikaram*, the Tamil equivalent of the *Odyssey*, are still present, they're offset by the reek of petrol and piss.

Tourists, Indian and foreign, usually come here to see the temple of Sri Meenakshi Amman, a labyrinthine structure that ranks among the greatest temples of India. Otherwise, Madurai, perhaps appropriately given its age, captures many of India's most glaring dichotomies: a city centre dominated by a medieval temple, an economy increasingly driven by IT, all overlaid with the energy and excitement of a typically Indian city slotted into a much more manageable package than Chennai's sprawl.

If you're here in spring, try to catch you catch the Chithrai Festival, when temple images are paraded throughout the city (p389).

History

Tamil and Greek documents record the existence of Madurai from the 4th century BC. It was popular for trade, especially in spices, and was also the home of the *sangam*, the academy of Tamil poets. Over the centuries Madurai has come under the jurisdiction of the Cholas, the Pandyas, Muslim invaders, the Hindu Vijayanagar kings, and the Nayaks, who ruled until 1781. During the reign of Tirumalai Nayak (r 1623–55), the bulk of the Sri Meenakshi Temple was built, and Madurai became the cultural centre of the Tamil people, playing an important role in the development of the Tamil language.

Madurai then passed into the hands of the British East India Company. In 1840 the company razed the fort, which had previously surrounded the city, and filled in the moat. Four broad streets – the Veli streets – were constructed on top of this fill and to this day define the limits of the old city.

Orientation

The main post office, tourist office and many hotels are conveniently wedged between the train station and the temple.

Information

BOOKSHOPS

Malligai Book Centre (11 West Veli St; ☪ 9am-2pm & 4.30-9pm Mon-Sat) Opposite the train station; the left-hand side has a decent selection of English-language titles.

Turning Point Books (75 Venkatesh Towers, Town Hall Rd; ☪ 10am-9pm Mon-Sat) A 4th-floor bookshop opposite New College with a good selection, especially the shelves on Indian religion.

INTERNET ACCESS

You can't walk without tripping over an internet cafe, including several 24-hour Sify i-ways, but the following is our favourite:

Chat Club (75 Venkatesh Towers, Town Hall Rd; per hr Rs20; ☪ 9am-11.30pm) Below Turning Point Books, these guys are exceedingly accommodating.

LANDSCAPES OF LOVE

Tamil is one of the world's oldest languages, and it has produced one of the world's great bodies of literature. Poetry – both short verse and some of the longest epics in the human canon – was practised here before societies in other parts of Earth had developed reading and writing. This is a legacy the Tamils are justifiably proud of, and it is still a sign of the highest education – and dedicated Tamil pride, with connotations of nationalism – to be able to quote some of the great poems of the past. The 'Golden Age' of Tamil literature, as it were, was the Sangam period in 300 BC. During this time thousands of scholars, poets and authors (the Sangam, or academy) contributed to a huge body of work that has since become a bedrock of Tamil culture.

There is no easily identifiable theme to Tamil classical literature, which (like any good writing) spans the human experience. In contrast with the Sanskrit texts of North India, almost all Tamil work deals with the secular, rather than ritual and concepts like spiritual advancement. But passion, perhaps ironically for a people whose culture is so traditionally linked to concepts like renunciation, figures strongly into a lot of the text.

The world of the Tamil classical poem is one of great deeds, exceptional heroes and big gestures. This is what happens in Tamil epic land when someone asks a mother where her warrior son is:

> I don't really know
> My womb is only a lair
> for that tiger
> You can see him
> Only in battlefields

> *Kamil Zvelebil, Puram no. 86*

Passion, of course, isn't limited to violence. There's lots of erotic undertones to Sangam writing, and the earthy language can be surprising amid modern Tamil culture, which can be quite prudish. Unabashed appeals for sex and lusty compliments seem more common in ancient Tamil Nadu than modern Chennai.

MONEY

ATMs are plentiful.

Canara Bank ATM (West Perumal Maistry St)
HDFC Bank ATM (West Veli St)
ICICI Bank ATM (North Chitrai St)
State Bank of India (West Veli St) Has foreign-exchange desks and an ATM.
VKC Forex (Zulaiha Towers, Town Hall Rd; ☾ 9am-7pm) An efficient place to change travellers cheques and cash.

POST

Main post office (West Veli St; ☾ 9am-5pm Mon-Sat, parcel office 9.30am-7pm)

TOURIST INFORMATION

Madurai tourist office (☎ 2334757; 180 West Veli St; ☾ 10am-5pm Mon-Fri, 11am-1pm Sat) Helpful staff when they're there, with brochures and maps. Tourist counters of sorts are also at the train station and airport.

Sights
SRI MEENAKSHI TEMPLE

The **Sri Meenakshi Temple** (camera Rs30; ☾ 6am-12.30pm & 4-9pm), abode of the triple-breasted, fish-eyed Goddess Meenakshi Amman ('fish-eyed' is an adjective for perfect eyes in classical Tamil poetry), is considered by many to be the height of South Indian temple architecture, as vital to the aesthetic heritage of this region as the Taj Mahal is to North India. It's not so much a temple as a 6-hectare complex enclosed by 12 *gopurams*, the highest of which towers 52m over Madurai, and all of which are carved with a staggering array of gods, goddesses, demons and heroes.

According to legend, the beautiful Meenakshi was born with three breasts and this prophecy: her superfluous breast would melt away when she met her husband. The event came to pass when she met Shiva and took her place as his consort. The temple of the cosmic couple was

Oh pray, be careful not to break
your waist, too frail to bear the weight
of young breast growing opulent!

Silappatikaram

But it is love – along with war, to the point that the classical Tamil canon is often referred to as 'Poems of Love and War' – that is the central plot-mover in long epics and the main subject of discussion in short verse. This is one of the most famous quotes from Kuruntokai, written between 200 BC and 200 CE.

What could my mother be
to yours?
What kin is my father
to yours anyway?
And how
did you and I meet ever?
But in love our hearts are as
Red earth and pouring rain:
mingled beyond parting.

Kuruntokai

Notice that nice use of allegory between scenery, weather and emotion? Sangam love poems rely on a strict set of rules that link landscape to feelings, terrain to mood and geography to the state of love. The conventions make a sonnet or haiku look like simplicity itself, but as a traveller, it's interesting to see which parts of the landscape are associated with which feelings in different parts of this vast state. A pining heroine, for example, is always clad in jasmine blooms and comes from the forest; she is associated with late summer. Every emotion, breakup, reunion and character in the epics possesses these multiple layers of meaning and signifiers. It can be tough for non-Tamils to appreciate, but if you're interested in the above, look for a copy of the *Silappatikaram*, the greatest of the great Tamil epics, akin in these parts to something like the *Iliad* and *Odyssey* rolled into one.

designed in 1560 by Vishwanatha Nayak and built during the reign of Tirumalai Nayak, but its history goes back 2000 years to the time when Madurai was a Pandyan capital.

Much of the temple is off-limits to non-Hindus, but lay people can enter the **Puthu Mandapa** in the east, which forms a long and impressive entrance hall that leads to the eastern *gopuram*. From here you can see the outer rings of the concentric corridors that enclose the sanctums of Meenakshi and Shiva, worshipped here as Sundareswarar, the beautiful lord. Be on the lookout for statues of deities encrusted in small balls of butter, thrown at the gods as offerings from their devout worshippers.

Also within the temple complex, housed in the 1000-Pillared Hall, is the **Temple Art Museum** (admission Rs7; 7am-7pm). It contains painted friezes and stone and brass images and good exhibits on Hindu deities.

Allow plenty of time to see this temple and be warned: shorts and socks are not allowed. Early mornings or late evenings are the best times to avoid crowds, and there's often classical dance somewhere in the complex at the weekends. 'Temple guides' charge negotiable fees, rarely below Rs200, so prepare to negotiate and be aware that they are often fronts for emporiums and tailor shops.

TIRUMALAI NAYAK PALACE
What the Meenakshi Temple is to Nayak religious architecture, the Tirumalai **palace** (Indian/foreigner Rs10/50, camera/video Rs30/100; 9am-1pm & 2-5pm) is to the secular. Unfortunately it's in a state of rot today, but the shell that remains is still impressive. The main event is the entrance gate, main hall and Natakasala (Dance Hall), with their faded yellow plasterwork, lion and *makara* (crocodile-elephant creature) sculptures and a series of fabulous murals

MADURAI

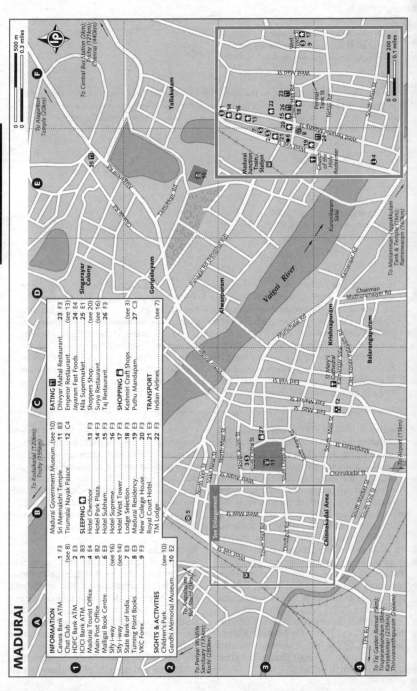

INFORMATION

Canara Bank ATM	1 F3
Chat Club	(see 8)
HDFC Bank ATM	2 E3
ICICI Bank ATM	3 B3
Madurai Tourist Office	4 E4
Main Post Office	5 B2
Malligai Book Centre	6 E3
Sify i-way	(see 16)
Sify i-way	7 E3
State Bank of India	8 E3
Turning Point Books	9 F3
VKC Forex	

SIGHTS & ACTIVITIES

Children's Park	(see 10)
Gandhi Memorial Museum	10 E2
Madurai Government Museum	(see 10)
Sri Meenakshi Temple	11 B3
Tirumalai Nayak Palace	12 C4

SLEEPING ⌂

Hotel Chentoor	13 F3
Hotel Park Plaza	14 F3
Hotel Subham	15 F3
Hotel Supreme	16 F3
Hotel West Tower	17 F3
Lodge Selection	18 F3
Madurai Residency	19 F3
New College House	20 F3
Royal Court Hotel	21 F3
TM Lodge	22 F3

EATING ⌂

Dhivyar Mahal Restaurant	23 F3
Emperor Restaurant	(see 13)
Jayaram Fast Foods	24 E4
Nila Supermarket	25 E1
Shoppers Shop	(see 20)
Surya Restaurant	(see 16)
Taj Restaurant	26 F3

SHOPPING ⌂

Kashmiri Craft Shops	(see 3)
Puthu Mandapam	27 C3

TRANSPORT

Indian Airlines	(see 7)

that hints at the opulence the Nayak rulers once enjoyed. The rectangular courtyard, 75m by 52m, is known as Swargavilasa (Celestial Pavilion), and while time has taken its toll, you still get the sense the plaza fully deserved the name. The Indo-Saracenic palace was built in 1636 by the ruler whose name it bears.

There's a nightly **sound-and-light show** (Rs50; 😌 English 6.45pm, Tamil 8pm) which can be fun; the mosquitoes and people carrying on conversations throughout come at no extra cost. The palace is a 20-minute walk from the temple.

MUSEUMS

Housed in the *tamukkam* (old exhibition pavilion) of the Rani Mangammal is the excellent **Gandhi Memorial Museum** (admission free, camera Rs50; 😌 10am-1pm & 2-5.30pm), set in spacious and relaxing grounds. The maze of rooms contains an impressively moving and detailed account of India's struggle for Independence from 1757 to 1947, and the English-language signs pull no punches about British rule. Included in the exhibition is the blood-stained dhoti (long loincloth) that Gandhi was wearing at the time he was assassinated in Delhi in 1948; it's here because he first took up wearing the dhoti as a sign of native pride in Madurai in 1921. The **Gandhian Literary Society Bookstore** (😌 Mon-Sat) is behind the museum.

The **Madurai Government Museum** (Indian/foreigner Rs10/100; 😌 9.30am-5.30pm Sat-Thu) is next door in the same grounds. Inside is a neglected collection of archaeological finds, sculpture, bronzes, costumes and paintings. A shady **children's park** (admission Rs2; 😌 10am-8pm) with pay-as-you-go rides and slides is alongside the museums' entrance driveway.

MARIAMMAN TEPPAKKULAM TANK

This vast tank, 5km east of the old city, covers an area almost equal to that of Sri Meenakshi Temple and is the site of the incredible **Teppam (Float) Festival** (p389), held in January/February, when the Meenakshi temple deities are taken on a naval tour of their kingdom. The evening culminates in Shiva's seduction of his wife, whereupon the icons are brought back to the temple to make love and in so doing, regenerate the universe (Meenakshi's diamond nose stud is even removed so it doesn't irritate her lover). As exciting as that all sounds the tank is empty for most of the year and primarily serves as a cricket ground for local kids. It

was built by Tirumalai Nayak in 1646 and is connected to the Vaigai River by underground channels.

Tours

The tourist office organises half-day sightseeing tours that include the Tirumalai Nayak Palace and Gandhi Memorial Museum, and finish at the Sri Meenakshi Temple. Tours start at 7am and 3pm and cost Rs125 per person (minimum six people).

Sleeping

Most of Madurai's accommodation is concentrated in the area between the train station and Sri Meenakshi Temple.

BUDGET

Town Hall Rd, running eastwards from the train station, has a knot of cheap and not-so-cheerful hotels. All budget choices have squat toilets.

Lodge Selection (☎ 2342625; 70 Town Hall Rd; s/d Rs190/250) This is one of the better choices amid the budget hotels clustered around Town Hall Rd. The upper rooms have alright views and while the rooms aren't ritzy, they're as good as you'll get for this price.

Hotel Subham (☎ 2342022; 61 West Perumal Maistry St; s/d Rs200/320) Some rooms here are clean, slightly airy and a good deal, but the darker, dingier ones are definitely worth a pass.

TM Lodge (☎ 2341651; www.maduraitmlodge.com; 50 West Perumal Maistry St; s/d Rs200/320, d with AC & TV Rs550; 🖭) TM is efficiently run with clean linen and reasonably well-kept rooms. The upper rooms are definitely lighter and airier, some with private sit-outs.

New College House (☎ 2342971; collegehouse_mdu@ yahoo.co.in; 2 Town Hall Rd; r from Rs240, with AC from Rs660; 🖭) FYI: it's spelled 'Neww College House' in case you get confused. There's some 250 rooms scattered over this concrete complex. Some are quite nice, some not-so-much, and street noise often permeates, so try and get something away from the bustle.

MIDRANGE & TOP END

Madurai's best-value accommodation is the midrange hotels along West Perumal Maistry St near the train station. Rooms without AC are a bargain and worth making that step up from the budget joints, especially if you're not travelling alone. Most have rooftop restaurants with temple and sunset views.

Hotel West Tower (☎ 2346098; 42/60 West Tower St; r Rs350-525, with AC Rs700-800; ⚇) On the line between budget and midrange, and in spitting distance of the temple, the West Tower has clean rooms, friendly service and a location that can't be beat.

Madurai Residency (☎ 2343140; www.madurai residency.com; 15 West Marret St; s/d Rs425/490, r with AC from Rs850; ⚇ ▣) The service is stellar and the rooms are lovely and fresh at this winner, which has the highest rooftop restaurant in town. There's 24-hour internet in the lobby, and breakfast is included in the room rates.

Hotel Supreme (☎ 2343151; www.supremehotels.com; 110 West Perumal Maistry St; s/d from Rs550/680, r with AC from Rs1200; ⚇) This is another large, well-presented hotel that is very popular – although sometimes overcrowded – with domestic tourists. You can't miss the chance to walk into Apollo, a bar built to look like a spaceship, and wonder if someone laced your lassi last night. There's good feed at the on-site Surya Restaurant.

Hotel Chentoor (☎ 3042222; www.hotelchentoor.com; 106 West Perumal Maistry St; s/d Rs650/700, with AC from Rs950/1050; ⚇) Chentoor has spick-and-span rooms, some of which have great temple and city views; a busy, cheap rooftop restaurant (right); and what surely must be the dimmest lit bar in India on the ground floor.

Hotel Park Plaza (☎ 3011111; www.hotelparkplaza .net; 114 West Perumal Maistry St; s/d Rs1075/1350; ⚇) The Plaza's lobby is slightly more upmarket than its neighbours, and rooms are standard midrange: comfortable and simply furnished. The front rooms have temple views from the 3rd floor up. There's a good rooftop restaurant and the (inappropriately named) Sky High Bar – on the 1st floor.

Royal Court Madurai (☎ 4356666; www.royalcourt india.com; 4 West Veli St; s/d Rs2800/3100; ⚇ ▣) The Royal Court manages to blend a bit of white-sheeted, hardwood-floored colonial elegance with a whole mess of modern amenities, such as wi-fi in all rooms, that makes it an excellent, centrally located top-end choice for someone who needs a bit of spoiling.

Eating

Along West Perumal Maistry St the rooftop restaurants of a string of hotels offer breezy night-time dining and temple views; most also have AC restaurants open for breakfast and lunch.

Jayaram Fast Foods (5-8 Nethaji Rd; mains Rs25-75; ⚇ lunch & dinner) There's a busy (and yummy) bakery downstairs, and a crisp and clean restaurant up top that does a nice line in Indian fare, plus burgers and pizzas. While the latter aren't winning any awards, this is as good a piece of pie as you'll find in Madurai.

Taj Restaurant (☎ 2343650; 55 Town Hall Rd; mains Rs30-64; ⚇ lunch & dinner) This non-veg extravaganza is packed with happily masticating families in the evening, no doubt enjoying specials like the Mughal biryani (only available Sundays) and the intriguing, occasionally offered pigeon masala.

Emperor Restaurant (☎ 2350490; 106 West Perumal Maistry St; mains Rs30-80) It's all veg all the time at Hotel Chentoor's rooftop restaurant, but that karmic goodness is a bit undone by the fact this spot basically becomes a very popular bar come nightfall.

Dhivyar Mahal Restaurant (☎ 2342700; 21 Town Hall Rd; mains Rs30-92; ⚇ lunch & dinner) One of the better multicuisine restaurants not attached to a hotel, Dhivyar Mahal is clean and bright. The usual curries go down a treat, and where else are you going to find roast leg of lamb in Madurai?

Surya Restaurant (110 West Perumal Maistry St; mains Rs45-110; ⚇ dinner) The rooftop restaurant of Hotel Supreme offers a superb view over the city and a nice pure-veg menu, but the winner here has got to be the cold coffee, which might as well have been brewed by God when you sip it on a dusty, hot (ie every) day.

Taj Garden Retreat (☎ 2371601; www.tajhotels.com; 40 TPK Rd; mains from Rs150; ⚇ breakfast, lunch & dinner) This indoor-outdoor restaurant is perched in the gardens above the city, with stunning sunset views. If you're hankering for spag and salad in relaxed surrounds, this is the place to come.

Street stalls selling sweets, dosas, *idli* and the like are ubiquitous, especially near the train station. **Shoppers Shop** (Town Hall Rd; ⚇ 8am-11pm) and **Nila Supermarket** (Algarkoil Rd; ⚇ 7am-11pm) are well-stocked grocery stores including a good selection of Western foods.

Shopping

Madurai teems with cloth stalls and tailors' shops, which you may notice upon being approached for the umpteenth time by a tailor tout. A great place for getting cottons and printed fabrics is **Puthu Mandapa**, the pillared former entrance hall at the eastern side of Sri Meenakshi Temple. Here you'll find rows of tailors, all busily treadling away and capable of whipping up a good replica of whatever you're wearing in an hour or two. Quality, designs and prices vary greatly depending on the material and complexity of the design, but you can have a shirt made up for Rs150. Every driver, temple guide and tailor's brother will lead you to the **Kashmiri craft shops** in North Chitrai St, offering to show you the temple view from the rooftop – the views are good, and so is the inevitable sales pitch.

Getting There & Away

AIR

Indian Airlines (☎ 2341234, airport 2690771; West Veli St; ✆ 10am-5pm Mon-Sat) flies daily to Mumbai and Chennai. Jet Airways also flies daily to Chennai, as does newcomer **Paramount Airways** (☎ 1800 1801234; www.paramountairways.com). Air Deccan flies daily to Bengaluru. None of these last three airlines has an office in town, but airport counters open at flight times.

BUS

Most long-distance buses arrive and depart from the **central bus station** (☎ 2580680; Melur Rd), 6km northeast of the old city. It appears chaotic but is actually a well-organised 24-hour operation. Local buses shuttle into the city every few minutes for Rs2. There's a fixed-rate autorickshaw stand just outside the station (you'll inevitably be waved there); the fee to the train station (where most of the hotels are located) is Rs79, plus a Rs2 service charge.

Private bus companies offer super-deluxe coaches with video services to Chennai and Bengaluru (Rs220 to Rs300), but the state bus companies have similar services and while travel agencies sell tickets – often at

an inflated price – you may end up on a state bus anyway. The boxed text (left) lists prices for government buses; some express services run to Bengaluru, Chennai, Mysore and Puducherry.

The Arapalayam bus stand, northwest of the train station on the river bank, has hourly buses to Kumili (Rs45, 4½ hours) for the Periyar Wildlife Sanctuary. There are regular services to Coimbatore (Rs75, six hours). Buses leave for Kodaikanal at 2.30pm and 8.30pm (Rs40, four to five hours), and to Palani every half-hour (Rs35, five hours).

TRAIN

Madurai Junction train station is on the main Chennai–Kanyakumari line. There are at least nine daily trains to Chennai, and three daily services to Kanyakumari.

Other services include Madurai to Coimbatore (2nd class/sleeper Rs62/98, 6½ hours) and Bengaluru (sleeper/3AC Rs179/502, six hours), as well as Trivandrum and Mumbai.

Getting Around

The airport is 12km south of town and taxis cost Rs200 to the town centre. Autorickshaws ask around Rs100. Alternatively, bus 10A from the central bus station goes to the airport, but don't rely on it being on schedule.

Central Madurai is small enough to get around on foot.

KANYAKUMARI (CAPE COMORIN)

☎ 04652 / pop 19,739

The end of India has more appeal than being the end of the road. There's a whiff of accomplishment (along with dried fish) upon making it to the tip of the country, the terminus of a narrowing funnel of rounded granite mountains – some of India's oldest – green fields plaided with silver-glinting rice paddies and slow-looping wind farms. Like all edges, there's a sense of the surreal here. You can see three seas mingle, the sunset over the moonrise and the Temple of the Virgin Sea Goddess within minutes of each other. But beyond that, Kanyakumari is a genuinely friendly village that makes a nice respite from the dust of the Indian road.

Orientation & Information

The main temple is right on the point of Kanyakumari and leading north from it is a

BUSES FROM MADURAI			
Destination	**Fare (Rs)**	**Duration (hr)**	**Frequency**
Bengaluru	182	12	4 daily
Chennai	144-186	10	every 30min
Chidambaram	85	8	3 daily
Kochi	144	8	2 daily
Kanyakumari	90	6	hourly
Mysore	260	16	1 daily (via Ooty)
Puducherry	105	8	2 daily
Rameswaram	59	4	every 30min
Trichy	40	3	every 10min
Trivandrum	215	9	2 daily

small bazaar lined with restaurants, stalls and souvenir shops.

Janaki Forex (☼ 9.30am-6pm Mon-Sat) Off South Car St. Change cash and travellers cheques here.

Post office (Main Rd; ☼ 8am-6pm Mon-Fri) About 300m north of the tourist office.

Tamil Mercantile Bank ATM (Main Rd)

Tony's Internet (Sannathi St; per hr Rs50; ☼ 10am-8pm) Friendly and relatively fast.

Tourist office (☎ 246276; Main Rd; ☼ 8am-6pm Mon-Fri) Get a useful, free *In and Around Kanyakumari* brochure here. If anyone's in the office.

Sights & Activities

KUMARI AMMAN TEMPLE

We can't claim to have written the first review of this place; let's go back to the 1st-century *Periplus of the Erythraean Sea*, by an unknown Greek merchant:

> …there is another place called Comari, at which are the Cape of Comari and a harbour; hither come those men who wish to consecrate themselves for the rest of their lives, and bathe and dwell in celibacy; and women also do the same; for it is told that a goddess once dwelt here and bathed.

The legends say the *kanya* (virgin) goddess Kumari, a manifestation of the Great Goddess Devi, single-handedly conquered demons and secured freedom for the world. At this **temple** (☼ 4.30am-12.30pm & 4-8pm) pilgrims give her thanks in an intimately spaced, beautifully decorated temple, where the nearby crash of waves from three oceans can be heard through the twilight glow of oil fires clutched in vulva-shaped votive candles (a reference to the sacred femininity of the goddess). Men must remove their shirts to enter and cameras are forbidden.

GANDHI MEMORIAL

Poignantly and appropriately placed at the end of the nation Gandhi fathered is this **memorial** (admission by donation; ☼ 7am-7pm), which purposely resembles an Orissan temple embellished by Hindu, Christian and Muslim architects. The central plinth was used to store some of the Mahatma's ashes, and each year, on Gandhi's birthday (2 October), the sun's rays fall on the stone. Guides may ask for an excessive donation, but Rs10 is enough; try and keep an air of silence (even if locals don't).

KAMARAJ MEMORIAL

Just next to the Gandhi memorial is this **shrine** (☼ until dark) to K Kamaraj, known as 'the Gandhi of the South'. One of the most powerful politicians of post-independence India, Kamaraj held the chief ministership of both Madras State and latter-day Tamil Nadu and was instrumental in bringing Lal Bahadur Shastri and Indira Gandhi into the prime minister's seat. You can also thank the Tamil leader for school lunch, since he instituted the first free ones in Tamil Nadu in 1956. Unfortunately, the shrine is nothing but a collection of dusty blown-up photographs with barely any space given to context or explanation.

VIVEKANANDA EXHIBITION & VIVEKANANDAPURAM

This **exhibition** (Main Rd; admission Rs2; ☼ 8am-noon & 4-8pm) details the life and extensive journey across India made by the philosopher Swami Vivekananda (the 'Wandering Monk'; 1863–1902), who developed a synthesis between the tenets of Hinduism and concepts of social justice. The storyboards are a bit over-detailed; if you're overwhelmed, concentrate on enjoying the photos and Swamiji's letters, which detail his growth during his *prabrajya* (period of wandering). A more pictorial and interesting exhibition can be found at **Vivekanandapuram** (☎ 247012; admission free; ☼ 9am-1pm & 5-9pm), an ashram 3km north of town that provides a snapshot of Indian philosophy, religion, leaders and thinkers.

VIVEKANANDA MEMORIAL

Four hundred metres offshore is the rock where Swami Vivekananda meditated and chose to take his moral message beyond India's shores. A **memorial** (admission Rs10; ☼ 8am-5pm) was built in Vivekananda's memory in 1970, and reflects architectural styles drawn from all over India. It can be a loud place when packed with tourists, but the islet is big enough to provide moments of seclusion. If you really need quiet, there's a meditation chamber focused on a glowing Om symbol.

The huge **statue** on the smaller island, which looks like an Indian Colossus of Rhodes, is not of Vivekananda but Tamil poet Thiruvalluvar. India's 'Statue of Liberty' was the work of more than 5000 sculptors. It was erected in 2000 and honours the poet's 133-chapter work *Thirukural* – hence its height of exactly 133ft (40.5m).

KANYAKUMARI (CAPE COMORIN)

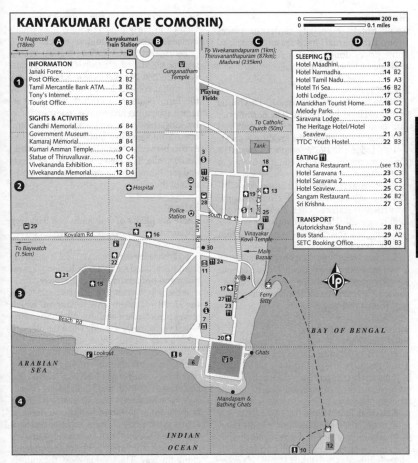

INFORMATION	
Janaki Forex	**1** C2
Post Office	**2** B2
Tamil Mercantile Bank ATM	**3** B2
Tony's Internet	**4** C3
Tourist Office	**5** B3

SIGHTS & ACTIVITIES	
Gandhi Memorial	**6** B4
Government Museum	**7** B3
Kamaraj Memorial	**8** B4
Kumari Amman Temple	**9** C4
Statue of Thiruvalluvar	**10** C4
Vivekananda Exhibition	**11** B3
Vivekananda Memorial	**12** D4

SLEEPING	
Hotel Maadhini	**13** C2
Hotel Narmadha	**14** B2
Hotel Tamil Nadu	**15** A3
Hotel Tri Sea	**16** B2
Jothi Lodge	**17** C3
Manickhan Tourist Home	**18** C2
Melody Parks	**19** C2
Saravana Lodge	**20** C3
The Heritage Hotel/Hotel Seaview	**21** A3
TTDC Youth Hostel	**22** B3

EATING	
Archana Restaurant	(see 13)
Hotel Saravana 1	**23** C3
Hotel Saravana 2	**24** C3
Hotel Seaview	**25** C2
Sangam Restaurant	**26** B2
Sri Krishna	**27** C3

TRANSPORT	
Autorickshaw Stand	**28** B2
Bus Stand	**29** A2
SETC Booking Office	**30** B3

Ferries shuttle between the port and the islands between 8am and 4pm; the cost is Rs20 round trip.

GOVERNMENT MUSEUM

This **museum** (Main Rd; Indian/foreigner Rs5/100; 9.30am-5.30pm Sat-Thu) is overpriced and underwhelming. There's a blah display of archaeological finds and temple artefacts and some freak-show paraphernalia, like the foetus of a four-legged goat and (gasp!) a three-chambered coconut.

SEAFRONT

There's a crowded beach here and **ghats** that lead down to a lingam half submerged in a wave-driven tidal pool. Past the ice-cream and *chaat* (snack) sellers above the beach is a somewhat blasé **memorial** to victims of the 2004 tsunami.

BAYWATCH

Tired of temples? This impressive **amusement park** (☎ 246563; www.baywatch.co.in; adult/child Rs240/180; 10am-7pm) is a great way to spend the day, especially if you've got kids in tow. The entry ticket gives unlimited access to a wave pool with water slides (women should swim in at least knee-length shorts and shirt for propriety). The adjacent **wax museum** (adult/child Rs50/40), filled with Indian politicians and celebrities, promises to 'Make You Feel at London!' The park is just 1.5km west of the town centre – a rickshaw ride shouldn't be more than Rs80.

TAMIL NADU

Sleeping

Some hotels, especially midrange places around the bazaar, have seasonal rates, so some prices double during April and May, and late October to January.

BUDGET

TTDC Youth Hostel (☎ 246257; dm Rs50) This hostel is part of Hotel Tamil Nadu. The dormitories and common bathrooms are foul, but you can't beat the price and the location is great.

Jothi Lodge (☎ 246316; Sannathi St; r from Rs150) Offers rooms for as low as Rs150, but they're pretty dingy.

Hotel Narmadha (☎ 246365; Kovalam Rd; r Rs200-250) This big concrete block conceals some very friendly staff and cheapo rooms that are kept reasonably clean and comfy; it's popular with pilgrims and set to the west of the main bazaar, next to Hotel Tri-Sea.

Saravana Lodge (☎ 246007; Sannathi St; r Rs250-450) If you opt for a room without TV you can cut a pretty good deal at this place just outside the temple entrance. All rooms have private bathrooms with squat toilets.

MIDRANGE & TOP END

Hotel Tamil Nadu (☎ 246257; Beach Rd; r Rs450, with AC Rs750; ✹) Despite the usual quirks of a government-run hotel, this is a great location if you want to get away from the (slight) bustle of town; balcony rooms have ocean, though not temple, views.

Manickhan Tourist Home (☎ 246387; East car St; d Rs450, with AC Rs1100; ✹) This very friendly hotel is professionally run and a real pleasure to doss in; the large rooms are all outfitted with clean bathrooms, satellite TV and, if you're willing to shell out a bit, superb sea views.

Hotel Maadhini (☎ 246787; East Car St; d Rs450, with AC Rs1100; ✹) Next door to Manickhan, this place offers almost the exact same experience (and rates).

Hotel Tri Sea (☎ 246787; Kovalam Rd; r from Rs500, with AC from Rs1200; ✹) As you walk west of town you can't miss the high-rise Tri Sea, which has huge, airy rooms, most with balconies facing the ocean. The doors of some of the bathrooms seem to have been painted by a bored, drugged-up graphic artist, but hey, all in the name of quirky character.

Melody Parks (☎ 247667; Sannathi St; r from Rs1000, with AC from Rs1500; ✹) The enthusiastic staff here make you feel well at home in one of Kanyakumari's few true top-end places. In this case, you're getting an extra dose of spoiling, if much the same views and fairly plusher rooms than what's available at the nearby midrange spots.

Heritage Hotel/Hotel Seaview (☎ 247841; seaview@ sancharnet.in; East Car St; d without/with AC Rs1400/1950, with sea view Rs1750/2550; ✹) Welcome to Kanyakumari's attempt at colonial luxury (ironically run by the Tamil Nadu government). It's a good attempt at creating luxurious if snooty exclusivity: king-sized beds, dark wood furniture and oceanfront views in a building that looks like a cross between a Victorian mansion and drug dealer's villa. The tiled floors, plasticky sheets and semi-dim lighting detract from the poshness of the place.

Eating

There are plenty of fruit stalls and basic veg restaurants in the bazaar area, open for breakfast, lunch and dinner.

Sri Krishna (Sannathi St; mains Rs25-85) If you need fresh juice, good ice cream or Indian takes on pizza and burgers, try this clean, busy cafe.

Archana Restaurant (East Car St; mains Rs25-95) At the Hotel Maadhini, this restaurant, which serves predictable if well-executed Indian fare, is best visited in the evening when the pleasant garden area provides open-air ambience.

Hotel Seaview (East Car St; mains Rs30-150) This upmarket hotel has an excellent AC multicuisine restaurant specialising in fresh local seafood and posh takes on North and South Indian faves.

Sangam Restaurant (Main Rd; mains Rs40-170) It's as if the Sangam started in Kashmir, trekked across the entirety of India, and stopped here to open a restaurant that features top culinary picks culled from every province encountered along the way. The food is good, the joint is bustling, and the menu must be one of the biggest in Tamil Nadu.

Hotel Saravana has two clean, busy veg restaurants with thalis (Rs25) and good chai.

Getting There & Away

BUS

The surprisingly sedate bus stand is a 10-minute walk west of the centre along Kovalam Rd and there's a handy **SETC booking office** (☉ 7am-9pm) on Main Rd. For details of services, see the boxed text (opposite).

TRAIN

The train station is about 1km north of the bazaar and temple. The daily *Chennai Egmore Express* departs for Chennai (sleeper/2AC/

BUSES FROM KANYAKUMARI (CAPE COMORIN)

Destination	Fare (Rs)	Duration (hr)	Frequency
Bengaluru	333	15	1 daily
Chennai	280	16	6 daily
Kodaikanal	132	10	1 daily
Kovalam	40	3½	1 daily
Madurai	76	6	8 daily
Rameswaram	108	9	2 daily
Trivandrum	31	3	2 daily

3AC Rs189/321/1026, 13 hours) at 5.15pm and the 6.35am *Tiruchirappalli-Howrah Express* to Chennai departs on Saturday. The same trains stop at Madurai and Trichy.

There are two daily express trains to Trivandrum (2nd class/3AC Rs33/183, two hours, 87km).

For the real long-haulers or train buffs, the weekly *Himsagar Express* runs all the way to Jammu Tawi in Jammu & Kashmir, a distance of 3734km, in 66 hours – the longest single train ride in India.

THE WESTERN GHATS

Deep blue skies, pine sap breezes, dollops of purple and gold splashed from a wildflower palette and the crackle of a wood fire on perpetual late autumn nights.

The British built their summer homes here, seeking what we might call 'colonial air-con'. Because let's face it: Tamil Nadu can be as hot as hell, and even the plushest rooms can't cool you off as you wander the dust clouds on the plains. Solution? The lush mountains of the Western Ghats, offering some of the most welcome hill heat relief in India. Rising like an impassable bulwark of evergreen and deciduous tangle from the north of Mumbai to the tip of Tamil Nadu, the Western Ghats (with an average elevation of 915m) contain 27% of all India's flowering plants, 60% of its medicinal plants and an incredible array of endemic wildlife. Although it's not just the air and (relative) lack of pollution that's refreshing, either – there's also a general acceptance of quirkiness and eccentricity in the hills that is hard to find in the lowlands.

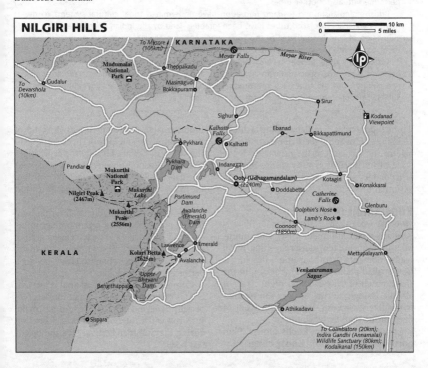

NILGIRI HILLS

TAMIL NADU

HILL TRIBES OF THE NILGIRI

For centuries, the Nilgiris have been home to hill tribes. While retaining integrity in customs, dress and language, the tribes were economically, socially and culturally interdependent. The British concept of exclusive property rights disenfranchised many tribespeople, as did exploitative commercial practices that undermined their barter-based economy. Today, many eke out a living in poverty gathering honey or herbs for the ayurvedic industry.

The Toda tribe's social, economic and spiritual system centred on the buffalo, whose milk and ghee was integral to their diet and used as currency – in exchange for grain, tools and medical services. Most importantly, the dairy produce provided offerings to the gods as well as fuel for the funeral pyre. It was only at the ritual for human death that the strictly vegetarian Toda killed a buffalo, not for food but to provide company for the deceased.

The Badagas are believed to have migrated to the Nilgiris from the north around 1600 AD, in the wake of Muslim invasions in the north, and are thus not officially a tribal people. With knowledge of the world outside the hills, they became effective representatives for the hill tribes. Their agricultural produce, particularly grain, added a further dimension to the hill diet.

The Kotas lived in the Kotagiri area and were considered by other tribes to be lower in status. They still undertake ceremonies in which the gods are beseeched for rains and bountiful harvests.

The Kurumbas inhabited the thick forests of the south. They gathered bamboo, honey and materials for housing, some of which were supplied to other tribes. They also engaged in a little agriculture, and at sowing and harvest times they employed the Badaga to perform rituals entreating the gods for abundant yields.

The Irulus, also from the southern slopes, produced tools and gathered honey and other forest products that they converted into brooms and incense. They are devotees of Vishnu and often performed rituals for other tribes.

British colonialism and lowland migration have undermined tribal cultural systems to the point of collapse. Displaced tribes have been 'granted' land by the Indian government, but the cultivation of land is anathema to the Toda, who see themselves as caretakers of the soil – for them, to dig into the land is to desecrate it.

Today many tribal people have assimilated to the point of invisibility. Some have fallen into destructive patterns associated with displacement and alienation. Others remain straddled across two cultures, but the tribes are in a precarious state. Although the Indian government claims 5000 hill people remain, tribal censuses put the number at 1700.

Think hippie cafes, handlebar-moustachioed trekking guides and tiger-stripe earmuffs for sale in the bazaar. On the downside is the state of local tribal groups whose identity is in danger of both over-exploitation and assimilation.

KODAIKANAL (KODAI)

☎ 04542 / pop 32,969 / elev 2100m

Kodai is small, intimate, misty and mountainous; there are few more refreshing Tamil Nadu moments than boarding a bus in the heat-soaked plains and disembarking in the sharp pinch of a Kodaikanal night. It's not all cold though; during the day the weather is positively pleasant, more reminiscent of deep spring than early winter.

Located in the Palani knolls some 120km northwest of Madurai, Kodai clings to a mountainside draped in *sholas* (forests) of pine, gum trees and *kurinji* shrub, unique to the Western Ghats. The light, purple-blue-coloured blossoms flower every 12 years; next due date 2018. If you don't feel like waiting, the many treks by nearby dark rock faces and white waterfalls are still rewarding.

The renowned Kodaikanal International School provides a bit of cosmopolitan influence and scenes like a French teenager getting a light for his *bidi* off a Punjabi classmate, before they discuss in English Heath Ledger's performance as the Joker.

Compared to Ooty, Kodaikanal is relaxed, but it's still popular with Indian tourists (especially honeymooners). If it's summer, make sure you catch the horse races and boating during the Summer Festival (see the boxed text p389).

Orientation & Information

For a hill station, Kodai is remarkably compact and the central town area can easily be explored on foot. There are several internet cafes, and a State Bank of India ATM near the Carlton Hotel.

Alpha Net (PT Rd; per hr Rs40; ⏰ 9am-10pm) By far the friendliest and fastest internet in town.

Apollo Communications (Anna Salai; per hr Rs40; ⏰ 9am-8pm) Internet access.

Indian Bank (Anna Salai; ⏰ 10am-2pm & 2.30-3.30pm Mon-Fri, 10am-12.30pm Sat) With foreign-exchange desk.

Kurinji Tours & Travel (☎ 240008; kurinjitravels@ sancharnet.in; Club Rd; ⏰ 9am-6pm) Reliable help with onward travel arrangements.

Tourist office (☎ 241675; Anna Salai; ⏰ 10am-5.45pm)

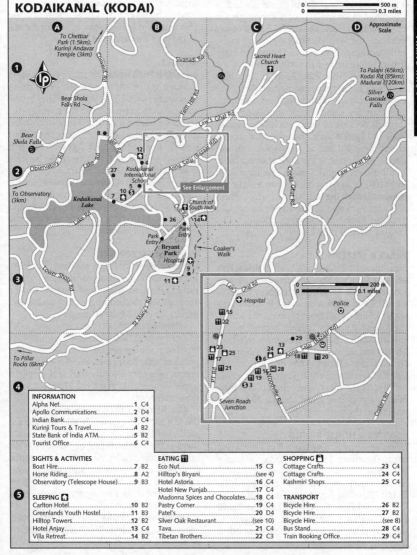

KODAIKANAL (KODAI)

TAMIL NADU

Sights & Activities

WALKING & TREKKING

Assuming it's not cloaked in opaque mist, the valley views along paved **Coaker's Walk** (admission Rs2, camera Rs5; ⊙ 7am-7pm) are superb. There's no plastic allowed on the pathway, a rule flagrantly flaunted by locals, and a small **observatory** (admission Rs3) with telescope at the southern end. You can start near Greenlands Youth Hostel or Villa Retreat – where **stained glass** in the nearby Church of South India (CSI) is stunning in the morning light – and the stroll takes all of five minutes. The 5km **lake circuit** is pleasant in the early morning when you can count the king-fishers before the tourist traffic starts.

The views from **Pillar Rocks**, a 7km hike (one-way beginning near Bryant Park), are excellent (again, assuming fine weather), and there are some wonderful hiking trails through pockets of forest, including **Bombay Shola** and **Pambar Shola**, that meander around Lower Shola Rd and St Mary's Rd. You will need a guide; talk to the staff at Greenlands Youth Hostel (right). Guides (per hour Rs70 to Rs100) of varying quality can also be arranged through the tourist office while others will approach you in the street; its booklet *Trekking Routes in Kodaikanal* details walks ranging from 8km to 27km.

PARKS & WATERFALLS

Near the start of Coaker's Walk is **Bryant Park** (admission Rs5; ⊙ 9.30am-5pm), landscaped and stocked by the British officer after whom it's named. **Chettiar Park** (admission free; ⊙ 8.30am-5pm), about 1.5km uphill from town on the way to the Kurinji Andavar Temple, is small, pretty and landscaped. Both get crowded with school groups and canoodling couples. Nearby waterfalls include **Silver Cascade**, on the road outside Kodai and often full of interstate tourists bathing on the rocks, and compact **Bear Shola Falls**, in a pocket of forest about a 20-minute walk from the town centre.

BOATING & HORSE RIDING

If you're sappy in love like a bad Bollywood song, the thing to do in Kodai is rent a pedal boat (Rs20 to Rs40), rowboat (Rs100) or Kashmiri *shikara* (covered gondola; Rs140 including boatman) from either the Kodaikanal Boat & Rowing Club or Tamil Nadu Tourist Development Corporation; screechy crooning to your significant other is strictly optional.

There's a few horse-hire stands on the lake. The rate is Rs180 per hour unaccompanied or Rs300 with a guide but you can take a short ride for Rs80. Some of the horses here are in bad shape.

Sleeping

Hotel prices can jump by up to 300% during high season (from 1 April to 30 June). Prices listed here are low-season rates.

Most hotels in Kodai have a 9am or 10am checkout time in high season, but for the rest of the year it's usually 24 hours.

BUDGET

Greenlands Youth Hostel (☎ 240899; www.greenlands kodaikanal.com; dm Rs100, d Rs200-800) With cheap rooms and sweeping views of the valley below, this excellent lodge remains the number-one choice for budget travellers. There's a crowded dormitory and a range of rooms from basic doubles to more spacious digs with balcony, fireplace and TV. Staff are cheery, the location is peaceful and treks can be arranged.

Hotel Anjay (☎ 241809; Anna Salai; www.hotelanjay .com; d Rs400-650) The Anjay is a well-kept box of comfy, clean rooms with basic beds and amenities. Management is friendly and the hotel is centrally located.

MIDRANGE & TOP END

Strawberry Park (☎ 242340; Anna Salai; r from Rs500) Who wouldn't be attracted to a hotel with a name that sounds like a Beatles single? Rooms are huge and the bedding is thick and warm, perfect for cold Kodai evenings.

Hilltop Towers (☎ 240413; www.hilltopgroup.in; Club Rd; d/ste from Rs890/1500) Although it comes off as big, boxy and corporate, rustic accents like polished teak floors and wooden embellishments, plus very friendly staff and excellent upper-floor views, make the Hilltop a midrange standout.

Villa Retreat (☎ 240940; www.villaretreat.com; Club Rd; r Rs1089-2250, cottages Rs2813) The terrace garden of this lovely old stone-built hotel at the northern end of Coaker's Walk offers awesome valley views. The best rooms, somewhat overpriced, are the cottages with panoramic views. Most rooms have fireplaces and TV, and there's a cosy restaurant. Prices include taxes.

Carlton Hotel (☎ 240056; www.krahejahospitality .com; Lake Rd; d/cottages Rs7000/10,000) The cream of Kodai's hotels is a magnificent five-star colonial mansion that overlooks the lake and the international school. Rooms are bright, spacious and some have private balconies with lake views. The lobby and grounds very much succeed at recreating hill-station ambience, with stone walls, dark-wood flooring and roaring fireplaces that make you want to demand a scotch now, dammit, from the eager staff.

Eating
RESTAURANTS
PT Rd is the best place for cheap restaurants and it's here that most travellers and students from the international school congregate. The once-vaunted Manna Bake, a bakery popular with granola-types and backpackers, was closed at the time of research.

Madonna Spices and Chocolates (☎ 245461; Anna Salai) Friendly as hell, our favourite chocolate stall in town sells big blocks of the good stuff, along with a good array of oils, lotions, ointments, sacks of spice and assorted herbal goodness culled from the surrounding hills. We like the dark chocolate with nuts, although several travellers swore by the fruit and nut.

Tava (PT Rd; mains Rs30; ⏰ lunch & dinner Thu-Tue) A clean, fast and cheap veg option, this place has a wide menu; try the cauliflower-stuffed *gobi paratha* (spicy cauliflower bread) and *sev puri* (crisp, puffy fried bread with potato and chutney).

Hotel Astoria (☎ 240524; Anna Salai; mains Rs30-50, thalis Rs35-60) This veg restaurant is always packed with locals and tourists, especially come lunchtime when it serves excellent all-you-can-eat thalis.

Hotel New Punjab (PT Rd; mains Rs30-100; ⏰ lunch & dinner) For North Indian and tandoori dishes (and any non-veg curries in general), this is the best place in Kodai.

Patel's (Anna Salai; mains Rs40; ⏰ lunch & dinner) Locals and Gujaratis craving a taste of their state's delicious vegetarian cuisine crowd into this barren yet bustling cafe come dinner time.

Royal Tibet (PT Rd; mains Rs40-80; ⏰ lunch & dinner) If you're missing Tibetan food, come here for the chewy but tasty *momos* (dumplings). A nearby competitor, Tibetan Brothers, offers almost the exact same menu, and while their *momos* aren't up to scratch, they do a superior *thukpa* (noodle soup).

Hilltop's Biryani (Club Rd; mains Rs55-80; ⏰ lunch & dinner) There's a huge range of biryani available

here, from hot Hyderabadi-style to an intriguing seafood version of the spicy rice dish.

Silver Oak Restaurant (☎ 240056; Lake Rd; buffet lunch & dinner Rs450) The restaurant at the Carlton Hotel puts on lavish buffet meals, serving everything from steak to lasagne to paneer *makhani* (paneer cooked in creamy tomato gravy), though you might feel a bit out of place in hiking gear.

SELF-CATERING
Eco Nut (☎ 243296; PT Rd; ⏰ 10am-5pm Mon-Sat) This interesting shop sells a wide range of locally produced organic health food – whole-wheat bread, muffins, cheese, salad greens – and essential oils, herbs and herb remedies.

Pastry Corner (Anna Salai; ⏰ 9am-9pm) Pick up great picnic sandwiches and yummy brownies (Rs5; after 3pm) here, or squeeze onto the benches with a cuppa to watch the world go by.

Excellent homemade chocolates and dried fruit are sold all over town.

Shopping
The many handicraft stores stock good craftwork, and several reflect the local low-key but long-term commitment to social justice.

Cottage Crafts (☎ 240160; PT Rd; ⏰ 10am-8pm) Run by the voluntary organisation Coordinating Council for Social Concerns in Kodai (Corsock), these shops sell goods crafted by disadvantaged groups; about 80% of the purchase price returns to the craftspeople. There's a second hand shop on Anna Salai.

On PT Rd you'll find small Kashmiri shops and South Indian handicrafts stalls.

Getting There & Away
The nearest train station is Kodai Rd, at the foot of the mountain, where taxis (around Rs1000) and buses (Rs15) wait. There's a **train booking office** (Anna Salai; ⏰ 9am-5pm Mon-Sat, 1.30pm-5pm Sun) in town.

Don't expect a bus to be leaving from Kodaikanal in the next five minutes. Tickets for private buses can be booked at travel agents near the bus stand. For details of main bus departures from Kodaikanal see the boxed text (p460).

Getting Around
The central part of Kodaikanal is compact and very easy to get around on foot. There are no autorickshaws (believe it or not) but plenty of taxis willing to take you to various sightseeing

TAMIL NADU

BUSES FROM KODAIKANAL (KODAI)

Destination	Fare (Rs)	Duration (hr)	Frequency
Bengaluru	283	11	1 daily
Bengaluru *	450	11	1 daily
Chennai	450	11	2 daily
Coimbatore	50	5	1 daily
Kochi*	400	8	1 daily
Madurai	34	3½	hourly
Madurai*	150	3	2 daily
Ooty	250-400	8	1 daily
Palani	20	2	8 daily
Trichy	57	5	3 daily

*private buses

points. Charges are fixed and relatively high; sightseeing tours cost from Rs650 to Rs1500 for a day trip.

If you fancy a ride around the lake or you're fit enough to tackle the hills, mountain bikes can be hired from several **bicycle stalls** (per hr/day Rs10/75; ☉ 8am-6pm) around the lake.

AROUND KODAIKANAL

One of the better high-end escapes in the hills, about three hours' drive below Kodaikanal off the Palani–Dindigul road, is the fabulous **Cardamom House** (☎ 0451-2556765, 09360-691793; www.cardamomhouse.com; r from Rs3000). Created with love and care by a retired Brit, this comfortable guest house – at the end of a scenic road beside bird-rich Lake Kamarajar – runs on solar power, uses water wisely, farms organically, trains and employs only locals (who produce terrific meals), and supports several village development initiatives. You'll need to book well in advance, hire a driver to take you there, and prepare for some serious relaxation.

INDIRA GANDHI (ANNAMALAI) WILDLIFE SANCTUARY

The largest of the three wildlife sanctuaries in the Western Ghats along the Tamil Nadu–Kerala border, this misty mountain park covers almost 1000 sq km of mostly teak forest and evergreen jungle. It's home to elephants, gaurs (Indian bison), tigers, panthers, spotted deer, wild boars, bears, porcupines and civet cats, and the Nilgiri tahr – commonly known as the ibex. The endangered lion-tailed macaque may also be spotted. The park has a renowned medicinal plant garden and in-

terpretive centre (check out the astrological medicine chart and beauty hints if you're feeling travel-weary), and is home to the tribal group of Kada people, many of whom work here. The park's elephant training centre can be visited on the guided vehicle tour.

The **park reception centre** (per person Rs50, camera/video Rs10/50; ☉ day visitors 6.30am-6pm) at Topslip, where trekking guides can be arranged and where there are several lodges, is about 35km southwest of Pollachi. Wildlife is often seen on the drive in, and you can wander around the reception-centre surroundings. Access to the inner forest has traditionally been limited to tours (Rs625 for a 25-seater bus, irrespective of numbers, one hour) or guided treks (Rs70, maximum four people, four hours), but as of research private vehicles were being permitted into the park; this may be your best bet for covering the large area free of minders. Other tours and treks run on demand.

Sleeping & Eating

Forest accommodation is available at and near Topslip. It *must* be booked in advance in Pollachi at the **Wildlife Warden's Office** (WWO; ☎ 04259-2225356; Meenkarai Rd; ☉ 9am-5pm Mon-Fri), but hours and service can be erratic. Rooms in several simple lodges at Topslip are Rs300; the somewhat more comfortable New Tree Tops lodge is Rs1000; and dorm beds are available for Rs30 at Ambulli Illam, 2km from the reception centre. There's a basic canteen at Topslip.

It's a fairly good bet you'll need to overnight in Pollachi; try **Sakthi Hotels** (☎ 04259-223050; sakthi fibreproducts@vsnl.net; Coimbatore Rd; d Rs200, with AC Rs495; ☒). You can also try to stay in Valparai, a hill town about 64km south of Pollachi that is trying to sell itself as the Nilgiris' next big tourism thing. There's the usual setting of cool valleys, tea plantations and several guest houses. These range from the serviceable **Green Hills** (☎ 04253-222262; State Bank Rd; r from Rs300; ☒) to the posh, Victorian comfort of the **Stanmore Bungalow** (☎ 422-4351500; www.teabungalows.com; r from Rs300; ☒), a converted British villa with suited-up butlers, tea-plantation views from the verandah and all the other paraphernalia that reminds you there will always be some corner of this land that is forever cashing in on colonial nostalgia.

Getting There & Away

The sanctuary is between Palani and Coimbatore. Regular buses travelling from both places stop at the nearest large town, Pollachi, which is also on the Coimbatore–Dindigul train line.

From Pollachi, buses leave the bus stand for Topslip at 6.15am, 11.15am and 3.15pm, returning at 9.30am, 1pm and 6.30pm. A taxi from Pollachi to the sanctuary costs around Rs800 one way. Buses from Pollachi to Valparai run throughout the day.

COIMBATORE
☎ 0422 / pop 1.46 million
Coimbatore may be one of the largest cities in Tamil Nadu, but most travellers use it as either a step towards getting into Ooty, or out of the hills and into Kerala. Which isn't a bad idea; this is a large business and junction city that's friendly enough, but short on sights. Sometimes known as the Manchester of India for its textile industry, it has plenty of accommodation and eating options if you need to spend the night.

Information
Blazenet (Nehru St; per hr Rs20; ⏰ 9am-12.30pm) Internet access.

HSBC ATM (Racecourse Rd) Next to Annalakshmi Restaurant.

ICICI ATM (Avanashi Rd) Opposite Nilgiri's Nest.

Main post office (Railway Feeder Rd; ⏰ 10am-8pm Mon-Sat, 10am-2pm Sun) A few hundred metres northwest of the train station, reached via a pedestrian underpass from the platforms.

Tourist office (⏰ 10am-5.45pm) Small office inside the train station.

Sleeping
Hotel Shri Shakti (☎ 2234225; Sastri Rd; s/d Rs195/280) There's not much character here, but there are a lot of rooms; if you need a cheap, basic place to crash that's adjacent to the bus stands, look no further.

Hotel AP (☎ 4392777; hotelap@yahoo.com; s/d from Rs195/420, d with AC Rs750; ❄) Again: cheap, basic rooms, in this case located across from the train station. The AP's tucked into some back alleys, but you'll recognise it by its oddly cubist, Gaudi-esque exterior.

Hotel Blue Star (☎ 2230635; 369A Nehru St; s/d from Rs400/600, with AC from Rs600/850; ❄) A sprawling hotel, this has simple, clean rooms; the top floor is much nicer than downstairs. Management is friendly and it's convenient for the bus stands.

Legend's Inn (☎ 4350000; legends_inn@yahoo.com; Geetha Hall Rd; s/d Rs700/800, with AC Rs950/1100; ❄)

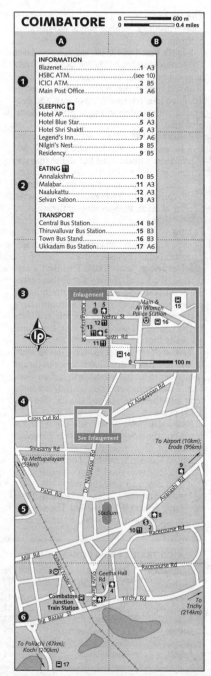

COIMBATORE   0 ━━━━ 600 m
0 ━━━━ 0.4 miles

INFORMATION
Blazenet..............................1	A3
HSBC ATM........................(see 10)	
ICICI ATM..........................2	B5
Main Post Office..................3	A6

SLEEPING 🏠
Hotel AP.............................4	B6
Hotel Blue Star....................5	A3
Hotel Shri Shakti.................6	A3
Legend's Inn.......................7	B6
Nilgiri's Nest.......................8	B5
Residency...........................9	B5

EATING 🍴
Annalakshmi......................10	B5
Malabar............................11	A3
Naalukattu.........................12	A3
Selvan Saloon....................13	A3

TRANSPORT
Central Bus Station............14	B4
Thiruvalluvar Bus Station....15	B3
Town Bus Stand..................16	B3
Ukkadam Bus Station.........17	A6

The Legend is, well, a legend, with comfortable furnishings, bamboo blinds and sparkling bathrooms.

Nilgiri's Nest (☎ 4505500; nilgiriscbe@gmail.com; 739A Avanashi Rd; s/d from Rs1500/2600; 🕱) This lovely large complex feels like a vaguely kitschy hotel plunked out of the West; rooms are well-designed in a '60s mod kind of way, and decorated with Audubon-esque prints of local bird life.

Residency (☎ 2201234; www.theresidency.com; 1076 Avanashi Rd; s/d from Rs4700/5000; 🕱 🖳 🕱) Coimbatore's finest hotel has all the five-star trimmings, along with friendly staff and immaculate rooms. There's a well-equipped health club and pool, two excellent restaurants, a coffee shop and a bookshop in the lobby.

Eating

There's a fast-food hall and supermarket underneath Nilgiri's Nest (above).

Selvan Saloon (Sastri Rd; Rs20) This isn't a restaurant; it's a stall. But it's a stall that serves the best street food we had in South India: an incredibly rich and spicy mushroom curry that would shame some of the pricier dishes in the country. Look for the long lines, and get ready for bliss.

Malabar (7 Sastri Rd; mains Rs50-120; 🕑 lunch & dinner) In the KK Residency Hotel, this restaurant specialises in Keralan and North Indian food. The Malabar chicken roast (Rs100) is a spicy treat and there are seafood choices like tandoori pomfret.

Naalukattu (Nehru St; mains Rs50-130; 🕑 lunch & dinner) For the price, this is a rather gorgeous restaurant that resembles a dark-wood-accented Keralan verandah. The Malayalam-inspired food is all good, but it's the fish curry that goes down an absolute treat.

Annalakshmi (☎ 2212142; 106 Racecourse Rd; set meals Rs150; 🕑 lunch & dinner Tue-Sun) The top veg restaurant in town, this is run by devotees of Swami Shatanand Saraswati; the price of your meal helps support the Shivanjali educational trust for underprivileged children.

Getting There & Away

AIR

The airport is 10km east of town. There are flights from here to Mumbai (US$100 to US$160), Delhi (US$110 to US$309), Kozhikode (Calicut; US$65 to US$100), Chennai (US$130) and Bengaluru (US$60 to US$90). Airlines include the following:

Air India (☎ 2399833)
Jet Airways (☎ 2243465)
Kingfisher Airlines (☎ 2214075)
Paramount Airways (☎ 3256822)
SpiceJet Airlines (☎ 1800 1803333)

BUS

There are three bus stands in the city centre.

From Central Bus Station services depart to nearby northern destinations such as Ooty (Rs50, 3½ hours, every 30 minutes) and Mettupalayam (Rs13, one hour, every 10 minutes). From Thiruvalluvar bus station you can catch state and interstate buses to Bengaluru (Rs180 to Rs225, nine hours, 10 daily), Mysore (Rs70 to Rs95, five hours, every hour) and Chennai (Rs275, 11½ hours, seven daily). The town bus stand is for local city buses.

Ukkadam bus station, south of the city, is for buses to nearby southern destinations including Palani (Rs30, three hours, every 20 minutes), Pollachi (Rs15, one hour, every five minutes) and Madurai (Rs70, five hours, every 30 minutes).

TRAIN

Coimbatore Junction is on the main line between Chennai and Ernakulam (Kerala). For Ooty, catch the daily *Nilgiri Express* at 5.15am; it connects with the miniature railway departure from Mettupalayam to Ooty at 7.10am. The

MAJOR TRAINS FROM COIMBATORE

Destination	Train name	Fare (Rs)	Duration (hr)	Departure
Bengaluru	Kanyakumari-Bangalore Exp	148-416	9	10.35pm daily
Chennai	Kovai Exp	116-404	7½	1.40pm daily
	Cheran Exp	116-404	8½	10pm daily
Kochi	Sabari Exp	93-261	5	8.50am daily
Madurai	Coimbatore-Madurai Exp	60-102	6	10.45pm daily
Ooty	Nilgiri Exp (via Mettupalayam)	22-35	7	5.15am daily
Pollachi	Pollachi-Podanur	24	1½	5 daily

TAMIL NADU

whole trip to Ooty takes about seven hours. For train services see the boxed text (opposite).

Getting Around

For the airport take bus 20 from the town bus stand or bus 90 from the train station (Rs4). Many buses ply between the train station and the town bus stand (Rs1.50). Autorickshaw drivers charge around Rs40 between the bus and train stations.

AROUND COIMBATORE
Isha Yoga Center

This **ashram** (☎ 0422-2515345; www.ishafoundation .org; ☯ 6am-8pm), in Poondi, 30km west of Coimbatore, is also a yoga retreat and place of pilgrimage. The centrepiece is a multireligious temple housing the Dhyanalingam, said to be unique in that it embodies all seven chakras of spiritual energy. Visitors are welcome to the temple to meditate, or to take part in one- to two-week Isha yoga courses, for which you should register in advance.

Mettupalayam

This commercial town is the starting point for the miniature train to Ooty. There's little of interest for travellers, but if you want to avoid the 7.20am connection, there is plenty of accommodation. Try **Nanda Lodge** (☎ 04254-222555; Ooty Main Rd; r from Rs231), which is basic but clean and right opposite the bus station, through which there's a short cut to the train station. **Hotel EMS Mayura** (☎ 04254-227936; 212 Coimbatore Rd; r Rs680, with AC Rs1150; ❷), a decent enough midrange hotel, is 2km from the train station.

COONOOR

☎ 0423 / pop 101,000 / elev 1850m

Coonoor is one of the three **Nilgiri hill stations** – Ooty, Kotagiri and Coonoor (see the Nilgiri Hills map, p455) – that lie above the southern plains. Like Kotagiri, Coonoor is a place for quiet and isolation, which can be found in any of Upper Coonoor's accommodation, 1km to 2km above the town centre. From here you can look down over the sea of red tile rooftops to the slopes behind and soak up the peace, cool climate and beautiful scenery. Just note you get none of the above in central Coonoor, which is a bustling, honking mess.

Sights & Activities

In Upper Coonoor the 12-hectare **Sim's Park** (adult/child Rs5/2, camera/video Rs25/250; ☯ 8.30am-6pm)

is a peaceful oasis of manicured lawns and more than 1000 plant species, including magnolia, tree ferns and camellia. Buses heading to Kotagiri can drop you here.

There are several popular viewpoints around Coonoor. **Dolphin's Nose**, about 10km from town, exposes a vast panorama encompassing Catherine Falls across the valley. On the way back, drop into **Guernsey Tea Factory** (☎ 2230205; admission Rs10; ☯ 8am-6pm) and take a short guided tour of the fragrant processing plant. Afterwards, stop at **Lamb's Rock**, named after the British captain who created a short path to this favourite picnic spot in a pretty patch of forest, for some more amazing views past the hills into the hazy plains. The easiest way to see these sights – all on the same road – is on a rickshaw tour for around Rs400. If you're feeling energetic, walk the 6km or so back into town from Lamb's Rock (it's mostly, but not entirely, downhill).

Sleeping & Eating

You'll need a rickshaw (or good legs) to reach all these places.

Hotel Vivek Coonoor (☎ 2230658; www.hotelvivek .com; Figure of Eight Rd; dm Rs100, r Rs400-700) Many of the wide range of rooms here have balconies (screened to avoid the 'monkey menace') from which you can hear the tea-pickers plucking leaves below you. There's also a monster dormitory.

YWCA Wyoming Guesthouse (☎ 2234426; s/d Rs275/550) This ramshackle guest house, a hillstation gem of a structure nestled into an upslope of Upper Coonoor, is a budget favourite. Although ageing and draughty, the 150-year-old colonial house oozes character with wooden terraces and serene views over Coonoor.

Taj Garden Retreat (☎ 2230021; www.tajhotels .com; Church Rd; s/d from US$70/85) Right: you come to a hill station to feel like you're a tweedy colonialist with a ridiculous moustache and – dammit, this gin and tonic needs ice! Such is the ambience at this hilltop…well, retreat, snuggled besides the All Saints Church. Besides occupying a green corner of some lovely gardens, the enormous colonial-style rooms all come with polished floorboards, bathtubs and open fireplaces, while the 'superior' rooms even have a separate sitting room for the memsahib. Sadly, there are no pith helmets There's an excellent multicuisine restaurant and bar on-site, and for the more health conscious, a gym, ayurvedic and yoga centre.

TAMIL NADU

Tryst (☎ 2207057; www.trystindia.com; d incl breakfast & dinner Rs4000) If you're looking for a gregarious accommodation experience that's quirky and classy, check out the website of this extraordinary guest house and book ahead. It's beautifully located in a former tea plantation manager's bungalow.

Your best bet for eating is your hotel restaurant, though there are forgettable restaurants in the town centre.

Getting There & Away

Coonoor is on the miniature train line between Mettupalayam (28km) and Ooty (18km) – see p470. Buses to Ooty (Rs6.50, one hour) and Kotagiri (Rs8, one hour) leave roughly every 15 minutes.

KOTAGIRI

☎ 04266 / pop 29,184

The oldest of the three Nilgiri hill stations, Kotagiri is about 28km from Ooty. It's a quiet, unassuming place with a forgettable town centre, but we're assuming you're not here for the nightlife. Rather, the appeal is the escape from Ooty's overdevelopment: red dirt tracks in the pines, blue skies and the high green walls of the Nilgiris.

From Kotagiri you can visit **Catherine Falls**, 8km away near the Mettupalayam road (the last 3km is by foot only, and the falls only flow after rain), **Elk Falls** (6km) and **Kodanad Viewpoint** (22km), where there's a view over the Coimbatore Plains and Mysore Plateau. A half-day taxi tour to all three will cost around Rs600. The scenery on the road to Mettupalayam is gorgeous, so you may want to detour this way if you're heading down from Ooty.

A couple of very basic lodges are in the small town centre and a splendid 1915 colonial building, **Stone House Retreat** (☎ 273300; www.naharhotels.com; r Rs2000), offers fabulous views and atmosphere but charges like a wounded bull for all extras.

Also located here are the offices of the **Keystone Foundation** (☎ 272277; Groves Hill Rd; www.keystone-foundation.org), an NGO that works to improve environmental conditions in the Nilgiris while working with, and creating better living standards for, indigenous communities. For more info, see the boxed text (below).

Buses stop at the edge of town, about 1km from the centre. Buses to Ooty depart hourly (Rs15, two hours), crossing one of Tamil Nadu's highest passes. Buses to Mettupalayam leave every 30 minutes and to Coonoor every 15 minutes.

OOTY (UDHAGAMANDALAM)

☎ 0423 / pop 93,921 / elev 2240m

Ah, Ooty. It may be a bit bustling for some tastes, but most travellers quickly fall in love

---

NATURE, NATIVES & THE NILGIRIS

What are the challenges facing tribal communities in the Nilgiris today? In proportion to the rest of the population they are a minority population. They are flaunted as museum pieces. They had a tremendous synergy. But that has been lost now. The government says 5000 Adivasis are left – the Adivasis say 1700. There is an awareness among them that they are in danger of disappearing in a generation. We need to work on education and healthcare.

Is it true parts of the ayurveda industry get many of their herbs from the Nilgiris while employing tribal peoples at exploitative wages? That industry needs good manufacturing practices. If, from the demand side, people said they want certain requirements like fair compensation for herb gatherers, that will happen on the supply side. I very much believe the consumer has a voice here.

Can you speak about environmental campaigns here, and the challenges they've faced? There was a very good effort here to rid the Nilgiris of plastic. [The antiplastic movement] had gotten the public on their side. But you need a solution – you just can't say 'ban plastic' without providing paper or cloth bags. And you need enforcement. Just a few raids on plastic in the markets caused such a stir. With Indian tourists there's no enforcement, so they feed monkeys, toss trash and talk loudly in quiet areas.

How does tourism impact the Nilgiris? Both sides. Tourism is positive in that it keeps the economy going, especially when tea is in the dumps. The negative is what you see – pollution etc. When tourists come up, they need to be sensitised to our unique conditions then and there.

Mathew John is director of the Keystone Foundation (above).

with this pine-clad retreat, where trekkers congregate in front of roaring fires before setting out into the surrounding green dream. Even the typical chaos of India becomes somehow subdued in the shadow of the hills. Therein lies Ooty's charm, especially when you throw in its quirks: a jumble of Hindu temples and ecotourism, overlaid by a veneer of manicured British aesthetic and, for the hell of it, a garden dedicated to thread.

This is South India's most famous (and certainly best-named) hill station, established by the British in the early 19th century as the summer headquarters of the then-Madras government and memorably nicknamed 'Snooty Ooty'. Development ploughed through a few decades ago, but somehow old Ooty survived. The quiet, wildflower-shaded boulevards left behind by the English (think Dorset-Upon-Ghat) and the surprisingly cosmopolitan town centre (thanks, crowds of travellers and local international school students) have ended up complementing, rather than clashing with, each other.

The journey up to Ooty on the miniature train is romantic and the scenery stunning – try to get a seat on the left-hand side where you get the best views across the mountains. With that said, even the bus ride is pretty impressive (if not nearly as relaxing). From April to June (the *very* busy season) Ooty is a welcome relief from the hot plains, and in the colder months (October to March) you'll need warm clothing – which you can buy cheap here – as overnight temperatures occasionally drop to 0°C.

The Summer Festival, when the hills explode in colour and parties, is a great time to visit (see the boxed text, p389).

Orientation & Information

The train station and bus station are next to the racecourse, which is surrounded by cheap hotels. Further downhill is the lake, while the valley slopes up on either side, studded with colonial houses and guest lodges with good views. From the bus station it's a 10-minute walk to the bazaar area and a 20-minute walk to Ooty's commercial centre, Charing Cross.

BOOKSHOPS
Higginbothams Commercial Rd (☎ 2443736; ☺ 9.30am-1pm & 3.30-7.30pm Mon-Sat); Commissioner's Rd (☎ 2442546; ☺ 9am-1pm & 2-5.30pm Mon-Sat) OK

selection of contemporary English-language Indian and other fiction.

INTERNET ACCESS
Global Net (Commercial Rd; per hr Rs25; ☺ 9.30am-9pm)
Internet cafes Church Hill Rd (per hr Rs30; ☺ 10am-9pm); Commercial Rd (per hr Rs20; ☺ 10am-10pm)

LIBRARY
Nilgiri Library (Bank Rd; temporary membership Rs350; ☺ 9.30am-1pm & 2.30-6pm, reading room 9.30am-6pm, Sat-Thu) Quaint little haven in a crumbling 1867 building with a collection of more than 40,000 books, including rare titles on the Nilgiris and hill tribes.

MONEY
Canara Bank ATM (Commercial Rd)
State Bank of India (Bank Rd; ☺ 10am-4pm Mon-Fri, 10am-2pm Sat) Changes travellers cheques and has an ATM.
State Bank of India ATM (Commercial Rd)
UK Forex (Commercial Rd) Changes travellers cheques and cash.
UTI Bank ATM (Ettines Rd)

NATIONAL PARK INFORMATION
Wildlife Warden's Office (WWO; ☎ 2444098; ☺ 10am-5.45pm Mon-Fri) Manages Mudumalai National Park, including advance booking for park accommodation.

POST
Charing Cross post office (Ettines Rd; ☺ 9.30am-5.30pm Mon-Fri)
Main post office (Havelock Rd; ☺ 9am-5pm Mon-Sat) Diagonally opposite St Stephen's Church.

TOURIST INFORMATION
Tourist office (☺ 2443977; ☺ 10am-5.45pm Mon-Fri) Maps, brochures and tour information.

Sights
ST STEPHEN'S CHURCH
Perched above the town centre, the immaculate **St Stephen's Church** (Church Hill Rd; ☺ 10am-1pm & 3-5pm Mon-Sat, services 8am & 11am Sun), built in 1829, is the oldest church in the Nilgiris. Throughout its history, St Stephens has racially shifted from hosting an exclusively British congregation to an Anglo-Indian orphanage to falling under the auspices of the Church of South India. Look out for lovely stained glass, huge wooden beams hauled by elephant from the palace of Tipu Sultan some 120km away, and the sometimes kitschy, sometimes touching,

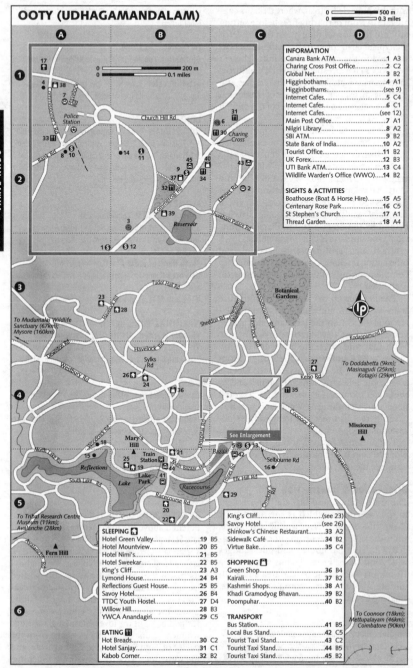

OOTY (UDHAGAMANDALAM)

0 ————— 500 m
0 ————— 0.3 miles

INFORMATION
Canara Bank ATM.....................1 A3
Charing Cross Post Office...........2 C2
Global Net...............................3 B2
Higginbothams..........................4 A1
Higginbothams.......................(see 9)
Internet Cafes.........................5 C4
Internet Cafes.........................6 C1
Internet Cafes......................(see 12)
Main Post Office........................7 A1
Nilgiri Library...........................8 A2
SBI ATM..................................9 B2
State Bank of India...................10 A2
Tourist Office..........................11 B2
UK Forex...............................12 B3
UTI Bank ATM..........................13 C4
Wildlife Warden's Office (WWO)....14 B2

SIGHTS & ACTIVITIES
Boathouse (Boat & Horse Hire)....15 A5
Centenary Rose Park................16 C5
St Stephen's Church..................17 A1
Thread Garden........................18 A4

SLEEPING 🏠
Hotel Green Valley...................19 B5
Hotel Mountview.....................20 B5
Hotel Nimi's...........................21 B5
Hotel Sweekar........................22 B5
King's Cliff.............................23 A3
Lymond House........................24 B4
Reflections Guest House.............25 B5
Savoy Hotel...........................26 B4
TTDC Youth Hostel...................27 D4
Willow Hill.............................28 B3
YWCA Anandagiri....................29 C5

EATING 🍴
Hot Breads............................30 C2
Hotel Sanjay..........................31 C1
Kabob Corner.........................32 B2
King's Cliff..........................(see 23)
Savoy Hotel........................(see 26)
Shinkow's Chinese Restaurant.....33 A2
Sidewalk Café.........................34 B2
Virtue Bake...........................35 C4

SHOPPING 🛍
Green Shop............................36 B4
Kairali.................................37 B2
Kashmiri Shops.......................38 A1
Khadi Gramodyog Bhavan..........39 B2
Poompuhar............................40 B2

TRANSPORT
Bus Station...........................41 B5
Local Bus Stand......................42 C5
Tourist Taxi Stand...................43 C2
Tourist Taxi Stand...................44 B5
Tourist Taxi Stand...................45 B2

To Mudumalai Wildlife
Sanctuary (67km);
Mysore (160km)

Botanical
Gardens

To Doddabetta (9km);
Masinagudi (25km);
Kotagiri (29km)

Missionary
Hill

See Enlargement

To Tribal Research Centre
Museum (11km);
Avalanche (28km)

Fern Hill

To Coonoor (18km);
Mettupalayam (46km);
Coimbatore (90km)

Church Hill Rd

Charing
Cross

Police
Station

Reservoir

Commissioner Rd

Bank Rd

Commercial Rd

Ettines Rd

Shoreham Palace Rd

Tudor Hall Rd

Sheddon Rd

Havelock Rd

Woodcock Rd

Kodappamund Rd

Havelock
Rd

Sylks
Rd

Kelso Rd

Coonoor Rd

Thalaivarmund Rd

Mary's
Hill

Bazaar

Selbourne Rd

Train Station

Main Bazaar

Elk Hill Rd

Reflections

Lake
Park

Racecourse

Orchard Rd

Racecourse Rd

South Lake Rd

North Lake Rd

Westbury Rd

Devanhu Rd

Woodcock Rd

Lake

Reflections

Ettines Rd

TAMIL NADU

slabs and plaques donated by colonial-era churchgoers. In the quiet, overgrown cemetery you'll find headstones commemorating many an Ooty Brit, including the wife and daughter of John Sullivan, the town's founder.

BOTANICAL GARDENS

Established in 1848, these lovely **gardens** (adult/child Rs10/3, camera/video Rs10/100; ☺ 8am-6.30pm) are a living gallery of the natural fauna of the Nilgiris. Look out for a fossilised tree trunk believed to be around 20 million years old, and on busy days, roughly 20 million Indian tourists.

CENTENARY ROSE PARK

With its terraced lawns and colourful flower-beds – best between May and July – this terraced **rose garden** (Selbourne Rd; adult/child Rs10/5, camera/video Rs30/50; ☺ 9am-6.30pm) is a pleasant place for a stroll. There are good views over Ooty from the hilltop location.

THREAD GARDEN

Your appreciation of the **Thread Garden** (☎ 2445145; North Lake Rd; admission Rs10, camera/video Rs15/30; ☺ 8.30am-7.30pm) rests on your love of irony and kitsch. If that threshold is low, you'll be disappointed. If it's decent, you may, if you're in a good mood, enjoy the 'miracle' (official description and just *slight* hyperbole) that is 150 species of 'plants' from around the world meticulously re-created using 'hand-wound' thread. The technique was perfected by Keralan artist Anthony Joseph and the work took 50 craftspeople 12 years to complete, which is either very impressive or kinda sad.

DODDABETTA LOOKOUT

This is it: the highest point (2633m) of the Nilgiris and one of the best **viewpoints** (admission Rs2; ☺ 7am-6pm) around, assuming, as usual, the day is clear. It's about 10km out of town; go early for better chances of a mist-free view. Any Kotagiri buses will drop you here.

TRIBAL RESEARCH CENTRE MUSEUM

It's hard to say why you should love this **museum** (admission free; ☺ 10am-5pm Mon-Fri) more: for its decently executed exhibits on Nilgiri and Andaman tribal groups, or the decomposing corpses of badly stuffed local wildlife, including a rotting mongoose that just arrived from hell's deepest pit and a 'python' apparently made from several socks, a blanket and those googly eyes you buy at the local crafts store. OK: seriously, the artefacts are fantastic – you may never get the chance to hold a Stone Age bow in your life again – and descriptions of the tribes are good, if written by anthropologists with no filter from academia to normal English. The guides are either researchers who can give you an enthusiastic account of their expeditions, or some hapless local staffer who shouts 'Spear! Spear!' while gesturing at a spear. The museum is just beyond the village of M Palada, 11km from Ooty on the way to Emerald. Catch any of the frequent buses heading to M Palada and walk from there, or hire a rickshaw from Ooty for around Rs300 return.

Activities

TREKKING

Trekking is pretty much de rigueur in Ooty and the reason most travellers come here. On day trips you'll have a wander through evergreen forest, tea plantations, over lookouts, into local villages and, generally, catch a bus back to town. Most guest houses will set you up with guides, or you can hire your own – plenty will offer their services to you. Expect to pay depending on the size of your group, Rs300 to Rs900 for a full-day trek. For other nearby hiking options, consider the resorts near Mudumalai National Park (see p471).

HORSE RIDING

Alone or with a guide, you can hire horses outside the boathouse on the north side of the lake; the rides mostly consist of a short amble along bitumen, although you can explore the woods and hills for more money. Prices run from Rs70 for a short ride to Rs150 to Rs200 for an hour, which takes you partway around the lake. Try not to pick a horse that looks too tired, as many do.

BOATING

Rowboats can be rented from the **boathouse** (☺ 9am-5.30pm) by the artificial lake (created in 1824). Prices start from Rs60 for a two-seater pedal boat (30 minutes) and go up to Rs250 for a 15-seater motorboat (20 minutes).

HORSE RACING

Ooty's racecourse dominates the lower part of the hill station between Charing Cross and the lake. The horse-racing season runs from mid-April to June and on race days the town is a hive of activity; it's an event you can't miss if you're in town. Outside the season, the 2.4km racecourse just becomes a cricket field–cum–trash dump–cum–public toilet.

Tours

The tourist office (p465) can put you in touch with agencies that run day trips to Mudumalai National Park via the Pykhara Dam (Rs200; minimum 15 people) starting at 9.30am and returning at 7pm, with just a quick spin through the park. Trips to Coonoor and surrounds are also possible.

A better alternative is to hire a taxi for the day and go as you please. Rates run for about Rs650 for a four-hour trip around Ooty, or Rs1200 to Rs1500 for a full day depending on where you're heading.

Sleeping

Ooty has some fantastic rustic lodges in the budget–midrange scale, gorgeous colonial residences at the high end, and even some decent backpacker dosses around the noisy bus stands. Be warned: it's a sellers' market in the high season (1 April to 15 June), when many hotel prices double and checkout time is often 9am. Prices listed here are for the low season when most places are good value.

Many lodges have open fireplaces in a central common area. There's generally a small charge for firewood and cleaning, but it's well worth it to get that toasty chalet-chic feel in the middle of South India.

BUDGET

YWCA Anandagiri (☎ 2442218; www.ywcaagooty .com; Ettines Rd; dm from Rs90, r & bungalow incl tax Rs264-906) This former brewery and sprawling complex of hill cottages, dotted with brilliant clouds of flower gardens and possessed of an almost Tuscan vibe, is one of the most attractive YWCAs we've ever seen. Throw in elegant lounges and fireplaces and you've got some seriously lovely budget accommodation going on.

TTDC Youth Hostel (☎ 2443665; Botanical Garden Rd; dm/d Rs100/350) This state-run hostel is reliably mediocre, clean and busy; you may want to call ahead to book a dorm bed if you're in the area.

Hotel Nimi's (☎ 2444552; s/d Rs200/300) Nimi's, opposite the train station, is a very basic lodge with rooms that are as cheap as attached-

bathroom accommodation comes in Ooty. It's clean, but otherwise, don't expect a lot.

Hotel Green Valley (☎ 2444219; North Lake Rd; s/d Rs250/350) With nice views of the lake and clean, cosy rooms, Green Valley offers most of what next-door Reflections possesses (minus the on-call cooking and busy common area) at roughly half the rate.

Hotel Sweekar (☎ 2442348; Race View Rd; d Rs300-350) Probably the best value for money in town, the Sweekar hosts guests in big, rustically touched-up rooms that carry a whiff of age and colonial class. The hotel occupies a traditional old Ooty cottage that sits at the end of a lavender-lined path, and is run by an incredibly friendly Bahai manager.

Reflections Guest House (☎ 2443834; North Lake Rd; d from Rs400-800) Reflections has a great common area that becomes an excellent spot for meeting other hill-bound travellers and trekkers. Unfortunately, service has suffered in inverse proportion to popularity, and the ladies who run the place can be curt in a 'Pay now' kinda way. But if you're looking to meet folks and enjoy the occasional home-cooked meal on demand, you're in the right spot.

MIDRANGE & TOP END

Hotel Mountview (☎ 2443307; Racecourse Rd; r Rs660) Perched on a quiet driveway directly above the bus station, these eight simple, enormous rooms, decked out in colonial hill-station chic, occupy an elegant old bungalow.

Willow Hill (☎ 2444037; www.willowhill.in; 58/1 Havelock Rd; d Rs900-1750) Sitting high above town, Willow Hill's large windows provide great views of Ooty. The rooms, all with wooden floors, have a distinct alpine-chalet-chic, with the most expensive rooms offering a private garden.

King's Cliff (☎ 2452888; www.kingscliff-ooty.com; Havelock Rd; d Rs1475-3575) High above Ooty on Strawberry Hill is this gorgeous residence, the sort of colonial house with wood panelling, antique furnishings and cosy lounge where you'd expect to find Kipling sipping a sherry. In point of fact the lobby is decorated with photos of Churchill, Hitchcock, Al Capone and…Jesus. Anyways, this place drips charm and Old World polish, so book ahead and live large, Raj-style.

Lymond House (☎ 2223377; thewildstay@yahoo .com; 77 Sylks Rd; r Rs3000) If Mucha and F Scott Fitzgerald partnered up to open a hotel in Ooty, it'd probably come out looking something like this delightful restored English villa. Rooms are all ensconced in Old World/Jazz Age opulence, the dining room and gardens are gorgeous, and the period atmosphere is thick enough to swim in, while alleviated by breaths of fresh air in the form of quirky embellishments like the owner's classic car.

Savoy Hotel (☎ 2444142; www.tajhotels.com; 77 Sylks Rd; s/d from Rs5800/6800) The Savoy is one of Ooty's oldest hotels, with parts dating back to 1829. Big cottages are arranged around a beautiful garden of flowerbeds, lawns and clipped hedges. The quaint rooms have large bathrooms, polished floors, log fires and bay windows. Modern facilities include a 24-hour bar, excellent multicuisine dining room and an ayurvedic centre.

Eating

Virtue Bake (☎ 2452788; Charing Cross) If you want to see Indian kids and international students talk like American valley girls while sipping posh coffee and snacking on excellent cakes and brownies, Virtue Bake is *totally* your scene.

Hotel Sanjay (☎ 2443160; Charing Cross; mains Rs35-85) This basic but bustling spot does excellent thalis; the Keralan-style fish meal is especially tasty.

Shinkow's Chinese Restaurant (☎ 2442811; 38/83 Commissioner's Rd; mains Rs50-150; ☺ lunch & dinner) Shinkow's is an Ooty institution and the simple menu of chicken, pork, beef, fish, noodles and rice dishes is usually pretty good, if kind of uninspired.

ourpick **Kabob Corner** (Commercial Rd; mains Rs50-200; ☺ lunch & dinner) Aaargh – let your inner carnivore scream in vicious exultation after enduring the non-stop veg of South India. Here you can tear apart perfectly grilled and spiced chunks of lamb, chicken and if you like, paneer (wussy). Sop up the juices with pillowy triangles of naan and revel in your messy return to the meat-eating fold.

Sidewalk Café (Commercial Rd; Rs80-250; ☺ lunch & dinner) A cross between an American diner and an Italian cafe is something you'd expect to find in Mumbai rather than the mountains, but it's a welcome change of scene. The fluorescent interior is oddly out of place in Ooty and the food is a bit overpriced, but if you're craving something Western, this is as good as it gets.

Both the **Savoy Hotel** (☎ 2444142; www.tajhotels.com; 77 Sylks Rd; mains from around Rs140; ☺ lunch & din-

ner) and **King's Cliff** (☎ 2452888; www.kingscliff-ooty.com; Havelock Rd; mains Rs80-200; ☺ lunch & dinner) have atmospheric restaurants with log fires and quality multicuisine food. The latter has no alcohol permit, but you can BYO.

QUICK EATS

There are plenty of basic veg places on Commercial and Main Bazaar Rds and you can get a spicy biryani for Rs10 at street stalls near the bus stand. Otherwise, repair down any small side street and look for the stalls where locals line up.

Hot Breads (Charing Cross; ☺ 8am-10pm) This is a popular bakery turning out a huge range of breads, pastries, pies and sweets – go early for the fresh stuff. (Don't be put off by the Chinese shopfront; it's advertising the upstairs restaurant.) An afternoon of munching small pizzas, sipping coffee and munching more pizza while people-watching from the shop front is an Ooty afternoon well spent in our books.

Like Kodai, Ooty is famous for its delicious **homemade chocolates** (per 100g around Rs50).

Shopping

Ooty can be a fun place to shop, but don't expect anything out of the ordinary. The main places to shop are along Commercial Rd, where you'll find Kashmiri shops as well as government outlets for Kairali and Khadi Gramodyog Bhavan. Poompuhar is on Comercial Rd. The Keystone Foundation (see boxed text, p464) runs the **Green Shop** (☎ 2441340; Club Rd), which sells honey and organic produce harvested by local and indigenous farmers.

Getting There & Away

Without doubt the most romantic way to arrive in Ooty is aboard the miniature train, and you'll need to book ahead in the high season. Buses also run regularly up and down the mountain, both from other parts of Tamil Nadu and from Mysore in Karnataka.

BUS

The state bus companies all have **reservation offices** (☺ 9am-5.30pm) at the busy bus station. There are two routes to Karnataka – the main bus route via Gudalur and the shorter, more arduous route via Masinagudi. The latter is tackled only by minibuses and winds through 36 hairpin bends! Frequent buses leave for Mettupalayam and Coimbatore, and there's daily service to Chennai, Bengaluru and Mysore.

Connect with trains to Chennai or Kochi (Cochin, Kerala) at Coimbatore.

To get to Mudumalai National Park (Rs27, 2½ hours, 12 daily), take one of the Mysore buses that will drop you at park headquarters at Theppakadu, or one of the small buses that go via the narrow and twisting Sighur Ghat road. Some of these rolling wrecks travel only as far as Masinagudi (Rs14, 1½ hours), from where there are buses every two hours to Theppakadu.

Local buses leave every 30 minutes for Kotagiri (Rs10, two hours) and every 10 minutes to Coonoor (Rs6.50, one hour).

TRAIN

The miniature train – one of the Mountain Railways of India given World Heritage status by Unesco in 2005 – is the best way to get here. There are fine views of forest, waterfalls and tea plantations along the way, especially from the front 1st-class carriage; the steam engine pushes, rather than pulls, the train up the hill, so the front carriage leads the way. Departures and arrivals at Mettupalayam connect with those of the *Nilgiri Express,* which runs between Mettupalayam and Chennai. The miniature train departs Mettupalayam for Ooty at 7.20am daily (1st/2nd class Rs117/12, five hours, 46km). If you want a seat in either direction, be at least 45 minutes early or make a reservation (Rs25) at least 24 hours in advance.

From Ooty the train leaves at 3pm and takes about 3½ hours. There are also two daily passenger trains between Ooty and Coonoor (1½ hours).

Getting Around

Plenty of autorickshaws hang around the bus station – a ride from the train or bus stations to Charing Cross costs about Rs30, and a list of autorickshaw fixed prices is on a sign at the steps on Commercial Rd leading to the tourist information office.

Taxis cluster at several stands in town. There are fixed fares to most destinations including Coonoor (Rs400), Kotagiri (Rs600), Gudalur (Rs800), Mudumalai National Park (Rs800) and Coimbatore (Rs800).

There's a jeep hire near the main bazaar, although its best to rent these out in groups; expect to pay about 1.5 times more than local taxi fares.

MUDUMALAI NATIONAL PARK
☎ 0423

In the foothills of the Nilgiris, this 321-sq-km **park** (admission Rs35; ⏲ 6.30-9am & 3-6pm) is like a classical Indian landscape painting given life sans trash: thin, spindly trees and light-slotted leaves concealing spotted chital deer and slow herds of gaur (Indian bison). Somewhere in the hills are tigers, although you're very lucky if you spot one.

Part of the Nilgiri Biosphere Reserve (3000 sq km), the park is the best place for spotting wildlife in Tamil Nadu, although there's still a good chance you won't see more than some deer and kingfishers. Vegetation ranges from grasslands to semi-evergreen forests to foothill scrub; besides the above species, panthers, wild boars, jackals and sloth bears prowl the reserve. Otters and crocodiles both inhabit the Moyar River, and the park's wild elephant population numbers about 600.

This may be the best spot in the state for getting out of doors – trekking in the jungle, jeep safaris, night safaris and birdwatching. Many resorts provide a pick-up service from nearby towns such as Ooty (starting from Rs500), otherwise hire any jeep in Masinagudi. It's best to book rooms in advance, particularly in the high season. Each resort offers a range of services including visits to Mudumalai National Park, hikes with a guide, fishing and horse riding, all of which cost extra.

A good time to visit is between December and June although the park may be closed during the dry season, February to March. Heavy rain is common in October and November.

The admission price includes a Rs20 minibus tour.

Orientation & Information

The main service area in Mudumalai is Theppakadu, on the main road between Ooty and Mysore. Here you'll find the park's **reception centre** (☎ 526235; ⏲ 6.30-9am & 3-6pm) and some park-run accommodation.

The closest village is Masinagudi, 7km from Theppakadu.

Tours

It's not possible to hike in the park and tours are limited to sanctuary minibuses; private vehicles are not allowed in the park except on the main Ooty–Mysore road that runs through it. Most people see the park via 45-

minute **minibus tours** (per person Rs35, incl Rs15 park entry fee) that run between 7am and 9am and 3pm and 6pm. The tour makes a 15km loop through part of the park; passengers are told not to wear bright clothes and remain quiet, but in the land of loud saris and louder cell phones, this very rarely happens.

A much better bet is to hire a guide for a foot **trek** outside the park boundaries. Talk to the guys who hang around the park entry station, or ask at your resort – all have their own knowledgeable, English-speaking guides who charge around Rs150 for a couple of hours and Rs300 to Rs400 for a four-hour walking or combined jeep-and-walking tour. Don't forget you'll need a permit to trek in some parts of the park; reputable guides should already possess the right paperwork.

Elephant rides are occasionally offered for Rs400 per group of four.

Sleeping & Eating

All budgets are catered for – there are budget and midrange lodges inside the park at Theppakadu; budget rooms and midrange cottages in Masinagudi; and midrange jungle resorts in Bokkapuram (4km south of Masinagudi). For meals at the resorts, expect to pay from Rs400 per person per day.

IN THE PARK

For most accommodation in the park, book in advance, in person, with the WWO in Ooty (p465). In low season, you *may* be able to get accommodation if it's available by asking directly at the park reception centre. The following three park-run places are walking distance from park reception and on the banks of the river.

Minivet Dormitory (per person Rs35) A clean place, with two four-bed rooms, each with private bathroom with cold water only.

Theppakadu Log House (d/q Rs330/560) and **Sylvan Lodge** (d/q Rs330/560) are the pick of the places in the park. Overlooking the river, they're comfortable, well maintained and good value. There's a kitchen at Sylvan Lodge that prepares meals for booked guests.

The government-run **Tamil Nadu Hotel** (☎ 252 6580; dm/d/q Rs75/295/495) is in the same cluster of buildings; it provides basic accommodation and basic meals. Near Masinagudi, try **Bamboo Banks Farm** (☎ 2526211; www.bamboobanks.in; cottages s/d Rs825/1125), which lies a couple of kilometres out of town towards Bokkapuram. There are four big, comfortable private cottages in the

lush gardens of the family-run property. The landscape is beautiful but tamed; you'll need transport to travel the few kilometres to wilderness areas.

BOKKAPURAM

This area south of Masinagudi is home to a gaggle of fine forest resorts, mostly family-run businesses with a warm, homely atmosphere, high standards and breathtaking views.

Forest Hills Guest House (☎ 2526216; www.foresthills-resort.com; s/d from Rs1400/1700, huts Rs1250) Forest Hills is a family-run, family-sized guest house (10 rooms on 5 hectares) with a few cute bamboo huts, some clean spacious rooms and a fabulous watchtower for wildlife- and bird-watching. There's a slight colonial air here with a gazebo-style bar, games rooms and a barbecue pit.

Safari Land Farm and Guest House (☎ 2526937; r from Rs1800) You can get Swiss Family Robinson in this jungle complex of well-decked-out tree houses. The views into the surrounding jungle hills are stunning, but the pace, for all the dramatic scenery, is supremely relaxed.

Jungle Retreat (☎ 2526469; www.jungleretreat.com; dm Rs473, bamboo huts/standard r Rs1969/2532, tree house Rs4500) This is one of the most stylish resorts in the area, with lovingly built stone cottages decked out in classic furniture, and sturdy bamboo huts, all spread out to give a feeling of seclusion. It's possible to camp, and there's a dormitory for groups. The bar, restaurant and common area are great places to meet fellow travellers and the owners are knowledgeable and friendly with a large area of private forest at their disposal. All prices include taxes.

Getting There & Away

Buses from Ooty to Mysore and Bengaluru stop at Theppakadu (Rs24, 2½ hours, 11 daily). Bus services run every two hours between Theppakadu and Masinagudi.

The longer route that these buses take to or from Ooty is via Gudalur (67km). The direct route to Masinagudi, however, is an interesting 'short cut' (Rs10, 1½ hours, 36km) which involves taking one of the small government buses that make the trip up (or down) the tortuous Sighur Ghat road. The bends are so tight and the gradient so steep that large buses simply can't use it. Private minibuses heading to Mysore also use this route but if you want to get off at Masinagudi, you'll have to pay the full fare (Rs125).

Andaman & Nicobar Islands

Andaman & Nicobar Islands

On old maps, the Andamans and Nicobars were the kind of islands whose inhabitants were depicted with dog heads or faces in their chests, surrounded by sea serpents coiled around a tempest-lashed sea known to Indians as Kalapani: The Black Waters. These were the islands that someone labelled, with a shaky hand, 'Here be Monsters'.

Likely, those maps were drawn by an early traveller who realised they had found a Very Good Thing and didn't want to share it with the rest of us.

Because the Andaman and Nicobar Islands are, unambiguously and without hyperbole, tropical bliss. If it weren't for the tragic fact their indigenous populations have largely been wiped out and displaced, they'd be practically perfect. That depressing addendum aside, what's the attraction here?

Blue, blue, blue and blue: oceans and skies, streaked with silver sheets of flying fish. Primeval jungle cut by muddy rivers that run past villages as old as India itself, where some inhabitants still live in the Stone Age. Snow-white beaches melting under flame-and-purple sunsets, all populated by a friendly masala of South and Southeast Asian settlers and their laid-back descendants.

Unfortunately the Nicobars are off limits to tourists, but that still leaves hundreds of islands to explore. When you do choose to wander, it will likely be by ferry. When the salt cuts the waves and dolphins shimmer in front of the next oncoming Eden, you'll know you've found a wholly unexpected island allure to India.

HIGHLIGHTS

- Regress to infantile laziness and happiness on **Neil Island** (p488)
- Snorkel and socialise on **Havelock Island** (p486)
- Interact with a small town yet multicultural cast of Indians in **Port Blair** (p480)
- Take a road trip through the jungle heart of the Andamans around **Mayabunder** and **Diglipur** (p489)
- Find Butler Bay; call God; say thanks for paradise on **Little Andaman** (p490)

★ Diglipur

★ Mayabunder

★ Havelock Island
★ Neil Island
★ Port Blair

Little Andaman
★

History

The date of initial human settlement in the Andamans and Nicobars is lost to history. Anthropologists say stone tool crafters have lived here for 2000 years, and scholars of human migration believe local indigenous tribes have roots in Negrito and Malay ethnic groups in Southeast Asia. Otherwise, these specks in the sea have been a constant source of legend to outside visitors.

Even the name 'Andaman' is thought to derive from 'Hanuman'; the Hindu monkey god supposedly used the islands as a stepping stone between India and Sri Lanka. The 10th-century Persian adventurer Buzurg Ibn Shahriyar described an island chain inhabited by cannibals, a story Marco Polo repeated with the slight embellishment that the natives had dog heads. With that said, stories of cannibalism may have been inflated by Malay pirates, who liked to use the archipelago as a secret raiding base. Tablets in Thanjavur in Tamil Nadu named the archipelago Timaittivu: The Impure Islands.

None of the above was exactly tourism brochure stuff, but visitors kept coming: the Marathas in the late 17th century and 200 years later, the British. The latter used the Andamans as a base for invading Burma during the first Anglo-Burmese War and as a penal colony. During the British Raj, Indian political dissidents and freedom fighters found themselves on lockdown with 'normal' criminals in Port Blair's cellular jail. When WWII rolled around, some islanders greeted the invading Japanese as liberators, but despite installing Indian politicians as (puppet) administrators, the Japanese military proved to be far harsher occupiers than the British.

Following Independence in 1947, the Andaman and Nicobar Islands were incorporated into the Indian Union. Since then, massive migration from the mainland has inflated their population from a few thousand to more than 350,000; many of these arrivals were Bengali refugees fleeing the chaos

---

FAST FACTS

Population 356,265

Area 8248 sq km

Telephone code ☎ 03192

Main language Hindi, Bengali, Tamil

When to go December to early April

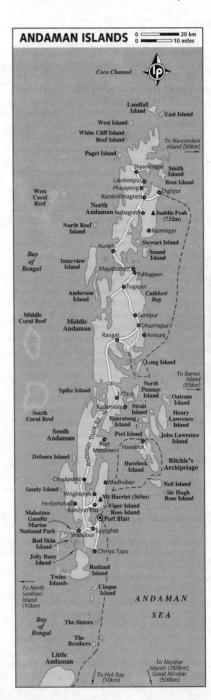

ANDAMAN & NICOBAR ISLANDS

of Partition. During this influx, tribal land rights and environmental protection were often disregarded, and while some conditions are improving, the indigenous tribes remain largely in decline.

Many of the aftershocks of the 2004 Indian Ocean earthquake were concentrated off the coast of the Andaman and Nicobars, which were doubly devastated by the resulting tsunami and vibrations from the actual quakes. The Nicobars were especially hard hit; some estimate a fifth of the population was killed. Small islets were swallowed by the sea, and Trinket Island was literally split in two by seismic activity and flooding. Numerous outer island residents were relocated to Port Blair after the tsunami, and many have yet to return to their homes. But by and large normalcy has returned here, along with tourists, although places like Little Andaman remain practically deserted by visitors (so visit). There may even be an air route opening between Port Blair and Phuket in the future (Thailand is far closer than India); if so, it may be time to kiss the Andamans' quirky, family-owned huts and hotels farewell.

You might notice quite a few Indian military men in paradise. That's because China-aligned Myanmar is increasingly allowing its large neighbour to the north more access to the Indian Ocean via Myanmar ports, a move that makes India a little wary.

Climate

Sea breezes keep temperatures within the 23°C to 31°C range and the humidity at around 80% all year. The southwest (wet) monsoons come to the islands between roughly mid-May and early October, and the northeast (dry) monsoons between November and December. Be warned: bad weather can seriously muck up your travel itinerary since ferry services are cancelled if the sea is too rough.

Geography & Environment

The islands form the peaks of the Arakan Yoma, a mountain range that begins in Western Myanmar (Burma) and extends into the ocean running all the way to Sumatra in Indonesia. The majority of the land area is taken up by the Andamans, at 6408 sq km. The Nicobars (1841 sq km) begin 50km south of Little Andaman.

The isolation of the Andaman and Nicobar Islands has led to the evolution of many endemic plant and animal species. Of 62 identified mammals, 32 are unique to the islands. Among these are the Andaman wild pig, the crab-eating macaque, masked palm civet and species of tree shrews and bats. Almost 50% of the islands' 250 bird species are endemic, and include eagles, ground-dwelling megapodes, *hawabills* (swiftlets), doves, teals, hornbills and the emerald Nicobar Pigeon. The isolated beaches provide excellent breeding grounds for turtles, and inland rivers are prowled by saltwater crocodiles. While dolphins are frequently sighted, the once abundant dugongs have all but vanished, although they are the official animal of the Union Territory.

Mangroves are an important aspect of the landscape, offering a natural protective barrier to both land and sea. Further inland the tall evergreen and moist deciduous forests contain important tree species, including the renowned padauk – a hardwood with light and dark colours occurring in the same tree.

CAREFUL WITH THE CORAL!

In general, you should only snorkel during high tide in the Andamans. During low tide it's very easy to step on coral, which irreparably damages the delicate organisms. Even the sweep of a strong flipper kick can harm coral. You're also risking a painful sea urchin spine if you set your feet on the seabed. Divers need to be extra cautious about descents near reefs; colliding with the coral at a hard pace with full gear is environmentally disastrous.

THE GREAT PIGEON QUEST

Perhaps the coup for a birdwatcher in India is to spot the Nicobar Pigeon, a near extinct bird from uninhabited islands in Indonesia and the Nicobars. The brilliant dark grey and neon green creature can occasionally be spotted in Indian zoos, but it's every ornithologist's dream to spot one in the wild, on a jungle trek. If you do spot a Nicobar Pigeon, give yourself a big bird-watching pat on the back, as you've seen one of the rarest of the rare in its very remote endemic environment.

Information

Even though they're 1000km east of the mainland, the Andamans still run on Indian time. This means that it can be dark by 5pm and light by 4am; people here tend to be very early risers. The peak season is December and January, and in September and October tourists can fill literally every bed in Port Blair; book accommodation in advance if you're travelling at these times. The wet monsoon season runs from roughly June to August, and while the weather can be foul, you'll essentially have the islands to yourself.

Andaman & Nicobar Tourism (A&N Tourism; Map p481; ☎ 232747; www.tourism.andaman.nic.in; Kamaraj Rd, Port Blair; ⏰ 8.30am-1pm & 2-5pm Mon-Fri, 8.30am-noon Sat) is the main tourism body for the islands.

ACCOMMODATION

In the low season there are great deals on simple beach huts on Neil and Havelock Islands; some huts with shared toilet run for as low as Rs50, although you'll generally pay somewhere between Rs150 and Rs250 (still a steal!). High-end resorts, on the other hand, are almost uniformly overpriced.

Prices shoot up in the peak season (15 December to 15 January). Prices given in this chapter are for midseason (1 October to 30 April, excluding peak). May to September is low season. Camping is currently not permitted on public land or national parks on the islands.

PERMITS

Most civil servants come to Port Blair on two-year postings from the mainland. With such a turnover of staff, be aware rules and regulations regarding permits are subject to sudden changes.

All foreigners need a permit to visit the Andaman Islands, and it's issued free on arrival. The 30-day permit (which can be extended to 45 days), allows foreigners to stay in Port Blair. Overnight stays are also permitted on South and Middle Andaman (excluding tribal areas), North Andaman (Diglipur), Long Island, North Passage, Little Andaman (excluding tribal areas), and Havelock and Neil Islands.

The permit also allows day trips to Jolly Buoy, South Cinque, Red Skin, Ross, Narcondam, Interview and Rutland Islands, as well as The Brothers and The Sisters.

To obtain the permit, air travellers simply present their passport and fill out a form on arrival at Port Blair airport. Permits are usually issued for as long as you ask, up to the 30-day maximum.

Boat passengers will probably be met by an immigration official on arrival, but if not should seek out the immigration office at Haddo Jetty immediately. Keep your permit on you at all times – you won't be able to travel without it. Police frequently ask to see it, especially when you're disembarking on other islands, and hotels will need permit details. Check current regulations regarding boat travel with the following:

Andaman & Nicobar Tourism (A&N Tourism; Map p481; ☎ 238473; www.tourism.andaman.nic.in; Kamaraj Rd, Port Blair; ⏰ 8.30am-1pm & 2-5pm Mon-Fri, 8.30am-noon Sat)

Foreigners' Registration Office Chennai (☎ 044-23454970, 044-28278210); Kolkata (☎ 033-22470549, 033-22473300)

Shipping Corporation of India (SCI; www.shipindia .com) Chennai (☎ 044-5231401; Jawahar Bldg, 6 Rajaji Salai); Kolkata (☎ 033-2482354; 1st fl, 13 Strand Rd); Port Blair (Map p481; ☎ 233347/233590; Aberdeen Bazaar)

National Parks & Sanctuaries

Additional permits are required to visit some national parks and sanctuaries. To save a lot of running around, take advantage of the 'single window' system for permits and information at the A&N Tourism office (p480) in Port Blair, where there's now also a **Forestry Department Desk** (⏰ 8.30-11am & 2.30-4.30pm Mon-Sat). Here you can find out whether a permit is needed, how to go about getting it, how much it costs and whether it is in fact possible to get one (it's not always).

If you plan to do something complicated, you'll be sent to the **Chief Wildlife Warden** (CWW; Map p481; ☎ 233321; Haddo Rd; ⏰ 8.30am-noon & 1-4pm Mon-Fri) where your application should consist of a letter stating your case, the name of the boat and the dates involved; all things being equal, the permit should be issued within the hour.

For most day permits it's not the hassle but the cost. For areas such as Mahatma Gandhi Marine National Park, and Ross and Smith Islands near Diglipur, the permits cost Rs50/500 for Indians/foreigners. For Saddle Peak National Park, also near Diglipur, the cost is Rs25/250.

Students with valid ID often only pay minimal entry fees, but must produce a letter from

ISLAND INDIGENES

The Andaman and Nicobar Islands' indigenous peoples constitute just 12% of the population and, in most cases, their numbers are decreasing.

Onge

Two-thirds of Little Andaman's Onge Island was taken over by the Forest Department and 'settled' in 1977. The 100 or so remaining members of the Onge tribe live in a 25-sq-km reserve covering Dugong Creek and South Bay. Anthropologists say the Onge population has declined due to demoralisation through loss of territory.

Sentinelese

The Sentinelese, unlike the other tribes in these islands, have consistently repelled outside contact. For years, contact parties arrived on the beaches of North Sentinel Island, the last redoubt of the Sentinelese, with gifts of coconuts, bananas, pigs and red plastic buckets, only to be showered with arrows, although some encounters have been a little less hostile. About 150 Sentinelese remain.

Andamanese

Now numbering only about 40, it seems impossible the Andamanese can escape extinction. There were around 7000 Andamanese in the mid-19th century, but friendliness to colonisers was their undoing, and by 1971 all but 19 of the population had been swept away by measles, syphilis and influenza epidemics. They've been resettled on tiny Strait Island.

Jarawa

The 350 remaining Jarawa occupy the 639-sq-km reserve on South and Middle Andaman Islands. In 1953 the chief commissioner requested an armed sea plane bomb Jarawa settlements and their territory has been consistently disrupted by the Andaman Trunk Rd, forest clearance and settler and tourist encroachment. Hardly surprisingly, most Jarawa remain hostile to contact.

Shompen

Only about 250 Shompen remain in the forests on Great Nicobar. Semi-nomadic hunter-gatherers who live along the riverbanks, they have resisted integration and avoid areas occupied by Indian immigrants.

Nicobarese

The 30,000 Nicobarese are the only indigenous people whose numbers are not decreasing. The majority have converted to Christianity and been partly assimilated into contemporary Indian society. Living in village units led by a head man, they farm pigs and cultivate coconuts, yams and bananas. The Nicobarese, who probably descended from people of Malaysia and Myanmar, inhabit a number of islands in the Nicobar group, centred on Car Nicobar, the region worst affected by the 2004 tsunami.

An Indian anthropologist tells us expeditions to the Sentinelese (a traditional pastime of visiting dignitaries who want to be seen roughing it in the Andamans) have ceased, which may be a good thing, as contact with the 'civilised' world continues to devastate other tribes. In 2008, eight Onge died after drinking washed-ashore chemicals they mistook for alcohol, evidence of the danger of alcoholism in the native community. In the same year, violent encounters flared between the Jarawa and poachers and intruders who illegally entered their reserve, resulting in the deaths of both settlers and Jarawas.

the Chief Wildlife Warden in Port Blair authorising the discount.

The Nicobar Islands are normally off limits to all except Indian nationals engaged in research, government business or trade.

Activities
DIVING

The Andaman Islands are considered one of the world's great diving locations, as much for their relative isolation as for their crystal-clear waters, superb coral and kaleidoscopic marine life.

The main dive season – depending on the monsoon – runs from roughly November to April, but trips still occur during the summer wet season, from roughly June to August (you'll just be closer to shore). And diving conditions are generally fine in September and October; there's just rain to contend with.

Centres offer fully equipped boat dives, discover scuba-diving courses (around US$100), open water (US$350) and advanced courses (US$300), as well as Divemaster training. Prices vary depending on the location, number of participants and duration of the course, but diving in the Andamans runs around Rs2000/3000 for a single/double boat dive. In national parks there's an additional cost of Rs1000 per person per day payable directly to the park.

Havelock Island is far and away the main diving centre in the islands, although some outfits were expanding onto Neil at the time of research.

Barefoot Scuba (Map p486; ☎ 282181; www.barefoot india.com) Based at Café del Mar at No 3 Village, this dive operation is connected with Barefoot at Havelock resort.
Blue Lagoon Divers (Map p486; ☎ 091-9933201327; www.divingandaman.com) Based out of Eco Villa at No 2 Village.

Dive India (Map p486; ☎ 091-9932082204; www .diveindia.com) Based at Island Vinnie's Tropical Beach Cabanas, midway between Nos 3 and 5 Villages.

SNORKELLING
Much easier and cheaper to arrange than diving, snorkelling can be highly rewarding. Havelock Island is one of the best, and certainly easiest, places for snorkelling as many accommodation places organise boat trips out to otherwise inaccessible coral reefs and islands, and you can snorkel offshore on Neil Island.

The closest place to Port Blair for snorkelling is North Bay. Other relatively easily accessible snorkelling sites include Red Skin and Jolly Buoy, near Wandoor.

SURFING
Intrepid surfing travellers have been whispering about **Little Andaman** since it first opened up to foreigners several years ago. Although the island is still quite remote, surfers continue to drift here for the reliable waves off the east coast. **SEAL** (http://seal-asia.com) offers a couple of live-aboard surfing charters a year, with pick-up and drop-off in Port Blair, between mid-March and mid-May.

FISHING
The Andamans also have game fishing opportunities. The occasional charter boat out of Phuket (Thailand) makes **live-aboard trips**

ISLAND LIFE

Most people don't visit the Andamans for their culture, unless they're interested in researching the islands' tribal populations. But there is a just-as-fascinating 'new' home-grown culture here born of the settlement of pioneers from across India and nearby Myanmar (Burma). You'd be hard pressed to find such a cosmopolitan mix of South and Southeast Asians in what amounts to a series of small towns and villages, rather than large, multicultural cities; it comes as quite a relaxing surprise to see Bengalis, Keralans, Telugus and Karens (from Myanmar) chatting and sharing tea amid swaying palms.

And locals appear to appreciate their idyllic surrounds. Today, most residents of the Andamans are native born, although many have travelled to the mainland for hospital visits or schooling. Mostly, they seem to loathe it. It's not uncommon to hear comments such as 'I can't stand the mainland'. One local said to us, 'I was born here, raised here, and I'll die here. Whenever I step on the mainland, I just want to be back in the islands.'

Andamaners and Nicobarans are generally laid-back, friendly and fair-minded, as the following episode illustrates.

I was taking an autorickshaw in Rangat and hadn't agreed to a price beforehand. Not feeling like arguing, I handed the driver Rs20 at the end of the ride – more, I thought, than I owed.

As I walked away, the driver yelled, 'Sir! Sir!' I sighed, not wanting to argue, and turned around – to see the auto driver holding out Rs5 change.

Adam Karlin

(www.andamanisland-fishing.com), usually around March.

Getting There & Away

AIR

There are daily flights to Port Blair from Delhi, Kolkata (Calcutta) and Chennai (Madras), although flights from Delhi and Kolkata are often routed through Chennai. Fares run between US$250 and US$400 round-trip depending on how early you book; some airlines offer one-way flights for as low as US$50, but these need to be booked months in advance. At the time of research, **Kingfisher Airlines** (☎ 18002093030; www.flykingfisher.com) had the cheapest last-minute flights to the islands. Other options include **Air India** (Chennai ☎ 044-285554747; Kolkata ☎ 033-22822356; Port Blair ☎ 230949; www.airindia.com) and **JetLite** (Chennai ☎ 044-22560909; Kolkata ☎ 033-25110901; Port Blair ☎ 244364; www.jetlite.com).

There's been talk for some years about direct flights from Phuket (Thailand) to Port Blair, but for now, it's still talk. Check the **A&N Tourism** (www.tourism.andaman.nic.in) website for updates.

BOAT

Ah, the infamous boat to Port Blair. Depending on who you ask, it's either 'the only *real* way to get to the Andamans, man' or a hassle and a half. The truth lies somewhere in between; the ferry from the mainland is probably nicer than you expect, but it ain't Carnival Cruise lines. There are usually four to six sailings a month between Port Blair and the Indian mainland – fortnightly to/from Kolkata (56 hours) and weekly (in high season) to/from Chennai (60 hours) on vessels operated by **Shipping Corporation of India** (SCI; www.shipindia.com; Chennai ☎ 044-5231401; Kolkata ☎ 033-2482354; Port Blair Map p481; ☎ 233347/233590; Aberdeen Bazaar). The schedule is erratic, so call SCI in advance. Updated schedules and fares can be found at www.and.nic.in/s psch/sailing.htm.

Take sailing times with a large grain of salt – travellers have reported sitting on the boat at Kolkata harbour for up to 12 hours, or waiting to dock near Port Blair for several hours. With hold-ups and variable weather and sea conditions, the trip can take three to four days. The service from Chennai goes via Car Nicobar once a month, taking an extra two days, but only residents may disembark. There is usually a service once a month from

Visakhapatnam in Andhra Pradesh (see p314 for more details).

If you're buying your return ticket in Port Blair, go to the 1st floor of the A&N Tourism office where they can reserve you a berth under the tourist-quota system; you then take the approval letter to the Directorate of Shipping Services' ticket office at Phoenix Bay Jetty. This process can take some days, so it's simpler to arrange return tickets on the mainland when purchasing your outward ticket.

Classes vary slightly between boats, but the cheapest is bunk (Rs1700 to Rs1960), followed by 2nd class B (Rs3890), 2nd class A (Rs5030), 1st class (Rs6320) and deluxe cabins (Rs7640). The MV *Akbar* also has AC dorm berths (Rs3290). Pricewise, higher-end tickets cost as much, if not more, than a plane ticket. If you go bunk, prepare for waking up to a chorus of men 'hwwaaaaching' and spitting, little privacy and toilets that tend to get…unpleasant after three days at sea. That said, it's a good way to meet locals.

Food (tiffin for breakfast, thalis for lunch and dinner) costs around Rs150 per day and pretty much consists of glop on rice. Bring something (fruit in particular) to supplement your diet. Some bedding is supplied, but if you're travelling bunk class, bring a sleeping sheet. Many travellers take a hammock to string up on deck.

There is no official ferry between Port Blair and Thailand, but if there are yachts around you could try to crew. Some travellers wonder

---

FESTIVALS IN THE ANDAMAN ISLANDS

The 10-day **Island Tourism Festival** is held in Port Blair, usually in January. Dance groups come from surrounding islands and the mainland, and various cultural performances are held at the Exhibition Complex. One of the festival's more bizarre aspects is the Andaman dog show, but there's also a flower show, a baby show and a fancy-dress competition! For information, check the **A&N Tourism** (www.tourism.andaman.nic .in) website.

Subhash Mela is held every January on Havelock to celebrate the birthday of freedom fighter Subhas Chandra Bose; expect a fun week of dance, readings and other cultural bric-a-brac.

THE TALE OF JACK

Reports of the Andamaners being one of the last uncontacted peoples on Earth are not entirely true. In the days of the Indian Uprising, one inhabitant of these islands did make a journey that sent him further away from home than any of his people have likely been before or since.

On 31 December 1857, the East Indian Company ship *Pluto* was sailing home to Calcutta from the site of what would one day be Port Blair. When island natives were spotted on South Reef Island, longboats were sent from the British ship to make contact. European ship and native canoe approached each other, and disaster ensued – someone shot someone first (accounts are disputed), several natives were killed, and one Andamaner, mysteriously, ended up on a British boat.

The islander was named 'Jack' by his captors/hosts, dressed in cabin boys' clothes (Andaman Islanders still rarely grow over 1.5m (5ft) tall), and it was decided he would be brought back to Calcutta for the sake of research. Jack reportedly looked wistful and homesick as the boat steamed away from his island; his one comfort, despite never having seen a dog before, was to make fast friends with the ship's pet, Neptune.

Jack became something of a minor celebrity in Calcutta, causing a stir among the entire colonial administration, but after less than two weeks he came down with cholera. Although he was successfully treated, an inflammation of the lungs followed, and it was decided he should be sent back to his home. And so Jack was given presents – pots, pans, tools and the like – and steamed back to South Reef Island, where was left alone and naked with a pile of home and kitchenware, possibly wondering what the hell just happened.

if it's possible to get from the Andamans to Myanmar (Burma) by sea. Legally, you can't, although we hear it's been done by those with their own boats. Be aware you are risking imprisonment or worse from the Indian and Burmese navies if you give this a go.

Getting Around

All roads – and ferries – lead to Port Blair, and you'll inevitably spend a night or two here booking onward travel. The main island group – South, Middle and North Andaman – is connected by road, with ferry crossings and bridges. Cheap state and more expensive private buses run south from Port Blair to Wandoor, and north to Bharatang, Rangat, Mayabunder and finally to Diglipur, 325km north of the capital. The Jarawa reserve closes to most traffic at around 3pm; thus, buses that pass through the reserve leave from around 4am up till 11am. Private jeeps and minivans connect many villages; these are hop-on, hop-off affairs, but you can hire a whole vehicle for an inflated price.

A boat is the only way to reach most islands, and while ferry travel is romantic, ferry ticket offices will become the hell of your life. Expect the worst: hot waits, slow service, queue-jumping and a rugby scrum to the ticket window. To hold your spot and advance in line you need to be a little aggressive (but don't be a jerk). Or be a woman; the queues for ladies

are a godsend if you can join them, but they really only apply in Port Blair. You can buy tickets the day you travel by arriving at the appropriate jetty an hour beforehand, but this is risky during high season and not a guarantee on Havelock any time of year. In towns like Rangat, ferry ticket offices usually open between Never-O'clock and Go-to-Hell.

There are regular boat services to Havelock and Neil Islands, as well as Rangat, Mayabunder, Diglipur and Little Andaman. If all else fails, fishermen may be willing to give you a ride for around Rs2000 between, say, Port Blair and Havelock. A schedule of sailing times can be found at www.and.nic.in/spsch/iisailing.htm.

A subsidised inter-island helicopter service runs from Port Blair to Little Andaman (Rs1488, 35 minutes, Tuesday, Friday and Saturday), Havelock Island (Rs850, 20 minutes or 40 minutes via Neil Island, Tuesday, Saturday via Neil Island) and Diglipur via Mayabunder (Rs2125 or Rs1915 from Mayabunder, one hour, Tuesday). Bookings must be made through the **Civil Aviation Office** (☎ 230480) in Port Blair.

Mainland train bookings can be made at the **Railway Bookings Office** (⊗ 8am-12.30pm & 1-2pm), located in the Secretariat's office south of Aberdeen Bazaar; your hotel owners should also be able to help with any onward rail enquires.

PORT BLAIR

pop 100,186

Port Blair deserves more credit than it receives from the mobs of travellers who rush through it on the way to Havelock Island. Green, laid-back and surprisingly cosmopolitan, it's an incredibly attractive town that sprawls over jungly hills culled from Jurassic Park and several deep-blue bays that fuzz into a soft-focus seascape horizon. You'd be hard pressed to find such a vibrant mix of Indian Ocean inhabitants – Bengalis, Tamils, Nicobarese, Burmese and Telugus – anywhere, let alone in what's basically a very friendly small town. Whatever your opinions on the place, you're inevitably here for a day or two as 'PB' is the only place to reliably access the internet, withdraw money and book onward travel in the islands.

Orientation

Most of the hotels, the bus stand and inter-island ferries from Phoenix Bay Jetty are around the Aberdeen Bazaar area. The airport is about 4km south of town.

Information

EMERGENCY

Aberdeen Police Station (☎ 232400, 232100; MG Rd)
GB Pant Hospital (☎ 232102; GB Pant Rd)
Secretariat Office (A&N office; ☎ 232579; Rajbhawan Secretariat Complex, Kamraj Rd)

INTERNET ACCESS

There are quite a few internet places in Aberdeen Bazaar; try **Net World** (per hr Rs40; ◑ 9am-8.30pm), by the Clock Tower.

MONEY

Port Blair is the only place in the Andamans where you can change cash or travellers cheques, and find an ATM. There's a Western Union office by the post office.
Axis Bank ATM (MA Rd)
Canara Bank (Clock Tower)
ICICI Bank ATM (cnr Foreshore & MA Rds)
Island Travels (☎ 233358; islandtravels@yahoo.com; Aberdeen Bazaar; ◑ 9am-1pm & 2-6pm Mon-Sat)
One of several travel agencies with foreign-exchange facilities.
State Bank of India (MA Rd; ◑ 9am-noon & 1-3pm Mon-Fri, 10am-noon Sat) Travellers cheques and foreign currency can be changed here.
UTI Bank ATM (cnr MG & Haddo Rds; Aberdeen Bazaar)

POST

Main post office (MG Rd; ◑ 9am-5pm Mon-Sat)

TOURIST INFORMATION

Andaman & Nicobar Tourism (A&N Tourism; ☎ 232747; www.tourism.andaman.nic.in; Kamraj Rd; ◑ 8.30am-1pm & 2-5pm Mon-Fri, 8.30am-noon Sat)
This is the main island tourist office, and the place to book government accommodation (between 8am and 11.30am or 2pm and 3pm) and get wildlife permits. Staff are helpful, if laid-back.
India Tourism (☎ 233006; 2nd fl, 189 Junglighat Main Rd; ◑ 8.30am-12.30pm & 1-5pm Mon-Fri)

Sights & Activities

CELLULAR JAIL NATIONAL MEMORIAL

A former British prison that is now a shrine to the political dissidents it once jailed, **Cellular Jail National Memorial** (GB Pant Rd; admission Rs5, camera/video Rs10/50; ◑ 9am-12.30pm & 1.30-5pm Tue-Sun) is worth visiting to understand the important space the Andamans occupy in India's national memory. Built over a period of 18 years in 1890, the original seven wings contained 698 cells radiating from a central tower. Like many political prisons, Cellular Jail became something of a university for freedom fighters, who exchanged books, ideas and debates despite walls and wardens.

A **sound-and-light show** (adult/child Rs20/10) consisting of voice-over conversations between the 'spirit' of the jail and its former inhabitants borders on being powerful, if it weren't for frequent interruptions by cheesy synthesiser riffs and patriotic song recitals sung by a Bollywood backup ensemble. It's still worth seeing; shows are in Hindi nightly at 6pm and English at 7.15pm, but check ahead. No refunds for bad weather.

ANTHROPOLOGICAL MUSEUM

The best **museum** (☎ 232291; MG Rd; Indian/foreigner Rs10/50; ◑ 9am-1pm & 1.30-4.30pm Fri-Wed) in Port Blair provides a thorough and sympathetic portrait of the islands' indigenous tribal communities. The glass display cases may be old school, but they don't feel anywhere near as ancient as the simple geometric patterns etched into a Jarawa chest guard, a skull left in a Sentinelese lean-to or the totemic spirits represented by Nicobarese shamanic sculptures. Pick up a pamphlet (Rs20) on indigenous culture, written by local anthropologists, in the gift shop.

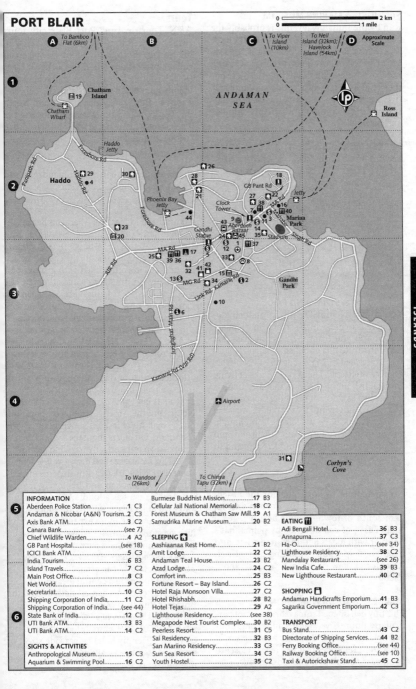

PORT BLAIR

INFORMATION

Aberdeen Police Station	**1** C3
Andaman & Nicobar (A&N) Tourism	**2** C3
Axis Bank ATM	**3** C2
Canara Bank	(see 7)
Chief Wildlife Warden	**4** A2
GB Pant Hospital	(see 18)
ICICI Bank ATM	**5** C3
India Tourism	**6** B3
Island Travels	**7** C3
Main Post Office	**8** C3
Net World	**9** C2
Secretariat	**10** C3
Shipping Corporation of India	**11** C2
Shipping Corporation of India	(see 44)
State Bank of India	**12** C3
UTI Bank ATM	**13** B3
UTI Bank ATM	**14** C2

SIGHTS & ACTIVITIES

Anthropological Museum	**15** C3
Aquarium & Swimming Pool	**16** C2
Burmese Buddhist Mission	**17** B3
Cellular Jail National Memorial	**18** C2
Forest Museum & Chatham Saw Mill	**19** A1
Samudrika Marine Museum	**20** B2

SLEEPING

Aashiaanaa Rest Home	**21** B2
Amit Lodge	**22** C2
Andaman Teal House	**23** B2
Azad Lodge	**24** C2
Comfort inn	**25** B3
Fortune Resort – Bay Island	**26** C2
Hotel Raja Monsoon Villa	**27** C2
Hotel Rhishabh	**28** C2
Hotel Tejas	**29** A2
Lighthouse Residency	(see 38)
Megapode Nest Tourist Complex	**30** B2
Peerless Resort	**31** C5
Sai Residency	**32** B3
San Mariino Residency	**33** C3
Sun Sea Resort	**34** C2
Youth Hostel	**35** C2

EATING

Adi Bengali Hotel	**36** B3
Annapurna	**37** C3
Ha-O	(see 34)
Lighthouse Residency	**38** C2
Mandalay Restaurant	(see 26)
New India Cafe	**39** B3
New Lighthouse Restaurant	**40** C2

SHOPPING

Andaman Handicrafts Emporium	**41** B3
Sagarika Government Emporium	**42** C3

TRANSPORT

Bus Stand	**43** C2
Directorate of Shipping Services	**44** B2
Ferry Booking Office	(see 44)
Railway Booking Office	(see 10)
Taxi & Autorickshaw Stand	**45** C2

SAMUDRIKA MARINE MUSEUM

Run by the Indian Navy, this is probably the best science **museum** (☎ 232012, ext 2214; Haddo Rd; adult/child Rs10/5, camera/video Rs20/40; 9am-5.30pm Tue-Sun) in Port Blair (which isn't saying much). The exhibits could be flashier, but they're at least largely accurate and informative, especially as concerns the islands' ecosystem, tribal communities, plants, animals and marine life.

FOREST MUSEUM & CHATHAM SAW MILL

Located on Chatham Island (reached by a road bridge), the **saw mill** (admission Rs2; 8am-2.30pm Mon-Sat) was set up by the British in 1836 and was one of the largest wood processors in Asia. Inside is the forest museum, which displays locally grown woods, including padauk, and has displays on the history of timber milling on the island. It may not be to everyone's taste – especially conservationists – but it gives a different perspective on the islands' history and economy.

AQUARIUM & SWIMMING POOL

You found Nemo! Or his formaldehyde-preserved corpse, which screams in silent accusation at you from the rows of glass jars that constitute this ghoulish **aquarium** (Mahabir Singh Rd; adult/child Rs5/3; 9am-1pm & 2-4.45pm Thu-Tue, closed 2nd Sat of month). There's also tanks of living tropical fish lining the walls that are about as impressive as a decent pet shop. Opposite the aquarium, the Olympic-sized public **swimming pool** (admission Rs25; Mon-Sat) is clean enough, and open to men only 6.30am to 8am and 5pm to 6pm, to women only 4pm to 5pm, and to families 6pm to 7pm.

CORBYN'S COVE

No one comes to Port Blair for the beach, but if you need a sand fix, Corbyn's Cove, 7km south of town, is your best bet. It's a small curve of coast backed by palms that's popular with locals and Indian tourists, and it's a good spot for swimming and sunset. An autorickshaw ride from town costs about Rs200.

BURMESE BUDDHIST MISSION

This tiny bell-shaped stupa (shrine) is not particularly impressive, but it's an incongruous example of Burmese Buddhist architecture in India and a reminder that you're way closer to Southeast Asia than the subcontinent.

Tours

A&N Tourism runs Port Blair city tours (Rs52), as well tours to Ross Island (Rs75), Mt Harriet (Rs157), Wandoor via spice and rubber plantations (Rs105), Corbyn's Cove (Rs52), Chiriya Tapu (Rs105), snorkelling trips to Jolly Buoy and Redskin Islands (Rs450), and a tour of Ross and Viper Islands and North Bay (Rs360). Trip times vary throughout the week; check with the A&N Tourism office (p480) for full details.

Sleeping

Prices are higher than the mainland, and you need to book ahead in high season.

BUDGET

Many cheap lodges line Aberdeen Bazaar.

Youth Hostel (☎ 232459; dm/d Rs50/100) Opposite the stadium, this YHA only offers discounts for students (Rs30). It's still the cheapest place around but it's often filled with groups, and while some rooms are clean, others are in pretty worn states of dinginess. Management can also be unwilling to accommodate foreigners, but if you're truly penny conscious, this is your cheapest bet.

Azad Lodge (☎ 242646; MA Rd, Aberdeen Bazaar; r Rs200) Probably the best budget option in town, Azad's rooms are clean, cheap and come with attached bathrooms including sit-down flush toilets – what more do you need?

Comfort Inn (☎ 91 9932086969; 36 MA Rd; r Rs300) No, it's not the American motel corporation, but a small hotel located above Temptations restaurant. Quality is about the same as the US chain: so-so but perfectly passable rooms.

 Aashiaanaa Rest Home (☎ 0947 4217008; Marine Hill; r Rs300-700;) Run by the incredibly friendly Shadab and his lovely family, the Aashiaanaa has a lot of 'As' in the name and love in its heart. Rooms are spotless and spacious, and the more expensive ones have nice views over town. It's conveniently just up the hill from the main jetty.

Sai Residency (☎ 212737; r Rs400, with AC Rs600;) This small, family-run affair has some spick-and-span rooms in a central location; it's behind a cluster of mechanics' stalls behind the Burmese Buddhist Mission.

Hotel Raja Monsoon Villa (☎ 241133; s/d Rs400/550, with AC Rs550/900;) Centrally located, this tatty, clean and friendly hotel is in a side street of small shops and tea stalls opposite the town's main mosque.

Andaman Teal House (☎ 232642; Haddo Rd; d Rs400, with AC Rs800; 🌂) The local government guest house sprawls over a garden onto a hill that offers some nice sea views, but a lot of the rooms, particularly non-AC ones, are worn down. Bookings must be made through A&N Tourism.

MIDRANGE

San Mariino Residency (☎ 9434282717; MG Rd; r Rs500-800; 🌂) Run by a very friendly if slightly overbearing manager, this hotel offers crisp sheets, well-kept if characterless facilities, a strangely spelled title and a central location near the Anthropological Museum. Some of the spotless rooms have good views out over the best part of Port Blair (where the jungle meets the ocean); others have not quite as nice views onto the street.

Amit Lodge (☎ 230657; Medical Rd; r Rs600-750; 🌂) Service could use a swift kick and a lesson in smiling, but otherwise this is a fine hotel with breezy balconies that overlooks a bluff near Cellular Jail.

Hotel Tejas (☎ 230360; hotel_tejas@yahoo.co.in; Haddo Rd; d Rs650, with AC Rs950; 🌂) Sparkling rooms of the linoleum-floor-and-comfy-enough-bed sort perch over a hill, a tangled clump of jungle and a sweeping view of Haddo Jetty.

Hotel Rhishabh (☎ 238223; hotelrishabh@yahoo.co.in; Marine Hill; d Rs950, with AC Rs1400; 🌂) On top of Marine Hill, the Rhishabh primarily caters to well-heeled Indian families on holiday. The rooms and facilities are bright white and comfortable, if kind of boring, and some have good views over town.

Ligthouse Residency (☎ 238918; ashraf.lhresidency@gmail.com; MA Rd, Aberdeen Bazaar; r from Rs1000-1200; 🌂) On top of the restaurant of the same name, the Lighthouse is a bit overpriced for what it offers, which are perfectly pleasant rooms with TVs and, at the more expensive end, good views of the waterfront.

Sun Sea Resort (☎ 238330; www.sunsearesort-andamans.com; MG Rd; s/d from Rs1500/2000; 🌂) Despite there being no sea anywhere nearby, this hotel is still a winner, as plush as (if not plusher than) most of the high-end resorts for about half the price.

TOP END

Major credit cards are accepted at the following and prices include breakfast.

Megapode Nest Tourist Complex (☎ 232076, 232207; aniidco@vsnl.com; off Haddo Rd; s/d from Rs2000/2500, cottages Rs3500; 🌂) Despite having a name that sounds like a villain's lair in a Nintendo game, this is the best top-end deal in town, primarily because the prices allow it to straddle the mid-range border. A complex of rooms and cottages slopes down to the sparkling sea, with the best ones styled like traditional Nicobari huts.

Peerless Resort (☎ 22172153; www.peerlesshotels .com; s/d Rs3000/3900, cottage d Rs5000; 🌂) The location is the main plus for Peerless Resort – just back from Corbyn's Cove Beach. Rooms have undergone a fairly major renovation, but they're still overpriced for what you get; they're clean and that's about it.

Fortune Resort – Bay Island (☎ 234101; www.fortune hotels.in; Marine Hill; s/d from Rs4500/5000; 🌂 🍴) Port Blair's top hotel boasts a great location, perched above the ocean with fine sea views from its terraced garden and balcony restaurant. The rooms, while comfortable with polished floors, balconies, and island bric-a-brac, are small; make sure to ask for a sea-facing room.

Eating

Port Blair has a good range of North and South Indian restaurants, reflecting its diverse population of settlers from across India.

New India Cafe (MA Rd; mains from Rs30) There's not terribly much 'new' about this rather worn locals' favourite, but then – it's a locals' favourite. There's well-done veg and non-veg from across India, and breakfast omelettes are surpassingly scrumptious.

Adi Bengali Hotel (MA Rd; mains from Rs30) This energetic canteen does a brisk stock-in-trade in spicy fish curries and other West Bengal staples. Everything's prepared pretty well, if the usual clientele of silent, satisfied Bengali labourers is any proof.

Annapurna (MG Rd; from Rs40) Annapurna is an extremely popular veg option that looks like a high-school cafeteria and serves consistently good karma-friendly fare, ranging from crisp southern dosas (paper-thin lentil-flour pancakes) to rich North Indian–style curries.

Lighthouse Residency (MA Rd, Aberdeen Bazaar; mains Rs45-140; 🕐 lunch & dinner) The Lighthouse is lit like a fluorescent nightmare, but the AC's cranked, the beer's cold and Thai and Chinese dishes make a welcome addition to the Indian favourites. Try the fish tikka – well-grilled goodness, if dinky portions.

Ha-O (MG Rd; mains Rs60-140) The on-site restaurant for Sun Sea Resort is one of the better upmarket eateries in town, well-regarded for its tandoori grill and excellent North Indian of the heavy Punjabi curry sort.

New Lighthouse Restaurant (Marina Park; mains Rs80-250, seafood Rs150-400) The New Lighthouse is the sort of open-air seafood place autorickshaw drivers recommend because they assume this is what Port Blair tourists are looking for. Unfortunately, it's breezy and open air because it's kind of falling apart, but hey: if you want fresh, whole grilled fish, lobster or crab, they got you covered here.

Mandalay Restaurant (Marine Hill) If you need to splurge, you can do a lot worse than the Mandalay's excellent buffet (breakfast Rs200, lunch and dinner Rs350), heavy with Indian and Western faves served on either an attractive deck or in a not-quite-as-appealing Burmese-themed interior.

Shopping

Aberdeen Bazaar is lined with stalls selling cheap clothing and household goods. 'Island' crafts (the same tiki tat you can find anywhere) are available from a handful of emporiums and speciality shops. Most of the shells on sale are collected legally – a good emporium can show proof of this – but, as always, be aware of your home country's restrictions on importing them.

Andaman Handicrafts Emporium (☎ 240141; MG Rd, Middle Point; 10am-7pm)

Sagarika Government Emporium (MG Rd, Middle Point; 10am-7pm)

Getting There & Away

See p478 for details on transport to and from the Andaman Islands.

BOAT

Most inter-island ferries depart from Phoenix Bay Jetty. Advance tickets for boats can be purchased from the ticket counters at the ferry booking office between 9am and 4pm the day before travel. On some boats tickets can be purchased on the boat, but in high season you risk missing out.

From Chatham Wharf there are hourly passenger ferries to Bamboo Flat (Rs3, 15 minutes).

BUS

There are four daily buses to Wandoor (Rs10, 1½ hours). Daily buses run at 4.30am to Diglipur (Rs150, 12 hours) and at 5am and 10.30am to Mayabunder (Rs110, nine hours) via Rangat. The above represents a mix of private and government services; private buses are inevitably more expensive and generally more comfortable. Their 'offices' (a guy with a ticket book) are located across from the main bus stand; they'll likely find you if you look confused enough.

If you want to take the scenic 48km road trip to Bamboo Flat and Mt Harriet, there's a bus at 8.15am and 4pm (Rs18, 1½ hours); returning by ferry will take only 15 minutes.

Getting Around

The central area is easy enough to walk around, but to get out to Corbyn's Cove, Haddo or Chatham Island you'll need some form of transport. A taxi or autorickshaw from the airport to Aberdeen Bazaar costs around Rs60. From Aberdeen Bazaar to Phoenix Bay

---

THE DYING DUGONG

In the Andamans you'll see all kinds of promotional material associated with dugongs – large, slow aquatic mammals and herbivores that look like a cross between a seal and a tuskless walrus. Sadly, the dugong are dying out in the Andaman Islands, and by the time you read this they may only be referenced in these parts in the past tense.

Everything about the dugong seems unhurried and ponderous (although they are actually immensely lithe and strong creatures), from its 70-year lifespan to slow reproduction rate to gentle, vacuum-esque seagrass eating habits. Unfortunately these attributes have made the animal susceptible to predators like sharks, crocodiles, and most dangerous of all, humans. Habitat destruction, hunting and fishing accidents have taken a heavy toll on the dugong, and while it has been an officially protected species for some time now – it's even become something of the wildlife mascot for the islands – the species' future is in doubt.

The first underwater sightings and behaviour observations of the animals in Indian waters were published in 2009 – three dugong were spotted in Havelock, Neil and South Andaman islands. If dugong numbers do not climb appreciably in the future via extensive habitat protection, this mascot may be only that: a symbol rather than an environmental reality.

Jetty is about Rs20 and to Haddo Jetty it's around Rs35.

Bicycles are good for getting around the town and the immediate Port Blair area. They can be hired from stalls in Aberdeen Bazaar for around Rs40 per day.

AROUND PORT BLAIR & SOUTH ANDAMAN

Ross Island

Visiting Ross Island feels like discovering a jungle-clad Lost City, à la Angkor Wat, where the ruins happen to be Victorian English rather than ancient Khmer. The former administrative headquarters for the British in the Andamans, **Ross Island** (admission Rs20) is an essential half-day trip from Port Blair. In its day, little Ross was fondly called the 'Paris of the East' (along with Pondicherry, Saigon etc…). But the cute title, vibrant social scene and tropical gardens were all wiped out by the double whammy of a 1941 earthquake and the invasion of the Japanese (who left behind some machine-gun nests that are great fun to poke around in).

Today the old English architecture is still standing, even as it is swallowed by a green wave of fast-growing jungle. Landscaped paths cross the island and most of the buildings are labelled. There's a small museum with historical displays and photos of Ross Island in its heyday, and a small park where resident deer nibble on bushes.

Ferries to Ross Island (Rs16, 20 minutes) depart from the jetty behind the aquarium in Port Blair at 8.30am, 10.30am, 12.30pm and 2pm Thursday to Tuesday; check when you buy your ticket, as times can be affected by tides.

Viper Island & North Bay

The afternoon boat trip to **Viper Island** (admission Rs5) is worthwhile to see the sobering remains of the ochre-coloured brick jail and the gallows built by the British in 1867. The formidable name comes from a wrecked 19th-century British trading ship nearby. Harbour cruises leave from the jetty behind the aquarium daily at 3pm (Rs60 to Rs75, 45 minutes each way); there are more frequent boats on Wednesday. **North Bay** is the most easily accessible snorkelling bay to Port Blair. A **combined boat tour** (per person Rs300; ⏱ 9.30am-5pm) to Ross and Viper Islands and North Bay leaves daily from the aquarium jetty, allowing 2½ hours to snorkel and explore the bay.

Mt Harriet

Mt Harriet (365m) is across the inlet, north of Port Blair, and there's a road up to the top with good views and birding. To reach Mt Harriet, take the Bamboo Flat passenger ferry (Rs3, 15 minutes) from Chatham Jetty. From Bamboo Flat the road runs 7km along the coast up the summit. Taxis will do the trip for around Rs250 if you don't want to walk.

Wandoor

Wandoor, a tiny speck of a village 29km southwest of Port Blair, is the jumping-off point for **Mahatma Gandhi Marine National Park** (Indian/foreigner Rs50/500), which covers 280 sq km and comprises 15 islands of mangrove creeks, tropical rainforest and reefs supporting 50 types of coral. The marine park's snorkelling sites at **Jolly Buoy** and **Red Skin** islands are popular day trips from Wandoor Jetty (Rs300). That said, if Havelock or Neil Islands are on your Andamans itinerary, it's probably easier and cheaper to wait until you reach them for your underwater experience; unless you're willing to pay through the nose, boats simply don't linger long enough for you to get a good snorkelling experience.

Buses run from Port Blair to Wandoor (Rs8, 1½ hours). About 2km beyond the Wandoor Jetty are quiet, sandy beaches with some excellent snorkelling.

Chiriya Tapu

Chiriya Tapu, 30km south of Port Blair, is a tiny village of beaches, mangroves, and about 2km south, some of the best snorkelling outside Havelock and Neil Islands. There are seven buses a day to the village from Port Blair (Rs8, 1½ hours) and it's possible to arrange boats from here to Cinque Island. Port Blair's zoo was in the process of moving its animals to a new **biological park** here at the time of research; it should be open by the time you read this.

Cinque Island

The uninhabited islands of North and South Cinque, connected by a sandbar, are part of the wildlife sanctuary south of Wandoor. The islands are surrounded by coral reefs, and are among the most beautiful in the Andamans.

Only day visits are allowed, but unless you're on one of the day trips occasionally organised by travel agencies, you need to get permission in advance from the Chief Wildlife

Warden (p475). The islands are two hours by boat from Chiriya Tapu or 3½ hours from Wandoor, and are covered by the Mahatma Gandhi Marine National Park permit (Indian/foreigner Rs50/500).

HAVELOCK ISLAND

If you're coming to the Andamans, chances are you're making a beeline from Port Blair direct to Havelock. With snow-white beaches, teal shallows, dark jungle hills, a coast crammed with beach huts and backpackers from around the world (including roughly a division of Israeli Defence Force leavers), Havelock's one of those budget-travel tropical gems that, in a few years, will have the same cachet as Ko Pha Ngang. If not the nightlife, there are quietly buzzing social scenes concentrated around the common area of the beach-hut resorts, but nothing approaching full-moon party madness. Besides for doing nothing, Havelock is a popular spot for snorkelling and diving. Most travellers make a beeline here from Port Blair.

Inhabited by Bengali settlers since the 1950s, Havelock is about 54km northeast of Port Blair and covers 100 sq km. Only the northern third of the island is settled, and each village is referred to by a number. Boats dock at the jetty at No 1 Village; the main bazaar is 2km south at No 3 Village; and most of the accommodation is strung along the east coast between villages No 2 and No 5. Internet access was spotty at time of research; some small shops offers unreliable link-ups, but don't expect to stay connected here.

Sights & Activities

The prettiest and most popular sweep of sand here is **Radha Nagar Beach**, also known as **beach No 7**. It's a beautiful curve of sugar fronted by perfectly spiralled waves, all backed by native forest that might have grown out of a postcard. And the sunsets? Pretty damn nice. The drive out to the beach, located on the northwestern side of the island about 12km from the jetty, runs through the green dream that is inland Havelock (autorickshaws will take you for about Rs150). Ten minutes' walk along the beach to the northwest is the gorgeous **'lagoon'**, another gem of sheltered sand and crystalline water, and in peak season you can take an **elephant ride** (adult/child Rs20/10) through the jungle.

Elephant Beach, where there's good snorkelling, is further north and reached by a

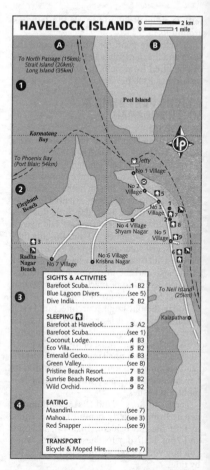

HAVELOCK ISLAND

0   2 km
0   1 mile

To North Passage (15km);
Strait Island (20km);
Long Island (35km)

Peel Island

Karmatang Bay

To Phoenix Bay
(Port Blair; 54km)

Jetty
No 1 Village

No 2 Village

No 3 Village

No 4 Village
Shyam Nagar No 5 Village

Elephant Beach

Radha Nagar Beach No 7 Village

No 6 Village
Krishna Nagar

To Neil Island
(25km)

Kalapathar

SIGHTS & ACTIVITIES
Barefoot Scuba......................1 B2
Blue Lagoon Divers..............(see 5)
Dive India.............................2 B2

SLEEPING
Barefoot at Havelock...........3 A2
Barefoot Scuba...................(see 1)
Coconut Lodge.....................4 B3
Eco Villa...............................5 B2
Emerald Gecko......................6 B3
Green Valley.........................(see 8)
Pristine Beach Resort............7 B2
Sunrise Beach Resort.............8 B2
Wild Orchid..........................9 B2

EATING
Maandini.............................(see 7)
Mahoa.................................(see 3)
Red Snapper........................(see 9)

TRANSPORT
Bicycle & Moped Hire...........(see 7)

40-minute walk through a muddy elephant logging trail; it's well marked (off the cross-island road), but hard going after rain. The beach itself virtually disappeared after the tsunami and at high tide it's impossible to reach – ask locally. Lots of snorkelling charters come out this way, and there are lifeguards who will reprimand anyone who litters – God bless them.

A highlight of Havelock is **snorkelling** or **fishing**, and the best way to do either is on a boat trip organised by your hotel. Trips cost from Rs1000 to Rs2000, depending on the number of people going, distance involved etc – if you go with a good-sized group you may pay as low as Rs250 per head. Snorkelling gear is widely available on Havelock from resorts and small restaurants, and is generally very low quality. Havelock is also the premier spot for **scuba diving** on the Andamans; see p476 for more information.

Some resorts can organise guided **jungle treks** for keen walkers or birders, but be warned: the forest floor turns to glug after rain. The inside rainforest is a spectacular, emerald cavern, and the **birdwatching** – especially on the forest fringes – is rewarding; look out for the blue-black racket-tailed drongo trailing his fabulous tail feathers and, by way of contrast, the brilliant golden oriole.

About 5km beyond No 5 Village is Kalapathar, where an **elephant training camp** is sometimes open to visitors. Beyond Kalapathar the road passes another pristine beach and then peters out into forest.

The local **bazaar** in No 2 Village is a good spot for an evening stroll; it's like being back in mainland India, except you can crank the chaos down from an anarchic '10' to a tropically languid '5'.

Sleeping & Eating

Most hotels in Havelock are of the cluster-of-beach-hut genre. They all claim to be 'eco' huts ('eco' apparently meaning 'cheap building material'), but they are great value for money, especially in low season.

There are occasional crackdowns on booze here, but you can almost always buy grog at the 'wine shop' in No 1 Village. Unless otherwise noted, all listed accommodation have passable menus of backpacker-oriented Western and Indian food. If you desire something more authentically Indian, head to the cheap food stalls in town (No 1 Village) or the main bazaar (No 2 Village).

The following listings run north to south.

Eco Villa (☎ 091-9933201327; huts Rs200-1500) The thatch and hut complex for Blue Lagoon Divers (p476) has a spacious feel to it and gets pretty damn romantic at night, when the moon rises over deep-blue ocean. Larger, midrange huts are very good, two-storey value for money.

Barefoot Scuba (☎ 282181; www.barefootindia.com; cabanas Rs4100-10,600; ❄) Barefoot's main diving centre (p476) has some of the best upmarket accommodation on the island: well-endowed Nicobari cottages, AC Andaman villas and semi-contemporary split-level apartments that face directly over the sea.

Pristine Beach Resort (☎ 282344; alexpristine@ hotmail.com; huts Rs100-150, cottages Rs250-400) One of the better beach-hut options; Pristine's beach really is just that, and the hammock-to-hut-to-tree ratio is scientifically sound. The nearby restaurant Maandini (mains Rs30 to Rs60) was a popular hang-out of the pasta-and-curry genre during research.

Green Valley (☎ 99-33298075; huts from Rs50) Green Valley is the only beach-hut complex that's not actually on the water. Instead, it's set back in a copse of palm and coconut trees that provide nice shade over the cheapest lodging in town. The huts are exactly the same as the ones you'll find in the standard beach resorts, although bathrooms are shared.

Sunrise Beach Resort (huts Rs150-400) Sunrise offers the same thatched goodness as every other resort on Havelock – what sets it apart is a long, awning-topped communal hall where everyone eats and does arts and crafts. It kinda feels like kindergarten for budget travellers.

Wild Orchid (☎ 282472; www.wildorchidandaman .com; d cottages from Rs2500, with AC from Rs2500; ❄) Set back from a secluded beach, this is a mellow, friendly place with tastefully furnished cottages designed in traditional Andamanese style. The restaurant, Red Snapper (mains Rs100 to Rs350), is one of few genuinely good places to eat on the island and scores on ambience. Fresh seafood is usually available (often caught by the owner or guests!).

Emerald Gecko (☎ 282170; www.emerald-gecko.com; huts Rs500-2000) This is a step up in quality from other hut resorts. There are four comfortable double-storey huts with open-roofed bathrooms, lovingly constructed from bamboo rafts that drifted ashore from Myanmar. There are some budget huts too, and a restaurant with a menu designed by the same folk as Wild Orchid.

Coconut Lodge (huts Rs150-300) These huts are arranged in a weird circular outlay that directs everyone to a raised, concrete platform where the entire lodge usually ends up carousing.

Barefoot at Havelock (☎ 282151, in Port Blair 237656; www.barefootindia.com; cottages Rs3600-5300; ❄) For the location alone – ensconced in bird-filled forest grounds just back from Radha Nagar Beach – this is Havelock's most luxurious resort, boasting beautifully designed timber and bamboo-thatched cottages. Nearby Mahoa (mains Rs200 to Rs500), set on a raised thatched platform, serves good if small-proportioned Italian food that, when combined with a blue night and some ambient music, makes for a nice romantic splurge.

Getting There & Away

Ferry times are changeable, but there are always direct sailings to Havelock from Port Blair at least once daily, and often twice or more (tourist ferry Rs150, 2½ hours). You'd best book tickets at least a day in advance. The ticket office is open between 9am and 11am. Several ferries a week link Havelock with Neil Island and with Rangat in Middle Andaman, where buses continue north to Diglipur.

Getting Around

A local bus connects the jetty and villages on a roughly hourly circuit, but having your own transport is useful here. You can rent mopeds or motorbikes (per day from Rs250) and bicycles (per day Rs40 to Rs50) from the shop outside Pristine Beach Resort, from the stall with the sign in Village No 3, or ask at your hotel.

An autorickshaw from the jetty to No 3 Village is Rs30, to No 5 is Rs50 and to No 7 is Rs150 to Rs200.

NEIL ISLAND

Gbknjbhnm. Sorry, that's what happens when you fall asleep on your keyboard, or in the sand, a hammock or wherever. Because that's life on Neil Island: you arrive, say 'Nice!', and then you either dive or become more indolent than a Roman emperor after lunch. You're about 40km from Port Blair, a short ferry ride from Havelock and several universes away from life at home. Oh OK, it's not all torpor; you can swim, snorkel, bike, go on jungle treks, bdbjdkbnbmzzzzzzzzz.

Whoops.

Sights & Activities

Neil Island's beaches are numbered 1 to 5, and the road distance between them is 8km. **No 1** is the prettiest and most accessible, a 40-minute walk west of the jetty and village. Most of the accommodation places are close to here and the island's best **snorkelling** is around the coral reef at the far (western) end of this beach. There's a good sunset viewpoint out this way that becomes a communal spot in the sand for tourists and locals come early evening. At low tide it's difficult getting over the coral into the water; conversely, at high tide the beach is underwater (it's kind of ironic how hard it can be to swim here given you're in the middle of the ocean).

No 2 Beach, on the north side of the island, has a natural bridge formation in the water; a cycle ride and short walk will take you to it. A track up the small hill behind Gyan Garden Restaurant leads to a **viewpoint** across the island and out to sea. At time of research, beaches No 3 and 4 were undeveloped. **No 5 Beach**, reached via the village road to the eastern side of the island, is an enclosed stretch with a bit of swell. It's a pleasant bike ride out here (about 5km from the village); just cycle to the end of the road, and walk 50m or so straight ahead to the beach.

You might be able to hire snorkelling gear around town (per day Rs100), but don't bank on it. Hire of a fishing boat to go to offshore snorkelling or fishing spots will cost between Rs1000 and Rs2000 depending on how far out you want to travel, how long you choose to snorkel etc; several people can usually fit on board. Bicycles are available for hire at several shops in the village (per day Rs40).

Sleeping & Eating

In the village there's a market, a few shops, a couple of basic restaurants and the A&N Tourism guest house. West of the jetty along No 1 Beach are three small 'resorts'; all have great locations and serve mediocre food.

The first place you come to, about 500m from the village market, **Cocon Huts** (☎ 282528; huts Rs50, cottages Rs350-400) has a good waterfront ambience. It was closed for renovation during our visit and has a reputation as a local drinking hole, but still comes recommended by travellers.

Tango Beach Resort (☎ 270364; huts Rs50-250, cottages Rs500) and **Pearl Park Resort** (☎ 282510; huts Rs100-250, cottages & r Rs400-1000) are technically two different resorts, but their proximity and same-same-ness makes them feel like identical sides of a double-headed coin. They both offer nice thatch huts, less interesting if more comfortable concrete rooms, flower-bedecked gardens, friendly communal areas and good service. OK, there is one difference: Tango has pet kittens; Pearl Park keeps puppies.

For a charmless, government-run hotel, **Hawa Bill Nest** (☎ 282630; dm Rs150, d Rs800; 🐾) offers pretty cosy digs. Five minutes' walk from the village beach, it's convenient if not as atmospheric as the other options; book at A&N Tourism (p480) in Port Blair.

Providing somewhat erratic service out of season, but popular when/if they're up and running, Gyan Garden Restaurant and Green Heaven Restaurant are two informal and relaxed outdoor eateries and hang-outs between the village and No 1 Beach.

Getting There & Around

A ferry makes a round trip each morning from Phoenix Bay Jetty in Port Blair (Rs36, two hours). Twice a week the Rangat ferry calls at Neil after Havelock, which is useful if you want to visit both islands.

An autorickshaw will take you to No 1 Beach from the jetty for Rs50.

MIDDLE & NORTH ANDAMAN

The Andamans aren't just sun and sand. They're also jungle that feels as primeval as the Jurassic and thick as the Amazon, a green tangle of ancient forest that could have been birthed in Mother Nature's subconscious. This shaggy, wild side of the islands can be seen on a slow, loping bus ride up the Andaman Trunk Rd (ATR). Going to Diglipur by road thrusts you onto bumpy roads framed by antediluvian trees and roll-on, roll-off ferries that cross red-tannin rivers prowled by saltwater crocodiles.

But there's a negative side to riding the ATR: the road cuts through the homeland of the Jarawa and has brought the tribe into incessant contact with the outside world. Modern India and tribal life do not seem able to coexist – every time Jarawa and settlers interact, misunderstandings have led to friction, confusion and at worst, violent attacks and death. Indian anthropologists and indigenous-rights groups like Survival International have called for the ATR to be closed; its status is under review as of this writing (see p476).

The first major town north of Port Blair is Rangat. There's not much here, but you could hire a private dinghy to take you to **Long Island**, which has a couple of good beaches that will very likely be deserted – namely Lalaji and Marg Bay. Expect to pay Rs500 to Rs800 for boat hire. **Hawksbill Nest** (☎ 279022; 4-bed dm Rs600, d Rs450, with AC Rs850; 🖾) is about 15 minutes north of Rangat, and any northbound bus will drop you there; bookings must be made at A&N Tourism (p480) in Port Blair. Hawksbill turtles do nest on the beaches of nearby Cuthbert Bay between November and February.

If you need to stay in town there are several awful lodges that charge from Rs150 to Rs300

a night. You can get to Rangat several times a week from Port Blair or Havelock Island by ferry (Rs80/25, nine hours) or daily by bus (Rs90, eight hours). Ferries are more likely to cancel due to bad weather here. The ticket office, with fickle hours (ostensibly 10am to 3pm), is on the north edge of town.

Mayabunder & Around

In 'upper' Middle Andaman, there are several villages inhabited by Karen, members of a Burmese hill tribe that were relocated here during the British colonial period. In Mayabunder, stop at **Sea'n'Sand** (☎ 273454; r Rs200-500), a simple lodge, restaurant and bar overlooking the water, 1km south of the town centre. Run by an extended Karen family, it's low-key and will appeal to travellers looking for an experience away from the crowds. You can go on a range of **boat-based day tours** (per tour from Rs500-2500) that, depending on the season, may include visits to **Forty One Caves** where *hawabills* make their highly prized edible nests; snorkelling off **Avis Island**; or a coast-and-forest-wilderness experience on **Interview Island**.

Mayabunder, 71km north of Rangat, is linked by daily buses from Port Blair (Rs120, 10 hours) and by once- or twice-weekly ferries.

Diglipur & Around

Don't expect too much out of Diglipur, three hours by road above Mayabunder and the northernmost major town in the Andamans. It's basically a muddy bazaar and you'll likely head straight for Kalipur, where you'll find lodging and vistas of the ocean and outlying islands. Ferries arrive at Aerial Bay Jetty from where it's 11km southwest to Diglipur, the bus stand and Administration Block, where boat tickets can be booked. Kalipur is on the coast 8km southeast of the jetty.

SIGHTS & ACTIVITIES

Like lovely tropical counterweights, the twin islands of **Smith** and **Ross** are connected by a narrow sandbar. Since this is designated as a marine sanctuary, you must get a permit (Indian/foreigner Rs50/500) from the **Forest Office** (🕙 6am-2pm Mon-Sat) opposite Aerial Bay Jetty to visit. You can charter a boat to take you for the day from the village for around Rs700.

At 732m, **Saddle Peak** is the highest point in the Andamans. You can trek through subtropical forest to the top and back from Kalipur in about six hours; the views from the peaks onto the archipelago are incredible. Again, a permit is required from the Forest Office (Indian/foreigner Rs25/250) and a local guide will make sure you don't get lost – ask at Pristine Beach Resort. **Snorkelling** is possible behind the small island off the beach near Pristine Beach Resort, and just around the coast at Radha Nagar.

Leatherback and green turtles nest along the Diglipur coastline between December and March.

SLEEPING & EATING

There are two places to stay opposite each other at Kalipur, 8km southeast of the Aerial Bay Jetty. Buses run along this route (Rs8); an autorickshaw costs about Rs100.

Pristine Beach Resort (☎ 201837; huts Rs200-700) Huddled among the palms between paddy fields and the beach, Pristine is a pretty spot with several simple bamboo huts on stilts, a restaurant and friendly owners. It gets very busy in peak season.

Turtle Resort (☎ 272553; r Rs400, with AC 800; ❄) Set on a small hill with rural views from the balconies, this A&N Tourism hotel is comfy if a little musty. It's best to book ahead through A&N Tourism (p480) in Port Blair, though you'll likely be able to get a room on-site if one's available.

GETTING THERE & AWAY

Diglipur, about 80km north of Mayabunder, is served by daily buses to/from Port Blair (Rs150, 12 hours), as well as buses to Mayabunder (Rs30 to Rs50, 2½ hours) and Rangat (Rs70, 4½ hours). There are also daily ferries from Port Blair to Diglipur, returning overnight from Diglipur (seat/berth Rs81/150, 10 hours).

LITTLE ANDAMAN

Named Gaubolambe by the indigenous Onge, Little Andaman is as far south as you can go in the islands. There's an end of the world

(in tropical paradise) feeling here: barely any tourists visit, the locals are so friendly they feel like family and the island itself is a gorgeous fist of mangroves, jungle and teal plucked from a twinkle in nature's eye.

Located about 120km south of Port Blair, the main settlement here is Hut Bay, a pleasant small town that primarily produces smiling Bengalis and Tamils. North of here you'll find isolated beaches as fresh as bread out of the oven. **Netaji Nagar Beach**, 11km north of Hut Bay, and **Butler Bay**, a further 3km north, are gorgeous and great for surfing. Inland, the **White Surf** and **Whisper Wave waterfalls** offer a forest experience; they're pleasant falls and you may be tempted to swim in the rock pools, but beware local crocodiles. The **Andaman and Nicobar Islands Forest Plantation Development Corporation** (ANIFPDC; ☎ 232752) runs much of the tourism on Little Andaman and may or may not be staffing Rs20 ticket booths at the above locations. They also, ostensibly, operate elephants treks into the jungle, boating and birdwatching fun near Butler Bay creek, and a Red Oil Palm plantation 11km north of Hut Bay.

There are plenty of cheap thali and tiffin places in Hut Bay (we recommend the unnamed Bengali eatery across from the police station). Sleepingwise there's only a few places to stay on the island. Vvet House, Cozy Cave and Green Grace lodges are all operated by ANIFPDC and offer comfy if uninspired rooms running from Rs150 to Rs300; you can get an AC room in Green Grace for Rs300/600 (single/double) and there's a Rs100 dorm in Cozy Cave. The independent **Sealand Tourist Home** (☎ 284525) next to Vvet House, offers much the same prices and accommodation as above.

Ferries land at Hut Bay Jetty on the east coast; from there the beaches lay to the north. Buses (Rs10) leave when they want for Butler Bay, or you can hire a local jeep (Rs100). Boats sail to Little Andaman from Port Blair daily – the trip there is eight hours, while the return is a six-hour speedboat trip.

Directory

CONTENTS

ACCOMMODATION

South India has accommodation to suit all budgets, from squalid dives at rock-bottom prices, to flashy five-star offerings. Most big towns and tourist centres have a wide range of options, but rates vary from state to state, making it best to see this book's individual chapters ('Sleeping' sections) for accommodation costs in the areas you intend visiting. Also see p493. Keep in mind that popular tourist centres usually witness a significant price hike during the tourist season and can fill up fast at these times, making advance reservations wise.

Room quality can vary considerably *within* hotels so try to inspect a few rooms first. Avoid

carpeted rooms at cheaper hotels unless you like the smell of mouldy socks. For the lowdown on hotel bathrooms, read p492. Sound pollution can be irksome (especially in urban hubs); pack good-quality earplugs and request a room that doesn't face a busy road. It's a good idea to keep your door locked, as some staff can have the annoying habit of knocking and automatically walking in without first seeking your permission.

Credit cards are accepted at most top-end hotels and many midrange places; budget hotels invariably require cash. Most hotels ask for a deposit at check in – ask for a receipt and be wary of any request to sign a blank impression of your credit card. If the hotel insists, consider going to the nearest ATM and paying cash. Verify the check-out time when you check in – some hotels have a fixed checkout time (usually 10am or noon), while others give you 24-hour check out. Reservations by phone without a deposit are usually fine, but call to confirm the booking the day before you arrive.

Be aware that in tourist hot spots, hotels may 'borrow' the name of a thriving competitor to confuse travellers, paying commissions to taxi and rickshaw drivers who bring them unsuspecting customers. Make sure that you know the *exact* name of your preferred hotel, and confirm that you have indeed been taken to the right hotel before you pay the driver (also see p498).

Accommodation Options

As well as conventional hotels, there are some charming family-run guest houses and unique boutique-style possibilities. Standout options are indicated with the Our Pick icon – **our pick** – in this book's regional chapters.

BOOK YOUR STAY ONLINE

For more accommodation reviews and recommendations by Lonely Planet authors, check out www.lonelyplanet.com/hotels. You'll find the insider lowdown on the top places to stay. Best of all, you can usually book online.

DIRECTORY

BUDGET & MIDRANGE HOTELS

Apart from some character-filled exceptions – such as traditional guest houses – most budget and midrange hotels tend to be modern-style concrete blocks. Shared bathrooms (often with squat toilets) are usually only found at the cheapest lodgings. Most rooms have ceiling fans, and better rooms have electric mosquito killers and/or window nets, though cheaper rooms may lack windows altogether. Bringing your own sheet (or a sleeping-bag liner) is a sound policy – some cheap hotels have sheets with more holes and stains than a string vest at an oyster-eating contest! Apart from that, many budget hotels don't provide a top sheet so you could find yourself sleeping under (dodgy) bedcovers that haven't been washed for years. Away from tourist areas, cheaper hotels may not take foreigners because they don't have the necessary foreigner-registration forms.

Midrange hotels usually offer extras such as cable/satellite TV and air-conditioning, although some just have (noisy) 'air-coolers' that cool air by blowing it over cold water. They're better than nothing, but no comparison to real air-conditioning, especially during the monsoon.

Note that some hotels lock their front doors at night. Members of staff may sleep in the lobby but waking them up can be a challenge. Let the hotel know in advance if you'll be arriving or coming back to your room late in the evening.

CAMPING

There are few official camping sites around South India, but travellers with their own vehicles can usually find hotels with gardens where they can park and camp for a nominal charge that includes communal bathroom facilities.

GOVERNMENT ACCOMMODATION & TOURIST BUNGALOWS

The Indian government maintains a network of guest houses for travelling officials and public workers, known variously as rest houses, dak bungalows, circuit houses, PWD (Public Works Department) bungalows and forest rest houses. These places may accept travellers if no government employees need the rooms, but permission is sometimes required from local officials and you'll probably have to find the *chowkidar* (caretaker) to open the doors.

'Tourist bungalows' are run by state governments – rooms are usually midpriced (some with cheap dorms) and have varying standards of cleanliness and service. Details are normally available through the state tourism office.

HOMESTAYS/B&BS FOR PAYING GUESTS

Known as homestays, or B&Bs, these family-run guest houses will appeal to those seek-

---

GET TO KNOW YOUR BATHROOM

Most of South India's midrange hotels and all top-end ones have sit-down toilets with toilet paper and soap supplied. In ultra-cheap hotels, and in places off the tourist trail, squat toilets are the norm and toilet paper is rarely provided. Squat toilets are variously described as 'Indian-style', 'Indian' or 'floor' toilets, while the sit-down variety may be called 'Western' or 'commode' toilets. In a few places, you'll find the curious 'hybrid toilet', a sit-down version with footpads on the edge of the bowl.

Terminology for hotel bathrooms varies across India. 'Attached bath', 'private bath' or 'with bath' means that the room has its own ensuite bathroom. 'Common bath', 'no bathroom' or 'shared bath' means communal bathroom facilities.

Not all rooms have hot water. 'Running', '24-hour' or 'constant' water means that hot water is available round-the-clock (not always the case in reality). 'Bucket' hot water is only available in buckets (sometimes for a small charge).

Many places use wall-mounted electric geysers (water heaters) that need to be switched on up to an hour before use. Note that the geyser's main switch can sometimes be located outside the bathroom.

Hotels that advertise 'room with shower' may be misleading – sometimes the shower is just a pipe sticking out of the wall. Meanwhile, some hotels surreptitiously disconnect showers to cut costs, while showers at other places render a mere trickle of water.

In this book, hotel rooms have their own private bathroom unless otherwise indicated.

PRACTICALITIES

■ Electricity is 230V to 240V, 50 Hz AC, and sockets are the three-round-pin variety (two-pin sockets are also found). Blackouts are common, particularly during summer and the monsoon.

■ Officially India is metric. Terms you're likely to hear are: lakhs (one lakh = 100,000) and crores (one crore = 10 million).

■ Major English-language dailies include the *Hindustan Times, Times of India, Indian Express, Hindu, Statesman, Telegraph, Daily News & Analysis (DNA)* and *Economic Times*. Regional English-language and local-vernacular publications are found nationwide.

■ Incisive current-affairs reports are printed in *Frontline, India Today,* the *Week, Tehelka* and *Outlook.*

■ The national (government) TV broadcaster is Doordarshan. More people watch satellite and cable TV; English-language channels include BBC, CNN, Cartoon Network, Star Movies, HBO, Discovery and MTV. TV programme (and radio) details appear in most major daily newspapers.

■ Government-controlled All India Radio (AIR) nationally transmits local and international news. There are also private FM channels broadcasting music, current affairs, talkback and more.

---

ing a small-scale, uncommercial setting with home-cooked meals. Standards range from mud-and-stone huts with hole-in-the-floor toilets to comfortable middle-class homes. Contact the local tourist office for a full list of participating families.

Some travellers love the experience, while others have reported feeling stifled by the often close tabs kept on them by overprotective (usually for caring reasons) families, and/or obliged to return home at a reasonable hour of night because they aren't given a key.

RAILWAY RETIRING ROOMS

Most large train stations have basic rooms for travellers in possession of an ongoing train ticket or Indrail Pass. Some are grim, others are surprisingly pleasant, but all are noisy from the sound of passengers and trains. Nevertheless, they're useful for early morning train departures and there's usually a choice of dormitories or private rooms (24-hour checkout).

TEMPLES & PILGRIMS' REST HOUSES

Accommodation is available at some ashrams (spiritual retreats), gurdwaras (Sikh temples) and *dharamsalas* (pilgrims' guest houses) for a donation, but these places have been established for genuine pilgrims so please exercise judgment about the appropriateness of staying. Always abide by any protocols.

TOP-END HOTELS

Found in South India's larger cities and tourist traps, top-end hotels range from swanky five-star chains to less glamorous four-star properties. Most have swimming pools, fancy restaurants and assorted amenities (gyms, beauty salons, business centres etc). Most top-end hotels have rupee rates for Indian guests and separate US dollar rates for foreigners (including Non-Resident Indians, or NRIs). Officially, you are supposed to pay the dollar rates in foreign currency or by credit card, but many places will accept rupees adding up to the dollar rate.

While the luxury chain hotels are all pretty predictable, there are some unique places worth seeking out, such as the heritage hotels in Puducherry (Pondicherry), resort hotels in Goa and Kerala, colonial-era mansions in Ooty (Udhagamandalam) and the sublime Taj Mahal Palace & Tower in Mumbai (Bombay; p131).

Costs

Given that the cost of budget, midrange and top-end hotels varies so much across South India it would be misleading of us to provide a 'national' price range for each category. The best way to gauge accommodation costs for the regions you intend visiting is to go directly to the 'Sleeping' sections of this book's regional chapters. Keep in mind that most establishments raise tariffs annually, so the prices are likely to have risen by the time you read this. Regional chapters will also proffer *specific* details about locally relevant factors such as seasonal cost variations.

Accommodation listings in this book are arranged in price order, from cheapest to most expensive. Tariffs don't include taxes unless otherwise stated. All room costs include en suite bathrooms unless otherwise mentioned.

As blackouts are common (especially during summer and the monsoon), double check that the hotel has a back-up generator if you're paying for electric 'extras' such as air-conditioners and TVs.

SEASONAL VARIATIONS

In popular tourist hangouts (hill stations, beaches, places of pilgrimage etc) most hoteliers crank up their high-season prices. Tourist hubs such as Goa can triple their rates in season – advance bookings are often essential at these times.

The definition of the high and low seasons varies depending on location. For beaches such as Goa and Kerala high season is basically one month before and two months after Christmas; in the hill stations it's usually from around April to July when domestic tourists flock to the hills for some cool relief. Some hotels charge higher rates for the Christmas and New Year period, or over major festivals, such as Diwali (for festival details see p19; the 'Festivals In…' boxed texts at the start of regional chapters focus on local events). For any major festival, make advance accommodation arrangements. Conversely, in the low season, prices at even normally expensive hotels can be delightfully affordable. It's always worth asking for a better rate if the hotel doesn't seem busy.

Regional chapters have details on seasonal rates for individual areas.

TAXES & SERVICE CHARGES

State governments slap a variety of taxes on hotel accommodation (except at the cheaper hotels), and these are added to the cost of your room. Taxes vary from state to state and are detailed in the regional chapters. Many upmarket hotels also levy an additional 'service charge' (usually around 10%). Rates quoted in this book's regional chapters exclude taxes unless otherwise indicated.

BUSINESS HOURS

Official business hours are from 9.30am to 5.30pm Monday to Friday, but many offices open later and close earlier. Apart from Sundays, government offices in many states remain closed on alternate (usually second and fourth) Saturdays. Most offices have an official lunch hour from around 1pm. Shops generally open around 10am and operate until 6pm or later; some close on Sunday (or another day of the week; see regional chapters). Airline offices generally stick to standard business hours, Monday to Saturday (regional chapters provide exact timings).

Most banks are open from 10am to 2pm on weekdays (until 4pm in some areas), and from 10am to noon (or 1pm) on Saturday. Exact branch hours vary from town to town so check locally. Foreign-exchange offices may open longer and operate daily.

Main post offices are open from around 10am to 5pm on weekdays (though some postal services may not be offered in the afternoon), and until noon on Saturday. Some larger post offices have a full day on Saturday and a half-day on Sunday.

Restaurant timings vary regionally – most open from around 8am to 10pm daily. Exceptions are noted in the regional chapters.

CHILDREN

India is wonderfully accepting of children, however, extra caution is needed in hot and crowded conditions. Pay particular attention to hygiene and be *very* vigilant around traffic. It's also advisable to keep children away from monkeys and stray dogs, which can carry all sorts of diseases. See Lonely Planet's *Travel with Children,* and the travelling with children section of Lonely Planet's **Thorn Tree travel forum** (www.lonelyplanet.com/thorntree) for more detailed advice.

Practicalities
ACCOMMODATION

Many hotels have 'family rooms' and almost all will provide an extra bed for a small additional charge, though cots are less common. Upmarket hotels may offer babysitting facilities and/or kids' activity programmes and should also have cable TV with English-language children's channels (many cheaper hotels have cartoons only in Hindi).

DISCOUNTS

On Indian trains, children aged under four travel for free and those aged five to 11 pay half-price. Most airlines charge 10% of the adult fare for infants (under two years) and 50% for under-11s.

Many tourist attractions have a reduced entry fee for children under 12 (see regional chapters).

FOOD & DRINK

Children are welcome at most restaurants, but usually it's just upmarket places and fast-food chains that have highchairs and children's menus. Across India, nappy-changing facilities are usually restricted to the (often cramped) restaurant toilet.

Unfamiliar food may initially present a hurdle for some kids, but Western fast food is widely available and snacks such as pakoras (deep-fried battered vegetables) and dosas (savoury crepes) should appeal. As long as it's peeled or washed in purified water, fruit is also good. Bottled water, cartons of fruit juice and soft drinks are easily found. Some children will enjoy sweet milky chai (tea).

HEALTH

Avoiding tummy upsets can be a daily challenge – see p539 for more advice. Note that rabid animals can also pose a risk. If your child takes special medication it's wise to bring along an adequate stock. Check with a doctor before departure about recommended jabs and drug courses for children.

TRANSPORT

Long-distance road travel should include sufficient food and toilet stops as travel sickness can be a problem, particularly on rough roads. On public transport, children may be expected to give their seat to adults, meaning long journeys with a child on your lap. Note that child seats in rented cars are rare (inquire when booking).

Trains are usually the most comfortable mode of transport, especially for long trips. Internal air travel can save time and tempers.

TRAVEL WITH INFANTS

Standard baby products such as disposable nappies (diapers), wet wipes and milk powder can be bought in most large cities and tourist centres, but aren't reliably found elsewhere (so stock up). If you've got a finicky baby, consider bringing powdered milk or baby food from home. Also bring along high-factor sunscreen, a snug-fitting wide-brimmed hat and a washable changing mat for covering dirty surfaces. Breastfeeding in public is generally not condoned by Indian society.

Sights & Activities

It's a good idea to allow a few days for your child to simply acclimatise to India's explosion of sights, sounds, smells and tastes before launching into any big trips around the country.

In terms of attractions, there are numerous options that will keep kids happy, from beaches and wildlife parks to planetariums and sound-and-light shows – see regional chapters for details.

South India's bounty of festivals may also capture your child's imagination, although some may be overwhelmed by the crowds. For festival details see p19, and the 'Festivals in…' boxed texts at the start of regional chapters.

CLIMATE CHARTS

South India has a largely tropical climate that can be roughly divided into two distinct seasons – the wet (monsoon) and the dry. For details see p15.

COURSES

You can pursue all sorts of courses in South India, from yoga and meditation to cooking and learning to speak Tamil. To find out about new courses, inquire at tourist offices, ask fellow travellers and browse local newspapers and noticeboards. Also see p100 and, for cooking courses, p78.

Arts & Crafts

One recommended option is in Mumbai at the **Khatwara Institute** (p125), which offers assorted courses (for women only), including *mehndi* (henna) and block printing.

Languages

The following places offer language courses; some require a minimum time commitment.

Kerala Short courses in Malayalam, Hindi and Sanskrit at Vijnana Kala Vedi Cultural Centre (p351).

Mumbai Beginners' courses in Hindi, Marathi and Sanskrit at Bharatiya Vidya Bhavan (p125).

Tamil Nadu Hindi and Tamil courses in Chennai (p398).

Martial Arts

Courses are available in the traditional Keralan martial art of *kalarippayat* – a form of sword and shield fighting incorporating elements of Ayurveda and *marma* (the precursor to Chinese acupressure massage). Major centres include the Vijnana Kala

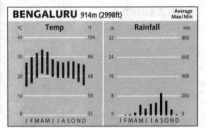

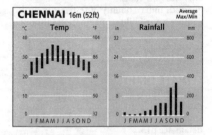

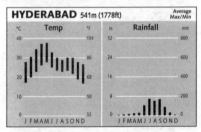

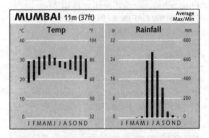

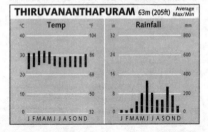

Vedi Cultural Centre (p351) near Kottayam, the CVN Kalari Sangham Centre (p327) in Thiruvananthapuram (Trivandrum) and Ens Kalari (p371) in Ernakulam.

Music & Performing Arts

Allow at least several weeks to derive any real benefit from music courses. Most centres provide instruments, but perhaps invest in your own if you intend to play back home.

Karnataka Classical Indian dance classes at Nrityagram (p249) in Hessaraghatta, and tabla classes at Shruthi Musical Works (p253) in Mysore.

Kerala Courses in Kathakali (traditional Keralan dance opera) and *kootiattam* (traditional Sanskrit drama) in Trivandrum (p327), Kathakali and Kathakali make-up in Fort Cochin (p365), and dance centres near Thrissur (p378) and around Kottayam (p351).

Tamil Nadu Courses in *bharatanatyam* (classical dance), singing and various musical instruments in Puducherry (p423); Kalakshetra Arts Village (p403) in Chennai offers courses in classical Tamil dance and music.

Yoga & Holistic Therapies

India has thousands of yoga centres offering long courses and daily classes as well as courses in Ayurveda, meditation and other therapies. See p104 for details about what's on offer in South India.

CUSTOMS

Visitors are allowed to bring 1L each of wine and spirits and 200 cigarettes or 50 cigars or 250g of tobacco into India duty free. Officials sometimes ask tourists to enter expensive items such as video cameras and laptop computers on a 'Tourist Baggage Re-export' form to ensure they're taken out of India at the time of departure.

Technically you're supposed to declare any amount of cash/travellers cheques over US$5000/10,000 on arrival. Indian rupees shouldn't be taken out of India, however, this is rarely policed. There are additional restrictions on the export of antiques and products made from animals; see p510.

DANGERS & ANNOYANCES

India – more the north than the south – has its fair share of scams, but most problems can be avoided with a bit of common sense and an appropriate amount of caution. Scams change as tricksters try to stay ahead of the game, so chat with travellers and tourism officials to keep abreast of the latest cons. Have a look at the India branch of Lonely Planet's **Thorn Tree travel forum** (www.lonelyplanet.com/thorntree), where travellers often post timely warnings about problems they've encountered on the road.

Also read the Dos & Don'ts boxed text on p47. Women travellers should see p516.

Contaminated Food & Drink

In past years, some private medical clinics have provided patients with more treatment than necessary to procure larger payments from travel insurance companies – get a second opinion if possible.

Most bottled water is legit, but always ensure the lid seal is intact and check that the bottom of the bottle hasn't been tampered with. Crush plastic bottles after use to prevent them being misused later or, better still, bring along water-purification tablets or a filtration system to avoid adding to India's plastic-waste mountain.

Drugs

Possession and use of drugs is illegal in India. A few towns allow the legal (controlled) sale of bhang (marijuana) for religious reasons, but elsewhere courts treat possession of cannabis as severely as possession of heroin. Don't assume strangers are harmless because they share your interest in drugs. See also p502.

Festivals

The sheer mass of humanity at many of India's festivals provides an incredible spectacle, but every year pilgrims are crushed or trampled to death in temple processions and on train platforms. Be extra careful around large crowds at these times, and travel on conventional trains rather than special pilgrim services.

Care is also needed during the Holi festival (see p19) when foreigners get doused with water and coloured dye like everyone else; a few people have been scarred by dodgy chemicals. Consider buying a cheap set of throwaway clothes specifically for this festival. There's also a tradition of guzzling alcohol and bhang during Holi, and female travellers have been hassled by spaced-out blokes; it's wise for women to avoid venturing onto the streets alone at the time.

Overpricing & Photography

There are circumstances where it's best to agree on prices beforehand so as to avoid being overcharged, whether it's eating in places without menus or flagging down an autorickshaw. Apart from the money issue, prior price-setting could also deflect potentially ugly misunderstandings later.

On the photographic front, something to be aware of – apart from propriety issues (see the Photography Etiquette section in the Dos & Don'ts box on p47) – is that some travellers have reported getting approval when photographing a person, only to have that same individual demand money afterwards. Use your instincts and when uncertain avoid taking pictures of people.

Scams

There are various scams, predominantly in tourist hubs, designed to separate travellers from their money. Don't be fooled – any deal that sounds too good to be true invariably is, though in the south thankfully you won't find as much of the gem and carpet scams that are rampant up north. The main places to be wary in South India are big cities, such as Mumbai and Chennai, and at tourist centres, such as Goa and parts of Kerala.

Be highly suspicious of strangers' claims that you can purchase goods cheaply in India and sell them easily at a profit elsewhere. Precious stones and carpets are favourites for this long-running con. Operators who practise such schemes are deceptively friendly, pouring out sob stories about not being able to obtain an export licence etc. And therein lies the opportunity for you to 'get rich quick' – by carrying or mailing the goods home and selling them to the trader's (non-existent) overseas representatives at a profit. Some may show you (forged) testimonials from other travellers. Without exception, the goods are worth a fraction of what you paid and the 'representatives' never materialise.

It also pays to be cautious when sending goods home. Shops have been known to swap high-value items for junk when posting goods to home addresses. If you have any doubts, send the package yourself from the post office. Be careful when paying for souvenirs with a credit card. Government shops are usually legitimate; private souvenir shops have been known to surreptitiously run off extra copies of the credit-card imprint slip, and use it for phoney transactions later. Insist that the trader carries out any credit-card transaction on the counter in front of you. Alternatively, take out cash from an ATM to avoid this risk altogether.

While it's only a minority of traders who are involved in dishonest schemes, many souvenir vendors are knee-deep in the commission racket (see right).

TRANSPORT SCAMS

Unscrupulous travel agencies may make extra money by scamming travellers for tours and travel tickets. Make sure you are clear about what is included in the price of any tour (get this in writing) to avoid charges for hidden 'extras' later on.

When buying a bus, train or plane ticket anywhere other than the registered office of the transport company, make certain you're getting the ticket class you paid for. It's not uncommon for travellers to book a deluxe bus or AC train berth and arrive to find a bog-standard ordinary bus or a less comfortable sleeper seat.

Swimming

Dozens of locals and foreigners drown every year on Goa's beaches alone, even confident swimmers who venture into (deceptively) calm seas – see p188. Be aware that the sea can have very dangerous rips, undertows and currents; always inquire locally to find safe places to swim and preferably have someone keep watch while you take a paddle. Apart from the ocean, there are also deceptively strong currents in many rivers, including the Ganges.

Never venture into the water after consuming alcohol.

Theft & Druggings

Theft is a risk in India, as anywhere else. On buses and trains, keep luggage securely locked (minipadlocks and chains are available at most train stations) and lock your bags to the metal baggage racks or the wire loops found under seats; padlocking your bags to the roof racks on buses is also a sensible policy.

Thieves tend to target popular tourist train routes, such as Mumbai to Goa. Be extra alert just before the train departs; thieves often take advantage of the confusion and crowds. Airports are another place to exercise caution; after a long flight you're unlikely to be at your most alert.

Occasionally tourists (especially those travelling solo) are drugged and robbed during train or bus journeys, although reports of this are relatively rare in South India. A friendly stranger strikes up conversation, offers you a spiked drink (to send you to sleep) then makes off with your valuables. It's often best to politely decline drinks or food offered by strangers (use your instincts) – stomach upsets are a convenient excuse.

Unfortunately some travellers make their money go further by helping themselves to other people's – take extra care in dormitories. For lost credit cards, immediately call the international lost/stolen number; for stolen/lost travellers cheques, contact the closest local branch or the American Express/Thomas Cook offices in Mumbai (p113), Chennai (p392) or Delhi (see p504).

A good travel-insurance policy is essential (see p501) – keep the emergency contact details handy and familiarise yourself with the claims procedure. Keep photocopies of your passport, including the visa page, separate from your passport, along with a copy of your airline ticket, or email scans to yourself.

PERSONAL SECURITY

The safest place for your money and your passport is next to your skin, either in a concealed money belt or a secure place under your shirt. If you carry your money in a wallet, keep it in your front trouser pocket, never the back pocket.

It's wise to peel off at least US$100 and store it separately from your main stash; however, keep your main stash and other valuables on your person. Also, separate big currency notes from small bills so you don't publicly display large wads of cash when paying for services or checking into hotels.

In hotels, *never* leave your money or valuable documents in your room (no, not even under mattresses) when you go out. At better hotels you can expect a safe for valuables. For peace of mind, you may also want to use your own padlock at hotels where doors are locked with a padlock (common at cheaper hotels). If you cannot lock your hotel room securely from the inside at night, stay somewhere else.

Touts & Commission Agents

With so many businesses dependent on tourism, competition is cut-throat. Many hotels and shops drum up extra business by paying commission to local fixers who bring tourists through the doors. These places tend to be unpopular for a reason – prices will invariably be raised (by as much as 50%) to pay the fixer's commission. To get around this, ask taxis or rickshaws to drop you at a landmark rather than at your intended destination, so you can walk in alone and pay the normal price.

Train and bus stations are often swarming with touts – if anyone asks if this is your first trip to India, say you've been here several times, as this is usually a ruse to gauge your vulnerability. You'll often hear stories about the hotels that refuse to pay commissions being 'full', 'under renovation' or 'closed'. Check things out yourself. Be very sceptical of phrases like 'my brother's shop' and 'special deal at my friend's place'.

A good way to avoid tout hassles is to arrange hotel pick-ups where possible, especially when arriving in a big city for the first time.

On the flip side, touts can be beneficial if you arrive in a town without a hotel reservation when some big festival is on, or during the peak season – they'll know which places have beds.

Trekking

Trekking off the beaten track always carries risks and India is often poorly set up for independent trekkers. We strongly recommend hiring local guides and porters or joining an organised trek before heading off into potentially dangerous terrain; see p103 for more information.

DISCOUNTS
Seniors

Some airlines offer discounts (of up to 50%) on domestic air travel for Indian citizens aged 65 or over (inquire when booking). However, promotional fares and internet tickets on airlines are often cheaper than discounted full fares. Anyone over 60 is entitled to a 30% discount on the cost of train travel (foreigners should bring passports as proof of age).

Student & Youth Travel

Student cards are of limited use nowadays as most concessions are based on age. Hostels run by the Indian Youth Hostels Association are part of the HI network; an HI card sometimes entitles you to discount rates. YMCA/ YWCA members also receive discounts on accommodation.

Foreigners under 30 years of age receive a 25% discount on some domestic air tickets (inquire when booking). This applies to full-price tickets, so standard fares for budget airlines may be cheaper still.

EMBASSIES & HIGH COMMISSIONS IN INDIA

Most foreign diplomatic missions are based in Delhi, but several nations operate consulates in other Indian cities (see websites, where provided, in the following Delhi addresses). Many missions have certain timings for visa applications, usually mornings, but phone for details.

These are just some of the many foreign missions found in India.

Australia Chennai (Map p396; ☎ 044-28601160; 512 Raheja Towers, 177 Anna Salai, Anna Salai); Delhi (☎ 011-41399900; www.ausgovindia.com; 1/50G Shantipath, Chanakyapuri); Mumbai (Map pp110–11; ☎ 022-66692000; 36 Maker Chambers VI, 3rd fl, 220 Nariman Point)

Bangladesh Delhi (☎ 011-24121394; www.bhcdelhi .org; EP39 Dr Radakrishnan Marg, Chanakyapuri); Kolkata (☎ 033-22475208; 9 Circus Ave)

Bhutan (☎ 011-26889230; Chandragupta Marg, Chanakyapuri, Delhi)

Canada Chennai (Map pp394–5; ☎ 044-28330888; 18 D Khader Nawaz Khan Rd); Delhi (☎ 011-41782000; www .dfait-maeci.gc.ca/new-delhi; 7/8 Shantipath, Chanakyapuri); Mumbai (Map p118; ☎ 022-67494444; 6th fl, Fort House, 221 Dr DN Rd)

France Delhi (☎ 011-24196100; www.france-in-india .org; 2/50E Shantipath, Chanakyapuri); Mumbai (Map pp110–11; ☎ 022-66694000; 7th fl, Hoechst House, Nariman Point)

Germany Chennai (Map pp394–5; ☎ 044-24301600; 9 Boat Club Rd, RA Puram); Delhi (☎ 011-26871837; www .new-delhi.diplo.de; 6/50G Shantipath, Chanakyapuri); Kolkata (☎ 033-24791141; 1 Hastings Park Rd, Alipore); Mumbai (Map pp110–11; ☎ 022-22832422; 10th fl, Hoechst House, Nariman Point)

Israel Delhi (☎ 011-30414500; http://delhi.mfa.gov .il; 3 Aurangzeb Rd); Mumbai (Map pp110–11; ☎ 022-22822822/22819993; Earnest House, 16th fl, NCPA Marg, Nariman Point)

Italy Delhi (☎ 011-26114355; www.ambnewdelhi .esteri.it; 50E Chandragupta Marg, Chanakyapuri); Mumbai (Map pp110–11; ☎ 022-23804071; Kanchanjunga, 1st fl, 72G Deshmukh Marg, Kemp's Corner)

Japan Chennai (Map pp394–5; ☎ 044-24323860; 12/1, Cenetoph Rd, 1st St, Teynampet); Delhi (☎ 011-26876564; www.in.emb-japan.go.jp; 50G Shantipath, Chanakyapuri); Mumbai (Map pp110–11; ☎ 022-23517101; 1 ML Dahanukar Marg, Cumballa Hill)

Malaysia Chennai (Map pp394–5; ☎ 044-28226888; 44 Tank Bund Rd, Nungambakkam); Delhi (☎ 011-26111291; www.kln.gov.my/perwakilan/newdelhi; 50M Satya Marg,

Chanakyapuri); Mumbai (Map p130; ☎ 022-26455751/2; Notan Plaza, 4th fl, Turner Rd, Bandra West)

Maldives Chennai (Map pp394-5; ☎ 044-24331696; Balaji Dental & Craniofacial Hospital, 30, KB Dasan Rd, Teynampet); Delhi (☎ 011-41435701; www.maldiveshigh com.in/; B2 Anand Niketan); Kolkata (☎ 033-22485400; ground fl, Hastings Chambers, KS Roy Rd) Hidden around the side of the building down an alley off KS Roy Rd; Mumbai (Map p118; ☎ 022-22078041; 212A Maker Bhawan 3, New Marine Lines, Churchgate); Trivandrum (Map p326; ☎ 0471-2558189; 13/1245 TC, Kumarapuram)

Myanmar Delhi (☎ 011-24678822; 3/50F Nyaya Marg); Kolkata (☎ 033-24851658; 57K Ballygunge Circular Rd)

Nepal Delhi (☎ 011-23327361; Barakhamba Rd); Kolkata (☎ 033-24561224; 1 National Library Ave, Alipore)

Netherlands Chennai (Map pp394-5; ☎ 044-43535381; 76 Venkatakrisha Rd, Mandaveli); Delhi (☎ 011-24197600; http://india.nlembassy.org/; 6/50F Shantipath, Chanakyapuri); Mumbai (Map p118; ☎ 022-22194200; Forbes Bldg, Home St, Fort)

New Zealand Chennai (Map pp394-5; ☎ 044-28112472; Rane Engine Valves Ltd, 132 Cathedral Rd); Delhi (☎ 011-26883170; www.nzembassy.com; 50N Nyaya Marg, Chanakyapuri); Mumbai (Map pp110-11; ☎ 022-23520022; Aashiana, 1st fl, Breach Candy)

Pakistan (☎ 011-24676004; 2/50G Shantipath, Chanakyapuri, Delhi)

Singapore Chennai (Map pp394-5; ☎ 044-28158207; 17-A North Boag Rd, T. Nagar); Delhi (☎ 011-46000915; www.mfa.gov.sg/newdelhi; E6 Chandragupta Marg); Mumbai (Map pp110-11; ☎ 022-22043205; Maker Chambers IV, 10th fl, 222 Jamnalal Bajaj Rd, Nariman Point)

South Africa Delhi (☎ 011-26149411; www.dha.gov .za; B18 Vasant Marg, Vasant Vihar); Mumbai (Map pp110–11; ☎ 022-23513725; Gandhi Mansion, 20 Altamount Rd, Cumballa Hill)

Sri Lanka Chennai (Map pp394-5; ☎ 044-24987896; 196 TTK Rd, Alwarpet); Delhi (☎ 011-23010201; www.new delhi.mission.gov.lk; 27 Kautilya Marg, Chanakyapuri); Mumbai (Map p118; ☎ 022-22045861; Mulla House, 34 Homi Modi St, Fort)

Switzerland Delhi (☎ 011-26878372; www.eda.admin .ch; Nyaya Marg, Chanakyapuri); Mumbai (Map pp110-11; ☎ 022-22884563-65; 102 Maker Chambers IV, 10th fl, 222 Jamnalal Bajaj Marg, Nariman Point)

Thailand Chennai (Map pp394-5; ☎ 044-42300730; 21/22 Arunachalam Rd, Kotturpuram); Delhi (☎ 011-26118104; www.thaiemb.org.in; 56N Nyaya Marg, Chanakyapuri); Kolkata (☎ 033-24407836; 18B Mandeville Gardens, Gariahat); Mumbai (Map pp110-11; ☎ 022-22823535; Dalamal House, 1st fl, Jamnalal Bajai Marg, Nariman Point)

UK Chennai (Map pp394-5; ☎ 044-42192151; 20 Anderson Rd); Delhi (☎ 011-26872161; www.ukinindia.com; Shantipath, Chanakyapuri); Kolkata (☎ 033-22885172; 1 Ho Chi Minh Sarani); Mumbai (Map p130; ☎ 022-

66502222; Naman Chambers, C/32 G Block Bandra Kurla Complex, Bandra East)

USA Chennai (Map pp394-5; ☎ 044-28574242; Gemini Circle, 220 Anna Salai); Delhi (☎ 011-24198000; http:// newdelhi.usembassy.gov; Shantipath, Chanakyapuri); Kolkata (☎ 033-39842400; 5/1 Ho Chi Minh Sarani); Mumbai (Map pp110-11; ☎ 022-23633611; Lincoln House, 78 Bhulabhai Desai Rd, Breach Candy)

FOOD

Sampling the local cuisine is undoubtedly one of the highlights of a visit to South India. To get a taste of what's on offer read p71 and the Eating sections of the regional chapters. For opening hours see p494 and the book's Eating sections.

GAY & LESBIAN TRAVELLERS

Technically, homosexual relations for men are illegal in India and the penalties for transgression can theoretically be as high as life imprisonment. There's no law against lesbian sexual relations.

Foreigners are unlikely to be targeted by India's homosexuality laws, but members of the Indian community have been campaigning against this legislation for years. The campaign to repeal 'Section 377' has recently attracted some high profile supporters – for more information read p48.

There are low-key gay scenes in a number of cities including Mumbai and Bengaluru (Gay Pride marches have been held at some of these centres).

However India is, broadly speaking, a conservative society and public displays of affection are generally frowned upon for heterosexual couples as well as gay and lesbian couples. In fact, men holding hands can be more commonly seen than heterosexual couples doing the same, though this is generally a sign of friendship rather than sexual orientation.

Publications & Websites

To tap into Delhi's gay scene, join the Gay Delhi email list: send a blank email to gaydelhi-subscribe@yahoogroups.com. There are regular socials and this is also a point of contact for the Delhi Frontrunners & Walkers, a weekly running and walking group.

Details about the Mumbai publication *Bombay Dost* can be found in the 'Support Groups' section (Humsafar Trust), opposite.

For further information (including local events) have a look at **Indian Dost** (www.indian

dost.com/gay.php), **Gay Bombay** (www.gaybombay .org), **Humrahi** (www.geocities.com/WestHollywood/ Heights/7258) and **Humsafar Trust** (www.humsafar .org).

Support Groups

There are support groups in a number of South Indian cities; a selection follows.

Several organisations exist in Bengaluru: **Good As You** (www.sawnet.org/orgns/good_as_you.html) is a support group for gay, lesbian, bisexual and transgender people. Meanwhile, the NGO **Swabhava** (☎ 080-22230959; http://swabhava_trust .tripod.com; 4th fl MS Plaza, No 1, Old No 566, 13th A Cross, 4th Main, Sampangiramnagar) works directly with issues affecting lesbians, gays, bisexuals and transgender people in ways that include publications, advocacy, counselling and training programmes. It also operates the **Sahaya Helpline** (☎ 080-22230959). Volunteer opportunities exist. **Sangama** (☎ 080-23438840; 23438843; www.sangama .org; 9 Ababil Patil Cheluvappa St, JC Nagar) deals with crisis intervention and provides a community outreach service for gay and bisexual men and women, transgenders and *hijras* (transvestites and eunuchs).

In Chennai, **Sahodaran** (☎ 044-8252869; www.sa hodaran.faithweb.com; 127 Sterling Rd, 1st fl, Nungambakkam) is a support group for gay men. It holds social-group meetings and activities.

In Mumbai, the **Humsafar Trust** (☎ 022-26673800; www.humsafar.org; Old BMC building, Vakola Post Office, Nehru Rd, Vakola, Santa Cruz East) runs gay and transgender support groups and advocacy programs. Their drop-in centre in Santa Cruz East hosts workshops and has a library; it's also the place to pick up a copy of the pioneering gay-and-lesbian magazine *Bombay Dost* and is one of the venues for 'Sunday High', a monthly screening of queer-interest films (also see p137).

HOLIDAYS

In India there are officially three national public holidays: Republic Day (26 January), Independence Day (15 August) and Gandhi Jayanti (2 October). Every state celebrates its own official holidays, which cover bank holidays for government workers as well as major religious festivals – usually Diwali, Dussehra and Holi (Hindu), Nanak Jayanti (Sikh), Eid al-Fitr (Muslim), Mahavir Jayanti (Jain), Buddha Jayanti (Buddhist) and Easter and Christmas (Christian). For more on religious festivals, see p19.

Most businesses (offices, shops etc) and tourist sites close on public holidays, but transport is usually unaffected. It's wise to make transport and hotel reservations well in advance if you intend visiting during major festivals.

INSURANCE

Every traveller should take out travel insurance – if you can't afford it, you can't afford the consequences if something does go wrong. Make sure that your policy covers theft of property and medical treatment, as well as air evacuation. Be aware that some policies place restrictions on potentially dangerous activities such as scuba diving, skiing, motorcycling, trekking, paragliding and climbing. When hiring a motorcycle in India, make sure the rental policy includes at least third-party insurance; see p528.

There are hundreds of different policies so read the small print carefully and make sure your activities are covered. In some areas, trekking agents may only accept customers who have cover for emergency helicopter evacuation. Some policies pay doctors and hospitals directly; others expect you to pay upfront and claim the money later (keep all documentation for your claim). It's crucial to get a police report in India if you've had anything stolen; insurance companies may refuse to reimburse you without one. Also see p534.

For insurance recommendations, click www.lonelyplanet.com/travel_services.

INTERNET ACCESS

Internet cafes are widespread in South India and connections are usually reasonably fast, except in more remote areas. Bandwidth load tends to be lowest in the early morning and early afternoon. Internet charges vary regionally (see regional chapters), usually falling anywhere between Rs20 and Rs65 per hour and often with a 15- to 30-minute minimum.

It's a good idea to write and save your messages in a text application before pasting them into your browser – power cuts can be common and all too often your carefully crafted email can vanish into the ether. Be wary of sending sensitive financial information from internet cafes; some places are able to use key-stroke-capturing technology to access passwords and emails. Using online banking on any non-secure system is generally unwise.

If you're travelling with a laptop some internet cafes can supply you with internet access over a LAN Ethernet cable, or you can join an international roaming service with an Indian dial-up number, or take out an account with a local Internet Service Provider (ISP); inquire locally. Make sure your modem is compatible with the telephone and dial-up system in India (an external global modem may be necessary).

Another useful investment in India is a fuse-protected universal AC adaptor to protect your circuit board from power surges. Plug adaptors are widely available throughout India, but bring spare plug fuses from home. Wi-fi access is available in an ever-increasing number of hotels (mostly top-end properties and a growing number of midrange ones) and some coffee shops in larger cities but, again, avoid sending credit-card details or other personal data over a wireless connection. For more information on travelling with a portable computer try www.teleadapt.com.

In this book, hotels offering internet access to guests are marked with the internet icon 🖳. See p18 for useful India-specific web resources.

LAUNDRY

Almost all hotels (of every budget) offer a same- or next-day laundry service. Most employ the services of dhobi-wallahs – washermen and women who will diligently bash your wet clothes against rocks and scrubbing boards, returning them spotlessly clean and ironed, but possibly missing a button or two. If you don't think your clothes will stand up to the treatment, wash them yourself or give them to a drycleaner. Washing powder can be bought cheaply virtually everywhere. Note that some hotels ban washing clothes in their rooms.

Most laundries and hotels charge per item (you'll usually be required to submit a list with your dirty clothes). It can take longer to dry clothes during the (humid) monsoon.

LEGAL MATTERS

If you're in a sticky legal situation, immediately contact your embassy (p499). However, be aware that all your embassy may be able to do is monitor your treatment in custody and arrange a lawyer. In the Indian justice system, the burden of proof can often be on the accused and stints in prison before trial are not unheard of.

You should always carry your passport; police are entitled to ask you for identification at any time.

Antisocial Behaviour

Recent laws have made smoking any form of tobacco in public illegal throughout India. The punishment (which is variably enforced) for breaking this rule is a fine of at least Rs200. People are free to smoke inside their homes and in most open spaces such as streets (heed any signs stating otherwise). A number of Indian cities have also banned spitting and littering.

Drugs

Possession of any illegal drug is regarded as a criminal offence. If convicted, the *minimum* sentence is 10 years, with very little chance of remission or parole.

Cases can take months (even several years) to appear before a court, while the accused may have to wait in prison, and there's usually a hefty monetary fine on top of any custodial sentence. The police have been getting particularly tough on foreigners who use drugs, so you should take this risk very seriously.

Marijuana grows wild in various parts of India, but consuming it is still an offence, except in towns where bhang is legally sold for religious rituals.

MAPS

Maps available inside India are of variable quality. Some of the better map series include TTK Discover India, **Nest & Wings** (www.nestwings .com), **Eicher** (http://maps.eicherworld.com) and **Nelles** (www.nelles-verlag.de). The **Survey of India** (www.sur veyofindia.gov.in) also publishes decent city, state and country maps, but some titles are rather frustratingly restricted for security reasons. All of these maps are available at good bookshops, or you can buy them online at **India Map Store** (www.indiamapstore.com).

Throughout South India, most state-government tourist offices stock basic local maps. These are often dated and lacking in essential detail but fine for general orientation purposes.

MONEY

The Indian rupee (Rs) is divided into 100 paise (p), but paise coins are becoming increasingly rare. Coins come in denominations of 5p, 10p, 20p, 25p and 50p, and Rs1, Rs2 and Rs5;

notes come in Rs5, Rs10, Rs20, Rs50, Rs100, Rs500 and Rs1000 (this last one is handy for large bills but can pose problems in regards to getting change for small services). The Indian rupee is linked to a basket of currencies and its value is generally stable; see the inside front cover of this book for exchange rates.

ATMs linked to international networks are common in most urban centres throughout India. However, carry cash or travellers cheques as backup in case the power goes down, the ATM is out of order, your card is rejected, or you lose or break your plastic.

You need to present your passport whenever you officially change currency or travellers cheques (don't forget to keep money-exchange receipts in case you need to change excess rupees into foreign currency before departing India; see p504). Commission for foreign exchange still exists but is usually nominal. For information about costs, see p15.

Read p498 for tips on keeping money safe during your trip.

ATMs

Modern 24-hour ATMs are found in most urban centres across the country, though the ATM may not always be in the same place as the bank branch. The most commonly accepted cards are Visa, MasterCard, Cirrus, Maestro and Plus. Some banks in India that accept foreign cards include Citibank, HDFC, ICICI, HSBC and the State Bank of India. Away from major towns, always carry cash or travellers cheques as backup.

Banks usually impose higher charges on international transactions, but this may be cancelled out by the favourable exchange rates between banks. Reduce charges by making larger transactions less often. Before your trip, check whether your card can reliably access banking networks in India and ask for details of charges. Some travellers have reported their home banks blocking use of cards, making it advisable to notify your bank that you'll be using it in India (provide dates); also take along your bank's phone number (as even some prewarned banks have automated programmes that detect and block nonroutine banking).

Note that some ATMs can snatch back money if you don't remove it within around 30 seconds. Conversely, other machines can take more than 30 seconds to actually release

cash, so don't panic if the money doesn't appear instantaneously.

The ATMs listed in this book's regional chapters accept foreign cards (but not necessarily all types of cards). Always keep the emergency lost-and-stolen numbers for your credit cards in a safe place, separate from your cards, and report any loss or theft immediately.

Cash

Major currencies such as US dollars, UK pounds and euros are easy to change throughout India, although some bank branches insist on travellers cheques only. Quite a few banks also accept other currencies such as Australian and Canadian dollars, and Swiss francs. Private moneychangers deal with a wider range of currencies, but Pakistani, Nepali and Bangladeshi currency can be harder to change away from the border. When travelling off the beaten track, always carry an adequate stock of rupees.

Whenever changing money, check every note. Banks staple bills together into bricks, which puts a lot of wear and tear on the currency. Don't accept any filthy, ripped or disintegrating notes, as these may be difficult to use.

It can be tough getting change in India (particularly at small shops, taxis etc) making it wise to maintain a stock of smaller currency. Try to stockpile Rs10, Rs20 and Rs50 notes.

Officially, you cannot take rupees out of India, but this is laxly enforced. However, you can change any leftover rupees back into foreign currency, most easily at the airport (some banks have a Rs1000 minimum). You may be required to present encashment certificates (p504) or credit-card/ATM receipts, and you may also have to show your passport and airline ticket.

Credit Cards

Credit cards are accepted at a growing number of shops, upmarket restaurants, and midrange and top-end hotels, and you can also usually use them to pay for flights and train tickets. However, be wary of scams; see p497. Cash advances on major credit cards are also possible at some banks without ATMs. MasterCard and Visa are the most widely accepted cards; for details about whether you can access home accounts in India, inquire at your bank before leaving.

DIRECTORY

Encashment Certificates

By law, all foreign currency must be changed at official moneychangers or banks. For every (official) foreign exchange transaction, you'll receive an encashment certificate (receipt), which will allow you to re-exchange rupees into foreign currency when departing India. You'll need to have encashment certificates totalling the amount of rupees you intend changing back to foreign currency. Printed receipts from ATMs are also accepted as evidence of an international transaction at most banks.

Traditionally, money-exchange receipts have also been required when paying for tourist-quota train tickets in rupees, but this requirement has been relaxed.

International Transfers

If you run out of money, someone back home can wire you cash via moneychangers affiliated with **Moneygram** (www.moneygram.com) or **Western Union** (www.westernunion.com). A fee is added to the transaction. To collect cash, bring your passport and the name and reference number of the person who sent the funds.

Moneychangers

Private moneychangers are usually open for longer hours than banks, and they're found almost everywhere (many also double as internet cafes and travel agents). Compare rates with those at the bank and, as elsewhere, check you are given the correct amount. Upmarket hotels may also change money, but their rates are usually not as competitive as the banks/private moneychangers.

Tipping, Baksheesh & Bargaining

In tourist restaurants or hotels, a service fee is usually already added to your bill and tipping is optional. Elsewhere, a tip is appreciated. Hotel bellboys and train/airport porters appreciate anything around Rs50 to carry heavy bags, and hotel staff should be given similar gratuities for services above and beyond the call of duty. It's not mandatory to tip taxi or rickshaw drivers, but it's good to tip drivers who are honest about the fare. If you hire a car with driver for more than a couple of days, a tip is recommended for good service – details on p525.

Baksheesh can loosely be defined as a 'tip', and it covers everything from alms for beggars to bribes.

Many Indians implore tourists not to hand out sweets, pens or money to children, as it encourages them to beg. To make a lasting difference, donate to a reputable school or charitable organisation (see p514).

When it comes to shopping, apart from fixed-price shops (such as government emporiums and fair-trade cooperatives), bargaining is the norm; read the Art of Haggling boxed text, p509.

Travellers Cheques

All major brands are accepted in India, but some banks may only accept cheques from American Express (Amex) and Thomas Cook. Pounds sterling and US dollars are the safest currencies, especially in smaller towns. Charges for changing travellers cheques vary from place to place and bank to bank.

Always keep an emergency cash stash in case you lose your travellers cheques, and keep a record of the cheques' serial numbers separate from your cheques, along with the proof-of-purchase slips, encashment vouchers and photocopied passport details.

To replace lost travellers cheques, you need the proof-of-purchase slip and the numbers of the missing cheques (some places require a photocopy of the police report and a passport photo). If you don't have the numbers of your missing cheques, Amex (or whichever company has issued them) will contact the place where you bought them.

If you do lose your cheques, contact the Amex or Thomas Cook office in the closest city, or call the head offices in Delhi:

American Express (Amex; ☎ 011-23719506; A-Block, Connaught Place, Delhi; ⊘ 9.30am-6.30pm Mon-Fri, to 2.30pm Sat)

Thomas Cook (☎ 011-23342171; Hotel Janpath, Janpath; ⊘ 9.30am-7pm Mon-Sat)

For Thomas Cook office locations in Mumbai see p113, and for Chennai see p392.

PHOTOGRAPHY

For useful tips and techniques on travel photography, read Lonely Planet's travel photography guides, including *Travel Photography*, *Wildlife Travel Photography* and *People Travel Photography*.

Digital

Memory cards for digital cameras are available from photographic shops in most large cities and towns. However, the quality of memory cards is variable – some don't carry the advertised amount of data. Expect to pay upwards of Rs500 for a 1GB card. To be safe, regularly back up your memory card to CD; internet cafes may offer this service for Rs60 to Rs110 per disk. Some photographic shops make prints from digital photographs for roughly the standard print-and-processing charge.

Print & Slide

Colour-print film-processing facilities are readily available in most urban centres. Film is relatively cheap and the quality is usually good, but you'll only find colour-slide film in the major cities and tourist traps. On average, developing costs around Rs5 per 4x6 print, plus Rs20 for processing. Passport photos are available from many photo shops for around Rs100 to Rs125 (four visa-size shots).

Always check the use-by date on local film and slide stock. Make sure you get a sealed packet and that you're not handed a roll that's been sitting in a glass cabinet in the sunshine for the last few months. Be wary of buying film from street hawkers – unscrupulous characters have been known to load old/damaged film into new-looking canisters. It's best to only buy film from reputable stores – and preferably film that's been refrigerated.

Restrictions

India is touchy about anyone taking photographs of military installations – this can include train stations, bridges, airports, military sites and sensitive border regions. Photography from the air is officially prohibited, although airlines rarely enforce this.

Many places of worship – such as monasteries, temples and mosques – also prohibit photography. Respect these proscriptions and always ask when in doubt as to taking photographs of forbidden images can cause serious offence. See p47 for etiquette about photographing people.

POST

Mail and poste restante services are generally good, although the speed of delivery will depend on the efficiency of any given office. Airmail is faster and more reliable than sea mail, although it's best to use courier services (such as DHL) to send and receive items of value; expect to pay around Rs3000 per kilo to Europe, Australia or the USA. Private couriers are often cheaper, but goods may be repacked into large packages to cut costs and things sometimes go missing.

Receiving Mail

To receive mail in India, ask senders to address letters to you with your surname in capital letters and underlined, followed by 'poste restante', GPO (main post office), and the city or town in question. Many 'lost' letters are simply misfiled under given/first names, so check under both your names and ask senders to provide a return address in case you don't collect your mail. Letters sent via poste restante are generally held for around one to two months before being returned. To claim mail, you'll need to show your passport. It's best to have any parcels sent to you by registered post.

Sending Mail

Posting letters/aerogrammes to anywhere overseas costs Rs20/15, while Rs12 is the usual cost for international postcards. For postcards, stick on the stamps *before* actually writing on them, as post offices can give you as many as four stamps per card. Sending a letter overseas by registered post adds Rs15 to the stamp cost.

In terms of posting parcels, some post offices can be relatively straightforward while others involve multiple counters and lots of queuing. Some services are only offered at certain times of the day (often mornings, but check locally).

Prices vary depending on weight (including packing material) and you have a choice of airmail (delivery in one to three weeks), sea mail (two to four months), or Surface Air-Lifted (SAL) – a curious hybrid where parcels travel by both air and sea (around one month). Parcels must be packed up in white linen and the seams sealed with wax. Local tailors offer this service, or there may be a parcel-packing service at the post office itself. Carry a permanent marker to write on the parcel any information requested by the desk. The post office can provide the necessary customs declaration forms and these must be stitched or pasted to the parcel. If the contents are a gift under the value of Rs1000, you won't have to pay duty at the delivery end.

Parcel post has a maximum of 20kg to 30kg depending on the destination, and charges vary depending on whether you go by air or sea (prices on application).

A small package costs Rs40 (up to 100g) to any country and Rs30 per additional 100g (up to a maximum of 2000g; different charges apply for higher weights than this). You also have the option of the EMS (express mail service; delivery within three days) for around 30% more than the normal airmail price.

Books or printed matter can go by (inexpensive) international book post for Rs350 (maximum 5kg), but the package must be wrapped with a hole that reveals the contents for inspection by customs – tailors are experienced in creating this in such a way that nothing falls out. The website for **India Post** (www.indiapost.gov.in) has an online calculator for assorted domestic and international postal tariffs.

Be cautious with places that offer to mail things to your home address after you have bought them. Government emporiums are usually fine, but for most other places it pays to do the posting yourself.

SHOPPING

You'll find a treasure trove of things to buy in South India, from exquisite textiles and carpets to stunning jewellery and handicrafts. Specialities from all over the country can be sourced. Rajasthani crafts, such as sequinned and mirrored embroidery or colourful saris, and Kashmiri shawls, carpets and carvings, can be found almost everywhere, especially at tourist-oriented markets (such as the Anjuna flea market in Goa, see p216) and city shopping centres. Kashmiris especially are among India's most ubiquitous traders.

Be cautious when buying items that include delivery to your country of residence, and be wary of being led to shops by smooth-talking touts (see p498). Exporting antiques is prohibited (read p510).

Unless you're at fixed-price shops (such as fair-trade cooperatives and government emporiums), you'll invariably have to bargain – see the boxed text, p509.

Opening hours for shops vary – exceptions to standard hours are indicated in the shopping listings in regional chapters.

Only a small proportion of the money brought to India by tourism reaches people in rural areas. You can make a greater contribution by shopping at community shops and cooperatives, set up to protect and promote traditional cottage industries and provide education, training and a sustainable livelihood for rural families. Many of these projects focus on refugees, low-caste women, people with disabilities and other socially disadvantaged groups. Prices are usually fixed and a share of the money goes directly into social projects such as schools, healthcare and training. Shopping at the national network of Khadi & Village Industries emporiums will also contribute to rural communities.

Bronze Figures, Metalwork, Stone Carving & Terracotta

Bronze figures of various deities are available around South India, especially in and around major temple towns. The bronze makers (called *shilpis*) still employ the centuries-old lost-wax method of casting, a legacy of the Chola period when bronze sculpture reached its apogee in skill and artistry. A wax figure is made, a mould is formed around it and the wax is melted and poured out. Molten metal is poured in and when it's solidified the mould is broken open. Figures of Shiva as Nataraja (lord of the cosmic dance) are among the most popular. Small copper bowls, cigarette boxes and paan containers are still handmade in Hyderabad, while bell metal lamps are a particularly good buy in Thrissur.

Bidriware is a craft named after the town of Bidri (in northern Karnataka) where silver is inlaid into gunmetal (an alloy of zinc, copper, lead and tin). Hookah pipes, lamp bases and jewellery boxes are made in this manner. Bidri employs the technique of sand-casting, where artisans make a mould from sand, resin and oil (also see the boxed text, p290).

In Mamallapuram (Tamil Nadu) craftspeople have revived the ancient artistry of the Pallava sculptors using local granite and soapstone – souvenirs range from tiny stone elephants to enormous deity statues weighing half a tonne. Tamil Nadu is also known for the bronzeware from Thanjavur and Trichy (Tiruchirappalli).

At temples across South India you can buy small terracotta or plaster effigies of assorted deities.

Carpets

The majority of carpets you'll see for sale in South India come from Kashmir, Rajasthan or Uttar Pradesh. Kashmiri rugs are either made of pure wool, wool with a small percentage of silk to give them a sheen (known as 'silk touch') or pure silk. The latter are more for decoration.

CARPETS & CHILD LABOUR

Children have been employed as carpet weavers in the subcontinent for centuries, and many childcare charities from within and beyond India are campaigning against the use of child labour by the carpet industry. Although it's impossible to get accurate figures, various published reports suggest there are upwards of 100,000 child carpet weavers in India.

Unfortunately, the issue is more complicated than it first appears. In many areas, education is often not an option, for both economic and cultural reasons, and the alternative to child labour may not be school but hunger for the whole family. We encourage travellers to buy from carpet weaving cooperatives that employ adult weavers *and* provide education for their children, breaking the cycle of child labour.

India's **Carpet Export Promotion Council** (www.india-carpets.com) is campaigning to eliminate child labour from the carpet industry by penalising factories that use children and by founding schools to provide an alternative to carpet making. Ultimately, the only thing that can stop child labour is compulsory education for children. However, the economic and social obstacles are significant, often making new initiatives difficult to implement.

Unfortunately for the buyer, there's no easy way of knowing whether a carpet has been made by children. Shops are unlikely to admit using child labour and most of the international labelling schemes for carpets have been discredited. The carpets produced by Tibetan refugee cooperatives are almost always made by adults, while Uttar Pradesh is known as the capital of child labour in India. Most government emporiums and charitable cooperatives are usually the best places to buy.

The price of a carpet will be determined by the number and size of the hand-tied knots, the range of dyes and colours, the intricacy of the design and the material. Silk carpets cost more and look more luxurious, but wool carpets usually last longer. Expect to pay upwards of US$200 for a good quality 90cm by 1.5m (or 90cm by 1.8m, depending on the region) wool carpet, and around US$2000 for a similar sized carpet in silk. Tibetan carpets are cheaper, reflecting the relative simplicity of the designs; many refugee cooperatives sell 90cm by 1.5m carpets for around US$100 or less.

Most places can ship carpets home for a fee – though it may be safest to ship things independently to avoid scams – or you can carry them in the hold (allow 5kg to 10kg of your baggage allowance for a 3ft by 5ft carpet).

Kashmir and Rajasthan produce coarsely woven woollen *numdas* (or *namdas*), which are much cheaper than knotted carpets. Various parts of India produce flat weave *dhurries* (kilim-like cotton rugs). Kashmiris also produce striking *gabbas* made from chain-stitched wool or silk. All these types of carpets can also be found for sale in South India.

Jewellery

South India's most significant jewellery-making centres include Hyderabad, Bengaluru,

Mysore, Ooty, and Thanjavur (Tanjore). South Indian jewellery is generally distinguished from that made in the north by its use of motifs inspired by nature – lotus buds, flowers, grass stalks and, in Kerala, birds. Throughout South India you can find finely crafted gold and silver rings, anklets, earrings, toe-rings, necklaces and bangles. Pieces can often be crafted to order.

Virtually every town in South India has at least one bangle shop. These sell an extraordinary variety ranging from colourful plastic and glass to shiny brass and silver.

Pearls are produced by most seaside states. They're a speciality of Hyderabad (Andhra Pradesh) and pearls are crafted into jewellery in many other areas. You'll find them at most state emporiums. Prices vary depending on the colour and shape – you pay more for pure white pearls or rare colours like black. Perfectly round pearls are generally more expensive than misshapen or elongated pearls however the quirky shapes of Indian pearls can actually be more alluring than the perfect round balls. A single strand of seeded pearls can cost as little as Rs300, but better-quality pearls start at around Rs700.

Leatherwork

As the cow is sacred in India, leatherwork here is made from buffalo-hide, camel, goat or some other substitute. Most large cities offer a smart range of modern leather footwear at very reasonable prices, some stitched with zillions of sparkly sequins – marvellous partywear!

Chappals, those wonderful (often curly-toed) leather sandals, are sold throughout India but are particularly good in the Maharashtran cities of Kolhapur, Pune and Matheran.

In the larger cities, such as Chennai, Bengaluru and Mumbai, you'll find impressive, moderately priced leather handbags, wallets and other leather accessories.

Musical Instruments

Quality musical instruments are available in the larger South Indian cities, but there tends to be more variety in North Indian centres such as Delhi. Prices vary according to the quality – and sound – of the instrument.

Decent tabla sets with a wooden tabla (tuned treble drum) and metal *doogri* (bass tone drum) cost upwards of Rs3000. Cheaper sets are generally heavier and sound inferior.

Sitars range anywhere from Rs4000 to Rs20,000 (possibly even more). The sound of each sitar will vary with the wood used and the shape of the gourd, so try a few. Note that some cheaper sitars can warp in colder or hotter climates. On any sitar, make sure the strings ring clearly and check the gourd carefully for damage. Spare string sets, sitar plectrums and a screw-in 'amplifier' gourd are sensible additions.

Other popular instruments include the *shehnai* (Indian flute), the sarod (like an Indian lute), the harmonium and the *esraj* (similar to an upright violin).

Paintings

Reproductions of Indian miniature paintings are widely available, but quality varies – the best are almost as good as the real thing, while cheaper ones have less detail and use inferior colours. Beware of paintings purported to be antique – it's highly unlikely and, in addition, paintings more than 100 years old can't be exported from India.

In Kerala and Tamil Nadu, you'll come across miniature paintings on leaf skeletons depicting deities as well as domestic and rural scenes. Meanwhile, in Andhra Pradesh you can buy lovely cloth paintings called *kalamkari,* portraying deities and historic

events – see www.kalamkariart.org for more on this interesting art form.

A traditional craft practised in some villages is that of carving dried palm leaf sections with a fine stylus, after which the incisions are dyed with a wash of colour. There's an artists' colony, adopting similar styles, at the Cholamandal Artists' Village (p407) south of Chennai in Tamil Nadu.

Throughout the country (especially in capital cities) look out for shops and galleries selling brilliant contemporary paintings by local artists. Mumbai is the centre of the flourishing Indian contemporary art scene; you can see some of this art at the National Gallery of Modern Art (p116); also read the box, p137.

Papier Mâché

Artisans in Srinagar (Kashmir) have been producing lacquered papier mâché for centuries and papier-mâché ware is now sold right across India. The basic shape is made in a mould from layers of paper (often recycled newsprint), then painted with fine brushes and lacquered for protection. Prices depend upon the complexity and quality of the design and the amount of gold leaf used. Many pieces feature delicate patterns of animals and flowers, or hunting scenes from Mughal miniature paintings. You can find papier-mâché bowls, boxes, letter holders, coasters, trays, lamps and Christmas decorations (stars, crescent moons, balls and bells).

Shawls, Silk & Saris

Indian shawls are famously warm and lightweight – they're often better than the best down jackets. Shawls are made from all sorts of wool, from lambswool to fibres woven from yak, goat and angora-rabbit hair. Many are embroidered with intricate designs. However it's illegal to buy *shahtoosh* shawls, as rare Tibetan antelopes are killed to provide the wool.

The undisputed capital of the Indian shawl is the Kullu Valley in Himachal Pradesh, which has dozens of women's cooperatives producing sublime woollen varieties. Ladakh and Kashmir are major centres for *pashmina* (wool shawl) production – you'll pay at least Rs6000 for the authentic article – however be aware that many so-called *pashmina* shawls are actually made from a mixture of yarns.

Aurangabad in Maharashtra, is the traditional centre for the production of *himroo* shawls, sheets and saris, which are made from a blend of cotton, silk and silver thread. Silk and gold-thread saris produced at Paithan (near Aurangabad) are some of India's finest – prices range from around Rs6000 to a mind-blowing Rs300,000.

Saris are a very popular souvenir, especially given that they can be easily adapted to other purposes (from cushion covers to skirts). Real silk saris are the most expensive, and the silk usually needs to be washed before it becomes soft. The 'silk capital' of India is Kanchipuram in Tamil Nadu.

Textiles

Textile production is India's major industry and around 40% takes place at the village level, where it's known as *khadi* (homespun cloth) – hence the government-backed *khadi* emporiums around the country. These inexpensive superstores sell all sorts of items made from homespun cloth, including the popular Nehru jackets and kurta pyjamas (long shirt and loose-fitting trousers) with sales benefiting rural communities.

You will find a truly amazing variety of weaving and embroidery techniques around the country. In tourist centres, such as Goa, textiles are stitched into shoulder bags, wall hangings, cushion covers, bedspreads, clothes and much more.

Appliqué is an ancient art in India, with most states producing their own version, often featuring abstract or anthropomorphic patterns. The traditional lampshades and *pandals* (tents) used in weddings and festivals are usually produced using the same technique.

Batik can be found throughout South India, especially in the larger cities such as Mumbai. It is often used for saris and *salwar kameez* (dresslike tunic and trouser combination). *Kalamkari* cloth from Andhra Pradesh is an associated but far older craft. It traditionally emerged around South India's temples – the designs reflect elements of temple murals, and are largely used as decorative cloths during devotional ceremonies and festivals.

Big South Indian cities, such as Mumbai, Bengaluru and Chennai, are top spots to pick up *haute couture* (high fashion) by talented Indian designers, as well as moderately priced Western fashions.

Block-printed and woven textiles are sold by fabric shops all over India, often in vivid colour combinations. Each region has its own speciality. The India-wide chain-store **Fabindia** (www.fabindia.com) strives to preserve traditional patterns and fabrics, transforming them into highly accessible items for home decoration and Indian and Western-style fashions.

Woodcarving

Woodcarving is an ancient art form throughout India. Mysore is known as South India's main centre of sandalwood carving. While

---

THE ART OF HAGGLING

Government emporiums, fair-trade cooperatives, department stores and modern shopping centres almost always charge fixed prices. Anywhere else you need to bargain. Shopkeepers in tourist hubs are accustomed to travellers who have lots of money and little time to spend it, so you can often expect to be charged double or triple the 'real' price. Souvenir shops are generally the most notorious.

The first 'rule' to haggling is never to show too much interest in the item you've got your heart set upon. Secondly, resist purchasing the first thing that takes your fancy. Wander around and price items, but don't make it too obvious – if you return to the first shop the vendor will know it's because they are the cheapest (resulting in less haggling leeway).

Decide how much you would be happy paying and then express a casual interest in buying. If you have absolutely no idea of what something should really cost, start by slashing the price by half. The vendor will, most likely, look utterly aghast, but you can now work up and down respectively in small increments until you reach a mutually agreeable price. You'll find that many shopkeepers lower their so-called 'final price' if you head out of the store saying you'll 'think about it'.

Haggling is a way of life in India and is usually taken in good spirit. It should never turn ugly. Always keep in mind exactly how much a rupee is worth in your home currency to put things in perspective. If a vendor seems to be charging an unreasonably high price, simply look elsewhere.

PROHIBITED EXPORTS

To protect India's cultural heritage, the export of certain antiques is prohibited. Many 'old' objects are fine, but the difficulties begin if something is verifiably more than 100 years old. Reputable antique dealers know the laws and can make arrangements for an export-clearance certificate for any old items that you're permitted to export. If in doubt, contact Delhi's **Archaeological Survey of India** (☎ 011-23010822; www.asi.nic.in; Janpath; ◷ 9.30am-1pm & 2-6pm Mon-Fri) next to the National Museum. The rules may seem stringent but the loss of artworks and traditional buildings in places such as Ladakh, Himachal Pradesh, Gujarat and Rajasthan, due to the international trade in antiques and carved windows and doorframes, has been alarming. Look for quality reproductions instead.

The Indian Wildlife Protection Act bans any form of wildlife trade. Don't buy any products that endanger threatened species and habitats – doing so can result in heavy fines and even imprisonment. This includes ivory, *shahtoosh* shawls (made from the down of rare Tibetan antelopes), and anything made from the fur, skin, horns or shell of any endangered species. Products made from certain rare plants are also banned.

Note that your home country may have additional laws forbidding the import of restricted items and wildlife parts. The penalties can be severe so know the law before you buy.

sandalwood was once purely reserved for carving deities, nowadays all manner of things are made, from solid pieces of furniture to keyrings and delicate fans. Sandalwood carvings of Hindu deities is one of Karnataka's specialities, but you'll pay a kings' ransom for the real thing – a 10cm-high Ganesh costs around Rs3000 in sandalwood, compared to Rs300 in kadamb wood. However, the sandalwood will release fragrance for years. Rosewood is used for making furniture, and carving animals is a speciality of Kerala. The religious icons produced from wood inlay in Goa also have a certain chintzy appeal.

Kerala, along with coastal Karnataka, is a centre for marquetry, which uses woods of various hues (including rosewood) and, in Mysore, ivory substitutes. Carved wooden furniture and other household items, either in natural finish or lacquered, are also made in various locations. Woodcarvers' skills are very much in evidence in the major temple towns of Tamil Nadu.

Wooden boxes and chests, once major dowry items, are available in the antique shops of Fort Cochin in Kerala. Although the wooden versions are still made by local artisans, metal cupboards and trunks are replacing them and they are becoming rarer. Dowry boxes are usually made from the wood of the jackfruit tree (sometimes rosewood), and are reinforced with brass hinges and brackets.

Wooden toys are also produced in many regions of South India; brightly painted buses and trucks are a highlight of Thiruvananthapuram (Trivandrum).

Other Buys

It's little surprise that Indian spices are snapped up by tourists. Virtually all towns have shops and bazaars selling locally made spices at great prices. Karnataka, Kerala and Tamil Nadu produce most of the spices that go into garam masala (the 'hot mix' used to flavour Indian curries).

Attar (essential oil mostly made from flowers) shops can be found right around the country. Mysore (Karnataka) is especially famous for its sandalwood oil, while Mumbai is a major centre for the trade of traditional fragrances, including valuable *oud,* made from a rare mould that grows on the bark of the agarwood tree. Ooty and Kodaikanal (both in Tamil Nadu) produce aromatic and medicinal oils from herbs, flowers and eucalyptus.

Indian incense is exported worldwide, with Bengaluru and Mysore being major producers, and incense from Auroville (near Puducherry) also well regarded.

Meanwhile, a speciality of Goa is feni (liquor distilled from coconut milk or cashews) – a head-spinning spirit that often comes in decorative bottles. Excellent Indian tea is also widely sold in South India.

Fine-quality handmade paper – often fashioned into cards, boxes and notebooks – is worth seeking out, with good places to start including Puducherry (see the Sri Aurobindo Handmade Paper Factory, p427).

India has a phenomenal range of books at very competitive prices, including gorgeous leather-bound titles. Music CDs by local musicians are also red-hot value.

So much to buy, so little luggage space... Happy shopping!

SOLO TRAVELLERS

Perhaps the most significant issue facing solo travellers is cost. Single-room rates at guest houses and hotels are sometimes not much lower than double rates; some midrange and top-end places don't even offer a single tariff. However, it's always worth trying to negotiate a lower rate for single occupancy.

In terms of transport, you'll save money if you find others to share taxis and autorickshaws. This is also advisable if you intend hiring a car with driver for longer trips. Solo bus travellers may be able to get the 'co-pilot' (near the driver) seat on buses, which not only has a good view out front, but is also handy if you've got a big bag.

Although most solo travellers experience no major problems in South India, some less honourable souls (locals and travellers alike) view lone tourists as an easy target for theft. Don't be paranoid, but like anywhere else in the world, it's wise to stay on your toes in unfamiliar surroundings.

The main traveller hotels and restaurants are good places to swap stories, get up-to-the-minute travel tips and find people to travel with. You may also be able to find travel companions on Lonely Planet's **Thorn Tree travel forum** (www.lonelyplanet.com/thorntree).

It's worth noting that there have been muggings on single men wandering around isolated areas, even during the day. Information specific to women can be found on p516.

TELEPHONE

There are few payphones in India, but private PCO/STD/ISD call booths do the same job, offering inexpensive local, interstate and international calls at lower prices than calls made from hotel rooms (especially top-end ones). These booths are found extensively around the country, many open 24 hours. A digital meter displays how much the call is costing and usually provides a printed receipt when the call is finished. Faxes can be sent from quite a few call centres.

Recent years have seen phone costs slide, thanks to competition. There are variations (depending on the operator and destination).

Some booths also offer a 'call-back' service – you ring home, provide the phone number of the booth and wait for people at home to call you back, for a fee of around Rs10 on top of the cost of the preliminary call.

Useful online resources include the **Yellow Pages** (www.indiayellowpages.com) and **Justdial** (www.justdial.com).

Note that getting a line can be difficult in remote country and mountain areas – an engaged signal may just mean that the exchange is overloaded, so keep trying.

Mobile Phones

India is mobile-phone crazy and there's roaming coverage for international GSM phones in most cities and large towns. Mobile phone numbers in India usually have 10 digits, typically starting with a 9. To avoid expensive roaming costs (often highest for incoming calls), get hooked up to the local mobile-phone network. Note that mobiles bought in some countries may be locked to a particular network; you'll have to get the phone unlocked, or buy a local phone (available from Rs2000) to use an Indian SIM card.

Getting connected is inexpensive and, overall, relatively straightforward (larger cities are easiest). Foreigners need to supply one passport photo (take two, just in case) and a photocopy of their passport identity and visa pages (some places will do the photocopying for you).

In most Indian towns you simply buy a prepaid mobile-phone kit (SIM card and phone number, plus an allocation of calls) from around Rs150 from a phone shop or local PCO/STD/ISD booths, internet cafes or grocery stores. Thereafter, you must purchase new credits on that network, sold as scratch-cards in shops and call centres. Credit must usually be used within a set time limit and costs vary with the amount of credit on the card. The amount you pay for a credit top-up is not the amount you get on your phone – state taxes and service charges come off first. For some networks, recharge cards are being replaced by direct credit, where you pay the vendor and have the credit deposited straight to your phone – ask which system is in use before you buy.

Calls made within the state or city in which you bought the SIM card are cheap – Rs1 per minute – and you can call internationally for less than Rs10 per minute. SMS messaging is even cheaper. The more credit you have on your phone, usually the cheaper the call rate. However, some travellers have reported unreliable signals and problems with international texting (with messages or replies being delayed or failing to get through).

The most popular (and reliable) companies include Airtel, Vodaphone and BSNL. Note that most SIM cards are state specific; they can be used in other states, but you pay for calls at roaming rates and you'll be charged for incoming calls as well as outgoing calls. If, for example, you buy a SIM card in Delhi, calls ex-Delhi will be around Rs1.50 per minute, while the charge to receive a call from anywhere in India (ex-Delhi) is Rs1 per minute.

As the mobile-phone industry continues to evolve, mobile rates, suppliers and coverage are all likely to develop over the life of this book.

Phone Codes

Regular phone numbers have an area code followed by up to eight digits. The government is slowly trying to bring all numbers in India onto the same system, so area codes may change and new digits may be added to numbers with limited warning.

To make a call *to* India from overseas, dial the international access code of the country you're in, then 91 (international country code for India), then the area code (drop the initial zero when calling from abroad), then the local number.

To make an international call *from* India, dial 00 (international access code from India), then the country code of the country you're calling, then the area code and the local number.

Also available is the Home Country Direct service, which gives you access to the international operator in your home country. For the price of a local call, you can then make reverse-charge (collect) or phonecard calls. The number is typically constructed ☎ 000 + the country code of your home country + 17. Some countries and their numbers:

Country	Number
Australia	☎ 0006117
Germany	☎ 0004917
Italy	☎ 0003917
Japan	☎ 0008117
Netherlands	☎ 0003117
New Zealand	☎ 0006417
UK	☎ 0004417
USA	☎ 000117

TIME

India is 5½ hours ahead of GMT/UTC, 4½ hours behind Australian Eastern Standard Time (EST) and 10½ hours ahead of American EST. The local standard time is known as IST (Indian Standard Time), although some affectionately dub it 'Indian Stretchable Time'. The floating half hour was added to maximise daylight hours over such a vast country.

TOILETS

Public toilets are most easily found in major cities and tourist sites. The cleanest toilets (usually with sit-down and squat choices) are most reliably found at modern restaurants, shopping complexes and cinemas. It's always a good idea to carry your own toilet paper, just in case.

When it comes to effluent etiquette, especially beyond urban centres, locals may use the 'hand-and-water' technique, which involves cleaning one's bottom with a small jug of water and the left hand.

Also see p492.

TOURIST INFORMATION
Local Tourist Offices

In addition to the Government of India tourist offices (also known as 'India Tourism'), each state maintains its own network of tourist offices. These vary in their efficiency and usefulness – some are run by enthusiastic souls who go out of their way to help, others are basically a vehicle for the sale of State Tourism Development Corporation tours. Most of the tourist offices have free brochures and often a free (or inexpensive) local map (for further map information see p502).

The first stop for information should be the tourism website of the Government of India, **Incredible India** (www.incredibleindia.org); for details of its regional offices around India, click on the 'Help Desk' tab at the top of the homepage.

See regional chapters for contact details of relevant tourist offices.

Tourist Offices Abroad

The Government of India operates the following tourist offices abroad.

Australia (☎ 02-9221 9555; info@indiatourism.com .au; Level 5, 135 King St, Glasshouse Shopping Complex, Sydney, NSW, 2000)

Canada (☎ 416-962 3787; info@indiatourismcanada.ca; 60 Bloor St, West Ste 1003, Toronto, M4 W3 B8)

China (☎ 86-1065686294; beijing@indiatourism.org.cn; 29th fl, East Tower, LG Twin Towers, B-12 Jianguomenwai Dajie, Chaoyang District)

Dubai (☎ 971-4-2274848; goirto@eim.ae; NASA Building, AL Maktoum Rd, Deira, UAE)

France (☎ 01 4523 3045; indtourparis@aol.com; 11-13 Bis Blvd Haussmann, F-75009 Paris)

Germany (☎ 069-2429490; office@india-tourism.com; Basler Strasse 48, D-60329 Frankfurt Am-Main 1)

Italy (☎ 02-8053506; info@indiatourismmilan.com; Via-Albricci 9, Milan 20122)

Japan (☎ 03-3571 5062; indtourt@smile.ocn.ne.jp; Art Masters Ginza Bldg, 6th-9th fl, 6-5-12 Ginza, Chuo-Ku, Tokyo 104-0061)

Netherlands (☎ 020-6208991; info@indiatourism amsterdam.com; Rokin 9/15, 1012 KK Amsterdam)

Singapore (☎ 65-6235 3800; indtour.sing@pacific.net .sg; 20 Kramat Lane, 01-01 United House, 228773)

South Africa (☎ 011-3250880; goito@global.co.za; Craighall 2024, Hyde Lane, Lancaster Gate, Johannesburg 2000)

UK (☎ 0207-4373677; london5@indiatouristoffice.org; 7 Cork St, London W1S 3LH)

USA Los Angeles (☎ 213-380 8855; indiatourismla@aol .com; Suite 204, 3550 Wilshire Blvd, California 900102485); New York (☎ 212-586 4901; ny@itonyc.com; Suite 1808, 1270 Ave of Americas, NY, 10020)

TRAVEL PERMITS

Even with a visa, you're not permitted to travel everywhere in South India. Some national parks and forest reserves require a permit if you intend to go trekking, and a permit is required to visit the Andaman Islands (see p475) and another to visit Lakshadweep (p386).

TRAVELLERS WITH DISABILITIES

India's crowded public transport, crush of humanity and variable infrastructure can test even the hardiest able-bodied traveller. If you have a physical disability or you are vision impaired, these can pose even more of a challenge.

India has a very limited number of wheelchair-friendly hotels (almost exclusively top end), making it highly advisable to make pre-trip inquiries and book ground-floor rooms at hotels that lack adequate facilities. Some restaurants and offices have ramps, but most tend to have at least one step. Staircases are often steep and lifts frequently stop at mezzanines between floors. Footpaths and pavements, where they exist, can be riddled with holes, littered with debris and packed with pedestrians, hindering movement. If you use crutches, bring along spare rubber caps for the tips as they're likely to wear down quickly.

Given these challenges, if your mobility is considerably restricted you may like to ease the stress by travelling with an able-bodied companion. Additionally, hiring a car with driver will make moving around a whole lot easier (see p525); if you use a wheelchair, make sure the car-hire company can provide an appropriate vehicle to carry it.

To obtain further advice pertaining to your specific requirements, consult your doctor before heading to India. A number of organisations may also be able to proffer further information or at least point you in the right direction – good places to start include **Mobility International USA** (MIUSA; www.miusa.org), **Access-Able Travel Source** (www.access-able.com), **Global Access News** (www.globalaccessnews.com), **Royal Association for Disability & Rehabilitation** (RADAR; www.radar.org.uk) and **Accessible Journeys** (www.disabilitytravel.com).

VISAS

You must get a visa *before* arriving in India and these are available at Indian missions worldwide. Most people travel on the standard six-month tourist visa. Student visas and business visas have strict conditions (consult the Indian embassy for details). An onward travel ticket is a requirement for most visas, but this isn't always enforced (check in advance). Note that your passport needs to be valid for at least six months beyond your intended stay in India.

Six-month multiple-entry tourist visas (valid from the date of issue) are granted to nationals of most countries regardless of whether one stays that long or not. You can enter and leave as often as you like, but you can only spend a total of 180 days in the country, starting from the date of issue. There are additional restrictions on travellers from Bangladesh and Pakistan, as well as certain Eastern European, African and Central Asian countries. Check any special conditions for your nationality with the Indian embassy in your country.

Visas are priced in the local currency and may have an added service fee (contact your country's Indian embassy for current prices).

Extended visas are possible for people of Indian origin (excluding those in Pakistan and Bangladesh) who hold a non-Indian passport and live abroad.

For visas lasting more than six months, you're supposed to register at the Foreigners' Regional Registration Office (FRRO; see below) within 14 days of arriving in India; inquire about these special conditions when you apply for your visa.

Visa Extensions

Fourteen-day visa extensions are theoretically possible at the discretion of the **Ministry of Home Affairs** (☎ 011-23385748; Jaisalmer House, 26 Man Singh Rd, Delhi; ✆ inquiries 9-11am Mon-Fri) but don't get your hopes up. The only circumstances where this might conceivably happen are in *extreme* medical emergencies or if you were robbed of your passport just before you planned to leave the country (at the end of your visa). If you run low on time, consider doing the 'visa run' over to Bangladesh or Nepal and applying for another tourist visa there.

If you do find yourself needing to request an extension (again, there has to be a very good reason), you should contact the **Foreigners' Regional Registration Office** (FRRO; ☎ 011-26195530; frrodelhi@hotmail.com; Level 2, East Block 8, Sector 1, Rama Krishna (RK) Puram, Delhi; ✆ 9.30am-5.30pm Mon-Fri), just around the corner from the Hyatt Regency hotel. This is also the place to come for a re-placement visa if you've had your lost/stolen passport replaced (required before you can leave the country). Note that regional FRROs are even less likely to grant an extension.

Assuming you meet the stringent criteria, the FRRO is permitted to issue an extension of 14 days (free for nationals of most countries; inquire on application). You must bring your confirmed air ticket, one passport photo (take two, just in case) and a photocopy of your passport identity and visa pages. Note that this system is designed to get you out of the country promptly with the correct official stamps, not to give you two extra weeks of travel.

VOLUNTEERING

Many charities and international aid agencies work throughout India and there are numerous opportunities for volunteers. However, you're much more likely to be of help if you commit for at least a month. Better international volunteer agencies will work to make sustainable changes, letting the process be guided and informed by local people. It may be possible to find a placement after you arrive in India, but charities and NGOs normally prefer volunteers who have applied in advance and been approved for the kind of work involved.

Agencies Overseas

There are scores of international volunteering agencies, and it can be bewildering trying to assess which ones have ethical policies. Agencies that offer short projects in lots of different countries whenever you want to go are almost always tailoring projects to the volunteer rather than finding the right volunteer for the work that needs to be done. Look for projects that will derive benefits from your existing skills.

The organisation **Ethical Volunteering** (www .ethicalvolunteering.org) has some excellent guidelines for choosing an ethical sending agency.

There are some tried and tested international projects, such as Britain's **Voluntary Service Overseas** (VSO; www.vso.org.uk), that volunteer in various professional roles, though the time commitment can be up to several years. The international organisation **Indicorps** (www.indicorps.org) matches volunteers to projects across India in all sorts of fields, particularly social development. There are special fellowships for people of Indian descent living outside India.

Many Indian NGOs also offer volunteer work; for listings click on www.indian ngos.com.

To find sending agencies in your area, read Lonely Planet's *Volunteer*, the *Gap Year Book* and the *Career Break Book*, or use the internet – some good starting sites include **World Volunteer Web** (www.worldvolunteerweb.org), **Working Abroad** (www.workingabroad.com) and **Worldwide Volunteering** (www.worldwidevolunteering.org.uk).

Aid Programmes in South India

Following are listings of programmes in South India that may have opportunities for volunteers. It's best to contact them in advance, rather than turning up on the doorstep expecting to automatically be offered a position. Donations of money or clothing may also be welcomed. Note that unless otherwise indicated, volunteers are expected to cover their own costs (accommodation, food, transport etc).

Some of the organisations below may have other branches in India; see websites for details.

ANDHRA PRADESH
Blue Cross of Hyderabad (☎ 040-23544355; www .bluecrosshyd.in; Rd No 35, Jubilee Hills, Hyderabad) runs a

2-acre shelter with 600 animals at the western edge of Hyderabad. It works to rescue and adopt sick animals and vaccinate and sterilise stray dogs. Volunteers can help in the shelter, grooming, feeding and caring for shelter animals, or in the office.

The **Confederation of Voluntary Associations** (COVA; ☎ 040-24572984; www.covanetwork.org; 20-4-10, Charminar, Hyderabad) is an umbrella organisation for around 800 NGOs in Andhra Pradesh working with women, children, civil liberties and sustainable agriculture. Volunteers are matched to programmes that need their skills (long-term volunteers preferred).

With an animal hospital and sanctuary, **Karuna Society for Animals & Nature** (☎ 08555-287214; www.karunasociety.org; 2/138/C Karuna Nilayam, Prasanthi Nilayam Post, Anantapur) rescues and treats sick, abandoned and mistreated animals. Volunteers can help with caretaking operations; a one-month, full-time minimum commitment is needed, as are vaccinations.

GOA

Goa's leading environmental group, the **Goa Foundation** (☎ 08322256479; www.goafoundation.org; G-8 Feira Alta, Mapusa) runs occasional voluntary programmes, including litter cleanups (contact them for current details).

The British-based organisation **Children Walking Tall** (☎ 09822-124802; www.childrenwalkingtall .com; 'The Mango House,' near Vrundavan Hospital, Karaswada, Mapusa) has opportunities for volunteer child carers, teachers and medics at its projects for homeless children and orphans near Mapusa. The minimum placement is three months and every volunteer needs a criminal background check.

For more possibilities read the box, 'Get Involved' on p204.

KARNATAKA

Bengaluru's **Ashoka Trust for Research in Ecology & the Environment** (ATREE; ☎ 080-23533942; www.atree .org; 659 5th A Main Rd, Hebbal, Bengaluru) is committed to sustainable development issues related to conservation and biodiversity. It takes volunteers with experience or a keen interest in conservation and environmental issues.

Equations (☎ 080-25457607; www.equitabletourism .org; 415, 2nd C Cross, 4th Main Rd, OMBR Layout, Banaswadi Post, Bengaluru) works to promote 'holistic tourism' and protect local communities from exploitation through lobbying, local training programmes and research publications.

Family India (☎ 9844026222; www.thefamilyindia .org; 68, 2nd fl, Transpade Towers, Koramangala Industrial Layout, Jyothi Nivas College Rd, Bengaluru) runs a school for slum kids – it's possible to visit on weekends to help out. It also runs programmes in Delhi and Mumbai – contact them for further details.

It may be possible to volunteer at the Bengaluru gay-and-lesbian support group Swabhava – see p501.

KERALA

The UK-registered charity **Kerala Link** (www .kerala-link.org) places volunteers at one of its partner institutions in rural Kerala, including a special needs children school. Contact them online for current volunteer opportunities lasting from six weeks to six months.

MAHARASHTRA

Based near Phaltan, the **Nimbkar Agricultural Research Institute** (☎ 02166-222396; www.nariphaltan .org; Phaltan-Lonand Rd, Tambmal, Phaltan) has a focus on sustainable development, animal husbandry and renewable energy. Volunteer internships lasting two to six months are available for agriculture, engineering and science graduates to assist with the research.

Located 30km from Pune is **Sadhana Village** (☎ 020-25380792; www.sadhana-village.org; Priyankit, 1 Lokmanya Colony, Pune), a residential-care centre for intellectually disabled adults. Volunteers (prepared to commit to at least two months) assist in workshops, cultural activities and community-development programs for women and children. Meals and accommodation are provided but the organisation receives no government funding so donations are appreciated.

Anandwan (http://mss.niya.org; mss@niya.org; Maharogi Sewa Samiti, Waroa, Chandrapur) Volunteering options are available at this ashram, founded by social activist Baba Amte, and its satellite ashrams in the region. However do write in advance. Also see the box on p166.

MUMBAI

In Mumbai, **Child Rights & You** (CRY; ☎ 022-23063647/51; www.cry.org; 189A Anand Estate, Sane Guruji Marg, Mahalaxmi) fundraises for more than 300 projects India-wide, including ones that help deprived children. Volunteers can assist with campaigns (online and on the ground), research, surveys and media. A six-week commitment is required.

The **Vatsalya Foundation** (☎ 022-24962115; www
.thevatsalyafoundation.org; Anand Niketan, King George
V Memorial, Dr E Moses Rd, Mahalaxmi) works with
Mumbai's street children, focusing on rehabilitation into mainstream society. There are
long- and short-term opportunities in teaching and sports activities.

Volunteers can support English and art
classes, design workshops or do research or
data analysis at **Apne Aap Women Worldwide**
(☎ 022-32015597; www.apneaap.org; Chandramani Budh
Vihar Municipal School, 4th Floor, 13th Lane, Kamatipura),
an anti-trafficking organisation that works
in legal protection and provides learning and
livelihood training to women's and teenage
girls' groups. There are also volunteer possibilities with their offices in Kolkata, Bihar
and Delhi.

Concern India Foundation (☎ 022-22852270;
www.concernindia.org; 3rd fl, Ador House, 6 K Dubash Marg)
supports development-oriented organisa-
tions working with vulnerable members of
the community. The focus is on establishing
sustainable projects run by local people. The
foundation can arrange volunteer placements
matched to your skills and interests in Mumbai
and around India (six months minimum).
Many of the field jobs require Hindi.

Saathi (☎ 022-23009117; www.saathi.org; Agripada
Municipal School, Farooque Umarbhouy Lane, Agripada)
works with adolescent youths living on the
street. Volunteers should be willing to commit to at least three months and work full-
time (six days per week) for the organisation.
There's a range of volunteering possibilities,
but those interested in working directly with
adolescents should speak some Hindi. The
organisation also gives information sessions
and tours of the neighbourhoods where it
works with a Rs1000 donation.

The **Welfare of Stray Dogs** (☎ 022-23733433,
9819100808; www.wsdindia.org; H1 Chambers, B Bharocha
Rd, Kala Ghoda) works to improve the lives of
street dogs by eradicating rabies, sterilising,
educating the public about strays and finding
adoptive homes. Volunteers can walk dogs,
mind kennels, treat street dogs (training and
rabies shot required), manage stores, educate
kids in school programs or fund-raise.

TAMIL NADU
In Chennai, there are volunteer opportunities
at the **Missionaries of Charity** (☎ 044-25956928; 79
Main Rd, Royapuram, Chennai), which is part of Mother
Teresa's Kolkata-based care operation.

The **Freedom Foundation** (☎ 044-25567228; www
.thefreedomfoundation.org; 15 United Colony, Red Hills Rd,
Kolathur, Chennai) provides services to people
living with HIV/AIDs, including treatment
at its clinic and work-skills training. It also
campaigns for HIV education and prevention. There are opportunities for counsellors,
trainers, teachers and carers.

The international eye-care charity **Unite for
Sight** (www.uniteforsight.org/intl_volunteer) has regular
month-long openings for volunteer assistants,
teachers, nurses and optical-health professionals to help at its partner eye-care clinics
in Chennai and around India; see the website
for details.

The NGO **Rural Institute for Development
Education** (RIDE; ☎ 04112-268393; 46 Periyar Nagar, Little
Kanchipuram) works with numerous villages in
Kanchipuram to remove children from forced
labour and into transition schools. Volunteers
can contribute in teaching, administrative and
support roles.

In Chennai, the **Rejuvenate India Movement**
(RIM; ☎ 044-22235133; www.india-movement.org; A1
Monisha Sriram Flats, 9 Kulothungan Cross St, Chittlapakkam,
Chennai) can arrange short- and long-term
placements for skilled volunteers on development projects run by partner NGOs in over
a dozen villages in Tamil Nadu. There are also
opportunities in Karnataka. Spoken Hindi
is an asset.

In Kotagiri is the **Keystone Foundation** (www
.keystone-foundation.org), an NGO that strives
to improve environmental conditions in
the Nilgiris while working with, and creating better living standards for, indigenous
communities.

WOMEN TRAVELLERS

Broadly speaking, India is a conservative society, and the skimpy clothing and culturally
inappropriate behaviour of a minority of foreign women appears to have had somewhat
of a ripple effect on the perception of foreign
women in general. One unfortunate consequence of this is that many female travellers
have reported some form of sexual harassment while in India – predominantly lewd
comments and invasion of privacy, sometimes
groping. Most cases are reported in urban
centres of North India and prominent tourist
towns elsewhere.

While there's no need to be paranoid, you
should be aware that your behaviour and dress
code is under scrutiny, particularly away from

cosmopolitan cities like Mumbai and the tourist-accustomed beaches of Goa. Getting constantly stared at is something you'll have to live with. Don't allow it to get the better of you. It's best to refrain from returning male stares, as this may be considered a come-on; dark glasses can help, while MP3 players and books are useful accessories for averting unwanted conversations.

Other harassment women have encountered includes provocative gestures, jeering, getting 'accidentally' bumped into on the street and being followed. Exuberant special events such as the Holi festival can be notorious for this (see p19). Women travelling with a male partner are less likely to be hassled. However, mixed couples of Indian and non-Indian descent may get disapproving stares, even if neither individual actually lives in India.

Ultimately, there are no sure-fire ways of shielding yourself from sexual harassment, even if you do everything 'right' – use your own judgement and instincts, and err on the side of caution if you're unsure.

On the personal hygiene front, sanitary pads are widely available but tampons are usually restricted to pharmacies in big cities and some tourist towns (even then, the choice may be limited). Carry additional stocks for travel off the beaten track.

Clothing

Warding off sexual harassment is often a matter of adjusting your behaviour to match the prevailing social norms. Avoiding culturally inappropriate clothing can help enormously. Steer clear of sleeveless tops, shorts, miniskirts (ankle-length skirts are recommended) and any other skimpy, see-through or tight-fitting attire. Baggy clothing that masks the contours of your body is the way to go. Strategically draping a dupatta (long scarf) over T-shirts is another good way of staving off unwanted stares.

In some areas, such as Goa and Mumbai, there's generally a more liberal attitude towards dress. But away from these areas, take your cues from local women. Most Indian women wear saris, salwar kameez, or long shorts and a T-shirt whenever swimming in public view. When returning from the beach, use a sarong to avoid stares and glares on the way back to your hotel.

Wearing Indian-style clothes makes a positive impression and can considerably deflect harassment. The salwar kameez is regarded as respectable attire and wearing it will show your respect for local dress etiquette. This elegant, flowing outfit is also surprisingly cool in the hot weather, and the dupatta worn with it is very handy if you visit a shrine that requires your head to be covered. If you don't wish to wear a salwar kameez, a smart alternative is a kurta (long shirt) worn over jeans or trousers.

Going into public wearing a choli (sari blouse) or a sari petticoat (which some foreign women mistake for a skirt) is rather like strutting around half dressed – avoid it. You can read personal experiences proffered by fellow women travellers at www.journeywoman.com.

Staying Safe

Women have reported being molested by masseurs and other therapists, especially in tourist centres. No matter where you are, try to check the reputation of any teacher or therapist before going to a solo session. If you feel uneasy at any time, leave. For gynaecological health issues, most women prefer to seek out a female doctor.

To keep conversations with unknown men short, get to the point as quickly and politely as possible – getting involved in an inane conversation with someone you barely know can be misinterpreted as a sign of sexual interest. Questions and comments such as 'Do you have a boyfriend?' or 'You're looking very beautiful' are indicators that the conversation may be taking a steamy tangent. Some women prepare in advance by wearing a pseudo wedding ring, or by announcing early on in the conversation that they're married or engaged (regardless of the reality).

If you still get the uncomfortable feeling that a guy is encroaching on your space, he probably is. A firm request to keep away usually does the trick, especially if your tone is loud and curt enough to draw the attention of passers-by. Alternatively, the silent treatment (not responding to questions at all) can be remarkably effective.

When interacting with men on a day-to-day basis, follow the cue of local women and instead of shaking hands say namaste – the traditional, respectful Hindu greeting.

Female filmgoers will probably feel more comfortable (and lessen the chances of potential harassment) by going to the cinema with a companion. At hotels, get into the habit of keeping your door locked, as staff (particularly at budget places) can knock and automatically walk in without waiting for your permission.

Lastly, it's wise to arrive in towns before dark. Don't walk alone at night and avoid wandering alone in isolated areas even during daylight.

Taxis & Public Transport

Officials recommend that solo women prearrange an airport pick-up from their hotel if their flight is scheduled to arrive after dark. If that's not possible, in some cities you can avail of a prepaid radio cab service (see regional chapters) – it's more expensive than the regular prepaid taxis, but promotes itself as a safe service, with drivers that have been vetted as part of their recruitment. If you do catch a regular prepaid taxi, make a point of (in front of the driver) writing down the car registration and driver's name, and giving it to one of the airport police.

Avoid taking taxis alone late at night (when many roads are deserted) and never agree to have more than one man (the driver) in the car – ignore claims that this is 'just my brother' or 'for more protection'. Women are advised against wearing expensive-looking jewellery as it can make them a target for muggers.

On trains and buses, being a woman has some advantages. Women are able to queue-jump without consequence, and on trains there are special women-only carriages. Solo women have reported less hassle by opting for the more expensive classes on trains, especially for overnight trips. If you're travelling overnight in a three-tier carriage, try to get the uppermost berth, which will give you more privacy (and distance from potential gropers).

On public transport, don't hesitate to return any errant limbs, put some item of luggage in between you, be vocal (so as to attract public attention, thus shaming the fellow), or simply find a new spot.

Transport

CONTENTS

GETTING THERE & AWAY

South India is most easily accessed via its major international airports of Mumbai (Bombay) and Chennai (Madras). Some countries also offer charter flights to Goa. For details, see right. The South can also be reached overland from elsewhere in India – for details, see p522.

The following sections contain information on transport to and around South India. Flights, tours and other tickets may also be booked online at www.lonelyplanet.com /bookings/index.do.

ENTERING THE COUNTRY

Entering India by air or land is relatively straightforward, with standard immigration and customs procedures (p496). It's wise to pre-arrange an airport pick-up if arriving at night.

Passport

To enter India you need a valid passport, visa (see p513) and an onward/return ticket. Your passport should be valid for at least six months beyond your intended stay in India.

If your passport is lost or stolen, immediately contact your country's representative (see p499). Keep photocopies of your airline ticket and the identity and visa pages of your passport in case of emergency. Check any special conditions that may exist for your nationality with the Indian embassy in your home country.

AIR
Airports & Airlines

India is a big county so it makes sense to fly into the nearest airport to the area you want to visit. The main international airports in South India are Mumbai's Chhatrapati Shivaji International Airport (see p140) and Chennai's Anna International Airport (see p403), however, there are a number of other cities servicing (fewer) international carriers – for details see regional chapters and www .indianairports.com.

Direct charter flights from the UK, Russia and certain parts of Europe land at Goa's Dabolim Airport and, while you can get some cheap deals, you must also return via a charter flight (see p189 for details).

India's national carrier is **Air India** (www .airindia.com), of which the former state-owned domestic carrier, Indian Airlines, is now part of following a merger deal. The well-regarded private airline, **Jet Airways** (www.jetairways .com), also operates a number of international flights, as do several other Indian carriers (see p523). Consult the websites for current route and fare information. For details about India's domestic airlines, see p523.

> **THINGS CHANGE...**
>
> The information in this chapter is particularly vulnerable to change. Check directly with the airline or a travel agent to make sure you understand how a fare (and the ticket you may buy) works and be aware of the security requirements for international travel. Shop carefully. The details given in this chapter should simply be regarded as pointers and not as a substitute for your own careful, up-to-date research.

CLIMATE CHANGE & TRAVEL

Climate change is a serious threat to the ecosystems that humans rely upon, and air travel is the fastest-growing contributor to the problem. Lonely Planet regards travel, overall, as a global benefit, but believes we all have a responsibility to limit our personal impact on global warming.

Flying & climate change

Pretty much every form of motorized travel generates CO_2 (the main cause of human-induced climate change) but planes are far and away the worst offenders, not just because of the sheer distances they allow us to travel, but because they release greenhouse gases high into the atmosphere. The statistics are frightening: two people taking a return flight between Europe and the US will contribute as much to climate change as an average household's gas and electricity consumption over a whole year.

Carbon offset schemes

Climatecare.org and other websites use 'carbon calculators' that allow travellers to offset the level of greenhouse gases they are responsible for with financial contributions to sustainable travel schemes that reduce global warming – including projects in India, Honduras, Kazakhstan and Uganda.

Lonely Planet, together with Rough Guides and other concerned partners in the travel industry, support the carbon offset scheme run by climatecare.org. Lonely Planet offsets all of its staff and author travel.

For more information check out our website: www.lonelyplanet.com.

Other airlines flying to and from India (websites have updated contact details):

Aeroflot (www.aeroflot.org)
Air Canada (www.aircanada.com)
Air France (www.airfrance.com)
Alitalia (www.alitalia.com)
American Airlines (www.aa.com)
Austrian Airlines (www.aua.com)
Biman Bangladesh Airlines (www.biman-airlines.com)
British Airways (www.british-airways.com)
Cathay Pacific Airways (www.cathaypacific.com)
Drukair (www.drukair.com.bt)
El Al Israel Airlines (www.elal.co.il)
Emirates (www.emirates.com)
Finnair (www.finnair.com)
Gulf Air (www.gulfairco.com)
Japan Airlines (www.jal.com)
Kenya Airways (www.kenya-airways.com)
KLM – Royal Dutch Airlines (www.klm.com)
Kuwait Airways (www.kuwait-airways.com)
Lufthansa (www.lufthansa.com)
Malaysia Airlines (www.malaysiaairlines.com)
Nepal Airlines (www.royalnepal-airlines.com)
Pakistan International Airlines (www.piac.com.pk)
Qantas Airways (www.qantas.com.au)
Qatar Airways (www.qatarairways.com)
Singapore Airlines (www.singaporeair.com)
South African Airways (www.flysaa.com)
Sri Lankan Airlines (www.srilankan.aero)
Swiss International Airlines (www.swiss.com)
Thai Airways International (www.thaiair.com)

Departing India

Most airlines no longer require reconfirmation of international tickets, although it's still a good idea to call to check that flight times haven't changed. The majority of airlines ask you to check in three hours before international departures – remember to factor in the Indian traffic when planning your trip to the airport.

Most Indian airports have free luggage trolleys, but porters will eagerly offer to lug your load for a negotiable fee. For flights originating in India, checked bags must be passed through the X-ray machine in the departures hall and baggage tags are required for the security check for all cabin bags, including cameras.

Tickets

An onward or return air ticket is usually a condition of the Indian tourist visa, so few visitors buy international tickets inside India. Only designated travel agents can book international flights, but fares may be the same if you book directly with the airlines. Departure tax and other charges are included in airline tickets.

Given the fluctuating prices of international travel to India, it's best to contact a travel agent or surf the web to get up-to-the-minute fares and flight schedules. Note that internet fares often offer the best deals – here are some good places to start:

Ebookers (www.ebookers.com)
Expedia (www.expedia.com)

Flight Centre (www.flightcentre.com)
Flights.com (www.tiss.com)
STA Travel (www.statravel.com)
Travelocity (www.travelocity.com)
Yatra (www.yatra.com)

Africa

There are direct flights to India from South Africa and East Africa. **Rennies Travel** (www.rennies travel.com) and **STA Travel** (www.statravel.co.za) have offices throughout Southern Africa. Check their websites for branch locations.

Asia

STA Travel has branches in Bangkok (www.sta travel.co.th), Singapore (www.statravel.com .sg), Hong Kong (www.statravel.com.hk) and Japan (www.statravel.co.jp). Another resource in Japan is **No 1 Travel** (www.no1-travel.com); in Hong Kong try **Four Seas Travel** (www.fourseastravel.com). At least one airline offers flights to India from Bangladesh, the Maldives, Myanmar, Nepal, Pakistan and Sri Lanka; consult local travel agencies or the internet for current details.

Australia

Most flights from Australia involve a stop-over, the destination depending on the carrier. Popular agents include **STA Travel** (www.statravel .com.au) and **Flight Centre** (www.flightcentre.com.au). Also see www.travel.com.au.

Canada

From eastern and central Canada, most flights go via Europe; from Vancouver and the west coast, flights go via Asia. **Travel Cuts** (www.travel cuts.com) is Canada's national student travel agency. For online bookings try www.expedia .ca and www.travelocity.ca.

Continental Europe

There are connections to Indian cities from most European capitals, either directly or with a stop. For discount fares, try the agencies below or visit the big online ticket agencies. **STA Travel** (Austria www.statravel.at; Denmark www.sta travel.dk; Germany www.statravel.de; Norway www.statravel.no; Sweden www.statravel.se; Switzerland www.statravel.ch) and **Last Minute** (www.last-minute.co.uk) have regional websites for nations across Europe.

FRANCE

Recommended agencies:
Anyway (www.anyway.fr)
Lastminute (www.lastminute.fr)

Nouvelles Frontières (www.nouvelles-frontieres.fr)
OTU Voyages (www.otu.fr)
Voyageurs du Monde (www.vdm.com)

GERMANY

Recommended agencies:
Expedia (www.expedia.de)
Just Travel (www.justtravel.de)
Lastminute (www.lastminute.de)
STA Travel (www.statravel.de)

ITALY

One recommended agent is **CTS Viaggi** (www .cts.it).

NETHERLANDS

A recommended agency is **Airfair** (www.air fair.nl).

SPAIN

One recommended agency is **Barcelo Viajes** (www.barcelo viajes.com).

Middle East

Recommended agencies:
Al Rais Travel (www.alrais.com) In Dubai.
Egypt Panorama Tours (www.eptours.com) In Cairo.
Israel Student Travel Association (www.issta.co.il) In Jerusalem.
Orion-Tour (www.oriontour.com) In Istanbul.

New Zealand

Flights between India and New Zealand go via Southeast Asia. Both **Flight Centre** (www .flightcentre.co.nz) and **STA Travel** (www.statravel.co.nz) have branches throughout the country.

South America

Recommended agencies include the following:
ASATEJ (www.asatej.com) In Argentina.
Ividiomas (www.ividiomas.com) In Venezuela.
Student Travel Bureau (www.stb.com.br) In Brazil.

UK & Ireland

Discount air travel is big business in London. Advertisements for many travel agencies appear in the travel pages of the weekend broadsheet newspapers, in *Time Out*, the *Evening Standard* and in the free online magazine **TNT** (www.tntmagazine.com).

Recommended travel agencies include the following:
Ebookers (www.ebookers.com)
Flight Centre (www.flightcentre.co.uk)

> **STOP PRESS: DOMESTIC AIRLINE CHANGES!**
>
> Recent years have seen various domestic airline mergers and name changes in India – these were still unfolding at the time of going to press, so be aware that there may be changes over the life of this book. We've used airline office names that were applicable on the ground at the time of research.
>
> Keep in mind that although Air India and Indian Airlines have merged, some offices across the country may still be using the old name of Indian Airlines. Kingfisher Airlines and Air Deccan have also merged, with their offices now going by the names of Kingfisher Airlines and, its budget carrier, Kingfisher Red. Meanwhile, JetLite (which used to be known as Air Sahara) is a subsidiary of Jet Airways.
>
> Be aware that some dodgy travel agents may try to confuse travellers with name changes.

North South Travel (www.northsouthtravel.co.uk)
Quest Travel (www.questtravel.com)
STA Travel (www.statravel.co.uk)
Trailfinders (www.trailfinders.co.uk)
Travel Bag (www.travelbag.co.uk)

USA

Discount travel agents in the USA are known as consolidators (although you won't see a sign on the door saying 'Consolidator'). San Francisco is the ticket consolidator capital of America, although some good deals can certainly be found in Los Angeles, New York and other big cities.

Recommended for online bookings:
American Express Travel (www.itn.net)
CheapTickets (www.cheaptickets.com)
Expedia (www.expedia.com)
Lowestfare.com (www.lowestfare.com)
Orbitz (www.orbitz.com)
STA Travel (www.sta.com)
Travelocity (www.travelocity.com)

LAND

It's possible, of course, to get to South India overland via the long haul through North India. The classic hippie route from Europe to Goa involves travelling via Turkey, Iran and Pakistan. Other overland options are via Bangladesh or Nepal. For more on these routes, consult Lonely Planet's *Istanbul to Kathmandu*, or see the 'Europe to India overland' section on www.seat61.com/India-over land.htm.

If you enter India by bus or train you'll be required to disembark at the border for standard immigration and customs checks. You *must* have a valid Indian visa in advance as no visas are available at the border. The standard Indian tourist visa allows multiple entries within a six-month period – see p513.

Drivers of cars and motorbikes will need the vehicle's registration papers, liability insurance and an international drivers' permit in addition to their domestic licence.

You'll also need a *Carnet de passage en douane*, which acts as a temporary waiver of import duty. To find out the latest requirements for the paperwork and other important driving information, contact your local automobile association.

For details on travelling through South India by motorcycle, see p527.

Consult the relevant embassy for countries you plan crossing into from India (see p499).

Even though the security situation in Nepal has improved greatly over recent years, officials advise that travellers check the current security status before crossing into Nepal by land – local newspapers and international news websites are good places to start. Political and weather conditions permitting, there are five land border crossings between India and Nepal: Sunauli (Uttar Pradesh) to Bhairawa (central Nepal); Raxaul (Bihar) to Birganj (central Nepal); Panitanki (West Bengal) to Kakarbhitta (eastern Nepal); Jamunaha (Uttar Pradesh) to Nepalganj (western Nepal); and Banbassa (Uttaranchal) to Mahendranagar (western Nepal). The Sunauli to Bhairawa route is the most popular travellers' crossing.

Given the rocky relationship between India and Pakistan, crossing by land depends on the current state of relations between the two countries – check locally. Assuming the crossings are open, there are routes into Pakistan from Delhi, Amritsar (Punjab) and Rajasthan by bus or train. However, clearing the border formalities can take anywhere between two and five hours – compared to one or two hours if you travel independently. The bus route from Srinagar to Pakistan-administered Kashmir is currently only open to Indian citizens.

For those travelling from India to Bangladesh, there are many daily bus services from Kolkata (Calcutta) to Dhaka, which is the most convenient option. There's also a train link between Kolkata and Dhaka.

Phuentsholing is the main entry and exit point between India and Bhutan; you need a Bhutanese visa to enter the country and are required to book a tour with a registered tour operator in Bhutan, which can be done directly through an affiliated travel agent abroad. As entry requirements need advance planning and are subject to change, we recommend you consult a travel agent or Bhutanese embassy for up-to-the-minute details. Also see www.tourism.gov.bt and Lonely Planet's *Bhutan*.

SEA

There are several sea routes between India and surrounding islands but none leave Indian sovereign territory – see p524. There has long been talk of a passenger ferry service between southern India and Colombo in Sri Lanka but this has yet to materialise. Inquire locally to see if there has been any progress.

GETTING AROUND

AIR

South India is well serviced by domestic airlines, with air connections to the major cities as well as dozens of smaller towns. India has a competitive domestic airline industry. Airline seats can be booked directly by telephone, through travel agents, or cheaply over the internet. Domestic airlines set rupee fares for Indian citizens, while foreigners may be charged US-dollar fares (usually payable in rupees).

Reconfirmation is normally only required if your ticket was bought outside India, but it doesn't hurt to call a few days ahead to be safe. Airlines may issue a replacement for lost tickets at their discretion, but refunds are rare. For details of airfare discounts see p499.

Recommended check-in for domestic flights is an hour before departure and hold luggage must be X-rayed and stamped before you check in. Every item of cabin baggage needs a baggage label, which must be stamped as part of the security check (don't forget to collect tags at the check-in counter). Flights to sensitive destinations (eg Kashmir and Ladakh) have extra security restrictions: cabin baggage may be completely prohibited and batteries usually need to be removed from all electronic items and placed in the hold. You may also need to identify your bags on the tarmac before they are loaded on the plane. Officially, photography at airports and from the air is prohibited.

The usual baggage allowance is 20kg (10kg for smaller aircraft) in economy class, 30kg in business.

Airlines in South India

Recent years have witnessed a surge in domestic flights (and resulting price wars) around the country due to industry deregulation. Two well-established players are Air India (of which Indian Airlines is now a part) and Jet Airways. Then there are India's new budget airlines, offering discounted fares on a variety of domestic sectors.

Competition among carriers means that fares frequently change and airlines are constantly adopting all sorts of promotional offers. It's advisable to consult travel agents and the web for up-to-the-minute details about the best fares and routes. One useful site for booking domestic flights online is www.makemytrip.com.

Taxes can add a considerable amount to airfares. At the time of writing, the airlines listed below were operating across various destinations in India – see regional chapters for specifics about routes, fares and booking offices.

Air India (www.airindia.com) India's national carrier (which now includes Indian Airlines) operates many domestic and international flights.

GoAir (www.goair.in) Low-cost carrier.

IndiGo (www.goindigo.in) Another budget airline.

Jagson Airlines (www.jagsonairline.com) Among other destinations, it uses tiny Dornier planes to access small runways in Himachal Pradesh.

Jet Airways (www.jetairways.com) Rated by many as India's best airline, with growing domestic and international services.

JetLite (www.jetlite.com) Jet Airways budget carrier.

Kingfisher Airlines (www.flykingfisher.com) Yep, it's an airline owned by a beer company, offering domestic flights and a few international ones.

Kingfisher Red (www.flykingfisher.com/kingfisher-red.aspx) Kingfisher Airlines low-cost option.

Spicejet (www.spicejet.com) Budget carrier.

BICYCLE

South India offers loads of variety for the cyclist, from pretty coastal routes to winding roads passing fragrant spice plantations and breezy coconut groves.

There are no restrictions on bringing a bicycle into the country, but those sent by sea can take a few weeks to clear customs in India, making it better to fly bikes in. Having said that, it may actually be cheaper – and less of a hassle – to hire or buy a bicycle in India itself. Mountain bikes with off-road tyres give the best protection against India's many potholed and puncture-prone roads. Roadside cycle mechanics abound but you should still bring spare tyres and brake cables, lubricating oil and a chain repair kit, and plenty of puncture repair patches. Bikes can often be carried for free, or for a small luggage fee, on the roof of public buses – handy for uphill stretches. Contact your airline for information about transporting your bike and customs formalities in your home country.

Read up on bicycle touring before you travel – Rob Van Der Plas' *Bicycle Touring Manual* and Stephen Lord's *Adventure Cycle-Touring Handbook* are good places to start. Consult local cycling magazines and cycling clubs for useful information and advice. The **Cycling Federation of India** (www.cyclingfederationof india.org) can provide local information.

Road rules are virtually nonexistent throughout most of India, and cities and national highways can be hazardous places to cycle, so stick to back roads where possible. Be conservative about the distances you expect to cover – an experienced cyclist can manage around 60km to 100km a day on the plains, 40km to 60km on sealed mountain roads and 40km or less on dirt roads.

Hire

Tourist centres and other places where travellers congregate are the easiest spots to find bicycles for hire – simply inquire locally. Prices vary, with most places charging anywhere between Rs30 and Rs80 per day for a roadworthy, Indian-made bicycle (mountain bikes, where available, are usually upwards of Rs350 per day). Hire places may require a cash security deposit (avoid leaving your airline ticket or passport).

Purchase

Mountain bikes from reputable brands that include **Hero** (www.herocycles.com) and **Atlas** (www .atlascyclesonepat.com) generally start at around Rs3000. Reselling is usually fairly easy – ask at local cycle or hire shops or put up an advert on travel noticeboards. You should be able to get around 50% back of what you originally paid if it was a new bike and is still in reasonably good condition.

BOAT

Scheduled ferries connect mainland India to Port Blair in the Andaman Islands (see p478). The trip takes around 60 hours from Chennai (see p405) or around 56 hours from Kolkata. There are also sporadic ferries from Visakhapatnam (Andhra Pradesh) to the Andaman Islands (p314).

Between October and May, there are boat services from Kochi (Cochin; Kerala) to the Lakshadweep Islands (see p386).

There are also numerous shorter ferry services across rivers, from chain pontoons to wicker coracles, and various boat cruises – see the regional chapters and the Activities chapter for more information.

BUS

Bus travel in South India is comprehensive, inexpensive and effectively fills the gaps not served by trains (trains are preferable for long-distance journeys). Services are fast and frequent, and buses are the only way to get around many mountainous areas. However, roads in curvaceous terrain can be especially perilous, buses are often driven with wilful abandon and accidents are always a risk. Avoid night buses unless there's no alternative, as driving conditions are more hazardous and drivers may also be suffering from lack of sleep. All buses make snack and toilet stops (some more frequently than others), providing a break from the rattle and shake but possibly adding hours to journey times.

Buses run by the state government bus companies are usually the most reliable option (if there's a breakdown, another bus will be sent to pick up passengers), and seats can usually be booked up to a month in advance. Private buses tend to be either more expensive (but with greater comfort) or, cheaper, but drivers can be notorious speed-demons and conductors tend to cram as many passengers on as possible to maximise profits. On top of that, there's usually no backup plan for private buses – if your bus breaks down, you may be waiting for an awfully long time. Earplugs are a boon on all long-distance buses to muffle the often deafening music. On any bus, try to sit between the axles to minimise the bumpy effect of potholes.

Luggage is either stored in compartments underneath the bus (sometimes for a small fee) or it can be carried on the roof (arrive at least an hour ahead of the departure time, as some buses cover the roof-stored bags with a large sheet of canvas, making it inconvenient/impossible for last-minute additions). If your bags go on the roof, make sure they're securely locked and tied to the metal baggage rack – some unlucky travellers have seen their belongings go bouncing off the roof on bumpy roads! Theft is a minor risk so keep an eye on your bags at snack and toilet stops and *never* leave your day pack or valuables unattended inside the bus.

Classes

Both state and private companies offer 'ordinary' buses – ageing rattletraps, often with wonky windows that blast in dust – or more expensive 'deluxe' buses, which range from less decrepit versions of ordinary buses to flashy Volvo tour buses with AC and reclining two-by-two seating. Travel agents in many tourist towns offer relatively expensive private two-by-two buses, which tend to leave and terminate at conveniently central stops. Be warned that agents have been known to book people onto ordinary buses at superdeluxe prices. If possible book directly with the bus company – many state tourist offices run their own reliable deluxe bus services. Timetables and destinations may be displayed on signs or billboards at travel agencies and tourist offices.

Costs

The cheapest buses are 'ordinary' government buses but prices vary from state to state (consult regional chapters). Add around 50% to the ordinary fare for deluxe services, double the deluxe fare for AC, and triple or quadruple the fare for a two-by-two service.

Reservations

Most deluxe buses can be booked in advance – usually up to a month in advance for government buses – at the bus station or local travel agents. Reservations are rarely possible on 'ordinary' buses and travellers often get left behind in the mad rush for a seat. To maximise your chances of securing a seat, either send a travelling companion ahead to grab some space, or pass a book or article of clothing through an open window and place it on an empty seat. This 'reservation' method rarely fails. If you board a bus midway through its journey, you'll often have to stand until a seat becomes free.

At many bus stations there's a separate women's queue, although this isn't always obvious as signs are often in Hindi and men frequently join the melee. Women have an unspoken right to elbow their way to the front of any bus queue in India, so don't be shy, ladies!

CAR

Few travellers to India bother with self-drive car rental not only because of the challenging driving conditions, but also because hiring a car with driver is wonderfully affordable, particularly if several people share the cost. Seatbelts are either non-existent or of variable quality where they exist.

Hiring a Car & Driver

Hiring a car with driver is an excellent way to see several places in one day, and the cost slides if you find other travellers to split the fare. Most towns have taxi stands or car-hire companies where you can arrange short or long tours (see regional chapters).

Be aware that not all hire cars are licensed to travel beyond their home state. Even those vehicles that are licensed to enter different states have to pay extra (often hefty) state taxes, which will add to the rental charge – confirm the amount when booking so you don't get a nasty surprise later!

Ask for a driver who speaks some English and knows the region you intend visiting. Try to see the car and meet the driver before paying any money. For multi-day trips, the charge should cover the driver's meals and accommodation. Drivers should make their own sleeping and eating arrangements.

Finally, it's *essential* to set the ground rules from day one. Many travellers have complained of having their holiday marred by their driver. To avoid anguish later, respectfully but firmly let the driver know from the outset that you're the boss.

COSTS

The cost of charter trips depends on the distance and the terrain (driving on mountain roads uses more petrol, hence the higher cost). One-way trips usually cost the same as return ones (to cover the petrol and driver charges for getting back to base). Petrol should be included in the quoted price.

Hire charges vary from state to state. Some taxi unions set a time limit or a maximum kilometre distance for day trips – if you go over, you'll have to pay extra. To avoid potential misunderstandings later, ensure you get *in writing* what you've been promised (quotes should include petrol, sightseeing stops, all your chosen destinations, and meals and accommodation for the driver). If a driver asks you for money to pay for petrol en route because he is short of cash, get receipts so you can be reimbursed later.

For sightseeing day trips around a single city, expect to pay anywhere upwards of Rs700/800 for a non-AC/AC car with an eight-hour, 80km limit per day (extra charges apply beyond this).

A tip is customary at the end of your journey; Rs125 per day is fair (more if you're really pleased with the driver's service).

Self-Drive Hire

Self-drive car hire is possible in South India's larger cities, but given the hair-raising driving conditions most travellers opt for a car with driver. International rental companies with representatives in India include **Budget** (www.budget.com) and **Hertz** (www.hertz.com); you'll need an international driver's permit and your domestic licence.

HITCHING

Hitching is not much of an option in South India, as the concept of a 'free ride' – considering the inexpensive public transport options available – is relatively unknown.

Travellers who decide to hitch should understand that they are taking a small but potentially serious risk. As anywhere, women are strongly advised against hitching alone or even as a pair. Always use your instincts.

LOCAL TRANSPORT

Buses, cycle-rickshaws, autorickshaws, taxis, boats and urban trains provide transport throughout South India. On any form of transport without a fixed fare, agree on the price *before* you start your journey and make sure that it covers your luggage and every passenger. If you don't, you're likely to en-

counter a heated altercation when you get to your destination. Even where local transport is metered, drivers may refuse to use the meter, demanding an elevated 'fixed' fare. If this happens, insist on the meter and if that fails, find another vehicle.

Costs for public transport vary from town to town (consult regional chapters). Fares usually increase at night (by up to 100%) and some drivers charge a few rupees extra for luggage. Carry plenty of small bills for taxi and rickshaw fares as drivers rarely have change.

Many taxi/autorickshaw drivers are involved in the commission racket – for more information read p498.

Autorickshaw, Tempo & Vikram

The Indian autorickshaw is basically a three-wheeled motorised contraption with a tin or canvas roof and sides, providing room for two passengers (although you'll often see many more bodies than that squeezed in) and limited luggage. You may also hear autorickshaws being referred to as autos, scooters, riks or tuk-tuks. Autorickshaws are mostly cheaper than taxis and are usually metered, although getting the driver to turn the meter on can be a challenge.

Travelling by auto is great fun, but the clunky two-stroke engines can be smelly and noisy, and the open windows allow blasts of air in – which can be a boon or a curse, depending on the ambient temperature and the level of pollution outside.

Tempos and *vikrams* are basically outsized autorickshaws with room for more passengers, running on fixed routes for a fixed fare. In country areas, you may also see the fearsome-looking 'three-wheeler' – a crude, tractor-like tempo with a front wheel on an articulated arm.

Boat

Various kinds of local boats offer transport across and down rivers in South India, from big car ferries to wooden canoes and wicker coracles – see regional chapters for details. Most of the larger boats carry bicycles and motorcycles for a fee. Kerala is especially renowned for its breathtaking backwater boat cruises (see the boxed text, p346).

Bus

Urban buses, particularly in the big cities, are fume-belching, human-stuffed, mechanical monsters that travel at breakneck speed (except during morning and evening rush hours, when they can be endlessly stuck in traffic). It's usually far more convenient and comfortable to opt for an autorickshaw or taxi.

Cycle-Rickshaw

Cycle-rickshaws are becoming scarce in South India these days, but you'll still find them in some cities, such as Puducherry (Pondicherry). A cycle-rickshaw is a pedal cycle with two rear wheels, supporting a bench seat for passengers. Most have a canopy that can be raised in wet weather, or lowered to provide extra space for luggage. Most of the big cities have phased out (or reduced) the number of cycle-rickshaws, but they are still a major means of local transport in many smaller towns. Fares must be agreed upon in advance – it's a good idea to speak to locals to get an idea of what a fair price is for the distance you intend travelling. Tips are always appreciated given the slog involved.

Taxi

Most South Indian cities and towns have taxis, and these are usually metered. However, getting drivers to use the meter can be a major hassle. Drivers often claim that the meter is broken and proceed to request a hugely elevated 'fixed' fare instead. Threatening to get another taxi will often miraculously fix the meter. In tourist areas especially, some taxis flatly refuse to use the meter – if this happens, just find another cab. To avoid fare-setting shenanigans, use prepaid taxis where possible (regional chapters contain details).

Getting a metered ride is only half the battle. Meters are almost always outdated, so fares are calculated using a combination

---

PREPAID TAXIS

Most Indian airports and many train stations have a prepaid-taxi booth, normally just outside the terminal building. Here, you can book a taxi for a fixed price (which will include baggage) and thus avoid commission scams. However, officials advise to hold onto the payment coupon until you reach your chosen destination, in case the driver has any other ideas! Smaller airports and stations may have prepaid autorickshaw booths instead.

---

of the meter reading and a complicated 'fare adjustment card'. Predictably, this system is open to abuse. If you spend a few days in any town, you'll soon get a feel for the difference between a reasonable fare and a blatant rip-off. Be aware that many taxi drivers supplement their earnings with commissions – see p498.

Other Local Transport

In some towns, tongas (horse-drawn two-wheelers) and *victorias* (horse-drawn carriages) still operate. Mumbai and Chennai, among other centres, have suburban trains that leave from ordinary train stations. See regional chapters for further details.

MOTORCYCLE

In terms of motorcycles as public transport, Goa is the only place in South India where they are a licensed form of conveyance. They take one person on the back and are a quick, inexpensive way to cover short distances.

Despite the traffic challenges, India is an amazing country for long-distance motorcycle touring. Motorcycles generally handle the pitted roads better than four-wheeled vehicles, and you'll have the added bonus of being able to stop when and where you want. However, motorcycle touring can be quite an undertaking – there are some popular motorcycle tours (see p528) for those who don't want the rigmarole of going it alone.

The classic way to motorcycle round India is on an Enfield Bullet, still built to the original 1940s specifications. As well as making a satisfying chugging sound, these bikes are fully manual, making them easy to repair (parts can be found almost everywhere in India). On the other hand, Enfields are often less reliable than many of the newer, Japanese-designed bikes.

Weather is an important factor to consider – for the best times to visit different areas see the Fast Facts boxes at the start of regional chapters. To cross from neighbouring countries, check the latest regulations and paperwork requirements from the relevant diplomatic mission.

Driving Licence

To hire a motorcycle in India, you're technically required to have a valid international drivers' permit in addition to your domestic licence. In tourist areas, some places may rent out a motorcycle without asking for a driving permit/licence, but you won't be covered by insurance in the event of an accident, and may also face a monetary fine.

Fuel & Spare Parts

Spare parts for Indian and Japanese machines are widely available in South Indian cities and towns. If you intend to travel to remote regions, ensure you carry enough extra fuel (seek local advice about fuel availability before setting off). At the time of writing, petrol cost around Rs56 per litre. If you're going to remote regions it's also important to carry basic spares (valves, fuel lines, piston rings etc).

For all machines (particularly older ones), make sure you regularly check and tighten all nuts and bolts, as Indian roads and engine vibration tend to work things loose quite quickly. Check the engine and gearbox oil level regularly (at least every 500km) and clean the oil filter every few thousand kilometres. Given the road conditions, the chances are you'll make at least a couple of visits to a puncture-wallah – start your trip with new tyres and carry spanners to remove your own wheels.

Hire

If you are planning an independent trip, motorcycles can be rented throughout South India, with tourist magnets, such as Goa, having the widest options (see also p191).

Japanese and Indian-made bikes in the 100cc to 150cc range are cheaper than the big 350cc to 500cc Enfields. As a deposit, you'll need to leave a large cash lump sum (ensure you get a receipt that also stipulates the refundable amount), your passport, or air-ticket; it's strongly advisable to avoid leaving your air-ticket and passport, the latter of which you'll need to check in at hotels and which the police can demand to see at any time. A standard 500cc Enfield costs around Rs17,000, a European-style is Rs22,000 and a 350cc costs Rs15,000 for three weeks. See the regional chapters for recommended rental companies.

Insurance

Only hire a bike with third-party insurance – if you hit someone without insurance, the consequences can be very costly. Reputable companies will include third-party cover in their policies. Those that don't probably aren't reputable.

You must also arrange insurance if you buy a motorcycle (usually you can organise this through the person selling the bike). The minimum level of cover is third-party insurance – available for Rs400 to Rs500 per year. This will cover repair and medical costs for any other vehicles, people or property you might hit, but no cover for your own machine. Comprehensive insurance (recommended) costs upwards of Rs500 per year.

Organised Motorcycle Tours

Dozens of companies offer organised motorcycle tours with a support vehicle, mechanic and guide. Below are some reputable outfits (see websites for details) offering tours within and/or beyond South India:

Blazing Trails (www.blazingtrailstours.com)
Classic Bike Adventure (www.classic-bike-india.com)
Ferris Wheels (www.ferriswheels.com.au)
H-C Travel (www.hctravel.com)
Himalayan Roadrunners (www.ridehigh.com)
Indian Motorcycle Adventures (http://homepages.ihug.co.nz/~gumby)
Lalli Singh Tours (www.lallisingh.com)
Moto Discovery (www.motodiscovery.com)
Royal Expeditions (www.royalexpeditions.com)
Saffron Road Motorcycle Tours (www.saffronroad.com)
Shepherds Realms (www.asiasafari.com)
Wheel of India (www.wheelofindia.com)

Purchase

If you are planning a longer tour while in South India, consider purchasing a motorcycle. Second-hand bikes are widely available and the paperwork is a lot easier than buying a new machine. Finding a second-hand motorcycle is a matter of asking around. Check travellers' noticeboards and approach local motorcycle mechanics and other bikers. Because of the number of bikes and the fact that locals are accustomed to foreigners, Goa is the best place in South India to start your search.

A decent firm in Mumbai is **Allibhai Premji Tyrewalla** (☎ 022-23099313; www.premjis.com; 205 Dr D Bhadkamkar (Lamington) Rd; Mumbai), which sells new and second-hand motorcycles with a buy-back option.

Real enthusiasts should check out the Enfield Factory in Chennai (see the boxed text on p398).

COSTS

A well-looked-after, second-hand 350cc Enfield will cost anywhere from Rs18,000 to

ROAD DISTANCES (KM)

	Bengaluru (Bangalore)	Chennai (Madras)	Mumbai (Bombay)	Panaji (Panjim)	Thiruvananthapuram (Trivandrum)
Bengaluru (Bangalore)	---				
Chennai (Madras)	337	---			
Mumbai (Bombay)	995	1332	---		
Panaji (Panjim)	576	913	540	---	
Thiruvananthapuram (Trivandrum)	635	716	1526	986	---

Rs40,000, while a more modern version, with European-style configuration, costs Rs40,000 to Rs50,000; the 500cc model is Rs45,000 to Rs75,000. A useful website for Enfield models is www.royalenfield.com.

It's advisable to get any second-hand bike serviced before you set off. When re-selling your bike, expect to get between half and two-thirds of the price you paid if the bike is still in reasonable condition. Shipping an Indian bike overseas is complicated and expensive – ask the shop you bought the bike from to explain the process.

As well as the cost of the bike, you'll have to pay for insurance – see opposite. Helmets are available for Rs500 to Rs2000, and extras like panniers, luggage racks, protection bars, rear-view mirrors, lockable fuel caps, petrol filters and extra tools are easy to come by. One useful extra is a customised fuel tank, which will increase the range you can cover between fuel stops. An Enfield 500cc gives about 25km/L: the 350cc model gives slightly more.

OWNERSHIP PAPERS

There's plenty of paperwork associated with owning a motorcycle. The registration papers are signed by the local registration authority when the bike is first sold and you'll need these papers when you buy a second-hand bike. Foreign nationals cannot change the name on the registration. Instead, you must fill out the forms for a change of ownership and transfer of insurance. If you buy a new bike, the company selling it must register the machine for you, adding to the cost.

For any bike, the registration must be renewed every 15 years (for around Rs5000) and you must make absolutely sure that it states the 'fitness' of the vehicle, and that there are no outstanding debts or criminal proceedings associated with the bike. The whole process is complicated and it makes sense to seek advice from the company selling the bike. Allow around two weeks to tackle the paperwork and get on the road.

Road Conditions

Given the varied road conditions, India can be challenging for novice riders. Hazards range from cows and chickens crossing the carriageway to broken-down trucks, pedestrians on the road, and perpetual potholes and unmarked speed humps. Rural roads sometimes have grain crops strewn across them to be threshed by passing vehicles – a serious sliding hazard for bikers.

Try not to cover too much territory in one day and avoid travelling after dark – many vehicles drive without lights, and dynamo-powered motorcycle headlamps are useless at low revs while negotiating around potholes. On busy national highways expect to average 50km/h without stops; on winding back roads and dirt tracks this can drop to 10km/h.

For long hauls, transporting your bike by train can be a convenient option. Buy a standard train ticket for the journey then take your bike to the station parcel office with your passport, registration papers, driver's licence and insurance documents. Packing-wallahs will wrap your bike in protective sacking for around Rs150 to Rs250 and you must fill out various forms and pay the shipping fee – around Rs2000 to Rs3500 – plus an insurance fee of 1% of the declared value of the bike. Bring the same paperwork to collect your bike from the goods office at the far end. If the bike is left waiting at the destination for more than 24 hours, you'll pay a storage fee of around Rs50 to Rs100 per day.

Road Rules

Traffic in India is officially required to stick to the left but, in reality, most people drive all over the road – stay alert! Observe local speed limits (these vary from state to state) and give way to any larger vehicles.

TRANSPORT

TRANSPORT

SHARE JEEPS

In mountain areas, such as those around Aurangabad in Maharashtra, share jeeps supplement the bus service, charging similar fixed fares. Although nominally designed for five to six passengers, most share jeeps squeeze in many more people. Jeeps run from jeep stands and 'passenger stations' at the junctions of major roads; ask locals for directions. See this book's regional chapters for routes and fares. In some states, jeeps are known as 'sumos' after the Tata Sumo, a popular 4WD.

TOURS

Tours are available all over South India, run by tourist offices, local transport companies and travel agencies. Organised tours can be an inexpensive way to see several places on one trip, although you rarely get much time at each place. If you arrange a tour through the local taxi office (or any reputable car-hire outfit), you'll have more freedom about where you go and how long you stay (also see p525).

Drivers often double as guides, or you can hire a qualified local guide for a fee. However, be wary of (often ill-informed and pushy) touts claiming to be professional guides in tourist towns. Ask the local tourist office about recommended (approved) guides and ask to see evidence from guides who claim to be accredited.

See the Tours sections in the regional chapters of this book for details about local tours. For more information about treks and tours, read the Activities chapter (p100).

International Tour Agencies

Many international companies offer tours to India, from straightforward sightseeing trips to adventure tours and activity-based holidays. To find current tours that match your interests, quiz travel agents and surf the web. Some good places to start your tour hunt include the following:

Dragoman (www.dragoman.com) One of several reputable overland tour companies offering trips on customised vehicles.

Exodus (www.exodustravels.co.uk) A wide array of specialist trips, including tours with a holistic, wildlife and adventure focus.

India Wildlife Tours (www.india-wildlife-tours.com) All sorts of wildlife tours, plus jeep/horse/camel safaris and birdwatching.

Indian Encounter (www.indianencounters.com) Special-interest tours that include wildlife-spotting, trekking, river-rafting and ayurvedic treatments.

Intrepid Travel (www.intrepidtravel.com) Appealing possibilities, from wildlife tours to sacred rambles.

Peregrine Adventures (www.peregrine.net.au) Popular cultural and trekking tours.

Sacred India Tours (www.sacredindia.com) Includes tours with a holistic focus such as yoga and ayurveda, as well as architectural and cultural tours.

World Expeditions (www.worldexpeditions.com.au) An array of options that include trekking and cycling tours.

TRAIN

Travelling by train is a terrific way to traverse India. Trains offer a smoother ride than buses, and are especially recommended for long journeys that include overnight travel. India's rail network is one of the world's most extensive, prices are reasonable, and the experience of travelling on an Indian train is a reason to travel all by itself.

An estimated 18–20 million people travel by train in India *every day* and Indian Railways is the largest utility employer on Earth, with roughly 1.5 million workers. There are around 6900 train stations scattered across India.

At first, the process of booking a seat can seem bewildering, but behind the scenes things are astonishingly well organised – see Reservations (p532) for tips on buying a ticket. Some cities also have suburban train networks, although these can get very crowded during peak hours.

TOP TRAIN JOURNEYS

If you have a passion for train travel, don't miss these…

■ Mountain Railway – the miniature steam train from Mettupalayam to Ooty (Udhagamandalam) climbs up through the stunning Nilgiri Hills (p470)

■ Konkan Railway – the trip from Mumbai (Bombay) to Goa passes between the scenic coast and the Western Ghats (see p190)

■ Matheran Toy Train – a miniature diesel train running from Neral (north of Mumbai) to the hill station of Matheran (p170)

■ Visakhapatnam to the Araku Valley through the Eastern Ghats – a superb ride from the coast through the rugged Eastern Ghats to the tribal communities in Araku Valley (p315)

Train services to certain destinations are often increased during major festivals, but almost every year people tragically get crushed to death in stampedes on overcrowded platforms. Something else to be mindful of is passenger drugging and theft – see p498. Be aware that train trips can be delayed at any time of the journey, making it wise to factor in some leeway to your travel plans to avoid stress.

We've listed useful trains throughout this book but there are hundreds more services. The best way of sourcing updated railway information is to use relevant internet sites such as **Indian Railways** (www.indianrail.gov.in) and the useful www.seat61.com/India.htm. There's also *Trains at a Glance* (Rs35), available at many train-station bookstands and better bookshops/newsstands, but it's published annually so not as up-to-date as websites. Nevertheless, it offers comprehensive timetables covering all the main lines.

Big stations often have English-speaking staff who can help with choosing the best train. At smaller stations, mid-level officials such as the deputy station master usually speak English. It's also worth approaching tourist-office staff if you need advice about booking tickets, deciding train classes etc. The nationwide railways inquiries number is ☎ 139.

Classes

Trains and seats come in a variety of classes. Express and mail trains usually have general (2nd class) compartments with unreserved seating – usually a real free-for-all – and a series of more comfortable compartments that you can reserve. On day trains, there may be a chair-car with padded reclining seats and (usually) AC, or an executive chair car, with better seats and more space.

For overnight trips, you have several choices. 'Sleeper' berths are arranged in groups of six, with two roomier berths across the aisle, in air-cooled carriages. Air-conditioned carriages have either three-tier AC (3AC) berths, in the same configuration as sleepers, or two-tier AC (2AC) berths in groups of four on either side of the aisle. Some trains also have flashier 1st-class AC (1AC) berths, with a choice of two- or four-berth compartments with locking doors.

Bedding is provided in all AC sleeping compartments and there is usually a meal service, plus regular visits from the coffee- and chai-wallah. In sleeper class, bring your own bedding (a warm Indian shawl is perfect for the job). In all sleeping compartments, the lower berths convert to seats for daytime use. If you'd rather sleep, book an upper berth. Note that there is usually a locked door be-

TRANSPORT

RAILWAY RAZZLE DAZZLE

If you're seeking a luxurious way of seeing parts of South India, the following rail journeys should tickle your fancy. Fares usually include accommodation on board, tours, admission fees and all or most meals, and there are normally child concessions – inquire when booking.

In Maharashtra, the *Deccan Odyssey* offers seven nights of luxury covering the main tourist spots of Maharashtra and Goa. The train leaves from Mumbai, heading south through the resorts and fort towns of the Konkan Coast to Goa, then looping inland to Pune, Aurangabad (for Ellora), Jalgaon (for Ajanta) and Nasik. From October to March, fares per person per night start at US$540/390/320 for single/double/triple occupancy (US$415/320/260 in September and April). You can do the trip for a minimum of three days; the seven-day package costs an extra US$100 for guided tours of Mumbai and Goa. Make reservations through Mumbai's **Maharashtra Tourism Development Corporation** (MTDC; ☎ 022-22845678; www.maharashtratourism.gov.in; Madame Cama Rd, Nariman Point, Mumbai).

The **Golden Chariot** (www.thegoldenchariot.co.in) takes visitors through Karnataka (with a brief stop in Goa) in style. Three different tour packages are available: Bengaluru–Bengaluru (Monday to Monday); Bengaluru–Goa (Monday to Sunday); and Goa–Goa (Sunday to Sunday): all of them visit Karnataka's major sights including Bengaluru, Mysore, Belur, Halebid, Kabini, Hampi and Badami, with a pit stop in Goa. It runs throughout the year. Rates per person per night start at single/double/tripleRs15,800/11,800/9600(ApriltoAugust)andRs19,400/14,000/11,400(September to March). Bookings can be made online or at the **Karnataka State Tourism Development Corporation (KSTDC)** Badami House (☎ 080-22275883; Badami House, Kasturba Rd); Karnataka Tourism House (☎ 080-41329211; Karnataka Tourism House, 8 Papanna Lane, St Mark's Rd) offices in Bengaluru.

tween the reserved and unreserved carriages – if you get trapped on the wrong side, you'll have to wait until the next station to change.

There are also special train services connecting major cities. *Shatabdi* express trains are same-day services with seating only, in AC executive chair and AC chair cars. Both classes are comfortable, but the tinted-glass windows can cut down the views a fair bit. The clearest views are from the barred but unglazed windows of non-AC sleeper and general carriages.

Rajdhani express trains are long-distance overnight services between Delhi and state capitals, with a choice of 1AC, 2AC, 3AC and 2nd class. Reserved tickets on both *Shatabdi* and *Rajdhani* trains are a bit more expensive but fares include meals. Prices of all tickets reflect the level of comfort – see the Costs section, below. In all classes, a padlock and a length of chain are useful for securing your luggage to the baggage racks.

For a very helpful description of the various train classes (including pictures) see www.seat61.com/India.htm#classes.

Costs

Fares are calculated by distance and class of travel – as shown in the boxed text, below. *Rajdhani* and *Shatabdi* trains are slightly more expensive, but the price includes meals. Most air-conditioned carriages have a catering service (meals are brought to your seat). In unreserved classes it's a good idea to carry portable snacks. Seniors can avail of discounted train tickets – see p499.

To find out which trains travel between any two destinations, go to www.trainenquiry.com and click on 'Find Your Train' – type in the name of the two destinations (you may then be prompted to choose from a list of stations) and you'll get a list of every train (with the name, number and arrival/departure times). Then,

armed with these details, you can find the fare for your chosen train by going to www.indianrail.gov.in and clicking on 'Fare Enquiry'.

Major stations offer 'retiring rooms', which can be handy if you have a valid ongoing ticket or Indrail Pass – see p493. Another useful facility is the left-luggage office (cloakroom), where locked bags (only) can be stored for a small daily fee if you have a valid train ticket. For peace of mind, chain your bag to the baggage rack and check the opening times to make sure you can get your bag back when you need it.

Reservations

No reservations are required for general (2nd class) compartments. You can reserve seats in all chair-car, sleeper, and 1AC, 2AC and 3AC carriages up to 60 days in advance at any station with a computerised booking system. Advance bookings are strongly recommended for all overnight journeys.

The reservation procedure is reasonably straightforward – obtain a reservation slip from the information window and fill in the name of the departure station, the destination station, the class you want to travel in and the name and number of the train (this is where *Trains at a Glance* comes into its own, or see the Costs section, left, for how to get the required details on the net). You then join the long queue to the ticket window, where your ticket will be printed. Women should avail of the separate women's queue – if there isn't one, go to the front of the regular queue.

In larger cities, there are dedicated ticket windows for foreigners and credit-card payments. Elsewhere, you'll have to join a general queue and pay in rupees, cash. A special tourist quota is set aside for foreign tourists travelling between popular stations. These seats can only be booked at dedicated reservation offices in major cities (details are given in

EXPRESS TRAIN FARES IN RUPEES

Distance (km)	1AC	2AC	3AC	Chair car (CC)	Sleeper (SL)	Second (II)
100	542	322	158	122	56	35
200	794	430	256	199	91	57
300	1081	556	348	271	124	78
400	1347	693	433	337	154	97
500	1613	830	519	404	185	116
1000	2628	1352	845	657	301	188
1500	3328	1712	1070	832	381	238
2000	4028	2072	1295	1007	461	288

this book's regional chapters), and you need to show your passport and visa as ID. The government has fairly recently changed the rules, allowing foreigners to pay for tourist quota seats in rupees, British pounds, US dollars or euros, in cash or Thomas Cook and American Express travellers cheques (change is given in rupees). However, quite a few offices still ask to see foreign exchange certificates before accepting payment in rupees.

Trains are frequently overbooked, but many passengers cancel. You can buy a ticket on the 'wait list' and try your luck. A refund is available if you fail to get a seat – ask the ticket office about your chances. Refunds are available on any ticket, even after departure, with a penalty – the rules are complicated so check when you book.

If you don't want to go through the hassle of buying a ticket yourself, many travel agencies and hotels will purchase your train ticket for a commission, although beware of ticket scams (eg being sold a cheaper class than requested, at a higher class fare).

Internet bookings are also possible on the website www.irctc.co.in, and you can choose an e-ticket, or have the ticket sent to you within India by courier. The website www.seat61 .com/India.htm has some excellent advice on online bookings – scroll down to the 'How to buy tickets – from outside India' heading.

Reserved tickets show your seat/berth number (or wait-list number) and the carriage number. When the train pulls in, keep an eye out for your carriage number written on the side of the train (station staff can point you in the right direction if you get confused). A list of names and berths is also posted on the side of each reserved carriage – a beacon of light for panicking travellers!

It's wise to book well ahead if you plan on travelling during Indian holidays or festivals, when seats can fill up incredibly fast.

Train Passes

The Indrail Pass permits unlimited rail travel for the period of its validity, but it offers limited savings and you must still make reservations. Passes are available for one to 90 days of travel and you can book through certain overseas travel agents, or station ticket offices in major Indian cities – click on the Information/International Tourist link on www.indianrail.gov.in for further details, including prices. There's no refund for either lost or partially used tickets.

TRANSPORT

Health

CONTENTS

There is huge geographical variation in India, from tropical beaches to soaring mountains. Environmental issues such as heat and altitude can cause significant health problems. Hygiene is generally poor in most parts of India so food and water-borne illnesses are common. Many insect-borne diseases are present, particularly in tropical regions. Medical care is basic in many areas (especially beyond cities) so it's essential to be well prepared before you travel.

Travellers tend to worry about contracting infectious diseases when in the tropics, but these rarely cause serious illness or death in travellers. Pre-existing medical conditions and accidental injury (especially traffic accidents) account for most life-threatening problems. Becoming ill in some way, however, is very common. Fortunately most travellers' illnesses can be prevented with some common sense behaviour or treated with a well-stocked traveller's medical kit – however, never hesitate to consult a doctor while on the road, as self-diagnosis can be hazardous.

The following advice is a general guide only and certainly does not replace the advice of a doctor trained in travel medicine.

BEFORE YOU GO

Pack medications in their original, clearly labelled containers. A signed and dated letter from your physician describing your medical conditions and medications, including generic names, is very useful. If carrying syringes or needles, be sure to have a physician's letter documenting their medical necessity. If you have a heart condition, bring a copy of your ECG taken just prior to travelling.

If you take any regular medication, bring double your ordinary needs in case of loss or theft. You'll be able to buy quite a few medications over the counter in India without a doctor's prescription, but it can be difficult to find some of the newer drugs, particularly the latest antidepressant drugs, blood-pressure medications and contraceptive pills.

INSURANCE

Even if you are fit and healthy, do not travel without health insurance – accidents do happen. Declare any existing medical conditions you have – the insurance company will check if your problem is pre-existing and will not cover you if it is undeclared. You may require extra cover for adventure activities such as rock climbing and scuba diving. If your health insurance doesn't cover you for medical expenses abroad, you should consider getting extra insurance. Keep in mind that if you are uninsured emergency evacuation is expensive; bills of over US$100,000 are not uncommon.

It's a good idea to find out in advance if your insurance plan will make payments directly to providers or if it will reimburse you later for overseas health expenditures (in India, doctors usually expect immediate payment in cash). Some policies offer lower and higher medical-expense options; the higher ones are chiefly for countries that have extremely high medical costs, such as the USA. You may prefer a policy that pays doctors or hospitals directly rather than you having to pay on the spot and claim from your insurance company later. However, be aware that most medical facilities in India require immediate payment. If you do have to claim later, make sure you keep all relevant documentation. Some policies ask that you telephone back (reverse charges) to a centre in your home country where an immediate assessment of your problem will be made.

MEDICAL CHECKLIST

Recommended items for a personal medical kit:

- Antifungal cream, eg Clotrimazole
- Antibacterial cream, eg Muciprocin
- Antibiotic for skin infections, eg Amoxicillin/Clavulanate or Cephalexin
- Antihistamine – there are many options, eg Cetrizine for daytime and Promethazine for night
- Antiseptic, eg Betadine
- Antispasmodic for stomach cramps, eg Buscopam
- Contraceptive method
- Decongestant, eg Pseudoephedrine
- DEET-based insect repellent
- Diarrhoea medication – consider an oral rehydration solution (eg Gastrolyte), diarrhoea 'stopper' (eg Loperamide) and antinausea medication (eg Prochlorperazine). Antibiotics for diarrhoea include Norfloxacin or Ciprofloxacin; for bacterial diarrhoea Azithromycin; for Giardia or amoebic dysentery Tinidazole.
- First-aid items such as scissors, elastoplasts, bandages, gauze, thermometer (but not mercury), sterile needles and syringes, safety pins and tweezers
- Ibuprofen or another anti-inflammatory
- Indigestion tablets, eg Quick Eze or Mylanta
- Iodine tablets (unless you are pregnant or have a thyroid problem) to purify water
- Laxative, eg Coloxyl
- Migraine medication if you suffer from them
- Paracetamol
- Pyrethrin to impregnate clothing and mosquito nets
- Steroid cream for allergic/itchy rashes, eg 1% to 2% hydrocortisone
- High-factor sunscreen and wide-brimmed hat
- Throat lozenges
- Thrush (vaginal yeast infection) treatment, eg Clotrimazole pessaries or Diflucan tablet
- Ural or equivalent if prone to urine infections

VACCINATIONS

Specialised travel-medicine clinics are your best source of up-to-date information; they stock all available vaccines and will be able to give specific recommendations for you and your trip. The doctors will take into account factors such as past vaccination history, the length of your trip, activities you may be undertaking and underlying medical conditions, such as pregnancy.

Most vaccines don't give immunity until *at least* two weeks after they're given, so visit a doctor well ahead of departure. Ask your doctor for an International Certificate of Vaccination (otherwise known as the 'yellow booklet'), which will list all the vaccinations you've received.

Recommended Vaccinations

The World Health Organization (WHO) recommends these vaccinations for travellers to India (as well as being up to date with measles, mumps and rubella vaccinations):

Adult diphtheria and tetanus Single booster recommended if none in the previous 10 years. Side effects include sore arm and fever.

Hepatitis A This vaccination provides almost 100% protection for up to a year; a booster after 12 months provides at least another 20 years' protection. There are mild side effects such as a headache and sore arm which occur in 5% to 10% of people.

Hepatitis B Now considered routine for most travellers. Given as three shots over six months. A rapid schedule is also available, as is a combined vaccination with Hepatitis A. Side effects are mild and uncommon, usually headache and sore arm. In 95% of people lifetime protection results.

Polio Only one booster is required as an adult for lifetime protection. Inactivated polio vaccine is safe during pregnancy.

Typhoid Recommended for all travellers to India, even those only visiting urban areas. The vaccine offers around 70% protection, lasts for two to three years and comes as a single shot. Tablets are also available, however, the injection is usually recommended as it has fewer side effects. Sore arm and fever may occur.

Varicella If you haven't had chickenpox, discuss this vaccination with your doctor.

These immunisations are recommended for long-term travellers (more than one month) or those at special risk (seek further advice from your doctor):

Japanese B Encephalitis Three injections in all. Booster recommended after two years. Sore arm and headache are the most common side effects. Rarely, an allergic reaction comprising hives and swelling can occur up to 10 days after any of the three doses.

Meningitis Single injection. There are two types of vaccination: the quadravalent vaccine gives two to three years' protection; meningitis group C vaccine gives around 10 years' protection. Recommended for long-term backpackers aged under 25.

Rabies Three injections in all. A booster after one year will then provide 10 years' protection. Side effects are rare – occasionally headache and sore arm.

Tuberculosis (TB) A complex issue. Adult long-term travellers are usually recommended to have a TB skin test before and after travel, rather than vaccination. Only one vaccine given in a lifetime.

Required Vaccinations

The only vaccine required by international regulations is yellow fever. Proof of vaccination will only be required if you have visited a country in the yellow-fever zone within the six days prior to entering India. If you're travelling to India from Africa or South America, check to see if you require proof of vaccination.

INTERNET RESOURCES

There is a wealth of travel health advice on the internet – www.lonelyplanet.com is a good place to start. Some other suggestions:

Centers for Disease Control and Prevention (CDC; www.cdc.gov) Good general information.

MD Travel Health (www.mdtravelhealth.com) Provides complete travel health recommendations for every country, updated daily.

World Health Organization (WHO; www.who.int/ith/) Its helpful book *International Travel & Health* is revised annually and available online.

FURTHER READING

Lonely Planet's *Healthy Travel – Asia & India* is a handy pocket size and packed with useful information, including pre-trip planning, emergency first aid, immunisation and disease information, and what to do if you get sick on the road. Other recommended references include *Travellers' Health* by Dr Richard Dawood and *Travelling Well* by Dr Deborah Mills – check out the website of **Travelling Well** (www.travellingwell.com.au).

IN TRANSIT

DEEP VEIN THROMBOSIS (DVT)

Deep vein thrombosis (DVT) occurs when blood clots form in the legs during plane flights, chiefly because of prolonged immobility. The longer the flight, the greater the risk. Though most blood clots are reabsorbed uneventfully, some may break off and travel through the blood vessels to the lungs, where they may cause life-threatening complications.

The chief symptom of DVT is swelling or pain of the foot, ankle or calf, usually but not always on just one side. When a blood clot travels to the lungs, it may cause chest pain and difficulty in breathing. Travellers with any of these symptoms should immediately seek medical attention.

To prevent the development of DVT on long flights, walk about the cabin, perform isometric compressions of the leg muscles (ie contract the leg muscles while sitting), drink plenty of fluids, and avoid alcohol and tobacco.

JET LAG & MOTION SICKNESS

Jet lag is common when crossing more than five time zones; it results in insomnia, fatigue, malaise and/or nausea. To avoid jet lag try drinking plenty of fluids (nonalcoholic) and eating light meals. Upon arrival, seek exposure to natural sunlight and readjust your schedule (for meals, sleep etc) as soon as possible.

Antihistamines such as dimenhydrinate (Dramamine), promethazine (Phenergan) and meclizine (Antivert, Bonine) are usually the first choice for treating motion sickness. Their main side effect is drowsiness. Ginger (a hebal alternative) works wonders for some people.

IN SOUTH INDIA

AVAILABILITY OF HEALTHCARE

Medical care is hugely variable in India, especially beyond the big cities. Some cities now have clinics catering specifically to travellers and expatriates. These clinics can be more expensive than local medical facilities, but are worth it as they should offer a higher standard of care. They also understand the local system, and are aware of the most reputable local hospitals and specialists. They may also liaise with insurance companies should you require evacuation. Recommended clinics are listed under Information sections in the regional chapters of this book. It is usually difficult to find reliable medical care in rural areas.

Self-treatment may be appropriate if your problem is minor (eg traveller's diarrhoea), you are carrying the relevant medication and you cannot attend a recommended clinic. However, if you suspect you may potentially have a serious disease, especially malaria, do not waste time; travel to the nearest quality facility to receive attention. It is always better to be assessed by a doctor than to rely on self-treatment.

Before buying medication over the counter, always check the use-by date and ensure the packet is sealed. Don't accept items that have been poorly stored (eg lying in a glass cabinet exposed to the sunshine).

INFECTIOUS DISEASES
Avian Flu

'Bird Flu' or Influenza A (H5N1) is a subtype of the type A influenza virus. This virus typi-

cally infects birds and not humans; however, in 1997 the first documented case of bird-to-human transmission was recorded in Hong Kong. Currently very close contact with dead or sick birds is the principal source of infection and bird-to-human transmission does not easily occur.

Symptoms include high fever and typical influenza-like symptoms with rapid deterioration leading to respiratory failure and death in many cases. Early administration of antiviral drugs (eg Tamiflu) is recommended to improve the chances of survival. At this time it's not routinely recommended for travellers to carry Tamiflu with them, but immediate medical care should be sought if bird flu is suspected.

There is currently no vaccine available to prevent bird flu. For up-to-date information check these two websites:

- www.who.int/en/
- www.avianinfluenza.com.au

Coughs, Colds & Chest Infections

Around 25% of travellers to India will develop a respiratory infection. This usually starts as a virus and is exacerbated by environmental conditions, such as pollution in the cities, or cold and altitude in the mountains. Commonly a secondary bacterial infection will intervene – marked by fever, chest pain and coughing up discoloured or blood-tinged sputum. If you have the symptoms of an infection seek medical advice or consider commencing a general antibiotic.

Dengue Fever

This mosquito-borne disease is becomingly increasingly problematic in the tropical world, especially in the cities. As there is no vaccine available it can only be prevented by avoiding mosquito bites. The mosquito that carries dengue bites day and night, so use insect avoidance measures at all times. Symptoms include high fever, severe headache and body ache (dengue was previously known as 'breakbone fever'). Some people develop a rash and experience diarrhoea. There is no specific treatment, just rest and paracetamol – do not take aspirin as it increases the likelihood of haemorrhaging. Make sure you see a doctor to be diagnosed and monitored.

Hepatitis A

A problem throughout the region, this food- and water-borne virus infects the liver, causing jaundice (yellow skin and eyes), nausea and lethargy. There is no specific treatment for hepatitis A, you just need to allow time for the liver to heal. All travellers to India should be vaccinated against hepatitis A.

Hepatitis B

The only sexually transmitted disease that can be prevented by vaccination, hepatitis B is spread by body fluids. The long-term consequences can include liver cancer and cirrhosis.

Hepatitis E

Transmitted through contaminated food and water, hepatitis E has similar symptoms to hepatitis A, but is far less common. It is a severe problem in pregnant women and can result in the death of both mother and baby. There is currently no vaccine, and prevention is by following safe eating and drinking guidelines.

HIV

HIV is spread via contaminated body fluids. Avoid unsafe sex, unsterile needles (including in medical facilities) and procedures such as tattoos. The growth rate of HIV in India is one of the highest in the world – also see p46.

Influenza

Present year-round in the tropics, influenza (flu) symptoms include fever, muscle aches, runny nose, cough and sore throat. It can be severe in people over the age of 65 or in those with medical conditions such as heart disease or diabetes – vaccination is recommended for these individuals. There is no specific treatment, just rest and paracetamol.

Japanese B Encephalitis

This viral disease is transmitted by mosquitoes and is rare in travellers. Like most mosquito-borne diseases it is becoming a more common problem in affected countries. Most cases occur in rural areas and vaccination is recommended for travellers spending more than one month outside of cities. There is no treatment, and a third of infected people will die while another third will suffer permanent brain damage. Ask your doctor for further details.

Malaria

For such a serious and potentially deadly disease, there is an enormous amount of misin-

formation concerning malaria. You must get expert advice as to whether your trip actually puts you at risk. For most rural areas, especially, the risk of contracting malaria far outweighs the risk of any tablet side effects. Before you travel, seek medical advice on the right medication and dosage for you.

Malaria is caused by a parasite transmitted by the bite of an infected mosquito. The most important symptom of malaria is fever, but general symptoms, such as headache, diarrhoea, cough or chills, may also occur. Diagnosis can only be properly made by taking a blood sample.

Two strategies should be combined to prevent malaria – mosquito avoidance and antimalarial medications. Most people who catch malaria are taking inadequate or no antimalarial medication.

Travellers are advised to prevent mosquito bites by taking these steps:

- Use a DEET-containing insect repellent on exposed skin. Wash this off at night, as long as you are sleeping under a mosquito net. Natural repellents such as citronella can be effective, but must be applied more frequently than products containing DEET.
- Sleep under a mosquito net impregnated with pyrethrin
- Choose accommodation with proper screens and fans (if not air-conditioned)
- Impregnate clothing with pyrethrin in high-risk areas
- Wear long sleeves and trousers in light colours
- Use mosquito coils
- Spray your room with insect repellent before going out for your evening meal

There are a variety of medications available. The effectiveness of the chloroquine and Paludrine combination is now limited in many parts of South Asia. Common side effects include nausea (40% of people) and mouth ulcers.

The daily tablet doxycycline is a broad-spectrum antibiotic that has the added benefit of helping to prevent a variety of tropical diseases, including leptospirosis, tick-borne disease and typhus. The potential side effects include photosensitivity (a tendency to sunburn), thrush (in women), indigestion, heartburn, nausea and interference with the contraceptive pill. More serious side effects include ulceration of the oesophagus – you can help prevent this by taking your tablet with a meal and a large glass of water, and never lying down within half an hour of taking it. It must be taken for four weeks after leaving the risk area.

Lariam (mefloquine) has received much bad press, some of it justified, some not. This weekly tablet suits many people. Serious side effects are rare but include depression, anxiety, psychosis and having fits. Anyone with a history of depression, anxiety, other psychological disorders or epilepsy should not take Lariam. It is considered safe in the second and third trimesters of pregnancy. Tablets must be taken for four weeks after leaving the risk area.

The newer drug Malarone is a combination of atovaquone and proguanil. Side effects are uncommon and mild, most commonly nausea and headache. It is the best tablet for scuba divers and for those on short trips to high-risk areas. It must be taken for one week after leaving the risk area.

Rabies

This uniformly fatal disease is spread by the bite or possibly even the lick of an infected animal – most commonly a dog or monkey. You should seek medical advice immediately after any animal bite and commence postexposure treatment. Having pre-travel vaccination means the postbite treatment is greatly simplified. If an animal bites you, gently wash the wound with soap and water, and apply iodine-based antiseptic. If you are not prevaccinated you will need to receive rabies immunoglobulin as soon as possible, and this is very difficult to obtain in much of India.

STDs

Sexually transmitted diseases most common in India include herpes, warts, syphilis, gonorrhoea and chlamydia. People carrying these diseases often have no signs of infection. Condoms will prevent gonorrhoea and chlamydia but not warts or herpes. If after a sexual encounter you develop any rash, lumps, discharge or pain when passing urine, seek immediate medical attention. If you have been sexually active during your travels, have an STD check on your return home.

Tuberculosis

While TB is rare in travellers, those who have significant contact with the local population

(such as medical and aid workers and long-term travellers) should take precautions. Vaccination is usually only given to children under the age of five, but adults at risk are recommended pre- and post-travel TB testing. The main symptoms are fever, cough, weight loss, night sweats and fatigue.

Typhoid

This serious bacterial infection is also spread via food and water. It gives a high and slowly progressive fever, headache, and may be accompanied by a dry cough and stomach pain. It is diagnosed by blood tests and treated with antibiotics. Vaccination is recommended for all travellers who are spending more than a week in India. Be aware that vaccination is not 100% effective, so you must still be careful with what you eat and drink.

TRAVELLER'S DIARRHOEA

This is by far the most common problem affecting travellers in India – between 30% and 70% of people will suffer from it within two weeks of starting their trip. In over 80% of cases, traveller's diarrhoea is caused by a bacteria (there are numerous potential culprits), and therefore responds promptly to treatment with antibiotics. Treatment with antibiotics will depend on your situation – how sick you are, how quickly you need to get better, where you are etc.

Traveller's diarrhoea is defined as the passage of more than three watery bowel actions within 24 hours, plus at least one other symptom, such as fever, cramps, nausea, vomiting or feeling generally unwell.

Treatment consists of staying well hydrated; rehydration solutions like Gastrolyte are the best for this. Antibiotics such as norfloxacin, ciprofloxacin or azithromycin should kill the bacteria quickly.

Loperamide is just a 'stopper' and doesn't get to the cause of the problem. It can be helpful, though (eg if you have to go on a long bus ride). Don't take loperamide if you have a fever, or blood in your stools. Seek medical attention quickly if you do not respond to an appropriate antibiotic.

Amoebic Dysentery

Amoebic dysentery is very rare in travellers but is often misdiagnosed by poor-quality labs. Symptoms are similar to bacterial diarrhoea, ie fever, bloody diarrhoea and generally feeling unwell. You should always seek reliable medical care if you have blood in your diarrhoea. Treatment involves two drugs: Tinidazole or Metronidazole to kill the parasite in your gut and then a second drug to kill the cysts. If left untreated complications such as liver or gut abscesses can occur.

Giardiasis

Giardia is a parasite that is relatively common in travellers. Symptoms include nausea, bloating, excess gas, fatigue and intermittent diarrhoea. The parasite will eventually go away if left untreated but this can take months; the best advice is to seek medical treatment. The treatment of choice is Tinidazole, with Metronidazole being a second-line option.

ENVIRONMENTAL HAZARDS
Air Pollution

Air pollution, particularly vehicle pollution, is an increasing problem in most of India's urban hubs. If you have severe respiratory problems, speak with your doctor before travelling to India. This pollution also causes minor respiratory problems, such as sinusitis, dry throat and irritated eyes. If troubled by the pollution, leave the city for a few days and get some fresh air.

Diving & Surfing

Divers and surfers should seek specialised advice before they travel to ensure their medical kit contains treatment for coral cuts and tropical ear infections, as well as the standard problems. Divers should ensure their insurance covers them for decompression illness – get specialised dive insurance through an organisation such as **Divers Alert Network** (DAN; www.danasiapacific.org). Have a dive medical before you leave your home country – there are certain medical conditions that are incompatible with diving.

Food

Eating in restaurants is generally the biggest risk factor for contracting traveller's diarrhoea. Ways to avoid it include eating only freshly cooked food, and avoiding shellfish and food that has been sitting in buffets. Peel all fruit, cook vegetables and soak salads in iodine water for at least 20 minutes. Eat in busy restaurants with a high turnover of customers. Also read the box, p76.

DRINKING WATER

- Never drink tap water

- Bottled water is generally safe – check the seal is intact at purchase

- Avoid ice unless you know it has been safely made

- Be careful of fresh juices served at street stalls in particular – they may have been watered down or may be served in unhygienic jugs/glasses

- Boiling water is usually the most efficient method of purifying it

- The best chemical purifier is iodine. It should not be used by pregnant women or those with thyroid problems.

- Water filters should also filter out viruses. Ensure your filter has a chemical barrier such as iodine and a small pore size, eg less than four microns.

Heat

Many parts of India, especially down south, are hot and humid throughout the year. For most people it takes at least two weeks to adapt to the hot climate. Swelling of the feet and ankles is common, as are muscle cramps caused by excessive sweating. Prevent these by avoiding dehydration and excessive activity in the heat. Take it easy when you first arrive. Don't eat salt tablets (they aggravate the gut); drinking rehydration solution or eating salty food helps. Treat cramps by stopping activity, resting, rehydrating with double-strength rehydration solution and gently stretching.

Dehydration is the main contributor to heat exhaustion. Symptoms include feeling weak, headache, irritability, nausea or vomiting, sweaty skin, a fast, weak pulse and a normal or slightly elevated body temperature. Treatment involves getting out of the heat and/or sun, fanning the sufferer and applying cool wet cloths to the skin, laying the sufferer flat with their legs raised and rehydrating with water containing one-quarter teaspoon of salt per litre. Recovery is usually rapid and it is common to feel weak for some days afterwards.

Heat stroke is a serious medical emergency. Symptoms come on suddenly and include weakness, nausea, a hot dry body with a body temperature of over 41°C, dizziness, confusion, loss of coordination, fits, and eventually collapse and loss of consciousness. Seek medical help and commence cooling by getting the person out of the heat, removing their clothes, fanning them and applying cool wet cloths or ice to their body, especially to the groin and armpits.

Prickly heat is a common skin rash in the tropics, caused by sweat being trapped under the skin. The result is an itchy rash of tiny lumps. Treat it by moving out of the heat and into an air-conditioned area for a few hours and by having cool showers. Creams and ointments clog the skin so they should be avoided. Locally bought prickly heat powder can be helpful.

Tropical fatigue is common in long-term expatriates based in the tropics. It's rarely due to disease and is caused by the climate, inadequate mental rest, excessive alcohol intake and the demands of daily work in a different culture.

High Altitude

If you are going to altitudes above 3000m, you should get information on preventing, recognising and treating Acute Mountain Sickness (AMS). The biggest risk factor for developing altitude sickness is going too high too quickly – you should follow a conservative acclimatisation schedule such as can be found in all good trekking guides – and you should *never* go to a higher altitude when you have any symptoms that could be altitude related. There is no way to predict who will get altitude sickness and it is often the younger, fitter members of a group who succumb.

Symptoms usually develop during the first 24 hours at altitude but may be delayed up to three weeks. Mild symptoms include headache, lethargy, dizziness, difficulty sleeping and loss of appetite. AMS may become more severe without warning and can be fatal. Severe symptoms include breathlessness, a dry, irritated cough (which may progress to the production of pink, frothy sputum), severe headache, lack of coordination and balance, confusion, irrational behaviour, vomiting, drowsiness and unconsciousness.

Treat mild symptoms by resting at the same altitude until recovery, which usually takes a day or two. Paracetamol or aspirin can be taken for headaches. If symptoms persist or become worse, however, immediate descent is necessary; even 500m can help. Drug treatments should never be used to avoid descent or to enable further ascent.

The drugs acetazolamide and dexamethasone are recommended by some doctors for the prevention of AMS; however, their use is controversial. They can reduce the symptoms, but they may also mask warning signs; severe and fatal AMS has occurred in people taking these drugs.

To prevent Acute Mountain Sickness:

■ Ascend slowly – have frequent rest days, spending two to three nights at each rise of 1000m.

■ It is always wise to sleep at a lower altitude than the greatest height reached during the day, if possible. Also, once above 3000m, care should be taken not to increase the sleeping altitude by more than 300m per day.

■ Drink extra fluids. The mountain air is dry and cold, and moisture is lost as you breathe.

■ Eat light, high-carbohydrate meals.

■ Avoid alcohol and sedatives.

Insect Bites & Stings

Bedbugs don't carry disease but their bites can be very itchy. They live in the cracks of furniture and walls and then migrate to the bed at night to feed on you. You can treat the itch with an antihistamine. Lice inhabit various parts of your body but most commonly your head and pubic area. Transmission is via close contact with an infected person. They can be difficult to treat and you may need numerous applications of an antilice shampoo such as pyrethrin. Pubic lice are usually contracted from sexual contact.

Ticks are contracted after walking in rural areas. Ticks are commonly found behind the ears, on the belly and in armpits. If you have had a tick bite and experience symptoms such as a rash at the site of the bite or elsewhere, fever or muscle aches, you should see a doctor. Doxycycline prevents tick-borne diseases.

Leeches are found in humid rainforest areas. They do not transmit any disease but their bites are often intensely itchy for weeks afterwards and can easily become infected. Apply an iodine-based antiseptic to any leech bite to help prevent infection.

Bee and wasp stings mainly cause problems for people who are allergic to them. Anyone with a serious bee or wasp allergy should carry an injection of adrenalin (eg an Epipen) for emergency treatment. For others, pain is the

HEALTH

main problem – apply ice to the sting and take painkillers.

Skin Problems

Fungal rashes are common in humid climates. There are two common fungal rashes that affect travellers. The first occurs in moist areas, such as the groin, armpits and between the toes. It starts as a red patch that slowly spreads and is usually itchy. Treatment involves keeping the skin dry, avoiding chafing and using an antifungal cream such as clotrimazole or Lamisil. *Tinea versicolor* is also common – this fungus causes small, light-coloured patches, most commonly on the back, chest and shoulders. Consult a doctor.

Cuts and scratches become easily infected in humid climates. Take meticulous care of any cuts and scratches to prevent complications such as abscesses. Immediately wash all wounds in clean water and apply antiseptic. If you develop signs of infection (increasing pain and redness), see a doctor. Divers and surfers should be particularly careful with coral cuts, as they become easily infected.

Sunburn

Even on a cloudy day sunburn can occur rapidly. Always use a strong sunscreen (at least factor 30), making sure to reapply after a swim, and always wear a wide-brimmed hat and sunglasses outdoors. Avoid lying in the sun during the hottest part of the day (10am to 2pm). You can get burnt very easily when you are at high altitudes so be vigilant once above 3000m. If you become sunburnt, stay out of the sun until you have recovered, apply cool compresses and, if necessary, take painkillers for the discomfort. One-percent hydrocortisone cream applied twice daily is also helpful.

WOMEN'S HEALTH

In most places in India, supplies of sanitary products (pads, rarely tampons) are readily available. Birth-control options may be limited, so bring adequate supplies of your own form of contraception. Heat, humidity and antibiotics can all contribute to thrush. Treatment is with antifungal creams and pessaries such as clotrimazole. A practical alternative is a single tablet of Fluconazole (Diflucan). Urinary tract infections can be precipitated by dehydration or long bus journeys without toilet stops; bring suitable antibiotics. For gynaecological health issues, seek out a female doctor.

Pregnant women should receive specialised advice before travelling. The ideal time to travel is in the second trimester (between 16 and 28 weeks), when the risk of pregnancy-related problems is at its lowest and pregnant women generally feel at their best. Always carry a list of reputable medical facilities available at your destination and ensure you continue your standard antenatal care at these facilities. Avoid rural travel in areas with poor transport and substandard medical facilities. Most of all, ensure that your travel insurance policy covers all pregnancy-related possibilities, including premature labour.

Malaria is a high-risk disease for pregnant women, and WHO recommends that they do *not* travel to areas with Chloroquine-resistant malaria. None of the more effective antimalarial drugs are completely safe in pregnancy.

Traveller's diarrhoea can quickly lead to dehydration and result in inadequate blood flow to the placenta. Many of the drugs used to treat various diarrhoea bugs are not recommended in pregnancy. Azithromycin is generally considered safe.

Language

CONTENTS

There is no one 'Indian' language as such. The constitution recognises 18 official languages, including English. The non-English varieties fall roughly into two main groups: Indic (or Indo-Aryan) and Dravidian. There were also over 1600 minor languages and dialects.

The native languages of the regions covered in this book are Tamil, Kannada, Konkani, Malayalam, Marathi, Oriya, and Telugu. They mostly belong to the Dravidian language family, although these have been influenced to varying degrees during their development by Hindi and Sanskrit. As the predominant languages in specific geographic areas they have in effect been used to determine the regional boundaries for the southern states.

Major efforts have been made to promote Hindi as the 'official' language of India, and to gradually phase out English. While Hindi is the predominant language of the north, it bears little relation to the Dravidian languages of the south; subsequently very few people in the south speak Hindi. Resistance to change has been strongest in the state of Tamil Nadu, and as a result, Tamil is still very much the predominant language of South India. English is also widely spoken.

TAMIL

Tamil is the official language in the South Indian state of Tamil Nadu and the Union Territory of Puducherry.

Tamil is classed as a South Dravidian language, and is one of the major Dravidian languages of South India. The exact origins of the Dravidian family are unknown, but it is believed to have arrived in India's north west around 4000 BC, gradually splitting into four branches with the passage of time. Tamil became isolated to India's south as the Indo-Aryan language varieties such as Hindi became more dominant in the north.

Along with Sanskrit, Tamil is recognised as one of the two classical languages of India. It has a very rich historical tradition dating back more than 2000 years. Since then three forms have been distinguished: Old Tamil (200 BC to AD 700), Middle Tamil (AD 700 to AD 1600) and Modern Tamil (AD 1600 to the present).

Modern Tamil is diglossic in nature, meaning that it has two distinct forms: literary or classical (used mainly in writing and formal speech), and spoken (used in everyday conversation). The spoken form has a wide range of dialects, varying in social, cultural and regional dimensions. Irrespective of the differences, a common variety called Standard Spoken Tamil is widely used in mass media and by all Tamils in their day-to-day life.

Tamil has its own alphabetic script, which isn't used in this language guide. Our transliteration system is intended as a simplified method of representing the sounds of Tamil using the Roman alphabet. As with all such systems it's not exact and should be seen only as an approximate guide to the pronunciation of the language.

PRONUNCIATION
Vowels

a	as the 'u' in 'run'
aa	as in 'rather'
e	as in 'met'
i	as in 'bit'
ee	as in 'meet'
o	as in 'hot'
oo	as in 'boot'
u	as in 'put'

Vowel Combinations

ai	as in 'aisle'
au	as the 'ow' in 'how'

Consonants

g	as in 'go'
k	as in 'kit'
ñ	as the 'ni' in the word 'onion'; as in the Spanish *señor*
s	as in 'sit'
zh	as the 's' in 'pleasure'

Retroflex Consonants

Some consonants in Tamil and the other languages of India are a little more complicated because they represent sounds not found in English. The most common variants are called 'retroflex' consonants, where the tongue is curled upwards and backwards so that the underside of the tip makes contact with the alveolar ridge (the ridge of tissue on the roof of the mouth a little behind the teeth). Retroflex consonants are represented in this guide by a dot below the letter (in Tamil, these are ḷ, ṇ and ṭ). If the lingual gymnastics prove too much you'll find that you can still make yourself understood by ignoring the dot and pronouncing the letter as you would in English.

ACCOMMODATION

hotel	*hotal/vituti*
guest house	*viruntinar vituti*
youth hostel	*ilaiñar vituti*
camping ground	*tangumitam*

Do you have any rooms available?	*araikal kitaikkumaa?*
for one/two people	*oruvar/iruvarukku*
for one/two nights	*oru/irantu iravukal*
How much is it per night/per person?	*oru iravukku/oru nabarukku evallavu?*
Is breakfast included?	*kaalai sirruṇṭiyuṭan serttaa?*

CONVERSATION & ESSENTIALS

Hello.	*vaṇakkam*
Goodbye.	*poyiṭṭu varukiren*
Yes/No.	*aam/illai*
Please.	*tayavu ceytu*
Thank you.	*nanri*
That's fine, you're welcome.	*nallatu varuka*
Excuse me.	*mannikkavum*
Sorry/Pardon.	*mannikkavum*
Do you speak English?	*neenkal aankilam pesuveerkalaa?*
How much is it?	*atu evvalavu?*
What's your name?	*unkal peyar enna?*
My name is ...	*en peyar ...*

NUMBERS

0	*boojyam*
1	*onru*
2	*irantu*
3	*moonru*
4	*naanku*
5	*aintu*
6	*aaru*
7	*ezhu*
8	*ettu*
9	*onpatu*
10	*pattu*
100	*nooru*
1000	*aayiram*
2000	*irantaayiram*
100,000	*latsam* (written 1,00,000)
1,000,000	*pattu latsam* (written 10,00,000)
10,000,000	*koti* (written 1,00,00,000)

SHOPPING & SERVICES

bank	*vangi*
chemist/pharmacy	*aruntukkataikkaarar/ maruntakam*
... embassy	*... tootarakam*
market	*maarkkeṭ*
medicine	*maruntu*
newsagent	*niyoos ejensi*
post office	*tabaal nilayam*
public telephone	*potu tolaipesi*
stationers	*elutuporul vanikar*
tourist office	*surrulaa seyti totarpu aluvalakam*
What time does it open/close?	*tirakkum/mootum neram enna?*
big	*periya*
small	*siriya*

TIMES & DAYS

What time is it?	*mani ettanai?*
day	*pakal*
night	*iravu*
week	*vaaram*
month	*maatam*
year	*varutam*
today	*inru*
tomorrow	*naalai*

yesterday	*nerru*
morning	*kaalai*
afternoon	*matiyam*

Monday	*tinkal*
Tuesday	*sevvaay*
Wednesday	*putan*
Thursday	*viyaazhan*
Friday	*velli*
Saturday	*sani*
Sunday	*ñaayiru*

TRANSPORT

Where is a/the ...?	*... enke irukkiratu?*
Go straight ahead.	*neraaka sellavum*
Turn left/right.	*valatu/itatu pakkam tirumbavum*
near	*arukil*
far	*tooram*

What time does the	*eppozhutu atutta ...*
next ... leave/arrive?	*sellum/varum?*
boat	*paṭaku*
bus (city)	*peruntu (nakaram/ulloor)*
bus (intercity)	*peruntu (veliyoor)*
tram	*traam*
train	*rayil*

I'd like a ... ticket.	*enakku oru ... ṭikkeṭ veṇum*
one-way	*vazhi*
return	*iru vazhi*
1st class	*mutalaam vakuppu*
2nd class	*irantaam vakuppu*

SIGNS – TAMIL

வழி உள்ளே	Entrance
வழி வெளியே	Exit
திறந்துள்ளது	Open
அடைக்கப்பட்டுள்ளது	Closed
தகவல்	Information
அனுமதி இல்லை	Prohibited
காவல் நிலையம்	Police Station
மலசலகூடம்	Toilets
ஆண்	Men
பெண்	Women

left luggage	*tavara vitta saamaan*
timetable	*kaala attavanai*
bus stop	*peruntu nilayam*
train station	*rayil nilayam*

I'd like to hire a ...	*enakku ... vaatakaikku venum*
car	*kaara*
bicycle	*saikkil*

KANNADA

Kannada (also known as Kanarese) is also a Dravidian language and it is the official language of the state of Karnataka in India's south west. After Telugu and Tamil it's the third most common Dravidian language of South India.

The earliest known example of Kannada literature is Kavirajamarga, which dates back to the 9th century AD, and today the modern language is represented by a thriving tradition covering all literary genres.

See the pronunciation guide in the Tamil section of this chapter for an explanation of the retroflex consonants (ḍ, ḷ, ṇ, ṣ and ṭ).

CONVERSATION & ESSENTIALS

Hello.	*namaste* or *namaskaara*
Excuse me.	*kṣamisi*
Please.	*dayaviṭṭu*
Thank you.	*vandanegaḷu*
Yes/No.	*havdu/illa*
How are you?	*hege ideeri?*
Very well, thank you.	*bahaḷa oḷḷeyadu vandanegaḷu*
What's your name?	*nimma hesaru enu?*
My name is ...	*nanna hesaru ...*
Do you speak English?	*neevu ingliṣ mataaḍteeraa?*
I don't understand.	*nanage artha aagalla*
Where is the hotel?	*hoṭel ellide?*
How far is ...?	*... eṣṭu doora?*
How do I get to ...?	*naanu allige hogodu hege?*
How much?	*eṣṭu?*
This is expensive.	*idu dubaari*
What is the time?	*gaṇṭe eṣṭu?*

medicine	*auṣadhi*
big	*dodda*
small	*cikka*
today	*ivattu*
day	*hagalu*
night	*raatri*
week	*vaara*
month	*tingalu*
year	*varṣa*

NUMBERS

1	*ondu*
2	*eradu*
3	*mooru*
4	*naalku*
5	*aydu*
6	*aaru*
7	*elu*

LANGUAGE

8	*entu*
9	*ombhattu*
10	*hattu*
100	*nooru*
1000	*ondu saavira*
2000	*radu saavira*
100,000	*lakṣa* (written 1,00,000)
1,000,000	*hattu lakṣa* (written 10,00,000)
10,000,000	*koti* (written 1,00,00,000)

KONKANI

After a long and hard-fought battle Konkani was finally recognised in 1992 as the official language of the small state of Goa on India's southwest coast. Until then, argument had raged that Konkani was actually no more than a dialect of Marathi, the official language of the much larger neighbouring state of Maharashtra.

Even though Konkani is virtually the only universally understood language of Goa, centuries of colonial rule, significant dialectal variation and as many as five different scripts meant that defining it as an official language would always be problematic. The issue was further complicated by the varying loyalties of Goa's population: the high caste and predominantly Catholic and Hindu Brahmin families who spoke Portuguese, English and Konkani, and the lower caste, mainly Hindu families who tended to speak Marathi as a first language and some Konkani as a second language. Despite these obstacles Konkani went on to be added to the Indian Constitution as the country's 18th national language.

CONVERSATION & ESSENTIALS

Hello.	*paypadta*
Excuse me.	*upkar korxi*
Please.	*upkar kor*
Thank you.	*dev borem korum*
Yes/No.	*oi/naah*
How are you?	*kosso assa?* (m)
	kossem assa? (f)
Very well, thank you.	*bhore jaung*
What's your name?	*tuje naav kide?*
Do you speak English?	*to English hulonk jhana?*
I don't understand.	*mhaka kay samzona na*
Where is a hotel?	*hotel khoy aasa?*
How far is ...?	*anig kitya phoode ...?*
How do I get to ...?	*maka kashe ... meltole?*
How much?	*kitke poishe laqthele?*

This is expensive.	*chod marog*
What's the time?	*vurra kitki jali?*
medicine	*vokot*
big	*hodlo*
small	*dhakto*
today	*aaj*
day	*dees*
night	*racho*
week	*athovda*
month	*mohino*
year	*voros*

NUMBERS

1	*ek*
2	*don*
3	*tin*
4	*char*
5	*panch*
6	*sou*
7	*sat*
8	*att*
9	*nov*
10	*dha*
20	*vis*
30	*tis*
40	*chalis*
50	*ponnas*
60	*saatt*
70	*sottor*
80	*oixim*
90	*novodh*
100	*xembor*
200	*donshe*
1000	*ek hazaar*
2000	*don hazaar*
100,000	*lakh* (written 1,00,000)
10,000,000	*crore* (written 1,00,00,000)

MALAYALAM

Like Tamil, Malayalam belongs to the Dravidian language family. Though there are obvious lexical links between the two languages, with many words sharing common roots, Malayalam includes a far greater number of borrowings from ancient Indian Sanskrit. Its divergence from Tamil began some time after the 10th century AD, with the first official literary record of it dating back to Ramacharitam, a 'pattu' poem written in the late 12th century. The modern form of the Malayalam script developed from the 16th century literary works of Tuñcatt Ezuttacchan.

Malayalam is the official language of the state of Kerala on India's far southwestern coast.

See the pronunciation guide in the Tamil section of this chapter for an explanation of the retroflex consonants (ḍ, ḷ, ṇ, ṛ, ṣ and ṭ).

CONVERSATION & ESSENTIALS

Hello.	namaste
Excuse me.	ksamikkoo
Please.	dayavucheytu
Thank you.	nanni
Yes/No.	aanaate/alla
How are you?	sukhamaaṇo?
Very well, thank you.	sukham tanne
What's your name?	ninnaluṭe pera entaaṇua?
My name is ...	ente peru ...
Do you speak English?	ninnaḷ ingleeṣa samsaarikkumo?
I don't understand.	enikka aṛiyilla
Where is the hotel?	hottal eviṭeyaaṇa?
How far is ...?	... vetra dooramaaṇa?
How do I get to ...?	... aviṭe ennane pokaṇam?
How much?	etṛa?
This is expensive.	vila kootutal aaṇa
What's the time?	mani etṛayeyi?

medicine	marunnu
big	valiya
small	cheṛiya
today	inna
day	divasam
night	raatṛi
week	aalca
month	maasam
year	vaṛsam

NUMBERS

1	onna
2	raṇḍa
3	moonna
4	naala
5	ancha
6	aaṛa
7	ela
8	eṭṭa
9	ombata
10	patta
100	nooṛa
1000	aayiram
2000	raṇḍaayiram
100,000	lakṣam (written 1,00,000)
1,000,000	patta lakam (written 10,00,000)
10,000,000	koṭi (written 1,00,00,000)

MARATHI

Marathi is the official language of the state of Maharashtra and is one of India's national languages. Like its close linguistic relative, Konkani (the official language of Goa), it belongs to the Indo-Aryan language family. As a result of linguistic influences from neighbouring regions you may notice considerable dialectal variation in Marathi as you move around Maharashtra.

CONVERSATION & ESSENTIALS

Hello/Goodbye.	namaskar
Excuse me.	maaf kara
Please.	krupaya
Yes.	ho
No.	nahi
How are you?	tumhi kase aahat?
Very well, thank you.	mee thik aahe, dhanyawad
What's your name?	aapla nav kai aahe?
Do you speak English?	tumhala english yeta ka?
I don't understand.	mala samjat nahi
Where is a hotel?	hotel kuthe aahe?
How do I get to ...?	... kasa jaycha mhanje sapdel?
How much?	kevdhyala?/kai kimmat?
This is expensive.	khup mahag aahe
What's the time?	kiti vajle?

medicine	aushadh
big	motha/mothi (m/f)
small	lahan
today	aaj
day	divas
night	ratra
week	aathavda
month	mahina
year	varsha

NUMBERS

1	ek
2	don
3	tin
4	char
5	pach
6	saha
7	sat
8	aath
9	nou
10	daha
100	shambhar
200	donshe
1000	ek hazar

LANGUAGE

2000	*don hazar*
100,000	*ek lakh* (written 1,00,000)
10,000,000	*daha koti* (written 1,00,00,000)

TELUGU

Telugu is a Southeast Dravidian language spoken mainly in the state of Andhra Pradesh on India's east coast; it became the state's official language in the mid-1960s. With around 70 million speakers it is the most predominant of South India's four major Dravidian languages. Its literary history dates back to the 11th century AD when the poet Nannaya produced a translation of parts of the Mahabharata. While Sanskrit has played a major role in Telugu literature over the centuries, there is an increasing tendency for written works to reflect the more colloquial variety of Modern Standard Telugu. See the pronunciation guide in the Tamil section of this chapter for an explanation of the retroflex consonants (ḍ, ḷ, ṇ and ṭ).

CONVERSATION & ESSENTIALS

Hello.	*namaste/namaskaaram*
Excuse me.	*ksamińchaṇḍi*
Please.	*dayatsesi*
Thank you.	*dhanyawaadaalu*
Yes.	*awunu*
No.	*kaadu*
How are you?	*elaa unnaaru?/*
	elaa baagunnaaraa?
Very well, thank you.	*baagunnaanu dhanyawaadaalu*
What's your name?	*mee peru emiṭi?/nee peru emiṭi?*
My name is ...	*naa peru ...*

Do you speak English?	*meeku anglam waccha?*
I don't understand.	*naaku artham kaawaṭamledu*
Where is the hotel?	*hoṭal ekkada undi?*
How far is ...?	*... enta dooram?*
How do I get to ...?	*... nenu akkaḍiki weḷḷaṭam elaa?*
How much?	*enta?*
This is expensive.	*idi chaalaa ekkuwa*
What's the time?	*gaṇṭa enta?/ṭaym enta?*

medicine	*awsadham/mandu*
big	*pedda*
small	*tsinna*
today	*eeroju/eenaaḍu/neḍu*
day	*pagalu*
night	*raatri*
week	*waaram*
month	*nela/maasam*
year	*eḍu/samwatsaram*

NUMBERS

1	*okaṭi*
2	*reṇḍu*
3	*mooḍu*
4	*naalugu*
5	*aydu/ayidu*
6	*aaru*
7	*eḍu*
8	*enimidi*
9	*tommidi*
10	*padi*
100	*nooru/wanda*
1000	*weyyi/weyi*
2000	*reṇḍuwelu*
100,000	*laksa* (written 1,00,000)
1,000,000	*padilaksalu* (written 10,00,000)
10,000,000	*koṭi* (written 1,00,00,000)

Glossary

This glossary has some words and terms you may encounter during your South Indian wanderings. For food and drink definitions, see p78 and for an overview of the various vernaculars spoken in South India, see p543.

abbi – waterfall
Adivasi – tribal person
agarbathi – incense
Agni – major deity in the *Vedas*; mediator between men and the gods; also fire
ahimsa – discipline of nonviolence
AIR – All India Radio, the national broadcaster
air-cooler – noisy water-filled cooling fan
amrita – immortality
Ananta – serpent on whose coils *Vishnu* reclined
Annapurna – form of *Durga*; worshipped for her power to provide food
apsara – heavenly nymph
Aranyani – Hindu goddess of forests
Ardhanariswara – *Shiva's* half-male, half-female *(Parvati)* form
Arjuna – *Mahabharata* hero and military commander who married Subhadra (*Krishna's* incestuous sister), took up arms and overcame many demons; he had the *Bhagavad Gita* related to him by Krishna, led Krishna's funeral ceremony and finally retired to the Himalaya
Aryan – Sanskrit for 'noble'; those who migrated from Persia and settled in northern India
Ashoka – ruler in the 3rd century BC; responsible for spreading Buddhism throughout South India
ashram – spiritual community or retreat
ASI – Archaeological Survey of India; an organisation involved in monument preservation
attar – essential oil; used as a base for perfumes
autorickshaw – noisy, three-wheeled, motorised contraption for transporting passengers, livestock etc for short distances; found throughout the country, they are cheaper than taxis
Avalokiteshvara – in *Mahayana* Buddhism, the *bodhisattva* of compassion
avatar – incarnation, usually of a deity
ayurveda – the ancient and complex science of Indian herbal medicine and healing
azad – free (Urdu), as in Azad Jammu & Kashmir

baba – religious master or father; term of respect
babu – clerk
bagh – garden

baksheesh – tip, donation (alms) or bribe
banyan – Indian fig tree; spiritual to many Indians
Bhagavad Gita – Hindu Song of the Divine One; *Krishna's* lessons to *Arjuna*, the main thrust of which was to emphasise the philosophy of bhakti; it's part of the *Mahabharata*
bhajan – devotional song
bhakti – surrendering to the gods; faith
bhang – dried leaves and flowering shoots of the marijuana plant
bhangra – rhythmic Punjabi music/dance
Bharata – half-brother of *Rama;* ruled while Rama was in exile
bhavan – house, building; also spelt *bhawan*
Bhima – *Mahabharata* hero; he is the brother of *Hanuman* and renowned for his great strength
bidi – small, hand-rolled cigarette
bindi – forehead mark (often dot shaped) worn by women
BJP – Bharatiya Janata Party; political party
bodhisattva – literally 'one whose essence is perfected wisdom'; in Early Buddhism, bodhisattva refers only to the Buddha during the period between his conceiving the intention to strive for Buddhahood and the moment he attained it; in *Mahayana* Buddhism, it is one who renounces nirvana in order to help others attain it
Bollywood – India's answer to Hollywood; the film industry of Mumbai (Bombay)
Brahma – Hindu god; worshipped as the creator in the *Trimurti*
Brahmin – member of the priest/scholar caste, the highest Hindu caste
Buddha – Awakened One; the originator of Buddhism; also regarded by Hindus as the ninth incarnation of *Vishnu*
bund – embankment or dyke

cantonment – administrative and military area of a Raj-era town
Carnatic music – classical music of South India
caste – a Hindu's hereditary station (social standing) in life; there are four castes: the *Brahmins*, the *Kshatriyas*, the *Vaishyas* and the *Shudras;* the Brahmins occupy the top spot
chaitya – Sanskrit form of 'cetiya', meaning shrine or object of worship; has come to mean temple, and more specifically, a hall divided into a central nave and two side aisles by a line of columns, with a votive *stupa* at the end
chandra – moon; the moon as a god
chappals – sandals or leather thonglike footwear; flip-flops

charas – resin of the marijuana plant; also referred to as 'hashish'

chillum – pipe of a *hookah;* commonly used to describe the pipes used for smoking *ganja* (dried flowering tips of the marijuana plant)

chinkara – gazelle

chital – spotted deer

choli – sari blouse

chowk – town square, intersection or marketplace

chowkidar – night watchman; caretaker

crore – 10 million

dagoba – see *stupa*

Dalit – preferred term for India's *Untouchable* caste

dargah – shrine or place of burial of a Muslim saint

darshan – offering or audience with someone; auspicious viewing of a deity

Deccan – meaning 'South', this refers to the central South Indian plateau

devadasi – temple dancer

Devi – *Shiva's* wife; goddess

dhaba – basic restaurant or snack bar; especially popular with truck drivers

dharamsala – pilgrims' rest house

dharma – for Hindus, the moral code of behaviour or social duty; for Buddhists, following the law of nature, or path, as taught by the Buddha

dhobi – person who washes clothes; commonly referred to as *dhobi-wallah*

dhobi ghat – place where clothes are washed by the *dhobi*

dhol – traditional double-sided drum

dholi – people-powered portable 'chairs'; people are carried in them to hilltop temples etc

dhoti – like a *lungi,* but the ankle-length cloth is then pulled up between the legs; worn by men

dhurrie – rug

dowry – money and/or goods given by a bride's parents to their son-in-law's family; it's illegal but still exists in many arranged marriages

Draupadi – wife of the five Pandava princes in the *Mahabharata*

Dravidian – general term for the cultures and languages of the deep south of India, including Tamil, Malayalam, Telugu and Kannada

dupatta – long scarf for women often worn with the *salwar kameez*

durbar – royal court; also a government

Durga – the Inaccessible; a form of *Shiva's* wife, *Devi,* a beautiful, fierce goddess riding a tiger/lion

dwarpal – doorkeeper; sculpture beside the doorways to Hindu or Buddhist shrines

Emergency – period in the 1970s during which Indira Gandhi suspended many political rights

Eve-teasing – sexual harassment

filmi – slang term describing anything to do with Indian movies

gaddi – throne of a Hindu prince

Ganesh – Hindu god of good fortune and remover of obstacles; popular elephant-headed son of *Shiva* and *Parvati,* he is also known as Ganpati; his vehicle is a ratlike creature

Ganga – Hindu goddess representing the sacred Ganges River; said to flow from *Vishnu's* toe

garbhagriha – the inner, or 'womb' chamber of a Hindu temple

Garuda – man-bird vehicle of *Vishnu*

gaur – Indian bison

geyser – hot-water unit found in many bathrooms

ghat – steps or landing on a river, range of hills, or road up hills

giri – hill

gopuram – soaring pyramidal gateway tower of *Dravidian* temples

gumbad – dome on an Islamic tomb or mosque

gurdwara – Sikh temple

guru – holy teacher; in Sanskrit literally *goe* (darkness) and *roe* (to dispel)

Guru Granth Sahib – Sikh holy book

haj – Muslim pilgrimage to Mecca

haji – Muslim who has made the *haj*

Hanuman – Hindu monkey god, prominent in the *Ramayana,* and a follower of *Rama*

hartal – strike

haveli – traditional, often ornately decorated, residences

hijra – eunuch, transvestite

hindola – swing

hookah – water pipe used for smoking *ganja* (dried flowering tips of the marijuana plant) or strong tobacco

imam – Muslim religious leader

IMFL – Indian-made foreign liquor

Indo-Saracenic – style of colonial architecture that integrated Western designs with Islamic, Hindu and Jain influences

Indra – significant and prestigious Vedic god; god of rain, thunder, lightning and war

Jagannath – Lord of the Universe; a form of *Krishna*

jali – carved lattice (often marble) screen, also refers to the holes or spaces produced through carving timber or stone

jhula – bridge

ji – honorific that can be added to the end of almost anything as a form of respect; thus 'Babaji', 'Gandhiji'

jootis – traditional, often pointy-toed, slip-in shoes

jyoti linga – most important shrines to *Shiva,* of which there are 12

Kailasa – sacred Himalayan mountain; home of *Shiva*

kalamkari – designs painted on cloth using vegetable dyes

Kali – the ominous-looking evil-destroying form of *Devi*; commonly depicted with dark skin, dripping with blood, and wearing a necklace of skulls

kameez – woman's shirtlike tunic

Kannada – state language of Karnataka

karma – Hindu, Buddhist and Sikh principle of retributive justice for past deeds

khadi – homespun cloth; Mahatma Gandhi encouraged people to spin this rather than buy English cloth

Khalistan – former Sikh secessionists' proposed name for an independent Punjab

Khalsa – Sikh brotherhood

Khan – Muslim honorific title

kolam – elaborate chalk, rice-paste or coloured powder design; also known as *rangoli*

Konkani – state language of Goa

Krishna – *Vishnu's* eighth incarnation, often coloured blue; he revealed the *Bhagavad Gita* to *Arjuna*

Kshatriya – Hindu caste of soldiers or administrators; second in the caste hierarchy

kurta – long shirt with either short collar or no collar

lakh – 100,000

Lakshmana – half-brother and aide of *Rama* in the *Ramayana*

Lakshmi – *Vishnu's* consort, Hindu goddess of wealth; she sprang forth from the ocean holding a lotus

lama – Tibetan Buddhist priest or monk

lingam – phallic symbol; auspicious symbol of *Shiva*; plural 'linga'

lungi – worn by men, this loose, coloured garment (similar to a sarong) is pleated at the waist to fit the wearer

maha – prefix meaning 'great'

Mahabharata – Great Hindu Vedic epic poem of the Bharata dynasty; containing approximately 10,000 verses describing the battle between the Pandavas and the Kauravas

mahal – house or palace

maharaja – literally 'great king'; princely ruler

maharani – wife of a princely ruler or a ruler in her own right

mahatma – literally 'great soul'

Mahavir – last *tirthankar*

Mahayana – the 'greater-vehicle' of Buddhism; a later adaptation of the teaching which lays emphasis on the *bodhisattva* ideal, teaching the renunciation of nirvana (ultimate peace and cessation of rebirth) in order to help other beings along the way to enlightenment

mahout – elephant rider or master

maidan – open (often grassed) area; parade ground

Makara – mythical sea creature and *Varuna's* vehicle; crocodile

mala – garland or necklace

Malayalam – state language of Kerala

mandapa – pillared pavilion; a temple forechamber

mandir – temple

Mara – Buddhist personification of that which obstructs the cultivation of virtue, often depicted with hundreds of arms; also the god of death

Maratha – central Indian people who controlled much of India at various times and fought the *Mughals* and *Rajputs*

marg – road

masjid – mosque

mehndi – henna; ornate henna designs on women's hands (and often feet), traditionally for certain festivals or ceremonies (eg marriage)

mela – fair or festival

mithuna – pairs of men and women; often seen in temple sculpture

Mohini – *Vishnu* in his female incarnation

moksha – liberation from *samsara*

mudra – ritual hand movements used in Hindu religious dancing; gesture of Buddha figure

Mughal – Muslim dynasty of subcontinental emperors from Babur to Aurangzeb

Naga – mythical serpentlike beings capable of changing into human form

namaskar – see *namaste*

namaste – traditional Hindu greeting (hello or goodbye), often accompanied by a respectful small bow with the hands together at the chest or head level

Nanda – in Hinduism, cowherd who raised *Krishna*; in Buddhism, *Buddha's* half-brother

Nandi – bull, vehicle of *Shiva*

Narasimha – man-lion incarnation of *Vishnu*

Narayan – incarnation of *Vishnu* the creator

Nataraja – *Shiva* as the cosmic dancer

nilgai – antelope

nizam – hereditary title of the rulers of Hyderabad

NRI – Non-Resident Indian

Om – sacred invocation representing the essence of the divine principle; for Buddhists, if repeated often enough with complete concentration, it leads to a state of emptiness

paise – the Indian rupee is divided into 100 paise

palanquin – boxlike enclosure carried on poles on four men's shoulders; the occupant sits inside on a seat

Pali – the language; related to Sanskrit, in which the Buddhist scriptures were recorded; scholars still refer to the original Pali texts

Parasurama – *Rama* with the axe; sixth incarnation of *Vishnu*

Parsi – adherent of the Zoroastrian faith

Partition – formal division of British India in 1947 into two separate countries, India and Pakistan

Parvati – a form of *Devi*

PCO – Public Call Office from where to make local, interstate and international phone calls

pietra dura – marble inlay work characteristic of the Taj Mahal

Pongal – Tamil harvest festival

pradesh – state

pranayama – study of breath control; meditative practice

prasad – temple-blessed food offering

puja – literally 'respect'; offering or prayers

Puranas – set of 18 encyclopaedic Sanskrit stories, written in verse, relating to the three gods, dating from the 5th century AD

purdah – custom among some conservative Muslims (also adopted by some Hindus, especially the *Rajputs*) of keeping women in seclusion; veiled

Purnima – full moon; considered to be an auspicious time

qawwali – Islamic devotional singing

Radha – favourite mistress of *Krishna* when he lived as a cowherd

raga – any of several conventional patterns of melody and rhythm that form the basis for freely interpreted compositions

railhead – station or town at the end of a railway line; termination point

raj – rule or sovereignty; British Raj (sometimes just Raj) refers to British rule

raja – king; sometimes *rana*

Rajput – Hindu warrior caste, former rulers of north-western India

rakhi – amulet

Rama – seventh incarnation of *Vishnu*

Ramadan – the Islamic holy month of sunrise-to-sunset fasting (no eating, drinking or smoking); also referred to as Ramazan

Ramayana – the story of *Rama* and *Sita* and their conflict with *Ravana* is one of India's best-known epics

rana – king; sometimes *raja*

rangoli – see *kolam*

rani – female ruler or wife of a king

rathas – rock-cut Dravidian temples

Ravana – demon king of Lanka who abducted *Sita*; the titanic battle between him and *Rama* is told in the *Ramayana*

rickshaw – small, two- or three-wheeled passenger vehicle

sadhu – ascetic, holy person; one who is trying to achieve enlightenment; often addressed as *swamiji* or *babaji*

sagar – lake, reservoir

sahib – respectful title applied to a gentleman

salwar – trousers usually worn with a *kameez*

salwar kameez – traditional dresslike tunic and trouser combination for women

samadhi – in Hinduism, ecstatic state, sometimes defined as 'ecstasy, trance, communion with God'; in Buddhism, concentration; also a place where a holy man has been cremated/buried, usually venerated as a shrine

sambar – deer

samsara – Buddhists, Hindus and Sikhs believe earthly life is cyclical; you are born again and again, the quality of these rebirths being dependent upon your karma in previous lives

Sangam – ancient academy of Tamil literature; means literally 'the meeting of two hearts'

sangha – community of monks and nuns

Saraswati – wife of *Brahma*; goddess of learning; sits on a white swan, holding a *veena*

Sati – wife of *Shiva*; became a *sati* ('honourable woman') by immolating herself; although banned more than a century ago, the act of *sati* is still (very) occasionally performed

satyagraha – nonviolent protest involving a hunger strike, popularised by Mahatma Gandhi; from Sanskrit, literally meaning 'insistence on truth'

Scheduled Castes – official term used for the *Untouchables* or *Dalits*

sepoy – formerly an Indian solider in British service

shahadah – Muslim declaration of faith ('There is no God but Allah; Mohammed is his prophet')

Shaivism – worship of *Shiva*

Shaivite – follower of *Shiva*

Shakti – creative energies perceived as female deities; devotees follow Shaktism

shikara – covered gondola-like boat used on lakes

Shiv Sena – Hindu nationalist political party

Shiva – the Destroyer; also the Creator, in which form he is worshipped as a lingam

Shivaji – great Maratha leader of the 17th century

shola – virgin forest

Shudra – caste of labourers

sikhara – Hindu temple-spire or temple

Sita – the Hindu goddess of agriculture; more commonly associated with the *Ramayana*

sitar – Indian stringed instrument

Sivaganga – water tank in temple dedicated to *Shiva*

Skanda – Hindu god of war, *Shiva's* son

stupa – Buddhist religious monument composed of a solid hemisphere topped by a spire, containing relics of the Buddha; also known as a *dagoba* or pagoda

Sufi – Muslim mystic

Sufism – Islamic mysticism

Surya – the sun; a major deity in the *Vedas*

swami – title of respect meaning 'lord of the self'; given to initiated Hindu monks

tabla – twin drums

Tamil – language of Tamil Nadu; people of *Dravidian* origin

tandava – *Shiva's* cosmic victory dance

tank – reservoir; pool or large receptacle of holy water found at some temples

tempo – noisy three-wheeler public-transport vehicle; bigger than an autorickshaw

theertham – temple tank

Theravada – orthodox form of Buddhism practiced in Sri Lanka and Southeast Asia that is characterised by its adherence to the *Pali* canon; literally, 'dwelling'

tikka – a mark Hindus put on their foreheads

tilak – auspicious forehead mark of devout Hindu men

tirthankars – the 24 great Jain teachers

tonga – two-wheeled horse or pony carriage

toy train – narrow-gauge train; mini-train

Trimurti – triple form; the Hindu triad of *Brahma*, *Shiva* and *Vishnu*

Untouchable – lowest caste or 'casteless', for whom the most menial tasks are reserved; the name derives from the belief that higher castes risk defilement if they touch one; now known as *Dalit*

Vaishya – member of the Hindu caste of merchants

Varuna – supreme Vedic god

Vedas – Hindu sacred books; collection of hymns composed in preclassical Sanskrit during the second millennium BC and divided into four books: Rig-Veda, Yajur-Veda, Sama-Veda and Atharva-Veda

veena – stringed instrument

vihara – Buddhist monastery, generally with central court or hall off which open residential cells, usually with a Buddha shrine at one end

Vijayanagar empire – one of South India's greatest empires; lasted from the 14th to 17th century

vikram – *tempo* or a larger version of the standard tempo

vimana – principal part of Hindu temple; a tower over the sanctum

vipassana – the insight meditation technique of *Theravada* Buddhism in which mind and body are closely examined as changing phenomena

Vishnu – part of the *Trimurti*; Vishnu is the Preserver and Restorer who so far has nine avatars: the fish Matsya, the tortoise Kurma, the wild boar Naraha, *Narasimha*, Vamana, *Parasurama*, *Rama*, *Krishna* and *Buddha*

wallah – man; added onto almost anything, eg *dhobi*-wallah, chai-wallah, taxi-wallah

yali – mythical lion creature

yatra – pilgrimage

zakat – tax in the form of a charitable donation; one of the five 'Pillars of Islam'

zenana – area of a home where women are secluded; women's quarters

The Authors

SARINA SINGH
Coordinating Author

After finishing a business degree in Melbourne, Sarina bought a one-way ticket to India where she completed a corporate traineeship with the Sheraton before working as a freelance journalist and foreign correspondent. After four years in the subcontinent she returned to Australia, pursued postgraduate journalism qualifications and wrote/directed an award-nominated documentary that premiered at the Melbourne International Film Festival. Sarina has worked on around 30 Lonely Planet books, is the author of *Polo in India,* and has also written for many international publications including *National Geographic Traveler.* For this book, Sarina wrote Destination South India, Getting Started, Itineraries, Events Calendar, History, The Culture, Activities, Food & Drink, Environment, Directory, Transport, Glossary and the Scrumptious South India section.

AMY KARAFIN
Mumbai (Bombay), Andhra Pradesh

Indian in several former lives, Amy Karafin headed straight to India after university for an extended trip that would turn out to be karmically ordained. She spent the next few years alternating between New York and faraway lands until, fed up with the irony of being a travel editor in a Manhattan cubicle, she relinquished her MetroCard and her black skirts to make a living on the road. She's been freelancing seminomadically ever since, spending big chunks of time in Senegal, Ghana, Guinea and India. She lives mostly in Brooklyn now, but also sometimes in Mumbai and Dakar.

ADAM KARLIN
Tamil Nadu, Andaman & Nicobar Islands

Adam was a 23-year old backpacker in South India when the Tamil bandit Veerappan was killed near his hostel. The next day he filed his first international news story on the 'Jungle Cat's' death. A month later, Adam was being interrogated by Tamil Tigers while reporting on the Sri Lankan Civil War. The Tamils and their homeland have had a place in his heart ever since, and he jumped at the opportunity to go back to South India for Lonely Planet. While he'll always love Tamil Nadu, he was pleasantly surprised to discover Eden umpteen times during his first visit to the Andamans, too.

LONELY PLANET AUTHORS

Why is our travel information the best in the world? It's simple: our authors are passionate, dedicated travellers. They don't take freebies in exchange for positive coverage so you can be sure the advice you're given is impartial. They travel widely to all the popular spots, and off the beaten track. They don't research using just the internet or phone. They discover new places not included in any other guidebook. They personally visit thousands of hotels, restaurants, palaces, trails, galleries, temples and more. They speak with dozens of locals every day to make sure you get the kind of insider knowledge only a local could tell you. They take pride in getting all the details right, and in telling it how it is. Think you can do it? Find out how at **lonelyplanet.com**.

ANIRBAN MAHAPATRA — Maharashtra, Karnataka

Six years into his career as an Indian journalist, Anirban Mahapatra has almost perfected the art of selling outlandish story ideas to his editors to routinely beat the confines of his office cubicle and scoot off to far-flung corners of the country. Now based in Delhi, he's trundled through Maharashtra and Karnataka several times in the past, once even in a mad-hat attempt to retrace the steps of 15th-century Russian explorer Afanasy Nikitin. His primary reason for going south, however, is to significantly endanger the local marine life (oh the crabs!) while he's there, and wash it all down with some fresh draught in beer-town Bengaluru. He's also a writer and photographer, and this is his second Lonely Planet assignment.

AMELIA THOMAS — Goa

Amelia Thomas is a writer and journalist working throughout India and the Middle East. She has worked on numerous Lonely Planet titles, and her book *The Zoo on the Road to Nablus,* telling the true story of the last Palestinian zoo, was published in 2008. Her four small children, aged between 10 months and five years, enjoy accompanying her on assignments – particularly the Goan kind, which sees them conducting their own research into sandcastles, rock pools and Indian ice cream. Her forthcoming book, *'Hypnosis!'* tells the incredible, colourful tale of Abbé de Faria, Goan priest and hypnotist extraordinaire.

RAFAEL WLODARSKI — Kerala, Tamil Nadu (Chennai section)

After completing degrees in marketing and psychology in Melbourne, Rafael vowed never to use them and set off on a short around-the-world trip. Nine years and five passports later and he is yet to come home. Rafael spent his entire 20s travelling overland through the Middle East, the Indian subcontinent, and North and South America. He managed to get lost in India for six months along the way, and relished coming back to Kerala to update this Lonely Planet. He currently lives somewhere between San Francisco, London and Zanzibar.

Behind the Scenes

THIS BOOK

This is the 5th edition of South India. Sarina Singh coordinated the project and wrote the front and back material and the colour sections. The other authors on this book were Amy Karafin (Mumbai and Andhra Pradesh), Adam Karlin (Tamil Nadu, Andaman & Nicobar Islands), Anirban Mahapatra (Maharashtra and Karnataka), Amelia Thomas (Goa) and Rafael Wlodarski (Kerala, and Chennai). The 4th edition was based on our 12th edition of India, which was coordinated by Sarina Singh and Joe Bindloss. Dr Trish Batchelor wrote the Health text. This guidebook was commissioned in Lonely Planet's Melbourne office, and produced by the following:

Commissioning Editors Will Gourlay, Shawn Low, Suzannah Shwer, Sam Trafford
Coordinating Editor Elisa Arduca
Coordinating Cartographer Peter Shields
Coordinating Layout Designer Wibowo Rusli
Managing Editors Sasha Baskett, Brigitte Ellemor, Bruce Evans
Managing Cartographer David Connolly
Managing Layout Designer Laura Jane
Assisting Editors Nigel Chin, Helen Koehne, Helen Yeates
Assisting Layout Designer Paul Iacono
Cover Image research provided by lonelyplanetimages .com

Project Manager Chris Girdler
Thanks to Lucy Birchley, Sally Darmody, Martin Heng, Lauren Hunt, John Mazzocchi, Susan Paterson, Adrian Persoglia, Alison Ridgway, Averil Robertson, Laura Stansfeld, Gina Tsarouhas, Juan Winata

THANKS
SARINA SINGH

In India, thanks to those kind souls who made life on the road less bumpy, especially Hitender, Kalpana Kumari and Janmejaye Singh, for adopting me as family; and Mamta, Anup and Abhinav Bamhi, for being first-rate stress banishers. Kudos to all at Lonely Planet who worked their magic on the manuscripts, with heartfelt thanks, especially, to the tenacious authors for months of slog – I'm deeply grateful. At Lonely Planet, special thanks to Sam Trafford, Suzannah Shwer and Elisa Arduca. This book is dedicated to my parents, for strength and love during every twist and turn that life has tossed up.

AMY KARAFIN

My sincere thanks go to the people of Andhra Pradesh and Bombay for putting up with my questions and for having created such fascinating places. I'm also deeply grateful to Akash Bhartiya, assistant researcher, Hindi tutor and loyal kulfi part-

---

THE LONELY PLANET STORY

Fresh from an epic journey across Europe, Asia and Australia in 1972, Tony and Maureen Wheeler sat at their kitchen table stapling together notes. The first Lonely Planet guidebook, *Across Asia on the Cheap*, was born.

Travellers snapped up the guides. Inspired by their success, the Wheelers began publishing books to Southeast Asia, India and beyond. Demand was prodigious, and the Wheelers expanded the business rapidly to keep up. Over the years, Lonely Planet extended its coverage to every country and into the virtual world via lonelyplanet.com and the Thorn Tree message board.

As Lonely Planet became a globally loved brand, Tony and Maureen received several offers for the company. But it wasn't until 2007 that they found a partner whom they trusted to remain true to the company's principles of travelling widely, treading lightly and giving sustainably. In October of that year, BBC Worldwide acquired a 75% share in the company, pledging to uphold Lonely Planet's commitment to independent travel, trustworthy advice and editorial independence.

Today, Lonely Planet has offices in Melbourne, London and Oakland, with over 500 staff members and 300 authors. Tony and Maureen are still actively involved with Lonely Planet. They're travelling more often than ever, and they're devoting their spare time to charitable projects. And the company is still driven by the philosophy of *Across Asia on the Cheap*: 'All you've got to do is decide to go and the hardest part is over. So go!'

ner; Mom and Dad; Manik and Surekha Bhartiya; Sarina Singh, Sam Trafford and Will Gourlay; Malini and Hari Hariharan; Jayasree Anand and Sandhya Kanneganti; Raghu Raman; Sunjoy Monga; Zehra Jumabhoy; the original members of the Barry Karafin International Executive Club; Hervé, Charlie and Hernan; and SN Goenka and everyone at Dhamma Pattan, Dhamma Nagajjuna, Dhamma Vijaya, and Dhamma Khetta. Bhavatu sabba mangalam.

ADAM KARLIN
Thanks: Abi in Trichy, Santosh in Coonoor, Mani in Kumbakonam, Kumar in Mamallapuram, Selvam in Tirumayam, Shadab, BK Das and DK Das in Port Blair, the Indian Army men in Diglipur and Rakesh and Anthony in Chennai. Huge ups to Prabil and Amit in Little Andaman. Also: cheers to Stephanie et Francois, Em, Ellie and Becky, Simone, Moran, Charlie, Danny and Sophie, Lara and Andy and every other companion met on the road.

ANIRBAN MAHAPATRA
Many thanks to editors Sam Trafford, Shawn Low, Will Gourlay and Suzannah Shwer; carto Adrian Persoglia and the entire team at Lonely Planet; and my fellow authors, who put their heads and hearts into this book. Sarina, thanks a ton for your help and guidance – I owe you many beers! On the ground, thanks to the wonderful people of the Deccan, the energetic Mrs Ramu at the Bengaluru KSTDC office, fellow scribes Bishakha Sarkar, Abhijit Mitra, Swagata Sen and Nirmala Ravindran, Shama Pawar for her help in Hampi and Anegundi, and Sivakumar, Gajanan and Ashok, for their enthusiastic driving. Finally, to Shohini for her help, patience and encouragement, and to our house dogs, for generally making life a breeze!

AMELIA THOMAS
Many thanks, first, to Pinky and her fabulous family, without whom everyday life would have been impossible. Thanks, too, to Tanya, Shubangi and Pinky#2, who do such wonderful work, and to Sharon Salman and family for becoming great friends. Thanks to Sarina, Sam, Will, Alison, the other authors, and the team at Lonely Planet for being great to work with, to Nich and Cheryl for the morning *bhaji paus* and evening G&Ts, and to Cassidy, Tyger, Cairo, Gal and Zeyah for forsaking the Middle East to set up camp, instead, on the shores of the Arabian Sea.

RAFAEL WLODARSKI
Thanks goes out to all the helpful folk who smoothed my speedy path through India, par-

ticularly the staff at tourist and KTDC offices far and wide. A big bucket of thanks goes out to the people who went beyond the call of duty to help make this book possible: Dayar, taxi driver MK Sekhran in Kottayam, Prabhath (Joseph) in Kollam, Rottu in Trivandrum, Saji in Kovalam, Siddharth from Locadives, and a huge thanks to PJ Varghese, Kurien and Mr Vanu. Thanks also to Sarina Singh for her steady captainship and to Sam Trafford for sending me to India. Very special thanks are reserved, as always, for Suzanna, and for my mum.

OUR READERS
Many thanks to the travellers who used the last edition and wrote to us with helpful hints, useful advice and interesting anecdotes:

Stephanie Aicher, Fiona Anderson, Helen Atkinson, Melissa Branfman, Thomas Braunschweig, Mark Brayne, Andrew Burke, Marlene Caplan, Mark Chew, David Cobb, Isabel Cordero Padillla, Lou Elliott, Warren Ezekiel, Pia Fischer, Michelle Fitzpatrick, Kerstin Forsman, Gerald Gregory, Stefan Hagel, Hiroshi Hemmi, Esko Hurme, Margriet Huussen, Zohar Itzhaki, Hannah Jones, Sheila Kay, Carol Kempe, Julia Kozitsyna, Jan Kronhede-Jensen, Kate Lyons-Priker, Wolfram Machatsch, Yogeeta Manjdadria, Eloise Markwell-Butler, Brian Mccusker, Bruce Moon, Eddie Moore, David Moran, Mark Oakley, Jan Painter, David Peck,

SEND US YOUR FEEDBACK
We love to hear from travellers – your comments keep us on our toes and help make our books better. Our well-travelled team reads every word on what you loved or loathed about this book. Although we cannot reply individually to postal submissions, we always guarantee that your feedback goes straight to the appropriate authors, in time for the next edition. Each person who sends us information is thanked in the next edition – and the most useful submissions are rewarded with a free book.

To send us your updates – and find out about Lonely Planet events, newsletters and travel news – visit our award-winning website: **lonelyplanet.com/contact**.

Note: we may edit, reproduce and incorporate your comments in Lonely Planet products such as guidebooks, websites and digital products, so let us know if you don't want your comments reproduced or your name acknowledged. For a copy of our privacy policy visit lonelyplanet.com/privacy.

Inna Petrakova, Morven Pinkerton, Laurence Pinturault, Andy Prince, Michael Randall, Jamie Raskin, Liz Rhodes, Marcello Rizzi, Merfyn Roberts, Paul Rooney, Franz Schiele, Karsten Staehr, Alfred Strohmeier, Willi Suter, Jan Willem Ten Dolle, Juha Valimaki, Jolanda Van Bokhorst, Kim Van Den Broek, Franc Walsh, Hannah Wilde, Helena Yang

ACKNOWLEDGMENTS
Many thanks to the following for the use of their content:

Globe on title page ©Mountain High Maps 1993 Digital Wisdom, Inc.

Excerpt from *Shilappadikaram* (The Ankle Bracelet) by Prince Iiango Adigal, translated by Alain Daniélou, copyright ©1965 by Alain Daniélou. Reprinted by permission of New Directions Publishing Corp.

Excerpt from *Puram* (The Smile of Murugan on Tamil literature of South India) by Kamil Zvelebil, published by BRILL.

Excerpt from *Kuruntokai,* adapted from The Song of Songs and Ancient Tamil Love Poems by Abraham Mariaselvam, published by Biblical Institute Press.

Index

INDEX

Greendex

The following organisations have been selected by our authors because they demonstrate a commitment to sustainability. We've listed these businesses and not-for-profits for diverse reasons: some refill water bottles with safe, drinkable water and use local produce, funnelling profits back into the community; others support refugees by providing them with employment or reinvest profits into local groups. Ecolodges and trekking organisations that take care of the natural environment and minimise our impact on it are also mentioned here.

If you think we've omitted someone here, email us at www.lonelyplanet.com/contact. For more information about sustainable tourism and Lonely Planet, see www.lonelyplanet.com/responsible travel.

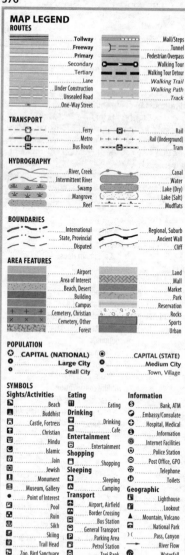

MAP LEGEND

ROUTES
.............Tollway
.............Freeway
.............Primary
.............Secondary
.............Tertiary
.............Lane
.............Under Construction
.............Unsealed Road
.............One-Way Street
.............Mall/Steps
.............Tunnel
.............Pedestrian Overpass
.............Walking Tour
.............Walking Tour Detour
.............Walking Trail
.............Walking Path
.............Track

TRANSPORT
.............Ferry
.............Metro
.............Bus Route
.............Rail
.............Rail (Underground)
.............Tram

HYDROGRAPHY
.............River, Creek
.............Intermittent River
.............Swamp
.............Mangrove
.............Reef
.............Canal
.............Water
.............Lake (Dry)
.............Lake (Salt)
.............Mudflats

BOUNDARIES
.............International
.............State, Provincial
.............Disputed
.............Regional, Suburb
.............Ancient Wall
.............Cliff

AREA FEATURES
.............Airport
.............Area of Interest
.............Beach, Desert
.............Building
.............Campus
.............Cemetery, Christian
.............Cemetery, Other
.............Forest
.............Land
.............Mall
.............Market
.............Park
.............Reservation
.............Rocks
.............Sports
.............Urban

POPULATION
CAPITAL (NATIONAL)
Large City
Small City
CAPITAL (STATE)
Medium City
Town, Village

SYMBOLS
Sights/Activities
.............Beach
.............Buddhist
.............Castle, Fortress
.............Christian
.............Hindu
.............Islamic
.............Jain
.............Jewish
.............Monument
.............Museum, Gallery
.............Point of Interest
.............Pool
.............Ruin
.............Sikh
.............Skiing
.............Trail Head
.............Zoo, Bird Sanctuary

Eating
.............Eating
Drinking
.............Drinking
.............Cafe
Entertainment
.............Entertainment
Shopping
.............Shopping
Sleeping
.............Sleeping
.............Camping
Transport
.............Airport, Airfield
.............Border Crossing
.............Bus Station
.............General Transport
.............Parking Area
.............Petrol Station
.............Taxi Rank

Information
.............Bank, ATM
.............Embassy/Consulate
.............Hospital, Medical
.............Information
.............Internet Facilities
.............Police Station
.............Post Office, GPO
.............Telephone
.............Toilets
Geographic
.............Lighthouse
.............Lookout
.............Mountain, Volcano
.............National Park
.............Pass, Canyon
.............River Flow
.............Waterfall

LONELY PLANET OFFICES

Australia
Head Office
Locked Bag 1, Footscray, Victoria 3011
☎ 03 8379 8000, fax 03 8379 8111
talk2us@lonelyplanet.com.au

USA
150 Linden St, Oakland, CA 94607
☎ 510 250 6400, toll free 800 275 8555
fax 510 893 8572
info@lonelyplanet.com

UK
2nd fl, 186 City Rd,
London EC1V 2NT
☎ 020 7106 2100, fax 020 7106 2101
go@lonelyplanet.co.uk

Published by Lonely Planet Publications Pty Ltd
ABN 36 005 607 983

© Lonely Planet Publications Pty Ltd 2009

© photographers as indicated 2009

Cover photograph: Tea plantation workers carry the day's harvest in Munnar (the Western Ghats, Kerala), Anders Blomqvist/Lonely Planet Images. Many of the images in this guide are available for licensing from Lonely Planet Images: www.lonelyplanetimages.com.

Printed by SNP Security Printing Pte Ltd, Singapore.

Mixed Sources
Product group from well-managed forests and other controlled sources
www.fsc.org Cert no. SGS-COC-005002
© 1996 Forest Stewardship Council

Although the authors and Lonely Planet have taken all reasonable care in preparing this book, we make no warranty about the accuracy or completeness of its content and, to the maximum extent permitted, disclaim all liability arising from its use.